Women and Capital Punishment
in the United States

Women and Capital Punishment in the United States
An Analytical History

DAVID V. BAKER

McFarland & Company, Inc., Publishers
Jefferson, North Carolina

LIBRARY OF CONGRESS CATALOGUING-IN-PUBLICATION DATA

Names: Baker, David V., author.
Title: Women and capital punishment in the United States :
an analytical history / David V. Baker.
Description: Jefferson, North Carolina : McFarland & Company, Inc., 2016 |
Includes bibliographical references and index.
Identifiers: LCCN 2015035341| ISBN 9780786499502 (softcover :
acid free paper) | **ISBN 9781476622880 (ebook)**
Subjects: LCSH: Capital punishment—United States—History. |
Women death row inmates—United States—History. | Discrimination
in criminal justice administration—United States—History.
Classification: LCC HV8699.U5 B35 2015 | DDC 364.66082/0973—dc23
LC record available at http://lccn.loc.gov/2015035341

BRITISH LIBRARY CATALOGUING DATA ARE AVAILABLE

© 2016 David V. Baker. All rights reserved

*No part of this book may be reproduced or transmitted in any form
or by any means, electronic or mechanical, including photocopying
or recording, or by any information storage and retrieval system,
without permission in writing from the publisher.*

Front cover image: *La Peine de Mort en Amérique* from *Le Petit Journal*,
April 9, 1899 © Look and Learn

Printed in the United States of America

*McFarland & Company, Inc., Publishers
Box 611, Jefferson, North Carolina 28640*
www.mcfarlandpub.com

For my son, Jeremy David Baker.
No father is more proud!

Table of Contents

Introduction   1
    Organization   2

Part I. Theoretical and Empirical Frameworks

1. Theoretical Frameworks 6
   Chivalry Theory   6
   Evil Woman Theory   7
   Equality Theory   9
   A Critical Perspective   10
   Capital Justice and the U.S. Supreme Court   12
   Capital Justice and Women in the Modern Era   18
   Concluding Remarks   30

2. Empirical Frameworks 31
   Data   31
   Characteristics   33
   Historical Contours   40
   Concluding Remarks   42

Part II. Historical Context

3. The First Historical Trend, 1630s–1750s 64
   Executions of White Women   65
   Executions of Black Women   83
   Executions of American Indian Women   90
   Concluding Remarks   91

4. The Second Historical Trend, 1760s–1890s 92
   Executions of White Women   92
   Executions of Black Women   107
   Executions of Mexican Women   128
   Executions of American Indian Women   130
   Execution of a Native Hawaiian Female   132
   Correcting the Historical Record   132
   Concluding Remarks   132

5. The Third Historical Trend, 1900s–2010s 134
   Executions of White Women   136
   Executions of Black Women   160
   Execution of an American Indian Woman   169
   Correcting the Historical Record   170
   Contrasting Lynchings and Executions   170
   Concluding Remarks   171

Table of Contents

Part III. Wrongful Convictions, Judicial Commutations, Executive Clemency and Women on Death Row Today

6. Wrongful Convictions in Potentially Capital Cases 174
   - *Data* 175
   - *Factors Contributing to False Convictions* 180
   - *Predatory Murder* 184
   - *Spousal Murder* 201
   - *Child Murder* 206
   - *Shaken Baby Syndrome* 220
   - *Medical Neglect Cases Motivated by Religion* 222
   - *Manslaughter* 223
   - *Concluding Remarks* 227

7. Judicial Reversals of Capital Convictions 229
   - *Early Cases of Judicial Reversals* 233
   - *Judicial Reversals Post-Furman* 239
   - *Concluding Remarks* 288

8. Executive Clemency of Condemned Women 290
   - *Clemency and Gender* 292
   - *Women on Death Row Granted Clemency* 292
   - *Clemency in the 18th Century* 298
   - *Clemency in the 19th Century* 302
   - *Clemency in the 20th Century* 314
   - *Concluding Remarks* 333

9. The Female Death Row Population 335
   - *Institutional Indifference* 337
   - *Women Foreign Nationals* 338
   - *Deaths of Condemned Women by Natural Causes* 339
   - *Characteristics of the Female Death Row Population* 340
   - *Predatory Murderers* 341
   - *Child Murderers* 356
   - *Spousal Murderers* 364
   - *Life Without Parole* 370
   - *Concluding Remarks* 372

Conclusion 373
- *The First Historical Trend* 373
- *The Second Historical Trend* 375
- *The Third Historical Trend* 376

Chapter Notes 381

Bibliography 394

Index 425

Introduction

Pulitzer Prize winning author Louis "Studs" Terkel often commented, "There's no yesterday in this country." Terkel's frequent observation is singularly instructive to understanding the contextual history of American women and capital justice. Scholars have afforded scant attention to gender issues in capital sentencing with most investigators narrowly constructing inquiries on gender and capital justice to the post–*Gregg* period—commonly known as the modern era of capital punishment. Consequently, the extant literature offers little in the way of comprehensive studies on the historical contexts of systemic oppression in female capital justice. Few scholars have linked the atrocities committed against women by contemporary justice practitioners to corresponding forms of maltreatment experienced by women in the centuries of gender oppression preceding the modern era in capital justice. In this regard, one researcher is misguided when she writes, "Since colonial times there have been numerous studies developed which focus on the execution of women." Certainly some scholarship has outlined the historical evolution of women and capital sentencing, but there are no publications that specifically chronicle the execution of American women while emphasizing the contexts of the penalty's history to women as an artifact of gender oppression. In all likelihood, the lack of historical and contextual discussions on female executions stem from women's executions not comprising a large enough population to justify their independent study. Yet, as one commentator suggests, "to fully understand the history of women in our criminal justice system, we need to look at women who have been given the death penalty and at the circumstances surrounding their sentencing and deaths."

To recognize the social, political, and economic contexts in which justice officials have put women to death, the present work furthers understanding of the intersection of capital justice and systemic gender oppression by examining the contextual history of American female executions. The historical record makes clear that challenging the patriarchal repression of women accentuates female executions in the United States. That is, female executions are a consequence of women's "economic deprivation, social vulnerability, and political powerlessness" in United States society. Poor and marginalized bonded servants and slaves typify most women executed historically. Social outcasts convicted of witchcraft, infanticide, spousal murder and predatory killings accent white women executions. In contrast, mostly slaves and domestic workers convicted of murdering oppressive slave masters, mistresses, overseers, employers and destroying the ill-gotten gains of white masters' property derived from slave repression accent black female executions. Similar demographics distinguish the execution of American Indian and Mexican women. One of the more enduring features of capital justice in the United States is that the social attributes of women executed in more modern eras correspond closely to women executed in earlier periods in the history of American capital justice. Today, though executed females are no longer servants and slaves, executed women remain largely social outcasts marginalized by poverty, sexual orientation, extreme drug and alcohol addiction, and severe psychological and psychiatric afflictions resulting from their violent victimization as children and young adults.

The history of executed women is largely "unknown, ignored, and discounted." An objective of this book then is to bring voice to this "forgotten population" victimized by the interlocking systems of race, gender, and class oppression in American capital justice. The study of executed women is important because the master narrative on judicial killings has focused on men to the virtual exclusion of women, rendering the historical picture of capital punishment in the United States incomplete and distorted. To correct for this unfinished portrait of American executions, the present work provides a historical and contextual narrative on the population of executed women. To that end, the discussions that follow *do not* adopt a comparative analysis with a contextual history of male executions because to compare women's experience to men's experience in the context of capital punishment "would be comparing apples to oranges" since men and women are not similarly situated in the patriarchal order of American society. Besides, the scholarly literature abounds with understanding the complexities of male judicial killings. The present work moves beyond an accounting of women executed in the United States and includes discussions on the historical contours of condemned women granted executive clemency, women given judicial commutations, an inquiry into women falsely convicted of potentially capital cases, and a profile of the current female death row population.

Organization

With these concerns at the forefront of understanding the contextual history of American women and capital justice, the book spans 10 chapters over four parts. Part I explores the theoretical and empirical frameworks accenting the investigation of women and capital punishment in the United States. Research on the capital sentencing of American women lacks a coherent theoretical structure appropriate to explaining the historical realities of gender oppression. To fill this void in the research record, the first chapter provides a brief examination of the extant yet defective theories on women executions and puts forth the notion that the *chivalry*, *evil woman*, and *equality* frameworks are incompatible with the objective historical reality of female executions in this country. Essentially, these theories are flawed because they ignore the patriarchal order of American society accenting white male domination and female subordination. In this regard, the theories overlook the idea that the criminal justice system is the enforcement arm of the American patriarchal order. The chapter puts forward a critical perspective as an alternative explanation on the history of women and capital punishment. From a critical perspective on female executions, imposition of the death penalty is a historically based device designed to control women who directly challenge the white male-controlled structure of American society. The chapter also explains that the U.S. Supreme Court has overlooked gender inequities in capital sentencing and has failed to implement practical protections to ensuring adequate funding of indigent defense services, restraining the discretion and blatant lawlessness of state prosecutors in marginalizing female capital defendants, protecting insane women and women with intellectual disabilities from execution, and prohibiting judicial override of biased judges in female capital cases.

The second chapter provides the empirical context of women executions and constructs an inventory of 702 female executions in the United States since 1632 when Virginia hanged June Champion for infanticide. The chapter presents a descriptive profile of women executions within the historical context in which they took place. Besides profiling the socio-demographic information on women's executions, analysis of the registry reveals three well-defined historical trends in female executions distinguished by the race of executed women. The analysis furthers understanding of female executions as occurring in a societal system of male domination and female subordination and illustrates, in a graphic sense, the brutality of female executions rooted in American society's racist and sexist social fabric, roots so deeply engrained in the nation's gender relations that they prevent change.

Part II explores the contextual history of female executions within the above-mentioned trends. The third chapter provides a descriptive profile and contextual discussion of events giving rise to female executions from 1632 to 1750 when jurisdictions mostly executed white women for witchcraft and infanticide. The fourth chapter entails discussions on female executions from 1760 to 1900 when jurisdictions executed mostly black women during antebellum slavery, Reconstruction, and the early Jim Crow period. The fifth chapter concerns female executions since 1900 when justice officials executed mostly white women for predatory murder though black women continued suffering executions in the late Jim Crow period, the civil rights period, and the modern post–*Gregg* period.

Part III provides inventories and contextual histories of women wrongfully convicted of potentially capital crimes, afforded judicial commutations, death row women granted executive clemency, and women currently residing on the nation's death rows. The sixth chapter examines cases of women wrongfully convicted of capital crimes as early as 1651 when Middlesex County officials in Massachusetts hanged British American Elizabeth Kendall for bewitching a child to death though a nurse was actually responsible for the killing and did not involve an accusation of witchcraft. The seventh chapter investigates cases of condemned women granted clemency by state governors in the 18th, 19th, and 20th centuries. The eighth chapter examines cases of condemned women where appellate courts have commuted their death sentences since the 1830s. The ninth chapter probes the current death row population of condemned women convicted of predatory murder, child murder, and spousal murder. The narrative also concerns the institutional indifference toward death row women, foreign-national women on death row, the death of condemned women from natural causes, and discussion of the increased use of life without parole as an alternative measure to seeking the death penalty against women and young girls.

Lastly, the Conclusion addresses some important questions about the contextual history of women and capital punishment: Why is it important to understand the circumstances of female death sentences and executions to appreciate the history of women in our criminal justice system? Why is it important that the capital justice system sentences women to death given the infrequency with which the event takes place? What are the policy implications arising from the historical record on female executions? What is the direction research on women and the death penalty should take in the future, and how might that that research help the plight of women on death row?

Part I

Theoretical and Empirical Frameworks

> "To fully understand the history of women in our criminal justice system, we need to look at women who have been given the death penalty and at the circumstances surrounding their sentencing and deaths."[1]

1

Theoretical Frameworks

This chapter puts forth the notion that the prevailing theories on female executions are inconsistent with the objective historical reality of female executions in the United States. In the alternative, a critical perspective on female executions more effectively complements the historical reality of judicial authorities putting women to death. Scholars studying gender in the American capital justice system typically advance the traditional theories of *chivalry theory*, *evil woman theory*, and *equality theory* as leading explanations of disparity in executions among men and women. After all, women comprise a modest percentage of persons put to death under civil authority in the United States since the early 17th century. Despite the allure of these theories to death penalty scholars, the theories remain deficient explanations of the systemic inequity accenting female executions historically. In this regard, death penalty researchers should focus less on explanations of gender disparity in capital punishment and concentrate more on the historical contexts and current processes under which jurisdictions have and continue to put women to death for capital offenses. The oppression of American women in the use of capital punishment is not found in its gender disparity but in the discrete historical stories of women's executions.

Chivalry Theory

In the context of capital justice, chivalry is "the reluctance to inflict harm on a woman accompanied by an unwillingness to believe that a woman could really be a criminal."[2] Chivalry theory holds that jurisdictions sentence to death and execute far fewer women relative to men because American society maintains a stereotypical view of women as weak, passive, and requiring male protection. Scholars often use differential statistics to validate chivalry theory. Data show, for instance, that since 1973 women account for 10 percent of persons arrested for murder and non-negligent manslaughter, for slightly more than 2 percent of death sentences imposed at the trial level, for just under 2 percent of persons currently on death row, and for less than 1 percent of persons actually executed. These figures suggest that the capital justice system effectively shields most female murderers from actual execution. Scholars explain that women receive sentence leniency in capital cases because "their crimes are often excused as aberrations, caused by a mental defect or some weakness of character or by circumstances beyond their control ... women are helpless and, like children, the mentally retarded, and the insane, they should not be punished like men."[3]

Chivalry theory explains that "[i]t is difficult for the actors in the capital justice system to condemn female offenders to death, even those who may have committed crimes just as heinous as any male offender."[4] Chivalry is an important explanation among crime evaluators who hold benevolent notions of women, though it has little explanatory impact to crime evaluators that do not hold such views of women. That is, the chivalrous treatment of female capital offenders does not have an overall societal effect; alternatively, notions of chivalry appear *individualistic* and *contextual*. One measure of chivalry in the historical treatment of death qualified female offenders, for instance, are comments of state governors concerning clemency of death row women often published in regional and national newspapers. Official comments by state governors on clemency historically show that chivalry in female capital justice has been sporadic and infrequent. Most state governors have not afforded clemency to condemned women or commuted women's death sentences to prison terms based upon their sentimental and chivalrous beliefs about female murderers. More accurately, state governors have afforded clemency to female capital offenders historically when doing so has been politically expedient.

Chivalry theory has a disparaging effect upon marginalized women. Chivalry is an unsuitable explanation to marginalized women facing capital sentencing since "[p]roper femininity is found more easily in white women than in women of color, in heterosexual women instead of lesbians, and in middle-class women rather than poor women."[5] As one commentator explains, chivalry is "a racist and classist concept ... reserved for the women who are least likely to come in contact with the criminal justice system: the ladies, or white middle-class women."[6] Chivalry theory gives moral authority to explaining why affluent heterosexual white women are largely immune from capital punishment. As one scholar points out, "Black women have never been placed on a pedestal; the cages in which they have been held have been real, not metaphoric."[7] One can make the same claim concerning other marginalized women of color—dominant societal attitudes are equally contemptuous against American Indian women and Latinas. Far removed from any notions of chivalry is the historical reality of womanhood for many marginalized white women, black women, American Indian women, and Mexican women. Interestingly, only one judicial officer has ever moved to impede the death sentence of a black woman. In late 1876, after a District of Columbia jury had convicted Johanna Turbin of killing her husband and dismembering the body, Judge MacArthur sentenced Johanna to death because the law compelled him to do so but then took measures to secure a commutation of Johanna's death sentence. Judge MacArthur explained that Johanna had committed an atrocious crime for which she deserved the death penalty but he loathed hanging a woman. A *New York Times* article explains that Judge MacArthur beseeched President Grant who ultimately commuted Johanna's death sentence to "hard labor for life."[8] Johanna's commuted death sentence was met with stark criticism. An editorial in the *Indiana Progress* commented:

> Now that it is settled that no woman can be hanged for murder, we should also exempt the sex from punishment for lesser crimes.... The chivalry which refuses to hang a woman for murder, but which punishes her for theft is inconsistent. What is wanted is an amendment to the Constitution guaranteeing to women the full enjoyment of theft, arson, forgery and other crimes. The world will then know that we are the most chivalrous people in existence.[9]

Evil Woman Theory

The antithesis to chivalry theory is the evil woman theory. This argument proposes that capital justice agents treat women offenders as harshly as men when they commit heinous murders that challenge conventional notions of "womanliness." One scholar explains, for instance, that because these women commit "unladylike" crimes, they "relinquish the benefits and protections afforded their sex and become evil incarnate. In this new role such women are not only eligible for the death sentence, but there is social pressure to execute them."[10] These are often women whose cases involved violations of gender-specific roles such as mother, wife, or caregiver. The Texas execution of Karla Faye Tucker in 1998 embodies the evil woman construct. In Karla's case, the single most important factor troubling the jury, criminal appeals courts, and the public was that in the immediate aftermath of Karla and Danny Garret's savage hammer and pickax killing of Jerry Dean and Deborah Thorton, Karla reportedly boasted to her friends that "every time she picked Jerry, she looked up and she grinned and got a nut and hit him again."[11] That is, viciously murdering a person with a pickax was a sordid sexually gratifying experience for Karla Tucker. Although she adamantly denied ever making the statement though officials apparently had recorded the statement during their murder investigation, an appeals court nevertheless explained that Karla's sexual pleasure while pick axing Jerry Dean to death lays bare the "most dangerous aberration of character."[12] One newspaper described Karla as "an animal driven by impulse and not conscience,"[13] and the state's attorney stated that Karla unduly embellished her "masculine proclivity for sex and violence."[14]

The evil woman concept is inexplicable to the execution of poor and marginalized women of color because crime evaluators' perceptions of these women have never allowed such women to rise to the privileged position as that of affluent white women in the United States—"white womanhood, pure and noble, was to be honored, black womanhood was something animalistic."[15] Historian Winthrop Jordan explains, for instance, that very early in the formation of white attitudes toward black females, whites largely perceived Africans as linked to apes, bestiality, and devoid of humanness. Black women were at the core of this irrationality; early American attitudes perceived the sexual union of apes and Negroes as involving female Negroes and male apes in that apes had intercourse with Negro women, and that this association functioned to maintain social distance between the Negro and white men. The notion that black women are devoid of "womanliness" remains today. White men in American society view black women as having less social value than have white women. Interviews with black middle-class women about their encounters with white men consistently reveal that white men still refer to black women in disparaging racist terms. Critical scholars also recognize that academics lack a decisive moral compass when using such disparaging historical stereotypes of black women as *mammy, matriarchal, welfare mom,* and *Jezebel*. As Huey and Lynch explain,

> The treatment of Black women in criminology is indicative of the interplay of patriarchy and racism that has dominated Western thought in the United States. Theoretical distortions are not accidental, but are a function of and necessity of domination. We need to be cognizant of the fact that criminologists, like others, influenced by systems of domination, reproduce these relations and myths in theoretical explanations involving Black female offenders and victims.[16]

Deeply embedded in American colloquial thinking are similarly offensive stereotypes defying the "womanliness" of Mexican and American Indian women. As a colonizing power in the northernmost territories of Mexico, Anglo Americans used ethnic chauvinism as an ideological justification for repressing Mexicans in the southwest with executions, vigilante violence, and the expulsion of Mexicans from territories in the region. Interestingly, Anglos did not meet Mexicans at the outset with neutral and impartial attitudes. One scholar traces the nature and history of Anglo intolerance toward Mexicans to the anti–Catholicism and irrational fears of anything Spanish accenting 16th century Elizabethan England.[17] The early colonists to the British mainland settlements apparently carried fixed notions of Mexican Indian inferiority to the New World. Puritan colonists received an abundance of literature from England critical of the racial and cultural fusion of Mexican Indians and the Spanish. Most European writers depicted Spanish Mexico as a decadent and indolent society. Consequently, Anglos conditioned their initial responses to early encounters with Mexicans in the borderlands of the southwest upon the two European traditions of "anti–Catholicism" and "Hispanophobia." In keeping with their position as conquerors and colonizers of northern Mexico, Anglos venerated upper-class Mexican women for the ulterior motive of land procurement but marginalized lower-class Mexican females as "sexually promiscuous women of ill repute."[18] This perception of poor Mexican women gave way to powerful anti–Mexican sentiments that justified the killing of Mexican women early in the region's history.

Anglos have also burdened their historical perceptions of American Indian woman as *savages*, *heathens*, *pagans*, and as *primitive* and *uncivilized*. Despite the fictional image of Pocahontas produced by the Disney Corporation, the Anglo perception of American Indian women as *squaws* (a vulgar and disparaging label) has been stereotyped historically with traits of "drunkenness, stupidity, and thievery." Pocahontas—her real name was "Matowa"—was actually a pre-teen child subjected to "kidnapping and rape by white men, a trip to England, a marriage to a white planter, and early death from disease."[19] Negative perceptions of American Indian women unquestionably became a moral justification for their outright murder by Anglo Americans and the U.S. Calvary in the conflicts associated with the westward expansionism of the United States into territories held by indigenous populations. That defenseless women and children accounted for sizeable percentages of the dead in military campaigns is one reason why Indian populations so dramatically waned in the 18th and 19th centuries. As Stannard writes, "The European habit of indiscriminately killing women and children when engaged in hostilities with the natives of the Americas was more than an atrocity. It was flatly and intentionally genocidal. For no population can survive if its women and children [are] destroyed."[20] In a related context, white men sexually assaulted Indian women with impunity since the rape of an Indian woman historically was not a crime. Indian women had no legal standing; "an Indian woman's testimony regarding rape meant nothing in a white court of law. Her testimony could not convict a white man."[21] The law essentially rendered Indian women easy targets for sexual attack; they were sexually *violable* and *rapable*. Anglo rape of Indian women was integral to the colonial conquest of tribal natives. Still, unlike the historical record compiled from narratives of sexual violence experienced by bonded black servants of white planters during slavery, similar testaments are few for Indian women. American Indian women continue to have excessively high rates of homicide, rates of rape and sexual violence and other physical assaults mostly perpetrated by Anglo men. Interestingly, Mexican and American Indian women remain the predominant victims of sex trafficking in the United States.

Equality Theory

As a middle ground theory, equality theory claims that gender-neutral factors account for female executions. Equality theory explains that death penalty jurisdictions execute fewer women than men because female murderers are less death-eligible than are male murderers since women commit fewer murders than do men; women usually commit homicides that do not typically lead to capital sentences. In this regard, the capital justice system limits imposition of the death penalty to women who commit the most heinous predatory killings. For women whose crimes juries perceive as callous as male crimes, "she loses the advantage of her gender and is more harshly punished because of her violation of stereotypical gender expectations."[22] One scholar adds to this notion by first conceding that "it is clear that the death penalty does not sanction the most heinous crimes, but, rather, participates in the management of certain hierarchies of power," and then argues, "once convicted of capital murder, some are more likely to land on death row than others not because they committed the worst crimes as defined by statutory law, but because they do not properly enact a feminine gender identity."[23] Still, equality theory is no more applicable to explaining women executions than are chivalry and the evil woman theories. The historical record on women executions paints a tarnished portrait of only the most heinous female murderers suffering capital punishment. The objective reality of female executions throughout American history is that justice agents have executed women when they have challenged the sexist exploitation of white men. The executed women profiled in the chapters to this work reveal that gender-neutrality is incongruent with the contextual history of oppression accenting female executions in the United States.

A Critical Perspective

The more troubling limitation of the extant theories to the study of female executions in the United States is that the schemes overlook systemic *gender oppression* as a paradigmatic theme in the history of American capital justice; that the underlying function of gender oppression in American capital justice historically has been to severely punish women who challenge male supremacy in the patriarchal social order. Scholars have afforded negligible attention to gender and capital sentencing and therefore have developed theories devoid of the contextual history of gender oppression. The extant theories fail to account for the brutality of female state executions using sadistic killing methods, the disparate execution of black females, the execution of women wrongly convicted of capital crimes, the purposeful killing of innocent fetuses when executing pregnant women, the execution of convicted women already dead from suicide, and the monstrous mutilation of women's corpses after execution. The theories do not explain the countless women viciously murdered by slave masters with legal impunity, the prevalence of black female executions in Reconstruction and the neo-slavery of Jim Crow, or the cruelty experienced by women executed in the early civil rights movement. What's more, the theories fail to provide any rationalization to the sexist prosecutorial discretion in selecting capital cases; the unlawful prosecutorial use of peremptory challenges that systematically exclude marginalized women from juries in capital cases; the judicial override by trial judges in female capital cases; the unrelenting prosecutorial misconduct; the exploited mental incapacities of female capital defendants; the ineffective and frequently dismal assistance of defense lawyers in female capital cases; and wrongful convictions due to prosecutorial lawlessness, police coerced false confessions, and faulty forensic evidence.

A critical perspective views American society as a patriarchal system of male domination and female subordination wherein men maintain social, political, and economic dominance over women. As one scholar makes clear, the United States is a male-dominated society with men controlling every key institution: "military, industry, technology, universities, science, political office, and finance—in short, every avenue of power within the society."[24] Arguably, one can incorporate the capital justice system into this registry of key institutions. The capital justice system is a male-dominated institution designed to maintain the patriarchal social order by controlling women with the imposition of lethal violence—the ruthlessness of white male supremacy is a historically enduring feature of American capital justice. Gender inequality distinguishing American society results from patriarchy. One noted scholar defines patriarchy as "the manifestation and institutionalization of male dominance over women and children in the family and the extension of male dominance over women in society in general. It implies that men hold power in all the important institutions of society and that women are deprived of access to such power."[25] Gender inequality within the institutional structure of society is the product of *gender stratification* denoting the class hierarchy in American society. Society allocates access to valued resources and opportunities given one's placement in the social hierarchy; that is, the higher one's position in the social hierarchy the more access one has to valued resources and societal opportunities. Men largely occupy superior ranks at the top of the class hierarchy and have access to the greater share of social opportunities and resources, while women mostly occupy inferior ranks in the class hierarchy and have far less access to social opportunities and resources. The resources valued in a society are those that allocate societal privilege: material wealth, social status or social prestige, and political power. The dynamics of the gender stratification system are rooted in a disproportionate distribution of valued resources and result in two culturally distinct gender groups: a culturally dominant group of men and a culturally subordinate group of women. The dominant group maintains its elevated class position by controlling the production and distribution of valued resources. Men control access to valued resources such as education, jobs, and income, while women are largely unable to improve their position within the class hierarchy because they lack access to the necessary resources.

Structured gender inequality defines a social arrangement patterned socially and historically that is rooted in a sexist ideology (the belief that men are superior to women) that legitimates and justifies the subordination of women—meaning that social inequality is institutionalized. That is, gender inequality is structured: "stratification is not random, with groups and individuals occupying different positions by chance; rather, social institutions such as government, the economy, and education operate to assure the position of various groups"—meaning that the patterns of gender stratification are deliberate and purposeful.[26] A sexist ideology accents a historical record of consistent patterns of institutionalized gender discrimination in the United States. Because of this discrimination, American society systematically denies women full and equal participation in the major societal institutions. That is, men and women are *not* similarly situated in the economic, political, and social spheres of American society. In contrast to men, women fall far below national averages in levels of educational attainment, placement in the occupational structure, and income and poverty levels. The discrimination and segregation experienced by women in the patriarchal system results in narrow educational and occupational opportunities and limited economic growth for women. Female-headed households, for instance, comprise the largest proportions of impoverished persons in the United States. One explanation for high poverty rates among women is that their annual median incomes are significantly less than the annual median incomes of men. Lower female incomes result from women's lower placement in the occupational structure of the United States—women are traditionally overrepresented in lower-paying jobs as librarians, registered nurses, elementary school teachers, secretaries, stenographers, typists, receptionists, and private household workers, while men are overrepresented in higher-paying jobs as engineers, lawyers and judges, physicians, dentists, in precision production jobs and craft workers. Gender discrimination in the American workplace ensures the occupational segregation of women to lower paying jobs and thereby limits competiveness with men for higher-paying jobs. That is, the dynamics of discrimination and segregation confine women to a subordinate position in United States society because it continually produces and reproduces the deeply embedded sexist relations that privilege white males while concomitantly leaving females disadvantaged. The intersection of sexism, gender bias, and structured gender inequality is *gender oppression*.

Social control of subordinate groups is essential to societal systems of intergroup domination and subordination. In such systems the dominant group implements repressive institutional strategies to control subordinate groups. In effect, the law is *a repressive institution that utilizes criminal justice as a systemic tool for maintaining differential power relations between the dominant group and subordinate groups*. State sanctioned violence is integral to the control, domination, and exploitation of subordinate groups. As one scholar puts forward, "the coercive power of the state, embodied in law and legal repression, is the traditional means of maintaining the social and economic interests of the dominant group."[27] Sentencing a person to death is an absolute "flexing of state power."[28] The capital justice system has evolved into American society's most tyrannical institution in engaging the brutality of lethal punishment against women to maintain white male dominance. Essentially, criminal justice is "the strong arm of the stratification system."[29] Despite the righteous rhetoric of judges, prosecutors, and other judicial officers to the constitutional cannons of equity, fairness, and evenhandedness in capital justice processes, the capital justice system furthers gender oppression in the United States. Since the earliest periods of American colonial history, female death penalty cases offer persuasive evidence that gender bias in capital sentencing has been purposeful, deliberate, and calculating—individual and institutional biases against women are entrenched and routinized historically in capital sentencing.

It follows that the dominant group defines as *criminal* those activities of subordinate group members that the dominant group perceives as a threat to its interests. One commentator explains the arrangement this way: "The ruling caste defines those acts as crimes that fit its needs and purposes and characterizes as criminal individuals who commit certain kinds of illegal acts, while similar acts are exempted from persecution and escape public disapprobation because they are not perceived as criminal or a threat to society."[30] The law, and its repressive use of the death penalty perpetuates a structuration of inequality that criminalizes individuals of marginalized groups.[31] Critical theory explains that persons who are economically and socially disadvantaged in the greater society are those persons who are differentially processed through the criminal justice system. Sexist imposition of capital punishment remains an artifact of the justice system because the discriminatory conduct of justice professionals is built into the system's structure and legitimated by American cultural beliefs and legal codes. In this regard, the gender animus upon which criminal justice practitioners make their decisions becomes the moral justification for imposing differential punishment on women. From a critical perspective, the United States criminal justice system uses the death penalty against those persons and groups of persons whose crimes victimize members, interests, or institutions of the powerful or dominant group in society.[32] The consequences of institutional sexism are not obscure and tangential aberrations of rogue justice administrators. Sexism is not fragmented and isolated in the system of justice; rather, the research record on the history of gender and capital sentencing shows clearly that sexism is endemic, integral, and central to its processes and procedures.

Capital Justice and the U.S. Supreme Court

For most of its history, the U.S. Supreme Court deferred to states' rights concerning capital punishment. During Earl Warren's tenure as Chief Justice of the Supreme Court, however, the court began examining the constitutionality of procedural and substantive rules on capital punishment when it set out to incorporate much of the Bill of Rights (the first 10 amendments to the federal constitution) as directives to states under the selective incorporation doctrine—"the process by which certain of the guarantees expressed in the Bill of Rights become applicable to the states through the Fourteenth Amendment."[33] The Court used the due process clause of that amendment to guarantee that states observe individual rights by ensuring that states make no laws abridging civil liberties and basic freedoms. The Court ultimately incorporated all of the assurances under the Bill of Rights to states *except* the right to keep and bear arms under the Second Amendment, the right to a grand jury indictment under the Fifth Amendment, the requirement of 12 jurors on a criminal jury under the Sixth Amendment, and the right to a civil jury under the Seventh Amendment.

The vast majority of U.S. Supreme Court decisions concerning application of the death penalty involve fashioning new *procedural* rules to state and federal government capital punishment schemes. Some of the more important procedural decisions in the use of capital punishment include the implementation of procedural safeguards against arbitrary and capricious imposition of the penalty, the elimination of judicial override schemes in capital cases, the exclusion of statistical studies proving racial bias in capital cases, death qualified juries, instructions ensuring that jurors understand the meaning of a life sentence, and that death penalty schemes allow for the admissibility of mitigating factors concerning capital defendants. In contrast, the Court has rendered relatively few *substantive* decisions barring death sentences to particular categories of defendants; prohibiting the execution of criminals in the absence of a victim's death, prohibiting the execution of mentally retarded persons, prohibiting the execution of juveniles and adult offenders for crimes committed as juveniles, and prohibiting the execution of insane persons.

The U.S. Supreme Court has never specifically addressed gender bias in capital sentencing despite the recognition of some Justices that partiality accents capital punishment imposition. Justice Douglas recognized that historically death penalty jurisdictions have imposed the punishment selectively based on "race, religion, wealth, social position, and class."[34] Justice Marshall remarked that there is "overwhelming evidence that the death penalty is employed against men and not women." To Marshall, "[i]t is difficult to understand why women have received such favored treatment since the purposes allegedly served by capital punishment seemingly are equally applicable to both sexes."[35] And the dissenters in one case worried that a "claim that racial bias has impermissibly tainted the capital sentencing decision, could be extended to apply to claims based on unexplained discrepancies that correlate to membership in other minority groups, and even to gender."[36] The Court has essentially limited its concern on arbitrariness in the administration of capital punishment to race and factually ignored gender bias. One critical commentator has explained the dilemma facing scholars in analysis of the equal protection of the law to women in American society:

> When we look at how women have been defined in U.S. law, we learn that we cannot separate the construction of race from the construction of gender. The ways in which women have been thought of in mainstream U.S. culture and in Supreme Court interpretations of the Constitution are very closely linked to the thinking that has shaped constructions of race.[37]

The more important decisions in death penalty cases include the implementation of procedural safeguards protecting capital defendants against race biased imposition of the penalty. In the aftermath of the Civil War and the emancipation of nearly four million former slaves, black defendants needed protection from a racist Southern judiciary that convicted impoverished and illiterate blacks, sending them to the gallows recurrently on fictitious charges and after unfair trials. Jim Crow–era Supreme Court cases proved effective in providing procedural safeguards to black defendants even if the Court did not take to task capital punishment substantively. Sentencing poor blacks to death ensured white domination over black people particularly in southern states. The Supreme Court reversed black defendants' convictions where trial courts violated procedural due process and equal protection. Klarman explains the similarities among many of the cases:

> Southern blacks were charged with serious crimes against whites: rape or murder. The defendants were nearly lynched before trial. Mobs consisting of hundreds or thousands of whites surrounded the courthouses, demanding that the defendants be turned over for execution. No change of venue was granted.... Lynchings were avoided only because state militiamen armed with machine guns surrounded the courthouse. Serious doubt existed—at the time of the trials, not just in retrospect—as to the guilt of the defendants. [Defendants] were tortured into confessing. Lawyers were appointed only a day or even less before trial, without adequate opportunity to consult clients, interview witnesses, or prepare defense strategy. Trials took place soon after the crime to avoid lynchings.... Trials lasted only a few hours ... and juries, from which blacks were intentionally excluded, deliberated only a few minutes before imposing death sentences.[38]

Despite procedural safeguards established throughout the 1920s and 1930s, race bias plagued capital sentencing well into the 1970s. It was then that the U.S. Supreme Court devised a rational structure of procedural safeguards ostensibly designed to curb discretion in capital sentencing. The Court developed these strategies in two landmark decisions: *Furman v. Georgia* and *Gregg v. Georgia*. In *McCleskey v. Kemp*, however, the Court recognized the failure of procedural safeguards to eliminate racial arbitrariness in capital cases and "acknowledged that a racially discriminatory—and in this way arbitrary—death penalty is an inevitable risk."[39]

Furman v. Georgia

Social scientists and legal scholars had amassed an impressive research record on racial bias in capital sentencing by the time the U.S. Supreme Court heard the *Furman* case in 1972. Studies on race and capital sentencing clearly demonstrated that jurisdictions applied the death penalty in a racially discretionary and discriminatory manner. The research record reveals that even in the earliest studies on race and capital punishment, the *race of the defendant* and the *race of the victim* were significant factors in jurisdictions imposing the death penalty. The defendant in *Furman* argued that his death sentence should be set aside because the jury had such complete and unbridled discretion in imposing the death penalty that it violated his constitutional rights to the "equal protection of the law" and against "cruel and unusual punishment." The case is important because it is not only the first time in the Court's history that it set aside a death sentence, but the case also represents the first instance in which the Court undertook the question of race bias in capital sentencing.

Furman involved the death sentence of William Henry Furman, Jr., a black man and sixth grade dropout with mild mental deficiencies and prone to epileptic seizures, shot and killed William J. Micke, Jr., a white Coast Guard petty officer and father of five, during a burglary of Micke's home in August 1967 in Savannah, Georgia. When Micke discovered Furman in the house, Furman tripped and fell and the gun that he was carrying went off and killed Micke. Furman quickly left the house but police found him a short time later under the porch of his father's house. A jury convicted Furman of murder and sentenced him to death. The Court agreed with Furman's contention that his jury's discretion in imposing the death penalty violated constitutional protections. A lower court eventually commuted Furman's death sentence to a life prison term. Correctional authorities paroled Furman in April 1984, but in 2004 he pleaded guilty to burglary and a Georgia court sentenced him to 20 years in prison. Furman remains incarcerated in state prison with a possible release date of March 2016.

There was no single opinion of the Court in *Furman*; many scholars hallmark the case as an exceedingly complex opinion with each of the nine Justices writing separate opinions either concurring or dissenting with the Court's judgment. A majority of the Justices supported Furman's position and held that Georgia's process of sentencing defendants to death denied condemned prisoners' equal protection of the law and amounted to cruel and unusual punishment. The Court was concerned with the extent to which standardless sentencing had informed capital cases. The Justices made it clear that death penalty jurisdictions had to devise procedural strategies restricting the unbridled discretion of juries remanding prisoners to death. Initially, many scholars interpreted *Furman* as the abolition of the death penalty in the United States, but nowhere in the decision did the Court hold capital punishment *per se* unconstitutional. Rather, it was the arbitrary and capricious imposition of the death penalty that the Court found constitutionally troubling. In the aftermath of *Furman*, the Justices vacated hundreds of cases immediately before the Court and other cases involving death row inmates. The decision rendered defective the death penalty statutes of 39 states, the District of Columbia, and the federal government. As one commentator explains,

> Two thirds of the condemned were on Southern death rows, the most by far in Florida and Texas, with Georgia and Louisiana close behind. All of the eighty-one who had been condemned for rape were in the South, nearly one-third of them in Florida, with Georgia and Louisiana tied for second place. Fifty-five percent of the capital offenders were black, 43 percent white, 1 percent His-

panic. Records also showed that juries had rarely allowed the men's backgrounds to have any mitigating effect on their sentences. True, most had previously committed crimes, but these were usually property crimes. Nearly three-fourths had never been convicted of a violent crime. Only 39 percent had ever before been in an adult court.[40]

Gregg v. Georgia

Researchers conducted studies on racial bias in capital sentencing during the period after the U.S. Supreme Court decided *Furman*, but before the Court handed down its decision in *Gregg*. These studies show that the Supreme Court's holding in *Furman* had no diminishing effect on the extent to which jurisdictions subjected black capital offenders to racial bias in imposing capital punishment, especially in cases involving black defendants who victimized white persons. Not surprisingly, analyses conducted since *Gregg* reveal further that the guidelines established in the case have failed to eliminate racial disparities in capital cases. *Gregg* marks the beginning of the modern era in capital punishment when the U.S. Supreme Court affirmed the constitutionality of the death penalty for aggravated murder. The question before the Court in *Gregg* was whether the Eighth and Fourteenth Amendments to the federal Constitution prohibit imposition of capital punishment under Georgia's revised death penalty statute.

The case resulted from Troy Leon Gregg's participation in the armed robbery and murder of Fred Edward Simmons and Bob Durwood Moore in 1973. Gregg admitted to police that he killed Simmons and Moore by shooting them in the head and then robbing them and stealing their car. A Georgia jury convicted Gregg of murder and sentenced him to death. On appeal, the U.S. Supreme Court affirmed Gregg's conviction and death sentence based on Georgia's revised death penalty statute that provided for bifurcated trials, consideration of mitigating circumstances of the defendant and the crime, and appellate review of capital sentences. The Court affirmed these guidelines because Georgia intended them to prevent biased imposition of the death penalty. In other cases decided the same day as *Gregg*, the Court declared North Carolina and Louisiana's death penalty statutes unconstitutional because the provisions in these statutes allowed no room for consideration of individual mitigating circumstances, and the jury's power to determine the degree of the crime in light of the mandatory penalty for first-degree murder did not safeguard against the biased imposition of the death sentences. Interestingly, Troy Gregg escaped with four other death-row prisoners the night before his execution and patrons of a "biker bar" in North Carolina beat him to death.

McCleskey v. Kemp

In 1978, a Fulton County jury in Georgia convicted a black man named Warren McCleskey for murdering a white police officer during an armed robbery of the Dixie Furniture Store. The evidence presented at McCleskey's trial indicates that he entered the front of the store and three accomplices entered the rear. McCleskey rounded up the customers and forced them to lie face down on the floor. The other three rounded up employees in the rear and tied them up with tape. During the course of the robbery, a police officer, answering a silent alarm, entered the store through the front door. As he was walking down the center aisle of the store, one or more of the assailants fired two shots with both bullets striking the police officer and one hitting him in the face and killing him. Police arrested McCleskey weeks later in connection with an unrelated crime. McCleskey confessed that he had participated in the furniture store robbery, but denied that he had shot the police officer. At trial, state prosecutors introduced evidence that at least one of the bullets that struck the officer came from a .38-caliber Rossi revolver, forensically matched to the gun McCleskey carried during the robbery. Georgia also introduced testimony from two witnesses who had heard McCleskey admit to the shooting.

McCleskey's conviction conformed to Georgia's capital statute prohibiting juries from sentencing a defendant to death for murder without first finding that the defendant had aggravated the crime by at least one of 10 circumstances. McCleskey failed to present any mitigating evidence and the jury sentenced him to death. On appeal to the U.S. Supreme Court, McCleskey claimed that Georgia administered its capital sentencing process in a bias manner in violation of the Eighth Amendment protection against cruel and unusual punishment, and that the biased sentencing system violated his Fourteenth Amendment guarantee to equal protection of the law. In support of his claim, McCleskey proffered the results of one of the most methodologically powerful studies of racial bias in capital sentencing to date. In this study, Iowa University Professor David Baldus and his associates analyzed nearly 2500 murder and non-negligent manslaughter cases in Georgia between 1973 and 1979. Baldus had controlled for some 230 nonracial variables and found that none of the variables could account for disparities in capital sentences among different defendant-victim racial categories. Baldus maintained that the state jurisdictions under study were 4.3 times more likely to sentence to death convicted murders of whites than convicted murders of blacks, and these jurisdictions were 1.1 times more likely to sentence black defendants to death than other defendants.[41] Accordingly, McCleskey claimed that race bias had infected the administration of the death penalty in Georgia in two distinct ways: (1) that jurisdictions were more likely to sentence murderers of whites to death than were murderers of blacks; and (2) that jurisdictions were more likely to sentence black murderers to death than white murderers. McCleskey alleged that Georgia's system of imposing the death penalty discriminated against him as a black man who killed a white man.

The question before the U.S. Supreme Court in *McCleskey* was whether a complex statistical study indicating a risk that racial consideration enters into capital sentencing determinations is unconstitutional under the Eighth and Fourteenth Amendments. In April 1987, Justice Powell, joined by Justices Rehnquist, White, O'Connor, and Scalia, delivered the opinion of the Court concerning McCleskey's claims. Justice Powell held that the Baldus study did not prove that Georgia's capital punishment system was unconstitutional. The court held that a defendant who alleges an equal protection violation has the burden of proving the existence of purposeful discrimination, and that the purposeful discrimination had a discriminatory effect on him. To the court, then, McCleskey had to prove that the jury in his particular case acted with a discriminatory purpose. To establish only that a pattern of racial discrimination in imposing the death penalty to a select group of defendants is not sufficient to support an equal protection claim. Further, the court held that McCleskey's claim of cruel and unusual punishment failed: McCleskey could not prove a constitutional violation by demonstrating that other defendants who may have been similarly situated did not receive the death penalty. The Court found that Georgia's sentencing procedures were sufficient to focus discretion on the particularized nature of the crime and the particularized characteristics of the individual defendant, and that it cannot, therefore, be presumed that McCleskey's death sentence was "wantonly and freakishly" imposed.

Essentially, the Court argued that discrimination in capital sentencing was negligible. The Court found that there are acceptable standards of risk of discrimination in imposing the death penalty. Accordingly, empirical studies simply showing that a discrepancy appears to correlate with race in imposing death sentences do not prove that race enters into any particular capital sentencing decision or that race is a factor in the petitioner's case. [This is the same rationale prohibiting male defendants from arguing sex discrimination in capital cases; the male defendant would have to show that sex or gender was part of the sentencing decision in their particular case.] Admittedly, the court was concerned that a finding for the defendant would open other claims extending to other types of penalties and to claims based on unexplained discrepancies correlating to membership in other minority groups including gender. Justice Powell feared that racial bias is systemic in the justice system and that formally recognizing that fact would undermine the legitimacy of the system:

> McCleskey's claim, taken to its logical conclusion, throws into serious question the principles that underlie our entire criminal justice system. The Eighth Amendment is not limited in application to capital punishment, but applies to all penalties. Thus, if we accepted McCleskey's claim that racial bias has impermissibly tainted the capital sentencing decision, we could soon be faced with similar claims as to other types of penalties. There is no limiting principle to the type of challenge brought by McCleskey. The Constitution does not require that a State eliminate any demonstrable disparity that correlates with a potentially irrelevant factor in order to operate a criminal justice system that includes capital punishment.

Justices Brennan, Blackmun, and Stevens filed dissenting opinions, with whom Justice Marshall joined in part. The dissenting justices claimed that McCleskey had clearly demonstrated that his death sentence violated the Eighth and Fourteenth Amendments. They found that nothing could convey more powerfully the reality of capital sentencing in the United States: "the effort to eliminate arbitrariness in the infliction of that ultimate sanction is so plainly doomed to failure that it and the death penalty must be abandoned altogether." The dissenters argued that whether McCleskey can prove discrimination in his particular case is irrelevant in evaluating his claim of a constitutional violation since the Court had long recognized that establishing a pattern of substantial risk of arbitrary and capricious capital sentencing suffices for a claim of unconstitutionality. The dissenting justices also called into question the effectiveness of the statutory safeguards designed to curb discretionary use of the death penalty. Justice Brennan specifically argued, "While we may hope that a model of procedural fairness will curb the influence of race on sentencing, we cannot simply assume that the model works as intended; we must critique its performance in terms of its results." The dissenting justices were particularly dismayed by the court's fear that finding McCleskey's claim sufficient would "open the door to widespread challenges to all aspects of criminal sentencing." To Justice Brennan, the court's rejection of McCleskey's evidence of discrimination in imposition of the death penalty on the basis that it would open further challenges to criminal sentencing "is to ignore both the qualitatively different character of the death penalty and the particular repugnance of racial discrimination." As one commentator on the *McCleskey* decision put it: "It is unimaginable that the U.S. Supreme Court, an institution vested with the responsibility to achieve equal justice under the law for all Americans, could issue an opinion that accepted the inevitability of racial bias in an area as serious and final as capital punishment. However, it is precisely this acceptance of bias and the tolerance of racial discrimination that has come to define America's criminal justice system."[42] In a speech at Columbia University in 2007, Anthony G. Amsterdam, who worked on the *McCleskey* case, stated that "*McCleskey* is the *Dred Scott* decision of our time—it is a decision for which our children's children will reproach our generation and abhor the legal legacy we leave them."[43] Georgia officials electrocuted Warren McCleskey in September 1991.

The most apparent conclusion one can draw from the historical record on capital sentencing is that the U.S. Supreme Court has failed miserably in its attempt to eliminate race bias in capital punishment. As Steiker and Steiker explain, "[t]he Supreme Court's death penalty law, by creating an impression of enormous regulatory effort while achieving negligible regulatory effects, effectively obscures the true nature of our capital sentencing system" and in so doing "legitimates the imposition of capital punishment both for participants in the legal system and for the public at large."[44] The Court formally recognized the pervasiveness of racial prejudice in capital sentencing in *Furman* and attempted to create a rational structure of procedural safeguards to curb racial arbitrariness and capriciousness capital sentencing in *Gregg*. The Court, however, summarily rejected the notions of fairness and evenhandedness in capital sentencing when it discarded in *McCleskey* exceptionally plausible evidence that racially discriminatory patterns remain in capital sentencing. Yet, even in the face of overwhelming statistical proof that race-based discrimination typifies the imposition of capital punishment in the United States, the elimination of prejudice, inequality, and caprice in capital sentencing has yet to move to the forefront of judicial thinking on capital punishment.

Capital Justice and Women in the Modern Era

The historical record on gender and capital sentencing reveals that the United States justice system has fully institutionalized sexism in capital sentencing. Indeed, imposition of capital punishment is integral to the United States maintaining its hierarchical social relations of gender-based privilege and perpetuating the inequality of women. As such, the death penalty is an exceptionally effective means in oppressing women and preserving white male interests—as one commentator put it, "capital punishment works as a social practice of oppression."[45] Major obstacles to implementing procedural and substantive protections designed to minimize gender bias in capital sentencing in today's capital justice system include: the chronic underfunding of indigent defense services by state and local governments; the unbridled discretion of state prosecutors in filing capital charges against women; the consistent marginalization of lesbian defendants to juries by prosecutors; the prosecution of mentally retarded and insane women in capital cases; prosecutorial lawlessness in female capital cases; and the use of judicial override in capital cases.

Poverty

Impoverished women disproportionately populate death rows because they are too poor to pay for private attorneys and must rely on public defenders or other appointed lawyers. It is axiomatic that if women overly represent the indigent capital defense population, then women unduly suffer poor lawyering in the capital justice system. Vick explains the problem:

> Approximately ninety percent of those charged with capital murder are indigent when arrested, and virtually all are indigent by the time their cases reach the appellate courts. These defendants are entirely dependent on others for the resources necessary to develop and present a defense at trial and to pursue an appeal. While the ultimate constitutional responsibility for providing indigent defense services in capital cases rests with the state, state governments have rarely regarded this constitutional responsibility as one that carries with it significant financial obligations. Most states have shifted the economic cost of defending the poor in criminal cases to individual lawyers asked to represent criminal defendants for woefully inadequate compensation or to severely underfunded public defender offices. This policy has had a disastrous impact on the quality of defense services provided in capital cases.[46]

The U.S. Supreme Court recognized in *Furman* that "one searches our chronicles in vain for the execution of any member of the affluent strata of this society."[47] Justice Marshall specifically commented: "It is the poor, and the members of minority groups who are least able to voice their complaints against capital punishment. Their impotence leaves them victims of a sanction that the wealthier, better-represented, just-as-guilty person can escape." The Pennsylvania Committee on Racial and Gender Bias in the Justice System pointed out in its report that one cannot separate race, ethnic, and gender bias from the issues of poverty: "Unless the poor, among whom minority communities are overrepresented, are provided adequate legal representation, including ample funds for experts and investigators, there cannot be a lasting solution to the issue of racial and ethnic [and gender] bias in the capital justice system."[48] Poverty is an aggravating factor for female capital defendants because they cannot afford private attorneys who often succeed in mitigating capital sentences. Poor female capital defendants must rely on court appointed lawyers or public defenders. Fogelman explains the inherent deficiencies in legal representation for indigent defendants.

> The poor are often represented by inexperienced lawyers who view their responsibilities as a burden and who have no real inclination to assist their clients. Other significant problems that plague indigent defense services include fee caps for appointed counsel; enormous caseloads and overworked public defender offices; low prestige and a lack of public support; and insufficient funding to pay necessary expert witnesses. Compounding these obstacles facing defendants, some defense attorneys often fail to request aid to which indigent defendants are entitled under certain circumstances. Because the indigent disproportionately receive appointed counsel, they risk being stuck with an attorney who is incapable of zealously advocating on their behalf, and, in some instances, who will fall asleep during trial, thus depriving them of their Sixth Amendment rights.[49]

An analysis by the *Associated Press* reveals that the Sixth U.S. Circuit Court of Appeals has overturned 61 percent of death sentences in Ohio since 1981 for ineffective assistance of counsel. The Ninth U.S. Circuit Court of Appeals has overturned 48 percent of death sentences for attorney incompetence in California. In one case, a Texas Court of Criminal Appeals ruled that a defendant's attorney did not deprive his client of effective assistance of counsel though the attorney slept through much of the *voir dire* and through most other critical stages of the capital trial. Besides sleeping during the trial, the attorney spent only four hours preparing for trial and "did not examine the crime scene, interviewed no witnesses, prepared no motions, did not request that any subpoenas be issued, relied solely on what was in the prosecutor's file, and visited his client only twice."[50] Florida Supreme Court Justice Raoul Cantero has openly criticized the quality of private lawyers handling appeals for death row inmates. Justice Cantero claims that Florida attorneys have botched cases, muddled and omitted key arguments, and performed the worst lawyering he has ever seen.

A disturbingly high percentage of capital defense lawyers representing indigent defendants are subject to disciplinary actions. North Carolina's state bar has sanctioned more than *one in six* trial attorneys representing death row inmates for committing felonies, embezzling money, intentionally prejudicing clients or failing to represent clients diligently. Disciplined attorneys represented four of the 21 defendants executed in North Carolina since the state reinstated capital punishment in 1977. Texas officials discipline trial lawyers representing death row inmates at a rate *eight times* the rate of lawyers generally. Tennessee's state bar has disciplined 39 trial lawyers representing capital defendants. Virginia trial lawyers representing capital defendants are subjected to disciplinary proceedings at a rate *six times* that of other lawyers. Lawyers that officials later disbarred or suspended have represented 25 percent of Kentucky's death row inmates. To one reporter, people facing a death sentence in Washington are frequently represented by some of the state's worst lawyers. Reports by judges to the Washington Supreme Court on state lawyer disciplinary records reveal that "one-fifth of the 84 people who have faced execution in the past 20 years were represented by lawyers who had been, or were later, disbarred, suspended or arrested."[51] And in a *New York Times* article, Anthony Lewis, the author of *Gideon's Trumpet*, pointed out that disbarred or suspended lawyers represented four of the 13 exonerated capital defendants in Illinois between 1987 and 2000. Studies in other states reveal similar results of incompetent death penalty lawyers.

Clearly, the Sixth Amendment right to counsel does not equate to competent counsel for poor defendants. Indeed, "tales of the pathetically inadequate representation many capital defendants receive are legion."[52] In *Gregg*, the U.S. Supreme Court touted bifurcated trials in capital cases as a procedural devise calculated to eradicate capricious and arbitrary imposition of the death penalty. Bifurcated trials give defense lawyers an opportunity to present mitigating evidence to persuade juries to spare the convicted defendant's life. Yet, as Justice Marshall noted, federal reporters are filled with stories of lawyers who failed to present mitigating evidence on behalf of their clients simply because the lawyer did not know what to offer, how to offer it, or because the lawyer had not read the state's sentencing statute.[53] Justice Ginsburg has explained, "I have yet to see a death case among the dozens coming to the Supreme Court on eve-of-execution stay applications in which the defendant was well represented at trial.... People who are well represented at trial do not get the death penalty."[54]

Ineffective defense lawyers perpetuate gender bias in capital sentencing when they fail to challenge procedures that preclude fairness to defendants in capital trials. Procedural errors involving bias claims are unsuccessful for defendants because defense lawyers fail to raise the claims at required times. Defense lawyers often fail to present evidence in domestic murder cases involving black women in abusive relationships. In the case of Louise Harris, for instance, defense counsel failed to provide the jury with evidence that Louise had a long history of abuse and trauma:

> She had been sexually assaulted at age 11; she had witnessed her older sister die suddenly of a seizure in her arms, leaving Louise, at age 14, to raise her younger siblings; she had seen her younger brother being pulled from a lake after he drowned, and she had been the one to discover the body of her father, who was murdered. She had also been beaten severely and regularly by her first husband, John Wesley Robinson; she had been abused for years by her husband common-law husband Jesse Lee Hall and then by her husband Isaiah Harris, resulting in multiple trips to the hospital; and she was also abused by the man from whom she had sought comfort, Lorenzo McCarter. This abuse and trauma resulted in Louise suffering from Post-Traumatic Stress Disorder, Battered Women's Syndrome and Dissociative Disorder.[55]

Other cases show that women convicted of capital crimes often receive inadequate representation at trial. The trial attorney that represented Blanche Kiser Taylor Moore in her capital case, for instance, while suffering from severe depression and other mental health problems. Wanda Jean Allen's defense counsel recognized his inability to competently represent Wanda and sought to be removed the case or to have assistance from the state public defender's office, or at the very least to be assigned an experienced investigator. But an Oklahoma court turned down these requests and, as a result, Wanda's attorney failed to introduce well-documented evidence of her mental retardation and consequently the court never fully litigated the issue. Defense lawyers in Sabrina Butler's case, a black woman who spent five years on Mississippi's death row for killing her infant son, failed to support their contention with adequate evidence that the child's injuries resulted from Sabrina's attempts to resuscitate the child. A jury later acquitted Sabrina of murder at a second trial when a defense lawyer proffered corroborated evidence from a neighbor who tried to help Sabrina revive the child, and an admission from the autopsy physician of shoddy forensic work. Frances Elaine Newton repeatedly requested that the trial court dismiss her count-appointed attorney. Frances's defense attorneys maintained in a clemency petition that her attorney failed to investigate claims that authorities found a second gun at the crime scene, and accounts from a relative of Frances's that a cellmate bragged about going to Frances's house the night of the killings to collect a drug debt "with orders to kill everybody present if the man did not have the money."[56] What's more, at least three jurors that heard Frances's case argued that they would not have convicted Frances had they known of all the evidence. Texas executed seven previous death penalty clients represented by France's attorney and the Texas Defenders Service found that the lawyer failed a required certification exam to become eligible for appointment to capital murder cases.

Scholars place much of the blame for the ineffective assistance of counsel in cases involving poor defendants at the doorstep of the U.S. Supreme Court. Astoundingly, the Supreme Court has found ineffective assistance of counsel in only three capital cases throughout its history. And as one appellate lawyer points out, "Despite the parade of drunk, sleeping, unprepared, inexperienced, and otherwise inadequate attorneys that fill the pages of digests and regional reporters, the Court has ... given no indication that it believes there to be a serious problem with the quality of capital representation."[57] The Court recognized more than 80 years ago in *Powell v. Alabama* that ineffective assistance of counsel violates an indigent defendant's constitutional rights, but the Court did not actually define ineffective assistance of counsel until 1984 in *Strickland v. Washington*. There, an appeals court found ineffective assistance of counsel when confessed murderer David Leroy Washington's attorney failed to investigate the circumstances of the crime and Washington's life history, reputation, level of intelligence, and psychology. There, the U.S. Supreme Court held that to support a claim of ineffective assistance of counsel a capital defendant must show (1) that the defense lawyer's representation fell below acceptable standards of legal practice, and (2) that the lawyers incompetence prejudiced the outcome of the trial—"that there is a reasonable probability that with better counsel, the outcome of his trial would have been different."[58]

Until *Wiggins v. Smith* in 2003, the Supreme Court had not reversed a single capital case on grounds of ineffective assistance of counsel. In *Wiggins*, the Court expanded its view of ineffective assistance of counsel in capital cases to include defense lawyers' failure to investigate a defendant's social history and to do a proper penalty phase investigation. Then, in 2005 in *Pompilla v. Beard*, the Court ruled that defense counsels' failure to investigate mitigating evidence amounted to ineffective assistance of counsel. Trial lawyers failed to adequately investigate Rompilla's school records, history of alcohol dependence, juvenile and adult incarceration records, and a prior rape conviction. Scholars argue that the ineffective assistance of counsel occurs in capital cases involving mentally retarded defendants when trial lawyers fail to recognize and present evidence of the defendant's mental retardation. In any event, the future does not look bright for poor female capital defendants waging claims of ineffective assistance of counsel beyond *Strickland* given newer appointments to the Court. Justice Alito, for instance, often dissented while on the Third Circuit Court Appeals in cases involving ineffective assistance of counsel and frequently disagreed with his brethren on issues of bias in jury selection.

Prosecutorial Discretion

Arguably, state and federal prosecutors possess unbridled discretion in filing criminal charges against persons accused of crime. As some scholars argue, while the courts are willing to impose formidable restrictions on the discretionary powers of police, sentencing judges, parole boards, and correctional officers, they are unwilling for the most part to restrict prosecutorial discretion. As U.S. Supreme Court Justice Brennan so fittingly argued in his dissent in *DeGarno v. Texas*, "The decision whether to prosecute, what offense to prosecute, whether to plea bargain or not to negotiate at all are made at the unbridled discretion of individual prosecutors. The prosecutor's choices are subject to no standards, no supervision, no controls whatsoever."[59] Indeed, the charging discretion of prosecutors remains largely unregulated, unreviewable, and for the most part, there is no public accountability. Prosecutors alone determine the seriousness of criminal charges brought against suspects.

The power of prosecutors to determine which cases to prosecute is not absolute, however. As Superior Court Judge Arthur L. Burnett for the District of Columbia explains, "Prosecutors have an affirmative duty to make sure that racial and national origin bias, as well as gender bias and prejudice, do not enter into their charging decisions. In the course of the trial of the case, prosecutors must ensure that they do not *consciously* or *unconsciously* inject racial, national origin, or gender biases and prejudices into the trial" [emphasis added].[60] Whereas the adversarial nature of criminal proceedings ostensibly offers impartiality in state and federal prosecutions, *fairness* in selective prosecution remains elusive in capital cases. Repeatedly, prosecutors breach ethical rules of professional conduct and deliberately deny indigent defendants constitutional protections. A central finding of empirical studies on the impact of prosecutorial discretion in seeking the death penalty in homicide cases is that prosecutors' bias attitudes shape the administration of capital punishment. Essentially, arbitrariness and discrimination characterize prosecutors' exercise of their unfettered discretion to select death penalty cases. Prosecutors often seek the death penalty based on legally inappropriate factors such as race, gender, and geographic location. A recent study by the American Bar Association found that prosecutors, in direct violation of a defendant's Sixth Amendment right to counsel, knowingly seek waivers of counsel and guilty pleas from unrepresented persons, and that judges accept and even encourage waivers of counsel where defendants have not knowingly, voluntarily, and intelligently waived counsel.

Jurisdictions commonly consign decisions to seek the death penalty exclusively to the discretion of prosecutors, and no jurisdiction has implemented guidelines to control how prosecutors decide on seeking the death penalty. Most state prosecutors are white males in death penalty states, and certainly the pervasiveness of white male prosecutors presupposes an unconscious bias toward marginalized persons that influences charging decisions in capital cases. White male prosecutors, for instance, undoubtedly have absorbed the cultural stereotype of *black inferiority* and perceive black defendants as more *violent* and more *dangerous* than white defendants. Prosecutorial decision-making fraught with bias surely challenges the idea that prosecutors seek the death penalty *objectively*. But prosecutors deny that bias effects prosecutorial decision-making. Nunn makes it clear that prosecutors are a major source of systemic bias in the criminal justice system primarily because they refuse to deal with the problem.

> Though prosecutors assert that there is no racial bias in the exercise of prosecutorial discretion, they have done little to verify this belief, or dispel the concerns of others. Prosecutors have rarely commissioned studies, promulgated internal guidelines, or made attempts to keep voluntary statistics on prosecutorial racial bias. Few prosecutors have taken it upon themselves to maintain a dialogue on these issues within their offices. There is little effort to sensitize prosecutors or provide diversity training. Even more disappointing than the lack of prosecutorial effort to determine the extent of racial bias in prosecutorial decision-making, is that prosecutors actively oppose the efforts of others to do so. Prosecutors have vehemently opposed legislative attempts to gather information regarding bias in the imposition of death sentencing and in automobile stops.[61]

Commentators deny that conscious bias permeates prosecutorial decision-making. Others concede that prosecutors suffer from unconscious bias when seeking capital charges against black defendants. Pokorak explains it this way:

> [U]nconscious bias may creep into the prosecutors' decisions to seek the death penalty. The predominantly white prosecutors may perceive violent crimes against whites as more serious than similar crimes against minorities and thus seek the death penalty more frequently against defendants accused of killing white victims. Conversely, white prosecutors may have an unconscious perception of blacks as inferior and may view violent crimes against blacks as less serious and less worthy of the death penalty than similar crimes against whites.[62]

One result of bias prosecutorial discretion in selecting capital cases is that 81 percent of all capital cases tried by prosecutors involve white victims, while nationally only half of all murder victims are white. Nearly two-thirds of women currently residing on the nation's death row murdered white persons. Execution data show similar disparities. Since 1976, death penalty officials have executed 20 white defendants for killing blacks but 275 black defendants for killing whites—revealing that authorities are nearly *14 times more likely to execute black defendants with white victims than white defendants with black victims*. Bias infiltrates the federal death penalty system as readily as it does state capital justice systems; federal prosecutors are excessive in selecting blacks for capital punishment as well—nearly three-quarters of federal and U.S. military death-row inmates are black. A U.S. Department of Justice study of federal death penalty prosecutions between 1995 and 2000, for instance, found that the attorney general approved death penalty prosecution for 72 percent of the cases involving non-white defendants. Moreover, federal prosecutors were twice as likely to seek the death penalty for black defendants with nonblack victims as for black defendants with black victims. Some scholars suggest reforming prosecutorial discretion with race impact studies by prosecutors, and others have recommended jury nullification and the hiring of more black prosecutors.

Prosecutorial Homophobia

One contemptible feature of gender oppression in capital justice is that mostly male prosecutors consistently marginalize lesbian defendants. Indeed, the capital justice system is a major location of homophobic-based oppression in United States society. Consequently, homophobia often informs prosecutorial decisions to seek the death penalty and defendants' sexuality recurrently becomes central to capital trials involving lesbian defendants. A result of prosecutors exploiting lesbianism to denigrate women in capital cases is that lesbians disproportionately occupy death row. Prosecutors use lesbian women's transgression of feminine stereotypes to show the *dangerousness* of lesbian capital defendants and that lesbian killers deserve the death penalty. While more than half the women on death row are lesbian, one national study finds that only slightly more than 3 percent of the American population is lesbian. This means that lesbians are represented on death row more than *81 times* their proportionate representation in the greater society. Some 40 percent of women accused of murder must contend with prosecutorial assertions of lesbianism to purposefully masculate and dehumanize lesbians. Prosecutors resort to prejudices and stereotypes to marginalize female defendants and render them executable to jurors.

Disparaging lesbian capital defendants is largely successful since lesbians rarely sit as jurors. The U.S. Supreme Court has ruled that race and gender are unconstitutional rationales for excluding persons as jurors, but the Court has yet to find the same protection for sexual orientation. Interestingly, negative stereotypes toward lesbians significantly influence jurors' beliefs. Jurors are more than *three times* as likely to think they could not be fair or impartial toward a lesbian defendant as toward a defendant from other minority groups, such as Blacks, Hispanics, or Asian-Americans. Predictably, positive attitudes toward the death penalty correlate significantly with negative attitudes toward women and higher levels of homophobia, racism, and sexism. A poll by the *National Law Journal* found that about 17 percent of prospective jurors admitted to a bias which would make it impossible for them to be fair and impartial in a case in which one of the parties was homosexual. Other surveys show that roughly two-thirds of persons believe that homosexual relationships are "always wrong." To one commentator, "it is therefore not surprising that the jury trial has been called one of the most standardless operations in our entire judicial system."[63]

Prosecutors resort to marginalizing prejudices and stereotypes to render lesbian defendants more executable to jurors. This was the case when Wanda Jean Allen's lesbianism overwhelmed the state's case against her for the murder of her lesbian lover Gloria Leathers. Wanda shot and killed Leathers after pleading with her to continue their two-year relationship when the couple had been fighting over a welfare check at a local grocery store. During the trial, the prosecutor made erroneous assertions that Wanda dominated her lover when actually Wanda and Leathers fought frequently and often mistreated one another. To show that Wanda was the aggressive person in the relationship while Leathers was more passive, the prosecution inaccurately yet purposefully portrayed Allen as wearing "the pants in the family," that she was the masculine one in the relationship, and even urged the trial court's rejection of defense motions outlining Leathers' violent nature. The state's attorney also solicited testimony from Wanda's mother that Wanda used the male spelling of her middle name. Wanda's sexuality played a prominent role in her trial and "evidences again that when a woman acts out from society's gender expectations, she faces harsher penalties."[64] Wanda's case also provides a particularly egregious illustration of how prosecutorial racism taints capital cases. During closing argument, the prosecutor compared Wanda to an ape by showing the jury a greeting care belonging to Wanda with the picture of a gorilla on the cover and a caption that read "patience my ass, I'm going to kill something." While showing the card to the jury, the prosecutor said, "That's Wanda Allen in a nutshell."[65] Wanda was poor, black, lesbian, mentally challenged, and because of these characteristics, an Oklahoma prosecutor won her execution by lethal injection in January 2001.

> Allen was convicted on the basis of a rash of stereotypes about lesbians which, combined with stereotypes about black people and poor people, played off juror biases to portray Allen as an aggressive offender so dangerous to society that the only recourse was execution. One observer proposed that had Allen been a middle class, white heterosexual woman who killed her boyfriend, the jury would probably have been more sympathetic and Allen's sentence would have been considerably lighter.[66]

Prosecutorial homophobia was central in the 1999 murder trial of Bernina Mata, a Latina lesbian, in Boone County, Illinois. During Bernina's trial where the state claimed that she had killed a man she had met at a bar after making unwanted sexual passes at her, the prosecutor paraded no less than 10 witnesses before the jury testifying to Bernina's lesbianism and introduced innocuous books found at her home as proof that Bernina was a lesbian. The state's homophobic prosecutor made reference to Bernina's lesbianism on 17 different occasions throughout her trial. He argued that Bernina was "overly homosexual," of "flaunting her sexuality," of "proclaiming her sexuality to anyone who would listen," that she was "a hard core lesbian," and that a heterosexual woman would not have resorted to murder under the circumstances. All this, in light of the state's stipulation before trial of Bernina's lesbianism. But, as capital defense attorney Joey Mogul has made clear, "they wanted to repeatedly flaunt Miss Mota's lesbianism in front of this jury because they knew that some jurors in Boone County would find it distasteful, while others would deem her to be sick, perverted, and deserving of death."[67]

Mentally Impaired Defendants

Though the ruling came too late for Wanda Jean Allen to contest her mental impediments at trial, the U.S. Supreme Court declared in 2002 that the execution of mentally retarded defendants is unconstitutional. In *Atkins v. Virginia,* the court held that imposition of the death penalty on mentally retarded persons constitutes cruel and unusual punishment. There, the Court found that American society had reached a national consensus against executing mentally retarded inmates since most death penalty states and the federal government prohibited executing such defendants. The Court surmised that it was time to stop a practice that most Americans found repugnant. The case stems from Daryl Reynard Atkins' and William Jones' conviction in the August 1996 shooting death of Eric Nesbitt, a 21-year-old aviator stationed at Langley Air Force Base in Virginia, after kidnapping Nesbitt and forcing him to withdraw money from an automatic teller machine. In 2008, Judge Prentiss Smiley of the York County Circuit Court, after learning that prosecutorial misconduct occurred in Atkins original trial when state attorney's failed to turn over evidence to defense lawyers, commuted Atkins' death sentence to life in prison. In 2009, the Virginia Supreme Court upheld Judge Smiley's decision to commute Atkins' death sentence. Atkins remains jailed at the Wallens Ridge State Prison in Big Stone Gap, Virginia.

The impact of *Atkins* in capital justice in the United States remains uncertain. One concern is whether state procedures used for determining retardation fall in line with *Atkins*. Another question is whether pretrial hearings before a judge on the determination of mental retardation violate the Court's holding in *Ring v. Arizona* that only a jury can decide critical issues in death penalty cases. Still another concern is the establishment of a legal standard for determining mental retardation since *Atkins* did not provide a standard. The actual number of death row inmates across the country affected by *Atkins* is unknown, but one commentator asserts that *Atkins* is the "most sweeping limitation of capital punishment since the Supreme Court restored execution in 1976" and estimates that the death sentences of some 300 mentally retarded inmates on death rows in 20 states may commute to life.[68] Not surprisingly, one study has found that well over two-thirds of exonerated defendants with mental disabilities, many of them juveniles, falsely confess to crimes they did not commit. In many of the cases, police had coerced false confessions. One scholar has identified some 75 persons with intellectual disabilities who have falsely confessed to authorities to murders they did not commit. Cases involving female defendants include 17-year-old Paula Gray who suffered two nights of intense interrogation. Paula confessed to killing a couple along with four other men, two of whom went to death row. It took authorities 17 years to find that Paula's DNA and that of the four other men did not match the real killer who eventually confessed.

Executing *mentally retarded* persons contravenes the federal Constitution, but the Supreme Court has not barred state and federal jurisdictions from executing persons with *mental illnesses* unless the mental illness renders the inmate insane and exempt from the death penalty. One study found that 88 death row inmates that have *volunteered* for execution from 1973 to 2003 had documented mental illness and/or substance abuse. Significant racial disparities exist among this volunteer death row subpopulation; black males are 42 percent of the death row population, but only 3.0 percent of those having volunteered for execution, while white males are 45 percent of the death row population and constitute 87 percent of those having volunteered for execution. Regarding gender, though no black females have volunteered for executions, Arkansas (Christina Riggs), Alabama (Lynda Lyon Block), and Florida (Aileen Carol Wuornos) have executed three white females that volunteered for execution in the same period.

Demographic, intellectual, educational, neurological, and psychological profiles of death row women are seriously lacking in the academic literature. Not surprisingly, many death row women suffered harrowing physical, sexual, and psychological abuse as children and developed subsequent neuropsychological abnormalities as adults. A protracted report by Amnesty International on the execution of mentally ill defendants in the United States revealed that Betty Lou Beets, for instance, executed in Texas in February 2000 for the killing her husband, "had a lengthy history of well-documented head injuries, including repeated blows at the hands of abusive men, as well as a near-fatal car accident in 1980" that trial lawyers never presented to the sentencing jury. Post-conviction proceedings revealed that Betty "suffered from posttraumatic stress disorder, battered women's syndrome and organic brain damage and that she was learning disabled and hearing-impaired." These mental and physical incapacities "left her with gravely impaired judgment and extremely dependent on others." At the time she killed her husband, Betty was an alcoholic and addicted to diet pills. And Christina Riggs, executed in Arkansas in May 2000 for killing her two children, suffered from extreme mental illness including depression.[69]

The harsh conditions of death row experienced by women surely exacerbate condemned women's mental disorders. In one of only a few studies on death row women and mental illness, scholars explain that death row women are not only intellectually limited and academically wanting, but also suffer "histories of significant neurological insult" and psychological disorders with developmental histories of trauma, family disruption, and substance abuse.[70] There are no definitive figures available on the proportion of female death row inmates suffering from mental health disorders. For the overall condemned inmate population, some estimates put the figure at 70 percent of inmates suffering from schizophrenia and other severe mental illnesses; more conservative estimates put the figure as low as 10 percent. One clinical examination of the neuropsychiatric status of condemned inmates concludes that "if our fifteen subjects are representative of death row inmates ... then we must conclude that many condemned individuals in this country probably suffer a multiplicity of hitherto unrecognized psychiatric and neurological disorders that are relevant to considerations of mitigation."[71] Scholars define mental illness as "any of various conditions characterized by impairment of an individual's normal cognitive, emotional, or behavioral functioning, and caused by social, psychological, biochemical, genetic or other factors."[72] Mental incapacities among the nation's death row population include conditions accented by impairment of an individual's normal cognitive, emotional, or behavioral functioning—bipolar disorders, personality disorders, post-traumatic stress disorders, schizoaffective disorders, schizophrenia, depression, and suicidal tendencies. What's more, the number of persons on death row with disabling mental health conditions has increased steadily over the past several decades.

Some organizations are concerned about the mental status of death row inmates that they have called upon states to suspend executing capital defendants until justice professionals can develop more accurate methods of determining guilt in consideration of defendants' mental status. Mental Health America claims, for instance, that given the failure of the current system of fact-finding in capital cases to identify among those convicted and sentenced to death that actually have a mental health condition, surely judicial authorities have unwittingly executed persons with mental illness though mental illness is a mitigating factor in capital cases. Worse yet, capital defendants with severe psychiatric and neurological impairments are less capable than other defendants to obtain competent legal counsel or to report their conditions to trial attorneys for mitigation purposes. In any event, a sizable proportion of death row inmates suffer from extreme mental deficiencies that experts argue should preclude their execution. One scholar explains:

> Most mentally ill people who are convicted on capital charges should not be executed, for one of three reasons. First, such executions would violate equal protection of the laws in any jurisdiction in which execution of children and people with mental retardation is barred. Second, many death sentences imposed on people with mental illness violate due process because their mental illness is treated by the fact finder as an aggravating factor, either directly or to bolster a separate aggravating circumstance. Third, many mentally ill offenders who are sentenced to death will be so impaired at the time of execution that they cannot emotionally appreciate the significance of their punishment and thus cannot be executed under the Eighth Amendment; the latter conclusion is required even if they are restorable through treatment, given the unethical and medically inappropriate role in which such treatment casts mental health professionals.[73]

Judicial Override

The American capital justice system traditionally has assigned responsibility for expressing community sentiment on death penalty cases to juries. As one scholar explains, "Throughout its history, the jury determined which homicide defendants would be subject to capital punishment by making factual determinations, many of which related to difficult assessments of the defendant's state of mind. By the time the Bill of Rights was adopted, the jury's right to make these determinations was unquestioned."[74] In the 1970s, mostly in response to the *Furman* decision and the U.S. Supreme Court's concerns about arbitrariness in the imposition of capital punishment, some states removed death sentencing authority from juries to judges. Jury's decisions became merely advisory though states required judges "to give a jury's recommendation 'great weight' and could exercise override only when the justification for a death sentence was 'so clear and convincing that virtually no reasonable person could differ.'"[75] The Supreme Court upheld judicial override in *Harris v. Alabama* trusting that judges will give proper weight to jury recommendations. In *Ring v. Arizona*, however, the Court held that judges cannot add aggravating factors in their calculations of mitigating and aggravating circumstances determined by juries—aggravating factors must be submitted to a jury and proven beyond a reasonable doubt. The Court also held that the decision was not retroactive.

Today, Alabama, Delaware and Florida allow for judicial override of jury sentencing recommendations in capital cases. Alabama's use of judicial override in capital cases is notorious; 20 percent of the cases of the nearly 200 death row inmates currently on state's death row involved judicial override. When an Alabama jury sentenced Louise Harris, a black woman, to life in prison for killing her husband, the presiding judge overruled the jury recommendation and sentenced Harris to death. Besides Louise Harris, judicial override was at issue in appellate court reversals of other women's death sentences, including Doris Ann Carlson in Arizona, Carla Ann Caillier in Florida, and Judith Ann Neelley and Christie Michelle Scott in Alabama. As in the *Harris* case, judicial override allowed trial judges to disregard jury recommendations and use their own biased discretion in sentencing female offenders to death.

Prosecutorial Lawlessness

In an intense election campaign for district attorney in a large southern California county recently, the incumbent prosecutor and former state assembly member Rod Pacheco remarked, "Any prosecutor can *convict the guilty*, but it takes a great prosecutor to *convict the innocent*."[76] Fortunately for the county's residents, Mr. Pacheco lost the election. It remains unimaginable, however, that a judicial officer and former state legislator would make a comment so repugnant to the integrity of American criminal justice. Even if made lightheartedly, the menacing comment embodies an extremely troubling mindset among public officials charged with ensuring "justice" for the criminally accused. Regrettably, when an organizational culture of encouraging lawlessness pervades state prosecutors' offices it often leads to wrongful convictions. "Political ambitions, media pressures, and a culture of prosecutorial infallibility" tend to embolden prosecutors to engage in unethical conduct in pursuing capital convictions.[77] As one commentator recently put it, "Tragic consequences can result from when prosecutors put aside their ethic obligations in their zeal to win convictions. Yet far too often their misdeeds go unpunished."[78] Though legal scholars cite prosecutorial misconduct as a key factor in appellate courts dismissing charges and reversing convictions or reducing prison sentences, errant prosecutors remain largely immune from criminal and civil liability. Judicial officers and the disciplinary arms of regional and national bar associations rarely penalize prosecutors for their lawlessness. It is even more astounding that jurisdictions often elevate prosecutors who knowingly engage in wrongdoing to state judgeships, to Congress, to chief counsel for state lawyer disciplinary boards, or to notoriety as a national television host, namely HLN's Nancy Grace.

Prosecutorial lawlessness in capital cases is the product of systemic bias in the justice system. Scholars have studied appellate court review of thousands of capital cases and found that courts reverse capital sentences primarily because of prosecutorial misconduct. One national study on capital cases learned that nearly all death penalty jurisdictions in the United States have excessive error rates stemming mostly from severe forms of prosecutorial misconduct. In Ohio, nearly a third of capital cases involve severe ethical issues of prosecutorial misconduct. Another study of wrongfully convicted capital defendants found that prosecutorial misconduct was one of the most significant factors leading to conviction in seven defendants' cases in Illinois. In one of the cases, Illinois executed Jesse Tafero who prosecutors convicted upon much of the same evidence that exonerated Sonia Jacobs, a white female. While these studies did not separately study the reversible error involved in female capital cases, Streib has calculated an error rate in female capital cases at 58 percent. Still, many white conservatives in Congress want to speed up executions in the United States with passage of the "Streamline Procedures Act of 2005" effectively limiting defendant's ability to seek federal habeas corpus review of their capital convictions. Critics contend that the legislation would restrict federal courts from considering petitions from state prisoners claiming constitutional violations or from presenting evidence of innocence. The National Conference of Chief Justices from state courts overwhelmingly passed a resolution suggesting that the U.S. Senate not support the proposed legislation. There has been no action on the bill.

One common form of prejudicial error in capital cases is prosecutorial suppression of evidence that defendants are innocent of the capital offense or that defendants do not deserve the death penalty. That is, state prosecutors frequently suppress exculpatory evidence, knowingly use false testimony, intimidate witnesses, give improper closing arguments, give false statements to the jury, and fabricate evidence. A former federal prosecutor and special counsel to the U.S. Senate and House Judiciary Committees recently noted problems in Virginia's criminal justice system that lead to convicting innocent persons; "the government is concealing or destroying evidence that is exclusively within its possession that demonstrates, or tends to demonstrate, that the accused is innocent or his accusers are not reliable."[79] A *Chicago Tribune* investigation found hundreds of homicide cases in which the prosecutors concealed or fabricated evidence. A Texas study of cases involving serious prosecutorial misconduct revealed that state prosecutors have "used threats against defendants or their family members to coerce confessions."[80] Undoubtedly, prosecutorial misconduct weighs most heavily against black offenders since blacks are over-represented as capital defendants. In Wanda Jean Allen's case, for example, the state's prosecutor withheld evidence at trial and later made false statements to the Parole and Pardon Board. In fact, the prosecutor in Wanda's case engaged in seven separate instances of misconduct, including instances of biased behavior. Other studies have focused on prosecutors' use of racist remarks while trying capital cases involving black defendants. The literature reveals that courts are frustrated over the frequency in which prosecutorial misconduct occurs, yet courts are unwilling to overturn cases on grounds of racial bias and, in the alternative, assess the relative weight of the statements to other evidence or otherwise explain away the prosecutors' remarks. One commentator identified the problem of prosecutorial racism this way:

> Many courts refuse to recognize the more discrete and arguably more insidious uses of racism that occur during the criminal trial. Instead, they choose to focus solely on overt expressions of racial bias. Nonetheless, the subtler racial references made by a prosecutor are more difficult to detect, and are precisely those that are most difficult to prove. Thus, in order to protect a defendant's due process right to a fair trial, courts must look beneath the surface to discover the race-based stereotypes on which prosecutors so cleverly rely.[81]

Efforts to deter prosecutorial misconduct have proven largely ineffective. The U.S. Supreme Court held in *Brady v. Maryland* that prosecutors are under a constitutional duty to disclose evidence favorable to the accused. But numerous studies attest to the futility of *Brady*. Authorities have not convicted any prosecutor of criminal conduct in all the documented cases of prosecutorial misconduct, though there are some ongoing investigations. In fact, Arizona is the only state that has even disbarred a prosecutor for wrongdoing. There, officials expelled Pima County prosecutor Kenneth Peasley from practicing law when he intentionally presented false evidence against three men in a triple-murder death penalty case. Also, a problem with prosecutorial accountability for misconduct is that they enjoy absolute immunity from civil liability.

The case of Ellen Reasonover typifies prosecutorial misconduct in capital cases involving wrongfully convicted black females. St. Louis County prosecutor Steven Goldman indicted Ellen for the murder of a white male service station attendant in January 1983 after she voluntarily reported to police that she had been at the service station after hearing about the robbery-murder on television. Goldman lacked a confession, eyewitness testimony, physical evidence, or motive with which to prosecute Ellen, and relied exclusively upon two jailhouse informants who claimed Ellen had admitted to them that she had killed the attendant. Both inmates had credibility problems and unknown to defense lawyers or the jury was that Goldman had made secret deals of leniency with the informants. One of the informants later recanted her testimony and the other committed suicide. Goldman used leading questions consistently and blatantly in extracting testimony from the two informants, and won the conviction from an all-white jury despite a substantial minority population in St. Louis County. An investigation by Centurion Ministries revealed Goldman's misconduct and subsequent injustice to Ellen, and the federal judge that released Ellen in 1999 concluded that without question Ellen had been the victim of prosecutorial misconduct. Ellen Reasonover spent 16 years in prison for a crime she never committed, while St. Louis County voters elected Goldman to a state court judgeship.

Peremptory Challenge

In remarks made at an American Bar Association awards dinner in Illinois, U.S. Supreme Court Justice John Paul Stevens called attention to the fairness of the jury selection process in capital cases that removes potential jurors who oppose the death penalty. State and federal prosecutors use the peremptory challenge as a procedural devise to remove potential jurors during *voir dire* for unexplained reasons. While prosecutors must give a reason when challenging jurors for cause, the peremptory challenge requires no justification and is "exercised without a reason stated, without impunity, and without being subject to the court's control."[82] It is the capricious nature of the peremptory challenge, however, that effectively masks racial discrimination in jury selection by allowing prosecutors to intentionally discriminate against black female jurors. As one Colorado judge put it, the peremptory challenge is "the last best tool of Jim Crow."[83]

The U.S. Supreme Court first visited racial discrimination in jury selection in 1880 in *Strauder v. West Virginia* when the Court invalidated a state statute prohibiting blacks from serving on grand or petit juries. The Court reasoned that "the very fact that colored people are singled out and expressly denied by a statute all right to participate in the administration of the law, as jurors, because of their color ... is practically a brand upon them, affixed by the law, an assertion of their inferiority."[84] A century later in *Batson v. Kentucky*, the Court reaffirmed its position in *Strauder* and argued that prosecutors are prohibited from using the peremptory challenge to strike potential jurors solely on account of race because it denies the defendant the protection that a trial by jury is intended to secure under the Constitution. The Court expanded *Batson* to include women in 1994 in *J.E.M. v. Alabama*.

Despite the Court's holdings in these and other cases involving prosecutorial abuse of the peremptory challenge, state attorneys continue to use the peremptory challenge in capital cases to openly discriminate against black women in jury selection. Veteran prosecutors in Philadelphia, for instance, use training tapes to instruct new assistant district attorneys how to exclude *young black women* from juries. One prosecutor believed that black women who dye their hair blonde are undesirable as jurors because they are "not cognizant of their own reality and experience."[85] The same prosecutor found white women who wear "Jeri curls" unsuitable for jury service. A former Alameda County (California) prosecutor claimed that he conspired with a trial judge to exclude *black women* from capital juries over a 20-year period from the 1970s to the early 1990s because they are reluctant to support the death penalty for black defendants. In a two-year investigation of 108 non-capital felony cases tried in 2002 involving some 6,500 jurors, *The Dallas Morning News* found that Texas prosecutors exclude eligible blacks from juries at more than twice the rate they reject eligible whites; "in fact, being black was the most important personal trait affecting which jurors prosecutors rejected."[86]

Women could not sit on juries until 1975 most likely because prosecutors generally found women untrustworthy. Some courts hold that striking black women as jurors does not amount to racist exclusion. In one case, a trial judge told a defense lawyer objecting to a prosecutor striking black women: "You have got women on the jury. What function does a Black woman fulfill that the White woman doesn't?"[87] Remarkably, prosecutors generally prefer white jurors to black jurors in capital cases because they believe that white juries are more prone to convict black defendants. Research shows that black women on capital juries does not influence sentencing outcomes, but in most cases, racism nevertheless pervades jury decisions since most white juries are far more punitive toward black defendants generally—particularly in cases involving black defendants accused of killing white victims. Still, it is difficult for defense lawyers to make the case of racial discrimination when prosecutors abuse peremptory challenges because courts allow "almost any conceivable justification for peremptory challenges, however arbitrary or irrational, while ignoring evidence that such challenges were exercised in a racially discriminatory manner."[88] Federal prosecutors also use peremptory challenges to exclude black jurors in capital cases. In *Batson*, Justice Marshall called for the elimination of peremptory challenges because he doubted that prosecutors could ever overcome their racist use of the devise. He argued:

> A prosecutor's own conscious or unconscious racism may lead him easily to the conclusion that a prospective black juror is sullen, or distant, a characterization that would not have come to his mind if a white juror had acted identically. Prosecutors' peremptories are based on their seat-of-the-pants instincts as to how particular jurors will vote. Yet seat-of-the-pants-instincts may often be just another term for racial prejudice. Even if all parties approach the Court's mandate with the best of conscious intentions, that mandate requires them to confront and overcome their own racism on all levels—a challenge I doubt all of them can meet.[89]

Concluding Remarks

This chapter explains that traditional theories on women and capital punishment are inapplicable to female executions in the United States because the theories are incompatible with the objective historical reality gender oppression in imposition of the penalty to women. Gender oppression is an artifact of gender stratification which, in turn is a product of sexism. The historical record on female executions reveals that imputing the death penalty to women has furthered the patriarchal structure of United States society. In this regard, a critical perspective is far more suited to understanding the history of American women and capital punishment. The chapter also explores the lack of attention afforded women by the U.S. Supreme Court in the context capital punishment—race has been at the forefront of the Court's interest in discerning bias in application of the punishment. Yet, there remain substantive barriers to implementing procedural and substantive protections designed to minimize bias in female capital sentencing. These impediments include the chronic underfunding of indigent defense services by state and local governments, the unbridled discretion of state prosecutors in filing capital charges against women, the consistent marginalization of lesbian defendants to juries by prosecutors, the prosecution of mentally retarded and insane women in capital cases, prosecutorial lawlessness in female capital cases, and the use of judicial override in capital cases. Until these institutional obstructions are recognized by the Supreme Court as impediments to due process and equal protection of the law to women in capital cases, women will continue to suffer gender biased processes assuring their convictions and subsequent executions.

"Documenting older executions of female offenders is quite challenging."[1]

2
Empirical Frameworks

Constructing a comprehensive inventory of female executions in the United States is a necessary first step to investigating the contextual history of criminal justice jurisdictions executing American women. Accessing information on female executions is not a straightforward task since social researchers and government agencies have largely overlooked female executions in the history of American capital justice. One could suggest that death penalty researchers discount women executions because the number of female executions does not comprise a sufficient population to justify their study, women are less than three percent of executions conducted historically in the United States. Like other criminological issues confronting American women, the sexist ideology entrenched within capital justice studies may render the history of women's executions unimportant of academic attention relative to the study of men's executions.

Data

M. Watt Espy's index of executions performed under civil authority in the United States since the early 17th century—commonly referred to as *The Espy File*—provides a starting point for the construction of a historical inventory of female executions.[2] In 1970, Espy began collecting data on public executions from his home in Headland, Alabama. The inventory consists of information on executions collected from prison officials and departments of correction, contemporary newspaper coverage of crimes, trials, and executions, actual court records of trials and various appeals, and through contact with local historians, historical societies, museums, and county clerks. Espy eventually moved the data collection project to the University of Alabama Law Center in Tuscaloosa, Alabama, under the directorship of John Ortiz Smykla and the Inter-University Consortium of Political and Social Research (ICPSR) where researchers confirmed existing executions in the file and documented new cases. Years later, Espy moved the research project back to Headland where he continued to document capital punishment cases until his death in August 2009. The School of Criminal Justice at the State University of New York in Albany now houses the archive. The most recent version of Espy's inventory released by the ICPSR for public use contains information on nearly 15,000 executions in the United States, of which 357 are female executions. The index is an impressive registry though it is far from complete and plagued with coding problems and burdening discrepancies, especially for colonial Maryland and post–Civil War Louisiana.

Construction of the female execution inventory has benefited significantly from law professor Victor L. Streib's compilation of 567 female executions since the early 17th century.[3] The registry provides the names of executed female offenders, the date of execution, the race and age of offenders, the criminal offense and state of execution. Other scholars have investigated archives and constructed comprehensive registries of executed prisoners for individual states that correct for much of the incompleteness in Espy's inventory. These academic sources include Kathleen O'Shea's work in *Women and the Death Penalty in the United States, 1990–1998* with accompanying narratives on the crimes of female prisoners though the carelessness with which the author treated sources burdens the undertaking.[4] In *The Penalty of Death: U.S. Newspaper Coverage of Women's Executions*, Marlin Shipman discusses specifics of female executions derived from historical newspapers but admittedly overlooks much about women of color.[5] Elizabeth Rapaport and Victor Streib identify female executions in North Carolina from 1720 to 1984 and Lewis L. Laska provides a comprehensive inventory of executions in Tennessee from 1782 to 2009.[6] Daniel Allen Hearn provides narratives on female executions in New England colonies, New Jersey, New York, and North and South Carolina since the early 17th century.[7] In his work on the *Legacy of Violence*, John D. Bessler surveyed executions in Minnesota, while Sheila O'Hare and her associates constructed a registry of executions in California though the work overlooks executions before statehood in 1851.[8] Harriet Frazier accounts for Missouri executions, and West Gilbreath and Robert Tórrez provide histories of crime and punishment in territorial New Mexico wherein they note female executions.[9] In two works, L. Kay Gillespie identifies female executions in the 19th through the 21st centuries in the United States.[10] Kerry Segrave compiled information on the execution of condemned women from 1840 to 1899 in both the United States and Canada.[11] George C. Wright identifies female executions in Kentucky from 1872 to 1939, and Negley Teeters inventoried female executions in early colonial Pennsylvania from 1682 to 1834.[12] Ann Jones' stimulating work in *Women Who Kill* provides contextual narratives on several executed women and Mary Welek Atwell provides an exceptional analysis of women executed in the modern period.[13] Victor Streib provides a descriptive profile of women executed in Ohio.[14] Unpublished doctoral dissertations also identify executed females historically in the United States.

Besides academic sources, many state correctional departments have digitized archives on condemned prisoners that contain information on executed female offenders. Newspaper articles archived by Heritage Microfilm provide first-hand information on executed women and the Colonial Williamsburg Foundation has archived digital copies of *The Virginia Gazette* from 1736 to 1780 containing information on colonial executions of women.[15] The Accessible Archives at The College of William and Mary contain full text searchable databases on primary source material from 18th and 19th century periodicals.[16] The Digital Library on American Slavery at the University of North Carolina, Greensboro, identifies female slave execution data extracted from such historical documents as legislative petitions, county court petitions, depositions, court proceedings, and amended petitions, and other sources.[17] The factual circumstances of female capital offenses are often obtainable from appellate court cases and the published works of legal historians. Newspaper stories on female executions are also available through commercial digitized newspaper archives.[18] The Death Penalty Information Center (DPIC) in Washington, D.C. is a vital source on more contemporary female executions.[19] The DPIC makes publicly available a continuously updated index of prisoners executed in the United States since January 1977. The DPIC register identifies executed prisoners' names and the date, state, method of execution, and the race of the defendant. The DPIC has recorded the race of victim(s) since 1982 and the ages of executed prisoners beginning in 2000.

Exploiting these various sources on female executions resulted in an inventory of 702 female executions in the United States from 1632 when Virginia hanged British American June Champion for infanticide, to late September 2015 when Georgia executed Kelly Renee Gissendaner by lethal injection for the murder of her husband. Table 2-1 (see end of chapter) contains the inventory of these female executions. One should note that 45 cases identified in Streib's inventory of female executions remain unconfirmed. There are also six cases where a definitive execution date is unknown or otherwise unavailable. An added dimension to female slave executions

2. Empirical Frameworks

in the United States is that states occasionally compensated slave owners for the loss of a slave executed for a capital offense. A jury usually assessed the compensation paid to slave owners that typically amounted to less than the full value of the slave to the owner. As Stampp explains, "since the execution of a slave resembled the public seizure or condemnation of private property, most of the states recognized the justice of the owner's claim."[20] Alabama, Kentucky, Mississippi, North Carolina, South Carolina, Texas and Virginia compensated owners for the execution of 20 female slaves. The inventory notes cases of wrongful convictions of executed female offenders, cases of appellate review before the U.S. Supreme Court's holding in *Gregg v. Georgia*, and cases of female execution where mental retardation of the condemned was present in the case.

Characteristics

Table 2-2 provides a summary of characteristics of female executions across the three historical periods discussed above. The table includes the race, age, sex, and occupation of executed

Table 2-2: Characteristics of Female Executions in the United States by Historical Trends, 1632–2014

Characteristics of Condemned Women	First Historical Period in Women Executions 1632–1759 N=196 (27.9%)		Second Historical Period in Women Executions 1760–1899 N=445 (63.4%)		Third Historical Period in Women Executions 1900–2014 N=55 (8.7%)		Totals in Women Executions 1632–2014 N=702[1] (100.0%)	
	N	%	N	%	N	%	N	%
Race of Offender								
White	125	63.8	68	15.3	36	65.5	229	32.6
Black/Mulatto	59	30.1	352	79.1	19	34.5	436	62.1
Native American	4	2	6	1.4	0	0	10	1.4
Spanish/Mexican	0	0	5	1.1	0	0	5	0.7
Hawaiian	0	0	1	0.2	0	0	1	0.1
Missing Data	8	4.1	13	2.9	0	0	21	3
Criminal Offense[2]								
Murders	36	18.4	229	51.5	22	40	292	41.6
Infanticide/Child Murder	56	28.6	41	9.2	3	5.5	100	14.2
Spousal Murder	4	2	28	6.3	10	18.2	42	6
Burglary	9	4.6	6	1.3	0	0	15	2.1
Conspiracy to Commit Murder	1	0.5	3	0.7	3	5.5	7	1
Slave Revolt	4	2	3	0.7	0	0	7	1
Witchcraft	33	16.8	0	0	0	0	33	4.7
Robbery-Murder	1	0.5	7	1.6	14	25.5	22	3.1
Accessory to Murder	2	1	1	0.2	0	0	3	0.4
Robbery	1	0.5	3	0.7	0	0	4	0.6
Arson	12	6.1	39	8.8	0	0	51	7.3
Spying-Espionage	0	0	0	0	1	1.8	1	0.1
Kidnapping-Murder	0	0	0	0	1	1.8	1	0.1
Arson-Murder	0	0	1	0.2	0	0	1	0.1
Adultery	2	1	0	0	0	0	2	0.3
Poisoning	6	3.1	27	6.1	0	0	33	4.7
Unspecified Felony	3	1.5	4	0.9	0	0	7	1
Attempted Murder	2	1	22	4.9	0	0	25	3.6
Forgery	2	1	0	0	0	0	2	0.3
Theft-Stealing	5	2.5	4	0.9	0	0	9	1.3
Violating Banishment	1	0.5	0	0	0	0	1	0.1
Criminal Assault	0	0	1	0.2	0	0	1	0.1
Other	0	0	1	0.2	0	0	1	0.1
Missing Data	16	8.2	25	5.6	1	1.8	42	6

I. Theoretical and Empirical Frameworks

Characteristics of Condemned Women	First Historical Period in Women Executions 1632–1759 N=196 (27.9%)		Second Historical Period in Women Executions 1760–1899 N=445 (63.4%)		Third Historical Period in Women Executions 1900–2014 N=55 (8.7%)		Totals in Women Executions 1632–2014 N=702[1] (100.0%)	
	N	%	N	%	N	%	N	%
Method of Execution								
Hanging	139	70.9	37	69	9	17	455	64.8
Electrocution	0	0	1	0.2	25	47.2	26	3.7
Asphyxiation (Gas Chamber)	0	0	0	0	7	13.2	7	1
Lethal Injection	0	0	0	0	12	22.6	13	1.9
Burned to Death	14	7.1	11	2.5	0	0	25	3.6
Hung in Chains	0	0	1	0.2	0	0	1	0.1
Gibbeted	3	1.5	0	0	0	0	3	0.4
Missing Data	40	20.4	125	28.1	0	0	172	24.5
Regions of Executions[3]								
New England States	71	36	10	2.2	1	1.8	82	11.6
Middle Atlantic States	29	14.7	65	14.6	10	18.2	104	14.8
East North Central States	0	0	4	0.9	4	7.3	8	1.1
West North Central States	0	0	10	2.2	1	1.8	13	1.9
South Atlantic States	95	48.7	234	52.6	11	20	343	48.8
East South Central States	0	0	77	17.3	9	16.4	87	12.3
West South Central States	1	0.5	37	8.3	14	25.5	52	7.4
Mountain States	0	0	5	1.1	1	1.8	6	0.9
Pacific States	0	0	3	0.6	4	7.3	7	1
Place of Execution								
City	0	0	3	0.6	0	0	3	0.4
County	193	98.5	440	98.9	10	18.2	649	92.5
State	0	0	2	0.4	45	81.8	47	6.7
Other	3	1.5	0	0	0	0	3	0.4
Jurisdiction of Execution								
State	0	0	368	82.7	52	94.5	421	59.9
Federal	0	0	2	0.4	2	3.6	4	0.6
Territorial	0	0	3	0.6	1	1.8	3	0.4
Military	196	100	72	16.2	0	0	274	39
Age of Offenders								
12 years of age	0	0	4	0.9	0	0	4	0.6
13 years of age	0	0	3	0.6	0	0	3	0.4
14 years of age	1	0.5	2	0.4	0	0	3	0.4
15 years of age	0	0	5	1.1	0	0	5	0.7
16 years of age	1	0.5	6	1.3	0	0	7	1
17 years of age	1	0.5	3	0.6	1	1.8	5	0.7
18 to 29 years of age	21	10.7	35	7.9	12	21.8	68	9.6
30 to 39 years of age	6	3.1	9	2	12	21.8	27	3.8
40 to 49 years of age	1	0.5	8	1.8	13	23.6	22	3.1
50 to 59 years of age	6	3.1	4	0.9	10	18.2	20	2.8
60 to 69 years of age	5	2.6	1	0.2	2	3.6	8	1.1
70 to 79 years of age	2	1	1	0.2	0	0	3	0.4
Mean Age	35.6	—	25.9	—	39.4	—	32.2	—
Missing Data	152	77.6	364	81.8	5	9.1	527	75.1
Race of Victim								
White	94	48	176	39.6	43	78.2	313	44.6
Black	10	5.1	28	6.3	10	18.2	48	6.8
American Indian	3	1.5	2	0.4	0	0	5	0.7
Latino	0	0	4	0.9	0	0	4	0.6
Hawaiian	0	0	1	0.2	0	0	1	0.1
Missing Data	89	45.4	234	52.6	2	3.6	331	47.2
Occupation of Offender								
Bar Maid	1	0.5	0	0	0	0	1	0.1
Boarding House Owner	0	0	0	0	1	1.8	1	0.1

Characteristics of Condemned Women	First Historical Period in Women Executions 1632–1759 N=196 (27.9%)		Second Historical Period in Women Executions 1760–1899 N=445 (63.4%)		Third Historical Period in Women Executions 1900–2014 N=55 (8.7%)		Totals in Women Executions 1632–2014 N=702[1] (100.0%)	
	N	%	N	%	N	%	N	%
Convict	0	0	2	0.4	0	0	2	0.3
Criminal	0	0	0	0	1	1.8	1	0.1
Domestic Cook	0	0	0	0	1	1.8	1	0.1
Domestic Servant	2	1	6	1.3	4	7.3	12	1.7
Domestic Worker	0	0	2	0.4	0	0	2	0.3
Farm Hand	0	0	2	0.4	0	0	2	0.3
Fence	0	0	1	0.2	0	0	1	0.1
House Maid	0	0	1	0.2	1	1.8	1	0.1
Housekeeper	0	0	0	0	3	5.5	3	0.4
Housewife	47	24	26	5.8	16	29.1	89	12.7
Indentured Servant	1	0.5	0	0	0	0	1	0.1
Innkeeper	1	0.5	1	0.2	0	0	2	0.3
Landlady	0	0	1	0.2	0	0	1	0.1
Maid	0	0	0	0	2	3.6	2	0.3
Nurse	0	0	0	0	5	9.1	5	0.7
Parolee	0	0	0	0	1	1.8	1	0.1
Petty Crook	0	0	1	0.2	0	0	1	0.1
Pirate	0	0	1	0.2	0	0	1	0.1
Prostitute	0	0	0	0	6	10.9	6	0.9
School Teacher	0	0	0	0	1	1.8	1	0.1
Servant	21	10.7	7	1.6	0	0	28	4
Slave	54	27.6	309	69.4	0	0	367	52.3
Store Owner	0	0	0	0	1	1.8	1	0.1
Tavern Owner	0	0	0	0	1	1.8	1	0.1
Teacher	0	0	1	0.2	0	0	1	0.1
Textile Worker	0	0	0	0	1	1.8	1	0.1
Waitress	0	0	1	0.2	3	5.5	4	0.6
Widow	7	3.6	0	0	0	0	7	1
Missing Data	61	31.1	83	18.7	7	12.7	154	21.9

1. Total includes six cases where the year is unknown or otherwise unavailable.   2. **Infanticide/Child Murder**—concealing the birth or death of an infant, killing an infant, killing an older child.   3. **New England States**—Maine, New Hampshire, Vermont, Massachusetts, Rhode Island, Connecticut; **Middle Atlantic States**—New York, New Jersey, Pennsylvania; **East North Central States**—Ohio, Indiana, Illinois, Michigan, Wisconsin; **West North Central States**—Minnesota, Iowa, Missouri, North Dakota, South Dakota, Nebraska, Kansas; **South Atlantic States**—Delaware, Maryland, District of Columbia, Virginia, West Virginia, North Carolina, South Carolina, Georgia, Florida; **East South Central States**—Kentucky, Tennessee, Alabama, Mississippi; **West South Central States**—Arkansas, Louisiana, Oklahoma, Texas; **Mountain States**—Montana, Idaho, Wyoming, Colorado, New Mexico, Arizona, Utah, Nevada; **Pacific States**—Alaska, California, Hawaii, Oregon, Washington.

female offenders, and the date, place, jurisdiction, offense, method of execution, and the victim's race. Interestingly, though death penalty jurisdictions have kept women far removed from capital punishment relative to men, the racial proportions of executed women correspond closely to the historical percentages of male executions.

Race of Offenders

The inventory shows that black women comprise slightly more than 62 percent (436) of all women executed historically in the United States and white women are nearly 33 percent (229). Jurisdictions have executed black women at almost *twice* the rate than they have executed white women. American justice officials have been far less likely to execute other non-white women; American Indian women are slightly more than 1 percent (10), Latinas are less than 1 percent (5), and the one executed Hawaiian woman put to death in 1846 constitutes a negligible

0.1 percent of female executions. The race of 3.0 percent (21) of executed women is unknown or otherwise unavailable.

One should note that there is confusion in the historical record as to the gender and race of one female offender, namely, that of Shellie McKeithen. Pennsylvania officials electrocuted McKeithen in January 1946. One newspaper refers to McKeithen as an Asian woman executed for murder in Allegheny County,[21] but another claims that McKeithen was a 48-year-old black male sentenced to die for the robbery and brutal hammer slaying of Tucker Boxley in Pittsburg in March 1944. Authorities sentenced McKeithen to the electric chair in Rockview Penitentiary, while an accomplice, a black man named Clinton Harrill, received a lengthy prison term for voluntary manslaughter.[22] In an another instance, though inventories show that Mississippi officials executed a black female named Carrie McCarty in April 1921 for the murder of an unnamed victim in Mississippi, the *Biloxi Daily Herald* claimed that authorities actually sentenced Carrie to a life prison term.[23] The Mississippi Supreme Court affirmed McCarty's conviction without comment. In several other cases, the execution record fails to show that state governors granted executive clemency to women ostensibly executed.

Criminal Offenses

Historically, women offenders have committed an array of capital offenses. About half of executed women committed crimes of murder including murder, conspiracy to commit murder, accessory to murder, attempted murder, and murders aggravated by robbery, kidnapping, and arson. Some 14 percent (100) of female executions were for offenses of concealing the birth or death of an infant, killing an infant, or killing older children. Women executions for spousal murder of largely abusive husbands are 6 percent (42) of female executions. Roughly 12 percent (81) of female executions involved property crimes of burglary, arson, robbery, theft stealing, and forgery. Much lower percentages of women committed capital offenses involving slave revolt, witchcraft, adultery, poisoning, unspecified felonies, violating banishment, and criminal assault. About 6 percent (42) of female executions were for unknown crimes.

There is considerable racial variation in the types of capital offenses committed by women. Death penalty jurisdictions executed 29 percent of white women for murders including robbery-murder, arson-murder, conspiracy to commit murder, accessory to murder, and kidnapping-murder. Some 14 percent of white bonded servant women killed abusive masters. In contrast, roughly 65 percent of executed black women committed predatory murders mostly for the killing of abusive masters, mistresses, overseers, and other servants. Jurisdictions executed far more white women than black women for infanticide and child murder; officials put to death 29 percent of white women and about 7 percent of black women for infanticide and child murders. Executed white women almost exclusively killed their own children while executed black women more often killed the children of oppressive slave masters. Jurisdictions also executed far more white women than black women for spousal murder; authorities executed nearly 13 percent of executed white women and about 3 percent of executed black women for spousal murders. Judicial officers executed American Indian women for predatory murder, infanticide, and spousal murder, while they put to death Latinas mostly for predatory murder. The one executed Hawaiian woman murdered her husband. Regarding other criminal offenses, the historical record shows that authorities executed white and black women in roughly equal numbers for burglary, slave revolt, robbery, and theft stealing. On the other hand, jurisdictions put to death far more black women than white women for arson and poisoning, and executed white women exclusively for witchcraft, adultery, forgery, and violation of banishment. Six percent of the criminal offenses committed by executed women are unknown or otherwise unavailable, black women comprise 75 percent of executed females where the offense is unknown.

Age

The ages of 75 percent of executed female prisoners at the time of execution are unavailable or otherwise unknown. Information on the ages of executed white women is missing in about 54 percent of cases, and information on the ages of black women is unavailable for 85 percent of the cases. The ages of four of the eight executed American Indian women and four of the five executed Latinas are unavailable. The age of the only Hawaiian female executions is also unavailable. Consequently, contrasting racial differences in the ages of executed women historically is at best conjectural. Even so, the available information on the ages of executed women suggests that jurisdictions executed women of color at much younger ages than white women. The mean age of executed white women is 38 years old whereas the average age of executed black women is 14 years younger. American Indian women are 18 years younger than are executed white women. The mean age of black women at the time of execution is slightly older than 24 years old and the mean age of the four executed American Indian women for which information is available is slightly older than 20 years old. The only executed Latina for whom age is available was 28 years old when executed, some 10 years younger than the mean age of white women.

Methods

Death penalty jurisdictions used a variety of methods to put women offenders to death, including hanging, firing squad, electrocution, asphyxiation (gas chamber), lethal injection, burning to death, hung in chains, and gibbeting. Hanging has been the most popular method of executing women prisoners in the United States. Jurisdictions hanged nearly 65 percent of executed women, including 83 percent of executed white women and 86 percent of executed black women. All 10 executed American Indian women hanged for their crimes. Death penalty jurisdictions used asphyxiation and electrocution as execution methods more often to put white women to death than black women and used burning to death, hung in chains, and gibbeting mostly to execute black slave women. Twenty-three slave women suffered burning to death as an execution method. Contrary to popular notions, however, burning to death was not an execution method reserved exclusively to slave women. New Castle County officials in Delaware burned to death a white housewife named Catharine Bevans for spousal murder in 1741, and Kent County authorities in Maryland burned to death a white servant woman named Esther Anderson for murder in May 1746. Hung in chains was not a favored execution method for women. One scholar notes, for instance, that Maryland executioners never used "hung in chains" as an execution method: "People were hanged first and then 'hung in chains,' which might usually have been iron straps rather than chains."[24] The same is probably the case with quartering as an execution method. Executioners used quartering after hanging slave woman Judith for killing her owner, Edward Harris, in March 1741 in Queen Anne County in Maryland. Slave woman Mol (most likely Molly) suffered quartering after she hanged for murdering her owner, Jeremiah Pattison, in April 1742. One white woman and two slave women suffered gibbeting as an execution method in the early colonial period of female executions.

Regions

There is also considerable regional variation in female executions historically. South Atlantic states put to death nearly 49 percent of women executed in the United States, followed by Middle Atlantic States at nearly 15 percent, East South Central and New England states at nearly 12 percent. In New England states, Massachusetts alone executed about 22 percent of executed white women, the Middle Atlantic States of New York and Pennsylvania put to death about 24 percent of executed white women, and the South Atlantic states executed nearly 22 percent of white women. In contrast, the overwhelming majority of black women executions occurred in South Atlantic states, Middle Atlantic States, and East South Central states. Collectively, these regions account for about 47 percent of black women executions. In the South Atlantic states, Virginia alone executed more than *one in four* of black women put to death in the United States. Significant numbers of black women executions have occurred in North Carolina, South Carolina and Georgia. New York in the Middle Atlantic region and Alabama in East South Central region account for large numbers of black women executions as well. The New England states of Connecticut, Maine, and Massachusetts executed most American Indian females though jurisdictions in Michigan and New York each executed an American Indian woman. Jurisdictions in the American Southwest account for all Latina executions. Hawaii accounts for the sole native Hawaiian woman execution.

Places

The task of carrying-out executions in the United States historically involved the transfer of responsibility from local (city and county) to state jurisdictions. With development of state prison systems, states began requiring officials to conduct executions exclusively under state authority using execution facilities in state prisons. The U.S. Supreme Court sanctioned the requirement that states use prison facilities to execute condemned inmates in *Rooney v. North Dakota* in January 1905. The rational for isolating executions in prison facilities was to avoid the public fanfare that often characterized public executions. As one early death penalty scholar put it, "the crowds often assumed the characteristics of a mob, and often indulged in the wildest and most unrestrained orgies."[25] Some officials believed, however, that public executions achieved a greater deterrent effect than executions conducted behind prison walls. Authorities used local facilities to execute three women: in January 1779 the small town of Pueblo Cochiti in New Mexico hanged Maria Josefa and her daughter Maria Francisca for the murder of Francisca's husband, Washington, D.C., hanged Mary Surratt in July 1865 for her alleged involvement in the assassination of President Lincoln, and local authorities in Hawaii hanged native Kaomali in August 1846 for spousal murder. States did not begin to use state prison facilities to execute women until March 1883 when Vermont hanged Emeline Meaker at the state prison in Washington County. Even then, it would be another 13 years before state officials began regularly executing women prisoners in state prisons. In this regard, authorities used state prison facilities to execute less than 7 percent of executed females. As a result, jurisdictions put to death about 93 percent of executed women using local and county facilities, usually a jail courtyard. In three cases, merchant ship's captains hanged women aboard ships bound from England to Virginia and Maryland. Today, all jurisdictions execute condemned female inmates under private, antiseptic conditions in state prisons.

Jurisdictions

Jurisdictions have used state, federal, territorial, American military and colonial British and Spanish authority to execute women in the United States historically. State jurisdictions commissioned nearly 60 percent of female executions, federal jurisdictions sanctioned less than 1 percent of women executions, territorial officials authorized less than 1 percent of women executions, and British, American, and Spanish military authorities account for 39 percent of women executions. Federal authorities have executed four women: Mary O'Cammon and Kate McShane were hanged in California in July 1890 for an unknown crime; Ethel Rosenberg died by electrocution in New York for espionage in June 1953; and Bonnie Brown Headley died in

December 1953 in Missouri's gas chamber for kidnapping and murdering a young child. The western territorial governments of Oklahoma, Arizona and New Mexico together authorized the executions of three women for predatory murders between 1861 and 1903: New Mexico hanged Pablita Sandoval in 1861; Arizona territorial officials hanged Dolores Moore in 1865; and Oklahoma hanged Dora Wright in 1903. The British military had legal authority over one-third of female executions in the early colonial period until Massachusetts used its state authority to hang Bathsheba Ruggles Spooner in July 1778. Spanish military commissioned the hangings of María Francisca and María Josefa in the New Mexico territory in 1779. Pursuant to British Courts of Admiralty, merchant ship captains authorized the hanging of Mary Lee, Elizabeth Richardson, and Katharine Grady aboard British ships in 1654, 1658, and 1659 respectively. Hawaii hanged a native woman Kaomali pursuant to Kingdom authority.

Race of Victims

Slightly more than 47 percent of the information on the race of the victims harmed by women executed for capital crimes in the United States is unknown or otherwise unavailable. Still, enough information exists in the historical record to advance some observations about the racial victimization patterns of women capital offenders. First, more information exists on the race of victims harmed by condemned white women, American Indian women, and Latinas than by executed black women offenders. The race of the victim is available for 67 percent of executed white women, for 46 percent of executed black women, for 80 percent of executed American Indian women. All of the victims harmed by executed Latinas and the one executed Hawaiian woman are available. Second, condemned women victimized white persons more than they victimized persons of color. Of the 371 victims harmed by executed women, whites are nearly 84 percent of known victims, blacks are roughly 13 percent, American Indians are 1.3 percent, Latinas are 1 percent, and the sole Hawaiian victim constitutes 0.2 percent of known victims. Third, only executed white women exclusively victimized persons of the same race. That is, of all 154 executed white women where the race of the victim is known victimized only other white persons. The known victims of executed black females were 76 percent (153) white, 24 percent (48) black, and less than 1 percent (1) Latina. About 37 percent (3) of the known victims of executed American Indian women were white and 62 percent (5) were other American Indians. Of the known victims of executed Latinas, 40 percent (2) were white and 60 percent (3) were other Latinos. The only executed female Hawaiian murdered her Hawaiian native husband.

Occupations of Offenders

There exists limited insight into the occupations of executed female prisoners since the occupations of nearly 22 percent of executed women prisoners in the United States are unavailable. Where occupation status is available, executed white women were mostly housewives (57 percent) and domestic workers (13 percent), while executed black women were overwhelmingly slaves (92 percent) and domestic workers and servants (4 percent). Information on the occupations of five of the eight executed American Indian women remains unavailable, but Patience Sampson who hanged in Maine in 1735 was a servant, Katherine Garrett who hanged in 1738 in Connecticut was a servant, and an unidentified Indian woman who hanged in 1761 in Michigan was a slave. Information on the occupations of two Mexican women reveals that Pablita Sandoval (Paula Angel) was a seamstress at the time of her hanging in New Mexico and Chipita Rodriquez was an innkeeper when Texas hanged her in 1863. The occupations of executed women prisoners of a marginal nature included convicts, fences, criminals, petty crooks, and prostitutes, while others were entrepreneurs, such as boarding house owners, tavern owners, and innkeepers. Some executed women prisoners had professional occupations as teachers and nurses.

Historical Contours

Figure 2-1 provides a graphic depiction of three distinct historical trends accenting the execution of American women by the race of female offenders. The first broad trend in female executions took place in the early 1630s through the 1750s and corresponds largely to the early colonial period when jurisdictions put to death slightly more than 28 percent of American women executed historically. Chapter Three provides a contextual history of the social, political, and economic issues surrounding these executions. In the first historical trend, white female executions outweighed black female executions by a margin of nearly *two to one*. White women were nearly 64 percent of female executions in the period and black women were about 30 percent. There are no confirmed Mexican women executions during this period, but the four executed American Indian women constitute 2 percent of female executions in the period. The race of eight executed women in the period is unknown or otherwise unavailable.

Accenting the first broad historical period in female executions are three well-defined peaks in the number of white women executions in the 1650s, 1690s, and 1730s. While executions for witchcraft accented a preponderance of white women executed in the 1650s and 1690s, jurisdictions executed white women in the 1730s mostly for infanticide and predatory murders. Charleston officials in South Carolina hanged an unnamed slave woman for arson as early as 1641 when planters grew increasingly dependent on African slave labor. Otherwise, throughout much of the 17th century Chesapeake planters relied largely on indentured white servants. As one scholar explains, "In York County, for example, one-third of unfree workers were black

Figure 2-1. Historical Trends in Female Executions by Race in the United States, 1630s–2010s

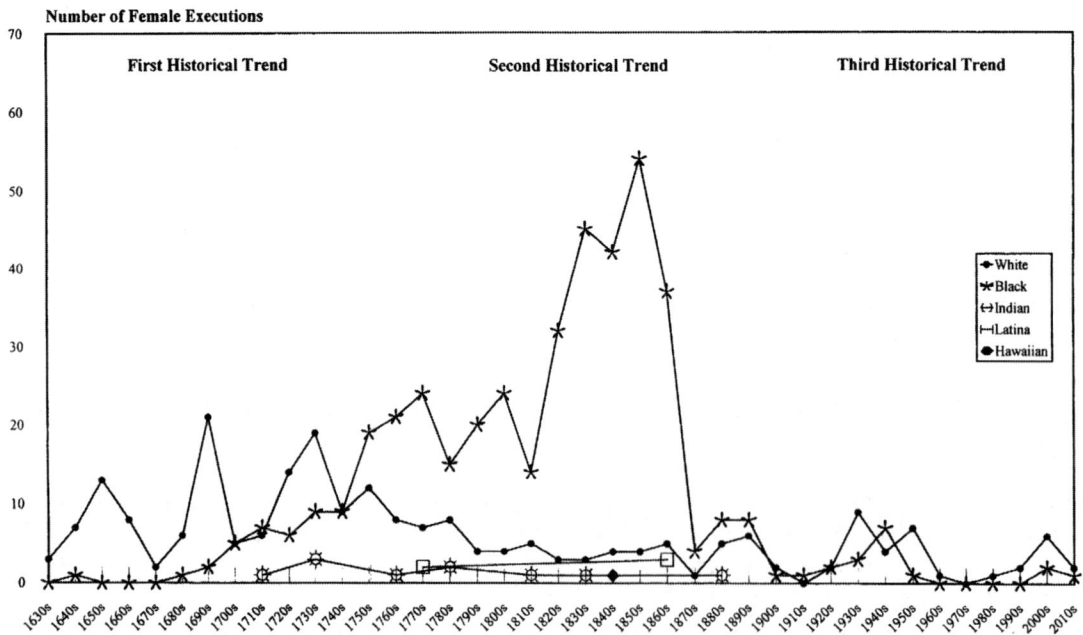

slaves in the 1670s, four-fifths by 1680, and 95 percent by the 1690s. This shift was accompanied by a decline in freedmen's status and prospects as the amount of inexpensive, available land dwindled."[26] Except for the 1710s and 1750s, the number of white women executions exceeded the number of black women executions throughout the period. Black women executions increased from one execution in the 1640s to seven black women executions in the 1710s. After the 1710s, black female executions decreased to five executions in the 1720s, increased to eight executions in the 1730s and 1740s, and increased again in the 1750s to 19 black female executions. Still, in no decade apart from the 1710s and the 1750s did black female executions exceed white women's executions over the period. Jurisdictions executed black women in the first historical period largely for murder, infanticide, arson, and slave revolt. Death penalty jurisdictions executed one American Indian woman in the 1710s and three in the 1730s for spousal murder, infanticide and child murder.

Chapter Four entails discussions of female executions in the second historical trend of women executions from the 1760s through the 1890s. Female executions in this period account for slightly more than 63 percent of women's executions historically. White women's executions occurred sporadically and generally decreased throughout the period. The downward trend in white women executions in the period involved a high of eight executions in the 1760s to a low of one execution in the 1870s. White female executions increased to six in the 1890s. Slightly more than 15 percent of female executions in the period were of white women and 79 percent were of black women. One plausible reason for the dramatic decrease in white women's executions in the period is that local and state governments concentrated their activities on controlling black slave women; death penalty jurisdictions executed black slave women by a margin of slightly *five to one* over white women in the period. White women largely escaped the apartheid history involving the oppressive strategies of gendered racism accenting the later period of colonial slavery (1750–1790), antebellum slavery (1790–1865), Reconstruction (1866–1877), and the early Jim Crow period (1877–1900). White women were largely not subjected to the brutal racial violence accenting these historical periods; white women endured less of the murderous assaults, lynching, and social and political repression that acted as a related means of imposing lethal punishment to black women—*six times* as many black women died from vigilante violence than white women in the period. White women hanged mostly for spousal killings of abusive husbands and predatory killings aggravated mostly by robbery. Executed white women were highly marginalized and impoverished females striking out against the gendered oppression of American society.

Accenting black women's executions are four historical peaks occurring in the 1770s, 1800s, 1830s, and 1850s. These peaks represent increased black female executions throughout the period mostly for murdering oppressive masters and their families, poisoning masters and their families, and the destruction of the ill-gotten property gains of white slave owners. Five Latinas (two Spanish women and three women of Mexican origin) went to the gallows in the 1770s and the 1860s. Six American Indian women also suffered state sanctioned executions, one in the 1760s, two in 1780s, and one in the 1810s, one in the 1830s, and one in the 1880s. The only confirmed Hawaiian woman execution in the history of female executions took place in 1846.

Chapter Five explains the contextual dynamics of women executions in the third historical trend in the late Jim Crow period, the civil rights period of the 1950s and 1960s, to the modern era since 1976. White female executions have exceeded black female executions in this period; white women are about 65 percent and black women are roughly 34 percent of female executions in the period. White female executions exceeded black female executions by a margin of nearly *two to one*. There are no confirmed Latina, American Indian, or Asian and Pacific Islander female executions in this period. The decrease in female executions after the 1950s had little to do with criminal justice policy disfavoring imposing women with the irrevocable punishment, however.

No jurisdiction conducted executions in the United States during a ten-year moratorium on executions from 1966 to 1976 when federal courts reviewed constitutional challenges to the death penalty. Accenting white female executions in the third historical period were 19 executions for predatory murders, one federal execution for espionage, and two child murder cases. Authorities executed one white female in the 1980s, two in the 1990s, five in the 2000s, and two in the 2010s. Over the same period, justice officials executed four black women, Wanda Jean Allen in 2001, Francis Elaine Newton in 2005, Kimberly McCarthy in 2013, and Lisa Ann Coleman in 2014.

Concluding Remarks

Inaccuracy in the historical record plagues investigations on female executions. A goal of the following chapters is to ensure that the historical record on female executions in the United States reflects past events as accurately as possible. The project has uncovered hundreds of female executions not included in the Espy file and corrects for many of the historical inaccuracies in the record concerning female executions. Utilizing a variety of sources including scholars' inventories and archived newspaper stories, this work goes far to confirm cases of female executions though there is often little in the historical record; this is particularly the case in accounting for black female executions in the 17th and 18th centuries. The inventory of female executions does not account for the entire population of executed women in the United States; certainly there are cases yet discovered in the historical record. But for those cases where the historical is clear, this chapter provides basic information on females executed in the United States since earliest colonial period.

[Following is the lengthy Table 2-1]

Table 2-1: Female Executions in the United States, 1632–2014

Name of Condemned Prisoner (Slave Owner)	Age at Death	Offense of Defendant	Race	Execution Date	Method of Execution	State of Execution	County of Execution	Occupation of Defendant	Place of Execution	Jurisdiction of Execution	Race of Victim
Unnamed (Calvert)^		Murder	Black	Unknown	Unknown	Arkansas	Unknown	Slave	Unknown	Unknown	Unknown
Unnamed (Gross)		Murder	Black	Unknown	Unknown	Georgia	Unknown	Slave	Unknown	Unknown	Unknown
Unnamed (Oglethorpe)		Attempted Murder	Black	1780s	Unknown	Georgia	Unknown	Slave	Unknown	Unknown	Unknown
Betty		Murder	Black	Unknown	Unknown	Louisiana	Unknown	Unknown	Unknown	Unknown	Unknown
Unnamed (Mills)		Murder	Black	Unknown	Unknown	Georgia	Unknown	Slave	Unknown	Unknown	Unknown
Unnamed^		Murder	Black	Unknown	Unknown	Tennessee	Unknown	Unknown	Unknown	Unknown	Unknown
Champion, June		Infanticide	White	JUN 1632	Hanged	Virginia	James City	Housewife	County	British	White
Hatch, Margaret		Infanticide	White	24 JUN 1633	Hanged	Virginia	James City	Housewife	County	British	White
Talbye, Dorothy		Infanticide	White	6 DEC 1638	Hanged	Massachusetts	Suffolk	Housewife	County	British	White
Unnamed		Arson	Black	JUL 1641	Hanged	South Carolina	Charleston	Slave	County	British	Unknown
Latham, Mary	18	Adultery	White	21 MAR 1643	Hanged	Massachusetts	Suffolk	Housewife	County	British	None
Cornish, Goodwife		Spousal Murder	White	1644	Hanged	Maine	York	Housewife	County	British	White
Martin, Mary	22	Infanticide	White	18 MAR 1647	Hanged	Massachusetts	Suffolk	Servant	County	British	White
Youngs, Alse		Witchcraft	White	26 MAY 1647	Hanged	Connecticut	Hartford	Unknown	County	British	None
Bishop, Alice (Allis)		Infanticide	White	4 OCT 1648	Hanged	Massachusetts	Plymouth	Housewife	County	British	White
Martin Clark	32	Witchcraft	White	15 JUN 1648	Hanged	Massachusetts	Suffolk	Housewife	County	British	None
Jones, Margaret		Witchcraft	White	7 DEC 1648	Hanged	Connecticut	Hartford	Servant	County	British	None
Johnson, Mary		Witchcraft	White	1650	Hanged	Massachusetts	Suffolk	Servant	County	British	None
Lake, Alice		Witchcraft	White	JUN 1651	Hanged	Connecticut	Fairfield	Housewife	County	British	None
Bassett, Goodwife		Witchcraft- Murder	White	1651	Hanged	Massachusetts	Middlesex	Housewife	County	British	White
Kendall, Elizabeth**	67	Witchcraft	White	1 APR 1651	Hanged	Connecticut	Hartford	Housewife	County	British	None
Carrington, Joan		Witchcraft	White	29 MAY 1651	Hanged	Massachusetts	Suffolk	Infanticide	County	British	White
Parsons, Mary		Witchcraft	White	NOV 1653	Hanged	Connecticut	Fairfield	Housewife	County	British	None
Knapp, Elizabeth		Witchcraft	White	1654	Hanged	Maryland	None	Servant	Naval Ship	Admiralty	None
Lee, Mary		Witchcraft	White	15 DEC 1654	Hanged	Connecticut	Windsor	Unknown	County	British	None
Gilbert, Lydia		Witchcraft	White	19 JUN 1656	Hanged	Massachusetts	Suffolk	Widow	County	British	None
Hibbens, Ann		Witchcraft	White	1658	Hanged	Maryland	None	Unknown	Naval Ship	Admiralty	None
Richardson, Elizabeth		Theft-Stealing	White	1658	Hanged	Maryland	Unknown	Housewife	County	British	White
Williams, Mary		Theft-Stealing	White	1658	Hanged	Maryland	Unknown	Housewife	County	British	White
Clocker, Mary		Witchcraft Violate	White	1659	Hanged	Virginia	None	Unknown	Naval Ship	Admiralty	None
Grady, Katharine											
Dyer, Mary Barrett		Banishment	White	1 JUN 1660	Hanged	Massachusetts	Suffolk	Housewife	County	British	None
Greensmith, Rebecca		Witchcraft	White	25 JAN 1663	Hanged	Connecticut	Hartford	Housewife	County	British	None
Barnes, Mary		Witchcraft	White	25 JAN 1663	Hanged	Connecticut	Hartford	Unknown	County	British	None
Sanford, Mary		Witchcraft	White	25 JUN 1662	Hanged	Connecticut	Hartford	Housewife	County	British	None
Greene, Elizabeth	30	Infanticide	White	8 JUL 1664	Hanged	Maryland	St. Mary's	Servant	County	British	White
Briggs, Ruth	30	Infanticide	White	1 JUN 1668	Hanged	Connecticut	Hartford	Unknown	County	British	White
Unnamed		Infanticide	White	OCT 1668	Hanged	Massachusetts	Essex	Unknown	County	British	White
Hendricks, Angel	28	Infanticide	White	17 JUL 1669	Hanged	New York	Manhattan	Unknown	County	British	White

*Compensation to slave owner or estate. **Wrongful execution. ***Appellate review of capital cases before Gregg v. Georgia in 1976. ****Mental retardation. ^Unconfirmed

Name of Condemned Prisoner (Slave Owner)	Age at Death	Offense of Defendant	Race	Execution Date	Method of Execution	State of Execution	County of Execution	Occupation of Defendant	Place of Execution	Jurisdiction of Execution	Race of Victim
Colledge, Joan		Infanticide	White	18 OCT 1671	Hanged	Maryland	Calvert	Spinster	County	British	White
Yausley, Isabella		Infanticide	White	17 APR 1671	Hanged	Maryland	Anne Arundel	Spinster	County	British	White
Marja (Joshua Lambe)	28	Child Murder-Arson	Black	22 SEP 1681	Burned	Massachusetts	Suffolk	Slave	County	British	White
Lake, Henry Mrs.		Witchcraft	White	1684	Hanged	Massachusetts	Unknown	Housewife	County	British	None
Axell, Mary		Infanticide	White	7 DEC 1684	Hanged	Maryland	Unknown	Housewife	County	British	White
Fowler, Rebecca		Witchcraft	White	9 OCT 1685	Hanged	Maryland	Calvert	Housewife	County	British	None
Unnamed		Infanticide	White	27 OCT 1687	Hanged	Rhode Island	Bristol	Unknown	County	British	White
Roe, Judith		Robbery-Murder	White	15 MAR 1688	Hanged	Delaware	Kent	Unknown	County	British	White
Glover, Ann		Witchcraft	White	16 NOV 1688	Hanged	Massachusetts	Suffolk	Housekeeper	County	British	None
Unnamed		Infanticide	Unk	1692	Hanged	Virginia	Unknown	Unknown	County	British	Unknown
Nurse, Rebecca Towne	71	Witchcraft	White	19 JUL 1692	Hanged	Massachusetts	Essex	Housewife	County	British	None
Martin, Susannah North	66	Witchcraft	White	19 JUL 1692	Hanged	Massachusetts	Essex	Housewife	County	British	None
Howe, Elizabeth Jackson	54	Witchcraft	White	19 JUL 1692	Hanged	Massachusetts	Essex	Housewife	County	British	None
Wildes, Sarah Averill	65	Witchcraft	White	19 JUL 1692	Hanged	Massachusetts	Essex	Housewife	County	British	None
Carrier, Martha Allen	38	Witchcraft	White	19 JUL 1692	Hanged	Massachusetts	Essex	Housewife	County	British	None
Parker, Mary Ayer	55	Witchcraft	White	22 SEP 1692	Hanged	Massachusetts	Essex	Unknown	County	British	None
Parker, Alice		Witchcraft	White	22 SEP 1692	Hanged	Massachusetts	Essex	Unknown	County	British	None
Easty, Mary Towne	51	Witchcraft	White	22 SEP 1692	Hanged	Massachusetts	Essex	Housewife	County	British	None
Corey, Martha	65	Witchcraft	White	22 SEP 1692	Hanged	Massachusetts	Essex	Housewife	County	British	None
Pudeater, Ann Greenslit	65	Witchcraft	White	22 SEP 1692	Hanged	Massachusetts	Essex	Midwife	County	British	None
Reed, Wilmot	55	Witchcraft	White	22 SEP 1692	Hanged	Massachusetts	Essex	Housewife	County	British	None
Scott, Margaret	72	Witchcraft	White	22 SEP 1692	Hanged	Massachusetts	Essex	Unknown	County	British	None
Bishop, Bridget	60	Witchcraft	White	22 SEP 1692	Hanged	Massachusetts	Essex	Tavern Owner	County	British	None
Good, Sarah	38	Witchcraft	White	22 SEP 1692	Hanged	Massachusetts	Essex	Unknown	County	British	None
Unnamed		Unknown	Unk	NOV 1692	Unknown	Virginia	Unknown	Unknown	County	British	Unknown
Kimball, Abigail		Unknown	White	DEC 1692	Unknown	Maryland	Unknown	Unknown	County	British	Unknown
Lunt, Mary		Infanticide	White	MAY 1693	Hanged	Maryland	Unknown	Housewife	County	British	White
Emerson, Elizabeth	27	Infanticide	White	8 JUN 1693	Hanged	Massachusetts	Suffolk	Unknown	County	British	White
Grace (James Taylor)		Infanticide	Black	8 JUN 1693	Hanged	Massachusetts	Suffolk	Slave	County	British	Black
Lewis, Elizabeth^		Unknown	Unk	1694	Unknown	Virginia	Unknown	Unknown	County	British	Unknown
Andrews, Susanna	20	Infanticide	White	5 APR 1696	Hanged	Massachusetts	Plymouth	Unknown	County	British	White
Andrews, Esther	45	Infanticide	White	5 APR 1696	Hanged	Massachusetts	Plymouth	Unknown	County	British	White
Threeneedles, Sarah	19	Infanticide	White	17 NOV 1698	Hanged	Massachusetts	Suffolk	Unknown	County	British	White
Smith, Sarah	30	Infanticide	White	25 AUG 1698	Hanged	Massachusetts	Suffolk	Unknown	County	British	White
Rogers, Esther	21	Infanticide	White	31 JUL 1701	Hanged	Massachusetts	Essex	Servant	County	British	White
Tandy, Ann		Infanticide	White	1702	Hang/Gibbet	Virginia	King & Queen	Unknown	County	British	White
Ward, Margaret		Murder	White	7 MAY 1703	Hanged	Maryland	Anne Arundel	Servant	County	British	White
Bridget (Page)		Arson	Black	5 JUL 1705	Unknown	Virginia	Unknown	Slave	County	British	Unknown
Sarah (Custis)		Arson	Black	16 JUN 1705	Hanged	Virginia	Northampton	Slave	County	British	Unknown
Mary		Grand Larceny	Black	13 SEP 1706	Hanged	New York	New York	Slave	County	British	Unknown
Caine, Margaret		Murder	White	MAY 1707	Unknown	Maryland	Charles	Unknown	County	British	White
Thompson, Abigail	37	Spousal Murder	White	27 MAY 1708	Hanged	Connecticut	Hartford	Housewife	County	British	White
Unnamed (William Hallett)		Murder	Black	7 FEB 1708	Burned	New York	Queens	Slave	County	British	White

2. Empirical Frameworks—Table 2-1

Name of Condemned Prisoner (Slave Owner)	Age at Death	Offense of Defendant	Race	Execution Date	Method of Execution	State of Execution	County of Execution	Occupation of Defendant	Place of Execution	Jurisdiction of Execution	Race of Victim
Bowen, Anne		Unknown	White	24 MAR 1708	Hanged	New York	New York	Innkeeper	County	British	Unknown
Unnamed		Arson	Black	1709	Burned	South Carolina	Unknown	Slave	County	British	White
Williams, Elizabeth		Burglary	White	APR 1710	Unknown	Maryland	Unknown	Unknown	County	British	Unknown
Degoe, Hannah	14	Infanticide	Black	29 NOV 1710	Hanged	Rhode Island	Bristol	Servant	County	British	Black
Waisoiusksquaw		Spousal Murder	Indian	MAY 1711	Hanged	Connecticut	Hartford	Unknown	County	British	Indian
Betty (Isaac Winslow)		Infanticide	Black	7 MAY 1712	Hanged	Massachusetts	Suffolk	Slave	County	British	Black
Abigail (Gysbert Vaninburgh)		Accessory to Murder									
Sarah (Stophel Pell)		Accessory to Murder	Black	SEP 1712	Hanged	New York	New York	Slave	County	British	White
Elizabeth Gordon		Murder	Black	19 APR 1712	Hanged	New York	New York	Slave	County	British	White
Tracy, Sarah		Unknown	White	27 OCT 1712	Unknown	Virginia	Unknown	Unknown	County	British	Unknown
Spurrier, Elizabeth		Murder	White	NOV 1713	Unknown	Maryland	Unknown	Unknown	County	British	Unknown
Gryce, Deborah		Murder	White	NOV 1713	Unknown	Maryland	Unknown	Unknown	County	British	White
Callogharne, Margaret		Infanticide	White	17 DEC 1714	Hanged	New York	Long Island	Unknown	County	British	White
Unnamed		Infanticide	White	9 JUN 1715	Hanged	Massachusetts	Suffolk	Servant	County	British	White
Unnamed		Infanticide	Black	1 JAN 1715	Hanged	New York	Long Island	Free	County	British	Black
Hagar (James Sherron)		Murder	Black	2 JAN 1717	Burned	New York	Albany	Slave	County	British	White
Atwood, Elizabeth		Murder	Black	16 APR 1717	Burned	New Jersey	Salem	Slave	County	British	White
Collar, Magdalen		Infanticide	White	25 AUG 1720	Hanged	Massachusetts	Ipswich	Unknown	County	British	White
Unnamed		Infanticide	White	1720	Hanged	North Carolina	Unknown	Poor woman	County	British	White
Horne, Frances		Adultery	White	25 MAY 1721	Unknown	Massachusetts	Unknown	Unknown	County	British	Unknown
Jones, Elizabeth		Burglary	White	MAY 1721	Unknown	Maryland	Unknown	Unknown	County	British	Unknown
Bell, Christiana		Theft-Stealing	White	NOV 1721	Unknown	Maryland	Unknown	Unknown	County	British	Unknown
Robinson, Anne		Infanticide	White	21 NOV 1721	Hanged	New Jersey	Gloucester	Servant	County	British	White
Moore, Eleanor		Burglary	White	OCT 1722	Unknown	Maryland	Unknown	Unknown	County	British	Unknown
Reed, Mary		Infanticide	White	9 MAY 1722	Hanged	Delaware	New Castle	Unknown	County	British	White
Carrah, Eleanor		Theft-Stealing	White	MAY 1723	Unknown	Maryland	Unknown	Unknown	County	British	Unknown
Hannah (Galloway)		Burglary	White	MAY 1723	Unknown	Maryland	Unknown	Unknown	County	British	Unknown
Burrass, Mary		Murder	Black	MAY 1723	Gibbeted	Maryland	Annapolis	Slave	County	British	White
Mounting, Mary		Theft-Stealing	White	OCT 1723	Unknown	Maryland	Unknown	Unknown	County	British	Unknown
Murphy, Elizabeth		Theft-Stealing	White	OCT 1723	Unknown	Maryland	Unknown	Unknown	County	British	Unknown
Unnamed		Infanticide	White	13 JUL 1724	Hanged	Pennsylvania	Delaware	Unknown	County	British	White
Jackson, Mary		Murder	White	MAR 1727	Hanged	Maryland	Kent	Servant	County	British	Unknown
Colson, Elizabeth		Infanticide	Black	25 MAY 1727	Hanged	Massachusetts	Plymouth	Unknown	County	British	Black
Hannah (George Walker)		Unknown	Black	JUN 1727	Unknown	Virginia	Elizabeth City	Slave	County	British	Unknown
Sarah (Blair)		Arson	Black	17 APR 1728	Unknown	Virginia	Unknown	Slave	County	British	Unknown
Babb		Felony	Black	17 JUN 1729	Unknown	Maryland	Kent	Unknown	County	British	Unknown
Unnamed		Slave Revolt	Black	JUN 1731	Hanged	Louisiana	Orleans	Slave	County	British	White
Bevan, Catharine	51	Spousal Murder	White	10 SEP 1731	Burned	Delaware	New Castle	Housewife	County	British	White
Hannah (Moses Atwater)		Murder	Black	15 SEP 1731	Hanged	Connecticut	New Haven	Slave	County	British	White
Pettifer, Ann	51	Spousal Murder	White	7 NOV 1732	Hanged	North Carolina	Unknown	Unknown	County	British	White
Unnamed		Murder	White	1732	Unknown	Pennsylvania	Lancaster	Unknown	County	British	Unknown
Unnamed		Revolt	Black	1732	Hanged	Louisiana	New Orleans	Slave	County	British	None
Westerdon, Jemmina		Infanticide	White	28 MAY 1733	Hanged	New Jersey	Newark	Unknown	County	British	White

Name of Condemned Prisoner (Slave Owner)	Age at Death	Offense of Defendant	Race	Execution Date	Method of Execution	State of Execution	County of Execution	Occupation of Defendant	Place of Execution	Jurisdiction of Execution	Race of Victim
Chamblitt, Rebecka	27	Infanticide	White	27 SEP 1733	Hanged	Massachusetts	Suffolk	Servant	County	British	White
Unnamed		Burglary	Unk	26 NOV 1734	Unknown	Pennsylvania	Chester	Unknown	County	British	Unknown
Ryley, Alice		Murder	White	19 JAN 1735	Hanged	Georgia	Chatham	Irish Servant	County	British	White
Sampson, Patience	23	Child Murder	Indian	31 JUL 1735	Hanged	Maine	York	Servant	County	British	White
Gross, Margaret^		Robbery	Unk	OCT 1736	Hanged	New York	Unknown	Unknown	County	British	Unknown
Greenley, Elizabeth		Murder	White	26 NOV 1736	Hanged	Virginia	Williamsburg	Servant	County	British	White
Unnamed		Unknown	Unk	1737	Unknown	Virginia	Unknown	Unknown	County	British	Unknown
Cloe		Unknown	Black	27 MAY 1737	Hanged	Maryland	Anne Arundel	Slave	County	British	Unknown
Finmore, Mary		Unknown	White	1 JUN 1737	Hanged	Maryland	Queen Anne	Servant	County	British	Unknown
Comfort, Abiah		Infanticide	Indian	31 AUG 1737	Hanged	Massachusetts	Sherburne	Unknown	County	British	Indian
Unnamed		Infanticide	White	7 SEP 1737	Hanged	New York	Albany	Unknown	County	British	White
Connor, Catharine (Prudden)	23	Burglary	Black	2 JUL 1737	Burned	Pennsylvania	Philadelphia	Unknown	County	British	Unknown
Ann (John Easton)	16	Murder	Black	25 FEB 1737	Hanged	Virginia	Nansemond	Slave	County	British	White
Garrett, Katherine	27	Infanticide	Indian	4 NOV 1737	Hanged	Rhode Island	New Port	Servant	County	British	White
Blair, Elizabeth		Unspecified Felony	White	3 MAY 1738	Hanged	Connecticut	New London	Servant	County	British	Indian
Chamberlain, Sarah		Infanticide	White	5 MAY 1738	Hanged	Virginia	Williamsburg	Servant	County	British	White
Bess (John Beale)	27	Attempted Murder		1738	Hanged	South Carolina	Charleston	Unknown	County	British	White
Unnamed		Unknown	Black	7 JUN 1738	Unknown	Maryland	Prince George	Slave	County	British	Unknown
Unnamed	20	Unknown	White	1739	Hanged	Maryland	Unknown	Unknown	County	British	Unknown
Unnamed		Murder	White	1739	Hanged	Maryland	Unknown	Unknown	County	British	Unknown
Judy (Plater)	20	Conspiracy to Murder	Black	1739	Hanged	Maryland	Unknown	Slave	County	British	Unknown
Simpson, Sarah		Infanticide	Black	30 MAR 1739	Hanged	Maryland	St. Mary	Slave	County	British	Black
Kenney, Penelope		Infanticide	White	27 DEC 1739	Hanged	New Hampshire	Rockingham	Widow	County	British	White
Sullivan, Catharine		Infanticide	White	27 DEC 1739	Hanged	New Hampshire	Rockingham	Servant	County	British	White
Twopence, Elizabeth	27	Infanticide	White	26 FEB 1739	Hanged	North Carolina	Chowan	Unknown	County	British	White
Maze, Elizabeth	20	Infanticide	White	4 MAY 1739	Hanged	Virginia	Williamsburg	Unknown	County	British	White
Judith (Harris)		Murder	Black	2 NOV 1739	Hanged	Virginia	Williamsburg	Unknown	County	British	White
Kate (Varambaut)		Arson-Slave Revolt		13 MAR 1741	Hang/Quarter	Maryland	Queen Anne	Slave	County	British	White
Sorubiero, Margaret		Slave Revolt	Black	JUL 1741	Unknown	South Carolina	Charleston	Slave	County	British	White
Hughson, Sarah	22	Slave Revolt	White	12 JUN 1741	Hanged	New York	New York	Bar Maid	County	British	White
Kerry, Sarah		Slave Revolt	White	12 JUN 1741	Hanged	New York	New York	Housewife	County	British	White
Mol (Jeremiah Pattison)		Murder	White	12 JUN 1741	Hanged	New York	New York	Bar Maid	County	British	White
			Black	28 APR 1742	Hang/Quarter						
Lucy (Richard Randolph)		Murder	Black	30 JUN 1742	Hanged	Maryland	Calvert	Slave	County	British	White
Otley, Ann		Murder	White	SEP 1742	Unknown	Virginia	Goochland	Slave	County	British	White
Plunkett, Anne		Murder	White	26 NOV 1742	Unknown	Pennsylvania	Unknown	Unknown	County	British	Unknown
Fennison, Margaret		Infanticide	White	14 APR 1743	Hanged	Virginia	Unknown	Housewife	County	British	Unknown
Kate (Thomas Belding)		Infanticide	Black	16 NOV 1743	Hanged	Connecticut	Hartford	Slave	County	British	Black

2. Empirical Frameworks—Table 2-1

Name of Condemned Prisoner (Slave Owner)	Age at Death	Offense of Defendant	Race	Execution Date	Method of Execution	State of Execution	County of Execution	Occupation of Defendant	Place of Execution	Jurisdiction of Execution	Race of Victim
Moss, Rebecca		Infanticide	White	7 OCT 1745	Hanged	Pennsylvania	Lancaster	Unknown	County	British	White
Eve (Peter Montague)		Murder	Black	23 JAN 1745	Burned	Virginia	Orange	Slave	County	British	White
Shaw, Elizabeth	22	Infanticide	White	18 DEC 1745	Hanged	Connecticut	Windham	Unknown	County	British	White
Catherine (Kieves)^		Unknown	Black	1746	Burned	Maryland	Unknown	Slave	County	British	Unknown
Anderson, Esther		Murder	White	13 MAY 1746	Burned	Maryland	Kent	Servant	County	British	White
Wakefield, Elizabeth		Infanticide	White	8 OCT 1747	Hanged	Massachusetts	Middlesex	Widow	County	British	White
Bett (Wilhelmus Houghtaling)		Burglary	Black	23 JUL 1748	Hanged	New York	Kingston	Slave	County	British	Unknown
Unnamed		Unknown	Black	1749	Unknown	Massachusetts	Unknown	Slave	County	British	Unknown
Robinson, Elizabeth		Burglary	White	1 FEB 1750	Hanged	Pennsylvania	Philadelphia	Criminal	County	British	Unknown
Kitt (Thomas Miles)		Poisoning	Black	1750	Hanged	South Carolina	Charleston	Slave	County	British	Unknown
Margaret Borden^		Burglary	Unk	1751	Unknown	Delaware	Unknown	Unknown	County	British	Unknown
Unnamed (Simmons)		Poisoning	Black	1751	Unknown	South Carolina	Unknown	Slave	County	British	Unknown
Alice Cunningham		Murder	White	8 FEB 1752	Unknown	Delaware	Unknown	Unknown	County	British	Unknown
Mary		Unknown	Black	1757	Hanged	North Carolina	New Hanover	Slave	County	British	Unknown
Phillis (John Greenleaf)	17	Child Murder	Black	16 MAY 1751	Hanged	Massachusetts	Boston	Slave	County	British	White
Unnamed		Unspecified	Black	1751	Hanged	Virginia	James City	Slave	County	British	White
Unnamed^		Felony	Unk	1751	Unknown	Maryland	Unknown	Unknown	County	British	Unknown
Jenny (Joseph Galloway)		Murder	Black	3 APR 1751	Hanged	Maryland	Anne Arundel	Slave	County	British	White
Grace (Joseph Galloway)		Arson	Black	3 APR 1751	Hanged	Maryland	Anne Arundel	Slave	County	British	White
Perry, Mary		Arson Burglary & Felony	White	22 OCT 1752	Hanged	Maryland	Queen Anne	Spinster	County	British	White
Jenny (Hugh Anderson)		Poisoning	Black	1752	Hanged	South Carolina	Charleston	Slave	County	British	Black
Unnamed (Cattrell)		Poisoning	Black	1752	Unknown	South Carolina	Charleston	Slave	County	British	Black
Bassett, Martha		Murder	White	10 JAN 1752	Hanged	Maryland	Baltimore	Servant	County	British	White
Powell, Mary		Accessory to Murder	White	10 JAN 1752	Hanged	Maryland	Baltimore	Servant	County	British	White
Molly (Pope)		Unknown	Black	6 JUN 1752	Unknown	Virginia	Unknown	Slave	County	British	Unknown
Unnamed (Drayton)		Poisoning	Black	1753	Unknown	South Carolina	Unknown	Slave	County	British	White
Sue (Connor)		Murder	Black	5 FEB 1753	Unknown	Virginia	Unknown	Slave	County	British	Unknown
Bramble, Sarah		Infanticide	White	21 NOV 1753	Hanged	Connecticut	New London	Servant	County	British	White
Buzard, Anne		Infanticide	White	13 JUL 1754	Hanged	New Jersey	Gloucester	Widow	County	British	White
Unnamed (Childermas Croft)		Arson	Black	24 JUN 1754	Burned	South Carolina	Charleston	Slave	County	British	White
Unnamed (Childermas Croft)		Arson	Black	24 JUN 1754	Burned	South Carolina	Charleston	Slave	County	British	White
Pegg (Pitman)		Murder	Black	17 DEC 1754	Unknown	Virginia	Unknown	Slave	County	British	Unknown
Schmidt, Eve Mary		Murder	White	1755	Unknown	Pennsylvania	Unknown	Unknown	County	British	White
Phillis (Captain John Codman)		Poisoning	Black	18 SEP 1755	Burned	Massachusetts	Suffolk	Slave	County	British	White
Unnamed (Derek Day)		Unknown	Black	MAY 1755	Burned	New Jersey	Bergen	Slave	County	British	Unknown
Murray, Mary		Murder	White	23 MAY 1755	Hanged	Virginia	Williamsburg	Unknown	County	British	White

Name of Condemned Prisoner (Slave Owner)	Age at Death	Offense of Defendant	Race	Execution Date	Method of Execution	State of Execution	County of Execution	Occupation of Defendant	Place of Execution	Jurisdiction of Execution	Race of Victim
Jenny (Jeremiah Chase)		Attempted Murder	Black	4 JUL 1755	Hang/Gibbet	Maryland	Port Tobacco	Slave	County	British	White
Plenty (Field)		Poisoning	Black	1756	Unknown	South Carolina	Unknown	Slave	County	British	Unknown
Tida (Ephraim Glover)		Attempted Murder	Black	6 APR 1757	Hanged	Maryland	Anne Arundel	Slave	County	British	White
Sexton, Margaret		Child Murder	White	4 JUN 1757	Hanged	Delaware	Sussex	Housewife	County	British	White
Mary		Unknown	Black	1757	Hanged	North Carolina	Unknown	Slave	County	British	Unknown
Unnamed^		Murder	Black	1758	Unknown	Massachusetts	Unknown	Unknown	County	British	Unknown
Grauel, Elizabeth Learch		Infanticide	White	10 MAR 1759	Hanged	Pennsylvania	Berks	Widow	County	British	White
Jenny (Strother)		Murder	Black	25 OCT 1760	Hanged	Virginia	Unknown	Slave	County	British	Unknown
Eleanor Evans^		Murder	Unk	1761	Hanged	Delaware	Unknown	Unknown	County	British	Unknown
Unnamed (Fickling)		Murder	Black	14 JAN 1761	Hanged	South Carolina	Charleston	Slave	County	British	White
Rachel (Grymes)		Poisoning	Black	8 MAY 1761	Unknown	Virginia	Unknown	Slave	County	British	Unknown
Rachael (John Hamilton)		Attempted Murder	Black	7 OCT 1761	Hanged	Maryland	Calvert	Slave	County	British	White
Unnamed (Clapham)		Murder	Indian	APR 1763	Hanged	Michigan	Wayne	Slave	County	British	White
Lettice		Murder	Black	1763	Hanged	North Carolina	Perquimans	Slave	County	British	Unknown
Nan (Robert Munford)		Unknown	Black	28 APR 1763	Hanged	Virginia	Caroline	Slave	County	British	Unknown
Phoebe (Joseph Richardson)		Burglary	Black	5 MAR 1764	Hanged	Pennsylvania	Chester	Slave	County	British	White
Betty (William Smith)		Poisoning	Black	20 JUN 1764	Hanged	Maryland	Calvert	Slave	County	British	White
Unnamed		Infanticide	White	30 DEC 1765	Hanged	New Jersey	Somerset	Unknown	County	British	Black
Ewing, Jane		Infanticide	White	19 JAN 1765	Hanged	Pennsylvania	Delaware	Unknown	County	British	White
Yates, Mary^		Theft-Stealing	Unk	8 FEB 1765	Hanged	New York	Unknown	Unknown	County	British	Unknown
Bellow (Mosby)		Poisoning	Black	18 JUN 1765	Unknown	Virginia	Unknown	Unknown	County	British	Unknown
Erwin, Elizabeth		Infanticide	White	26 SEP 1765	Hanged	Pennsylvania	York	Unknown	County	British	White
Unnamed^		Arson	Black	1766	Unknown	Maryland	Unknown	Unknown	County	British	Unknown
Beck (Joseph Smith)		Arson	Black	4 JUN 1766	Hanged	Maryland	Calvert	Slave	County	British	White
Vaughn, Elizabeth		Infanticide	White	2 JUN 1766	Hanged	New Jersey	Burlington City	Spinster	County	British	White
Sukey (Eppes)		Murder	Black	4 JUL 1766	Unknown	Virginia	Unknown	Slave	County	British	Unknown
Dent, Elizabeth		Theft-Stealing	Unk	NOV 1766	Hanged	New York	Unknown	Unknown	County	British	Unknown
Floyd, Elizabeth^		Theft-Stealing	Unk	NOV 1766	Hanged	New York	Unknown	Unknown	County	British	Unknown
Rose (Rabour)*		Arson	Black	6 NOV 1766	Hanged	North Carolina	Halifax	Slave	County	British	White
Venus (Catherine Ball)	17	Burglary	Black	9 FEB 1767	Hanged	New York	New York	Slave	County	British	White
Kreps, Catharine		Infanticide	White	19 DEC 1767	Hanged	Pennsylvania	Berks	Unknown	County	British	White
Esther (Wise)		Murder	Black	19 MAY 1767	Unknown	Virginia	Accomack	Slave	County	British	White
Sharp, Martha		Infanticide	White	JUN 1767	Unknown	Virginia	Williamsburg	Unknown	County	British	White
Jenny (Chapman)^		Murder	Black	OCT 1767	Unknown	Rhode Island	Unknown	Slave	County	British	Unknown
Bronson, Catherine	25	Theft-Stealing	White	23 NOV 1767	Hanged	New York	New York	Unknown	County	British	White
Malone, Frances^		Unknown	Unk	23 NOV 1767	Hanged	New York	Unknown	Unknown	County	British	Unknown
Betty (Smith)		Conspiracy to Murder	Black	21 DEC 1767	Unknown	Virginia	Unknown	Slave	County	British	Unknown
Blay, Ruth	25	Infanticide	White	30 DEC 1768	Hanged	New Hampshire	Rockingham	Teacher	County	British	White

2. Empirical Frameworks—Table 2-1

Name of Condemned Prisoner (Slave Owner)	Age at Death	Offense of Defendant	Race	Execution Date	Method of Execution	State of Execution	County of Execution	Occupation of Defendant	Place of Execution	Jurisdiction of Execution	Race of Victim
Kennedy, Mary		Murder	White	24 DEC 1768	Hanged	Pennsylvania	York	Irish Servant	County	British	White
Winny (John Knox)		Murder	Black	11 JUL 1769	Hanged	Virginia	Stafford	Slave	County	British	White
Dolly (Sands)		Murder	Black	28 JUL 1769	Burned	West Virginia	Jefferson	Slave	County	British	White
Dolly (James Sands)		Child Murder	Black	1769	Burned	South Carolina	Charleston	Slave	County	British	White
Jenny		Murder	Black	1770	Hang/Chains	Maryland	Unknown	Slave	County	British	White
Bolton, Elizabeth^		Unknown	Unk	1770	Unknown	Virginia	Unknown	Unknown	County	British	White
Sarah (Carter)		Burglary	Black	24 OCT 1770	Unknown	Virginia	Unknown	Slave	County	British	Unknown
Unnamed (Ward)		Murder	Black	11 DEC 1770	Hanged	North Carolina	Onslow	Slave	County	British	White
Annis (Henry Ormond)*		Murder	Black	11 DEC 1770	Burned	North Carolina	Beaufort	Slave	County	British	White
Phyllis (Henry Ormond)*		Murder	Black	11 DEC 1770	Hanged	North Carolina	Beaufort	Slave	County	British	White
Lucy (Wyriot Ormond)*		Murder	Black	11 DEC 1770	Hanged	North Carolina	Beaufort	Slave	County	British	White
Eve (James Chamberlaine)		Arson	Black	15 MAR 1771	Hanged	Maryland	Queen Anne	Slave	County	British	Unknown
Unnamed (Nathaniel Smith)		Arson-Murder	Black	1771	Burned	New York	Smithtown	Slave	County	British	White
Dailey, Mary		Robbery	White	10 MAY 1771	Hanged	New York	New York	Petty Thief	County	British	Unknown
Siggins, Margaret		Burglary	White	24 MAY 1771	Hanged	New York	New York	Unknown	County	British	White
Rauch, Margaret		Infanticide	White	1772	Hanged	Pennsylvania	Northumberland	Unknown	County	British	White
Judith (Harrison)		Poisoning	Black	26 JUN 1772	Burned	Virginia	Brunswick	Slave	County	British	Unknown
Sall (Loftain)		Murder	Black	11 JAN 1773	Hanged	Virginia	Brunswick	Slave	County	British	Unknown
Fanny (Charlton)		Murder	Black	18 JUN 1773	Unknown	Virginia	Unknown	Slave	County	British	Unknown
Sitty (Johannes Nellis)		Arson	Black	30 MAR 1774	Burned	New York	Montgomery	Slave	County	British	White
Elizabeth		Infanticide	Mulato	30 APR 1774	Hanged	Pennsylvania	Philadelphia	Unknown	County	British	White
Unnamed (William Crafts)		Arson	Black	18 NOV 1774	Hanged	New York	Westchester	Slave	County	British	White
Peppers, Catharine		Infanticide	White	3 JUN 1774	Hanged	Virginia	Williamsburg	Unknown	County	British	White
Unnamed		Arson	Black	18 NOV 1774	Hanged	New York	Unknown	Unknown	County	British	Unknown
Unnamed		Murder	Black	1 JAN 1775	Hanged	New York	Unknown	Free Woman	County	British	Unknown
Frazier, Susannah		Infanticide	White	13 JAN 1775	Hanged	Virginia	Williamsburg	Unknown	County	British	White
Jenny (Betty Williamson)		Murder	Black	17 NOV 1775	Hanged	Maryland	Calvert	Slave	County	British	Unknown
Unnamed		Murder	Black	7 DEC 1775	Burned	Georgia	Andrews Parish	Slave	County	British	White
Unnamed		Murder	Black	7 DEC 1775	Burned	Georgia	Andrews Parish	Slave	County	British	White
Unnamed		Arson	Black	1776	Unknown	Maryland	Unknown	Unknown	County	British	White
Synor (Downing)		Arson	Black	20 JAN 1776	Unknown	Virginia	Unknown	Slave	County	British	Unknown
Frances (Douglass)		Murder Conspiracy to	Black	3 SEP 1776	Unknown	Virginia	Unknown	Slave	County	British	Unknown
Jenny (Lewis)		Murder	Black	1777	Unknown	Virginia	Unknown	Slave	County	British	Unknown
Rachel (Collier)		Murder	Black	1777	Unknown	Virginia	Unknown	Slave	County	British	Unknown
Wyley, Ann		Robbery	Black	26 MAR 1777	Hanged	Michigan	Wayne	Unknown	County	British	White
Spooner, Bathsheba Ruggles	32	Spousal Murder	White	2 JUL 1778	Hanged	Massachusetts	Worcester	Housewife	County	State	White

Name of Condemned Prisoner (Slave Owner)	Age at Death	Offense of Defendant	Race	Execution Date	Method of Execution	State of Execution	County of Execution	Occupation of Defendant	Place of Execution	Jurisdiction of Execution	Race of Victim
Francisca, Maria		Spousal Murder	Spanish	26 JAN 1779	Hanged	New Mexico	Pueblo Cochiti	Unknown	City	Spanish	Spanish
Josefa, Maria		Spousal Murder	Spanish	26 JAN 1779	Hanged	New Mexico	Pueblo Cochiti	Unknown	City	Spanish	Unknown
Esther (Blount)		Unknown	Black	APR 1779	Hanged	North Carolina	Unknown	Slave	County	State	White
Fisher, Catherine		Infanticide	White	5 JUN 1779	Hanged	Pennsylvania	Lancaster	Unknown	County	State	Black
Poll (Bobbit)		Infanticide	Black	22 JAN 1779	Hanged	Virginia	Sussex	Slave	County	State	White
Jenny (Bryan)		Murder	Black	18 NOV 1780	Burned	North Carolina	Johnston	Slave	County	State	White
Sucky		Arson	Black	7 JUL 1780	Hanged	Pennsylvania	Cumberland	Slave	County	State	White
Violet (Sawyer)		Arson	Black	4 APR 1780	Hanged/Dec	Virginia	Dickenson	Slave	County	State	Unknown
Hall, Mary		Burglary	White	DEC 1781	Hanged	Pennsylvania	Unknown	Unknown	County	State	Unknown
Glass, Marie	35	Murder	Black	26 JUL 1781	Hanged/Dec	Louisiana	Orleans	Free	County	Military	White
Penelope (Copeland)		Unspecified									
Judith (Crawford)		Felony	Black	4 APR 1781	Hanged	Virginia	Charles City	Slave	County	State	Unknown
Belle		Arson	Black	26 JUN 1782	Hanged	Maryland	Unknown	Slave	County	State	Unknown
Bess (Joseph Warnock)		Murder	Black	1 MAR 1783	Hanged	New Jersey	Burlington	Slave	County	State	Unknown
Rose (Tyson)		Murder	Black	1783	Hanged	South Carolina	Charleston	Slave	County	State	White
Molly (Clark)		Murder	Black	1783	Burned	North Carolina	Pitt	Slave	County	State	White
		Unspecified									
Martin, Bridget		Felony	Black	1783	Unknown	Virginia	Dinwiddie	Slave	County	State	Unknown
Unnamed		Murder	White	23 JUL 1784	Hanged	Maryland	Unknown	Unknown	County	State	Unknown
Stillwell, Barbara		Child Murder	Black	1784	Hanged	Tennessee	Cocke County	Slave	County	State	Black
Peggen, Hannah		Infanticide	White	22 JUN 1784	Hanged	New York	New York	Unknown	County	State	White
Unnamed (Gerard)		Infanticide Attempted	Indian	JUL 1785	Hanged	Massachusetts	Northampton	Unknown	County	State	Indian
Ocuish, Hannah	12	Murder	Black	5 NOV 1785	Unknown	South Carolina	Unknown	Slave	County	State	Unknown
Wilson, Elizabeth**	27	Child Murder	Indian	20 DEC 1786	Hanged	Connecticut	New London	Servant	County	State	White
Kirk, Sarah		Infanticide	White	3 JAN 1786	Hanged	Pennsylvania	Delaware	Waitress	County	State	White
Converse, Abiah	23	Spousal Murder	White	5 DEC 1787	Hanged	Delaware	New Castle	Unknown	County	State	White
Dinah (Peter Damon)		Infanticide	White	17 JUL 1788	Hanged	Massachusetts	Northampton	Unknown	County	State	White
Connelly, Ann		Arson	Black	17 OCT 1788	Hanged	New Jersey	Somerset	Slave	County	State	White
Wall, Rachel	29	Robbery-Murder	White	11 JUN 1788	Hanged	South Carolina	Charleston	Criminal	County	State	White
Nelly (Captain Daniel Braine)		Robbery	White	8 OCT 1789	Hanged	Massachusetts	Suffolk	Pirate	County	State	White
Creese (Fisher)		Arson	Black	15 OCT 1790	Hanged	New York	Long Island	Slave	County	State	White
Molly (Marshall)		Arson	Black	14 MAR 1789	Unknown	Virginia	Northampton	Slave	County	State	White
		Unspecified									
Beck (Sarah Taylors)		Felony	Black	8 JUL 1791	Hanged	Virginia	Fauquier	Slave	County	State	White
Daphne (Edward Travis)		Poisoning	Black	1793	Hanged	North Carolina	Nash	Slave	County	State	White
Nelly (Edward Travis)		Murder	Black	19 JUL 1793	Hanged	Virginia	James City	Slave	County	State	White
Dinah (Dow)		Murder	Black	4 OCT 1793	Hanged	Virginia	James City	Slave	County	State	White
Bett (Philip Van Rensselaer)	12	Arson	Black	27 NOV 1793	Hanged	New York	Unknown	Slave	County	State	Unknown
Dean (Volkert Douw)	14	Arson	Black	14 MAR 1794	Hanged	New York	Albany	Slave	County	State	White
		Arson	Black	14 MAR 1794	Hanged	New York	Albany	Slave		State	White

2. Empirical Frameworks—Table 2-1

Name of Condemned Prisoner (Slave Owner)	Age at Death	Offense of Defendant	Race	Execution Date	Method of Execution	State of Execution	County of Execution	Occupation of Defendant	Place of Execution	Jurisdiction of Execution	Race of Victim
Lucy (Kirby)		Murder	Black	MAY 1794	Hanged	Virginia	Dinwiddie	Slave	County	State	White
Polly (Ragsdale)		Poisoning	Black	22 AUG 1794	Unknown	Virginia	Unknown	Slave	County	State	Unknown
Arden		Murder	Black	SEP 1795	Hanged	South Carolina	Unknown	Unknown	County	State	Spanish
Molly (Shubrick)		Arson	Black	5 SEP 1795	Unknown	South Carolina	Unknown	Slave	County	State	Unknown
Ardner, Sally		Spousal Murder	White	20 OCT 1795	Hanged	South Carolina	Charleston	Housewife	County	State	White
Chloe (Randolph)		Murder	Black	27 NOV 1795	Hanged	Virginia	Prince Edward	Slave	County	State	Unknown
Molly (Stanfield)		Murder	Black	12 NOV 1796	Hanged	Virginia	Halifax	Slave	County	State	White
McKay, Hannah (Glare)		Murder	Black	1797	Hanged	North Carolina	Robeson	Slave	County	State	White
Jenny (Haywood)		Poisoning	Black	7 JUL 1797	Unknown	Virginia	Unknown	Slave	County	State	Unknown
Polly Milles		Murder	Black	23 MAR 1798	Hanged	Virginia	York	Slave	County	State	Unknown
Wood, Sylvia		Spousal Murder	White	29 JUN 1798	Hanged	New York	Fort Stanwix	Housewife	County	State	White
Mary (Edward Tash)		Arson	Black	JUL 1798	Hanged	South Carolina	Charleston	Slave	County	State	Unknown
London, Catherine		Murder	White	10 MAY 1798	Unknown	Kentucky	Franklin	Spinster	County	State	Unknown
Millay (Robe)		Arson	Black	1 SEP 1798	Hanged	West Virginia	Monongalia	Slave	County	State	Unknown
Clark, Sarah	32	Murder	White	30 OCT 1799	Hanged	Pennsylvania	Cumberland	Servant	County	State	White
Amey (Gresham)		Murder	Black	15 JUN 1799	Hanged	Virginia	King & Queen	Slave	County	State	Unknown
Fanny (Field)		Murder	Black	3 AUG 1799	Unknown	Kentucky	Unknown	Slave	County	State	Unknown
Chainey (Lafferty)		Murder	Black	1800	Hanged	Virginia	Highland	Slave	County	State	Unknown
Polly (Baker)		Arson	Black	1800	Hanged	Georgia	Wilkes	Slave	County	State	White
Mrs. Walleck^		Murder	White	1801	Unknown	Kentucky	Unknown	Unknown	County	State	Unknown
Chloe (Carothers)		Child Murder	Black	18 JUL 1801	Hanged	Pennsylvania	Cumberland	Slave	County	State	White
Nan (Smith)	18	Unspecified									
Sarah (Mills)		Felony	Black	10 APR 1801	Hanged	Virginia	King George	Slave	County	State	Unknown
Chasity (Lawson)		Assault	Black	15 JUL 1803	Unknown	Virginia	Unknown	Slave	County	State	Unknown
		Poisoning	Black	28 OCT 1803	Hanged	Virginia	Beach				
Dayon (Abraham Bruyn)		Child Murder	Black	8 AUG 1803	Hanged	New York	Kingston	Slave	County	State	Unknown
Kate (Fowler)		Murder	Black	8 MAY 1805	Hanged	Maryland	Unknown	Slave	County	State	White
Unnamed (Jernegan)		Murder	Black	13 JUL 1805	Burned	North Carolina	Wayne	Slave	County	State	Unknown
Unnamed (Pierre Chouteau)	16	Arson	Black	1805	Hanged	Missouri	St. Louis	Slave	County	State	White
Hannah (Miller)		Infanticide	Black	1 AUG 1805	Hanged	Pennsylvania	Chester	Slave	County	State	Black
Unnamed (Myhan)		Murder	Black	28 MAR 1806	Hanged	North Carolina	Sampson	Slave	County	State	White
Barclay, Polly		Spousal Murder	White	30 MAY 1806	Hanged	Georgia	Wilkes	Housewife	County	State	White
Fanny (Goode)		Poisoning	Black	28 FEB 1806	Hanged	Virginia	Charlotte	Slave	County	State	Unknown
Charlotte (Pentross)		Murder	Black	15 MAR 1806	Hanged	Virginia	Caroline	Slave	County	State	White
Sally (Morrisett)		Murder	Black	MAY 1806	Hanged	Virginia	Chesterfield	Slave	County	State	White
Creasy (Morrisett)		Murder	Black	MAY 1806	Hanged	Virginia	Chesterfield	Slave	County	State	White
Elizabeth (Rimby)		Unknown	Black	3 SEP 1806	Unknown	Pennsylvania	Unknown	Slave	County	State	Unknown
Molly (Holcomb, Holevine)		Child Murder	Black	20 MAR 1807	Hanged	Tennessee	Williamson	Slave	County	State	Black
Phoebe (Rainey)		Murder	Black	1808	Hanged	Kentucky	Garrard	Slave	County	State	White
Nancy (Rhodes)		Arson	Black	30 SEP 1808	Hanged	Kentucky	Scott	Slave	County	State	Unknown

Name of Condemned Prisoner (Slave Owner)	Age at Death	Offense of Defendant	Race	Execution Date	Method of Execution	State of Execution	County of Execution	Occupation of Defendant	Place of Execution	Jurisdiction of Execution	Race of Victim
Unnamed		Murder	Black	1808	Hanged	Kentucky	Jefferson	Unknown	County	State	Unknown
Unnamed		Murder	Black	1808	Unknown	Tennessee	Unknown	Slave	County	State	Unknown
Sue		Arson	Black	7 APR 1809	Hanged	South Carolina	Unknown	Slave	County	State	Unknown
Moore, Elizabeth		Infanticide	Mulatto	27 MAY 1809	Hanged	Pennsylvania	York	Servant	County	State	Mulatto
Cox, Susannah	24	Infanticide	White	10 JUN 1809	Hanged	Pennsylvania	Berk	Servant	County	State	White
Flora (Jackson)		Murder	Black	5 MAY 1809	Hanged	Virginia	Frederick	Slave	County	State	Black
Nance (Chapman)		Murder	Black	4 AUG 1809	Hanged	Kentucky	Unknown	Slave	County	State	Unknown
Phoebe (Rumsey)		Infanticide	Black	1812	Hanged	Kentucky	Christian	Slave	County	State	Black
Cole, Mary		Murder	White	26 JUN 1812	Hanged	New Jersey	Sussex	Housewife	County	State	White
Amy (Tate)	21	Murder	Black	11 DEC 1812	Hanged	Virginia	Augusta	Slave	County	State	White
Betsy (Taggart)^		Murder	Black	1813	Unknown	North Carolina	Unknown	Slave	County	State	Unknown
Isabelle (Hildreth)	15	Murder	Black	8 AUG 1814	Unknown	Kentucky	Unknown	Slave	County	State	Unknown
Antoine, Mary	20	Murder	Indian	30 SEP 1814	Hanged	New York	Madison	Unknown	County	State	Indian
Sally (Cohen)	15	Arson	Black	26 AUG 1814	Unknown	South Carolina	Unknown	Slave	County	State	Unknown
Hannah (Nicholas Summer)	15	Arson	Black	NOV 1814	Hanged	South Carolina	Newberry	Slave	County	State	White
Tygart, Jane	70	Murder	White	18 NOV 1814	Unknown	West Virginia	Unknown	Unknown	County	State	Unknown
Jenny (Stratton)		Murder	Black	23 FEB 1816	Unknown	Virginia	Unknown	Slave	County	State	Unknown
Delphy (Mitchell)		Attempted Murder	Black	26 JUL 1816	Unknown	Virginia	Unknown	Slave	County	State	Unknown
Clara (Shelton)		Murder	Black	4 OCT 1816	Hanged	Virginia	Spotsylvania	Slave	County	State	Unknown
Seaborn, Margaret		Murder	White	OCT 1817	Hanged	Georgia	Camden	Housewife	County	State	Unknown
Gillespie, Ellenor		Spousal Murder	White	26 JUL 1817	Hanged	Kentucky	Henderson	Housewife	County	State	White
Houghtaling, Margaret**	25	Infanticide	White	17 OCT 1817	Hanged	Virginia	Columbia	Prostitute	County	State	White
Unnamed	18	Infanticide	Black	1818	Hanged	Virginia	Unknown	Slave	County	State	Black
Cary (Vaughan)		Murder	Black	30 JAN 1818	Hanged	Virginia	Brunswick	Slave	County	State	White
Sarah (Berkeley)		Murder	Black	10 JUL 1818	Hanged	Virginia	Chesterfield	Slave	County	State	White
Unnamed		Murder	Black	FEB 1819	Hanged	Tennessee	Sumner	Slave	County	State	White
Unnamed (Reynolds)^		Attempted Murder	Black	1820-1821	Unknown	Georgia	Unknown	Slave	County	State	Unknown
Martin, Eve		Murder	Unk	1820	Unknown	Tennessee	Unknown	Unknown	County	State	Unknown
Fisher, Lavinia	27	Robbery	White	18 FEB 1820	Hanged	South Carolina	Charleston	Gang Member	County	State	White
Butler, Rose (William Morris)	19	Arson	Black	9 JUL 1819	Hanged	New York	New York	Servant	County	State	White
Chaney (Barnes)		Conspiracy-Murder	Black	21 JAN 1820	Hanged	Virginia	Madison	Slave	County	State	Unknown
Cela (Wyat Smith)		Infanticide	Black	22 APR 1820	Hanged	South Carolina	Pendleton	Slave	County	State	White
Unnamed (Alexander Roach)		Murder	Black	31 JUN 1820	Hanged	North Carolina	Rockingham	Slave	County	State	Unknown
Kitty (Baker)	16	Murder	Black	2 MAR 1821	Hanged	Maryland	Frederick	Slave	County	State	Unknown
Jenny (Dashiell)	19	Murder	Black	19 OCT 1821	Hanged	Maryland	Unknown	Slave	County	State	Unknown
Celia (Daughtry)		Murder	Black	15 AUG 1821	Hanged	Virginia	Southampton	Slave	County	State	White
Pat (Farris)		Murder	Black	3 NOV 1821	Unknown	Virginia	Charlotte	Slave	County	State	Unknown
Owens, Elizabeth^		Unknown	Unk	1823	Unknown	North Carolina	Unknown	Unknown	County	State	Unknown
Vina (Joseph Wynn)*		Child Murder	Black	SEP 1823	Hanged	North Carolina	Tyrrell	Slave	County	State	White

2. Empirical Frameworks—Table 2-1

Name of Condemned Prisoner (Slave Owner)	Age at Death	Offense of Defendant	Race	Execution Date	Method of Execution	State of Execution	County of Execution	Occupation of Defendant	Place of Execution	Jurisdiction of Execution	Race of Victim
Unnamed (Roe)		Murder	Black	25 APR 1824	Unknown	South Carolina	Unknown	Slave	County	State	Unknown
Anaca (Ellis Palmer)*		Infanticide	Black	1824	Hanged	South Carolina	Union	Slave	County	State	Black
Unnamed^		Murder	Unk	1824	Unknown	Kentucky	Unknown	Unknown	County	State	Unknown
Patsy (Gorman)		Murder	Black	10 JUN 1825	Hanged	Alabama	Perry	Slave	County	State	Unknown
Facteau, Peggy		Infanticide	White	18 MAR 1825	Hanged	New York	Clinton	Housewife	County	State	White
Unnamed (Stuckey)		Murder	Black	24 FEB 1825	Hanged	South Carolina	Sumter	Slave	County	State	Unknown
Rebecca (Coalter)	11/12	Murder	Black	JUN 1825	Hanged	West Virginia	Monroe	Slave	County	State	Unknown
Unnamed (Mulford)^		Murder	Black	1826	Unknown	North Carolina	Unknown	Slave	County	State	Unknown
Unnamed		Child Murder	Black	1826	Hanged	Tennessee	Henderson	Slave	County	State	White
Maria (Stuart)^		Murder	Black	SEP 1826	Unknown	New Jersey	Unknown	Slave	County	State	Unknown
Milley (Hanley)		Infanticide	Black	15 JUN 1826	Hanged	Virginia	Patrick	Slave	County	State	Black
Judy (Ware)	17	Murder	Black	26 JAN 1827	Hanged	Virginia	Fluvanna	Slave	County	State	Unknown
Rachel (Montgomery)^		Murder	Black	25 MAY 1827	Unknown	Alabama	Unknown	Slave	County	State	Unknown
Hannah		Poisoning	Black	1 JUN 1827	Unknown	South Carolina	Unknown	Slave	County	State	Unknown
Molly (Long)		Child Murder	Black	20 JUN 1827	Hanged	North Carolina	Cabarrus	Slave	County	State	White
Huldah (James Cason)		Murder	Black	1828	Hanged	South Carolina	Fairfield	Slave	County	State	White
Eave (Richard Jones)		Poisoning	Black	NOV 1828	Hanged	South Carolina	Colleton	Slave	County	State	Unknown
Nelly (Shield)		Murder	Black	17 MAR 1828	Hanged	Virginia	Southampton	Slave	County	State	Unknown
Annice (Jeremiah Prior)		Infanticide	Black	23 AUG 1828	Hanged	Missouri	Clay	Slave	County	State	Black
Unnamed^		Murder	Black	10 JUL 1829	Unknown	Louisiana	Unknown	Slave	County	State	Unknown
Sandy (Boyer)		Murder	Black	28 AUG 1829	Unknown	Virginia	Unknown	Slave	County	State	Unknown
Unnamed^		Murder	Black	26 SEP 1829	Unknown	Louisiana	Unknown	Slave	County	State	Unknown
Hughes, Polly	24	Spousal Murder	White	13 NOV 1829	Hanged	Tennessee	Hardin	Housewife	County	State	White
Jenny Jones)		Arson	Black	4 DEC 1829	Hanged	Georgia	Richmond	Slave	County	State	Unknown
Cashiere, Catharine		Murder	Black	7 MAY 1829	Hanged	New York	New York	Tavern Girl	County	State	Black
Annis (Green)		Attempted Murder	Black	21 JAN 1829	Hanged	Virginia	Amelia	Slave	County	State	Unknown
Mary (Caldwell)		Murder	Black	4 SEP 1830	Unknown	Kentucky	Unknown	Slave	County	State	Unknown
Cinda (Lubbock)		Arson	Black	6 JUN 1830	Hanged	Georgia	Richmond	Slave	County	State	Unknown
Dinah		Murder	Black	25 MAY 1830	Hanged	Kentucky	Greensup	Slave	County	State	White
Harriett (Lewis)^		Murder	Black	1831	Unknown	Kentucky	Unknown	Slave	County	State	Unknown
Henny (Insley)		Murder	Black	JUN 1831	Hanged	Maryland	Dorchester	Slave	County	State	White
Johnson, Mary**	22	Murder	White	OCT 1831	Hanged	Massachusetts	Gloucester	Servant	County	State	White
Lucy (Barrow)		Slave Revolt	Black	24 OCT 1831	Unknown	Virginia	Unknown	Slave	County	State	Unknown
Elizabeth (Allen)		Poisoning	Black	9 MAR 1832	Unknown	Virginia	Unknown	Slave	County	State	Unknown
Catharine (Pearce)		Murder	Black	19 OCT 1832	Hanged	Kentucky	Unknown	Slave	County	State	Unknown
Lucy (Bouligny)		Poisoning	Black	NOV 1832	Hanged	Louisiana	Jefferson	Slave	County	State	Unknown
Freeman, Elizabeth	50	Spousal Murder	Black	20 JUL 1832	Hanged	New Jersey	Burlington	Free	County	State	Black
Mary (Hilhouse)		Murder	Black	JAN 1832	Unknown	Arkansas	Unknown	Slave	County	State	Unknown
Eliza (Anna Ward)		Burglary	Black	JAN 1832	Hanged	Virginia	Norfolk City	Slave	County	State	White
Renah (Dawson)		Poisoning	Black	5 JAN 1832	Hanged	Virginia	Prince Edwards	Slave	County	State	Unknown
Fanny (Dawson)		Poisoning	Black	5 JAN 1832	Hanged	Virginia	Prince Edwards	Slave	County	State	Unknown

Name of Condemned Prisoner (Slave Owner)	Age at Death	Offense of Defendant	Race	Execution Date	Method of Execution	State of Execution	County of Execution	Occupation of Defendant	Place of Execution	Jurisdiction of Execution	Race of Victim
Amy (Dodson)		Child Murder	Black	28 JUL 1832	Hanged	North Carolina	Caswell	Slave	County	State	White
Lucy (Wells)		Murder	Black	28 SEP 1832	Hanged	West Virginia	Tyler	Slave	County	State	Unknown
Unnamed		Unknown	Black	1833	Unknown	Mississippi	Unknown	Unknown	County	State	Unknown
Cassy (Grey)		Murder	Black	2 JAN 1833	Hanged	Kentucky	Christian	Slave	County	State	Unknown
Aurelia (Chase)		Poisoning	Black	20 DEC 1833	Unknown	Maryland	Baltimore	Slave	County	State	Unknown
Sophie (White)		Murder	Black	26 APR 1833	Hanged	Georgia	Unknown	Slave	County	State	White
Nancy (Moss)*		Poisoning	Black	2 MAR 1833	Unknown	Mississippi	Unknown	Slave	County	State	White
Silver, Frances Stewart	18	Spousal Murder	White	12 JUL 1833	Hanged	North Carolina	Mitchell	Housewife	County	State	White
Mary (Pond)		Attempted Murder	Black	21 JUN 1833	Hanged	Virginia	Southampton	Slave	County	State	Unknown
Harriet (James H. Shepperd, Jr.)	13	Child Murder	Black	23 AUG 1833	Hanged	Tennessee	Hardeman	Slave	County	State	White
Nannah (Hazelwood)		Child Murder	Black	30 APR 1834	Hanged	Kentucky	Henderson	Slave	County	State	White
Andrews, Mary (Treenberg)		Infanticide	White	30 APR 1834	Hanged	Missouri	Lafayette	Unknown	County	State	White
Nelly (Wheat)		Murder	Black	1 AUG 1834	Hanged	Virginia	Bedford	Slave	County	State	Unknown
Jane McCormick		Murder	Black	1835	Unknown	Florida	Unknown	Slave	County	State	Unknown
Unnamed (LeBlanc)		Arson	Black	NOV 1835	Hanged	Louisiana	St. Martin	Slave	County	State	Unknown
Amy (Murren)		Murder	Black	27 NOV 1835	Unknown	Georgia	Unknown	Slave	County	State	Unknown
Judah (Bayne)	14	Murder	Black	16 JAN 1835	Unknown	Maryland	Unknown	Slave	County	State	Unknown
Unnamed (Holley)*		Murder	Black	9 JAN 1836	Hanged	Alabama	Covington	Slave	County	State	Unknown
Unnamed (Holley)*		Murder	Black	9 JAN 1836	Hanged	Alabama	Covington	Slave	County	State	Unknown
Katy (Murren)^		Murder	Black	APR 1836	Unknown	Georgia	Unknown	Slave	County	State	Unknown
Fanny (Stevenson)		Attempted Murder	Black	20 DEC 1836	Hanged	Alabama	Perry	Slave	County	State	Unknown
Phoebe (Lumpkin)		Murder	Black	12 MAY 1836	Hanged	Virginia	Essex	Slave	County	State	White
Jane (Sarah Hight)		Murder	Black	26 MAY 1836	Hanged	New Jersey	Morris	Slave	County	State	White
Caroline (Roberts)		Unknown	Black	31 MAY 1836	Unknown	Kentucky	Unknown	Slave	County	State	Unknown
Delsey (Harkins)*		Unknown	Black	30 JUN 1836	Hanged	Alabama	Lauderdale	Slave	County	State	Unknown
Hughes		Murder	White	1837	Unknown	Tennessee	Unknown	Unknown	County	State	Unknown
Bella (Warren)		Murder	Black	1837	Hanged	Georgia	Effingham	Slave	County	State	Unknown
Sarah (Dye)		Murder	Black	29 APR 1837	Unknown	Kentucky	Unknown	Slave	County	State	Unknown
Jane (Gorman)	19	Murder	Black	AUG 1837	Hanged	Louisiana	St. Helena	Slave	County	State	Unknown
Unnamed^		Murder	Indian	31 AUG 1837	Unknown	Massachusetts	Unknown	Unknown	County	State	Unknown
Unnamed^		Unknown	Black	1838	Unknown	Georgia	Unknown	Slave	County	State	Unknown
Unnamed (Randolph)		Murder	Black	10 JAN 1838	Unknown	Louisiana	Unknown	Slave	County	State	Unknown
Eliza		Attempted Murder	Black	17 JUL 1838	Hanged	Mississippi	Unknown	Slave	County	State	White
Mary (John Brinker)	16	Child Murder	Black	11 AUG 1838	Hanged	Missouri	Crawford	Slave	County	State	White
Lucinda (Mayse)		Murder	Black	24 SEP 1838	Hanged	Virginia	Bath	Slave	County	State	Unknown
Unnamed (Florence)^		Murder	Black	MAY 1839	Unknown	Missouri	Unknown	Slave	County	State	Unknown
Martha (Risk)		Attempted Murder	Black	4 JAN 1839	Hanged	Kentucky	Unknown	Slave	County	State	White
Unnamed (Wilson)^		Murder	Black	1840	Unknown	North Carolina	Unknown	Slave	County	State	Unknown
Unnamed (Jones)*		Murder	Black	5 FEB 1840	Hanged	Kentucky	Scott	Slave	County	State	White

2. Empirical Frameworks—Table 2-1

Name of Condemned Prisoner (Slave Owner)	Age at Death	Offense of Defendant	Race	Execution Date	Method of Execution	State of Execution	County of Execution	Occupation of Defendant	Place of Execution	Jurisdiction of Execution	Race of Victim
Betsy (Wilson)		Murder	Black	5 SEP 1840	Hanged	Virginia	Fauquier	Slave	County	State	White
Unnamed (Hyde)		Poisoning Master	Black	JUL 1841	Hanged	Florida	St. Augustine	Slave	County	State	White
Biddy (Carter)		Unknown	Black	8 FEB 1843	Unknown	Alabama	Unknown	Slave	County	State	Unknown
Ellen (Alexander)		Murder	Black	1842	Unknown	Kentucky	Unknown	Slave	County	State	Unknown
Unnamed (Bisland)		Attempted Murder	Black	14 OCT 1842	Unknown	Louisiana	Unknown	Slave	County	State	Unknown
Fanny (Harman Garrett)		Murder	Black	25 AUG 1843	Hanged	South Carolina	Laurens	Slave	County	State	Unknown
Mary (Smith)*		Murder	Black	11 FEB 1843	Hanged	Alabama	Unknown	Slave	County	State	Unknown
Harriet		Child Murder	Black	19 MAY 1843	Hanged	North Carolina	Raleigh	Slave	County	State	White
America (Hiram Beasley)		Murder	Black	10 JUN 1843	Hanged	Missouri	St. Louis	Slave	County	State	White
Unnamed^		Attempted Murder	Black	30 JUN 1843	Unknown	Louisiana	Unknown	Slave	County	State	Unknown
Susan (Rosa Ann King)		Murder	Black	7 JUL 1844	Hanged	Missouri	Callaway	Slave	County	State	White
Nancy (Beasley)		Attempted Murder	Black	MAR 1844	Hanged	Alabama	Montgomery	Slave	County	State	Unknown
Hannah (Smith)		Murder	Black	11 APR 1844	Unknown	Kentucky	Unknown	Slave	County	State	Unknown
Keen, Rosanne	16	Murder	Black	26 APR 1844	Hanged	New Jersey	Cumberland	Housemaid	County	State	White
Lucy (James W. Haley)		Murder	Black	22 JUN 1844	Hanged	Tennessee	Madison	Slave	County	State	White
Amy		Murder	Black	30 NOV 1844	Unknown	Kentucky	Unknown	Slave	County	State	Unknown
Foster, Hester		Murder	Black	9 FEB 1844	Hanged	Ohio	Franklin	Convict	County	State	White
Burnett, Lavinia (Veny)		Robbery-Murder	White	8 NOV 1845	Hanged	Arkansas	Washington	Unknown	County	State	White
Emaline		Murder	Black	10 MAY 1845	Hanged	Georgia	Marion	Slave	County	State	Unknown
Reed, Elizabeth Betsey	40	Spousal Murder	White	23 MAY 1845	Hanged	Illinois	Lawrence	Housewife	County	State	White
Sophie (Hayes)		Murder	Black	30 MAY 1845	Unknown	Georgia	Unknown	Slave	County	State	Unknown
Lize (Wilson Turnar Meador)		Child Murder	Black	1845	Hanged	Tennessee	Macon	Slave	County	State	White
Unnamed		Unknown	Black	1845	Unknown	New Jersey	Unknown	Unknown	County	State	Unknown
Unnamed (John Henry Bayne White)		Child Murder	Black	1846	Hanged	Maryland	Prince Georges	Slave	Slave	County	State
Unnamed (Hamilton)^		Murder	Black	1846	Unknown	Kentucky	Unknown	Slave	County	State	Unknown
Kaomali		Spousal Murder	Hawaii	14 AUG 1846	Hanged	Hawaii	O'ahu	Unknown	City	Kingdom	Hawaiian
Claricy (William Dawson)		Infanticide	Black	3 AUG 1846	Hanged	Tennessee	Franklin	Slave	County	State	Black
Pauline (Rabbeneck)		Attempted Murder	Black	28 MAR 1846	Hanged	Louisiana	New Orleans	Slave	County	State	White
Lucy (Colcomb)		Murder	Black	11 DEC 1846	Hanged	Louisiana	St. James	Slave	County	State	Unknown
Van Valkenburgh, Elizabeth	47	Spousal Murder	White	26 JAN 1846	Hanged	New York	Montgomery	Housewife	County	State	White
Runkle, Mary Alice	50	Spousal Murder	White	9 NOV 1847	Hanged	New York	Oneida	Housewife	County	State	White
Sarah (Catherine Smith)		Murder	Black	15 JUN 1848	Hanged	Tennessee	Rutherford	Slave	County	State	White
Jane (Dukes)		Poisoning	Black	10 AUG 1848	Unknown	South Carolina	Unknown	Slave	County	State	Unknown
Celia (Bryan)		Murder	Black	22 SEP 1848	Hanged	Florida	Duvall	Slave	County	State	White
Adaline (Nelson)		Murder	Black	27 OCT 1848	Unknown	Mississippi	Unknown	Slave	County	State	Unknown

I. Theoretical and Empirical Frameworks

Name of Condemned Prisoner (Slave Owner)	Age at Death	Offense of Defendant	Race	Execution Date	Method of Execution	State of Execution	County of Execution	Occupation of Defendant	Place of Execution	Jurisdiction of Execution	Race of Victim
Lucy (Hamilton)		Murder	Black	1 JUN 1848	Hanged	Kentucky	Meade	Slave	County	State	Unknown
Maria (Brooks)		Unknown	Black	1848	Unknown	Mississippi	Unknown	Slave	County	State	Unknown
Cassily (Hamilton)^		Attempted Murder	Black	1849	Unknown	Kentucky	Unknown	Slave	County	State	Unknown
Unnamed^		Murder	Black	1849	Unknown	North Carolina	Unknown	Slave	County	State	Unknown
Pherebe (Shepherd)*	25	Murder	Black	11 DEC 1849	Hanged	Alabama	Fayette	Slave	County	State	Unknown
Margarette (James)		Murder	Black	25 MAY 1849	Hanged	North Carolina	Caswell	Slave	County	State	White
Eliza (Griffin)		Poisoning	Black	12 JAN 1849	Hanged	Virginia	Brunswick	Slave	County	State	Unknown
Roberta (Ezell)		Poisoning	Black	12 JAN 1849	Hanged	Virginia	Brunswick	Slave	County	State	Unknown
Sally (Kirkland)		Murder	Black	27 APR 1849	Unknown	Kentucky	Unknown	Slave	County	State	Unknown
Cyrina (Wilson)		Unknown	Black	26 OCT 1849	Unknown	Louisiana	Unknown	Slave	County	State	Unknown
Clarissa (Holley)		Attempted Murder	Black	11 MAY 1849	Unknown	Mississippi	Unknown	Slave	County	State	Unknown
Unnamed (Kirkpatrick)^		Murder	Black	1850	Unknown	South Carolina	Unknown	Slave	County	State	Unknown
Agnes (Gerard Mason)		Murder	Black	16 JUL 1850	Hanged	Virginia	Prince William	Slave	County	State	White
Cicily (Longgon)		Murder	Black	22 MAY 1850	Hanged	Mississippi	Tippah	Slave	County	State	Unknown
Jeanette (Villere)		Murder	Black	1851	Unknown	Louisiana	Unknown	Slave	County	State	Unknown
Unnamed (Watson)^		Arson	Black	13 JUN 1851	Unknown	South Carolina	Unknown	Slave	County	State	Unknown
Unnamed (Watson)^		Arson	Black	13 JUN 1851	Unknown	South Carolina	Unknown	Slave	County	State	Unknown
Mily (Fox)		Poisoning	Black	JUL 1851	Hanged	Mississippi	Unknown	Slave	County	State	White
Malinda (Burns)		Murder	Black	24 OCT 1851	Unknown	Georgia	Unknown	Slave	County	State	Unknown
Ellen (Chancedec)		Murder	Black	27 NOV 1851	Unknown	Louisiana	Unknown	Slave	County	State	Unknown
Sue (Burnaman)		Murder	Black	28 NOV 1851	Unknown	Mississippi	Unknown	Slave	County	State	Unknown
Worms, Pamela Lee	37	Spousal Murder	White	30 JAN 1852	Hanged	Pennsylvania	Allegheny	Housewife	County	State	White
Anarchy (Burnaman)		Murder	Black	22 FEB 1852	Unknown	Mississippi	Unknown	Slave	County	State	Unknown
Martha (Bingham)		Murder	Black	18 JUN 1852	Unknown	Mississippi	Unknown	Slave	County	State	Unknown
Hoag, Anna	31	Spousal Murder	White	30 JUL 1852	Hanged	New York	Dutchess	Housewife	County	State	White
Mahalia (Mason)		Murder	Black	14 MAY 1852	Hanged	Virginia	Giles	Slave	County	State	Unknown
Molly (Champion)		Attempted Murder	Black	10 SEP 1852	Hanged	Virginia	Sussex	Slave	County	State	Unknown
Jane (Depp)		Murder	Black	10 SEP 1852	Hanged	Virginia	Powhatan	Slave	County	State	Unknown
Jane Joseph Winston		Murder	Black	10 SEP 1852	Hanged	Virginia	Richmond City	Slave	County	State	White
Margaret (Buckner)		Murder	Black	12 SEP 1852	Hanged	Virginia	Culpeper	Slave	County	State	White
Unnamed (Davis)		Murder	Black	1853	Unknown	Arkansas	Unknown	Slave	County	State	Unknown
Unnamed^		Murder	Unk	1853	Unknown	Kentucky	Unknown	Slave	County	State	Unknown
Rose^		Unknown	Black	1853	Unknown	South Carolina	Unknown	Unknown	County	State	Unknown
Elkins, Jane		Murder	Black	27 MAY 1853	Hanged	Texas	Dallas	Slave	County	State	White
Ailey (Elijah McMichael)	18	Murder	Black	APR 1854	Hanged	Georgia	Jasper	Slave	County	State	White
Mary Jane (Swayze)	16	Murder	Black	28 JUN 1854	Unknown	Mississippi	Unknown	Slave	County	State	White
Martha		Unknown	Black	1855	Unknown	Kentucky	Unknown	Slave	County	State	Unknown
Martha (McKeller)		Arson	Black	MAR 1855	Hanged	Alabama	Dallas	Slave	County	State	Unknown
Melvaine (Frilvox)		Murder	Black	26 FEB 1855	Hanged	Louisiana	St. Charles	Slave	County	State	Unknown

2. Empirical Frameworks—Table 2-1

Name of Condemned Prisoner (Slave Owner)	Age at Death	Offense of Defendant	Race	Execution Date	Method of Execution	State of Execution	County of Execution	Occupation of Defendant	Place of Execution	Jurisdiction of Execution	Race of Victim
Phyllis (Smith)		Murder	Black	13 JUL 1855	Unknown	South Carolina	Unknown	Slave	County	State	Unknown
Clarissa (Wilson)		Murder	Black	2 NOV 1855	Unknown	South Carolina	Unknown	Slave	County	State	Unknown
Celia (Robert Newsome)	19	Murder	Black	21 DEC 1855	Hanged	Missouri	Callaway	Slave	County	State	White
Minerva (Mayes)		Arson	Black	9 FEB 1856	Hanged	Kentucky	Trigg	Slave	County	State	Unknown
Elizabeth (Leince)		Murder	Black	16 APR 1856	Unknown	Louisiana	Unknown	Slave	County	State	Unknown
Anna (Wilson)		Arson	Black	20 JUN 1856	Hanged	Virginia	Charles City	Slave	County	State	Unknown
Amelia (Clarke)		Murder	Black	12 SEP 1856	Hanged	Virginia	Caroline	Slave	County	State	Unknown
Eliza (Burrows)		Unknown	Black	4 MAR 1857	Unknown	Louisiana	Unknown	Slave	County	State	Unknown
Fanny		Murder	Black	27 MAR 1857	Hanged	North Carolina	Pitt	Slave	County	State	White
Massy (Norwood)		Spousal Murder	Black	8 MAY 1857	Hanged	North Carolina	Granville	Slave	County	State	Unknown
Nelly (George E. Green)	60	Murder	Black	13 FEB 1857	Hanged	Virginia	Prince William	Slave	County	State	White
Betsey (George E. Green)		Murder	Black	13 FEB 1857	Hanged	Virginia	Prince William	Slave	County	State	White
Catharine (Thompson)		Murder	Black	21 SEP 1857	Hanged	Virginia	Louisa	Slave	County	State	Unknown
Nancy (Brothers)		Attempted Murder	Black	20 NOV 1857	Hanged	Virginia	Nansemond	Slave	County	State	Unknown
Unnamed (Belvins)^		Murder	Black	1858	Unknown	Georgia	Unknown	Slave	County	State	Unknown
Unnamed (Belvins)^		Murder	Black	1858	Unknown	Virginia	Unknown	Slave	County	State	Unknown
Fannie^		Arson	Black	1858	Unknown	Louisiana	Unknown	Slave	County	State	Unknown
Margaret (Barrows)	21	Murder	Black	JAN 1858	Hanged	Pennsylvania	Allegheny	Unknown	County	State	White
Jones, Charlotte	35	Robbery-Murder	White	12 FEB 1858	Hanged	Pennsylvania	Montour	Unknown	County	State	White
Twiggs, Mary	35	Spousal Murder	White	22 OCT 1858	Hanged	Texas	Galveston	Slave	County	State	White
Lucy (Joseph Dougherty)*	46	Murder	Black	5 MAR 1858	Hanged	Virginia	Arlington	Slave	County	State	White
Jenny (Hall)	30	Murder	Black	26 FEB 1858	Hanged	Georgia	Meriwether	Slave	County	State	White
Sarah (Benjamin Gates)		Murder	Black	9 JUL 1858	Unknown	Mississippi	Unknown	Slave	County	State	Unknown
Eliza (Chamberlain)		Murder	Black	11 JUN 1858	Unknown	Virginia	Bedford	Slave	County	State	Unknown
Jane (Musgrove)		Murder	Black	10 SEP 1858	Hanged						
Sarah (Benjamin Williams)		Attempted Murder									
Rose (Singleton)		Attempted Murder	Black	14 OCT 1858	Hanged	Georgia	Harris	Slave	County	State	White
Rebecca (McCormick)	18	Murder	Black	4 MAR 1859	Unknown	Louisiana	Unknown	Slave	County	State	Unknown
Fanny (Stewart)		Murder	Black	24 JUN 1859	Unknown	Maryland	Unknown	Slave	County	State	Unknown
Nancy (Frizzell)*		Poisoning	Black	15 JUL 1859	Unknown	South Carolina	Unknown	Slave	County	State	Unknown
Angelina (Shacklefor)		Murder	Black	25 NOV 1859	Hanged	Alabama	Pike	Slave	County	State	Unknown
Nelly (William Rogus)		Arson	Black	30 SEP 1859	Hanged	Virginia	Culpeper	Slave	County	State	Unknown
Caroline (William Rogus)		Murder	Black	1860	Hanged	Georgia	Laurens	Slave	County	State	White
Josephine (William Rogus)		Murder	Black	1860	Hanged	Georgia	Laurens	Slave	County	State	White
Emma		Murder of Master	Black	1860	Hanged	Georgia	Laurens	Slave	County	State	White
Eliza (McCann)		Murder	Black	4 JAN 1860	Hanged	Texas	Fannin	Slave	County	State	White
Modeste (Thibodeaux)	21	Arson	Black	MAR 1860	Hanged	Mississippi	Yazoo City	Slave	County	State	White
		Murder	Unk	2 APR 1860	Unknown	Louisiana	Unknown	Unknown	County	State	Unknown
Patience (Edclon)		Unknown	Black	24 APR 1860	Unknown	Louisiana	Unknown	Slave	County	State	Unknown

Name of Condemned Prisoner (Slave Owner)	Age at Death	Offense of Defendant	Race	Execution Date	Method of Execution	State of Execution	County of Execution	Occupation of Defendant	Place of Execution	Jurisdiction of Execution	Race of Victim
June (Jones)		Murder	Black	13 JUL 1860	Hanged	Alabama	Montgomery	Slave	County	State	Unknown
Frances (Berry)		Attempted Murder	Black	7 SEP 1860	Hanged	Kentucky	Franklin	Slave	County	State	Unknown
Bilansky, Mary Ann	34	Spousal Murder	White	23 MAR 1860	Hanged	Minnesota	Ramsey	Housewife	County	State	White
Ann (William S. Croxton)	20	Murder	Black	23 MAR 1860	Hanged	Virginia	Essex	Slave	County	State	White
Eliza (William S. Croxton)	32	Murder	Black	23 MAR 1860	Hanged	Virginia	Essex	Slave	County	State	White
Jane (Smith)		Murder	Black	14 DEC 1860	Hanged	Kentucky	Unknown	Slave	County	State	Unknown
Malina		Arson	Black	1861	Hanged	Virginia	Caroline	Slave	County	State	White
Lizzie (Jones)*	26	Unknown	Black	18 JUN 1861	Hanged	Alabama	Montgomery	Slave	County	State	Unknown
Sandoval, Pablita	19	Murder	Mexican	26 APR 1861	Hanged	New Mexico	San Miguel	Seamstress	County	Territorial	Mexican
Harriet (Cooley)		Murder	Black	1861	Unknown	Virginia	Unknown	Unknown	County	State	Unknown
Rhodie (Witherspoon)		Murder	Black	JAN 1861	Hanged	South Carolina	Darlington	Slave	County	State	Unknown
Silvy (Witherspoon)		Murder	Black	JAN 1861	Hanged	South Carolina	Darlington	Slave	County	State	Unknown
Unnamed (Woodruf)		Child Murder	Black	23 FEB 1861	Hanged	North Carolina	Northampton	Farm Hand	County	State	Black
Unnamed		Attempt Slave Revolt	Black	JUN 1861	Hanged	Arkansas	Monroe	Slave	County	State	Unknown
Mary (Naylor)		Murder	Black	8 OCT 1861	Unknown	Maryland	Unknown	Slave	County	State	Unknown
Unnamed (Mavry)		Arson	Black	25 SEP 1861	Unknown	Mississippi	Unknown	Slave	County	State	Unknown
Carolina (Cobb)		Murder	Black	25 JUL 1862	Unknown	Louisiana	Unknown	Slave	County	State	Unknown
Ann (Whittington)		Unknown	Black	8 AUG 1862	Unknown	Louisiana	Unknown	Slave	County	State	Unknown
Ann (Clara)		Murder	Black	23 MAY 1862	Unknown	Virginia	Unknown	Slave	County	State	Unknown
Mary (Naylor)		Murder	Black	8 OCT 1861	Hanged	Maryland	Anne Arundel	Slave	County	State	Unknown
Chloe (Harris)		Unknown	Black	20 FEB 1863	Hanged	Louisiana	Unknown	Slave	County	State	Unknown
Rodriquez, Chipita		Robbery-Murder	Mexican	13 NOV 1863	Hanged	Texas	San Patricio	Innkeeper	County	State	White
Margaret (Mrs. Mary M. Butt)	20	Child Murder	Black	10 DEC 1863	Hanged	Virginia	Richmond City	Slave	County	State	White
Caroline (Dement)^		Murder	Black	17 AUG 1863	Unknown	Kentucky	Unknown	Slave	County	State	Unknown
Bet (Dillard)*		Murder	Black	MAY 1863	Hanged	Virginia	Lynchburg	Slave	County	State	White
Jane (Dillard)*		Murder	Black	MAY 1863	Hanged	Virginia	Lynchburg	Slave	County	State	White
Sarah (Dillard)*		Murder	Black	MAY 1863	Hanged	Virginia	Lynchburg	Slave	County	State	White
Mary Jane		Attempted Murder	Black	1863	Unknown	Virginia	Unknown	Unknown	County	State	Unknown
Alsie (Bane)		Attempted Murder	Black	1863	Unknown	Virginia	Unknown	Slave	County	State	Unknown
Margaret (Butt)	20	Murder	Black	9 JAN 1863	Unknown	Virginia	Unknown	Slave	County	State	Unknown
Unnamed (Finney)		Murder	Black	1864	Unknown	Georgia	Unknown	Slave	County	State	Unknown
Eliza (Banting)*		Unknown	Black	27 FEB 1864	Hanged	Alabama	Marengo	Slave	County	State	Unknown
Emma (Cabell)	16	Attempted Murder	Black	11 MAR 1864	Unknown	Virginia	Unknown	Slave	County	State	Unknown
Agnes (Harper)		Attempted Murder	Black	23 SEP 1864	Unknown	Virginia	Unknown	Slave	County	State	Unknown
Moore, Dolores		Murder	Mexican	1865	Hanged	Arizona	Pima	Unknown	County	Territorial	White

2. Empirical Frameworks—Table 2-1   59

Name of Condemned Prisoner (Slave Owner)	Age at Death	Offense of Defendant	Race	Execution Date	Method of Execution	State of Execution	County of Execution	Occupation of Defendant	Place of Execution	Jurisdiction of Execution	Race of Victim
Surratt, Mary**	42	Accessory to Murder	White	7 JUL 1865	Hanged	Washington, DC	Washington	Landlady	City	Military	White
Amy (Spain)	17	Robbery	Black	10 MAR 1865	Hanged	South Carolina	Darlington	Slave	County	Military	White
Grinder (Gunder), Martha	50	Murder	White	19 JAN 1866	Hanged	Pennsylvania	Allegheny	Housewife	County	State	White
Durgan, Bridget	22	Murder	White	30 AUG 1867	Hanged	New Jersey	Middlesex	Servant	County	State	White
Miller, Lena**	40	Spousal Murder	White	13 NOV 1867	Hanged	Pennsylvania	Clearfield	Housewife	County	State	White
Susan [Eliza]	12	Child Murder	Black	7 FEB 1868	Hanged	Kentucky	Henry	Servant	County	State	White
Purnell, Lucy	13	Murder	Black	28 FEB 1868	Hanged	Maryland	Worcester	Unknown	County	State	Black
Mrs. Moses Dean		Murder	Black	NOV 1868	Unknown	Arkansas	Unknown	Unknown	County	State	Unknown
Bradley, Sarah Jane		Child Murder	Black	14 DEC 1869	Hanged	Delaware	Sussex	Unknown	County	State	Black
Wallis, Mary	17	Child Murder	Black	10 FEB 1871	Hanged	Maryland	Prince Georges	Unknown	County	State	White
Eberhart, Susan	19	Murder	White	2 MAY 1873	Hanged	Georgia	Stewart	Servant	County	State	White
Hunt, Ann	25	Murder	Black	1 MAY 1874	Hanged	Georgia	Elbert	Servant	County	State	White
Harris, Alcee	24	Spousal Murder	Black	26 NOV 1875	Hanged	Louisiana	Ouachita	Unknown	County	State	Black
Osgood, Ellen		Murder	Black	19 DEC 1878	Hanged	Georgia	Liberty	Unknown	County	State	Black
Meierhoeffer, Margaret Klem	39	Spousal Murder	White	6 JAN 1881	Hanged	New Jersey	Essex	Housewife	County	State	White
Miller, Catherine	29	Spousal Murder	White	3 FEB 1881	Hanged	Pennsylvania	Lycoming	Housewife	County	State	White
Fowlkes, Lucinda		Spousal Murder	Black	22 APR 1881	Hanged	Virginia	Lunenberg	Unknown	County	State	Black
Moore, Ella		Murder	Black	20 OCT 1882	Hanged	Georgia	Dodge	Unknown	County	State	White
Carter, Matilda		Spousal Murder	Black	13 JAN 1882	Hanged	North Carolina	Rockingham	Farm Hand	County	State	Black
Teasdale, Lucinda	22	Spousal Murder	Black	23 JUN 1882	Hanged	South Carolina	Williamsburg	Unknown	County	State	Black
Harris, Margaret	18	Child Murder	Black	19 OCT 1883	Hanged	Georgia	Gordon	Servant	County	State	White
Meaker, Emeline Lucy***	43	Child Murder	White	30 MAR 1883	Hanged	Vermont	Washington	Housewife	State	State	White
Miller, Barbara	29	Spousal Murder	Black	14 SEP 1883	Hanged	Virginia	Henrico	Unknown	County	State	Black
Jones, Matilda		Robbery-Murder	Black	31 JUL 1885	Hanged	Louisiana	Franklin	Servant	County	State	White
Unnamed		Murder	Indian	MAY 1887	Unknown	Missouri	Unknown	Unknown	County	State	Unknown
Druse, Roxalana	40	Spousal Murder	White	28 FEB 1887	Hanged	New York	Herkimer	Housewife	County	State	White
McCoy, Pauline	22	Child Murder	Black	15 OCT 1888	Hanged	Alabama	Bullock	Unknown	County	State	White
Whiteling, Sarah Jane	51	Spousal Murder	White	25 JUN 1889	Hanged	Pennsylvania	Philadelphia	Housewife	County	State	White
O'Cannon, Mary		Murder	White	JUL 1890	Hanged	California	San Francisco	Unknown	County	Federal	Unknown
McShane, Kate		Murder	White	JUL 1890	Hanged	California	San Francisco	Unknown	County	Federal	Unknown
Potts, Elizabeth Atherton		Robbery-Murder	White	20 JUN 1890	Hanged	Nevada	Elko	Housewife	County	State	White
Mrs. Wiginton		Murder	White	MAR 1891	Hanged	Kentucky	Montgomery	Housewife	County	State	White
Murrell, Henrietta		Infanticide	Black	29 SEP 1891	Hanged	Virginia	Charlotte	Unknown	County	State	Black
Unnamed	15	Poisoning	Black	1892	Hanged	Louisiana	Unknown	Unknown	County	State	White
Shipp, Caroline	18	Infanticide	Black	22 JAN 1892	Hanged	North Carolina	Gaston	Servant	County	State	White
Brown, Mildry	13	Child Murder	Black	7 OCT 1892	Hanged	South Carolina	Spartanburg	Unknown	County	State	White
Tribble, Amanda		Infanticide	Black	7 JAN 1892	Hanged	South Carolina	Newberry	Unknown	County	State	Black
Lashley, Margaret		Spousal Murder	Black	22 JAN 1892	Hanged	Virginia	Danville City	Unknown	County	State	Black
Hiers, Ada		Murder	White	28 JUL 1893	Hanged	South Carolina	Waterboro	Housewife	County	State	Black
Cody, Amanda		Spousal Murder	Black	22 NOV 1895	Hanged	Georgia	Warren	Unknown	County	State	Black
Snodgrass, Mary	28	Infanticide	White	6 JUL 1896	Hanged	Virginia	Wise	Unknown	State	State	White

Name of Condemned Prisoner (Slave Owner)	Age at Death	Offense of Defendant	Race	Execution Date	Method of Execution	State of Execution	County of Execution	Occupation of Defendant	Place of Execution	Jurisdiction of Execution	Race of Victim
Place, Martha Savacool***	44	Child Murder	White	20 MAR 1899	Electrocution	New York	Kings	Dressmaker	State	State	White
Wright, Dora	38	Child Murder	Black	17 JUL 1903	Hanged	Oklahoma	Pittsburg	Servant	State	Territorial	Black
Rogers, Mary Mabel***	19	Spousal Murder	White	8 DEC 1905	Hanged	Vermont	Bennington	Servant	State	State	White
Farmer, Mary O'Brien***	27	Robbery-Murder	White	29 MAR 1909	Electrocution	New York	Jefferson	Housewife	State	State	White
Christian, Virginia	17	Robbery-Murder	Black	16 AUG 1912	Electrocution	Virginia	Hampton City	Servant	State	State	White
Perdue, Hattie		Robbery-Murder	Black	13 AUG 1921	Hanged	Mississippi	Wayne	Unknown	State	State	White
Knight, Ann		Spousal Murder	Black	22 OCT 1922	Hanged	Mississippi	Green	Unknown	State	State	Black
Snyder, Ruth Brown***	33	Spousal Murder	White	12 JAN 1928	Electrocution	New York	Queens	Housewife	State	State	White
LeBoeuf, Ada Bonner	38	Spousal Murder	White	1 FEB 1929	Hanged	Louisiana	St. Martin	Housewife	State	State	White
Gilmore, Silena		Murder	Black	24 JAN 1930	Electrocution	Alabama	Jefferson	Unknown	State	State	Black
Dugan, Eva***	57	Robbery-Murder	White	21 FEB 1930	Hanged	Arizona	Pima	Housekeeper	State	State	White
Schroeder, Irene Crawford***	22	Robbery-Murder	White	23 FEB 1931	Electrocution	Pennsylvania	Lawrence	Waitress	State	State	White
Antonio, Anna***	28	Spousal Murder	Italian	9 AUG 1934	Electrocution	New York	Albany	Housewife	County	State	Italian
Carey, May Hitchens	55	Murder	White	7 JUN 1935	Hanged	Delaware	Sussex	Housewife	State	State	White
Moore, Julia (Powers, Williams)		Murder	White	8 FEB 1935	Hanged	Louisiana	East Carroll	Unknown	State	State	White
Coo, Eva***	41	Murder	White	27 JUN 1935	Electrocution	New York	Otsego	Brothel Owner	State	State	White
Creighton, Mary Frances***	36	Murder	White	16 JUL 1936	Electrocution	New York	Nassau	Housewife	State	State	White
Holmes, Mary	35	Robbery-Murder	Black	29 APR 1937	Hanged	Mississippi	Clay	Cook	State	State	White
Porter, Marie	38	Murder	White	28 JAN 1938	Electrocution	Illinois	St. Clair	Confectionary	State	State	White
Hahn, Anna Marie	32	Murder	White	7 DEC 1938	Electrocution	Ohio	Hamilton	Housekeeper	State	State	White
Spinelli, Eithel Juanita Leta***	52	Murder	White	21 NOV 1941	Asphyxiation	California	Sacramento	Criminal	State	State	White
Henry, Toni Jo (Annie Beatrice)	26	Murder	White	28 NOV 1942	Electrocution	Louisiana	Calcasieu	Prostitute	State	State	White
Phillips, Rosana Lightner***	25	Robbery-Murder	Black	1 JAN 1943	Asphyxiation	North Carolina	Durham	Maid	State	State	White
Logue, Sue Stidham***	43	Murder	White	15 JAN 1943	Electrocution	South Carolina	Lexington	Teacher	County	State	White
Johnson, Mildred Louise	23	Murder	Black	19 MAY 1944	Electrocution	Mississippi	Jefferson City	Unknown	State	State	Black
Fowler, Helen***	37	Robbery-Murder	Black	16 NOV 1944	Electrocution	New York	Niagara	Housewife	State	State	White
Williams, Bessie Mae***	19	Robbery-Murder	Black	29 DEC 1944	Asphyxiation	North Carolina	Mecklenburg	House Maid	State	State	Black
Baker, Lena ***	44	Murder	Black	5 MAR 1945	Electrocution	Georgia	Randolph	Laundry	State	State	White
Sykes, Corrine**/***	22	Robbery-Murder	Black	14 OCT 1946	Electrocution	Pennsylvania	Philadelphia	Maid	State	State	White
Peete, Louise L.***	66	Murder	White	11 APR 1947	Asphyxiation	California	Los Angeles	Housekeeper	State	State	White
Stinette, Rosa Marie***	49	Spousal Murder	Black	17 JAN 1947	Electrocution	South Carolina	Florence	Servant	State	State	Black
Beck, Martha Seabrook***	29	Robbery-Murder	White	8 MAR 1951	Electrocution	New York	Bronx	Nurse	State	State	White
Dennison, Earle C. ***	55	Child Murder	White	4 SEP 1953	Electrocution	Alabama	Elmore	Nurse	State	State	White
Heady, Bonnie Brown	41	Kidnapping-Murder	White	18 DEC 1953	Asphyxiation	Missouri	Jackson	Prostitute	State	Federal	White
Rosenberg, Ethel**	38	Espionage	White	19 JUN 1953	Electrocution	New York	New York	Housewife	State	Federal	None
Dean, Dovie Blanche	55	Spousal Murder	White	15 JAN 1954	Electrocution	Ohio	Clermont	Housewife	State	State	White
Butler, Betty Evelyn	25	Murder	Black	12 JUN 1954	Electrocution	Ohio	Hamilton	Unknown	State	State	Black

2. Empirical Frameworks—Table 2-1

Name of Condemned Prisoner (Slave Owner)	Age at Death	Offense of Defendant	Race	Execution Date	Method of Execution	State of Execution	County of Execution	Occupation of Defendant	Place of Execution	Jurisdiction of Execution	Race of Victim
Graham, Barbara Elaine***	32	Robbery-Murder	White	3 JUN 1955	Asphyxiation	California	Los Angeles	Prostitute	State	State	White
Martin, Rhonda Belle***	48	Spousal Murder	White	11 OCT 1957	Electrocution	Alabama	Montgomery	Waitress	State	State	White
Duncan, Elizabeth Ann***	58	Murder-Conspiracy- Murder	White	8 AUG 1962	Asphyxiation	California	Ventura	Housewife	State	State	White
Barfield, Velma Margie	52	Murder	White	2 NOV 1984	Injection	North Carolina	Robeson	Nurse	State	State	White
Buenoano, Judy Ann	54	Murder	White	30 MAR 1998	Electrocution	Florida	Orange	Salon Owner	State	State	White
Tucker, Karla Faye	38	Robbery-Murder	Latina	3 FEB 1998	Injection	Texas	Harris	Office Worker	State	State	White
Riggs, Christina Marie	28	Child Murder	White	2 MAY 2000	Injection	Arkansas	Pulaski	Nurse	State	State	White
Beets, Betty Lou	63	Spousal Murder	White	24 FEB 2000	Injection	Texas	Henderson	Waitress	State	State	White
Allen, Wanda Jean****	41	Murder	Black	11 JAN 2001	Injection	Oklahoma	Oklahoma	Parolee	State	State	Black
Plantz, Marilyn****	40	Spousal Murder	White	1 MAY 2001	Injection	Oklahoma	Oklahoma	Housewife	State	State	White
Smith, Lois Nadean	61	Murder	Indian	4 DEC 2001	Injection	Oklahoma	Sequoyah	Unknown	State	State	White
Block, Lynda Lyon	54	Murder	White	10 MAY 2002	Electrocution	Alabama	Lee	Housewife	State	State	White
Wuornos, Aileen Carol	46	Robbery-Murder	White	9 OCT 2002	Injection	Florida	Volusia	Prostitute	State	State	White
Newton, Francis Elaine	40	Murder	Black	14 SEP 2005	Injection	Texas	Harris	Housewife	State	State	Black
Lewis, Teresa Wilson Bean	41	Spousal Murder	White	23 SEP 2010	Injection	Virginia	Pittsylvania	Textile worker	State	State	White
McCarthy, Kimberly	52	Murder	Black	26 JUN 2013	Injection	Texas	Dallas	Nursing home	State	State	White
Basso, Suzanne Margaret	44	Murder	White	5 FEB 2014	Injection	Texas	Harris	Office clerk	State	State	White
Coleman, Lisa Ann	38	Child Murder	Black	17 SEP 2014	Injection	Texas	Tarrant	Laborer	State	State	Black
Gissendaner, Kelly Renee	47	Spousal Murder	White	30 SEP 2015	Injection	Georgia	Dallas	Unknown	State	State	White

PART II
Historical Context

> "The model English woman was weak, submissive, charitable, virtuous, and modest. Her mental and physical activity was limited to keeping the home in order, cooking, and bearing and rearing children, although she might occasionally serve the community as a nurse or midwife."[1]

3

The First Historical Trend, 1630s–1750s

Women were about one-fifth of executions conducted in colonial America from 1632 to 1759. The infrequency with which officials executed women relative to men suggests that colonial governments favored less severe forms of corporal punishment for women in the period. The extant literature supports the notion that women committed far less violent crimes than did men and judicial officials were more likely to acquit women and dismiss their cases than men. Plausible explanations for authorities using the death penalty so guardedly toward colonial women had little to do with chivalrous notions about executing the gentler sex, however. Low rates of women executions in the early colonies likely stemmed from short supplies of female labor—there were severe disparities in male to female sex ratios in the early colonies. The adult sex ratio in most colonies was more than *two to one*; it was *four to one* in Virginia and as high as *six to one* in Maryland. Interestingly, women were just 14 percent of the more than 2,000 passengers that embarked from London to Virginia in 1635.

Planters relied on indentured servants throughout much of the 17th century. African slavery had yet to gain a foothold in the British mainland colonies and the enslavement of American Indians proved less than satisfactory to fulfilling the labor needs of the early colonies. Female labor was crucial to preindustrial colonial America since the work required to maintain even a subsistence level of existence was momentous. As one social historian put it, "In the period of colonial American history, from 1620 to the 1750s or 1760s, Puritan women were figures of unquestioned worth and importance, partners with their husbands in the economy of the farm."[2] Labor needs were moderated somewhat by the many unmarried Irish women that immigrated to the early British colonies as indentured house servants when crop failures, rising rents, and declines in the linen industry forced thousands to flee Ireland from 1717 to 1719, from 1726 to 1728, and again from 1740 to 1741. Excessive rates of natural female mortality also contributed to the shortage of women in American colonial society. Consequently, women convicted of serious crimes in the early colonies typically did not hang for their offenses. As one commentator explains, "[P]enal measures were characterized by the desire to preserve labor necessary for the development of the community, not to take lives except for behavior which was perceived as constituting the most undeniable threat to the security of the group."[3]

Still, it is interesting that colonial governments used capital punishment so sparingly toward women since many female immigrants to the early British mainland colonies beginning in 1615 comprised a highly marginalized lot. For one, women were among the thousands of indentured servants that ship owners treated ruthlessly and sold into slave-like bondage in early America. Young and corrupt women were roughly two thirds of the thousands of convicts and prisoners transported as part of the white slave trade from the British Isles before the end of the eighteenth century. These early colonial women came to America "not of their own free will, but kidnapped, shanghaied, impressed, duped, beguiled, and yes, in chains."[4] Many female transports were poor, abandoned and illegitimate girls, prostitutes, thieves, and murderers who suffered extreme hardships in England. One ship's captain referred to transported women as "a villainous and demoralized lot."[5] Unscrupulous entrepreneurs engaged in the lucrative enterprise of transporting young kidnapped women to Virginia and Maryland. The French too sent thousands of kidnapped and "shanghaied" women to colonial Louisiana, many of whom were "poor, diseased, or criminal women shipped from the notorious Salpêtrière prison," as well as the Paris almshouses and hospitals of Bicêtre, Pitié, Hôpital Général, and the Enfants Trouvées. Known for its "scenes of horror," the Salpêtrière prison housed "the sick, the criminal, the homeless, and the insane" with inmates "regularly flogged, bound in chains, and subjected to stupefying hygienic conditions."[6] Not surprisingly, early colonists made little distinction in their attitudes and treatment of felons and indentured servants comprising an impoverished and marginalized class. As one scholar explains,

> The poor creatures who have been inducted to indent themselves are in situations the most pitiable; they are treated by their masters in a similar manner to the felons formerly transported from England to Virginia. And the self-indentured woman, like her convict sister, was likely to be unhappy.[7]

Of course, other women came to the mainland colonies not as convicts, prisoners, indentured servants or slaves, but as the wives of immigrant freemen. Still, the contempt that 17th century planters held toward the Irish is epitomized in a letter to the trustees of one company: "Please don't send us any more Irishmen. Send us some Africans, because the Africans are civilized and the Irish are not."[8]

Executions of White Women

American jurisdictions put to death roughly 30 percent of women executed historically from the early 17th to the mid–18th centuries, and white women were about 70 percent of this condemned population. New England colonies account for about two-thirds of white women executions in the first historical period. Convicted largely of infanticide, witchcraft, and spousal murder, these women were typically poor housewives and domestic servants. Scholars concede that white women executions in early colonial New England resulted, either directly or indirectly, from three major social crises of the period—the Antinomian controversy of 1636, the Quaker intrusion into Massachusetts in the late 1650s, and the witchcraft hysteria of the Salem witch trials in 1692. Critical scholars view these crises as *crime waves* accenting "power struggles between those who ruled and those who were ruled."[9] In this era, as social historian Mary Beth Norton explains, there was no separation of the Puritan church from the secular state and both were so closely aligned and mutually supportive that early colonists found it difficult to distinguish the superior authority.[10] Another critical commentator explains, "[t]he creation of a stable economic and political environment and the establishment of a moral society were seen by many early colonial leaders as a single task. Laws governing matters of personal moral behavior were enforced not only with a view toward protecting the souls of colonists but the stability of the social order."[11] Consequently, corporal punishment imputed to white women in this early colonial period resulted largely from women openly challenging the authority of Puritan leaders to maintain control over prevailing religious beliefs, real and personal property, and the gender order of colonial society. Sheldon explains that early Puritan leaders singled out women for prosecution of such religious-based offenses as heresy, blasphemy, Quakerism, and violation of the Sabbath: "Women were considered property and lived in existence of servitude and compliance. When they failed to comply with these vigors, they were brought before the court."[12]

The Antinomian Controversy

A major crisis in early colonial New England was Boston's antinomian controversy in which out-spoken women challenged the theological, political, and gender order of early American society—the crime was *sedition*. Antinomianism is "an old heresy which technically means opposition to the law, [and] embodies the view that since men can be set free from sin by grace alone, obedience to the law is irrelevant to salvation."[13] Anne Hutchinson, Jane Verrin, Deborah Moody, Eleanor Trusler, Dorothy Talbye, Mary Oliver and other women gave attention to the church, courts, and the colonial leadership as dissenters challenging the religious and secular orthodoxy of early society—these women posed a subversive threat "to the authority, power, and economic well-being of the ruling elite" of early American society.[14] Church leaders labeled these women antinomians to discredit their opposition to established ruling class doctrine and "were ruthless in punishing any kind of opposition or heterodoxy."[15] Mary Oliver, for instance, "was sentenced to prison for heretical speeches to a group of new immigrants ... [and] several years later she was tied to the whipping post with a slit stick on her tongue for saying that all the ministers in the country were bloodthirsty men."[16] Church leaders ultimately excommunicated Mary and she returned to England in 1650. The historical significance of trying antinomian women in New England was to control women and curtail religious dissent.

Though the historical record fails to corroborate the notion that the antinomian movement resulted directly in women executions, antinomianism had a profound societal impact on early colonial women of increasing the female criminal conviction rates. While women were about 2 percent of convicted criminals in the first five years of the Puritan settlement, the percentage of female criminal convictions increased *fourfold* from 1635 to 1639 and *sixfold* from 1640 to 1644. The sizeable increase in female criminal conviction rates during the antinomian period lends credence to the contention that imprisoning women initially evolved to control female behavior challenging the gendered order of early America. Early colonies had yet to develop prison systems, but undoubtedly, these unmanageable women populated overcrowded and unsanitary jails or goals.

An inextricable link between female witchcraft indictments, women's public dissent, and orthodox perceptions of female criminality accented early Puritan society. This is no less the case with Anne Hutchinson who was pivotal in challenging the patriarchy of early New England society. Hutchinson was an admired spiritual advisor in her congregation and held weekly meetings with congregants in her home to deride clerics' sermons and their colonial leadership even after church authorities banned the gatherings. At the center of the controversy between Hutchinson, her followers, and orthodox ministers was the "covenant of works" versus the "covenant of grace." Hutchinson instructed congregants to the idea of the covenant of grace—that God's good grace redeems souls—and rejected the covenant of works—that God redeems soul's through righteous living. To Hutchinson, "the Covenant of Works had a deadening effect on the spiritual life of the community because it encouraged too much scrutiny of behavior and led to formalism or legalism in establishing rules of behavior."[17] Though Hutchinson had won favor with influential political and religious leaders, much of the church leadership feared her teachings were fragmenting the colony at a time when it was under attack from outside foes, namely, the Pequot Indians. It was not so much that Hutchinson's theology troubled colonial leadership; rather, it was that her ideas violated the Puritan cannon that women were to obey men and not to teach theology. Indeed, her unorthodox ideas challenged patriarchal control over the gender order and ultimately the stability of colonial society—"ministers and magistrates ... sharply criticized Anne for not fulfilling her ordained womanly role."[18] Antinomian women rejected the conventional notion of womanhood in early colonial New England:

The model English woman was weak, submissive, charitable, virtuous, and modest. Her mental and physical activity was limited to keeping the home in order, cooking, and bearing and rearing children, although she might occasionally serve the community as a nurse or midwife. She was urged to avoid books and intellectual exercise, for such activity might overtax her weak mind, and to serve her husband willingly, since she was by nature his inferior.... [S]he was to hold her tongue in church and be careful not to teach, nor to usurp authority over the man, but to be in silence.... The female role definition that the Massachusetts ministers and magistrates perpetuated severely limited the assertiveness, the accomplishment, the independence, and the intellectual activity of Puritan women.[19]

Boston's antinomian movement of female resistance to theological and secular doctrines reached a high point in 1638 when Hutchinson's ecclesiastical trial for blasphemy and her secular trial for sedition took place. One scholar claims that the surviving record of Hutchinson's trial verbatim reveals it as a "trial by examination, the very essence of Star Chamber method."[20] There, Hutchinson claimed revelation from God and warned the court "if you go on this course you will bring a curse upon you and your posterity."[21] The court convicted her on these words alone, for "if Anne Hutchinson was hearing voices, they were the revelations not of God, but of Satan."[22] Hutchinson's outspokenness ended when the colony's governor, John Winthrop, excommunicated Hutchinson and banished her and many of her followers from the colony as witches, heretics, and criminals. It did not help matters that Winthrop knew Hutchinson had given birth to a stillborn and extremely deformed infant resulting from a hydatidiform mole; Winthrop maliciously maligned Hutchinson with her personal misfortune as confirmation of her wickedness and heterodoxy. Winthrop's efforts to directly associate Hutchinson with witchcraft, however, mostly failed because at that time "the idea of the witch as a female challenger of the religious system never permeated colonial consciousness."[23] Hutchinson moved to Rhode Island in 1638 with her husband William who died in 1640. Distraught over her husband's death, Hutchinson sought refuge in New York where in August 1643 Siwanoy Indians slaughtered her and five of her younger children, most probably in corroboration with Puritan authorities. One of her children, young Susanna Hutchinson, survived the attack and the Siwanoy Indians held her captive for four years.

The Quaker Intrusion

Though no confirmed female executions resulted directly from Anne Hutchinson's contest with colonial leaders, her ordeal in Massachusetts went far to usher in another major crisis— the Quaker intrusion into Boston that began in 1656 and whose religious activism provoked the "witchcraft alarm among the clerical authorities." Most New England colonies had strong anti–Quaker measures, but Massachusetts was particularly callous in its intolerance of Quakers and their religious orthodoxy. The Puritan community underwent a severe crisis during this period as it grew increasingly bewildered and isolated by events in England: "After years of civil war the English had tired of theological conflict and a new mood of religious toleration was taking hold in the motherland, the Puritans responded swiftly and harshly to the new heresies propounded by the Quaker sect."[24] Massachusetts had banished Quakers from the colony by 1658 and prescribed death to persons who held their religious beliefs. Quaker women often endured the pillory, whippings, and such common physical tortures as "having their ears hacked off, their noses slit, and their tongues pierced with hot needles."[25] One scholar explains, "[d]efenseless women, maidens and matrons, were stripped naked to the waist, and, thus exposed to the public gaze, were beaten with whips of threefold knotted cord until the blood ran down their bare backs and bosoms."[26] The intrusion resulted in Quaker women threatened with death for challenging the patriarchal colonial authority of Puritan ministers and magistrates. Some

Quakers remained in the colony opposing the religious bigotry of Puritan authorities. Mary Barrett Dyer and three male companions (William Robinson, Marmarduke Stevenson, and William Leddra) are the most notable of those who chose to stay in Massachusetts and suffered dire consequences as a result. Mary Dyer was an intimate friend and follower of Anne Hutchinson who, as Winthrop observed from living across the street, frequently attended religious meetings at Hutchinson's home. Like Hutchinson, Mary Dyer had given birth to a premature, stillborn child that Winthrop depicted as fiendish and which he reasoned proved her a witch. Actually, Dyer's stillborn child was anencephalic with spinal bifida and had other abnormalities. Colonial authorities hanged Robinson and Stevenson in October 1659 while Dyer earned a reprieve on condition that she leave and stay out of Massachusetts. Dyer went to Rhode Island with her husband and eldest son after witnessing the execution of her friends but returned to Massachusetts within seven months. It was then that authorities arrested and condemned Dyer to death a second time. Refusing to abide her banishment, Massachusetts officials hanged Dyer in June 1660. A year later, her friend William Leddra met the same fate. Shortly after Mary Dyer's hanging, coupled with his growing frustration with the treatment of Quakers in the British colonies, England's King Charles II ordered an end to the death penalty for Quakers.

Witchcraft

European societies executed some 300,000 persons for witchcraft from the 1400s to the 1700s, most of whom were women. The persecution of women for witchcraft stretches back to the 11th century in European history; Joan of Arc was the most legendary of executed "witches" burned at the stake in May 1431. The Roman Catholic Church was at the vanguard of burning to death anyone, especially women, who violated church doctrine. Sheldon points out that the infamous witch hunts in Europe and the American colonies "stand as classic examples of the use of the legal system to punish women who dared challenge the male power structure."[27] Witchcraft was a capital offense in the early American colonies and though jurisdictions hanged several men for witchcraft during the period, women were far more vulnerable to accusation, trial, conviction, and execution. In this early period of colonial history "the idea that witches were women seems to have been more strongly held by local authorities, magistrates, and juries—men who had the power to decide the fate of the accused—than it was by accusers as a whole."[28] In colonial America, women were roughly 80 percent of witchcraft executions, but unlike Europe, authorities mostly *hanged* women for witchcraft rather than *burning* them to death. Belief in the existence of witches was so widespread throughout early colonial New England "that disbelief was itself suspect." Women executions for witchcraft were not limited to the notorious Salem ordeal of 1692, however. Seventy percent of witchcraft cases took place before 1658.

Women persecution for witchcraft "terrorized the Connecticut river valley and western Connecticut shore" as early as 1647.[29] Alse Youngs of Windsor was the first confirmed female execution for witchcraft in Connecticut, as well as in all of colonial New England. Historians know little of the events leading to the execution of Alse Youngs' hanging in May 1647 since court records of her case are long lost. Scholars know only that she was married to a carpenter named John Youngs, she was the mother of Alice Youngs Beamon of Springfield (Massachusetts), and that she had a son.[30] In another case, the confession of a domestic servant woman named Mary Johnson of her "familiarity with the devil" was enough for early Connecticut authorities to hang her for witchcraft in December 1648. Mary was unhappy with her plight in life and likely suffered from severe mental depression. An added justification for her witchcraft execution to Cotton Mathers was that Mary "confessed that she was guilty of the murder of a child and that she had been guilty of uncleanness with men and devils."[31] Other early women executions for witchcraft in Connecticut included Goodwife Bassett, the wife of Thomas Bassett who fought in the Pequot War, hanged in June 1651 in Stratford after confessing to witchcraft. [Early colonialists addressed women as "Goodwife" when referencing a woman of low socioeconomic status, and reserved the term "Mistress" for "the wealthiest and most prominent women."][32] An impoverished woman named Goodwife (Elizabeth) Knapp hanged in November 1653 in Fairfield after officials convicted her of witchcraft. At Elizabeth's burial "a crowd of curiosity seekers gathered around it ... they stripped the clothing from the corpse and rudely pawed it over" looking for devil teats but found none.[33] Hartford authorities also hanged servant woman Joan Carrington in April 1651 for witchcraft the circumstances of which are lost to history. In the case of Lydia Gilbert, peculiar events surrounding the death of Henry Stiles brought an accusation of "aggravated" witchcraft against Lydia who hanged in Hartford in December 1654. She reportedly had bewitched Thomas Allyn into killing Stiles that otherwise was an accidental killing.

Connecticut officials indicted no women for witchcraft for nearly a decade after hanging Lydia Gilbert, but in the early 1660s witchcraft prosecutions resurfaced in the colony "that bore tragic consequences not only for the parties involved but for their community in general."[34] Colonial authorities hanged three women during this period for witchcraft. The first hanging in June 1662 involved Mary Sanford charged with "having illegal clairvoyant powers bestowed on her by the devil."[35] Another hanging was that of Rebecca Greensmith indicted for witchcraft in June 1662 who languished in jail for six months before her trial and admitted to having "familiarity with the devil." Greensmith reportedly became irrational and weak of mind while imprisoned in "squalid conditions, loathsome food, and callous warders exasperated her plight through the long months of durance. Interrogations wore her down. She was baited and badgered by curiosity seekers and hounded incessantly by ecclesiastics. Eventually she was pushed beyond the limits of human frailty."[36] Greensmith hanged in January 1663. Another early Connecticut witchcraft case involved Mary Barnes who hanged with Rebecca Greensmith. Scholars know little about Mary's execution other than officials indicted her and a jury found her guilty of witchcraft.

Massachusetts authorities hanged women convicted of witchcraft long before the Salem ordeal as well. The 1640s proved a restless period for Massachusetts—crop failure, economic woes, out-migration, epidemics, and strained relations with the Pequot Indians all acted as evidence that the "Devil's work was at hand."[37] The first female witchcraft execution in the colony was that of housewife Margaret Jones whose strange behaviors aroused suspicion of witchery. A formal complaint brought her before the Court of Assistants where a customary physical examination by matrons of women accused of witchcraft found teats on the "secret parts" of her body believed to suckle evil spirits. Equally damning was her demeanor at trial where she disparaged her accusers, defied the judges, insulted the jury, and "reviled all who testified against her."[38] The Court found her guilty of witchcraft and ordered her hanged on the Boston gallows in June 1648. Alice Stratton, a friend to Jones, stated that Margaret "died wrongfully ... and her blood would be required at the magistrates' hands."[39]

Some historical information survives Massachusetts' hanging of Alice Lake and Elizabeth Kendall for witchcraft in 1650. Alice was an indentured servant who, after manumission, married Henry Lake and had four children. Court records concerning Alice Lake are lost, but a witness to her execution said that Alice Lake denied "all matters of witchcraft" but deemed herself worthy of execution since years earlier she had aborted an illegitimate child while a single woman. Massachusetts wrongly executed Elizabeth Kendall for bewitching to death a child that reportedly died from hypothermia. A nurse that testified against Elizabeth actually was responsible for the child's death. Years later, the nurse died in prison for adultery where she delivered a stillborn illegitimate child. Anne Hibbins was another early casualty of the Massachusetts witch scare. Her case is unusual since Anne was married to a successful merchant and a magistrate of the Massachusetts Court of Assistants and thus a member of Boston's affluent class. Despite her social position, Anne "had a haughty, domineering, argumentative and abrasive way about her."[40] Anne lost the protection of her husband when he died in 1654 and she became even more disgruntled, often openly chastising persons about her. A formal charge of witchcraft brought Anne before the Court in 1655; she hanged on the Boston gallows in June 1656.

Anne Glover was the last woman hanged in Massachusetts for witchcraft before the Salem tragedy. Anne was born in Ireland in the early 17th century, and sometime during the 1650s, Oliver Cromwell's forces captured her and her family and sold them as slaves in Barbados where her husband died because he would not renounce his Catholic faith. In 1680, John Goodwin of Boston employed Anne and her daughter as housekeepers. In the summer of 1688, four of the five Goodwin children fell ill which a physician diagnosed as "nothing but a hellish Witchcraft could be the origin of these maladies." One of the children, young Martha Goodwin, claimed that she and her siblings became ill after an argument with Anne when Martha discovered Anne's daughter stealing linen. Authorities arrested and tried Anne for witchcraft. To one recent work, "Anne had victim written all over her: she was beached in a foreign land run by English Puritans, whose idea of a good time was to hunt out demons and Catholics."[41] Overshadowing her trial was Anne's inability to speak English (she spoke Gaelic and some Latin) and she refused to renounce her Catholicism. Speculation of her "possession" increased at her trial when she could only recite the Lord's Prayer in Gaelic and Latin, but not English. Cotton Mathers characterized Anne as "a scandalous old Irishwoman, very poor, a Roman Catholic and obstinate in idolatry." Robert Calef, a Boston merchant who knew Anne, wrote that she "was a despised, crazy, poor old woman, an Irish Catholic who was tried for afflicting the Goodwin children. Her behaviour at her trial was like that of one distracted [most likely because she couldn't speak a word of English]. They did her cruel. The proof against her was wholly deficient. The jury brought her guilty."[42] Officials hanged Anne in November 1688.

Interestingly, European societies did not stop executing women for witchcraft until 1782 when village authorities in Mollis, Switzerland, beheaded Anna Goeldi for "causing a girl to spit pins and convulse." Religious authorities recently exonerated Anna, some 226 years after her execution.[43] In contrast, American colonies stopped executing women for witchcraft nearly a century earlier when the Salem witch trials in the summer and spring of 1692 resulted in the hanging of 14 women for witchcraft. In July, Puritan authorities hanged Rebecca Nurse, Susannah Martin, Elizabeth Howe, Sarah Wilde, and Martha Carrier, and in September, they hanged Mary Parker, Alice Parker, Mary Easty, Martha Corey, Ann Pudeater, Wilmot Reed, Margaret Scott, Bridget Bishop, and Sarah Good. Church officials even imprisoned Sarah Good's four-year-old daughter, Dorcas Good, for eight months causing the young girl severe mental anguish and leading to extreme psychoses that left the young child hopelessly dependent on other's care for the remainder of her life. Contributing to her mental state undoubtedly was the loss of her infant sister who died during Sarah Good's confinement.

Modern scholars have put forth a myriad of explanations why Salem residents underwent such a ruinous witch craze resulting in the execution of mostly poor, marginalized, and unpopular women. The Salem ordeal stemmed from the bizarre behaviors of eight young girls that a village physician concluded were witchcraft in origin since he found no physical abnormalities of the children. The young girls denounced many of the townspeople as bewitching them into eccentric and uncontrollable behaviors. Modern speculation has it that the girls responsible for the witchcraft accusations against Salem women suffered from hysteria and psychogenic, convulsive ergotism or encephalitis lethargica through agricultural poisoning, or even fraud and sexual abuse.[44] The historical record gives credibility to these claims, but a far less speculative reason for the Salem tragedy is that Puritan society was in complete and utter chaos during the period. As one leading scholar explains, "There were ongoing battles with the French and their Native American allies. Disease was rampant, religions were in conflict, neighbors were engaged in disputes, and death was a constant presence, afflicting not only the aged but the young and apparently robust as well."[45] Whether Barbados slave woman Tituba influenced impressionistic young minds with experiences of witchery, the young girls contracted pathogens, they fraudulently tricked adults into a frenzy, or adults reduced the girls to objects of sexual perversion, the clearest indication of societal catastrophe in Salem is that "the power to point out witches complied with the interests of the ruling class by accusing underlings as witches and carefully avoided accusing any of the ruling elites."[46] That power was so great that even colonial women believed "they were damned and more likely to think of themselves as utterly depraved, as rebellious wretches against God, bonded to Satan and bound for hell."[47]

Demographics accented much about women's persecution and execution for witchcraft. Witchcraft was a gender-related crime; women comprised the vast majority of the 342 persons accused of witchcraft in colonial New England. Officials suspected that about half of the men accused of witchcraft were through their associations with women suspects—"they were the husbands, sons, other kin, or public supporters of female witches."[48] What's more, men were three-fourths of the witnesses against women accused of witchcraft. Women prosecuted, convicted, and executed for witchcraft were largely "disagreeable women, at best aggressive and abrasive, at worst ill-tempered, quarrelsome, and spiteful."[49] These were "disorderly women who failed to, or refused to, abide by the behavioral norms of society." They were mostly older women ostensibly engaged in "magical powers by which to cast spells, pronounce curses, and cause accidents, storms, sickness and death."[50] What's more, colonial leaders assured that members of the ruling class did not suffer witchcraft accusations. As Chambliss points out, "So long as the special assistants of the courts who had the power to point out witches complied with the interest of the ruling class by accusing underlings as witches are carefully avoided accusing any of the ruling elites, their word was followed and criminal sanctions were imposed."[51]

In discerning the types of evidence colonial magistrates relied upon to convict women of witchcraft, one scholar contends that courts never executed women who had confessed to "having made a covenant with Satan." It may not have been the case that women who *confessed* to dealing with the Devil survived judicial persecution and execution, however; ministers and magistrates consistently pressured women to admit to their arrangements with Satan. In contrast, courts did not generally coerce men to confess to covenants, and if men did confess, Puritan leaders often punished them as "liars." The evidence is clear that women hanged for witchcraft even when they admitted their covenants.

> Mary Johnson succumbed to this insistence in 1648, admitting that she and the Devil provided many services for one another, she was convicted of familiarity with Satan and hanged. After Rebecca Greensmith described the nature of her covenant with Satan in Hartford in 1662, she too was executed. Similarly, confession doomed the widow Glover in Boston in 1688. Except during the Salem events, when the magistrates decided to put off the executions of people who admitted their guilt until all local witches were discovered, women who incriminated themselves were almost all punished in accordance with the biblical injunction, "Thou shall not suffer a witch to live."[52]

Women's economic status in early New England explains much about their persecution and ultimate execution for witchcraft. Inheritance rights to real and personal property lay at the heart of most accusations of witchcraft. As Barstow explains, "This was a society designed to keep property in the hands of men; when a woman had no husband, brother, or son and therefore inherited in their stead, she was liable to harassment of various kinds, including arraignment for witchcraft. And once arrested, she was more likely than other suspects to be condemned and executed."[53] Karlsen supports this position with empirical evidence that women with no legitimate male heirs in their immediate families in New England were 61 percent of women *accused* of being witches, 64 percent of women *tried* as witches, 76 percent of women *convicted* of being witches, and 89 percent of women *executed* as witches. Thus, women accused of witchcraft in colonial society were largely "daughters of parents who had no sons (or whose sons had died), women in marriages which brought forth only daughters (or in which the sons had died), or women in marriages with no children at all."[54] Accusations of witchcraft against women without sons began very early: "Alice Young, Mary Johnson, Margaret Jones, Joan Carrington, and Mary Parsons, all of whom were executed in the late 1640s and early 1650s, were women without sons when the accusations were lodged. Elizabeth Godman, brought into court at least twice on witchcraft charges in the 1650s, had neither brothers nor sons. Decade by decade, the pattern continued."[55] Women executed in Salem were largely women of property. "Dower" ostensibly protected a widow's inheritance to real and personal property—the right of a widow to the lifetime uses of one-third of a deceased husband's estate. Yet, labeling widows without male heirs as witches and executing them for witchcraft provided a legitimate strategy for Puritan leaders to gain valued property. Women executions for witchcraft in the colonial period were essentially "part of an ongoing attempt by men ... to ensure the continuance of male supremacy."[56] In effect, the accusations of being a "witch" or practicing "witchcraft" amounted to convenient labels reserved for recalcitrant women challenging Puritan authority in colonial New England. Colonial leaders could brand as a witch and execute any woman for witchcraft that violated the gender order.

In southern colonies, women suffered allegations for witchcraft as early as 1626 but most ended in acquittals since southern courts did not take witchcraft accusations as seriously as in New England. Still, Maryland authorities called for the execution of Rebecca Fowler for witchcraft. A grand jury indicted Rebecca and the Calvert County court found her guilty of "being led by the instigation of the devil into doing certain evil and diabolical arts, called witchcraft, enchantments, charms, and sorceries."[57] Rebecca hanged in October 1685. Women occasionally underwent physical ordeals: "a woman suspected of witchcraft was ... stripped naked and cross bound, the right thumb to the left toe, and the left thumb to the right toe, and cast into some deep water. It was believed that she would sink if innocent."[58]

Unlike the accused Salem women about whom scholars have exhausted the historical record, much less is familiar about the events surrounding Grace White Sherwood, the daughter of a carpenter, who lived with her planter husband James and three sons in what is now Virginia Beach, Virginia. Neighbors had misgivings about Grace and consistently tormented her after the death of her husband in 1701; "she was an independent woman who didn't remarry after her husband died, she wore long trousers, and she was skilled in the use of herbs as medicinal remedies." Neighbors accused Grace of "blighting gardens, causing livestock to die, and influencing the weather." Neighbors were resentful toward Grace largely because she inherited some 200 acres from her father and she proved a more successful farmer than her fellow townspeople. At one point, Grace won a legal action against Luke Hill and his wife after Mr. Hill "trespassed, attacked and caused great bodily harm to her." Court records show that Grace received 20 shillings in damages against the Hills. Neighbors took Grace to court on at least 12 separate occasions to answer for a variety of false accusations. Finally, there was evidence that Grace "was in league with the devil" though the Princess Anne County court and the attorney general refused to prosecute the case. County officials conceded, however, and the 46-year-old Grace agreed to trial by ducking. Bound and thrown from a boat, Grace survived the dunking ordeal when she worked herself free and swam to the surface. This meant, of course, that Grace was guilty of witchcraft and officials moved quickly to jail her indefinitely. After seven years in jail, authorities released Grace in 1713. She is the only woman ever convicted in Virginia of witchcraft by a "witch dunking trial." After the ordeal, Grace returned home to her three sons and lived to about 80 years of age. She died in the autumn of 1740. In July 2006, Virginia Governor Tim Kaine formally pardoned Grace on the 300th anniversary of her witchcraft conviction.[59]

On at least three occasions during the early colonial period, maritime justice aboard merchant ships bound to Maryland and Virginia from England resulted in the execution of women for witchcraft. In the first instance, crewmembers of the *Charity*, destined for Maryland in 1654, rumored that Mary Lee was a witch and demanded the captain try her "to assuage storms supposedly caused by the malevolence of witches."[60] The ship was leaking badly and in trouble, but the captain refused. Seamen then searched Mary and exposed a witch's mark. The crew tied Mary to the capstall, got a confession, hanged the elderly woman, and afterwards threw her body overboard. Fearing a mutiny, the captain did not intervene. In the second instance, Elizabeth Richardson hanged for witchcraft aboard the ship *Sarah Artch* sailing to Maryland in 1658. There, President George Washington's great-grandfather, John Washington, accused ship owner Edward Prescott of hanging Elizabeth as a witch. Officials charged and prosecuted Prescott for Elizabeth's hanging but a court acquitted him since the ship's captain, John Green, was actually responsible for the killing. In the third instance, the ship's master, Captain Bennett, ordered the hanging of Katharine Grady for witchcraft on a ship bound to Virginia in 1659.

Infanticide and Child Murder

One consequence of relatively few women in early colonial America was that men lusted after women. Consequently, *fornication* and *adultery* were among the most prosecuted offenses in colonial America. Roughly one-third of prosecuted sexual offenses involved mothers of illegitimate children in Massachusetts, and nearly two-thirds of prosecuted moral offenses in Pennsylvania involved bastardness. Rape and sexual brutality by strangers, neighbors, masters, fathers, husbands, and others were pervasive in colonial women's lives and added considerably to the rates of child illegitimacy. The murder of unwanted infants was common in colonial America. Pennsylvania officials tried 78 percent of unmarried women involved in killing their infants between 1682 and 1801. Though premarital pregnancy rates varied among the colonies, about one-third of women were pregnant at marriage. Many of the women tried for bastardy "came from the most profligate classes in England, and upon their arrival in this country found conditions which did not help in their reformation."[61] Courts recurrently imposed fines and whippings on young married couples "for premarital fornication after they produced the presumptive evidence: a 7-month baby."[62] Sexual relations outside of marriage were prevalent mostly among poor, young and uneducated indentured servant girls whose masters commonly prohibited them from marrying fearing the loss of their labor from pregnancy. As one commentator explains,

> Women servants suffered uniquely from the indignities of patriarchal control over their personal lives. The sexual double standard often put them literally in a double bind: powerless to resist advances, and even rapes, by their masters and other men, they were nevertheless given the entire blame for being caught in violation of conventional sexual morality. At the same time ... women servants were frequently kept from respectability because their employment did not allow them marriage.[63]

Masters often fined pregnant servants and whipped those who could not pay the fine. These servant women usually "served an extra twelve to twenty-four months to repay her master for the 'trouble of his house' and labor lost, and the fathers often did not share in this payment of damages."[64] Masters themselves were often the fathers of illegitimate children born to servant women. In other cases, however, masters sued to recover damages from men for impregnating their women servants. An early Virginia statute provided, for instance, that "each woman servant got with child by her master shall after her indenture is expired be sold for two years by the church wardens." One renowned legal scholar explains the inherent vulnerability and powerlessness of servant women in the biased statute:

While conception of a child required a male's involvement and while often the father may even have been the master of the mother, it was the mother only who had the additional burden of servitude. Furthermore, the psychological forces affecting the female indentured servant may raise the question as to how voluntary her act was, if it involved the master. Yet, the master or male's act was clearly voluntary and he was at least equally culpable. Nevertheless the male had no additional penal burden. The society economically profited by obtaining a servant for two years without cost for her labor. The child of the union suffered the social stigmatization of being a bastard.[65]

One misguided notion among death penalty scholars is that early colonial jurisdictions executed white women largely for witchcraft. The historical record reveals, however, that colonial jurisdictions hanged white women mostly for infanticide before 1760. Colonial officials selectively prosecuted infanticide laws and bastard concealment laws, "depending on the wealth, position and former reputation of the woman involved. Married women were almost never convicted, and likewise unmarried women of hitherto good character, especially if they were not servants."[66] Consequently, officials prosecuted mostly poor, young, and unmarried servant women for murdering their illegitimate children. One scholar identifies women convicted of infanticide as largely "servants, women on the fringes of society, often Irish, Indian, or Black, the very persons who would have been most likely to have been beaten and abused themselves."[67] One striking figure shows that 90 percent of murdered newborns in the early colonies were illegitimate. Colonial leaders criminalized illegitimacy to ensure that bastard children did not burden public coffers; illegitimate slave children were never wards of public expense but that of their masters. In explaining the motivation for infanticide, Hoffer and Hull contend, "It is not enough to say that the vast majority of murdering mothers did away with their newborn bastards to avoid the shame and difficulty of rearing unwanted illegitimate children."[68] These scholars concede that the reasons behind women killing their children are as varied as their personalities—"social ostracism, shame, loss of employment and reputation, and forcible intercourse, were certainly motives for the crime, [but] these influences had to pass through the filter of individual character and perception."[69]

Many young unmarried pregnant women committed suicide "believing that no other escape from ignominy lay open to them."[70] Scholars discount the more obvious reasoning for infanticide—high infanticide conviction rates did not result from a general severity of colonial courts, they did not derive from a special affection for children, "nor from Puritan magistrates' attempts to enforce class distinctions, nor from the harshness of biblical codes of laws."[71] Rather, Puritan judges found the severity of infanticide to social order in the concealment of sin, prior sexual wantonness, and "the disobedience of women to community standards."[72] Women executions for infanticide and child murder accent yet another major social crisis or "crime wave" in colonial America that remains largely unidentified in the criminal justice literature. In early America, colonial authorities prosecuted women who killed their children under common law murder and infanticide statutes. Given the presumption of innocence at common law, murder statutes burdened prosecutors with proving a woman guilty of killing an infant. If prosecuted under infanticide statutes that presumed a woman's child was born alive, the burden of proving blamelessness shifted to the woman. Where a mother claimed her dead child was stillborn, infanticide statutes required at least one witness to substantiate the mother's claim of a dead birth. Scholars argue that the infanticide statute made it easier to prosecute women for killing newborns since colonies made it a capital offense to simply conceal the death of a newborn even if stillborn. Moreover, the law had an added effect—"sentencing innocent women to death in many cases where a woman attempted to conceal her childbirth [where] the fetus was stillborn or died of natural causes."[73] Still, in cases where juries believed mothers sufficiently demonstrated remorse by shedding tears or "preparing any way for the coming of the child [e.g., benefit-of-linen] acquittal ordinarily followed."[74]

More than two-thirds of the women executed for murder in this period involved infanticide or child killings and *white* women were 80 percent of these executions. The earliest recorded white female execution for infanticide in the United States took place in 1632 when James City County officials in Virginia hanged June Champion; many contemporary sources mistakenly refer to June Champion as "Jane" Champion. June was the wife of Percival Champion, but it appears from the historical record that June's child was the product of an adulterous affair with William Gallopin. In June 1630, authorities indicted, convicted, and sentenced June and William for murdering and concealing the death of June's infant. There is no evidence that William hanged for the child's death though the historical record claims officials sentenced him to hang: "In 1630, Wm Gallopin & June Champion wife of Percival Champion Indicted by Gd. Jury for murder & Concealing ye death of ye sd. June's Child supposed to be got by ye sd. Wm. pleaded, found guilty by petty Jury & sentenced to be hang'd."[75]

The following year in June 1633, the same county officials in Virginia hanged Margaret Hatch for infanticide. As with June Champion, social historians know little about Margaret Hatch or why she murdered her infant. The available information shows that Margaret attempted to put off her hanging by claiming she was pregnant by "pleading her belly" and that officials could not execute her until she delivered the child. The colonial governor and Council of Virginia brought forth a jury of matrons, and after a physical examination reported that Margaret was not pregnant. She hanged shortly thereafter. Virginia also hanged an unnamed woman (race unknown) in 1692 for infanticide but the historical record is silent on the circumstances of the execution. There is also little historical information about the Virginia hanging of Ann Tandy in 1702 for killing her illegitimate child. Nearly four decades passed before Virginia hanged another woman for infanticide. Then, in May and November 1739, Williamsburg County officials hanged Elizabeth Maze and Elizabeth Twopence for the killing of their illegitimate children.

Maryland, North Carolina, and South Carolina are the only other southern jurisdictions that executed women for infanticide before the 1760s. Few facts, however, survive from the historical record about these hangings. In Maryland, the sheriff of St. Mary's County hanged Elizabeth Greene, an unmarried indentured servant to the John Gary household, in July 1664, after witnesses testified at her trial that upon giving birth to a male child Elizabeth threw the newborn into a fire. In Calvert County, the Provincial Court sentenced Joan Colledge, a spinster, to hang for the killing of her bastard infant in 1669. Joan most likely hanged in October 1671. The sheriff of Anne Arundel County also hanged Isabella Yausley for infanticide of her newborn son in April 1671. One scholar makes the point that these cases "indicate that women in Maryland accused of infanticide and not represented by a strong man, who either implicitly or explicitly vouched to control her and any subversive threats that her lawlessness presented to the young province, were condemned to death by the nascent Maryland elite."[76] Maryland archives make known a December 1684 case in which "a woman named Mary Axell appears to have been hanged for the murder of her child."[77] At the time of her trial for killing her daughter Elizabeth, Mary was pregnant and her execution postponed until after she delivered the child. The historical record is also silent on the Middlesex County hanging of widow Elizabeth Wakefield for infanticide in October 1747 as well as for Mary Lunt who hanged in May 1693 for infanticide. Magdalen Collar was the first woman executed in North Carolina in an unknown county in 1720. The colonial record of North Carolina reveals that Magdalen hanged for concealing the death of a bastard child. Chowan County officials in February 1739 hanged Catherine Sullivan for infanticide. Sarah Chamberlain is the only confirmed women execution in South Carolina for infanticide. She hanged in Charleston in 1738.

Massachusetts accounted for more than a third of white women executions for infanticide and child murder during the period. The earliest recorded female hanging for child murder in the colony was Dorothy Talbye in December 1638. She was a poor woman who found daily survival difficult since her husband John failed to provide adequately for the family. Dorothy became deeply depressed, despondent, and increasingly disillusioned with life over the years. She began acting irrationally; she broke with the Sabbath, quarreled with neighbors and clergy, and refused to perform her household tasks "claiming that God had commanded her to eschew all domestic duties."[78] When church elders ex-communicated Talbye, she began physically abusing John and in late 1637, the Essex County court ordered her "chained to a post for frequent laying hands on her husband to the danger of his life, and condemning the authority of the court."[79] Officials publicly whipped Dorothy in July 1638 again for abusing John. Dorothy's posture toward her husband may not have been entirely her own doing, however; John most likely contributed to Dorothy's violent inclinations since a year later the church censured John for "much pride and unnaturalness to his wife."[80] Dorothy snapped in November 1638 when she claimed divine revelation commanded her to kill her husband and children. Consequently, Dorothy attacked and killed her three-year-old daughter. John was most likely Dorothy's intended victim and would have killed him rather than her daughter had she been strong enough instead to break his neck. Charged with "the unnatural and untimely death of her daughter," Dorothy hanged in Salem in December 1638. Dorothy did not admit to her daughter's murder until threatened by church elders with *peine forte et dure* (death by crushing) and even then, she never repented.[81] To the church, her obstinacy proved Satan possessed her; Governor Winthrop believed that Satan made Dorothy delusional causing her to kill her child.

Suffolk County officials in Massachusetts hanged young Mary Martin sometime in 1646 for infanticide after her merchant father returned to England and abandoned Mary and her younger sister in Casco Bay, Maine, to fend for themselves after a business failure. Reputed to be a "very proper maiden ... of modest behaviour," Mary went to work as a servant for the Mitton household.[82] Mr. Mitton took a liking to Mary and soon the two were having sexual relations. After several months, Mary left the Mitton house and went to work in Boston for a dowager named Mrs. Bourne. Soon after arriving at Mrs. Bourne's house, Mary learned she was pregnant with Mitton's child. She concealed her pregnancy by wearing oversized clothes and denied her pregnancy to suspicious townspeople who often ridiculed and taunted her. Mary succumbed to the pressure and admitted her condition to the local goodwives. Mary gave birth to a baby girl alone in a backroom of Mrs. Bourne's house in December 1646. She murdered the baby and hid it in a chest where it remained until found by a suspicious midwife. Colonial officials arrested Mary, held a coroner's inquest, and brought Mary before a grand jury. Mary confessed after touching the baby and it bled. A jury found her guilty of murdering her newborn and Mary hanged at the Boston gallows in March 1647. The hangman botched the affair requiring Mary to hang twice. Cotton Mathers reported that the first hanging left Mary "to merely dangle in the air." The hangman remedied the noose by turning the knot of the rope backwards and Mary soon strangled to death.

In October 1648, Plymouth officials hanged Alice (Allis) Martin Clark Bishop for the unexplained murder of her four-year-old daughter Martha. Alice killed her child with a butcher knife while her husband was away on business. Alice cut the child's throat from ear to ear while the child slept in her bed. The historical record shows that Alice did not fully comprehend the consequences of the killing and made no protest when accused of the murder. She confessed to the killing in court but remained silent when asked why she had murdered her child. Most likely, Alice suffered from severe mental illness and postpartum depression. Authorities tried and convicted her for the child's murder. In another case, Suffolk County authorities hanged Mary Parsons for infanticide in May 1651 after she admitted responsibility for killing her young son Joshua. Mary's husband, Hugh Parsons, was abusive to Mary and caused her such mental anguish that scholars concede she had lost her mind and became delusional. Mary had endured much in her marriage and the death of her three children reportedly put her in a state of physical and emotional exhaustion. Boston authorities tried Mary for witchcraft (given her deranged behavior) but acquitted her of that charge in 1645 but later found her guilty of Joshua's murder. In other cases, Essex and Bristol county officials in Massachusetts hanged two unidentified white women in October 1668 and 1687 for murdering their children. In the first instance, scholars know little about the case other than a published report in *Bradstreet's Journal* that accomplices to the child's killing were the unknown woman's mother and a physician who "were made to sit on the gallows with ropes around their necks, each flanking the dangling form of the executed woman."[83] In the second instance, a young unmarried woman killed her newborn child stemming from a sexual liaison with an American Indian. She killed the infant "because she was ashamed of the way it was conceived."[84]

Plymouth Colony hanged Elizabeth Emerson, an unmarried woman who had an adulterous affair with a married man named Samuel Ladd and became pregnant, giving birth to twin girls. Emerson suffocated the newborns in a pillowcase that she stuffed into her hope chest. Authorities discovered the murdered children and executed Elizabeth in June 1693. Three years later in April, Plymouth Colony hanged unmarried Susanna Andrews, along with her mother Esther as an accomplice, to the killing of Susanna's newborn boy and girl twins. Unmarried Sarah Threeneedles hanged in November 1698 after leaving her newborn baby in an open field where it died from exposure. Historical records show "Sarah was a precocious girl who liked to sleep around" and who had given birth years earlier to another illegitimate child.[85] At her trial, Sarah accused shopkeeper Thomas Savage for abandoning her after she informed him she was pregnant. Savage denied the accusation and the court ignored Sarah's claim; some found it telling that jail officials discovered Sarah having sexual intercourse with another prisoner while awaiting execution.

Sarah Smith was a young woman when she married a much older Martin Smith. The couple moved to Deerfield, Massachusetts, in 1693, and in October of that year, Indians seized Martin while walking home from a nearby fort and held him captive in Canada until June 1698. A year after Martin's absence, sentry John Evans posted to protect residents against Indian raids at night raped Sarah. She filed charges against the soldier but authorities made no arrest most likely because Evans' wife and children would have become wards of the community. Years later, Sarah became pregnant after a romantic involvement with another soldier in the community. Alone, Sarah gave birth to the illegitimate child in January 1698 but the baby died shortly thereafter. Sarah hid the child's body under the bed and when discovered, officials claimed that Sarah had smothered the child. Judges of the Superior Court from Boston tried her in August 1698 in Springfield and a jury found her guilty of the child's murder. Justice Winthrop sentenced her "to be hanged by the neck till she was dead, on the 25th of August."[86]

Young servant girl Esther Rogers killed two of her newborns three years apart. Esther gave birth to a baby girl whose father was an African slave in the same household. Esther smothered the baby and buried it in a vegetable garden but authorities never learned of the killing. Three years later and pregnant again by the same man, Esther delivered another illegitimate baby in a field that she covered with dirt and snow, suffocating the infant. This time authorities discovered the crime and tried Esther before the Essex County Assizes where she confessed to both child murders. Esther hanged in July 1701, and to some accounts of the hanging, Ipswich officials afterwards gibbeted Esther's dead body.

Fourteen years passed before Massachusetts again executed a young unmarried white mother for infanticide. In June 1715, Boston hanged servant woman Margaret Callogharne for infanticide after she left her illegitimate newborn exposed to the winter weather and it died from hypothermia. Other young women hanged for infanticide in Massachusetts included Elizabeth Atwood and Rebeckah Chamblitt. In August 1720, Ipswich officials hanged young Atwood for infanticide after she had given birth to a baby boy alone in her bedroom. A summoned nurse grew suspicious after she examined Atwood and called upon authorities to investigate. Atwood claimed that the child was stillborn, but "it was also proven that she had attempted to conceal not only the birth itself but the disposal of the dead infant as well. This last fact was a capital crime in itself because it implied foul play."[87] In the case of Rebeckah Chamblitt, Boston authorities hanged the young servant woman in September 1733 for infanticide when Chamblitt gave birth to a baby boy and "then she threw the infant down into the feculent depths of the privy."[88] In the winter of 1739, Rockingham County Sheriff Thomas Packer in New Hampshire hanged widow Sarah Simpson and a young servant girl named Penelope Kenny for "feloniously concealing the death of a[n] ... infant bastard child." Simpson reportedly claimed that she miscarried her child, but "she still fell under a law making a capital crime of covering up the death of a baby."[89] Their hangings "drew together a vast concourse of people ... because these were the first executions that ever were seen in this province."[90] In a Massachusetts case, authorities in Malden County hanged Margaret Fennison in April 1743 for bludgeoning to death her 11-month-old baby boy with a rock after an adulterous affair with another man when her husband went to sea.

Ruth Briggs was the first woman executed in Connecticut for infanticide. One scholar claims that Ruth "was reputed to be the most shameless woman of her time. Her story, which begins in a dysfunctional home and ends at the gallows, is a sordid tale of moral and physical breakdown through years of violence, deprivation, promiscuity and general turpitude."[91] Ruth was the oldest surviving daughter of Nicholas and Elizabeth Pinion who were illiterate and poorly suited for parenthood. Both served jail time for spousal abuse and other behaviors punishable by the courts. As a young woman, Ruth served as a "concubine" for a group of local ironworkers that she reportedly enjoyed. Ruth became pregnant because of her promiscuity with the ironworkers. One of the men, Patrick Moran, was allegedly the child's father. While under indictment on a stolen property charge, officials accused Ruth of concealing her pregnancy. Ruth denied the accusation and violently resisted the magistrate's order that she undergo a physical examination. Matrons found Ruth's breasts enlarged with milk. Authorities also confronted Ruth with a petticoat used as a swaddling cloth. She denied ownership of the garment. A family member, however, testified that Ruth indeed had given birth. Ruth eventually admitted that she had given birth to a stillborn baby and had buried it in a nearby swamp that officials recovered. The Court of Assistants tried Ruth for murdering her child and she hanged in June 1668.

Years later, Windham authorities in Connecticut hanged young, unmarried Elizabeth Shaw for the murder of her newborn baby boy. In June 1745, Elizabeth went to the woods near her house and gave birth to an infant that she later stowed away in a rock crevasse covering it with leaves. Hearn notes that the baby either smothered to death or died from exposure. In any case, authorities summoned a committee of matrons who confirmed that Elizabeth had given birth. The Superior Court of Windham County tried and convicted Elizabeth of murder and ordered her hanged on December 1745.

In November 1753, New London officials in Connecticut hanged an unmarried servant woman named Sarah Bramble for killing her newborn daughter after two trials. In the first trial, the court declared a mistrial (a deadlocked jury) in which a preponderance of jurors believed Sarah's testimony that the baby was stillborn. Sarah remained in jail for a year awaiting a second trial. In that trial, the prosecutor focused on Sarah's conduct of hiding the dead baby as an act of foul play and convinced an otherwise favorable jury of Sarah's culpability for the death of her child and the court ordered Sarah to hang.

Pennsylvania and New York colonies also executed women for infanticide and child murder. The earliest recorded female infanticide execution in Pennsylvania was that of Elizabeth Murphy in July 1724. There is little in the historical record of Elizabeth's execution other than she "was indicted for murder and found guilty by ye Petty Jury and must be hanged by ye neck until she is dead. And ye Sherif is ordered to Execute her accordingly on ye 13th of 7 month 1724."[92] Two decades later in October 1745, Lancaster County hanged Rebecca Moss of Conestoga Township for killing her bastard child. In March 1759, Berk County officials in Pennsylvania hanged widow Elizabeth Learch Grauel for killing her illegitimate child. Recently discovered documents cast doubt on exactly for what crime authorities executed Elizabeth Grauel. The Berk County Historical Society claims that officials held her in the Berk County jail for several months awaiting the birth of her illegitimate daughter. Some speculate that Elizabeth Grauel killed one illegitimate child only to become pregnant with another illegitimate child while awaiting trial. Apparently, the King of England ordered town directors to care for Elizabeth's child "until she should become old enough to be bound out of service."[93]

New Jersey executed white women for infanticide. Christiana Bell, a domestic servant living in Gloucester County hanged in November 1721 for killing her illegitimate child. Seventeen years earlier, Christiana had escaped the death penalty for the same offense when the royal governor of New York and New Jersey, Lord Cornbury, gave her a full pardon. Newark authorities hanged Jemmina Westerdon in May 1733 after a coroner's inquest determined that she had killed her illegitimate newborn when a search for the child found it "with its mouth most barbarously crammed full of leaves and its hands filled with leaves, gasping for life."[94] In another case, controversy continues whether Gloucester County officials in New Jersey actually hanged Anne Buzard for killing her illegitimate newborn female child that she ostensibly concealed in a hog pen belonging to Samuel Coles, the reputed father of the child. Mary Coles (the elder), Mary Coles (the younger), and Keziah Roberts testified against Anne. The county court found her guilty of the child's death and issued a warrant for her execution in July 1754 in Gloucester City. Despite the death warrant, there is no direct evidence that Anne Buzard actually hanged, though it is more than likely that authorities executed her.

New York officials hanged Angel Hendricks in July 1669 for the murder of her illegitimate baby that she lowered down a well in a weighted basket. Condemned for killing her illegitimate child and confessing to the crime after her conviction, Deborah Gryce hanged in December 1714 in Jamaica, Long Island. Authorities permitted Gryce's other children to visit her in prison; thus, she was either married or widowed at the time of her execution. As one early commentator explained, "As an instance of the barbarity of those times it may be mentioned that the children of this unfortunate woman visited her in prison, and when she would have embraced them, she could not for the iron chains that were upon her arms."[95] In still another case, an unidentified woman hanged in Albany in September 1737 for killing her illegitimate child.

Spousal Murder

Household brutality in the early colonies often resulted from women crossing gender boundaries and exercising overreaching authority. As one commentator points out, "This retaliatory violence was gendered and aimed to contain white women who were perceived to have overstepped their proper sphere of influence."[96] Colonial women often lashed out against patriarchal authority when it became physically or psychologically abusive. Marriage in early colonial society was largely an "impromptu, tempestuous, and temporary affair," and husbands were often the focus of their wives violent conduct, as well as married women's children, servants, slaves, and acquaintances. One historian found that married women comprised 69 percent of women defendants accused of assault in early Philadelphia.[97] Scholars have discerned similar figures on assaults committed by women in other early colonies. In some cases, women assaults ended in a victim's death. Most colonies adopted the English common law of spousal murder as *petit treason*: servants killing masters, wives killing husbands, and clergymen killing ecclesiastical superiors were all acts of petit treason. One scholar explains that the crime effectively drew a parallel between subversion of state power (treason) and rebellion against a husband or master's power over households or the authority of the church. Petit treason demanded harsh and often brutal punishments, though it was slave women that mostly burned at the stake in such cases.

Justice officials in Maine, Connecticut, and Delaware executed white women for spousal murder during the early colonial period. Maine hanged Goodwife Cornish in 1644 for bludgeoning to death her husband Richard Cornish who officials found impaled on a stake and floating in the York River. A lover most likely aided Goodwife Cornish in her husband's murder. Reputed to be a "lewd woman," Goodwife Cornish despised her husband and had several adulterous affairs including the town mayor Roger Garde. Goodwife Cornish steadfastly denied murdering her husband, but when forced to undergo *trial by touch*—a bizarre ritual requiring a suspected murder to touch a dead person's corpse and who authorities presumed guilty of causing the death should the corpse bleed—her husband's corpse "bled abundantly"—a conclusive sign to the religiously devout that Goodwife Cornish killed her husband. Historians have derived little about Goodwife Cornish's execution from Winthrop's "meager account" which "cannot be verified because the Court of Assistants records are incomplete for that year and no mention of the case appears in the General Court records."[98]

Officials in Connecticut hanged Abigail Thompson for killing her husband, Thomas, an unassuming man of small stature who suffered Abigail's wrath of quick temper and violent hostility. Abigail was a masculine woman who dominated her husband and whose stepchildren despised her. She often physically and emotionally abused Thomas by constantly screaming and swearing at him, throwing stones and household objects at him, and at times chasing him out of the house with a butcher knife. During one tirade, Abigail threw a pair of scissors at Thomas that lodged in his head and he died several days later. Charged with Thomas' murder, Abigail had such a bad reputation for abusing her husband that no one appeared in her defense at trial. "Instead, one witness after another told of her brutal nature, her acts of violence, her hatred for her husband and her threats to his life."[99] There is nothing in the historical record suggesting why Abigail was seemingly such a wretched person toward Thomas and her children, though mental illness may be a logical explanation. A Hartford jury found Abigail guilty of murder and the court's chief justice sentenced Abigail to hang. After several years of legislative debate on whether Abigail had committed negligent homicide or intentional murder, she hanged in May 1708.

New Castle authorities in Delaware executed Catharine Bevan in June 1731 for murdering her husband, Henry. At the time of Henry's death, Catharine was having an affair with a much younger family servant named Peter Murphy. Henry often complained to friends and neighbors that Catharine and Peter abused him. At Henry's funeral, a suspicious magistrate in attendance ordered the nailed coffin opened and discovered that Henry's body looked badly beaten. A coroner's jury found that Henry had died a violent death. Peter admitted that he had severely beaten Henry and afterwards Catharine twisted a handkerchief around Henry's neck to strangle him. The court sentenced Peter to hang, and in an unusual move, sentenced Catharine to burn alive since her crime was *petite treason*. A rope tied around Catharine's neck was to strangle her before the fire could touch her. However, "the fire broke out in a stream directly on the rope around her neck, and burnt off instantly, so that she fell alive into the flames, and was seen to struggle there."[100]

Adultery

Sexual offenses were pervasive in the early colonies. The majority of cases that came to the attention of courts involved "consensual sex before marriage, but there were also cases of adultery, incest, attempted rape, sex between master and servant, and sex between servants."[101] Women suffered punishments for sexual offenses including stocks, fines, and whippings. A double standard of sexual morality existed in the early colonies where early colonial authorities meted out the majority of punishments to women. There are no records of officials accusing married men of infidelity, "whereas married women were often accused of and punished for adultery."[102] As Feinman points out, "The adulteress threatened familiar and secular stability ... and was considered a dangerous person, and subject to punishment by both the church and the state."[103]

Adultery was a capital offense in most jurisdictions. There are two known cases of female executions in the United States for adultery. There is little in the historical record concerning the Massachusetts execution of an unnamed white woman for adultery in May 1721. There is more historical information concerning Boston officials' execution of young Mary Latham and her playboy lover. Mary was an attractive girl from an affluent and devoutly religious family in Weymouth, Massachusetts. Mary had chosen to marry an older man after a much younger man with whom she had fallen deeply in love scorned her. The marriage to the older man was a disaster and left Mary longing for yet another younger man. Shortly after her marriage, Mary began frequently abusing her elderly husband and at one point threatened to kill him. Mary often engaged in drinking parties resulting in sexual intercourse with several married and unmarried men. One of her suitors was a young professor named James Britton who had recently arrived from England. Townspeople quickly learned of their liaison and Britton confessed to the adulterous affair that ended with county authorities trying, convicting, and hanging both Mary and James in March 1644. Puritan leaders hanged Mary Latham for adultery while at the same time many other women involved in similar conduct went unpunished. According to one commentator, Mary's hanging most likely resulted from Winthrop so intensely denouncing "the sinfulness of the defendant's conduct in this case." Puritan authorities almost certainly hanged Mary Latham for no other reason than to satisfy Winthrop's fanatical penchant for strict moral guidance when he found it beneficial to do so.

Murder of Abusive Masters

Servants were excessively violent—nearly one-half of criminal charges against indentured servants in 1660 were for violence. Chapin claims that the most common homicides among early colonist stemmed from the abuse of indentured servants and apprentices, "clear evidence of the extreme tensions that the master-servant relationship could generate."[104] Indeed, early colonial authorities put to death several servant women for killing their abusive masters. Kent County authorities in Maryland burned to death servant woman Esther Anderson for the murder of her master Richard Waters in May 1746. Esther was an Irish Catholic who immigrated to Maryland as an orphaned apprentice girl from southwest England. Along with two other servants, Hector Grant and an Irishman named James Horney of the same household, Esther conspired to murder Waters. Hector and James killed Waters with several blows to the head with an axe as he lay in bed drunk one night. Esther admitted to the conspiracy and a jury convicted the three of capital murder; Hector and James hanged while Esther burned to death. Authorities convicted all three of *petite treason*. Nothing less than a double standard of justice explains why the Special Court of Oyer and Terminer sentenced Esther to a far more brutish death than her male co-conspirators since nothing in the historical record alludes to an explanation.

Another case involved the Baltimore County, Maryland, hangings of servant women Martha Bassett and Mary Powell in January 1752 for the bludgeoning murder of their owner Mrs. Sarah Clark and the attempted murder of her husband John Clark as they slept in their beds. The *Maryland Gazette* dedicated nearly half a page of its November 27, 1751, edition to the murder. The newspaper reported that a week earlier, in the early morning of November 19, Martha Bassett carrying an axe and Mary Powell holding a candle went into the Clark's bedroom and struck several blows to Mrs. Clark's head, splitting her skull, and killing her instantly. Martha then struck Mr. Clark in the same manner but he survived the attack. The *Gazette* explains that John Berry, a son-in-law to the Clarks, conspired with Martha, Mary, and a young servant boy to murder the Clarks so he could inherit their estate and marry an orphan girl named Sarah Catcham who John Clark had raised with his first wife. Berry promised to set the servants free and give the boy a horse and saddle. The county court tried and convicted Berry along with Martha and Mary. The County Sheriff hanged Martha and Mary on the same day, and John Berry a few days later. Officials hanged Berry in chains after his execution.

Alice Ryley was an indentured servant woman who immigrated to Georgia as an Irish transport in December 1733 indentured to Richard Cannon. Alice became the first female executed in the colony of Georgia when she hanged in Chatham County in January 1735 for her part, along with her boyfriend Richard White, in murdering their master William Wise in March 1734. Known as "an Irishman of shady character" and a "cruel and heartless man," who became severely disabled shortly after arriving in Savannah from Ireland. According to historical records, Wise had long hair and had White comb it while he reclined in bed and leaned his head over the rail for the combing. One morning while combing Wise's hair, White choked Wise with handkerchief around his neck while Alice took a bucket of water and plunged his head down into the water drowning Wise. Although Ryley and White both claimed their innocence, a county court tried and convicted the two of Wise's murder and sentenced them to hang. White hanged immediately, but officials postponed Ryley's hanging for eight months until she delivered her baby boy named James Ryley fathered by William Wise. Ryley hanged two days after delivering her baby on January 19, her body remained hanging on the gallows for three days. Her baby died several weeks later.

Predatory Murder

Throughout the first historical period in women executions jurisdictions hanged several white women for killing unknown victims and for unspecified crimes. The historical record remains far from complete concerning the crimes of many of these executed women in the early colonial period. This is not the case with Judith Roe, however. Judith hanged in March 1688 for the robbery-murder of Mr. Hambleton and was the first female executed in the Delaware colony after the Duke of York granted the counties to William Penn in 1682. Officials reportedly convicted Judith on her son's testimony that she struck the man with an axe, as he lay asleep in bed and then robbed him of his money. The boy also testified that Judith then tied a rope around the midsection of the man and dragged him by his own horse to a nearby creek. At trial, Judith "had an arrogant smirk and a detectable hint of insanity in her eye." William Penn refused to pardon Judith because he thought her a "murderous woman and her crime notorious and barbarous."[105]

The historical record reveals little about Maryland's execution of Margaret Caine for murder in May 1707, as well as Virginia's hanging of Mary Murray for murder in May 1755. All that the record shows about Anne Bowen's execution in New York City in March 1708 was that she hanged for an unknown crime and that she was "an innkeeper who ran a hospice for convalescing soldiers."[106] In another case, the *Journals of the House of Burgesses* note without comment the 1712 execution of Elizabeth Gordon in Virginia. The same is true of Maryland's execution of Sarah Tracy and Elizabeth Spurrier for murder in November 1713. Similarly, social historians know little of Virginia's 1736 execution of Elizabeth Greenley other than she had killed a fellow servant. We know little of the Pennsylvania execution of Ann Ottley for murder in September 1742 or the Virginia execution of Anne Plunkett for murder in November of that year. Other female executions for murder where the historical record is mostly silent are Alice Cunningham

(Delaware) in February 1752 and Eve Mary Schmidt (Pennsylvania) in 1755. The historical record is more forthcoming on Catherine Connor hanged in Philadelphia in July 1737 for burglary, however. Authorities postponed the hanging for a short period after sentencing since Catherine claimed she was pregnant. An impaneled jury of matrons "found her not quick with Child." *Minutes of the Provincial Council of Philadelphia* of June 23, 1737, shows that one consideration of the court for hanging Catherine was that authorities had previously convicted her of a burglary. One source claims that a court convicted and sentenced Catherine to death for "carnal intercourse" in 1735, but officials pardoned her when they discovered she was pregnant.[107] Elizabeth Robinson hanged in February 1751 as an accomplice to the burglary of a shopkeeper in Philadelphia. Elizabeth was likely an English émigré transported as a sentenced criminal to Maryland aboard the ship *Alexander* in 1723. The *Proceedings of the Council of Maryland, 1732–1753* show that officials sentenced Mary Perry (Maryland) to hang in October 1752 for burglary and felony. A jury of matrons, however, found Mary "to be with child but not then quickened" and advised that Mary's execution be respited until the delivery of her child.[108] There is no evidence of Mary's actual execution, however.

Slave Insurrection

New York executed two white women for slave revolt in the early colonial period. John Hughson, a shoemaker and keeper of a disreputable tavern, his wife Sarah Hughson, and Margaret Sorubiero (alias Salingburgh, alias Kerry, commonly called Peggy, or the Newfoundland Irish beauty), a waitress and prostitute employed by the Hughson's at their tavern, hanged for conspiring to incite a slave rebellion in New York City. Hughson aspired to expand his organized crime activities in the city by using fires and thefts as part of a larger scheme "to topple the government and free the slaves." A court tried and convicted Hughson for inciting a slave rebellion in New York City and condemned Sarah and Margaret as accomplices in the affair. All three hanged in July 1741 and afterwards authorities gibbeted John's body. John Ury reportedly was the mastermind behind Hughson's seditious activities. Ury was a schoolmaster who authorities falsely accused of being an agent of the intensely hated Roman Catholic Church and using his religious teachings to incite a slave insurgency. Historians agree that John Ury's trial was a disaster and that the case against him "was weak, based on hearsay testimony of witnesses of dubious reputation and character."[109] Still, a jury found Ury guilty of sedition and he hanged in August the same year.

Executions of Black Women

The gendered racism accenting the lives of black women in the United States commenced when European slavers transported some 650,000 Africans from West African coastal nations to colonial enterprises in British North America. The Atlantic slave trade involved an estimated 40,000 ships, carrying an average of 80 persons a day for more than 400 years. The astounding profits from this trade fueled the industrial revolution in Europe and the United States. Limited numbers of black slave women populated the early colonies before 1760 and may account for far lower execution rates than white women. The scarcity of slave women in the early colonies resulted from American slaveholders' preference for adult males given their greater "strength and versatility." Slave men far outnumbered slave women in most regions of early America; the average male to female sex ratio among slaves in the British mainland colonies was roughly *two to one*. One historian suggests that the ratio of slave women to slave men in early communities was so low that it dramatically inhibited male slaves from finding companions. In Virginia, the ratio among slaves was roughly 145 men to 100 women in the 1670s and 1680s, but increased to two to one in the 1690s and 1700s. In South Carolina, the ratio of male slaves to female slaves in the early 1730s was 180 to 100. In Maryland, the ratio of male to female slaves was *eight to one* in the 1690s and *five to one* in the 1740s. Sex ratios did not even out for most southern colonies until the late antebellum period.

One reason for so few slave women in the early colonies was that a common rule among slavers was to limit the number of female captives because most slavers disliked purchasing women and young girls since young males garnered much higher market prices. One captain's directive, for instance, was to "buy no girls, and few women." Consequently, females were less than 40 percent of slave imports to mainland British colonies. Slavers began transporting more females once planters learned that slave women produced significant work yields. As experienced by white female transports from Europe in the early colonial period, slave women were susceptible to the vicious maltreatment of white slavers. Slavers commonly subjected black women to rape, sexual assault, and vicious attacks against their pregnancies and motherhood. For one, traders did not place female slaves in ship holds with shackled males; rather, slave traders typically positioned female slaves on quarterdecks where they could move freely and were far more accessible to the sexual perversions of officers who "were permitted to indulge their passions."[110]

Rape was a common torture for captured, disobedient slave women aboard slave ships. This was true even of young slave girls; Captain David Wilson of the *Eagle* delighted in raping African female slaves as young as eight and nine years old. Traders often branded slaves once aboard ship to denote their ownership, and crewmembers ruthlessly beat slave women who resisted stripping naked for the practice. Ship's crews particularly "ridiculed, mocked, and treated contemptuously" slave women with children.[111] Slavers sadistically abused slave children just to watch the mothers' anguish, and if a child died from the cruelty, slavers forced the mother to throw their child overboard under threat that slave mothers would suffer even more brutality. Slavers were as barbaric toward captured pregnant slave women. Aboard the American ship *Pongas* carrying some 250 mostly pregnant slave women, for instance, females "who survived the initial stages of pregnancy gave birth aboard ship with their bodies exposed to either the scorching sun or the freezing cold."[112] Even if a newborn survived the ordeal, captured mothers often smothered to death their babies fearing the child would grow up in slavery. One cannot overstate the cruelty suffered by African women aboard slave ships:

> Another captain facing a rage for suicide seized upon a woman as a proper example to the rest. He ordered the woman tied with a rope under her armpits and lowered into the water: When the poor creature was thus plunged in, and about half way down, she was heard to give a terrible shriek, which at first was ascribed to her fears of drowning; but soon after, the water appearing red all around her, she was drawn up, and it was found that a shark, which had followed the ship, had bit her off from the middle.[113]

Despite obvious danger to their lives, slave women regularly participated in slave ship insurrections as resistance against their white oppressors. One scholar has documented at least 392 cases of shipboard revolts by slaves with most occurring from 1698 to 1807 though slave ship uprisings continued through March 1865. Some 1000 slaves lost their lives in slave ship insurrections, many of them slave women. It was the accessible and unshackled female slaves who posed the most formidable threat to seamen, however; slave women recurrently incited and aided in seditious acts aboard slave ships. As one scholar explains, "women were often accommodated close to the officers' quarters as well as to weapon stores and keys."[114] Although unsuccessful, a mutiny of the *Roberts* in 1721 resulted from a woman slave aiding two male slaves in killing several sailors and wounding many others. The woman assisting the male slaves served as a lookout, alerted the male slaves to the number of sailors on the deck, and stole all the weapons used in the revolt. To "create terror among the rest of the enslaved aboard the vessel," Captain Harding killed one of those marginally involved in the conspiracy "and made the others eat his heart and liver." Harding severely punished the female slave: "The Woman he hoisted up by the Thumbs, whipp'd, and slashed her with Knives, before the other Slaves till she died."[115] In another incident in 1785, slave women attacked a ship's captain and tried to throw him overboard but his crew saved him.

A similar incident took place aboard the Rhode Island *Thames* years earlier. There, two slave women helped several slave men and slave boys in an attempted mutiny. The revolt was spontaneous, thereby limiting the role of the women in the insurrection. The ship's physician reported in a letter written years after the event, however, that the mutiny would certainly have been successful had the men had more time to organize with the women. Interestingly, government officials at times made paltry efforts to hold traders accountable for the maltreatment and killing of slave women. Admiralty Court, for instance, prosecuted Captain John Kimbler of the African slave ship *Recovery* for beating and torturing to death two female slaves transported from Africa in June 1792, one was a 14-year-old girl unable to eat or exercise because of gonorrhea and lethargy. Captain Kimbler had the slave girl punished for her supposed stubbornness: "flogged her, and had her raised up by pullies from the deck, so that the tortures she endured, caused her to languish for a few days, until she died."[116] A court acquitted Captain Kimbler. One scholar characterized the wretched experiences of slave women during the Atlantic crossing:

> They conceived children, had miscarriages, gave birth and had their children taken from them. The rhythms continued aboard a slave ship, set surreally against the looming specter of death. Let the distress and sorrow of many be represented by the known few. On the *Liberty* a woman died in childbirth, and the child surviving its mother was fed on flour and died two days later. A woman aboard the *Hudibras* had an abortion after being severely beaten. Another lost her nine-month-old child, who was flogged and burned to death, and then she herself was beaten when she refused to throw the body overboard. On the *Neptune* the boatswain requested to throw a six week old baby overboard because its crying disturbed him. The suffering was endless.[117]

The historical record is clear—in the earliest periods of initial contact with Africans, American slave traders viciously mistreated their female captives. African women suffered excessively from the "brutalization and terrorization" of the slave trade. The horridness of the slave trade did not cease once slave women were in the mainland colonies; they continued to suffer the sadistic wrath of white slaveholders and the slave state. At slave auctions, for instance, enslavers forced women to undergo the humiliation of stripping naked before white crowds while "bidders would come up and feel the women's legs, lift up their garments and examine their hips, feel their breast, and examine them to see if they could bear children."[118]

Slavery was a societal system of domination, degradation, and subordination, with an especially rigid legal structure allowing privileged, landowning whites to manage African women as chattel. The concerted efforts of colonial legislatures, judicial officers, regional sheriffs, and local constables, formed the justice system of slavery. Slave historian Ira Berlin distinguishes "colonial slavery" (before 1790) from "antebellum slavery" (after 1790) to acknowledge the variant forms of slavery that developed in discrete regions of the United States at differing times and for separate reasons.[119] Despite this delineation of slave history and its resulting regionalization, scholars find it difficult to develop much understanding of the legal frameworks in which slave women lived out their lives in the early colonial period because not much exists in the historical record about the treatment of slave women. There is so little in the record on slave women in early colonial history that one legal historian refers to the period as "the dark ages of American law."[120] As one distinguished slave historian explains, "[r]ecords of offenses by slaves are scant because on the one hand they were commonly tried by somewhat informal courts whose records are scattered and often lost, and on the other hand they were generally given sentences of whipping, death or deportation, which kept their names out of the penitentiary lists."[121] Still, existing records reveal sufficient evidence that early colonial jurisdictions executed slave women for crimes committed largely in response to white male oppression.

During early colonial slavery, death penalty jurisdictions put to death 13 percent of black females executed historically in the United States. Most black women executed in the period were slaves and domestic servants. Notably, historians have largely excluded black women from studies on slave resistance. To fill this void in the historical record, one scholar examined the gendered nature of slave conflict using ex-slave oral interviews conducted during the 1930s to illustrate the myriad of ways in which slave women directly challenged institutional slavery. Largely defending their needs as slaves, "slave women resisted sex assaults, feigned illness, were insolent, participated in work slowdowns and overt rebellions, murdered their masters, performed acts of sabotage, joined maroon colonies, and fled North to freedom."[122] Early colonial slave jurisdictions all along the eastern seaboard put to death slave women and domestic black servants in the first historical period of women executions for acts of open resistance. Most jurisdictions hanged, burned, or gibbeted black women for their participation in killing abusive masters, but slave women also suffered gruesome executions for burglary, arson, theft, slave revolts, and infanticide. Slave women mostly committed these offenses in resistance to the oppression of white masters, their families, and overseers. Examining the contextual peculiarities giving rise to black slave women executions since the earliest periods of American colonial slave history furthers understanding of the intersection of gendered racism, capital punishment, and the systemic oppression of black women.

Murder of Abusive Masters

Challenging the fierce exploitation of white masters accented black female executions in early colonial slavery. Slave women revolted violently against the brutal treatment of white masters, and early colonial governments used vicious execution methods to kill slave women. New York authorities, for instance, put to death an unidentified slave woman in February 1708 by roasting her alive "over a slow fire for several hours with a vessel of cool water held near her mouth. When she finally expired her body was burnt to ashes."[123] The slave woman had participated in axing to death her owner William Hallett, Jr., his pregnant wife, and five children while they slept. The reason for the slave woman aiding in murdering the Hallett family "was said to be resentment on the part of the guilty parties for not being allowed to move about freely on Sundays"—a sacred activity among slaves.[124] In another case, Albany officials in New York in January 1717 roasted to death an unidentified slave woman over a slow fire for her involvement in the murder of a white man named Trucax, most likely the slave woman's master or overseer. A Salem County sheriff in New Jersey dragged slave woman Hagar and her slave accomplice Ben on a wooden sledge through town to their executions after a Special Court of Magistrates and Freeholders had convicted them of murdering their master, lawyer James Sherron. With a white indentured servant named John Hunt, the three conspired to kill Sherron in April 1717 while inspecting his fields. Distracted by Hagar's purposeful small talk, Hunt hacked Sherron to death with a hatchet after Ben had retrieved the murder weapon from a tool shed. At the execution site, "Hagar was chained to a stake and burned to ashes—probably while still alive and conscious. Ben was hanged by his neck until dead. After that, his body was dipped in tar and set in a wrought iron frame [a gibbet]. This was hung aloft from a derrick pole for all to see. It probably remained there for many years, that being the custom."[125] Hunt hanged a month later.

The historical record reveals little of the May 1723 gibbeting death of an unnamed slave woman for murdering her master in Maryland, but Nansemond County officials in Virginia burned to death an unnamed slave woman belonging to Prudden in February 1737 who confessed to axing to death her mistress, Prudden's wife. Remarking on the case, Schwarz explained, "If voluntary, her confession suggests either that she would rather die than tolerate her mistress any longer or perhaps that she subsequently regretted a moment of explosive passion."[126] Maryland executed an unknown slave woman in 1739 for an axe murder, most likely of an overseer, in which the court ordered that "her head was to remain in public 'until she be rotten.'"[127] Virginia authorities also burned to death slave woman Eve for poisoning her master Peter Montague with a glass of milk in 1746. Eve's executioner afterwards quartered her burned body and displayed it publicly. There is nothing in the historical record explaining why Eve killed her master, but to Schwarz, "Eve died because of common law, her status as a slave, and her identity as a woman."[128]

The ferocious ill-treatment accenting the lives of slave women was not always a public affair. As one scholar points out, "In a closed system like slavery, where those in bondage found themselves judged and punished daily and privately without appeal or recourse by their masters and mistresses, mistreatment often occurred outside the public's eye."[129] Consider the following:

> In a particularly horrendous incident, Dr. Mathew Hardy, colonial North Carolina's "evil physician," conducted a petit feu in front of his assembled slaves and their families. In Northampton County in 1743, Hardy had Lucy, a young female slave who presumably refused his advances or who angered him by his actions, tied to a crude triangular ladder. He then made some of her friends whip her, and, in a particularly hateful act, forced her own mother to set fire to the straw gathered at her feet. After a few torturous minutes, Hardy, at gunpoint, orders another slave to drag Lucy's entire body "through the fire." He then refused supplies and aid to her. She died a few days later from her burns and injuries. Since it was not a felony to kill a slave by the Code of 1741, Hardy appeared in court, offered no explanation for his action, answered some questions concerning his "breach of the peace," and went back to his rounds as the county's physician, treating the ailments and injuries of both freemen and slaves.[130]

Early colonial authorities executed black slave women for killing white persons other than their masters. In September 1712, New York hanged slave woman Abigail belonging to Gysbert Vaninburgh for her part in the murder of Henry Brasier, a white man to whom Vaninburgh leased slaves—a common practice among slave owners. Since Abigail was pregnant at the time, authorities granted her a reprieve until the child's birth thereby ensuring Vaninburgh's property interest in the child. New York hanged slave woman Sarah belonging to Stophel Pell for accessory to murder of a white man named Augustus Grasset, a merchant and government official, during a slave uprising in New York City in 1712. Slave woman Lucy belonging to Richard Randolph of Goochland County, Virginia, hanged for killing a white man named John Lee in 1742.

Slave women waged acts of vengeance against their white oppressors by murdering their masters' white servants. In September 1731, slave woman Hannah belonging to Moses Atwater of Wallingford, Connecticut, hanged for murdering a young white girl, Jemima Beecher, a servant to the Atwater household, and seriously injuring Hannah Merriman, a niece to Mr. Atwater, who was residing at Atwater's house. For some unexplained reason, the slave woman crept into the girls' bedroom, stabbed Jemima in the throat with a large butcher knife killing her instantly, and then stabbed Hannah in the chest where one of her ribs deflected the knife and she survived the attack. Tried in New Haven and found guilty of murdering the Atwater servant, the county sheriff dragged the slave murderess through the street, to the gallows, hanged her and then buried her body beneath the gallows.

Infanticide and Child Murder

Killing their newborns was yet another desperate act of slave women against their white oppressors. Early colonial jurisdictions *convicted* slave women of infanticide excessively compared to white women accused of the crime—"a rate one and a half times the rate of white women."[131] Even so, in the first trend in women's executions there were relatively few slave women *executed* for infanticide—jurisdictions were *five times* more likely to execute white women for infanticide than black women in the period. Jones explains the racial disparity in female executions for infanticide: "Black slaves, if detected in infanticide, often were punished by their masters; consequently public records of such cases are rare. Undoubtedly the women were severely punished, but because they were valued as property they probably were not killed."[132] In many black infanticide cases, masters and their sons fathered the illegitimate newborns; the identities of slave baby's father were not part of the official record, however.

There is no historical record of black infanticide executions in southern states in early colonial slavery, most probably the result of slave women's low numbers. New England and Middle Colony jurisdictions exclusively executed black women for infanticide in the period. Suffolk County in Massachusetts put to death the first slave woman in June 1693 for infanticide when authorities hanged Grace belonging to Boston merchant James Taylor. Grace had murdered her newborn baby boy by dumping it down a latrine. The earliest confirmed execution of a juvenile female offender occurred in late November 1710 when Bristol County officials in Rhode Island (now part of Massachusetts) hanged Hannah Degoe, a 14-year-old black servant girl to Joseph Barney, for infanticide. Hannah has the dubious distinction of being the only confirmed juvenile female executed for infanticide in the United States. In April 1710, the "unmarried mulatto woman" reportedly killed her newborn infant when she dumped it into "some rubbish that had accumulated behind the chimney" at the Barney house. Joseph Barney discovered the dead child and contacted authorities. When confronted by local midwives concerning the child's death, Hannah confessed to "her maternity" and to concealing the dead child. At the September session of the Bristol County Assizes, officials found young Hannah guilty of a 1696 law making it a capital offense to conceal the birth or death of a child born out of wedlock. There is no reference in the historical record as to the father of her child; it may have been Joseph Barney himself. In other cases, slave woman Betty belonging to Isaac Winslow hanged in May 1712 in Suffolk County after authorities found her "guilty of feloniously concealing the death of a bastard child born of her" and "privately burying and disposing of the said child."[133] New York authorities hanged an unidentified free black woman in January 1715 for killing her illegitimate child. Elizabeth Colson hanged for infanticide in Plymouth in May 1727 after pleading guilty to killing her illegitimate child. Slave woman Kate belonging to Thomas Belding hanged in November 1743 at Hartford (Connecticut) for suffocating her newborn baby boy with a curtain sash.

In early November 1737, Newport County officials in Rhode Island hanged Ann, a 16-year-old mulatto girl, for killing an 11-year-old white servant girl named Alice Allen. Ann and Alice were both "apprentice domestics" to John Easton. Earlier in March, while Easton was visiting family across town, Ann had a young boyfriend over to the house and to whom she gave a drink of rum from Easton's private liquor stock. Alice threatened Ann with reporting the event to Easton. Ann became enraged at young Alice and locked her in a closet while she became romantic with her boyfriend. Ann soon broke out of the closet and ran outside the house. Ann captured Alice and during a scuffle broke her neck. Frightened, Ann threw Alice's limp body into a well in the backyard where another house servant drawing water found the body. Officials assumed that Alice had accidentally fallen into the well and soon buried her body. Ann changed her story about Alice's killing when Easton later questioned her and reported the foul play to authorities. Officials exhumed Ann's body and discovered her broken neck, then charged Ann with felony murder. Ann had no legal counsel at trial and the court found her guilty of Alice's murder and sentenced her to death. Authorities in Boston hanged 17-year-old slave woman Phillis belonging to John Greenleaf in May 1751. Phillis had murdered Greenleaf's one-year-old son with arsenic. Greenleaf was a druggist. Displeased by having to care for the young child, Phillis stole arsenic from Greenleaf's shop and mixed the poison in the child's milk. The young boy died two days later. Tried and convicted for the child's death, a court sentenced Phillis to death. On the day the court sentenced Phillis to hang, her mother collapsed from a nervous breakdown and died suddenly.

Slave Insurrection

Slave women's resistance in the early colonial period was not limited to setting destructive fires during insurrections; slave women also manifested rebellion by stealing and committing burglary, larceny, and other such crimes. Arson convictions brought severe penalties for slave women in the early colonial period. Arson was a crime appealing to slave women since they often "did not have the physical strength to confront their white enemies," and arson was a "powerful way to deprive whites of their property and injure their economic well-being."[134] Slave women burned their master's houses, jails, shops, wheat stacks, and agricultural buildings such as mills and barns. Slave women comprised significant numbers of individuals convicted of arson in Virginia in the period; in Georgia, slave women were 28 percent of persons convicted of arson between 1740 and 1785.

It is likely that an unnamed black slave woman hanged for arson in Charleston, South Carolina, in July 1641 was the first slave woman hanged for insurrection against her white oppressors. Four decades later in September 1681, however, Boston authorities burned alive slave woman Marja for the arson of her master's (Joshua Lambe) house and the accidental killing of Lambe's baby daughter who died in the fire. Before torching Lambe's house in Roxbury, Marja had set fire to a neighbor's house, that of Thomas Swan. Some argue that Marja's sentence was severe because of the infant's death and that residents were increasingly concerned over a rash of fires occurring in and around Boston at the time. If that were the rationale for burning Marja alive, then authorities would not have simply banished two of her black male accomplices (Cheffaleer and "Jack Pemberton's Negro") from the colony and hanged another accomplice (Negro Jack) but imputed the far more painful execution method of burning at the stake. It is more likely that Marja burned to death "because her actions were instigated by the devil ... the punishment traditionally used when the defendant was thought to be possessed by the devil."[135] In other early cases, Sarah, belonging to the Curtis household in Northampton, Virginia, hanged for arson in 1705. Charleston, South Carolina, suffered rebellious slave activity in 1740 and 1741 in which devastating fires destroyed hundreds of buildings. In July 1741, Charleston officials executed an unknown slave woman "as punishment for having set fire to a house with the evil intent of burning down the remaining part of the town."[136]

Records on female slaves executed for open insurrection are circumspect since Aptheker writes of hundreds of slave executions for uprisings that are largely unaccounted for in death penalty inventories. Of the three confirmed slave women executions for slave revolt, two took place during colonial slavery and one during the antebellum slave period in 1830. New Orleans hanged a slave woman for insurrection in June 1731. She remains nameless, but she was one of eight slaves executed after officials in colonial Louisiana uncovered a widespread conspiracy to kill slaveholders. The historical record reveals that an intoxicated French soldier demanded a slave woman retrieve needed wood for his fire but she refused to do so because she was too weary and wanted to eat her lunch. It was then that the soldier gave the slave woman a violent slap across the face. Angry, the insolent slave woman shouted to the French soldier that he would not slap blacks for much longer. Suspicious of her comment, bystanders seized her and took her before the governor who imprisoned her and launched an inquiry into the possibility of a slave conspiracy to insurrection. Officials soon learned that a plot was indeed in the making wherein "[t]he nègres planned to get rid of all the French and establish themselves in their place, taking over the Capital and all we owned."[137] Eight conspirators eventually confessed, "after which the eight negroes were condemned to be broke on the wheel, and the woman to be hanged before their eyes; which was accordingly done, and prevented the conspiracy from taking effect."[138]

In the only grand larceny case in the period, slave woman Mary "pled guilty to a charge of masterminding a sizable theft of goods" and hanged in September 1706 while authorities whipped her confederate Tom (race unknown) for his participation in the crime. Kingston County officials in New York hanged slave woman Bett belonging to Wilhelmus Houghtaling for burglary in July 1748. There are no details of the crime, but Hearn claims Bett hanged with a male accomplice. In other cases, jurisdictions executed slave women for crimes where the historical record remains silent. Elizabeth City County officials executed a slave woman named Hannah belonging to George Walker for an unknown offense sometime in 1729.

In 1730, a slave woman in New Orleans hanged for revolt aboard a ship bound for Louisiana and carrying a slave named Samba who French officials had condemned to slavery after planning a slave revolt. Samba planned to kill the ship's crew and take over the ship. He and seven other men were broke on the wheel. Officials in Andrews Parish, Georgia, burned alive two slave women who participated in killing their overseer and his wife during a slave revolt in 1775. In June 1861, slaves in Monroe County, Arkansas, planned an insurrection that resulted in the hanging of a young girl.

Executions of American Indian Women

The history of American Indian women executions is nested within a sociopolitical context of genocidal colonialism calculated to dispossess American Indians of their Indianism by removing them from their sacred tribal territories, disrupting their traditional cultures, and continuing their marginalized status in United States society. It is not so surprising that jurisdictions executed so few American Indian women in the early colonial period given the genocidal practices engaged in by early colonial governments.

Four American Indian women executions took place in the first historical period of female executions in the United States; during this period colonial jurisdictions executed 50 American Indian males. Connecticut executed the first Indian woman put to death under civil authority in the United States in May 1711 when Hartford County officials hanged a Mohegan-Pequot Indian woman named Waisoiusksquaw for disemboweling her husband, Wawisungonot, with a butcher knife during an impassioned argument. Colonial authorities also hanged two American Indian women during the period for infanticide: Massachusetts hanged Abiah Comfort, a Nantucket Indian woman, for killing her infant daughter in August 1737, and Connecticut hanged a Pequot woman named Katherine Garrett, a house servant to William Worthington, in May 1738 for bludgeoning to death her newborn baby girl. Garrett's hanging attracted a large size crowd: "She was surrounded with a vast Circle of people ... more numerous, perhaps, than Ever was gathered together before, on any Occasion, in this Colony. Ministers vied to deliver sermons from the scaffold."[139] Despite these two executions, colonial officials usually acquitted Indian women involving cases of infanticide since, as one scholar put it, "Indians were not a ready source of labor nor potential breeders of negotiable property. The Indians among the colonists were not so closely watched as the blacks, making it more difficult to find witnesses and evidence against the former."[140]

Courts may have exonerated some Indian women charged with murdering their own children, but this was certainly not the case when Indian women killed white children. In at least one confirmed case, officials hanged young Patience Sampson for murdering eight-year-old Benjamin

Trott in July 1735. Benjamin was the son of her master's neighbor who Patience reportedly strangled for an unknown reason and then hurled him down a well. Abandoned at a young age, Patience grew up on the streets of Barnstable, Massachusetts, supporting herself through charity, thievery, and prostitution. She later went to work as a servant for Elisha Thatcher and had an illegitimate child fathered by a house slave belonging to Thatcher. Patience murdered the 7-week-old child for whom officials prosecuted her but a jury acquitted. She later moved to Maine where she murdered young Benjamin.

Concluding Remarks

The early colonial period clearly accents the notion that British mainland colonial leaders used the developing legal system to punishment women who challenged the patriarchal power structure. White women executions largely accented the first historical period in female executions in the United States. White women executions surpassed black women executions by a significant margin and by an even larger margin in contrast to American Indian female executions. One substantive observation regarding gender and capital punishment in the first historical period of women executions is that, very early in the development of colonial governments, judicial imposition of death was a powerful means of controlling women who challenged the patriarchal religious and secular authority of colonial New England society. In the context of controlling white women within the first historical period of women executions, the judicial killings of white women stemmed from critical societal developments accenting the period. In Puritan society, the power of religious and political leaders to maintain social order drew an inextricable link between the growth of antinomianism, the spread of Quaker's religious passion, the witchcraft frenzy, and the storm of infanticide. In a practical sense, these events were highly interconnected and were the moral and legal justification for executing marginalized white women. Antinomian women questioned the prevailing views of the existing religious order that in turn openly opposed the control of Puritan leadership as a superior gendered authority that set the stage for witchcraft accusations as a means to discredit outspoken women. Physical violence met the religious passion of Quakers that endangered the religious orthodoxy of Puritan leadership. Puritan fathers linked infanticide to these struggles as an affront to social order. The thinking of colonial leaders was that women who killed their children were unmanageable women who pandered to the sexual debauchery of Satan that in turn brought about social disruption. These events were brutal campaigns of gendered oppression designed to further the political, economic, and social interests of powerful church leaders against challenges from unconventional and nonconforming women. Branding these dissenting women as witches and heretics and criminals of the state necessitated their execution in the eyes of religious leaders to ensure the patriarchal dominance of early colonial society.

Black women suffered uniquely under the institutional confines of early colonial slavery. One reason for the lower number of black women executions relative to white female executions is that there were relatively few slave women in the colonies during this period and the legal framework of slavery was in its infancy. Still, the historical record makes clear that very early in the development of institutional slavery women fought back viciously against the physical and sexual brutality of white masters by killing their owners, members of their owner's families, and destroying the ill-gotten gains of slave owner's property. Slave women responded to the violence of white masters by intentionally aborting pregnancies and at times killing their own children. The retort of the state to the rebellious undertakings of brutalized slave women was judicial murder. The historical record also shows that colonial governments had little interest in the behavior of American Indian women unless their conduct challenged the greater societal interests of white male hegemony.

> "*The sheriff was forced to put the wagon beneath her a second time, to cut her down, retie the rope amid the jeers and catcalls, properly secure her hands and feet, and to repeat the process. She did not survive her second hanging.*"[1]

4

The Second Historical Trend, 1760s–1890s

From the 1760s through the 1890s, jurisdictions put to death nearly 64 percent of American women executed historically in the United States. Accenting this period were excessive numbers of black female executions; black women were 79 percent of female executions and white women were roughly 15 percent. American Indian and Mexican women comprised much smaller percentages of female executions, and Hawaiian officials executed one native woman in the period. Black women executions exceeded white women executions by a margin of more than *five to one*. White women executions waxed and waned throughout the decades but their numbers decreased sharply over the first historical period. White women executions decreased from a high of eight executions in the 1760s, dropped to a low of three executions in the 1820s and 1830s, increased slightly to five executions in the 1860s, dropped again to one execution in the 1870s, and then increased to six executions in the 1890s.

Black women executions increased from 21 executions in the 1760s to a high of 54 executions in the 1850s. The 1860s brought a decrease to 37 executions of black women and decreased even more sharply to four executions in the immediate postbellum period of Reconstruction in the 1870s. Executions of black women increased slightly to eight executions in the early decades of Jim Crow in the 1880s and 1890s. Executed white women in the period were mostly poor, marginalized housewives while executed black women were overwhelmingly slaves. Jurisdictions in the Middle Atlantic States of New York and Pennsylvania executed roughly half of all white women in the period largely for spousal murder, infanticide, and predatory murders. Mostly southern jurisdictions executed slave women for predatory murders, arson, and poisoning. Women executed in the period mostly victimized whites.

Executions of White Women

It is interesting that death penalty jurisdictions did not execute far more white women during the second historical trend in female executions given the economic hardships experienced by many white women in the late 18th century and throughout much of the 19th century. As one scholar explains, "[c]onsidering the hardships of the dependent and working poor, amazingly few resorted to activities defined as criminally deviant by their society."[2] The economic conditions of the poor deteriorated dramatically in these decades. Free blacks and poor whites competed for few manufacturing jobs especially in the industrial Northeast. Women and young girls were the vast majority of workers in New England textile mills in the early 19th century. It was during this period that the largest migration of impoverished Irish took place; some 3.2 million Irish immigrated to the United States to escape the devastation and famine in their home country attributed mostly to diseased ridden potato crops. Women were more than half of Irish immigrants to the United States at the time. Most Irish émigrés settled in ethnic enclaves accented by wretched living conditions and unrelenting unemployment because they were far too poor to begin farming enterprises. Given their impoverishment, the Irish would work for any wage that made them competitive in the labor market. Even so, one scholar describes the Irish as represented heavily among the poor, even the "extremely poor, living the most sordid wretchedness, in dirty hovels of mud and straw, and clothed in rages."[3] Immigrant Irish women often worked as domestics in hotels and middle class households; in Boston alone in 1850, there were some 2,300 Irish women working as servants. Scholars have deplored the conditions of ethnic immigrant workers of the period; "industrial workers [were] victimized by low wages, company stores, blacklisting, arbitrary dismissals, forced overtime, sexual exploitation, company spies, police brutality, and a host of other ills."[4] One commentator describes the plight of urban ghettos in Pittsburgh: "Situated in what is known as the Dump of Schoenville runs a narrow dirt road. Frequently strewn with tin cans and debris, it is bereft of trees and the glaring sun shines pitilessly down on hundreds of ragged, unkempt, and poorly fed children."[5] Workers in New York lived in "an urban jungle of exploitation, family disintegration, crime, and human degradation."[6]

The dire impoverishment of Irish immigrants may explain why they comprised some 40 percent of all criminal convictions in Philadelphia in the late 1790s, and that roughly half the prostitutes in New York City in the 1850s were Irish women. One distressing outcome of impoverished families' was their inability to support their children. Many poor parents indentured their children at very early ages during the period; roughly 40 percent of child indentures were young girls. Illiterate and economically disadvantaged parents bound their daughters at about nine years of age, but often girls were much younger. Rachel Rowlens indentured her nine-year-old daughter Sarah to Martha F. Willmard, Mary Reading's parents bound her to Joseph and Marissa Froth on her ninth birthday, Martha Hoopes's parents indentured her to Amos Worthington when she was five years old, and Phyllis Gromley's parents indentured her at six years old to Waters Dewes. Black parents indentured their daughters as well, and in slightly larger numbers than white parents, who were unable to care for their young daughters because of their impoverished social condition. In one case, justice officials compelled Flora Dickerson to bind her 14-year-old daughter Juliett. It would be women akin to these young, illiterate, and poor indentured servant girls whose parents left them in a maligned and misguided world that years later would occupy jails and prisons and ultimately swing from the gallows.

Jurisdictions executed white women in the second historical period mostly for predatory murder, spousal murder, and infanticide; officials executed far fewer women for property crimes involving burglary, robbery, and theft. One would expect much higher proportions of white women executions for property offenses given the deplorable economic conditions in which white women lived out their lives in the period. Executed white women were characteristically no different from those put to death in previous decades; they were largely marginalized, poor, and illiterate immigrant women. The crimes of executed white women were undeniably a response to the horrors of their social condition. In many cases, the extreme economic and social hardships challenged women's mental stability that precipitated murders. The malevolence of criminal justice officials imposing death to females resulted in authorities not only executing mentally deficient women, but also executing women already dead from suicide, innocent women, and pregnant women.

Spousal Murder

Troubled marital relations in impoverished times occasioned spousal murder. Jurisdictions executed more than *six times* as many white women for spousal murder in the second historical period of female executions than in the first historical period. Death penalty jurisdictions executed 20 white women for killing their abusive and sadistic husbands. If domestic violence cases resulting in divorce in New England counties from 1793 to 1866 are any indication, significant percentages of women suffered "intolerable severity" from their husbands that intensified with years of marriage.

One of the earliest recorded cases of a female execution for spousal murder in the period took place when Massachusetts officials hanged Bathsheba Ruggles Spooner in 1778 in Worcester County. Bathsheba's state killing was the first female execution pursuant to American jurisdiction than under British authority. Also unique about Bathsheba's execution was that "of the hundreds of female defendants who have been legally put to death throughout the course of American history, Bathsheba Spooner was probably the most socially prominent."[7] Bathsheba was a member of the colonial aristocracy; her father was Brigadier General Timothy Ruggles who became a lawyer and Chief Justice of the Court of Common Pleas in Worcester. One commentator described Bathsheba as "beautiful, smart, well educated, high spirited, and a remarkable horsewoman."[8] At her father's behest, Bathsheba married Joshua Spooner whose father emigrated from England and was a wealthy commodities merchant. The couple had four children during their 12-year marriage that deteriorated with Joshua's frequent drunkenness and severe physical abuse of Bathsheba.

Ezra Ross, a 16-year-old soldier assigned to a regiment under George Washington, passed by the Spooner house while making his way home. Ross was terribly ill and over several weeks Bathsheba nursed him back to health. Ross returned home but revisited the Spooner's months later while on his way to rejoin his regiment. Four months later, Ross went again to the Spooner home and stayed on as a boarder. Ross and Bathsheba soon were lovers and she became pregnant ostensibly with Ross' child though some argue Bathsheba had several young lovers. To rid her of Joshua, Bathsheba urged Ross to kill her husband. Ross refused, but Bathsheba was able to convince two wayward British soldiers she boarded to kill Joshua. The soldiers, James Buchanan and William Brooks, attacked Joshua one evening after he returned home from an evening of drinking. Along with Ross, the three beat and strangled Joshua and then threw his dead body down a well. Authorities arrested Brooks, Buchanan, and Ross after they found the three drunk and in possession of Joshua's silver shoe buckles and wearing his clothes. They confessed and implicated two house servants, Sarah Stratton and Alexander Cummings. A grand jury returned indictments "charging Brooks with assaulting Joshua Spooner and inflicting the wounds from which he died, Buchanan and Ross with aiding and abetting in the murder, and Bathsheba Spooner with inciting, abetting, and procuring the manner and form of the murder."[9]

A one-day trial found all four guilty of the crimes and the court ordered their hangings. Stratton and Cummings had turned state's evidence and testified for the prosecution. Authorities postponed the hangings until matrons could examine Bathsheba whose spiritual advisor, Reverend Thaddeus McCarty, claimed she was pregnant. A first examination found that Bathsheba was not pregnant, but the trial court ignored the findings of a second examination that supported Bathsheba's claim of being "quick with child." Officials hanged all four defendants in July 1778 before a crowd of more than 5,000 spectators. An autopsy performed at Bathsheba's request confirmed that she was five months pregnant with a perfectly formed male fetus. Bathsheba Spooner's execution continues to plague the academic community with nagging questions about her execution and the political intrigue of the families and personalities caught in the turmoil and loyalties of the American Revolution.[10] What's more, the judicial killing of Bathsheba's unborn child attests to the illusion that the American criminal justice system does not execute innocent persons—Bathsheba's unborn child was legally and factually innocent.

There is little in the historical record about Sarah Kirk's hanging in New Castle County in Delaware in 1787 for petite treason; Sarah had murdered her husband. The trial court found

Sarah guilty of the crime in June 1787 but granted her a new trial "because one of the jury had not taken the oath of fidelity to the state." In the following October, the court of Oyer and Terminer again tried Sarah for "petty treason, in murdering her husband; when she was found guilty and condemned to be hanged." Sarah hanged in December; "she behaved with those sentiments of penitence and resignation."[11] It is also noteworthy that in a 1963 judicial challenge to the constitutionality of a state statute providing whipping for crimes, the Delaware Supreme Court observed that in June 1787 the province had changed the law that warranted the 1731 burning to death of Catherine Bevan for petit treason to death by hanging just in time to save Sarah Kirk from being executed by burning.

Little information survives concerning the October 1795 hanging of Sally Ardner by Charleston officials in South Carolina for killing her husband. Citing an issue of the Charleston *City Gazette*, one scholar points out that Sally "persisted to the last in declaring herself to be innocent of the crime for which she suffered, and forgave those whom she said had been the cause of her unjust condemnation. She nevertheless met her fate with a surprising degree of fortitude or boldness."[12] In April 1798, housewife Sylvia Wood killed her husband, Major Wood of Augusta, with a shotgun when he refused his alcoholic wife another drink. Strangely enough, Fort Stanwix County officials in New York hanged Sylvia though she was already dead from having committed suicide the morning of her scheduled execution. Not only did the state execute a dead woman, but events following Sylvia's hanging also made her case even more bizarre. According to W. H. Tippetts in an 1885 book about capital crimes in Fort Stanwix County,

> After the execution a number of medical students obtained possession of the body, and during the succeeding night carried it to a small island in the West Canada creek. Previous to this a large cauldron, or kettle, had been taken to the island. This was filled with water, a fire started underneath, and as soon as the water reached a boiling temperature pieces of the body thrown therein. The students kept the fire burning until the flesh was completely separated from the bones. These were carefully fished out of the "devil's broth," cleaned, polished and the skeleton put together. Old citizens state that the skeleton remained in possession of the students for many years, but was finally broken up and destroyed.[13]

One commentator states that Polly Barclay was the first white woman hanged in Georgia, though that dubious distinction actually goes to Alice Ryley, an Irish indentured servant executed in 1735 for killing her master. Georgia hanged Polly Barclay in late May 1806 after a trial and conviction for the murder of her husband upon his return from a cotton-selling trip to Augusta. Polly apparently hired two gunmen, her brother William Nowland and her lover Mark Mitchum, to kill her husband after she had called him out to the barn one night. A Wilkes County jury acquitted Nowland of the murder and Mitchum escaped whom authorities never apprehended, leaving only Polly to account for the killing. It seems that Polly paid the two gunmen $200 to murder her husband because she wanted to be with her lover and wanted the money Mr. Barclay had just earned from selling cotton in Augusta.

There is little in the historical record about the spousal murder execution of Ellenor Gillespie. The record reveals only that Henderson County officials in Kentucky hanged the housewife in July 1817 for the murder of her husband. Ellenor attempted to escape wearing a man's clothes but a guard arrested her as she was leaving the jail. Authorities in rural Hardin County, Tennessee, hanged Polly Hughes in November 1829 for the axe murder of her husband David Hughes "as he lay sleeping in a drunken stooper." At trial, Polly claimed that David seriously abused her and often threatened her life. Polly had apparently laid out David's burial clothes before she killed him which sealed her fate to the court that convicted her of premeditated murder and sentenced her to death. Polly sobbed while taken to the gallows in a wagon and several thousand people witnessed her hanging. According to one account of the execution, "The scene was awful, indeed—and the sympathies of the crowd greatly excited, not only for the wretched woman, but the hapless offspring, who are of tender years, and very poor."[14] Polly Hughes is the only white woman ever lawfully executed in Tennessee.

One novelist described the Frankie Silver story as a case that was "really about poor people as defendants and the rich people as officers of the court, about Celt versus English values in developing America, about mountain people versus the flatlanders." To this author, the Celts were oppressed victims within the Southern class and racial hierarchy.[15] In December 1832, an 18-year-old Appalachian, illiterate Celtic girl named Frances "Frankie" Silver (Stewart) hanged in Morganton, North Carolina, for killing her husband Charles Silver. Frankie and Charles had a troubled two year marriage; Charles often beat and abused Frankie. One evening in December 1831, Charles went to get liquor for a Christmas celebration and when he returned home drunk hours later an argument ensued between Charles and Frankie. During the quarrel, Charles reportedly threatened to shoot Frankie and their 13-month-old daughter Nancy if she did not stop nagging him about her suspicions of infidelity with another man's wife. In response to the threat, Frankie hit Charles in the head with an axe, and once he stumbled to the floor, she used the axe again to decapitate his body. That night, Frankie, along with her mother Barbara and brother Blackston, dismembered Charles' body and burned portions of it in an open fireplace in the cabin where the couple lived. Suspicious of Charles whereabouts, a neighbor checked the cabin when Francis was out and found bones in the fireplace and the head and torso outside the cabin. The county Sheriff soon arrested Frankie, her mother and brother on murder charges. After Frankie's father filed a habeas corpus petition, a county court ordered the release of Barbara and Blackston, but Frankie stood trial before an all-male jury for Charles' murder. The jury convicted Frankie and the court ordered her executed in July 1832 without ever hearing testimony from Frankie—North Carolina did not permit defendant testimony in felony cases at the time. Frankie's lawyer appealed to the North Carolina Supreme Court concerning the conduct of the jury. The appeal claimed that the after the jury had deadlocked favoring acquittal jurors asked to rehear some witnesses. Frankie's lawyers objected claiming that the witnesses by then had had an opportunity to communicate with each other and discuss the case. The judge overruled the objection and permitted a rehearing of witnesses. It was then that the jury voted to convict. The state's Supreme Court rejected the appeal and the state's governor refused a pardon. North Carolina hanged Frankie in July 1833 on a hill overlooking the courthouse. Her family took possession of the body and buried it an unknown grave somewhere about nine miles outside Morganton. Others buried Charles Silver in three separate gravesites.

Lawrence County officials in Illinois hanged Elizabeth "Betsey" Reed for the arsenic poisoning of her husband Leonard. It seems that Leonard became ill in the summer of 1844 and Elizabeth summoned a physician who examined Leonard and claimed, "The feeble old man couldn't live long." After Leonard's funeral, Eveline Deal, a 16-year-old relative who helped care for Leonard, explained to the county sheriff that she saw Elizabeth put a white powdery substance into Leonard's tea. The sheriff learned that Elizabeth had purchased arsenic from a local drug store and arrested Elizabeth. She had a good defense team and her trial lasted three days. A jury nevertheless convicted her for the murder and the court ordered her hanged. Executed in May 1845, Elizabeth became the first white woman hanged in Illinois before several thousand spectators. Reportedly, the executioner drove Elizabeth to the gallows in an oxcart while she sat atop her coffin. Authorities buried Elizabeth in a shallow grave beneath the gallows, but later that night relatives returned to the site and reburied her next to her husband.

Elizabeth van Valkenburgh killed two husbands with arsenic. In her handwritten confession to the murder of her second husband, Elizabeth admitted to killing her first husband while living in Vermont in 1833. Elizabeth claimed she poisoned her first husband because he drank too much. Elizabeth was born in 1799, orphaned as a five-year-old child, married at 20 years old, and had four children by her first husband in six years. She married her second husband

John shortly after murdering her first husband and had two more children. John was abusive to Elizabeth and the children and squandered what little money they had on excessive drinking. Elizabeth was poor, had six children, an abusive husband, and her life was unbearable. She saw that the only way out of her wretched marriage was to kill John and accept her eldest son's offer to buy her a house and to provide for her and his younger siblings. Elizabeth laced John's evening brandy with arsenic from which he died. Authorities tried and convicted Elizabeth for John's death and she hanged in January 1846 in Montgomery County, New York. A unique aspect of her hanging is that because of a broken leg and her obesity, the executioners carried Elizabeth to the gallows in a rocking chair in which she was sitting when the trap door sprung.

A year later, Oneida County officials in New York hanged 50-year-old Mary Alice Runkle for bludgeoning to death her husband John while he slept. Sources maintain that years earlier Mary had drowned her two young children; she believed it was necessary to kill the children to prevent the discovery of a peddler she killed who once passed by her house. Mary claimed she killed her husband John because he was abusive. She hanged in the Whitesboro jail in November 1847, but "[t]o spare her the sight of the gallows, a hole was cut in the upstairs floor and the rope passed down to the office below where she sat waiting tied to a chair." Friends from Whiteboro County claimed her body.[16]

Pennsylvania put white women to death for spousal murder, but the historical record is largely silent in many of the cases and in other cases it is unclear whether an actual execution took place. While some sources claim, for instance, that Pamela Lee Worms hanged in Pittsburgh in January 1852 for the poisoning death of her husband Moses Worms, others suggest that Pamela died of natural causes while awaiting her execution. A letter from Allegheny County Sheriff Richard Storm to the Reverend Augustus Dimick, who had written a private history and confession dictated by Pamela, noted that Pamela died on January 19 from a burst blood vessel perhaps self-inflicted to commit suicide. Pamela confessed also to drowning her eight-year-old stepson, poisoning her 10-year-old stepdaughter, poisoning a relative of her husband's named Mrs. Brock, and poisoning an elderly housekeeper named Anne Thomas. In her confession, Pamela believed she had become mentally ill.

New York hanged Anna Hoag after she confessed to poisoning her husband so she could be with another man, William Sumners. Abandoned by her parents as an infant "and left foundling in the public streets," Henry Taylor, a man of means adopted infant Anna and raised her as his own providing her with a good education. At 18 years old, Anna married Nelson Hoag with whom she had five children. Authorities stayed Anna's hanging until July 1852 because she had become pregnant with Sumners' child. In her 70-page confession, Anna implicated Sumners as an accomplice in Nelson's murder and authorities jailed him as an accessory. There is no record that officials executed Sumners.

In another case in October 1858, the Court of Oyer and Terminer of Montour County ordered the hanging of Mary Twiggs, an Irish immigrant woman, for aiding and abetting William John Clark, her peddler paramour, in the arsenic poisoning murder of his wife, Catharine Ann Clark, in the spring of 1857. Twiggs may have worked as a domestic for the Clarks since she lived in their house. Catharine Clark continued to nurse her new born while being poisoned by Mary and William and eventually the baby died from the same poisoning. Twiggs did not appeal her conviction and death sentence, but the Pennsylvania Supreme Court upheld the judgment of the county court in William Clark's case. He hanged in September 1858 when Governor Packer refused a pardon.

Circumstantial evidence was enough for a Minnesota court to convict Mary Ann Bilansky of murder. Executed a short two years after statehood, Mary Bilansky was the only white woman ever executed in Minnesota. Prosecutors accused Mary of poisoning her Polish émigré husband Stanislaus with arsenic. One newspaper characterized Stanislaus Bilansky as a man of violent disposition, and abusive and jealous who had taken several wives, the last of which left him because of his constant abuse and ill-treatment. A coroner's inquest initially determined that her husband died from natural causes, but authorities later arrested Mary and John Walker after "highly incriminating evidence omitted from the inquest" came to the attention of police. John Walker was Mary's nephew with whom she reportedly had a lurid love affair. The omitted evidence implicated that Mary failed to summon medical attention for her husband, that a nurse caring for Stanislaus witnessed Mary undress in front of John, and that when Mary had purchased arsenic to rid the house of rats she made an offhand comment to a friend that she should probably give the poison to her husband. Physicians could not determine whether the cause of death was poisoning or natural causes. The forensic evidence was "muddled and inconclusive ... about as unsatisfactory as it was possible to make." Despite the lack of definitive forensic evidence, a second coroner's jury claimed, "The deceased came to his death by the effects of arsenic administered by the hands of Mrs. Bilansky."[17] Authorities released John Walker for lack of evidence but bound Mary over for trial on first-degree murder charges. Much of the evidence used to prosecute her was innocuous: there were inconsistent toxicological reports on the cause of death; the nurse that witnessed Mary undress in front of John slept in the same bedchamber as Mary and John; Stanislaus was in financial ruins; and the purported torrid affair between Mary and John was most likely the manifestation of Stanislaus' jealousy. Some even suspected that Stanislaus committed suicide in light of his financial difficulties. Yet, as Jones puts it, the jury knew that Mary had purchased arsenic and they wanted to know what happened to that poison.[18] The Minnesota Supreme Court denied Mary a new trial finding that her defense attorneys had based the petition for review on bogus legal arguments. The state's governor refused clemency and Mary hanged in the Ramsey County jail yard in March 1860. A double standard accented Minnesota's capital justice system at the time; on the very day that the court pronounced Mary's death sentence, "a *man* convicted of manslaughter after he beat, clubbed, stomped, and kicked his wife to death was sentenced to five years in the Stillwater prison."[19]

In a later case in February 1881, Catharine Miller and George Smith hanged for killing Catharine's husband, Andrew Miller. Catharine and George had an adulterous affair for nearly two years before the murder. Raised in a poor family, Catharine had one year of schooling and could barely read and write. Andrew was some 30 years older than Catharine; they had two young daughters, Mary and Jennie. Authorities found Andrew hanging from a beam in the barn with his skull crushed. Catharine and George each held the other responsible for Andrew's murder and in one instance both accused a black man, John Brown, for the crime but there was no evidence supporting Brown's connection in the case. As Shipman notes, "In 1880, as in Boston in the 1980s and in South Carolina in the 1990s, white criminals knew that accusing a black man of a crime might shift blame from themselves."[20] George Smith exonerated Brown in a confession shortly before his execution.

Herkimer County officials in New York hanged Roxalana Druse. The "diabolical character" of Roxalana's crime made her execution one of national interest. The Druse family included George, his wife Roxalana, mentally retarded Mary, a 19-year-old daughter, George, a 10-year-old son, and Frank Gates, a 14-year-old nephew. The *Newark Daily Advocate* explained after George and Roxalana had argued at the breakfast table, Roxalana left the room and returned moments later with a loaded revolver under her apron.[21] Roxalana dismissed the boys from the room while Mary crept upon behind her father and threw a rope around his neck. It was then that Roxalana shot George twice in the chest. Roxalana called the boys to the room and under a threat of killing Frank; she made the young boy shoot her abusive elderly husband. Roxalana then seized an axe and decapitated George. She then had the boys and Mary help her dismember the body, burn it in a cook stove, and then put the ashes in a pigsty. Officials convicted and sentenced Roxalana to death. At her hanging in a jail yard, it took Roxalana 15 minutes to strangle to death. The sight was so disconcerting to authorities that state officials immediately moved to adopt the electric chair as the official execution method. Roxalana died in February 1887 and was the last woman *hanged* in New York. For her part in the murder, the same court sentenced Roxalana's daughter to life in prison. A *New York Times* article on Roxalana's hanging explained that persons stole her body before its burial—"It is well known that more than one physician would like to examine the brain of such a woman, and there are spirits here who are not adverse to rendering science all the assistance in their power in this particular case."[22] Interestingly, Governor Hill respited Roxalana's execution after he received commutation petitions from several women's groups and to give the state's legislature time to consider an act abolishing the death penalty for women. Roxalana's hanging took place shortly after the legislature defeated the bill.

New Jersey executed one woman for spousal murder. Essex County officials hanged Margaret Klem Meierhoeffer and her lover Frank Lammens for the murder of Margaret's husband John Meierhoeffer. Margaret was from a very poor immigrant German family living in the slums of New York. She was illiterate and spent most of her formative years as a young nanny caring for the children of affluent families. She ultimately went to work as a house servant for a prominent New Jersey family where she met John Meierhoeffer, a middle-aged bachelor 30 years her senior who worked as a sharecropper and who also was a German émigré. A romance blossomed and the two married in March 1859. After acquiring a modest parcel of land, John joined a New Jersey regiment and fought in the Civil War for four years. In his absence, Margaret began hiring young men to work the farm and with whom she often had lurid relations that earned her a reputation of a common prostitute. When John discharged from the military and arrived home, he was dismayed at his wife's many affairs but mental fatigue from the war had changed his personality and he quickly succumbed to Margaret's outlandish control. In the summer of 1879, a young wayward Dutchman named Frank Lammens who spoke fluent German arrived at the home for work and a meal. Soon he and Margaret were openly cohabitating in the house while John lived in the barn. The two discussed killing John. At some point when John entered the house Lammens kicked him down the cellar stairs and shot him in the back of the head with a large caliber gun. Margaret and Frank stashed the body under the cellar stairs. Feigning that Lammens had also victimized her, Margaret reported her husband's death to authorities who arrested the couple. The court found the two guilty of John's murder and sentenced them to die together on the gallows in the Essex County jail in January 1881.

In June 1889, Philadelphia officials hanged Sarah Jane Whiteling for the arsenic poisoning of her husband John, her two-year-old son Willie, and her nine-year-old daughter Bertha. Sarah had led a troubled life; her first husband had died in prison convicted of robbery, and Bertha was born after Sarah's marriage to John, a Philadelphia saloonkeeper. She also had a 15-year-old son to whom Sarah never revealed she was his mother. Sarah and her family were poor and apparently, life insurance money was the motive for the murders. Physicians believed the deaths resulted from natural causes, but a coroner's inquiry and subsequent police investigation demanded exhumation of the bodies that "revealed large quantities of arsenic in each victim."[23] After Sarah's arrest, a local newspaper published her full confession and a jury rejected her claim of insanity associated with menopause. After her execution, physicians performed an autopsy under the auspices of determining her sanity. Officials buried Sarah next to her murdered family members.

Infanticide and Child Murder

Infanticide "was perceived as a woman's crime, an act committed to conceal the birth of an illegitimate child."[24] Colonial officials rarely indicted fathers for infanticide even when they murdered in concert with the mother. Infanticide was an offense for which jurisdictions prosecuted women, but in most cases, jurisdictions did not execute women charged with the crime. Of the 34 women prosecuted for infanticide in Pennsylvania between 1763 and 1790, for instance, authorities executed five of the women. One scholar identified some 38 cases of infanticide in two Ohio counties from 1806 to 1879 in which officials imposed no death penalty. Even so, white women executions for child murder and infanticide remained proportionately high during the second historical trend in female executions; some 29 percent of white women executions in the period were for killing their own children, the same percentage of white women executed for spousal murder. Abortions took place, but the historical record is almost nonexistent on the subject in colonial America. Working class mothers usually kept their children born to them out of wedlock, but either had to work to support their children or enter an almshouse. Smith points out, for instance, that over a 20-year period from the late 18th century to the early 19th century roughly 58 percent of the 354 deserted women who entered the Philadelphia Almshouse "were pregnant or had young children with them. In the almshouse, though, children were often separated from mothers and could be bound out without their permission."[25]

Young, unmarried women rather than wives mostly committed infanticide. Some young women facing public disgrace for an illegitimate pregnancy and out of wedlock childbirth believed suicide was a viable alternative. Rowe explains,

> Young women, pregnant and desperate, at times chose to take their own lives as well as those of their unborn children. Suicide among young women was not unusual in eighteenth-century Pennsylvania. Six such suicides occurred in Philadelphia in 1773–1774 alone. Because autopsies generally were not performed on victims of suicide, or families successfully covered up such tragedies, no careful conclusions regarding which victims were pregnant, and which were not, can be reached. But unquestionably, pregnancies prompted some of the suicides of young mothers believing that no other escape from ignominy lay open to them. The suicide of a servant girl reported in the *Pennsylvania Gazette*, it was said, had been "with a Design, as 'tis thought, to haunt a young Fellow who had refus'd to marry her."[26]

Authorities in seven states executed 16 white women for infanticide and child murder in the second period of female executions. The New England colonies of New Hampshire, Vermont, and Massachusetts executed women for infanticide and child murder. In one New Hampshire case, Rockingham County Sheriff Thomas Packer hanged a young unmarried schoolteacher named Ruth Blay in December 1768 for infanticide. After delivering her stillborn baby alone, one of Ruth's students witnessed her bury the infant under the floorboards of the schoolhouse. The student reported the incident to her parents who in turn informed authorities. Tried and convicted for concealing the child's birth, county court officials ordered Sheriff Packer to hang Ruth in late December 1768 from the same tree he had decades earlier hanged Sarah Simpson and Penelope Kenny. Knowing that the colonial governor had issued a reprieve, Sheriff Packer proceeded with the hanging while callously ignoring pleas from the townspeople to wait for the reprieve. As the story goes (a common theme in female executions), officials carted Ruth across town and "her screams were heart wrenching as she pleaded her innocence."[27] A rider carrying the reprieve arrived moments after Ruth's hanging. Hostile townspeople met Sheriff Packer and burned his body in effigy believing he acted heartlessly in not waiting for the reprieve that he knew was forthcoming. In Vermont, published accounts of Emeline Meaker's hanging at Windsor Prison in March 1883 reveal, "she was a boorish virago who estranged everyone with whom she came into contact. Even her own husband and children disdained her to a point where they would not accept her body for burial."[28] State authorities hanged Emeline Meaker for the vicious killing of eight-year-old Alice Meaker, her husband's half-sister's daughter rescued from a state-funded orphanage that arranged for a $400 stipend for the child's care. Emeline insisted to the last that she did not commit the murder of young Alice. Hanged at Vermont State Prison in Washington County, Emeline was the first women hanged in a state prison in the United States.

Northampton County officials in Massachusetts also hanged a young, unmarried servant named Abiah Converse in July 1788 for killing her newborn child. Abiah had concealed the infant "by rolling it up in a ball of spinning wheel tow."[29] The prominent family for whom she was a domestic servant informed authorities and Abiah confessed to the crime after officials found the dead child.

The Middle Colonies of Pennsylvania, New York and New Jersey executed women for infanticide and child murder in the second historical period of women executions but the historical record is largely silent about most of these cases. In June 1766, Burlington County officials in New Jersey hanged an unmarried white woman named Elizabeth Vaughn after a search for her new born daughter revealed "it was crammed into the glovebox of a sleigh where it had either suffocated or succumbed to frostbite."[30] Delaware County officials in Pennsylvania hanged Jane Ewing in January 1765 after the court of Oyer and Terminer found her guilty of murdering her illegitimate male child in which "there was not a single circumstance in her favour but on the contrary at the Tryal she showed no kind of remorse."[31] Later that same year in September 1765, York County officials in Pennsylvania hanged Elizabeth Erwin for infanticide of her female newborn. Berks County officials hanged Catharine Kreps in December 1767 for murdering her infant male child. In June 1767, Williamsburg officials in Virginia hanged Martha Sharp from Chesterfield for child murder although she denied killing the child and claimed that the father actually did the killing.

Margaret Rauch of Northumberland County hanged for murdering her infant child in 1772 and buried it in a dung pit. Apparently, her brother informed authorities. Williamsburg authorities also hanged Catherine Peppers in June 1774 and Susannah Brazier in January 1775 for infanticide. In June 1779, Lancaster County officials in Pennsylvania hanged Catherine Fisher for infanticide. It appears from the historical record that Fisher's "defiance of the court and its personnel, her unrepentant utterances, and the undeniable damage done to her infant's skull doubtless account for her execution."[32] Some commentators have put forward that Catherine hanged for killing an adult rather than for killing her child. Historical accounts of Pennsylvania's executions of Elizabeth Wilson and Susannah Cox are more informative, however. In the case of Elizabeth Wilson, it appears certain that authorities wrongfully executed young Elizabeth. Delaware County officials hanged Elizabeth from the back of a cart in January 1786 after a murder conviction for killing her twin illegitimate sons 10 weeks after their birth. Elizabeth was the daughter of a poor but respected Tory farmer in East Bradford Township and often visited the Indian Queen Inn in Philadelphia operated by a relative. Elizabeth was quite sexually active and had previously given birth to three illegitimate children before the birth of the twins. There she met a young boarder named Joseph Deshong with whom she developed a relationship and was soon pregnant. Elizabeth gave birth to the twins after returning to her father's farm. Once the children were born, Elizabeth met with Deshong and demanded financial support but "Elizabeth's intended husband seized the children from her and crushed the infants to death beneath his heavy boot and compelled Elizabeth to remain silent concerning the matter."[33] Authorities charged Elizabeth with killing the infants after discovering the bodies. While jailed for nearly a year awaiting trial, Elizabeth continued her silence and refused to reveal the truth about the children's death. She maintained that she had abandoned the children along a public road. As a result, Elizabeth gave the trial judge no alternative but to sentence her to hang at Gallows Hills. On the day before her hanging though, Elizabeth conceded the truth and told authorities how her lover killed the children. Her brother William obtained a stay of execution from the Supreme Executive Council until January 3, 1786, but on his return from Philadelphia with yet another execution stay, William arrived 20 minutes too late to save his sister from hanging. There is nothing in the record of what fate befell the actual murderer.

Susannah Cox was born in Berks County, Pennsylvania, in 1785, and as a young teenager, her parents sold her as a domestic servant to the Schneider family in Oley Township, Pennsylvania. The eldest daughter of the Schneider family, Esther, married Jacob Geehr and Susannah raised the Geehr's three children. Esther eventually became physically disabled and Jacob turned his affections to Susannah. They began a sexual relationship and Susannah was soon pregnant but hid her pregnancy from family members. In February 1809, Susannah gave birth to an infant son that she insisted was stillborn. Jacob Geehr found the baby frozen to death in an outbuilding on the property. A forensic examination revealed that the baby's lower jaw had been broken, the child's tongue torn loose and thrust back, and that the baby died from strangulation from a wad of flax forced down its throat. Authorities soon arrested Susannah and held her in the regional jail until her trial. Represented by a competent team of lawyers, Susannah insisted that the baby was born dead and that she hid the birth because she feared losing her service with the Geehr family. A county jury found Susannah guilty of the child's death and sentenced her to hang in June. On the execution day, a wagon containing Susannah's coffin stood under the gallows with Susannah standing atop the coffin with a noose around her neck and a mask over her face. After her execution that lasted 17 minutes, authorities placed Susannah's body in the coffin, drove her to her brother-in-law's farm where he buried her. Strangely, in May 1905, someone exhumed Susannah's remains and they have been forever lost.

New York authorities put to death three white women for infanticide in the period. Barbara Stillwell hanged in New York City in June 1784 for the murder of a three-year-old boy named Benjamin Carpenter. Young Benjamin belonged to a family of Tories who fled from New York at the time of the British evacuation. Not wanting to have the child undergo the perils of traveling, the parents left the child in Stillwell's care until they resettled. Hearn explains, "Figuring that the Tory parents would never dare to be seen in New York again, [Stillwell] subjected the child to such mistreatment that it perished."[34] In another infanticide case, authorities in New York executed the wrong woman. The unjust execution took place when Columbia County officials hanged Margaret Houghtaling in October 1817 for killing Lewis Spencer, a 15-month-old mulatto child. Margaret was a prostitute who roomed with another young prostitute named Caty Ostrander, Lewis' mother. Caty grew tired of the child that undoubtedly was affecting her lifestyle. To rid herself of the child, Caty gave Lewis "enough poison to kill a dozen men" and left the child with Margaret.[35] Authorities blamed Margaret for the child's death, tried her for murder, and after winning a conviction sentenced Margaret to death. Margaret hanged at Hudson weeks later. The record shows that Caty "succumbed to a certain disease common among her profession and freely admitted just before her death that she had really poisoned the baby and that she had falsely sworn away her roommate's life."[36] There is little in the historical record concerning another New York case in which authorities hanged Peggy Facteau in March 1825 for killing her illegitimate baby.

Martha Savacool Place had a troubled life. At 23 years old, she may have suffered a brain injury from which her brother claimed she never fully recovered. Sarah was initially a dressmaker living in New Jersey with her first husband Wesley Savacool when she abandoned him and went to work as a house servant for the widower William W. Place. She soon married Place who had a 17-year-old daughter named Ida Place who Martha hated and with whom she rivaled for William's affection. Martha's embitterment turned to violence in February 1898 when she threw sulphuric acid in Ida's face and then "sat back for a while and relished the scene as the young girl thrashed about in agony, her face a mass of dripping flesh."[37] Martha then smothered Ida to death with a pillow and waited for William to return home from work. Martha attacked William with two hard hits with an axe when he arrived. Williams survived the attack, but authorities found Ida's body in her upstairs bedroom. Martha confessed her crimes to the police and a New York court tried, convicted, and sentenced her to die in the electric chair in Sing Sing Prison in March 1899. Lawyers for Martha appealed her conviction and death sentence but the Court of

Appeals rejected her plea. Then Governor Theodore Roosevelt refused to intervene on Martha's behalf claiming no reasonable doubt to her guilt and the severity of the crime. Martha was the first female put to death in New York's electric chair.

South Carolina hanged Sarah Chamberlain for killing her illegitimate child in 1738. Sarah was the first woman executed in the colony. In June 1757, New Castle County (Delaware) hanged Margaret Sexton for murdering her four-year-old stepson, "a most barbarous and willful act," and unknown county officials in Maryland hanged Mary Arnett for infanticide in February 1761.[38] Missouri hanged Mary Andrews in Lafayette County in April 1834 for killing her infant child. She was the common-law wife of Leland Tromley whom county officials hanged just a few short weeks before Mary's execution for killing James Stephens. At Leland's murder trial, Mary refused to testify against him claiming marital privilege. The court held her in contempt and jailed her with her 10-month-old daughter Sara. While in jail, Mary strangled young Sara claiming that she killed her daughter because "her mother had turned her out of doors, ... her sisters would not speak to her, and Tromley the father of the child was about to be hung, and she had no means of taking care of her."[39] In another Missouri case in 1836, Parmelia Yarber killed her infant daughter. After failing to appear on the murder indictment, a Scott County judge ordered that the "outlaw" Parmelia hanged on the indictment. Frazier explains that there is no record of Parmelia's arrest or her hanging although it is unlikely that she escaped the gallows. Virginia is the only other southern jurisdiction that put to death white females in the period for killing their children, yet the historical records reveal little about the cases. Mary Snodgrass hanged in July 1896 in Coeburn, Virginia, for murdering her baby by burning it in a fireplace.

Murder of Masters and Mistresses

Historically, American's believed that "[t]he next lowest thing to a black woman in the American hierarchy was an Irishwoman of the servant class. On the whole they were thought to be stupid, sluggish, thoroughly undependable. Too many of them are unsettled, reckless, slovenly; some dishonest, and some intemperate."[40] The historical record on women executions reveals that authorities executed women for killing their white employers. It was anti–Irish sentiment that accented the judicial murder of Bridget Durgan in August 1867 for killing her mistress. As a teenager, Bridget Durgan ran away from home after her father forbade a courtship with a young delivery boy. Bridget stole £20 from her father and immigrated to the United States in 1865. She worked as a domestic servant in and around New York City for several years, eventually working for the Coriell household in Plainsfield, New Jersey. Dr. Coriell was married to Mary Ellen Coriell and had an 18-month-old daughter named Mamie. Mary Ellen was a petite woman who distrusted her new Irish housemaid and suspected her physician husband of infidelity with young Bridget. After four months of service, Mary Ellen demanded that Bridget leave the household. According to one interpretation of the events, Bridget misinterpreted Dr. Coriell's remorse at terminating her employment as wishing "to be rid of his wife so he could be free to marry his housemaid."[41] One night in February 1867, while Dr. Coriell was away on a house call and after putting young Mamie to bed, Bridget burst into Mary Ellen's bedroom with an oil lamp and a butcher knife. Bridget immediately smashed the oil lamp in Mary Ellen's face, stabbed, and slashed her body with the knife, beat her severely with a wooden baby chair, and then set the bed on fire. Jones describes the beating suffered by Mary Ellen:

> There were scratches and just cuts all over the body, two dozen stab wounds up and down the spine, deeps wounds in the thighs and shoulders, a dozen jagged tearing wounds in the neck from unsuccessful attempts to cut the throat, scratches and teeth marks on the face. Her hair was torn

in clumps from her scalp. Her face, both arms, and her right leg were terribly bruised and swollen—a grim detail of great importance, for swelling does not occur after death. Mary Ellen Coriell's struggle with her attacker had been fierce—and long.[42]

After savagely beating and stabbing Mary Ellen to death, Bridget wrapped Mamie in a blanket and ran to a neighbor's house carrying the baby claiming that burglars had stormed the house and murdered Mary Ellen. Police arrested Bridget the next day after inconsistencies in her story. Additionally, investigators found blood on Bridget's nightclothes and the discarded and blood-encrusted butcher knife in a privy behind the Coriell's home. Bridget all but admitted to the killing and Middlesex County officials hanged her in the local jail yard on August 30, 1867, before what an eyewitness described as "the roughest, rudest and most ungentlemanly crowd of men we ever saw."[43] Jones concedes that there is little doubt that Bridget Durgan was a mentally ill woman with the very lowest level of human intelligence:

> It seems clear in retrospect that she suffered from frequent, severe grand mal epileptic seizures, and that she probably killed Mary Ellen Coriell while suffering what modern medicine calls a seizure of psychomotor or temporal lobe epilepsy—a type of seizure often characterized by rage, physical violence, and amnesia.[44]

In an earlier case in the period, Massachusetts wrongfully hanged an innocent 22-year-old servant woman named Mary Johnson for the murder of her elderly master and mistress, John and Anna Robinson, while they lay in bed. Mary was a faithful servant to the elderly couple for seven years who had retired to a small cottage after having kept the largest inn in Gloucester. Over the years, Mary had several suitors, among them a young man named Thomas Smith whom the Robinson had favored. On a Sunday evening in October 1831, Mary and Thomas sat at the kitchen fire when Mary left the kitchen for a short time, and when she returned Thomas was gone. It was then that Mary heard a noise coming from the Robinson's bedroom and ran upstairs where she found "her master and mistress lay with their throats cut from ear to ear, and the blood gushing in torrents from the wounds." Mary immediately ran to a neighbor's house for help who found no one other than Mary in the house. A court tried, convicted, and sentenced Mary to death for the killings and ordered "her body given to the surgeons for dissection." At the gallows and once Mary had made the drop, Thomas yelled out, "Take her down—I am the murderer." Officials immediately took Mary down from the hangman's rope and a physician attempted to revive her while she lay on the scaffold. Mary died two minutes later. Thomas made a full confession to the killings stating that he wanted to rob the Robinsons of a large sum of money. He also confessed that he had planned to kill Mary as well. There is no record of Thomas Smith's execution for the Robinsons' murder.[45]

Property Crimes

Pennsylvania, New York, Massachusetts, and Virginia together hanged five white women for property crimes in the period. There is little in the historical record concerning Mary Hall's hanging in Pennsylvania in December 1781 for burglary. Mary Dailey, a habitual petty thief, suffered public whippings totaling 60 stripes for numerous convictions of petty theft over a one-year period. After a fourth conviction involving robbery, New York hanged Mary in May 1771. New York also hanged Margaret Siggins in May 1771 for burglary of clothes and money from the home of Mrs. Mary Williams. Catherine Bronson hanged in New York City in November 1767 for grand larceny. Though most of the details of Catherine's crime are lost, scholars know that "clemency was denied her because she had already been allowed the 'benefit of clergy' after a prior felony conviction. An incorrigible prisoner, she became hysterical on the day of her execution and had to be dragged to the gallows."[46] Williamsburg County officials in Virginia hanged Sarah Matts along with Constantine Matthews in November 1739 for robbery.

The historical record is much more informative concerning the hanging of Rachel Wall in January 1789 for robbery. Rachel was born Rachel Schmidt in 1760 on a farm outside Carlisle, Pennsylvania, to a Presbyterian farming family. At the age of 16, Rachel traveled with her mother to Harrisburg to attend the funeral of her grandfather Joseph Kirsch. There, Rachel met a Boston angler named George Wall with whom she eloped and moved to Boston. Rachel took housemaid jobs in Beacon Hill and George worked as an angler. Squandering their earnings on party and drink, Rachel and George borrowed or stole a ship and began pirating off the Isles of Shoals on the New Hampshire and Maine coasts where "they lured in passing ships by pretending to be in distress, but when their would-be rescuers arrived they found only death at the hands of the Walls and their unsavory crew. Once all valuables were removed to their own ship, the pirates would then sink the captured ships and all those aboard."[47] In one year (1781–1782), they reportedly sank 12 ships, murdered 24 sailors, and stole some $6,000 worth of goods. In 1782, George drowned in a storm and ending Rachel's piracy. She continued stealing from ships docked in the Boston harbor, but some doubt her prowess as a thief aboard ships and argue that Rachel most likely became a prostitute and stole from her clients once they were asleep. In 1789, Sheriff Joe Robinson captured Rachel and a court tried and convicted her for robbing young Margaret Bender of a bonnet and then attempting to rip out the victim's tongue. Authorities suspected Rachel of murdering a sailor found dead on the waterfront. A court sentenced Rachel to death for highway robbery and hanged her with two other criminals in October 1789. Rachel Wall was the last woman put to death under civil authority in Massachusetts.[48]

Predatory Murder

That jurisdictions executed several white women for predatory murders involving murder, robbery-murder, and accessory to murder during the period challenges the notion that "predatory crimes by strangers was not a major problem in colonial America."[49] In the 1780s, colonial authorities implemented harsh measures to counter rising crime that local newspapers of the period blamed on poor whites including vagrants, sailors, and soldiers. As one scholar explains, "It is therefore not surprising that almost half the white people ... condemned in Charleston in the second half of the eighteenth century were executed in the late 1780s. Thirteen were hanged in 1788 alone and eleven of those over a period of five days."[50] Pennsylvania hanged a runaway Irish servant woman named Mary Kennedy, along with an Englishman named Henry Smith, in York County in December 1768 for the murder of Baltzer Klotzer in Manchester in July of the same year. Kennedy was a servant to Thomas Waters and Smith a servant to William Peters. Klotzer's killing is most likely related to Kennedy and Smith breaking out of a workhouse in Chester County in June of that year. Waters and Peters had earlier advertised a reward for Mary and Henry's return in the *Pennsylvania Gazette* in July 1768.

In June 1788, Pennsylvania authorities hanged Ann Connelly (along with Robert Stacy, Josiah Jordan, John George, Edward Hatcher, and Thomas Smith) for the robbery and murder of Nicholas John Wightman. Sarah Clark, a young servant woman to the John Douglas family hanged in Cumberland County, Pennsylvania, for the poisoning deaths of Captain John Carothers and his wife Mary and the crippling for life of their son Andrew. Sarah (called Sallie) Clark was obsessed with Douglas' young son (unknown name) but he was interested in Ann Carothers who lived nearby. Determined to kill Ann and win over the young man, Sarah went to work for the Carothers family and ultimately put arsenic in a pot of leaven that the family ate. Ann survived. County officials hanged young Sarah in October 1799.

In January 1817, Camden County officials in Georgia hanged Margaret Seaborn for the murder of an unidentified victim. Considerable myth surrounds the lives, crimes, and execution of Lavinia Fisher and her husband John. According to legend, 27-year-old Lavinia Fisher hanged with her husband in South Carolina as serial killers for the robbery and murders of guests at a hotel known as the Six Mile House. The story also has it that Lavinia, supposedly a beautiful woman, wore her white wedding dress for her execution. Contrary to popular understanding, the Fishers did not own the Six Mile House, they were not serial killers, and Lavinia did not wear her wedding dress on execution day. Scholars explain that in 1819 wagon traders began suffering losses from outlaw gangs in and around Charleston, South Carolina, when a cavalcade of citizens began patrolling the backcountry to end the robberies. One of the patrol's first stops was the Six Mile House just outside Charleston known to be a hideout for marauding gangs. The citizen's group evicted the residents without incident and left young David Ross the guard the property. When he awoke the next morning, he found himself surrounded by gang members. The gang assaulted David and threw him outside where Lavinia choked him and shoved his head through a window. A few hours later, John Peoples, accompanied by Zachariah Carwell, stopped by the hotel to water his horses when a gang of several men and Lavinia assaulted Peoples with guns and clubs and robbed him of $40. The vicious Lavinia beat Peoples about the face with a stick. Peoples made his way back to Charleston after the attack and informed authorities about the event and that he could identify several members of the gang including Lavinia. A judge ordered an arrest warrant and the county sheriff went to the hotel and made arrests of the most of the gang members including John and Lavinia Fisher. Officials tried and convicted the two and ordered them hanged on February 18, 1820, for highway robbery. The state's governor refused clemency and an appellate court denied an appeal. At the gallows, John and Lavinia wore long white robes over their clothes and the sheriff had to drag Lavinia up the stand. Lavinia died quickly but John struggled for several minutes. Lavinia's last words were reportedly, "If any of you have a message for the Devil, give it to me, for I am about to meet him!"[51]

Charlotte Jones hanged in Pittsburgh, Pennsylvania, in February 1858 alongside Henry Fife for the robbery-murder of Jones' aunt and uncle, George Wilson and Elizabeth McMasters. In April 1857, Charlotte and Henry reportedly killed the elderly couple who were brother and sister to get money so they could be married. Charlotte's role in the double murder was to get the elderly couple to answer the door, gain entrance to the cabin in which in the elderly couple lived, and then summon Henry by whistling. Henry did the actual murder by knifing George to death with a long dagger and beating Elizabeth to death with a fireplace poker. Authorities tried Charlotte and Henry before a Pittsburg jury that found them both guilty of first-degree murder. Charlotte collapsed on the gallows and the executioner had to support her on the trap while readying her for the hanging. Henry hanged in the same prison yard at the same time as Charlotte. In 1845, Washington County officials in Arkansas hanged Lavinia Burnett and her husband Crawford for the robbery-murder of a bachelor named Jonathan Selby who kept large sums of money in his house. The Burnett's 15-year-old daughter, Minerva, reportedly confessed to authorities that while her parents planned Selby's murder that it was their son John who actually did the killing. Court officials tried Lavinia and Crawford separately and juries in each case returned guilty verdicts. Crawford and Lavinia hanged on November 8, 1845. John had disappeared to Missouri but officials returned him to Arkansas, where they tried and convicted him of Selby's murder, he hanged the day after Christmas.

Mary Elizabeth Jenkins Surratt, a 42-year-old widow, is the only woman executed in the United States by a federal military commission for complicity in the assassination of President Abraham Lincoln. She hanged in July 1865 at the Washington Arsenal Penitentiary in Washington, D.C. Mary Surratt apparently owned a boarding house where her son John, a confederate spy, and John Wilkes Booth often stayed with other members of the conspiracy to kill President Lincoln. Mary supposedly supplied the pistol that Booth used to murder the president. There is still considerable debate over the culpability of Mary Surratt. Some have argued that Surratt's conviction was a convenient scapegoat for a military tribunal that had no constitutional authority to prosecute suspected conspirators in the killing of the president and that President Johnson should have pardoned her. Some scholars have questioned the evidence of Mary Surratt's involvement in the conspiracy that should have rendered her a not guilty verdict. One scholar puts it this way:

> Most historians have long accepted that Surratt's trial was arguably extralegal—that under the Constitution, the trial of the Lincoln conspirators should have been a trial by jury, not by military tribunal. They have also long sympathized with Surratt, a woman poorly represented by two junior attorneys in the actual courtroom and tried amidst the hysteria engendered by the death of Lincoln and the vengeful desire of the nation to find a scapegoat.[52]

Newspapers characterized Martha Grinder as a "'homicidal monomaniac'—killing without feeling or intent, seeming indiscriminately, poisoning people for no apparent reason"—a serial killer.[53] Pennsylvania hanged 50-year-old Martha Grinder in January 1866 for her confessed poisoning to death of two women, newlywed Mary Caroline Caruthers who lived next door to Martha and a young Irish servant girl named Jane R. Buchanan who worked for Martha. Officials suspected that Martha might have been responsible for some 20 deaths, including "two of her husband's brothers, a child left with her by a poor woman, and one of her own children."[54] Martha made a signed confession that the County Sheriff released to press after her hanging to killing Caruthers and Buchanan but adamantly denied poisoning any other persons. In another case, young Susan Eberhart hanged in Webster County, Georgia, in May 1873 for her role in Enoch Ferdinand Spann's killing of his wife Sarah Spann. Poor, illiterate, and "ignorant as a horse," Susan worked as a servant in the Spann's home helping Sarah who was 12 years older than Ferdinand and "disabled" having had a leg amputated years earlier. Apparently, Ferdinand strangled Sarah with "a common plow-line tightly drawn about her neck" and Susan "forced a handkerchief into Spann's throat, strangling her."[55] County Sheriff Matthews arrested Susan and her paramour Ferdinand six days after the murder and hanged the two less than a month after the murder before a crowd of 700 witnesses; Susan strangled to death since the fall did not break her neck.

English émigré Elizabeth Potts hanged with her husband Josiah in Elko County, Nevada in June 1890 for killing Miles Faucett two years earlier. George Brewer found Faucett's remains while remodeling the basement of his house he had purchased earlier from the Potts when they moved to Wyoming. Josiah Potts reportedly had dismembered Faucett's body and unsuccessfully tried to burn the remains. Officials arrested the Potts in Wyoming and returned them to Nevada for trial for murdering Faucett. Bigamy was apparently the motive for murdering Faucett. It seems that while on vacation in San Francisco in 1886, an English woman named Elizabeth Atherton had married Miles Faucett. After their marriage, Faucett learned that Elizabeth had a husband living in Carlin, Nevada. The couple separated and Elizabeth went back to her husband in Carlin. Faucett soon followed Elizabeth to Carlin to be closer to her. Scholars surmise that the Potts' killed Faucett to keep him from reporting Elizabeth's bigamy (a federal crime) to authorities, which he had threatened to do if the Potts' did not repay a debt owed Faucett. A jury found no reasonable doubt that the Potts murdered Faucett and the county court sentenced both to death. They appealed their convictions and capital sentences to the Nevada Supreme Court, which the court denied. The presiding judge in the case appealed to the Board of Pardons for a commutation of their death sentence to life in prison but to no avail.

Executions of Black Women

One scholar explains that slavery was horrible for men but it was far more dreadful for women—"superadded to the burden common to all, [slave women had] wrongs, and sufferings, and mortifications peculiarly their own."[56] The severe punishments associated with the oppression of slave women remained unabated once in the British colonies. What's more, the severity of the punishments increased for bondwomen as institutional slavery expanded throughout the colonies in the antebellum period. Death penalty jurisdictions executed more than *six times* as many slave women in antebellum slavery (1790–1865) than in colonial slavery (before 1790). Authorities undoubtedly executed far more slave women than what the historical record reveals. In his analysis of county court proceedings in colonial Virginia, Schwarz verifies more than 150 actual hangings of nearly 600 cases where officials sentenced slaves to death. But the state may have condemned as many as a thousand slaves and hanged 400 to 800. Schwarz identifies only *two* slave women executions during this period "including one slave burned to death after being convicted of poisoning her master in 1746 [most probably slave woman Eve] and another female slave burned to death after conviction for murder in 1737 [most likely an unnamed slave woman belonging to Prudden]."[57] Schwarz also shows that Virginia hanged more than 600 slaves in the antebellum period but historical accounts do not distinguish female from male slave executions. Surely, female slaves comprised a significant percentage of these executions. Hindus claims that women were roughly 10 percent of the nearly 300 slaves executed in antebellum South Carolina.[58] In the apartheid of Jim Crow, black women crimes of resistance against white male violence paralleled those of slave women decades earlier. Death penalty jurisdictions put to death roughly half of all executed slave women for murder, conspiracy to murder, and attempted murder in the late colonial period, the figure increased to nearly three-quarters in the antebellum period.

Late Colonial Slavery

The historical record reveals 71 slave women executed in the late colonial slave period from the 1750s through the 1780s. Many of these executed slave women strangled, clubbed, stabbed, burned, shot, poisoned, or hacked to death their white masters, mistresses, overseers, and their owner's children. Schwarz claims that whites were largely the victims of slaves condemned to hang in colonial Virginia though the state's historical record does not distinguish between male and female slaves involved in these killings. Of the homicides identified by Schwarz, slaves largely murdered their masters or members of their masters' families as well as other white persons of authority, including overseers, hirers, and constables.[59] Some 62 percent of murder victims of slaves in Georgia were master-class victims.

It was slave women's reaction to white oppression accenting their conditions under slavery that largely brought about slave women's vicious killing of their owners, and frequently their mistresses, overseers, and owners' other slaves. In 1750, for instance, South Carolina officials hanged slave woman Jenny belonging to Hugh Anderson for the poisoning murder of another slave woman belonging to John Matheringham. One historian contends that there were questions about the evidence against Jenny; it seems the mistress of the slave girl who died had intimidated Jenny's daughter into testifying against her mother. Officials nevertheless executed Jenny and the Commons House of Assembly awarded £50 to Hugh Anderson and £30 to John Matheringham. In September 1755, Suffolk County officials in Massachusetts burned slave woman Phillis alive while they hanged and gibbeted her accomplice Mark for the poisoning murder of their master, Captain John Codman. Codman was a sea captain and merchant of Charlestown and the owner of several slaves that he employed as mechanics, laborers, and house servants. Among his slaves, Mark and Phillis found Codman's rigid discipline unbearable. Several years before Codman's murder, the two slaves set fire to his workshop hoping that Codman would sell them. Their sale was not forthcoming and instead Mark and Phillis poisoned Codman to death. Mark's body remained on display for some 20 years.

Port Tobacco authorities in Maryland hanged slave woman Jenny and then gibbeted her body in July 1755 for killing her master. Charleston authorities in South Carolina hanged an unidentified slave woman belonging to George Fickling in January 1761 for poisoning her master. She hanged alongside Abraham, a male accomplice owned by John Gibbons. Slave woman Esther belonging to Wise in Accomack County, Virginia, died by an unknown execution method for the murder of her master in May 1767. Another slave woman named Jenny hanged in chains for poisoning to death her mistress in Maryland in 1770—"a horrible punishment that amounted to slow starvation" beyond the state's law.[60] West Virginia burned slave Dolly belonging to slave owner Sands in July 1770 for Sand's murder.

In December 1770, however, North Carolina authorities across five counties hanged 19 persons for murder, including three whites, three slave women, and 13 slave men. The white participants were most likely indentured servants with unidentified masters, but the three slave women were Annis and Phyllis belonging to Henry Ormond and slave woman Lucy belonging to Wyriot Ormond (brother to Henry Ormond). Along with two slave male confederates, the slave women killed Henry Ormond earlier in the summer. A Beaufort County slave court found the slave women and their accomplices guilty of Ormond's murder and sentenced Annis to burn at the stake and for Mary and Phyllis to hang on the gallows. Their male confederates also hanged. Henry Ormond's estate received £70 compensation for Annis and £20 for Phyllis, while North Carolina paid Wyriot Ormond £65 for the loss of Lucy. Henry Ormond was excessively abusive toward his slaves and garnered no mercy when his slave women sought revenge for his cruelty:

> Sometime in July 1770 the slaves conspired against their master, and on the Sunday night he was said to have rode from home in quest of one of his slaves who was missing, the conspirators, after their master was abed, went up to his room and with an handkerchief attempted to strangle him, which they thought they had effected, but a little time after they left him, he recovered, and began to stir, on hearing which they went up again, and told him he must die, and that before they left the room; he begged very earnestly for his life, but one of them, his house wench, told him it was in vain, that as he had no mercy on them, he could expect none himself, and immediately threw him between two feather beds, and all got on him till he was stifled to death.[61]

The historical record is often silent on the victims of predatory killings committed by slave women. In June 1820, for instance, an unnamed 16-year-old slave girl belonging to Alexander Roach hanged in Rockingham County, North Carolina, for murdering an unknown victim. Slave women in the late colonial slave period often hanged, however, for killing their master's children. Slave woman Dolly belonging to James Sands burned to death on the workhouse green in Charleston (South Carolina) in 1769 for poisoning her master's infant. Her accomplice Liverpoole, belonging to slave owner Price, burned to death as well. Four years later in 1773, authorities in Charleston tried, convicted, and executed slave woman Bess and her male slave accomplice Charlie, both owned by Joseph Warnock, for poisoning members of Warnock's family including Warnock, his wife, and two of his children. Warnock petitioned the Court of Justices and Freeholders for compensation for the executions of Bess and Charlie.[62]

Slave women hanged for the murder of their own children in late colonial slavery as well. Somerset County officials in New Jersey hanged an unidentified black woman for infanticide sometime in 1765. Some slave women murdered their own children when owners threatened to separate slave women from their children and grandchildren. A Tennessee case more than illustrates the horrors slave women suffered when slave owners broke apart slave families. In Cocke County, an unnamed slave woman was present at the auction sale of her eight-year-old grandson. Once bidding on the young boy began, the slave woman swore the buyer would never get him, grabbed her grandson and attempted to swim a nearby river with the boy hanging on to her back. Reportedly, the young boy lost his grip and drowned. County officials convicted the woman of her grandson's death and hanged her sometime in 1784.

Besides murdering slave masters and their families in retribution for their brutal oppression, jurisdictions in the late colonial slave period put to death several slave women for other types of predatory killings. Maria Glass, a free black (quadroon) woman of property, lived with her husband John Glass, a deserter from the British army, on a small farm near Baton Rouge. Touted as one of the most gruesome cases in colonial Louisiana, Maria Glass tortured to death a 15-year-old white indentured servant girl named Mary Emily Davis belonging to William Walker. The witnesses against Maria Glass included whites, free blacks, slaves, and three Choctaw Indians who testified that she often brutally whipped young Davis. Three slave men helped Maria bury Davis. A Baton Rouge judge sentenced Glass to a gruesome death in July 1781: "to have her right hand cutt off under the Gallous, then immediately to be hanged ... and when cutt down, her head to be severed ... and stuck up upon a pole at her former residence ... and her right hand to be nailed to the same Post." For his complicity, authorities sentenced John Glass to five years in the fortress prison of San Juan de Ulua.[63]

Slave women reacted to their oppression by committing property offenses in the late colonial slave period. Arson was a crime appealing to slave women in late colonial slavery since they "did not have the physical strength to confront their white enemies," and arson was a "powerful way to deprive whites of their property and injure their economic well-being."[64] Slave women burned their master's houses, jails, shops, wheat stacks, and agricultural buildings such as mills and barns. Slave women were 30 percent of slaves convicted of arson in colonial Virginia. Accordingly, this figure "gives some perspective on the method these women employed to counter the power of their masters."[65] Maryland officials executed Jenny and Grace, two slave women belonging to Joseph Galloway, for arson in 1751. Accordingly, the "Justices ... had passed Sentence of Death upon Negro Jenny and Negro Grace the slaves of ... Galloway ... for willfully burning a Tobacco House belonging to the said Galloway; It is ordered ... that Warrants issue for their Execution."[66] Charleston County officials in South Carolina burned to death two unidentified slave women belonging to Childermas Croft in June 1754 "for setting fire to their master's dwelling house and the outbuildings, all of which were destroyed."[67]

Slave woman Rose belonging to the Rabour household hanged in Halifax County, North Carolina, for house-burning in November 1766. New York burned to death an unidentified slave woman to Nathaniel Smith for arson resulting in a murder sometime in 1771. Slave woman Sitty belonging to Johannes Hellis burned at the stake in March 1774 after confessing that the devil possessed her to set fire to her owner's barn. Authorities executed an unidentified slave woman to William Crafts by an unknown means for arson of Mr. Craft's house in November 1774. Maryland executed an unidentified slave woman in 1776 "for destroying by fire her master's house, his outhouses, and tobacco house."[68] Cumberland County in Pennsylvania hanged slave woman Sucky for arson of her master's property in July 1780 though Sucky's codefendant, a white woman named Margaret Matthews, received a pardon from colonial governor John Dickinson. Virginia hanged Violet belonging to Sawyer in 1780 for burning Sawyer's house; the August County court that convicted Violet demanded that her "severed head was to remain on display on a pole near Staunton."[69] Dinah, a slave woman to Peter Damon, hanged in Somerset County, New Jersey, in October 1788 for poisoning Damon's wife and burning down his barn. Fifteen-year-old slave girl Hannah, belonging to Nicholas Summer of Newberry, South Carolina, hanged for arson in November 1814.

At least two slave women and one free black woman hanged in Michigan, New York, and Pennsylvania for property offenses in late colonial slavery. Phoebe belonging to Joseph Richardson and young Venus belonging to Catherine Ball hanged in 1764 and 1767 respectively for burglary. In June 1776, officials in Detroit arrested Ann Wyley and John Coutincineau for the robbery of a store of $50 in furs and hardware. Wyley was a free Negro woman at the time, but she was a former slave to Abbott and Finchley. Coutincineau was a French Canadian and a former servant. Authorities tried, convicted, and sentenced the two to hang for the robbery. On the execution date in March 1777, however, officials could find no hangman given the pettiness of the offense. Consequently, authorities offered to spare Wyley's life if she acted as hangman for Coutincineau. Wyley hanged Coutincineau but botched the execution so bad and "in such a clumsy fashion that the spectators were horrified at the struggles of the victim as he slowly strangled to death."[70] Officials reneged on their offer of leniency and hanged Wyley the same day.

At times, the historical record is less than forthcoming on information about slave women's crimes. Some slave women in late colonial slavery hanged for unknown or unspecified felonies. Virginia hanged an unnamed slave woman in 1751 for an unspecified felony against a white person. Beren County authorities in New Jersey hanged an unnamed slave woman belonging to Derek Day for an unknown offense against an unknown victim in May 1755. North Carolina hanged slave woman Mary for unknown offense in New Hanover County in 1757. In one case, slave woman Nan belonging to the Sutton estate hanged sometime in 1763 in Caroline County, Virginia, for an unknown crime. Slave woman Esther belonging to Blount hanged in April 1779 in North Carolina for an unknown offense. Charles City officials hanged slave woman Penelope belonging to the Copeland household for an unspecified felony in April 1781. Authorities in Dinwiddie County hanged slave woman Molly of the Clark household sometime in 1783 for an unspecified felony.

Antebellum Slavery

Jurisdictions executed 264 black women in the antebellum slave period from 1790 to the end of the Civil War in 1865 of which 250 were slave women. In May 1793, Virginia slave women Daphne and Nelly belonging to Edward Travis attacked and killed their overseer Joel Gathright who had accused the pregnant Nelly of leaving a gate open and allowing sheep to get into a cornfield. Nelly denied it, and for her brazenness, Gathright beat her severely until Daphne went to her defense. The two women beat Gathright with their fists, sticks, and rocks, leaving him dead with a crushed skull. The James City County court tried the two slave women separately, denying both the benefit of legal counsel. The court convicted Daphne and Nelly of Gathright's murder and sentenced them to hang. Daphne hanged on July 19, but authorities reprieved Nelly's hanging until October 4 after she had delivered her baby.

One of the earliest female slave executions in the antebellum period took place in 1797 in Robeson County, North Carolina. Slave woman Hannah McKay used an axe to murder her master and mistress, Stephen and Mollie Glare. Officials hanged Hannah with an unnamed black man from "the limb of a large yellow pine" near the Lumber River. Newspaper stories tell that Mollie Glare had promised Hannah her freedom upon Mollie's death, but Hannah had "grown tired of waiting and picked her chance to kill her mistress." Hannah hit Mollie in the head with an axe, put Mollie's dead body in the master bedroom, and then went in search of Stephen. Hannah told Stephen that his wife had taken ill. "When he found her in bed and she failed to answer his call, he stooped over the bed and as he did so Hannah is said to have brained him." Stephen Glare's will notes that he indeed promised to emancipate Hannah upon his death and several *Robesonian* news articles explain Hannah's murder of her owners and her subsequent hanging.[71]

Slave woman Sarah and five male confederates hanged in Virginia in 1818 after they beat their owner, Dr. Robert Berkeley, to death and then burned his body in a cabin fireplace. Shortly before Berkeley's murder one of the killers confessed to a friend "his master was a bad master and he would sooner die than serve him."[72] That same year, slave woman Caty murdered her owner Linah Harwell who had referred to Caty as "a bitch and a strumpet [prostitute]."[73] Two years later, slave woman Celia, along with Abel, axed to death Mr. and Mrs. James Powell and then set their house on fire with them in it, though they managed to save the couples infant child. Celia and Abel's owner, a man named Daughtry, hired out Abel to James Powell who repeatedly whipped Abel. Southampton County officials hanged the two for the murders in August 1821. Slave woman Susan hanged in November 1844 in Callaway County (Missouri) for axing to death her mistress, Rosa Ann King, while she napped. Susan killed King because she wanted to return to her previous owner. Slave woman Pauline belonging to the Rabbeneck household hanged in March 1846 at the "parish prison ... for cruelty to her mistress."[74]

In March 1848, slave woman Lucy belonging to Mrs. Maria Dougherty hanged for beating her owner to death. In retaliation for punishment from Dougherty for some minor infraction, Lucy set a minor fire in the Columbia Hotel where she lived with Dougherty who owned the "ramshackle wooden structure." Dougherty punished Lucy severely for setting the insignificant fire and Lucy swore vengeance against her. Lucy made good on her threat, authorities found Dougherty's body floating in an underground brick cistern with her head crushed from repeated blows from a club. Lucy admitted killing Dougherty and vowed she would do it again. Indicted for murder, Judge Peter Gray assigned counsel to defend Lucy, but a jury found her guilty and Judge Gray sentenced Lucy to death by hanging. Sheriff Westerlage hanged Lucy shortly after noon. Joseph Dougharty requested that the Texas legislature pay him $460 in reimbursement for the execution of his property.[75] Lucy was the first woman hanged in Texas and the only woman ever hanged in Galveston County.

Jasper County Superior Court Judge Robert V. Hardeman in Georgia sentenced slave woman Ailey to hang in April 1854 for the strangulation murder of her mistress, Mrs. Edna McMichael, in November 1853. Edna McMichael was 8 months pregnant at the time. Reportedly, Ailey had been weaving when Edna threatened to punish Ailey if she did not repair several broken stitches and then slapped her. "Ailey stood up, grabbed her mistress by the throat, covered her nose and mouth, and threw her to the floor, holding her there for some time."[76] Ailey confessed to killing Edna to two jailers who later testified against Ailey. There was some speculation that Edna's husband Elijah may have conspired with his slaves to kill his wife. In any event, Ailey hanged for the crime. Also in Georgia, three women were among five slaves hanged in the summer of 1860 in Laurens County for the strangulation death of their owner William Rogus while he slept off a night of drinking. While slave woman Nelly stood watch outside Rogus' bedroom, Dick, Caroline, Josephine, and Bibb grabbed Rogus from his bed, choked him to death with a cord, and then "planted a bottle of laudanum on the bed, to create the impression that Rogus had died from a drug overdose. The group went back to the field and pretended that nothing had happened."[77]

Slave women were vicious in killing their white oppressors. Morris County officials in New Jersey hanged 15-year-old Jane Huff, a slave girl belonging to 62-year-old Sarah Hight in May 1837. Sarah "nagged and scolded Jane about almost everything" and at times "struck Jane with household objects." Jane was often indifferent to Sarah's concerns and disobeyed her orders prohibiting Jane to see her young boyfriend. One night after Sarah had fallen asleep in a chair, Jane hit Sarah between the eyes with a fire poker severely stunning her. Jane then dragged Sarah over to a fireplace where meat was boiling in a kettle, removed the meat, and then thrusted Sarah's head into the boiling water—"Jane did not release her grip until Sarah Hight's head was cooked like a lobster."[78] In March 1860, Essex County officials in Virginia hanged two young slave women named Ann and Eliza for killing their elderly master Dr. William S. Croxton ostensibly for chastising them. The two women confessed that while their master used a grinding stone in the kitchen, Eliza struck him with a hoe from behind and Ann then seized an axe and struck Croxton with a blow to the head. The two women then threw his body into the kitchen fire that they kept burning strong all day. Authorities found among the ashes pieces of human bone, a jack knife, spectacles, and buttons.

Eighteen-year-old slave woman Chloe hanged in Cumberland County, Pennsylvania, in July 1801 for murdering the two young daughters of her owners Andrew and Mary Carothers. On a Saturday afternoon in January of that year, Chloe drowned four-year-old Lucetta Carothers in a nearby creek, and on the next Saturday, she drowned six-year-old Polly Carothers in the same creek. Chloe was mentally retarded and emotionally unstable, the young woman was so maltreated as a child that she was unmanageable; Chloe had several different masters over the years. Authorities tried Chloe for the two murders before the county Court of Oyer and Terminer that found her guilty and sentenced her to death by hanging. Chloe confessed to the killings to Reverend James Smith who visited Chloe in jail just days before her scheduled execution. To one commentator, the Court most likely ignored Chloe's cognitive disabilities, that before her arrest Mrs. Carothers beat Chloe daily with a cowhide whip while stripped naked, and that Chloe had no legal counsel present during her trial. Below is a rephrased statement by Chloe concerning the killings later printed in a local newspaper:

> The reason why I killed them was not because I had any spite or malice against them; on the contrary, I loved them both. My motive was this: I knew that the children were compelled by my mistress to give information respecting some parts of my conduct for which I was severely corrected far beyond the demerit of the fault. To cut off this means of information was the first end I promised myself but my second and greatest motive was to bring all the misery I possibly could upon the family—and particularly upon my mistress.... I entirely forgot what I had done until about an hour after, being at the run, above where she lay, my master calling to me to know if Lucetta was with me? I answered no. This was the first of my recollecting what I had done! I was much whipped by my master to extort a confession but I was much more lashed by my own conscience. At length I confessed and was committed. On my trial, I cried Not Guilty though still my conscience spoke within me to the contrary. The voice of the blood of two innocent children cries against me from the ground. Is my sin too great for the mercy of God to pardon? I trust that His unbounded goodness will not suffer me to perish.[79]

Kingston County officials in New York executed 16-year-old Dayon belonging to Abraham Bruyn in July 1803 for killing her master's infant child because she was angry over having to care for the child. In another case, Missouri hanged a 16-year-old slave girl named Mary when she confessed to beating and drowning Vienna Jane Brinker, one of her owner's children, in September 1837 because she did not want to be sold. Virginia hanged slave woman Jane Williams in September 1852 for slashing to death with a hatchet the wife and infant of her master Joseph P. Winston while they slept. The Winston's badly mistreated Jane and had threatened to sell Jane without also selling her child. A newspaper at the time characterized Jane as "a fiend" and "a wretched murderess" and that she would die "without the smallest particle of sympathy from any human being possessed of the ordinary feelings of justice."[80] An estimated 6,000 people watched Jane's hanging. Her husband John died alongside her for the same crime although Jane denied her husband's involvement in the killings claiming that he was asleep at the time she committed the killings. The state compensated Joseph Winston $500 for his property.

Joseph and Anne Wynn pleaded to the General Assembly of North Carolina in December 1823 for reimbursement of expenses incurred from the jailing, prosecution, conviction, and execution of slave woman Vina. Along with two slave male accomplices Charles and Jack, Vina murdered the Wynn's young daughter Mary on the day after Christmas in 1822. All three slaves hanged in Tyrell, North Carolina, in September 1823.[81] The Hustings Court of Richmond in Virginia authorized the hanging Margaret Ann Hutter, a 20-year-old mulatto slave belonging to Mrs. Mary M. Butt, in early December 1863 for the beating death of Francis Deane Tardy, the infant child of Mr. Samuel C. Tardy. Another slave woman testified against Margaret, but Margaret denied the accusation and blamed the child's death on the woman who testified against her.

Slave women committed predatory murders in the antebellum period. In September 1795, the Court of Common Pleas for South Carolina affirmed the conviction of a black woman named Arden for the murder of a Spanish seaman named Jewets. A county court had tried Arden separately from her accomplice, Campbell, and found that she was guilty of murder for stabbing Jewets in the throat and chest with a pair of scissors. A jury found Campbell guilty of manslaughter for severely beating the victim with a club or stick. The court postponed Arden's hanging after she claimed to be pregnant. A matron of 12 women found her not pregnant and immediately executed Arden.

In a later case, Dallas County officials in Texas tried, convicted, and sentenced to death slave woman Jane Elkins for killing her employer John Windom, a widower with two children, with an axe to the head as he slept in 1853. The historical record reveals little of the events surrounding Elkins' crime other then she worked for the victim as a house servant. Elkins was indifferent to her predicament and slept through much of her trial, and upon her conviction, Judge John H. Reagan sentenced her to death. On the night of her hanging members of a medical fraternity exhumed Elkins' body "for the grisly purpose of serving as a medical cadaver."[82] In early May 1829, New York hanged a black Manhattan tavern girl named Catharine Cashiere for stabbing to death another black woman named Susan Anthony in a scuffle.

In at least one case, a black woman convict and her white male confederate committed murder, Esther Foster hanged in Franklin County, Ohio, in February 1844 for murdering a white female inmate named Louisa White who she beat to death with a fire shovel while serving a prison sentence at the Ohio State Penitentiary. Years later a newspaper reported a bizarre aspect of Esther's execution: "The Foster woman was not mentally bright and the chronicles of those days tell that she sold her body to a surgeon for all the candy she could eat from the time of the making of the bargain until she was hanged."[83] Some claim that Esther's killing of Louisa White was not premeditated and therefore the county court should not have convicted her of first-degree murder. In another case, Judge Henry Goldthwaite determined that Nancy, a slave woman, hang in Montgomery County, Alabama, in March 1844 for assaulting with intent to kill Mary Beasley, a white woman.

Slave women often acted in concert with male slaves in response to white oppression. Some 48 percent of slave women executed in colonial and antebellum slavery involved multiple executions occurring on the same day for the same crime. Slave women confederates were usually one or two slave men. For instance, Virginia hanged Winney and her accomplice Phill for murdering their master John Knox "most barbarously" near Fredericksburg in July 1769. In several multiple execution cases slave women acted with one or two other slave women to commit murder or poisoning in retaliation for their mistreatment from white owners. In Virginia, Chesterfield County officials hanged Creasy and Sall for killing their mistress Mrs. Morrisett who had been repeatedly violent toward Creasy. Both female slaves earned reprieves in April 1806 due to their pregnancies, yet hanged in May. Melvaine, a female slave belonging to Florentine Frivaz, and Melvaine's slave brother Mango belonging to William Elien Kinair, hanged in February 1855 in the St. Charles Parish, Louisiana, jail yard for killing young Wesley Latham, the son of the overseer of the plantation of Mr. Lanfear. Frivaz was engaged to Latham, and Melvaine feared that Latham would usurp her authority in the household.

Scholars have identified several cases of multiple executions where authorities hanged groups of slaves (four or more persons) at the same time for the same crime—referred to as "mass legal executions." Some of these multiple execution cases involved slave women. Virginia hanged four male slaves and a slave woman named Poll belonging to Bobbitt for murder in January 1779. In antebellum North Carolina, Wayne County officials hanged four male slaves and burned to death an unknown slave woman belonging to Jernegan for slave revolt in 1805.

In August 1829, while traders led some 100 slave men, women, and children from Maryland to points south for sale, two of the slave men abruptly dropped their shackles that they had filed through and began fighting as a pretense to attacking and killing the traders. Upon recapturing the entire group of slaves, the circuit court tried, convicted, and sentenced six of the leaders of the uprising to hang for the murder of the traders. Among them was a slave woman named Dinah who was "pregnant and quick with child." The court delayed her execution until the delivery of her child, and on May 25, 1830, Dinah hanged in the courthouse yard at Greensup, Kentucky. South Carolina hanged four slave men and two slave women, Rhodie and Silvy belonging to Witherspoon, for murder in Darlington County in October 1861.

Slave women account for all female executions in the United States for arson, assault, attempted arson, and petty treason. Poisoning and arson, however, were the most prevalent methods slave women used to kill their white oppressors and destroy property unjustly gained through slave labor. Some alleged poisonings and related attempted murders by slave women resulted from unintentional acts, however; even if poisoning was "well-suited to women's resistance because of their duties as cooks and nurses on the plantation."[84] Cases of poisoning typically involved an accusation of poisoning food prepared by slave women for the owner's family that mostly resulted from a lack of safe food preparation methods than intentional acts of harm. Other cases involved slaves unknowingly administering poisonous medicine or unlawfully administering medicines.

Poisoning slave masters as resistance to their oppression warranted the death penalty for slave women. Common law classified poisoning one's master as *petit treason*, a capital offense. Poisoning of masters and master's families was more prevalent in the antebellum period where execution inventories show mostly southern jurisdictions executing numerous slave women for poisoning. Slave women were roughly a third of slave executions for poisoning in the period, although the rate of slave women executions for poisoning was significantly lower outside of Virginia. Schwarz, for instance, identifies 179 slaves tried for poisoning whites in colonial Virginia; authorities acquitted 28 of these slaves, but court records reveal that colonial officials actually executed 14 slaves for poisoning, four of whom were women.

In 1793, Sheriff Archibald Griffin of Nash County petitioned the North Carolina legislature for fees he incurred in hanging slave woman Beck belonging to Sarah Taylor for poisoning her husband and two sons.[85] Even an attempted poisoning of a slave master warranted execution. In June 1764, for instance, Calvert County officials executed slave Betty along with two accomplices named Sambo and Toby for attempting to murder their owner Mr. Smith and his wife by poisoning. Interestingly, the court gave the slave owners in this case a choice to either export the slaves out of the province (a common practice in colonial America called "transportation") or for the state to execute the slave—the owners chose to execute Betty and her accomplices.

In February 1806, Charlotte authorities in Virginia hanged slave woman Fanny for poisoning. Jefferson Parish in Louisiana hanged slave woman Lucy belonging to Bouligny in November 1832 for poisoning. Other cases of slave women executions for poisoning include Prince Edward County authorities in Virginia hanging slave women Renah and Fanny belonging to Dawson in January 1832. In 1833, Mississippi hanged 18-year-old slave woman Nancy for poisoning two members of her owner's family. Maryland hanged Auriela Chase, a slave woman, in Baltimore City just before Christmas in 1833 for poisoning. In 1849, Brunswick County officials in Virginia hanged slave woman Eliza belonging to Griffin, and slave woman Roberta belonging to Ezell, for poisoning. Louisiana also hanged slave woman Mily belonging to Fox in July 1851 for poisoning. In October 1858, Harris County officials in Georgia hanged slave woman Sarah belonging to Benjamin Williams for poisoning the family's breakfast with strychnine she had acquired from her white lover William Howell. Williams whipped Sarah into confessing to the crime which itself became a much disputed legal argument in later court proceedings. Sarah's case is unique given the interracial nature of the crime—"a free white man and a black slave woman had conspired to kill a white family."[86] Justice authorities in Franklin County, Kentucky, also hanged slave woman Frances belonging to Berry for poisoning in September 1860.

Slave jurisdictions executed juvenile female slaves for poisoning as well. Virginia hanged slave woman Chasity, along with male slave accomplice George, both belonging to Lawson for poisoning in October 1803. Missouri hanged 16-year-old Rosanne Keen for poisoning her owner, Enos Seeley, a former clerk for Cumberland County. Rosanne reportedly poisoned both Mr. and Mrs. Seeley with arsenic borrowed from a neighbor that she mixed with butter and served to the couple. Both victims became seriously ill but only Mr. Seeley succumbed to the poison. Authorities believed Seeley died of natural causes, but when a neighbor told authorities that she had given the poison to young Rosanne, suspicions escalated and officials exhumed Seeley's body. Analysis confirmed Seeley had died from arsenic poisoning, and officials tried, convicted, and sentenced Rosanne to death for murder. Local authorities hanged Rosanne in a jail yard in April 1844. Rosanne apparently was motivated to kill the Seeley's so she could steal jewelry and possessions. Some argue that Rosanne was "deficient in intellect."

Women were roughly a third of slave executions for arson, and mostly southern jurisdictions hanged or burned to death slave women for the offense. New York hanged Nelly belonging to Daniel Braine for burning Jeremiah Vanderbilt's house in October 1790. Slave woman Creese to the Fisher household hanged in Northampton County, Virginia, in March 1789 for arson. Fires in Albany, New York, destroyed 26 houses and did more than $200,000 in damage in 1793. Three slaves were involved in setting the fires including two female slave teenagers: 12-year-old Bett belonging to Philip Van Rensselaer, and 14-year-old Dean belonging to Vokert A. Douw. Both hanged in March 1794 and their accomplice, a male slave named Pompey belonging to Mathew Visscher, hanged a month later. West Virginia hanged slave woman Millay belonging to the Robe household in September 1798 for arson. St. Louis hanged an unidentified slave woman belonging to Pierre Chouteau, the patriarch of the most prominent French family in Missouri at time, for "wilfully and maliciously burning her owners dwelling, barn, or stable" in 1805.[87] Scott County officials hanged slave woman Nancy belonging to Rhodes for arson in September 1808. Young black servant woman Rose Butler hanged before some 10,000 spectators in July 1819 in New York for an attempted arson of her mistress's house. Rose was employed by William Morris. Rose had apparently scattered hot coals on three steps of the stairwell, but the court was more concerned with her intent to burn the house than the amount of actual damage. In December 1829, Richmond County hanged slave woman Jenny belonging to Jones for arson, and six months later in June 1830, the same county officials hanged slave woman Cinda belonging to Lubbock for arson. Caroline County authorities in Virginia hanged slave woman Malina in 1861 along with her confederate Andrew for burning their master's barn, stable, corn house, and tobacco house.

Most female slave insurrections amounted to day-to-day resistance that took on a variety of forms, including "malingering; self mutilation; suicide; destruction of owner's crops, tools, and livestock; running away; or criminal activity like stealing and violent insurrection."[88] Slave women often manifested resistance to bondage by assaulting and poisoning overseers and owners, breaking tools, pilfering, and burning barns. Female slave resistance also included controlling reproductive and maternal functions such as inducing abortions and committing infanticide. One Tennessee physician confirmed that slave women used medicines, violent exercise, and external and internal manipulations as rudimentary birth control or to effect miscarriages.

Even so, jurisdictions rarely executed black women for infanticide. In most cases, slave women "killed their children because they did not want them be slaves," and thus, infanticide was part slave women's resistance to their oppression in slavery.[89] Of some 118 female slave executions identified by Streib, seven slave women murdered their own children. Schwarz identified three slave women sentenced to death for infanticide during the antebellum period in Virginia but none during the colonial period. In Missouri, historical records show that Annice drowned five slave children belonging to her owner Jeremiah Prior. A Clay County court found Annice guilty of pushing "one Ann a negro child slave ... into a certain collection of water of the depth of five feet and there choked, suffocated, and drowned of which ... the said Ann instantly died."[90] Annice also drowned slave children Phoebe, Nancy, Bill, and Nelly. Five-year-old Bill and two-year-old Nelly were Annice's children. Annice hanged in August 1828. Undoubtedly, Annice wanted to deprive her master the value of the children; she was the only slave woman put to death in Missouri for infanticide.

Hannah Miller hanged in Chester County, Pennsylvania, in August 1805 for infanticide; she is the only confirmed black woman hanged after 1700 in a northern state for infanticide. Some 2,000 spectators watched her execution. Southern states executed most black women put to death for infanticide. Sussex County officials in Virginia hanged slave woman Poll belonging to Bobbitt for infanticide in January 1779. A Virginia court also found an 18-year-old slave woman guilty of murdering her newborn infant and sentenced her to hang in 1818. Kentucky hanged an unknown slave woman belonging to Rumsey for infanticide in 1812. Servant woman Elizabeth Moore, "a mulatto," hanged in May 1809 in York County for poisoning to death her nine-year-old son who she reportedly wanted in Heaven with his younger sister whom Moore murdered years earlier. Moore was born a slave in York County but ran away to Maryland where she became a free domestic. "She had a son by another man whom she had placed in an almshouse and for whom she seemed to have had a distorted feeling of affection and concern."[91] While in jail awaiting execution, Elizabeth became pregnant and delivered the child before her execution. White recounts several cases where slave women committed infanticide out of concern for the well-being of their children. In one case, an Alabama slave woman killed her baby because her master was the father; her mistress knew it and treated the child callously. The slave mother confessed to killing her baby claiming that she wanted to save the child from further cruelty. One slave woman killed her newborn to keep her master from selling the child as he had her other three children. In another case, Wyat Smith sought compensation for his female slave Cela that Charleston authorities executed in April 1820 for infanticide. Records of the General Assembly for South Carolina reveal that in 1824 Ellis Palmer solicited for reimbursement for the execution of slave woman Anaca for the murder of her two children.[92] Slave woman Milley belonging to Hanley hanged in Patrick County, Virginia, for infanticide in 1826.

White people generally interpreted black women's killing of their own children as evidence that slave women lacked maternal feelings. This is surprising when one considers that white females committed far higher rates of infanticide than black females. Infanticide was mostly an aberrant behavior of slave mothers, and in most cases, infant deaths were accidental with mothers' inadvertently overlaying and suffocating infants while sleeping. Smothering accounted for more than 60,000 slave infant deaths during the antebellum period. This explanation troubles slave historians as well as contemporary medical practitioners, however. Johnson suggests that most reported cases of slave mothers suffocating their children might have been "crib deaths," or what the medical community today refers to as Sudden Infant Death Syndrome (SIDS).[93] Malnutrition and planters overworking pregnant slave women surely contributed to infant sudden deaths. In some cases, slave women rendered psychotic raised reasonable doubts as to the culpability of women for killing their children. A Powhatan County Court in Virginia sentenced Jenny to death, for instance, for drowning her three young children even though the judge found her insane. Lucy, a 22-year-old slave woman belonging to Thomas Balton, believed to have killed her mulatto child, actually abandoned the child or it was born dead and not intentionally killed. Frantic about running away from her abusive master, one Virginia slave woman killed her four-year-old child. Clearly, as Schwarz points out, "slavery played a crucial role in the paternity, birth, or death of these unfortunate children. Slavery was like an unindicted co-conspirator or a perpetrator in many infanticides committed by slave women."[94]

Runaway slaves posed a far more menacing problem to southern planters. Masters imposed harsh punishments to runaways including branding recaptured slaves. Slaves often ran away from abusive masters to "avoid punishment or to get revenge for punishments already received."[95] Slave women were far less likely to runaway even from abusive masters because of their "restricted mobility associated with childbearing and childrearing responsibilities."[96] Most fugitive slaves were between 16 and 35 years old, the ages when most slave women were either pregnant, nursing an infant, or caring for a young child. Even if a slave woman fled the confines of slavery by running away, she rarely left without her children. As White notes, "Of the same one hundred fifty-one fugitive women advertised for in the 1850 New Orleans newspapers, none was listed as having run away without her children."[97]

Sexual control over slave women by white owners was critical to slavery and owners relied upon the routine sexual abuse of slave women as much as they did other forms of brutality. Slave law disregarded slave women's rights to control their own bodies, and as a result, slave owners sexually attacked females with legal immunity; the rape of a slave woman was not a crime. One scholar explains, "Forced sexual exploitation of the black woman under slavery was no offhand enterprise. Total control over her reproductive system meant a steady supply of slave babies, and slave children."[98] Also in place was the notion that "sexual coercion was an essential dimension of the social relations between slave master and slave—the right claimed by slave owners over the bodies of female slaves was a direct expression of their presumed property right over black people as a whole."[99]

A staunch reality of slave life for bonded females was that they were at once agricultural workers and the primary mode for increasing domestic slave populations, especially after Congress prohibited traders from importing slaves after 1808. Planters valued slave women that produced children; child-producing female slaves were generally worth 25 percent more than were childless slave women. Planters considered female slaves *breeders*, but not *mothers* since slave women had no legal control over their own children. Masters considered a slave woman a "good breeder" if she had 15 to 20 pregnancies during her productive years. Still, planters expected pregnant slave women to maintain their normal work schedules and production yields. Planters did not exempt pregnant women or mothers with infants from fieldwork. Consequently, miscarriages among slave women were common and infant mortality high. Slave mothers often left their infants lying on the ground next to them as they worked while other mothers worked with their babies fastened to their backs. Some slave women left their infants in the care of young children or older women, and nursing mothers were frequently unable to feed their babies and suffered the excruciating pain of swollen breasts. Undaunted, overseers regularly punished nursing mothers that fell behind in their work. As one slave narrative explains, "I have seen the overseer beat them with raw hide, so that the blood and milk flew mingled from their breasts."[100] Planters treated disobedient pregnant slave women harshly but somewhat guardedly to ensure the survival of unborn infants. One account explains that "a woman who gives offense in the field, and is large in a family way, is compelled to lie down over a hole made to receive her corpulency, and is flogged with the whip or beat with a paddle."[101] One can only speculate at the numbers of slave women inadvertently put to death by such cruelty.

Given the occupational distribution of plantation slaves in the United States, planters regularly consigned slave women to domestic work as house servants; some 17 percent of women slaves were domestics. Consequently, many slave women worked in close proximity to their white owners who often sexually abused and raped them. Sexual relations with white owners were a routine feature of life for slave women that were "both deeply traumatic and destructive of family life."[102] Most slave women victimized by white sexual aggression were unmarried, and sexual assaults on slave girls as young as 12 years old was common. Married slave women largely escaped white rape because white men knew slave husbands would revenge the rape of their wives; they "would rather die than stand idly by."[103]

White rape of bondwomen was pervasive in the southern slavocracy. One crude measure of the prevalence of white rape of slave women is that the father was white in *one out of every six* female-headed households, roughly 10 percent of slave children in 1860 were mulatto. Owners' perversions toward slave women rendered them powerless not only to resist the sexual advances of masters, but also those of masters' sons and overseers. One southern planter vulgarly declared that white rape of slave women explained the "absence of Southern prostitution and the purity of white women."[104] Actually, white and mulatto prostitution was widespread during slavery, but there is no evidence that slave women were prostitutes.

Slave women often reacted violently to sexualized brutality, what one historian refers to as "soul murders." Accordingly, the sexual abuses of young slave children often lead to "psychological depression, hatred of the abuser, or other forms of at risk behavior" that resulted in their killing abusers. Today, the legal and medical communities denote such victimization as "rape trauma," "battered women syndromes," and "post-traumatic stress disorders."[105] Celia's hanging in Missouri was one such case. Seventy-year-old widower Robert Newsom bought 14-year-old Celia at an 1850 auction in neighboring Audrain County and forced sexual relations upon her immediately and repeatedly. Newsom had fathered two children, Vina and Jane, with Celia by the time she was 19 years old. One night in August 1855, Newsom went to Celia's cabin to abuse her. Celia was pregnant for the third time by Newsome and was very ill when he approached her. Celia struck Newsom with a stick, killing him, and afterwards Celia burned Newsom's body in her fireplace and hid bone fragments under her cabin floor. Celia disposed of the ashes with the help of Newsome's young grandson. At her trial, defense lawyers offered legal reasoning why Celia had a right to defend herself against her master's assault. The trial judge, William Augustus Hall, made it clear that Celia did not have that right. To the court, Celia had no sexual rights over her own body because she was Newsom's property and she ought to have submitted to Newsom's demands. Judge Hall instructed the jury find Celia guilty of murder, "If Newsom was in the habit of having intercourse with the defendant who was his slave and went to her cabin on the night he was killed to have intercourse with her or for any other purpose."[106] Accordingly, Celia had no legal defense to killing Newsom and the jury must find her guilty of the murder. The jury found Celia liable for Newsom's murder and she hanged four days before Christmas in 1855. In a similar case, incestual victimization provoked one slave woman to kill her master, Jacob Bryan, who she battered to death with a hoe. Bryan was the slave woman's father and the father of her four children.

The rape charge also demonstrates the status difference between white women and slave women. Scholars can find no reported cases of a white man prosecuted for the rape or attempted rape of a slave woman. Thus, it is not surprising to find absent in the historical record white prosecutions for raping slave women. One reason for the dearth of such cases was that southern slave law prohibited slaves from testifying against whites in court. Essentially, slave women had no rights that white men could violate. What's more, as Tarpley points out, "the assumption of promiscuous Negro sexuality and the assertion of white male dominance over blacks in the sexual sphere would have inclined white male prosecutors not to prosecute, and white male juries not to convict."[107] White men generally viewed black women as "jezebels," "sexual temptresses," and "the embodiment of female evil and sexual lust." White masters also worried little about fathering mulatto children since state laws defined children born to slave women as slaves. Finkelman explains that rather than discouraging relations between slave women and white men, and discouraging miscegenation, such laws had the opposite effect and encouraged white men to sexually exploit slave women:

> By predetermining the status of a possible offspring, white men might be less concerned about the outcome of their sexual adventures. Slave owners were unlikely to bring bastardy charges against white fathers, because the masters after all, would gain the value of a new slave. Furthermore, the main social (as opposed to moral) reason for bastardy laws was to make sure that illegitimate children would be fed, clothed, housed, educated, and prepared for adult life. The 1662 law obviated all these problems for the bastard children of slave women and white men: the owner of the woman would pick up the tab, and be handsomely recompensed by the value of the new slave. Thus, rather than discouraging immoral relations between slave women and white men, as well as discouraging miscegenation, this law could have easily led to the opposite result.[108]

The gendered-racism of slavery also empowered white mistresses to brutalize slave women sexually involved with their husbands. In many slaveholding households, white women whose husbands sexually assaulted female slaves tortured and persecuted slave women. In one case,

> a white mistress returned home unexpectedly from an outing, opened the doors of her dressing room, and discovered her husband raping a thirteen-year-old slave girl. She responded by beating the girl and locking her in a smokehouse. The girl was whipped daily for several weeks. When older slaves pleaded on the child's behalf and dared to suggest that the white master was to blame, the mistress simply replied, "She'll know better in the future. After I've done with her, she'll never do the like again through ignorance."[109]

Among the accounts of beatings and whippings suffered by slave women, William Byrd recounts how his wife "cause[d] little Jenny to be burned with a hot iron."[110] Silvia Dubois recalled the abuse she suffered at the hands of her mistress, "Why, she'd level me with anything she could get hold of—club, stick of wood, tongs, fire-shovel, knife, ax, hatchet."[111] One scholar recites the story of a mistress who beat her cook's head in with a fire shovel because she had burned the dinner.

There was little regional variation in slave women executions in the colonial and antebellum slave periods. Mostly southern states hanged and burned to death capital offending female slaves. One reason for southern dominance in slave women executions is that slavery mostly flourished in the South after 1790; Virginia alone accounted for 38 percent of all female slave execution. Jurisdictional authority for female slave executions lied mostly with military officials in the early colonial period and almost exclusively with state authorities in the antebellum period. Actual executions took place in county facilities, mostly in jail courtyards. Black women suffered uniquely under the institutional confines of colonial and antebellum slavery. The historical record makes clear that slave women fought back viciously against the sexualized brutality of white masters by killing their owners, members of their owners' families, and destroying their owners' property. Slave women responded to the violence of white masters by intentionally aborting pregnancies and at times killing their own children. The retort of the state to the rebellious undertakings of brutalized slave women was judicial murder.

At least four Virginia slave women hanged in the second period of female executions for unspecified felonies. Fauquier County officials hanged slave woman Molly belonging to the Marshall household in July 1791 for an unspecified felony against a white person. In addition, King George County officials hanged slave woman Nan belonging to Smith in April 1801 for an unspecified felony against an unknown person. In other early cases, slave woman Phoebe belonging to Joseph Richardson hanged in Chester County, Pennsylvania, in 1764 for "burglariously entering the house of Thomas Barnard and stealing divers goods."[112] Richardson received

£55 for the loss of his chattel property. New York authorities hanged young slave woman Venus belonging to Catherine Ball in February 1767 for burglary and stealing "several articles from the house of a Mr. Forbes, a resident of New York City."[113] As late as March 1865, South Carolina hanged 17-year-old slave girl Amy in part for stealing "linens, sheets, pillow cases, flour, sugar, lard, and some furniture" from her master Major A.C. Spain. More likely, Darlington townspeople ushered Amy to the gallows for openly proclaiming her satisfaction of the approaching Union army when she clasped her hands and shouted, "Bless the Lord the Yankees have come!"

Reconstruction

Jurisdictions executed far fewer black women in the immediate postbellum period than in the previous decades of colonial and antebellum slavery. Authorities in southern states put to death seven black females for murder, including the killing of white children, and in one case a predatory murder against another black. The dramatic decrease in black women executions during Reconstruction resulted from what some scholars insist was a period of positive social relations and a growing complacency in criminal justice policy toward "dangerous classes." There is little historical evidence supporting this proposition, however. In fact, emancipation ushered in one of the most turbulent and violent periods in United States racial history. As law professor Denise Morgan points out, "The system of racial segregation and subordination that prevailed in the United States from the end of the Civil War through the middle of the twentieth century was maintained by the ever present threat and the consistent reality of violence."[114] Although the demise of slavery brought about critical developments in black "political rights," blacks found improving their "social rights" a far more formidable task. In effect, legal emancipation did not move southern society appreciably toward racial equality during Reconstruction; the South remained as segregated with a strict racial caste order as it had during slavery. The Reconstruction Amendments had introduced an ambiguity into black-white race relations, and keeping "blacks in their place" had become more difficult to enforce and often resulted in chaotic and unpredictable forms of racial domination over blacks. To white planters, the loss of nearly four million bonded workers profoundly threatened the South's economic and political viability, and immediately after emancipation, southern states limited black rights by adopting laws similar to those used to regulate blacks in slavery. Poor whites viewed the gains made by blacks during Reconstruction as rebellious and launched violent retaliations against blacks. By 1866, all southern states had enacted civil and criminal regulations known as *black codes* to regulate black lives with Mississippi and South Carolina enacting the first and harshest codes. Southern states sought to keep blacks subordinated to whites by imposing these discriminatory measures precluding blacks from voting, serving on juries, and testifying in court cases involving whites.

One result of the continued subjugation of blacks in this period was the loss of their labor value after emancipation. But southern justice systems quickly recognized the pecuniary benefit of black prisoners as lessees to private and public enterprises, thereby taking advantage of the exception in the Thirteenth Amendment allowing involuntary servitude as punishment for crime. Black prisoners comprised large numbers (90 percent) of leased prison work gangs for mining and railroad interests and on prison farms that was unprecedented in slavery. These prisoners included black women convicted of contrived charges, which along with their male counterparts "were routinely starved and brutalized by corporations, farmers, government officials, and small-town businessmen intent on achieving the most lucrative balance between the productivity of captive labor and the cost of sustaining them."[115] Fewer black female executions during the period resulted from the increase in black women prison populations in southern states immediately following the Civil War. Before emancipation, southern states rarely incarcerated slaves since planters' production needs made few slaves eligible for public punishment.

In the immediate aftermath of the war, however, newly freed black women swelled the ranks of southern prison populations with black females comprising between 40 to 70 percent of females committed to southern penitentiaries. Black female incarceration rates increased because many black women had significant contact with whites as domestic servants and housemaids thus rendering them especially prone to crime accusations. Although imprisoned black women committed mostly property crimes, violent crimes were still common among black females. Many black women confined as prisoners on convict farms went to work as servants and housekeepers to local residents and escaped the daily terror of overseer's punishment. Still, black women often endured horrifying punishments such as "the horse." There, prison guards forced women to straddle "an ax-handle-size peg driven into a vertical wooden stake. Guards fastened their victims to the stake so they could not squirm away and let gravity press the peg into their genitals."[116]

The reduction in the execution of black women in the immediate postbellum period is also attributable to the increase in white violence directed toward black people as a related means of imposing corporal punishment. Black lynchings became commonplace during this period. Racial violence was an insidious and pervasive feature of everyday life for blacks with southern whites employing the selective and deliberate strategies of such vigilante groups as the Ku Klux Klan, the Red Shirts, and the Knights of the White Camellias to terrorize blacks. Assaulting, murdering, lynching, politically repressing, and executing black men, women, and children continued throughout the postbellum period. One scholar notes that the Klan killed as many as 20,000 people from 1868 to 1871.[117]

The vulnerability of black women to white male sexual violence was actually greater in the postbellum period than it had been during slavery. The sexual brutalization of black women continued with white men raping, shooting, scalping, and cutting off the ears of black women that resisted their sexual advances. Black women who resisted white men's sexual attacks "were frequently thrown into prison to be further victimized by a system which was a return to another form of slavery."[118] But challenging white authority in any manner was enough to garner the brutality of white terrorism. In his chronicle on the hidden history of racial cleansing in the United States, Pulitzer Prize winning author Elliot Jaspin tells that when Mary Turner threatened to swear out arrest warrants against a mob that, the day before, had lynched her husband Hayes Turner and left his body hanging for two days: "[T]he mob grabbed Mary, eight months pregnant, hung her upside down from a tree, doused her with gasoline, set her on fire, then disemboweled her and tore out her fetus. The baby made a feeble cry before a member of the mob stomped it to death."[119]

In Texas, more than 1,500 acts of violence against blacks took place between 1865 and 1868. Nearly 200 of these incidents involved the victimization of black women. Perkinson, for instance, tells of a horrific case of violence on a plantation in Huntsville. After local slaves had heard of their emancipation and celebrated with excitement and jubilation, "a white man on horseback appeared. He had a rag tied over his face and a sword, and when he rode by a Negro woman, he just leaned over in his saddle and cut her nearly half in two."[120] After liberation from slavery but in an attempt to keep black women subordinated to the racial caste system, white employers beat black women for "using insolent language," for refusing to call her employer "master," and "for crying because he whipped my mother." White mobs whipped, flogged, beat, assaulted, castrated, and murdered black children as well. Whites killed nearly 300 blacks in Caddo Parish in Louisiana between 1865 and 1876, and in 1865 alone whites killed more than 2,000 blacks including women and children near Shreveport, Louisiana. Whites set fire to an entire black settlement in 1866 and lynched 24 blacks including women and children. Rioting white mobs in cities in Tennessee and Mississippi "raped black women as they went on an antiblack rampage."[121] Mississippi, Alabama, Louisiana, and Georgia—the black belt states—had the worst lynching records.

Black female executions in the immediate aftermath of slavery attest to the systemic racist and sexist brutality suffered by black women. It was in this era that state authorities executed one of the youngest black females put to death in United States history. Henry County officials in Kentucky hanged 12-year-old servant girl Susan in February 1868 for killing Walter Graves, a two-year-old white child under her care as a babysitter. Susan confessed to the killing after the white neighbors of the Graves' threatened her with lynching. Officials arrested and tried Susan for Walter's murder. Though the trial judge rendered her confession involuntary and inadmissible given the lynching intimidation, a jury nevertheless convicted Susan for the white boy's death. Susan reportedly "writhed and twisted and jerked many times" during her hanging. Many witnesses to Susan's hanging acquired pieces of the hanging rope.

In another case, Maryland hanged 16-year-old domestic servant Mary Wallis in the jail yard in Marlboro in February 1871 for poisoning the infant child of the Read family—Albert M. Read was a clerk in the U.S. Treasury Department in Washington, D.C. Mary was born into slavery and belonged to Richard D. Hall. After the Civil War, she worked as a house servant for several families, among them the Reads. Mary reportedly poisoned the infant's milk with strychnine killing the child but hoping to blame the murder on the baby's nurse with whom Mary had difficulties. A trial jury found Mary guilty of first-degree murder, but because of her age and mental deficiency, the jury recommended leniency in sentencing Mary. But as many white trial judges did at the time, he overruled the jury's suggestion and sentenced Mary to death.

There is no public information concerning the December 1869 hanging of Sarah Jane Bradley in Sussex County, Delaware, for killing an unidentified white child. The historical record is also silent in explaining why an unnamed black servant woman, as well as young Susan and Sarah Bradley killed innocent white children. These cases of black female violence most likely resulted from what one scholar explains as higher levels of violence accenting the gendered racism of southern society that rendered black women more likely to murder. These black women undoubtedly were responding to the brutalization of whites accenting much of slavery. The violent reaction of black women to killing white children may have been individual responses to "the stress generated by their dislocation, isolation, and economic marginality."[122]

There are a few cases of black women killing their spouses in retaliation for domestic maltreatment in the decades immediately following emancipation and little information is forthcoming in the historical record about these spousal murders. One of the earliest cases of spousal murder in the period was Elizabeth Freeman's killing of her husband David. No record indicates any reason for Elizabeth slitting David's throat with a razor, the killing was most likely the predictable outcome of their acute alcoholism. Elizabeth admitted her guilt on the gallows and hanged in July 1832 in Burlington County, New Jersey, before several thousand people.[123] In another case in May 1874 involving a common law marriage, authorities in Elberton, Georgia, hanged 25-year-old Ann Hunt for an interracial murder. Ann and a white man named John R. Fortson lived together and had five children. John apparently had a romantic interest in Elizabeth Brawner against whom Ann conspired with a friend, America Burden, to murder Brawner. America gave Burden a flask of whiskey laced with strychnine, which, in turn Burden gave to Brawner who died soon after consuming the whiskey. Authorities arrested Ann and Burden and indicted John as a co-conspirator but he had left the country. The punishment dealt Burden is unclear, but Ann hanged for involvement in Brawner's murder. In still another case, Ouachita County authorities in Louisiana hanged 24-year-old Alcee Harris in November 1875 for her part in the killing of her husband Henry Harris. Alcee and Henry had been arguing and she was afraid Henry was going to kill her. Alcee convinced Toney Nellum to kill Henry with an axe. Alcee and Toney confessed to their respective parts in the killing of Henry and hanged together before some 5,000 spectators. Alcee died immediately, but Toney strangled to death because the drop was too short. Lunenburg County in Virginia in April 1881 hanged Lucinda Fowlkes in the county facility for murdering her husband with an axe "because he was mean to her and consistently beat and abused her." Newspaper reports at the time claim that Isaac Dean, with whom Lucinda was intimate, conspired with Lucinda to kill her husband.

Scholars know little of two female predatory murderers hanged in the early part of the postbellum period. A simple footnote to history shows that Lucy Purnell hanged in Worcester County, Maryland, in February 1868 for the confessed murder of a black man named Hanson Robbins with whom she and her two young daughters lived. Apparently, Robbins aggressively demanded sex from Lucy one night, she refused, and after another try at seducing her, Lucy hit Robbins in the head with a nearby tool rendering him unconscious. Lucy dragged Robbins to the side of a road, dug a whole, and buried Robbins while he was still alive.

Early Jim Crow

The execution of black women accents the brutality and violence suffered by black women in the early Jim Crow period of American race relations from 1877 to 1890. Mostly southern jurisdictions executed black women for predatory killings of white employers. Black women worked in close proximity to white employers as domestic servants and housemaids since the white urban industrial workplace excluded black women who had little or no formal education and few technical skills. The horrid manner in which southern black female domestics killed their oppressive white employers is suggestive of the way slave women killed their violent white masters.

Whites in postbellum society harbored a gross intolerance toward marginalized persons, and the legal system proved the most effective apparatus to ensuring white's social, political, and economic supremacy. Jim Crow segregation took hold as an institutional means of subordinating blacks with the collapse of Reconstruction, and by 1890 southern society had fully established the legal separation of blacks. Congress and the U.S. Supreme Court were complicit in sanctioning the institutionalization of white supremacy in the post–Reconstruction era. As Sitkoff explains:

> Congress permitted the white South to reduce blacks to a state of peonage, to disregard their civil rights, and to disenfranchise them by force, intimidation, and statute. So did the Supreme Court. Writing into the Constitution its own beliefs in the inferiority of blacks, the late–nineteenth-century high court tightened every possible shackle confining the ex-slaves.[124]

Legal separation was not limited to the Jim Crow South. Litwack describes the legal segregation governing northern blacks during the period:

> In virtually every phase of existence, Negroes found themselves systematically separated from whites. They were either excluded from railway cars, omnibuses, stagecoaches, and steamboats or assigned to special "Jim Crow" sections; they sat, when permitted, in secluded and remote corners of theaters and lecture halls; they could not enter most hotels, restaurants, and resorts, except as servants; they prayed in "Negro pews" in the white churches, and if partaking of the sacrament of the Lord's Supper, they waited until the whites had been served the bread and wine. Moreover, they were often educated in segregated schools, punished in segregated prisons, nursed in segregated hospitals, and buried in segregated cemeteries.[125]

Beginning with the *Civil Rights Cases* (1883) that struck down the provisions of the Civil Rights Act of 1875, a series of U.S. Supreme Court decisions effectively dismantled the federal civil rights protections put in place during Reconstruction and ushered in the constitutionalization of white hegemony in United States society. The court struck down the provisions of the Civil Rights Act as beyond the power of Congress to enact under the Thirteenth and Fourteenth Amendments since private discrimination was not tantamount to state action controlled by the amendments. *Plessey v. Ferguson* constitutionally recognized an 1890 Louisiana statute separating blacks and whites on passenger trains, and such cases as *Williams v. Mississippi* (1898) and *Giles v. Harris* (1903) legitimated black voting restrictions with poll taxes, literacy tests, secret ballots, multiple-box laws, and residency requirements. These judicial mandates effectively replaced laissez-faire segregation and brought about complete legal domination of black people. As a result, whites had the full force of law behind them in their social, political, and economic dominion of black people.

The social instability of Jim Crow ushered in a bloody era in United States history for black people. Legal and extralegal forms of the death penalty killed more than 8,100 black persons during the period; death penalty jurisdictions killed 4,708 black prisoners and lynch mobs killed 3,445 black victims. Rates of legal and extralegal black executions increased in southern regions where higher concentrations of blacks precipitated economic competition between the races. Regarding extralegal executions, torture, mass attendance, and burning were the three main indicators of the ritualistic character of black lynchings. The lynching mindset was pervasive among whites throughout the United States to the extent that it was "exemplary" and "symbolic." Indeed, black lynchings were a fundamentally different, socially constructed event from white lynchings since the violence waged against poor white victims seldom involved torture or mutilation. Black lynchings were augmented with brutality and ritualistic savagery and entailed "a bestiality unknown even to the most remote and uncivilized parts of the world."[126] Of the 416 blacks lynched between 1918 and 1927, white mobs burned 42 alive, burned 16 after death, and beat to death or cut to pieces eight others.

In the early postbellum period, mostly southern jurisdictions put 17 black women to death for predatory murder, robbery-murder, spousal murder, child murder, infanticide, and poisoning. Liberty County officials in Georgia hanged Ellen Osgood along with her brother Raymond for the beating death a black man named Sam Gauldin in December 1878. Apparently, Goulden went to the Osgood home to inquire about a debt that Goulden owed Simon Osgood, Ellen's father. A dispute broke out and three of Simon's sons and his daughter Ellen beat Goulden to death with sticks, fence rails, and a hoe. A jury convicted Raymond and Ellen of first degree murder and sentenced them to hang, but found the other siblings guilty of involuntary manslaughter and sentenced them to the state penitentiary. The Georgia Supreme Court affirmed the conviction and death sentence stating that Ellen Osgood inflicted unnecessary blows with clubs and hoes to a man prostrate and unable to defend himself and that the victim died as a result. Officials had to postpone the hanging because Raymond and Ellen escaped from the county jail for a short time. More revealing is the hanging death of black woman Ella Moore who hanged along with four black men (Kiddick Powell, Simon O. Guinn, Joseph King and Robert Donaldson) in the Dodge County jail yard in Georgia in October 1882 for the shooting and beating death of James Q. Harwood, a white man.

It was unusual for blacks to attack whites in the South; the South was in turmoil in the 1880s and 1890s when political and economic instability often resulted in open conflict between whites and blacks when whites mostly attacked blacks. But in the Eastman Race Riot in late summer 1892 in Dodge County, Georgia, blacks violently confronted whites. Accounts from the period explain that thousands of blacks had gathered in Eastman for a religious revival (often referred to as a "camp meeting") with many of those attending openly drinking and gambling. An argument between two black men (one named Jake Tarrapin) ensued when one of the men who had wagered his watch in a gambling game demanded its return. When Tarrapin refused to give the watch back to its owner, the man reported his lose to Marshal Pete Harrell (white) who quickly arrested Tarrapin. While escorting Tarrapin to jail, Marshal Harrell ended up in a nearby ditch and Tarrapin ran off, but the man who had complained to Marshal Harrell shot and killed Tarrapin. Blacks attending the revival became violent over the killing and mistakenly believed that Marshal Harrell had killed Tarrapin. A mob attacked Marshal Harrell and one of his deputies but they escaped unharmed. The mob became frenzied and yelled out for killing whites and burning their houses. The mob killed James Harwood who was not involved in the mêlée. Police eventually quieted the mob and began making arrests. Authorities arrested, indicted, and in a 30-day trial convicted Ella Moore and the four men with whom she hanged, as well as 17 other black men sent to prison with life sentences. Ella Moore had no appeal.

At least one black woman hanged for robbery-murder in this period. In this case, Franklin County officials in Louisiana hanged black servant woman Matilda Jones in July 1885 for her confessed role in the robbery and strangling death of her employer, 70-year-old white widow Mrs. Henrietta Cole. Her deceased husband was a county judge. One commentator reported that Jones' part in the murder was to lead three black accomplices (George Wilson, Charles Davis, and Sol Price) to the house, "showing them how to enter, and revealing where Cole kept her money, jewelry, and other valuables hidden."[127] Wilson and Davis hanged with Matilda who actually hanged herself when she fainted and fell over the edge of the scaffold strangling to death. There is no record that authorities ever apprehended Price.

Several black women hanged for spousal murder. Farm worker Matilda Carter hanged along with two black male accomplices named Eldridge Scales and Joe Hayes in Rockingham County in North Carolina in January 1882 for the murder of Matilda's husband Nash Carter. Some 5,000 people witnessed the execution. In another case, South Carolina hanged Lucinda Teasdale in June 1882 along with her half sister's husband, Anderson Singleton, for the murder of Phoebe Teasdale. Lucinda claimed she killed Phoebe in self-defense. Sheriff Southward of Henrico County in Virginia hanged Barbara Miller in September 1883 for conspiring with her paramour, Charles Henry Lee, to kill her husband. Barbara was born a slave to a well-known planter in the county and in due course married Daniel Miller, a man 20 years her senior. Charles killed Daniel with an axe and then left the body on the railroad tracks where a train so mutilated the body that it was almost unrecognizable. Barbara confessed to the killing when arrested with Charles. The county court tried Charles first, found him guilty, and sentenced him to hang a month before Barbara hanged; Barbara's confession went far toward the conviction of Charles. Barbara hanged before several thousand people surrounding the jail yard; the Sheriff bungled the hanging by providing too long of a drop and Barbara strangled to death. One testament to Barbara's level of impoverishment was that after her hanging, Barbara's mother had to solicit donations from the crowd to pay funeral expenses. Virginia also hanged Margaret Lashley in January 1892 as an accessory to murder for her role in the killing of Margaret's husband by James Lyles, her boyfriend. Little information exists about the Georgia hanging of Amanda Cody and her male lover, Florence English, for the murder of Amanda's husband Cicero in November 1895.

Jurisdictions put to death six black women in the early Jim Crow period for child murder. In the first instance, 18-year-old Margaret Harris bound over as an indentured servant since she was a child to widow Nancy Barnwell in Fairmount, Georgia. In an attempt to relieve herself of her indenture, Margaret confessed to poisoning Barnwell and her two grandchildren at a dinner meal, but it was young Lela Lewis that died from the poisoning. A court tried and convicted Margaret for the child's death and sentenced her hanged in October 1883 before some 5,000 onlookers. As was usually the case with newspapers referencing executed black females, a *New York Times* article gave an unsavory description of Margaret as "coal black, five feet two inches in height, heavily built, and weighted one hundred fifty pounds. She had only one eye, the right one being put out, and altogether her face was not pleasant to look upon. Added to this she had very large hands and feet, which made her appearance even worse looking."[128] Margaret implicated her accomplice David Duke as the killer; Duke received a life sentence for his involvement.

Margaret claimed she was innocent but that the dead child's father extorted a confession from her after he and another man named Chapman who lived on the Barnwell estate took her to an old house, put a rope around her neck, hanged, and whipped her until they forced her to swear that she had administered the poison. The men reportedly told Margaret that if she would confess to the crime that she would not be hurt and would have a good home as long as she lived. Margaret Harris made a final statement on the gallows:

> Gentlemen, Ladies, Friends, and All: I hope the congregation will be quiet while I make this last statement on the facts in this case. I am going to tell the truth before God—the holy truth. I hope you all take warning from my fate, and none of you ever stand on the gallows as I do this morning. I am innocent of the charge. I did not poison Lela Lewis, and I hope to meet her in heaven. My kin people brought me to this and I want them to pray for me in heaven as there is no parting there. I have heard that they said hanging is too good for me, I ought to be burned. I hope they will repent like me, and meet me in heaven, for there is no forgiveness here. Every tub must stand on its own bottom here, but up there I will get justice. I am innocent, and my people are to blame because I stand where I do today. I hope you will all raise your children so as to meet me in heaven, and never stand on the gallows. Farewell all. I am going to die. Farewell all. Good bye. I must die. I hope this poor man is released, as he is innocent, before God. He is innocent.[129]

Alabama hanged young Pauline McCoy in October 1888 for murdering Annie Jordan, a 14-year-old white girl, for her shoes. There was speculation that Pauline may not have committed the murder, however. Annie Jordan was mentally retarded ("half-witted" and "demented" to use the language of the day) and had wandered away from home. Days later, authorities found her unclothed body in a pine thicket and discovered that she had been strangled to death. Officials questioned Pauline when they found her with the dead girl's shoes. Pauline immediately accused her father of killing young Annie; it is likely that Pauline's father had killed her after sexually assaulting the child. Some speculate that Pauline lacked the upper body strength to kill Annie. Even so, a trial court convicted Pauline of the murder and sentenced her to death. About 5,000 people witnessed Pauline's hanging after the state's governor denied clemency.

Fifteen-year-old Milbry Brown hanged in early October 1892 for the murder of W.C. Carpenter's one-year-old child in Spartanburg, South Carolina. Her hanging took place within the walls of the jail yard with about 20 persons witnessing the execution. Milbry's hanging was supposed to take place earlier in September but citizens petitioned Governer Tillman for an investigation into her hanging. "After a painstaking inquiry he decided that no sufficient showing had been made before him to warrant his arresting the due course of law by pardon or commutation of the sentence."[130]

There is little public information concerning the hanging of a black woman named Henrietta Murrell in September 1891 at Smithville in Charlotte County, Virginia, for the confessed drowning of her eight-year-old child because she was out of work and unable to support the child. Regional newspapers gave more attention to the case of Caroline Shipp, a poor, illiterate black girl no more than 18 years of age at her hanging. Caroline's parents treated her badly as a young child and both died when Caroline was in her early teens. Caroline had two children by different men at a young age, but the first child died from injuries suffered in a fall. Authorities in Gaston County, North Carolina, hanged Caroline in January 1892 for poisoning to death her 11-month-old son named James. A jury had found her guilty of the crime though Caroline always denied killing James claiming that her boyfriend Mack Farrar was responsible for poisoning the child. Jurors acquitted Farrar based on an alibi but convicted Caroline. Though authorities presented very weak evidence of her culpability at her trial, Caroline's defence lawyers believed she was guilty which undoubtedly influenced their ability to adequately defend her against the murder charge. There was no appeal. Once on the gallows, Caroline held a white handkerchief that she dropped after she asked if the Sheriff was ready. Caroline's hanging was a particularly perverse execution since officials botched her hanging with too short of a drop to kill instantly and two spectators had to pull on Caroline's legs to break her neck. It took Caroline 20 minutes to die. What's more, Caroline may have miscarried an unborn child at the gallows. The execution was so ghastly that newspaper reporters had to look away. What's more, Sheriff Officials did not immediately remove Caroline from the gallows for burial but left her body hanging all day.

In another southern case in 1892, Louisiana hanged an unidentified 15-year-old black child for poisoning a white person. Newberry County authorities hanged Anna Tribble also in October 1892 after a conviction for murdering her illegitimate newborn son. There was no appeal. Anna proclaimed her innocence and conflicting reports show either that she deserted the child in a field or that she had thrown the infant into a stream next to which she had given birth. Anna did not go to the gallows willingly; Sheriff Riser had to hold Anna down while he fastened the knot and adjusted the rope about her neck.

Executions of Mexican Women

After Spain's conquest of the Aztecs in the first half of the 16th century, the European power ignored the Mexican territory for nearly 200 years. Then, in 1769, the Spanish government dispatched Visitor-General José de Gálvez to establish a colony in Alta California. Gálvez selected Gaspar de Portolá to lead an expedition and to serve as governor of California who, in turn directed Junípero Serra, a Franciscan priest, to oversee construction of military presidios and Catholic missions in California to 1800. At first, Spain's occupation of California was exclusively a military expedition comprised of soldiers "dispatched to defend the frontier against European incursions, to protect the missionaries, and to pacify the Indians."[131] In his social history of *mestiza* women in Alta California from 1770 and 1821, Castañeda explains that it was during this period that Serra recruited Spanish-speaking women from Mexico to work in the missions of Alta California. In December 1773, eight women boarded the Spanish supply ship *Santiago* at San Blas, a small fishing village on the Pacific Coast of Mexico, and sailed to Monterey and became the first Spanish-speaking women in Alta California. These women included Ana María Hurtado and her two daughters, 20-year-old Cipriana and 18-year-old María del Carmen. Also boarding the *Santiago* were a young servant girl, María Teresa Ochoa, and María Josefa Davila. Three other women came with their husbands, Josefa María Góngora, María Arroyo Herrera, and Doña Josefa. These women were the "wives, daughters, and kinswomen of blacksmiths, carpenters, a storekeeper, and a surgeon."[132] By the end of the Spanish era in the northern territories, Spain had developed four major outpost clusters—Nuevo México, Pimería Alta, Tejas, and Alta California.

Spanish authorities used capital punishment to maintain order in its outermost posts. The Spanish used the death penalty sparingly against their own but routinely punished native Indians that rebelled against the exploitative labor system established in the region with hanging, flogging, and dismemberment. When Spanish officials used the death penalty against their own, "the government made executions a public spectacle, one that was so grisly, viewers never forgot what they witnessed."[133] Six short years after the first Spanish-speaking women arrived in the northern most territories of what is now Mexico, the first Latina executions took place in January 1779 in Santa Fe when Governor Juan Bautista De Anza of colonial New Mexico ordered two Cochiti Pueblo women, María Francisca and her mother María Josefa, hanged after confessing to the murder of Francisca's abusive husband, Agustín, a native of Pueblo Tesuque. The two women apparently tied a sash around Agustín's neck while he napped and then pulled on opposite ends of the sash strangling Agustín to death. María Josefa then slit Agustín's throat with a knife and stabbed him several times. While executed persons commonly remained hanging for several days, Governor De Anza ordered the women taken down and buried the same day.

Mexico remained a protectorate of Spain for three centuries until 1810 when the province began a protracted war for independence, proclaiming its autonomy in 1821. Mexico executed no females while in control over its northernmost territories. This was not the case, however, when the United States conquered the Mexican territory. The American conquest of the northernmost territories of Mexico began in May 1846 after United States and Mexican troops clashed at the border. President James K. Polk sent Zachary Taylor to protect the border when Mexican troops attacked his military entourage in a disputed part of the frontier. This event gave the staunch expansionist Polk the necessary pretext to invade Mexico. After nearly two years of a brutal and violent campaign against Mexico where some 20,000 soldiers and civilians lost their lives, the United States secured nearly a half million square miles of new territory, including what are now the states of Arizona, California, Colorado, New Mexico, Nevada, Texas, and Utah and parts of Kansas, Oklahoma, and Wyoming. Mexico signed the Treaty of Guadalupe Hidalgo ending the war in February 1848 and the United States paid Mexico $15 million. As noted by one observer, Mexico had fallen prey "to a *genocidal war* that was calculated to solidify the theft of vast stretches of their territories."[134] Mexican women were undoubtedly victims of the holocaust.

Mexican women in the southwestern borderlands committed far less crime than did Mexican men. One reason for the gender disparity in crime was the sex ratio; men far outnumbered women in Mexican communities well into the 1930s. Mexican female criminals mostly engaged in prostitution and cottage industry crimes such as the illegal manufacturing and distribution of liquor (bootlegging). Mexican women committed few violent crimes and were largely the victims of aggressive activities. Southwestern jurisdictions executed two Mexican women in the decades immediately following the Mexican War. In the first instance, some historical documentation survives New Mexico's hanging of Paula Angel in April 1861. Paula Angel, a 19-year-old Mexican woman, is the only female executed in New Mexico while it was still a territorial possession of the United States. There is some debate about Angel's actual name and age; some reports put her age at 26 or 27 years old and her name may have been Pablita Martin or Pablita Sandoval. Sheriff Herrera hanged Angel in San Miguel County for the murder of her married boyfriend, Juan Miguel Martin. Angel reportedly killed Martin by stabbing him in the back with a butcher knife after Martin, wanting to end his extramarital affair with Angel, told her that he did not intend to leave his wife and five children. Much of the controversy surrounding Angel's execution questions why the state executed her in the first place and how the Sheriff managed to botch the execution. In the first instance, it's troubling that a jury convicted Angel of first-degree murder for a crime of passion when today such a finding usually warrants a second-degree murder charge or even voluntary manslaughter, neither of which were capital offences. But at her trial, Judge Benedict left no alternative available and "instructed the jury prior to deliberations that the jury must either find Paula Angel guilty of first-degree murder or not find her guilty of any crime."[135] In the second instance, Sheriff Herrera bungled Paula Angel's execution and actually had to hang her twice. One commentator explains the execution this way:

> When it came time to launch Angel into eternity, the sheriff did not build a gallows. He selected a sturdy cottonwood tree outside of town. Paula Angel was driven there on a wagon, forced to ride on her own coffin to the site of her execution, which was witnessed by ranchers and townsmen. The sheriff fixed the rope to the tree, garlanded her with hemp, and then resumed his seat on the wagon and hawed the horses. But he'd made an error. He forgot to tie her hands behind her.
>
> Paula Angel managed to get her fingers underneath the rope in a last pitiful effort to save her own neck, and she struggled on the end of the rope.... The sheriff was forced to put the wagon

beneath her a second time, to cut her down, retie the rope amid the jeers and catcalls, properly secure her hands and feet, and to repeat the process. She did not survive her second hanging.[136]

Much about the trial and execution of Chipita Rodríguez execution verges on legend. As one commentator explains, "She is the subject of dramatic ghost stories, is said to haunt the San Patricio area over the years, and appears whenever a woman is to be executed as a specter with a noose around her neck roaming the river bottoms."[137] What's more, many of the facts surrounding Chipita's life and state killing are not verifiable because all but a week of the trial transcripts burned in a courthouse fire or were lost in a flood in 1889. Chipita Rodríguez was most likely Josefa Rodríguez, the daughter of Pedro Rodríguez who fled Antonio López de Santa Ana's army and joined the Texas forces. Mexican soldiers killed Pedro Rodríguez in the ensuing conflict of Texas' independence from Mexico. Some speculate that Chipita was Tejano—born in Texas of Mexican parents. More exactly, Chipita's father brought her from Mexico and they lived in the San Patricio de Hibernia area in Texas as early as the 1830s. After her father's death, she took up with a cowboy drifter and had a son, but the man soon left Chipita and kidnapped the infant. She eventually settled down in a lean-to shack on the Arkansas River where she would provide travelers with a meal and a cot on the porch. One August night in 1863, a horse trader named John Savage and another man stayed at Chipita's shack. That night Chipita became convinced that Savage's companion was her long-lost son. By morning, both men had disappeared along with $600 in gold that Savage had in his saddlebags. Servants from a nearby ranch washing clothes in the river downstream from Chipita's shack found Savage's body wrapped in burlap. The assailant had killed Savage with an axe to the head. Last seen at Chipita's shack, Sheriff "Pole" Means investigated and found blood on the front porch, Chipita claimed it was chicken blood. Sheriff Means arrested Chipita and her mentally deficient helper, Juan Silvera, for robbery and murder. Silvera explained to the sheriff that he had helped Chipita dump the body in the river after wrapping it in burlap. There is some speculation that Savage's companion was the murderer and that Chipita believed she was helping her son when she disposed of the body.

Unquestionably, Chipita's trial was a sham by any standard. The judge was Captain Benjamin F. Neal who had taken leave from General Nathaniel Banks' infantry to preside over the trial. The state's prosecutors were John S. Givens and T. H. O'Callaghan. The irregularities in Chipita's trial included Sheriff Means serving as foreman of the grand jury that indicted Chipita, there was no list of qualified jurors, at least three members of the grand jury served on the petite jury, four members of the jury had been indicted on felony charges (one for murder), and the jury foreman was a close friend of the sheriff. The trial lasted one morning and the jury returned with a verdict by noon the following day. Just before the trial, the saddlebags and the gold turned up intact. Nevertheless, the jury found Juan Silvera guilty of second-degree murder and Chipita guilty of first-degree murder. The jury assessed Silvera's penalty at five years in the state penitentiary and recommended leniency for Chipita because of her age—she was probably in her late sixties. Ignoring the jury's recommendation of mercy, the judge sentenced Chipita hanged. Another person confessed to the murder shortly after Chipita's execution. As a result, Chipita's execution at the hands of a racist court stands as an execution of an innocent woman.

Executions of American Indian Women

Jurisdictions put to death six American Indian women in the second historical period of female executions in the United States. The first recorded American Indian female execution took place in the period in April 1763 when Wayne County authorities in Michigan hanged an unidentified Pawnee Indian slave woman for murdering her owner Mr. Clapham. Clapham was an English trader on his way to Detroit with two Pawnee slaves, a man and a woman, when the

Indians decapitated Clapham and threw his body into a nearby river. An Indian party captured the Pawnee slaves and delivered them to authorities who tried and convicted them for Clapham's murder. British Major Henry Gladwin sentenced them to death. The male Indian slave escaped from custody leaving only the unnamed Pawnee woman to hang.

Hannah Peggin succumbed to hanging in Northampton, Massachusetts, in July 1785 for infanticide of her illegitimate male child. Hannah apparently "took a length of flax from a nearby loom and knotted it tightly around the baby's throat. The result was fatal strangulation."[138] In another case, Madison County officials in New York hanged young Mary Antoine, an Oneida Indian, in September 1814 for fatally stabbing another Indian woman with whom Mary's native boyfriend had developed a relationship after ending his interest in Mary. An account of Mary's execution explains,

> The witness whose testimony at trial most helped convict her was a local farmer named John Jacobs. He figured also in her apprehension for the crime. Appearing unremorseful about her violent act, Mary was quoted as saying that the victim deserved to die for taking away her boyfriend. On the day of execution, authorities had arranged for her father, Abram, and brother who lived on a farm near Siloam to say their good-byes to her. They did so on the scaffold, stoically shaking hands without sign of emotion and then walking away without looking back. However, Abram had openly vowed before and after his daughter's execution that he would kill Jacobs whom he blamed for Mary's death. For years, Jacobs stayed away from Madison County. But reportedly after receiving assurances transmitted to him from Abram that no harm would befall him, Jacobs returned. One day when Jacobs was hoeing a field with a group of men, Abram approached in a friendly manner, shaking hands in greeting each one in turn. But as he greeted Jacobs, Abram pulled a knife and fatally stabbed him. Eventually apprehended, Abram was tried, convicted and sentenced to death. Exactly nine years to the month after his daughter's execution, the 73-year-old warrior—he had fought on the American side during the Revolution—was hanged for killing the prosecution's chief witness against her.[139]

Connecticut holds the dubious distinction of executing the youngest condemned American Indian female prisoner in United States history. Officials in Groton hanged Hannah Ocuish, a 12-year-old mentally retarded Pequot Indian girl for killing six-year-old Eunice Bolles, the daughter of an affluent white family to whom Hannah was a servant. Hannah's alcoholic mother had abandoned her at a young age and Hannah lived in various foster homes. The sentencing judge was concerned that not executing young Hannah would send the message that "children might commit such atrocious acts with impunity." More likely, the sentencing judge was concerned more with accounting for the affluence and race of Eunice and her parents in contrast to that of a young Indian servant girl. Authorities hanged Hannah three months before her thirteenth birthday in late December 1786. One commentator gave the following account of Hannah's case:

> On the 21st of July, 1786, at about 10 o'clock in the morning, the body of the murdered child was found in the public road leading from New-London to Norwich, lying on its face near to a wall." The document went on to trace the investigation that followed: The neighborhood turned out to hunt for the murderer; Hannah was questioned and claimed that she had seen four boys near the scene of the crime. When a search failed to turn them up, Hannah was interrogated again, and then taken to the Bolles home to be charged with homicide in the presence of the dead child. She burst into tears and confessed.... Five weeks earlier, Eunice had reported Hannah for stealing fruit during the strawberry harvest, and Hannah had plotted revenge. Catching sight of her young enemy headed for school one morning, Hannah had lured Eunice from her path with a gift of calico, then beat and choked her to death.[140]

There is little in the historical record concerning two other American Indian female executions. The record is silent on the Massachusetts execution of an unnamed American Indian woman for murder in August 1837 and the Missouri execution of an American Indian woman for murder in May 1887.

Execution of a Native Hawaiian Female

Before Hawaii became a territorial possession of the United States, a native Hawaiian woman named Kaomali hanged at Oahu Prison with her paramour Ahulika for the murder of Kaomali's husband Kawao. Ahulika and Kaomali hanged under local authority in August 1846 when Hawaii was an independent kingdom under the rule of King Kamehameha III. Kaomali's execution took place some 50 years before the U.S.-led overthrow of the Hawaiian monarchy. Although Hawaii did not become a territorial possession of the United States until 1893, American missionaries and planters were well established in Hawaii by the mid–19th century and wreaked political, cultural, economic and religious havoc on the kingdom.

Correcting the Historical Record

There is at least one mistaken case of a white female execution occurring in this period. The historical record shows that Eve Martin, most likely white, supposedly hanged in Hawkins County, Tennessee, for accessory to murder in 1820. Mrs. Eve Martin was actually a murder victim killed by Robert Delap and Mitchell Marcum. Delap, a wealthy landowner, was married to Marcum's sister, Tabitha Marcum. Marcum was a farm hand who probably worked for Delap. It seems that Delap had Marcum kill Eve because she was going to testify against Delap in a counterfeiting case. Marcum shot Eve in her cabin and he hanged in June 1821 for the murder. A Campbell County jury convicted Delap of assessory to murder and Judge Samuel Powel sentenced him to death. Delap hanged in April 1823 after two failed appeals to the state's supreme court.

In an another case, one scholar claims that a woman named Francesca Mesca hanged for the murder of William Pickles in October 1783. Actually, Mesca was a Portuguese male named Francisco Mesca and hanged with Petro Jacobi, Matteo Bratelli, and Antonio Rasso for the stabbing murder of Captain William Pickles of the Continental Navy. A jury acquitted a fifth man named Jean Bautist le Jour for lack of sufficient evidence.

Concluding Remarks

State killings of black slave women accented the second historical period in women executions from the 1760s through the 1890s. Female slaves hanged largely for killing abusive white masters, their mistresses, and occasionally their masters' children. The poisoning of whites and the arson of their property also account for significant numbers of black female executions in the period. Undoubtedly, the capital crimes of black women resulted from their oppression in late colonial slavery and antebellum slavery, and the ruthless violence against black women accenting Reconstruction and the early Jim Crow periods. Black lynchings peaked in the 1890s and may explain why southern jurisdictions executed fewer black women in Reconstruction and the Jim Crow eras than in the antebellum decades.

In contrast, jurisdictions executed far fewer white women in the second historical period than in the first historical period of female executions. White women put to death in the period were largely marginalized, poor, and illiterate immigrant women whose capital offenses were certainly responses to the social hardships of extreme poverty during the period. Spousal murders resulting from abusive domestic relations increased for white women during the period. The impoverishment that immigrant women endured in the period often resulted in extreme mental disorders and may explain much about spousal murders among white females in the period. Mexican and American Indian female executions account for very few of the women executed in the period. Still, their state killings resulted from the Anglo extremism against marginalized groups in the period.

> "Her trial attorneys—do you know what they did to help her lately? Know what? One of them wrote to me, saying he'd like four invitations to her execution. That's the kind of defense she had."¹

5

The Third Historical Trend, 1900s–2010s

The immigrant population more than doubled in the first few decades of the 1900s when nearly 23 million foreign-born persons entered the United States. Southern, eastern, and central Europeans comprised the vast majority of new arrivals that landed in the industrial northeast and ultimately displaced skilled and unskilled native workers as preferred laborers since foreign-born workers exacted far lower wages. Consequently, many occupations assumed a distinct ethnic makeup: "Italians and Jews in the clothing industry; Italians and Portuguese in New England's textile manufacturing; Irish in the transportation field; eastern Europeans in the production of steel; Germans in printing and machine tooling; and Scotch-Irish and English in the skilled section of steel fabrication of by-products."² Some two million immigrant child laborers also worked in fields, factories, mines, and workshops. The influx of foreign-born immigrants in the period had a profound effect on poverty rates; some 40 percent of the working population earned poverty wages, joblessness was widespread, and the cost of living increased dramatically. Joblessness rose to 25 percent in the 1930s; 60 percent of rural households and 82 percent of farmers were poor in 1939. Foreign-born workers effectively displaced black workers; the black poverty ratio to that of whites was 176 to one in the late 1930s.

Alarmingly high poverty rates gave way to raging labor activism in the early decades of the 20th century when one of the worst workplace disasters in American history took place. The event called into question the unsafe working conditions of immigrant workers when industrial accidents claimed the lives of at least a hundred workers daily; workplace accidents often threw the working poor into the ravages of poverty with lost incomes. Low wages, long hours, and unhealthy and hazardous working conditions marked the appalling conditions for sweatshop workers. The disaster at the *Triangle Shirtwaist Factory* on the ninth floor of the Asch Building in New York City in March 1911 involved a garment factory fire that killed 146 workers, mostly young immigrant Russian Jewish, Italian, German, and Hungarian women and girls. Some of the girls killed in the fire were as young as 12 years old. The fire started when a gas lamp used for lighting ignited a bin holding fabric scraps. Supervisors had locked workrooms to keep workers from taking unauthorized breaks or stealing materials, and because of those locked factory doors, workers were unable to escape the fire and were burned alive. More than a third of the workers jumped to their deaths from window ledges. Adding to the calamity were cramped workspaces in the factory, ineffective fire escapes that crumpled in the fire, and deficient fire department equipment. Shortly after the fire, New York City District Attorney Charles Whitman indicted Max Blanck and Isaac Harris on manslaughter charges but a jury acquitted the building owners. Blanck and Harris settled civil suits three years later by paying $75 for each dead worker. What's more, two years after the fire, safety inspectors charged Max Blanck with locking a door to the factory during working hours and a court fined him $20, the judge in the case reportedly apologized to Blanck for any inconvenience the case may have caused him.

Economic disengagement profoundly affected the lives of American workers in the early 1900s. Women's wages were far below men's wages, which meant that women were more employable than were men; nearly 25 percent of women were in the labor force by 1900. "Female clerks, secretaries, maids, and waitresses earned much less than male factory workers, but their jobs were more likely to survive hard times."[3] Others argue that many women's jobs were more unstable, temporary, and seasonal than men's jobs. Unemployed men undoubtedly suffered psychological and emotional volatility in their inability to support their families that surely culminated in family instability and troubled domestic relations that at times resulted in spousal murders.

The economic depression of the 1930s was particularly disenfranchising to women. In southern states, an unemployment rate of 26 percent burdened both black and white women. In northern states, however, the rate of black female unemployment was nearly twice that of white females. Slightly more than 23 percent of white women were unemployed while black women suffered a staggering unemployment rate of 43 percent. The unemployment rate among black women in northern states resulted largely from mass layoffs of black women in service and manufacturing jobs. White women began replacing black women as traditional domestic workers such as cooks, house cleaners, nurses, and laundresses. Many skilled and educated black women desperate for jobs "actually offered their services at the so-called 'slave markets'—street corners where Negro women congregated to await white housewives who came daily to take their pick and bid wages down."[4] Homelessness among black women was pervasive during the depression era. The demand of homeless shelters for women increased *twentyfold* over a 12-year period ending in 1932; women seeking shelter increased by 270 percent over a one-year period from 1929 to 1930.

High levels of impoverishment undoubtedly fueled the social conditions ripe for increased rates in criminal conduct. Homicides among women increased appreciably in the early to mid-decades of the 20th century. Women were 8.7 percent of arrests for criminal homicide in the early 1930s but the percentage more than doubled by the late 1950s. Despite the growth in female homicide rates, jurisdictions executed few women; roughly 57 percent of murdering women received less than life in prison. Women were only 0.5 percent of the more than 8,000 executions in the United States throughout the 20th century though public sentiment toward capital punishment for women increased over the period. In the late 1930s, 58 percent of the population favored capital punishment for women, but by the early 1950s, some 75 percent of those who favored the death penalty favored it for women. In the early 2000s, 68 percent of Americans favored capital punishment for women but opposed the penalty for juveniles, mentally retarded persons, and the mentally ill.

Since 1900, death penalty states executed 54 women. White women executions exceeded black women executions by a margin of *two to one*. It was only in the 1940s that black female executions marginally exceed white female executions. Black women executions increased ever so slightly from one execution in the 1900s to a high of seven executions in the 1940s, but dropped again to one execution in the 1950s. There were no black women executions for four decades beginning in the 1960s. Black female executions resumed in the 2001 when Oklahoma executed Wanda Jean Allen. Texas executed Francis Elaine Newton in 2005 and Kimberly McCarthy in 2013. No jurisdiction put to death a Latina or American Indian woman in the period.

In contrast, state officials executed two white women in the 1900s and none in the 1910s. Authorities increased white women executions from two in the 1920s and to 10 in the 1930s, the number decreased to four in the 1940s, but increased to seven executions in the 1950s. White women executions dropped to one execution in the 1960s, to none in the 1970s, to one execution in the 1980s, and to two executions in the 1990s. White women executions increased to six executions in the 2000s though the number dropped to one female execution in 2010. There were no women executions in the United States from 1962 when California asphyxiated Elizabeth Ann Duncan to 1984 when North Carolina executed Velma Margie Barfield by lethal injection. The last white woman execution took place in September 2015 when Georgia put to death Kelly Renee Gissendaner for spousal murder. Predatory murder, spousal murder, infanticide and child murders are the major capital crimes committed by executed women since 1900. Roughly half of the 23 women executed over the last century for predatory murders involved murders aggravated by conspiracy, robbery, and kidnapping.

Executions of White Women

In the third historical period of female executions in the United States, jurisdictions executed 36 white women largely for crimes of predatory murder, robbery-murder, kidnapping-murder, spousal murder, conspiracy to commit murder, and child murder. The federal government executed one white woman for espionage after a federal court found her guilty of spying for the former Soviet Union. Death penalty officials used electrocution to put to death more than half of executed white females in the period, the remaining executions involved hanging, asphyxiation (gas chamber), and lethal injection. New York accounts for 20 percent of white women executions while California executed about 12 percent. Roughly half of white women executed were homemakers and housekeepers; others included criminals, nurses, prostitutes, schoolteachers, waitresses, and business owners. All but one of these executed women victimized other whites. The most consistent feature of white female killers is that they were poor and marginalized women. Many of them suffered from severe mental disabilities resulting from extremely troubled childhoods often involving sadistic physical, sexual, and psychological abuse that predisposed them to lives accented by violent criminality as adult women.

Predatory Murder

Predatory murders dominated white women executions beginning in the 1900s. Mary O'Brien Farmer became the first white woman executed in the third historical period for a predatory murder when, in March 1909, New York authorities electrocuted Mary at Auburn State Prison for axing to death Sarah Brennan. Mary, a poor and ignorant woman with a facial paralysis, came to the United States from Ireland in 1900 and most probably landed in the urban ghetto populated by millions of southern and eastern European immigrants in New York. During this period, women were more than half of Irish immigrants to the United States and most worked as house servants. Mary worked as a housekeeper for the Binghamton family, but soon moved to Buffalo and married millwright James D. Farmer. The couple had one son, Peter. They moved to Jefferson County, a predominantly Irish immigrant community, where James worked at a local mill and the family lived in a ramshackle house. The family lived in one of two properties owned by Sarah Brennan. Sarah was married to Patrick Brennan who was James' immediate supervisor at the mill. It infuriated Mary that the Brennan's were so financially better off than her family and she contrived a scheme to defraud Sarah Brennan of the house. Mary visited an attorney, feigned being Sarah Brennan, and had the deed to both the Brennan's houses transferred to her husband James. After learning of the improper transfer, Sarah demanded return of the deeds. It was then that the Farmers transferred the forged deeds to their son Peter in hopes that he would have a better life. When Sarah went to Mary and demanded return of the deeds, Mary killed her with several axe blows to the head and then stuffed Sarah's butchered body into a trunk. The Farmers took up residence at the Brennan's house after they evicted Patrick.

Soon a local sheriff investigated the events surrounding Sarah's disappearance and found

Sarah's body in the trunk located in a back room of the Brennan's house. Sheriff Bellinger arrested James and Mary believing that the two had conspired to murder Sarah. James and Mary went to trial, an all-male jury convicted them of Sarah's murder, and the court sentenced them to die in the state's electric chair. At trial, the defense claimed that Mary was insane at the time of the killing. Though a New York Court of Appeals believed Mary had "an inferior and untrained intellect and that her moral perceptions were of a low order," the Court argued that these character flaws did not rise to a legal standard of insanity. Just before her execution, Mary confessed to the murder and exonerated James. Immediately following Mary's execution, Drs. Edward Spitzka of Philadelphia and Charles Lambert of the Pathological Institute at Wards Island in New York performed an autopsy and took possession of Mary's brain for analysis. In 1910, a jury acquitted James of forgery of the Brennan's deeds and he spent the rest of his life as a mill worker in Brownville.

Eva Dugan survived a tortuous childhood to become an uneducated woman with no skills though early on she was a cabaret singer in Alaska during the Klondike gold rush. She married five times and four of her husband's mysteriously disappeared. Eva married her first husband at the age of 16 who abandoned her and her two small children, a son and a daughter. Eva turned to prostitution to survive with her children. In her fifties, Eva moved to Tucson, Arizona, where rancher Andrew J. Mathis hired her as a housekeeper and caregiver. Mathis soon disappeared and Eva reportedly left the Mathis ranch with a young hired hand named Jack in Mathis's Dodge coupe. While investigating Mathis's disappearance, Pima County Sheriff Jim McDonald discovered Mathis's house nearly stripped of everything, Eva had sold Mathis's belongings to neighbors. Eva gave conflicting reports to neighbors of Mathis's whereabouts; McDonald suspected foul play and began searching for Eva. McDonald discovered that while posing as Mrs. Mathis, Eva sold Mathis's Dodge coupe for $600 in Kansas City. Eva's grown daughter lived in White Plains, New York, and Eva's father, William McDaniel's, lived in Ceres, California, but neither had seen her for several years. McDonald found Eva living in White Plains and working in a mental institution. McDonald arrested Eva, arranged for her extradition, and returned her to Arizona in March 1927. A court found Eva guilty of grand larceny and sentenced her to prison.

Almost a year after Eva's imprisonment, a tourist (J.F. Nash) camping just off the Mathis ranch uncovered Mathis' decomposing body in a shallow grave. The skull revealed that Mathis had died a violent death; the body had encrusted with lime and a gag was still in his teeth. Arizona officials charged Eva with Mathis's murder. The evidence against Eva was circumstantial; there were no fingerprints, no witnesses; the only thing Eva admitted was that she and Mathis had quarreled. While testifying on her own behalf at trial, Eva blamed the killing on Jack who accidentally killed Mathis after he struck Jack on the head for refusing to milk a cow. In fact, two letters exonerated Eva of the Mathias killing: one arrived at the jail from Agua Prieta, Mexico, and the other letter arrived just a few days later from Fort Worth, Texas, claiming that a "Bob" had seen Jack kill Mathias. A jury found Eva guilty of first-degree murder and the court sentenced her to hang. The Arizona Supreme Court rejected Eva's contention, among other claims, that the evidence did not support a guilty verdict. Interestingly, physicians testified at trial that Eva's 30-year syphilis infection had compromised her mental state. Eva Dugan hanged at the Arizona State Prison in February 1930, but the executioner botched the hanging: "When Mrs. Dugan plunged through the trap door and hit the end of the rope with a bounding jolt, her head snapped off and rolled into a corner."[5]

In late February 1931, Pennsylvania authorities electrocuted Irene Crawford Schroeder and her paramour Walter Glenn Dague for killing state police officer Corporal W. Brady Paul. Schroeder was born in West Virginia in 1909, one of 12 children. The family was very poor, forcing Irene to work at a young age. She dropped out of school in the eighth grade and at the age of 15 married Homer Schroeder with whom she had a son, Donnie. Soon after giving birth to Donnie, Irene left her husband and moved to Wheeling, West Virginia, where she worked as a waitress. It was there that she met Walter Glenn Dague, an insurance sales representative and Sunday school superintendent. Irene eventually divorced her husband for a life with Dague who abandoned his wife and three children. Dague soon lost his job and money was a problem. In the months preceding December 1929, Irene and Dague engaged in a series robberies. Irene's brother, Tom Crawford, soon joined them and the three robbed a grocery store in Butler, Pennsylvania. Corporal Brady Paul of the state police and Ernest C. Moore, a motorcycle officer of the highway patrol, stopped a car fitting the description of the car used in the robbery. A shootout ensued with the officers wherein Irene shot and killed Corporal Paul and one of the others shot and seriously wounded Patrolman Moore.

The three then headed west robbing stores in the day and service stations at night. They eluded capture by the St. Louis police and proceeded west through Oklahoma and Texas, eventually arriving in Arizona, where they picked up an ex-convict named Wells and kidnapped Sheriff Chapman who tried to apprehended the fugitives. As they drove through Chandler, Arizona, other law enforcement officers gave chase and another shootout took place in which Sheriff Lee Wright died from wounds he suffered in the mêlée. A sheriff's posse captured the trio after they had abandoned their car and continued on foot for a few miles. Pennsylvania extradited Irene and Dague where authorities tried and convicted the two for the Paul's murder. The state tried them separately, and in March 1930, a jury found the two guilty of first-degree murder and the court sentenced them to death in the state's electric chair. Authorities executed Irene at the Rockview Penitentiary in Center County, Pennsylvania, and days later Dague met the same fate. There is little in the historical record of Irene's life before Irene met Dague, but there is evidence that she suffered a personality disorder when she fell and injured her head about the age of ten. She attempted suicide on several occasions. At trial, her attorney put this evidence forward in an insanity plea that the jury denied, and similarly, the Pennsylvania Supreme Court rejected evidence of an uncontrollable impulse to commit murder.

A postscript to Irene and Walter's executions is that Marshall County officials in West Virginia indicted and tried Frank and Norma Howell for the robbery of Jack Cott's filling station down the road from where the Howells lived with their three children. Cott was a farmer who operated a filling station. Cott positively but erroneously identified the Howell's as the robbers. Cott's identification of the Howells matched almost exactly that of Irene and Walter. Despite concrete alibis, a grand jury indicted the Howells for the Cott's robbery. Officials tried Frank Howell first, a jury found him guilty and the court sentenced him to 15-years in the state penitentiary. A different jury hearing the same evidence presented at Frank's trial acquitted Norma Howell of the Cott's robbery. Immediately afterwards, officials arrested and extradited Norma to Cadiz, Ohio, for the robbery of an Inn. A Harrison County jury acquitted Norma; she returned home and found a waitress job to support herself and her children. Exoneration of the Howells for any wrongdoings was not forthcoming until Irene and Walter signed a confession to the robbery of Cott's filling station. The state's governor pardoned Frank Howell in January 1931.

The murder of an elderly bachelor auto mechanic named Robert R. Hitchens remained unsolved for seven years until police arrested the man's young nephew, Lawrence Carey, in December 1937 for a home burglary. Police investigators asked if he knew anything about the death of his uncle. His response was that he "knew plenty" and proceeded to implicate his mother, May (Mary) H. Carey, and two older brothers, 16-year-old James and 20-year-old Howard, in the murder. Reportedly, the three surprised Hitchens when he arrived home one evening and used a club and hammer about his head, shot him, and then poured liquor down his throat in an attempt to make the killing look like the result of drunken brawl. Hitchens's head and face took more than 200 stitches to make the body presentable for burial. The murderers returned home after the killing, burned their clothes, and buried the sledge hammer used to kill Hitchens in some nearby woods. The motive for murdering Hitchens "was to acquire possession of his small estate and the proceeds of life insurance policies."[6] A Sussex County jury deliberated for three hours and found May and Howard guilty of first-degree murder with a recommendation for mercy, the same jury found James guilty of second-degree murder and the court sentenced him to life in prison. There was no mercy forthcoming for May and Howard when Justice Daniel J. Layton ordered the two hanged. All three defendants filed motions for new trials and but the Sussex County court rejected their appeals. In June 1935, May went to the gallows first but the executioner botched her hanging and she strangled to death after 17 minutes. Howard died next when authorities used the same rope that they had used to hang his mother.

Eva Coo was the oldest of six daughters born in Ontario, Canada. Eva became the owner and operator of an inn outside Cooperstown, New York, an establishment "known for its rowdiness and for its powerful visitors ... [including] politicians, doctors, and lawyers."[7] The establishment was unquestionably a brothel. New York executed Eva in June 1935 for the murder of Harry Wright, a slow-witted handyman that she took under her wing when his mother died. Wright entrusted his inheritance of a few thousand dollars and the family home to Eva. She went through Wright's estate rather quickly; his house mysteriously burned down and the insurance money spent. Eva took out a dozen policies on Wright's life with an estimated payout of $6,000 with a double indemnity clause if he died in an accident. Along with one of her employees, Martha Clift, the two devised a plan to kill Wright and get the insurance proceeds. In mid–June 1934, Eva and Martha drove the hapless Wright to an isolated spot outside Oneonta, New York, where Eva hit him with a mallet and Martha drove the car over his unconscious body. The two women dumped Wright's body beside a busy highway to make it look like a hit and run accident. After their arrests for the murder, Martha testified against Eva with a grant of immunity. Martha apparently lied, lost her immunity, and received a second-degree murder charge. To coerce a confession from Eva, local police exhumed Wright's body without a court order and forced her to reenact the crime using his dead corpse. A jury found her guilty of the murder and the court sentenced her to die in the state's electric chair. The Court of Appeals for New York affirmed Eva's conviction without comment. A year nearly to the day after the killing, authorities electrocuted Eva Coo. Warden Lawes of Sing Sing Prison commented on Eva's defense:

> I don't know if she was innocent or guilty. But I do know that she got a rotten deal all around. Rotten. She told me that after her arrest she signed a power of attorney for a lawyer so that he could collect three thousand dollars a man owed her. She gave them everything to defend her. I suppose I ought not to say anything. My job was to kill the woman, not defend her. And I'm not defending her—she may be guilty as well, but she got a raw deal. Her trial attorneys—do you know what they did to help her lately? Know what? One of them wrote to me, saying he'd like four invitations to her execution. That's the kind of defense she had.[8]

In June 1937, New York authorities electrocuted Mary Frances Creighton for the poisoning death of Ada Applegate. Years earlier, New Jersey officials unsuccessfully prosecuted Mary and her husband John Creighton for the poisoning deaths of Mary's teenage brother Raymond and John's mother Anna Creighton. Authorities suspected the two in the poisoning death of John's father-in-law, Walter Creighton, as well. The Creighton's had a teenage daughter named Ruth. Shortly after the Creighton's moved to Long Island to escape the publicity surrounding their murder trial, Everett Applegate, his wife Ada, and their teenage daughter, Agnes, moved-in with the Creighton's. Soon Everett began a sexual relationship with Mary and Ruth and Ada Applegate began telling neighbors of Everett's lurid relationships. Many believed Mary to be an unfit mother, and it was then that Mary turned her murdering skills against Ada and gave her large amounts of arsenic poison. A physician ruled Ada's death from natural causes, but an informed police detective suspected otherwise. An autopsy showed arsenic poisoning and the focus of the investigation turned quickly to the three other adults in the household. After hours of interrogation, Mary confessed that she and Everett had schemed to kill his wife in part so he could marry Ruth who was now pregnant with his child. After a trial that found both Mary and Everett guilty of Ada's murder, the court sentenced them both to die in the state's electric chair. The state's governor denied clemency and it was then that Mary confessed to the earlier murders in New Jersey. There is considerable evidence that Everett had nothing to do with the murder and New York may have executed an innocent man. The evidence was overwhelming as to Mary's guilt for Ada's murder, however. It seems that Mary was unconcious at the time of her electrocution. One source reports that Mary was in a morphine induced coma when officials put her to death. "Mrs. Creighton gave no slightest sign of life or consciousness when she was brought into the execution chamber in a wheelchair. The 24 official witnesses, 22 of them newspaper men, agreed that she was completely unconscious."[9]

Anna Marie Hahn was born in Fussen, Germany, in 1906 and immigrated to this country in 1929 with her husband, a physician from Vienna who died shortly after their arrival. Anna gave birth to a son named Oscar shortly afterwards and a year later she married Phillip Hahn. Ohio electrocuted the immigrant school teacher in December 1938 for the poisoning deaths of an undetermined number of elderly German men in and around Cincinnati although the state prosecuted her only for the poisoning murder of Jacob Wagner. Anna's motive for the killings was economic gain by access to the men's finances. The trial jury of 11 women and one man took roughly three hours to deliberate Anna's guilt with no recommendation for mercy. Anna appealed her case to the Ohio Court of Common Pleas for a new trial alleging that the state improperly admitted evidence, there was prosecutorial misconduct in the case, and that the verdict was unsupported by the evidence. The court denied her motion for a new trial and the state's governor refused to intervene. One unusual aspect of Anna's case is that her young son Oscar visited her every day while she was on death row.

San Quentin prison officials asphyxiated Eithel Spinelli for the murder of Robert Sherrard. Eithel headed a motley gang involved in robberies, drunk-rolling, high-jacking, manufacturing blackjacks, and murder. Eithel, the mother of three children, had a harrowing childhood that included incest, pregnancy at the age of 13, and troubled relationships with men as an adult. San Quentin warden Clinton T. Duffy referred to Eithel as "the coldest, hardest character, male or female that he had ever known, and utterly lacking in feminine appeal."[10] As a member of the gang, Sherrard had become too troublesome for Eithel and she had two other members of the gang, Mike Simeoni and Gordon Hawkins, kill Sherrard. The men laced a glass of whiskey with chloral hydrate (a sleeping agent) and while he was semi-conscious threw Sherrard from a bridge into a river in Sacramento where he drowned. Simeoni and Hawkins confessed to killing Sherrard once apprehended by police but claimed Eithel masterminded the murder. A jury found all three defendants guilty of Sherrard's murder and a court sentenced them to die in the state's gas chamber. Eithel died in San Quentin's death chamber on November 21, 1941, and Simeoni and Hawkins died a week later. Eithel was the first woman asphyxiated in a gas chamber in the United States.

Marie Porter, the mother of four daughters, died along with Angelo Ralph Giancola in Illinois' electric chair in January 1938 for the murder of Porter's brother, William Kappen, for a $3,300 life insurance policy. Marie, Angelo and John Giancola kidnapped William on his wedding day. William had earlier informed his sister that he would change the beneficiary on the life insurance policy from his sister Marie to his new wife, Irene Traub. The news upset Marie who claimed to have helped William through some rough economic times during the depression. Before he could change the beneficiary on the policy, Marie and her accomplices abducted William, Angelo shot him in the head on Marie's orders, and the three dumped his body in a vacant field. Marie had promised the Giancola brothers $800 of the insurance proceeds for helping her kill William. All three defendants confessed to the murder once arrested. Remarkably, police allowed newspaper reporters to sit in during the confessions and interview the defendants at will. A court sentenced Marie and Ralph to execution and John to 99 years in prison. There was no appeal, and Governor Henry Horner denied clemency to Marie though he had earlier commuted the death sentences of three other women for murder, namely, Gertrude Puhae (1934), Minnie Mitchell (1937) and Mildred Bolton (1937).

Annie Beatrice Henry, also known as Toni Jo Henry (Hood), was born Annie Beatrice McQuiston in January 1916 to a family of five children in Shreveport, Louisiana. Annie's mother died of tuberculosis when she was a young child and her father often beat the children. Unhappy in her father's house, Annie left and by the time she was 16 years old she was addicted to drugs and a prostitute. It was then that she began using the name Toni Jo Hood. While working full time in a brothel in Shreveport in 1939, Annie met ex–prize fighter Claude "Cowboy" Henry with whom she quickly became infatuated and they married that year. While vacationing in the southern California, Claude received notice from a Texas court to answer charges on the barroom killing of a former San Antonio police officer named Arthur Sinclair. Claude returned to Texas and a court convicted him of murder and sentenced him to 50 years in the Texas State Penitentiary at Huntsville. Annie promised to get Claude out of jail.

To further her ill-fated scheme, Annie met up with an ex-convict and Army deserter named Horace Finnon Burks who claimed to know the design of the prison. The two armed themselves with guns, planned to steal a car and rob a bank. They hitchhiked to Arkansas under the guise of newlyweds to rob a bank in a small town known to Horace. In Orange, Texas, they hitched a ride from Joseph P. Calloway who was delivering a new Ford Coupe for a friend to a customer in Jennings, Louisiana. Calloway was married and had a nine-year-old daughter. The three drove toward Jennings when well into the countryside Annie pulled a gun on Calloway and ordered him to stop the car. Annie ordered Calloway to undress and to get into the trunk of the car. Horace drove the car a distance further when Annie had him stop the car. They ordered Calloway out of the car, and Annie pulled him across a field with pliers tugging at his penis. She then ordered Calloway to kneel and pray and then she shot him in the forehead. After killing Calloway, the two registered into a roadside hotel but Horace left with the car while Annie slept. The next morning she took a bus to Shreveport where she relayed the killing to Sergeant David Walker, a colleague of her brother who was also a police officer. Walker arrested Annie and eventually found Calloway's body and the stolen car. Lake Charles courts tried Annie three times for Calloway's murder. The first appeal to the Louisiana Supreme Court granted Annie a new trial given the amount of publicity and courtroom rancor surrounding her case. In his concurring opinion, Justice Odom claimed:

> The populace clamored for the death penalty. They demanded the life of the accused and clearly manifested their desires to the jury by signs and gestures which could not be misunderstood. The trial was attended by throngs. Hundreds more than could be seated crowded into the courthouse. The courtroom was literally packed and jammed with spectators. The judge says that more than 150 either stood or were seated within the railing which separated his stand from the space reserved for spectators. The record clearly shows that they were present not merely through interest, but for the purpose of letting it be known that they demanded the death penalty instead of punishment by life imprisonment. The members of the jury unquestionably knew what they were there for, because it is shown that they heard outcries and observed in the courtroom and on the streets certain signs and gestures which clearly showed that public sentiment against the accused was at fever heat and that no punishment inflicted upon the accused except that of death would appease the wrath of the throng.[11]

The state Supreme Court granted Annie a second trial on legal technicalities and the trial court again found her again guilty of Calloway's murder and sentenced her death. On her third appeal, the court affirmed the conviction, sentence, and the state's governor refused to consider clemency. Louisiana executed Annie in late November 1942 in a portable electric chair in the basement of the Lake Charles jail. Horace Burks died in the same chair in March 1943.

In the wake of a family feud riveting an entire South Carolina county in the early 1940s, state authorities electrocuted schoolteacher and farmer's wife, Sue Stidham Logue, in January 1943 for her part in arranging for the murder of Davis W. Timmerman who killed her husband, J. Wallace Logue, in an intense argument about a yearling calf kicked by a mule belonging to Timmerman. A jury found Timmerman acted in self-defense and acquitted him of Wallace's murder. Seeking revenge for her husband's death, Sue apparently recruited Joe Frank Logue to hire Spartanburg police officer Clarence Bagwell to murder Timmerman for $500. Bagwell apparently told police about the killing. When Sheriff W.D. Allen and Deputy W.L. Clark served arrest warrants on George Logue (Wallace's brother) and Sue Logue at Sue's home, a gunfight broke out and both police officers and a sharecropper to the Logue's farm named Fred Dorn died. There was a standoff with police and reportedly, it took Strom Thurmond, then a county judge, to convince Sue and George to surrender. According to one source, Thurmond had had an affair with Sue when he was a superintendent at the school where Sue worked as a teacher: "The stories still whispered in Edgefield tell of Strom's long affair with Sue, who campaigned for him when he ran for county superintendent of education and whom he allowed to teach in the county schools despite unwritten rules generally excluding married women from teaching positions. Her reputation for sexual prowess was such that men told stories of her reputed vaginal muscular dexterity. The lore includes a tale of her and Strom found *flagrante delicto* in the superintendent's office." The source also reports,

> Randall Johnson, a black man who supervised "colored help" at the State House and often served as driver and messenger, drove Sue from the women's penitentiary to the death house at the main penitentiary in Columbia. In the back seat with her, he said many years later, was Thurmond, then an Army officer on active duty. They were "a-huggin' and a-kissin' the whole day," said Johnson, whom Thurmond later as governor considered a trusted driver... In whispered "graveyard talk"—the kind of stories not to be told outsiders—the word around SLED (State Law Enforcement Division) was that Joe Frank said his aunt Sue was the only person seduced on the way to the electric chair.[12]

Sue became the first woman in South Carolina history to die in state's electric chair. The state executed George Logue and Clarence Bagwell on the same day as Sue.

Unlike most women executed throughout American history, Louise Peete was not born poor or burdened with the mental sufferings resulting from years of childhood abuse and neglect. Louise was born Lofie Louise Preslar in Bienville, Louisiana, in September 1880, the daughter of a wealthy newspaper publisher. Her family's prominence enabled Louise to attend the finest schools until misguided transgressions with young men warranted her expulsion. To her own admission, Louise had a good upbringing, yet her passion for destroying the lives of people around her, including her own, belies the integrity of her childhood—she became a serial killer. In 1903 and in her early twenties, Louise married traveling salesman Henry Bosley who, after three years of marriage, discovered Louise's infidelity with another man. Some commentators hold that Bosley was so distraught over his wife's betrayal that he committed suicide. Others claim that Bosley divorced Louise in 1912. Louise moved to Shreveport where she worked as a prostitute to save enough money to relocate to Boston. There, Louise serviced wealthy men, stole, and fenced their wives' expensive jewelry. Threatened with exposure, Louise moved to Waco, Texas, where she met oilman Joe Appel whom she killed with a bullet to the head one week later. Louise asserted self-defense claiming that Appel had attempted to rape her; a jury acquitted her of the murder. Louise left for Dallas where she married a hotel desk clerk named Harry Faurote who also found Louise's infidelity emotionally devastating and hanged himself in the hotel basement shortly after their marriage. In 1915, Louise moved to Denver where she married Richard Peete and had a daughter a year later. Louise left her husband and daughter and moved to Los Angeles in 1920; reportedly, Richard had become seriously ill and unable to work and support Louise to her liking.

In California, Louise met mining executive and widower Jacob Denton while looking for a house to rent. Denton rented a separate house on the same property to Louise who quickly became his live-in companion. Two weeks after renting the house, Louise killed Denton with a shot to the back of the neck and buried his body in the basement. Louise continued living in the house, hold lavish parties, and providing excuses for Denton's absence. Troubled by her father's disappearance, Denton's daughter contacted a private investigator and Denton's lawyer. They contacted police who discovered Denton's body. In the interim, Louise returned to Denver where police found her again living with Peete. Los Angeles authorities tried and convicted Louise of first-degree murder and sentenced her to life in prison. With no contact with Louise for several years after her imprisonment, Peete committed suicide. Louise served 18 years of her life sentence where she befriended Margaret Logan who was instrumental in Louise's parole in 1939. State officials paroled Louise to a Mrs. Latham in 1943 and she worked at a canteen servicing military personnel. During her employment, an elderly female co-worker vanished whom authorities suspected Louise had killed but never investigated the woman's disappearance after Louise revealed that the co-worker had died from injuries sustained from a fall. Louise then married Lee Borden Judson and Logan disappeared shortly thereafter. Louise and Judson had moved into Logan's house and Louise's parole officer became suspicious of forged periodic status reports from Logan. Officials found Logan's body buried in the backyard of her house. Louise confessed to the murder and was tried, convicted, and sentenced to death. Judson committed suicide shortly after his own acquittal for Logan's killing by throwing himself down a 13-story building stairwell. San Quentin prison officials asphyxiated Louise in April 1947. Authorities believe that Louise had murdered four people during her lifetime.

By the time Martha Jule Seaborn (Beck) was 10 years old, she was a fully matured young girl owing to a glandular problem that also caused her to grow obese at an early age. She suffered ridicule from family members and classmates. Her brother raped her when she as a youngster and her mother beat Martha when she told her about the incidents claiming that the abuse was Martha's fault. One commentator explains, "Throughout her teenage years, Martha was the focus of cruel jokes and insults which drove her further within herself. She became reclusive, withdrawn and had virtually no friends her own age."[13] Martha graduated from high school and then from nursing school and eventually moved to California where she landed a job as a nurse in an Army hospital. She began patronizing bars where she would have sex with wayward soldiers. She became pregnant and gave birth to a daughter, Willa Dean, in 1944. She eventually married a bus driver named Alfred Beck, had a second child, and then divorced Beck. Martha abandoned both children to the Salvation Army and moved to Florida. She had left two previous marriages.

Martha met Raymond Martinez Fernandez in 1947 and became instrumental in his fraudulent scheme of procuring lonely women's bank accounts. Fernandez solicited women through the Lonely Hearts correspondence club; some commentators suggest that Raymond defrauded more than 100 women of their homes and bank accounts. One such incident in late 1948 involved a 66-year-old widow named Janet J. Fay who had written to Fernandez inviting him to New York. Janet eventually withdrew funds exceeding $4,000 that she turned over to Raymond. Martha and Raymond later strangled and bludgeoned Janet to death in her New York apartment. The next victim was Delphine Downing, a young widow with a two-year-old daughter, Rainelle. Delphine and Raymond soon became lovers and moved into the Downing home in Michigan with her child. Martha and Raymond robbed Delphine of money and possessions and afterwards forced sleeping pills down her throat and shot the unconscious woman through the head. Martha drowned Rainelle in a bathtub to keep her from crying. The two then buried Delphine and Raninelle in the cellar of Delphine's home. Neighbors contacted police after noticing the mother and daughters disappearance. After their arrests, Martha and Raymond confessed to the killings of Janet, Delphine and Rainelle, but officials suspected the two of killing 17 other women. New York electrocuted Martha and Raymond at Sing Sing prison in March 1951.

Bonnie Brown Heady was born on a Missouri farm in 1923. Her mother died when she was young and an aunt raised Bonnie. Eventually she married Vernon Heady, a livestock merchant. The couple was married for 17 years and had no children. In 1950, the marriage failed because of Bonnie's excessive drinking. Soon after her divorce from Vernon Heady, Bonnie met a man who convinced her to put her love-making skills to work. They transformed a bedroom in the Heady home that she got from her marriage to Vernon into a parlor and she began servicing men. The federal government executed Bonnie Brown Heady and her male accomplice Carl Austin Hall in December 1953 for kidnapping and murdering six-year-old Robert Cosgrove Greenlease, Jr., of Kansas City. Hall apparently masterminded a scheme whereby Heady posed as Bobby's aunt and took the child from his Catholic school, Notre Dame de Sion in Hyde Park, ensuring nuns that the boy's mother had suffered a heart attack. Shortly after the kidnapping, Heady and Hall demanded a $600,000 from Bobby's father, Robert Greenlease, a multimillionaire Cadillac dealer, who paid the ransom a week later. Unknown to Greenlease, Hall had already shot young Bobby in the head and buried his body in a shallow grave behind Heady's house. With money in hand, Hall quickly abandoned Heady. St. Louis police officer Louis Shoulders arrested Hall after a local cab driver reported Hall's spending spree as he drove him around St. Louis. Reportedly, a mobster named Joe Costello owned the cab company and may have informed Shoulders about Hall for part of the ransom money since authorities never recovered more than $303,000 of the money. Several criminal indictments against police officers followed.

Scholars continue to debate the guilt and innocence of Barbara Graham, asphyxiated in California in June 1955 along with accomplices John Albert Santo and Emmett Raymond Perkins. State officials executed the three for the brutal beating and strangulation murder of Mabel Monahan; a 64-year-old partially disabled widow thought to be holding hundreds of thousands of dollars in cash in her Burbank home for a former son-in-law connected with Las Vegas gambling interests. As with so many other women executed in this country, Barbara Graham had a wretched childhood. She was born Barbara Elaine Wood in 1923 to an unwed teenage mother, Hortense Wood, in a dilapidated boarding house in Oakland, California. Two years after Barbara's birth, a juvenile court deemed Hortense incorrigible and committed her to the Ventura State School for Girls. Hortense's extended family cared for young Barbara until her release years later, after which Hortense gave birth to two more illegitimate children and afforded little to no attention to Barbara. Long after her arrest for murder, Barbara commented to a *San Francisco Chronicle* reporter, "My mother never cared whether I lived or died, so long as I didn't bother her." Another newspaper reporter writing a story about a welfare worker that wanted to adopt young Barbara stated, "The poor little kid never had anyone who really loved her" and believed Hortense intensely hated young Barbara. As a young teenager, Barbara became promiscuous and incorrigible so Hortense turned her over to juvenile authorities who, in turn sent her to the same boarding school attended by her mother. To one commentator, "Graham never had a chance because ... she was put into a reform school for girls, where she learned to be a prostitute, a drug user, a forger, and a murderer. Society shared guilt because a 13-year-old-child was discarded by society and her feet planted firmly on a road that led, almost inevitably, to the gas chamber at San Quentin."[14]

After her release from reform school, Barbara tried to put her life on a more positive track by attending a business college, she married a young man also attending a business college and had her first child at 17 years old. A second pregnancy strained the marriage, the couple soon divorced and a court granted full custody of the children to Barbara's husband. She became deeply depressed after her divorce, moved to San Diego, and became a full-time prostitute. She married another man but after four months he learned of Barbara's checkered past and annulled the marriage. Barbara returned to San Francisco as a professional call girl. There she met two men about to go to trial on theft charges who asked Barbara to testify as an alibi witness. She agreed, but the prosecution proved Barbara was not in San Francisco at the time of the theft and she ended up with a conviction for perjury and served a year in jail. With that conviction, Barbara now had a criminal record for prostitution, vagrancy, disorderly and lewd conduct, and for writing fraudulent checks.

In 1948 at the age of 25, Barbara moved to Reno, Nevada, and went to work as a nurse in a county hospital. There she married her third husband; a sales clerk for an auto supply store, but Barbara left the marriage unexpectedly and made her way to the Los Angeles area where she again worked as a prostitute. It was there that Barbara became entangled with a bartender named Henry Graham who she married in 1952 and had her third child. Graham was a drug addict and soon Barbara became a "full-blown junkie, with a hypodermic needle and spoon in her purse at all times." Barbara soon left her third husband and the child to move in with a man introduced to Barbara by her husband, Emmett Perkins. To one commentator, Barbara Graham

> was a beautiful and strangely charming young woman, she was also utterly amoral. She had no conception of the difference between right and wrong. She did what she pleased, never taking time to think, never worrying about the consequences. She neither knew nor cared whether or not an act was criminal, indecent, or immoral. If she had never done it before, she wanted to try it, and if she found it interesting, she wanted to repeat it.[15]

In March 1953, Barbara, along with four men including Santo and Perkins, tricked their way into Monahan's home to steal the money ostensibly kept in the house by Monahan's former son-in-law Tutor Scherer. They bound, gagged, and pistol-whipped Monahan who died by asphyxiation from a pillowcase put over her head, but found no money in the house. Soon afterwards, Los Angeles and Burbank police officers arrested Emmett Perkins, John Santo, Barbara Graham, and John True and a trial ensued for Monahan's murder. John True turned state's evidence and testified that Barbara was Monahan's actual killer. The jury convicted the three defendants of Monahan's murder after a 5-week trial, and two weeks later, the trial judge sentenced them to die in the state's gas chamber at San Quentin Prison. The California Supreme Court denied Barbara a new trial and affirmed her conviction and death sentence. Officials executed Barbara first, and then three hours later executed Perkins and Santos together.

Considerable controversy remains about Barbara Graham's conviction and execution. One legal commentator challenges much about the police procedures used to convict Barbara of the murder:

> If Barbara Graham was ... an innocent victim of circumstance, the governmental termination of her life is an unspeakable perversion of justice. If Barbara Graham was guilty of Mrs. Monaghan's murder, premising her conviction for that crime upon information acquired by illegal, abusive and reprehensible law enforcement tactics sabotages fundamental principles of respect for the dignity of the individual—even the individual criminal—and for her inviolable constitutional rights.[16]

In a tasteless attempt to vilify and disparage Barbara to the jury in her murder trial, the state's prosecutor read letters Barbara had written to a lesbian lover she met while in jail and awaiting trial.

> Leavy brought out the love notes exchanged between Mommy and Candy Pants, and forced Barbara to read them aloud to the jury. It was a mortifying experience for Barbara, but she braced up and tried to get through it. When one letter got particularly intimate, she could not continue.

Leavy offered to read it for her. Barbara blinked back tears, looking stricken. "Mr. Leavy, do you have to read that'" she implored.

Leavy, a relentless prosecutor who believed to his very core that the woman before him helped kill elderly, frail, helpless Mabel Monohan, had not an iota of mercy for her. He read aloud, "'I do love you, honey. You are so lovely and desirable, sweetheart. I want so much to show you how I love you. I am sure I can make you happy—'"

The note went on, a heartfelt expression of the love of one woman for another, by someone who, perhaps, had never really felt deep, sincere love from anyone—not even her own mother. But the revelation made Barbara squirm; this was 1953, when homosexual love in America was not only predominantly in the closet, but the closet was locked as well. For Barbara, it was an excruciatingly humiliating few minutes.[17]

Elizabeth Ann Duncan was one of five children born to a chiropractor and his wife who lived around mining camps in the southwest. Elizabeth had a turbulent life. She had reached the fourth-grade when her parents demanded she leave school to care for her younger siblings. At the age of 14, Elizabeth married and had three children with a man who left her for another woman; as a result, Elizabeth turned over custody of her children to her mother-in-law. Soon thereafter, Elizabeth married again and gave birth to Frank Patrick Duncan. She also had a daughter that suddenly died when 15 years old. Duncan married no less than 11 times, spent considerable time in a sanitarium, became addicted to seconal, charged with forgery in San Diego, and for running a house of prostitution in San Francisco. Elizabeth had a perverted relationship with her son Frank to whom she was completely devoted. The two lived together for nearly 30 years. When Frank demanded that his mother move out of their shared house, Elizabeth attempted suicide with an overdose of seconal and was hospitalized. It was there that Frank met Olga Kupczyk, a nurse working in the hospital where physicians were treating Elizabeth. The two married in June 1958, and almost immediately Elizabeth began planning her murder of Olga. She had contacted eight persons with proposals to kill Olga when she finally met Augustine Baldonaldo and Luis Moya who agreed to murder Olga for $6,000. The two men went to Olga's apartment, kidnapped her, pistol whipped her, took turns strangulating her, and then buried her in a shallow grave at a dam construction site. A coroner later reported that Olga, eight months pregnant, was most likely alive when the two killers buried her. Upon their arrest, Baldonado and Moya confessed to crime and that Elizabeth had solicited the killing. Trials throughout 1959 found all three guilty of murder and sentenced to death, appellate courts affirmed the judgments. San Quentin authorities executed Baldonado and Moya together in the state's gas chamber in August 1962, and Elizabeth died in the same chamber several hours later.

Velma Barfield was the first woman executed in the United States after the U.S. Supreme Court's landmark decision in *Gregg v. Georgia*. Why the state of North Carolina put to death Velma Barfield is more perplexing to some commentators than why Velma killed her victims. Velma was yet another in a long line of women offenders that suffered the brutal violence of men. Velma was born into rural South Carolina poverty and was the second oldest of nine children and the oldest daughter. Her father, Murphy Bullard, was a small tobacco and cotton farmer who lost his farm shortly after Velma's birth in October 1932. As a child, Velma suffered the scorn of her classmates because of her poverty. Velma's life of abuse from men began at 13 years old when her father sexually assaulted and viciously raped young Velma. She dropped out of high school in her junior year, married Thomas Burke at 16 years old, and had two children by the time she was 21 years old. She had a hysterectomy in 1963 that left her severely emotionally scared. Suffering from depression after an automobile accident and unable to work, Burke became progressively violent and abusive. He died in a house fire in 1968. At the time of Thomas' death, Velma was sole financial support for her family, working two jobs and had become addicted to tranquilizers and sedatives. Two years later Velma married a retired civil servant inflicted with diabetes, emphysema and heart disease, Jennings Barfield, who died eight months after their marriage. After a stay in the hospital from a drug overdose, Velma became addicted to several psychotropic drugs used to curb her depression. Over the next several years Velma was either in jail or prison for passing fraudulent checks to support a drug habit that put her in the hospital on a few occasions. Working as a nurse's aide for the elderly, Velma met her employer's nephew Stewart Taylor, a wealthy tobacco farmer, alcoholic and widower who was 10 years older than Velma. They planned to marry but Steward died. An autopsy showed that Stewart died from arsenic poisoning. Attention focused on Velma who admitted to poisoning Stewart, his mother and three elderly persons—Montgomery Edwards, Dollie Edwards, John Henry Lee—she had once nursed. Authorities also suspected Velma of poisoning to death her late husband Thomas whose body officials exhumed and found that it contained arsenic. Admittedly, Velma's motivation for the killing was to conceal her forging checks to support her drug habit. A North Carolina jury convicted her of Taylor's murder and recommended the death penalty without ever hearing mitigating evidence of Velma's drug addiction, troubled childhood, or her ability to judge right from wrong, or that at least one medical professional had treated Velma for schizophrenia. For this reason, Robert Jacobson, Velma's court-appointed lawyer proved incompetent. What's more, Jacobson had never before tried a death penalty case. After a team of defense lawyers had exhausted all appeals and the state's governor who was in a fervently contested Senate race denied clemency, officials at the Central Prison in Raleigh executed Velma in November 1984 by lethal injection.

In June 1983, Karla Faye Tucker and Daniel Ryan Garrett broke into Jerry Lynn Dean's apartment in northeast Houston to steal motorcycle parts. Confronting Dean in the bedroom of the apartment, Garrett began beating him about his head with a hammer. Tucker struck Dean in the back with a pickax found in the room so he would stop making a "gurgling sound." Tucker found Deborah Ruth Davis Thornton, a companion to Dean, under the bed and Garrett hacked her to death leaving the pick-ax embedded in her chest. Karla Tucker exemplified the poverty and backwardness of most women on death row today. At 23 years old she committed a heinous crime while delirious on drugs. At trial, expert testimony revealed that Karla began to use marihuana at the age of eight and was already using heroin intravenously by age ten. She continued to use drugs until she was arrested for Jerry Dean's murder. Karla used drugs so extensive that one expert stated she had probably been off drugs for only two weeks out of her entire life. During the two days before the killings, Karla had taken Valium, Placidyl, Percodan, Soma, Wygesic, Dilaudid, and methamphetamine. Karla was a prostitute, introduced to her at a very young age by her mother. Yet the single most important factor troubling not only to the jury, the criminal appeals court, and the public concerning Tucker's case was that in the immediate aftermath of Karla and Garrett's savage hammer and pickax beating to death of Dean and Thornton, Tucker boasted to her friends that "every time she picked Jerry, she looked up and she grinned and got a nut and hit him again."[18] Though Karla denied ever making the comment, investigators had taped the statement. Many of the more than 550 newspaper reports on the case referenced Tucker's supposed sexual gratification in pickaxing Dean to death. The criminal appeals court explained that Tucker's sexual gratification while pick axing Jerry Dean to death lays bare the "most dangerous aberration of character."[19] One commentator referred to Tucker as "an animal driven by impulse and not conscience."[20] In response to Tucker's declarations of rehabilitation while in prison, Deborah Thornton's husband claimed that Tucker simply wants "back on the streets" and "in the bedroom with her husband." Unquestionably, Karla Tucker's jailhouse conversion from evil woman to pious Christian fundamentalist prompted affirmations from conservative religious leaders (most notably, Pat Robertson, Pope John Paul II, Cardinal O'Connor, and Sr. Helen Prejean) that Tucker was no longer the person who committed the ghastly killings and that Texas justice officials should show leniency and allow her to live. Joining the chorus were the United Nations and European Parliament. Meanwhile, Texas Governor George W. Bush ridiculed Karla Faye Tucker's pleads for life and sneeringly mocked her words: "Pleeease don't kill me." Texas executed Karla by lethal injection in early February 1998.

In August 1992, Lynda Cheryle Lyon Block and her common-law husband, George Everette Sibley, lived in Orlando, Florida, where police arrested and charged the two for aggravated battery and burglary in the stabbing of Lynda's elderly former husband. A county court set a sentencing hearing in early September 1993, but the couple failed to appear and the court issued warrants for their arrests. They fled the state with Lynda's nine-year-old son. In early October 1993, while stopped at a Big B Drugs in Pepperell Corners Shopping Center in Opelika, Alabama, Lynda used a pay telephone outside the store and Sibley stayed near the car with Lynda's son. A passerby named Ramona Robertson heard the child ask for help. Robertson was worried that the child was in danger and was afraid the family was living in their car. She watched the Ford Mustang as Sibley moved it to a different location in the parking lot near the entrance to a Wal-Mart. At that point, Opelika Police Sergeant Roger Lamar Motley had just finished lunch and was running an errand for the police department. When he came out of a store in the shopping center, Robertson reported to him what she had observed. After Robertson reported the situation, Motley radioed to the Opelika Police Department of his activities about the incident. Motley pulled his cruiser behind the Mustang. Sibley was in the car with the boy and Motley asked Sibley for his driver's license. Sibley said he didn't need one and while trying to explain, Motley put his hand on his service revolver. Sibley reached into the car and pulled out a gun. Motley took cover behind his cruiser and Sibley crouched by the bumper of the Mustang. As the men were firing at each other, Lynda dropped the phone, pulled a pistol from her handbag and ran toward the scene, firing. Motley turned and Lynda shot him in the chest. Motley had several gunshot wounds and he died later that afternoon in a nearby hospital. Lynda and Sibley sped away from the parking lot and a high speed chase ensued and ended when the coupled stopped a roadblock. The couple surrendered to police after a four-hour standoff. A police search of their car revealed several weapons and a large quantity of ammunition. Alabama tried, convicted, and sentenced Lynda to death. Authorities electrocuted her on April 18, 2002, and put Sibley to death by lethal injection on August 4, 2005.

In October 2002, Florida put to death Aileen Carol Wuornos by lethal injection at the Broward Correctional Institution for murdering seven men. Florida tried Aileen for the murder of Richard Mallory but she eventually pleaded guilty to the other killings though she claimed she killed the men in self-defense. Aileen was born Aileen Carol Pittman in February 1956 to Diane and Leo Pittman, but her maternal grandparents raised her from about the age of two after being abandoned by her mother. Serving a life sentence for kidnapping and raping an adolescent child, Leo Pittman committed suicide while in prison. Aileen had an exceedingly troubled childhood that entailed abandonment by her mother, suicide of her father, incestual victimization by her brother and grandfather, and was fully engaged in prostitution by the age of eleven. These experiences left Aileen devoid of emotions, a low IQ, a long criminal history, an alcoholic, drug abuser, and with an illegitimate child the product of a rape by the age of 14. A juvenile case worker described young Aileen as immature and impulsive. After her arrest for the murder and armed robbery of Richard Mallory, the press almost immediately labeled Aileen a "man-hating lesbian." The assumption about her sexuality was based on her 4-year romantic relationship with Tyria Moore whom she called her wife. As Atwell points out, "Themes of lesbianism, man-hating, deceitfulness, greed, deviance, and manipulativeness characterize Wuornos' trial in the Mallory case."[21] Aileen dropped all appeals in October 2002, essentially volunteering for execution.

A Harris County jury convicted Suzanne Margaret Basso of the 1998 brutal killing of a 59-year-old mentally retarded man named Louis "Buddy" Musso whose diminished intellectual capacity was that of an eight-year-old child. District Judge Mary Lou Keel sentenced Suzanne to death. Despite his mental incapacities, Musso lived independently in an assisted living home, held a job at a grocery store, and handled his own financial affairs. In June 1998, Musso left New Jersey where he met Suzanne and went to live with her in Texas under the pretense that she would marry him. Soon after moving to Texas, Basso took a $6,000 life insurance policy out on Musso and drafted a will that left Musso's entire estate to Suzanne. Trial evidence shows that Musso suffered tremendous abuse at the hands of Suzanne and five co-defendants in the days leading to his death. Suzanne took Musso to the apartment of James O'Malley, Bernice Ahrens, Craig Ahrens, Hope Ahrens, and Terence Singleton, where they forced Musso to remain seated or in a kneeling position on a plastic mat in the hallway for hours after breaking a Disney figurine. Whenever Musso attempted to get off the mat, O'Malley would beat or kick him. O'Malley, Singleton, Bernice, and Craig beat Musso, and O'Malley, while wearing combat boots, kicked him repeatedly. Suzanne beat Musso with a baseball bat on the buttocks, back, and groin area, and both she and Hope struck him with a belt and buckle. After hearing that Musso had been "misbehaving" while she was away from the apartment, Suzanne, who weighed over 300 pounds, repeatedly jumped on top of Musso while he was on his hands and knees, causing him to fall flat on the ground. Members of the group often bathed Musso in a solution of bleach and Pine-Sol cleaning fluid, using a wire brush on his body. Musso died during one of these baths.

A jogger found Musso's body on a morning in late August 1999 dumped near a roadway and contacted authorities. A county medical examiner reported an astonishing number of injuries to Musso's body and was unable to count the literally hundreds of bruises covering Musso's body. The palms of Musso's hands and the soles of his feet were bruised, his back and buttocks showed numerous lash marks showing that someone had whipped him, and Musso's severely blackened eyes resulted from a "hinge fracture" to his skull, which probably was caused by a blow to the back of the head. Musso sustained broken bones in his nose, ribs, and throat. Musso also exhibited burn marks on his back from a cigarette or a hot poker. The medical examiner also found skin abrasion attributable to contact with a cleaning solution or scrub brush. The cause of death was a skull fracture from an object that left a large, X-shaped laceration in Musso's scalp. After her arrest, Suzanne confessed in a written statement to police to have driven Bernice Ahrens's car, with Musso's body in the trunk, to the site where O'Malley, Singleton, and Craig Ahrens dumped the body. She also admitted driving the car to the dumpster where the others disposed of additional incriminating evidence, including bloody clothes and rubber gloves, which the police had found as a result of O'Malley's confession. Suzanne explained that Musso's death at the hands of her and her five confederates was the final act of abuse that Basso had inflicted on her family and the outcasts she brought home over the years. Hardy said that her mother had been practicing on her kin and honing her abusive techniques. The Texas Court of Criminal Appeals and the U.S. Supreme Court denied Suzanne any relief from her conviction or death sentence. As for the other defendants, James David O'Malley received a life prison term, Bernice Ahrens received an 80-year prison term, Craig Ahrens received a 60-year prison term, Hope Ahrens pleaded guilty to murder and received a 20-year prison sentence, and Terence Singleton received a life term.

In his review of an abundance of newspaper stories on Suzanne, David Krajicek of the *New York Daily News* showed that Suzanne led an extremely turbulent life since childhood.[22] Suzanne was one of eight children and the youngest of three girls. Suzanne's troubled life began when her alcoholic parents subjected her and her siblings to grotesque physical and sexual abuse. Suzanne was a delinquent teenager engaging in sex, truancy, and theft, and eventually landed in a reform school. After completing high school, Suzanne married James Peek with whom she had a daughter and son. Sexual deviance accented the Peek marriage. Suzanne and Peek were promiscuous; Suzanne often had sexual relations with other men in the home. North Carolina officials convicted James Peek of molesting his daughter and spent nearly a year in jail. Suzanne's own daughter, Christiana Hardy, asserted during the penalty phase of her mother's trial that her life too was plagued with horrors of child victimization, "There was sexual abuse, mental abuse, emotional abuse, physical abuse. Any kind of abuse she could inflict." Christiana recalled that once Suzanne forced her and her brother to undress for two maintenance men and Suzanne watched as the men fondled her then-seven-year-old daughter. Suzanne had sexual relations with her son and often forced him to eat on the floor. Suzanne's defense lawyer claimed that she was mentally incompetent and delusional at the time of her executions. What's more, there were claims that the chief medical examiner involved in the case "fabricated credentials and hypothesized expansively."[23] Texas put Suzanne to death by lethal injection in early February 2014.

Ethel Rosenberg

In the 1950s era of McCarthyism and its communist witch hunts, the federal government put Ethel Rosenberg, along with her husband Julius Rosenberg, to death by electrocution at New York's Sing Sing Prison in June 1953 for conspiracy to commit espionage between 1944 and 1945. To some commentators, the Korean War "heightened the anti-communist witch hunt that led to Ethel and Julius Rosenberg's lynching in the electric chair on June 19, 1953."[24] Yet, to trial judge Irving R. Kaufman who heard the case against Julius and Ethel Rosenberg, spying was a "crime worse than murder."[25] Ethel Greenglass (Rosenberg's maiden name) was the only daughter of low-income Jewish immigrants from Russia who was born in New York City in September 1915. Ethel's father was a sewing machine technician who provided poorly for his family. Ethel was an exceptionally intelligent girl and graduated from high school at the age of 15. After completing school, Ethel became a clerk for a shipping company but terminated her employment shortly after joining the American Communist Party where she met Julius Rosenberg at a New Year's Eve benefit. They married in the summer 1939. The couple had two sons, and Ethel became a homemaker caring for her children.

There is still considerable debate on the extent to which Ethel Rosenberg was involved in the espionage for which the government tried, convicted, and executed Ethel on the perjured testimony of Ruth Greenglass, Ethel's sister-in-law. In 1945, Igor Gouzenko defected from the Soviet Union to Canada and claimed to have evidence linking Ethel Rosenberg's brother, David Greenglass, to an espionage ring centered in Great Britain. At this time, David Greenglass was stationed in Los Alamos and was associated with the Manhattan Project. The FBI arrested Greenglass in July 1950 who confessed to spying for the Soviet Union and named Julius Rosenberg as a contact to whom he gave atomic secrets. He implicated his wife Ruth Greenglass as a courier, but David Greenglass clearly denied any involvement of Ethel Rosenberg in the espionage ring. The government quickly arrested and interrogated Julius Rosenberg but he implicated no other persons of spying for the Soviets. Hoping to get Julius to detail his espionage activities and to bring favorable publicity to the FBI, Director J. Edgar Hoover ordered Ethel arrested and intimidated both Julius and Ethel to name others. Meanwhile, the FBI re-interrogated David Greenglass and offered him a deal of leniency and not to charge his wife Ruth with espionage if he were to name Ethel as part of the Soviet spy ring. As a result, Greenglass changed his original position that Ethel had nothing to do with the spying and stated that he gave secreted information to the Rosenberg's in their apartment. Ruth claimed that Ethel typed notes for Julius about the secreted information given to them by David.

In March 1950, the federal government began its espionage trial against the Rosenbergs and the federal court in New York that quickly convicted and sentenced the Rosenbergs to death. They remained on death row in Sing Sing Prison for 26 months. Commentators contend that the government would never have executed the Rosenbergs had they confessed and implicated others. To Nobel Laureate Jean-Paul Sartre, the Rosenberg case amounted to "a legal lynching which smears with blood a whole nation."[26] In a recent expose, Tom Ely denounces the Rosenberg executions as "a savage act by the U.S. government calculated to terrorize the population."[27]

Ethel Rosenberg's actual execution remains controversial since it took five consecutive attempts to kill her. Obviously appalled by Rosenberg's execution, U.S. Supreme Court Justice Brennan commented in his dissent in *Glass v. Louisiana*, "After the *fourth* (shock) guards removed one of the two straps and the two doctors applied their stethoscopes. But they were not satisfied that she was dead. The executioner came to them from his switchboard in a small room 10 feet from the chair. 'Want another?' he asked. The doctors nodded. Guards replaced the straps and for the *fifth* time electricity was applied."[28] Chief Justice William Rehnquist working as a Supreme Court clerk at the time of the Rosenberg's case stated in a memorandum, however, "the Rosenbergs were fitting candidates for the electric chair and that it is too bad that drawing and quartering has been abolished."[29]

Evidence supporting Ethel Rosenberg's innocence surfaced recently when newspapers reported that the only known Soviet intelligence officer alive with personal knowledge of the Rosenberg case, Alexander Feklisov, claims that Ethel Rosenberg had nothing to do with the espionage. Ethel Rosenberg was innocent though she probably knew of her husband's involvement in the case. Since 1975, the government has released information and documents on the Rosenberg case under the Freedom of Information Act. These documents show that Ethel's involvement in the espionage case was at best marginal. Cold War scholars at the National Security Achieve, the American Historical Association, and Georgetown University Law center among other agencies solicited the government to study the secret grand jury testimony of some 46 witnesses in the government's case against Ethel Rosenberg that tend to confirm a frame-up of Ethel Rosenberg. Those grand jury transcripts show that Ruth Greenglass testified that she wrote the notes and that she did not testify that she witnessed Ethel Rosenberg type the secret notes. To Law Professor David Vladeck, "Ruth Greenglass' pretrial testimony confirms that her husband's trial claim was a fabrication."[30] In recent years, David Greenglass recanted his testimony that Ethel Rosenberg typed the notes. David Greenglass died in July 2014 at the age of 92; he had been living in nursing home under an assumed name. Ethel Rosenberg's execution unquestionably raises the specter that the federal government not only botched her execution but that it executed a wrongfully convicted woman. Noted lyricist Abel Meeropol and his wife Anne adopted the Rosenberg's two young sons, Michael and Robert, in 1957. In a recent *Los Angeles Times* editorial, the Rosenberg's sons examined the lessons learned from the government's action against their parents:

> This case provides a crucial warning about the tendencies of our government to manufacture and exploit public fear, to trample civil rights and to manipulate judicial proceedings. In our current political climate, the targets being vilified have changed, but the tactics of those in power remain much the same.[31]

Robert Meeropol more recently pointed out in a *Los Angeles Times* editorial that his analysis of more than 300,000 previously secret files reveals, "We now know that my parents' trial judge collaborated with the prosecution, that witnesses perjured themselves and that evidence was fabricated."[32]

Spousal Murder

The often-troubled backgrounds of young women manifested pathologies years later in unhappy marriages, at times resulting in women killing their abusive husbands. From the later decades of the 19th century to the early decades of the 20th century, however, jurisdictions did not execute most white women who killed their husbands. From 1875 to 1920 in Chicago, for instance, juries found guilty and courts sentenced to prison terms only two of 80 white women prosecuted for murdering their husbands; authorities generally limited the affirmative defense of self-defense in spousal abuse cases to older, wealthier white women "who refused to submit to extreme domestic abuse."[33] This trend existed in all the major industrializing cities in the United States and essentially was a defense limited to white women who protected themselves against sadistic husbands. Accordingly, "the new unwritten law gave a woman the right to use lethal force in resisting an abusive husband. In order to secure an acquittal (on the ground of self-defense), the woman had to demonstrate that she had been the victim of wife beatings. Having established a history of abuse, she was then legally justified in killing her husband."[34] In a 1908 California case,

> Margaret Finn shot and killed J.E. Mahaffey on a crowded Los Angeles Street. Finn and Mahaffey were engaged to be married. Moreover, Finn was pregnant with Mahaffey's child. But Mahaffey was having second thoughts. He was running out of money, he told her, and wanted to postpone the wedding indefinitely. Devastated by the scoundrel's betrayal, Finn found a revolver, tracked Mahaffey down, and shot him dead. She claimed that she could not remember firing the gun. Her mind had gone totally blank: what happened was "a mystery." Still, she refused to apologize: "I had placed my honor and my life in his trust and he betrayed that trust...." Mahaffey "deserved death for the way he treated me." The judge agreed. He dismissed the case against her without trial.[35]

In one of the few cases of convicted women in the period, the defendant was a poor, young dressmaker from Mississippi that "lacked the dignity and respectability of older, wealthier defendants."[36] Here, a jury did not accept Virginia Troupe's self-defense claim because she murdered her husband for beatings involving "an appropriate reason—for accepting 'the attentions of other men.'"[37] The other case concerned a middle-aged Swedish immigrant who stabbed her husband after he attacked her with a knife. Evidence showed that Hilda Exlund had a powerful physique and consistently brutalized her husband of a much smaller stature. These women likely served a term of years in prison because there is no evidence of their executions. Southern judges were especially reluctant to send white women to prison even for the most grievous of crimes. In the 1929 case of a 25-year-old white woman named Marion Drew, for instance, a Mississippi judge accepted a guilty plea from Marion for killing her husband Martin and then released her without bond. "She would remain free, he ordered, if she behaved herself in the future."[38] Mississippi never prosecuted Marion for her husband's murder.

Despite the availability of the unwritten defense, jurisdictions executed several white women for spousal murder in the third historical trend in female executions. Mary Mabel Rogers was the illegitimate child of a criminal father and a mentally deficient mother. She was orphaned at six months old and reared by Johanna Callahan. As one news reporter explained, "Suffice it to say that Mary Rogers was probably mentally deficient, virtually uneducated and not intelligent enough to cover the least of her tracks in the clumsy plotting of her husband's death."[39] Mary and an accomplice, described as a "half-witted boy," killed her husband Marcus Meritt Rogers in August 1902 for a $1,000 life insurance policy and so she could marry another man. Mary was 15 years old when she married Marcus who was 10 years her senior and with whom she had a baby daughter who died from a fractured skull at six months old. Marcus was a farm worker and the couple lived in perpetual poverty. Mary left Marcus four years after their marriage and began "a promiscuous lifestyle and cultivated a reputation that was nothing short of abominable."[40] At the time, Mary went to work as a servant for Emmett and Laura Perham who had two young sons—Levi and Leon Perham—with whom she soon became sexually involved. She also began a sexual liaison with a boarder in the household named Morris Knapp. To rid her of Marcus and gain the insurance proceeds, Mary coaxed Marcus to meet with her at a picnic grounds near the Little Walloomsac River under the pretense of mending their marriage and returning to Marcus who had all but forgiven her. At the meeting, Mary and Leon attacked Marcus, rendered him unconscious with chloroform, and then beat him so severely that they crushed his skull. The two then rolled Marcus into the river where he drowned. An investigation into Marcus' disappearance led to Mary and Leon. Authorities arrested them and a grand jury indicted both for capital murder. Leon turned state's evidence against Mary and a county court found them guilty of the crime, sentencing Leon to life in prison and Mary to the gallows. Mary appealed her capital sentence to the Vermont Supreme Court and the U.S. Supreme Court, both courts upheld the sentence. Just before her hanging in December 1905, Mary claimed that she was pregnant by another inmate, a convicted rapist named Vernon Rogers. The Sheriff ignored her claim and proceeded with the hanging that he botched; the rope reportedly used to hang Mary was too long and her shoes touched the ground after she fell through the trap door. The Sheriff and an attending physician pulled on the rope and let Mary strangle to death. Justice authorities again proved incompetent and callous not only in botching Mary's execution but also possibly killing yet another innocent unborn child.

Ruth Brown Synder was born Ruth Brown in 1895 to a working-class Swedish-Norwegian couple in upper Manhattan. Ruth attended public schools and after the eighth grade, she left school for a job with the telephone company. She attended night school and took courses in shorthand and typing that enabled her to eventually land a job as a stenographer with *Cosmopolitan* magazine in 1914 at the age of 19 where inadvertently she met Albert Synder, the art director at *Motor Boating* magazine. The couple married in 1915 and soon had a daughter. After 12 years of marriage, Ruth tired of relationship with Albert and reportedly had extra-marital affairs with some 28 men during her marriage. Much of Ruth's marital disharmony is directly attributable to Albert's emotional abuse. Albert reportedly hung a picture of Jessie Guishard, a deceased fiancée, in the couple's home. Albert named a boat after Jessie and consistently reminded Ruth that Jessie was the finest woman he had ever known. One of Ruth's sexual suitors was Henry Judd Gray, a Syracuse sales representative for Bien Jolie Corset Company. The two planned and carried out Albert's murder. A substantial life insurance policy secretly paid for by Ruth was an issue in the case. Both confessed to the murder and died in the electric chair in Sing Sing Prison in New York in January 1927.

The 1929 hanging of Ada Bonner LeBoeuf, and her paramour Thomas E. Dreher, for the murder of Ada's husband, James L. LeBoeuf, two years earlier in St. Mary Parish, involved one of the most notorious murder cases in Louisiana history—though now long forgotten. One reason for its notoriety at the time is that Ada LeBoeuf was an unusual candidate for murder and execution. While women who eventually met the gallows were mostly marginalized persons, Ada was a well-thought-of 38-year-old mother of four and married to the superintendent of the city's utility company. James was ill-tempered and occasionally beat Ada. Her paramour was a prosperous, well regarded physician, married with three children. Apparently, it was common knowledge among the Morgan City townspeople that Ada LeBoeuf and Dr. Dreher were having an affair. Ada and Thomas confessed to James' murder though they pleaded not guilty at trial. Ada admitted that she lured her husband onto Lake Palourde for a midnight boat ride and past the place where Thomas and James Beadle (a hunter and trapper) were waiting to kill him. James was shot to death but he had a long incision in his abdomen when found by men cruising in a motorboat. The killers tied two railroad angle irons to James' head and feet. The state's governor, Huey P. Long, would not grant clemency and Ada and Thomas hanged on February 1, 1929. The trial court sentenced James Beadle to life in prison and Angola Prison officials released him April 1939.

Anna Antonio ostensibly contracted for the murder of her extremely abusive husband. Anna married Salvatore Antonio when she was a 16-year-old child and he was a 30-year-old man. Anna was married to Salvatore for 11 years and had four children, three-year-old Frank, nine-year-old Phyllis, and six-year-old Marie. Salvatore's violence toward his family caused the death of a fourth child (name and age unknown). Salvatore was a drug dealer who was "rude, crude, lewd, and not averse to using his tiny wife [Anna weighed less than 100 pounds] as a punching bag."[41] Salvatore dominated every aspect of Anna's life and confined her largely to the house. There are conflicting versions of the crime. In one account Anna solicited two local Italian rogues named Vincent Saetta and Samuel Feraci to kill her husband in return for $800 of a $5,000 life insurance policy on Salvatore. In this description of the events Saetta and Feraci implicated Anna's involvement in soliciting the murder. Another version of the crime has it that Saetta and Feraci simply informed Anna that they were going to kill Salvatore because he owed Saetta an unpaid debt of $75 and that they expected a share of the insurance money. Anna's reply to Saetta and Feraci's intent to kill her husband was "I don't care what you do. I am only interested in the children."[42] Saetta, in fact, later signed an affidavit claiming that "Mrs. Antonio in no way asked me to kill her husband, in no way encouraged me to kill her husband and never at any time promised me any money to kill her husband."[43]

In March 1932, Saetta and Feraci persuaded Salvatore to join them for a night on the town drinking and patronizing a brothel. On their return to Albany, and while Salvatore stood on the side of the road urinating, the two culprits shot Salvatore five times and stabbed him 15 times, leaving his body on the side of the road. Attesting to the clumsiness of the murder, the actual cause of death was a concussion Salvatore suffered when he fell to the ground. The case against Anna hinged on the prosecution's claim that she conspired with Saetta and Feraci to kill her husband despite Saetta's written statement exonerating Anna of any culpability in the killing. Three separate appeals to the New York Court of Appeals argued that the case "presents no points overlooked or misapprehended by the court on the original decision."[44] Anna was the only woman on death row in New York at the time and three female guards hired to care for Anna became her friends and protected here while she remained imprisoned. Governor Lehman granted several stays of execution while lawyers pursued attempts to prove Anna's innocence. Interested parties solicited help from President Franklin Roosevelt, Cardinal Hayes of New York, and even the famed attorney Clarence Darrow. In August 1934, New York electrocuted 28-year-old Anna for the contract killing of her husband. Minutes later state authorities electrocuted Vincent Saetta and Samuel Feraci. One commentator points out that "[m]ore than anything else it was [Anna's] lack of widow's grief that doomed her."[45] Yet, it is difficult to imagine that Anna would regret the death of a violently sadistic husband that had murdered one of her children. As one scholar points out, rarely do women murderers of abusive husbands express a "widow's grief"; they more often find solace, and at times actually hearten in their husband's death.[46] Undoubtedly, that Anna was an Italian American during a period of harsh anti–Italian sentiment played a significant role in her execution.

Before her marriage to Hawkins Dean, Dovie was poor and worked as a domestic servant. After Hawkins' first wife died, he hired Dovie to work as a housekeeper and they soon married. That her marriage to Hawkins was more a business arrangement than anything else became clear when she stated to authorities that "he needed a housekeeper and I needed a home."[47] Dovie had a wretched life. She had been married once before but the marriage ended when authorities sent her husband to a West Virginia prison for seven years for raping one of their daughters who later died at childbirth. Dovie also had a son who died in a boiler explosion and her youngest daughter drowned. Hawkins was a prosperous farmer with a sizable estate that he willed to Dovie soon after their marriage. Five months later, Hawkins was dead and an autopsy revealed enough arsenic poisoning in his body to kill three men. After an investigation, Dovie made a full confession claiming that she had put arsenic poison in Hawkins' milk. A jury found her guilty of murder and a court sentenced her to die in the state's electric chair in January 1954.

Several appeals failed and the state's governor refused clemency. Scholars argue that there are several reasons why Dovie may have wanted to kill Hawkins: access to the estate, Hawkins was impotent, Dovie was romantically involved with her son-in-law, or Dovie was mentally imbalanced.

In another case involving more than just spousal murder, Alabama officials electrocuted 49-year-old waitress Rhonda Bell Martin in October 1957 for the arsenic poisoning of her mother, two husbands, three of her seven children, and two other children that took place over three decades. Rhonda poisoned her fifth husband, Ronald Martin, formerly her son-in-law, but he survived. It was during an investigation of Ronald's poisoning that officials exhumed the body of Rhonda's fourth husband, 51-year-old Claude Martin, Ronald's father, who died in 1951. Forensics discovered fatal levels of arsenic poisoning. Suspicions then aroused over the deaths of several other members of Rhonda's family—the death of Rhonda's four-year-old daughter in 1934, her first husband George Garrett in 1937, four other children and her mother's death in 1944. There was considerable publicity of Martin's murders long before her trial including her confession to the crimes; undoubtedly public disclosure of such evidence influenced the jury that convicted Martin. At least one psychiatrist claimed Rhonda suffered from schizophrenia, but other psychiatrists found no evidence of mental incapacity.

Judy Ann Buenoano (Welty) was the daughter of an itinerant farm worker. Her mother died of tuberculosis when she was two years old and she and her infant brother went to live with their grandparents. Years later she reunited with her father but found herself the object of extreme abuse from her father and his second wife. Both parents beat, starved, and burned Judy with cigarettes. Judy Ann Buenoano murdered her husband Sergeant James E. Goodyear, a boyfriend named Bobby Joe Morris, her partially paralyzed 19-year-old son Michael, and she attempted the murder of her fiancé John Gentry. In August 1984, an Orange County jury in Florida found her guilty of the 1971 arsenic poisoning of her husband and recommended the death penalty. Finding four aggravating circumstances and no mitigating factors, Circuit Court Judge Emerson R. Thompson sentenced Judy to death. Florida electrocuted Judy in March 1998. Trial evidence showed that James Goodyear began suffering from nausea, vomiting and diarrhea shortly after returning from military duty in South Vietnam. Hospitalized at a naval hospital, James complained that he had been ill with the symptoms for about two weeks. Physicians could not determine any medical reason for the symptoms, attempts to stabilize James failed, and he died from cardiovascular collapse and renal failure. At the time of his death, medical personnel did not perform any toxicological tests on James because there was no reason to suspect toxic poisoning.

Debra Sims lived with Judy and James and testified that James became progressively ill and experienced hallucinations, but that Judy was slow to take James to the hospital. Two of Judy's friends also testified that Judy had discussed with them the killing of a person with arsenic poison added to food, and had admitted to them that she killed James. Evidence presented at trial also showed that Bobby Joe Morris, with whom Judy lived after James' death, became ill and died after exhibiting the same symptoms of vomiting, nausea, fever and hallucinations that James exhibited before his death. Judy and John Gentry began living together after Bobby's death and later became engaged. Gentry testified that in November 1982 he caught a cold, and Judy began giving him vitamin C capsules. Gentry checked into a hospital in mid–December after experiencing extreme nausea and vomiting. Gentry returned home after his recovery and on the same day Judy again gave him vitamin C. His symptoms of nausea and vomiting quickly returned. Gentry had the capsules chemically analyzed revealing that they contained the poison paraformaldehyde. In 1984, authorities exhumed James and Bobby's bodies and analyses of tissue samples revealed acute arsenic poisoning in both victims. Judy collected $33,000 in life insurance proceeds and $62,000 in dependency indemnity compensation from the Veterans Administration.

Judy also collected $23,000 in life insurance proceeds from Bobby Joe Morris. Buenoano owned life insurance on Gentry's life totaling $510,000 in benefits, and she was a 50 percent beneficiary under his will. In 1988, the Florida Supreme Court affirmed Judy's conviction and death sentence. The U.S. Court of Appeals vacated a denial of habeas corpus relief for Judy who was entitled to an evidentiary hearing on her claims of ineffective assistance of counsel, and that the district court either unduly restricted the evidence allowed or failed to hold a hearing at all on these issues. The court remanded her case for a full hearing. In 1996, the U.S. Court of Appeals found no validity to Judy's claims of ineffective assistance of counsel or that she actually suffered physical, sexual, and emotional abuse or was mentally ill. The U.S. Supreme Court denied Judy certiorari and Florida executed her in March 1998.

The execution of Betty Beets is a particularly horrific example of the brutality and vindictiveness of the death penalty. In February 2000, two weeks before her sixty-third birthday, Texas put to death by lethal injection Betty, a cashier and waitress, for murdering her husband Jimmy Don Beets in 1983. The prosecution claimed that Betty killed her husband to benefit from his pension fund and life insurance, but Betty did not learn of these entitlements for more than a year after her husband's death. Two years after the murder, authorities found Jimmy's body buried under a wishing well in the yard of her mobile home in Gun Barrel City, Texas. Officials also found the body of another man married to Betty who had disappeared in 1981, Doyle Wayne Barker, buried under a wooden storage building on the property. Betty apparently killed both of the men execution-style with gunshots to the back their heads. Authorities discovered the bodies after reports from family members. Betty had previously pleaded guilty to a misdemeanor charge of aggravated assault against another husband she shot, Billy York Lane, but who survived to marry Betty a second time though they soon divorced. Raised in extreme poverty, Betty suffered from the violence of an alcoholic father and a mentally ill mother. Betty was raped when she was five years old, she suffered near deafness from meningitis at six years old, was a mother at 16 years old and a grandmother by 30 years old. Speaking out against her execution, Amnesty International claimed that the record of Betty's life was a virtual chronicle of uninterrupted physical, sexual, and emotional abuse. Betty was married to five different men, all of whom brutally beat and sexually abused her.

> Beets has a lengthy history of well-documented head injuries, including repeated blows at the hands of abusive men, as well as a near-fatal car accident in 1980. Expert testimony in post-conviction proceedings established that she suffers from Post-Traumatic Stress Disorder, Battered Women's Syndrome and Organic Brain Damage and that she is both learning disabled and hearing-impaired. According to defense experts, her multiple disabilities have left her with gravely impaired judgment and extremely dependent on others. At the time of the offense, she was abusing alcohol and diet pills, further impairing her already limited judgment.[48]

Betty's attorney, E. Ray Andrews, epitomized attorney incompetence in defending his client's constitutional rights. Andrews admitted, for instance, that he did not investigate Betty's traumatic background of physical and sexual abuse experienced from an early age and thus never presented expert testimony of the disabilities suffered by Betty at trial. Andrews failed to present any mitigating evidence during the sentencing phase of Betty's trial. On separate occasions state and federal appellate courts rejected claims from Betty's appellate lawyers that the jury never heard mitigation claims. Andrews also engaged in unethical behavior involving a conflict of interest when he refused to withdraw himself from the case so that he could testify that Betty had no prior knowledge of her husband's death benefits and thus the collection of benefits could not have been Betty's motive for killing Jimmy. Andrews obtained media rights to Betty's story. Andrews was also an alcoholic at the time of Betty's ordeal drinking "between one-half and three-quarters of a fifth of Wild Turkey per night."[49]

Oklahoma executed Marilyn Plantz by lethal injection in May 2001 for her part in killing her husband, James Earl Plantz, ostensibly for a $300,000 life insurance policy. Marilyn became sexually involved with a young black man named William Clifford Bryson[51] whom she would entertain with drugs and alcohol in the evenings while her husband was at work. In August 1988, after an evening of drinking and smoking crack cocaine and while Marilyn waited in her bedroom, Bryson and another teenager named Clinton McKimble beat James Plantz to death with baseball bats after he arrived home from work. The two killers then put James in the bed of his pickup truck, drove the body to an isolated area, doused the truck and James' body with gasoline, and set it on fire. There is some speculation that James was still alive when the culprits set the truck on fire. When apprehended by police, both Bryson and McKimble confessed to the murder and disclosed Marilyn's part in planning the murder. Authorities tried Marilyn and Bryson together and a jury took three hours to convict them of first-degree murder and another five hours to sentence them to death penalty. McKimble pleaded guilty to first-degree murder and received a life sentence in exchange for his testimony against Plantz and Bryson. Robert Macy tried the capital case against the defendants together ensuring the jury's consistent reminder that Marilyn had had sexual relations with a young black man that culminated in the murder of Plantz's white husband.

As with other women put to death in this period, Marilyn claimed in a habeas corpus petition to the United States Court of Appeals for the Tenth District that she had ineffective court-appointed trial counsel that failed to investigate adequately mitigating evidence concerning Marilyn's background and her extremely disturbing childhood. Her trial lawyer failed to bring forth evidence that Marilyn's brother forced her to masturbate him, that Marilyn's father beat her, and that before her marriage to James Plantz, he savagely raped 15-year-old Marilyn. She argued that her "trial counsel should have informed the jury of her difficult and impoverished childhood and her father's racial prejudice and strictness, causing his children to leave home as soon as possible." Marilyn claimed further that counsel failed to seek a mental health evaluation of Marilyn before her trial. A post-conviction evaluation found that Marilyn was borderline mentally retarded with an IQ of 76. The mental health professional who evaluated Marilyn found it highly improbable that Marilyn was capable of creating a scheme to murder her husband. In another development, the Federal Bureau of Investigation found serious errors in much of Joyce Gilchrist's work as a chemist for the Oklahoma City Police Department and who testified in Marilyn's murder trial. According to Jack Dempsey, an attorney and representative for the Oklahoma Criminal Defense Trial Lawyers Association, "If one juror was convinced to give the death penalty to Marilyn Plantz due to the testimony of Ms. Gilchrist, Marilyn should not be executed."[50] A professional crime scene reconstruction association had previously expelled Gilchrist for unethical behavior. To one commentator, "In light of the cloud that has been cast over the role of Gilchrist in capital trials, it is unconscionable to execute without determining the extent to which her misconduct influenced the outcome of these cases."[51] Apparently state officials in Oklahoma did not much care about how Gilchrist did her job so long as she helped gain capital convictions. Still, the Court found little merit in Marilyn's claims and held that ineffective counsel had not prejudiced her case. William Clifford Bryson died by lethal injection a month after Oklahoma executed Marilyn Plantz.

After waiving her right to a jury trial in May 2003, 41-year-old Teresa Wilson Bean Lewis pleaded guilty in the Circuit Court for Pittsylvania County in south-central Virginia to two counts of capital murder-for-hire in the killing of her 51-year-old husband, Julian Clifton Lewis, and 25-year-old stepson, National Guardsman Charles J. Lewis, set to deploy to Iraq. The state portrayed Lewis as masterminding the murders despite evidence that she lacked the mental capacity to do so. Since her trial, a letter surfaced from one of her two accomplices that it was he and not Lewis who masterminded the murders. Circuit Court Judge Charles Strauss found that Teresa's "conduct was outrageously or wantonly vile, horrible, or inhumane and sentenced her to death for both capital murder offenses."⁵² Judge Strauss sentenced Teresa to death because he believed that she was the ringleader ("the head of the serpent") and more culpable than the actual shooters. Teresa's defense lawyer did little to curb this portrayal of Lewis. The judge sentenced her two co-defendants, the actual killers who pled guilty to the murders, to life imprisonment and her daughter to five-years in prison.

Teresa grew up poor and in a repressive home environment in a small town where she also met her husband, Teresa's supervisor at the Dan River Inc. textile plant. Teresa met two young men named Rodney L. Fuller and Matthew Jessie Shallenberger while waiting in the customer service line at a Wal-Mart store. She and Shallenberger soon became lovers and before long discussed the possibility that Shallenberger and Fuller would kill Julian and Charles for a share in the life insurance proceeds. On occasion, Teresa and her 16-year-old daughter, Christie Lynn Bean, met Shallenberger and Fuller in a parking lot where Christie had sexual intercourse with Fuller and Teresa had sexual intercourse with Shallenberger in another vehicle. At other times, Teresa performed a lingerie show for the two men at her home and had sexual intercourse with both men. In October 2002, Teresa met the two men at a shopping center after she had gone to a bank and withdrew $1,200 in cash that she gave the men to purchase firearms with which to kill Julian and Charles. Shortly after midnight on the day of the killings, the two men crept into the Lewis' trailer through a backdoor that Teresa left unlocked armed with shotguns. The two men roused Teresa and told her to wait in the kitchen while Shallenberger and Fuller shot to death Julian and Charles. Shallenberger shot Julian several times and Fuller shot Charles three times with the shotguns. Teresa waited about an hour before calling police to report the shooting. Police found Julian still alive when they arrived on the scene, and he said that Teresa knew who had shot him before he died at the residence.

During a police interview in early November 2002, Teresa admitted to her role in the murders, she told authorities where to find the two shooters, and that her daughter played a role in the murders. On appeal, attorneys argued that Teresa's cognitive testing showed an IQ of 72 (verbal IQ was 70 and performance IQ was 79) and that these figures put Teresa in the borderline range of mental retardation. According to mental health experts who examined Teresa, she performed below the level of mental retardation on tests designed to measure "planning." Teresa also had a dependent personality disorder among other mental disabilities and a long history of drug addiction. The Supreme Court of Virginia affirmed Teresa's double murder conviction and death sentence and the U.S. Supreme Court denied certiorari with only Justices Ruth Bader Ginsburg and Sonia Sotomayor voting for a stay of execution; recently appointed Justice Elena Kagan voted against the stay. Teresa exhausted her appeals and the state's governor, Bob McDonnell, refused clemency. He stated, "Having carefully reviewed the petition for clemency, the judicial opinions in this case, and other relevant materials, I find no compelling reason to set aside the sentence that was imposed by the Circuit Court and affirmed by all reviewing courts. Accordingly, I decline to intervene and have notified the appropriate counsel and family of my decision."⁵³ Virginia authorities put Teresa to death by lethal injection in late September 2010. Shallenberger committed suicide while in prison in 2006. To her post-conviction appellate lawyer, James Rocap, the courts that heard Teresa's case overlooked the nuances of her intellectual disability. "There has to be a much higher level of appreciation in courts of what low-level functioning is, even if it's not specifically mental retardation."⁵⁴ In this regard, Teresa's execution stands as testament that mentally impaired inmates still face the risk of execution despite the Supreme Court's holding in *Atkins*. Teresa spent her years in death row at the Fluvanna Correctional Center for Women. A particular point of contention is that Teresa Lewis, executed in Virginia in September 2010, received a death sentence while her two co-defendants received life sentences. One commentator put it this way: "The fact that someone like Teresa can be executed, while her more culpable codefendant has received a life sentence, illustrates why the death penalty is wrong: its use is not limited for people who are the worst of the worst."[55]

Child Murder

In September 1953, Alabama officials electrocuted Earle Dennison after an all-male jury convicted her of the arsenic-poisoning murder of her two-year-old niece, Shirley Dianne Weldon. Earle was a widow employed as a head nurse at the General Hospital in Wetumpka, Alabama. Authorities also suspected Earle of the arsenic killing of her three-year-old niece Polly Ann Weldon after a visit with her aunt over two years earlier. Authorities charged Earle with that crime but never prosecuted her for killing Polly. Earle's motive for murdering young Shirley was $6,000 in life insurance, a premium upon which Earle paid while Shirley laid in the hospital dying from the poisoning. Earle was the sole beneficiary to the life insurance policy. After her arrest, Earle signed two confessions to the crime and explained that she had mixed the poison with an orange drink she gave to Shirley. The Supreme Court of Alabama affirmed the judgment of the trial court and found no prejudicial trial error. Governor Gordon Persons denied clemency to Earle and she died at Kelby Prison in Montgomery. Earle was the first white woman executed in the state.

The plight of Christina Marie Riggs is yet another wretched story of "how poor, single mothers, many of whom are women of color, are turning to violence towards themselves and their children to escape the desolation and despondency they feel from raising their children alone in America."[56] Christina came from a family troubled with a long history of chronic depression, mental illness and suicidal tendencies; a cousin successfully committed suicide, an older sister attempted suicide, and her grandmother was in and out of mental institutions. Christina was molested by a family member as a young child and was pregnant at 15 years old, a child she put up for adoption. Christina had become increasingly depressed and suicidal after her divorce from John Riggs who left her alone to raise two children in a poor financial situation. Undoubtedly, these difficulties caused Christina to agonize over painful childhood memories.

In early November 1997, Christina killed her two young children, five-year-old Justin Dalton Thomas and two-year-old Shelby Alexis Riggs. She sedated the children with an antidepressant, Elavil, which she obtained from the Arkansas Heart Hospital in Little Rock where she worked as licensed practical nurse. She obtained morphine and potassium chloride, the same drug used by state executioners to put condemned prisoners to death. After the children were asleep, Christina injected Justin with the potassium chloride but he awoke in pain. She then gave him morphine and smothered him with a pillow. Not wanting to inject Shelby, she proceeded to smother her with a pillow. She carried both children to her bed and laid them in it. She then wrote a suicide note to her mother and took a large quantity of anti-depressant pills and injected herself with potassium chloride concentrate. Not being diluted, it ate a hole in her arm, collapsing her vein and never reached her heart. She was discovered the next morning and taken to hospital where she was stabilized in intensive care and kept under police guard. Her family hired a lawyer, but before the lawyer arrived police took an eight-minute taped confession from Christina. Much of her statement was inaudible as she was crying throughout, and towards the end appeared to be hallucinating. At her trial, expert witnesses testified that her actions resulted from severe depression. To her, the children's deaths were an act of love and an extension of her own suicide. One psychologist said: "The pathological suicidal depression that she was in ... effectively precluded her from being able to do something more reasonable, something more appropriate. From the outside looking in, the death of two children like this is pretty horrible. From the inside looking out, it looks like an act of mercy."[57] For the state, a psychiatrist and a psychologist did not dispute that her suicide bid was genuine, but testified that they did not believe that she was sufficiently depressed to justify the defense of not guilty by reason of mental impairment. The jury agreed and convicted her of capital murder after less than an hour of deliberation. At the sentencing, Christina refused to have any evidence presented on her behalf and asked the jury for a death sentence: "I want to die. I want to be with my babes. I started this out seven months ago. And I want you to give me the death penalty. I don't want you to feel guilty."[58] Having been granted her wish, she then refused to appeal her sentence. On May 2, 2000, Arkansas authorities executed Christina Riggs by lethal injection.

Executions of Black Women

Criminal justice officials have executed 18 black women since 1900. Jurisdictions executed 15 black women in the pre-modern period (before 1976) and three black women in post-modern period (after 1976). Mostly southern jurisdictions executed the women for predatory murder, robbery-murder, and spousal murder. One result of white society excluding black women "with little or no formal education and few technical skills ... from the urban industrial workplace" is that most black women executed during the period were domestic servants and housemaids whose offenses involved crimes of resistance against white aggression similarly experienced by slave women generations earlier.[59] The horrid manner in which southern black female domestics killed their oppressive white employers corresponds notably to the means used by slave women to kill their abusive white masters. One such case represents an all too familiar story of black women in southern society during the period—Virginia Christian's killing of her white employer Ida Virginia Belote. As one study characterized the killing: "The social position and popularity of the victim stood in stark contrast to Christian's family background, unkempt appearance, and rude manner in describing the crime."[60] Young Virginia Christian was a poor, mentally retarded black girl whose family were sharecroppers on Belote's farm and for whom Christian was a laundress. She was one of eight children whose father's meager wages failed to adequately support the family. Christian's mother was enfeebled who had a reputation for dishonesty; some argue that Christian had "adopted her mother's habits of immorality, dishonesty, and thievery," but Christian was not a hardened criminal.[61] In contrast, Ida Belote was an older white woman and one of the town's "white aristocracy by way of her father's prominence as the owner of a large grocery."[62]

Belote frequently mistreated Christian, and in March 1912 a violent argument ensued between the two in which Belote accused Christian of stealing a locket and a skirt. Belote hit Christian with a cuspidor ("spittoon") that sent Christian into a violent frenzy. The altercation escalated when Christian and Belote ran for two broom handles Belote used to prop up her bedroom windows. Christian grabbed one of the broom handles and struck Belote on the forehead. In an attempt to stifle Belote's screams, Christian stuffed a towel down Belote's throat and she died by suffocation. When Christian left the house, she stole Belote's purse containing money and a ring. One newspaper reported that police found Belote's body "laying face down in a pool of blood, and her head was horribly mutilated and a towel was stuffed into her mouth and throat."[63] Police soon arrested Christian, and during questioning she admitted to hitting Belote but was shocked that Belote was dead. Christian claimed she had no intent in killing Belote. With a lynch mob looming in the background, an Elizabeth City County Court tried and convicted Christian for murder and the trial judge sentenced her to death in the state's electric chair. One day after her seventeenth birthday in August 1912, a short five months after the crime, Virginia authorities executed Christian at the state penitentiary in Richmond. The state's medical school took possession of Christian's body since her parents were too poor to transport the body home. Years later, prominent activist and intellectual leader W.E.B. DuBois poignantly accented the social context of Christian's judicial killing:

Virginia Christian was a product of Virginia far more than of the colored race. It was the social organization of white Virginia that made this girl what she was and then brutally killed for it. The State pushed her down into poverty despite the hard-earned pennies of her father; the State refused to educate her or even to let Northern philanthropy do it; the State put her as a servant, body and soul, into the hands of her mistress and constituted that mistress judge and jury over this ignorant, wayward child. At the age of sixteen ... this child was convicted of murder, when there is not a white man in the nation who after impartial review of the facts would not have to admit that every circumstance shows lack of premeditation with a strong case of self-defense. Make this child as brutal, immoral and irresponsible as you will and the black fact remains that a civilized community made her and then murdered her for being herself. And that community was Christian Virginia![64]

Another early black (some argue she was actually of American Indian origin) female execution took place in the period when territorial officials in Oklahoma hanged Dora Wright in July 1903 for the murder and mutilation of a black orphan girl in her care, seven-year-old Annie Williams. It seems that Dora viciously beat young Annie to death. There was post-mortem evidence that Annie had suffered severe beatings for more than a month and had brandings made with a red-hot poker. Dora was a domestic servant and there is no published reason for Annie's murder. The jury took 20 minutes for deliberation and recommended death. Dora's attorney twice visited President Theodore Roosevelt seeking clemency for his client. The President denied clemency claiming that, "If that woman was mean enough to do a thing like that, she ought to have the nerve to meet her punishment."[65] Hundreds of people in McAlester viewed the execution.

Pattie Perdue hanged along with Leon Viverett in Wayne County, Mississippi, for the robbery-murder of a white man named Alton Page in August 1921. Newspaper reports of the period reveal that Perdue and her male accomplice killed Page, dismembered and burned his body in a stove, and then buried the remains in a Negro cemetery. It appears from reports that a fight between Viverett and Page in Hattie's house resulted in Viverett killing Page. Some reports claim that Perdue proclaimed her innocence on the gallows while others claimed the two confessed to the murder. Though Pattie and Viverett were represented by court appointed attorneys, a local newspaper reported that "little or no defense was attempted."[66] There is nothing in the historical record explaining why Pattie and her companion murdered the victim other than the robbery.

In another case, Mississippi hanged Ann Knight along with Will Gray in October 1922 for killing Ann's husband John. News reports of the day explain little more than the details of the hangings and nothing about the facts of the case. An appeal to the Mississippi Supreme Court noted nothing more other than Ann committed "a foul murder of her husband." Gray appealed the voluntariness of his confession.

Alabama electrocuted Selina Gilmore at Kirby Prison in January 1930 for the shotgun killing of Horace Johnson, a white Birmingham restaurant owner who quarreled with Selina over a food order. Apparently, after several hours of drinking corn whiskey, Selina went to a restaurant and ordered take out. She ordered sandwiches, brains, and eggs, but only got the sandwiches since the kitchen help had yet to cook the remainder of the order. Selina became difficult when Johnson told her she would have to wait for her order, but soon he demanded that Selina leave the restaurant. Selina went home, retrieved a loaded shotgun, returned to the restaurant, cornered Johnson and shot and killed him. Selina went to the state's electric chair singing spiritual hymns. There is no record of an appeal of Selina's conviction and death sentence.

Mary Holmes was the last woman hanged in the United States. Mississippi hanged Holmes in April 1937 along with her black male accomplice Selmon Brooks for the robbery-murder of

E. W. Cook, a prominent white planter and businessman in Sharkey County for whom Holmes worked as a cook. Newspaper reports reveal that while Cook was preparing the week's payroll, Mary and Brooks brutally beat him, scalped him, and dismembered his body. Afterwards, the two burglarized the house and set fire to it to conceal the crime. The two stole $850 from Cook. They confessed to the crime when police arrested them but later recanted their confessions. A local newspaper doubtlessly overstated Cook's relationship with Mary when it claimed she deserved to hang because Mary had betrayed a friendship. It is cynical to believe that Cook and Mary had such familiarity given Cook's status as a wealthy white southern planter and that of Mary's social position as a poor black cook. There is no record that Mary appealed her conviction and death sentence, but the Supreme Court of Mississippi affirmed Brooks' conviction and death sentence stating the Brooks' confession to the murder should stand. Mary hanged shortly before Brooks.

Like most other cases of black female executions during the period, the case of Rosana Lightner Phillips more than illustrates "the manner in which gender, race, and status operated dialectically to shape the historical social construction of the southern Negro female offender."[67] Rosana was born into rural southern poverty, she was illegitimate and born to a mother who dropped out of school in the sixth grade to give birth to Rosana. Her mother gave Rosana and a sister to her grandmother to raise. After her grandmother's death, Rosanna moved back to live with her mother at the age of six years old. Rosana became sexually promiscuous at an early age and by the time she was 14 years old she dropped out school and gave birth to the first of two illegitimate children. As a young teenager, Rosana worked as a nurse and house cleaner earning $2 a week. Rosana developed a criminal record during this time that included arrests for drunkenness and violent assault on a police officer; by the time she was 17 years old, Rosana faced a two-year prison sentence for larceny. After leaving prison in 1937, she met her husband Daniel Phillips who was a farmer and textile worker with a fifth grade education earning $60 a month. At that time she gave birth to her second illegitimate child that was not Daniel's. The Phillips had a tumultuous marriage accented by relentless violence.

Rosana and Daniel went to work as domestics for Harry F. Watkins in early 1942 and moved into a tenant dwelling on Watkins' property. In September of that year, authorities found Watkins' decomposed body at the bottom of a well with a wound on the back of his head and another wound through the front of the neck that nearly severed the head. Suspicion immediately focused on the Phillips who had recently abandoned Watkins property for a nearby town. Officials arrested Rosana and Daniel and the state's prosecutor filed felony murder charges against the two with robbery as the underlying cause of the killing. Their Orange County trial lasted 13 hours and it took the all-white male jury less than an hour to render a unanimous guilty verdict against the "Negro farm tenants." The North Carolina Supreme Court affirmed the trial court's judgment and dismissed the appeal. Both admitted complicity in the murder yet implicated the other as the actual killer. There is nothing in the historical record indicating why the Phillips killed Watkins other than stealing Watkins' wallet. But if one were to trust Rosana's claim, she had nothing to do Watkins' killing and watched Daniel commit the murder from the kitchen window where she stood washing the morning dishes. The state's governor refused to intervene and North Carolina executed Rosana and Daniel Phillips by lethal gas on the same day in November 1942. Rosana was the first woman put to death in the state's gas chamber.

Mississippi electrocuted Mildred Louise Johnson (James) in May 1944 for killing Annie Laura Conklin, her elderly white landlady who lived alone in Vicksburg. Mildred savagely beat Conklin to death with a stick, a fireplace poker, and a pair of tongs. Before her trial and conviction, Mildred confessed to Conklin's killing and implicated Jessie James, Mildred's common law husband, and Charles H. Barley, Mildred's father-in-law. But at her arraignment, Mildred denied that the two had anything to do with the killing. The trial court granted severance and tried James and Barley separately. It is unclear why Mildred and her accomplices murdered Conklin. Still, Jim Crow southerners needed not much more justification than the murder of an elderly white woman to execute a poor black woman. The Warren County jury deliberated Mildred's fate in 12 short minutes and County Judge R. B. Anderson sentenced Mildred to death. The Mississippi Supreme Court affirmed the trial court's conviction and death sentence. Regarding Jessie James and Charles Barley, there is no record that either appealed their conviction nor is there any record of their executions.

Helen Ray Fowler was a black woman who by the age of 37 had married several times and had five children and one grandchild. She supported herself, her children and a nephew by prostitution. In fact, Helen lived in a neighborhood known as one of the nation's most notorious red-light districts. She was poor and uneducated. Conflicting testimony revealed no clear picture of the crime at her trial. Even the state's attorney, David Marsh, failed to identify or produce a murder weapon, had no clear theory of the facts surrounding the case, and after 30 witnesses produced no evidence that Helen actually committed the killing of William Fowler (no relation), a service station owner. But her defense lawyer, Earl W. Brudges, did little more than call two witnesses. In early summer 1943, with cash and several uncashed checks totaling about $1,000 in hand, William and his cousin, Lee Clark, patronized several local gin mills and William somehow ended up at Helen's house. In December of that year, William's bloated and badly decomposed body washed up on the shore of the Niagara River.

Most likely, George Knight, a black man who lived with Helen, killed William during a brawl in Helen's house. Knight admitted as much to police after his arrest; he claimed that he beat Williams after robbing him, hit him in the back of the head with a hammer, and then he and Helen dumped the body. Helen's defense counsel claimed that Helen was guilty of any number of crimes, none of which had the state prosecuted her, but she was not liable for first-degree murder. Even so, an all-white jury convicted her and George Knight of killing William Fowler. New York electrocuted Helen and George on the same day in November 1944. Jon Getz, a New York attorney provides some idea why the state executed Helen Fowler: "I think race may have played a strong factor—you've got two black people killing a white guy. [Helen] was a disposable person in [the jury's] mind. I think they threw her in for good measure, so to speak. She certainly didn't get her fair day in court, and so she died an early death. The system is supposed to be about fairness."[68] Without comment, the Court of Appeals of New York affirmed the convictions of Fowler and Knight.

Bessie Mae Williams was 19 years old when North Carolina executed her and her 18-year-old accomplice Ralph Thompson by lethal gas in December 1944. Along with Cleve Bryant Johnson and 14-year-old Annie Mae Allison, the defendants robbed and stabbed to death Charlotte taxi driver Mack Minyard. The defendants admitted being in Minyard's taxi and gave police details as to what happened. Officials arraigned the defendants and entered pleas of not guilty, Johnson plead guilty to second-degree murder and received a prison sentence. After her arrest, an intake worker at the detention center described Bessie Mae as economically destitute, of low mentality, and a grouchy nature. The clerk also noted that Bessie Mae was illiterate and moronic. A Mecklenburg County trial court found Williams, Thompson, and Allison guilty of murder and sentenced them to die in the state's gas chamber. On appeal, the Supreme Court of North Carolina found that the trial judge and the attorneys appointed by the court to represent the defendants were extremely careful to safeguard the rights of the defendants and found the confessions given by the defendants to be lawful. The state's governor refused to intervene in the executions of Bessie Mae and Thompson, but commuted Annie Mae's death sentence because of her age at the time of the murder.

Authorities rarely exonerated black women of capital crimes and executed black women despite doubts of guilt or legal culpability. Such is the case of Lena Baker, a black woman born in 1900 to the daughter of Georgia slaves who spent her formative years in a two-room slave cabin without running water and electricity in Cuthbert—not unlike most poor black southerners. To support her three illegitimate children, Lena picked cotton, washed white people clothes, and cleaned white people's houses. As one commentator put it, all Lena had "ever known was the cruelty of poverty, the drudgery of eking out a meager and mean existence—a life lived in utter hopelessness."[69] Lena was illiterate, and when 20 years old, she was tried and convicted of prostitution and operating a "Lewd House." She spent 10 months as a prisoner in the "dehumanizing and brutal women's convict-lease system" working on a farm. Lena's life remained unchanged after her prison stay until May 1944 when an all-white, all-male jury convicted Lena in a one-day trial for the shooting death of 67-year-old gristmill owner Ernest B. Knight. Lena reportedly had killed Knight with a pistol she pulled from him when he threatened her with a metal pipe. Lena had an intimate yet violent relationship with Knight and the two often drank together. Judge Worrill sentenced Lena to death for Knight's killing and officials electrocuted Lena in March 1945 that some have called a "legal lynching." There is no record of an appeal, but 60 years after her execution in the state's electric chair, the Georgia Board of Pardons and Paroles pardoned Lena Baker for the murder claiming that her execution was "a grievous error." While the pardon does not declare Baker innocence, the Board suggested, "She could have been charged with voluntary manslaughter, rather than murder" and received a 15-year prison term and not death. Given the racial hostility of the Jim Crow South, however, a black woman killing a white man demanded execution.[70]

In the 1940s, poor young black girls from North Philadelphia often stood on street corners in prominent neighborhoods waiting for affluent housewives to hire them as housemaids—what one commentator referred to as the "slave markets." In one such case, Mrs. Freda Wodlinger, a 45-year-old public school teacher and housewife from a prominent white family in West Oak Lane, hired 22-year-old Corrine Sykes. Corrine was shy and petite, had low intelligence, and was illiterate and inclined to hysteria. A psychiatrist that examined Corrine before her trial claimed she was psychopathic, and, "according to her school records, she had a mental age of an eight-year-old when she was nearly thirteen years old."[71] Three days after Corrine's hire, police found Wodlinger dead from multiple stab wounds; there was a terrific struggle with the killer hacking Wodlinger to death with a heavy kitchen knife. Missing from the house was $50 in cash, $2,000 in jewelry, and a sable fur piece. Suspicion immediately turned to Corrine who police arrested after an extensive search. Corrine gave conflicting stories but in the end signed a written confession despite her illiteracy. A jury convicted Corrine of first-degree murder and the trial judge sentenced her to death by electrocution. Pennsylvania executed Corrine Sykes in the Rockview Penitentiary in October 1946.

Troubled by doubts that Corrine was Wodlinger's killer, some believe Corrine's judicial killing was a wrongful conviction and execution. There are several uncertainties that continue to plague Corrine's case. For one, immediately upon her arrest Corrine implicated her boyfriend, Jaycee Kelly, who threatened to kill her and her mother if she refused to steal the valuables. More pronounced, Corrine's defense lawyers claimed that she had been living with the notorious bootlegger with a long criminal record for about six months. It seems he induced Corrine to steal valuables from Mrs. Wodlinger and turn them over to him. Others find it strange that when Corrine's boyfriend learned of her arrest "he raced to his boarding house, burned the sable, and dumped the diamonds."[72] Another point is that Corrine was far too small to have inflicted the severity of the knife wounds that killed Wodlinger. There is also speculation that years after Corrine's execution Wodlinger's husband made a deathbed confession that he had killed his wife. Whatever happened, Corrine's execution had a profound impact on North Philadelphia's black community. Some 10,000 people attended Corrine's viewing though it was open only to family members and close friends. On the day of her execution, most domestics in the city went home early from their jobs. According to a woman whose grandmother worked as a domestic in North Philadelphia at the time, city buses were full of black housemaids going home early on that day and an uncanny quite settled over the city. What's more, employers would no longer allow housemaids' boyfriends or husbands in their houses; an increasing mistrust accented the relations between white employers and black domestics.

Rose Marie Stinette died in South Carolina's electric chair in January 1947 for the contract murder of her husband for an insurance policy. Roy Singletary and two other men had bludgeoned Stinette's husband to death; authorities found his mutilated body beside a railroad track. The trial judge, L. D. Lide, sentenced Rose and Singletary to death even though 11 of the 12 jurors in the case sought clemency for the two defendants. Judge Lide sentenced the other two accomplices to life sentences. The day before Rose and Singletary's execution, however, the state's governor granted Singletary a reprieve leaving only Rose Stinette to answer for the killing by execution although it was the three men who actually did the killing. There is no record of an appeal. During her electrocution, a fuse blew from the surge of electricity required for the execution. One newspaper reported, "Witnesses then saw sparks from the woman's head and arms dimly illuminating the death scene."[73] Prison officials typically buried poor executed black women in a Potter's Field whose families could not afford to claim prisoners' bodies, and such was the case with Rose Marie Stinette.

Betty Evelyn Butler was the last black woman executed during Jim Crow. Butler reportedly strangled and drowned Evelyn Clark with whom Butler had a lesbian relationship. Butler left her husband and her two young children and moved to Cincinnati to start a new life. She met Clark, had a sexual relationship, and then became repulsed by the lesbian affair and apparently tried to break off the relationship. Trouble began when Clark apparently propositioned Butler by offering her money for sex. Butler became so irate that she tried to strangle Clark but was unsuccessful. Later in the day, she pulled Clark to the edge of the water where they had been fishing and drowned her in the lake. Some commentators suggest that Butler killed Clark in a rage over her attention to another woman. In any event, a Hamilton County court convicted Butler of first-degree murder and sentenced her to death. Ohio officials electrocuted Butler in June 1954.

The Modern Era

The rise of Black Nationalism, the Student Nonviolent Coordinating Committee, the Southern Christian Leadership Conference, and the Congress of Racial Equality brought organization to black protests against white dominion in the civil rights period. Black resistance to racial inequality in the period succeeded in effecting legislative and legal reforms. Congress passed the 1964 Voting Rights Act assuring black voter rights and the 1965 Civil Rights Act prohibiting discrimination in employment, housing, and public accommodations. One of the more significant legal challenges to the segregation accenting the modern era was the U.S. Supreme Court's holding in *Brown v. Board of Education* overturning *Plessy*'s long-standing "separate, but equal" doctrine. But these reforms have had little impact on the burden of blackness in United States society. As critical sociologist Joe R. Feagin explains,

> Civil rights laws and desegregation decisions have been overwhelmed by the massiveness of racial discrimination. [T]hese laws were crafted by the liberal wing of the white elite—mostly in the face of grass roots protests in the period from 1954 to 1972—with only modest concern for the group interests of African Americans. The laws were never intended to uproot systemic racism. While they have gotten rid of legal segregation, they are for the most part ineffective in regard to much informal discrimination and segregation.[74]

Although blacks made political and economic gains in the early periods of the civil rights struggle, societal institutions began reversing these gains in the 1980s during the Reagan administration. One reason for the "massiveness of racial discrimination" in American society today is that the federal government continued backpedaling on civil rights and failed to implement needed reforms. Essentially, the federal government has proven powerless in reducing entrenched discrimination, expanding civil rights for disadvantaged groups, or promoting access to federal programs and services for underserved populations on such issues as voting rights, equal educational opportunity, affirmative action, fair housing, environmental justice, racial profiling, hate crimes, immigration, women's rights, and gay rights. Mistakenly, most Americans believe that the aims of the civil rights movement alleviated the inequities suffered by racial minorities and that marginalized groups are no longer denied equal participation in societal institutions. Unquestionably, the continued debate regarding white persons as the new victims of reverse discrimination and disadvantagement has fostered and encouraged this misconception.

The gendered racism of mostly white judicial officers in the modern era renders black women ever more vulnerable to the death penalty even supposing a national civil rights agenda ostensibly diminishing the racialized sexism troubling the lives of black women. Jurisdictions put to death three black women in the modern era: Wanda Jean Allen in 2001, Francis Elaine Newton in 2005, and Kimberly McCarthy in 2013. Oklahoma's execution of Wanda Jean Allen for murdering her lesbian lover is instructive on the legal troubles facing condemned black women today. Criminal justice investigators cannot relegate the relevance of Allen's case to pervious historical periods accenting systemic gendered racism in the execution of black women to the "race of the defendant" versus the "race of the victim" connection even if Allen victimized a black person. Instead, the overwhelming importance of Allen's case is the blatant gendered racism and homophobia deliberately employed by the state prosecutor and the gross incompetence of her defense lawyer that denied Allen evenhandedness and fairness in her capital trial. Allen was poor, uneducated, and a troubled black woman that the state prosecutor exploited to gain a capital conviction and execution. Allen is a contentious figure in the imposition of capital punishment because her case symbolizes how poverty, mental health, race, and sexuality accent capital sentencing distinctively to black lesbian women. These social characteristics distinguished Allen as executable to the sentencing jury because state prosecutors successfully portrayed Allen erroneously, yet decisively, as "disobedient, dangerous, a threat to society, immoral, manly, and sexually deviant."[75] What's more, the evidence in Allen's case staunchly reveals that state judicial authorities should have never permitted the execution to take place.

Allen was the second of eight children born to a mother who suffered from alcoholism and mental retardation; she drank excessively during her pregnancy with Wanda. Acting as a surrogate mother to her younger siblings after her father abandoned the family, Wanda regularly stole food and clothing for the children that led to several juvenile arrests. Allen performed poorly in school, and at the age of 15 officials diagnosed her as mentally retarded. Years later, while serving a prison term for a manslaughter conviction—a case so dubious that she was able to plead guilty and receive a minimum sentence—Allen met Gloria Leathers with whom she began a lesbian relationship. After their release from prison, Allen and Leathers lived together and had a tumultuous relationship. In late 1988, the two women argued at a grocery store over a welfare check. A police officer escorted the women to their house and watched as Leathers collected her belongings and moved out. Afterwards, Leathers went to the police station to file a complaint against Allen who followed her hoping to talk to Leathers. One account has it that Allen shot Leathers in the abdomen with a handgun as she exited the car she drove to the police station. Allen's account is that she shot Leathers in self-defense after Leathers attacked Allen with a rake. During an argument earlier the same day, Leathers had attacked Allen and slashed her face with a garden rake. Allen also feared Leathers because she had killed a woman 10 years earlier in Tulsa, Oklahoma. Leathers died two hours after police arrested Allen. Oklahoma tried Allen and after a short deliberation, a jury convicted her of capital murder and recommended the death penalty.

At most, Allen's killing of Leathers was a heat-of-passion manslaughter that would not warrant a death sentence. Yet, the state prosecutor successfully convinced the jury that Allen posed a significant societal danger because she was a lesbian killer. Allen's lesbianism and her alleged "dangerousness" overwhelmed the state's case. The state prosecutor freely, yet erroneously asserted that Allen dominated her lover when factually she and Leathers largely mistreated each other. The state prosecutor won the trial court's rejection of defense motions outlining Leathers' violent nature. The prosecution inaccurately, yet purposefully portrayed Wanda as wearing "the pants in the family" and that she was the masculine one in the relationship. The state's attorney even solicited testimony from Allen's mother that Allen used the male spelling of her middle name (Gene). Wanda's sexuality played a prominent role in her trial and "evidences, again, that when a woman acts out from society's gender expectations, she faces harsher penalties."[76] Even Oklahoma's black churches rebuffed efforts for leniency for Allen from the state's governor because she was a lesbian. As one commentator explained,

> Allen was convicted on the basis of a rash of stereotypes about lesbians which, combined with stereotypes about black people and poor people, played off juror biases to portray Allen as an aggressive offender so dangerous to society that the only recourse was execution. One observer proposed that had Allen been a middle class, white heterosexual woman who killed her boyfriend, the jury would probably have been more sympathetic and Allen's sentence would have been considerably lighter.[77]

Allen's case provides a particularly egregious illustration of how prosecutorial gendered racism taints capital cases involving black women. During closing arguments the prosecutor depicted Allen as a black monster deserving of the death penalty by comparing Allen to a gorilla. The prosecutor produced a greeting card belonging to Allen with the picture of a gorilla on the cover with a caption that read, "Patience my ass, I'm going to kill something." While showing the card to the jury, the prosecutor said, "That's Wanda Allen in a nutshell." The sole purpose of the prosecutor showing the picture to the jury was to portray Allen as an aggressive beast. Such racist derogations in prosecutors' closing arguments in capital cases involving black women defendants illustrate what law professor Sheri Lynn Johnson contends are forms of petite apartheid that continue to plague the capital justice system.[78] An appeals court, however, found no prejudicial error in the prosecutor's racist tactic. The racist scheme employed by the prosecutor to denigrate Allen was especially effective since "the definition of Allen as a brutal beast undeserving of mercy persisted long after her trial."[79] At her clemency hearing, for instance, Allen was mostly concerned with dispelling the way the racist prosecutor had characterized her during the trial.

Allen's indigence was a significant factor leading to her execution because poor black women accused of capital crimes cannot afford private attorneys and rely on court appointed lawyers or public defenders who are largely ineffective in mitigating capital cases. As a poor black woman, Allen relied on a court appointed lawyer, Robert Carpenter, who denied Allen her Sixth Amendment right to competent counsel and an adequate legal defense. Carpenter, who had never tried a capital case, sought to recuse himself or to have assistance from the state's public defender's office, or at least the assistance of an experienced investigator. The Court rejected these requests. Carpenter's most severe error was failing to introduce well-documented evidence of Allen's mental retardation. Had Carpenter adequately investigated Allen's troubled and delinquent childhood, he would have discovered that she had an IQ of 69 (within the range of low-functioning, mild mental retardation) resulting from brain damage incurred from a head injury suffered in an automobile accident when Allen was 12 years old. She had also endured a stab wound to the temple as a teenager that certainly exacerbated her problem. Allen never completed high school and it is doubtful she functioned intellectually even at an eighth-grade level. Carpenter's incompetence precluded the trial court from fully litigating Allen's mental retardation; her mental impediments surely would have kept Allen from execution since the U.S. Supreme Court ruled shortly after her judicial killing that executing mentally retarded defendants is unconstitutional.

In September 2005, Texas executed Frances Elaine Newton after a Harris County jury convicted Newton of killing her husband, a drug addict and dealer, and her two young children allegedly for $100,000 in insurance proceeds in April 1987. Newton always maintained her innocence and claimed that drug dealers killed her family. More than for any other reason, Texas succeeded in executing Newton because her court-appointed trial lawyer was grossly incompetent. Newton repeatedly requested that the court dismiss her lawyer, but without a hearing on the issue the trial court summarily rejected her pleas. Her appellate attorneys maintained that her trial lawyer failed to competently investigate the case, to include reasonable allegations that the murders were committed by someone else, to interview witnesses, to challenge the state's mishandling of evidence, and to introduce mitigating circumstances. The attorneys further determined that Newton's defense lawyer had a dubious history and a record of professional incompetence. Commentators assert, "There is no doubt that Newton was prejudiced by [her trial lawyer's] ineffectiveness: no reasonable juror would have found her guilty beyond a reasonable doubt had she received competent counsel."[80]

In November 1998, a Dallas County jury (all white but one) convicted Kimberly Lagayle McCarthy for the 1997 robbery and bludgeoning death of a 71-year-old retired psychology professor named Dorothy Booth. Kimberly was a college graduate with a degree in occupational therapy from Texas Woman's University and a therapist at a nursing home. At the sentencing phase of Kimberly's trial, prosecutors introduced DNA evidence showing that she also was responsible for the brutal murders 81-year-old Maggie Harding and 85-year-old Jettie Lucas a decade earlier. Harding was stabbed and beaten with a meat tenderizer and Lucas was beaten with a claw hammer and stabbed. In murdering Dorothy Booth, Kimberly feigned her way into Booth's house on the pretense of borrowing sugar and immediately began attacking Booth with a butcher knife and stabbed the woman five times. Kimberly robbed her and severed a finger to take Booth's diamond and gold wedding ring. Before leaving the house, Kimberly smashed the woman's face with a candelabra so hard that it knocked out teeth and bone. Her motive for the murder was to get money for her crack cocaine habit. Police found a ten-inch butcher knife matching the wounds suffered by Booth in a cupboard above Kimberly's refrigerator. After the murder, Kimberly drove Booth's Mercedes Benz station wagon to a house near Fair Park to buy drugs. She pawned the wedding ring for $200 and police apprehended Kimberly after using Booth's credit cards. Supposedly, Kimberly was raised in a loving family, attended Catholic schools as a youngster, and was a staunch Christian and an active member of her church. Despite these claims, trial testimony revealed that Kimberly's father, who had a troubled childhood, had been incarcerated several times and battled alcohol problems. Kimberly suffered feelings of insecurity by losing her father after her parents divorced and her stepfather was abusive to her. Kimberly battled a crack cocaine addiction since 1986 and was in and out of drug treatment facilities.

In 2001, the Texas Court of Criminal Appeals remanded Kimberly's case for retrial because a statement taken shortly after her arrest in July 1997 by a Dallas police detective violated her constitutional rights against self-incrimination. The court held that there was no evidence that Kimberly consulted with a lawyer before a police detective questioned her. Likewise, there is no evidence that Kimberly herself affirmatively reinitiated conversations with law enforcement. At Kimberly's retrial, a Dallas County jury found her guilty of Booth's murder and District Judge Henry Wade again sentenced Kimberly to death. The U.S. Supreme Court rejected her claims while the Court of Criminal Appeals of Texas reviewed Kimberly's record and adopted the trial judge's findings and denied Kimberly relief. More recently, Dallas County District Court Judge Larry Mitchell postponed Kimberly's execution date from late January 2013 to April 2013 to give Kimberly's attorneys time to present evidence of racial discrimination in selection the jury that convicted her in a retrial in 2002; there was only one black juror in a county that is comprised of 22.5 percent black Americans. In June 2013, Texas court of criminal appeals dismissed her claim. The court denied the appeal ruling that Kimberly's claims were untimely and should have been raised earlier. Texas executed Kimberly McCarthy by lethal injection on June 26, 2013.

In July 2004, Marcella Williams, Lisa Ann Coleman's partner, called emergency personnel when she found her nine-year-old son, Davontae Marcel Williams, unconscious on the bathroom floor. When paramedics arrived at Williams' apartment, they found young Davontae clad in a disposable diaper, emaciated and appeared to be as if only three to five years old. The child's body was in full rigor mortis despite claims from Williams and Lisa that they had just fed Davontae Pediasure and that the child was breathing when they summoned paramedics. An autopsy revealed that the child's death was a homicide from malnutrition and pneumonia. Davontae weighed less than 40 pounds and had infected exterior injuries comprising open wounds on his wrists and ankles indicating that the child had been continuously bound. A pediatrician testified at trial that Davontae had at least 250 distinct injuries including cigarette or cigar burn wounds and that the child had been intentionally starved to death. Lisa confessed to police investigators that she often beat Davontae with a belt and that on several occasions she and Williams tied up the child. Child protection services investigators had removed Davontae from Williams' home in 1999 and placed him foster care because Lisa physically abused the child, but returned the child to Williams a year later. Because of Davontae's death and that of several other children in the care of child protective services, the state's governor launched an investigation into the state agency. In 2006, a Tarrant County jury took less than an hour to convict Lisa of capital murder in the starvation death of Davontae and the trial court sentenced her to death. The jury rejected defense attorneys' mitigating factors that Lisa was the product of incest, neglected by her mother, and bounced through foster homes, and repeatedly raped by an uncle. In 2009, the Court of Criminal Appeals of Texas affirmed Lisa's conviction and death sentence. Marcella Williams pleaded guilty to avoid a death sentence and is serving a life prison term and will have to serve 40 years before authorities allow her parole. She is eligible for parole in July 2044. In 2013, Lisa lost a federal appeal to the Fifth U.S. Circuit Court of Appeals asserting that she had incompetent trial counsel and that she was actually innocent of the child's death. John Stickels, Lisa's appellate attorney, filed a clemency application on August 2014 asserting that Lisa was not guilty of capital murder and that Governor Rick Perry commute her sentence to life in prison but the clemency board voted unanimously not to recommend commutation or a reprieve of Lisa's sentence. The U.S. Supreme Court rejected Lisa's final appeal for a stay of execution. Texas officials executed Lisa by lethal injection in September 2014 at the Huntsville facility. According to her attorney, state prosecutors punished Lisa with the death penalty because she had the audacity to exercise her constitutional right to a jury trial. Prosecutors never offered Lisa a plea bargain as they did Williams. To Stickels, "The state singled Lisa out and figured some way to get her the death penalty because she was black, a lesbian and an easy target ... it was a slam dunk."[81]

Execution of an American Indian Woman

A Sequoyah County jury in Oklahoma convicted a Cherokee Indian woman named Lois Nadean Smith of first-degree murder in December 1982 and District Court Judge Bill Ed Rogers sentenced her death. The trial evidence reveals that Lois, her son James Gregory Smith and friend Teresa Baker DeMoss picked up 21-year-old Cindy Baillee at a motel. Cindy was Gregory's ex-girlfriend. While in the car, Lois confronted Cindy that she had threatened to tell law enforcement officials about Gregory's involvement with illegal drugs and that Cindy had arranged to have Gregory killed. When Cindy denied the allegation, Lois stabbed Cindy in the throat with a knife. After arriving at Jim Smith's house, Lois' ex-husband and Gregory's father, Lois forced Cindy to sit in a recliner chair. Lois then threatened Cindy with a pistol and apparently fired a shot from the pistol into the recliner nearly Cindy's head. Lois then emptied the pistol into Cindy and she fell to the floor. While Gregory reloaded the pistol, Lois jumped repeatedly on Lois' neck and fired four more bullets into her body. An autopsy showed that Lois shot Cindy five times in the chest, twice in the head, and once in the back. There is evidence that Lois suffered extreme physical abuse by her alcoholic husband and had suffered a head injury. What's more, the federal courts refused to consider whether Lois' counsel was negligent for not introducing evidence of her physical abuse and not having had a psychological evaluation performed. Counsel also excluded evidence that pointed to Greg's culpability in Cindy's murder. Lois was under the influence of alcohol and drugs at the time of the murder. After exhausting her appeals, Oklahoma officials executed the 61-year-old Lois Nadean Smith by lethal injection in December 2001. A separate jury convicted Gregory of murder and the trial judge sentenced him to life in prison. Teresa testified against Lois and Gregory in exchange for immunity from prosecution.

Correcting the Historical Record

Historical state prison records in Louisiana failed to note the sex of persons executed, thus researchers are uncertain as to how many women state officials have actually put to death. There was little publicity of the hanging of Julia Moore in East Carroll Parish Louisiana in February 1935. Louisiana executed Julia (also known as Julia Powers and Julia Williams) for the murder of Elliot E. Wilson. It is likely that a condemned prisoner named Ed Dunn may have been an accomplice to Wilson's murder since he hanged in the same parish on the same day for the same crime as Julia. Some sources claim that Julia was an Asian female while other sources assert she was black and still others maintain she was white. Julia was most likely black since newspapers of the day commonly gave considerable attention to white female executions.

Contrasting Lynchings and Executions

There is a robust historical association between lawful female executions and unlawful female lynchings in the United States though scholars continue to debate the merits of that relationship. Most investigators understand that executions and lynchings are *not* mutually exclusive forms of social control; both share striking similarities—both are actions of the community to punish social transgressors, both are forms of vengeance, both ostensibly deter like conduct, both employ similar methods of imposing death, and both have attracted public exhibition and fanfare.[82] One can argue that lynchings are inconsistent with executions since justice officials impose the death penalty pursuant to civil authority while lynch mobs had no such legal license. Yet, the collusion of public officials, law enforcement, court officials, and the national government in malign indifference toward vigilante violence belies the notion that mobs acted illegitimately.

Contrasting women's executions with female lynchings across decades reveals that the power to put women to death shifted periodically from the hands of the state to the hands of lynch mobs. Table 10-1 shows the number of female executions and lynchings by decades from the 1830s to the 1960s. Nearly 83 percent of all female lynchings were black women over these decades. The remaining percent of female lynchings involved whites, Latinas, American Indians and the killing of one Chinese woman. In contrast, black women were slightly more than 77 percent of female executions. The remaining percent were whites, Latinas, American Indians, and one Asian-Pacific Islander female execution. As a result, the trends in female executions and female lynchings illustrated in Table 10-1 represent mostly black female killings by the state or the result of mob violence.

One scholar frames the historical connection between executions and lynchings in rather simplified terms: "Did these lethal punishments complement each other or serve as alternatives? Did their numbers rise and fall in tandem (the 'reinforcement' effect), or did an increase in one mean a decrease in the other (the 'substitution' effect)? Or was there no correlation at all?"[83] The data in Table 10-1 suggest that the power to put women to death never fully resided in either the state or lynch mobs, evidenced by the fact that both female executions and lynchings took place throughout the entire period. The dominant power to execute women shifted from the state to lynch mobs when vigilante violence took more female lives than did state executioners. Overall trends in the data show that female lynchings increased throughout the period while female executions decreased. Women's executions surpassed female lynchings by a margin of nearly *10 to 1* in the antebellum slave period from the 1830s through the 1860s. The 1850s was the peak decade of female executions when death penalty jurisdictions hanged more than 8 percent of women lawfully executed historically. Female lynchings exceeded female executions during Reconstruction and the Jim Crow periods from the 1870s through the 1920s at a ratio of about *four to one*. The peak decade in female lynchings occurred at the height of Jim Crow in the 1890s when vigilante violence accounted for slightly more than 23 percent of female lynchings historically. From the 1930s through the 1950s, women's executions exceeded female lynchings at a margin of just over *two to one*, and in the civil rights period of the 1960s, female lynchings surpassed female executions at a ratio of *fifteen to one*.

The trends in female executions and lynchings support a substitution thesis; that is, female executions and female lynchings did not rise and fall concurrently and thus are *not* complementary means of gender control historically. Largely, female executions and female lynchings were alternative means of gender control; when female executions decreased, female lynchings increased. There are decades, however, when female executions and female lynchings increased and decreased in tandem. From the 1870s through the 1880s, both female executions and female lynchings increased. The same effect appears from the 1890s through the 1900s when both female executions and female lynchings decreased. In these decades, it may be fitting to view the two lethal devices as acting in concert to effect gender control. Mostly, however, the historical relationship between female lynchings and female executions is that the increased use of lynching as a mechanism of gender control in the United States effected a decline in state executions of women.

Concluding Remarks

One can make several observations about female executions since 1900. A larger number of white female executions than black female executions accent the third historical trend in American women and capital punishment. Despite the racial disparity in women executions, females executed in the period were largely impoverished and marginalized women and many of them suffered extreme mental anguish as adults resulting from troubled childhoods of extreme physical, sexual, and psychological abuse. Many of the women had severe intellectual deficiencies. Still, jurisdictions were compelled to execute these women. Many condemned women put to death in the period suffered the same excruciating violence in execution methods that condemned women experienced in previous periods. Sheriff's deputies decapitated Eva Dugan during her

Table 10-1: Female Executions and Female Lynchings, 1830s–1960s

Decades	Female Executions N=263 (54.9%)		Female Lynchings N=216 (45.1%)		Totals N=479 (100%)	
	N	%	N	%	N	%
1830s	52	19.7	3	1.3	55	11.4
1840s	48	18.2	0	0.0	48	10.0
1850s	59	22.4	8	3.7	67	13.9
1860s	52	19.7	11	5.0	63	13.1
1870s	5	1.9	15	6.9	20	4.1
1880s	14	5.3	20	9.2	34	7.0
1890s	14	5.3	50	23.1	64	13.3
1900s	3	1.1	28	12.9	31	6.4
1910s	1	0.3	32	14.8	33	6.8
1920s	4	1.5	20	9.2	24	5.0
1930s	11	4.1	7	3.2	18	3.7
1940s	11	4.1	2	0.9	13	2.7
1950s	8	3.0	5	2.3	13	2.7
1960s	1	0.3	15	6.9	16	3.3

hanging and May Carey strangled to death for 17 minutes. Police officials forced Eva Cool the horrific task of reenacting her killing with the victim's exhumed corpse and Mary Frances Creighton was unconscious from a morphine injection during her electrocution. And in the case of Mary Rogers, the executioner and attending physicians strangled Mary to death by pulling on the hanging rope. Mary may also have been pregnant at the time of her execution. State officials also botched Rose Marie Stinette's electrocution when a surge of electricity caused sparks at her head and arms. An unsavory event also took place when the future longest-serving U.S. Senator, Strom Thurmond, seduced Sue Logue on the way to her electrocution and became the only known circuit court judge in South Carolina history to bed a condemned murderess as she was being transferred to the execution chamber from state prison. It is also noteworthy that the power of state to execute women involved state prosecutors using defendant women's lesbianism to vilify and denigrate them to juries so to render the women executable. This was the case in the trials of Barbara Graham, Aileen Wuornos, Betty Butler, Wanda Allen and Lisa Coleman. Lastly, there is significant evidence that Georgia committed an injustice when it executed Lena Baker for the self-defense killing of her white employer in the mid–1940s.

Part III

Wrongful Convictions, Judicial Commutations, Executive Clemency and Women on Death Row Today

> "In a society whose foundations were built upon the guarantee of justice to every citizen, the conviction of an innocent person represents a serious and egregious violation of such guarantee."[1]

6

Wrongful Convictions in Potentially Capital Cases

Wrongful convictions in capital cases have troubled western scholars since at least 1816 when Samuel March Phillipps published his treatise on the *Theory of Presumptive Proof*. In the 1820s, prominent legal scholar and statesman Edward Livingston expressed uneasiness about wrongfully convicted prisoners in the United States. Others carried the notion of innocent persons suffering unjustified convictions throughout the 19th and 20th centuries, namely Charles C. Burleigh, Horace Greeley, William Howells, Lewis Lawes and the American League to Abolish Capital Punishment. In the early 1930s, Yale law professor Edwin Montefiore Borchard identified 65 cases where justice officials wrongfully prosecuted, convicted, and incarcerated innocent persons because of eyewitness misidentification, perjured testimony, and police and prosecutorial misconduct.[2] Some argue that the importance of Borchard's "then-pioneering research was to shift the research question away from whether factually innocent individuals are wrongfully convicted in the American criminal justice system to *why* they are wrongfully convicted and *what* can be done to remedy the problem."[3] Despite the acuity of Borchard's thinking about factual innocence, scholars gave limited attention to faulty convictions over the next several decades. It was not until 1987, when Hugo Bedau and Michael Radelet published a major study in the *Stanford Law Review*, that there was a renewed interest in wrongful convictions. In it, the authors identified hundreds of wrongful convictions in potentially capital cases between 1900 and 1985. Of those false convictions, authorities had sentenced some defendants to death, actually executed other prisoners, and still other prisoners came within hours of their executions before officials established their innocence. Scholars researched wrongful convictions in the decades following Bedau and Radelet's work. One analysis of more than 300 exonerations including 13 women from 1989 to 2003 found that 60 percent of exonerations involved erroneous convictions for murder with 22 percent of those convictions involving death sentences.[4] According to the study, exonerations are heavily concentrated among capital cases because of "the extraordinary pressure to secure convictions for heinous crimes; the difficulty of investigating many homicides because, by definition, the victims are unavailable; extreme incentives for the real killers to frame innocent fall guys when they are facing the possibility of execution."[5] There have been hundreds of capital cases involving wrongfully convicted defendants since 1900. One study accounts for nearly 900 exonerations from 1989 to 2012 including 57 women.[6] A new study that recently appeared in the esteemed *Proceedings of the National Academy of Sciences*, sought to determine the number of innocent people on death row in the United States. Using a sophisticated biostatistics method called "survival analysis" and data from three independent sources, researchers estimate that one in 25 death row inmates may be innocent; a 4 percent rate of wrongful conviction.[7]

Data

A "wrongful conviction" occurs when a convicted woman is factually innocent of the charges or where procedural error violates a woman's constitutional rights. A wrongful conviction, however, does not necessarily result in "exoneration." In fact, the vast majority of wrongful convictions never result in exonerations. Still, roughly two-thirds of falsely convicted women in potentially capital cases result in exonerations. Exonerations only arise when new evidence warrants a judicial finding of innocence of a woman convicted of a crime. Observers have identified a host of factors that predispose jurisdictions to wrongly convict persons of capital crimes. Social critic Alan Berlow, for instance, identifies several features of the justice system that increase the prospects that jurisdictions may wrongly convict innocent prisoners: Death-qualified juries, a "take-no-prisoners" mindset of jurists and politicians, the lack of resources required to fund public defender organizations, an ever-increasing public condemnation of heinous criminality, an indifference of jurists to the possibility of wrongful convictions, the incompetence of defense counsel, the lawlessness of police officers and prosecutors in suppressing exculpating evidence, and the increasing complexity of the appeals process have all added to the equation that the capital punishment scheme in the United States is faulty, impractical, and ineffectual.[8] Similarly, legal scholars acknowledge several *systemic myths* about the criminal justice system that, if corrected, would go far to ensure that innocent women are not unjustly convicted. These flawed assumptions include the notions that every woman receives effective assistance of counsel, that police properly collect, handle, preserve, and analyze forensic evidence, that cross examination produces the truth, that jury instructions cure trial error, that innocent woman do not confess to crimes they did not commit, and that women escape on technicalities because they are protected by too many rights.[9]

Another fiction brought forward by one legal critic is that appellate courts ensure that justice prevails for disadvantaged groups such as the wrongfully convicted. Accordingly, state and federal appellate courts further the victimization of innocent women by their reliance on "the harmless error rule to dismiss the grounds upon which a wrongful conviction or prosecution is challenged," and on unpublished opinions designed "to minimize attention given to an appeal and to conceal the details of the appeal's resolution."[10] In one of the most in-depth statewide reviews of prosecutorial misconduct in the United States, the Northern California Innocence Project reviewed more than 4,000 state and federal appellate rulings between 1997 and 2009 and showed that prosecutors committed misconduct in more than 700 cases. In 77 percent of those cases involving prosecutorial misconduct, state and federal courts upheld the convictions and ruled that the misconduct was harmless error. In the remaining cases, courts found the misconduct harmful and "either set aside the conviction or sentence, declared a mistrial or barred evidence." The study reveals that state and federal courts fail to "report prosecutorial misconduct (despite having a statutory obligation to do so), prosecutors deny that it occurred, and the California State Bar almost never disciplines it."[11] Studies in New York, Pennsylvania, and Texas show similar findings.

Justice authorities have long histories of wrongly convicting women and at times executing falsely convicted women. Besides the recorded cases of female miscarriages of justice in the witchcraft trials of 17th-century New England, other early confirmed wrongful female convictions include cases where officials executed the wrong woman responsible for another's death. In 1651, for instance, Middlesex County officials in Massachusetts hanged British American Elizabeth Kendall for bewitching a child to death though a nurse was actually responsible for the killing that did not involve an accusation of witchcraft. Delaware County authorities in Pennsylvania hanged Elizabeth Wilson in 1786 for the murder of her infant twin daughters though the children's father was the real killer. Columbia County officials in New York hanged

Margaret Houghtaling in 1817 for killing a 15-month-old mulatto child left in her care, yet it was the child's mother who was actually responsible for the death. Massachusetts wrongfully hanged an innocent 22-year-old servant woman named Mary Johnson for the murder of her elderly master and mistress. At Mary's hanging, the actual perpetrator confessed to the murders once Mary had made the hangman's drop and died shortly thereafter. A German woman named Lena Miller ostensibly poisoned her husband Xavier with arsenic and hanged in November 1867 in the jail yard of the Brookville prison in Pittsburgh before several hundred onlookers. Although Lena confessed to the murder, a chemical investigation found no arsenic in her husband's stomach. Lena was most likely innocent of the charges and falsely confessed to the killing. In other cases, the historical record reveals that state and federal officials convicted and executed at least two women despite serious doubts of their guilt—the U.S. military hanged Mary Surratt in 1865 for her role in the assassination of President Lincoln and Pennsylvania electrocuted Corrine Sykes in 1946 for killing her white employer. Oddly enough, military authorities based Mary Surratt's conviction upon much of the same evidence that later acquitted her brother.

Though an innocence movement has developed over the past few decades, it has largely left women behind. Women escape scholarly concern as victims of wrongful convictions most likely because they comprise such a small proportion of wrongful convictions in the United States relative to wrongly convicted men. The National Registry of Exonerations reveals that women are slightly more than 8 percent of the some 1,670 known exonerations in the United States.[12] To correct for the oversight of academic attention on falsely convicted women, Table 6-1 comprises an inventory of 89 women wrongly convicted in potentially capital cases since 1908 when an Illinois court falsely convicted Margaret Lucas of a predatory murder based upon perjured eyewitness testimony. *Potentially capital cases* are cases that might have culminated in a death sentence "except for some relatively adventitious factor: the verdict of the trial court (second-degree rather than first-degree murder), the sentencing decision of the trial court (life imprisonment rather than death), or the jurisdiction in which the crime occurred (an abolition state rather than a death penalty state)."[13]

The registry derives from several sources of wrongful convictions available to researchers. The National Registry of Exonerations, a joint project of the University of the Michigan Law School and the Center on Wrongful Convictions at Northwestern University School of Law, maintains a comprehensive inventory of wrongful convictions leading to exonerations. The registry accounts for wrongful convictions leading to exonerations since 1989.[14] Of these cases, the registry accounts for 51 women wrongly convicted of murder and nine women wrongly convicted of manslaughter. The Innocence Project maintains an inventory of persons exonerated with DNA evidence that contains information on 317 exonerations in 35 states and the District of Columbia, four of the cases involve female exonerations for murder. The Death Penalty Information Center in Washington, D.C., maintains information on false convictions. The center identifies 144 innocent persons in 26 states released from death row since 1973 including one female—Sabrina Butler. Hans Sherrer maintains a comprehensive list of more than 5,000 persons wrongly convicted worldwide since the 15th century. Included in the database are nearly 3,000 cases in the United States, including 287 wrongful convictions of women, 66 of those false convictions concerned homicides. There is other information available from narratives posted on websites at Life After Exoneration Program, Truth in Justice, and Victims of the State. Individual scholars have constructed inventories of the wrongfully convicted though they focus on contemporary cases. Samuel Gross and Michael Shaeffer account for 57 female exonerations in the United States from 1989 through 2012, 24 of those convicted of murder. In her work on the consequences of wrongful conviction for women, Zieva Dauber Konvisser identifies 49 innocent women wrongly convicted of murder and manslaughter. Mitch Ruesink and Marvin Free examined

Table 6-1: Wrongful Female Convictions in Potentially Capital Cases

Name of Defendant	Race/ Ethnicity	Age at Conviction	State of Conviction	Criminal Offense	Years in Prison	Sentence Imposed by Court	Year of Conviction/ Released from Custody	Contributing Factors to Wrongful Convictions									
								FWI	FC	PER	FFE	OM	ILD	SBS	CS	NC	IE
Tayshea Aiwohi	Hawaiian	32	Hawaii	Manslaughter	1 year	10 years	2004/2005									X	
Candice Anderson	White	21	Texas	Manslaughter	None	Probation	2007/2014										
Eunice M. Baker	White	23	New York	Child Murder	4 years	15 years to life	2000/2004		X			X					
Nissa Baillie*	White	20	Florida	Manslaughter	4 years	15 years	1997/2001					X				X	
Victoria Banks	Black	27	Alabama	Child Murder	4 years	15 years	1999/2003		X								
Delphine Bertrand	White	54	Connecticut	Predatory Murder	2 years	10-15 years	1945/1946		X								
Yeidja Bostick*	White	21	Pennsylvania	Manslaughter	3 years	5-10 years	1990/1993			X		X					
Debra Brown*	White	36	Utah	Predatory Murder	17 years	Life Sentence	1995/2011			X		X	X				
Joyce Ann Brown*	Black	33	Texas	Predatory Murder	9.5 years	Life Sentence	1980/1989	X		X		X					
Sheila Bryan*	White	43	Georgia	Predatory Murder	2 years	Life Sentence	1998/2000				X	X				X	
Kristine Bunch*	White	21	Indiana	Child Murder	17 years	60 years	1996/2012				X	X				X	
Louise Butler	Black	Unknown	Alabama	Child Murder	2 months	Life Sentence	1928/1930		X	X							
Sabrina Butler*	Black	17	Mississippi	Child Murder	6 years	Death Penalty	1990/1995		X	X						X	
Lana Canen*	White	45	Indiana	Predatory Murder	8 years	55 years	2005/2012			X		X					
Patricia Cohen	White	Unknown	New York	Spousal Murder	1 year	20 years to life	1979/1983			X		X	X				
Norma Jean Croy*	Am. Indian	23	California	Predatory Murder	18 years	Life Sentence	1979/1997			X			X				
Lynn M. DeJac*	White	31	New York	Child Murder	13.5 years	25 years to life	1994/2008					X				X	
Margaret A. Earle*	White	41	Massachusetts	Child Murder	5 years	Life Sentence	2005/2010										
Audrey Edmunds*	White	34	Wisconsin	Child Murder	11.5 years	18 years	1996/2008				X			X		X	
Elizabeth Ehlert	White	32	Illinois	Child Murder	14 years	58 years	1991/2004										
Ella Mae Ellison	Black	27	Massachusetts	Predatory Murder	4 years	Life Sentence	1974/1978			X							
Teresa Engberg-Lehmer	White	24	Iowa	Child Murder	1 year	15 years	1997/1998				X			X		X	
Judith Fritz*	White	35	Pennsylvania	Manslaughter	2 years	3 years	1994/1997	X					X			X	
Cynthia (Cindy) George	White	50	Ohio	Child Murder	2 years	Life Sentence	2005/2007				X					X	X
Kathy Gonzalez*^	Latina	24	Nebraska	Predatory Murder	4.5 years	10 years	1989/2009	X	X	X							

*Exoneration. ^Forensic DNA evidence central to establishing innocence. False Witness Identification (FWI)—Where a witness falsely identifies the defendant as the person the witness saw commit a crime; False Confession (FC)—the defendant made a false statement to authorities which was treated as a confession, authorities claimed that the defendant made such a statement but the defendant denied it, or the defendant made a statement that was not an admission of guilt, but was misinterpreted as such by the authorities; Perjury (PER)—A person other than the defendant falsely accused the defendant of committing the crime for which the defendant was later exonerated, either in sworn testimony or otherwise; False Forensic Evidence (FFE)—A forensic analyst or other forensic expert presented evidence that was either based on unreliable or unproven methods, expressed with exaggerated and misleading confidence, or fraudulent; Official Misconduct (OM)—Police, prosecutors, or other government officials significantly abused their authority or the judicial process in a manner that contributed to the defendant's conviction; Inadequate Legal Defense (ILD)—The defendant's lawyer at trial or on appeal provided obviously and grossly inadequate representation; Shaken Baby Syndrome (SBS)—The defendant was convicted of injuring or killing an infant by violent shaking, based on a medical diagnosis that is now highly controversial; Christian Scientist (CS)—Christian Scientist beliefs of not seeking medical attention for dependent children; No Crime (NC)—a judicial finding that the defendant committed no crime; Insufficient Evidence to Support the Conviction (IE)—Where the state has provided insufficient evidence to support the verdict. Source: Definitions adapted from the Glossary of terms at the National Registry of Exonerations available at http://www.law.umich.edu/special/exoneration/Pages/glossary.aspx.

Name of Defendant	Race/Ethnicity	Age at Conviction	State of Conviction	Criminal Offense	Years in Prison	Sentence Imposed by Court	Year of Conviction/Released from Custody	FWI	FC	PER	FFE	OM	ILD	SBS	CS	NC	IE
Paula Gray*^	Black	17	Illinois	Predatory Murder	18 years	60 years	1978/2002	X	X	X	X	X					X
Phyllis Elaine Hall	White	Unknown	Florida	Predatory Murder	2 years	25 years to life	1985/1987										X
Paula Hal*	White	36	Missouri	Predatory Murder	4 years	20 years	2009/2013		X			X					
Mary Kathryn Hampton	White	19	Louisiana	Predatory Murder	5.75 years	Life Sentence	1961/1966		X				X				
Tanya A. Harden	White	31	West Virginia	Spousal Murder	2 years	Life Sentence	2007/2009					X	X				
Nicole Harris*	Black	23	Illinois	Child Murder	8 years	30 years	2005/2013		X			X	X			X	
Ashley Nicole Hepburn	White	23	South Carolina	Child Murder	+33 months	45 years	2009/2013										X
Christine Hermanson	White	36	Florida	Child Murder	None	15 years prob	1986/1992								X		
Christina Hill	Black	17	Massachusetts	Child Murder	1 year	Youth Services	1990/1991			X							
Letha Hockersmith*	White	31	Oklahoma	Child Murder	4 years	Life Sentence	1995/1999										
Elicia Hughes*	Black	35	Mississippi	Spousal Murder	<1 year	Life Sentence	2007/2007				X		X				
Ernestine Audry James*	Am. Indian	42	Washington	Manslaughter	4 years	Probation	1995/1999										
Emma Jo Burton Johnson	White	32	Nevada	Predatory Murder	3 years	10 to 12 years	1951/1954										
Sophia Johnson*	Black	23	Washington	Predatory Murder	2 years	43 years	2003/2005		X			X					
Abere Karibi-Ikiriko*	Black	27	Maryland	Predatory Murder	2.8 years	15 years	2005/2007										
Gloria Killian*	White	35	California	Predatory Murder	16 years	32 years to life	1986/2002		X		X					X	
Susan Jean King*	White	32	Kentucky	Manslaughter	5.5 years	10 years	2008/2014		X		X	X					
Janine Kirby	Unknown	24	U.S. Military	Manslaughter	1 year	9 months	1983/1984										
Kriseya J. Labastida	Latina	26	Nevada	Child Murder	7 years	20 years	1993/2003		X			X					
Beth LaBatte*	White	24	Wisconsin	Predatory Murder	10 years	Life Sentence	1997/2006		X		X		X				
Marie LaPinta	Latina	47	New York	Spousal Murder	22 years	Life Sentence	1983/2005				X						
Bridget Lee	White	37	Alabama	Child Murder	0.75 year	Life Sentence	2006/2009				X	X					
Virginia LeFever*	White	37	Ohio	Spousal Murder	20 years	Life Sentence	1990/2011			X						X	
Mechele K. Linehan*	White	34	Alaska	Predatory Murder	3 years	99 years	2007/2012			X	X	X	X				
Debbie Loveless*	White	31	Texas	Child Murder	5 years	Life Sentence	1989/1994			X	X	X	X				
Margaret Lucas	White	Unknown	Illinois	Predatory Murder	1 year	Life Sentence	1908/1909										
Kimberly Mawson*	White	32	Rhode Island	Child Murder	5 years	35 years	2007/2012			X							
Susan Marie Mellen*	White	42	California	Predatory Murder	17 years	LWOP	1998/2014		X			X	X				
Debra Jean Milke*	White	25	Arizona	Predatory Murder	25 years	Death	1990/2015					X	X			X	
Beverly Anne Monroe*	White	54	Virginia	Predatory Murder	10 years	22 years	1992/2003		X		X	X	X				
Fredda Sue Mowbray*	White	39	Texas	Spousal Murder	10 years	Life Sentence	1988/1998		X		X	X	X				
Michelle Murphy*	White	16	Oklahoma	Child Murder	20 years	LWOP	1995/2014		X		X	X	X				
LaCresha Murray*	Black	11	Texas	Child Murder	5 years	20 years	1996/2001		X			X	X				
Sandra Ortiz*	Latina	30	New Jersey	Predatory Murder	2 years	Not sentenced	2001/2003					X				X	
Laverne Pavlinac*	White	57	Oregon	Predatory Murder	4 years	Life Sentence	1991/1995		X								
Carolyn June Peak*	White	39	Arizona	Spousal Murder	4 years	No sentence	2000/2003					X					

6. Wrongful Convictions in Potentially Capital Cases

Name of Defendant	Race/Ethnicity	Age at Conviction	State of Conviction	Criminal Offense	Years in Prison	Sentence Imposed by Court	Year of Conviction/Released from Custody	FWI	FC	PER	FFE	OM	ILD	SBS	CS	NC	IE
Leona Pettit*	White	27	Ohio	Predatory Murder	2 years	15 years to life	1999/2001						X			X	
Lisa Pineda*	Latina	26	California	Predatory Murder	4 years	40 years to life	2005/2009									X	
Tabitha Pollack	White	37	Illinois	Child Murder	6.5 years	36 years	1996/2002					X					
Julie Rea (Harper)*	White	28	Illinois	Child Murder	2 years	65 years	2002/2006					X					X
Ellen Reasonover*	Black	24	Missouri	Predatory Murder	17 years	Life Sentence	1983/1999			X							
Sierra Nichole Rigel*	White	17	Oregon	Manslaughter	None	Cmty Service	2011/2014			X	X	X	X				
Lisa Marie Roberts*	Black	37	Oregon	Manslaughter	10 years	15 years	2004/2014		X	X	X	X	X			X	
Debra Shelden*^	White	26	Nebraska	Predatory Murder	4.5 years	10 years	1989/2009		X	X							
Grace M. Smith	White	Unknown	Virginia	Spousal Murder	1 year	20 years	1945/1946										
Cynthia Sommer*	White	33	California	Spousal Murder	2 years	LWOP	2007/2008			X			X			X	
Patricia Stallings*	White	24	Missouri	Child Murder	1 year	LWOP	1991/1991			X			X			X	
Carol Stonehouse*	White	41	Pennsylvania	Predatory Murder	7 years	7-14 years	1983/1990						X			X	
Maude Cushing Storick	White	40	Michigan	Spousal Murder	27 years	Life sentence	1923/1949	X									
Ada JoAnn Taylor*^	White	21	Nebraska	Predatory Murder	4.5 years	10-40 years	1989/2009		X	X		X					
Cherice Thomas*	Black	18	California	Predatory Murder	3.0 years	25 years to life	2009/2012		X	X		X					
Teresa R. Thomas*	Black	29	Ohio	Predatory Murder	4 years	18 years to life	1993/1997	X									
Diane Bell Tucker	Black	37	Alabama	Child Murder	4 years	15 years	1999/2003	X								X	
Ginger Twitchell	White	34	Massachusetts	Child Murder	None	10 years prob	1990/1993								X		
Betty Tyson*	Black	24	New York	Predatory Murder	25 years	25 years to life	1973/1998		X	X		X					
Melonie K. Ware*	Black	31	Georgia	Child Murder	5 years	Life Sentence	2005/2009		X	X			X	X		X	
Merla Walpole	White	25	California	Child Murder	2 years	None	1974/1976										
Cathy Watkins*	Black	27	New York	Predatory Murder	15 years	25 years to life	1997/2012		X	X				X			
Mary C. Weaver*	White	41	Iowa	Child Murder	3 years	LWOP	1994/1997		X	X						X	
Shelia Wilson	White	26	Kentucky	Spousal Murder	4 years	20 years	1979/1983		X	X							
Megan Winfrey*	White	18	Texas	Predatory Murder	7 years	Life Sentence	2008/2013					X					
Cathy Woods*^	White	26	Nevada	Predatory Murder	35 years	LWOP	1980/2015	X									

42 women wrongly convicted in the United States from 1970 to 2005, including 15 women wrongly convicted of murder.

Table 6-1 provides information on the name, race, and offense of falsely convicted women, the state of conviction, the number of years imprisoned, the original sentence given the defendant, the year of conviction and release from custody, the causes of wrongful convictions, female defendant exonerations, and whether DNA was instrumental in determining a defendant's innocence. The data reveal that courts unjustly convicted roughly 43 percent of falsely convicted women for predatory murders involving strangers, acquaintances and adult intimates, slightly more than 36 percent for killing children, and about 14 percent for murdering spouses. Officials falsely convicted another 6 percent of women in manslaughter cases. Justice authorities have falsely convicted more white women than women of color in potentially capital cases; white women are 65 percent of female wrongful convictions, black women are roughly 26 percent, Latinas are about 5 percent, and Native American women (including one Native Hawaiian) are roughly 4 percent. In contrast, whites are 40 percent of the overall population of exonerated prisoners, blacks are 47 percent, Latinos are 11 percent, and Native Americans are less than 1 percent. That is, white women are far more represented among the wrongfully convicted than are other persons.

Factors Contributing to False Convictions

The contributing factors to wrongful female convictions include false witness identifications, false confessions, false forensic evidence, inadequate legal defense, official misconduct, perjury, and cases involving "Shaken Baby Syndrome" or Christian Scientists beliefs resulting in the death of a child. In some cases, female wrongful convictions involved cases where women had not committed a crime and in other cases the evidence was insufficient to support the verdict.

False Eyewitness Identification

Early forensic psychologists challenged the reliability of eyewitness identification. Borchard, for instance, found that eyewitness misidentification was the leading cause of wrongful convictions. Though eyewitness identification remains integral to police and prosecutors as a crime investigation device, studies confirm the imprecision of eyewitness identifications. Some 25 percent of exonerations are attributed to false or mistaken witness identification in homicide cases, and about 72 percent of convictions overturned by DNA evidence involve eyewitness misidentification. Eyewitness misidentification can take various forms including in-person line-ups, photo line-ups, one-on-one show-ups, one-on-one photos, voice identification, artist sketches, and hypnosis. Judicial officers have taken notice of the unreliability of eyewitness identification. In a recent U.S. Supreme Court, Justice Sotomayor outlined the "vast body of scientific literature" and "more than two thousand studies" that show that "eyewitness misidentification is the single greatest cause of wrongful convictions in this country." As she explained,

> Study after study demonstrates that eyewitness recollections are highly susceptible to distortion by post event information or social cues; that jurors routinely overestimate the accuracy of eyewitness identifications; that jurors place the greatest weight on eyewitness confidence in assessing identifications even though confidence is a poor gauge of accuracy; and that suggestiveness can stem from sources beyond police-orchestrated procedures.[15]

More recently, Justice Barbara Pariente of the Florida Supreme Court commented on the danger of mistake in eyewitness testimony and the importance of warning juries about the possibility of error. Her comments were made in a concurring opinion in *Petersen v. Florida*, a death penalty case. Justice Pariente opined that widely accepted scientific research, "convincingly demonstrates the fallibility of eyewitness identification testimony and pinpoints an array of variables that are most likely to lead to a mistaken identification." She lamented that in Florida "eyewitness misidentification has played a role in more than seventy-five percent of convictions that were subsequently overturned through DNA testing."[16] She suggested that courts allow experts to testify about the fallibility of such testimony. In contradiction to her warnings, however, Justice Pariente concurred with a majority of the court that the failure to utilize an eyewitness identification expert in the case did not constitute ineffective assistance of counsel.

Other studies support the notion that mistaken eyewitness testimony is the most important factor leading to faulty convictions, followed by police and prosecutorial misconduct, jailhouse informant testimony, junk science, false or coerced confessions, and such factors as questionable circumstantial evidence and hearsay. Yet, eyewitness misidentification is *not* a major source of female wrongful convictions in potentially capital cases. False eyewitness identification has played a role in the wrongful convictions of three female defendants inventoried in Table 6-1. In the case of Joyce Ann Brown, the murder victim's surviving wife gave a cross-racial misidentification of Joyce from a photograph. A man who lived in the same neighborhood as Paula Gray erroneously implicated her and four others in the murder of two people in a Chicago suburb. In the manslaughter case of Judith Fritz, a survivor of a deadly automobile accident falsely testified that Judith was the driver of the car that killed another passenger in the car.

False Confessions

Wrongly convicted female defendants are deemed to have falsely confessed to a crime when they fabricated a statement to authorities that officials treated as a confession, authorities claim that the defendant made such a statement but the defendant denied it, or the defendant made a statement that was not an admission of guilt but officials misinterpreted the statement as a confession.[17] False confessions are a significant factor in female wrongful convictions; slightly more than one-fifth of female wrongful convictions involve false confessions. White women are more likely to give false confessions than other racial categories of wrongly convicted female defendants; 53 percent of white women, 35 percent of black women, and 12 percent of Latinas wrongly convicted in potentially capital cases gave false confessions.

Delphine Bertrand, for instance, pleaded guilty to manslaughter in 1944 and falsely confessed to the killing of her fiancé because she did not want it revealed in a public trial that she was having a sexual encounter with another man in another part of the house when the murder took place. Laverne Pavlinac falsely confessed to killing an Oregon woman and implicated her boyfriend to escape from their abusive relationship. In 1928, Louise Butler falsely confessed to killing her niece who authorities later found living in a nearby county. Louise likely confessed to the murder in hopes of gaining leniency from an all-white jury in the Jim Crow south. Often, police violence during interrogations of suspects' results in false confessions. Despite no physical evidence linking Betty Tyson to the killing of a white businessman in 1973, white police officers tortured Betty for more than 12 hours before she confessed. Police also had no evidence that Paula Gray, an emotionally disabled and impoverished 17-year-old black girl, was an accomplice to the killing of two white people in Chicago in 1978, but the lack of evidence did not keep white police officers from torturing a confession from Paula for the killings. Sabrina Butler signed a declaration in 1990 stating that she had punched her baby in the abdomen when actually she was attempting to resuscitate the child who had fallen ill and eventually died from a kidney infection.

Perjury

Perjury or false accusations take place when a person falsely testifies that a female defendant committed a crime for which she is later exculpated of the crime.[18] Perjured testimony is a leading factor contributing to false convictions. Some 56 percent of all wrongful convictions involve perjured testimony but roughly 37 percent of female wrongful convictions in potentially capital cases embroil false accusations that the defendant committed the crime. Cases against women falsely convicted of predatory murders are far more likely to involve perjured testimony than in cases against women wrongly convicted of child murder and spousal murder. Of the 27 falsely convicted women cases involving perjury or false accusations, slightly more than 55 percent of the wrongful convictions concerned white women, 37 percent included black females, and 7 percent of Latina wrongful convictions.

Some of the more perverse cases where perjury or false accusations contribute to female wrongful convictions take place when police and state prosecutors threaten witnesses or make deals of punishment leniency with jail snitches to falsely testify against a female defendant. In the case of Beth LaBatte, for instance, a Wisconsin jury in Green Bay convicted Beth of the ghastly murders of two retired schoolteachers based entirely on the erroneous testimony of a jailhouse informant that she had confessed to the killings. Officials exonerated Beth of the killing with DNA evidence. And surprisingly, in at least one case a newspaper reporter coached young girls to testify untruthfully and influenced a verdict by the trial judge. In the case of Christina Hill, the trial judge based his guilty verdict against Christina in the death a young child on evidence provided by a newspaper reporter who had instructed two teenage girls to provide falsified incriminating evidence against Christina.

False Forensic Evidence

Junk science resulting in speculative testimony by forensic experts is yet another reason for wrongful convictions of women in the United States. In a groundbreaking study recently published in the *Virginia Law Review*, authors Brandon Garrett and Peter Neufeld explored erroneous scientific testimony by prosecution experts in the trials of defendants who officials later exonerated through post-conviction DNA testing. The research, entitled "Invalid Forensic Science Testimony and Wrongful Convictions," explored serological analysis, microscopic hair comparison, bite mark evidence, shoe prints, soil, fiber, fingerprint comparisons, and DNA analysis. The analysis found that in 60 percent of trials, the prosecution's forensic analysts provided invalid testimony with conclusions that misstated empirical data or was completely unsupported by empirical data. Flawed expert testimony was not an isolated issue stemming from a handful of analysts, however. In the 137 cases examined by researchers, 72 forensic experts, employed by 52 laboratories, practices, or hospitals in 25 states, delivered inaccurate testimony. What's more, the researchers found that defense lawyers rarely cross-examine analysts concerning invalid testimony and rarely obtain experts of their own. Still further, judges infrequently provide relief in cases that challenge invalid forensic science. Essentially, the study shows that our adversarial system of justice fails miserably to scrutinize erroneous testimony. To the authors,

> this evidence supports efforts to create scientific oversight mechanisms for reviewing forensic testimony and to develop clear scientific standards for written reports and testimony. The scientific community can through an official government entity promulgate standards to ensure the valid presentation of forensic science in criminal cases and thus the integrity and fairness of the criminal process.[19]

False or misleading forensic evidence occurs in female potentially capital cases when a forensic expert presents evidence that is either based on unreliable or unproven methods, expressed with exaggerated and misleading confidence, or fraudulently. Jurisdictions have used false or misleading forensic evidence to convict 22 percent of all exonerated defendants accounted for by the National Registry of Exonerations. Yet, officials have engaged in using false forensic evidence to convict nearly 38 percent of women wrongly convicted in potentially capital cases. In one troubling case, a police detective falsely identified a fingerprint found on a prescription pill bottle found at the murder scene of an elderly blind woman despite the fact that the detective had no formal training in latent fingerprint comparisons. Based on this evidence and the perjured testimony of a mentally retarded man, an Indiana jury convicted Lana Canen of the elderly woman's murder. A qualified latent fingerprint expert examined the pill container and determined that the print did not belong to Lana and a court vacated her conviction.

Official Misconduct

Official misconduct refers to the notion that police, prosecutors, or other government officials significantly abuse their authority or the judicial process in a manner that contributes to the female defendant's conviction. Nearly 60 percent of all exonerations in homicide cases involve official misconduct, but government officials have successfully condemned 30 percent of wrongfully convicted women in potentially capital cases with the abuse of their legal authority. In the 1960s case of Mary Kathryn Hampton, for instance, police interrogated young Mary for more than a month and state prosecutors threatened her with execution in the state's electric chair. Mary eventually pleaded guilty to murders she did not commit. Police investigators and state prosecutors used the threat of the death penalty to coerce false confessions from Ada JoAnn Taylor, Debra Shelden, and Kathy Gonzales.

Inadequate Legal Defense

An inadequate legal defense refers to the notion that the defendant's trial or appellate lawyer(s) provided grossly insufficient representation. Roughly 21 percent of all exonerated prisoners had poor legal representation at trial, but the figure is slightly more than 25 percent for women falsely convicted in potentially capital cases. Poor defense lawyering is more prevalent in female predatory and child murder cases than in spousal murder cases. Still, in many wrongful convictions of women in potentially capital cases, defense lawyers failed to raise "battered woman" as a legitimate defense of women's actions against violent husband or boyfriends.[20] The case of Carol Stonehouse stands out as particularly troubling. A court convicted Carol of killing her boyfriend. After Carol, a mother of two small children, broke off the relationship, her boyfriend began a campaign of abuse that included death threats and severe property damage to her home. Worse yet, Carol's boyfriend was a police officer and her complaints to local police about her boyfriend's violence were ignored. To the court, her trial lawyer provided inadequate legal representation to Carol since he should have waged a battered woman defense. The court argued, "We believe that expert testimony regarding battered women is admissible as the basis for proving justification in the use of deadly force where the defendant has been shown to be a victim of psychological and physical abuse."

No Crime Cases

In no crime cases, authorities convict female defendants of a crime that did not occur because the incident was an accident or a suicide or because the event was a fabricated crime that never took place. Nearly 25 percent of all exonerations involve cases where no crime occurred. In female exonerations, however, no crime occurred in 62 percent of the cases. This figure diminishes to 26 percent for women wrongfully convicted in potentially capital crimes. Of female wrongful convictions in potentially capital cases, nearly 43 percent involved child murders, nearly 29 percent involved predatory murders, slightly more than 14 percent concerned manslaughter, and roughly 9 percent were spousal murder cases.

Insufficient Evidence

In five cases of wrongfully convicted women in potentially capital cases there was insufficient evidence provided by state prosecutors to support a verdict. In the case of Cynthia George, an Ohio appellate court ruled that Cynthia's conviction for complicity to commit aggravated murder could not stand because the circumstantial evidence presented by prosecutors was insufficient to prove her guilt beyond a reasonable doubt. A Florida appellate court remanded the conviction of Phyllis Hall for aiding her boyfriend in a murder with instructions to vacate the judgment and sentence and to dismiss the charges. At a new trial for Paula Hall for her participation in a murder, a Missouri appeals court found not only perjury and official misconduct in Paula's first trial but that the state could not prove the elements of a second degree murder charge.

Forensic DNA Evidence

Forensic DNA evidence rarely establishes women's innocence leading to exoneration. DNA was central to establishing innocence in 22 percent of all exonerations in the United States since 1989. DNA evidence was present in 382 exonerations and was central to establishing innocence in 300 seven cases involving men. DNA evidence was vital to establishing innocence in only four female exonerations, namely Kathy Gonzales, Paula Gray, Debra Shelden and Ada JoAnn Taylor.

Predatory Murder

On Christmas Eve 1943, four men and Delphine Bertrand visited James Streeto with the intent to rob him at a summer hotel where he worked as a caretaker. The four men were Philip Contino, Marvin Beebe, Walter Johnson and Joseph Smith. Delphine was Streeto's fiancée. Unknown to Delphine, while she and one of the four men (either Johnson or Smith) were engaged in a romantic interlude in another part of the house, the other men killed Streeto. Contino claimed that Beebe shot and killed Streeto. Delphine falsely confessed to shooting Streeto during a quarrel over his refusal to marry her and pleaded guilty to manslaughter in April 1944. Several newspaper articles report that Delphine confessed to the killing because she preferred being branded a killer than to having her sex life publicly disclosed during a trial. It is far more plausible, however, that Delphine falsely confessed to the murder after the state's attorney threatened her with the death penalty if she did not confess. After the actual killers confessed to Streeto's murder, the state's attorney dismissed the indictment against Delphine in 1946.

In October 1995, a Cache County jury in Utah convicted Debra Brown of the November 1993 shooting death of Lael Brown, her unrelated employer. Lael was an older wealthy man who owned an abundance of rental properties and kept large amounts of cash in his home from collected rents. Debra told police investigators that Lael had been ill and when he failed to respond to her knocking on the front door to his house, Debra let herself into the house and found Lael's body with three gunshots wounds to the head. Debra contacted authorities. During the murder investigation, police discovered that Debra had forged nearly $3,000 in checks to herself drawn on Lael's accounts and alleged that Debra murdered Lael to conceal the fraudulent activities.

At trial, a medical examiner testified that Lael's murder occurred on a Saturday morning between 6:30 a.m. and 10:00 a.m.—a time when Debra had no alibi. Official misconduct occurred in Debra's case when the state's attorney and the medical examiner conspired to change the time of death to put Debra at the scene of the crime. Two people had seen Lael alive at a local restaurant on a Saturday afternoon hours after the state held Debra had killed Lael. The citing of Lael eliminated the possibility that Lael was killed Saturday morning, yet defense lawyers never called witnesses to testify. Though no physical evidence linked Debra to the murder, the jury convicted Debra and the trial judge sentenced her to life in prison. The Utah Supreme Court affirmed the conviction in 1997. But in 2002, the Rocky Mountain Innocence Center began investigating Debra's case that culminated in a hearing in January and March 2011 to determine Debra's innocence. Debra's case was the first to use Utah's Post-Conviction Remedies Act allowing inmates to challenge convictions based upon new evidence. There was evidence that Lael had evicted Bobbie Sheen, a resident of the complex with a troubled past that police had never investigated. Sheen began flashing around large amounts of cash near the time of Lael's death. Debra told police about Sheen's eviction, and one of Sheen's friends tried to tell police about the Sheen's angry comments and piles of money but was told to stay out of it. Sheen committed suicide in August 2007. In May 2011, District Judge Michael DiReda ruled Debra "factually innocent" and ordered her release from prison and ordered the state to pay Debra nearly $500,000 in compensation. Debra spent 17 years imprisoned in a state penitentiary for a crime she did not commit. In February 2012, the Utah Attorney General's office filed an appeal with the state's Supreme Court challenging Judge DiReda's ruling. On July 14, 2013, the Utah Supreme Court upheld Judge DiReda's finding of innocence.

An all-white jury convicted Joyce Ann Brown of murder in 1980 and sentenced her to life in prison based upon perjured testimony and prosecutorial misconduct. In Dallas, Texas, police suspected Joyce of robbing and killing Rubin Danziger, the proprietor of *Fine Furs by Rubin*. Apparently, another woman named Joyce Ann Brown of Denver had rented a car that she and Rene Michelle Taylor used in the murder of Danziger. Danziger's widow made a mistaken cross-racial eyewitness identification of Joyce from a photograph and Martha Bruce, a county jail inmate, falsely testified that Joyce had confessed to her involvement in the murder while the two were incarcerated together. A month after Joyce's trial, Martha Bruce received a reduced sentence for attempted murder. Six months after Joyce's conviction, police arrested Renee Taylor who eventually pleaded guilty to Danziger's murder. Though Taylor refused to identify a second woman involved in the crime, she testified that neither of the two Joyce Ann Browns were that person. A court sentenced Taylor to life in prison without the possibility of parole. It was another nine years before the Centurion Ministries obtained a judicial exoneration for Joyce; it was not until November 1989 that the Texas Court of Criminal Appeals overturned Joyce's conviction. According to her application for writ of habeas corpus, prosecutor Norman Kinne acted in concert with Dallas Police Officer T. J. Barnes to suppress evidence favorable to Joyce, intentionally used testimony which he knew or should have known was false and perjurious, and suppressed evidence that would have served to impeach Martha Bruce. Joyce spent nine and a half years in prison for a murder she did not commit. Texas officials denied her compensation for the wrongful conviction because Joyce "refused to apply for a pardon, asserting that she had done nothing and that, if anything, the state should ask her pardon. Her stand rendered her ineligible for compensation because a pardon is a prerequisite to payment under Texas law."[21]

In September 1998, a Colquitt County jury in Georgia found Sheila Bryan guilty of arson and murder in the death of her elderly mother, Freda Weeks. While taking a leisurely sightseeing drive through the countryside one Sunday afternoon, Sheila's Mercury Cougar ran off the road, down a large embankment, caught fire and burned Freda to death. The state prosecutor claimed through the testimony of arson investigators that the fire began on the floorboard in front of the driver's seat and spread to the passenger's side, the fire was intentionally set by someone using ignitable liquids, and that investigators had eliminated all other possible causes of the fire. What's more, the state's attorney claimed that her husband increased his automobile liability insurance three months before the fire. The trial court sentenced Sheila to 20 years in prison on the arson count and life imprisonment for her mother's murder. On appeal, the state Supreme Court reversed Sheila's conviction finding that the prosecution failed to present independent evidence of a nexus between Sheila's supposed crimes and the existence of the insurance policy. There was no independent evidence that Sheila knew about the increased insurance coverage. Without such evidence, the Court argued that the trial court erred in admitting evidence of the insurance coverage increase. The county prosecutor tried Sheila again in January 2000. This time, however, her defense lawyers retained Gerald Hurst, an arson expert from Austin, Texas, who testified that the car fire appeared to have been started by a faulty ignition switch, and what prosecution experts claimed were pour patterns of a combustible substance were actually the result of the burning of plastic that melted during the intense blaze. Hurst said the prosecution experts relied on outdated and disproven arson theories. On January 28, 2000, a jury deliberated for three hours and acquitted Bryan.

In August 2005, an Elkhart County jury in Indiana convicted Lana Canen and Andrew Royer of the November 2002 robbery and strangulation murder of 94-year-old Helen Sailor who was blind and lived in an apartment complex for the elderly and disabled. Judge Terry C. Shewmaker sentenced Lana to a 55-year prison term. A day after Helen had spent Thanksgiving with relatives, a health care provider and two relatives found Helen strangled to death in her apartment and the premises ransacked. With no suspects in the killing, the case was dormant until September 2003 when Royer, a mentally-impaired resident of the apartment complex, confessed to Elkhart police of strangling Helen with a rope and robbing her of jewelry and money. A year later, police learned from Royer that Lana was involved in the murder; Lana lived at the same apartment complex and was good friends with Royer who she easily influenced. Police questioned Lana but she denied any involvement in the crime. Police interviewed a heavy drug user neighbor who claimed that Lana had made incriminating statements concerning the crime. Police charged Lana as a co-defendant in Helen's murder after Detective Dennis Chapman mistakenly identified a fingerprint found on a prescription pill container in Helen's apartment as matching the little finger on Lana's left hand though Chapman had no formal training in latent fingerprint comparisons.

The Indiana Court of Appeals affirmed Lana's conviction and sentence. Lana's post-conviction lawyer, Cara Schaefer Wieneke, however, conducted an investigation in 2010 that included sending high-resolution photographs of the fingerprint to Kathleen Bright-Birnbaum, an expert fingerprint examiner at Arizona-based Desert Forensics. Bright-Birnbaum determined the fingerprint on the prescription pill container did not match the print found in Helen's apartment. Based on the new evidence, Wieneke filed a motion for a new trial asserting that Lana's defense trial was inadequate and that Lana was innocent. Wieneke also found the neighbor's testimony erroneous, and during an evidentiary hearing Chapman admitted that he had overstated his fingerprint examination experience during the trial. Wieneke filed a motion for Lana's immediate release from prison. The prosecution offered a plea agreement for time served but Lana refused to negotiate, and in September 2012 the district attorney's office arranged for Lana's release. In November 2012, an Elkhart County Court vacated Lana's conviction, dismissed the charges against her and ordered her immediate release from prison. Andrew Royer remains imprisoned because there is no new evidence exonerating him of the crime; an appeals court denied him relief in 2011. Remarkably, Detective Chapman continues working for the Elkhart County Sheriff's Department.

In Siskiyou County in northern California where Anglos are notoriously racist against

American Indians, an all-white jury wrongly convicted Norma Jean Croy, a young Shasta-Karok Indian, of conspiracy to commit murder in the killing of Yreka police officer Jessie J. (Bo) Hittson in a highly charged trial in 1979. The jury also convicted Norma's brother, Patrick (Hooty) Croy, and three cousins (Darrell Jones, Carol Thom, Jasper Alford) for their participation in Hittson's death. The trial judge sentenced Norma to life in prison, Patrick received a death sentence, and the cousins received lengthy prison terms. In the summer of 1978, after attending a party, the group drove to the Sports and Spirits Liquor Store in Yreka where a store clerk, John Thurman, known for hating Indians, became verbally abusive claiming that Patrick had short-changed him of $2 on an earlier visit to the store. After a scuffle broke out, a patrol car pulled into the store's parking lot and gave chase to the group who had just driven off. Police chased the group to a mountain cabin where they ran into the hills. They sought refuge at Norma's grandmother's cabin in an area known as Rocky Gulch. Some 27 police officers with automatic weapons went after the group of Indian youth. As they ran up a hill, a police officer shot Norma in the back. Hittson shot Patrick in the back while he attended to Norma, and it was then that Patrick turned and shot and killed Hittson. On appeal to the California Supreme Court, Chief Judge Rose Bird ordered a new trial for Patrick who then won an acquittal. The California Department of Corrections denied Norma parole several times, but U.S. Chief Judge Lawrence Karlton of the District Court in Sacramento vacated her conviction due to ineffective assistance of defense counsel in 1997. As a lesbian, many in San Francisco's gay and lesbian community organized events on her behalf and with the vigorous efforts of attorneys Diana Samuelson and Jim Thompson, Norma won a conviction reversal. The state's attorney general and county prosecutors declined to try Norma again. State officials released her from Central California Women's Facility at Chowchilla in February of that year.

Prosecutors convicted Ella Mae Ellison in 1974 in Massachusetts for a robbery-murder that she did not commit and for which she spent four years in a state penitentiary. It seems that in late November 1973, Nathaniel Williams, Anthony Irving, and Terrell Walker robbed Suffolk Jewelers, a pawnshop in Roxbury, during which Walker shot and killed Boston police officer John Schroeder in a struggle. Police apprehended Williams and Irving a day after the robbery with jewelry taken from the pawnshop. During questioning, the two suspects mentioned that an unnamed light-skinned black girl about 18 years of age drove the getaway car. Ella, the woman identified by Williams and Irving, was a single mother of four with no criminal record, dark-skinned, and 27 years old. No physical evidence linked Ella to the crime, but given the opportunity to plead to second-degree murder and escape the death penalty, Williams and Irving identified Ella as the getaway driver. Police apprehended Ella and a jury convicted her almost entirely upon the testimony of Williams and Irving. The trial court sentenced her to two concurrent life sentences. Ella petitioned the court for a new trial in 1976 based upon the presentation of new evidence on two issues: the prosecution had suppressed several early statements by Williams and Irving that supported the claim that Ella was not involved in the crime; and second, that Williams and Irving had recanted their testimony incriminating Ella and that they had driven themselves to the crime scene in a stolen car. The trial court denied Ella's motion for a new trial, but, in 1978 the Massachusetts Supreme Court vacated her conviction. The Court held unconstitutional "[t]he prosecutor's late, piecemeal, and incomplete disclosures" of earlier, exculpatory statements by the perpetrators, whose several conflicting versions of the crime made them "emerge as very willing to lie under oath." Following the court's reversal of her conviction, the state's attorney dropped all charges against Ella. According to one legal commentator, "Although neither the prosecutor's action nor the Supreme Judicial Court's decision can be said to manifest official exoneration of Ellison, her conviction was reversed in circumstances raising strong doubts about her factual guilt."[22]

In 2005, a Summit County jury in Ohio convicted Cynthia (Cindy) George of conspiracy to commit murder when her paramour, John F. Zaffino, fatally shot her former lover of 10 years, Jeff Zack, while he sat in his sport utility vehicle at a gasoline station. Though Cindy came from humble beginnings, she was the wife a well-known and wealthy Akron restaurateur. She lived in a sprawling mansion on 18 acres and had seven children, one of which Jeff Zack had fathered unbeknown to her husband, Edward George. Police arrested Zaffino about a year after the murder and in 2003 a court tried and sentenced him to life in prison. Arrested in 2005, Summit County Judge Patricia Cosgrove found Cindy guilty of complicity to commit aggravated murder and sentenced her to life in prison. On appeal to the Ohio Court of Appeals, the court ruled that the circumstantial evidence presented by prosecutors was insufficient to prove her guilt beyond a reasonable doubt. The Ohio Supreme Court upheld the dismissal of Cindy's conviction and authorities released her from custody in March 2007.

In 1989, state prosecutors in Gage County, Nebraska, wrongly convicted Kathy Gonzales, Debra Shelden and Ada JoAnn Taylor, and three male defendants (James Dean, Thomas Winslow and Joseph Edgar White) for the February 1985 rape and murder of 68-year-old Helen Wilson, a widow who lived alone in an apartment, despite the lack of any physical or forensic evidence linking the defendants to the murder. Allegedly, on the night of the murder the defendants forced their way into Mrs. Wilson's apartment when she responded to a knock on her door. The attackers knocked down Mrs. Wilson in her living room, forcibly took to her bedroom, and physically abused her when she refused to tell the intruders the location of her money. Afterwards, the assailants took Mrs. Wilson back to the living room and demanded that she reveal where she kept her money. Mrs. Wilson was held down by one of the women intruders while two of the men took turns raping and vilifying the victim. The woman attacker suffocated the victim with a pillow and at one point committed sexual acts on the victim while one of the men was committing rape. Following the brutal assault, Mrs. Wilson was either dead or near death and it was then that the intruders searched the apartment and found Mrs. Wilson's money. Ivan Arnst, Mrs. Wilson's brother-in-law, found her body the next morning; she had severe bone fractures, a fractured sternum, a vaginal tear, and numerous bruises, abrasions, and scratches. Her hands were tied with a towel.

It was the unscrupulous actions of former Gage County Prosecutor Richard Smith and officers of the Beatrice Sheriff's Department that led to the arrest and convictions of six innocent people; prosecutors and investigators had used the threat of the death penalty to coerce false confessions from the defendants and which became the basis of the state's case. Ada and Debra, as well as Dean, testified in detail at White's murder trial claiming that all six defendants were in the apartment the night of Wilson's killing though they later recanted their testimony. The prosecution went so far as to use a psychologist who told the accused that they had committed crimes so heinous they had blocked what they had done from their memories; Debra still believes she was somehow involved though the evidence overwhelmingly points to her innocence. Kathy Gonzales stated years later that since investigators had no suspects, "they found a bunch of disposal people—and that was us."

At sentencing, Joseph White received a life prison term without parole, Thomas Winslow pled no contest to second-degree murder and received a prison term from 10 to 50 years, Ada JoAnn Taylor pled guilty to second-degree murder and the court sentenced her to a 10- to 40-year prison term. James Dean, Kathy Gonzalez and Debra Shelden all pled guilty to second-degree murder and received 10-year prison terms each. After their convictions and while serving their respective prison terms, the case sat dormant for years until retired Beatrice Police Officer Burdette Searcey reopened the investigation as a private investigator and White and Winslow won court battles in 2008 to have DNA testing done on evidence from Wilson's apartment. None of the forensic evidence matched any of the persons convicted of the crime. Police had carefully preserved blood, saliva and pubic hair samples from Bruce Allen Smith, an original suspect in the case but a blood test done in 1985 cleared him of involvement in the killing. The DNA analysis matched that collected from Smith who died of AIDS at age 30 in an Oklahoma City hospital. In 2009, officials released all the defendants with full exonerations for a crime they did not commit and the state compensated some for the "Beatrice Six" for their wrongful convictions and incarcerations.

At the time of her conviction in 1978, Paula Gray had an IQ of 64, she was illiterate, had severe emotional problems, and could not tell time. One source noted that Paula Gray's IQ was in the mid–50s. Paula lived in Ford Heights, one of the most impoverished public housing developments in East Chicago. Charles McCraney, a man who lived in the same ramshackle housing project as Paula, reported to Cook County police that Paula and four black men were responsible for the shooting deaths and rape of a white couple—Lawrence Lionberg and Carol Schmal. Reportedly, Schmal was visiting her fiancé, Lionberg, at the gas station where he worked the late-night shift. Police found Lionberg's body the next day in a field and found Schmal's nude body in an upstairs room in a nearby abandoned building. An autopsy disclosed that attackers shot both victims to death execution-style with two bullets to the back of Lionberg's head and two bullets to Schmal's head at short range. Police interrogated Paula over two nights in a local hotel room where she confessed that she was with Kenneth Adams (her boyfriend), Verneal Jimerson, Willie Rainge, and Dennis Williams—later known as the "Ford Heights Four"—when they repeatedly raped Carol Schmal and killed both victims.

Paula's mental state "made her highly susceptible to being induced to falsely confess to a crime she knew nothing about and to implicate four innocent men."[23] Police were so forceful in her interrogation that Paula checked into a mental hospital shortly afterwards. There was no physical evidence linking the defendants to the crime, and what's more, police had learned within a week of the murders from an anonymous tip (later identified as Marvin Simpson) that they had arrested the wrong people. The unnamed witness identified other men (later acknowledged as Ira Johnson, Johnson's dead brother, Arthur Robinson, and another man named Johnson) that killed the victims, ran away from the scene, and the next day sold items taken from the victims. Northwestern University journalism Professor David L. Protess noted, however, that the police "already had four poor black men in custody, which they considered good enough regardless of the defendants' guilt or innocence." The identity of the actual killers lay dormant in a police file until discovered by Professor Protess in his 1995 investigation of the case—the prosecution had never turned over the police file to defense lawyers as required by law—a so-called *Brady* violation. A special investigation into the "Ford Heights Four" revealed that police and prosecutors perpetuated *tunnel vision* that kept them from pursuing the actual perpetrators of the crime. Former federal prosecutor and Judge Gino DiVito directed the independent investigation by the Federal Bureau of Investigation. Creating the myopic mentality of the Chicago police investigation of the "Ford Heights Four," according to Judge DiVito was contradictory testimony from a purported eyewitness, weak corroboration of another witness, questionable scientific evidence, and dubious testimony of a jailhouse informant. Chicago police failed to follow through on early reports that pointed to the actual killers. Exonerated in 1996 after 18 years in prison and on the state's death row, officials released Paula and the three men. In a civil suit brought against the Cook County Sheriff's Police for misconduct in the trial, the Ford Heights Four settled their claim for $36 million. Circuit Court Judge William D. O'Neal reversed Paula Gray's conviction and Illinois Governor Ryan pardoned Paula based upon innocence in November 2003. The pardon qualified Paula Gray for approximately $100,000 in compensation for wrongful imprisonment. Remarkably, a 4-year, $300,000 investigation of misconduct by prosecutors and police rendered them blameless of the wrongful convictions.

In 1985, an Escambia County jury found Phyllis Hall, an unemployed security officer, guilty of armed robbery and first-degree murder when she allegedly aided and abetted her boyfriend, Albert Freer, in killing a man named Perry. Judge William S. Rawley sentenced Phyllis to 25 years to life. At trial, the state's attorney claimed that Phyllis and Albert robbed Perry of $1,200 in night receipts from a bowling alley while on his way to deposit the money at a bank. Evidence showed that authorities found Perry shot to death and handcuffed to the inside of his truck in a ditch off a highway. The state based its case against Phyllis solely on the fact that persons had seen Phyllis with Albert before and after the robbery-murder of Perry. The state had no other evidence supporting her participation in Perry's murder though Phyllis had lied about her activities on the night of the murder. On appeal, the court argued that "here the evidence is wholly insufficient to justify a verdict of guilt" and that "the entire position of the state is based on stacking inference upon inference." The Court of Appeals of Florida reversed the trial court's position and remanded the case back to the court with instructions to vacate the judgment and sentence and to dismiss the charges. Authorities released Phyllis in 1987 after she spent two years incarcerated for a crime she did not commit.

In February 2009, a Christian County jury found Paula Hall guilty of second-degree murder in the November 2003 killing of Freda Heyn in Oldfield, Missouri, and Judge Michael J. Cordonnier sentenced her to a 20-year prison term. Heyn's family had reported the 68-year-old woman missing. Police found her trailer in disorder and blood spattered on the walls, floors, ceiling and furniture. DNA tests revealed blood samples from the trailer were those of Freda Heyn and that of an unknown male. Several months later, hikers found a skull at the bottom of a ravine in a nearby national park and dental records revealed it was Freda's remains. In 2006, police arrested David Epperson on an unrelated violent crime of assaulting a woman and took DNA as a part of that arrest that officials later determined matched the DNA found in Freda's trailer. Epperson, who was romantically involved with Paula, implicated her as an accomplice in Freda's killing. He claimed that during the attack Paula had repeatedly hit Freda in the head with a golf club. In 2011, Paula appealed her conviction and prison sentence claiming that the state's prosecutor withheld exculpatory evidence from her trial lawyers and that a prosecution witness was improperly coerced into testifying. The Missouri Court of Appeals granted Paul a new trial and prosecutors again tried her before Judge Cordonnier with no jury. At the conclusion of that trial, Cordonnier wrote; "Based on the Findings of Fact, the Court cannot conclude, beyond a reasonable doubt, that all necessary elements of the offense charged have been proven. Therefore, the Court finds Defendant, Paula Hall, NOT GUILTY of Murder in the Second Degree." The Missouri Court of Appeals upheld Judge Cordonnier's decision to overturn Paula's murder conviction.

Mary Hampton was 16 years old, a ninth-grade dropout with an I.Q. of 70, and one of eight children born to a rural Kentucky working-class family when she met up with a 31-year-old Emmitt Monroe Spencer. Unknown to Mary, Emmitt was an ex-convict who had just completed a 12-year sentence in a Kentucky prison for voluntary manslaughter. Mary and Emmitt took off together from Sandy Hook (Mary's hometown) and over the next 11 months traveled across the South to the Northwest and back again. During that time, Emmitt robbed and murdered John Hunt in Idaho, and Leon Hammell, Virginia Tomlinson, Ethel Little and John T. Keen in Florida. He also shot and wounded a State Highway Patrol officer in Central Florida. Authorities suspected Emmitt in the murders of Benjamin Yount and German immigrant and bar owner Hermine Fielder in Boutte, Louisiana. Police officials took Emmitt and Mary into custody following the shooting of the highway patrol officer. Louisiana re-arrested Mary in Kentucky where she had returned when Florida officials released her from custody. Louisiana police charged her and Emmitt with the murders of Yount and Fielder. Emmitt confessed to the killings, as well as some 48 other murders, to which he claimed Mary was an accomplice. Police had trouble verifying much of what Emmitt story, however. Police interrogated Mary for 43 days when she ultimately submitted to prosecutorial threats of execution in the state's electric chair and pleaded guilty to the killings. Death penalty expert Michael Radelet explains that Mary's false confession was the product of three critical factors: "[l]ies from a prisoner on death row, exhausting police interrogation, and terrible fear of a threatened death sentence."[24] There was no trial and Mary had incompetent lawyers, one of whom she met for the first time just moments before her sentence. Despite the lack of any substantive evidence linking Mary to the killings except Emmitt's fabricated testimony, a county court sentenced her to two life terms. Later evidence showed that Emmitt and Mary could not have committed the Yount and Fielder murders because they were hundreds of miles away at the time of the killings. Governor McKeithen commuted her sentence to time served and the parole Board released Mary in November 1966 after she had spent five years in the Louisiana Correctional Institution for Women for a crime she did not commit. In 1979, authorities transferred Spencer to a prison in Iowa where he died in 1996 of natural causes. Mary resides in Georgia.

Nevada authorities wrongly convicted Emma Johnson in 1951 for the second degree murder of her 72-year-old hotel landlady, Jane Jones. According to prosecutors, Mrs. Jones died after a violent altercation over mail with Emma who beat Mrs. Jones with a heavy can-opener so severely that she died from a blood clot to the brain two weeks later. Emma claimed she only grabbed Mrs. Jones by the hair in self-defense and she fell to the floor unconscious. A jury convicted Emma of the killing and Judge A. S. Henderson sentenced her to 10 to 12 years in prison. An investigation of Emma's case by attorney Erle Stanley Gardner (mystery story writer and creator of "Perry Mason" detective fiction thrillers) revealed that Emma's assault did not kill Mrs. Jones; rather she died from a brain tumor. At the time of her death, Mrs. Jones was under the care of a Las Vegas physiotherapist, Dr. T. V. Nendick, who diagnosed Mrs. Jones of needing immediate surgery to remove a brain tumor. Dr. Nendick and two leading pathologists later testified before a Board of Pardons that Mrs. Jones would have died regardless of the altercation with Emma. Amid considerable controversy from prosecutors, the state pardons board commuted Emma's sentence to time served and ordered her release. By then, Emma had spent nearly three years in prison for a crime she did not commit.

In 2003, a Clark County jury in Washington convicted Sophia Johnson for the bludgeoning death of Marlyne Johnson and Superior Court Judge Diane Woolard sentenced her to a 43-year prison term. A native of Guyana, Sophia was married to Brad Johnson, Marylne's son. A police investigation into the murder revealed that Marlyne had come home unexpectedly while Sophia and her brother Sean Correia were burglarizing Marylne's home for money. Sean falsely testified that Sophia bludgeoned Marlyne with fireplace tongs in return for a lenient prison sentence. After the killing, Jean and Sophia stole Marlyne's van, drove to Sophia's house to change their blood-spattered clothes, and then abandoned the van in a parking lot. In 2005, the Washington Court of Appeals reversed Sophia's conviction because Judge Woolard had improperly replaced a juror in the case with an alternate juror and that a bailiff had improperly communicated with the jury during deliberations. To the appeals court, "This error cannot be presumed harmless. We reverse and order a new trial before a different judge." At retrial before a new judge, a jury acquitted Sophia of the murder because forensic evidence proved that Sophia could not have been Marylne's attacker. The actual attacker was at least six inches taller than Sophia and was left-handed while Sophia was right-handed. Though acquitted of the murder, officials deported Sophia to Guyana because she had never become a U.S. citizen and was convicted of an unrelated felony of embezzlement of an employer.

In 2005, a Prince George County jury in Maryland convicted Abere Biobele Karibi-Ikiriko, a 23-year-old medical student and woman of Nigerian descent, of the second-degree murder in the shooting death of her ex-boyfriend, Okechukwu Ohiri, and Circuit Court Judge Richard H. Sothoron Jr. sentenced her to 15 years in prison. The couple had a troubled relationship and Abere had broken off the relationship because her boyfriend was visiting prostitutes. In an attempt to rekindle their relationship, Okechukwu approached Abere but she refused to discuss the matter. Angered by her rejection, Okechukwu became physical with Abere, the two struggled over a pistol that Okechukwu had retrieved from an upstairs room, it accidentally discharged and the bullet struck Okechukwu in the chest. At trial, the judge barred seven exculpatory letters and an email from Okechukwu to Abere showing that he was obsessed with Abere and tried to force himself on her at gunpoint. On appeal, however, a three-judge panel of the Maryland Court of Special Appeals reversed the conviction and ruled that the trial judge had incorrectly barred the letters and emails from Ohiri and remanded the case back to the trial court for a new trial. While awaiting a new trial, Abere attempted suicide in her cell at a county detention center. At a second trial, the defense was permitted to use the letters and emails and a jury acquitted her of the murder. Abere Karibi-Ikiriko died at the age of 35 in November 2012.

Authorities arrested Gloria Killian in 1983 for the robbery-murder of Edward Davies. In December 1981, Stephen DeSantis and Gary Masse disguised as telephone technicians, entered the suburban Sacramento home of an elderly couple named Mr. and Mrs. Davies. They ransacked the house, bound and hog-tied the couple, and then robbed them of six suitcases of silver coins—Mr. Davies was a collector and dealer of rare coins. During the robbery, the assailants shot and killed Mr. Davies execution style and seriously wounded Mrs. Davies. Shortly after the robbery and killing, Sacramento authorities in California received an anonymous phone call identifying Gary Masse and Stephen DeSantis as the assailants. Masse's wife Joanne told police during an investigation that Gloria had masterminded the robbery. Authorities arrested Gloria but a preliminary hearing resulted in a dismissal of charges. Masse surrendered to authorities and a court convicted him of first-degree felony murder in May 1983 and sentenced him to life in prison without parole. Masse approached prosecutors and struck a sentence reduction deal after he implicated DeSantis and Gloria in the killing. Police rearrested Gloria in June 1983, along with DeSantis who testified at his trial that Gloria was not involved in the Davies murder and that he had never met or even knew Gloria. At her 1986 trial, Masse testified that he had made no deal with state prosecutors, that Gloria had masterminded the Davies robbery and murder, and that she was involved in an earlier attempt to rob the Davies' house. Masse also testified that Gloria called him after learning of the robbery and murder to demand her share of the robbery proceeds. A court convicted Gloria of first-degree felony murder, robbery, and conspiracy; the court sentenced her to 32 years to life. In March 2002, however, the U.S. Court of Appeals for the Ninth Circuit overturned Gloria's conviction based upon the perjured testimony of Gary Masse—a "thoroughly discredited perjurer." To one veteran defense lawyer involved in the case, Gloria's plight amounts to "one of the most egregious and serious violations of a person's right to a fair trial that I have ever seen." After her release, Killian founded the Action Committee for Women in Prison.

In December 1996, authorities tried Beth LaBatte for the grisly murder of two retired schoolteachers in Green Bay, Wisconsin. Beth had a prior criminal history involving thefts from elderly people's homes, cashing stolen checks, and armed robbery. A Kewaunee County jury found Beth guilty of the November 1991 murder and armed robbery of 85-year-old Cecelia Cadigan and her 90-year-old sister, Ann Cadigan, in their rural home. Both women were severely beaten and stabbed in the head and chest and both had defensive wounds to the hands and arms. Neighbors discovered their bodies when they failed to show at a church memorial service for their brother. The court sentenced Beth to two consecutive terms of life imprisonment despite the fact there was no forensic evidence or eyewitness testimony that Beth committed the crime. Prosecutors relied entirely upon the erroneous testimony of a jailhouse informant that Beth had confessed to the killings. In a separate trial, a jury acquitted Charles Benoit, Beth's co-defendant boyfriend. In June 2005, DNA evidence failed to support Beth's conviction and officials released her from prison in August 2006, 10 years after her wrongful conviction and imprisonment. Beth died in an automobile accident while driving drunk in early September 2007 just over a year after being released from prison.

During a six-week trial in Anchorage, Alaska, ending in October 2007, a jury found Mechele Linehan (Hughes) guilty of first degree murder in the May 1996 shooting death of Kent Leppink, a commercial fisherman. Anchorage Superior Court Judge Philip R. Volland sentenced Mechele to a 99-year prison sentence. Mechele was romantically involved with three men at the same time — Scott Hilke, John Carlin and Kent Leppink — and supposedly the men knew of one another's relationships with Mechele. Alaska State Troopers interviewed Mechele, Hilke and Carlin about the Leppink murder but officers could not identify them as the killers. The murder remained unresolved until 2004 when troopers reopened the investigation and conducted new witness interviews and an examination of e-mails and other materials recovered from two computers. From this evidence, troopers surmised that Mechele solicited Carlin to shoot and kill Leppink to collect on a $1 million life insurance policy. Five days before his death, however, Leppink changed the beneficiary of the policy to his father. Based upon these findings, police arrested Mechele who by then was married to a physician and living in Olympia, Washington, under her married name of Linehan. In lieu of direct evidence to prove a murder case against Mechele Linehan (Hughes), state prosecutors used conjecture, speculation, suspicion, innuendo, and even gossip to falsely convict Mechele of the murder. One commentator described her trial as sensational, "full of tawdry details about her lifestyle and accusations about how she manipulated men she met while dancing at the Great Alaskan Bush Co. strip club in Anchorage." The media characterized Mechele as "a stripper-turned-soccer mom." That Mechele was an exotic dancer was important to the Alaska Court of Appeals when the court noted that reference to Mechele's work as an exotic dancer was relevant to explain her relationships with the various men involved in the case, and to explain the men's relationships with each other. To defense lawyers, it was prejudicial to the fairness of the trial to let the state use the label "exotic dancer" because people generally understand the phrase as a euphemism for "stripper." Defense attorneys also argued that most people assume that strippers are not just dancing with their clothes off, but "are involved in other acts that would be illegal [and] unsavory to most people." The defense also asserted that, despite the state's protestations, the state relied on the fact that Mechele worked as an exotic dancer to prove her character — specifically to prove that she was skilled at manipulating men for her own ends.

State prosecutors proffered a lengthy and detailed case against Mechele, but the case was primarily circumstantial with no direct evidence linking Mechele to Leppink's murder. Prosecutors painted a disturbing portrait of Mechele as "the kind of person who would conspire to have Leppink murdered." In doing so, prosecutors presented two forms of evidence — a letter and Mechele's statement about a movie she supposedly watched with a former co-worker and friend. First, prosecutors presented a letter that Leppink sent to his parents in Michigan in April 1996 stating that should he die under suspicious circumstances, Mechele, Carlin, and Hilke were most likely responsible. Second, prosecutors offered the testimony of Lora Aspiotis, with whom Mechele often watched movies, and that one of the movies was "The Last Seduction." According to Lora's testimony, after watching the movie, Mechele claimed that the "protagonist was her heroine, and that she wanted to be ... just like her." Lora described the film this way:

> [The story is about] a woman who's married to a doctor, and she ... talked him into doing [an illegal] drug deal, selling pharmaceutical cocaine, and he got $700,000. ... [Later,] while he was in the shower, she stole the money, [and she] took off and went to a small town where a young man lived

that she met at a bar. And she could tell right away that he was very naive, ... just [a] pretty innocent guy. And eventually she talked him into trying to murder her husband for the insurance. ... [In the movie, the innocent young man] ended up in prison, and she went free with all the money.

A separate jury convicted Carlin of Leppink's murder and the court sentenced him to 99 years in prison but prison inmates beat him to death in 2008 shortly after he arrived at a state facility. In early 2010, the Court of Appeals of Alaska overturned Mechele's conviction and held that Leppink's letter to his parents and Lora's testimony concerning Mechele's remarks about the movie was inadmissible evidence at her trial. According to the appeals court, "The unfair prejudice of this type of evidence is most acute in a prosecution like this one, where the State's case is based almost entirely on circumstantial evidence. The State's ability to secure a guilty verdict hinged on convincing the jury to view a large number of ambiguous facts in the light most favorable to Linehan's guilt." The court ordered a new trial but officials instead released Mechele on bond in May 2010.

In December 2011, Judge Philip R. Volland dismissed the indictment, and while prosecutors pondered whether to re-indict Mechele, her attorneys re-investigated the case and uncovered exculpatory evidence that prosecutors had failed to disclose to defense lawyers prior to Mechele's trial. The information included the fact that after the murder, some of Leppink's family members went to prosecutors and said that they suspected Leppink's father was involved in the killing. Family members had told defense attorneys that they informed state investigators that Leppink had embezzled significant sums of money from the family business and had borrowed tens of thousands of dollars more from the family to finance the purchase of a fishing boat. Leppink's father had been in Alaska at about the same time that Leppink was murdered, according to family members. The defense also discovered that the lead detective in the investigation was writing a book about the case at the time of the trial and was attempting to sell it to a publisher—evidence the defense contended was a financial motive to obtain a conviction. In August 2012, after Mechele's attorneys presented the newly discovered evidence to the prosecutors who abandoned its effort to seek a new indictment.

One of the earliest known wrongful convictions of a female offender was that of Margaret Lucas, the keeper of a riverfront dive, for the 1905 killing of Clyde Showalter, a young prosperous farmer in Wabash County, Illinois. At her trial in September 1908, the court imposed life sentences on both Margaret her son Jesse Lucas who was an accomplice. The killing took place after Showalter arrived in the small town of Mt. Carmel "with a large roll of bills [$600] to have a good time." Nearly a year after Showalter's disappearance, two men discovered his badly decomposed body in the Patoka creek. State witnesses Oma Johnson, Myrtle Mercer, Ruth Henson, and Richard Conrad had given perjured testimony that they had seen Jesse bludgeon Showalter to death with something similar to a baseball bat and then, with Margaret's help, carried the body to the nearby creek. All four witnesses were disreputable: Conrad exchanged his perjured testimony for an early release from prison stemming from a rape conviction of a 13-year-old girl; Johnson, Mercer and Henson were all prostitutes whom the county sheriff and state's attorney had threatened into cooperating. After their convictions, the trial court granted Margaret a new trial but the state's attorney dropped all charges against her. The state's Supreme Court, however, affirmed Jesse's conviction. Then, in 1932, authorities released Jesse from prison after George Pond, a former resident of Mt. Carmel, made a deathbed confession to Anna Smith, a woman with whom he attended church, that he had murdered Showalter. Smith transcribed Pond's dying words:

> I killed Showalter. I hit him over the head with a hammer on the southern bridge at Mt. Carmel. I thought I would get over $1,400, but all I got was $50. I threw him in the river first and later took

him over to Patoka Creek and buried him in a sand bar. Jesse Lucas is serving life for that murder, but I am the one who is guilty.[25]

In early March 1992, a wealthy art collector and notorious philanderer named Roger Zygmunt de la Burdé died from a single gunshot wound at his Powhatan County estate in Virginia. Beverly Monroe, Burdé's longtime girlfriend, and his groundkeeper, Joe Hairfield, found Burdé's body lying on a couch with a gunshot to his head from his own handgun. Although police and a medical examiner ruled Burdé's death a suicide, officials began focusing their attention on Beverly and suspected foul play. During an eight-hour interrogation wherein police threatened her with not being able to see her children, Beverly signed a confession. In November 1992, a jury convicted Beverly of first-degree murder and the trial court sentenced her to 20 years in prison for the murder and an additional two years for a firearm conviction. On appeal to the U.S. Court of Appeals for the Fourth Circuit, Senior U.S. District Judge Richard L. Williams granted Beverly a writ of habeas corpus and overturned her conviction. Beverly's lawyer proffered evidence that the prosecution had suppressed exculpatory evidence in the trial including impeachment material, leads implicating other suspects, official documents labeling Burdé's death a suicide, and statements suggesting that Burdé may have been suicidal—all in violation of Beverly's due process rights. Judge Williams called her case a "monument to prosecutorial indiscretions and mishandling."

In 2001, a Passaic County jury in New Jersey convicted Sandra Ortiz, a Columbian immigrant and nightclub manager, of the 1997 stabbing death of her boyfriend, Camel "Diego" Hammad. It seems Sandra had stabbed Camel during a violent confrontation wherein he lunged at Sandra and she stabbed him with a kitchen knife that pierced his heart. The couple had a troubled relationship and a history of domestic violence. The trial judge set aside the conviction claiming that the prosecution had made improper comments during closing arguments including a reference to about Sandra's decision not to testify at trial. At a second trial, forensic evidence showed that Sandra was the victim of battered woman syndrome and suffering from post-traumatic stress syndrome given Camel's history of violence toward her. A jury acquitted Sandra of the murder in 2003.

After serving four years of a life sentence in the Pocahontas Correctional Center for Women in Chesterfield County, Virginia, authorities released Laverne Pavlinac, along with her boyfriend and codefendant John Sosnovske from prison for the rape and strangulation death of Taunja Bennett. In January 1990, authorities found Bennett's beaten, raped and strangled body in a remote area of the Columbia Gorge just outside Portland, Oregon. Laverne read about the Bennett murder and decided she could use the case to end her long-term abusive relationship with her boyfriend, John Sosnovske. Laverne made anonymous tips to police that Sosnovske had bragged about the crime, but when she received no response, she called the detectives working on the case and told them about her abusive relationship and claimed Sosnovske had murdered Bennett. Laverne claimed that she and Sosnovske met Bennet at a bar in Portland and Sosnovske forced her to help him rape Bennet, kill her and then dispose of the body. Police arrested the couple in February 1990 and Laverne confessed to the killing. The state's prosecutor tried Laverne separately from Sosnovske. At trial, Laverne recanted her confession and claimed to have made up the story to escape from her relationship with Sosnovske. Her taped confession was compelling and in January 1991 a Multnomah County jury convicted her of felony murder and the Circuit Court judge sentenced her to life in prison with a minimum of 10 years. Sosnovske pleaded no contest to the murder to avoid the death penalty because of Laverne's confession.

Newspapers began receiving anonymous letters in 1994 from someone who claimed he had killed Bennett. A year later, Keith Jesperson, known as the "Happy Face Killer," confessed to killing Bennett and provided information to police that only the killer would know—the location of Bennett's purse. Jesperson pleaded no contest to murdering Bennett. In November 1995, based on Jesperson's confession and at the insistence of prosecutors, Circuit Court Judge Circuit Paul Lipscomb overturned both wrongful convictions. Judge Lipscomb stated, "There's no longer any doubt that these two individuals are innocent. The evidence is compelling." Judge Lipscomb, however, would not set aside Laverne's conviction for inventing the story though he released her from custody because to keep an innocent person in prison would have been cruel and unusual punishment. Famed death penalty expert Samuel Gross stated the case serves as an example of how "the threat of the death penalty can lead to an innocent man to forgo his day in court and accept a lesser sentence in exchange for not fighting the charge. Prosecutors, defense attorneys and judges need to recognize that risk and ensure the death penalty threat isn't made in a shaky case to exact a guilty plea."[26]

In 1999, a Vinton County jury in Ohio convicted Leona Pettit for the murder of her boyfriend, Charles Pettit, by driving a car into the back of a tractor mower he was driving along the side of the two-land highway. Charles died eight days later when taken off life support. The court sentenced Leona to 15 years to life in prison. At her first trial, the state presented testimony that Leona was upset with Charles for kicking her out of the house. Lawyers appealed the conviction to the Ohio Court of Appeals which reversed Leona's conviction because the trial court had improperly instructed the jury on the issue of intent thereby allowing the jury to essentially convict Leona on a negligence theory rather than a purposeful intent theory. The court also found troubling her trial counsel's failure to object to such a grievous error in the jury instructions. At her second trial in 2001, the jury acquitted Leona because expert forensic testimony showed that Charles had not died from a head injury resulting from the impact of the tractor flipping over when Leona hit it with the car, but because of a large dosage of morphine and sedatives essentially impaired his ability to breathe after being removed from life support.

In May 2005, a Los Angeles jury convicted 26-year-old Lisa Pineda of second-degree murder in the shooting death of 19-year-old Freddie Diaz, a member of a street gang in La Puente, California. The trial court sentenced Lisa to a 40-year to life prison term. Apparently, Lisa drove a car involved in the drive-by shooting in which Adrian Gudino, a rival gang member, killed Diaz. Also in the car was Francisco Rodriguez who pled guilty and testified for the prosecution. Lisa and Gudino had a troubled romantic relationship. Lisa claimed she had no idea that when she went to drive Gudino to a nearby store that he was going to shoot anyone. Lisa appealed her conviction and filed a state petition for a writ of habeas corpus in which she claimed she had received a constitutionally unfair trial because her trial lawyer had failed to call an expert to testify that Lisa had been so physically and emotionally abused by Gudino that she followed his orders for fear of being further abused. The California Court of Appeals reversed the conviction and ordered a new trial. The appeals court held that the trial judge had failed to instruct the jury on the lesser-included charge of involuntary manslaughter. Lisa went to trial a second time where the jury acquitted her of first-degree murder but was unable to reach a unanimous verdict on the involuntary manslaughter charge. Lisa's defense attorney offered expert testimony that the physical and emotional abuse Lisa suffered from Gudino had an adverse impact on her ability to resist Gudino. The trial judge declared a mistrial and the prosecution dismissed the manslaughter charge in April 2009.

Ellen Reasonover's case epitomizes the wrongful convictions of marginalized women resulting from prosecutorial misconduct. Ellen had gone to a service station for change while at a nearby Laundromat at about the same time as the killing of the station attendant. She heard about the murder on television and volunteered information to the police. Mistrusting the police, Ellen used an alias and told officers of two men and a vehicle she had seen while at the service station. Her initial fear of police reprisal came to fruition when, instead of investigating her claims, police arrested Reasonover for the killing. As one commentator put it, "As a poor black woman, she was helpless against the prosecutorial onslaught unleashed against her once she was charged with the murder."[27] Despite no confession, no eyewitness testimony, no physical evidence, no legitimate motive, and no real evidence that a robbery had occurred, prosecutors tried and convicted Reasonover of capital murder. The entire case against Ellen centered exclusively on the erroneous testimony of two jailhouse informants who claimed she had admitted to the killing shortly after her arrest. Unknown to defense lawyers or the jury, the prosecutor withheld exculpatory evidence, made cash payments and secreted deals of leniency with the informants. If not for the courage of one juror refusing to agree with the death penalty, the court would certainly have sentenced Ellen to death rather than 50 years in prison without possibility of parole that she received. An investigation by Centurion Ministries exposed the prosecutor's misconduct and flagrant lawlessness. A U.S. District Judge overturned Ellen's conviction, ordered her immediate release from prison, and concluded without question that she had been the victim of prosecutorial lawlessness. The District Judge described her trial as "fundamentally unfair" and an unashamed deprivation of Ellen's rights to due process. In August 1999, Ellen ended her 17-year stay in prison for a crime she never committed. Her case illustrates all too clearly how the white-male controlled justice system continues its long and sordid history of convicting poor, young, and vulnerable black women.

An Allegheny County jury in Pennsylvania found Carol Stonehouse guilty of the shooting death of her estranged boyfriend, William Welsh. On the night of Welch's murder, Carol shot him to death from the third-floor back porch of her apartment. Carol and Welsh were Pittsburgh police officers and began dating shortly after Carol joined the department in 1979. Carol was a single mother with two children and Welsh was married at the time. Carol broke off the relationship several months later. After the breakup, however, Welch began what can only be described as "a three-year campaign of abuse that included numerous death threats delivered with a gun pointed to her head." Welch's extreme violence and mistreatment of Carol involved not only death threats, but break-ins into Carol's apartment wherein Welch "threw food on the floors and walls, cut up her clothes, tore the curtains from the windows, urinated on and sliced the bed, ripped the wires out of the television, and soaked her shoes and clothes in hot water." Though Carol reported the violence and brutality she was suffering from Welsh to police, "Welsh's colleagues in the police department did little to protect appellant from Welsh's surveillance, harassment, acts of vandalism and assaults."[28]

The court sentenced Carol to seven to 14 years in prison, and the Superior Court of Pennsylvania affirmed Carol's conviction and sentence in 1986. Three years later, however, the Supreme Court of Pennsylvania reversed the order and remanded Carol's case for a new trial on the basis that she had an inadequate legal defense. To the court, Carol's trial lawyer should have waged a battered woman defense. The court argued, "We believe that expert testimony regarding battered women is admissible as the basis for proving justification in the use of deadly force where the defendant has been shown to be a victim of psychological and physical abuse." The court noted further, "The events culminating in Welsh's death are so bizarre that one would be tempted to dismiss them as the stuff of pulp fiction were it not for the corroboration of disinterested witnesses and for the fact that the literature on the 'battered woman syndrome' is replete with similar cases." In March 1990, Carol went on trial again wherein experts testified as to the effects of psychological and physical abuse and the trial judge acquitted Carol of the murder charge. Common Pleas Judge John W. O'Brien stated, "I find that the defendant, Carol Stonehouse, is a victim of the battered woman syndrome and in a frenzied state, and reasonably believed that she was in imminent danger of death at the time she fired her weapon at Welsh." The Pittsburgh police department eventually reinstated Carol and awarded her $129,000 in back pay.

One early morning in June 2007, Stanley Daniels, a member of a street gang named Rollin 30's Crips, died from a single gunshot wound to the abdomen in south-central Los Angeles. A witness to the killing claimed that the gunman was about the same height as the victim. The murder remained dormant for several weeks until a gang member, Chris Walker, told police upon his arrest for an unrelated shooting that the murder of Daniels was in retaliation for the shooting of a rival (Rollin 20's Crips) gang member in April. Walker claimed that he was at a meeting of the gang when the members decided to retaliate. He also claimed that Cherice Thomas was at the meeting. Police eventually arrested Cherice for her participation in the killing and charged her with first degree murder. A witness to the shooting of Daniels testified that the shooter was a man. The prosecution went to great lengths to prove Cherice was a gang member. A Los Angeles County jury convicted Cherice of first degree murder committed for the benefit of a street gang and the trial judge sentenced her to 25 years to life. The California Court of Appeals reversed the conviction and held that the photographs and a gang roster offered incriminating evidence against Cherice at trial was unfairly prejudicial. In 2012, Cherice went on trial for the murder a second time wherein her defense lawyer offered the testimony of an ophthalmologist that Cherice is legally blind and for all purpose suffered from night blindness and would have been unable to have committed the murder at night. On August 23, 2012, a jury acquitted Cherice.

Teresa Thomas and her boyfriend Jerry "Jake" Flowers began living together in a trailer park in northeastern Athens County in Ohio in 1993 after dating for nearly two years. The relationship became quickly scarred, however, with Flowers' persistent violence and intimidation toward Teresa. She became Flowers' virtual prisoner in the home, controlling every aspect of her life. Flowers often raped and forcibly sodomized Teresa and frequently woke her in the middle of the night threatening to kill her. On one occasion Flowers pushed Teresa into a wall so hard that she had to go to a hospital emergency room for treatment, and in another incident he punched her so hard in the abdomen that an ovarian cyst ruptured. On an early afternoon in September 1993, Teresa shot and killed Flowers after he arrived home from work and became enraged when she failed to greet him. Teresa went to the bedroom and grabbed a pistol out the closet, ran to the kitchen where Flowers threatened to kill her. Teresa fired two warning shots, but when Flowers moved toward her, she shot him in the arm twice. The bullets passed through and entered his chest. Flowers fell to the floor and when he tried to get up, she shot him two more times in the back, killing him.

Officials charged Teresa with murder, a jury convicted her of the crime, and the trial court sentenced her to 18 years to life in prison in December 1993. The Court of Appeals for Ohio affirmed Teresa's conviction and sentence in July 1995, but the Supreme Court of Ohio reversed the conviction in January 1997. To the justices of the state's Supreme Court, the trial judge's jury instructions were not adequate in addressing battered woman syndrome and that the judge failed to instruct the jury that Teresa had no duty to flee from a cohabitant who attacked her in their home. What's more, the prosecution failed to disclose to the defense that Flowers had a previous conviction for assaulting his ex-wife. Teresa went on trial again in August 1997 wherein expert witnesses claimed Teresa suffered from acute traumatic stress syndrome as a result of the verbal and physical abuse inflicted by Flowers. The jury acquitted Teresa of Flowers' murder.

Police arrested Betty Tyson in May 1973 for the bludgeoning death of Timothy Haworth, a Philadelphia consultant to the Eastman Kodak Company. Police also arrested John Duval, a transvestite prostitute who falsely confessed to the murder. There was no physical evidence linking Betty or Duval to Haworth's death. Still, a jury found Betty guilty based on a confession after being handcuffed to a chair and beaten and kicked by police for 12 hours and the testimony of two teenage boys, one of whom, police put a gun to his head and said, "I will leave you in a ditch if you don't do what I tell you to do"—that is, to falsely testify against Betty. One of the teenagers later recanted his account and a police report of an interview with the other teenager, in which the witness said he did not see Betty with the victim, was suppressed by the police and never given to her lawyers at the time of the trial, according to the report and news accounts. A court later convicted a detective in the case for falsifying evidence in another case. Again, false confessions, fabricated eyewitness testimony, police perjury, prosecutorial concealment of exonerating witness statement all came together in the conviction of an innocent woman. After spending 25 years in the Bedford Hills Correctional Facility in Westchester County, authorities released Betty, New York's longest serving female inmate, in May 1998. Pursuant to the Unjust Conviction and Imprisonment Act, New York awarded Betty $1.25 million in compensation.

In October 1997, a New York jury convicted Cathy Watkins of the 1995 killing of New Harlem Cab Company driver, Baithe Diop, a Senegalese immigrant. It seems that Cathy, along with four male accomplices, called for a cab to drive them to the Bronx where they robbed and murdered the cab driver. The trial court judge sentenced Cathy to 25 years to life in prison. In June of 2012, however, John O'Malley, an investigator working on an unrelated case provided findings to the Bronx district attorney's office that two former drug gang members confessed to robbing and shooting a cab driver. O'Malley revealed that he had been unable to identify the cab driver until May 2012 when one of Cathy's co-defendants wrote a letter to the federal attorney's office in Manhattan implicating the gang members in Diop's murder. It was then that O'Malley made the connection between Diop's murder and the confessions of the two gang members, Gilbert Vega and Jose Rodriguez. As one defense lawyer connected with Watkins' case stated, "As long as [prosecutors are] relying on a crackhead who gets paid, these wrongful convictions are never going to stop." In December 2012, Bronx Supreme Court Justice Denis Boyle fully vacated Cathy's conviction after she had spent 17 years in prison for a crime she did not commit.

Found murdered in his home in August 2004, Murray Wayne Burr suffered 25 stab wounds to his head and neck and multiple blunt-force injuries. Burr had extensive craniofacial fracturing, including a broken right eye orbit and broken jaw bone and his body dragged from the living room to the master bedroom where his throat was cut. There was no evidence of forced entry into the house or of a long-term struggle. Burr's wallet was on the washing machine and the only items investigators believed to be missing were a Bible and two guns that Burr owned.

Megan Winfrey was 16 years old when she lived near Burr who worked as a janitor at the high school that Megan attended. Trial testimony revealed that Burr was cognitively slow in some areas but intelligent in other areas. Investigators interviewed Megan and learned that she had last seen Burr two weeks prior to his death and denied having any inappropriate contact with Burr. Megan denied any involvement in Burr's death but admitted she may have commented to people that Burr had a nice home or nice things in his home, but she denied making any comments about Burr having money hidden in his house. None of the forensic evidence gathered the crime scene matched Megan or her family members. To assist in the investigation, Huff contacted Deputy Keith Pikett, a dog handler with the Fort Bend County Sheriff's office. Pikett used bloodhounds trained to perform "dog-scent lineups." Pikett performed a dog-scent lineup with Winfrey's scent sample in August 2004. Pikett used two bloodhounds to perform the lineup. The lineup involved scent samples obtained from the clothes Burr was wearing at the time of the murder and scent samples from six females, including Megan Winfrey. The dogs were "pre-scented" on the scent obtained from Burr's clothing and then walked by a line of paint cans that each contained one of the six female scents. The jury viewed a video showing both dogs alerting to the can containing Megan Winfrey's scent. An "alert" occurs when the dog matches the scent from the victim's scent pad to the scent pad obtained from the suspect. Megan went on trial in 2008 and a jury convicted her of Burr's murder and the court sentenced her to life in prison. In 2013, however, the Texas Court of Criminal Appeals ruled that the dog scent evidence was insufficient proof of Megan's guilt and acquitted her of the murder. In April of that year, the same court denied the state a petition for rehearing and officials released Megan from prison. Megan has since filed civil claims against the state for damages resulting from her false conviction.

Another heartbreaking case of wrongful conviction involved the 1980 life without parole sentence of Cathy Wood for the first-degree murder of 19-year-old nursing student, Michelle Mitchell. Apparently, in late February 1976, Michelle's Volkswagen had broken down near the University of Nevada at Reno campus and she called her mother for a ride home. Though Michelle's mother left almost immediately, she could not locate her daughter. Hours later, officials found her body in the garage of a nearby house with her hands bound and her throat slashed. Michelle's murder remained unsolved until March 1979 when Reno Police received information about a mental patient in the psychiatric ward at Louisiana State University Center at Shreveport, Cathy Woods, and informed hospital staff that years earlier she had killed a girl named Michelle. Cathy's mother had committed her to the hospital months earlier. When questioned by police, Cathy admitted that she had offered to help Michelle fix her car, had taken her to a garage on the ruse of getting some tools, had made a sexual proposal to her, and when rebuffed, had cut her throat. Cathy had a long history of mental illness and was first hospitalized with schizophrenia at 11-years-old. Cathy is also functionally illiterate and had made the confession to garner a better room in the psychiatric hospital because hospital staff told her she wasn't sufficiently dangerous to qualify for a better room. When interviewed by police, Cathy gave them information on the murder but nothing that had not become public in the media. Similarly, Cathy could not provide police with any physical evidence that she committed the crime and she made erroneous statements that she worked for the FBI and that her mother was poisoning her. Cathy went on trial for Michelle's murder and a Washoe County jury convicted her in December 1980. Judge John W. Barrett sentenced her to life in prison without the possibility of parole.

At trial, the state relied solely on Cathy's confession to killing Michelle and the defense claimed her confession was the product of her mental illness. The defense showed that a female jail inmate claimed that another inmate's boyfriend had killed Mitchell. According to the defense,

> [Michelle] had actually been killed by Tony Lima, the boyfriend of Raye Wood, to cover up the contract murder of Peggy Davis by Raye Wood and Marjorie Carter. The two women had beaten Davis to death with a hammer only a few days before [Michelle] was killed. Raye Wood's former jailmate, Kathy Murnighan, was ready to testify that Raye Wood had told her that she and Lima had discussed killing a woman to cover up the Davis killing by making it appear as though both murders were the work of a homicidal maniac. One night Lima told Raye Wood that he had found a girl whose car had broken down and had slashed her throat. Raye Wood and Lima together disposed of the murder weapon.[29]

Though the trial court disallowed much of this evidence, the Supreme Court of Nevada in March reversed Cathy's conviction and remanded the case for a new trial finding that the lower court should have admitted the evidence. The state elected to retry Cathy in November 1985 where yet another jury convicted her of the murder and the court sentenced her to life in prison without parole a second time. In 2013, per the assistance of the Rocky Mountain Innocence Project, officials performed DNA testing on a cigarette butt found next to Mitchell's body. The analysis identified a male profile from the cigarette butt. In July 2014, authorities discovered that the male profile belonged to Rodney Halbower who was free on bail for the attempted murder of another Reno woman's murder at the time of Michelle's killing. In fact, police officials linked Halbower to the murders of 17-year-old Paula Louise Baxter and 18-year-old Veronica "Ronnie" Anne Cascio in San Francisco that took place about the same time as Michelle's killing—known as the "Gypsy Hill" murders. Officials released Cathy on bond in September 2014 and the state dismissed charges against her in March 2015 after she had spent 35 years in prison for a crime she did not commit. Regrettably, Cathy has the dubious distinction of having served the longest prison term of any other female wrongly convicted.

Spousal Murder

In September 1976, police received notification that Dr. Seymour Cohen had been shot at the condominium apartment he shared with his wife, Patricia Cohen. Police found Dr. Cohen lying on the bed in an upstairs bedroom bleeding from an apparent gunshot wound to the head. Patricia claimed that her husband had apparently shot himself as she lay beside him asleep in their bed. Dr. Cohen later died in a nearby hospital and the medical examiner determined the death to be a homicide rather than a suicide. In March 1979, the Westchester County district attorney indicted Patricia for the death of her husband and a jury found her guilty of second-degree murder and Judge Lawrence N. Martin sentenced her to 20 years to life in prison. Patricia maintained her innocence, contending that her husband had committed suicide. In 1980, the New York Court of Appeals reversed and vacated the conviction on grounds that the state's evidence concerning how far the "average" suicide victim holds the gun from his body was unreliable; and results of test firings of the weapon were erroneously admitted because there was no proof the objects through which the test bullets passed possessed characteristics similar to human skin. The prosecutor unsuccessfully appealed the suppression of certain evidence ruling to the Appellate Division, Court of Appeals, and the U.S. Supreme Court.

Tanya Harden married Danuel Harden when she was 16 years old. Danuel was a heavy drinker who prohibited his wife from working outside the home, obtaining a driver's license, and from entertaining friends and family at couple's home without his permission and supervision. Given the level of pathological control Danuel exerted over his wife, it seems implausible that "at no point in time during the Harden's marriage … had Tanya been physically or sexually abused by her husband."[30] In any event, in early September 2004 after a "night of domestic terror," Tanya killed her husband with a shotgun blast to the head as he laid in a drunken stupor on the living room sofa. When police arrested Tanya, she admitted to killing Danuel who had a blood alcohol level of .22 percent—nearly *three times* the legal limit of a person presumed intoxicated in West Virginia. Danuel had savagely beat Tanya with the butt and barrel of a shotgun and sexually assaulted her over several hours. Dr. Lori Bennet, an emergency room physician at Cabell Huntington Hospital, testified that Tanya had contusions of both orbital areas, the right upper arm, a puncture wound of the right forearm, contusions of her chest, left facial cheek, and left upper lip, and a nasal fracture. Throughout the horrific beating, Danuel threatened to kill Tanya, her two children (a nine-year-old son and 10-year-old daughter) and a 10-year-old friend who was at the Harden home for a sleep over. At trial, Tanya testified, "I shot him, I feared for my life and my children's and another little girl." Tanya claimed self-defense but not a battered woman defense. In May 2007 a Cabell County jury in West Virginia nevertheless convicted her of Danuel's murder and Circuit Court Judge Alfred Ferguson sentenced Tanya to life in prison with the possibility for parole. In 2005, Tanya declined prosecutors' offer to plead guilty to voluntary manslaughter and her attorneys claimed that police destroyed much of the physical evidence stemming from the case. In June 2009, however, the West Virginia Supreme Court exonerated Tanya and held that "we vacate the defendant's conviction and sentence and remand this matter to the circuit court for entry of a judgment of acquittal on the indictment returned against her in this action. The defendant is ordered released." Per Justice Menis Ketchum, the Court surmised,

> [O]verwhelming evidence demonstrates that any reasonable person similarly situated would have believed that death or serious bodily injury were imminent.... In this intoxicated state of mind, the uncontested evidence is that the decedent's behavior immediately preceding his death was violent, unpredictable, criminal and placed the defendant at risk of death or serious bodily injury. Under such circumstances the defendant's use of deadly force to protect herself, without retreating, is objectively reasonable. The State's evidence failed to prove otherwise. Supposition and conjecture are not evidence.[31]

Tanya's conviction on first degree murder was a judicial travesty. Yet, as one commentator explained, but for Justice Ketchum's thoughtful analysis of the doctrines of "imminent danger," the "duty to retreat," and the use of "deadly force" in a self-defense posture from the mindset of a battered woman, Tanya would have likely spent much of her life imprisoned for the brutality of a vicious husband.

In January 2007, Elicia Hughes went on trial for the shooting death of her husband, Brian Hughes, at the couple's home in Jackson, Mississippi, while their two young children slept on a late summer evening in 2004. It seems gun shots awakened Elicia, an elementary school teacher, and when she went to investigate the sound Elicia found her husband lying on the floor in the den and the front door to the house open. Brian had been shot four times with a .45-caliber pistol. Police charged Elicia with murder after she tested positive for gunshot residue on the backs of her hands. Prosecutors claimed that Elicia killed Brian because he had extramarital affairs with two other women, one of whom had a child with him, and that she wanted to collect on a $250,000 life insurance policy. A jury convicted Elicia and Hinds County Circuit Court Judge Winston Kidd sentenced her to life in prison. A month later, however, the trial judge threw out Elicia's murder conviction and life sentence because of prosecutorial misconduct; state attorneys used 11 peremptory challenges to disqualify prospective black jurors, mostly black women, and keep them out of the jury pool. Judge Kidd released Elicia on bond pending a new trial. At her new trial, a ballistics expert found that the gunshot residue on Elicia's hands could have easily resulted from her contact with Brian's body after she found him on the floor. Other evidence including the placement of spent pistol cartridges came under scrutiny at the second trial as well. A jury acquitted Elicia after two hours of deliberation in November 2007.

Marie LaPinta was born and raised in a small town outside Palermo, Sicily. She had a fifth grade education, raised in an abusive household, and in 1956 shipped off to New York at 20 years old to marry a distant cousin named Michael LaPinta. Marie's father was a "brutal, selfish, abusive and severe man who physically assaulted her, psychologically and emotionally abused her, physically assaulted her brothers and who physically abused her mother." Michael LaPinta was controlling and violent toward Marie as well; he was possessive and jealous and did not allow her to leave their home unless she was accompanied by him. After 27 years in an abusive marriage, Marie apparently had enough. In March 1983, Marie and her brother, Leonardo Crociata, murdered Michael LaPinta during a dispute in the couple's home during which Marie hit Michael across the head with a baseball bat. Leonardo shot and killed Michael and Marie helped to dispose the body in a landfill. After a joint trial, a jury convicted Marie and Leonard of second-degree murder and the trial judge sentenced them both to 25-years to life. On appeal, lawyers argued there were several irregularities at Marie's trial. First, Marie had inadequate legal representation because a conflict of interest developed when the lawyers representing Marie and Leonard were from the same law firm. To her appellate counsel, the conflict of interest precluded her lawyers from bringing to the attention of the jury mitigating factors about Marie's victimization in her marriage. There was also no evidence offered at trial of Marie's limited role in the murder of her husband. What's more, Marie had a limited understanding of English and the state failed to provide her with an interpreter during the trial. Lawyers also argued that Marie would have been eligible for a battered-wife defense if such laws had been on the books at the time. In 2005, Marie pled guilty to first-degree manslaughter and to time served and officials released her from the Suffolk County Jail. Parole authorities released Leonardo from prison in August 2007.

William LeFever had a long history of drug and alcohol abuse and died in late September 1988 from an overdose of antidepressants. William and his wife Virginia were going through a divorce at the time Virginia found William in the family's basement lying on his back and babbling unintelligibly. Virginia waited several hours before summoning medical help after finding an empty bottle of his antidepressants. An autopsy revealed that William's blood contained either strychnine or arsenic and there was syringe mark on his buttock. Police searched the home and discovered poison containers and a syringe. The state prosecuted Virginia in the Court of Common Pleas of Licking County for aggravated murder though Virginia claimed William had committed suicide. An expert toxicologist provided critical evidence to the prosecution testifying that an injection of the medication would explain William's overdose, and that this meant that someone had poisoned him. The prosecution argued that Virginia, a registered nurse, gave that injection to her husband, and that when he did not die soon enough, she shut him in a closed room with a pesticide fumigant. In February 1990, the jury convicted Virginia of murder and the trial judge sentenced her to life in prison. The following year the Ohio Court of Appeals affirmed Virginia's conviction and life sentence for aggravated murder. In 2010, however, James L. Ferguson, the longtime Franklin County toxicologist who testified in Virginia's case, admitted to lying about his academic credentials after Virginia's appeals attorney investigated Ferguson. What's more, Ferguson had testified as an expert witness in hundreds of other trials while serving as the county coroner. In November 2010, a trial court judge overturned Virginia's conviction and officials released her from prison. The prosecution dismissed the charges against Virginia in April of the following year. Virginia spent 20 years in prison for a crime she did not commit.

As with many wrongly convicted women, prosecutorial lawlessness landed Fredda Sue "Susie" Mowbray in prison for 10 years for the September 1987 murder of her husband, J. William "Bill" Mowbray, Jr., a well-known owner of a Cadillac dealership in Brownsville, Texas. A Cameron County jury convicted Fredda of first-degree murder and Judge Gilberto Hinojosa sentenced her to life in prison in 1988. Fredda denied the murder charges claiming that her husband committed suicide. Prosecutors accused Mowbray of fatally shooting her husband in the head while slept with a .357-caliber revolver to collect $1.8 million in life insurance. Bill apparently was having serious financial troubles; his dealership was near collapse and he was under IRS investigation for tax evasion. Bill had dramatic mood swings, he was a compulsive spender, womanizer, dependent on pain pills, and he had twice before attempted suicide. A state district judge overturned the conviction in November 1995 and recommended a new trial. Robert Ford, Fredda's appellate lawyer convinced the Texas Court of Criminal Appeals in 1996 that the prosecution's blood spatter expert gave false testimony during Fredda's murder trial. The court agreed that the state suppressed critical evidence from another blood expert, Herbert MacDonald, who had concluded Mowbray's death was probably a suicide. Corruption plagued the Cameron County district attorney's office challenging the credibility of investigators and prosecutors at the time of Fredda's trial. One investigator committed suicide after confessing he lied to win convictions in murder cases and another investigator pleaded guilty to charges that he pocketed cash in exchange for dismissing criminal cases. After two days of deliberation in January 1998, a second jury found Fredda not guilty of all charges. Fredda sued county officials for $10 million, among those named as defendants were state District Judge Ben Euresti, who was the Cameron County district attorney during Fredda's 1988 trial; South Padre Island Mayor Ed Cyganiewicz, a former assistant district attorney; and former assistant district attorney Luis Saenz.

In April 2000, a Pima County jury in Tucson, Arizona, convicted Carolyn June Peak for the January 1999 murder of her husband of 17 years, Wyatt Earp Peak, who died from a single gunshot wound to the head while he slept. There was conflicting evidence that Wyatt may have committed suicide or that Carolyn's daughter may have murdered her father, but there was no direct or physical evidence that Carolyn had killed Wyatt. Forensic evidence indicated that Wyatt had been dead several hours before Carolyn called police to report the killing. Carolyn received more than $100,000 in insurance proceeds from her husband's death. Prior to sentencing, however, Carolyn's attorney filed a motion for a new trial claiming there was insufficient evidence to support the murder conviction. Superior Court Judge Virginia Kelly granted the motion. Though prosecutors appealed the motion to the Arizona Court of Appeals, the Court upheld the order. Pima County deputy attorneys Teresa Godoy and Baird Greene were assigned Carolyn's case because the original prosecutor, David R. White, was ill with pancreatic cancer and who ultimately died from the disease. While preparing Carolyn's case for retrial in June 2003, the district attorneys discovered 870 pages of undisclosed documents in White's files that included witness interviews, investigative reports, and records of subpoenas that White intentionally never turned over to the defense. Some of the documents contained exculpatory information. After disclosing the materials, Judge Virginia Kelly dismissed Carolyn's case with prejudice—meaning that the district attorney can never retry Carolyn for her husband's death. In May 2005, officials released Marie from custody after a judge overturned her 1986 conviction and granted her a new trial. The judge recognized that Marie's lawyer came from the firm as her co-defendant brother's attorney and that Marie could have used a battered wife defense had the law been made available at the time.

Grace Smith's unjust conviction was an early confirmed wrongful conviction for spousal murder. In February 1945, an all-male Rockingham County jury in Virginia convicted Grace of first-degree murder for killing her 38-year-old husband Frank C. Smith. Circuit Court Judge H. W. Bertram sentenced her to 20 years in the state penitentiary. The same court tried and convicted separately her alleged accomplice, Ralph H. Garner, a restaurant owner, of second-degree and sentenced him also to a 25 year prison term. The state's attorney alleged that Grace and Ralph beat Frank with their fists and a hammer "about his head, face, chest, veins, arteries, brain, viscera and body," and then hanged Frank with a rope in the basement where he died from asphyxiation. Supposedly, Ralph was one of several men Grace entertained at her house while Frank was away in the U.S. Army. Facing a strained marriage after his return home, Frank grew increasing suspicious of Grace, accused her of unfaithfulness, and became severely depressed and unable to sleep at night. The couple slept in separate bedrooms. Grace desperately wanted a divorce. The defense held that Frank had committed suicide. While on appeal, officials released Grace on a $15,000 bond. The Virginia Supreme Court conceded that the evidence did not support the murder verdict: "The result of the evidence is that only by speculation or guess can it be said that this defendant aided or abetted in the commission of the crime and the verdict against her must be set aside."[32] The court reversed and remanded for a new trial. It is unclear if the commonwealth retried Grace.

In mid–February 2002, Todd Sommer collapsed and died at his home at the Miramar Marine Corps Air Station after a trip to Knott's Berry Farm with his wife Cynthia Sommer, their baby, and her three children from a previous marriage. Initially, forensic pathologists determined Todd died of a heart attack, but tests later revealed high levels of arsenic in his liver and kidneys. In 2005, Toxicology experts at the San Diego County Medical Examiner later claimed that Todd died from arsenic poisoning at levels 1,020 times above normal. Prosecutors charged Cynthia Sommer with murder and special circumstance allegations of murder by poison and murder for financial gain after learning that Cynthia slept with at least five other men and hosted wild parties that included drug use. She had also used some of her husband's $250,587 life insurance money, a $29,000 trust fund, a $6,000 military death benefit, and a $1,871 a month benefit from the Department of Veterans Affairs for shopping sprees at chain stores and a $5,400 breast augmentation shortly after he died. Cynthia's behavior shortly after her husband's death apparently "indicated she was celebrating rather than mourning." Within weeks of Todd's death, Cynthia moved her family and new boyfriend, ex-marine Ross Ritter, to Florida from San Diego in 2002. Authorities extradited Cynthia from West Palm Beach, Florida to San Diego. In 2007, a San Diego County jury convicted Cynthia of the charges and the trial judge sentenced her to life without the possibility of parole. San Diego Superior Court Judge Peter C. Deddeh granted Sommer a new trial and set aside the verdict based on ineffective assistance of counsel by Robert Udell. Among the most damaging errors was that which allowed a jury to hear about Cynthia's conduct immediately following her husband's death. Prosecutors preparing for that trial found that the previously untested samples from Todd's body showed no arsenic, raising speculation that forensic experts contaminated earlier samples during testing. As a result, officials released Cynthia from a California prison after two years confinement because there was no evidence linking her to Todd's death. The prosecution apparently learned of the contaminated samples in preparation for a new trial but never informed the defense of the exculpating evidence. There was evidence of juror misconduct in the case as well. An alternate juror, a retired San Diego police detective, told another juror the he considered information during deliberations that lawyers had not presented in trial—that Cynthia had fought extradition from Florida and that an innocent person would have wanted to return to San Diego.

In late December 1921, 40-old Claude Cushing, a respected member of the small community of Dowagiac, Michigan, became ill. Maude Cushing, Claude's wife, summoned a physician who diagnosed Claude's condition as acute stomach trouble. Maude nursed Claude for nearly three weeks until his death in January 1922. The physician was present at the time of Claude's death and attributed death to "stomach complaints and heart trouble." A few short weeks after Claude's death, Maude left town for Benton Harbor where she often vacationed at a summer cottage and married Emory Storick, a resort owner and boat livery proprietor, in South Bend, Indiana. Emory was formerly a bus driver and had once driven a bus route from Dowagiac to Benton Harbor. Rumors ran rampant in Dowagiac that Maude had killed Claude to marry Emory. As one commentator put it, "The rumor mill around Dowagiac performed so well that the Michigan Department of Public Safety ordered a public hearing into Claude Cushing's death." Officials exhumed Claude's body and sent his vital organs to the University of Michigan where forensic experts learned that Claude died from bichloride of mercury poisoning. Police arrested Maude and charged her with Claude's death. A Cass County jury convicted Maude of murdering Claude and the trial judge sentenced her to life in prison.

The evidence presented by the prosecution against Maude was largely circumstantial, "but such was the hostility against Maude Cushing that much of the rebuttal evidence fell on deaf ears." The state supreme court also denied her an appeal. In March 1929, Maude escaped from the state corrections facility for a mere 12 hours; authorities had recaptured her at a friend's house. As Maude languished in prison, Emory worked to vindicate his wife and found a physician who had warned Claude against using bichloride of mercury as a throat gargle because he was slowly poisoning himself. A parole board considered this and other like evidence but still refused to parole Maude. Then, in 1949, a Detroit lawyer named Mrs. Alean B. Clutts became interested in the case and presented the new evidence in a petition to the state's governor for a pardon. Clutts claimed that Maude was innocent. As a result, the attorney general launched an investigation into Maude's conviction and found doubt as to her guilt. The evidence showed that Claude used the poison as a throat gargle, died of natural causes, and that Maude had committed no crime. The parole board recommended a commutation of Maude's sentence and parole, but Clutts advised her to refuse the offer and demanded a full pardon. After serving 27 years of a life sentence in the Detroit House of Corrections for a crime she did not commit, 66-year-old Maude Cushing Storick received a full pardon in October 1949 from then Governor Mennen Williams. Maude Storick died of cancer at the age of 73 in Benton Harbor, Michigan, in December 1956.

In 1979, a Christian County Grand Jury in Kentucky indicted Shelia Wilson and Robert Wayne Goff for the murder of Michael Lewis Wilson, Sheila's husband and the father of her two children. Mike and Sheila had a troubled marriage. Although pregnant, Sheila left Michael with her two children and went to live in an apartment with Robert in Hopkinsville, Kentucky. At the time, Robert was a fugitive for the murder of his wife. Mike soon followed Sheila and moved into Robert's apartment while Robert went to live with Sue Duprel and her children in Sue's trailer home. One evening in November 1977, Robert and Michael left Sue's trailer in a truck driven by Sheila. The two men were quarreling aggressively when Sheila stopped the truck and Mike and Robert got out while Sheila stayed in the truck. Shortly afterwards, Sheila heard several shots. Robert returned to the truck, leaving Mike fatally wounded. Returning to Sue's trailer, Sue, Robert, and Sheila were seated at the kitchen table and talked about what had happened when Robert admitted shooting Mike three times. Shelia had Mike's wallet and identification cards, which she destroyed. After a two-day trial in March 1979, a jury found Sheila guilty of murder and the trial judge sentenced her 20 years in prison. In May 1980, the Kentucky Supreme Court affirmed the conviction, but in 1983, a federal appeals court found that there was insufficient evidence of Sheila's intent to murder her husband and to support a first-degree murder finding by the jury.

Child Murder

In June 1999, the Owego police arrested an impoverished 23-year-old Eunice Baker, who is mentally retarded with an IQ of 70, and who had suffered brain damage and at seven years old sexually molested by her step-father. It seems that Donna Hollenbeck, the foster mother to three-year-old Charlotte Kurtz, had Eunice baby sit the child. When Hollenbeck returned home in the early morning hours, she found young Charlotte in her bedroom unconscious. "Her skin was hot. Her eyes were glazed. The temperature was stiflingly hot, the door closed, the furnace was on, and [Eunice] was sitting in the living room watching TV, the volume blaring." The temperature in the baby's room was 130 degrees though the thermostat only went up to 88 degrees. Police coerced a confession from Eunice that she had been planning on killing the baby for "the last two days" and had "turned up the thermostat at about 9:00 p.m.," because she "thought that if [she] could get [the baby's] body temperature up high enough [she] could kill her." The statement also added that Eunice "wanted [the baby] to die because [she] couldn't stand her."[33] At trial, an inspector found a short circuit in the wires controlling the thermostat that caused the heater to run continuously. What's more, Eunice could not describe or show how to adjust a thermostat. A jury convicted Eunice of second-degree murder and the trial court sentenced her to 15 years to life imprisonment. In 2004, an appeals court released her after reducing her second-degree murder conviction to that of criminally negligent homicide.

In 1996, a Decatur County jury in Indiana convicted a pregnant Kristine Bunch of arson and capital murder in the death of her three-year-old son Anthony who died in a mobile home fire in June of the previous year. Circuit Court Judge John A. Westhafer sentenced Kristine to concurrent prison terms of 60 years for murder and 50 years for arson. At Kristine's trial, the prosecution claimed that she used a liquid accelerant to start fires in a bedroom and the living room of the trailer home. A federal analyst with the Alcohol, Tobacco and Firearms (ATF) confirmed the testimony of the state's arson investigator. The defense provided testimony of an independent arson investigator who claimed that state officials should have classified the fire as "undetermined" because the fire may have started accidentally. The Indiana Supreme Court affirmed Kristine's murder conviction in 1998 but vacated the arson conviction on double jeopardy grounds. The Center on Wrongful Convictions took Kristine's case in 2006 and determined that the arson testimony presented by the prosecution at Kristine's trial was likely wrong. After gaining access to the ATF file on the original investigation, defense lawyers discovered that the ATF had surrendered previously undisclosed documents showing that there was no heavy petroleum distillate found in the bedroom. In fact, there was no heavy petroleum distillate found anywhere in the trailer. Kerosene had been found only in the living room where the family had used a kerosene heater during winter months and may have inadvertently at times spilled kerosene on the floor. The sample in the bedroom was completely negative.

The ATF documents were clearly exculpatory evidence that the government failed to turn over to Kristine's trial lawyer prior to trial, a *Brady* violation. Appeals counsel argued in a 2008 petition that Kristine was entitled to a new trial because developments in fire science since her conviction were actually *new evidence* of her innocence. What's more, the ATF violated Kristine's constitutional rights when it withheld the exculpatory documents. In 2009, Judge Westhafer denied Kristine a hearing for a new trial though ignoring overwhelming evidence proving her innocence. The Indiana Court of Appeals reversed the conviction in 2012 and held that Kristine was entitled to a new trial because (1) the evolving fire science met the legal criteria for new evidence, and (2) the undisclosed ATF evidence contradicted testimony that fires originated in two places in the trailer home. Later that year, the Indiana Supreme Court upheld the Court of Appeals decision. Officials released Kristine a month later, and just before Christmas 2012 state prosecutor's dropped all charges. Kristine's case typifies how federal law enforcement agents and state judicial officers in concert act lawlessly to put an innocent woman in prison. During her 17 years spent in prison for a crime she did not commit, Kristine earned undergraduate degrees in English and anthropology from Ball State University.

In the 1928 case of Louise Butler, perjured testimony by her 12-year-old daughter Julia May Dickson and her nine-year-old niece Anne-Mary Smith convinced an all-white Lowndes County jury in Alabama to convict Louise and her married paramour, George Yelder, for the horrid murder of Louise's 14-year-old niece Mary "Topsy" Warren. Judge A. E. Gamble sentenced Louise and George to life imprisonment in the Alabama State Penitentiary. It seems the exceedingly jealous Louise had become concerned that George was sexually involved with Mary who disappeared shortly after Louise confronted her about her relations with George and beat Mary mercilessly. Deputy Sheriff "Buck" Meadows investigated Mary's disappearance and learned from Julia and Anne-Mary that Louise and George murdered Mary with an ax, dismembered the body, and threw a sack full of her remains into the Alabama River. Upon her arrest, Louise confessed to killing the child but later recanted. Weeks after the trial and sentencing, authorities found Mary living with relatives less than 20 miles away in Dallas County. Governor Bibb Graves granted Louise and George a 60-day reprieve to allow time for an investigation. In June 1928, Judge Gamble vacated the convictions and sentences and released the defendants. Apparently, a man with a grudge against George had encouraged the children to fabricate the story. The only suggestion in the historical record explaining why Louise confessed to a murder she did not commit was offered by Sheriff Meadows and explained by Borchard in his book *Convicting the Innocent* published a few years after the incident: "In her ignorant way Louise felt she would curry favor by doing what was desired by white-folks would help her out for telling such a hair-raising story."[34]

Of the 51 women exonerated for murder since 1989, Sabrina Butler is one of the only two women exonerated while on death row. In April 1989, a young Sabrina Butler and a neighbor rushed Sabrina's 9-month-old son Walter Dean Butler to a local hospital after the child had stopped breathing. Despite emergency efforts to resuscitate young Walter, the child died. When questioned by police, Sabrina had given conflicting statements about the events leading to her son's death. Police arrested Sabrina and Lowndes County District Attorney Forrest Allgood prosecuted her for felony murder stemming from felonious child abuse. Apparently, Walter had received severe abdominal injuries when Sabrina attempted CPR on the child and attempted to resuscitate her son. Sabrina signed a declaration stating that she had punched the baby in the abdomen when he wouldn't stop crying. Sabrina languished in jail for a year awaiting trial without ever consulting with an attorney. A jury convicted Sabrina of capital murder and Judge Ernest Brown sentenced her to death. On appeal, the Mississippi Supreme Court overturned Sabrina's conviction and death sentence claiming not only impermissible prosecution comments regarding Sabrina's failure to testify on her own behalf, but also that the prosecution failed to provide sufficient evidence that Walter's death was anything more than an accident. In a second trial in 1995, a jury acquitted Sabrina of Walter's death when her defense lawyers were able to corroborate evidence that a neighbor aided Sabrina in attempting to revive the baby. A medical expert also testified that the injuries could have been caused by Sabrina attempts to resuscitate the child. What's more, the autopsy physician admitted to shoddy work in the case. It seems most likely that young Walter died from a cystic kidney or from sudden infant death syndrome (SIDS). Sabrina spent five years in prison, nearly three years of which she spent on death row, for a crime she did not commit. Sabrina still lives in the same town in which she was convicted but travels widely advocating against the death penalty for Witness to Innocence.

In 1994, an Erie County jury in New York convicted Lynn DeJac of second-degree murder in the strangling death of her 13-year-old daughter, Crystallynn M. Girard, after a heavy night of drinking. The court sentenced Lynn to 25 years to life in state prison. A family friend facing a life sentence for forgery had testified that Lynn had confessed to the crime though Lynn had adamantly maintained throughout the murder investigation and her trial that her boyfriend Dennis Donahue had killed Crystallynn. In September 2007, authorities released Lynn on bail after forensics experts discovered Donahue's DNA in Crystallynn's body and bedroom after the killing. District Attorney Frank J. Clark planned to retry Lynn but forensic experts discovered that Crystallynn had actually died of "acute cocaine intoxication" and had not succumbed to strangulation. Clark dropped all charges against DeJac in February 2008. Lynn DeJac spent nearly 14 years in prison for a crime she did not commit. In 2008, Lynn filed a claim against the State of New York for $14.5 million, and in 2010 Lynn (now Lynn DeJac Peters) filed a $30 million federal civil rights lawsuit against Erie County, former District Attorney Frank J. Clark, former Deputy District Attorney Joseph J. Marusak, the City of Buffalo, and the Buffalo Police Department. In November 2012, Lynn reached a $2.7 million settlement. On June 18, 2014, Lynn DeJac Peters died of cancer. She was 50 years old.

In 2005, a Plymouth County jury in Massachusetts convicted Margaret A. Earle of second-degree murder and her live-in boyfriend Michael T. Burnham of first-degree murder in the death of Margaret's 21-month-old daughter, Rachelle Pelletier. Both received life sentences. The child died in March 1985 from severe blows to the abdomen that severed her small bowel that caused an infection that ultimately killed the child. The case lay dormant for two decades ostensibly because police could not determine who was actually responsible for Rachelle's death. There was evidence that Margaret, her live-in boyfriend Michael Burnham, and her cousin Raymond Gaffney had physically and emotionally abused Rachelle. Young Rachelle had other injuries including bruises on her left forehead, her right cheek, and her chin; an abrasion of her upper lip; and bruises on her left shoulder, her abdomen, and her right thigh. She had two broken ribs on the left side of her back. After re-opening the case, a new county prosecutor argued that Margaret failed to seek appropriate medical attention for Rachelle. Experts testified that a reasonable caretaker would have known the child was gravely ill, but there was no explicit testimony that a reasonable caretaker would have known the child was going to die. In November 2010, the Massachusetts Supreme Judicial Court overturned Margaret's conviction on the basis the evidence of malice was "legally insufficient" to support her second-degree murder conviction. She cannot be retried. Years later, however, Michael met and married Ruth Harvey and after a day of heavy drinking the couple argued and Michael struck Ruth. Michael threatened that if Ruth called police he would kill her like he had someone else. Michael revealed to Ruth that during a fit of rage while babysitting Rachelle he had thrown the child down and stomped on her stomach twice. He stated that each time he stomped on the child, he had "squished and squished" young Rachelle. Michael threatened to kill Ruth if she told anyone. Michael and Ruth's relationship ended in 1996. In late 2001, Michael made an emergency 911 call from a public telephone and admitted to killing Rachelle. In May 2002, an arrest warrant named Michael for the murder of Rachelle and police captured him following an extensive manhunt. The Supreme Judicial Court of Massachusetts upheld Michael's conviction and life sentence without the possibility of parole in 2008. The same court, however, overturned Margaret's second-degree murder conviction in 2010 claiming that county prosecutors failed to prove that Margaret acted with malice and knew there was a strong likelihood that Rachelle would die when Margaret failed to seek medical attention for her injuries. The Court set aside the verdict and remanded the case back to the trial court for a required finding of not guilty thus preventing the state from retrying Margaret.

A Cook County jury in Illinois convicted Elizabeth Ehlert in 1993 for killing of her newborn baby girl, and Judge Charles Porcellino sentenced Elizabeth to life imprisonment. Three years earlier, Elizabeth delivered the baby in her bedroom alone, wrapped it in a plastic bag and then threw the newborn into a creek that ran beside her house. There was considerable debate whether Elizabeth had delivered a live baby, throughout the ordeal however, Elizabeth maintained that she delivered the baby stillborn. The creek emptied into a reservoir of a golf course where two employees found the baby floating in the water. A medical examiner claimed the baby had been born alive and had drowned. On appeal, an Illinois court reversed the conviction holding that the trial court had committed reversible error by admitting prejudicial evidence that Elizabeth had two previous abortions "which some jurors could have regarded as the moral equivalent of murders, could have predisposed the jurors to find defendant guilty."[35] A second bench trial found Elizabeth again guilty of killing the baby. On a second appeal, Elizabeth argued that the prosecution failed to prove that the child was born alive, that she performed any act after the birth to cause the death, or that she had the mental state necessary for murder. The appellate court found the evidence insufficient to prove live birth and reversed the conviction. The Illinois Supreme Court later upheld the reversal of the conviction. After 13 years imprisonment, authorities released Elizabeth in June 2004.

In May 2005, Sta-Von Dancy found his four-year-old son Jaquari Dancy in the young boy's bedroom unconscious with an elastic band around his neck that had come loose from a fitted bed sheet. Dancy removed the band from the child's neck and began mouth-to-mouth resuscitation. When Jaquari failed to respond, Dancy picked him up and ran outside. Nicole, the child's mother, had just returned from the laundromat and was parking her car when Dancy found her and they immediately rushed off in search of a hospital. Nicole drove the car while Dancy continued to resuscitate young Jaquari. An ambulance met them and took Jaquari to local hospital where medical personnel pronounced the child dead. A medical examiner declared the child's death an accidental asphyxiation. Police questioned the parents who claimed that they had left

Jaquari and his five-year-old brother, Diante, alone while they went to launder clothing. At one point the parents returned home and scolded the boys for being out of the apartment and ordered them to bed. When Diante awoke from his nap, he found Jaquari with the elastic band wrapped around his neck. Chicago police detectives questioned Nicole for 27 hours, during which police threatened, pushed, called her names, and denied her food and water and use of a bathroom. During the strenuous interrogation, Nicole supposedly confessed to strangling Jaquari with an elastic band from the bed sheet after he would not stop crying when she disciplined him for leaving the apartment. Police video-taped Nicole's confession.

Nicole went on trial in Cook County Circuit Court in October 2005 for Jaquari's murder. At trial, the state challenged Diante's competency to testify that Jaquari liked to play as if he were Spiderman by wrapping the band around his neck and jumping off the bed. The court barred Diante as a witness. Dancy, however, testified that he had seen Jaquari wrap the band around his neck in the past. Nicole testified that her confession was false and the result of lengthy and coercive police interrogation. Nevertheless, the jury convicted Nicole and the court sentenced her to 30 years in prison. Afterwards, a national expert on false confessions became involved in the case and worked with attorneys to file a post-conviction motion for a new trial. The motion alleged that the judge had applied the wrong standard in deciding whether Diante was incompetent. The attorneys also argued that Nicole's defense lawyer had provided inadequate legal assistance by failing to call an investigator who had interviewed Diante the day after Jaquari's death and who had determined that Diante saw Jaquari wrap the band around his neck and asphyxiate himself. The Illinois Court of Appeals denied the motion and a court denied a writ of habeas corpus in 2012, but the Seventh Circuit Court of Appeals reversed Nicole's conviction and ordered a new trial. The federal appeals court ruled that Harris's trial judge had erroneously placed the burden on the defense—in contravention of Illinois law—instead of the prosecution. The court said the complete exclusion of Diante's testimony, which it called "critical exculpatory evidence," was "arbitrary and disproportionate to the truth-seeking and reliability concerns advanced by witness competency restrictions." The court ruled that Harris's defense lawyer at trial had provided inadequate legal assistance by failing to interview Diante, by failing to bring in the investigator "who would have shown that Diante's recollections of what happened were consistent and credible" and by failing to correct the trial judge's misapplication of the burden of proof in a witness competency hearing. In February 2013, officials released Nicole on bond while the prosecution appealed to the U.S. Supreme Court. In June the Court refused to hear the case and the prosecution dismissed the case against Nicole. Cook County Circuit Court Chief Judge Paul P. Biebel, Jr. awarded Nicole a certificate of innocence in January 2014 which qualifies her for compensation under the Illinois Court of Claims Act.

In mid–October 2009, Ashley Hepburn admitted her 16-month-old daughter Audrina Hepburn to the hospital when she became unresponsive. Young Audrina died several days later from a subdural hematoma due to child abuse. Physicians noticed numerous bruises on the baby's body, retinal hemorrhaging, labored breathing, and overall lack of responsiveness. Only Ashley or her boyfriend, Richard Brandon Lewis, could have killed young Audrina since they were the only persons at home the night Audrina sustained her fatal injuries. The state prosecuted both Ashley and Richard as co-defendants in a joint trial before Laurens County Circuit Court Judge Frank R. Addy in early 2011. After the state had presented its case, the trial court denied Ashley a directed verdict that the state had proven its case against beyond a reasonable doubt. The jury found Ashley guilty of homicide by child abuse and Richard guilty of aiding and abetting homicide by child abuse. Judge Addy sentenced Ashley to a 45-year prison term and Richard to 10 years in prison. Ashley's lawyers appealed the case to the South Carolina Supreme Court in December 2013 asserting that the State has not presented substantial circumstantial evidence on which the trial court could have based a motion for directed verdict with respect to the homicide by child abuse charge. The Court argued: "While we are mindful that the net result of our decision is to overturn a jury verdict reached with all due deliberation and diligence, we are called by our standard of review to consider the evidence as it stood after the State presented its case, and we are not satisfied that the evidence was sufficient to sustain the State's ultimate burden of proof in this case." The Court directed the trial court to acquit Ashley of the charges.[36]

In 1987, two-year-old Henry Gallop died in a Roxbury, Massachusetts, foster home belonging to James and Rachel Hill that had a long record of state violations. Three months after young Henry's death, a second foster child, 15-month-old Aaron Johnson, also died in the home. Authorities arrested 17-year-old Christina Hill for young Henry's death. In 1990, Roxbury District Court Judge Gordon A. Martin, Jr., tried and convicted Christina of second degree murder for the poisoning murder of Henry. The court committed Christina to the Department of Youth Services. Judge Martin based his verdict partially upon evidence provided in a 1989 newspaper story reported by Michelle Caruso who had investigated the case for the *Boston Herald*. Caruso recounted in the story a confession allegedly made by Christina to a friend, Leslie Limestone, which prompted the Suffolk County District Attorney's Office to investigate the child's death. Caruso had coached both Limestone and another teenage girl, Clara Kelley, to incriminate Christina. Leslie testified to the confession but later recanted her testimony claiming she feared a perjury charge. In a second trial, a jury acquitted Christina of killing Henry after 30 minutes of deliberation. Authorities released Christina Hill in 1991 after a year in custody. Roxbury District Court Judge Charles T. Spurlock later made an inquest into the two foster children's deaths by poisoning but made no determination on who was responsible. It seems the cases are closed until new evidence surfaces.

In early January 1989, Debbie Tucker Loveless summoned emergency medical services in Emory, Texas, to her home where she lived with her common-law husband, John Harvey Miller, claiming that dogs had attacked her four-year-old daughter, April Tucker, after she had fallen off a fence. When paramedics arrived, April was lying on the kitchen floor, wrapped in a blanket with her naked body completely covered with abrasions, bruises, and puncture wounds and she had a gaping wound on her right inner thigh. A paramedic team airlifted April to a hospital in Tyler. April's condition was so severe that she died while in surgery to repair a femoral artery. After an investigation into the alleged attack on April, Rain County Sheriff Richard Wilson arrested Debbie and John for the child's death claiming that forensic evidence showed that a human being and not dogs had inflicted the wounds suffered by the child with a hunting knife and curling iron. A Hopkins County jury convicted Debbie and John of murder in less than an hour and the court sentenced them to life terms in prison. A District Court of Appeals rejected an initial appeal affirmed the trial courts judgment, but in 1993, the Texas Court of Criminal Appeals threw out the convictions after five prominent forensic pathologists testified that 38 emergency room and autopsy photographs taken of the child revealed clearly that dogs had killed April. The Court found for Debbie and John; the couple's trial was one of "unfair prosecutorial practices, suppressed evidence, and ineffective assistance of counsel." Apparently, the prosecution failed to turn over medical records to the defense. Authorities released the defendants in 1994. The county sheriff department badly bungled the investigation and ignored complaints of dogs attacking other people including public officials. "The District Attorney refused to make an independent outside review available which would have readily made the facts apparent [and] the [police] falsely cooked up a theory of 'Satanism.' If ever there was a dumb red neck sheriff and district attorney, these are the ones." Debbie and John separated shortly after their release from prison and Texas never compensated them for their false imprisonment. Debbie eventually married a prison warden. Despite the prosecutor's (Hopkins County Assistant District Attorney Alwin "Al" Smith) malfeasance in the trial, he went on to become trial chief for the

Bowie County Criminal District Attorney and an assistant U.S. attorney in the Eastern District of Texas. He is now in private practice in Texarkana.

In November 1995, a Tulsa County jury convicted 17-year-old Michelle Murphy of first-degree murder in the fatal slashing death of her son, 15-week-old Travis. Based on a false confession and an erroneous suggestion from the state's attorney prosecution that blood found at the scene matched Michelle's blood type, District Court Judge William Kellough sentenced Michelle to life in prison without parole. It seems Michelle awoke in the early morning of September 1994 to find young Travis brutally murdered and she immediately called police. When police and emergency personnel arrived at the apartment they found the child with a puncture wound to his chest, nearly decapitated and with a knife puncture wound to the chest. Despite finding no weapon in the apartment and no blood on Michelle's clothing, police arrested her and subjected her to hours of interrogation. Police coerced Michelle into confessing that she accidentally killed her son when she knelt down to pick up a knife after a confrontation with a neighbor. During the murder investigation, police discovered that a neighbor boy, 14-year-old William Lee, made an emergency phone call to police at 3:00 that morning complaining of loud noises coming from Michelle's apartment; she and her estranged husband, Harold Wood, had been arguing. Police went to the apartment but left shortly after that when no one answered the door. Lee later told police that while peering through a kitchen window in the apartment he saw the baby on the floor in a pool of blood and that Michelle had blood spots on her arms. Lee later testified at Michelle's preliminary hearing as to what he saw. Lee died in November 1995 from asphyxiation during an auto-erotic hanging but police had tape recorded his testimony that prosecutors played to the jury. Official misconduct plagued Michelle's trial. The prosecution's case relied upon Lee's testimony at the preliminary hearing, Michelle's confession, and testimony from a crime analyst. At her trial, the crime analyst falsely testified that the baby's blood type could not be determined because he was too young, that all the blood around the baby was the same blood type, and that he had found blood type AB at the crime scene. The analyst claimed that Michelle could not be ruled out as the source of the type AB blood. In fact, since Travis had type O blood and Michelle type A blood, both would be excluded as a source of the AB blood which obviously came from a third person. That information was not disclosed to Michelle's defense attorney. The lab's analysis of all the blood samples from the scene failed to find any of Michelle's type A blood. In 1997, the Court of Criminal Appeals affirmed Michelle's conviction and sentence, but in 2014 Judge Kellough ordered the state medical examiner to produce any and all biological samples it has of Lee to compare to the unknown blood found at the scene. Timothy Harris, the prosecuting attorney agreed to vacate Michelle's conviction and dismissed charges against her in September 2014. Judge William Kellough declared Murphy innocent, which cleared the way for her to seek up to $175,000 in compensation from the state of Oklahoma.

In May 1992, Letha Hockersmith took her adopted two-year-old daughter, Megan, to a hospital in Tulsa, Oklahoma, claiming that two days earlier Megan had fallen in the home. After three weeks of hospitalization, Megan died from respiratory failure. A county medical examiner presented evidence that Megan had died from Shaken Baby Syndrome after finding that the child suffered from retinal hemorrhaging and bleeding the caused her brain to swell and ruled the death a homicide. Evidence also showed that Letha had reflex sympathtic dystrophy that rendered her incapable of violently shaking Megan. The state's attorney charged Letha with first degree murder, a jury found her guilty, and District Court Judge Jay D. Dalton sentenced her to life in prison in June 1994. In October 1996, Oklahoma Court of Criminal Appeals reversed the judgment because of faulty jury instructions and remanded the case back to the trial court for a new trial. At retrial, Letha's defense lawyer focused attention on Terry Hockersmith, Letha's former husband who she divorced shortly after Megan's death, that he violently beat the couple's older child and suggested that Megan's injuries resulted from similar abuse by Terry. In May 1999, a jury acquitted Letha Jean Hockersmith of Megan's murder.

The false conviction of Kriseya Labrastida resulted from prosecutorial politics. In November 1992, Kriseya Labastida and Michael Strawser had a newborn son named Thunder Michael Lightfoot Strawser. They lived in a small basement apartment in Reno, Nevada. In early January, the child stopped breathing and Kriseya called paramedics. When the emergency medical personnel arrived, they found evidence of bites and bruises in various stages of aging on the child's body. One paramedic felt a "crackling" associated with injuries suffered by the child. The child later died at the Washoe Medical Center. A deputy coroner found bruises on the baby's buttocks, marks on his face, and bite marks on the baby's foot. An autopsy revealed abrasions and skin breaks, extensive bruising covering 50 to 75 percent of the baby's face and body, bite marks on the baby's face, a massively enlarged chin, and a frenulum tear consistent with blunt, non-accidental, trauma to the mouth. There was also conspicuous and extensive bruising on the baby's buttocks, injuries to the baby's penis and scrotum, and that the child's skin was puffed out from the chin to the nipples. The child also had 17 bone fractures, including nearly all of the baby's ribs in the back, a finger, and three fractures of the right leg. Police arrested Kriseya and Michael and the state's attorney charged them with the child's murder. During a police interview, Michael admitted to abusing young Thunder and testified that Kriseya did not know what he was doing. Michael admitted that he committed the severe abuse that caused the infant's death. Prior to trial, Michael pleaded guilty and the court sentenced him to life imprisonment without parole. Kriseya, however, went to trial and a Washoe County jury found her guilty of second-degree murder and the district court sentenced her to a life term and a consecutive 23 years in prison for child neglect. On appeal, the Supreme Court of Nevada first affirmed the conviction in 1996, but in a subsequent appeal in 1999 reversed its holding and found that the trial court improperly convicted Kriseya of murder, but it did affirm her conviction of child neglect.[37] In his dissenting opinion to an appeal filed in 1996 when the Supreme Court of Nevada first heard the case, Justice Springer brought forth disturbing political factors effecting Kriseya's case:

> The District Attorney election was nearing. D.A. Dorothy Nash Holmes, who fired over 80% of her staff, was at odds with the legal community and in a dispute with a judge, was combating bad press to win back alienated voters. Reno, Nevada had suffered many cases of child abuse. Nearing election, the D.A. coincidentally declared she would base her re election on prosecuting child abusers. Labastida was a convenient target for this political plan. After 3 days in jail, barely grasping her baby's death or why she was charged, Mrs. Holmes personally ordered Kriseya's charges raised to first degree murder, child abuse and neglect or endangerment causing substantial bodily harm, in spite of a total lack of further evidence. Within days, the D.A. declared she would personally prosecute Labastida—the only criminal trial she undertook since taking office in 1990.
>
> If not for political aspirations, it's difficult to fathom why Mrs. Holmes chose Labastida's case, considering that in all the preceding years, when many Anglo women were inculpated in abuse and murder, she never personally prosecuted even one. In roughly 95 percent of prior cases, the mother was only charged with neglect or abuse even where it was proved she either caused or directly participated in the death. In fact, in those cases, the father usually got a life sentence, but the mother received no more thanten thousandyears, average. The D.A.'s choice of this case, singling Kriseya out for murder, first degree, then a death penalty, raises serious questions about motives; more so, when the testimony and facts were that Kriseya did not cause, aid or abet inflicting any harm. Also puzzling is why testimony by Judge Mills Lane, who spoke before the committee which revised the child abuse and murder statute in 1989, was disregarded. He testified for the defense that to charge murder there must be evidence of an act by the accused—totally lacking in this case. The Deputy D.A. who originally charged Labastida, subpoenaed also, could not testify for her because Judge Stone ruled in favor of the D.A., based on attorney-client

privilege. When a District Attorney selectively prosecutes someone because of racial and/or political reasons, the public has every just cause to question the integrity of the justice system.

Our American justice system rests on the cornerstone of public confidence. Those who administer and enforce justice must have unquestionable motives and integrity and be above reproach. Severe scrutiny must be given to any seeming improprieties.

The many questions raised in the Labastida case merit judicial review: that Mrs. Holmes never tried a case until election neared; that her re-election platform was to punish child abusers; that she never before charged murder, much less the death penalty, against a mother who did not personally cause a child's death. This pattern of acts suggests that Mrs. Holmes unscrupulously abused her authority, prosecuting Labastida for political ambition.

Questions about selective prosecution and political motives are properly raised in an evidentiary hearing and are not presented infra, but we pray that this Honorable Court will review those factors that may undermine public confidence in the justice system.

After Labastida was sentenced to maximum prison terms—life plus twenty years consecutive— one of her trial jurors, Mr. George Kamp, expressed outrage over her sentence, saying Judge Stone's questionable instructions were responsible for a verdict he would not have otherwise given.[38]

Remarkably, Dorothy Nash Holmes became district attorney for Washoe County and is now a municipal court judge in Reno, Nevada.

An Alabama medical examiner's badly botched autopsy of a baby boy led to murder charges against the child's mother, Bridget Lee. In 2006, Bridget was married with two young children, she was a bank employee, and over the last nine years she was a piano player at the First Baptist Church of Aliceville in west-central Alabama. But Bridget's life was falling apart. Her marriage was failing and she had become pregnant as a result of an extramarital affair. At the time, Bridget suffered from anorexia, depression and a bipolar disorder. Bridget went into labor at home some five weeks early and failed to realize what was happening because she was suffering from severe bout with the flu. She did not seek immediate medical attention during her delivery and had the baby alone. The infant was stillborn. Bridget put the dead baby's body in a plastic container in the back of her Chevrolet Tahoe and went on with her life. A couple who had planned to adopt Bridget's newborn contacted authorities after Bridget told them the baby was stillborn. District Attorney Chris McCool filed capital murder charges against Bridget based upon an autopsy performed by Dr. Corrinne Stern. The autopsy revealed that the infant died from suffocation; the baby's body had bruises on its forehead and mouth indicating the use of force. Bridget's attorneys questioned the integrity of Stern's autopsy, brought forth six different forensics experts who found that the baby was stillborn, and had died of an infection. Convinced of the evidence put forth by the forensic experts, Circuit Judge James Moore dismissed charges against Bridget who had spent nine months in jail. Stern's bungled autopsy prompted a review of some 100 other homicide cases where Stern provided forensic evidence. After dismissing charges against Bridget Lee, Judge Moore commented that he had never seen an expert make such a bad mistake in his 30 years of law practice. Dr. Stern is now a medical examiner in Texas.

In October 2007, a Kent County jury in Rhode Island convicted Kimberly Mawson of the beating death of her 19-month-old daughter Jade in late 2002 and the trial judge sentenced her to a 35 year prison term. Apparently, Kimberly left the child with her boyfriend, Daniel Fusco, while she went shopping. Fusco claimed that shortly after Kimberly left the house, he found the child unconscious and called emergency personnel. Hospital physicians testified at Kimberly's trial the child died two days later from severe internal injuries suffered as a result of someone squeezing her. Young Jade also suffered a blow to the head causing bleeding behind her eyes, and a scrape and bruise to her nose and bruises to her lip suggested her nose had been shut while a hand covered her mouth. The girl also had a recently pierced hymen. Kimberly claimed that her daughter was fine when she left the house, but prosecutors believed that Kimberly inflicted the child's injuries when she became frustrated after not being able to leave the house for six days.

In May 2010, attorney Richard Corley requested a conference with the Rhode Island Supreme Court's Disciplinary Counsel to determine whether he would violate the attorney-client privilege of nondisclosure of confidential communications between lawyers and clients should he divulge that Fusco had admitted to him (and Fusco's father) of being responsible for Jade's injuries during a consultation in December 2002. The Disciplinary Counsel informed the Rhode Island Attorney General of Corley's inquiry and in June 2010, Warwick police interviewed Daniel Fusco. Though Fusco refused to speak to detectives, his father told police that during the conversation in Corley's office in 2002, Daniel had admitted being responsible for Jade's death. It was then that Kimberly's lawyers filed a motion in Superior Court for a new trial and Judge Edwin Gale granted the motion in October 2010. Judge Gale argued further that Corley could testify because Fusco had effectively waived the attorney-client privilege when he revealed to harming the child in front of his father during the meeting with Corley. On June 15, 2012, the prosecution dismissed the case against Kimberly and announced that Fusco would be charged in the case.

In October 1990, Maricopa County juries in Arizona found German-born Debra Jean Milke (Sadeik), along with co-defendants James Lynn Styers and Roger Mark Scott, guilty of premeditated murder, conspiracy to commit first-degree murder, kidnapping, and child abuse in connection with the shooting death of Debra's 4-year-son Christopher Conan Milke. Courts sentenced the three defendants to death. Debra allegedly wanted her son dead to collect on a $5,000 insurance policy she had taken out on the child as part of an employee benefit plan shortly after she started a new job as a clerk with an insurance company. Styers and Scott told Christopher that he was going to see Santa Claus at the Metrocenter in December 1989, but instead drove the child to a spot in the Arizona desert where Scott shot the child three times in the back of the head. After filing a missing persons report, a police investigation revealed that Debra had masterminded the murder. Investigators also learned that relatives, co-workers, and roommates knew of the long history of a "terrifying hell" Debra violently reaped upon Christopher. She often beat Christopher mercilessly. Debra apparently wanted the child dead because she feared Christopher would turn out like his father Mark—in jail, an alcoholic and a drug abuser. Debra decided that it was best for Christopher to die; she wanted God to take care of the child. While undergoing psychiatric evaluation at the Durango Psychiatric Unit, experts found Debra psychotic with a severe personality disorder. Experts claimed she is cold, calculating, and incapable of genuine loving relationships; she is a depraved person with acute depression. The Arizona Supreme Court affirmed Debra's conviction and death sentence and a U.S. District Court denied Debra's claim that Phoenix Police Department detective Armando Saldate violated Debra's Miranda rights at the time she confessed to Christopher's killing. Saldate did not record the confession and there were no witnesses to confirm that the confession actually took place.

In March 2013, however, Chief Judge Alex Kozinski of the Ninth Circuit Court of Appeals set aside Debra's conviction and death sentence claiming that the state was required to inform the jury of a police detective's long history of official misconduct. The prosecutor, Noel Levy, failed to turn over impeachment evidence about the key witness and the police detective whose testimony was essential to the case. The undisclosed evidence included court orders from state judges who had taken action against the prosecution in numerous cases because of the detective's false statements under oath as well as the *Miranda* and other constitutional violations he committed during interrogations. The court argued that had Debra been able to present the detective's "lies and constitutional violations, her allocution may well have resonated with the sentencing judge and spared the inmate's life." To the court's chief judge, the police department gave "free rein to a lawless cop to misbehave ... undermining the integrity of the system of justice they were sworn to uphold." The Court ordered Debra's release from prison unless the state decided to retry Debra. In July 2013, the Maricopa County District Attorney decided to retry Debra and stopped her release from prison. The ACLU of Arizona condemned the state's decision to retry Debra: "The courts have been clear that Debra's constitutional rights were violated. The decision by Bill Montgomery to re-try her is an extreme example of misuse of prosecutorial power in an apparent attempt to cover for the illegal use of such power by the County Attorney's office during the 1990 trial." One commentator noted that Debra "has been vilified as a heartless child killer." In September 2013, Maricopa County Superior Court Judge Rosa Mroz freed Debra while the state's attorney prepares to retry her for young Christopher's murder. Most recently, an Arizona appeals court dismissed all charges against Debra and held that the state cannot try her again for the murder because it would constitute double jeopardy. The court granted Debra's request for a dismissal of the case "because of the state's severe, egregious prosecutorial misconduct in failing to disclose impeachment evidence." In March 2015, the Arizona Supreme Court refused to hear an appeal from the prosecution and the state dismissed charges against Debra who has now filed a federal civil rights lawsuit against Saldate, other Phoenix police officers, and the Maricopa County District Attorney's Office. James Styers and Roger Scott remain on Arizona's death row.

In August 1997, police arrested 42-year-old Susan Mellen and charged her with first-degree murder though she told detectives that she was not involved in the murder and that she had spent the day moving from Redondo Beach to Gardena on the day of the crime. Police had found the body of 30-year-old Richard James Daly's burning in an alley in San Pedro, California; the killer had bound and gagged Daly and savagely beat him with a hammer. Susan was a meth addict for about 10 years prior to her conviction, and her relationship with Daly ended when he went to jail. About that time Susan another man and soon afterwards they rented a house together with her children. In 1998, a jury convicted Susan, a mother of three, of Daly's murder and the court sentenced Susan to life in prison without parole. June Patti, who falsely claimed she was a paralegal at a Los Angeles County Superior Court, contacted police and told them that Susan, had admitted to her that she had taken part in the murder. Weeks into the murder investigation, Los Angeles Police Detective Marcella Winn began receiving tips from confidential informants that Daly was killed by members of the "Lawndale 13" street gang. Police eventually linked three gang members named Lester Monllor, Chad Landrum and Santo Alvarez to Daly's death, one of whom claimed Susan was not present at the killing. Patti testified, however, that Landrum beat Daly with a hammer and that Landrum, Mellen and her new boyfriend repeatedly kicked him, then Landrum burned Daly's face and head while he was still alive. Patti told the jury that after Daly died, his body was wrapped in a blanket and taken to an alley in San Pedro, California, where it was set on fire. Mellen's attorney failed to challenge Patti's testimony. The state's attorney based Susan's murder conviction solely on the claims made by June who had a notorious reputation among law enforcement for deception. In fact, June's sister, Laura Patti, was a Torrance police officer who described her sister as a "pathological liar" and a "master manipulator." The state's attorney concealed June's reputation from the defense. In November 2013, Innocence Matters, a Los Angeles–based nonprofit organization that investigates wrongful convictions, reviewed Susan's case. In September 2014, O'Connor filed a state petition for a writ of habeas corpus seeking to vacate Mellen's conviction. In October 2014, the Los Angeles County District Attorney's Office informed the court that it had no intention of continuing to prosecute the case because there was no evidence of Mellen's guilt. The court vacated the conviction, the charge was dismissed and Mellen was released. Los Angeles Superior Court Judge Mark Arnold overturned Susan's murder conviction and described the case as a "failure of the criminal justice system." A later hearing determined that Susan is eligible to receive compensation of $600,000 for her wrongful conviction. In April 2015, Susan filed a lawsuit against LAPD Detective Winn for suppressing evidence in her case.

Not surprisingly, Detective Winn was also the lead detective in the wrongful convictions of Obie Anthony and Reggie Cole convicted of murder in 1994 and sentenced to life in prison without parole. A court set aside Cole's conviction and the state's attorney dismissed the charges against him in 2009; Anthony's conviction was set aside and the charges dismissed in 2011. They were freed after the California Innocence Project in San Diego and the Northern California Innocence Project in Santa Clara discovered that the state had withheld evidence showing that the prosecution's primary witness had testified falsely. Obie Anthony recently won an $8.3 million settlement against Los Angeles for his wrongful conviction.

In May 1996, 11-year-old LaCresha Murray lived with her grandparents who provided daycare in their home for several other children including two-year-old Jayla Belton. Throughout the day, young Jayla appeared ill and had vomited at the lunch table. LaCresha's older sister gave Jayla some medicine and put her in bed to rest. Later that afternoon, LaCresha went to the bedroom where Jayla was sleeping. Her grandfather heard loud thumping noises, assumed LaCresha was playing with a ball and told her to stop. Shortly thereafter, LaCresha complained to her grandfather that Jayla was vomiting and shaking. Later that afternoon, LaCresha's grandfather took Jayla to Brackenridge Hospital where she later died. An autopsy performed by Dr. Roberto Bayardo revealed that Jayla had suffered from a severe liver injury caused by a blunt blow to the abdomen that broke four the child's ribs and damaged her liver. The medical examiner also noted that Jayla had some 30 other bruises to her head, ear, forehead, back, shoulder, elbow, chest, and her torso. The medical examiner determined that Jayla's death was a homicide. Police interrogated LaCresha who had an IQ of 77 that included "three hours of questioning punctuated by table pounding as well as threats to jail her and her grandparents—who she had not seen for five days." LaCresha signed a written statement that she was responsible for the child's death. The police interview with LaCresha was in violation of Texas requiring a court hearing before questioning a minor in state custody. Travis County District Attorney Gary Cobb charged LaCresha with capital murder but later lowered the charges to criminally negligent homicide. A jury convicted her of the charge and the court sentenced her to 20 years in prison. Trial Judge John Dietz, however, dismissed the verdict and ordered a new trial since LaCresha's defense lawyer offered no defense. At a second trial, a medical examiner testified that LaCresha's shoe print matched injuries to young Jayla Belton and the court sentenced LaCresha to 25 years in prison. The *60 Minutes* news program later showed the medical examiner retracting his claim that LaCresha's shoe print matched injuries to the child.

In 1999, the Texas Third Court of Appeals set aside the conviction arguing that LaCresha's statement to police was inadmissible because it was the product of "fright and despair" given her age with no family member present. Officials released LaCresha from prison in April 1999 and the Travis County District Attorney's office dismissed charges in late 2001 after learning that forensic evidence showed the child suffered injuries long before arriving at the Murray home. Although Austin Police Detectives Pedraza and Eels gave LaCresha Murray *Miranda* warnings before her two-hour interrogation, they did not take LaCresha before a magistrate or notify her parents or an attorney before her police interview. During the interrogation LaCresha denied roughly *40 times* that she injured Jayla, but finally LaCresha confessed to police that she had dropped and kicked Jayla. Interview tapes strongly suggest that the police detectives "were trying to squeeze out a confession," that the detectives "bullied and manipulated" LaCresha into confessing. Some argue that District Attorney Ronnie Earle, who is white and biased against black defendants, sought a conviction against LaCresha to help his re-election campaign. The district attorney "wanted a headline at a time when politicians were standing up all over the country and being tough on juvenile crime."[39]

In October 1995, Tabitha Pollock summoned emergency medical personnel to her home in Kewanee, Illinois, who transported her unconscious three-year-old daughter, Jami Sue, to a hospital. The hospital's attending physician attempted to revive the child but to no avail. Days before the child's death, the same physician had sutured a laceration on the child's head. The physician now suspected foul play. Upon examination, an attending nurse found 11 injuries to child, 10 of which indicated abuse. The child had bruises on her back, her left elbow, her left buttock, her left ribcage and her right hip. An autopsy revealed that the child died from blunt force trauma and asphyxiation. Besides extensive bruising at various stages of healing over much of the child's body, there were curved claw marks on the child's chest, small ruptures of the blood vessels in the child's face, and 13 distinct hemorrhagic injuries to the child's skull. Tabitha's live-in boyfriend, Scott English, admitted to causing the child's injuries. Authorities tried and convicted Tabitha of the child's murder before a Henry County jury under a theory that she should have known that Scott was capable of killing the child. Judge Jay M. Hanson sentenced Tabitha to 36 years in prison. In 1999, the Illinois Appellate Court for the Third District affirmed Tabitha's conviction and sentence, but in October 2002, the Illinois Supreme Court reversed the conviction and held that "a person cannot be convicted of murder on the basis that what they should have known what someone else would do—but only on the basis of what they actually knew." According to the Court, "The evidence simply does not support the inference that Jami was the victim of an on-going pattern of abuse that the mother knew about and sanctioned." When officials released Tabitha from the Lincoln Correctional Center just before Christmas 2002, she had served six and half years in prison. A jury found Scott guilty of first-degree felony murder, aggravated battery of a child, and sentenced to life in prison.

With the help of the Illinois Innocence Project at the University of Illinois in Springfield, officials exonerated Julie Rea Harper in March 2002 for the October 1997 pre-dawn stabbing death of her 10-year-old son Joel Kirkpatrick as he slept in his bed in her Lawrenceville home. Joel had been stabbed 12 times. Julie testified that after being awakened by screams from her son's room, she encountered and fought off an intruder who fled on foot. The prosecution claimed that Julie was the only person in the house that she more likely killed her son as a result of a bitter custody battle with the child's father. A jury found Julie guilty of her son's murder and Lawrence County Circuit Court Judge Robert M. Hopkins sentenced her to 65 years in prison in March 2002. The Illinois Court of Appeals vacated Rea's murder conviction and prison sentence in 2004 because the trial court allowed special prosecutor Ed Parkinson to try the case over defense objections who had no authority to try the case. The court remanded the case for a new trial and a Clinton County jury acquitted Rea of the killing in 2006 after the actual killer, Illinois death row inmate and serial killer Tommy Lynn Sells, confessed to a several murders across several states. His crimes included killing several children, among them the decapitation and sexual assault of an unidentified girl about eight to 10 years old whose body officials found in the basement of an abandoned building. In a true-crime book about Sells written by Diane Fanning, Sells revealed to the author that he killed the boy in retaliation for Julie's rude treatment of Sells in a chance encounter in a convenience store. Officials exonerated Julie after she spent two years in prison for a crime she did not commit. The Illinois Court of Claims awarded Julie nearly $90,000 in compensation and a Certificate of Innocence in 2010.

The child murder case against Patricia Stallings is unusual because it was prosecuting attorney, George B. McElroy III, who sought justice for Patricia in the death of her 5-month-old son Ryan. In July 1989, Patricia took Ryan to the emergency room at Cardinal Glennon Hospital after finding him lethargic, unable to keep food down, and his breathing grew laborious. The emergency room physician performed several tests and found that Ryan had extremely high levels of ethylene glycol, a chemical found in antifreeze. After medical personnel discharged Ryan, the Missouri Division of Family Services immediately placed Ryan in foster care where he remained throughout the summer. Officials permitted Patricia to visit Ryan in September and during the supervised visitation, she fed Ryan a bottle. Ryan again became ill requiring hospitalization. Police later arrested Patricia and charged her with Ryan's murder after he died from allegedly ingesting ethylene glycol found in the bottle Patricia gave him during her visit. An investigation of the Stallings house discovered a gallon of antifreeze in the basement. McElroy grew troubled after news reports surfaced that Patricia's second baby; she was pregnant at the time of her imprisonment, suffered from a rare metabolic disease known as Methylmalonic Acidemia (MMA). McElroy contacted medical experts that confirmed through an autopsy that Ryan undoubtedly had the same disease but that Patricia most likely poisoned Ryan since no other explanation accounted for the elevated levels of ethylene glycol in the child's system. McElroy prosecuted the case against Patricia, a Jefferson County jury found her guilty of Ryan's death, and Circuit Court Judge Gary P. Kramer sentenced Patricia to life in prison. Several months after the trial, McElroy filed a motion with the court seeking a new trial for Patricia that the judge granted based upon new evidence in the case. McElroy apparently had consulted with renowned biochemists and molecular biologists that performed tests on Ryan's blood samples. McElroy contacted Dr. Piero Rinaldo, a renowned geneticist at Yale University, who concurred with other experts that Ryan died from MMA and not ethylene glycol poisoning. The lack of sophistication of the tests previously performed on the blood samples astounded Dr. Rinaldo. He found that the bottle used to feed Ryan did not contain traces of ethylene glycol, and that the treatment Ryan received at the hospital was grossly inappropriate for a child with MMA that actually furthered the child's death by giving Ryan an ethanol drip that caused high concentrations of brain crystals. Authorities released Patricia in September 1991 after she spent a year in prison. But not for the state's prosecutor, George McElroy, it is likely that Patricia would still be serving her life sentence. Patricia settled a multi-million dollar lawsuit against the labs and hospital in 1993.

One of the more outrageous cases of child murder involved the Choctaw Three—Victoria Bell Banks, her estranged husband Medell Banks, Jr., and Victoria's sister, Dianne Bell Tucker. All three persons are poor, black, and severely mentally challenged. Victoria has an IQ of 40 and dropped out of special education in the ninth grade to have the first of six children, for instance. It seems that Victoria feigned a pregnancy while incarcerated in the Choctaw County jail in Butler, Alabama, in October 1998 to garner an early release from a prison sentence. That conviction resulted in a 15-year sentence for physical and sexual violence toward her 11-year-old daughter whom she helped her boyfriend, George Bonner, rape. In February 1999, a jail physician examined Victoria and claimed she heard a fetal heartbeat. Victoria visited the same physician a month later and again the physician claimed the presence of a fetal heartbeat. Victoria told the sheriff that she wanted to be released from jail to have the baby and threatened litigation since she was not receiving prenatal care in jail. The county sheriff released Victoria in May 1999 and she returned to Butler and her job in a chicken processing plant. In August of the same year, the sheriff saw Victoria in town and asked about the baby. Victoria said she had lost the baby through a miscarriage. Troubled by the events, the sheriff took Victoria to the same physician who examined her while in jail where a nurse determined there was no physical evidence that Victoria had ever been pregnant. A few days later police took Victoria, Medell, and Dianne into custody to investigate what had happened to the baby. The three admitted that Victoria had fabricated the pregnancy as a ruse to get out of jail. They also explained that Victoria could not possibly have been pregnant since four years earlier Victoria had a tubal ligation in 1995. Nevertheless, after extensive and prolonged police interrogations without the presence of defense counsel, all three confessed to police that they had participated in the baby's killing and capital murder indictments followed in September. Threatened with the death penalty if convicted, police eventually pressured all three defendants to plead guilty to manslaughter. In 2000, Circuit Court Judge Lee McPhearson sentenced Victoria and Dianne to 15 years in prison and gave the same sentence to Medell in 2001.

Court appointed lawyers appealed Medell's conviction and prison sentence to the Alabama Court of Criminal Appeals in 2002. As part of the appeal, attorneys solicited a nationally renowned fertility expert to examine Victoria and found that she indeed had a tubal ligation, that she was sterile, and that "it was impossible for her to naturally conceive a child." As one commentator pointed out, "all three defendants were the innocent victims of a wrongful prosecution for the killing of a child that never existed." The Court of Appeals described the prosecution as a "manifest injustice" and reversed Judge McPhearson's initial rejection of Medell's motion to withdraw his guilty plea and requested a new trial. Officials released Victoria and Dianne from prison after they pleaded guilty to manslaughter, but Medell remained in prison until January 2003. Hans Sherrer aptly described the prosecution of the Choctaw Three as the result of the "vindictiveness of a petty small town prosecutor luxuriating in the limelight of national press attention for the one and only time it will occur in his lifetime."[40]

Merla Walpole and her common law husband Antonio Rivera were a poor Latino couple. Unable to care for their three-year-old daughter Judy who was seriously ill, the couple abandoned the child at a San Francisco gas station in 1965 hoping that someone would provide the care Judy needed. An Alameda County court tried and convicted Merla and Antonio for second-degree murder for killing the child in 1973 after authorities had found the skeletal remains of a young girl in a shallow grave close to where the couple had once lived. Just prior to sentencing, Judge Thomas M. Haldorsen reversed the convictions on a technicality and ordered a new trial. The trial judge also directed law enforcement to investigate the defendants' claim concerning the child. During retrial, San Bernardino District Attorney Investigator Timothy Martin found the child alive in San Francisco. Then 13, Judy Rivera strongly resembled her parents and blood tests and comparisons of bone formations confirmed that Judy was their daughter. Prosecutors dropped the charges in 1975. Authorities never identified the remains of the young girl found in the shallow grave.

Shaken Baby Syndrome

In 1996, a Dane County District Court jury convicted Audrey Edmunds for the death of 7-month-old Natalie Beard based on the "Shaken Baby Syndrome." Audrey was Natalie's care provider in Waunakee, Wisconsin, when the child's mother took their baby to Audrey' house early one morning in October 1995. Audrey had put the child in a bedroom with a bottle, and when she went to check on Natalie about a half-hour later Audrey found the child limp and unresponsive. She called emergency personnel who flew the child to University Hospital but doctors were unable to save the child and she died later that evening. Audrey denied shaking or striking Natalie, and claimed that Natalie's parents, Tom and Cindy Beard, must have injured the child. The court sentenced Audrey to 18 years in prison. The Court of Appeals affirmed the conviction in 1999, and the U.S. Court of Appeals denied Audrey' habeas corpus petition in 2002. Audrey had served nearly 11 years of her sentence when the Court of Appeals again reviewed her case and reversed her conviction arguing "a significant and legitimate debate in the medical community has developed in the past 10 years over whether infants can be fatally injured through shaking alone, whether an infant may suffer head trauma and yet experience a significant lucid interval prior to death, and whether other causes may mimic the symptoms traditionally viewed as indicating shaken baby or shaken impact syndrome."[41] To the court, the new medical testimony presented alternate theories explaining Natalie's injuries. Authorities released Audrey on bail in February 2008. After the Wisconsin Supreme Court decided not to disturb the lower court's decision to overturn Audrey's conviction, state attorneys declared in July 2008 that they would not retry the case and dismissed the charges against Audrey.

Teresa Engberg-Lehmer and her husband Joel Lehmer were so poor they could not afford a telephone or crib for their 3-month-old son, Jonathan. After feeding Jonathan on an early evening in April 1997, Teresa Engberg-Lehmer put him to sleep on a blanket on the floor in a back bedroom of their apartment in Council Bluffs, Iowa. The Lehmer's went to bed later that evening and in the morning when Teresa went to check on Jonathan and give him a bottle, she found him cold, unresponsive, and not breathing. Since she had no telephone, Teresa rushed to a neighbor's apartment and asked her to call 911. Emergency workers took Jonathan to Jennie Edmunson Hospital's emergency room where medical staff pronounced the child dead. State medical examiner, Thomas Bennett, performed an autopsy and declared Jonathan's death a homicide claiming that the cause of death was Shaken Baby Syndrome. Pottawattamie County District Attorney Rick Crowl charged Teresa and Joel with first-degree murder though both insisted they never shook the baby. In October 1997, Judge Timothy O'Grady of the Iowa District Court in Pottawattamie sentenced both Teresa and Joel to 15 years in prison after they pleaded guilty to manslaughter.

In November 1997, Teresa wrote to attorney Stephen Brennecke asking him to examine the case. Brennecke had successfully defended another person involving Shaken Baby Syndrome in March of that same year. In the other case, Brennecke uncovered medical evidence that the child died of a skull fracture inflicted days before the child's death. Brennecke sent the Jonathan's case file to Peter Stephens, an Iowa City pathologist, who determined there was no evidence of Shaken Baby Syndrome and that Jonathan had died from Sudden Infant Death Syndrome. In response to Dr. Stephens' findings, Pottawattamie County Attorney Rick Crowl sent Jonathan's file to Jerry Jones, an Omaha forensic pathologist who agreed that there was no evidence the baby had been shaken. In September 1998, Rick Crowl requested a hearing with Iowa District Court Judge Timothy O'Grady. With attorneys for Joel and Teresa present at the hearing, Dr. Jones testified to his findings and Crowl informed Judge O'Grady that Dr. Stephens concurred with Dr. Jones' findings. Judge O'Grady granted the state's motion to vacate the convictions and officials soon released Teresa and Joel from prison. It is noteworthy that Bennett resigned as medical examiner two weeks after the couple pled guilty in October 1997 amid an investigation of the administration of his office. Meanwhile, at least two other Shaken Baby Syndrome diagnoses made by Bennett had come under fire. In one case, the prosecution, faced with contradictory evidence, declined to bring charges. In the other, prosecutors dismissed the case almost immediately after the trial began.

Melonie Ware provided day-care in her home in Decatur, Georgia. In March 2004, Melonie was babysitting 9-month-old Jaden Paige when the child became unresponsive. She summoned medical personnel who took the child to a nearby hospital where the child died. Police arrested Melonie, DeKalb County prosecuted her for young Jaden's death and a jury found her guilty of felony murder while in the commission of cruelty to a child. The trial court imposed a sentence of life imprisonment. A local forensic pathologist testified at Melonie's trial that Jaden had died from "Shaken Baby Syndrome" that damaged his brain. After a protracted legal battle based upon ineffective legal representation, Melonie won reversal of her murder conviction and a new trial in 2009 wherein medical evidence suggested that shaking had nothing to do with the child's death. Two prominent physicians testified that Jaden had died from complications of sickle cell anemia. After five years in prison, a second jury acquitted Melonie of the murder. Melonie's case drew attention in investigations by *National Public Radio*, *ProPublica*, and *PBS Frontline* on how medical examiners and coroners frequently mishandle cases of infant and child deaths. Though Melonie won an acquittal for the Jaden's death, her life remains deeply troubled—her husband spent more than $700,000 on her defense, selling off and mortgaging real estate acquired over decades and Melonie has been unable to find employment largely because potential employers are frightened off by her time in jail.

In mid–1993, authorities charged Mary, a well-liked and deeply religious woman, with the first-degree murder of 11-month-old Melissa Mathes after the child died while in her care. Mary was Melissa's babysitter. Mary had picked up Melissa in the late morning from her mother's home and drove to Mary's house where she cared for the child. Mary called emergency services when Melissa stopped breathing. Paramedics revived her and rushed to a nearby hospital, but she died the following day. An autopsy showed that Melissa had sustained severe head injuries, including a massive skull fracture. Physicians detected a fresh bruise on the front of Melissa's brain and new bleeding around the brain and in her eyes. They claimed that the older injuries were not the cause of death and that the more recent injuries showed she had been shaken to death—Shaken Baby Syndrome.

Mary's first trial for Melissa's death ended in a mistrial because the jury was deadlocked on a verdict. In 1994, however, Mary Weaver waived her right to a jury trial and officials tried her case a second time before Marshall County District Court Judge Carl E. Peterson. Judge Peterson found Mary guilty of murder and sentenced her to life in prison without parole. The Iowa Court of Appeals upheld the conviction in 1995. In early 1996, Marshall County District Judge Allan Goode granted Mary a new trial based upon new evidence from Tessia's co-workers that Melissa had hit her head on a coffee table rather than a padded recliner and knocked the child unconscious. Expert medical testimony also showed that the child's "vulnerable neurological state on the morning she was picked up combined with the trauma described by the new witnesses offered a reasonable medical explanation for the acute conditions that precipitated the child's death." In early 1997, a jury acquitted Mary at a third trial. Authorities investigated state medical examiner, Thomas Bennett, who resigned from his position after several of his cases turned on dubious evidence. It was his claim that Melissa died from violent shaking and slamming the child's head against a hard surface. The state dropped charges in two other of Bennett's cases as a result of the erroneous findings provided in Mary's murder case.

Medical Neglect Cases Motived by Religion

In the 1989 case of Christine Hermanson, a Sarasota County jury in Florida convicted Christine and her co-defendant husband, William Hermanson, of third-degree murder when their seven-year-old daughter, Amy Hermanson, died from untreated juvenile diabetes. The trial judge sentenced the Hermansons to a 4-year suspended prison sentence and ordered the couple to serve 15 years' probation. In 1990, the Court of Appeals affirmed the lower courts conviction and sentence, but in 1992 the Florida Supreme Court quashed the decision of the district court of appeals and remanded the case with directions that the trial court's adjudication of guilt and sentence be vacated and the Hermansons discharged. The Supreme Court concluded that the state statute relied upon for the conviction failed to clearly indicate the point at which a parent's reliance on his or her religious beliefs in the treatment of his or her children becomes criminal conduct.

In April 1986, two-and-one-half-year-old Robyn Twitchell died from peritonitis caused by the perforation the bowel that was obstructed from an anomaly known as Merkel's diverticulum. Robyn was extremely ill for about five days before his death. Surgery could have corrected the condition, but young Robyn's parents David and Ginger Twitchell did not seek medical attention for Robyn. As practicing Christian Scientists who grew up in Christian Science families, the Twitchell's believed in healing by spiritual treatment and relied upon a church publication outlining the legal rights and obligations of Christian Scientists in Massachusetts. The publication essentially stated that remedial treatment by spiritual means satisfies state parental obligations not to neglect a child or to provide a child with physical care. Suffolk County prosecutors won a manslaughter conviction against David and Ginger Twitchell in 1990 for Robyn's death and the trial judge sentenced to couple to 10 years' probation. In 1993, however, the Massachusetts Supreme Judicial Court reversed the conviction and sentence and argued that while the spiritual-treatment provision in the law regarding willful failure and neglect does not shield parents from prosecution from manslaughter if a child dies as a result of the parents' "wanton and reckless" conduct in not seeking medical care, "the Twitchells reasonably believed that they could rely on spiritual treatment without fear of criminal prosecution. This affirmative defense should have been asserted and presented to the jury. Because it was not, there is a substantial risk of a miscarriage of justice in this case, and, therefore, the judgments must be reversed."[42]

Manslaughter

In July 2001, Tayshea Aiwohi, a mother of four, gave birth to her fifth child, Treyson Aiwohi, at Kaiser Moanalua Medical Center. A day after Tayshea and her son's release from the medical center, an ambulance rushed Treyson to Castle Hospital; the child had stopped breathing. Physicians pronounced the child dead from methamphetamine poisoning. Tayshea had admitted to investigators that she had used methamphetamines four days before and on the day of Treyson's birth. Tayshea had a long-standing and well-documented history of substance abuse for which she had received treatment from various programs. Tayshea breast fed her newborn. In October 2003, a grand jury indicted Tayshea for manslaughter in the death of her son, "the first case in Hawaii in which a mother [was] charged with killing her baby by smoking ice while pregnant."[43] Tayshea plead no contest to the charge and a judge sentenced her to 10 years' probation. She appealed the case to the Hawaiian Supreme Court. In November 2005, the court overturned her conviction ruling that she had not committed a crime by her behavior prior to her child's birth because a fetus is not a person, and therefore she could not have committed manslaughter.

In 1997, a Hillsborough County jury in Florida convicted 20-year-old Nissa Baillie and her two co-defendants, 19-year-old Christopher Cole and Thomas Miller, of manslaughter for the deaths of three 18-year-old men, Kevin Farr, Brian Hernandez and Randall White, when a semi-truck broadsided the car in which they were riding. The car carrying the young men failed to stop at the intersection because the three defendants ostensibly had stolen the stop sign from the intersection. The eight-ton truck had the right of way, which wasn't known by the oncoming car because the stop sign was lying out of sight beside the road. Police arrested in Baillie, Cole and Thomas Miller April 1996 and charged them with three counts of manslaughter and one count of grand theft. The grand theft charge was based on the accusation the three had stolen almost two dozen signs in the area and had taken down the stop sign at the fatal intersection. Nissa and her co-defendants admitted to police they had stolen some signs and thrown some in a creek, but not the stop sign at the intersection where the victims were killed. During the trial of Nissa and her co-defendants in the spring of 1997 the prosecution introduced a total of 21 signs recovered either in the creek or the trailer where the defendants lived. Larry Jarrard, a friend of the defendants, gave false testimony at the trial. A defense expert testified that he examined the stop sign post and believed something pushed it over. A man who was driving to a luncheon the day before the crash testified that as he pulled up to the intersection, he saw a semi-truck backing up across the road toward the sign. He said that when he came back after lunch, the stop sign was on the ground. Nissa and her co-defendants were convicted by the jury and Judge Anderson Mitcham sentenced the three defendants to 15-year prison terms. All three remained free on bond pending their appeal. In 1998, the three defendants filed a post-conviction motion for a new trial based on new witness evidence that the stop sign was down days before the accident. During an evidentiary hearing several witnesses testified that before the defendant's trial they reported to either Hillsborough County Sheriff's detectives or the prosecution that the sign had been down for days. One witness who said that after she told a prosecutor about the sign being down the state's attorney, Leland Baldwin, told her she intended to "burn their [the defendant's] ass." There were also claims that the prosecutor intimidated witnesses, failed to turnover exculpatory evidence to the defense, and that state investigators manipulated evidence. The motion for a new trial was denied by the trial court. In 2001 the Florida Court of Appeals ruled on the defendant's direct appeal and reversed the manslaughter convictions of all three defendants based on the prosecution misconduct of two prejudicial errors during closing arguments. The Hillsborough County District Attorney's Office dismissed the manslaughter charges. For the grand theft convictions the defendants were sentenced to perform community service and the convictions were dismissed after successfully completing their sentences.

In June 1990, a Philadelphia County Commons Pleas Court Judge John Poserina, Jr., convicted 21-year-old Yeidja Bostick of vehicular homicide, aggravated assault, five counts of recklessly endangering another person and three counts of simple assault and sentenced her to five to 10 years in prison. Yeidja's conviction stemmed from an automobile accident in August 1989 that occurred while state trooper Robert Debellis pursued a stolen Volvo that ran a stop light causing a three-vehicle collision, killing 56-year-old Audrey Fisher and injuring several others including four of her grandchildren. Yeidja was also seriously injured in the accident. The district attorney charged Yeidja with murder, vehicular homicide while under the influence of marijuana, aggravated assault, simple assault, reckless endangerment and receiving stolen property. Debellis who pursued the Volvo, other police officers, civilians and expert witnesses called by the prosecution claimed that Yeidja was driving the car at the time of the collision. Actually, a black man named Robert Hallman was the driver of the car.

In 1991, however, a reporter with the *Philadelphia Inquirer*, David Zucchino, while investigating Debellis' harassment of black motorists' during traffic stops, published an article that seriously challenged the state's case against Yeidja. Zucchino had discovered several witnesses claiming that Hallman was the driver the Volvo and Yeidja was a passenger in the car. None of these witnesses testified at the trial and police never investigated the witnesses' claims though Hallman had a criminal record of stealing cars. Other witnesses came forward claiming that Yeidja was in the passenger seat at the time of the accident. This and other evidence prompted Judge Poserina to conduct an evidentiary hearing in 1992 that eventually led to him vacating Yeidja's conviction and prison sentence and granting her a new trial. In December 1993, Common Pleas Judge Carolyn Temin acquitted Bostick of all the charges.

In March 1994, a car carrying three people went out of control on a rural highway in Lehigh County, Pennsylvania, and rolled some 50 feet and came to rest on its roof on top of some boulders. Rescue workers found 33-year-old Randy Schnyder dead and partially ejected from the vehicle. His live-in girlfriend, 35-year-old Judith Fritz, and Schnyder's live-in girlfriend, 30-year-old Robert Pribila, were injured, but survived. Shortly thereafter, police charged Judith with vehicular homicide, drunk driving, possession of cocaine, which police found in her purse. At her trial in May 1995, a pathologist testified for the prosecution that based on the position of Schnyder, Fritz and Pribila when authorities arrived at the scene, he believed that Judith was driving, Schnyder was a passenger in the front seat and Pribila was in the back seat. Pribila also testified that Judith was driving the ill-fated car. Judith testified and claimed that Schnyder was the driver and she was riding in the front passenger seat. She admitted that the three had been to three taverns that night. She admitted she had four drinks and had used cocaine, but said the cocaine found in her purse belonged to Schnyder. A jury convicted Judith of vehicular homicide, driving under the influence and, because she was the driver, possession of the cocaine in the vehicle. The trial court sentenced her to three years in prison, but allowed her to remain free on bond while the case was appealed.

Attorney Frederick Fanelli took on Judith's appeal and when reviewing the trial record discovered that Judith's trial attorney, a part-time pastor who handled divorce cases, had not consulted an expert to review the state pathologist's opinion on who was driving. Fanelli retrained an expert who, after studying photographs and other evidence of the accident, determined that Judith was not driving the car, rather the driver was Schnyder. Fanelli also located a witness that claimed that Schnyder got into the driver's seat when he saw the three co-defendants leave a bar not long before the accident. Fanelli then filed a motion for a new trial based on the new evidence of the expert and eyewitness. The court granted the new trial, the state appealed, but in August 1996, the Pennsylvania Superior Court upheld the decision and remanded the case for a new trial. A jury at the retrial acquitted Judith of the manslaughter charge in February 1997.

In July 1993, young teenager Jaylene Jeffries shot and killed David Ogden on the Lummi Indian Reservation on the northern coast of Washington state. After her arrest, Jaylene told police she shot and killed Ogden out of fear that she and her mother, Ernestine James, were in physical danger after Ogden had assaulted Jaylene's boyfriend in a drunken rage. David Ogden had a long history of violent assaults and often raped Ernestine if she refused to have sex with him when he was drunk. A state court convicted Jaylene of second-degree murder and sentenced her to a term of years in prison. In September 1995, a U.S. District Court tried and convicted Ernestine of aiding and abetting in Ogden's manslaughter since she provided the gun with which Jaylene had shot and killed Ogden. Judge William L. Dwyer sentenced Ernestine to five years' probation. In 1998, a three-judge panel of the U.S. Court of Appeals for the Ninth Circuit upheld the conviction. A year later, the Court of Appeals granted Ernestine's attorney's motion for the entire appeals court to rehear the case and the "en banc" panel reversed James's conviction arguing that the trial judge had erred on the admissibility of evidence, after which the prosecution dismissed the charges.

In July 2014, the Court of Appeals of Kentucky vacated Susan Jean King's guilty plea for the 1998 murder of her on-again, off-again boyfriend Kyle "Deanie" Breeden and ordered a new trial. The court held that Susan was entitled to a new trial based upon evidence of actual innocence. In a unanimous decision of the Court, Justice Jeff S. Taylor wrote, "In a society whose foundations were built upon the guarantee of justice to every citizen, the conviction of an innocent person represents a serious and egregious violation of such guarantee."[44] The Court dismissed the charges in October 2014. Spencer County Circuit Judge Charles R. Hickman had found Susan guilty of second-degree manslaughter after she had entered an Alford plea wherein she admitted guilt by conceding that the prosecution had sufficient proof to obtain a conviction. Otherwise, Susan faced life in prison if convicted of murder. Judge Hickman sentenced Susan to 10-years imprisonment that made her eligible for parole in two years though she spent nearly six years in prison for a crime she did not commit. Authorities released Susan in November 2012.

It seems that in November 1998, a fisherman found Breeden's body in the Kentucky River with two gunshots to the head made with .22 caliber gun and his legs bound with guitar amplifier cord. The murder remained unsolved until 2006 when Kentucky State Police Detective Todd

Harwood picked it up as a cold case. Within three weeks Harwood identified King as the chief suspect. The Kentucky Innocence Project investigated her case after Linda A. Smith, a supervising attorney of the project, concluded that it would have been physically impossible for Susan to have thrown Breeden's body off a bridge into the Kentucky River given that Susan has only one leg, is wheelchair bound and weighed 97 pounds at the time of the offense. Susan lost her leg in 1993 following a vehicle accident for which she was convicted of drunken driving. Forensic analyses of the several reasons that Detective Harwood took to a grand jury showing that Susan committed the murder proved untruthful. Later, while interrogating Richard Jarrell about an attempted murder charge for firing a shotgun into the home of a confidential police informant, Jarrell admitted to Harwood that he killed Breeden as well as committing two other murders in return for leniency for his brother who was facing federal drug charges in Arkansas.

The U.S. Army prosecuted and convicted Janine Kirby, wife of Army sergeant Geoffrey Kirby, for killing her 4-month-old infant daughter Katie in July 1983. Janine was an "excellent and caring mother" but claimed that she must have done something to her daughter—"there's no other way about it." The couple had taken Katie to the Dortmund British Military Hospital near Dortmund, Germany, after the child fell seriously ill and died in the hospital. Military police arrested Janine shortly thereafter. A military trial court sentenced Janine to 9-months in prison. The Court Martial Appeal Court in London overturned Janine's conviction in 1994 after Dr. Ian Turnbull, a consultant radio neurologist, established that the child's skull fracture occurred after the child left her mother's care. According to Dr. Turnbull, the skull injury occurred after hospital personnel admitted the child or in the ambulance that transferred the child to a specialist clinic. During her decade-long ordeal, Janine had two other children that social workers took control over immediate after their births and for years allowed the Kirbys only limited access to their children. Janine commented to reporters in 1994, "The majority of our married life has been spent in proving to others my innocence and our suitability and ability to care for our children. We hope we can now resume a normal life with our family and children."[45]

In May 2011, Sierra Nichole Rigel went on trial as a juvenile before Judge Cynthia Beaman without a jury for negligent homicide. The case stems from an automobile accident in which Sierra's Ford Excursion crossed the center divider of Highway 101 in Curry County, Oregon, and struck a motorcycle driven by Danny Michael Nudo, who was killed. Sierra was an honor student who was driving within the speed limit and had no alcohol or other illicit substances in her system. There was also no evidence that Rigel was distracted by being on a cell phone. At trial, the prosecution presented a transcript of a recorded interview Sierra gave to a police officer shortly after the crash wherein Sierra said, "So I—I knew I should have pulled off, so I—I was waiting for somewhere to sleep, but I couldn't (inaudible)." Judge Beaman convicted Sierra, noting that Sierra knew she should have pulled off the road but did not. "Those statements and … the fact that you're a bright person and knew that you needed to pull over and takes naps because you could possibly fall asleep … it's clear to me that you were aware of the risk and you consciously disregarded the risk," the judge declared. Judge Beaman sentenced Sierra to 100 hours of community service and her driver's license was revoked for life. In January 2014, the Oregon Court of Appeals reversed the conviction and dismissed the case. The Court admitted it had listened to the audio of Sierra's statement to police and determined that the transcript was incorrect. That is, the prosecution relied on a faulty understanding of what constituted reckless conduct sufficient to qualify as negligent homicide and the correct statement was exculpatory. Where the transcript quoted Sierra as saying, "So I—I knew I should have pulled off, so I—I was waiting for somewhere to sleep," the audio revealed that what she actually said was "I knew I shouldn't put it off, so I—I was looking for somewhere to—to sleep. But I couldn't find a turnoff." The Court held that Sierra's actual statement was not evidence of her disregarding a known risk and thus there was insufficient evidence to support a conviction for negligent homicide; Sierra had acted with reasonable care as required by the law because as soon as she felt drowsy she began to look for a place to pull off the highway to rest.

A woman walking with her daughter and dog on a Saturday morning in May 2002 found the naked body of 25-year-old woman named Jerri Lee Williams in a city park in north Portland, Oregon. An autopsy concluded that Williams had died by strangulation. Later that year, police arrested 37-year-old Lisa Marie Roberts, Williams' lesbian lover, and charged her with murder, assault, harassment and menacing. The state's attorney claimed that Williams was the victim of a volatile love triangle between Lisa and another woman, Terry Collins, with whom Lisa had had an eight-year relationship. Lisa had a history of domestic violence against Terry who had a history of prostitution and drug abuse. The prosecution maintained that Lisa strangled Williams, put her body in a sleeping bag with a pillowcase over her head and took the body to the Kelley Point Park in a pickup truck. Multnomah County District Attorney Rod Underhill declared that he had irrefutable evidence that Lisa used her cellphone within three miles of the park on the morning of the murder. Lisa denied she was near the park and said the call was made to a friend whom she was going to visit that morning. The prosecution also claimed that after police arrested Lisa and while she was being held in jail pending trial, Sarah Ater, a jail inmate, told authorities that Lisa solicited her to find someone to kill a man. "Ater told police that Roberts claimed the man was her boyfriend and that he had actually killed Williams." Lisa's attorney, William Brennan, convinced her that the state had a strong case against her and that a jury would probably convict her. Lisa pleaded guilty to manslaughter to avoid a life sentence and accepted a 15-year prison sentence.

In 2009, federal public defenders took Lisa's case and filled a writ of habeas corpus. The attorneys brought in technical experts who claimed that "it would have been virtually impossible to pinpoint a cellphone's location based on a signal logged by a single cell tower." The legal team also had experts retest DNA found on Williams' body that prosecutors never disclosed to Lisa's defense attorney. The analysis revealed that besides Lisa's DNA, several men's DNA showed up on the body that could have been Williams' murderer. One of those men discovered in a database search was Brian Lee Tuckenberry, a state inmate serving a prison term for sexual assault. Apparently, Tuckenberry had worked as a pimp and had a penchant for choking women while he having sex with them and had unsuccessfully attempted to recruit Williams. In April 2014, U.S. District Court Judge Malcolm Marsh granted the habeas petition and vacated Roberts's guilty plea and ordered a new trial. The judge ruled that William Brennan was constitutionally ineffective in his defense of Lisa because he failed to investigate the cell tower evidence and the DNA evidence identifying a man convicted of unrelated crimes as the likely killer. The judge held: "Despite the critical importance of the cell tower evidence, (Roberts's attorney) failed to take reasonable steps to collect the relevant data and independently evaluate the reliability of the (prosecution's) analysis before advising his client to plead guilty to manslaughter." Judge Marsh found the evidence against Tuckenberry "compelling." The District Attorney's Office wrote to Judge Marsh stating that although their re-investigation of the case led them to conclude that Lisa was guilty, they would not seek to further prosecute her because she was near the end of her sentence. In late May 2014, officials released Lisa from prison. The state's attorney dismissed charges against Lisa in June 2014 and has still not pursued a legal case against Tuckenberry for Williams' murder.

Concluding Remarks

The foregoing puts forth narratives on women wrongly convicted in potentially capital crimes. The chronicles involve false convictions of women for predatory murders, spousal murders, child murders and manslaughter. At times, child deaths occasioned Shaken Baby Syndrome or from medical neglect based upon religious beliefs. In other cases, falsely convicted women had actually committed no crime or the evidence in a particular case could not support a conviction. Beginning with the miscarriages of justice for women convicted of witchcraft in the 17th century, there is a history of justice administrators invoking blameworthiness to women innocent of crimes. The record is scattered, thus making unearthing female false convictions throughout criminal justice history difficult. For those cases where there is adequate documentation, the historical record reveals that several factors account for wrongful female convictions of crimes they did not commit: false witness identification, false confessions, perjury, false forensic evidence, official misconduct of police and state prosecutors, and inadequate legal representation. Regarding the race of wrongly convicted women, white women are represented among the falsely convicted more than women of color.

> "When the majority of death penalty sentences lead to reversal, the entire system itself must be called into question."[1]

7

Judicial Reversals of Capital Convictions

The federal Constitution does not provide a right to appeal in capital convictions. In federal courts, a criminal defendant had no right to appellate review until 1879. Scholars explain that the right to appeal state court decisions was largely limited until the late–1800s, but by the 20th century, the right to appeal lower court decisions in criminal cases was ubiquitous in federal and state criminal justice systems providing the right through statutory provisions and state constitutions. The U.S. Supreme Court argued in 1894 that states were not required to provide appellate review of state convictions. Once provided, however, guarantees of due process and equal protection of the law govern appellate review of capital convictions. Most states did not require automatic review of capital sentences until the 1930s. California, for instance, introduced automatic appeals in capital cases in 1935 and Alabama began the practice in 1943. Utah and most other death penalty states did not introduce automatic appeals until the U.S. Supreme Court's 1976 decision in *Gregg v. Georgia*. The Court in *Gregg*, however, did not require appellate review of capital cases, "it merely explained that it was one of a variety of factors that could be utilized to combat arbitrariness."[2] Though many jurisdictions afforded the opportunity for capital defendants to appeal, legal scholar Jack Greenberg explains that many defendants did not appeal capital cases because they were too poor to afford legal services—"virtually all capital defendants have been poor and free legal services have not been readily available."[3] What's more, it was not until the late 1960s that capital defendants began seeking federal habeas corpus review of their cases when the U.S. Supreme Court enforced rights of the criminally accused against states through incorporation of the Fourteenth Amendment. "Only then did capital convictions and sentences first begin to come under careful, systematic scrutiny in state courts, lower federal courts, and the U.S. Supreme Court."[4] It is not surprising, then, that the historical record reveals so few female capital cases subjected to appellate review before the late 20th century.

Table 7-1 identifies 110 confirmed cases of condemned women where appellate courts have reversed or commuted their death sentences since the 1830s. The table lists the name of female defendants, the defendant's age at the time of committing the crime, the offense for which trials courts convicted the women and sentenced them to death, the female defendants' race, the year of their original death sentence, the state and county of conviction, the year of their judicial reversal, the race and sex of their victims, and the reason for the judicial reversals. The inventory of female death sentence reversals is by no means exhaustive; with further research into appellate reversals, more cases should complement the inventory. In any event, the registry affords researchers an occasion to peer into the historical record of appellate review of female capital cases.

Historically, appeals courts have reversed the sentences of condemned white women (70 percent) far more often than condemned black women (26 percent) and other nonwhite women

Table 7-1: Judicial Reversals of Female Death Sentences

Name of Offender	Age at Crime	Criminal Offense	Race of Offender	Initial Sentencing Date	State of Sentencing	County of Sentencing	Year of Judicial Reversal	Race & Sex of Victim(s)	Reasons for Judicial Reversal
Shonda Nicole Johnson	28	Predatory Murder	White	22 OCT 1999	Alabama	Walker	2014	White male	Unknown
Debra Jeanene Bracewell	17	Predatory Murder	White	17 MAY 1978	Alabama	Covington	1978	White male	Procedural Error
Patricia Ann Thomas Jackson	32	Predatory Murder	Black	28 FEB 1981	Alabama	Tuscaloosa	1990	Black female	Prosecutorial Misconduct
Judy M. Haney	32	Spousal Murder	White	18 NOV 1988	Alabama	Talladega	1997	White male	Procedural Error
Altion Maxine Walker	—	Predatory Murder	White	17 NOV 1988	Alabama	Talladega	1992	White male	Prosecutorial Misconduct
Louise Harris*	25	Spousal Murder	Black	JUL 1989	Alabama	Montgomery	2011	Black male	Ineffective Trial Counsel
Patricia Hendrickson	40	Spousal Murder	White	10 MAR 1983	Arkansas	Clark	1984	White male	Police Misconduct
Mollie King	25	Spousal Murder	Black	24 JAN 1896	Arkansas	Sebastian	1897	White male	Procedural Error
Mary A. Kettenring	—	Spousal Murder	White	30 JUN 1894	Arkansas	Sebastian	1898	White female	Unknown
Doris Ann Carlson*	34	Predatory Murder	White	31 MAR 2000	Arizona	Maricopa	2002	White male	Procedural Error
Laura D. Fair	—	Predatory Murder	White	NOV 1870	California	San Francisco	1872	White male	Evidentiary Problems
Mabel Glenn	51	Spousal Murder	Black	25 OCT 1975	California	Santa Barbara	1979	Black male	Death Penalty Nullification
Marie Elaine Kozeak	22	Predatory Murder	White	4 OCT 1975	California	Riverside	1976	White male	Death Penalty Nullification
Susan Denise Atkins	21	Predatory Murder	White	29 MAR 1971	California	Los Angeles	1972	Tate-LaBianca Murders	Death Penalty Nullification
Leslie Louise Van Housten	20	Predatory Murder	White	29 MAR 1971	California	Los Angeles	1972	Tate-LaBianca Murders	Death Penalty Nullification
Patricia Krenwinkle	21	Predatory Murder	White	29 MAR 1971	California	Los Angeles	1972	Tate-LaBiance Murders	Death Penalty Nullification
Bessie Wakefield	24	Spousal Murder	White	23 JUN 1913	Connecticut	Middlebury	1914	White male	Evidentiary Problems
Amy E. Archer Gilligan	48	Predatory Murder	White	3 MAY 1916	Connecticut	Hartford	1918	White male + 40 others	Procedural Error
Linda Lou Charbonneau	53	Spousal Murder	White	4 JUN 2004	Delaware	Sussex	2006	2 White males	Procedural Error
Carla Ann Caillier*	24	Spousal Murder	White	19 MAR 1987	Florida	Hillsborough	1988	White male	Prosecutorial Misconduct
Dee Dyne Casteel	49	Predatory Murder	White	16 SEP 1987	Florida	Miami-Dade	1990	White male/white female	Prosecutorial Misconduct
Kaysie B. Dudley	24	Predatory Murder	White	27 JAN 1987	Florida	Pinellas	1989	White female	Evidentiary Problems
Deidre Michelle Hunt	20	Predatory Murder	White	13 SEP 1990	Florida	Volusia	1992	White male/white female	Prosecutorial Misconduct
Virginia Gail Larzelere	41	Spousal Murder	White	11 MAY 1993	Florida	Volusia	2005	White male	Ineffective Trial Counsel
Sonia Jacobs	28	Predatory Murder	White	9 OCT 1992	Florida	Broward	1992	2 White males	Confession of actual killer
Andrea Hicks Jackson	25	Predatory Murder	Black	10 FEB 1984	Florida	Duval	1997	Black male	Improper Jury Instructions
Irene Leverne Jackson	43	Spousal Murder	Black	24 APR 1962	Florida	Pasco	1964	Black male	Procedural Error
Ruby McCollum	43	Predatory Murder	Black	20 DEC 1952	Florida	Live Oak	1954	White male	Procedural Error
Marie Dean Arrington	35	Predatory Murder	Black	12 JUN 1968	Florida	Lake	1972	White female	Death Penalty Nullification
Rebecca Akins Machetti (Smith)	35	Predatory Murder	White	30 JAN 1975	Georgia	Bibb	1983	White male/white female	Jury Selection Bias
Emma Ruth Cunningham	27	Predatory Murder	Black	26 OCT 1979	Georgia	Lincoln	1983	White male	Judicial Error
Shirley Tyler	26	Spousal Murder	Black	5 OCT 1979	Georgia	Pike	1985	Black male	Incompetent Trial Counsel
Janice Buttrum	17	Predatory Murder	White	31 SEP 1981	Georgia	Whitfield	1989	White female	Procedural Error
Teresa Faye Whittington	20	Predatory Murder	White	7 MAY 1982	Georgia	Madison	1984	White female	Procedural Error
Martha Ann Johnson (Bowen)	35	Child Murder	White	5 MAY 1990	Georgia	Clayton	1992	2 White males/2 females	Unknown
Karla Yvonne Windsor	28	Predatory Murder	White	28 FEB 1984	Idaho	Canyon	1985	White male	Disproportionate Sentence

*Judicial override case

7. Judicial Reversals of Capital Convictions

Name of Offender	Age at Crime	Criminal Offense	Race of Offender	Initial Sentencing Date	State of Sentencing	County of Sentencing	Year of Judicial Reversal	Race & Sex of Victim(s)	Reasons for Judicial Reversal
Geraldine Smith	42	Predatory Murder	Black	20 FEB 1991	Illinois	Cook	1997	Black female	Disproportionate Sentence
Marilyn Mulero	21	Predatory Murder	Latina	11 NOV 1993	Illinois	Cook	1997	2 Latinos	Evidentiary Problems
Lois Ann Thacker	26	Spousal Murder	White	27 JUN 1985	Indiana	Dubois	1990	White male	Evidentiary Problems
Paula R. Cooper	16	Predatory Murder	Black	11 JUL 1986	Indiana	Superior	1989	Black female	Death Prohibited by Law
Cindy Lou Landress	30	Predatory Murder	White	23 APR 1988	Indiana	Superior	1992	White male	Evidentiary Problems
Angela Jane Johnson	29	Predatory Murder	White	20 DEC 2005	Iowa	Mason City	2012	2 White males & 3 females	Incompetent Trial Counsel
Laverne O'Bryan	43	Spousal Murder	White	12 SEP 1980	Kentucky	Jefferson	1982	White male	Evidentiary Problems
Lafonda Fay Foster	22	Predatory Murder	White	28 APR 1987	Kentucky	Fayette	1991	3 White males/2 females	Evidentiary Problems
Amanda Gutweiler	31	Child Murder	White	30 APR 2002	Louisiana	St. Landry	2006	2 White males/1 female	Faulty forensic evidence
Annette Louise Stebbing	19	Predatory Murder	White	31 AUG 1981	Maryland	Worcester	1985	White female	Disproportionate Sentence
Attina Marie Cannady	17	Predatory Murder	White	23 SEP 1982	Mississippi	Pontotoc	1984	White male	Disproportionate Sentence
Cecilia Ann Williamson	41	Spousal Murder	White	14 MAR 1984	Mississippi	Panola	1987	White male	Procedural Error
Susie Ann Balfour	48	Predatory Murder	Black	14 OCT 1989	Mississippi	Leake	1992	White male	Police Misconduct
Sabrina Butler	17	Child Murder	Black	14 MAR 1990	Mississippi	Lowndes	1995	Black male	False confession/evidence
Vernice Ballenger	46	Predatory Murder	White	13 JAN 1993	Mississippi	Oktibbeha	2000	White female	Faulty jury instructions
Kristi Leigh Fulgham	27	Spousal Murder	White	DEC 2006	Mississippi	Callaway	2010	White male	Evidentiary Problems
Michelle Byrom	42	Spousal Murder	White	NOV 2000	Mississippi	Tishomingo	2014	White male	Judicial misconduct
Slave woman Jane	—	Child Murder	Black	DEC 1830	Missouri	Callaway	1831	Black female	Error in the indictment
Slave woman Fanny	—	Child Murder	Black	SEP 1838	Missouri	Lincoln	1839	2 White males	Procedural error
Anna Nesenhener	—	Spousal Murder	White	JUL 1900	Missouri	Platte	1901	White male	Lack of evidence
Nila Jeanne Wacaser	39	Child Murder	White	31 MAY 1988	Missouri	Pettis	1990	2 White males	Jury selection bias
Virginia A. Twenter	49	Predatory Murder	White	6 JAN 1989	Missouri	Livingston	1990	White male/white female	Ineffective Trial Counsel
Faye Della Copeland	69	Predatory Murder	White	27 APR 1991	Missouri	St. Louis	1999	5+ White males	Evidentiary problems
Maria Isa	46	Child Murder	Brazilian	19 DEC 1991	Missouri	Greene	1993	Palestinian female	Procedural error
Shirley Jo Phillips	52	Predatory Murder	White	6 APR 1992	Missouri	Greene	1997	White female	Prosecutorial misconduct
Sheila Ann Summers	26	Predatory Murder	White	20 DEC 1983	Nevada	Clark	1986	White female	Procedural error
Sandy Lee Murphy	—	Predatory Murder	White	2000	Nevada	Clark	2004	White male	Procedural error
Marie Moore	35	Child Murder	White	19 NOV 1984	New Jersey	Camden	1988	White female	Legal insanity of offender
Leslie Ann Nelson	43	Predatory Murder	White	30 MAR 2001	New Jersey	Camden	2002	White male	Prosecutorial misconduct
Cynthia Buffum	40	Child Murder	White	1913	New York	Albany	1914	2 White males/ female	Prosecutorial misconduct
Mary Teresa (Koehler) Hartung	—	Spousal Murder	White	JUN 1858	New York	Albany	1860	White male	No execution method
Maria Barbella (Barberi)	22	Predatory Murder	Italian	26 APR 1895	New York	Edgecomb	1896	Italian male	Evidence & jury instruction
Mamie Lee Ward	21	Predatory Murder	Black	19 JUL 1973	N. Carolina	Anson	1976	Black male	Death Penalty Nullification
Rozell Oxendine Hunt	46	Spousal Murder	Indian	10 JUN 1974	N. Carolina	Johnston	1976	White male	Death Penalty Nullification
Margie C. Boykin	44	Spousal Murder	White	1 DEC 1975	N. Carolina	Martin	1976	White male	Death Penalty Nullification
Faye Beatrice Brown	22	Predatory Murder	Black	5 JAN 1976	N. Carolina	Forsyth	1977	White male	Death Penalty Nullification
Rebecca Case Detter	37	Spousal Murder	White	26 SEP 1978	N. Carolina	Robeson	1979	White male	Procedural Error
Donna Sue Cox	28	Predatory Murder	White	28 SEP 1987	N. Carolina	Lee	1992	White male	Procedural Error
Barbara Terry Stager	41	Spousal Murder	White	19 MAY 1989	N. Carolina	Alamance	1991	White male	Procedural Error

III. Wrongful Convictions, Commutations, Clemency, Death Row Today

Name of Offender	Age at Crime	Criminal Offense	Race of Offender	Initial Sentencing Date	State of Sentencing	County of Sentencing	Year of Judicial Reversal	Race & Sex of Victim(s)	Reasons for Judicial Reversal
Marylin Rudd Mahaley	35	Spousal Murder	White	17 DEC 1990	N. Carolina	Beaufort	1992	White male	Procedural Error
Yvette Gay	28	Predatory Murder	Black	10 AUG 1991	N. Carolina	Wilkes	1993	Black males/black female	Procedural Error
Melanie Sammons Anderson	33	Child Murder	White	26 SEP 1996	N. Carolina	Rockingham	2003	White female	Mental retardation
Christene Knapp Kemmerlin	32	Spousal Murder	White	18 OCT 2000	N. Carolina	Guilford	2002	White male	Disproportionate Sentence
Mary Elizabeth Roach	---	Child Murder	White	30 NOV 2007	N. Carolina	Guilford	2009	White female	Insufficient evidence
Christina Shea Walters	20	Predatory Murder	Indian	17 AUG 1998	N.Carolina	Cumberlain	2012	2 White females	Prosecutorial Misconduct
Patricia JoAnn Jennings (Wells)	47	Spousal Murder	White	5 NOV 1990	N. Carolina	Wilson	2013	White male	Ineffective Trial Counsel
Sandra Lockett	21	Predatory Murder	Black	APR 1975	Ohio	Franklin	1978	White male	Death Penalty Nullification
Alberta L. Osborne	22	Predatory Murder	White	2 JUN 1975	Ohio	Lucas	1978	Black female	Death Penalty Nullification
Patricia N. Wernert	32	Predatory Murder	White	22 NOV 1976	Ohio	Lucas	1978	2 White females	Death Penalty Nullification
Benita Smith	23	Predatory Murder	Black	30 OCT 1977	Ohio	Hamilton	1978	White male	Death Penalty Nullification
Sharon Faye Young	26	Predatory Murder	White	30 SEP 1983	Ohio	Lorain	1986	White male	Procedural Error
Nicole Diar	35	Child Murder	White	2 NOV 2005	Ohio	Lorain	2008	White male	Procedural Error
Janet M. Sanders (Miller)	29	Predatory Murder	White	26 AUG 1975	Oklahoma	Oklahoma	1997	White female	Prosecutorial Misconduct
Michelle Ann Binsz	32	Predatory Murder	White	23 OCT 1979	Oklahoma	Oklahoma	1984	White male	Procedural Error
Patricia Beth Jones	38	Predatory Murder	White	7 DEC 1989	Oklahoma	Oklahoma	1995	White male/white female	Prosecutorial Misconduct
Delpha Jo Spunaugle	46	Spousal Murder	White	31 MAR 1995	Oklahoma	Philadelphia	1997	White male	Procedural Error
Grace Giovanetti	45	Spousal Murder	White	28 SEP 1939	Pennsylvania	Philadelphia	1941	White male	Faulty jury instructions
Mattie Jones	---	Predatory Murder	Black	SEP 1923	Pennsylvania	Philadelphia	1925	Black male	Procedural Error
Louise Thomas	19	Predatory Murder	Black	SEP 1923	Pennsylvania	Philadelphia	1925	Black male	Procedural Error
Kelly O'Donnell	25	Predatory Murder	White	1 JUY 1993	Pennsylvania	Philadelphia	1999	White male	Procedural Error
Delores Rivers	35	Predatory Murder	Black	30 JAN 1988	Pennsylvania	Dauphin	2005	Black female	Ineffective Trial Counsel
Marilyn Ann Dobrolenski	20	Predatory Murder	White	6 JAN 1972	Pennsylvania	Cumberland	1972	2 White males	Death Penalty Nullification
Beth Ann Markman	34	Predatory Murder	White	6 NOV 2001	Pennsylvania	Philadelphia	2007	White female	Procedural Error
Donetta Marie Hill (Williams)	23	Predatory Murder	Black	9 APR 1992	Pennsylvania	Lebanon	2005	Asian/Black males	Procedural Error
Carolyn Ann King	28	Predatory Murder	Black	30 NOV 1994	Pennsylvania	Matagorda	2010	White male/white female	Ineffective Trial Counsel
Rebecca M. Smith (Ewell, Kline)	41	Spousal Murder	White	10 DEC 1990	S. Carolina	Tarrant	1992	White male	Procedural Error
Chelsea Lea Richardson	19	Predatory Murder	White	11 DEC 2003	Texas	Bexar	2012	White male/white female	Prosecutorial Misconduct
Mary Lou Anderson	35	Predatory Murder	White	29 AUG 1978	Texas	Harris	1982	White male/white female	Procedural Error
Linda Mae Burnett	35	Predatory Murder	White	20 MAR 1979	Texas	Jefferson	1983	3 White males/2 females	Ineffective Trial Counsel
Pamela Lynn Perillo	25	Predatory Murder	White	13 NOV 1984	Texas	Houston	1996	2 White males	Procedural Error
Kenisha Eronda Berry	21	Child Murder	Black	19 FEB 2004	Texas	Harris	2007	Black male	Procedural Error
Carolyn Ann Lima	17	Predatory Murder	White	JAN 1963	Texas	Houston	1965	White male	Prosecutorial Misconduct
Cathy Lynn Henderson	37	Child Murder	White	25 MAY 1995	Texas	Travis	2012	White male	Lack of evidence
Valerie Suzette Friend	43	Predatory Murder	White	May 2007	Federal (WV)	Mingo	2009	White female	Juror Misconduct
Angela Jane Johnson	29	Predatory Murder	White	21 JUN 2005	Federal (IA)	Cerro Gordo	2012	2 White males/3 females	Ineffective Trial Counsel

(4 percent) including a Latina and Brazilian, Italian and American Indian women. Additionally, appeals courts have commuted the death sentences of white women in cases involving the victimization of white males more frequently than in cases involving other gender and racial categories of offenders and victims. Appeals courts have reversed the death sentences of women historically largely for procedural error (30.0 percent), prosecutorial misconduct (11.8 percent) and evidentiary problems (11.8 percent). These reasons for appeal court reversals of condemned women alone constitute more than half of all cases. Cases involving predatory murder comprise nearly 62 percent of all judicial reversals, while 25 percent of judicial reversals involved spousal murder cases, and nearly 14 percent involved cases of child murder.

Early Cases of Judicial Reversals

The earliest appellate review of confirmed female capital cases involved slave women. Slaves generally had a right of appeal to state supreme courts by the 19th century. Maryland, Virginia, and South Carolina, however, provided no right to appeal to the state's highest court and Louisiana had no criminal appeals until 1847. After 1839, South Carolina allowed slaves to appeal to a single judge of the highest court but not to the entire court. Georgia limited slave appeals to the highest court in a county; Georgia had no supreme court until the early 1850s. South Carolina had roughly a half dozen appeals in the 1850s and 1860s. Missouri had 10 criminal slave appeals to the state's Supreme Court between 1822 and 1860, four of which involved female slaves. Virginia had one slave case in 1865.

One of the earliest confirmed cases of judicial reversal of a female capital sentence was that of slave woman Jane belonging to Henry Brite in Callaway County, Missouri. A county jury convicted Jane of smothering to death her infant daughter, Angeline, in December 1830 and the circuit court judge sentenced Jane to hang. The Missouri Supreme Court reversed the verdict finding error in the indictment. Accordingly, "the first count of the indictment was fatally defective because ... it averred that defendant 'then and there' choked the child, without referring to or identifying the precise day; the averments were thus too uncertain; in all indictments for felony, the indictment had to charge the acts to have been done feloniously or with the felonious intent; and the third count was thus bad because it did not did not charge defendant with having administered the medicine feloniously."[5] Jane's fate is unknown.

In 1839, the Missouri Supreme Court reversed the murder conviction of slave Fanny belonging to William C. Prewitt of Warren County. A jury found Fanny guilty of first-degree murder and a trial court sentenced her to death for the killing of two young white boys, eight-year-old William Florence and 10-year-old Thomas Florence, the sons of mill owner William Florence. Townspeople had found the young boys' naked bodies in a swamp; they were bludgeoned to death. After the boys went missing, the county sheriff arrested and took Fanny and her husband Ben into custody. The sheriff forced a confession from Fanny's son Ellick when "they then put a rope around his neck and hung him; that he then told them that his mother had told him that she had killed the children in the orchard, when they came for peaches."[6] The court reversed the circuit court's judgment and remanded the case for retrial because the court allowed for a change of venue without Fanny's consent and that Ellick's extorted confession was inadmissible. A jury acquitted Fanny at retrial.

In November 1870, Laura D. Fair, the widow of Sheriff Fair of Shasta County in California, shot Alexander Parker Crittenden, a prominent San Francisco attorney and judge while he and his wife and children were aboard a ferry steamer from Oakland to San Francisco. Crittenden died two days later. Laura and Crittenden had been lovers for seven years and she became outraged with jealously at the sight of Crittenden with his wife. Laura had a daughter from one of her many previous marriages. Authorities tried Laura for first-degree murder and waged a defense based upon "maniacal attacks" resulting from "delayed menstruation." A San Francisco County jury rejected the defense and found Laura guilty of the killing and the trial court sentenced her to hang in July 1871. The California Supreme Court, however, vacated the death sentence and remanded the case back to the trial court for a new trial because the trial judge had improperly admitted evidence that went to Laura's reputation and character of chastity or want of chastity. The Court argued that Laura "was not on trial for her chastity, virtue, or moral character. Her character was not in any aspect of the case in issue. She was being tried for her life. She and she alone, could have put her character in issue."[7] A second trial acquitted Laura. She later married a San Francisco lawyer and her daughter, Lillian Lorraine Hollis, became a well-known actor in New York and died in February 1913. Laura attempted suicide after the death of her daughter, but died of natural causes six years later at the age of 82 in San Francisco.

In April 1858, a New York German émigré and mother of two, Mary Teresa (Koehler) Hartung and her paramour and boarder William Rheimann murdered her husband, saloonkeeper and deliveryman Emil Hartung, by poisoning him with arsenic and phosphorus paste added to his soup. Four weeks after his death, authorities exhumed Emil's body and chemical analyses revealed excessive amounts of arsenic in his stomach and liver. After learning that the investigation into Emil's death focused on her, Mary left for New Jersey where she worked as a servant. Authorities soon arrested William in a saloon. Weeks later, officials arrested Mary and returned her to New York. An Albany jury convicted Mary of her husband's murder and Judge Ira Harris sentenced her to hang in late January 1859. There was considerable public outcry that Mary's death sentence was too severe since several men who had committed similar crimes upon their wives in the years surrounding Mary's capital sentence received lighter sentences. The state's Supreme Court stayed Mary's execution but affirmed the murder conviction. In 1860, the Court of Appeals of New York reversed the judgment and ordered a new trial. In the interim, the state assembly passed a revision to the death penalty statute that repealed hanging as the state's method of execution but substituted no other execution method. As a result, "there was no longer any statutory method provided for inflicting capital punishment, and hence the punishment by hanging, imposed upon [Mary], was unauthorized."[8] Justice Deodatus Wright directed a judgment discharging Mary but in 1862 a court of appeals denied the motion to dismiss the case. Mary took the case back to the appeals court the next year. There, the court reversed the prior holding with directions to discharge Mary after she had spent five years in prison. After Mary's conviction, New York tried William for Emil's murder but after the state had presented its case against him, Judge George Gould granted a defense motion that the evidence was insufficient to convict him and the trial judge discharged William.

The historical record is less forthcoming in revealing why judicial authorities reversed the trial court findings of two Arkansas women in 1897 and 1898. Judge Isaac C. Parker tried nearly 400 capital offenders during his tenure as a federal judge at Fort Smith, Arkansas. Only a few of these offenders were women and none hanged for their offenses. Among those were Elizabeth Owens, Fanny Echols, Elsie James, Mary A. Kettenring and Mollie King. A jury acquitted Elizabeth Owens and federal executive clemency kept Fanny Echols and Elsie James from the gallows. In the other two cases, judicial authorities reversed Judge Parker's convictions and death sentences. In the first instance, Mollie King was a hotel chambermaid and her husband Ed worked at a livery stable in the 1890s. Both were "Cherokee Freedmen" whose parents had been slaves to the Cherokee tribe before the Civil War. The couple had a very troubled relationship from the beginning of their marriage and eventually decided to live separately but not divorce; they had two children. Mollie soon became promiscuous with several men at the hotel where she worked and when Ed learned of Mollie's adventures constant arguing ensued. Mollie decided to kill Ed and persuaded him to take a day trip to her mother's house in the spring of 1894.

About a half mile from the couple's house, two men hired by Mollie, Alexander Martin and Barry Foremen, ambushed Ed and shot him several times, dragged his corpse through the woods and buried it in a shallow grave. Officials soon found Ed's half-naked body full of bullet holes and arrested Mollie and Foremen for murder and took the two to Fort Smith. Martin escaped and authorities never captured him. In late March 1896, a jury convicted Mollie and Foremen of Ed's murder and the infamous hanging judge at Fort Smith in Indian Territory, Judge Isaac C. Parker, sentenced the two to hang. In 1897, however, the two filed a writ of error based upon the federal prosecutor's confession of error and the Supreme Court remanded the case for retrial. Before the retrial, however, Judge Parker died and Congress changed the law to allow juries to either sentence persons convicted of murder or rape to death or to life in prison. A jury in the second trial in November 1897 acquitted Foremen but found Mollie guilty of murder and the court sentenced her to a life term at the Ohio State Penitentiary.

Judge Parker described Mary Kettenring's crime of murdering her husband at the hands of two accomplices as "one of the most wicked in the annals of crime." As Parker explained, "The details of the crime are shocking in the extreme. They show such wickedness, such brutality, and such total disregard of human life as to shock and sicken the stoutest heart."[9] It seems that in June 1894, Mary solicited the help of two men named George Washington Frazier and Richard Calhoun to murder her third husband, Andrew J. Kettenring, for which Judge Parker sentenced Mary to hang in October 1895. The case was largely circumstantial; the government claimed Mary's motivation was a $20,000 life insurance policy. There is speculation that Mary's acquittal in the murder of her first husband, Eugene McClintock, in 1871 swayed the jury to a guilty verdict. Mary was the third woman sentenced to death by Judge Parker during his tenure as a federal district judge. The Supreme Court, however, overturned her death sentence and a jury acquitted Mary and her accomplices of Andrew's murder in a retrial in 1898.

In late April 1895, Maria Barbella (Barberi) murdered her lover and betrayer Dominico Cataldo. According to several newspaper reports and the appellate court record, Maria and Cataldo were recent poor émigrés from Italy to New York. Maria worked at her father's tailoring business and Cataldo had a boot-blacking stand. Some two months before the murder, Cataldo had promised to marry Maria but then refused to do so though the couple cohabitated for a short time. Cataldo's refusal to marry Maria drove her to despair. On the day of the killing, Maria and her mother went to a saloon where Cataldo was playing cards and pleaded with him to marry her. On his reply that he would not marry her, Maria drew a razor and cut his throat. A jury convicted Maria of first-degree murder and the trial court sentenced her to death. While awaiting execution at Sing Sing Prison, Maria learned the New York Court of appeals had reversed the judgment of the trial court and remanded the case for a new trial. At her new trial, a jury acquitted Maria when expert witnesses proved that she was an epileptic and thus not responsible for the killing.

Other women received judicial reversals of their capital cases in the early 1900s. In 1901, a Marion County jury in Missouri convicted Anna Nesenhener of the July 1900 poisoning murder of her husband, Frank Nesenhener, a railroad worker. The couple had been married for 15 years. Judge Eby sentenced Anna to death. A post-mortem examination revealed that Frank had died from morphine poisoning. Anna faced the trial stoically and even nursed her 16-month-old baby during the proceedings. As one newspaper reported, "There was not a quiver in her voice and not a tear in her eye, but an unmistakable expression of self-confidence and determination."[10] There was also evidence that three of Anna's children had died under mysterious circumstances in the same year—three-year-old Mary, five-year-old Emma, and 11-year-old Ida. Along with her husband, each of the children had life insurance policies payable to Anna. Missouri Governor Alexander M. Dockery refused to commute Anna's death sentence. On appeal to the Missouri Supreme Court in November 1901, the justices reversed her conviction and ordered her immediate release claiming, "There was no direct proof of the fact of poisoning, or substantial evidence that the deceased, in fact, died of morphine poisoning." Moreover, the Court argued, "there was no evidence that defendant administered to deceased any medicine of any kind or character, or food, and no such inference can be drawn from the evidence, unless it be from the mere fact that they were man and wife, and lived together as such."[11] In June 1903, Anna's fourth child, Howard Nessenhener, suddenly died from carbolic acid poisoning. After Howard's death, Alice Nesenhener went to an asylum for the criminally insane.

Bessie J. Wakefield was one of 15 children born to Frank Webster and his wife in 1889. Bessie lived in poverty and her parents were illiterate and of "low mentality." The family lived in a one-room shack in the hills at the north end of a lake near Middlebury, Connecticut. At 14 years old, she worked as a laborer for local farmers' wives. In 1909, when Bessie was 17 years old, her parents forced her to marry 50-year-old William O. Wakefield. The couple eventually had two children, daughter Bessie Belle and son William George. There is evidence that William abused Bessie and his children, often threatened to kill Bessie and at times starved the children. One commentator pointed out that "the children were without shoes or stockings and their clothes were in rags. Wakefield bought nothing for them."[12] Bessie's mother told a reporter that William once kicked his son as an infant and chronic back pain required his mother to rub his back for hours before he could sleep. Bessie left William on three separate occasions but always returned, strangely enough, for the sake of her children. William was a farmhand and worked with a man named James Plew who soon became a boarder at the Wakefield home. Both men worked for Josh Burns, a wealthy farmer. James expressed a genuine kindness to Bessie and the children and soon the two became lovers and planned William's murder. [Interestingly, an investigation into James Plew's family history by a prison association of New York revealed that Plew was a descendant of the notorious "Jukes" family, who since 1710 comprised generations of "degenerates and criminals." At one time, New York state officials had 21 members of the Jukes family incarcerated in state penitentiaries].[13]

In furthering their plan to kill William, James went to the Wakefield's bedroom where he gave William chloroform but he awoke and two men struggled. James pulled a revolver, subdued William, and got him to walk several miles toward Bristol through the forest. There, James shot William six times in the back and stabbed him in the heart. James attempted to make the murder look like a suicide by using William's shoestrings to hang him from a tree. Authorities arrested Bessie and James for William's murder, and in November 1913, an all-male jury convicted Bessie Wakefield for her role in William's murder. Connecticut law demanded that Judge Lucien F. Burpee sentence Bessie to hang. James pled guilty and the trial court sentenced him to hang. There was considerable public outcry against hanging Bessie. Besides death threats condemning Judge Burpee for sentencing Bessie to hang, thousands of petitions from individuals and national women's associations flooded Governor Simeon Baldwin's office, the U.S. Department of Justice, and President Wilson and his wife. Most of the letters received by the Governor concerned the state putting a woman to death. New York newspapers made it a point that most of the letters "came from the presumably less sophisticated citizens of the West and Midwest."[14] The Connecticut Supreme Court reversed Bessie's conviction and death sentence and granted her a new trial claiming inadmissible hearsay evidence. In July 1914, a second jury found Bessie guilty of second-degree murder and Judge Joel H. Reed sentenced her to life in prison. The State Board of Pardons released Bessie from prison in 1933 after 17 appeals. James Plew hanged in March 1914.

In April 1917, Judge Gardiner Green sentenced Amy E. Archer Gilligan to death by hanging after a four-week trial for the poisoning murder of Franklin R. Andrews, a patient at her home for the elderly and chronic invalids. The state showed that at least four other elderly persons died by Amy's hands and that as many as 40 other persons died under peculiar circumstance.

Amy's motive was to profit on contracts she had made with inmates; she agreed to provide a comfortable home for them during the remainder of their lives for a specified sum. The Supreme Court of Errors of Connecticut reversed the verdict in 1918 on procedural grounds and remanded the cases back the county court for retrial. During a second trial in 1919, Amy pleaded guilty to second-degree murder and the court sentenced her to a life prison term. Officials incarcerated her at the state prison, but deemed her insane in 1928, authorities moved Amy to a state mental institution. Amy died of natural causes at 89 years old.

In late August 1913, Willis Buffum, a farmer, died of arsenic poisoning at his home near Little Valley in the town of Mansfield, Cattaraugus County, in New York. Authorities charged Cynthia Buffum, Willis Buffum's wife, with his death by means of arsenic administered throughout the month of July 1913. The couple had been married since Cynthia was 15 years old and they had six children. They were poor tenant farmers, deeply in debt and the family moved frequently following employment opportunities. Cynthia and Willis had a strained marriage; Willis often accused Cynthia of marital infidelity including incestual relations with her sons. Cynthia did become infatuated with Ernest Frahm, a young man who lived in the vicinity. There was also evidence that Cynthia may have poisoned to death her four-year-old son, Norris Buffum, and her young daughter, Laura Buffum. Other Buffum children suffered from arsenic poisoning but survived. Authorities arrested Cynthia, a Cattaraugus County jury convicted her of the first-degree murder of her husband, and the court sentenced her to death. Overburdened by his financial debt, the defense claimed that Willis suffered from severe depression and had contemplated taking his own life and the lives of his children. The New York Court of Appeals reversed the conviction and remanded the matter for a new trial because the state prosecutor had engaged in a "carefully planned scheme of falsehood, artifice and deception" to obtain a confession from Cynthia. At retrial, Cynthia pled guilty to second-degree murder and Justice Pound sent her to Auburn Prison to serve a 20-year prison term.

Pennsylvania judges issued 233 death warrants from 1914 to 1925. Courts commuted to life prison terms 58 prisoners, courts recalled the death sentences of four prisoners, four prisoners died in prison before their execution dates, and state authorities executed 167 prisoners. Louise Thomas and Mattie Jones were among the prisoners where appeals courts reversed their death sentences. In the first instance, a Philadelphia jury found Louise Thomas guilty of the gunshot murder Harrison Saunders, a detective in the city's police vice squad. Louise and Saunders were both married to other persons. Louise claimed that Saunders pulled a gun when she refused to reconcile with him, a struggle ensued, and she wrenched the gun from him and shot him five times. Judge Ferguson sentenced Louise to death and scheduled her execution for October 1929. On appeal, the Pennsylvania Supreme Court granted Louise a new trial after the court discovered procedural errors and officials commuted her sentence to a life prison term.

In mid–September 1923, a Philadelphia jury found Mattie Jones guilty of killing William Martin, a man with whom she had been living for about three years. The killing took place after the couple had attended a party and a struggle ensued when Mattie questioned William about a woman with whom he had been dancing at the party. After the shooting, Mattie voluntarily surrendered to police carrying the pistol she used to kill William and signed a written confession. At trial, Mattie claimed self-defense and that William often would come home drunk, that at times he would hit her in the eye with his fist. A confidant testified that Mattie repeatedly came to her with complaints about how William was cruel to her and beat her when he was drunk. The Pennsylvania Supreme Court granted Mattie a new trial because of trial error and in 1925 upheld her second conviction wherein the trial court sentenced her to life in prison.

During the depths of the Great Depression between 1932 and 1938, a murder-for-insurance scheme plagued Italian communities in Pennsylvania, New York, Delaware and New Jersey that eventually took the lives of more than 100 men and women though most victims were men.

Operating the moneymaking conspiracy were former spaghetti sales representative Herman Petrillo, tailor Paul Petrillo and cousin to Herman, obstetrician Horace Perlman, and Russian Jewish mystic Morris Bolber. These culprits enlisted disgruntled married women who wanted to rid themselves of an abusive husband. The women were poor, illiterate, non–English speaking Italian émigrés who obtained arsenic from the ringleaders; they poisoned their husbands, and then collected insurance proceeds once the belligerent husbands died. Newspapers at the time dubbed these women "poison widows" or "arsenic widows." Physicians treating the victims— mostly husbands in their thirties—noted the symptoms from arsenic poisoning as digestion problems. The husbands' deaths attracted little official attention since they were poor Italian immigrants living in working-class ghettos. The scheme began to fall apart in 1938 after the U.S. Secret Service learned of the operation while investigating counterfeiters. Confessions derived from many of the widows enhanced their prosecution; most of the women spoke little to no English and could not read the confessions officials forced them to sign. Insurance investigators eventually uncovered payments of between $50,000 and $100,000 linked to the ring. Poison was not the only method of killing, other methods involved drowning, beating to death with a lead pipe, and fake auto accidents. Herman and Paul Petrillo died in the state's electric chair at Rockview State Correctional Institution in Bellfonte, Pennsylvania, in March 1940 and October 1941, respectively.

Housewife Grace Giovanetti was an "arsenic widow." Philadelphia prosecutors secured a conviction and death sentence against Grace for the poison murder of her first husband, Pietro Piorolli, who died in 1935. Authorities exhumed Pirolli's body in 1939 and forensics revealed that the cause of death was arsenic poisoning. The Pennsylvania Supreme Court vacated her conviction and death sentence, however, finding that the evidence against Grace weak and inconclusive. The evidence also showed that another person could have administered the poison that killed her husband. What's more, the court determined that it was unclear whether Grace clearly understood the alleged confession since she was inept in English. The court noted that even if the defendant knew that another person had poisoned her husband, there was no evidence supporting a claim that Grace was an accomplice or an accessory after the fact for failing to report the murder. The court ruled that the trial judge should have informed the jury on circumstantial evidence and the requirement of an acquittal if the evidence could be explained on any other theory of Grace's guilt. Grace ultimately pled guilty to second-degree murder and received a five-year prison sentence.

Courts reversed the capital convictions of a few women in the 1950s and into the 1960s. The state of Florida tried Ruby McCollum, a black woman married to Sam McCollum, before an all-white, all-male Suwannee County jury that convicted her of murdering C. LeRoy Adams, a prominent white physician and state senator-elect in August 1952. Speculation has it that Dr. Adams had fathered one of Ruby's children. Ruby went to Dr. Adams' office after he had sent a bill for medical treatment to Ruby's husband. An argument broke out between the two concerning the bill. When Dr. Adams turned his back to walk away, Ruby shot him in the back. Ruby admitted to authorities of having the discussion with Dr. Adams but testified that she shot him in self-defense after he became angry and attacked her. The Florida Supreme Court overturned Ruby's murder conviction and death sentence and ordered a new trial because it was reversible error for presiding Judge Hal W. Adams not to be present when the jury toured the scene of the crime. Authorities never retried Ruby but determined her to be insane and committed her to a Florida state mental hospital. In January 1974, after spending 20 years in the mental hospital, officials released Ruby to live with her daughter. Ruby died from a stroke in May 1992 at the age of 82.

An early confirmed judicial reversal of a female death verdict owing to prosecutorial misconduct occurred in 1963 when Carolyn Ann Lima, a young prostitute, and her homosexual and professional female impersonator roommate Leslie Douglas Ashley murdered a real estate agent. The appeals record shows that in February 1961 the two shot to death Houston real estate agent Fred Tomes after he became violent during a three-party sexual encounter in Tomes' office. After shooting him six times, the two doused Tomes' nude body with gas and burned the corpse in a drainage ditch. Carolyn and Leslie fled to New York but officials soon apprehended the two and extradited them to stand trial in Texas. A trial court convicted them of Tomes' murder and Judge Marion A. Love sentenced them to death in the state's electric chair. In March 1963, and within just a few short hours of their executions, a U.S. Court of Appeals granted the two new trials claiming that the district attorney withheld psychiatric evidence regarding Carolyn and Leslie's competency to stand trial; the prosecution withheld mental test evidence from the defense. In a second jury trial, Carolyn testified against Ashley claiming he was the actual killer and that she had nothing to do with the murder. She received a five-year prison sentence but served two years. Officials discharged her from prison in April 1965. Psychiatrists found Ashley insane and committed him to a state asylum. He later received a pardon and authorities released him from custody. Ashley underwent sex transformation and is now named Leslie Elaine Perez living in Houston and involved in local politics.

In late November 1961, Irene Jackson, along with her boyfriend William Reddick and her son Willie Charles Hill, beat Johnnie Jackson, Irene Jackson's husband to death with a blunt instrument reportedly for life insurance money. Tried together, a Pasco County jury found the three defendants guilty of first-degree murder without recommendation. In March 1962, the trial judge sentenced each defendant to death in the electric chair. Irene appealed to the Florida Supreme Court and in December 1962, the Court reversed the murder conviction because the trial court abused its discretion in denying the motion of these defendants for severance of the cases. In 1964, the state retried Irene, the jury found her guilty of second-degree murder, and the trial court sentenced her life in prison. State prison authorities paroled Irene in 1972 and discharged her from parole in 1980.

While free on bond from a manslaughter sentence in the death of her husband, Marie Dean Arrington shot and killed 37-year-old Vivian June Ritter. Authorities discovered Vivian's badly decomposed body. Appeals records reveal that Marie went to the Public Defender's Office on the morning of April 22, 1968, to kill the public defender that had unsuccessfully defended Marie's two children on felony charges. Not finding the lawyer in his office, Marie kidnapped Vivian instead and drove away from the office in Vivian's car. A Hernando County jury found Marie guilty of first-degree murder and did not recommend mercy. The trial judge sentenced Marie to death and the Florida Supreme Court affirmed the conviction and death sentence. In March 1969, Marie escaped from death row at the Florida Correctional Institution for Women at Lowell by cutting through a heavy window screen and making her way past two barbed-wire fences and fleeing in her pajamas. Federal authorities arrested Marie in New Orleans in late December 1971. The Florida Supreme Court commuted Marie's death sentence to life in prison after rendering the state's death penalty statute unconstitutional in response to the U.S. Supreme Court's *Furman* decision. Marie remained incarcerated at the Lowell Correctional Institution until her death at 80 years old in May 2014.

Judicial Reversals Post-Furman

Appeals courts vacated the capital sentences of several women after the U.S. Supreme Court nullified state capital statutes in *Furman v. Georgia* in 1972. The aftermath of the Court's decisions proved to be the largest mass judicial commutation of death row inmates in the history of American capital justice. Greenberg estimates that *Furman* and pre–*Furman* anti-death penalty litigation vacated the death sentences of some 860 defendants including 629 defendants on death row at the time of *Furman*. Besides death row inmates housed at state and federal penitentiaries, there were also prisoners in county jails whose status had not been recorded. In pre–*Furman* litigation, the California Supreme Court found capital punishment unconstitutional in 1972 vacating the death sentences of 101 defendants. That same year, the New Jersey Supreme Court held capital punishment unconstitutional vacating the death sentences of 22 defendants. Pre-*Furman* cases in 1968 by the U.S. Supreme Court also vacated more than 100 death sentences in response to holdings in *Witherspoon v. Illinois* and *United States v. Jackson*. The Court's holding in *Gregg v. Georgia* and *Woodson v. North Carolina* vacated 414 death sentences imposed after *Furman*. Many of these commuted death sentences involved female defendants.

State and federal appeals courts have commuted in excess of one-third of the more than 8,000 death sentences of prisoners in the United States since 1973. These judicial commutations commonly involve invalidated state death penalty statutes, quashed convictions, and reversed death sentences. A recent study of nearly 6,000 capital cases revealed that almost all capital punishment jurisdictions in the United States have excessive error rates. Kentucky, Maryland, and Tennessee have error rates of 100 percent, followed closely by California (87 percent), Mississippi (91 percent), Montana (87 percent), and Wyoming (89 percent). On retrial, jurisdictions resentenced over 75 percent of all capital defendants to less than death, while authorities resentenced to death 18 percent of the cases. In 7 percent of the cases, a figure representing about 420 people, jurisdictions found capital defendants innocent of the charges altogether. There are a host of reasons why courts overrule capital convictions and reverse death sentences: procedural error involving improper trial arguments or tactics of prosecutors, withholding evidence from defense lawyers that frequently exculpate capital defendants, discrimination in jury selection, manipulating witnesses, speedy trial violations, subpoena errors, paying witnesses, improper pretrial tactics, perjured testimony, improper contact with a judge, goading a defendant into a mistrial, and destruction of evidence.

Appeals courts reversed the death sentences of 12 women prosecuted under pre–*Furman* statutes that the U.S. Supreme Court later held unconstitutional. Since 1973, state and federal jurisdictions have sentenced 178 women, and of these women, 61 were on death row awaiting execution. Of the remaining 117 women sentenced to death since that year, appeals courts commuted the death sentences of 86 women and state governors commuted the death sentences of another 23 women.

Courts of appeal in Alabama commuted the death sentences of six women between 1978 and 2014 for police and prosecutorial misconduct, procedural error, and incompetent defense counsel. In the earliest of these cases, a Covington County jury convicted 17-year-old Debra Bracewell of first-degree felony murder and Circuit Court Judge Murland Smith sentenced her to death. Debra had an eighth grade education, limited mental capacity, and was under the domination of her abusive husband, Charles Howard Bracewell. The picture that emerges from the record about Debra is that her husband led her on a three-month crime spree across several counties in two states. One of those crimes involved a robbery-murder at Carnley's Grocery in Covington County where the Bracewells knew that Rex Carnley, the owner of the local market, kept large amounts of cash in the store. Carnley was a reputed loan shark and held gambling events in the back of his store. Concerned about burglaries, Carnley locked himself in the store on the evening of the murder, but for some unknown reason let the Bracewells into the store to make a purchase. While the couple was talking with Carnley, Charles drew a handgun and held it on Carnley while Debra took a pistol from underneath a counter and, at her husband's direction, fired the pistol directly to the back of Carnley's head killing him instantly. Charles then fired several more shots into Carnley's head. They left the store with Carnley's billfold containing more $1,200. Early the next morning, authorities found Carnley's body lying in the store with nine gunshots fired into his head. Police arrested the Bracewells and Debra made a written confession to Carnley's robbery and murder.

On appeal to the Alabama Court of Criminal Appeals, attorneys argued that an evidentiary law rendered Debra's interrogation and subsequent written confession inadmissible. The law required the presence of an attorney or guardian when a criminal defendant 18 years of age or younger gives a confession. The appeals court agreed and granted Debra Bracewell a new trial. The same appeals court found Bracewell's second trial without error and affirmed the conviction but instructed the lower court to consider mitigating evidence as to her death sentence. In 1984, the Alabama Court of Criminal Appeals overturned Debra's death sentence based on a U.S. Supreme Court ruling that Alabama's 1975 death penalty statute under which the state prosecuted Debra was unconstitutional. A jury again convicted Debra of Carnley's murder and the trial judge sentenced her to life imprisonment without parole. The U.S. Supreme Court denied Debra a petition for certiorari in 2007. Debra remains incarcerated at Julia Tutwiler Prison in Oscala and Charles is serving life in prison without parole at the St. Clare Correctional Facility in Springville.

In October 1999, a Walter County jury convicted Shonda of capital murder in the shooting death of Randy McCullar who had testified against Shonda in a criminal proceeding. McCullar had a life insurance policy that paid Shonda in the event of his death. Shonda married William Hayward McIntyre in September 1995 with whom she had a son, Chad McIntyre. While still legally married to McIntyre, Shonda married McCullar. The relationship was short-lived and Shonda then married Timothy Richards, a co-defendant in McCullar's murder who was the state's main witness in a bigamy case against Shonda. McCullar's grand jury testimony against Shonda was motivated by his attempt to gain custody of his son. In late 1997, Shonda and Richards found McCullar at a lounge in Jasper. McCullar left the lounge and drove to an eatery. Shonda and Richards followed McCullar after he left the restaurant and ambushed him in a church parking lot where Richards shot McCullar to death. Upon her arrest for McCullar's murder, Shonda gave statements to police originally denying her marriage to McCullar or any involvement in his murder but "with each successive statement, she confessed to increased involvement in the murder, particularly as more evidence surfaced implicating her." Richards eventually admitted to being involved in the murder, though Shonda and Richards each implicated the other as the shooter. Richards eventually entered into a guilty-plea agreement with state prosecutors and testified against Shonda at her trial. The jury recommended Shonda's execution and the trial court sentenced her to death. On appeal, the Court of Criminal Appeals for Alabama granted Shonda a new trial in 2005, but the Supreme Court of Alabama later overruled that finding. The state's Supreme Court ultimately affirmed Shonda's murder conviction and death sentence and the U.S. Supreme Court denied her certiorari in 2013. According to the Alabama Department Corrections, however, authorities commuted Shonda's death sentence in July 2014 to life in prison without parole. She remains incarcerated at the Julia Tutwiler Prison for Women.

In February 1981, Patricia Ann Thomas Jackson stabbed her neighbor Bonnie Mae Walker in the chest during an argument about liquor that Patricia wanted to buy from Walker. Paramedics arrived at the scene and pronounced Walker dead from her wounds and Patricia voluntarily surrendered to police a day after the killing. An all-white Tuscaloosa County jury found Patricia, who is black, guilty of murder and recommended the death penalty. Circuit Judge Joseph A. Colquitt affirmed the conviction and sentenced Patricia to death. The Court of Criminal Appeals of Alabama affirmed Jackson's conviction and death sentence and both the Alabama Supreme Court and the U.S. Supreme Court denied her certiorari. Later, the U.S. District Court found that state prosecutors at the time of Patricia's trial used peremptory challenges unlawfully to exclude blacks from jury service in serious criminal cases in Tuscaloosa County and thereby denied Patricia equal protection rights. The Court granted Patricia a habeas corpus writ and ordered her conviction and sentence set aside. Authorities sentenced Patricia to life in prison with parole. Alabama appealed that ruling to the U.S. Court of Appeals in 1995 but the court ruled that Patricia provided overwhelming evidence that the discriminatory use of peremptory challenges by the Tuscaloosa County District Attorney's Office was widespread and systematic to keep blacks off juries. Statistics presented to the court showed that at the time of Patricia's trial, prosecutors were more than *two-and-one-half times* more likely to strike blacks from juries than whites, and that 65 to 70 percent of Tuscaloosa County's juries underrepresented blacks. Patricia also claimed that her lawyer failed to introduce mitigating factors of Jackson's personal hardships at the penalty phase of her trial—Patricia's father died when she was six years old, she suffered a brutal and abusive childhood at the hands of an alcoholic mother who essentially raised her in a whorehouse or "shothouse," she left school in the eighth grade to care for her mother dying of cancer, she became pregnant at 15 years old, and intelligence tests placed Patricia at the borderline range of intelligence, above mental retardation. Authorities paroled Patricia in April 2011.

In another Alabama case, a Talladega County jury found Altion Maxine Walker guilty of hiring her nephews, James Charles and Mack O'Neal Lawhorne, to kill her abusive lover, William Clarence Berry, in December 1988. Altion had apparently been trying to end her violent relationship with Berry. At trial, Altion testified that she was afraid Berry was going to kill her since he had already killed one woman with whom he had a sadistic relationship and served six years for manslaughter. Lawhorne shot Berry to death and a hunter later found Berry's body in a wooded area. An autopsy revealed that Lawhorne shot Berry 27 times. Juries convicted Altion and Lawhorne of Berry's death and courts sentenced them to death. Lawhorne remains in an Alabama prison serving life without parole. The Court of Criminal Appeals of Alabama reversed Altion's death sentence in 1992 due to prosecutorial misconduct in using peremptory challenges to exclude five black jurors. The trial court retried and convicted Altion in 2002 on a lesser offense of murder. The trial court sentenced her to life in prison; in 2009, the U.S. Court of Appeals affirmed the conviction. The Alabama Department of Corrections shows no record that Altion remains in prison; officials may have released her on parole.

The murder of Jerry Wayne Haney remained a cold case for nearly four years until the fall of 1987 when the wife of the killer came forward and admitted to police that her sister, Judy Haney, contracted with her brother-in-law, Jerry Paul Henderson, shortly after Christmas 1983 to kill her husband Jerry Haney for $3,000. As planned, Henderson drove to the Haney home and when Jerry stepped out of the house, Henderson shot him in the stomach with a shotgun. The blast knocked Haney to the ground, but he got to his feet and tried to escape. When Jerry fell to the steps of the house Henderson shot him again in the face. Under the ruse that she had not heard from her husband while visiting her sister, Judy called Jerry Haney's brother, Billy Haney, an officer with the Talladega Police Department, and told him that her husband was supposed to call her and to come get her but that she had not heard from him. Judy told Billy that she had been unable to reach him by telephone, and she asked him to check on her husband and call her back. Billy discovered the body and called Judy after notifying the authorities. Billy told her that Jerry was dead. A break in the investigation of Jerry's murder came when Martha Henderson, having separated from Jerry Paul Henderson, agreed to cooperate with the state, assisted the state in its investigation, and made a statement giving the details of the crimes. Authorities arrested Judy and Henderson for Jerry's murder. At trial, Judy testified in her own behalf and admitted to the murder-for-hire of her husband. Judy argued that she lacked the necessary intent to commit the crime because spousal abuse and fear of her husband impaired her judgment. She appealed to the court and jury to spare her life because of years of alleged torment by an abusive husband. There was evidence that Judy had visited the hospital from injuries suffered from her husband, but the jury never heard this mitigating evidence since her attorney,

Gould Blair, never introduced the evidence. Another measure of Gould Blair's incompetence is that during the trial he "came to court so drunk that the judge halted the proceedings and sent him to jail overnight to dry out."[15] The Circuit Court of Talladega County nevertheless convicted Judy of murdering her husband and the trial judge sentenced her death. The Court of Criminal Appeals of Alabama affirmed Judy's conviction for murder, but remanded the case to the trial court with instructions to resentence defendant because of procedural error. Judy received a life sentence without the possibility of parole and remains incarcerated at Tutwiler Women's Prison. A Talladega County jury found Jerry Paul Henderson guilty of capital murder arising out of the death of Jerry Wayne Haney and sentenced him to death. Appellate courts affirmed his conviction and death sentence and Alabama executed Henderson by lethal injection in June 2005.

In July 1989, a Montgomery County, Alabama, jury convicted Louise Harris of murder-for-hire of her husband, Isaiah Harris, a deputy sheriff who worked the night shift as a jailer. Court records show that Harris was sexually involved with Lorenzo McCarter while married to her husband. Louise and Isaiah had severe marital problems and to rid herself of Isaiah and collect on life insurance proceeds, Louise asked her paramour to find someone to kill Isaiah. McCarter hired Michael Anthony Sockwell and Alex Hood to do the killing. Sockwell followed Isaiah and while he stopped at an intersection on his way to work, Sockwell shot Isaiah directly in the face with a shotgun. "As a result, the lower half of the victim's face was blown off, leaving his teeth, tongue, and matter from his face blown across the car. After the shot, the victim's vehicle traveled slowly across the highway and came to a stop in a ditch." When police arrived at the Harris' house to notify Louise that her husband had been killed, she "began screaming and sobbing, but she shed no tears. Moreover, she became completely calm instantly in order to answer questions." According to one review of her case, Louise's defense lawyer failed to present much about her personal history at her trial—a testimony to attorney ineptitude often accenting women's defense in homicide cases. Not only was Louise raised in extreme poverty and the oldest of eight children, but she also had a long history of abuse and trauma in her life.

> She had been sexually assaulted at age 11; she had witnessed her older sister die suddenly of a seizure in her arms, leaving Louise, at age 14, to raise her younger siblings; she had seen her younger brother being pulled from a lake after he drowned, and she had been the one to discover the body of her father, who was murdered. She had also been beaten severely and regularly by her first husband, John Wesley Robinson; she had been abused for years by her common-law husband Jesse Lee Hall and then by her husband Isaiah Harris, resulting in multiple trips to the hospital; and she was also abused by the man from whom she had sought comfort, Lorenzo McCarter. This abuse and trauma resulted in Louise suffering from Post-Traumatic Stress Disorder, Battered Women's Syndrome and Dissociative Disorder. None of this evidence was presented at her trial.[16]

At trial, McCarter testified against Louise in exchange for a life prison term without parole. The jury found Louise guilty and recommended to the court to sentence her to life imprisonment without the possibility of parole. At her sentencing hearing, however, Montgomery Circuit Court Judge H. Randall Thomas overrode the jury's recommendation and sentenced Louise to death by electrocution finding that the aggravating circumstances outweighed the mitigating circumstances. In *Harris v. Alabama* in 1995, the U.S. Supreme Court upheld judicial override in capital cases. Juries sentenced Sockwell to life in prison but the trial judge rejected the jury recommendation and sentenced him to death as well. Sockwell remains on Alabama's death row while undergoing appeals of his death sentence.

The Supreme Court of Alabama and the Court of Criminal Appeals of Alabama both affirmed Harris' conviction and death sentence. In a dissenting opinion in the case, one justice of the state's Supreme Court found that the court should grant Louise a new trial because the prosecutor in the case violated Louise's constitutional rights under *Batson* during the jury selection process when "she [the prosecutor] challenged 71 percent of the black venire members but only 21 percent of the white venire members." What's more, Justice Adams argued, the Court of Criminal Appeals has observed that the prosecutor "has a history of using peremptory challenges to discriminate against black jurors." In 2004, the Court of Criminal Appeals of Alabama reversed the death sentence and remanded the case to the circuit court for a new penalty-phase hearing finding that Louise had ineffective assistance of counsel during the guilt phase of her trial. The trial court resentenced Louise to life in prison without parole and she is presently housed at the Tutwiler Prison for Women.

Modernly, Arkansas appeals courts have commuted the death sentence of only one female death row defendant. In March 1984, a Clark County jury found Patricia Hendrickson guilty of the 1983 capital murder of her husband, Orin Hendrickson, for financial gain of over $600,000 and the trial court sentenced her to death. Patricia conspired with Norma Foster, a college dormitory housemother at Ouachita Baptist University, and Mark Yarbrough, a student at the same university, to hire Howard Daniel Vagi, another student at the university, to kill her husband for $16,000. Patricia gave Vagi a picture of her husband, supplied him with a key to the Hendrickson house, showed him the house, and gave him a down payment of $5,000. Yagi bought a shotgun and on the afternoon of the murder went to the Hendrickson's house. He waited for Orin to come home later in the evening and then shot him twice in the chest. Vagi ransacked the house to make the killing appear to be part of a robbery. Patricia and Norma found Orin's body when they went to the house and notified police. About eight months after Orin's murder, police arrested all the principals in the killing. At trial, evidence showed that Patricia was intellectually and emotionally incapable of contriving the murder, and that her low I.Q. and personality traits made her highly susceptible to the influence or control of others. To one expert, Patricia was "a very feminine, mousey, passive, dependent kind of person who would be expected to be easily led." Vagi negotiated a plea agreement in return for a life sentence and testified about the crime.

The Supreme Court of Arkansas reversed Hendrickson's conviction because Clark Circuit Court Judge J. Hugh Lookadoo allowed prosecutors to introduce an incriminating statement by Hendrickson that the police had taken from her immediately after they warned her of her right to remain silent but said that she wanted to talk to her lawyer. At retrial, a jury again found Hendrickson guilty of capital murder but sentenced to life imprisonment without parole. The Supreme Court of Arkansas affirmed the second conviction and life prison sentence. Patricia Hendrickson, now 68 years old, is serving her life sentence without parole at the McPherson Correctional Facility in Newport, Arkansas. The U.S. Court of Appeals most recently denied Patricia habeas corpus relief. Authorities sentenced Norma Foster to life in prison and eventually tried her three times; her first trial resulted in a conviction which the state supreme court reversed and remanded for a new trial, a court declared a mistrial in the second trial, and the state's supreme court reversed her conviction on a third trial and dismissed the case. Officials never charged Mark Yarbrough with a crime.

Appeals courts reversed the capital sentences of two Arizona women in 2002 and 2013. In the first instance, Doris Ann Carlson and her husband David John Carlson lived with and were financially dependent on David's mother, Mary Lynne Carlson in Peoria, Arizona. Mary received monthly living payments from a trust fund valued at several thousand dollars. Mary also had two annuities with a combined value of about $140,000. Mary received monthly living installments from the first annuity and could draw on the principal from the second. David was beneficiary of the trust and both annuities. Mary had multiple sclerosis, confined to a wheelchair, and required home care. Doris was hostile toward Mary, claiming that her multiple sclerosis was a charade. Doris often suggested to David that they should kill Mary so they could inherit Mary's money. In July 1996, David moved his mother into a residential care facility since she required more care than he and Doris could provide for her at home. As a result, the trust accounts and annuities began supporting Mary's residential care leaving Doris and David without supporting funds. They mapped out a scheme to have Mary killed so David could inherit the trust accounts and annuity funds. In late 1996, Doris approached John Daniel McReaken, a boarder at the home, to kill Lynne for $20,000. In turn, McReaken solicited the help of Scott Christopher Smith who agreed to participate in the murder for half the money Doris and David was to give McReaken. Apparently, time was of the essence since Mary had refused to sign an annuity document to help Dora and David to pay the mortgage so they would not lose the house to repossession. In October 1996, Doris drove McReaken and Smith to Mary's residential care facility where they knifed Mary to death. A residential nursing assistant found Mary later that morning and summoned emergency medical personnel. Mary underwent several surgeries to repair her wounds suffered during the knife attack but died in April 1997. Less than a month after the attack on Mary, authorities arrested Doris and David and charged them with Mary's murder. A jury found Doris guilty of first-degree murder but called for leniency in sentencing.

Under Arizona law at the time, a judge could conduct the sentencing part of the trial without a jury and make factual findings to determine a sentence of death or life imprisonment. Maricopa County Superior Court Judge Peter T. D'Angelo found that the state's evidence in the case had proven three aggravating factors beyond a reasonable doubt: Doris procured Mary's murder by promise of payment of something of pecuniary value; Mary's murder was committed in expectation of Doris' pecuniary gain; and that Mary's murder was committed in an especially heinous, cruel, or depraved manner. The judge found mitigating factors but he believed those issues did not outweigh the aggravating evidence. Consequently, Judge D'Angelo ignored the jury's call for leniency and sentenced Doris to death. In 2002, however, the Arizona Supreme Court upheld Doris' conviction but reduced her death sentence to life in prison based the U.S. Supreme Court's holding in *Ring v. Arizona* permitting a trial judge to find facts as to the presence or absence of statutory aggravating factors in reaching an ultimate sentencing determination (judicial override) in capital cases unconstitutional. The court reduced Doris' sentence to life in prison without parole in June 2002 and she remains incarcerated at the Arizona State Prison Complex Perryville at Goodyear.

The California Supreme Court vacated the death sentences of five women from 1972 to 1979. A moratorium on capital punishment in the state began in 1964 when the Court ruled in *People v. Morse* that instructions to juries could not include statements that authorities could parole the defendant if a trial court did not impose the death penalty. In June 1968, the U.S. Supreme Court held in *Witherspoon v. Illinois* that "a sentence of death cannot be carried out if the jury that imposed or recommended it was chosen by excluding veniremen for cause simply because they voiced general objections to the death penalty or expressed conscientious or religious scruples against its infliction."[17] The Court made it clear that trial judges could only excuse jurors whose views on the death penalty prevented or substantially impaired the performance of their duties. The outcome of *Witherspoon* required that California retry the penalty proceedings of all condemned prisoners awaiting execution. In *People v. Anderson* in 1972, the California Supreme Court declared the state's death penalty unconstitutional, resulting in authorities commuting the death sentences of 107 condemned prisoners to life prison terms. Among the prisoners escaping execution were Susan Denise Atkins, Leslie Louise Van Housten, and Patricia Krenwinkle involved in the infamous killing of pregnant actress Sharon Tate and several others during a killing spree in 1969. Susan Atkins died of brain cancer in September 2009, but Leslie Van Housten and Patricia Krenwinkle remain incarcerated at the California Institution for Women in Chino. In their cases, the state's parole board continues to deny them parole because they pose an "unacceptable risk to public safety." Because of the judicial commutations, public opinion turned against the Court and in November 1972, more than two-thirds of the California electorate rejected the Court's holding in *Anderson* when voters approved a constitutional amendment restoring the death penalty later that year. In October 1975, however, the California Supreme Court invalidated the state's death penalty statute again because it did not comply with the U.S. Supreme Court guidelines established in *Furman*.

Because of these developments, authorities also commuted the death sentences of Marie Elaine Kozeak and Mabel Glenn to life prison terms in 1976 and 1979 respectively. In October 1976, a Riverside County jury found Marie Elaine Kozeak guilty of the robbery and murder of a Pomona man near Blythe in the eastern part of the county. Kozeak and her accomplices, Michael Ray Taylor and an unnamed juvenile, had shot Ronald Hunziker to death with a rifle and dismembered his body, officials found only Hunziker's torso. Hunziker apparently agreed to drive Marie and Taylor to Michigan since he was driving there any way to visit his mother. The trial court sentenced Marie to death and Taylor to life in prison. There is no record of an appeal; one can assume that the state's Supreme Court commuted Marie's death sentence to life in prison because of the court invalidating the state's death penalty statute in December 1976. Marie remains jailed at the Valley State Prison for Women in Chowchilla, California.

A Santa Barbara County jury found Mabel Glenn guilty of murder-for-hire of her husband, retired Army sergeant and postal worker Edgar Glenn, and Superior Court Judge Arden T. Jensen sentenced Mabel to death. A jury also found her accomplice, Willie Lee Henderson, guilty of murder and sentenced him to death as well. Municipal Court Judge Robert Trapp sentenced another accomplice, Kirk L. Douglas, to a five-year prison term after he turned state's evidence and pleaded guilty to second-degree murder for his part in Edgar's killing. A court tried another accomplice, Michael Steele, as a juvenile. Mabel had offered the men part of a $50,000 life insurance policy. Apparently, after heavy drinking in the living room of Edgar's home in March 1974, Mabel went to the kitchen, brought a skillet into the living room, and put it behind the couch. Edgar was drunk and could hardly sit up. Henderson told Douglass to hit Edgar on the head with the skillet. Douglass did not remember whether he did so. Henderson took the skillet from Douglass and hit Edgar in the head until the handle broke. Steele stabbed Edgar a few times. Henderson took a gun he had with him, put a pillow over the victim's head, and shot him. The California Supreme Court invalidated the state's death penalty statute, and the California Court of Appeals vacated Mabel and Henderson's death sentences to life terms in May 1978.

In the post–*Furman* period, the Supreme Court of Delaware reversed the death sentence of one woman, Linda Lou Charbonneau. Linda was the former wife of John Charbonneau with whom she had a troubled marriage. Linda later married William Sproates, John's nephew. Melissa Rucinski was Linda's daughter and John's stepdaughter, who married Willie Tony Brown, an ex-convict. John Charbonneau disappeared in September 2001 and William advised Delaware State Police that Linda, Melissa, and Willie were responsible for John's death. Then, in November 2001, William's relatives notified police that he had disappeared. Police investigated William's residence and found his body buried in a shallow grave. An autopsy revealed that William had died from multiple stab wounds, blunt force trauma, and asphyxiation. As part of the investigation into Williams' murder, police inspected the Charbonneau residence and cars and found John's blood in a Dodge van and ATM receipts for money withdrawn from John's bank account in a Chevrolet Lumina. A convenience store video tape showed that Melissa had withdrawn the money from John's account. Police also found John's driver license and social security card at the residence. Police questioned Linda, Melissa, and Willie about Williams' body in the backyard and about John. The three denied knowing anything about Williams or the whereabouts of John. In December 2001, however, John Rucinski, Melissa's former husband, told police that Linda and Melissa had asked him to kill John in the fall of 2000 and bury his body in the backyard or by hiding it a camper. In the summer of 2002, Willie admitted to police that he had killed John and led police to John's body. An autopsy revealed that John died by blunt force injury causing a fractured skull. Willie implicated himself, Linda, and Melissa in the murders of William and John and of disposing the bodies. Melissa pled guilty to second-degree murder and a trial court sentenced her to a 25-year prison term. Willie Brown pled guilty to the first-degree murders of both John and William and sentenced to two consecutive life sentences without parole. A Sussex County jury found Linda guilty of the murders and based upon the jury's recommendation of death, the trial judge sentenced Linda to die by lethal injection. In March 2006, the Supreme Court of Delaware reversed Linda's conviction and death sentence because of judicial error at trial. At a retrial, Linda pleaded guilty to second-degree murder to killing John and prosecutors dropped the murder charge involving William. Linda is serving her sentence at the Baylor Women's Correctional Institution and is due for parole in April 2020.

Florida appeals courts commuted the sentences of six death row women between 1984 and 1993. The first of these cases took place in May of 1983 when Andrea Hicks Jackson vandalized her own car; she broke out the windows and removed the car's battery, spare tire, and license plate. Neighbors notified Jacksonville police and Officers Burton Griffin and Gary Bevel arrived at the scene. Jackson told the officers that someone had destroyed her car. After Officer Bevel had spoken to witnesses that Jackson had damaged her own car, he arrested Jackson for filing a false police report. While placing Jackson under arrest and placing her in the back of his patrol car, Jackson assaulted Officer Bevel. Sitting in the back of the patrol, Jackson told Officer Bevel that she had dropped her keys. When Bevel stepped back and bent down to search for the keys, Jackson shot him six times, four times in the head, once in the shoulder and once in the back. Officer Bevel fell into Jackson's lap and she pushed him aside and ran from the scene. Following the shooting, Jackson went to Shirley Ann Freeman's home and washed her clothes. She told Freeman that she had shot a cop because she "wasn't going back to jail" and she didn't like men touching her. Freeman called a cab and gave Jackson money for the cab fare. While in the cab, the taxi driver saw that Jackson had a gun, struggled with her and threw the gun from the car. Jackson left the taxi, retrieved the gun, and shot at the back window of the cab. Officers arrested Jackson hours later outside her ex-husband's apartment. In 1984, a Duval County jury found Jackson guilty of first-degree and recommended the death penalty, and finding no credible mitigating factors in the case, Circuit Court Judge Donald R. Moran sentenced Jackson to death.

The murder case against Jackson presents a rather complex appellate record. On direct appeal, the Florida Supreme Court affirmed Jackson's murder conviction and death sentence and the state's governor, Bob Martinez, signed a death warrant in March 1989. Jackson sought post-conviction relief but the trial court denied the motion. Jackson appealed the motion's denial and petitioned the state's Supreme Court for a writ of habeas corpus. The court granted her petition for habeas corpus because the trial court had wrongly admitted victim impact statements. The Court then vacated Jackson's death sentence and remanded the case back to the trial court for a new hearing before a new jury. The Court again vacated Jackson's death sentence based on improper jury instructions and remanded the case to the trial court where again a jury sentenced Jackson to death. A federal appeals court ruled that the trial court should resentence Jackson because the court did not have all the pertinent evidence before it at Jackson's trial. Finally, in June 2000, Judge Moran resentenced Jackson to life in prison. One reporter put it this way: "Yesterday, Chief Circuit Judge Donald R. Moran—who maintained for more than 15 years that Jackson should die for killing Officer Gary Bevel—stunned a Jacksonville courtroom when he changed his sentence and ordered that she instead spend the rest of her life in prison."[18] She is serving that sentence in the Lowell Correctional Institute Annex in Ocala, Florida.

Andrea's case accentuates the notion that trial courts are often unconcerned with the abusive experiences suffered by death row women. Mental health professionals testified at Andrea's trial that she was mentally impaired by drugs and alcohol at the time of the shooting; that she suffered from post-traumatic stress disorder due to extended sexual abuse by her stepfather; that she had a flashback of a prior sexual assault when the police officer struggled with her; and that her "capacity to appreciate the criminality of her conduct or to conform her conduct to the requirements of law was substantially impaired and that she was under the influence of extreme mental or emotional disturbance at the time of the crime."[19]

In 1986, Carla Ann Caillier solicited her lover, ballroom dance instructor Ty Payne, to murder her husband, Louis J. Caillier, to gain access to $110,000 life insurance policy and an additional $25,000 in a bank account from the sale of a pet shop. Trial evidence revealed that Carla hated her husband because he verbally abused her. Louis had moved to Tampa from Louisiana to find work as a cabinetmaker and planned to move Carla and their son after he found work. After purchasing a handgun, Payne went to Tampa where he killed Louis, shooting him twice in the chest and once in the back. Police arrested Payne for the murder to which he confessed and implicated Carla, whom authorities charged with first-degree murder. A Hillsborough County jury found Carla guilty of the murder and recommended life in prison, but Circuit Court Judge Harry Lee Coe overrode the jury recommendation and sentenced Carla to death. Judge Coe sentenced Payne to a 25-year prison term in exchange for his testimony against Carla. On appeal, Carla challenged the verdict and imposition of the death penalty. The Florida Supreme Court found sufficient evidence to affirm Carla's conviction but supported her contention that the trial court erred by overriding the jury's recommendation of life. The Court vacated the death sentence and remanded the case for an imposition of a life-prison term without eligibility of parole for 25 years. In 1992, Carla received a four-year sentence to run concurrently with her life term when she planned an escape from the Broward Correctional Institution. Carla pleaded guilty to conspiracy to aid and abet in an escape and introduction of contraband into a state prison. She remains jailed at the Lowell Correctional Institution in Ocala.

Authorities tried together James Allen Bryant, Dee Dyne Casteel, Michael R. Irvine, and William E. Rhodes for numerous offenses including two counts of first-degree murder and a jury found each of them guilty of the 1983 murders of the wealthy Arthur Venecia and his elderly mother Bessie Fischer. Dade County Circuit Court Judge Ralph N. Person sentenced them to death. According to prosecutors, Bryant, the homosexual lover and managerial employee of Venecia's, instigated the murders, while Casteel, whom Bryant employed at Venecia's restaurant, procured the hit men, Irvine and Rhodes. The record does not reveal any motive of Casteel for the killings, but some have speculated. It seems that Casteel would do what Bryant asked since she loved him even though he was a homosexual, she went along with Bryant's scheme to keep her job at an International House of Pancakes in Naranja, Florida, where Bryant was the manager (other restaurants in area had fired her), and that Casteel needed the job to help support her alcoholic husband and drug addicted daughter. Probably the most important reason for Casteel to join Bryant's murder conspiracy was that it made it possible for her to keep drinking while at work which Bryant tolerated; Casteel was an alcoholic who drank upwards of a quart of liquor per day. Despite her alcoholism, Casteel was well liked and considered a hard worker. It seems that Bryant wanted Venecia killed because Venecia had found a new lover. The assailants strangled Venecia in his bedroom and stored his body in a shed near Venecia's house. A few weeks later, Bryant had Irvine and Rhodes kill Bessie, who lived in a trailer on the property to keep her from talking about her missing son. On appeal to the Florida Supreme Court, the defendants raised numerous issues including that the state's prosecutor utilized its peremptory challenges to systematically exclude blacks, and that the trial court erred in refusing to sever the trials. The Florida Supreme Court agreed, reversed their convictions and death sentences, and remanded the cases for new trials. While James Bryant, Michael Irvine, and William Rhodes are serving long prison terms, but Dee Dyne Casteel died in prison in October 2002.

The case of Kaysie B. Dudley shows again that judges often sentence women to death while the actual killers receive a different punishment. In late September 1985, Daytona Beach waitress Kaysie, along with a co-worker, a cook named Michael F. Sorrentino, murdered her mother's wealthy employer, 77-year-old widow Geneva Kane, after she had fired Kaysie's mother, Nancy Dene, who worked as a maid for Kane. Kaysie admitted to authorities that she and Sorrentino went to Kane's home to steal several expensive rings and that she engaged in a physical struggle with Kane when he attempted to choke her with a belt. Sorrentino took over choking Kane in the kitchen of her home and slit Kane's throat with a knife. After murdering Kane and while she lay in a pool of blood, Kaysie and Sorrentino pried diamond and emerald rings worth $19,000 off her fingers. A Pinellas County jury found Kaysie guilty of first-degree murder and recommended the death penalty. Pinellas County Circuit Court Judge James R. Case imposed the death penalty, finding that the murder was particularly heinous, atrocious, cruel, cold, calculated, and premeditated, and that Kaysie committed the murder during a robbery for financial gain. Without elaboration, the court referenced Kaysie's past medical and psychological problems as mitigating factors. In 1989, the Florida Supreme Court vacated Kaysie's death sentence and remanded the case back to the trial court to resentence Kaysie before a new jury; apparently the trial court had allowed hearsay testimony at the trial and prosecutors agreed to allow Kaysie to serve a life sentence in prison. Sorrentino pleaded guilty to second-degree murder and the court sentenced him to a 25-year prison term. Prison officials released Sorrentino in June 2007. Kaysie Dudley remains incarcerated at the Lowell Correctional Institute Annex in Ocala, Florida.

In late October 1989, Deidre Michelle Hunt, her lover Konstantino O. Fotopoulos, and a young transient named Mark Kevin Ramsey, drove out to an isolated wooded rifle range. Once there, Ramsey, who Deidre and Fotopoulos led to believe were initiating him into a "hunter and killer club," tied him to a tree. While Fotopoulos videotaped, Deidre shot Ramsey three times in the chest and once in the head with a .22 gauge rifle. The videotaping stopped and Fotopoulos shot Ramsey once in the head with an AK-47 assault rifle. Apparently, each member of the "hunter and killer club" was videotaped killing someone and the members would exchange tapes as "insurance policies" insuring that the members of the club would not report each other's activities to authorities. According to trial testimony, one reason for Deidre and Fotopoulos choosing Ramsey as a victim was that he was blackmailing Fotopoulos concerning Fotopoulos' alleged counterfeiting activities and his affair with Deidre. After Ramsey's murder, Deidre and Fotopoulos began soliciting members of the club to kill Fotopoulos' wife, Lisa Psaros, so he could collect on a $250,000 life insurance policy. Fotopoulos used the videotape of Deidre killing Ramsey to insure Deidre's participation in his plan to murder his wife. Deidre enlisted Bryan Chase to do the job for $10,000. In November 1989, Chase entered Fotopoulos' residence and shot Lisa once in the head; the shot was not fatal. After Chase shot Lisa, in accord with Fotopoulos and Deidre's plan to get rid of the assassin and to make Lisa's murder appear to have occurred during a robbery, Fotopoulos fatally shot Chase. Prosecutors indicted Deidre and Fotopoulos for the murders of Ramsey and Chase. At the sentencing hearing, the trial court found several aggravating factors associated with Deidre's killing of Ramsey and Chase. In mitigation to both murders, the court found that Deidre was physically, emotionally, and sexually abused as a child, she entered into physically and emotionally abusive relationships with men, and was a prostitute The court also found Deidre to be a sociopath, unstable with a history of alcohol and drug abuse. The trial court rejected Deidre's contention that she acted under extreme duress and substantial domination of Fotopoulos, who masterminded the murder plots. Volusia County Circuit Court Judge imposed the death penalty as to both murders. Deidre pleaded guilty to two counts of first-degree murder, two counts of attempted first-degree murder, two counts of solicitation to commit first degree-murder, one count of conspiracy to commit first-degree murder, and one count of burglary of a dwelling while armed. At the time of her plea, Deidre waived a penalty-phase jury. The Supreme Court of Florida, however, affirmed Deidre's convictions but vacated the death sentences and remanded the case back to the trial court for resentencing in 1992. It seems that the state prosecutors did not honor a plea agreement that the trial judge would sentence Deidre after Fotopoulos' trial was complete. Deidre remains incarcerated in Florida serving two life sentences at the Homestead Correctional Institute, and Fotopoulos is on death row.

A Volusia County jury convicted Virginia Gail Larzelere for the March 1991 murder of her husband, Norman Larzelere, a dentist and for whom she worked as an office manager in his practice. Trial evidence showed that early in the afternoon a masked gunman went into Norman's dental office and shot him to death. The gunman was supposedly Jason Larzelere, Virginia's son from a previous marriage with whom she conspired to kill Norman for a $2 million in life insurance policy and $1 million in other assets. Virginia proved to be the dominant motivator to securing seven different life insurance policies on Norman and that within the six months preceding his death, Virginia doubled the total amount payable on his life from $1 million to over $2 million. Volusia County Circuit Court Judge John W. Watson, III, followed the jury's recommendation and sentenced Virginia to death. In a separate trial, a jury acquitted Jason Larzelere of being the triggerman. On appeal, the Florida Supreme Court affirmed Virginia's conviction and death sentence, but Judge Watson vacated the sentence in 2005 claiming that her lawyers, John Howes and Jack Wilkins, had been ineffective during the penalty phase of Virginia's trial. It seems her lawyers failed to introduce evidence that Virginia was sexually abused as a child by her father and her uncle, she had a disadvantaged and deprived childhood due to lack of friends and social activities caused by her father's pedophilia, she had a history of medical problems such as Legionnaire's disease and pulmonary issues, she had alcohol or drug abuse issues, she had a disabled son, she was physically abused as an adult, and that she suffers from personality disorders, including narcissistic and histrionic personality disorders explaining her relationship troubles and cunning, manipulative behavior. Virginia suffers from post-traumatic stress disorder and an obsessive-compulsive disorder. In response to the Supreme Court upholding the incompetent defense counsel argument, Assistant Attorney General Barbara Davis claimed that Virginia tried to kill two prior husbands, embezzled from an employer, and that she exposed her own children to sexual abuse. There is also speculation that Norman sold illegal narcotics to some of his patients, that he had a long list of gay lovers, and that he would arrange sexual liaisons for Virginia. Resentenced to life in prison, Virginia Larzelere remains jailed at the Lowell Correctional Institute Annex in Ocala, Florida.

Florida officials tried, convicted, and sentenced to death Sonia "Sunny" Jacobs (also known as Sonia Kinder) and her boyfriend and father of her oldest child, Jesse Joseph Tafero, for the murder of Florida Highway Patrol trooper Philip Beck and vacationing Canadian trooper Donald Irwin. The two officers reportedly approached a car parked at a rest stop off an interstate highway in Broward County in which Jacobs, Tafero, their ten-month-old daughter, Jacob's six-year-old son, and a friend of Tafero's, Walter Norman Rhodes, were sleeping. Gunfire broke out between Rhodes and the two police officers once the troopers learned over a radio transmission that Rhodes had a criminal record. Rhodes had shot and killed both officers. Rhodes commandeered the patrol car but officials later captured the group when Rhodes lost control of the car while evading a police roadblock. At trial, Jacobs and Tafero claimed that Rhodes had shot the officers and Rhodes forced them to go with him after the shooting. Eyewitness testimony and forensic evidence supported Jacobs and Tafero's declarations. Rhodes had turned state's evidence and agreed to testify against Jacobs and Tafero for a reduced charge of second-degree murder and a sentence of life in prison. Brenda Isham, a jailhouse informant, also testified that Jacobs had confessed to the murders. Blatant prejudice overwhelmed the trial: all the jurors knew of the case, the jury was not sequestered, and the trial judge, M. Daniel Futch, Jr., kept a miniature replica of an electric chair on his desk. What's more, the judge rejected a jury recommendation of life in prison for Jacobs and instead sentenced her to death. On appeal, the Florida Supreme

Court commuted Jacobs' sentence to life in prison claiming that Judge Futch lacked the necessary evidence to override the jury's recommendation. In a writ of habeas corpus hearing before a federal court, Brenda Isham recanted her trial testimony and admitted to committing perjury under threats from the prosecution. Affidavits filed with the U.S. Circuit Court of Appeals by Micki Dickoff, a childhood friend of Jacobs, brought further claims of Jacobs' innocence. In October 1992, the state attorney released Jacobs after strong-arming her into entering a plea that did not admit guilt or she would face a re-trial and possible death sentence. Sonia had spent 16 years in prison for a crime she did not commit. State officials convicted Tafero on much of the same evidence used to exonerate Jacobs. Tafero underwent a ghoulish execution in Florida's electric chair in May 1990 during which flames and smoke shot out of Tafero's head, forcing executioners to interrupt his electrocution three times. Shortly after Tafero's botched execution, Florida moved to adopt lethal injection as the state's execution method.

Georgia appeals courts have overturned the death sentences of six women since the state revamped its death penalty statue in light of *Furman*. One of the women was Rebecca Machetti whom a Bibb County jury convicted in February 1975 for the shotgun murders of her ex-husband, Joseph Ronald Akins, and his new wife of 20 days, Juanita Knight Akins, in a secluded area of a new housing development in August 1974. A jury in a separate trial found Rebecca's then present husband, Anthony Isalldo Machetti, also guilty of the murders. Rebecca's jury recommended death and Superior Court Judge Morgan sentenced her accordingly. Trial evidence showed that the Machetti's, along with John Maree, planned the Joseph's death to redeem $20,000 in life insurance policy and other benefits of which Rebecca and her three daughters by her marriage to Joseph were beneficiaries. According to Maree's trial testimony, the Machetti's were to pay him $1,000 for his participation in the killings. He testified at Rebecca's trial that he and Anthony drove to Macon, Georgia, where they contacted Ronald and lured him to the housing development ostensibly to install a television antenna. When Joseph and his wife arrived at the location, Anthony killed both of them with a shotgun. Anthony and Maree then returned to Florida. The Georgia Supreme Court consolidated the cases against Rebecca and Anthony Machetti and affirmed the convictions and death sentences of both defendants.

Rebecca appealed to the U.S. Court of Appeals contending that the state had systematically excluded women from her jury. The Court found that Rebecca's jury comprised only 18 percent women despite census data showing that women were 54 percent of the Bibb County adult population. The grand jury list contained only 12 percent women. The Court argued that the absolute disparity between the adult female population of Bibb County and the grand jury list deprived Rebecca of her constitutional right to an impartial jury trial. It seems that at the time of jury selection for Rebecca's trial, state law provided for any woman who preferred not to serve on a jury could "opt-out" by sending written notice to the jury commissioners. Potential women jurors in Bibb County automatically received cards allowing them the opportunity to exempt themselves from service. A retrial found Rebecca guilty of the murder and the trial court sentenced her to life in prison; officials paroled Rebecca in July 2010 after she had served 36 years. Maree drew a life sentence after agreeing to testify for the prosecution and Georgia officials paroled him in 1987. Georgia put Anthony Machetti (also known as John Eldon Smith) to death by electrocution in December 1983.

In October 1979, a Lincoln County jury found Emma Cunningham, along with her husband James Cunningham, guilty of the January 1979 robbery-murder of a wealthy businessman named William Beall Crawford, found brutally beaten to death in his home. Superior Court Judge Stevens sentenced Emma Ruth to death even though she did not kill Crawford. Unlike many death row women, Emma's parents raised her in a loving and caring home though they were very controlling and overprotective. Emma ran away from home at 18 years old, dropped out of school, and married James Cunningham. Emma Ruth and James had befriended Crawford from whom the couple attempted to borrow money, but he refused a loan thereby inducing James to burglarize Crawford's house. While engaged in the burglary, Crawford startled James who then proceeded to savagely beat Crawford to death with a large wrench. Forensic evidence showed that both of the Crawford's forearms were broken, his lip was bruised, his nose was split, his cheekbones were fractured, and he suffered blows to the head that resulted in eight skull fractures. James confessed to assaulting Crawford during a burglary and robbery of his home, and that Crawford was lying on the floor moaning when he left the house. Based on an anonymous tip, police arrested Emma Ruth and James for Crawford's murder as they boarded on a bus for North Carolina to start a better life. Authorities prosecuted Emma Ruth based on a vicarious liability doctrine of conspiracy imputing the crimes of conspirators to all other conspirators. Pursuant to this doctrine, Emma Ruth was liable as James for Crawford's murder even though she did not participate in the killing. The Georgia Supreme Court argued, however, that the state had convicted and sentenced Emma to death based upon a conspiracy theory that could not stand because the evidence used by the court to substantiate the crime was inadmissible. The appeals court ruled that Emma Ruth was entitled to a new trial. Authorities re-sentenced Emma Ruth to life in prison in 1983 and paroled her in 1990.

In December 1979 after a two-day trial, an all-white Pike County jury convicted Shirley Tyler of the poison-murder of her husband, James Wilson Tyler, and Superior Court Judge Whalen sentenced Shirley to death. Earlier in October, James ate a large bowl of chili prepared by Shirley. About an hour later, James staggered over to his father's house next door showing physical symptoms identical to those he experienced on two other occasions for which he required hospitalized. His father summoned medical personnel, but James died in route to the hospital. An autopsy found that James died from a fatal ingestion of a toxic substance used in rat poison. In a police interview, Shirley admitted that she had scraped a spoonful of poison out of the cabinet drawer and had mixed it with the chili that James had eaten immediately prior to his death. She stated that her motive for killing James was to prevent him from hurting her son; James had a history of beating his wife and children. What's more, Shirley had James jailed on several occasions throughout their turbulent 12-year marriage for such maltreatment. Trial testimony showed that Shirley had occasionally been involved with another man. Shirley admitted to police that her husband had a life insurance policy valued at $15,000.

Not surprisingly for a poor and uneducated black woman living in a southern state, police had Shirley sign a written confession with no attorney present; she did not see her court-appointed lawyer until two weeks before trial. In 1981, the Supreme Court of Georgia affirmed Shirley's conviction and death sentence, but in February 1985, the U.S. Court of Appeals granted Shirley a writ of habeas corpus on her death sentence arguing that her attorney, Richard Bishoff, was ineffective because he failed to present mitigating evidence at the sentencing phase of Shirley's trial. To the federal court, Bishoff could have submitted the following mitigating factors: Shirley Tyler had no prior criminal record; she had a good work record and used her earnings to help care for her family; her husband was drunk and abusive at times and had knocked out some of her teeth when drunk; on one occasion she and her children moved away because he drank and beat her; on another occasion he put her out of the house in her night clothes; she was a good mother, crazy about her children, and kept them clean and cared for; her character and reputation as a wife and mother were good. The court reversed her death sentence to life in prison and after serving 17 years officials released Shirley in 1997.

Janice Buttrum had a troubling and exceptionally impoverished childhood, her upbringing epitomized child neglect. As explained by the U.S. Court of Appeals, Janice's alcoholic and unmarried mother gave her away as an infant to a middle-aged couple named Adcock, also alcoholics, in exchange for payment of her hospital maternity bill. The Adcock's sexually abused Janice who grew up in a three-room, unpainted house with no bathroom. The Adcock's moved to a one-bedroom trailer where Janice's slept in a broken-down van in the yard. The trailer was filthy, the floor covered with dirt, paper, beer bottles, and moldy food. The city dump provided most of Janice's clothing and her stepmother, often drunk, subjected Janice to physical and emotional abuse. The children at Janice's school ridiculed and ostracized her because young Janice was dirty, smelled horribly, had unfitting clothes, matted hair, a dirty face, filthy nails, and often went to school with no shoes to wear. One teacher stated, "She never carried on a conversation with anybody; she just always stood over to herself." Still, Janice posed no problem for school officials who described Janice as shy, passive, quiet, non-violent, withdrawn, a follower, and as having a passive personality but low self-image. While in her early teens, Janice ran away from her dilapidated home and befriended two older men who sexually assaulted her. Social services declared her a deprived child when she was 14 years old and shuttled between foster homes until finally placing her in a Youth Detention Center where she remained for six months. A year later, Janice returned home to her stepmother where she met Danny Buttrum, a 26-year-old divorced father of two. Danny was borderline mentally retarded and a drug dealer. Janice married Danny within a month and for the entire two-year marriage, Danny repeatedly beat her. Janice had a baby at 17 years old.

In August 1981, a Whitfield County jury found Janice Buttrum guilty of the sex torture and stabbing murder of 19-year-old Demetra Faye Parker that took place a year earlier. The jury found that Janice committed the murder in the course of a rape, that it was outrageous, vile, and inhuman, involving torture and depravity of mind. Superior Court Judge Pannell sentenced Janice to death. Testimony and evidence presented at trial revealed that Janice and her husband, Danny Buttrum, raped, sodomized, and stabbed Demetra 97 times with a small pocketknife while in her Country Boy Inn motel room. Demetra had recently moved to Georgia from Tennessee. Janice and Danny lived in the same motel and befriended Demetra. Danny had recently escaped from prison work camp in Cobb County. On the night of the murder, Demetra was in her motel room watching television with two male friends and saw Danny pacing back and forth in front of her room. Demetra told her friends she was afraid of him. Later in the evening, Demetra drove to her friend's home.

After her arrest, Janice gave inconsistent accounts of the initial events of the murder. In one account, Janice claims she and Danny went to Demetra's room to scare her. In another story, when the couple entered Demetra's room Danny threw her to the floor and Janice took a knife from Danny and stabbed Demetra to death while Danny masturbated. In still another account, Janice claimed she waited outside the room for several minutes after Danny entered and that when she entered the room, Danny was removing Demetra's underwear and believed the two were going to have intercourse. There is speculation that Janice had oral sex with Demetra as she was stabbing her to death. Not surprisingly, Janice's rumored sexual acts on Demetra became an integral part of the state's case against Janice. After the killing, Janice and Danny fled to Pensacola, Florida, were the FBI apprehended them in a restaurant.

An autopsy on Demetra showed that she incurred 67 stab wounds to her left chest, 24 stab wounds and cuts to her front neck area with several cuts to the windpipe, a spinal stab into the backbone, a gaping gash inflicted to Demetra's lower abdomen exposing her bowels, cut to her genital area, as well as damage to the vagina and rectum from forcible penetration. Demetra also suffered from hemorrhages and bruise marks on her scalp, nose, knees, and genital region. There was a bite mark on her neck, and a plastic toothbrush holder recovered from her vagina. The vast majority of injuries were around Demetra's vagina and anus, inflicted while she was still alive. Demetra reportedly died toward the end of the protracted assault. All the time the couple's young daughter Marlena was playing under a coffee table. Janice was also pregnant with a second child, Maria, who was born in prison.

At trial, Janice's defense lawyer asserted that Danny controlled Janice and cajoled her into participating in the murder. At the penalty phase of the trial, the state proffered the expertise of a psychiatrist who argued that Janice was a sexual sadist and posed a future threat. The defense presented Janice's background in mitigation of the death sentence. In the summer 1982, the Georgia Supreme Court affirmed Janice's conviction and death sentence, concluding that the crime against Demetra "can only be described as butchery and barbarism." The court found that passion, prejudice, or arbitrary factors did not influence the jury's decision to impose Janice with the death penalty. What's more, the Court found that Janice was not entitled to a jury instruction on "her deprived childhood, or her sad and complex life." The Court denied Janice's state petition for habeas corpus and she appealed to the federal courts. In 1989, however, the U.S. District Court denied Janice's petition on the murder conviction but granted her a new trial on the death sentence. The District Court found that when the lower court allowed psychiatric evidence from the state it prejudiced Janice in the penalty phase of her trial because the trial court prohibited defense funds for obtaining private psychiatric assistance. At the new hearing in 1991, Janice pled guilty to Demetra's murder and accepted a life sentence without the possibility of parole and remains in prison. Danny Buttrum committed suicide in his jail cell a week after the court sentenced him to death.

In May 1982, a Madison County jury convicted Teresa Whittington guilty of the shooting death of Cheryl Marie Soto and Superior Court Judge Bryant sentenced Teresa to death. After graduating from high school in May 1981, Teresa began working at a grocery store in Athens, Georgia, where she met Richard Soto (also known as Richard R. Miller) who was married to the murder victim. Cheryl, three months pregnant, discovered that Teresa and Richard were having a relationship. Richard and Teresa planned Cheryl's murder with Teresa to shoot Cheryl to death. Richard obtained a $50,000 life insurance policy on Cheryl with a double indemnity clause months before meeting Teresa. As planned, Teresa went into the Soto's house while Cheryl was bathing and shot her once in the neck with a handgun that Richard had purchased months before. Teresa left the house but returned when Richard demanded that she make sure Cheryl was dead. When Teresa re-entered the house, she found Cheryl standing in the living room and she shot Cheryl in the forehead while she begged for her life. Richard then ransacked the house under the ruse that a robbery had been committed. Richard went to a neighbor's house and asked that they call the police and get an ambulance. Sheriff's deputies found Cheryl's naked body on the living room floor. An investigation led police to Teresa. Once in custody, Teresa made and signed a confession to Cheryl's murder. Richard received a life sentence after the jury deadlocked on imposing the death penalty. In February 1984, the Georgia Supreme Court affirmed Teresa's murder conviction but overturned her death sentence because the state failed to show aggravating circumstances. The Court argued that Cheryl's murder was not outrageously and wantonly vile, horrible, and inhuman in that it did not involve torture to the victim or depravity of mind on the part Teresa. The trial court subsequently sentenced her to life in prison. The Idaho Commission on Pardons and Parole paroled Teresa in December 2004.

In separate incidents from 1977 to 1982, Martha Ann Johnson murdered her four children. The case lay dormant for some six years until a reporter for the *Atlanta Journal-Constitution* wrote an article challenging how the government handles deaths of juveniles. The report sparked a police officer to review the file and reopen the case in 1988. At the time of their deaths, medical authorities had determined the cause of death of the children as Sudden Infant Death Syndrome. The children were two-year-old James William Taylor, three-month-old Tibitha Janeel Bowen, three-year-old Earl Wayne Bowen, and 11-year-old Jenny Ann Wright. Once police reopened the case, Martha confessed to killing the children in 1977, 1980, 1981, and 1982, respectively. In May 1990, a Clayton County jury convicted Martha of the children's deaths and Judge Kilpatrick sentenced her death. The Georgia Supreme Court affirmed the conviction and death sentence in July 1991, but another appeal commuted Martha's death sentence to life in prison. Martha is currently serving her life sentence at the Pulaski State Prison.

Karla Yvonne Windsor had a troubled childhood. Karla's stepfather sexually molested her at a very young age that resulted in authorities placing her in a series of foster homes and group care facilities. Karla underwent clinical counseling for several years during her teens. Karla also spent time in shelter homes, juvenile hall, and at a school for incorrigible girls. Yet, Canyon County District Attorney Richard L. Harris was quick to point out that Karla's counseling "had negligible effect on her ability to conform her conduct to the requirements of the law." As an adult, Karla lived on the streets as a drug user and a prostitute. According to Harris, Karla's entire history "discloses that the defendant has been hardly anything more than a societal parasite." Harris won a murder conviction against Karla in February 1984 when a Canyon County jury returned a guilty verdict for Karla Yvonne Windsor to the charges of grand theft, second-degree burglary and the first-degree felony murder of Sterling Grammer. District Judge Edward J. Lodge sentenced Karla to death.

In September 1983, Karla and her co-defendant boyfriend, Donald Fetterly, had become acquainted with Sterling and showed up one evening without money, a vehicle, or a place to stay. Karla and Donald apparently sold most of their belongings to raise money to travel to adjacent states in search of work. There were several arrest warrants out on Karla and Donald. Sterling invited them for dinner and offered for them to stay the night since he had an extra bedroom. Early the next morning, Sterling, Karla, and Donald left the house together. Karla and Donald returned to Sterling's house later that afternoon and waited for him to arrive from work. When Sterling failed to arrive at home, Karla and Donald entered the house and waited for him. Sterling had spent the night elsewhere with a friend. When Sterling arrived the following morning, Karla and Donald asked him to give them a vehicle and money. When Sterling refused, the two hit him unconscious, bound his feet, hands, and face with duct tape, and left him lying on a bed. Gaining consciousness, Sterling struggled when Donald grabbed a knife he used to cut the duct tape and stabbed Sterling in the chest. Sterling continued to struggle and Donald stabbed him several more times in the chest. Afterwards, Donald and Karla dumped Sterling's body in the Snake River where anglers found it a few days later. Police took the couple into custody for questioning after seeing them driving around in Sterling's pickup truck. Karla and Donald proceeded to give detailed confessions to Sterling's murder. Based on that confession, officials indicted the two on charges of first-degree murder, burglary, grand theft and the use of a deadly weapon in the commission of a felony. In December 1983, a separate jury found Donald guilty of first-degree felony murder and the court sentenced him to life imprisonment without parole. In December 1985, the Supreme Court of Idaho affirmed Karla's murder conviction but vacated the death sentence and remanded the case for re-sentencing. The Court held that Karla's death sentence was excessive and disproportionate since Karla received the same death sentence as her co-defendant who actually committed the murder; Karla only participated in the burglary. The trial court sentenced Karla to a life prison term and prison officials paroled her in August 2004.

In the late evening on June 23, 1987, Eddie Williams shot Valerie McDonald in the head in front of her husband, Louia, and her two daughters, 16-year-old LaChina and eight-year-old Lakeya. Valerie died two days later. A police investigation into the shooting resulted in the arrests of Geraldine Smith, Marva Golden, and Eddie Williams. The investigation revealed that Geraldine and Louia were involved in an extramarital affair and that Geraldine gave birth to Louia's child in 1986 whom she named Louia McDonald, Jr. Trial testimony showed that the night of the murder Louia picked up his family after Valerie and her two daughters had attended church services had drove them home to family's Chicago apartment. As Louia and his daughters entered the building with Valerie trailing behind them, Eddie shot Valerie in the head and she collapsed on the sidewalk. Louia pursued Eddie but he escaped in a car belonging to Geraldine.

Marva identified Eddie to police as the person who shot Valerie and LaChina, who witnessed the actual shooting, identified Eddie from a lineup as the man who shot her mother. It seems Geraldine had Eddie kill Valerie for $500. Geraldine waived her right to a jury and Cook County Circuit Court Judge John W. Crilly sentenced Geraldine to death. The Illinois Supreme Court affirmed Geraldine's conviction but reversed her death sentence. According to the Illinois Department of Corrections, authorities paroled Geraldine Smith in February 2008 and her projected discharge date was February 2011. The Illinois Supreme Court vacated Eddie Williams' death sentence because the state's attorney misrepresented evidence and the law during closing arguments, and he remains incarcerated at the Statesville Correctional Facility. Marva Golden plead guilty to first-degree murder, served her sentence, and is no longer in custody.

Increasing rates of violence among young women may accent their resistance to gender inequality. A recent study finds a "disturbing trend of an increasingly violent society where women and young girls assume the role of perpetrator."[20] This may be the case of three young Latinas that shot and killed rival gang members in Chicago in the early 1990s. Stemming from Latino gang hostilities between the "Maniac Latin Disciples" and the "Latin Kings," a 21-year-old mother of two named Marilyn ("Mauri") Mulero, along with 15-year-old Jacqueline Montanez and 16-year-old Madeline Mendoza, murdered Jimmy Cruz and Hector Reyes with a small caliber hand gun in May 1992. Marilyn and her confederates killed Cruz and Reyes in a public bathroom in Humboldt Park. Jacqueline shot Reyes execution style with a bullet to the back of the head and then gave the gun to Marilyn who shot Cruz in the same manner. The shootings took place in the early morning hours of May 1992 in retaliation for the death of a gang member named Mudo killed by members of the Latin King Gang days earlier. Police arrested the three female suspects within hours of the killings. In September 1993, Marilyn pled guilty to the murders, a Cook County jury recommended the death penalty, and Circuit Judge Colleen McSweeney Moore sentenced Marilyn to death. In 1997, however, Marilyn won a new sentencing hearing after the Illinois Supreme Court found prosecutorial error in her 1993 trial. Subsequently, the trial jury recommended that the court sentence her to life in prison without parole. Marilyn remains in custody at the Dwight Correctional Center in Dwight, Illinois. Tried as an adult, Madeline Mendoza pleaded guilty to murder and the trial court sentenced her to a 35-year prison term in 1993. Officials paroled Madeline in August 2009 and her discharge date was August 2012. Circuit Court Judge John J. Mannion sentenced Jacqueline Montanez to life in prison with no parole. In June 1995, an Illinois appellate court granted Jacqueline Montanez a new trial because her confession to the murders was involuntary.

Indiana authorities reversed the death sentences of Paula R. Cooper in 1989 and Lois Ann Thacker in 1990. In first instance in May 1985 at the age of 15, Paula R. Cooper, along with Cooper's accomplice April Beverly, entered 78-year-old Ruth Pelke's house armed with a knife "to get money and jewelry and different things" under the ruse of learning the schedule of her Bible classes. While Ruth wrote down the information about her Bible classes, Paula grabbed Ruth from behind and pushed her to the floor. Paula then hit her over the head with vase, cut Ruth's arms and legs, and stabbed her in the stomach and chest. An autopsy revealed that Paula had stabbed Ruth 33 times. Paula and April stole $10 from the house and Paula's car. In July 1985, authorities charged the two girls with Ruth's murder, and in April 1986, Paula pled guilty and admitted that she had entered Ruth's house intending to commit robbery. The trial court found that Cooper's statements provided the factual basis to prove she had committed the crimes and entered a judgment of conviction. In July of that year, Judge James Kimbrough sentenced Cooper to death. On direct appeal to the Supreme Court of Indiana, Paula's attorneys argued that sentencing her to death violates the state and federal constitutions because Paula was a minor when she committed the crime. The Supreme Court of Indiana agreed with Paula's claim, vacated the death sentence, and remanded the case back to the trial court with instructions that the court sentence Paula to the maximum prison sentence of 60 years afforded by law for murder. Paula remained incarcerated at the Rockville Correctional Facility until her release in June 2013.

In the case of Lois Ann Thacker, trial evidence shows that Lois hired her cousin, Charles M. Music, to kill her husband, John Thacker, to collect on a $134,000 life insurance policy. The Thackers had a troubled marriage. In 1984, Charles hired two other assailants, Donald R. Buchanan and James L. Hart, to aid in John's murder. In November of that year, the three men drove a short distance from the Thacker's house, put a log across the road, and waited for John to come along. When John drove up in his truck and stopped to remove the log, Charles shot and killed John with a shotgun. A Dubois County jury convicted Lois for the murder of her husband and Circuit Court Judge Hugo C. Songer imposed a sentence of death. On direct appeal to the Supreme Court of Indiana, the justices affirmed Lois' conviction but vacated the death sentence and remanded the case to the trial court for resentencing to the maximum prison sentence allowed by law for murder. The court overturned the death sentence because the aggravating circumstance of murder for hire was not present; the court found that the defendant never offered to compensate the men for the murder, and the court affirmed the conviction because defendant caused the men to commit the murder. Thacker remains imprisoned at the Indiana Women's Prison and her earliest release date is November 2011. State authorities discharged James Hart in October 1996, Donald Buchanan in January 2001, and Charles Music in April 2008.

Cindy Lou Landress had a difficult childhood. Cindy's father abused and her brothers and their friends sexually molested Cindy, and her parents were alcoholics. Cindy's mother refused to believe her about her sexual abuse and would physically abuse Cindy herself when she was intoxicated. Cindy claimed that such constant abuse led her to marry at the age of 13 and to become addicted to drugs and alcohol. Cindy's suffering as a young child had no impact on the courts, but the abuse undoubtedly gave rise to Cindy's crime. In April 1988, a Lake Superior County jury found 31-year-old Cindy guilty of the felony murder of 46-year-old Leonard Fowler during a robbery and recommended a death sentence. Judge Richard Conroy sentenced Cindy to die in the state's electric chair. On direct appeal to the Supreme Court of Indiana, Cindy did not challenge the jury's finding of guilt, but disputed the imposition of the death penalty. The Court found that the evidence was insufficient to find that Cindy had the intent to kill, a requisite to the imposition of the death penalty. The Court vacated Cindy's death sentence and remanded the case for imposition of a new sentence. According to the appellate record, Cindy lived at Leonard's home, a former boyfriend, and was awakened mid-morning after William O. Lewellen had arrived. She and William began talking and drinking in the kitchen when William suddenly threatened Leonard with a knife and forced him to lie face down on the floor. Cindy obtained an extension cord that William used to tie up Leonard and robbed him of $1,000. He handed the wallet to Cindy and she removed the money. At that time, Cindy told William that Leonard had escaped to his bedroom and was loading a shotgun when William entered the room and stabbed Leonard to death. William stabbed Leonard 22 times. Cindy removed Leonard's truck keys from his pocket as instructed to by William. Using Leonard's truck, Cindy and William went to California where authorities arrested the two a few weeks later. Forensics found that Leonard died from multiple stab wounds to his abdomen that severed a large artery, causing him to bleed to death. To support its claim that Cindy lacked the requisite intent to kill to warrant a capital sentence, the state's Supreme Court that there was no direct evidence that Cindy inflicted a mortal wound or used the knife in a manner likely to cause great bodily injury. On remand, the trial court sentenced defendant to a 60-year prison term. Cindy appealed that sentence as inappropriate given the mitigating evidence she presented at trial. The Supreme Court affirmed the sentence. Cindy remains incarcerated at the Indiana Women's Prison but has a projected release date of October 2017. William pled guilty to murder to avoid the death penalty and a prison sentence at the Miami Correctional Facility. He has a projected release date of December 2018.

In late July 1993, Angela Johnson and her boyfriend Dustin Lee Honken murdered execution-style five people—Gregory Nicholson, Terry DeGeus, Lori Duncan (Nicolson's girlfriend), and Duncan's two children, 10-year-old Kandi and six-year-old Amber. Under a ruse, Angela and Honken stormed Duncan's house and extorted a videotaped statement from Nicholson exonerating Honken against a federal indictment for drug trafficking activities. Afterwards, Angela and Honken tortured, bound, gagged the victims and drove them to a wooded area southwest of Mason City. Honken took Duncan and Nicholson out of the car and shot them in the back of the head while Angela stayed in the car with the children. Honken then shot and killed the two children. Angela and Honken dumped all four bodies into a single grave dug earlier. In early November of that year, Angela lured Terry DeGeus to a meeting place where she and Honken beat him to death with a baseball bat and then shot him several times. Honken wanted Greg Nicholson and Terry DeGeus dead because they were witnesses in the federal drug trafficking case against Honken. Duncan and her children simply had the misfortune to be at home when Angela and Honken went looking for Nicholson. Subsequent to the deaths of Nicholson and DeGeus, the government dropped its case against Honken but continued its investigation. The government indicted Honken again in 1996 on other federal drug charges and sentenced him to a long prison term in February 1998. In July 2000, the government charged Angela with several non-capital crimes relating to the 1993 murders. While in custody awaiting trial on those charges, Angela drew maps to the grave sites and gave them to jailhouse informant Robert McNeese who turned them over to police. It was only then that law enforcement discovered the bodies.

Federal prosecutors indicted Angela and Honken on five capital murder charges in 2001. In June 2005, a federal jury in Cerra Gordo County, Iowa, found Angela guilty of aiding and abetting Honken in the killings and recommended the death penalty for Angela. U.S. District Judge Mark Bennett affirmed the conviction and imposed the death sentences on Angela. The capital cases against Angela generated more than two dozen published rulings on pre-trial, trial, and post-trial issues. Angela is at a medical center for female inmates in Fort Worth, Texas, and is the first woman sentenced to death by the federal government since executions resumed in 1976. In February 2007 the U.S. Court of Appeals for the Eighth District affirmed the conviction and death sentence. But in March 2012, Judge Bennett vacated Angela's death sentence ruling that her lawyers failed to introduce mental health evidence during the penalty phase of her trial that could have resulted in a different jury finding. Bennett's ruling did not affect Angela's guilty verdict. She remains incarcerated at a medical center in Fort Worth, Texas. In June 2012, the U.S. Attorney's Office stated that it will again seek the death penalty against Angela but her trial will be limited to the penalty phase. In April 2013, Bennett made it clear that he will instruct the new jury that if even one juror does not want to impose the death penalty he will sentence Johnson to life in prison without parole. Vacating her death sentences does not effect her convictions in the case. In December 2014, federal prosecutors abandoned seeking the death penalty against Angela and she will serve a life sentence without parole.

In early October 1979, Jefferson County authorities indicted LaVerne O'Bryan for the 1967 murder of a former boyfriend, Harold Sadler, the 1979 murder of her husband John O'Bryan, and the attempted murder of her sister-in-law, LeAnne O'Bryan. After a trial in the summer of 1980, a jury found LaVerne guilty of the murders and attempted murder and Circuit Judge S. Rush Nicholson sentenced her to death. In June 1979, John O'Bryan became violently ill and soon hospitalized with acute abdominal pain, vomiting, weakness, dizziness, kidney malfunction, and a deteriorating capacity. John died a day following his hospitalization. An autopsy revealed that John died because of acute arsenic poisoning. Police soon learned that Harold Sadler, with whom LaVerne had lived, died of similar complications in December 1967. Authorities exhumed Harold's body and found that he died from chronic arsenic poisoning. LaVerne also poisoned LeAnne while she waited in the hospital for John to recover. Police searched LaVerne's house and found arsenic in a bottle of horse medicine. The prosecution charged that LaVerne killed both husbands because she wanted their land holdings. On appeal to the Supreme Court of Kentucky in 1982, LaVerne alleged that there was no evidence that she furthered Harold Sadler's death and thus the trial court improperly admitted prejudicial evidence to that effect. The Court reversed LaVerne's murder conviction and death sentence and remanded the case back to the trial court with instructions to retry LaVerne. There is no record that LaVerne remains jailed.

Lafonda Fay Foster came from a highly dysfunctional family where she suffered physical and emotional abuse as a young child. She became a drug-addicted prostitute and eventually had a lesbian relationship with a woman named Tina Hickey Powell that prosecutors used heavily to demoralize Lafonda at her sentencing trial. One psychologist testified at Lafonda's trial that she "was an extremely emotionally disturbed child, was an extremely emotionally disturbed adolescent; she is an extremely emotionally disturbed and drug dependent adult." The appellate record shows that in April 1986, Lafonda and Tina murdered Carlos Kearns, his wife Virginia Kearns, Roger Keene, Theodore Sweet, and Trudy Harrell by shooting them in the back of the head, stabbing them relentlessly about their faces, chests, and necks, cutting their throats, and running over them with a car where the bodies became lodged and dragged considerable distances. In the case of one victim, Roger Keene, the two women shot him two times in the back of the head and once in the ear, and while pinned under the car, Lafonda and Tina set the car on fire. In April 1987, a Fayette County jury found Lafonda Foster and Tina Powell guilty of the five murders. Circuit Court Judge James E. Keller sentenced Lafonda to death and Tina to a life prison term. On direct appeal in 1991, the Supreme Court of Kentucky affirmed Lafonda's conviction but reversed her death sentence. The Court claimed that the trial court erred when it admitted evidence of prior acts of misconduct (that Lafonda had shot her husband, cut her brother with a knife, charged with carrying a concealed deadly weapon, involved in burglaries, and fought with other people), contents of letters written by Lafonda to Tina (showing a "great propensity for violence"), and evidence regarding the battered wife syndrome (that Tina feared Lafonda because she had beaten Tina on several occasions throughout their lesbian relationship). The state's attorney used these issues to "defeminize Foster and to portray her as a brutal, manly murderer." Together, the court argued, these errors prejudiced Lafonda's sentencing hearing and required reversal of her death sentence. Authorities resentenced Lafonda to life in prison without parole in 1999 and she currently resides at the Western Kentucky Correctional Complex in Fredonia. Tina Powell resides at the Kentucky Correctional Institute in Pewee Valley.

In late April 2002, a Rapides Parish grand jury indicted Amanda Gutweiler (Hypes, Kelly) on three counts of first-degree murder contending that she deliberately set fire to her family home in January 2001 with the intent of killing her three young children, ten-year-old Sadii Plumm, six-year-old Luke Hayden and three-year-old Jessica Gutweiler. The state sought the death penalty against Amanda and based the murder charges on a fire expert's analysis conducted more than a year after officials had razed the burnt-out house. Amand remained in jail for more than four years awaiting trial. In June 2006, however, a judge dismissed the indictment and ordered her released. The judge ruled that authorities based their initial arson findings "merely on an old wives' tale" and that "every shred of evidence to prove or disprove a possible crime was destroyed and placed in a pile."

In a pre-trial motion to squash the indictment filed with the court in February 2006, Amanda's attorneys alleged that the assistant district attorney confirmed that he had released grand jury testimony to the state's chief forensic arson expert, Dr. John DeHaan. The Third Circuit Court of Appeal and the state's Supreme Court upheld the dismissal. In 2008, however, the state's attorney charged Amanda with three lesser charges of second-degree cruelty to a juvenile. In February 2010, Amanda pleaded guilty to three counts of negligent homicide in the deaths of her three children.

Maryland rewrote its death penalty laws in 1975, but nobody sentenced to death since then has exhausted appeals in state courts. When those appeals are exhausted, appeals in the federal courts could begin. Annette Louise Stebbing was 19 years old in April 1980 when she and her much older husband, Bernard Lee Stebbing, raped and murder 19-year-old Dena Marie Polis, the stepdaughter of Bernard's brother and the daughter of Edna Stebbing. Annette was a runaway, a high school dropout with a below normal IQ, she used alcohol, marijuana and cocaine and was convicted of drug charges, larceny and eluding police before the age of 19. A Harford County jury convicted Annette of first-degree murder, rape, robbery, and sexual offense and in August 1981, Circuit Court Judge Albert P. Close of Harford County sentenced her to death in the state's gas chamber. Appellate records show that Annette and Bernard offered Dena a ride to a bus stop where she was to take a bus to see her boyfriend in another town. Instead, Annette and Bernard took Dena out into Harford County where Annette held the victim in the back of the van while Bernard raped her. Dena screamed during the altercation so Annette strangled Dena to death. Afterwards, Annette and Bernard turned Dena's body over and Bernard sodomized Dena's corpse. The two assailants went home, slept in the van with Dena in it, and carried her body around until the following day when they dumped it into a sewer. Upon reviewing the findings, sentencing reports and opinions in similar cases, the Maryland Supreme Court concluded in April 1984 that Annette's death sentence was not excessive or disproportionate; the court affirmed the conviction, vacated the death sentence, and remanded with instructions to enter the maximum prison sentence for murder provided for by law. Judge Close modified Annette's death sentence to life imprisonment in 1985. Annette remains incarcerated at the Patuxent Institution in Jessup, Maryland.

Attina Marie Cannaday had a disturbing childhood. She ran away from her broken home in Alabama at 13 years old, married and divorced by 14 years old, and worked as a dancer and barmaid in local clubs and supplemented her income by prostitution. Attina met 26-year-old Ronald Wojcik, a divorced father of two, at a lounge where he worked after his duties at Keesler Air Force Base. The two began a relationship and Attina soon moved in with Wojcik. They acted as a married couple until Wojcik learned her true age. Wojcik made Attina move out because the military disapproved of the relationship. Wojcik soon found himself another girlfriend, Sandra Sowash. In June 1982, Attina befriended David Gray, an unemployed man who lived out of his automobile. During that period, Attina and David were at a hotel lounge drinking where they met Dawn Bushart. As the lounge was closing, Cannaday asked Gray if he would go with her to Donald's apartment to get her van and some clothes. They approached the apartment, and David gave Attina and Dawn knives. David kept a butcher knife and a fourth knife that was strapped to his belt and order Dawn to stand out on the front porch. Attina and David entered the apartment and found Donald and Sandra asleep in bed. They then forced Donald and Sandra at knifepoint into Donald van and drove off. Once on the highway, Attina suggested that David have sex with Sandra, David then raped Sandra. Attina drove the van down a gravel road to a wooded area where David forced Donald into the woods. Sandra escaped the scene and found a nearby house from which she notified Harrison County Sheriff's Department. Authorities later found Donald's dead body about 50 feet from the road with 19 wounds to the face, neck, and chest and back. Police later found Attina asleep at a friend's house and took her into custody. Police arrested David with Donald's van. While being transported to the police station, Attina made unsolicited statements that David had used the knife to kill Donald and that she saw David grasp Donald's hair, pull his head back, and cut his throat. She eventually gave police a 14-page statement as to her involvement in the murder. Police arrested Dawn while she was walking along Highway 90 in Harrison County. Authorities indicted Attina, David, and Dawn for capital murder and tried them separately. A jury convicted David of the murder and testified against Attina. Dawn pled guilty to manslaughter. A jury found Attina Marie Cannaday guilty of capital murder and the trial judge sentenced to death. The Supreme Court of Mississippi affirmed Attina's conviction on appeal but vacated the sentence and remanded the case for a new sentencing trial. The court held that Attina's death sentence was disproportionate in a situation where she received the same death penalty sentence as David Gray in a separate trial though David had actually committed the murder and Attina only participated in the underlying burglary. A court resentenced Attina to life in prison in 1984 and the state granted her parole in March 2008.

In March 1984, a Pontotoc County jury deliberated for less than hour before convicting Cecilia Ann Williamson (also known as Cookie Williamson) of the capital murder of her husband James Williamson two years earlier and Circuit Court Judge George C. Carlson sentenced Cecilia to death. Cecilia paid Larry Sheldon Hentz and Owen Lee Harden from life insurance proceeds of $72,500 to kill James. Hentz and Harden brutally murdered James outside his home in Oakland, Mississippi, in the early morning hours of March 1982. An autopsy showed that the killers shot James in the back at close range with a shotgun and then burned the house to the ground with James in it. Trial evidenced revealed that Cecilia and Larry Hentz were involved in adulterous relationship before James' murder and that Cecilia moved in with Hentz shortly after James' murder. In 1987, the Supreme Court of Mississippi reversed Cecilia's conviction and death sentence and remanded the case back to the trial court for a new trial because the state denied Cecilia the right to confront and cross-examine witnesses presented against her at trial. The Mississippi Department of Corrections shows that only Larry Hentz remains incarcerated and serving a life sentence.

In December 1985, Desoto County jury convicted Judy Lane Houston of first-degree murder after a five-day trial for the murder of her 15-year-old daughter Paula Susanne Houston and recommended the death penalty. The trial judge sentenced Judy to death. Paula was a quiet teenager and an excellent ninth grade student with superior grades. She was poised to receive academic honors from her school at an upcoming graduation. Judy's voluntary confession to police the day after Paula's murder provided the trial court with most of the facts surrounding the case. It seems that Judy had found a letter from Paula to one of her girlfriends warning the girl about sexual intercourse with a boyfriend. The letter revealed that Paula had romantic feelings towards a boy as well. There was an argument between Judy and her husband, Larry Houston, a poor sharecropper and factory worker, about Judy reading Paula's personal letter. The next day Paula refused to go to school. After getting her younger children ready for school and off on the school bus, Paula went into her mother's bedroom and began berating her about Judy's marital infidelity. A struggle ensured and Judy strangled Paula with a pink macramé belt. Judy tried but could not revive Paula. Judy disrobed Paula, put her body in the trunk of her car, drove to a dump on the banks of the Yocona River in south Panola County, and threw Paula's body off the bank. It appears from trial testimony, however, that the struggle between Paula and Judy was much more perverse. One commentator noted, "Paula's mother had beaten Paula's face almost unrecognizable." There was also trial testimony to the effect that Judy had been physically abusing Paula since she was seven years old. "Documentation of beatings with belt buckles, hairbrushes and broom handles started when Paula was in the first grade at Pope and extended throughout the seven or so years she attended the school." It was this evidence that warranted Judy a new trial. On appeal of her conviction and death sentence, the Supreme Court of Mississippi vacated Judy's conviction and death sentence and remanded the case to the trial court for a new trial. The Court held that the probative value of this evidence was dubious and had a prejudicial effect upon Judy's trial. She remains incarcerated in Mississippi.

The culmination of several days of robbing convenient stores in the northern Mississippi countryside took place when authorities arrested Susie Ann Balfour and her boyfriend Lawrence Kirby Payne for the shooting death Southaven police officer Billy Lance who had stopped the two as they attempted to flee to Memphis after robbing a Circle K convenience store in early October 1988. As Lt. Lance attempted to handcuff Lawrence Payne, Susie retrieved a .38 caliber pistol and fired one fatal shot at the police officer who died some 30 minutes later at a local hospital. Upon her arrest, Susie gave a full confession to the shooting of Lt. Lance and admitted involvement in a string of convenience store robberies committed with her accomplice. A Loundes County jury convicted Susie of Billy Lance's murder and the trial judge sentenced her death by lethal injection. In March 1992, the Mississippi Supreme Court vacated Susie's capital murder conviction and death sentence and remanded the case to the trial court for a new trial. The Supreme Court had found Susie's right to counsel had attached before she made her confession and thus any statements obtained from the accused during subsequent police-initiated custodial questioning regarding the charge at issue were inadmissible. On retrial, Susie pled guilty and received a 45-year sentence in a Mississippi prison that she is presently serving. She has an expected release date of May 2024. Lawrence Payne is serving a 33-year sentence with an expected release date of September 2014.

In July 1983, Vernice Ballenger asked her estranged husband Mac Ballenger to rob her elderly aunt, Myrtle Ellis. Mac recruited James Head and Ronald Ritter to do the robbery for $10,000. Apparently, Vernice had learned that her aunt had large amounts of money after a newspaper reported on an automobile accident that involved Myrtle and for which she required hospitalization. Ritter and Head went to Myrtle's house while Mac stayed on the front porch. Once inside Ritter asked her where her money was and she replied she did not have any money. It was then that Ritter slapped Myrtle and she got mad and said her money was in the bank. Head pulled out a pistol; put the gun to Myrtle's head, pulled the trigger but the gun was not loaded. Head then hit her with the gun. Head and Ritter searched the house for the money but found none. The three returned to Ballenger's house and told her what had happened. Vernice suggested that they burn down Myrtle's house with her in it. Ritter, Head, and Ballenger then went back to the house and set the house on fire although Myrtle was lying outside the house. When fire fighters arrived, they transferred Myrtle to a hospital where she died, never regaining consciousness. An autopsy revealed that Myrtle died from internal injuries consistent with her being struck or kicked in the chest area. In January 1993, a Leake County jury convicted Vernice Ballenger for the capital murder of Myrtle Ellis while engaged in the commission of the crime of robbery and Circuit Court Judge Marcus D. Gordon sentenced Vernice to death by lethal injection. The Supreme Court of Mississippi found no reversible error in 1995 and affirmed both Vernice's conviction and sentence of death. In 2000, however, the same court vacated Vernice's conviction and sentence, and remanded for a new trial because the State did not offer an instruction on the elements of the underlying offense of robbery, and that Vernice's trial was sufficiently prejudiced to warrant a new trial. Vernice died at age of 65 in April 2002 at Whitfield Medical/Surgical Hospital in Whitfield, Mississippi. Authorities no longer incarcerate Head, but Ritter is serving a life sentence with no tentative release date.

Michelle Byrom's trial was "manifestly unconstitutional," plagued by prosecutorial misconduct, judicial misconduct, and the most "egregious" legal representation. In November 2000, a Tishomingo County jury in Mississippi found Michelle Byrom guilty of "masterminding" the murder of her husband, Edward "Eddie" Byrom, an electrician, a year earlier, and Circuit Court Judge Thomas J. Gardner sentenced Michelle to death. According to the state's case, Michelle allegedly contracted Joseph Dale Gillis to kill Edward for $15,000 that she would pay from life insurance proceeds totaling $350,000. Gillis shot Edward to death with a World War II relic Lugar nine-millimeter pistol. With full knowledge of the agreement between Michelle and Gillis, Edward's son, Byrom, Jr. (Junior), drove Gillis to a wooded area that led to a field beyond the Byrom home. Gillis had possession of the pistol, and some 30 minutes later Junior picked Gillis up where he had dropped him off earlier. Gillis had shot Edward twice in the chest. Junior took Gillis home, and then went to the hospital where Michelle was recuperating from pneumonia, and told his mother "it was done." Michelle then told Junior to return home to make sure Edward was dead. Junior went home and found his father dead. He then called 911 to report the murder. Arriving at the Byrom home, Sheriffs became immediately suspicious of Junior and took him into custody. During questioning, Junior confessed to the events surrounding the killing of her father. Police then interviewed Michelle and told her that Junior had confessed to everything. Michelle also confessed to the crime. Junior pled guilty to conspiracy to commit capital murder and Judge Gardner sentenced him to 50 years in prison with 20 years suspended. Gillis pled guilty to accessory after the fact to capital murder and conspiracy to commit capital murder and served a 15-year prison term. Authorities released Gillis and Junior from prison in 2009 and 2013, respectively.

In her appeal, Michelle argued that she killed Edward because she suffered physical and sexual abuse at the hands of her husband engaging in forced sexual acts that Edward made into home videos. Michelle's stepfather sexually abused her for years and forced her into prostitution. Michelle ran away from home to become a stripper at 15 years old and eventually married Edward who continued to abuse her. Part of the abuse involved forced sexual relations with other men that Edward videotaped. A forensic psychiatrist diagnosed Michelle with borderline personality disorder, depression, alcoholism, and Munchausen syndrome. In January 2006, the Mississippi Supreme Court rejected Michelle's claims on appeal and affirmed the conviction and death sentence. The U.S. Supreme Court refused to hear an appeal from Michelle Byrom in November 2006. In October 2013, the Mississippi Supreme Court heard arguments in Michelle's case seeking a new trial in the slaying of her husband based on claims that she is mentally ill from the decades of abuse. According to reports, Michelle Byrom says she deserves a new trial because her original lawyer failed to present what could have been mitigating evidence of physical and sexual abuse at the hands of her husband, as well as physical abuse as a child.

In late March 2014, in a two-page order, the Mississippi Supreme Court, per Justice Josiah D. Coleman, vacated Michelle's murder conviction and granted her a new trial based upon new evidence that Junior actually killed Edward because the abuse he suffered from his father. It seems that Junior confessed to Dr. W. Criss Lott, a forensic psychologist appointed by the trial judge, that he had killed his father. Dr. Lott, however, did not include Junior's confession in his report to the court but contacted Judge Gardner and asked him what he should do about the confession. Judge Gardner told Dr. Lott to keep the confession confidential. In reversing Michelle's conviction, the Mississippi Supreme Court referred to its action as "extraordinary and extremely rare" but dictated by the facts of the case. The courts ordered that the circuit court of Tishomingo County not assign the case to Judge Gardner. One commentator explains:

> It is the failure to disclose this confession at trial that has to be the central reason this petition was granted. It's a little odd though—Michelle's trial lawyers learned about it several months after the trial through hearsay (from Gillis's lawyers) and a newspaper report of a statement by an assistant district attorney. So it was sort-of-known. However, Lott refused to cooperate with every attempt to obtain an affidavit of or evidence about the statement, and Michelle's postconviction lawyers never got allowed discovery. What was not known that may have tipped the balance is that Lott had told the trial judge about the confession pre-trial."[21]

Nile Jeanne Accuser came from a troubled family. In 1965, her father committed suicide with an overdose of alcohol and sleeping pills, and as a teenager, Nile attempted suicide although she was not a substance abuser. In August 1987, Nila stabbed to death her 11-year-old son Jeremy

Williams and her eight-year-old son Eric Williams with a filet knife in a motel room hours after learning that her former husband, Bobby Lee Williams, had won a court order giving him full custody of the children. Nila had stabbed Jeremy 39 times in the chest and she stabbed Eric seven times in the chest and eight times in the back. In June 1988, a Platte County jury convicted Nila in the death of her younger son, and Circuit Court Judge John M. Yeaman imposed a death sentence after jurors were unable to decide whether to sentence Nila to death or life in prison without parole. Her defense lawyer described Nila as under tremendous stress that psychiatrists describe as a "dissociative state." Nila had been taking a controversial sleeping aid called Halcion and known to cause memory loss, depression, paranoia, and irrational actions. Britain had banned use of the drug. Confidential evidence of the drug's severe side effects was intentionally kept secret during Nila's trial. *Newsweek Magazine* explained in May 1992 that Nila's trial had produced evidence that Upjohn, the maker of Halcion, had ignored its own scientists' safety concerns. In July 1990, the Missouri Supreme Court reversed Nila's conviction on first-degree murder and remanded the case back to the trial court for a new trial because of jury selection bias. In May 1992, a Platte County jury found Nila guilty of her older son's murder. Before jurors could deliberate on the punishment for Nila, however, the trial judge informed them that Nila had committed suicide in her jail cell. Nila had apparently taken drugs.

In January 1989, a Pettis County jury found Virginia A. Twenter, a divorced mother of two, guilty of the shooting murders of her father, John D. Wells, and her stepmother, Marilyn K. Wells. The jury assessed life imprisonment without parole for 50 years for the murder of her father, and the death penalty for the murder of her stepmother. Circuit Court Judge Donald Barnes imposed the sentences. Earlier in May 1988, Anna Laas, found the John Wells' body in the living room of the Wells' home and authorities later found the body of Marilyn Wells eight miles from the Wells' home. Virginia had shot her father in the back and in the chest, and her stepmother once in the chest. Evidence showed that Virginia had killed the Wells with a .38 caliber pistol registered to Virginia's former husband, Hugo Twenter, who had discovered the gun missing from his pickup truck as he was leaving Virginia's house one evening in April of 1988 and reported the missing gun to police. It seems Virginia was in dire financial straits with all of her debts in arrears; her home was in foreclosure and a new car in repossession. Virginia used stolen checks totaling $8,400 from her father's business to pay down some of the debts. In October 1991, the Missouri Supreme Court remanded Virginia's case for a new trial and set aside the death penalty. The court held that Virginia had ineffective assistance of counsel because the lawyer failed to investigate and call family members at the punishment phase that justified remand for resentencing. A trial court reversed her sentences to two life terms without parole and she is presently serving her sentences at the Chillicothe Correctional Center.

In November 1990, a Livingston County jury convicted Faye Della Copeland for her complicity in the murders of five homeless transients between 1986 and 1989: Paul Jason Cowart, John W. Freeman, Jimmie Dale Harvey, Dennis Murphy and Wayne Warner. Circuit Court Judge E. Richard Webber sentenced Faye to death by lethal injection for the murders of Cowart, Freeman, Harvey, and Warner, and to life imprisonment without parole for the murder of Murphy. Trial evidence shows that Faye and her 76-year-old husband, Ray Copeland, committed the killings in a complex fraudulent check and cattle buying scheme. Authorities suspect the Copelands may have killed as many as 12 transients. Although appellate courts rejected Faye's claims of severe spousal abuse, there was expert testimony of battered wife syndrome and family members claimed that Ray abused Faye and her children. Faye was born poor to a good hard working family in Harrison, Arkansas. At 19 years old, Faye married Ray Copeland in 1940.

Apparently, as an appellate court explained, the Copeland's fraud schemes involved Ray enlisting a transient at a homeless shelter and bring him to the couple's rural Missouri farm home and the transient would open a post office box and checking account using the Copeland's money. The transient would then go to various livestock auctions where he would buy cattle at Ray's direction. The transient would purchase cattle using the newly obtained checks. The checking account did not have funds sufficient to cover the cattle purchases, and the Copelands would sell the cattle immediately after the purchase. The Copelands would then kill the homeless person before the checks would bounce and authorities could investigate. The scheme unraveled following a tip to police by a would-be victim. Police searched the Copeland farm and found clothes and luggage belonging to the murder victims, a piece of paper inside a Polaroid camera case which had a list of murder victims' names written by Faye, several shallow graves on a farm where Ray had done odd jobs, the body of Wayne Warner buried in a shallow grave beneath thousands of large round bales of hay, and the body of Dennis Murphy chained to a 40-pound concrete block at the bottom of a well. Autopsies showed that the victims died from gunshot wounds to the head. Police identified one of the bullets recovered from one of the victims as fired from a rifle found in the Copelands' home.

The Missouri Supreme Court upheld Faye's convictions and death sentence in August 1996, but per Justice Ortrie D. Smith of the U.S. District Court for the Western District of Missouri, the federal court affirmed the murder convictions but vacated Faye's death sentence in August 1999 and sentenced Faye to life in prison. The federal court vacated Faye's death sentence because of weaknesses in the case that Faye held any more than a minor role in the crimes and there was no evidence that she personally shot any of the victims. There was evidence that Faye was controlled by her husband, of prosecutorial misconduct, and ineffective trial counsel. In August 2002, Faye suffered a stroke that left her paralyzed and unable to speak. In September 2002, Missouri Governor Holden authorized a medical parole for Faye to Morningside Center nursing home in her hometown of Chillicothe, Missouri. Faye Copeland died from natural causes in late December 2003 at 82 years old. Besides her five children, Faye left behind 17 grandchildren and 25 great-grandchildren. Ray Copeland died from natural causes while awaiting execution.

A St. Louis jury convicted Maria Isa of the murder of her 16-year-old daughter, Palestina Isa, and recommended the death penalty. Circuit Court Judge Charles A. Shaw sentenced Isa to death. Palestina Isa was the youngest daughter of Zein and Maria Isa. Zein Hassan Isa was a Palestinian Muslim and Maria was a Brazilian Catholic. According to appellate records, the Isa family had rigid cultural traditions that became arguable between young Palestina and her parents. Palestina was an excellent student and athlete and her social life thrived, but her parents were concerned they could no longer control their daughter. Palestina's parents began to limit her activities. Yet, most of the difference between Palestina and her parents centered on her relationship with a young African American man named Cliff Walker. Her parents emphatically objected to the relationship because Cliff was black, and moved to withdraw Palestina from her high school to prevent her relationship with Cliff. During a meeting with school officials, Maria referred to daughter as tramp and a whore who had gone against her family. In November 1989, Zein Isa came to the attention of federal authorities for espionage activities and the FBI place a surveillance microphone in the Isa home. Those taped conversations provided authorities with information about Palestina's murder. Apparently, Palestina took a job at a local Wendy's Restaurant, and when she returned home about midnight after work, a physical altercation developed between Palestina and her parents wherein Maria held Palestina down while her father repeatedly stabbed her to death. An autopsy revealed that Palestina died from a knife wound through her breastbone and into her heart and a second fatal stab wound that entered her left lung. The court affirmed Maria's first-degree murder conviction but reversed her sentence of death on procedural error during the penalty phase of her trial. The Missouri Supreme Court remanded the case to the trial court for a new penalty-phase hearing and resentencing in 1993. The trial court sentenced Maria to life in prison without parole. She remains incarcerated at Women's Eastern Correctional Center in Vandalia, Missouri. Zein Isa died of diabetes in February 1997.

In April 1992, a Greene County jury convicted Shirley Jo Phillips (also known as Jo Ann Phillips) guilty of the shooting death of Wilma Plaster in early October 1989. Police determined that the gun used to kill Plaster belonged to Glenn Minister, Shirley's son, and that Wilma's garage, car, and house had the presence of human blood. Police discovered a bank statement in Wilma's mail that contained a canceled check for $4,050 payable to Shirley and endorsed by Joann Phillips. Evidence showed Wilma did not write the check and that her signature on the check was a forgery. Authorities found Wilma's dismembered body several feet from the side of a road. Witnesses put Shirley and Wilma together the night of Wilma's death. A neighbor found a gun and plastic bags containing bank statements, check registers, and other items containing Shirley's fingerprints. In February 1997, the Missouri Supreme Court affirmed Shirley's conviction for first-degree murder but reversed the death sentence because the exclusion of evidence that another person dismembered the victim's body was material. The Court remanded the case for a new penalty phase proceeding. According to the appeals court, Shirley claimed that the police withheld exculpatory evidence during her trial by failing to disclose an audiotape of a statement given by Joyce Hagar to the police. The audiotape revealed that Hagar said Shirley's son told her that he and his mom killed Wilma and that his mom drove while he scattered her body. He also told her that they threw Wilma's hands into the creek. To the court, the existence of this evidence was not disclosed to Shirley before trial despite numerous discovery requests, including a specific request for tapes of any interviews of any witnesses. The trial court resentenced Shirley to life in prison without parole. She is currently residing at the Chillicothe Correctional Center.

In late 2006, a Union County jury convicted Kristi Leigh Fulgham of the murder of her estranged husband, Joseph T. "Joey" Fulgham, whom Kristi left for another man, Kyle Harvey. Circuit Judge Lee Howard sentenced her to death. Another jury convicted Kristi's 13-year-old half-brother, Tyler W. Edmonds, of his role in the murder and Circuit Judge Jim Kitchens sentenced him to a life term in prison. In 2008, however, the Mississippi Supreme Court ordered a new trial after finding numerous errors by the judge in his first trial and a second trial ended in Edmonds' acquittal. Concerning Kristi's trial, the court argued that the trial court abused its discretion at the penalty phase in excluding the expert mitigation testimony of a licensed social worker and that the exclusion of that testimony denied the Kristi a fair sentencing hearing. The jury was convinced that Kristi Fulgham coerced Edmonds into confessing to the killing. In October 2010, the Mississippi Supreme Court overturned Kristi's death sentence and an Oktibbeha County Circuit Court judge sentenced her life in prison without the possibility of parole. Apparently, in May 2003, Kristi shot and killed Joey with a .22 caliber rifle in the back of the head as he slept. She then took her three children and drove to Jackson to pick up her boyfriend Kyle. Afterwards, the group drove to the Mississippi Gulf Coast and vacationed at the Beau Rivage on the beach. On their way back to Jackson, Kristi received a phone call from her mother that Joey had been murdered. Kristi and Tyler turned themselves in to the police where Kristi blamed the murder on Tyler. Kristi is serving her life sentence at the Central Mississippi Correctional Facility in Pearl, Mississippi.

In December 1983, a Clark County jury found Sheila Ann Summers guilty of first-degree murder. The jury found that Sheila's crime involved depravity of mind and District Court Judge John F. Mendoza sentenced her to death. In September 1982, authorities found Joy Spinney's body in the Nevada desert. It seems that Sheila and a friend named Joan Mack shot Joy to death. Las Vegas Police contacted Joy's husband about his wife's death. At that time, Joy's husband revealed that when he last spoke with Joy she was at Joan's trailer. Police arrested Mack in October 1982 in Florida for Joy's murder. Joan Mack committed suicide shortly before the start of her trial. At Sheila's trial, she testified that she and Mack were acquaintances and that she had once met Joy. She stated that Joan telephoned her and she drove to Joan's trailer. Joan answered the door with a revolver in her hand. She appeared drunk and disheveled. Behind Joan, Sheila saw Joy lying on the floor covered with a bloody sheet. When Sheila asked Joan what had happened, Joan told her that Joy was not going to interfere in her relationship with Charlie (Joan's boyfriend). Joan then told Sheila that if she talked to police she would harm Sheila's children. Sheila also testified that Joan forced her at gunpoint to drag Joy to Joy's car, place her in the back seat, and drive the car. Sheila tried to drive to Southern Memorial Hospital, but Joan pointed the revolver at her head and said, "No, you're not taking her there." Joan then directed Sheila at gunpoint to a deserted spot outside of Las Vegas. After Sheila stopped the car, Joan dragged Spinney several feet away from the car, shot Joy, and then ordered Sheila, once again at gunpoint, to drive back to Joan's trailer. The Nevada Supreme Court argued that the district court committed reversible error when it admitted into evidence a suicide note written by Joan that implicated Sheila in Joy's murder. As a result, the court reversed Joy's conviction and remanded the case for a new trial. The trial court sentenced Sheila to life in prison with parole. Sheila won parole in April 2010.

After a six-week trial in 2000, a Clark County jury in Nevada convicted Sandra Renee Murphy and co-defendant Richard Bennett Tabish of the 1998 robbery and suffocation/poisoning murder of Horseshoe Casino owner Lonnie Theodore "Ted" Binion at Binion's home in Law Vegas. Sandra was Binion's live-in girlfriend. The district attorney alleged that Sandra and Richard, who became lovers, robbed and murdered Binion at his house and then stole $8 million in silver coins and bars from an underground vault constructed by Richard at the Binion home. The trial judge, Joseph T. Bonaventure, sentenced Sandra to serve a life term in the Nevada State prison with the possibility of parole after 20 years and Richard to a life sentence as well. In July 2003, the Nevada Supreme Court overturned the murder conviction of Sandra and Richard for the robbery and murder of Binion. The court remanded the case back to the Clark County Superior Court for retrial because of due process rights violations. A jury acquitted the two defendants in November 2004 of Binion's murder but found them guilty of burglary and larceny. In 2008, the Nevada Supreme Court upheld Sandra's convictions on these charges. The justices believed that there were sufficient facts showing Murphy entered into an agreement with Tabish to commit burglary and larceny to steal the silver. The trial judge sentenced Sandra to one to five years for her part in stealing the silver collection. Officials have since released Sandra who moved to California.

The New Jersey Supreme Court reversed the death sentences of Marie Moore in 1988 and Leslie Ann Nelson in 2004. Regarding the reversal of Marie Moore's death sentence, it seems that in late December 1983 police searched an apartment where Marie had resided and discovered the partially mummified body of 12-year-old Theresa Feury, Marie's goddaughter, in a crawl space behind a bedroom wall 11 months after her death. An investigation into the young girl's death revealed that Marie and an adult friend living with Marie had sexually and physically abused both children over a two-year period. Marie lived in the apartment with her 12-year-old daughter Tammy Moore, a friend's 12-year-old daughter left in Marie's care named Harriet Bayne, and Marie's 50-year-old friend Mary Gardullo. In the summer of 1981, 14-year-old Ricky Flores, 12-year-old Theresa Feury, and 13-year-old Luis Mantalvo began visiting the apartment on a regular basis. Marie often took the children to beaches, amusement parks, and bowling alleys. The children enjoyed spending time in the Moore household, and developed a great affection for Marie. The household then began changing with Marie imposing physical and sexual torture to the children. Marie not only physically abused the children, but Mary Gardullo as well, and forced the children to abuse one another. Marie also had sexual relations with Ricky Flores who eventually became instrumental in abusing the other children. The ill-treatment culminated in Teresa's death and the arrest of Marie. An autopsy revealed that Teresa had suffered a blow to her head and face that killed her, but that she had been alive and in a coma for four to eight hours after her head injury. Theresa had been alive when wrapped in blankets and plastic and taped; she most likely suffocated to death from the wrapping. Marie admitted to police that she had witnessed Ricky kill Teresa. Prosecutors charged Flores as a juvenile with a maximum sentence term of three years. Flores agreed to testify against Moore. In November 1984, a Passaic County jury convicted Marie of Teresa's death and several other charges including aggravated sexual assault, kidnapping, and child endangerment and Superior Court Judge Vincent E. Hull sentenced Marie to die by lethal injection. The trial court overlooked expert testimony that Marie was a paranoid schizophrenic who had assumed multiple personalities including a male she called "Billy Joel." In 1988, Marie appealed her conviction and death sentence contending she was legally insane and not eligible for the death penalty. Given the expert testimony provided the court at Marie's trial, the Supreme Court of New Jersey agreed and reversed Marie's capital murder conviction and death sentence. The Court argued that it favored a sentence that would ensure Marie never becomes eligible for parole during her lifetime.

In April 1995, Leslie Ann Nelson shot and killed John McLaughlin, an investigator with the Camden County Prosecutor's Office, and Richard Norcross, a detective with the Haddon Heights Police Department. Leslie also severely wounded Richard's brother, John Norcorss, a police officer with the same department. The trial court sentenced Leslie to death and to life in prison with 30 years of parole ineligibility. The court also imposed a consecutive 10-year term with five years of parole ineligibility for second-degree assault. The shootings took place while the three officers attempted to execute a search warrant for guns in Leslie's bedroom of her parent's home in reference to a weapons violation. It seems that on the afternoon of the shootings, McLaughlin, Detective Norcross, and three other police officers, including Officer John Norcross, searched the house. When Leslie learned that police were to search her bedroom, she ran into the room, armed herself, and fatally shot McLaughlin as he ran after her toward the bedroom. Leslie shot and wounded Detective Norcross as he pursued her, though he managed to escape from the house. Leslie killed Officer Norcross when she shot at officers from an upstairs window during a 14-hour standoff with police.

At trial, Leslie asserted strong mitigating factors to counter the aggravating factors claimed by the prosecution. The mitigating factor all revolved around Leslie's mental illness and her sexual identity; Leslie was born male (Glen Nelson) but had sex transformation surgery. Mental health professionals diagnosed Leslie as severely depressed with schizoid and antisocial tendencies. Leslie suffered years of painful doubt about her sexual identity. In 1986, one doctor advised her to begin the sex-change process by taking estrogen and progesterone. In 1989, Leslie underwent psychological testing to determine if he would be a good candidate for sex-change surgery. Tests indicated that Leslie suffered from a depressive disorder, a dysthymic disorder, and paranoia. Although physicians denied Leslie the sex-change operation at that time, she began taking estrogen and progesterone. Leslie had breast augmentation surgery in 1991, changed her name to Leslie, and began to live and dress as a woman. Leslie's doctors described her as having "severe psychological problems" but approved the sexual reassignment because they feared Leslie would commit suicide without the surgery. Leslie has the sex-change operation in 1992. Afterwards, Leslie's depression actually worsened and she became obsessed with guns; Leslie spent hours in her bedroom polishing the guns. One defense psychiatrist testified that Leslie's mental condition had deteriorated significantly that caused an abnormal reaction to the threat of the police entering her bedroom.

The trial jury unanimously rejected Leslie's mitigating factors of "emotional disturbance" and "impaired capacity." After Leslie's sentencing, she learned that during the penalty-phase trial, Detective Norcross had filed a civil lawsuit against Leslie, the Borough of Haddon Heights Police Department, and the Camden County Prosecutor's Office, alleging that he was injured by Leslie because of "improper hiring, screening, training, and supervision" of Haddon Heights police officers. Leslie appealed for a new trial based the State's failure to reveal this information to her during trial. The trial court denied the motion. Leslie appealed her death sentence to the New Jersey Supreme Court and the court vacated the death sentence and remanded a new sentencing trial. In 2002, the Supreme Court again overturned the death sentence on faulty jury instructions and prosecutorial misconduct. In June 2007, Leslie accepted a sentence of life in prison after prosecutors agreed not to seek Leslie's execution. She is currently serving her sentence at the Edna Mahan Correctional Facility for Women in Clinton, New Jersey.

Mamie Lee Ward shot and killed her former boyfriend Frank Parker while he sat in the den of his home talking with his new girlfriend Lucy Taylor. Trial evidence showed that Mamie and Frank had lived together for more than two years, but when Mamie's daughter, Brenda Ward, returned from New Jersey with a baby in May 1973, the three moved into an apartment. On an early evening in mid–July 1973, Mamie walked over to Frank's house, went to the rear door, and entered through the kitchen. Frank saw her and motioned her into the rear bedroom, adjacent to the kitchen. From there Mamie went into the adjoining bedroom where Frank kept his guns. She got a shotgun from a rack on the wall and walked through the bedroom into the living room. There, she aimed the gun at Frank Parker and shot, left the house through the front door, called a cab from a friend's house, and went to the police station. The Supreme Court of North Carolina affirmed Mamie's conviction and death sentence. Authorities reversed Mamie's death sentence to life in prison when the state's death penalty statute became invalid. Mamie is no longer on parole.

Rozell Oxendine and her common law husband, Joe Hunt, lived in Anson County, North Carolina, along with an 18-year-old live-in named Brenda Jacobs. In late August 1973, Brenda witnessed Rozell purchase a small bottle of liquid rat poison and saw her mix the rat poison in a jug of tea especially prepared for Joe that he consumed during lunch. Joe became violently ill over the afternoon and into the night. The following morning, Joe went to the hospital where he died the next day. Six months after Joe's death, Brenda made statements to police implicating Rozell in Joe's killing. As a result, investigators exhumed Joe's body and an autopsy revealed that he had died of arsenic poisoning. A trial in 1974 found Rozell guilty of murder and sentenced her to death. In March 1976, the Supreme Court of North Carolina affirmed the trial court's conviction and death sentence. Officials resentenced Rozell to life in prison in 1976 and released her on parole in August 1992.

In August 1975, 44-year-old Margie C. Boykin hired 26-year-old Garland Sanders to kill her husband, Daniel S. Boykin for $2,000. Marge provided Sanders with gloves, masking tape, and a shotgun left at the back door on the night he was to kill Daniel, and she left the keys to her 1974 Electra Buick in the ignition switch. Margie also left the back door to the Boykin house unlocked and put out the floodlight. On the night of the killing, Garland had 17-year-old Johnny Edmondson drop him off at the Boykin house shortly before midnight. On schedule, Sanders entered the Boykin house through the backdoor and shot Daniel once in the arm and twice in the head with the shotgun. Sanders got in Margie's car. Later Sanders met Johnny Edmondson and abandoned Margie's car. Edmondson pawned the rifle and shotgun. A neighbor went to the Boykin home after receiving a frantic telephone call from Margie that an intruder had robbed her and Daniel and killed Daniel. About two weeks after the murder, Margie gave Sanders an envelope containing $1,000 in cash. Margie made no other payments to Sanders but promised him the balance out of the insurance proceeds. A Johnston County jury found Margie guilty of Daniel's for-hire murder and the trial court sentenced her to death in the state's gas chamber. Under a plea bargain arrangement with state prosecutors, Sanders received a life sentence in return for a guilty plea to second degree murder and Edmundson a sentence of 20 to 30 years in prison. On appeal, the North Carolina Supreme Court affirmed Margie's convictions for first-degree murder but vacated her death sentence. The court remanded the case back to the trial court with directions to substitute life imprisonment for the death penalty given the U.S. Supreme Court's holding in *Woodson*. Correctional authorities released Margie from prison in December 1994; she is now 79 years old. Officials released Garland Sanders in August 1993.

In January 1976, along with 24-year-old Frankie Jerome Squire and 21-year-old Joseph Seaborn, a jury convicted 22-year-old Faye Beatrice Brown of an armed robbery of a bank and trust company in Jamesville, North Carolina. Afterwards, Guy Thomas Davis, Jr., of the State Highway Patrol, stopped a brown Pontiac about 10 miles from the bank. Davis approached the automobile and spoke to the driver when Joseph Seaborn shot the trooper in the throat with a sawed-off shotgun. Davis died instantly and the robbers drove away. Police later found the car abandoned in a creek bottom. Officers began a search for the suspects in a field of soybeans not far from where they had discovered the car and soon had the suspects in custody. Police took the suspects to the police station in Williamston where they were interrogated by investigators during which the three suspects confessed to their participation in the robbery and to the shooting of Trooper Davis. The trial court sentenced all three suspects to death. The North Carolina Supreme Court, however, vacated the death sentence imposed on the defendants sentenced them to life imprisonment pursuant to the U.S. Supreme Court's ruling in *Woodson*. Faye Beatrice Brown is currently serving her sentence at the Raleigh Correctional Center for Women in Raleigh, North Carolina, with an expected released date of August 2055.

In late 1987, a Robeson County jury found Donna Sue Cox guilty of her role in the first-degree murder of Jerry Richardson with whom she lived for four years. The jury recommended execution and the trial court sentenced Donna to death, along with her accomplice, James Earl Willis. Trial evidence showed that Donna lived with Jerry and that he provided her with a telephone, an automobile, and credit cards. In January 1986, James began frequenting Donna's house when Jerry was not present. Together, they planned to kill Jerry. Then, in July 1986, along with Tony Owens and Roy Grooms, Donna and James put their plan into effect. James and Willis waited outside the house until Jerry left it at about midnight. Donna went outside with Jerry and stood on the porch as he drove down the driveway. When Jerry left his car to open the driveway gate, James, who had been hiding in the bushes, attacked Jerry and beat him to death with a crowbar. When James started to attack him, Jerry called to Donna who was on the front porch of the house, but she turned and walked into the house. On appeal to the North Carolina Supreme Court, Donna claimed several procedural errors. The Court held that there was error in the penalty phase of the trial when the trial judge instructed jury that it had to find unanimously a mitigating circumstance before it could consider a mitigating factor. The Court ordered Donna a new sentencing hearing. Authorities sentenced her to life in prison and she remains incarcerated at the Southern Correctional Institute in Troy, North Carolina.

In August 1989, it took less than an hour for a Lee County jury to convict Barbara Terry Stager of first degree of murder for killing her husband of 10 years, Allison Russell Stager, a popular high school baseball coach and teacher. The jury recommended a capital sentence and Superior Court Judge J.B. Allen imposed the death penalty. It appears that in early February 1988, Barbara's teenage son Jason summoned medical personnel to the family home claiming that Russell had suffered a gunshot wound. Paramedics found Russell lying on his bed. Barbara claimed the .25 caliber Beretta pistol gun had discharged as she was pulling it out from under the pillow. Russell Stager died around noon that day from a single gunshot wound to the middle of the back of his head. Trial evidence showed that Barbara had killed her husband for $100,000 in life insurance proceeds. The state also showed that Barbara had likely killed her first husband, Larry Ford, who died under similar circumstances as Russell. Barbara appealed the trial court's conviction and death sentence to the Supreme Court of North Carolina which concluded that errors during the sentencing proceeding required that the court vacate the sentence of death and remanded the case back to the Superior Court for a new sentencing proceeding. The Court had found that a jury instruction that the jury must unanimously find the existence of a mitigating circumstance before any juror could consider that circumstance in a capital sentencing decision amounted to harmful error. Barbara is serving a life term with the possibility of parole after 20 years at the Southern Correctional Institute in Troy, North Carolina. Prison authorities denied Barbara parole in March 2009 and she is scheduled for a new parole hearing in 2012.

In December 1990, an Alamance County jury convicted Marylin Rudd Mahaley for her part in the strangling murder of her husband, Roy Mahaley, and recommended a sentence of death. Superior Court Judge J.B. Allen affirmed the sentence and sent Marylin to death row. Trial testimony revealed that along with her accomplice boyfriend, Steven Randall Harris, and Eric Taylor, killed Roy to collect $200,000 in life insurance proceeds. Marylin had a history of illegal drug use and the theft of money and credit cards to support her habit, but otherwise, she had no criminal history. Marylin had met Steven at a drug rehabilitation center a few years before Roy's murder. Apparently, Marylin was in her bedroom when Steven and Eric strangled Roy with a cord and then put his body in the trunk of his car. The two men drove the car to Roy's place of employment and left the car in the company parking lot. Workers found Roy's body two days later. A trial court sentenced Steven to life plus 70 years, and Eric, who had testified against Marylin, plead guilty to second-degree murder. The court sentenced Eric to life in prison and prison officials released him on parole in September 2000. On appeal, the North Carolina Supreme Court upheld Marylin's conviction but reversed her death sentence and remanded the case for a new sentencing hearing. The Court had found that the trial court erred when it failed to submit to the jury the fact that defendant had no prior criminal convictions at the sentencing phase of her trial. The trial court sentenced Marylin to life in prison in July 1994. The North Carolina Court of Appeals reviewed the resentence and found no error. Marylin is eligible for parole in 2016. In the interim, she remains incarcerated at the Southern Correctional Institute in Troy, North Carolina.

A Beaufort County jury found Yvette Gay guilty of the first-degree murders of 40-year-old Louise Farris, 16-year-old Shamika Farris, and 13-year-old William Farris in August 1991. Superior Court Judge Weeks imposed the death sentence as recommended by the jury. Police found the three victims tied, gagged, and shot to death in their home. At the time of the murders, Yvette was involved in a five-year long relationship with Renwick Gibbs. Throughout their relationship, however, Renwick was married to Anne Farris. Renwick and Anne lived together in a mobile home but for about a month prior to the murders Anne lived in a battered woman's shelter. During the couple's separation, Renwick lived with Yvette, her two children, and her twin sister, Doris, in a converted bus. In late May 1990, Renwick murdered the members of Anne Farris's family. Police soon arrested Renwick and Yvette for the killings. Yvette testified that when Renwick returned to the bus on the day of the killings, he was angry after talking with Anne who told him to go back to his so-called "new wife" Yvette. He told Yvette he was going to kill the Farris family and made Yvette get dressed. Yvette told him she did not want to go, but he said that she had to go in order to see what it would be like if she left him. Once at the Farris house, Renwick cut the telephone wires. Renwick and Yvette entered the house and Renwick ordered the family into one room. He then ordered young William to tie up his mother and Shamika. Renwick then tied up William. In response to the pleas by the mother, Renwick told her that he was tired of her coming between him and his wife. After Renwick ordered Yvette to shoot the victims and she refused, Renwick shot and killed the family. He then turned the gun on Yvette told her he was going to kill her, her family, and "everybody that I was ever involved with. I'm going to kill all of you and then I'm going to kill myself." They left and returned to the bus. Renwick left after telling Yvette that he would kill her or her sister if she did anything. Psychiatric expert testimony offered at trial found that Yvette suffered from "atypical dissociative disorder" at the time of the murders that resulted from domination, mistreatment and abuse typical of battered spouse syndrome. Yvette was essentially a slave to Renwick. On appeal, the North Carolina Supreme Court affirmed Yvette's murder convictions, but remanded the case for a new capital sentencing proceeding because the trial court failed to instruct the jury that it could not use the same evidence to find more than one aggravating circumstance. That is, it was improper for the trial court to submit two aggravating circumstances supported by the same evidence. As a result, the trial court sentenced Yvette to life in prison without parole. She now resides at the Southern Correctional Institute. In October 2004, Beaufort Superior Judge William Griffin vacated Renwick's death sentence imposed a life sentence without parole; Renwick suffers from mental retardation and thus ineligible for the death penalty pursuant to *Atkins*. He is currently serving his sentence at the Scotland Correctional Institution in Laurinburg, North Carolina.

In September 1996, a Wilkes County jury convicted Melanie Sammons Anderson of the torture murder of two-and-one-half year old Tabitha Lynn Pierce in August 1994 and recommended the court sentence Melanie to death; the trial court entered a judgment accordingly. Melanie was the girlfriend of Ronald Eugene Pierce, Tabitha's uncle. In July 1994, Tabitha's parents agreed to let Tabitha leave her home in Pennsylvania and stay with Melanie and Ronald for a few weeks in North Carolina. Soon afterwards, Melanie and Ronald took an unconscious Tabitha to the Wilkes Regional Medical Center where medical personnel airlifted the child to a pediatric intensive care unit at Baptist Hospital. Tabitha died the next day once removed from life support.

Tabitha's injuries were severe. Trial evidence showed that the child had numerous injuries extending all over her body, including bruises on her face, cheeks and jaw, chin, forehead, sides of her neck, collarbones, over the front of her chest, on her back, over her right flank, her buttocks, upper and lower legs, her eyelid, and on her shins. Tabitha had patches of hair pulled out from her scalp, and she suffered injuries caused by a blunt trauma to the mouth. There was evidence of forceful pinching and grabbing and human adult bite marks on Tabitha's body. She had suffered a blunt trauma to her pubic area. A forensic pathologist found bruises in the forms of grab marks, belt marks, shoe marks, and marks from a radio antenna and a metal tray. A hemorrhage over the surface of the brain in the lining as well as a subdural hematoma between the skull bone and the brain caused Tabitha's brain to swell. There were retinal hemorrhages in the back of her eyes indicating violent shaking. The pathologist suggested that Tabitha's injuries resulted from inflictions imposed over time, the injuries would have been painful, and required considerable force. The consensus of medical experts is that Tabitha had received severe beatings and that Tabitha was a victim of the shaken-baby syndrome and the battered-child syndrome.

On appeal, Melanie claimed that her sentence was disproportionate to the crime she committed since Ronald received life in prison while Melanie received a death sentence. The Supreme Court of Ohio affirmed Melanie's conviction and death sentence and the U.S. Supreme Court denied certiorari. In April 2003, however, the Wilkes County Superior Court Judge Williams J. Wood vacated Melanie's death sentence and sentenced her to a life prison sentence without parole because evidence revealed that Melanie is mentally retarded with an IQ of between 67 and 75; states cannot executed mentally retarded defendants. Melanie is currently housed at the Southern Correctional Institution.

As with many women murderers, Christene Knapp Kemmerlin's childhood included sexual abuse and neglect. As a product of her maltreatment as a child, Christene suffered from a borderline personality disorder and a more acute and serious disorder of major depressive disorder as an adult. A trial court held, however, that Christene's adult disorders did not diminish Christene's capacity to appreciate the criminality of her conduct or her ability to conform her conduct to the requirements of law. In September 2000, a Rockingham County jury found Christene guilty of the March 1999 first-degree murder of her husband, Donald Wayne Kemmerlin, and recommended a sentence of death. The trial court entered a judgment in keeping with that recommendation. Trial evidence showed that in the summer of 1998, Christene hired William Antone Johnson to kill her husband. Once under arrest, Christene admitted to police investigators that she hired William to kill Donald and that she was involved in the events leading up to her husband's shooting. On appeal, the Supreme Court of North Carolina affirmed Christene's conviction but vacated the death sentence and sentenced her to life imprisonment without the benefit of parole. The Court held that the totality of the circumstances surrounding Christene's case did not warrant imposition of the death penalty. It was significant to the court that William received a life sentence without parole, but that the trial court sentenced Christene to death. Christene is currently housed at the Southern Correctional Institute.

In late November 2007, a Guilford County jury returned a guilty verdict against Mary Elizabeth Roach for first degree murder in the November 2005 death of three-year-old Hailey Rae Resch who at the time of her death was in Mary's care. It seems that Mary summoned paramedics to her home after Hailey stopped breathing and paramedics were unsuccessful in their attempts to revive Hailey. She had appeared well when her parents left her with Mary earlier in the day. At a regional hospital, emergency room physicians conducted a post-mortem examination of Hailey and discovered several small bruises of varying ages on Hailey's forehead but found no evidence of broken bones and no significant signs of trauma. There were, however, retinal hemorrhages in both of Hailey's eyes. An autopsy of the child revealed a variety of injuries to Hailey including five subgaleal hematomas; bilateral subdural neomembranes; contusions on the head, torso, and extremities; and bilateral retinal hemorrhages. There was no observable damage to the Hailey's brain and no bleeding inside the brain. All medical experts agreed that Hailey suffered a subdural hematoma sometime in the weeks preceding her death. At trial, state experts testified that the cause of Hailey's death was blunt force trauma to the head. Defense medical experts disagreed but could provide no precise cause of death. At the end of Mary's trial, her defense lawyers made a motion to dismiss and the trial court granted the motion as to murder under the theory of premeditation and deliberation but denied the motion as to felony child abuse and felony murder. In October 2009, however, the North Carolina Court of Appeals explained that the state did not present sufficient evidence that felonious child abuse was committed by Mary, and therefore a felony murder conviction is unsupportable. To the Court, the verdict in the case was "based on speculation and conjecture, not evidence, and cannot stand." The North Carolina Supreme Court upheld the appeals court holding in 2010.

In 1977, Rebecca Case Detter solicited persons to kill her husband, Don Gene Detter, for $5,000. Rebecca claimed that Don was cruel to the family; he was a heavy drinker, consuming three to four fifths of liquor per week. No one accepted Rebecca's offer and she tried killing Don over several months using arsenic poison from ant bait, lead from fishing weights, and various recreational drugs (PCP, cocaine, and acid). Don was eventually hospitalized and died in early June 1977. Physicians performed tests for heavy metal poisoning and treated Don for arsenic poisoning. An autopsy confirmed Don's death resulting from arsenic poisoning; his body contained 10 times the normal amount of arsenic. A Forsyth County jury found Rebecca guilty of first-degree murder and the trial judge sentenced her to death. In 1979, the North Carolina Supreme Court affirmed Rebecca's conviction, vacated the death sentence, and remanded the case back to the trial court for imposition of a life sentence. The Court argued that since the date of a murderous act rather than the date of death was the date that Rebecca murdered Don, the trial court erred when it imposed death upon Rebecca when the only sentence for murder at the time was life imprisonment. Authorities paroled Rebecca in September 1995.

In October 2001, a Cumberland County jury convicted Christina Shea Walters, a Lumbee Indian, of two counts of first-degree murder and recommended a death sentence. Superior Court Judge William C. Gore entered the sentence recommended by the jury, and in 2002, the North

Carolina Supreme Court upheld Christina's conviction and death sentence. Evidence at Christina's trial reveals that she was a leader of a local "Crips" gang, that the murders were part of a gang-initiation, and that the gang members chose the victims at random. In August 1998, the gang needed money and Christina and three others kidnapped and robbed Debra Cheeseborough. The group decided to take Debra to a nearby lake where Christina shot her eight times. Passersby found Debra the next day, paramedics took her a regional hospital, and she survived. After shooting Debra, the gang kidnapped and robbed two nightclub dancers, 18-year-old Tracy Rose Lambert and 21-year-old Susan Raye Moore, whom Christina killed execution style with a single bullet to the head. Myrtle Beach Police arrested two of the gang members in Debra's car and arrested three more members at a local motel the next day. A task force of 53 officers arrested the entire gang.

In December 2012, however, Cumberland County Superior Court Judge Gregory A. Weeks commuted Christina's death sentence to life in prison without the possibility of parole. Judge Weeks concluded that evidence presented over a four-week hearing showed prosecutors made a concerted effort to reduce the number of black jurors in Christina's original trial. "During the presentation of evidence," wrote Judge Weeks, "the court finds powerful and persuasive evidence of racial consciousness, race-based decision making in the writings of prosecutors long buried in the case files and brought to light for the first time during this hearing." The evidence apparently included prosecutors' handwritten notes indicating that they eliminated black jurors resulting in jury panels comprising overwhelmingly white jurors. North Carolina had implemented a Racial Justice Act allowing death row inmates to show that racial bias influenced their sentences. According to one commentator, the legislation banned racial discrimination in jury selection in capital cases and allows capital defendants "to use the same tool—statistical evidence of discrimination—that has allowed advocates to reform discriminatory housing, education, and employment practices."[22]

In October 1990, a Wilson County jury convicted Patricia Wells Jennings of murdering her 80-year-old husband, William Henry Jennings, and the trial court imposed a death sentence. Patricia had beat and tortured to death her husband in a hotel room at a Hampton Inn in Wilson, North Carolina, in September 1989. The jury found Patricia committed the murder while attempting the penetration of William's anus with an object, that the murder was committed for pecuniary gain, and that the murder was especially heinous, atrocious, or cruel. Patricia was a nurse at Westwood Manor Nursing Home where she met William, a retired businessman who counseled alcoholic patients at the home. They married, but throughout their marriage Patricia became increasingly violent toward William who admitted to his attorney when drafting a will that Patricia physically had beaten him, dragged him across the room, stomped him with her cowboy boots, and that she tried to have him institutionalized. Trial evidence showed that while at the hotel Patricia had summoned paramedics to the room who found William lying naked on the floor and Patricia performing CPR. Paramedics testified at trial that when they arrived at the hotel room William had been dead between five and six hours. An autopsy revealed that William had multiple bruises and scrapes on various parts of his head, scalp, face, neck, legs, arms and hands. There was a large bruise in the abdominal cavity caused by blunt force. The injuries appeared consistent with a kick or stomp to the abdomen. The autopsy also showed tiny cracks or splits in his anus, there were injuries to the head of William's penis in the form of sharply defined imprints, lacerations on the shaft of the penis, scrapes at the base of the penis, and a scratch on the scrotum. Patricia had sexually assaulted and tortured William to death. In 2013, however, Superior Court Judge Wayland Sermons granted a defense motion to vacate her death sentence and instead sentenced Patricia to life in prison. According to reports, defense lawyers claimed that Patricia received ineffective counsel when her original lawyers failed to request that jurors consider that she had no significant criminal history. What's more, the State Bureau of Investigation concealed favorable lab results and used false and unreliable evidence to win the murder conviction and death sentence against Patricia.

In mid–January 1975, Sandra Lockett participated in a robbery of a pawn shop in downtown Akron during which one of her accomplices shot and killed the owner of the shop, 61-year-old Sidney Cohen. A police investigation resulted in the arrests of Al Parker (the actual shooter), Nathan Earl Dew, and James Lockett (Sandra's brother). Sandra apparently sat outside the shop in a car while the three others actually robbed the store. A Summit County jury found Sandra guilty as an accomplice to the murder and the trial court sentenced her to death. Sandra had refused to plea bargain her case. As mitigating factors at her penalty hearing, Sandra's lawyer maintained that she was borderline mentally retarded, under the influence of methadone, and subject to the undue influence of the others at the time of the killing. The lawyers found that these factors should have precluded a death sentence although no expert testimony showed that Sandra's participation in the murder and robbery of Sidney Cohen was not the product of a psychosis or mental deficiency. As a result, according to one court, Sandra failed to meet the burden of proving that mitigating circumstances existed such as to preclude the imposition of capital punishment. At the time, Ohio's death penalty statute narrowly limited the consideration of "mitigating circumstances" to cases where the victim facilitated their own death, where the murder was under duress, or if the murderer suffered from a mental deficiency. The Court of Appeals for Summit County and the Supreme Court of Ohio affirmed the trial court's judgment against Sandra, but in 1978, the U.S. Supreme Court granted certiorari to Sandra Lockett and overturned her death sentence. Per Chief Justice Burger, the majority held that Ohio's death penalty statute was far too restrictive. "We conclude that the Eighth and Fourteenth Amendments require that the sentencer ... not be precluded from considering, as a mitigating factor, any aspect of a defendant's character or record and any of the circumstances of the offense that the defendant proffers as a basis for a sentence less than death." As a result of *Lockett v. Ohio*, the state resentenced 101 death row inmates to life in prison including three other women, Alberta Osborne, Patricia N. Wernett, and Benita Smith. After serving 19 years in prison, authorities paroled Sandra in 1993 and she served five years' probation. She returned to prison for a short period for parole violations. Al Parker, now 61 years old, remains at the Mansfield Correctional Institution under a life sentence. Seventy-three-year-old James Lockett is serving a life sentence at Trumbull Correctional Institution. Nathan Dew was adjudged mentally deficient and sentenced to life in prison.

Alberta L. Osborne and Edgel Ross had a five-year relationship that he ended in November 1974 after his wife, Hermalee, had learned of the adulterous affair. It was then that Alberta hired her son, Carl Edward Osborne, and James Kenneth Weind, Carl's friend, to kidnap and murder Hermalee Ross for $325. In mid–December of that year, Carl and James abducted Hermalee from the parking lot of an Ontario food store in Franklin County where Hermalee worked as a cashier. Authorities later found her body in an abandoned schoolhouse in Delaware County with bullet wounds to the back of her head and neck, to her ear and hand, and with numerous other abrasions and contusions apparently caused by repeatedly striking her with a blunt instrument. In June 1975, a Franklin County jury found Alberta guilty of Hermalee's kidnapping and murder and the trial court sentenced her to death. The state tried the principals in the killing separately. The Court of Appeals affirmed the judgment of the trial court, as did the Supreme Court of Ohio. Given the *Lockett* ruling, however, the court vacated her death sentence to life in prison. Alberta is no longer incarcerated. Carl Osborne remains incarcerated at the Madison Correctional Institution and has a parole hearing scheduled for March 2015. James Weind is an inmate at the London Correctional Institution and is schedule for a parole hearing January 2015.

A Lucas County jury found Patricia N. Wernert guilty for her participation in the November 1975 murder of her 67-year-old mother-in-law, Harriet Wernert, and her 97-year-old grandmother-in-law, Velma Bush. A superior court tried her co-defendants, Patricia's husband David Ernest Wernert, and friend Richard Wayne Arterberry, separately though simultaneously. Apparently, David helped smuggle Richard into the home where Harriett and Velma lived in an affluent community. He hid in the basement for a few hours and then bludgeoned the women to death with a crowbar and hammer. The motive for the killings was a $2 million inheritance David would receive upon their deaths. All three defendants confessed to the killings upon their arrests. The Lucas County Court of Common Pleas sentenced all three defendants to death. Pursuant to the *Lockett* decision, however, the defendants received life sentences and remain incarcerated. Patricia remains at the Franklin Pre-Release Center, and David Wernert and Richard Arterberry are serving life sentences at the Allen Correctional Institution. Officials have scheduled all three defendants with parole hearings in November 2010. A recent inmate search of the Ohio Department of Corrections does not show any of the three defendants remaining in prison.

In November 1977, a Lucas County jury convicted 23-year-old Benita Smith of her complicity in the robbery-murder of a store operational manager named Jules Vennedge as he made a bank deposit of the store's receipts. Benita's 20-year-old brother was the actual killer who shot Jules in the head. Tried separately, both juries recommended that Bentia and her brother die by electrocution. The trial court sentenced them accordingly. Police learned of the murder when two teenage sisters who Benita asked to drive one of two cars to a carryout restaurant while Benita and her brother robbed Jules found out about the killing. After the U.S. Supreme Court rendered Ohio's death penalty statute unconstitutional in *Lockett*, authorities resentenced Benita to life in prison. According to the Ohio Department of Corrections, Benita is no longer incarcerated.

At the time of her crime, Sharon Faye Young was a 26-year-old lesbian who was the product of a broken home and who suffered brutal and sadistic beatings by her father and stepfather. Sharon's stepfather sexually abused her as a child. Sharon later gave birth to a child that she gave up for adoption. Officials institutionalized Sharon during her youth for long periods, and she spent eight years incarcerated on two separate occasions during her late teens and early twenties for theft offenses. Sharon was an alcoholic and indulged in drugs that most likely precipitated a short temper and a history of fighting. Trial evidence also showed that Sharon suffered from a psychological bent for compulsive repetition. Sharon was never employed for more than six months although she received her high school GED diploma and did some college work. In June 1983, Sharon shot and killed Larry Smyrlakis, the owner of Patches Café, with a single gunshot to the back of the head after a night of heavy drinking. After the police discovered a burglar alarm sounding at the café, they found the door open with no one inside. Police learned that Larry had not returned home after his night shift and that a .38 caliber handgun was missing. Police later found Larry's body alongside a road. Police arrested Sharon driving Larry's car in Columbus and subsequently found the gun in the car that Sharon used to kill Larry. Evidence showed that Larry and Sharon were heavily intoxicated the night of the shooting and that others saw them together at the café in the early morning hours. Shortly after her arrest, Sharon made a recorded declaration to police that she and Larry drove from the café to an isolated road where Larry stopped the vehicle and she pulled the gun that she had stolen from under the bar at the café. Sharon told Larry to get out of the car and demanded his money. Larry threw his wallet on the front seat. As Sharon reached into the car to pick up the wallet, Larry lunged at Sharon and she fired the gun. She stated she did not mean to kill Larry or to hurt him and that she did not know how many shots she fired. Sharon also stated that she would not have shot Larry if he had not lunged toward her. Sharon fled the scene, throwing Larry's wallet and credit cards out of the car window but she kept $60 in cash. In September 1983, a Hamilton County jury found Sharon guilty of Larry's murder returned its recommendation to impose the death penalty. The trial court adopted the jury's recommendation of the death sentence.

On appeal, the Ohio Supreme Court reversed Sharon's murder conviction and death sentence and remanded the case back to the trial court for further proceedings. The Court held that the trial judge committed prejudicial error in refusing to instruct the jury on the lesser-included offense of involuntary manslaughter given Sharon's level of intoxication at the time Larry's killing. As in most cases involving lesbian capital defendants, there was prosecutorial misconduct in Sharon's case in the form of callous disregard for her sexuality. Apparently, while the prosecutor was holding the gun used to kill Larry, he remarked:

> You know, this is the same person the anti-gun crowd always refers to as a phallic symbol. Those of us who are gun collectors or gun enthusiasts, it's a symbol of our manhood that a person would have any interest or desire in having this. Here we have someone who God caused to be born as a woman. She wants to be a man. She dresses like one, she acts like one, she was Casey. Casey, tough person. No, she wanted the gun because she knew what it represented to her, what she could do, that it was her manhood, her power.[23]

Sharon's appellate lawyers claimed these statements go beyond the record; they are unsubstantiated by the evidence, and improperly create prejudice against Sharon for her admitted homosexuality. While the Court found the prosecutor's comments "totally lacking any degree of professionalism," it did not agree that the comments prejudiced Sharon trial. The Court found more troubling the prosecutor's misstatements of law and that the trial court should have given a corrective instruction. The jury in the second trial found Sharon guilty of murder, but did not recommend the imposition of capital punishment. The trial court ordered Sharon to serve a term of life imprisonment, with parole eligibility after 30 years. Sharon is presently serving a life sentence at the Ohio Reformatory for Women and her first parole hearing is in April 2016.

In November 2005, a Lorain County jury found Nicole guilty of murder and the trial court sentenced her to death. Apparently, an intentionally set fire seriously damaged Nicole's home and fire investigators found young Jacob's body in the bedroom to the home. Investigators determined that gasoline was used to start the fire and that Jacob was dead before the house fire began. Forensic experts were unable to determine the exact cause of Jacob's death, but they determined that the child had died before the fire because his mouth, nasal passages, and lungs were clear of any soot or debris. What's more, Jacob's clothing and the mattress pad tested positive for the presence of an "ignitable liquid." Coroner officials concluded that Jacob died as a result of "homicidal violence of an undetermined origin." Other testimony showed that Nicole frequently used babysitters when she went out at night, failed to leave emergency contact numbers with them, instructed babysitters to give Jacob codeine, stayed out late, she was a poor housekeeper and essentially neglected Jacob. Under the state's theory, Nicole killed her son because she was tired of being a parent. Nicole Diar is herself a burn victim. At age four, Diar's pajamas caught fire and she suffered terrible burns that left permanent scarring over much of her body. She underwent 61 operations over 14 years. According to the Ohio Supreme Court on appeal, the trial court erred in Nicole's case when it failed to instruct the jury that a solitary juror could prevent the imposition of the death penalty. The defense requested an instruction that if a single juror "concludes that the aggravating circumstances do not outweigh the mitigating circumstances, beyond a reasonable doubt, then [the jury must] go down to life without parole." The trial court refused to give this requested instruction. The State conceded that the trial court's failure to provide the solitary juror instruction constituted error and required the Court to remand Nicole's case to the trial court for a new mitigation hearing. Nicole Diar is serving a life sentence without the possibility of parole at the Ohio Reformatory for Women in Marysville.

The death row population of Ohio includes one woman named Donna Marie Roberts who a Trumbull County jury convicted of murdering her ex-husband, Robert Fingerhut, for which the Superior Court sentenced her to death. Robert and Donna were married in 1983 but soon divorced for financial and business reasons to protect assets in the event his business failed. Robert owned Greyhound bus terminals in Ohio. Despite the divorce, the couple continued as husband and wife and both considered themselves married. Donna began an affair with Nathaniel Jackson, a co-defendant in Robert's murder. Apparently, in early December 2001, Donna summoned emergency personnel to the couple's home claiming something was seriously wrong with Robert. Police found Robert's body on the kitchen floor. Forensic reports show that Robert had sustained lacerations and abrasions to his left hand and head, as well as multiple gunshot wounds to his head, chest, and back. Police investigators learned that Robert had taken out two life insurance policies on his life amounting to $550,000 and naming Donna as sole beneficiary. Letters recovered by police from the home indicated that Donna and Nathaniel had planned to murder Robert. Also, evidence from telephone conversations between Donna and Nathaniel while he was in prison for a short stay at the Lorain Correctional Institute revealed a plot to murder Robert. A grand jury indicted both Donna and Nathaniel for Robert's murder. The Ohio Supreme Court upheld both the verdict and death sentence of Nathaniel Jackson, however the court reversed Donna's death sentence and remanded her case back to the trial court for reconsideration of the death sentence. The court vacated Donna's death sentence because the trial judge permitted the state's prosecutor to help prepare his sentencing opinion on Donna. Apparently, while the court read aloud its sentencing opinion and imposed the death penalty, defense counsel noticed the prosecutor reading a document and was reading along with the trial judge. Defense counsel objected to the prosecution's involvement with the sentencing opinion. The trial judge conceded that the prosecution had participated in the drafting of the opinion without the knowledge of defense counsel. The trial judge apologized to defense counsel for not providing them with a copy of the opinion before the sentencing hearing. The justices of the Supreme Court unanimously ruled that the trial judge acted in violation of Ohio law. Donna remains on death row at the Ohio Reformatory for Women in Marysville, but in May 2013, Donna's defense attorneys argued before the Ohio Supreme Court that the trial judge failed to consider her mental illness, low intelligence, and other mitigating factors before sentencing her to death again in 2007. Donna's attorney claims that she suffers from bipolar disorder, depression, and that her I.Q. is 55. In October 2013, the Ohio Supreme Court overturned Donna's death sentence and remanded the case back to the trial court "to consider all mitigating evidence reflected in the record."[24] Officials hold Nathaniel on death row at the Ohio State Penitentiary.

In February 1975, Janet M. Sanders and her common law husband, Billie Roger Miller (married to Ann Miller), robbed and murdered a night clerk at a convenience store named Louise Bensen, who was shot five times in the face and neck at close range. The two emptied the store's cash register and took about $150 missing from a safe. An Oklahoma County jury convicted Janet and Billie of the robbery-murder and affixed the sentence at death by electrocution. Customers found Louise's body lying in a pool of blood behind the counter of the Time Store. After Sanders and Miller's arrests, each signed confessions. The confessions showed that Billie told Janet that he planned to rob the store and that she begged him to allow her to go along and drove him to the store in her car. After ensuring that Louise was alone inside the store, Billie went inside. When he returned to the car, Billie told Janet that he had shot Bensen. They drove back to her residence, packed some clothes, and drove to Dallas, Texas. The couple spent the night with Janet's relatives then returned to Oklahoma City. Along the way, they stopped and saw in a newspaper that police looking for the two in connection with the robbery-murder. Billie contacted Midwest City police who told him they would like to talk with him. As they drove to Oklahoma City, they disposed of the murder weapon in a lake and some money in a trash can. Police recovered the stolen money but not the gun. On appeal, the Court of Criminal Appeals of Oklahoma affirmed Janet and Billie's murder convictions but modified their sentences from death to life imprisonment because of the Court's holding in *Riggs v. Branch* finding the state's death penalty law unconstitutional after the U.S. Supreme Court's holding in *Furman*. Officials paroled Janet in June 1983. Billie is currently residing at the Lexington Correctional Center in Lexington, Oklahoma, and has a parole hearing scheduled for February 2011.

The District Court of Oklahoma County jointly tried Michelle Ann Binsz and her husband, Steven William Binsz, for the murder-for-hire of a state correctional employee named Robert Busch. The jury set the sentence for Michelle and Steven at death and Judge William R. Saied affirmed the penalties. The Court of Criminal Appeals of Oklahoma reversed the convictions because of prosecutorial misconduct. Apparently, at the Binszes murder trial, Carla Jo Rapp, also charged in the same murder, turned state's evidence and testified against the Binszes. In exchange for her testimony, the state's attorney agreed to dismiss a first-degree murder charge against Carla in exchange for Carla's guilty plea to conspiracy to commit murder and to serve two years in prison. When asked about the plea agreement at trial, however, Carla erroneously stated that the only promise she had received in the plea agreement was that the prosecutor would be fair with her and not put her in the same penitentiary as Michelle Binsz. The testimony of one of Carla's former cellmates, however, showed that Carla had bragged about her deal, that she described the very terms of the bargain, and that Carla had learned of the agreement several months before the Binsz trial. The Court of Criminal Appeals found that the prosecutor had thus ensured that the jury would not learn the true nature of the plea agreement and thereby misled the jury as to the reasons Carla testified against the Binszes. The Court found that the prosecutor effectively denied the Binszes due process of law under the Fourteenth Amendment. As the Court put it, "The State thusly joined the falsehood and used it to achieve murder convictions against the Binszes."[25] Officials commuted the Binszes death sentence to life in prison and both were paroled in 2012.

A District Court jury in Oklahoma County convicted Patricia Beth Jones on two counts of murder for the killing of 31-year-old Kim Gayleen Grant and her 37-year-old boyfriend named Harrell Lloyd "Rob" Robinson in March 1988. Judge Charles Owens sentenced Patricia to death on both murder counts. The state also charged Ronnie Lee Floyd, David Lee Flippo, and Alfredo "Pineapple" Omalza for their complicity in the murders. Police discovered the bodies of Kim and Harrell in a shallow grave in a ravine; they had been stabbed and beaten to death. According to the state's case, Patricia and Alfredo, her incarcerated boyfriend, conspired to kill Kim Grant who was about to testify against Patricia in a drug smuggling case whereby Patricia attempted to smuggle heroin into the Mabel Bassett Correctional Center. Alfredo ordered Ronnie and David to kidnap Kim and Harrell and scare Kim into recanting her preliminary hearing testimony against Patricia. Otherwise, the two were to kill Harrell and Kim. She refused to recant her testimony and died as a result. The Criminal Court of Appeals found procedural error in that the trial court abused its discretion when it denied Patricia continuances to prepare for trial after the state introduced new witnesses.

In March 1995, District Judge Nancy Coats sentenced Delpha Jo Spunaugle to death for the brutal murder of her husband, Dennis Spunaugle. It seems from the appellate record that Delpha Jo had tried for two years to find someone to kill Dennis. Then, on the evening of August 14, 1993, Delpha Jo asked her friend David Woodward to come over and be with her when Dennis came home from a night of drinking hoping that Dennis would not abuse her verbally if David were present. Apparently, David and Delpha Jo had been past lovers, and Delpha Jo revealed to David that Dennis was abusive to her and had molested her daughter. When Dennis arrived at home, he went to bed after some a brief verbal exchange with Delpha Jo. Later in the evening, David went into the bedroom where Dennis was sleeping hit him over the head with a baseball bat. A struggle ensued and David stabbed Dennis repeatedly. When Dennis had the upper hand in the struggle, Delpha Jo hit him with the bat. The two then got a rope, tied it around Dennis' neck, and pulled it from both ends until Dennis was dead. A passing truck driver found Dennis' maggot infested and partially skeletonized body in a dry creek bed. Upon their arrests, David confessed to the crime. Delpha Jo also confessed to Dennis' murder, but claimed that she did so because David was "possessed" during the assault on Dennis and threatened to harm her or her children if she did not help kill Dennis. Delpha Jo also asserted to police that David was a devil worshipper who licked Dennis' blood from his knife and threatened that his followers would hurt her if she reported the crime. Authorities tried and convicted Delpha Jo and David jointly, but Delpha Jo received a death sentence while the trial court sentenced David to life in prison without parole. On appeal, the Circuit Court of Criminal Appeals found that the trial court committed prejudicial error when it hampered Delpha Jo's duress defense, denied her all of her allowable peremptory challenges, and failed to remove a sleeping juror. The Court reversed the conviction and death sentence and remanded the case for a new trial. Delpha Jo is serving a life sentence with no parole at the Mabel Bassett Correctional Center.

Multnomah County prosecutors in Portland, Oregon, tried and convicted Karla Crosby in 2002 for the manslaughter death of her 76-year-old mother Sheila Crosby. Karla was Sheila's sole caregiver after her mother's health deteriorated in the 1990s. Sheila lived in the family's dilapidated home, refusing to go to a nursing home. When Sheila had difficulty swallowing in late 2001, Karla took her to a hospital emergency room where staff suspected abuse and neglect; Sheila was in an emaciated state suffering from, among other things, dehydration, muscle atrophy, malnourishment, and sepsis resulting from infection of a number of bedsores, some exposing bone. She was also covered with feces. A physician determined that Sheila was preterminal and transferred her to a convalescent home for hospice care and she died a few days later. Hospital staff reported Sheila's condition to the police for investigation of possible elder abuse. An autopsy concluded that Sheila had died of "infected decubitus ulcers with probable sepsis." To prosecutors, "it was the most graphic and horrifying case of elder abuse they had seen" though they conceded that there was no evidence Karla intended her mother's death. A state's appeals court affirmed Karla's conviction in February 2006. A year later, however, the Oregon Supreme Court overturned Karla's conviction on the basis that the trial judge improperly instructed the jury on the legal definition of killing a dependent person. Rather, the judge should have told the jury that it had to find that Karla had exhibited a reckless disregard of the risk of killing her mother.

In June 1972, Marilyn Ann Dobrolenski pled guilty to first-degree murder in the shooting deaths of Ronald L. Carey and David C. Yarrington, officers with the Delaware State Police. The shooting took place while the officers were investigating an armed robbery of the Tally-Ho Motor Lodge and noticed a suspicious vehicle with its engine left running at the nearby Concord Motel just over the state line in Pennsylvania. When they began to investigate the vehicle, they became engaged in a scuffle with Irving R. Hogg, a convicted felon from Ohio. Marilyn, Irving's accomplice, shot and killed both officers during the struggle. After the robbery and murders, Marilyn and Irving led police on a 14-hour manhunt through Pennsylvania and Maryland. The state police commissioner described the two fugitives as "a modern-day Bonnie and Clyde." Police suspected the two of several robberies in Ohio and Michigan. Police spotted the two in a stolen car and after a high speed chase, police shot and killed Irving and arrested Marilyn. The trial court sentenced Marilyn to die in the state's electric chair, but vacated the capital sentence in light of the *Furman* decision rendering the state's death penalty statute unconstitutional. Instead, the court imposed two consecutive life sentences. On appeal, the Pennsylvania Supreme Court affirmed the order of the lower court that imposed two consecutive life sentences and held that the imposition of the death penalty under the applicable statute violated the U.S. Constitution. A Delaware trial court sentenced Marilyn to an additional 10 years imprisonment for firearm-possession charges to run consecutively with an additional sentence of 20 years imprisonment for the robbery. The Supreme Court of Pennsylvania upheld the convictions and sentences. Marilyn remains at the State Correctional Institution in Pennsylvania in Muncie.

In July 1993, in the Court of Common Pleas of Philadelphia County, Judge Paul Ribner found Kelly O'Donnell, along with her boyfriend William Russell Gribble, guilty of the sadistic robbery-murder of Eleftherios Eleftheriou, a pizza parlor owner. After a bench trial and penalty-phase hearing, Judge Ribner sentenced Kelly, the mother of six and a drug user, to death. The appellate record reveals that in early November 1992, Kelly borrowed money from Eleftherios and made arrangements to meet later that evening. In a confession to police and admitted at trial, Kelly met with Eleftherios and took him back to a home where she was staying while the owner was gone on vacation. While Eleftherios looked out a window, Kelly struck him in the head with a hammer. Even after Eleftherios fell to the floor, Kelly continued to beat him with the hammer. Kelly claimed that she killed Eleftherios because he was a "pervert" and had previously sexually assaulted her. While he was still alive, Kelly took Eleftherios' body to the basement of the house and dismembered the body with a hacksaw. She put the body parts in trash bags. Kelly also cut off Eleftherios' penis and placed it in a pencil case. William helped Kelly dispose of the trash bags containing the body parts by dumping them in trash dumps along Delaware Avenue. Later that same evening, Kelly and William used Eleftherios' car and credit card to go shopping.

Philadelphia police received a report that someone had found body parts in a trash dump. When police responded they found the severed arms of a white male, a human torso with its head missing and a head with the left eye removed. Later, police also found Eleftherios' burned out car with body parts inside the car. A search of the basement revealed a kitchen knife, a chisel, and a claw hammer containing traces of human tissue and blood. Police also found a pencil case containing a human eyeball and penis stuffed inside a pipe. The Supreme Court of Pennsylvania affirmed Kelly's conviction but reversed the death sentence imposed by the trial court and remanded the case for a new penalty phase hearing because the trial court did not properly ensure that Kelly waived her right to a jury in the penalty phase of the trial. Kelly is serving a life sentence at the State Correctional Institute at Muncy where the state houses its female capital inmates. William is serving a life sentence at the State Correctional Institute in Green County where the state houses its male capital case inmates.

In March 1989, a Philadelphia County jury convicted Delores Rivers of the January 1988 brutal murder of 77-year-old Violet Burt, an amputee. The jury recommended the death penalty and Common Pleas Court Judge John J. Poserina sentenced Delores to death. She was Violet's home health-care worker responsible for cleaning, cooking, and feeding Violet under a contract with the Philadelphia Corporation for the aging. An autopsy determined that Violet suffered some 30 areas of trauma of beating and stabbing to death with a pocketknife about her neck and on the front of her body while in her home. Apparently, Delores murdered Violet while she and her boyfriend, Lawrence Flowers, robbed Violet of $6,000 to buy drugs. An inmate testified that Delores had admitted to her that she and her boyfriend killed Violet. Delores was crack cocaine addict at the time of Violet's murder. After many lost appeals and 16 years on death row, Delores won a reprieve after a federal judge in May 2005 granted Delores a new penalty phase hearing. In her appeal to U.S. District Judge Mary A. McLaughlin, Rivers argued that Delores's trial lawyer failed to present mitigating evidence to jurors before they imposed the death penalty. McLaughlin ordered a new penalty phase. Delores's trial attorney failed to investigate and present her history of sexual and physical abuse, her mental disturbances, and the effects of her long-term drug abuse, and that she had taken drugs on the night of the murder. Delores suffered from paranoid and explosive traits, chronic drug, and alcohol abuse. A court psychologist determined that Delores had a mixed personality disorder even though she did not suffer from a major mental illness. Philadelphia prosecutors chose not to seek another death sentence and

Delores plead guilty to murder and waived all future appeals. Judge Poserina resentenced Delores to life in prison without parole.

In April 1992, a Philadelphia jury convicted Donetta Hill of two counts of murder of the first degree and returned a death sentence on each murder. The trial evidence showed that in late June 1990, 72-year-old Nghia Quy Lu propositioned Hill to have sex with him for money. The two went to the basement of Mr. Lu's home and had sex. After their encounter, Donetta grabbed a hammer and struck Lu in the back of the head several times. Lu collapsed and died from his injuries. Donetta then ransacked the house and took several items. Several months later, 21-year-old Nairobi Dupont offered money to Donetta to have sex with him. Dupont, who was "mentally slow," had sex with Hill at his father's house. Afterwards, Donetta grabbed a hammer and struck Dupont repeatedly in the back of the head. As Dupont laid dead or dying on the floor, Donetta ransacked the house and took several items and fled the scene. Donetta soon learned that police wanted to question her about the murders, and it was then that Donetta went to her probation officer who accompanied her to the Philadelphia police department. Once there, Donetta was taken to an interview room and fully advised of her *Miranda* rights where she confessed to both murders signed a written confessions. The Pennsylvania Supreme Court upheld both verdicts and death sentences. In March 2012, the prosecution withdrew the capital status of the case and the Court of Common Pleas sentenced her to life imprisonment.

In November 1994, a Lebanon County jury convicted Carolyn Ann King, and her co-defendant Bradley A. Martin, of a September 1993 murder in the first degree. Court of Common Pleas Judge Robert J. Eby sentenced King to death. It appears that authorities gave Martin a two-hour visitation pass to leave the Lebanon County Correctional Facility where he was serving a sentence for parole violation. He met Carolyn, with whom he was romantically involved, and failed to return to prison. Instead, the two traveled to Palmyra, Pennsylvania, where they called upon Guy Goodman, with whom Martin was acquainted. Mr. Goodman, who was 74 years old, had written, telephoned and visited Martin in prison, identifying himself as Martin's friend. Trial testimony revealed that Goodman was attracted to young men and that Martin and Goodman were openly affectionate with one another. Soon after arriving at Goodman's home, Martin hit Goodman over the head with a vase from the hallway. Carolyn and Martin then bound Goodman's wrists, ankles and neck, wrapped a bathrobe around Goodman's head, placed a plastic bag over it, sealed the bag with duct tape, and wrapped a bedspread over the bag. Then the two carried Goodman into the basement, tying him more securely and leaving him to suffocate. Martin and Carolyn then stole Mr. Goodman's checkbook and credit card and drove away in his car. The couple fled across the country in Goodman's car, using his checks and credit card to pay their expenses. The couple was also accused of abducting and killing Donna Mae Martz from a motel parking lot in South Dakota. Police found Martz's body in a remote area just outside Elko, Nevada, with a single gunshot to the head. Arizona authorities captured the couple, and upon her arrest, Carolyn gave statements to federal and state police confessing to Goodman's murder. The Pennsylvania Supreme Court affirmed the verdicts and death sentences for Carolyn in 1998. Carolyn has mental and emotional difficulties stemming from a dysfunctional childhood; she suffers from post-traumatic stress disorder, sexual abuse, child abuse, domestic violence, depression, and drug abuse. But her attorney, M. Jannifer Weiss, did not present this mitigating evidence regarding past abuse and mental disorders present at Carolyn's sentencing hearing in 1994 claiming that she didn't have time to investigate the issues because the penalty phase began immediately after the verdict and that she didn't feel testimony on the matters would have helped her defense. In 2000, the U.S. Supreme Court refused to hear Carolyn's appeal, but in 2010, the Court of Common Pleas for Lebanon County granted her a new sentencing hearing. Officials have yet to publish the outcome of that sentencing hearing. Carolyn pled guilty to Martz's murder and received a life sentence.

In February 2002, Cumberland County Court of Common Pleas Judge George E. Hoffer sentenced Beth Ann Markman, along with her boyfriend co-defendant, William Howard Housman, to death for the murder of an 18-year-old photojournalism student named Leslie Rae White. Trial evidence shows that in the summer of 2000, White met Beth when both worked at a local Wal-Mart store and soon began an intimate relationship while Housman was living in a trailer park with Beth. About August 2000, Beth learned of a relationship between White and Housman, which had an adverse effect on Housman and Beth's relationship. Housman became increasingly violent with Beth and she demanded that Housman move out of the trailer. In mid–September 2000, Housman and Beth reconciled and he moved back into the trailer. Meanwhile, White began dating a fellow student from the College she attended. Under the ruse that he was distraught over the recent death of his father, Housman lured White to the trailer. Housman told White that Beth was out of town and that they would be alone. White went to the trailer, Housman and Beth subdued her, bound her feet and hands with speaker wire, placed a large piece of cloth in her mouth, and Housman strangled her with the speaker wire killing her. White died from asphyxiation. After killing White, Housman and Beth wrapped her body in a canvas tent and put her in the back of White's Jeep Cherokee. They drove the car to land owned by Housman's mother and placed White's body in the trunk of an abandoned car and discarded her personal effects. White's parents filed a missing persons report and through an investigation, officials tracked the jeep to Housman's father's house. Police went to the house to investigate and interviewed Housman and Beth concerning the jeep. Soon afterwards, they couple abandoned the jeep where they had disposed of White's body. Police soon discovered the jeep and White's partially decomposed body in the abandoned car. They arrested Beth and Housman at a friend's house October 2000 and both confessed separately to White's murder. At trial, Beth testified that Housman physically abused her during their relationship and that he terrorized her for the two days preceding the murder, during which time he cut her clothes off with a knife, repeatedly raped her, and threatened her if she did not do as he wanted. In 2007, the Pennsylvania Supreme Court overturned Beth's murder and kidnapping convictions and ordered her a new trial based on prosecutorial misconduct involving an altered tape recording of Housman's confession implicating Beth in White's murder. Moreover, the Court argued that "the jury should have been informed of the defense of duress and its recklessness exception, and allowed to resolve these factual issues—at least with respect to the charges of homicide, kidnapping and unlawful restraint." Beth remains on death row in Pennsylvania awaiting a new trial.

In December 1990, a Horry County jury convicted Rebecca M. Smith, a motel worker, of first-degree murder for the killing of her husband, 49-year-old Harold Smith, in July 1989. The jury recommended execution and Judge Dan F. Laney, Jr., imposed the death penalty. The appellate record shows that police went to a mobile home where Harold was staying while on a fishing trip and noticed the front door pried open. Police discovered Harold's dead body in the front bedroom. Harold died from blunt trauma to the head associated massive injury to the underlying brain, an injury consistent with strikes on the forehead with a baseball bat. Apparently, the night before police found Harold's body, Rebecca, her nephew Hank Locklear, her paramour Billy Ray McGee, and her son Brian went to the trailer where, about an hour after Rebecca and Brian went into the trailer carrying a baseball bat, Rebecca came running out, telling Billy and Hank to come into the trailer, that she had killed Harold. Hank saw Harold lying on the bed in a pool of blood, calling out for Rebecca. After Rebecca struck Harold with the baseball bat, Brian took the bat and hit him again to "make sure that he was dead." Billy then took the bat, hitting the trailer door to give the appearance of a break-in. Upon their arrests, Billy, Hank, and Brian pled guilty to various charges and received varying sentences—Hank received concurrent ten-year prison terms, and Billy and Brian each received 35-year prison terms. On appeal, the South Carolina Supreme Court granted Rebecca a new trial for procedural error when the trial court allowed irrelevant and prejudicial testimony in Rebecca's initial murder proceedings concerning her use of cocaine. A second jury unanimously voted to give Rebecca a life sentence. Accordingly to her trial lawyer, Bill Diggs, "jurors in the retrial didn't buy the 'Hannibal Lecter' image his client was given in the first trial." None of these defendants appears in the current records of the South Carolina Department of Corrections.

In August 1978, Texas officials tried Mary Lou Anderson for the murder of her father and stepmother. Her co-defendant was John Feryl Granger. Authorities tried Mary first and a Matagorda County jury found her guilty, and District Court Judge Neil Caldwell sentenced her to death. On appeal, judicial authorities granted Mary a new trial but instead she pled guilty to murder and received a reduced sentence of 50 years in prison. Mary testified at John's trial to the effect that John went to her apartment and told her that he was going to kill her father so Mary could collect on a $5,000 life insurance policy. Part of the motive to collect the insurance proceeds was in part to cover worthless checks for which authorities had prosecuted Mary who was facing a prison term unless she could cover the bad checks. To get Mary's support for the killings, John threatened Mary that if she did not cooperate in the killing he would kill her son. Shortly after they arrived at the home of Mary's parents, John put on gloves and loaded his pistol. He then went inside the Anderson home, bound and gagged them with adhesive tape, and then shot to death Steve Anderson, a county road maintenance worker, and Marjorie Anderson, a hospital bookkeeper. John shot Steve Anderson three times in the head and Marjorie Anderson five times in the head. A jury found John guilty of murder and sentenced him to life in prison. The Texas Department of Corrections shows no record that Mary Anderson or John Granger remains incarcerated.

In May 1978, Linda Mae Burnett, a homemaker and mother of three, along with her co-defendant Joe Dugas, conspired to kill Joe Dugas' in-laws, Bishop Neil Phillips and Esther Viola Phillips, and Linda's former husband, Hubert Miller. Elmer Phillips, his wife Martha Jean Phillips, and their three-year-old son Jason Blair Phillips, were visiting Elmer's parents (Bishop and Esther) at the time of the murders. Joe wanted to kill his in-laws because he believed they had broken-up his marriage. Linda and Joe planned a beach trip as an alibi, obtained weapons, and dug a large grave in which to bury the bodies. In early July of that year, Linda and Joe drove his car to a prearranged site where they left Joe's car and drove Linda's car to the Phillips' home. They entered the home by cutting through a front screen door. They held the Phillips family at gunpoint, ordered them into the son's car, and drove to the pre-dug grave. Linda shot and killed execution style the adult members of the family and in the same manner Joe shot and killed young Jason. They then disposed of the weapons and covered the grave. Dugas returned to the car the next day and burned it. George Phillips, who lived with his parents, Bishop and Esther, discovered the house abandoned when he returned from Houston and called police. Joe's brother Richard contacted police after Joe admitted to him that he and Linda had killed the Phillips family. A week after the killings, Joe led police to the bodies in the thick woods of southeastern Texas. Each of the victims was tied up and shot in the head at least once at close range. A trial court found Linda guilty of murder and Judge Larry Gist sentenced her to death. A psychiatrist believed Linda had a severe anti-social personality and that the slayings "were premeditated and precipitated by some kind of inner urge." Linda testified against Joe at his trial and a jury found him guilty of murder and the court sentence him to death. The Texas Court of Criminal Appeals overturned Linda's conviction in 1983 because the trial court improperly allowed into evidence a tape recording made of a hypnosis session with Linda. The Court granted Linda a new trial where again a jury convicted her of the murders and Judge Gist sentenced her to life in prison. The Texas Court of Criminal Appeals upheld Joe's conviction and death sentence. An investigator for the Jefferson County district attorney's office shot and killed Joe in June 1983 after he stabbed the investigator at a rest stop during a prisoner transport back to Huntsville. Linda Mae

Burnett remains incarcerated at the Mountain View Unit of the Texas Department of Criminal Justice in Gatesville, Texas.

Pamela Lynn Perillo grew up in an impoverished California family with an abusive father. She began using heroin at 10 years old and dancing in bars by the age of 21. In February 1980, Pamela joined Linda Joyce Fletcher and James Michael Briddle in Tucson, Arizona, after learning police had issued arrest warrants for Pamela, James, and another man for the robbery of a customer at the topless bar where Pamela worked in California. The trio found transportation with various truck drivers and eventually ended up in Houston, Texas. There, 30-year-old Robert Banks picked up the three near the Astrodome. Robert was in the process of moving to another house and the three hitchhikers assisted him in moving some of his belongings. Robert treated them to dinner. When Robert paid for the meal, Linda and Pamela observed he had several hundred dollars in his wallet. Pamela told James about the money. The three spent the night at Robert's house and then helped him move other belongings the next day. James learned that Robert had some guns. Robert took the three to a carnival and rodeo at the Astrodome. It was there that Pamela told James she wanted to kill Banks. After the rodeo, Banks took the others to dinner and returned to his house where they met 26-year-old Bob Skeens, a friend of Banks' from Louisiana. The next morning, armed with a shotgun and a handgun, James and Pamela made it clear to Robert and Bob that they were robbing them of their money. They tied-up the two men then took their wallets containing $800. Soon afterwards, the three drove to Dallas in Skeens' car where they abandoned it and took a bus to Colorado.

When Robert failed to appear for work for two days, Robert's supervisor went to his house to investigate. A man with the supervisor looked in a window and saw a body. The police who arrived at the scene found Robert and Bob's bodies. The murderers had bound each victim and tied ropes around their necks. The victims had died from asphyxia due to strangulation with a rope. After her arrest, Pamela gave a statement to Denver police and a description of James. With her consent, they entered a room at a hotel in Denver and found James, Linda, and two boys. A Houston detective went to Denver, interviewed James, and obtained an oral confession in which he told of his participation in the alleged offense. He admitted putting a rope around Robert's neck and pulling on it with Pamela until he was unconscious. He admitted he took the wallets, several hundred dollars, a machete, and a shotgun.

In 1982, a Harris County jury found Pamela guilty of the murders and the trial court assessed her punishment at death. In June 1983, the Court of Criminal Appeals reversed Pamela's murder conviction and death sentence, holding that the trial court committed reversible error when it failed to allow her the opportunity to question a juror the prosecution had dismissed for cause, the record did not indicate that the juror was incapable of rendering a fair decision. Texas tried and convicted Pamela a second time for the murders the trial court assessed her punishment at death. In March 1996, the Fifth Circuit Court of Appeals vacated the district court's ruling and remanded the case back to the trial court for appropriate discovery and an evidentiary hearing on an incompetent trial counsel claim. In June 1999, the U.S. District Court for the Southern District of Texas, per Judge Ewin Werlein, overturned Pamela's second conviction after finding incompetent trial representation; her attorney had a personal relationship with Linda Fletcher, the chief witness against Pamela. In March 2000, the Fifth Circuit Court of Appeals ordered Texas to give Pamela a new trial within four months or release her. Pamela plead guilty and received a life sentence, in July 2000 she received an additional 30-year sentence for the armed robbery of the persons she helped kill. Pamela was not eligible for parole for 10 years, but officials may have released her from prison since the Texas Department of Corrections has no record of her current incarceration. Texas executed 40-year-old James Michael Briddle in December 1995, and Linda Joyce Fletcher received five years' probation.

Four-day-old Malachi Berry died at the hands of his mother Kenisha Eronda Berry in

November 1998. She had duck taped his mouth, taped his arms around his abdomen, placed him inside a plastic trash bag, and put him in a dumpster at an apartment complex. Roy Black and his wife found the infant inside the dumpster while looking for aluminum cans. An autopsy revealed that the infant "died from asphyxia due to smothering" and forensic experts classified the death as a homicide. Infant Malachi's death remained unsolved until the summer of 2003 when police were investigating another case involving Kenisha Berry. During that investigation, Berry took officers to the dumpster where Roy Black and his wife had found Malachi five years earlier. A latent fingerprint found on the duck taped used on Malachi, as well as DNA analysis, confirmed the child belonged to Kenisha. She had four other children out of wedlock whose ages ranged from an infant to seven years old, all of whom were in protective custody. According to family members, Kenisha was a timid and weary child, who dropped out of high school but eventually earned her GED and became a prison guard and day care worker. She was indigent at the time authorities found young Malachi. In 2004, after about four hours of deliberation, a Jefferson County jury found Kenisha guilty of Malachi's murder and recommended the death penalty. District Judge Layne Walker sentenced her for execution. In May 2007, however, the Texas Court of Criminal Appeals affirmed Kenisha's murder conviction but reformed the sentence to life in prison because the state's attorney "did not meet its burden of proving beyond a reasonable doubt that there is a probability that [Kenisha], if allowed to live, would commit criminal acts of violence in the future so as to constitute a continuing threat, whether in or out of prison." In November 2007, the Jefferson County prosecutor filed charges against Kenisha for abandoning her infant daughter Paris in a roadside ditch in June 2003. Authorities were investigating the case when Kenisha showed police where she abandoned Malachi. It seems that 83-year-old Andrew Durham heard a baby crying as he walked along a road and found Paris lying naked on her back in a ditch with fire ants all over her body. Durham and his wife, a nurse, took Paris to the hospital. She had extensive ant bites and her eyes were swollen shut. Medical personnel gave Paris blood transfusions and the infant had seizures while hospitalized. Paris now resides in foster care. Kenisha is serving her life sentence at the Murray correctional unit in Gatesville and is eligible for parole in February 2044.

In 1995, a Travis County jury convicted Cathy Henderson of the capital murder of three-and-a-half-month-old Brandon Duane Baugh and the court sentenced her to death. Eryn and Melissa Baugh left Brandon with Cathy, their babysitter, one morning in late January 1994. Cathy kidnapped Brandon and the publicity over the kidnapping enabled law enforcement to capture Cathy in Kansas City, Missouri. At first, Cathy denied any knowledge of Brandon's whereabouts. Then Cathy claimed that the Brandon's grandmother had picked up Brandon in the afternoon after his parents had dropped him off. Only later did Cathy admit to killing Brandon but claimed the child's death was an accident. Cathy told police that she had buried the child in a wooded area near Waco. The trial judge scheduled Cathy's execution for June 2007, but a Texas Court of Criminal Appeals remanded her case back to the trial court to consider new scientific evidence challenging Texas' claim that Cathy intentionally killed Brandon. In December 2012, the court ordered a new trial. The appeals court based its decision largely on an affidavit by former Travis County medical examiner, Dr. Roberto Bayardo that Brandon's death may have resulted from an accidental fall. According to Dr. Bayardo,

> Since 1995, when I testified at Cathy Henderson's trial, the medical profession has gained a greater understanding of pediatric head trauma and the extent of injuries that can occur in infants as a result of relatively short distance falls.... I cannot determine with a reasonable degree of medical certainty whether Brandon Baugh's injuries resulted from an intentional act or an accidental fall. In fact, had the new scientific information been available to me in 1995, I would not have been able to testify the way I did about the degree of force needed to cause Brandon Baugh's head injury.[26]

Most recently, state prosecutors have decided not to seek the death penalty when they retry Cathy for capital murder, she faces a potential life prison sentence.

In August 2005, after two hours of deliberation, a Tarrant County jury convicted Chelsea Lea Richardson for the 2003 murder of Rick Wamsley and his wife, Suzanna Wamsley. The jury recommended a death sentence. Her co-defendant boyfriend, Andrew Wamsley, pleaded guilty to murder and a court sentenced him to life imprisonment. Co-defendant Susan Toledano testified against Richardson and Andrews in exchange for a life sentence. Another defendant who provided the gun used to kill the Wamsley's, Hilario Cardenas, pleaded guilty to conspiracy to commit murder and the district court sentenced him to 50 years in prison. The apparent motive for the killings was the Wamsley's $1.65 million estate and insurance proceeds that Andrew would inherit from his parents upon their deaths. In response to a 911 call, police discovered Rick and Susanna dead inside their house. Based upon testimony of Toledano, the three defendants entered the Wamsley's home and Toledano killed Suzanna instantly as she slept on the living room couch with a gunshot to her head. Suzanna also had post-mortem stab wounds. Immediately after, Toledano ran toward the Wamsley's bedroom and began firing at Rick Wamsley as he charged toward her, hitting him in the right temple. Rick forced Toledano back into the living room and fell on top of her, causing her to drop the gun. As the two struggled, Andrew intervened, trying to force Rick off Toledano, and Richardson joined the fray by shooting Rick in the back. As the three stood facing Rick as he sat on the floor, Rich pleaded to know why all of this was happening. Richardson thrusted a knife she had taken from the kitchen at him, stabbing his hand as he tried to block the attack. Soon after, Toledano stabbed him in the back with another kitchen knife as he lay on the ground. Rick Wamsley died, and the three left the residence. The Court of Criminal Appeals of Texas upheld Richardson's conviction and death sentence in January 2008. In a unanimous ruling, Judge Michael Keasler wrote, "In the light most favorable to the verdict, the testimony and evidence at trial showed that Richardson participated in the planning of the murders, aided in the two failed attempts to murder the Wamsleys, and was present during, encouraged, and participated in the final attempt during which the Wamsleys were killed."[27] The appeal also questioned the testimony of a jail inmate to whom Richardson implicated herself in the slayings. Also rejected by the court was the constitutionality of capital punishment in Texas. Susan Toledano pled guilty to murder and a Tarrant County court sentenced her to life in prison with the possibility of parole and will be eligible for parole in 2034. Andrew Wamsley was sentenced to life in prison and will be eligible for parole in 2044. Hilario Cardenas pled guilty to conspiracy to commit murder and received a 50-year sentence and is eligible for parole in 2014. As for Chelsea Richardson, a Tarrant County jury found her guilty of capital murder and unanimously voted the death penalty for Chelsea. On appeal, however, the Texas Court of Criminal Appeals found that misconduct of former prosecutor Mike Parrish in withholding evidence of a psychologist's report from defense lawyers affected the trial. A spokesperson for the district attorney's office stated that "this office will not be a party to the infliction of death as a punishment when there is even an appearance of impropriety on the part of a prosecutor who formerly worked in this office. If the death penalty is to be used, it must be obtained legally, fairly and honestly and without the hint of a possible injustice." In 2012, Judge Steve Herod sentenced Chelsea to life in prison. She must serve 40 years before she is eligible for parole.

Sonia Cacy moved to Fort Stockton, Texas, in October 1991 to live with and care for her 76-year-old uncle William R. Richarson. In November of that year, a fire broke out at William's residence wherein police later found his badly burned body. Sonia had escaped the fire through a back door to the house and summoned emergency services. A day after the fire investigators searched the house and found an amended will signed by William making Sonia sole heir to his estate. In April 1992, a Pecos County grand jury indicted Sonia for William's murder and in

February 1993 a jury found her guilty of the crime. The court sentenced Sonia to 99 years in prison. Sonia appealed her conviction and sentence to the Court of Appeals of Texas and the court reversed the prison sentence but affirmed the remainder of the judgment and remanded the case to the trial court for new sentencing proceedings. Authorities released Sonia on parole in 1998 after serving six years in prison.

There was significant controversy surrounding the forensic evidence used to convict Sonia. An autopsy of William's body showed that he had actually died from a heart attack and that he was dead before he inhaled any toxic fumes from the fire. Despite serious chain of custody issues surrounding William's clothing, the chief toxicologist for the Bexas County Crime Lab testified that there was gasoline on William's clothes. Based on this evidence alone, the county prosecutor surmised that Sonia had doused her uncle with gasoline and then set him on fire. Sonia's court appointed defense lawyer failed to challenge the toxicologist's findings with contradictory expert testimony. A court later convicted Sonia's defense attorney of complicity in a multi-ton marijuana smuggling operation. A Houston crime lab technician found no evidence of gasoline on Richardson's clothing. Other clothing remnants of Richardson's sent to a Houston crime lab found no evidence of gasoline. Arson expert Gerald Hurst reviewed the evidence against Sonia and wrote in a report: "The analysis has been reviewed by numerous independent experts in arson debris analysis who concur that the State's purported analyst erred in finding gasoline." Sonia continues to fight her conviction and sentence.

In 2004, the West Virginia State Police began an investigation into a major drug ring operation in Mingo County. As part of that investigation, Carla Collins became a federal informant about cocaine being sold out of a pizza parlor owned by George M. "Porgie" Lecco. In April 2005, Lecco arranged for Valerie Suzette Friend and Patricia Burton to murder Collins to protect his drug operations. Police later found her body in a makeshift grave near an abandoned burned-out trailer. The two murderers had beaten and shot Collins with a .38 caliber revolver who apparently begged for her life, asked to pray, and suggested to the killers that her children needed their mother. In May 2007, a jury recommended the death penalty for Valerie. Prior to sentencing, however, U.S. District Judge John T. Copenhaver, Jr., overturned the conviction because a juror, William Griffith, did not reveal that he was under federal investigation for possessing child pornography by the same U.S. Attorney's Office that was prosecuting Valerie. To avoid the death penalty, Valerie pleaded guilty to the killing of Collins in exchange for a life prison term and to testify against Lecco. Valerie is currently serving her prison term at the United States Penitentiary at Hazelton in Preston County, West Virginia, with an anticipated release date of January 2036. Patricia Burton received a 30-year sentence.

Concluding Remarks

Appellate review of capital cases is not a constitutional privilege in the United States. Even so, the historical records shows that when an appeal is afforded capital defendants, the appeals process must conform to capital procedural rules ensuring due process and equal protection rights. Some of the earliest appeals in female death cases involved slaves. It is more probable that the appeal went to slave owners to ensure the protection of their property interests in slaves and not to individual slaves. The inventory of confirmed judicial reversals of female death sentences provided in this chapter is by no means exhaustive, but it does allow for some insight into the reasons appeals courts have historically reversed women's death sentences. Procedural error by lower court judges accounts for about one-third of women's cases judicial reversal of death sentences, followed closely by death penalty nullification, prosecutorial misconduct and evidentiary problems. Ineffective assistance of counsel, improper jury instructions, jury selection process, juror misconduct, disproportionality of death sentences, and lack of evidence to support the verdict are also rationales for appeals courts to upset trial court death sentences to women. Many of the women whose death sentences appeals courts have reversed are women who suffered extreme violence as children and later as adults. Others are women with low intelligence and borderline mental retardation. Several women are mentally ill and have extreme personality disorders. Appeals courts treat these defects as mitigating factors that tend to qualify women for less than death as punishment for their crimes.

> *"Executive clemency has proved to be the 'fail safe' in our criminal justice system.... It is an unalterable fact that our judicial system, like the human beings who administer it, is fallible."*[1]

8

Executive Clemency of Condemned Women

Adopted from English common law and embraced by the British mainland colonies, clemency is an integral part of American criminal justice. Clemency is a broad government power that includes *pardons* (invalidating the guilt and punishment of a defendant), *reprieves* (temporarily postponing a defendant's punishment), and *commutations* (reducing the severity of a defendant's original sentence). Executive clemency is "standardless in procedure, discretionary in exercise, and unreviewable in result."[2] The design of executive clemency is threefold:

> The first is unrestrained mercy. Clemency is a free gift of the executive, needing no justification or pretense of fairness. The second is a quasi-judicial rationale suggesting that governors and clemency officials may consider factors that were not presented or considered by trial judges, juries, or appellate courts. The third rationale is a retributive notion of clemency, which is intended to ensure that only the most deserving among the convicted murderers are executed.[3]

Clemency had no restrictions in the early colonial period: "It was purely within the discretion of colonial and state governors, who could grant or deny a pardon for any reason or no reason."[4] Today, states have moderated the structure of executive clemency-granting authority than in earlier periods, but most death penalty jurisdictions still confer broad clemency powers to state governors.[5] Despite structural variations in clemency-granting powers across jurisdictions, the critical aim of clemency is to *promote justice*. Legal scholars explain that clemency furthers justice "where the reliability of the conviction is in question ... where the reliability of the sentence is in question, and ... where neither the reliability of the conviction nor the sentence is implicated."[6] Reasons for granting clemency in capital convictions may include a defendant's proven or likely innocence, bias and unfairness in trial or post-trial proceedings, a changed political, moral or legal climate, reward for exemplary character, or excessive sentencing. In this regard, courts have touted clemency as a "safety value" or "fail-safe" in capital cases accented by injustices. Incredibly, though the U.S. Supreme Court declared in *Herrera v. Collins* that habeas corpus relief is not available to capital defendants claiming actual innocence based upon newly discovered evidence, the Court recognized alternatively, that clemency "is the historic remedy for preventing miscarriages of justice where judicial process has been exhausted." As such, clemency provides "the fail safe in our criminal justice system" whereby capital defendants providing actual evidence of innocence can avoid an impending execution. For Leon Herrera, however, the purported "fail safe" of executive clemency proved ineffective. Despite evidence that Herrera's deceased brother killed two police officers, that the brother confessed to the murders to others including a former state judge, and that an eyewitness to the killings denied Herrera's presence at the shootings, Texas executed Herrera in May 1993 after Governor Ann Richards refused to grant Herrera's request for executive clemency. Here, neither the Court nor gubernatorial clemency remedied a terrible injustice. To one legal scholar, "clemency as a 'fail safe' in the killing state may do more to help legitimate judicial dismantling of various procedural protections than to point toward an efficacious device for correcting law's failures in the killing state."[7]

An added dimension to clemency is the petitions submitted to state governors on behalf of capital defendants. To Sarat, clemency petitions memorialize the injustices burdening the American capital justice system. Clemency petitions as narratives "provide an archive of stories of law's failures."[8] In his analysis of clemency petitions filed with Texas and Virginia governors from 1990 to 2002, Sarat identified claims recognized by lawyers that clemency should correct if it is a *failsafe* to injustices:

> factual error/innocence; police misconduct; prosecutorial misconduct; false/ unreliable witness testimony; incompetent/unethical expert witnesses; ineffective assistance of counsel; jury bias; errors or omissions in the mitigation phase of the original trial; unavailability of life without parole as an option at the time of sentencing; equity; error/procedural bar in the appellate or post-conviction process; remorse/religious conversions/post-sentencing rehabilitation/mercy.[9]

Yet, state executives regularly disregard the types of claims identified by Sarat and deny clemency to condemned prisoners. During his term as the governor of Texas, for instance, George W. Bush overlooked the claims in clemency petitions filed by 150 condemned men and two women who were eventually executed. Besides Bush's personal apathy to the circumstances and the law's failures surrounding cases of death row prisoners, the neglect of Bush's legal counselor Alberto R. Gonzales played a significant role in Bush's dismal record on clemency. Social commentator Allan Berlow explains that Gonzales's case summaries to Bush consisted mainly of a brief description of the facts of the crime, some personal background on the defendant, and a condensed legal history. Gonzales's abstracts had a strong prosecutorial bias and assumed that if appeals courts had rejected a defendant's claims there is no reason for Bush to intervene. As such, the abstracts often failed to apprise Bush of "crucial issues in the cases at hand: ineffective counsel, conflict of interest, mitigating evidence, even actual evidence of innocence." Yet, as Berlow points out, "this assumption ignores one of the most basic reasons for clemency: the fact that the justice system makes mistakes."[10]

In some cases, clemency has proven politically catastrophic for state governors. Arkansas Governor Mike Huckabee, for instance, pardoned a dozen murderers and one of the men he pardoned, Wayne Dumond, raped and killed two more women after his release and pardon. What's more, some state governors are calling for legislation to hasten executions. In California, three former state governors, George Deukmejian, Peter Wilson, and Gray Davis, none of whom granted clemency to death row prisoners while governor, recently took a controversial step and publicly announced their support of a proposed ballot measure to limit the state's lengthy death penalty process to five years. In Louisiana, Representative Kenny Havard wants to accelerate the process in that state as well. In Florida, the state legislature has put forward legislation requiring the state's governor to sign a death warrant within 30 days after a state Supreme Court review and the execution to take place within six months of the court's review. The Kansas legislature is also attempting to limit the death penalty appeal process.

According to a report recently released by the American Bar Association assessing the fairness and accuracy of death penalty imposition in 12 jurisdictions that account for some 65 percent of all executions in the United States since 1976, researchers identified "clemency" as one of a dozen procedural flaws that remain prevalent in the jurisdictions. These procedural deficiencies "create an unacceptably high risk of fundamental injustice and inadequate safeguards to minimize the potential that innocent persons will be executed."[11] The report found that state clemency processes do not serve as a final safeguard to prevent wrongful executions. Accordingly, there are four reasons for this: most states fail to require any specific type or breadth of review in considering clemency petitions; clemency decision-makers have denied clemency stating that all relevant issues have been vetted by the courts; states do not provide a right to counsel in clemency proceedings; and few states require the clemency decision-maker to meet with the inmate or the inmate's counsel.[12]

Clemency and Gender

Empirical studies on clemency and gender consistently show that state clemency processes favor women more than men. Early studies conducted mostly in the 1960s reveal that women's chances of clemency were high in the pre–*Furman* period. In an analysis of much of this early research comparing executed to commuted offenders between 1903 and 1972, researchers reveal that not only was it unusual for courts to sentence female capital offenders to death, but most women had their death sentences commuted to life in prison. Recent work on clemency and gender shows that in the post–*Furman* period death row women continue to fare better in garnering clemency from state executives than do men. More current studies show that death row women are *11 times* more likely to receive clemency than are men. Kramer, for instance, found that a gender effect is consistent with other studies on clemency and explains that a "greater propensity to commute women's sentences reflects, at least in part, differences in the sort of crimes that women commit compared to men, or mitigating factors that women are more likely to possess (such as a history of being abused by the person they killed)."[13] One scholar explains that there are likely as many male murderers as female murderers who have suffered abuse, but the capital system affords them less opportunity to tell their stories as women.[14] Other researchers suggest that there is no strong evidence that the merit of women's cases predicts higher clemency rates. In this regard, Argys and Mocan found that of the eight women accounted for in their study where state governors commuted women's death sentences, only two involved issues of "battered wife syndrome." Whether state governors commute the sentences of death row inmates depends less on the characteristics of the case, such as the presence of mitigation factors, and more on the political affiliation of the governor, and whether the governor is a lame duck.[15] Addressing the merits of empirical studies on women and clemency, Heise explains the findings this way:

> Ordinarily, one should be cautious in drawing firm conclusions from empirical results. Nonetheless, in light of the strong and robust findings from this study, their consistency with other empirical findings, and the overwhelming qualitative and anecdotal evidence illustrating how women's experience with clemency and death penalty processes differs from men's experience, it may be time to render at least a tentative verdict. Whether because of social norms or stereotypes, the unusualness of women sentenced to death, the different ways in which men and women murder, or a consistent run to extraordinary good luck and defies standard mathematical probabilities, the weight of existing evidence demonstrates that male and female death row inmates receive different treatment when it comes to clemency grants.[16]

Women on Death Row Granted Clemency

There is no national archive of clemency appeals, and without a definitive registry historical inquiry on the context and frequency of female clemency remains blurred. The registry put forth in this chapter provides nothing more than a portal to the past to gain some rudimentary sense of the history of female clemency. Certainly, there are far more condemned women granted clemency than those reported in the registry and continued research should reveal more cases. Table 8-1 includes the names of confirmed female offenders granted executive clemency in capital cases historically, the capital offenses for which jurisdictions sentenced women to death, the race of condemned women, the state of sentencing, the race of the victim(s) wronged by condemned female offenders, the year of clemency, the names of state governors that granted clemency and the governors' reasoning for granting women clemency.

Of the 127 women granted clemency by state governors historically, slightly more than 30 percent of committed predatory murders, just over 19 percent committed spousal murder, nearly 15 percent committed child murders or infanticide, and almost 12 percent committed property crimes (robbery, burglary, horse theft, conspiracy to revolt, arson, counterfeiting, receiving stolen goods). Just over 18 percent committed the colonial offense of witchcraft, and just fewer than 5 percent engaged in conspiracy to revolt during colonial slavery and other unidentified crimes. Regarding spousal murders, it is interesting that state governors were historically less likely to commute the death sentences of women convicted of killing their husbands than husbands convicted of murdering their wives. There is a clear racial disparity in executive clemency for women who murdered their husbands; of the 25 women granted clemency in spousal murder cases, nearly 70 percent were white women, nearly 22 percent were black women, and almost 9 percent were Mexican women. The racial distribution was far more equitable for women granted clemency for predatory murders and infanticide/child murders. Overall, however, white women are about 67 percent of all women granted executive clemency historically, black or mulatto women are about 25 percent, Latinas are slightly more than 2 percent, and American Indian woman are about 1 percent. The race of four women is unknown or otherwise unavailable and represents about 3 percent of women granted executive clemency. Surely, the race of women offenders and the race of their victims influenced state governors' decisions to grant clemency to death row women. State governors mostly commuted the death sentences of white women who victimized white males or females; they were far less likely to commute the death sentences of black women who murdered black males or females.

Interestingly, a tradition prevalent in the 19th century expressed the notion "that an outraged husband, father, or brother could justifiably kill the alleged libertine who had been sexually intimate with the defendant's wife, daughter, or sister."[17] Some states went so far as to institutionalize the practice in statutes protecting husbands who murdered their wives' paramours. The convention had a sexist and racist double standard, however, the rule was not applicable to wives who killed their husband's lovers, and there is evidence that capital juries willingly convicted "avengers who were from lower socio-economic strata, especially those who were black."[18]

State governors were slightly less likely to commute the death sentences of women in the 19th century than state and colonial governors were in the 18th century. Governors granted clemency to 40 women in the 18th century, 39 women in the 19th century, and 36 women in the 20th century. Governors granted clemency to 14 women in the 21st century, yet nearly half of these clemency decisions involved women convicted of witchcraft in colonial Massachusetts and Virginia. These figures tend to support claims that state executives are declining their use of clemency power particularly over the past several decades.

Regionally, state governors were more forthcoming in granting executive clemency to women in Mid-Atlantic States, East North Central states, and South Atlantic states. In contrast, governors in West North Central states, East South Central states, and West South Central states commuted the death sentences of far fewer women. While governors in Massachusetts granted executive clemency mostly to women convicted of witchcraft in the early colonial period, only Governor Eugene Foss commuted the death sentence of a woman convicted of a non-witchcraft crime. Arizona is the only mountain state where a governor granted clemency to a

Table 8-1: State Executive Clemency Granted to Death Row Women in the Unites States, 1711–2010

Name of Prisoner	Offense of Defendant	Race of Prisoner	State of Sentencing	Year of Commutation	Race/Sex of Victim(s)	State/Colonial Governor or U.S. President	Reason for Clemency
Mary Perkins Bradbury	Witchcraft	White	Massachusetts	1711	None	Joseph Dudley	Wrongful conviction
Martha Carrier (executed)	Witchcraft	White	Massachusetts	1711	None	Joseph Dudley	Wrongful conviction
Martha Corey (executed)	Witchcraft	White	Massachusetts	1711	None	Joseph Dudley	Wrongful conviction
Rebecca Eames	Witchcraft	White	Massachusetts	1711	None	Joseph Dudley	Wrongful conviction
Mary Easty (executed)	Witchcraft	White	Massachusetts	1711	None	Joseph Dudley	Wrongful conviction
Abigail Faulkner (executed)	Witchcraft	White	Massachusetts	1711	None	Joseph Dudley	Wrongful conviction
Anne Foster	Witchcraft	White	Massachusetts	1711	None	Joseph Dudley	Wrongful conviction
Sarah Good (executed)	Witchcraft	White	Massachusetts	1711	None	Joseph Dudley	Wrongful conviction
Dorcas Hoar	Witchcraft	White	Massachusetts	1711	None	Joseph Dudley	Wrongful conviction
Elizabeth Howe (executed)	Witchcraft	White	Massachusetts	1711	None	Joseph Dudley	Wrongful conviction
Mary Lacey	Witchcraft	White	Massachusetts	1711	None	Joseph Dudley	Wrongful conviction
Rebeccah Nurse (executed)	Witchcraft	White	Massachusetts	1711	None	Joseph Dudley	Wrongful conviction
Mary Post	Witchcraft	White	Massachusetts	1711	None	Joseph Dudley	Wrongful conviction
Elizabeth Proctor (executed)	Witchcraft	White	Massachusetts	1711	None	Joseph Dudley	Wrongful conviction
Sarah Wardell	Witchcraft	White	Massachusetts	1711	None	Joseph Dudley	Wrongful conviction
Sarah Wilde (executed)	Witchcraft	White	Massachusetts	1711	None	Joseph Dudley	Wrongful conviction
Unnamed slave woman	Conspiracy to revolt	Black	New York	1712	White residents	Robert Hunter	Prison sufficient punishment/health
Martha Underdown	Infanticide	White	Pennsylvania	1718	White infant	William Keith	"A fit object for mercy"
Anne Huson	Robbery	White	Pennsylvania	1720	Unknown	William Keith	"A weak ignorant woman"
Mary Woolvin	Burglary	White	Pennsylvania	1722	Unknown	William Keith	Unknown
Martha Hunt	Counterfeiting	White	Pennsylvania	1724	Unknown	William Keith	Unknown
Ann Mitchell	Burglary	White	Pennsylvania	1724	Unknown	William Keith	Pregnancy of offender
Margaret Shitts	Infanticide	White	Pennsylvania	1732	White infant	Patrick Gordon	Speculation of defendant's guilt
Susanna Holt	Infanticide	White	Maryland	1734	White infant	Charles Calvert	"Object of mercy"
Martha Cash	Burglary	White	Pennsylvania	1739	Unknown	William Keith	Remorse of offender
Sarah Matts	Robbery	White	Virginia	1739	Unknown	William Gooch	Unknown
Margaret Ingram	Burglary	White	Pennsylvania	1739	White resident	William Keith	Age of offender
Ann Bullingnee	Burglary	White	Maryland	1740	Unknown	Samuel Ogle	"Object of mercy"
Mary Spearman	Burglary	White	Maryland	1740	Unknown	Samuel Ogle	Not a notorious offender
Sarah Houghson	Conspiracy to revolt	White	New York	1741	White residents	George Clarke	Mental health of defendant
Slave Jenny (McNemara)	Unknown	Black	Maryland	1748	Unknown	George Clarke	Unknown
Elizabeth Collett	Horse Theft	White	Maryland	1749	Unknown	George Clarke	No reason given
Sarah Bevers (Beavers)	Infanticide	White	Maryland	1751	White infant	George Clarke	Unknown
Jane Parker	Theft	White	Maryland	1751	White male	George Clarke	Pregnant
Catherine Reynolds	Infanticide	White	Pennsylvania	1753	White infant	James Hamilton	"A fit object of mercy"
Margaretta Catherine Kirchin	Infanticide	White	Pennsylvania	1759	White infant	Judicial Pardon	Speculation of defendant's guilt
Slave Bet Pone	Poisoning	Black	Maryland	1761	White male	Horatio Sharpe	Justices recommend mercy
Sarah Reardon	Infanticide	White	Maryland	1761	White infant	Horatio Sharpe	Evidence uncertain
Slave Abigail	Attempted Poison	Black	Maryland	1761	White female	Horatio Sharpe	Pregnant
Slave Hannah	Burglary	Black	Maryland	1763	White male/female	Horatio Sharpe	Unknown

Name of Prisoner	Offense of Defendant	Race of Prisoner	State of Sentencing	Year of Commutation	Race/Sex of Victim(s)	State/Colonial Governor or U.S. President	Reason for Clemency
Slave Sue	Murder	Black	Maryland	1766	White male	Horatio Sharpe	Evidence vague and uncertain
Rachel Francisco	Infanticide	Mulatto	Pennsylvania	1767	Mulatto infant male	John Penn	"Object of mercy"
Elizabeth Horner	Horse Theft	White	Maryland	1769	White male	Robert Eden	Speculation of defendant's guilt
Jane Turner	Burglary	White	Maryland	1769	White male	Robert Eden	"Pregnant, a poor silly woman"
Mary Brian	Burglary	White	Pennsylvania	1770	White female	John Penn	Unknown
Slave Kate	Burglary	Black	Maryland	1771	White female	Robert Eden	Unknown
Elizabeth Grant	Burglary	White	Pennsylvania	1771	White male	John Penn	"Object of mercy"
Slave Hannah	Arson	Black	Maryland	1772	White male	Robert Eden	"Youth, first offense"
Mary Dickson	Murder	White	Pennsylvania	1772	White male	Richard Penn	Lack of intent to commit murder
Slave Hagar	Attempted Murder	Black	Maryland	1773	White male	Robert Eden	Unknown
Slave Judith	Arson	Black	Maryland	1774	White male	Robert Eden	Unknown
Rebecca McDonald	Murder	White	Maryland	1774	White female	Robert Eden	"Object of mercy"
Margaret Matthews	Arson	White	Pennsylvania	1780	White planter	John Dickinson	Public outcry for clemency
Mary Hall	Robbery	White	Pennsylvania	1782	Unknown	William Moore	Unknown
Mary Grover	Arson	White	Pennsylvania	1784	Unknown	John Dickinson	Unknown
Alice Clifton (slave)	Infanticide	Black	Pennsylvania	1787	Black female infant	Benjamin Franklin	Public outcry for clemency
Sarah Williams	Infanticide	White	Pennsylvania	1787	White infant	Peter Muhlenberg	"Object if mercy"
Sarah Craig (slave)	Rec'd stolen goods	Black	Pennsylvania	1790	White male	George Ross	Well behaved before conviction
Angelica Barnett	Murder	Black	Virginia	1793	White infant	Henry Lee	Public outcry for clemency
Elizabeth Rimby	Infanticide	White	Pennsylvania	1806	Black infant	Thomas McKean	Unknown
Slave woman Letitia ("Letty")	Infanticide	Black	Virginia	1822	Unknown	James Pleasant	Sale and banishment from County
Mary Martin	Murder	White	Pennsylvania	1827	Unknown	John Andrew Shultz	Unknown
Hannah Lewis	Murder	White	Pennsylvania	1828	Multiple victims	John Andrew Shultz	Unknown
Pamelia Dickenson Mann	Forgery	White	Texas	1840	White male	Mirabeau B. Lamar	Against hanging a widowed mother
Rebecca Hawkins	Spousal Murder	White	Missouri	1841	White male	Thomas Reynolds	Public outcry for clemency
Slave Nelly	Infanticide	Black	Missouri	1846	Black infant	John C. Edwards	Public outcry for clemency
Henrietta Robinson	Murder	White	New York	1855	White male & female	Myron H. Clark	Mental health of defendant
Elizabeth Harker	Spousal Murder	White	Pennsylvania	1855	White male & female	William Bigler	Sex and extreme age of the defendant
Sarah Haycraft	Murder	White	Missouri	1858	White male	Robert M. Seward	Influence of wealthy sister
Polly Frisch (Hoag)	Child Murder	White	New York	1859	White female	Edwin D. Morgan	Mental health of defendant
Agnes Agar	Unknown	Unknown	New York	1863	Unknown	Horasio Seymour	Mental health of defendant
Jane Brooks	Unknown	Unknown	New York	1863	Unknown	Horasio Seymour	Mental health of defendant
Catherine McCoy	Child Murder	Black	Missouri	1864	White female	Williard P. Hall	Mental health of defendant
Delores Moore	Murder	Latina	Arizona	1865	Unknown	Lewis Sumpter Owings	
Catherine Johnson	Murder	White	New York	1868	White female	Rueben Fenton	Unknown
Harriet Grier (Crittenden)	Murder	Black	Georgia	1869	White female	Rufus B. Bullock	Mental health of defendant
Hester Vaughn	Infanticide	White	Pennsylvania	1869	White infant	John W. Geary	Public outcry for clemency
Wilhemine Weick	Unknown	Unknown	New York	1869	Unknown	Samuel J. Tilden	Mental health of defendant

Name of Prisoner	Offense of Defendant	Race of Prisoner	State of Sentencing	Year of Commutation	Race/Sex of Victim(s)	State/Colonial Governor or U.S. President	Reason for Clemency
Elizabeth Garrabrant	Predatory Murder	White	New Jersey	1872	White male	Court of Pardons	Public outcry for clemency
Eveline Johnson	Unknown	Unknown	New York	1874	Unknown	John Adams Dix	Mental health of defendant
Anna Hallenschied	Predatory Murder	White	Missouri	1875	White male	Charles H. Hardin	Doubt of defendant's guilt
Johanna Turbin	Spousal Murder	Black	D.C.	1876	Black male	Pres. Ulysses S. Grant	Chivalry of sentencing judge
Lodicia Fredenburg	Predatory Murder	White	New York	1876	White male	Samuel J. Tilden	Lack of sufficient evidence
Catherine "Kate" Southern	Predatory Murder	White	Georgia	1878	White female	Alfred H. Colquitt	Public outcry over hanging a woman
Jennie R. Smith	Spousal Murder	White	New Jersey	1879	White male	George B. McClellan	Public outcry for clemency
Mary Booth	Predatory Murder	Black	Virginia	1882	White female	William E. Cameron	Defendant's young age (14 years old)
Fannie Echols	Predatory Murder	Black	Arkansas	1884	White male	President Chester Arthur	Life in prison sufficient punishment
Angenette B. Haight	Spousal Murder	White	New York	1884	White male	Grover Cleveland	Physical health of defendant
Annie E. Cutler	Predatory Murder	Black	Pennsylvania	1885	Black male	Robert E. Pattison	Public outcry for clemency
Chiara Cignarale	Spousal Murder	White	New York	1886	White male	David B. Hill	Victim of domestic violence
Axey Cherry	Predatory Murder	Black	South Carolina	1887	White infant	John Peter Richardson	Age and mental capacity of defendant
Margaret Given	Child Murder	Black	Mississippi	1888	Black infant	Robert Lowry	Public outcry for clemency
Milly Poteat	Infanticide	Black	North Carolina	1888	White property	Alfred M. Scales	Public outcry for clemency
Sarah M. Victor	Arson	White	Ohio	1888	White female	Joseph B. Foraker	Speculation of defendant's guilt
Elsie James	Predatory Murder	Chickasaw	Arkansas	1889	White male	Pres. Benjamin Harrison	Life in prison sufficient punishment
Emily Boon	Predatory Murder	White	Georgia	1890	White female	John B. Gordon	Public outcry over hanging a woman
Elizabeth "Lizzie" Carter	Predatory Murder	Black	Ohio	1890	Black male	James Edwin Campbell	Unknown
Elizabeth "Lizzy" Halliday	Spousal Murder	White	New York	1894	White male & others	Roswell P. Flowers	Mental health of defendant
Mrs. T. Elizabeth Nobles	Predatory Murder	White	Georgia	1895	White male	George Mathews	Unknown
Mary Garrett	Predatory Murder	White	Ohio	1899	2 White females	Asa S. Bushnell	Public outcry for clemency
Amanda Umble	Predatory Murder	Mulatto	Missouri	1893	Black female	William J. Stone	Public outcry for clemency
Sadie Hayes (Hill)	Predatory Murder	Mulatto	Missouri	1898	White male	Lawrence V. Stephens	Unknown
Pearl Waters	Predatory Murder	Black	Missouri	1899	Black female	Lawrence V. Stephens	Unknown
Maggie Meyers	Spousal Murder	Black	Missouri	1906	White female	Martin Sennett Conner	Public outcry for clemency
Valentina Madrid	Spousal Murder	Mexican	New Mexico	1907	Mexican male	James W. Raynolds	Testimony required from defendant
Alma Lyons	Acc to Murder	Black	New Mexico	1907	Mexican male	James W. Raynolds	Testimony required from defendant
Freida Hartmann Trost	Spousal Murder	White	Pennsylvania	1913	White male	John Tener	Unknown
Lena Cusumano	Spousal Murder	White	Massachusetts	1912	White male	Eugene Foss	Doubts of first-degree murder
Maddalena Ciccone	Spousal Murder	White	New Jersey	1913	White male	James F. Fielder	Public outcry for clemency
Kate Edwards	Spousal Murder	White	Pennsylvania	1914	White male	William C. Sproul	Sex and poverty of the defendant
Madeline Ferola	Spousal Murder	White	New York	1915	White male	Charles S. Whitman	Public outcry for clemency
Pearl Jackson	Predatory Murder	Black	Alabama	1925	White male	William W. Brandon	Disproportionate death sentence
Annie Mae "Billy" Jackson	Spousal Murder	White	Florida	1933	White male	John W. Martin	Victim of domestic violence
Eula Mae (Elrod) Thompson	Predatory Murder	Black	Georgia	1928	White male	Lamartine G. Hardman	No evidence to support verdict
Bertha Hall	Spousal Murder	White	Florida	1929	White male	John W. Martin	Victim of domestic violence
Harriet "Hattie" Evans	Predatory Murder	White	New Jersey	1931	2 White males	Morgan F. Larson	Defendant not the actual killer
Beatrice Ferguson Snipes	Predatory Murder	White	South Carolina	1933	White male	Ibra C. Blackwood	Public outcry for clemency

8. Executive Clemency of Condemned Women

Name of Prisoner	Offense of Defendant	Race of Prisoner	State of Sentencing	Year of Commutation	Race/Sex of Victim(s)	State/Colonial Governor or U.S. President	Reason for Clemency
Gertrude Puhae	Spousal Murder	White	Illinois	1934	White male	Henry Horner	Unknown
Nellie May Madison	Spousal Murder	White	California	1935	White male	Frank Finley Merriam	Victim of domestic violence
Sarah Ruth Dean	Predatory Murder	White	Mississippi	1935	White male	Joseph W. Folk	Chivalry of governor
Marguerite Fox Dolbow	Spousal Murder	White	New Jersey	1936	White male	Harold G. Hoffman	Flaw in death penalty law
Minnie Mitchell	Predatory Murder	Black	Illinois	1937	Black male	Henry Horner	Unknown
Mildred Mary Bolton	Spousal Murder	White	Illinois	1937	White male	Henry Horner	Unknown
Josephine Romulado	Spousal Murder	White	Pennsylvania	1941	White male	Gifford Pinchot	Life term "adequate justice"
Lena Baker	Predatory Murder	Black	Georgia	1944	White male	Board of Pardons	Unfair adjudication
Annie Mae Allison	Predatory Murder	Black	North Carolina	1945	Black male	J. Melville Broughton	Defendant's young age (14 years old)
Emma Oliver	Spousal Murder	Black	Texas	1951	Black male	Allan Shivers	Lack of a fair trial and mental illness
Opal Collins	Spousal Murder	White	Indiana	1956	White male	George N. Craig	Chivalry of governor
Ann Pudeator (executed)	Witchcraft	White	Massachusetts	1957	None	State Legislature	Wrongful conviction
Anjette Donovan Lyles	Child Murder	White	Georgia	1959	White female & others	Ernest Vandiver	Mental health of defendant
Edythe M. Klumpp	Predatory Murder	White	Ohio	1961	White female	Michael V. DiSalle	Doubt of defendant's guilt
Margaret "Maggie" Morgan	Predatory Murder	Black	Texas	1961	White female	Price Daniels	Disproportionate death sentence
Jeannace June Freeman	Child Murder	White	Oregon	1964	White male & female	Mark Hatfield	Death penalty abolished in state
Winnie Ruth Judd	Predatory Murder	White	Arizona	1971	2 White females	Jack Williams	Mental health of defendant
Catherine "Kitty" Dodds	Spousal Murder	White	Louisiana	1977	White male	Edwin W. Edwards	Disproportionate death sentence
Doris Ann Foster	Predatory Murder	Indian	Maryland	1987	Black female	Harry Hughes	Substantial mitigating factors
Debra Denise Brown	Predatory Murder	Black	Ohio	1991	Black female & others	Richard F. Celeste	Mental health of defendant
Rosalie Grant	Child Murder	Black	Ohio	1991	2 Black males	Richard F. Celeste	Doubt of defendant's guilt
Elizabeth Green	Predatory Murder	Black	Ohio	1991	Black female	Richard F. Celeste	Mental health of defendant
Beatrice Lampkin	Spousal Murder	Black	Ohio	1991	White male	Richard F. Celeste	Victim of domestic violence
Guinevere Falakassa Garcia	Spousal Murder	Mexican	Illinois	1996	Mexican male	Jim Edgar	Disproportionate death sentence
Judith Ann Neelley	Predatory Murder	White	Alabama	1999	2 White females	Forrest "Fob" James	No reason publicly given
Bridget Bishop (executed)	Witchcraft	White	Massachusetts	2001	None	Interim Gov. Jane Swift	Wrongful conviction
Alice Parker (executed)	Witchcraft	White	Massachusetts	2001	None	Interim Gov. Jane Swift	Wrongful conviction
Margaret Scott (executed)	Witchcraft	White	Massachusetts	2001	None	Interim Gov. Jane Swift	Wrongful conviction
Wilmot Redd (executed)	Witchcraft	White	Massachusetts	2001	None	Interim Gov. Jane Swift	Wrongful conviction
Susannah Martin (executed)	Witchcraft	White	Massachusetts	2001	None	Interim Gov. Jane Swift	Wrongful conviction
Dorothy Williams	Predatory Murder	Black	Illinois	2003	Black female	George Ryan	Unfair application of death penalty
Latasha Pulliam	Child Murder	Black	Illinois	2003	Black female	George Ryan	Unfair application of death penalty
Jacqueline Annette Williams	Predatory Murder	Black	Illinois	2003	2 Black females/1 male	George Ryan	Unfair application of death penalty
Bernina Mata	Predatory Murder	Mexican	Illinois	2003	White male	George Ryan	Unfair application of death penalty
Grace White Sherwood	Witchcraft	White	Virginia	2006	None	Tim Kaine	Unjust conviction
Gaile Kirksey Owens	Spousal Murder	White	Tennessee	2010	White male	Phil Bredesen	Disproportionate death sentence

condemned woman and only Oregon and California governors granted clemency to a female capital offender in any Pacific state, respectively.

A few studies have isolated the major themes of governors' declarations justifying commuting death sentences. In an early study, Johnson listed several factors given by state governors in North Carolina in commuting the death sentences of more than 200 murderers and rapists from 1909 to 1954; public officials and juries urged commutations, communities urged commutations, the age of offenders or their underprivileged status, dishonesty of the victim or their contribution to the crime, mental condition of the offender, or lack of proof to offenders' premeditation in committing the crime, and evidence that did not justify the death penalty or that the evidence was of a doubtful nature. Johnson also found that the proportion of governors' reasons for clemency changed over the five-decade period from "evidentiary problems" in a particular case to the "status of the offender."[19] There are several other reasons for state governors granting clemency over the past several years, but Adler and Lanier explain that the more common reasons for executive clemency decisions today involve "doubts about the offender's guilt, the offender's mental retardation or mental illness, and equitable considerations in light of less harsh sanctions imposed against other participants in the same crime."[20] Radelet and Zsembik identify six historical categories of humanitarian reasons for gubernatorial clemency, including unqualified mercy, lingering doubts of guilt, defendant's mental problems, proportionality, rehabilitation, and remorse.[21] In one study, the American Bar Association found that state governors have granted clemency to condemned inmates for humanitarian reasons—rather than legal technicality or judicial expedience—48 times since 1976. The leading reasons among these clemencies were possible innocence, disproportionate sentence, and opposition to the death penalty. Focusing on 19 clemencies granted to death row inmates between 1992 and 2002, the study revealed still more reasons why governors grant clemency: possible innocence, mental illness or juvenile status, unfair trials, disproportionate sentencing, rehabilitation, request from the Pope, and no reason.[22]

Table 8-2 shows the more common historically based reasons for state governors commuting the sentences of condemned women. Those reasons have included public outcry for clemency, characteristics of offenders (mercy, pregnancy, remorse, mental and physical health, sex, age and poverty), speculation of the guilt of offenders or of the evidence used to convict offenders, imprisonment sufficient punishment, chivalry of state governors against executing women, flaws in death penalty laws, wrongful or unjust convictions, unfair or disproportionate application of the death penalty, and victims of domestic violence. Governors have given other reasons (sale and banishment, testimony required from defendant), and in some cases no reason, for granting clemency to female capital offenders. In about 10 percent of women clemency cases, the historical record is unclear as to why a state governor granted clemency to a female capital offender. Overall, however, the data show that the most frequent reason given by state executives for granting female clemency has been the personal characteristics of offenders (23.8 percent), wrongful or unjust convictions (20.0 percent), and public outcry for clemency (15.3 percent). Other important reasons for governors granting clemency to condemned women include speculation of the guilt of the offender or the evidence used to establish guilt (10.7 percent), unfair or disproportionate application of the death sentence (6.9 percent), and that the offender was the victim of domestic violence (3.8 percent).

Clemency in the 18th Century

The historical record reveals that colonial and state governors commuted the death sentences of women in Pennsylvania, Maryland, Massachusetts, New York, North Carolina and

Virginia in the 18th century. Colonial women convicted and sentenced to prison terms or death for witchcraft were among the earliest female criminal defendants to receive executive pardons in the early 18th century. In May 1693, for instance, Massachusetts Governor Phips pardoned some 200 persons in prison for witchcraft, many of whom were women.[23] Pursuant to the *Petitions for Compensation and Decision Concerning Compensation, 1710–1711*, however, Massachusetts Governor Joseph Dudley pardoned 16 women convicted of witchcraft and sentenced to death or executed during the Salem Witch Trials.[24] These women were Mary Perkins Bradbury (jailed), Martha Allen Carrier (executed), Martha Rich Corey (executed), Rebecca Blake Eames (jailed), Mary Towne Easty (executed), Abigail Faulkner (executed), Anne Alcock Foster (jailed), Sarah Solart Poole Good (executed), Dorcas Hoar (jailed), Elizabeth Jackson Howe (executed), Mary Lacey (jailed), Rebeccah Towne Nurse (executed), Mary Post (jailed), Elizabeth Bassett Proctor (executed), Sarah Wardell (jailed), and Sarah Averill Wilde (executed). Some 264 years later, the Massachusetts legislature finally approved a resolution in 1957 exonerating Ann Greenslit Pudeator executed in the commonwealth for witchcraft, and in November 2001 state governor Jane Swift signed legislation exonerating Bridget Playfer Bishop, Alice Parker, Margaret Scott, Wilmot Redd and Susannah North Martin. In July 2006, 300 years after her trial, dunking, and eight-year imprisonment, Virginia Governor Tim Kaine pardoned Grace White Sherwood for her wrongful conviction for witchcraft in 1706.

Women were among New York's condemned prisoner population pardoned by colonial governors in the 18th century and among the one-quarter to one-third of the condemned prisoners' sentences officials commuted in the same

Table 8-2: Reasons for Governors Granting Clemency by Criminal Offense

Reasons for Governors Granting Clemency	Predatory Murder N=39 (30.7%)		Spousal Murder N=25 (19.6%)		Infanticide/Child Murder N=19 (14.9%)		Property Crimes N=15 (11.8%)		Witchcraft N=23 (18.1%)		Other Crimes N=6 (4.7%)		Totals N=127 (100.0%)	
	N	%	N	%	N	%	N	%	N	%	N	%	N	%
Public Outcry for Clemency	6	15.3	5	20	4	21	2	14.3	0	0	0	0	17	13.3
Characteristic of the Offender	8	20.5	4	16	8	42.1	6	42.8	0	0	5	71.4	31	24.4
Speculation of Guilt/Evidence	8	20.5	2	8	3	15.7	1	7.1	0	0	0	0	14	11
Imprisonment Sufficient Punishment	2	5.1	1	4	0	0	0	0	0	0	1	14.3	4	3.1
Chivalry Against Executing Female	1	2.5	2	8	0	0	0	0	0	0	0	0	3	2.3
Flaw in Death Penalty Law	0	0	1	4	1	5.2	0	0	0	0	0	0	2	1.5
Wrongful or Unjust Conviction	3	7.6	0	0	0	0	0	0	23	100	0	0	26	20.4
Unfair/Disproportionate sentence	5	12.8	3	12	1	5.2	0	0	0	0	0	0	9	7
Victim of domestic violence	0	0	5	20	0	0	0	0	0	0	0	0	5	3.9
Unknown	5	12.8	1	4	1	5.2	5	35.7	0	0	1	14.3	13	10.2
Other	1	2.5	1	4	1	5.2	0	0	0	0	0	0	3	2.3

Predatory murder includes accessory to commit murder. Property crimes—robbery, burglary, counterfeiting, horse theft, arson, forgery and receiving stolen property. Other crimes—conspiracy to revolt and unknown crimes. Other reasons for granting clemency include "sale and banishment," testimony required from defendant, and no reason publicly given.

period in Virginia. Certainly at least some of the cases where authorities in North Carolina commuted death sentences imposed from 1663 to 1776 involved women. New York's colonial governor Robert Hunter pardoned many of the slaves convicted of conspiracy in the aftermath of the 1712 New York slave revolt; he believed it was the "the blind fury" of people rather than the evidence that condemned the slaves. One of the convicted slaves was a woman who officials had scheduled for execution. After the woman *pleaded her belly*, Hunter stayed the woman's death sentence and confined her to jail until after the child's birth when he then pardoned the woman to time served. Hunter found the woman "in a woeful condition ever since, and I think she suffered more than death by her long imprisonment."[25] New York colonial governor George Clarke granted Sarah Houghson clemency as a conspirator in the New York slave revolt of 1741. Clemency was forthcoming to Sarah in hopes that she would volunteer information about other conspirators. It is far more likely, however, that Sarah's clemency was a product of her mental retardation, a condition commonly used to excuse female criminality.

Pennsylvania governors pardoned 138 persons, or roughly one-third of condemned prisoners in the colonial period. Twenty-nine condemned women were among those pardoned. Negley Teeters provides an annotated list of pardons, reprieves, and commutations in Pennsylvania. There, colonial governors pardoned six women for burglary, eight for infanticide, three for predatory murder, five for spousal murder, two for arson, one for robbery and one for counterfeiting.[26] Several governors based women's pardons largely on the notion that they were *fit objects of mercy*. Beginning with the case of Martha Underdown in 1718, Pennsylvania governors and colonial officials pardoned several women for infanticide. In Martha's case, Governor William Keith reprieved her from execution for one year and then found her "a fit object for mercy." In May 1732, Pennsylvania Lieutenant Governor Patrick Gordon pardoned Margaret Shitts for concealing the birth and burial of her bastard child. Apparently, there was evidence that the infant may been born dead. Governor James Hamilton pardoned Catherine Reynolds in April 1753 for the murder of her bastard child because of "sundry favourable circumstances ... a fit object of mercy."[27] A Lancaster jury in Pennsylvania convicted 17-year-old Margaretta Catherine Kirchin of killing her illegitimate infant child in 1759, but Margaretta received a judicial pardon in May of that year when the evidence of her guilt became unclear. In April 1767, Rachel Francisco of New Castle, a free and poor mulatto woman, received a pardon for the murder of her bastard male child. The pregnancy apparently resulted from her involvement with one of her mistress's sons. The *Minutes of the Provincial Council of Pennsylvania* show that justices found her to "be an object truly worthy of compassion and mercy."[28] In November 1787, a Philadelphia County court convicted Alice Clifton, a young and uneducated slave woman belonging to John Bartholomew, of murdering her female infant in April 1787. At her trial for infanticide, Alice testified,

> The child had been born dead; that she had cut the child's throat to keep it from crying and revealing its existence to her master; that she had killed it by command of the child's father, who had promised to purchase her and make her a fine lady if she would do so; and that she had cut the throat of her stillborn child so that the father would keep his promise to her.[29]

The court sentenced Alice to death but colonial Governor Benjamin Franklin pardoned her "because influential white citizens in Philadelphia rallied to her cause."[30] The last confirmed pardon in Pennsylvania during the 18th century for infanticide took place in November 1787 when colonial officials pardoned Sarah Williams for the murder of her infant child.

Pennsylvania executives commuted the death sentence of only one woman for predatory murder in the 18th century. In that case, Mary Dickson of Lancaster, along with her husband William, murdered their neighbor Alan Regan after an argument over the Dickson's behavior toward Regan's wife. Colonial Governor Richard Penn pardoned Mary in July 1772. Pennsylvania colonial governors also pardoned several condemned women for property crimes. In November 1720, Martha Hunt and her husband Edward received death sentences in Philadelphia for making and passing counterfeit dollars. Reportedly, the death sentences were the first imposed by officials in the colony for counterfeiting. Officials hanged Edward in November 1720 but spared Martha. After spending several years imprisoned on a life sentence for another offense, Governor William Keith pardoned Martha in March 1724. In August 1722, William Keith pardoned Mary Woolvin and Anne Huson for burglary. The governor pardoned Mary Woolvin along with her accomplice William Hill. Governor Keith also pardoned Anne Huson because her crime "showed her to be a weak ignorant woman."[31] Anne had pleaded guilty but the evidence against her apparently would have been difficult to sustain a conviction. In 1724, John Mitchell filed a petition on behalf of his wife Anne Mitchell who was under a death sentence for burglary. In October of that year, the deputy governor granted Anne a pardon because she was pregnant. Anne and John were to leave the colony and never return. Deputy Governor Patrick Gordon pardoned Catherine Connor in 1736 for burglary, but a year later in July 1737 colonial officials hanged Catherine along with her accomplice Henry Wildeman in Philadelphia after another burglary conviction. Five years before Deputy Governor George Thomas pardoned Martha Cash in May 1739 for a capital conviction for burglary, Martha suffered 40 lashes for stealing six yards of kersey. Governor Thomas pardoned Martha and Margaret Ingram on "condition that they would transport themselves out of the Province and not return to it again." The justices believed the extreme conditions of their impoverishment drove the two to commit the crimes. Martha was "very penitent" after pleading guilty to the crime, Margaret was "very aged."[32]

Colonial governors granted women less than 10 percent of all pardons awarded between 1726 and 1775. Early proceedings of the Council of Maryland reveal that colonial governors granted clemency to 19 free white women, white convict servants, and slave women for crimes of infanticide, burglary and theft crimes, arson, poisoning and attempted poisoning, and murder and attempted murder.[33] The earliest of these executive clemency cases involved Susanne Holt, a free white woman of Charles County, pardoned by Governor Charles Calvert in December 1734 after she pleaded guilty to killing her newborn child in early September. The colonial governor claimed she was "an object of mercy." Governor George Clarke pardoned white servant woman Sarah Bevers (Beaver) of Cecile County for infanticide in April 1751 after a coroner's jury found that her child was actually stillborn. Governor Horatio Sharpe pardoned a free white woman named Sarah Reardon of Kent County for infanticide in August 1761 when justices recommended mercy after determining that the evidence against her was uncertain.

Maryland colonial executives pardoned two women for predatory murders; one was a slave and the other was a free white woman. In January 1766, slave woman Sue, belonging to Constant Chapman of Charles County, murdered William Garner who was most likely an overseer or a planter that leased Sue from her owner. A county court convicted Sue in early March 1766 but Governor Horatio Sharpe pardoned her in late March because justices found the evidence against her uncertain and because exculpatory evidence discovered after her conviction supported her innocence. In the case of Rebecca McDonald, a free white woman of Baltimore County, Governor Robert Eden pardoned her for the beating death of Charity Stoble in September 1774; the justices and jurors in Rebecca's case recommended her as an "object of mercy" because they believed she was remorseful and never intended to kill the victim.

At least five women received early colonial gubernatorial pardons in Maryland for burglary. Governor Samuel Olge pardoned free white woman Ann Bullingnee of Anne Arundel County in April 1740 after finding her "an object of mercy" for breaking and entering the home of Robert Langford the previous September. Servant woman Mary Spearman also received a pardon in May 1740 for burglary. Interestingly, authorities in another colony had transported Mary to Maryland at the age of 17 in 1721 for a previous offense. Even so, Governor Samuel Olge found

Mary not to be "a notorious offender." Governor Horatio Sharpe pardoned slave woman Hannah belonging to Charles Clagget of Calvert County in 1763 for burglary. A county court convicted Hannah of stealing goods after burglarizing the homes of William Millhouse and Mary Parran. Justices recommended mercy for Hannah because of her young age, it was her first offense, and she regretted committing the crime and promised to reform. Governor George Clarke pardoned Jane Parker, an unmarried woman of Ann Arundel County, for stealing sundry goods from a planter named Henry Ainsley in 1751 because a jury of matrons determined that she was "quick with child." Governor Eden pardoned Elizabeth Horner in September 1769 for stealing a mare belonging to Levin Ballard. Officials apprehended Elizabeth some 20 miles away with the horse and goods belonging to Ballard. Elizabeth claimed to have acquired the horse and goods from another person. The judge thought that Elizabeth may not have committed the offense and petitioned Governor Eden for clemency. Governor Eden ordered Elizabeth transported from the province with orders never to return.

In Pennsylvania, the historical record reveals little of Mary Hall's pardon for her participation in a burglary. The record of Mary's conviction shows that Mary was to hang along with James Cannon, James Green, and James Jones convicted of robbery in November 1781. The commonwealth hanged Cannon and Green, but officials pardoned Mary and Jones in May 1782. Mary was to leave the state and never return. In April 1770, Lieutenant Governor John Penn pardoned Mary Brian for a November 1769 burglary of Susannah Moffat's house in Philadelphia.[34] While Penn was away in Great Britain, Lieutenant Governor James Hamilton pardoned Elizabeth Grant in April 1771 for felony and burglary of John Plankinhorn's house— she was the "object of mercy." Governor Gooch pardoned Sarah Matts in Williamsburg, Virginia, in November 1739 as an accessory to a robbery of her master's store, Colonel Woodford of Caroline County, but hanged her accomplice, Constantine Matthews. In June 1780, Governor John Dickinson pardoned Margaret Matthews for arson of a store where authorities found her inebriated. In February 1784, the governor also pardoned Mary Grover for arson after her confinement in the Lancaster jail. James Oellers of Philadelphia filed a petition on behalf of his slave Sarah Craig for a pardon. It seems Sarah Craig had knowingly received stolen goods from Alice Wiley, who in turn had taken them from John Fry. Because of the petition, Governor Ross granted her a pardon in October 1790 since before her conviction she behaved well.

An early female case clemency case took place in Virginia in 1793 when Governor Henry Lee pardoned a free young black woman, Angelica Barnett, for the murder of a white man name Peter Franklin. A Henrico County jury had convicted Angelica of Franklin's murder. In early September 1792, Peter and an associate named Jesse Carpenter captured a young runaway slave boy from Angelica's house. The next evening, Franklin and Carpenter went back to Angelica's house claiming that she harbored other runaway slaves. The two forced their way into the house during which Peter threatened to bludgeon Angelica to death. It was then that Angelica "grabbed an adze [an axe-type tool] from behind a trunk and drove its blade six inches deep into [Peter's] skull, fatally wounding him."[35] Angelica had a long history of respectful relations with elite whites in and around Richmond who petitioned Governor Lee to pardon Angelica. Reportedly, much of the Richmond bar petitioned the governor for Angelica's commutation. Interestingly, U.S. Supreme Court Chief Justice John Marshall was a signatory to the petition.

Clemency in the 19th Century

Massachusetts governors granted pardons to 12.5 percent of all prisoners sentenced from 1828 to 1866. Florida officials pardoned more than 1300 convicts from 1889 to 1919. It is unclear whether imprisoned women were part of these pardoning patterns, however. Some commentators assert that commutations were more frequent in the 19th century than in more modern decades. The District of Columbia, Georgia, Ohio, Pennsylvania, Mississippi, Missouri, New Jersey, New York, North Carolina, South Carolina, Texas, Virginia, and the Indian Country of Arkansas commuted the death sentences of 36 women in the 19th century. In December 1883, a jury in the Federal Court for the Western District of Arkansas convicted the unmarried Fannie Echols of the murder of John Williams, a man with whom she had been living. Fannie, "a bright young negro girl about 25 years old," lived in Eufaula in the Creek Nation and was the first woman to receive the death penalty from Judge Isaac Parker, the infamous hanging judge, at Fort Smith. It seems the couple had a troubled relationship; John had become very possessive of Fannie and often physically abused her. After one of their frequent arguments, Fannie shot John to death when he threatened to kill her. Fanny claimed self-defense but to no avail, Judge Parker sentenced Fanny to hang in July 1884 for the murder. Reportedly, however, some 300 citizens of Fort Smith and the Creek Nation signed a petition for executive clemency. District Attorney William Clayton and Judge Parker may have used the public's disfavor in hanging a woman as an excuse not to send Fanny to the gallows. The Attorney General wrote to President Chester Arthur claiming that Fannie's execution may help to curb crime in the Creek Nation but the President refused to overturn Fannie's death sentence. Judge Parker wrote to President Arthur declaring that life imprisonment would be an appropriate punishment for Fannie; to Parker, "the certainty of punishment rather than its severity" was enough to deter crime in the territory. Seemingly persuaded by Parker's argument, President Arthur granted Fannie a reduction in sentence to life imprisonment and officials sent her to the House of Corrections in Detroit, Michigan.

In February 1889, Judge Parker at Fort Smith tried a 60-year-old Chickasaw Indian woman named Elsie James and her daughter Margaret for the robbery and murder of an elderly unmarried white man named William Jones. Elsie and Margaret lived alone on a farm in the Chickasaw Nation and regularly employed men to work the farm's fields and tend to livestock. Jones was one of those men and a boarder with whom Elsie may have had "more than a working relationship." Jones disappeared a day after he had received $65 in the mail. One version of the story is that Elsie shot and killed Jones after he attacked her with a butcher knife. In another version, Elsie claimed that a man named Zeno Colbert shot and killed Jones in her house. Elsie and a man named Samson Alexander buried Jones' body. Deputy Marshal Heck Thomas arrested Elsie, Margaret, Colbert and Alexander and charged them with murder. Once officials exhumed Jones' body they discovered that he had not died from a gunshot wound but rather from a blunt instrument, a grinding stone used to smash Jones' skull. Marshal Thomas released Margaret, Alexander and Colbert. One commentator notes that the perpetrator killed Colbert once he returned home and that "it was assumed that he was killed at the behest of Elsie James, so he could not testify against her."[36] Judge Parker's court tried Elsie twice for Jones' murder; the first trial ended in a hung jury, and in the second trial a jury found her guilty and Judge Parker sentenced her to hang in July 1889. Shortly before her scheduled execution, however, President Benjamin Harrison commuted Elsie's death sentence to life in prison at the Ohio State Penitentiary. Apparently, the President thought a life prison term was sufficient punishment.

There is little in the historical record concerning the commutation of Johanna Turbin in 1876 for spousal murder. A *New York Times* article claims that Johanna had killed her husband and then dismembered his body, and that a District of Columbia jury convicted her of the murder but the trial judge refused to sentence her to death. Though the judge recognized that Johanna had committed "a most atrocious and revolting" crime and "if ever there was a case in which capital punishment was deserved" it was Johanna's case, he was repulsed at hanging a woman and promised to secure a commutation of the death sentence. The judge's chivalrous position was unusual because as a black woman Johanna did not warrant the mercy of the court. Had Johanna been white, the legal fiction was that pleading insanity for spousal murder exempted her from hanging was unavailable to black women. Nevertheless, in late November 1876, President Ulysses S. Grant granted a commutation of Johanna's death sentence to "imprisonment at hard labor for life."[37]

Georgia officials commuted the death sentences of Harriet Grier (Crittenden), Catherine "Kate" Southern, and Emily Boon for predatory murders in 1869, 1878 and 1890, respectively. In July 1869, Georgia Governor Rufus B. Bullock reprieved Harriet Grier, a poor black woman, for the robbery and axe murder of a young white girl named Nancy Wright in Macon earlier in March. Harriet had been born a slave to Oliver Crittenden in Americus, Georgia. Harriet had confessed to Wright's killing and Judge Cole sentenced her to death. It seems that while the two women were gathering wood to sell, Harriet hit Nancy three times in the head with the axe and then stole $3.20 from Nancy's pocket. Earlier, Harriet had been drinking in a bar and was likely highly intoxicated at the time. Governor Bullock postponed Harriet's execution until August 20 of that same year so "that she might have full opportunity for prayer and penitence," but there is no record of Harriet's execution after lifting the reprieve. It is likely that Governor Bullock commuted Harriet's sentence to life in prison.[38]

Catherine "Kate" Southern reportedly epitomized the rural southern Georgia white housewife. She was the mother of a young child and pregnant at the time of her offense. Scandalous rumours of her husband's affair with Narcissa Canart, however, wracked her marriage. During festivities at her father's house, Kate confronted Narcissa concerning the affair with her husband and stabbed Narcissa repeatedly with a penknife. Kate and Robert fled to North Carolina where officials soon captured the couple. Despite doubts of whether Kate or her sister actually stabbed Narcissa to death and evidence that the killing may have been in self-defense, a Pickens County jury in April 1878 convicted Kate of murder and the county court sentenced her to hang. Her case sparked debate throughout the South about the treatment of women in the criminal justice system. After her sentencing there was public outcry that if a man had committed the same crime he probably would have been acquitted under the theory that it was justifiable homicide to kill the seducer of an adulterous wife. Kate Southern's death sentence was eventually commuted by Governor Colquitt to 10 years imprisonment, but the governor later pardoned Kate under pressure from the state's legislature.

A Gordon County jury in Georgia had convicted Emily Boon and Rufus B. Collins for the murder of Collins' wife. Collins had paid $50 to a young black man named Steve Custer (or Curtis), who had worked for Collins years earlier in North Carolina, to do the killing. Custer had shot Collins' wife in the head and confessed to the killing shortly after his arrest. The presiding judge sentenced Custer to life in prison but sentenced Emily and Rufus to hang for the crime. On his last day in office, Governor John B. Gordon commuted Emily's death sentence to life in prison; apparently, the governor had succumb to the extensive public outcry against hanging a woman. There is no record of Rufus Collins' execution who may have received a term of years.

Ohio authorities commuted the death sentences of three women in the 19th century for predatory murder. In May 1868, in the Court of Common Pleas of Cuyahoga County, a jury convicted Sarah M. Victor of the first-degree murder of her brother, William Parquet, a soldier in the U.S. Army. Judge Foote sentenced her to hang in August of that year. Suspicion aroused about the young soldier's death in February 1867. A year after his death officials exhumed his body and found that he had died from arsenic poisoning. Authorities arrested Sarah when they discovered that she had a $3,600 life insurance policy on William. At her trial, Sarah exhibited outlandish conduct associated with mental disorders. During her imprisonment awaiting execution, Cuyahoga County Sheriff Felix Nicola became convinced that Sarah was insane and wrote Ohio Governor Rutherford B. Hayes soliciting executive clemency of Sarah's death sentence. The governor suspended Sarah's execution until November 1868 and authorities immediately confined her to the Northern Ohio Lunatic Asylum at Newbury. Later that same month, Governor Hayes commuted her death sentence to life imprisonment in solitary confinement in the state penitentiary and officials removed Sarah from the asylum and committed her to the penitentiary. In January 1876, Sarah refused the commutation and secured a habeas corpus petition against the prison warden claiming that she was entitled to her liberty. She sought to have the court carry out her original execution since she tired of living a secluded prison life and the Court of Common Pleas scheduled her to hang. In December 1877, the Ohio Supreme Court heard her case and held that authorities had retained Sarah in the penitentiary unlawfully. The Court argued that Sarah "was not entitled to be set at liberty" and the Court remanded her to the prison warden "to hold her in accordance with the governor's order." After nearly 20 years in prison, Ohio Governor Joseph B. Foraker granted Sarah a pardon based on considerable speculation that the arsenic found in her brother's body might have been the product of the undertaker in preparing the body for burial. What's more, the army had subjected William to arsenic therapy for venereal disease.

In 1890, a Hamilton County jury convicted Elizabeth "Lizzie" Carter in the poisoning death of her lover and the trial judge sentenced her to death. Lizzie appealed her case to the Court of Common Pleas after lawyers discovered juror misconduct at the trial. The juror, a white man named Stephenson, made derogatory comments concerning Lizzie's trial during the second week of the trial. He publicly made declarations in a streetcar and in the dining and bar rooms of the Keller House where he was staying during the trial. The statements included, "I think they will hang that woman. She is a big, brazen nigger, and she poisoned her husband. She ought to hang, because she poisoned her husband. We will certainly hang her. She looked like a very wicked woman, she sat up before the jury as brazen-faced as the very devil himself; that she was charged with poisoning her husband, and she ought to be hung." To the Court it was clear that Stephenson's misconduct and prejudice denied Lizzie a fair trial before an impartial jury. The Court vacated her conviction and death sentence and remanded the case for a new trial, but again a jury sentenced her to death. Ohio Governor James Edwin Campbell commuted Lizzie's death sentence to life imprisonment and officials eventually paroled Lizzie.

Alonzo Garrett had two older daughters from a previous marriage when he married Mary, 26-year-old Anna and 42-year-old Eva. Apparently, Mary married Alonzo for his money and she "plotted viciously against the lives of his daughters." Mary was able to send one of the daughters to the Imbecile Asylum in Columbus for a time but eventually sent them both to the poorhouse. On November 1, 1887, Mary burned down the house killing her two "idiotic stepchildren" when she locked them in their bedroom and started the blaze with oil-soaked rags thrown into the room. A Medina County jury in Ohio convicted Mary Garrett of Anna and Eva's deaths in the fall 1888 and authorities scheduled her hanging for January 1889. Mary entered the Ohio penitentiary in October 1888 "carrying a babe in her arms." Her condemnation aroused the public and Ohio Governor Asa Smith Bushnell pardoned Mary in December 1899 after she had served 10 years in prison. Some newspaper reports claimed the governor commuted Mary's death sentence to life in prison.[39]

Pennsylvania authorities commuted the death sentences of six women throughout the 19th century. In the first case, regional newspapers claimed that authorities had lawfully hanged Elizabeth Rimby in early September 1808. Newspapers, as well as scholars, erroneously referred to Elizabeth as the first woman executed in the United States. While there is little in the historical record on Elizabeth, her death sentence for infanticide was noted in the *Centinel* in September 1806, in Gettysburg, Pennsylvania: "Elizabeth Rimby was indifled at a late Court of Oyer and Terminer, held in Cbefter county, for the murder of her infant child; found guilty, and sentenced to be executed."[40] Indeed, Elizabeth received a death warrant from Chester County officials noting her scheduled execution in early September 1806, but according to Teeters' annotated list of pardons and reprieves of persons sentenced to death in Pennsylvania, colonial Governor Thomas McKean granted Elizabeth a pardon in September 1806. There is little in the historical record concerning the commutations of Mary Martin and Hannah Lewis. The executive minutes of Pennsylvania Governor John Andrew Shultz note that the governor pardoned Mary Martin in April 1827 for a first-degree murder conviction in Allegheny County. Governor Shultz pardoned Hannah Lewis of Lancaster County for first-degree murder in February 1828.

Hester Vaughn was a Welsh émigré married to a Welshman named John Harris. When the two arrived in the United States in 1866, her husband quickly deserted her for another woman. Hester worked as a domestic servant in and around Pottsville and eventually became a dairy maid in Jenkintown, Pennsylvania. There is some debate as to whether Hester suffered the seduction of her wealthy employer or whether he raped Hester while she was alone in her bedroom one night. In any event, Hester became pregnant and within a few months her pregnancy began to show and her employer put her out with $40. Hester moved to Philadelphia where she worked as a seamstress and slept in almshouses. She eventually rented a squalid room in a tenement house where alone she gave birth to a daughter. Hester suffered from severe malnutrition and exhaustion when she gave birth to the child. One historian described the events surrounding the baby's birth in February:

> The third-story garret was unheated and a blizzard raged. Hester, who had been without food for three days, began a violent labor. She crawled to the door to cry for help. Twenty-four hours passed before the landlady heard Hester's low moans. When she opened the door, Hester lay semiconscious on the rough wood floor in a pool of blood. Her dead baby was still attached to a crudely tied umbilical cord. The constables arrived an hour later and, since she could not walk, they carried her to prison. The newborn's body was so frozen that a portion of the skin stuck to the floor and was torn away as the corpse was lifted.[41]

Authorities arrested Hester and charged her with the murder of her child in December 1868. Five months after her arrest, an all-male jury convicted Hester and Judge James Ludlow sentenced her to hang. Hester had no legal representation at her trial and the court prohibited her from giving testimony because she was a woman. The judge sentenced Hester to death as an example to women who commit infanticide. Indeed, the discovery of "thousands of dead newborns ... in alleys, ash heaps, privies, rivers, and so on" in 19th-century Philadelphia confirmed the frequency of the crime. Judge Ludlow sent Hester to Moyamensing Prison to await execution. Hester quickly became emblematic of the plight of working class women criminalized by a patriarchal legal system and its sexual double standard that feminists continue to deliberate today. There was significant national protest of the brutality and unfairness Hester suffered at the hands of jailers. The leading voices of dissent at the time came from the suffragist movement's leadership, including such renowned persons as Horace Greeley, Susan B Anthony, Ernestine L. Rose, Eleanor Kirk, and Elizabeth Cady Stanton. The Workingwomen's National Association solicited an unconditional pardon from Pennsylvania Governor John W. Geary in May 1869. The Governor pardoned Hester on the condition that she returned to Wales. She left the United States penniless and was gravely ill during the Atlantic voyage home.

In Pennsylvania, Elizabeth Harker poisoned her husband sometime in 1852, and a year later, she poisoned her sister so she could marry her sister's husband. Authorities focused their investigation on Elizabeth shortly after her sister's death. Officials exhumed both bodies and forensic examinations revealed that both victims had excessively high levels of arsenic. Police arrested Elizabeth and a state court prosecuted her for the murders. After two hours of deliberation a jury found her guilty of first-degree murder, and the trial judge sentenced her to hang. While awaiting execution in the Huntington jail, Governor William Bigler determined that she should escape execution given Elizabeth's sex and "extreme age." The Governor withheld the death warrant; essentially commuting her death sentence to life imprisonment. Elizabeth died in prison in November 1855.

Annie E. Cutler, a poor black woman, received a commutation of her death sentence to eight years in the state penitentiary in December 1885. A Philadelphia court had convicted Annie of shooting to death William H. Knight, her paramour with whom she was engaged to be married. The court tried Annie without defense counsel; she pleaded guilty and Judge Mitchell sentenced her to hang. Annie was a cook in a Philadelphia saloon and William was a waiter for a private family. William had grown tired of Annie and secretly married another woman. Annie shot and killed William out of jealousy. The public had significant interest in her case and many prominent citizens of Philadelphia signed a petition for clemency to the Pennsylvania Board of Pardons and Governor Robert E. Pattison that resulted in Annie's commutation. As one commentator put it, "No girl, white or black, should be punished for killing the libertine who robs her of her honor."[42]

Margaret Given typified women sentenced to prison in post–Reconstruction Mississippi, in their early twenties, poor, black, and mostly convicted of killing husbands and lovers. In his work on the Parchman Penitentiary, historian David Oshinsky tells of Margaret, a 15-year-old black girl who was one of the first females sent to the infamous Parchman prison farm in 1876 after the demise of Reconstruction. A Clay County jury had convicted Margaret of killing her newborn, Belle Given, in a pond after Henry White, the child's father, promised to marry her if she did away with the child. A jury had found Margaret and White guilty of infanticide, but the presiding circuit court judge sentenced Margaret to death and White to a life prison term. There is no record of Margaret appealing her sentence, but a holding of the Mississippi Supreme Court in the case of White reversed the finding of the circuit court and awarded him a new trial. Mississippi Governor Robert Lowry commuted Margaret's death sentence to life in prison, and in 1888, Lowry pardoned Margaret after "reputable white citizens in Clay County petitioned the governor to overturn her life sentence and set her loose. They argued that Margaret had been tricked into the crime by the infant's father, a smart, shrewd black demon who had promised to marry her if she did away with the child."[43] The Parchman prison farm housed 26 black women in 1915 and 48 by 1925, only Margaret received clemency.

Seven women received clemency from Missouri governors in the 19th century. One of the earliest involved Rebecca Hawkins who served a prison term in Missouri for the December 1838 poisoning of her husband, mill-owner Williamson Hawkins. After Rebecca's release from prison for poisoning Williamson, the mother of eight hired George Goster (or Henry Garster) to murder her sadistic husband. Townspeople knew Rebecca as a "person of wicked mind and disposition" who maliciously poisoned her husband with arsenic tainted coffee with the aid of slaves Mary and Ned. Testimony at her trial also confirmed that townspeople knew Williamson as excessively abusive toward Rebecca. Late in 1838, George shot Williamson to death through an opening in the chimney as he sat at his fireplace. A Jackson County court tried Rebecca, Mary, and Ned for Williamson's murder but the jury acquitted all three defendants. The jury convicted George, however, and he hanged in May 1839 in Independence. In November 1841, Missouri Governor Thomas Reynolds pardoned Rebecca after hundreds of citizens petitioned the governor's office seeking clemency presumably because of her long-term spousal abuse and ill health. One letter described Rebecca's husband as a "brute who had exercised his cruelty by kicking and beating and other outrageous indignities, leaving large gashes on her head."[44]

Missouri Governor John C. Edwards pardoned 15-year-old slave girl Nelly for killing her newborn in October 1846. A mentally challenged girl, Nelly became pregnant after her owner

Henry Edwards raped her. The more than 100 white male citizens mostly from Warren County that signed a petition to the governor requesting Nelly's exoneration surely influenced the governor's decision. The white citizens of the community cited Nelly's young age and that she was mentally limited as reasons for the pardon. The townspeople, however, were perhaps less concerned with Nelly's welfare and more troubled by the prospect that "very respectable ladies [would] have to be examined as to the facts" of the case for reasons that are unclear.[45]

Missouri Governor Charles H. Hardin commuted the death sentence of a German woman named Anna Hallenschied to life in prison claiming that her sex and questionable guilt in Christian Alband's murder warranted clemency. The Governor reportedly had grave doubts of Anna's complicity in Alband's killing. A women's rights group had interceded on Anna's behalf with the Governor and brought forth the idea that a married woman could refuse her husband's will to participate in a crime. A Circuit Court of Gasconade County jury convicted Anna, her husband Henry Hallenschied, and the couple's daughter, Wilhelmina Alband, of the murder of their daughter's husband, Christian. Wilhelmina and Christian lived in a small log cabin with Anna and Henry after they married and Christian and Henry quarreled incessantly. Henry and Anna confessed to killing Christian after their arrest. It seems that in June 1875, when an altercation developed between Christian and Henry, the two women held Christian to the ground while Henry beat the young man to death. Officials found Christian's "horribly mutilated and battered remains" buried in shallow grave some 150 yards from the cabin. The jury convicted Anna and Henry of first-degree murder and the trial judge sentenced them both to hang in December 1875. Convicted of second-degree murder, the court sentenced Wilhelmina to 10 years in the Missouri State Penitentiary. Immediately following Anna's commutation, the Sheriff in Hermann hanged Henry Hallenschied. Wilhelmina died shortly after arriving at the state prison, but Anna lived long enough "to become the oldest inmate in the prison." She died in 1891.[46]

Missouri Governor Willard P. Hall commuted the death sentence of Catherine McCoy to life in prison in 1864 for the murder and dismemberment of a five-year-old girl in St. Louis County. A County Court of St. Louis had found Catherine guilty of the murder, sentenced her death, and the state Supreme Court confirmed the conviction and death sentence. Catharine reportedly took the young girl to her room and after killing her, mutilated the body by cutting off appendages to the child's body. Although the trial jury ignored her insanity defense, it was clear during the trial that Catharine suffered from a mental disorder. As one newspaper explained, "It is thought the woman insane. During her trial, she evinced the utmost indifference to what was passing around her, and heard the sentence to death passed upon her with stoical stolidity. When, however, any allusion was made in court to her insanity, she would at once deny it." Officials sent Catharine to the Missouri State Penitentiary for about year before transferring her to a mental asylum.[47]

Missouri Governor Sterling Price commuted Sarah Haycraft's death sentence to 25 years in prison shortly before her scheduled hanging. A St. Louis County jury had found Sarah guilty of the first-degree murder of her paramour Samuel Hudson in December 1855. The court sentenced Sarah to hang in April 1856 and the Missouri Supreme Court affirmed the conviction and death sentence. Sarah, who owned a house of prostitution in St. Louis, claimed that she killed Samuel after he beat her. Sarah's wealthy and influential sister spared no expense in soliciting the governor to free Sarah. Governor Robert M. Stewart pardoned Sarah in February 1858 conditioned upon that she leave and not return to Missouri.

New Jersey governors granted clemency to two women in the 19th century beginning in 1872 after a jury of the Passaic County Court in New Jersey found young Elizabeth "Libbie" Garrabrant guilty of the first-degree poisoning murder of her paramour Ransom F. Burroughs. Judge Bedle sentenced Libbie to hang. It seems from newspaper reports that Libbie may have been an accomplice to the murder rather than actual killer. A *New York Times* story shows that Libbie's lover, a man named Bogert Van Winkle, was the real criminal. In December 1871, after Burroughs showed signs of poisoning, Libbie volunteered to go for medical assistance but Bogert went instead. A physician never arrived at the house, however, and Burroughs died. In sentencing Libbie, Judge Bedle made his sexist thoughts clear:

> When once the female character is debased, and she allows herself to become a prey to the most vicious passions of her nature, terrible consequences may be the result. You seem to be lost to shame to a certain extent, and instead of abiding by the dictates of your conscience you took counsel from the violent impulses of your nature.

Almost immediately, concerned citizens began circulating a petition asking the New Jersey Court of Pardons to commute Libbie's sentence to life in prison. The Court comprised the state's Governor, Chancellor, and six Lay Judges of the Court of Errors and Appeals. The Court of Pardons commuted Libbie's death sentence to life in prison in 1872. Libbie served 35 years of her sentence at the New Jersey State Prison until the Court of Pardons released her from the life sentence in December 1905. Reportedly, Libbie was a feeble-minded girl and illiterate. Some commentators suggest that the state should have sent Libbie to a mental hospital rather than to prison.

A Hudson County jury in New Jersey convicted Jennie R. Smith and her paramour, Covert "Cove" D. Bennett, of killing Jennie's husband of five years, Police Officer Richard H. Smith of Jersey City in August 1878. Jennie struck two blows to Richard's head with an iron window-sash weight while he lay asleep and then stabbed him 18 times in the breast and side. Jennie's defense was that she had woken from a sound sleep and found the dead body of her husband at her side. She remembered a tall man administering chloroform to her before he killed her husband. The court tried Jennie and Covert together but there were two trials. The state tried Jennie and Covert twice since one of the jurors experienced severe mental problems during the first trial. In the second trial, Judge Knapp sentenced both defendants to hang in July 1879. There was public moral outcry that Jennie's death sentence was too severe and New Jersey Governor McClellan commuted the death sentences to life in prison. In the interim, several appeals courts reversed the conviction and death sentences. The state tried the couple a third time and a jury acquitted them.

The historical record reveals that only one Texas governor granted clemency to a woman in the 19th century. There is little in the historical record concerning Pamela (Pamelia) Dickinson Mann and much of the information available is conflicting. Pamela was born on a farm in Tennessee. She went to New York in 1826 to work in a brothel and later established her own brothel in New Orleans but fled to Galveston, Texas, in 1832 after killing a man who assaulted one of her girls. Pamela is known as the woman who chastised General Sam Houston for return of her yoke of oxen pulling the "Twin Sisters" cannons used by Houston's army during the Texas Revolution to destroy Mexican forces at San Jacinto in 1836. Years later, Pamela opened Houston's Mansion House Hotel where "she controlled various police, officials and politicians, and used bribery, blackmail and all forms of corruption." At the Mansion House, Pamela provided local clientele with "feminine companionship of a robust and none virtuous nature." Houston residents eventually turned against Pamela, burned down her hotel, "humiliated and whipped her girls, and forced them to leave town." Officials indicted Pamela for counterfeiting, forgery, fornication, larceny, and assault with the intent to kill. A court sentenced Pamela to death on the forgery charge, a conviction that carried a mandatory death penalty at the time. Pamela was the first woman sentenced to death in Texas. Mirabeau B. Lamar, the second president of the Republic of Texas granted Pamela clemency, however. Lamar believed he should show mercy to Pamela given "the peculiar situation of the accused, being a female, a mother, and a widow, and an old settler of the country." Pamela reportedly lost much of her fortune speculating during the California gold rush and died in San Francisco in November 1840 of yellow fever at the age of 72.[48]

In 1819, New York Governor Dewitt Clinton granted pardons to some 2,300 inmates. Less than 2 percent of these cases involved women convicted of non-capital property and money crimes. Governor Clinton commuted the sentences of two women convicted of violent crimes; the governor pardoned a white woman convicted of attempting to poison her husband and a black woman convicted of assault and battery with the intent to kill. In the first of five female death penalty cases in the period, however, New York Governor Horatio Seymour commuted the death sentence of Henrietta Robinson to life in prison at Sing Sing State Penitentiary in 1855. The trial judge and her defense lawyer sought Henrietta's commutation believing she suffered from a severe psychosis. Despite an insanity defense, a jury convicted Henrietta in 1854 of poisoning Timothy Lannagan, a shopkeeper and father of four. Henrietta also poisoned an unmarried houseguest of the Lannagan's who was Timothy's sister, Catherine Lubee, visiting from Albany at the time though she survived the poisoning. Henrietta poisoned Timothy after an altercation in his store where Henrietta often shopped. Henrietta apparently put arsenic in their beer during a dinner at the Lannagan's home. Authorities transferred Henrietta to the Auburn Prison in 1873 and in 1896 to the state asylum for the criminally insane at Mattawan, New York, where she died at the age of 73 in 1905.

Herkimer County authorities charged Lodicia Fredenburg, her son Albert Fredenburg, Albert's daughter Mary Davis, and Mary's husband Franklin Davis with the axe murder of Franklin's father Orlo Davis in June 1875. The state tried all four defendants before Judge Milton H. Merwin. The testimony against the Fredenburgs was particularly strong, a jury found them guilty of Davis' murder and the court sentenced both defendants to hang. The court dropped murder charges against Mary and Franklin Davis. Another court denied the Fredenburgs a new trial and affirmed the death sentences. New York Governor Samuel Tilden commuted the Fredenburg's death sentences to life imprisonment stating "that he would not hang a dog on such testimony." Lodicia Fredenburg served her life sentence at the insane asylum on Blackwell's Island where she died in 1884. Albert was an inmate at Auburn Prison for several years but officials eventually transferred him to a maximum-security prison in Clinton. After serving 27 years in prison for Davis' death, New York Governor Odell pardoned Albert who died in Little Falls, New York, in 1903 at the age of 64.

New York governor David B. Hill commuted the death sentence of an Italian woman named Chiara Cignarale to life in prison for the murder of her husband, Antonio Cignarale. Remarkably, the jurors that convicted Chiara signed a petition to Governor Hill to commute Chiara's death sentence to life imprisonment. Governor Hill had received scores of letters and telegrams, including one from Italian Ambassador Baron Fava, thanking him for commuting Chiara's death sentence. The murder trial showed that Chiara suffered "long-continued cruel and inhuman treatment" from her husband that most likely drove her to kill Antonio Cignarale. Chiara left her home with Antonio and moved in with her cousin and alleged paramour, Antonio D'Andrea, who promised to marry "the poor foreign woman" who spoke little English once she killed her husband. When Antonio Cignarale discovered that Chiara was living with D'Andrea, he followed her and an argument ensued. Chiara trailed her husband after the argument and "deliberately shot him from behind while he was walking ahead of her." Though the trial judge sentenced Chiara to death, another jury acquitted D'Andrea of first-degree murder "for having advised Chiara Cignarale to kill her husband."[49]

Angenette B. Haight shot and killed her husband, George W. Haight, in February 1883 in De Ruyter, New York, and a Madison County jury convicted her of first-degree murder a year later. Judge Murray sentenced her to death by hanging in April 1884. The prosecution claimed that Angenette shot her husband in the head with a pistol to collect on an $18,000 life insurance policy. There was speculation that Angenette had similarly killed two previous husbands who had substantial amounts of life insurance. The only evidence presented in the case was a dying declaration from George that he saw Angenette coming at him with a cloth draped over a gun, which she fired at his head. There was considerable elation in the courtroom and elsewhere after the reading of Angenette's guilty verdict. Apparently, George was well known and liked in the community. Some townspeople hanged Angenette in effigy. New York Governor Grover Cleveland commuted Angenette's death sentence to life in prison at the Onondaga County Penitentiary because of her age (she was 62 years old when convicted) and physical health. He stated, "The report of the medical examination made by my direction disclosed that her bodily ailments and infirmities are such that it is likely her life will not be long duration in any event."[50]

Polly Franklin (Hoag, Frisch) had eight children after marrying Henry Hoag in 1844, but only two of the children survived to adulthood. Polly's husband and six-year-old daughter Frances died in 1856. She married Otto Frisch the same year and lost custody of two of her children to Henry's relatives the same year but retained custody of her baby, Eliza Jane. The next year, Otto became ill and sought medical advice. He survived after being given an antidote to arsenic poison and afterwards left Polly for Canada. Eliza Jane died in late 1857 and authorities initiated a coroner's inquest. In late 1857, the Genesee County Sheriff arrested Polly for the murder of her young daughter. Authorities exhumed and autopsied Henry and Frances's bodies and found they had died from arsenic poisoning and indicted Polly on three counts of murder in the deaths of Henry Hoag and her two daughters Frances and Eliza Jane Hoag. County district attorneys tried Polly five times. In the first trial, the jury acquitted Polly of Henry's murder and in a second trial, a judge acquitted her of the Eliza Jane's murder with a directed verdict. A third trial for the murder of Frances resulted in a hung jury but in the fourth trial a jury found Polly guilty. Her attorney's appealed the verdict because of improper statements made to the jury by the judge and the verdict was overturned. In a fifth trial, Polly pleaded insanity but the jury found her guilty of Frances's murder and the trial judge sentenced her to death by hanging. At once, however, the jury petitioned the court and New York Governor Edwin D. Morgan for mercy. Governor Morgan commissioned a mental evaluation of Polly that found her insane resulting from epileptic disease. Governor Morgan immediately commuted Polly's death sentence to prison "for the term of her natural life." Polly remained at Sing Sing Prison until 1877 when officials transferred her to Kings County Penitentiary. In 1892, at the request of a physician at the prison, Governor Roswell P. Flower pardoned Polly and authorities released her after she had served more than 33 years in prison.

In March 1887, the *Orlean Democrat* noted that New York governors had commuted the death sentences of four women housed in the asylum for insane criminals attached to the King's county jail at Flatbush and the asylum at Auburn Prison. Accordingly, Governor Seymour commuted the death sentences of Agnes Agar and Jane Brooks to life in prison in 1863, Governor Tilden commuted the death sentence of Wilhemine Weick to a life term in 1869, and Governor Dix commuted the death sentence of Eveline Johnson in 1874 to life in prison. Other than the article published in the *Orlean Democrat*, no other newspaper sources confirm these commutations and reveal no other facts about the cases.

Catherine Johnson, a married woman with two young children, murdered her friend Bridget McDermot with an axe. It seems that Catherine and Bridget had been drinking with other friends for several days before the killing. A quarrel ensued between the two after a neighbor supplied Bridget a greater quantity of milk and beer than received by Catherine. A jury convicted Catherine of the murder and the court scheduled her execution for December 1868. New York Governor Rueben Fenton, however, commuted her death sentence to a life term undoubtedly based upon Catherine's mental health given that officials housed her in a mental health facility.

Elizabeth "Lizzie" Halliday was born Elizabeth Margaret McNally in County Antrim in Northern Ireland about 1864. She immigrated to the United States with her parents when she was three years old. Lizzie became a serial killer that some observers have compared to London's assassin "Jack the Ripper." Over a 14-year period beginning in 1879, Lizzie had married six different husbands and she had one son. All of her husbands were elderly, died suddenly, or deserted her after she attempted to poison them. She met an elderly Irish widower named Paul Halliday and became his housekeeper in Burlingham, New York. They married after living together for a short time. One commentator described Lizzie, as "a type of low humanity, [she] was ... an ignorant, mean, cunning and revengeful woman, with the belief that she possessed the power to deceive everybody she chose." Lizzie killed six people including two husbands whom she mutilated, Charles Hopkins and Paul Halliday, a crippled stepson, John Halliday, who died in a house fire set by Lizzie, two women housekeepers, Margaret McQuillan and Sarah McQuillan, a mother and daughter who she murdered about the same time as her husband Halliday, and then a nurse, Nellie Wickes, who attended to her in the Mattawan State Asylum for the Insane in New York. Officials suspected Lizzie of killing several other people including a roaming peddler. She also attempted to kill a nurse at the asylum named Catherine Ward. In July 1894, a Sullivan County jury convicted Lizzie of her husband's murder and that of the two McQuillan women. The presiding judge sentenced her to die in the state's electric chair. Governor Roswell P. Flowers commuted Lizzie's death sentence to life imprisonment based on her insanity, she remained at Mattawan State Asylum until her death at 58 years old in June 1918.

Elizabeth (Scarborough) and William H. "Billy" Nobles were poor southern farmers with daily regiments of hard fieldwork while living in squalor conditions on 300 acres just outside Jeffersonville, Georgia. The couple had two children, 18-year-old Debby and 10-year-old Jack. The family had troubled relations; "Mrs. Nobles complained that her husband cruelly mistreated her, but neighbors said the woman was anything but kind to her husband."[51] The family employed three black workers who lived on the property, Gus Fambles and his wife Mary, and Dalton Joiner. In June 1895, along with Debby, Gus, Mary, and Dalton, Elizabeth conspired to kill her husband William. Elizabeth offered $10 to her paramour Gus from William's small life insurance policy. Under a ruse that someone was stealing corn from the barn (a common problem in the area), Elizabeth rousted William from bed on an early Sunday morning to investigate. Once William was in the barn, Gus hit him from behind with a blow to his head with a hatchet. When William fell to the ground, Elizabeth took an axe and hit William again killing him. They buried William's body in a shallow grave. Authorities arrested the group and Gus and Elizabeth quickly confessed to the murder. In August, a Twiggs County jury convicted Gus and Elizabeth of William's murder and District Judge C.C. Smith sentenced them to death. The jury acquitted Dalton Joiner and Debby Nobles but convicted Mary and the court sentenced her to life in prison. Elizabeth's death sentence produced a schism across the state. Many pleaded for a commutation from the state governor citing strong sentiment that it was shameful to hang a southern white woman. Others claimed that her ignorance and poverty mitigated the crime. Still others argued that the state must uphold the law and hang Elizabeth. The Georgia Supreme Court, as well as the U.S. Supreme Court, upheld the conviction and death sentence. Governor Atkinson commuted Elizabeth's death sentence to life in prison upon the recommendation of the state's prison commission. Elizabeth died in prison in February 1916 at the age of 71.

In July 1887, Judge Hudson in Charleston, South Carolina, sentenced 12-year-old Axey Cherry to hang for killing an infant belonging to Amos Williams. Reportedly, Axey was a poor, "half-witted" black girl living with her parents in Barnwell County. It seems that Axey's mother sent her to watch over the baby but Axey begrudged having to do so. On one occasion while caring for the child, Mrs. Williams warned Axey to stay away from a concentration of poisonous lye. Mrs. Williams was using the concentration to scour floors. Mrs. Williams left the room, when she returned she was horrified to see that her baby's mouth was full of the concentration. It was then that Axey ran out of the house stating, "I don't reckon I will have to nurse that baby much longer now." The baby died from the poisoning. One report about Axey's trial explained,

> The young murderess all through her trial seemed to have no idea of the terrible nature of her deed, and when she was sentenced to be hanged she gazed steadily at the Judge and grinned as she played with the buttons on her dress. As she was being carried back to jail she saw her father and made an effort to go to him. She cried for the first time when told that she could not go home, but must go back to jail to await the day of her execution.[52]

Governor Richardson commuted Axey's death sentence to five years in prison in August 1887 most likely because of her age and her diminished capacity to understand the nature of the crime. Officials had scheduled Axey's hanging for the third Friday in September of 1887.

In August 1888, a Caswell County jury in North Carolina convicted a black woman named Milly (Millie) Poteat of the November 1887 arson and total destruction of James Henry Slade's house. The trial lasted one day and the all-white male jury found her guilty "without hesitation." Milly's paramour testified against her at trial and claimed that he and Milly plundered the house and then set it ablaze while James Slade was away. The trial judge sentenced Milly to death. North Carolina Governor Alfred M. Scales commuted Milly's death sentence to life imprisonment a day before her scheduled hanging.

In one of the earlier Virginia cases of executive action on a female death sentence, Governor James Pleasant commuted the execution of Letty, a 28-year-old slave woman belonging to Robert Hartford, for the murder of her mulatto newborn daughter. In July 1822, Letty murdered the infant by crushing its skull, wrapping her in a petticoat, and then leaving it for dead in nearby woods. Letty denied killing the child though she stated, "if the child had been one of her colour, she would not have done as she did." Letty may have been the victim of Hartford's sexual aggression. A unanimous jury found Letty guilty of the murder and a Brook County court sentenced to her to hang in early November. Shortly afterwards, a citizen's counsel petitioned the state's governor to commute Letty's sentence to "sale and banishment" from the county. One can equate banishment as a social death, however. As historian Wilma King explains:

> Separation from family and friends, whether living or dead, created a physical void and left deep emotional scars on those who were removed and on those who remained behind. Separating fictive or blood relations was one of the harshest aspects of southern bondage, and the slaves' fear of family dispersal gave owners their most powerful weapon of control.[53]

Mary Booth, a 14-year-old black girl, allegedly murdered the wife of R. C. Gray and an overseer named Tavis Jones with arsenic poison in April 1882 in Surrey County, Virginia. There was speculation that Mrs. Gray and Jones were lovers. Mary confessed to the killings and implicated Martha Jones, a black servant in the Gray household, and others in the murder. In July 1882, a county jury convicted Mary of the murders and the trial judge sentenced her to hang in November 1882. There was talk of lynching Mary. Governor William Evelyn Cameron commuted Mary's death sentence to life in prison because he was concerned with Mary's young age and that she "was only a tool in the hands of other unknown persons." The public was concerned that the evidence used to convict young Mary was "purely circumstantial." Mary's commutation apparently met with general approval. Mr. Gray eventually committed suicide.

In October 1883, a St. Louis jury convicted Sadie Hayes (Hill), a mulatto women and an alleged prostitute, for the murder of Pelatiah M. Jenks, a veteran sergeant with the St. Louis Police Department. Jenks was the father of five children. It seems that Sadie was drunk with a revolver and threatened to kill someone after a quarrel with a man named John Collins. She shot Jenks with a bullet to the head while he struggled to arrest Sadie. Jenks died later that evening. A large crowd "with a strong disposition to lynch" Sadie gathered in front of the jail where police held Sadie. The trial court sentenced Sadie to hang in January 1886. After losing an appeal to the St. Louis Court of Appeals, Sadie appealed her case to the Missouri Supreme Court, which overruled the lower court's decision and remanded the case back to the trial court for new jury instructions. She received a 99-year prison term. In November 1898, however, Missouri Governor Lawrence V. Sephens pardoned Sadie.

Weeks after her release from the Missouri State Penitentiary for an assault conviction, Pearl Waters killed a woman named Lillian Waddell in February 1897 during a heated quarrel over a ten-cent beer wherein Pearl plunged a "huge knife" into the victim. A jury convicted Pearl of first-degree murder and the trial court sentenced her to hang. One report noted, "When the verdict was read, Pearl Waters shrieked like a mad woman."[54] A court retried Pearl and sentenced her to life in prison for second-degree murder. Two years after Pearl began serving her prison sentence, Governor Lawrence V. Stephens pardoned Pearl in July 1899.

Clemency in the 20th Century

State governors commuted the death sentences of nearly 1400 prisoners from 1900 to 2002, but only 41 (3.0 percent) of these commutations involved condemned women. South Carolina Governor Cole L. Blease, for instance, paroled 52 prisoners convicted of murder and manslaughter in November 1913. Oklahoma Governor Lee Cruce commuted all death sentences during his administration from 1911 to 1915. From 1911 to 1914, Massachusetts Governor Eugene N. Foss pardoned 77 non-capital offenders in his first year of office and 55 prisoners the next year. Governor Foss was troubled when he found prisoners serving excessively long prison sentences and believed "the ends of justice have been served." In one case Governor Foss pardoned William E. Hill, a veteran of the Civil War who occupied a prison cell for 41 years. In another case, the Governor commuted the sentence of Stearns Kendall convicted in Middlesex County in October 1880. A court had sentenced Kendall to hang but Foss commuted his death sentence after discovering that Kendall was most probably innocent. In Oregon, Governor Robert D. Holmes commuted all death sentences that arose during his two-year term from 1957 to 1959. Governor Peabody of Massachusetts from 1962 to 1964 recommended commutations to an executive council of all death sentences during his tenure, and in 1971, Arkansas Governor Winthrop Rockefeller commuted the death sentences of 15 prisoners at the Tucker Prison Farm in 1970. State executives acting consecutively have resulted in the commutation of sentences to large numbers of death row prisoners as well. State governors in Massachusetts from 1900 to 1958 exercised executive clemency to commute the death sentences of 30 capital offenders. In North Carolina from 1903 to 1963, state governors commuted the death sentences of 234 defendants. Pennsylvania governors from 1914 to 1958 commuted the death sentences of 86 offenders. Four Maryland governors from 1936 to 1961 commuted 34 death sentences. State governors in Ohio from 1950 to 1959 moved to commute the death sentences of 22 offenders. The historical record on broad commutations reveals that few of these actions involved death row women.

A significant challenge to capital sentencing in the United States since the U.S. Supreme Court declared state and federal death penalty laws unconstitutional in *Furman v. Georgia* came when Illinois Governor George Ryan commuted the sentences of all 167 condemned death row prisoners in early January 2003. Ryan became concerned with the Illinois death penalty scheme when he took office as the state's governor and noted that in the time since Illinois had reaffirmed capital punishment, state authorities had conducted 12 executions and exonerated 13 death-row inmates with one exonerated inmate coming within 48 hours of execution. Ryan called for a state moratorium on capital punishment in January 2000 and ordered a blue-ribbon commission to study the state's death penalty system. The commission issued more than 80 recommendations that the state legislature failed to adopt and Ryan acted on his last days in office to commute the death sentences of all condemned inmates on the state's death row. Politicians from both mainstream political parties criticized Ryan's blanket commutation and many state attorneys "vowed to begin filling up the state's death row as soon as possible." Many commentators opposed Governor Ryan's blanket clemency as an insult to the integrity of American justice system. In claiming that the governor was unjustified in commuting the sentences of death row prisoners, for instance, one commentator referred to Governor Ryan's commutation as "cowardice masquerading as courage." Despite the disparagement launched against Ryan's broad commutation, no one addressed the findings of the state commission. Three black women and one Mexican woman were among the inmates with commuted death sentences. Four black women were among the commutations granted by Ohio Governor Richard Celeste in 1991. And in March 2011, Illinois Governor Patrick Quinn commuted the death sentences of 15 death row inmates to life in prison without parole when he signed legislation into law abolishing the state's death penalty though no women were among these last commutations.

State governors commuted the death sentences of 29 female capital defendants between 1900 and 1972. In the earliest of these cases, a Jackson County jury convicted Amanda Umble for the first-degree murder of another woman named Effie Jackson in April 1892. The trial judge, H. P. White, sentenced Amanda to hang and the Missouri Supreme Court affirmed the conviction and death sentence. Members of the Colored Woman's League solicited the state's governor to commute Amanda's death sentence because of her gender. The organization must have had a substantial impact on Governor William J. Stone because he commuted Amanda's death sentence to 50 years in the Missouri State Penitentiary in June 1893. Governor Alexander M. Dockery awarded Amanda a full pardon in July 1901 after serving an eight-year prison term. There is nothing in newspapers reports explaining why Governor Dockery pardoned Amanda. The murder apparently involved a lovers' quarrel. Amanda and Effie were both in love with William Jackson, a black porter in a saloon in Kansas City. Amanda was angry that William was spending considerable time with Effie. One night after William and Effie were returning home from a dance, Amanda accosted the two on the street. During the argument, Amanda struck Effie who then ran into an alleyway. Amanda pursued Effie and stabbed her numerous times. Amanda fled from the alley and police arrested her several days later. Effie died weeks afterwards from an infection attributed to the several stab wounds.

In February 1905, a Jackson County jury in Missouri convicted Maggie (Agnes or Aggie) Meyers for the murder of Clarence Meyers, Maggie's husband. Clarence was a supervisor at a printing office. The couple had been married about four years and had no children. Officials tried Maggie's 20-year-old paramour Frank Hottman separately after he won a change of venue to Clay County where a jury convicted him of the murder as well. Frank had confessed as an accomplice to the murder and voluntarily testified against Maggie. According to Frank's testimony, Maggie let him into the Myers' home at an early hour on May 10 and immediately gave Clarence a drug to make him sleep. Once Clarence was asleep, Frank went to his bed and hit him in the head with a billiard cue. The blow aroused Clarence, and while two men struggled, Maggie hit Clarence with a bed slat and cut his throat with a razor repeatedly. Afterwards, Maggie stabbed Clarence a half-dozen times in the chest with a pair of scissors. Judge Alexander sentenced Maggie to hang in August 1905. The Missouri Supreme Court stayed her execution until June 1906 to allow for appeals, and in July of that year, the same court upheld her conviction and death sentence. While attorneys appealed her case to the U.S. Supreme Court, Governor Folk commuted Maggie and Frank's death sentences to life imprisonment claiming, "Public morals would be benefited more by a life sentence than a death sentence in this case." Frank died in prison in 1923, and officials paroled Maggie in January 1925. Maggie eventually married a pharmacist and moved to Colorado.

In his work on crime and justice in the New Mexico territory, historian Robert J. Tórrez tells of the commutation of a black woman named Alma Lyons and a Mexican woman named Valentina Madrid for the poisoning murder of Valentina's husband, Manuel Madrid.⁵⁵ After two years of marriage, Valentina became infatuated with Francisco Baca and they soon began a sexual relationship. Manuel learned of the adulterous affair and demanded that Francisco stay away from his wife, but the affair continued. Francisco wanted Manuel dead and instructed the two young women on how to accomplish the murder with poison. Manuel succumbed after a week to the poison put in his morning coffee and a physician reported to authorities that Manuel died from arsenic poisoning. The county sheriff arrested Valentina, Alma, and Francisco for Manuel's murder. The two women confessed to the killing but insisted that Francisco "conceived the plan to poison [Manuel] and had threatened to kill them if they refused to carry it out."⁵⁶ The three defendants appeared before New Mexico District Court Judge Frank W. Parker. The court tried the women together but postponed Francisco's trial until the next term of the district court. A Sierra County jury convicted Valentina and Alma of first-degree murder after an hour's deliberation and Judge Parker sentenced them both to hang. In June 1907, Acting Governor James W. Raynolds, Governor Herbert J. Hagerman had resigned, commuted the women's death sentences to life in prison. Raynolds could have used "the overwhelming public support for a commutation due to the extenuating circumstances of the girl's age and alleged mental incompetence." Instead, he argued, "their execution would eliminate the only witnesses who could testify for the prosecution at [Francisco Baca's] upcoming trial.⁵⁷ Friends since childhood, both women were 16 years old, illiterate, and childlike mental incompetents who came from troubled backgrounds. In a letter to the state's governor seeking commutation for the young women, longtime county resident W. S. Hopewell knew well their respective upbringings. Tórrez explains the commentary:

> The conditions under which Alma was raised led him to concede that nothing but depravity and demoralizing results could be expected from one brought up under such adverse circumstances; and the result was that the girl developed into a woman of weak mind and very deficient morals. He likewise felt Valentina had been raised under the same conditions of depravity and that these were extremely unfavorable for the development of a morally responsible woman.⁵⁸

The two women served 13 years of their sentences at the New Mexico Territorial Penitentiary in Santa Fe until May 1919 when Governor Octaviano A. Larrazolo signed an executive order commuting Valentina and Alma's life sentences to time served, effective in early March 1920. The terms of the pardons showed Valentina and Alma could not leave New Mexico, they were to stay out of Sierra County, and they were to have offers of "honorable employment." After their release, Valentina Madrid moved to her brother's ranch near Hillsboro and Alma Lyons became a domestic worker in Santa Fe.

A Philadelphia jury convicted Freida Hartmann Trost, a tavern owner, in December 1912 for the arsenic poisoning murder of her husband, William Trost, shortly after they were married. The trial judge sentenced Freida to death by hanging. A separate jury acquitted Edmund Guenkel, a bartender employed by Freida, of the murder. Freida killed William to obtain possession of his property valued at $10,000 and life insurance proceeds to pay off heavy debts that she had acquired. Governor John K. Tener commuted Frieda's death sentence to life in imprisonment in November 1913, and in May 1938, Governor George E. Earle ordered Freida released from the Muncy Home for Women after she had spent 26 years in prison. Newspaper articles of the day are unclear as to any reason why the state governors commuted Frieda's sentences.

In September 1910, Lena Cusumano hired Enrico Mascioli (as known as Harry Marshall) to kill her husband Calagero Francisco Cusumano for $35. Enrico was a border in the Cusumano home and with whom Lena reportedly had relations. Police found Calagero's stripped body on a local beach with wounds from an axe and bound in wire. In February 1911, with the use of Italian interpreters, a Plymouth County jury convicted Lena and Enrico of first-degree murder and in March of that year Superior Court Judge Quinn sentenced them to death in the state's electric chair. Massachusetts authorities electrocuted Enrico at Charlestown State Prison in June 1912. The day after Enrico's execution, and upon the recommendation of Governor Eugene Foss, his executive council commuted Lena's death sentence to life in prison at the Reformatory for Women. Members of the executive council reasoned that additional information provided reasonable doubt as to Lena's guilt of first-degree murder.

In January 1913, a Newark jury in New Jersey found Maddalena Ciccone guilty of the first-degree poisoning murder of her husband, Leonardo Ciccone. Maddalena had mixed arsenic in coffee that she then served to her husband. When arrested, Maddalena implicated her paramour, Antonio Fiore, in the murder as an accomplice in procuring the poisoning. New Jersey authorities tried Maddalena and Antonio separately. The state tried Maddalena first and a jury convicted her of first-degree murder. The trial court sentenced Maddalena to death. In April 1913, in a special session of the Court of Pardons in Trenton, however, officials commuted Maddalena's death sentence to life in prison. State prosecutors argued that she was entitled to clemency since Antonio Fiore instigated the crime and it was upon her testimony that the state was able to prosecute Fiore for Leonardo's murder. The court of pardons in a special session commuted Maddalena's death sentence to life imprisonment under the approval of New Jersey Governor James F. Fielder in June 1915. A court convicted and sentenced to death Antonio for his part in aiding, abetting, and counseling Maddalena in the killing. An appeals court affirmed Antonio's conviction and death sentence and New Jersey electrocuted him in February 1914.

In 1905, a Berks County jury in Pennsylvania convicted Kate Edwards of murdering her husband John Edwards in July 1901 and the trial court sentenced her to death. Kate had killed her husband farmer with a mason's hammer while she was intoxicated. On several occasions John had threatened to kill Kate and her unborn child. Kate grew up in squalor and the "wretched conditions" of poverty. Kate's parents were illiterate and there was "an absence of intellectual and moral training" in the home. She had attended grade school for four months, and when eight years old her parents forced her to work. Kate married John when she was 16 years old and had a deeply troubled marriage. A Board of Parsons explained: "Edwards was a man of equally low social standing, and besides was a drunkard, and had the reputation of being a thief. It was a common thing for him and his wife and children and such visitors as happened at his home all to join in debaucheries of the vilest sort."[39] Kate had implicated her paramour, Samuel Greason, a black man in the murder but later recanted Greason's involvement. A court later acquitted Greason. Kate gave birth to Greason's daughter, Alma Edwards, while jailed. Governor Samuel W. Pennypacker originally signed her warrant but recalled the order and refused to issue another. He also refused to approve a pardon. Kate languished in jail for 12 years through the governorships of Edwin S. Stuart, John K. Tener, and Martin G. Brumbaugh who also refused to sign a death warrant out of concern of executing a woman. Finally, Kate's case went before the pardon board, Governor William C. Sproul approved the pardon, and authorities released Kate from prison in February 1914. Kate apparently had gone through a significant transformation while in jail where she learned to read and write. Interestingly, Booker T. Washington found a home for Alma Edwards when she was three years old. He apparently placed the child in an institution in Virginia. Kate petitioned the state pardon board for release:

> I was born in a board house with one room below and one above in a valley in the Welsh mountains in Lancaster County. Our house was in the woods far away from other houses, and a little stream ran by not three steps away.
> There were six of us in all, and my father left my mother, and she used to leave us alone and go away all day, working to keep us. I went to school two Winters, about two month each Winter.

The reason I did not get longer is because I had to walk three miles over the mountains, through the woods and across the fields to the school, when snow fell and the weather became too cold I could not go all Winter.

When I was eight years old I was put away to work for my clothes and board, and when I was not sixteen I was married. Then my eight children came, and had no time for anything but work. Since I have been here in jail I have learned more than I did in my life before. I have been treated kinder and better than ever in my life. I have tried to learn everything I could.

If I am pardoned I am told I have friends who will get me a chance to work and earn a living, and I know that I could work and give good service to someone if given a chance.

I have prayed for years for my release, and I hope and pray that the Board of Pardons will have mercy on me and give me my freedom again.[60]

In December 1913, Madeline Ferola stabbed to death Carmello Canestrale on a bridge overlooking the railroad tracks of the New York Central Railroad. She had stabbed Carmello in his chest penetrating the heart. Madeline kept a boarding house and Carmello had been a boarder. Madeline and Carmello planned to wed and accompanied by friends obtained a marriage license in Manhattan. Thereafter, they lived together for a few weeks until Carmello left Madeline and went to live with Salvatore Peragine. Madeline arranged for the wedding, but Carmello did not appear at the wedding. The following day, Carmello went to Madeline and claimed he refused to marry Madeline because she had insufficient money. Carmello's murder most likely resulted from the scornful Madeline. The trial record reveals that Salvatore most likely aided and incited Madeline to kill Carmello. Once arrested for the murder, Madeline made confessions to the killing at a coroner's inquest and to the district attorney. The state convicted Madeline of Carmello's murder and the trial judge sentenced her to death. The Court of Appeals of New York affirmed the conviction and death sentence. Within weeks of her pending execution in August 1915, Governor Charles S. Whitman commuted Madeline's death sentence to 20 years in prison. A delegation of a New York women's club and a plea from Assemblyman S. A. Cotillo representing the Italian Chamber of Commerce and some 40,000 persons of six Italian organizations undoubtedly influenced the Governor's decision for clemency.

From 1919 through 1924, some 18 people were axed to death on the streets of Birmingham, Alabama, and another 16 were seriously injured. Most of the dead and injured were immigrant storekeepers. Police eventually arrested five blacks in connection with the killings, 19-year-old Pearl Jackson, her common law husband O'Dell Jackson, Peyton "Foots" Johnson, Fred Gover and John Reed. They all confessed to the killings at the Birmingham jail after authorities injected with the drug scopolamine ("truth serum"). Jefferson County juries convicted the five but they received different sentences. While courts affixed death sentences to Pearl and O'Dell Jackson, the other defendants received long prison terms. In early August 1925, Alabama Governor William W. Brandon commuted the death sentences of Pearl and O'Dell to life imprisonment for the murder of John Robert Turner. Though Governor Brandon had an aversion to the death penalty, he claimed that the wide differences in sentences imposed by the juries influenced his decision to commute the sentences of the Jacksons.

In June 1926, a Duval County jury in Florida convicted Bertha Hall and her paramour, Gordon Denmark, of killing her husband, James H. Hall, a grocer. Judge Daniel A. Simmons sentenced Bertha and Gordon to death in the state's electric chair. Bertha has the dubious distinction of being the first woman sentenced to die in the Florida electric chair. News reports of the period explain that Bertha provided Gordon with a shotgun for killing James. Gordon, a plumber by trade, confessed to the killing and implicated Bertha as his accomplice and architect of the crime. Upon his confession, Gordon told detectives that he had become Bertha's slave and that she commanded him to do the slaying. He killed James Hall after several attempts "to hire a Negro to kill Hall for him." Bertha claimed that James drank and beat her and even shot her once. Gordon shot James to death as he laid drunk in front of his store. Florida Governor John W. Martin commuted both death sentences to life imprisonment in 1929. Authorities released Bertha in early 1935.

In February 1927, a Duval County jury convicted Annie Mae "Billy" Jackson of stabbing her roadhouse musician husband, Hugh Jackson, to death during an intense argument in their apartment. Circuit Court Judge Daniel A. Simmons automatically sentenced Annie to death in the state's electric chair when the jury did not recommend mercy. Governor John W. Martin commuted Annie's death sentence in June 1933 to life in prison. Officials released Annie in October 1934.

In early August 1927, Eula Mae Thompson, accompanied by her husband Clifford Thompson and a black man named Jim Hugh Moss, drove a Ford roadster to Chatsworth in northern Georgia from their home near Etowah in the Cohutta Mountains of southern Tennessee. The three were running whiskey into Georgia when the car ran out of gas near a store owned by Coleman Osborne. Clifford and Jim went to the store, leaving Eula in the automobile. Though the store had closed for the evening, Osborne offered to help and either Clifford or James shot him to death. Shortly afterwards, the two returned to the car and with Mrs. Thompson drove back to the Tennessee town. Police arrested them several days later. Though the case against Eula was largely circumstantial, a Murray County jury had found her guilty of conspiracy to commit murder without recommendation and Judge Claude C. Pitman sentenced Eula to die in the state's electric chair. Juries convicted Clifford Thompson and James Hugh Moss, a former baseball player with the Chicago American Giants, in a separate trial and both received death sentences. In August 1928, state authorities electrocuted Thompson and Moss at Georgia State Prison in Milledgeville. In late November 1928, Georgia Governor Lamaratine G. Hardman granted Eula a 60-day stay to study her case relative to a conspiracy. He ultimately concurred in the recommendation of the prison commission and commuted Eula's death sentence to life imprisonment because the records and evidence did not show a conspiracy to kill Osborne, but at most a conspiracy to rob Osborne. Governor Hardman noted that two Supreme Court justices had declared that the evidence was not sufficient to prove a conspiracy to murder Osborne on her part. The evidence was limited to the participation of Clifford Thompson and Jim Hugh Moss in the robbery and commission of the murder. Governor Eugene Talmadge pardoned Eula in December 1936 after she served eight years of her sentence.

Interestingly, Eula later made an unsuccessful $50,000 claim against Tennessee claiming that state officials had kidnapped her husband and illegally extradited him to Georgia. While in prison, officials denied Eula a request to marry Dan G. Harrison, an Atlanta butcher employed with L & N Railroad, whom she had met while being transferred to the state prison from county jail. In a related circumstance, Murray County officials in Georgia again jailed Eula in June 1941 along with Virgil Scott and Kermit Pritchett in connection to the stabbing death of Eula's brother Walker Elrod during an intense argument over a debt. A jury trial found Eula guilty of stabbing her brother and recommended mercy that automatically warranted a life term in prison. Eula died in September 1980 at the age of 76.

At the home of Robert and Harriet Evans in May 1930, Harriet aided and abetted in the murders of her husband Robert Evans and his friend Albert Duffy, while they celebrated in the kitchen their recent discharge from the Navy. Claude Carmichael and Lester Underdown actually did the killings and Madison E. Chapel participated in the murders. The three men were all with the U.S. Marines. They had struck Evans and Duffy on the head and then shot them to death. An Ocean County court tried Harriet and Lester together and all-male jury convicted them of first-degree murder with no claim for mercy, and the trial judge sentenced them to die in the state's electric chair. Claude and Madison won severance and tried separately, but another Ocean County court convicted them both of second-degree murder and sentenced Claude to

25 years in prison and Madison to ten-years in prison. Evidenced developed at trial showed that Harriet and Lester were lovers and wanted no interference from Robert. Harriet had threatened to get rid of Robert as soon as he returned stateside from the Navy. Also revealed was that Harriet masterminded the murder plot and induced Lester to kill Robert. Harriet was present at the time of the killing but took no part in the actual murder. The New Jersey Court of Appeals upheld both convictions and death sentences. New Jersey Governor Morgan F. Larson commuted Harriet and Lester's death sentences to life in prison.

In December 1932, a York County jury found former mill worker Beatrice Ferguson Snipes guilty of the shooting death of Elliot Harris, a married county police officer and father of one, without a recommendation of mercy. The verdict meant an automatic death sentence that Judge Thomas Sease affirmed but did not set an execution date. Beatrice was the mother of a young child. She was also in the advance stage of pregnancy and gave birth to the child while in prison. In January 1933, Governor Ibar C. Blackwood commuted Beatrice's death sentence to life in prison. Newspaper reports reveal that the governor likely granted clemency after succumbing to public pressure in the case and after Beatrice agreed to abandon all appeals. Authorities paroled Beatrice in April 1943 after she had served 12 years in prison.

The historical record is not forthcoming on Illinois Governor Henry Horner's commutation of Gertrude Puhae's death sentence. In May 1934, a Madison County jury fixed the death penalty to Gertrude, mother of two, and her lover Thomas Lehney for the confessed murder Gertrude's husband William Puhae, a steel worker. Lehney apparently shot William twice in the head as he lay in bed in his home. Police had interrogated Gertrude for two days to acquire the confession.

In October 1908, Nellie May Madison married the first of six husbands at the age of 13 when she eloped to Ogden, Utah. By 1933 Nellie had met and married her sixth husband Eric Madison after a short courtship. Eventually the couple moved by way of Salt Lake City to Burbank, California, where they worked in the commissary of Warner Brothers Studio and lived in an apartment across the street. Eric frequently battered Nellie until early March 1934 when Nellie shot and killed Eric and then drove to a ranch house where police arrested her days after the murder. A Los Angeles County jury convicted Nellie of Eric's murder with no recommendation for leniency; meaning that by law the judge was to sentence the defendant to death. Judge Charles W. Fricke sentenced Nellie to hang in early October 1935 but California Governor Frank Finley Merriam commuted Nellie's death sentence to life in prison after evidence showed that Eric victimized his wife. In March 1943, after nine years in prison at the California Institution for Women, Governor Culbert Olson had Nellie freed from prison. She married again and died of a stroke in July 1953 at the age of 58 in San Bernardino, California. To some commentators, the life and tribulations of Nellie helped "garner legitimacy to the abuse defense, a concept virtually unknown at the time, in criminal cases."[61]

After deliberating 13 hours, a Leflore County jury in Mississippi convicted Dr. Sarah Ruth Dean of the August 1933 poison murder of her clinical associate and fiancé Dr. John Preston Kennedy to prevent him from marrying his divorced wife. The trial court sentenced Sarah to a life term in the infamous Parchman prison. Sarah was a specialist in pediatrics and Kennedy was a surgeon. Kennedy reportedly gave a dying declaration that Sarah had given him an alcoholic beverage laced with bichloride of mercury. The state offered the testimony of a black servant named "Toodlums" who had seen the two together just before Kennedy's death. Other evidence revealed, however, Sarah had initiated an end to the relationship because she had become involved with another man. Sarah was to marry Captain Maull. There was speculation that Kennedy may have committed suicide. Authorities were so unclear of Sara's guilt that prison officials allowed her to remain at home while attorneys appealed her case. What's more, jurors were equally troubled at the prospect of sending Sarah to prison. One juror commented, "We wanted to make the punishment less severe, but could not under the verdict we had to decide on." Bessie Barry Kennedy, the surgeon's former wife, had much to gain by Sarah's conviction; Dr. Kennedy was heavily insured and if the state was to convict Sarah of murder, Mrs. Kennedy was assured a double indemnity life insurance award. Sarah remained free on bail while undergoing appeals of her murder conviction; actually, she spent much of the time convalescing in a hospital. The Mississippi Supreme Court ruled against Sarah stating that she had to serve the life term. Motivated by the Supreme Court's rendering of a three-to-three split decision in Sarah's appeal, Governor Martin Sennett Conner granted Sarah a full pardon in July 1935 claiming he was "being bombarded with mercy requests." He also claimed that he "had the benefit of information not available to the courts either in the original trial or on appeal" and that "she was wholly innocent of the charge upon which she was tried and convicted."[62] In contrast, one scholar claims that Governor Conner did not base his pardon decision upon her guilt or innocence but rather his chivalrous notions about sending a professional woman to prison; he had noted to friends that he could not send a woman like Sarah Dean to Parchman Prison no matter what she had done. Interestingly, Sarah Dean was the first woman to graduate from the University of Virginia's medical school where she received her medical degree in 1922.

In early August 1935, Marguerite Fox Dolbow, a former schoolteacher, lived with her wealthy farmer-husband, Harry Y. Dolbow, in Mannington Township in Salem County, New Jersey. The couple had a young daughter. Along with her paramour and childhood sweetheart, Norman Driscoll, Marguerite killed Harry in the barnyard of their farmhouse with blows to the head with a steel shaft. They wanted Harry dead so they could marry and collect on the $140,000 estate. Albert Drummond, a black farmhand who witnessed the killing, testified at the trial that Norman struck the fatal blows to Harry while Marguerite held a flashlight. The two concealed Harry's body in the barn. An investigation led to the arrest, indictment, and trial of Marguerite and Norman. Marguerite confessed to the murder shortly after her arrest, but later repudiated the statement. A Salem County jury found the two guilty of first-degree murder without recommendation of life imprisonment. Judge Frank E. Neutze sentenced the two to death in accordance with the state's death penalty statute. The judge sentenced them to die in the state's electric chair the week of March 15, 1936. Actually, the Salem County court tried Marguerite and Norman twice because Judge Neutze declared a mistrial in the first case. Apparently, a Mrs. Ella Holton attempted to influence her husband and juror on the case, Thomas Holton, when she passed him a note. Judge Neutze fined Mrs. Holton $250. The Court of Errors and Appeals of New Jersey affirmed Marguerite and Norman's conviction and death sentence. New Jersey Governor Harold G. Hoffman commuted their sentences to life in prison in 1936 most likely because of state's flawed death penalty statute that also earned Harriet Evans a commuted sentence.

In February 1937, Illinois Governor Henry Horner commuted the death sentences of Minnie Mitchell and Mildred Mary Bolton each to prison terms of 199 years. An East St. Louis jury had convicted Minnie and her husband Allen Mitchell of the insurance scheme murder of Sam Simpson. Governor Horner did not commute Allen Mitchell's death sentenced and he died in the electric chair the month that Governor Horner commuted Minnie's death sentence. Thirty-seven-year-old Mildred Bolton shot her husband Joseph Bolton to death in his insurance broker office.

In September 1941, upon the recommendation of the state's pardon board, Pennsylvania Governor Gifford Pinchot commuted the death sentence of Josephine Romualdo to a life prison term. A jury had convicted Josephine, a mother of two young children, of murdering her husband, lamplighter Antonio Romualdo, in September 1939. A native Brazilian and once a cigarette roller in a tobacco factory collected more than $10,000 in life insurance proceeds after she used arsenic to poison her husband. Josephine was one of two women sentenced to death in the mass murder insurance scheme in Philadelphia in the 1930s. In October 1952, Josephine solicited the state pardon board to commute her life sentence.

Lena Baker was a poor black woman unjustly convicted of murder by an all-white-male jury in Randolph County, Georgia, and executed in March 1945. Testimony from the one-day trial reveals that Lena shot and killed gristmill owner Ernest B. Knight during a struggle for a pistol she pulled from Knight when he threatened her with a metal pipe. Lena, a domestic servant and mother of three, apparently had an intimate relationship with Knight and the two often drank together that began after Knight hired her to care for him while he recovered from a broken leg. The struggle ensued when Lena attempted to break off the relationship. Lena never knew anything but poverty and hopelessness; she chopped cotton, cleaned houses, and took in laundry to support her mother and children. Some commentators have called the execution a "legal lynching." Sixty years after her execution in the state's electric chair, the Georgia Board of Pardons and Paroles pardoned Lena Baker for the murder claiming that her execution was "a grievous error." The pardon does not declare Lena's innocence, the Board simply suggested, "She could have been charged with voluntary manslaughter, rather than murder" and sentenced to 15 years in prison rather than sentenced to death. Given the white racial hostility toward blacks in the Jim Crow South, a black woman killing a white man, especially one with whom she had been sexually intimate, demanded execution. Lena Baker's last words before electrocution were "What I done, I did in self-defense or I would have been killed myself. Where I was, I could not overcome it. I am ready to meet my God."[63]

In April 1943, 18-year-old Bessie Mae Williams, 18-year-old Ralph Thompson, and 14-year-old Annie Mae Allison robbed and stabbed to death a Mecklenburg taxi cab driver named Mack Minyard in Charlotte. The three confessed to the killing and a county court judge sentenced the three to death. The state's Supreme Court upheld the convictions. Authorities executed Bessie Mae and Ralph in the state's gas chamber in December 1944. Governor J. Melville Broughton, however, commuted the death sentence of Annie Mae to life in prison the day before her scheduled execution. The governor commuted the death sentence because of Annie Mae's young age.

Emma Oliver had a long criminal record spanning over 20 years beginning in the 1930s that included more than 30 arrests for "vagrancy, prostitution, and acts of violence, including four arrests for murder, seven for aggravated assault, and one for attempted murder."[64] Emma served a short sentence for a murder conviction in the mid–1940s. Then in February 1949, a Bexar County jury convicted Emma of the knifing murder of a middle-aged black man named Herman Cohn with whom she had had a dispute over $3. The press tagged Emma as the "Straight Eight" for the eight-inch knife she used to kill her victims. When presiding judge W.W. McCrory sentenced Emma to death she became the first women sentenced to die in the state's electric chair. Emma appealed her conviction and death sentence to the Court of Criminal Appeals for Texas claiming, among other issues, that the prosecutor had made comments that amounted to prosecutorial misconduct, and racial bias in jury selection since "no member of the Negro race was appointed or served on the jury commission that selected the grand jurors, nor on the grand jury that indicted appellant." Finding no trial error, the court affirmed the conviction. There is evidence that Emma suffered from severe organic brain damage that manifested psychotic and delusional patterns. After Emma arrived on death row, a psychologist's report claimed, "It can be definitely stated that this individual is psychotic and in only limited contact with reality.... A delusional pattern is evidenced especially in the religious area. The emotions are confused and not in keeping with the situation.... The state of mental confusion and type of symptomology seem to indicate definite schizoid type of psychosis."[65] Convinced that Emma did not get a fair trial, a criminal court judge and county sheriff appealed the Texas Board of Pardons and Paroles for commutation of her death sentence. In June 1951,

Governor Allan Shivers commuted Emma's death sentence to life in prison. Emma died of cancer in prison in February 1963.

Another early female commutation took place when Indiana Governor George N. Craig commuted Opal Collins' death sentence to life in prison in December 1956. Earlier that May, an all-male jury convicted the newly married Opal of the murder of her husband, Benjamin Collins, Jr., while he sat in his wheelchair paralyzed from the shoulders down from an automobile accident suffered during Army service in 1947. Opal also killed her husband's mother, Mrs. Julia M. Collins, and her two young sisters-in-law, 14-year-old Martha Ann and 11-year-old Mary Sue. Opal killed the four with a .22 caliber rifle after Opal flew into a rage over a life insurance policy and the deed to a house that Opal wanted her husband to sign over to her. The couple had been married less than a month and the entire family lived in a small five-room bungalow in Hammond. The only source of income for the family was Benjamin's pension who had filed for divorce a few days before the killings. At Opal's trial in the Lake County Criminal Court building, Judge William J. Murray sentenced her to death. In a rare act of chivalry, Governor Craig commuted Opal's death sentence to a life term. He claimed, "The people of Indiana have never destroyed the life a woman. I fear if they did they would later be ashamed of it."[66]

In early June 1959, a Bibb County jury in Georgia convicted Anjette Donovan Lyles, a former Macon restaurant operator, of the poisoning murder of her first husband, Ben F. Lyles, Jr., in January 1952, her second husband, Joe Neal Gabber, in December 1955, her mother-in-law, Mrs. Lyles, Sr., in September 1957, and her nine-year-old daughter Marcia Elaine Lyles, in April 1958. Insurance proceeds garnered Anjette $32,000 that she spent mostly on a boyfriend. With no recommendation for leniency from the jury, the trial judge sentenced Anjette to death by electrocution. An appeals court upheld the conviction and death sentence. A state sanity commission confined Anjette to a mental hospital for the criminally insane; the commission deemed her "psychotic and insane." Psychiatrists, attorneys, and ministers sought a clemency hearing for Anjette and Governor Ernest Vandiver commuted her death sentence a life prison term at the Central State Hospital in Milledgeville. Anjette died at the hospital of natural causes at the age of 52 in December 1977.

In November 1958, two duck hunters stumbled over the body of Louise Bergen near a lake located about 50 miles northeast of Cincinnati, Ohio. A forensic examination of the body found that assailants had burned Louise's body while she was still alive. Louise was the mother of a young daughter. Police investigators learned that Louise was the wife of William Bergen but the couple had separated several months earlier. William was living with Edythe Margaret Klumpp, a 45-year-old divorcee and mother of four. William, Edythe and Louise met, and during the encounter a struggle developed over a gun that accidentally went off killing Louise. William and Edythe disposed of Louise's body later in the evening where the hunters had found the body. At William's encouragement, Edythe took the blame for the killing and in early July 1959, a Hamilton County jury convicted Edythe of Louise's murder and the trial court sentenced her to die in the electric chair. In January 1961, Ohio Governor Michael V. DiSalle, a strong opponent of capital punishment, commuted Edythe's death sentence to life in prison, and just before leaving office in January 1963, he commuted Edythe's first-degree murder to second-degree murder. The former governor explained the case against Edythe and his reason for commuting her conviction and death sentence in a series of articles published in newspapers in April 1969. After visiting Edythe in her prison cell at the women's reformatory at Maryville, the governor became convinced that William was actually responsible for Louise's death. Edythe remained at the Ohio Women's Reformatory until May 1971 when prison officials paroled her after serving 11 years. Edythe died of natural causes in Kentucky on Christmas Eve 1999.

Texas women who had their death sentences commuted to life in prison in the 1960s included a black fortuneteller and mother of three, Margaret "Maggie" Morgan. A jury convicted Maggie of orchestrating the 1959 murder of a Houston white woman named Wilma B. Selby. Wilma was the wife of an accountant named Joseph Selby who asked a worker at his favorite massage parlor, Patra Mae Bounds, to find him someone to kill his wife. Patra put Joseph in touch with Maggie who, in turn hired her long-time associate and black dockworker Clarence "Sack" Collins to kill Wilma for $1,600. Upon his arrest, Joseph admitted to police to attempting to hire someone to kill his wife and he implicated Maggie, who denied complicity in the killing. In fact, Maggie had masterminded the killing by first arranging for an acquaintance to work in the Selby home as a maid. On one occasion, Maggie went to his house to study the layout and plan the murder. After a candlelight dinner at a fashionable restaurant with his wife, Joseph had Wilma drop him off downtown and Wilma drove home. That night, Collins entered the Selby home and shot Wilma twice in the chest with a .22-caliber pistol. Maggie was the only principle involved in the murder who received the death penalty; courts sentenced Collins to 99 years in prison and Joseph Selby to life in prison. Governor Price Daniels commuted Maggie's death sentence in July 1961 citing the disproportionate sentence Maggie received compared to her co-defendants. Maggie died in prison in late 1970.

In May 1961, 19-year-old Jeannace June Freeman and her lover, 33-year-old Gertrude May Nunez Jackson, tossed the naked bodies of Gertrude's two young children, four-year-old Martha and six-year-old Larry, over a 350-foot cliff in Ogden State Park after Gertrude had bludgeoned the children to death with a tire iron. One report claims the children were interfering with the women's sexual relationship. Authorities determined that the children belonged to Gertrude and police arrested both women. A Jefferson County jury heard the case and found the women guilty of first-degree murder. In a plea bargain, Gertrude testified against Jeannace claiming she had actually killed Martha. Judge Robert H. Foley sentenced Gertrude to life in prison and authorities released her years later, while Jeannace received a death sentence. The Oregon Supreme Court affirmed Jeannace's guilty verdict and death sentence. Governor Mark Hatfield commuted Jeannace's death sentence to life in prison in 1964 after voters abolished the death penalty and officials released her from prison in July 1983. Jeannace changed her name to Wilma Lin Rhule after her release from prison. She received another jail sentence for pulling a knife on some acquaintances. Jeannace died in 2003.

In February 1932, a Maricopa County jury found Winnie Ruth (McKinnell) Judd guilty of the October 1931 murder of an openly bisexual couple, medical technician Agnes Ann LeRoi and schoolteacher Hedvig ("Sammy") Samuelson. Actually, Winnie's murder trial involved only the killing of Agnes, the court was to try Winnie later of Hedvig's murder but the trial never took place. Winnie was born the daughter of an Indiana Methodist preacher and became a homemaker in January 1905 when she married William C. Judd in 1924, a physician some 22 years older than was she. Six years later, Agnes and William were living apart, he in Mexico giving medical attention to the poor and she a medical secretary in Arizona. It was there that Winnie met and fell in love with a successful businessman named Jack Halloran with whom Agnes and Hedvig were also sexually involved. Soon, Winnie moved into the small studio-type duplex shared by Agnes and Hedvig. It appears that Winnie killed the two women because one or both of them became intimate with Jack. After killing the two women, Winnie dismembered the bodies and put the remains into two separate trunks that she shipped to Los Angeles. Police arrested Winnie when she went to claim the trunks at Union Station, which by that time had an offensive odor with blood leaking from the trunks. Winnie had shot both women with a .25-caliber gun. Police extradited Winnie to stand trial in Phoenix. Superior Court Judge Howard C. Speakman sentenced her to death by hanging, but the state adjudged Winnie insane and committed her to the Arizona State Mental Hospital where, and but for her seven escapes she spent nearly 40 years at the hospital. The state commuted her death sentence to life in prison in 1952, and upon recommendation of the Arizona Pardon Board, Governor John R. Williams commuted Winnie's sentence to time served in December 1971. Winnie Ruth Judd died in her sleep at the age of 93 in Phoenix in October 1998.

Clemency Post-*Gregg*

Since states resumed executions after the U.S. Supreme Court's decision in *Gregg v. Georgia*, some 22 state governors of both mainstream political parties have granted clemency to more than 150 battered women serving prison sentences for killing their abusive partners. One scholar has inventoried cases in which state governors have commuted women's prison sentences for killing abusive partners but where courts imposed a sentence less than death: Ohio Governor Richard F. Celeste granted clemency to 28 women, Maryland Governor William Schaefer commuted the sentences of eight women, Missouri Governor John Ashcroft reduced the sentences of two women, Iowa Governor Terry Brandstad commuted the sentence of one woman, California Governor Pete Wilson commuted the sentences of three women, Massachusetts Governor William Weld commuted the sentence of one woman, Colorado Governor Roy Romer reduced the sentences of three women, Florida Governor Lawton Chiles commuted the sentence of one woman, Kentucky Governor Brereton Jones commuted the sentences of nine women, New Hampshire Governor Steve Merrill gave a conditional pardon to one woman, New York Governor George Pataki reduced the sentence of one woman, Illinois Governor Jim Edgar reduced the sentence of one condemned woman, and Oregon Governor Barbara Roberts commuted the sentence of one woman.[67] Besides these commutations, Louisiana Governor Edwin Edwards who served from 1972 to 1980, and then again from 1984 to 1988, commuted the death sentence of Catherine Dodds to life in prison in June 1977, and then to 30 years in December 1986.

In the modern period of capital punishment, some state governors have declared moratoriums on state executions. In February 2014, for instance, Washington Governor Jay Inslee announced a moratorium on executions after he became convinced that the death penalty is "unequally applied" in the state. Though the governor has not commuted the sentences of the nine prisoners on death row or issued any pardons, he declared that he will issue a reprieve if presented with a death penalty for action. One reason for Governor Inslee's decision to reprieve death penalty cases that come before him is that, over the past several decades, some 60 percent of the 32 persons sentenced to die had their sentences overturned because of error. To Governor Inslee, "when the majority of death penalty sentences lead to reversal, the entire system itself must be called into question."[68] Seven other states besides Washington have governor- or court-ordered moratoriums; including California, Colorado, Maryland, North Carolina, Arkansas, Oregon and Kentucky. Together, these states have 25 female death row inmates awaiting execution. Besides challenging the fairness of states' capital justice systems, states are under moratoriums because of challenges to the lethal injection procedures. The status of capital punishment is unclear in 11 state death penalty systems and that of the federal government. Again, the unclear status of the death penalty in these states involves lethal injection challenges. In this regard, some state officials are contemplating the reintroduction of long-abandoned execution methods such as the firing squad, electric chair, and the gas chamber. Washington, for instance, has the only working gallows for hanging capital defendants in the country.

One of the more unusual cases of commutation in the post–*Gregg* era took place in January 1987 involving Catherine "Kitty" Dodds. In January 1975, a Baton Rouge jury convicted Catherine of the shooting death of her husband, Charles Dodds, a former New Orleans police sergeant outside his home as he stepped from his car after attending a night class at Loyola University. Police arrested Catherine at her husband's funeral. The court sentenced Catherine to die in the state's electric chair and officials sent her accomplice, Rodney Blackwell, to state prison on a life sentence. Apparently, Catherine hired the 18-year-old Blackwell to murder her husband for $1,000. Catherine claimed that her husband had brutally raped her. Several neighbors told police that Catherine was a battered wife who often sought refuge in their homes from an enraged Charles. There are conflicting reports as to whether the U.S. Supreme Court commuted Catherine's death sentence to life in prison in 1976 because of the *Furman* decision vacating capital sentences for persons on death row, or that then Governor Edwin Edwards commuted her death sentence to life in prison. In any event, Catherine escaped from a Baton Rouge hospital while serving her sentence at the Louisiana Correctional Institute for Women in August 1980. She became an accepted and quiet member of a small rural town (Peculiar) in Missouri where she adopted the name Linda Dee Winter from a tombstone and married a railroad worker named Charles Hayes. The FBI found Catherine in May 1982 after a local newspaper story exposed her for saving the life of an elderly man who had fallen into a ditch during a snowstorm. In December 1986, Governor Edwin Edwards commuted Catherine's life sentence to 30 years in prison and the state paroled her in 1992. A 1994 television movie, *The Conviction of Kitty Dodds*, tells Dodds' story. Catherine died in March 2009. Rodney Blackwell is serving his life sentence at the Louisiana State Penitentiary.

A Cecil County court in Maryland found Doris Ann Foster (also known as Nuketa Leah Ansara and Doris Ann Raven Darkwing Foster, an American Indian) guilty in February 1982 for the January 1981 robbery and fatal stabbing of Josephine Torres Dietrich, manager of the Maryland Manor Motel in northeast Maryland where Doris resided with her husband Tommy Foster. Doris reportedly stabbed Dietrich seven times in the heart and dumped her body into the Chesapeake and Delaware canal. Judge Donaldson C. Cole sentenced Doris to death. The Court of Appeals of Maryland reversed the trial courts judgment and remanded the case for a new trial in 1984 because Doris received an unfair trial when the court had erroneously excluded relevant evidence. In a second trial, a jury found Doris guilty of the robbery-murder and again sentenced her to death. In 1985, the Court of Appeals affirmed the lower court's finding and death sentence. Two years later Maryland Governor Harry Hughes commuted Doris's death sentence to life in prison without the possibility of parole, commenting "no other individual in recent memory has been sentenced to death in Maryland with as many mitigating circumstances."[69] Included among those mitigating factors was that Doris had a long history of alcohol and drug abuse. Spending the rest of her natural life in the Maryland Correctional Institution for Women may not have been an escape for Doris, however. In a 1983 *Time* article about Doris, the three-quarters Cherokee woman claimed she wanted to die: "I've put life in one hand and death in the other and weighted the two. To me, death is my only route to freedom."[70] Foster claimed that she had given her ordeal considerable thought and had even written the Maryland Court of Appeals and the U.S. Supreme Court requesting that the justices disregard any appeals on her behalf by lawyers. Doris wrote to the Chief Justice Warren E. Burger asking that she be executed immediately in the state's gas chamber than remain in "inhumane living conditions" at the Maryland Correctional Institution for Women at Jessup. Doris remains incarcerated at the Patuxent Institution Correctional Mental Health Center. Tommy Foster served a 12-year sentence for theft and obstruction of justice. Authorities have released him from prison.

Just prior to the expiration of his term as Ohio's Governor in January 1991, Richard F. Celeste commuted the death sentences of four black women to life in prison. These women were Debra Brown, Rosalie Grant, Elizabeth Green, and Beatrice Lampkin. To Governor Celeste, "the death penalty in cases involving women had not been administered fairly" in Ohio. Concerned with a "disturbing racial pattern" in sentencing women to death, Governor Celeste stated, "All of these women were black, three of the four were from Hamilton County, and to me it was absolutely clear that the death penalty in cases involving women had not been administered fairly. When the burden's falling that heavily on women of one race, heavily on women of one jurisdiction, it seemed to me compelling that they had been treated unfairly in terms of the law."[71] Incoming Governor George V. Voinovich challenged Celeste's granting of the commutation of eight inmates and one full pardon without reviewing any recommendations from the Ohio Adult Parole Authority and sought to void the pardons. The trial court held that the pardon and commutations were invalid, but the Court of Appeals for Franklin County reversed. The Ohio Supreme Court of upheld the Court of Appeals decision.

In June 1985, Hamilton County jury convicted Debra Denise Brown, along with Alton Coleman, for a serial murder crime spree across several states of the upper mid-west. Debra had confessed to her part in the murder of Tonnie Storey, Tamika Turks, Donna Williams, Virginia Temple, Rachelle Temple, and Marlene Walters, and that she participated in attempts to kill Annie Hillard, Palmer Jones, Frank Duvendack, Ralph Welch, and Harry Walters. The jury recommended the death penalty and the court imposed the punishment. Debra came to the attention of police in July 1984 when witnesses saw her and Alton with 15-year-old Tonnie Storey while on her way to summer school in Cincinnati. A realtor later found the partially decomposed body while showing a prospective buyer an abandoned building. Authorities identified the body as Tonnie Storey. Appellate courts affirmed the conviction and sentence. Ohio Governor Celeste, however, commuted her death sentence to life in prison without the possibility of parole in 1991 claiming that Debra is retarded (she has an IQ ranging from 59 to 74) and had a "master-slave" relationship with Alton.[72] Debra is currently serving two life sentences at the Ohio Reformatory for Women in Marysville. Ohio authorities executed Alton Coleman by lethal injection at the Southern Ohio Correctional Facility in April 2002.

As an unmarried welfare mother, Rosalie Grant had an exceedingly troubled childhood. Her mother, Wilma Grant, was a prostitute with an unpredictable, immature, and at times violent personality. She mistreated and often beat her children. Rosalie's father raped her when she was in her early teens, she was a high school dropout, and her mother stabbed her stepfather, Perry Ford, to death after forcing her children to hold Ford while she stabbed him. As one appellate justice put it, Rosalie was "raised in an environment where human life was not greatly valued." In April 1983, a Mahoning County jury convicted Rosalie after nine hours of deliberation on two counts of aggravated murder for the arson death of her two young sons, one-year-old Donovan and two-year-old Joseph. Arson investigators claimed Rosalie intentionally set fire to her boy's bedroom fueled by charcoal lighter fluid. Investigators later found her fingerprints on a can of the accelerant in a nearby vacant house. According to the coroner, the children died from shock and asphyxia due to their extensive burns and inhalation of smoke. The children also suffered thermal skull fractures, which occur when the brain boils and cracks the skull. Rosalie had purchased life insurance policies on the boys listing her as beneficiary two weeks before the fire. Judge Peter Economus sentenced Rosalie to death at the Marysville Reception Center and appellate courts affirmed her conviction and sentence. The Ohio Supreme Court affirmed the Court of Appeal's support for her conviction and death sentence. Governor Richard F. Celeste commuted Rosalie's death sentence to life imprisonment with no restriction as to parole eligibility. Rosalie remains incarcerated with a parole hearing scheduled for June 2018.

Elizabeth Green had a tormented childhood. As a three-year-old child, Green's mother tried to kill her and her alcoholic father often beat her. By the age of 13, authorities institutionalized Green at a juvenile facility, she suffered a miscarriage at 15 years old, and she turned to drugs and alcohol and was chemically dependent by the time she committed her capital offense. As developmentally impaired with an IQ of 66, Green could only function marginally. One psychiatrist described her as "ten, eleven, twelve; emotionally, much younger than that, more like seven or eight." In early January 1988, Elizabeth Green, along with Belinda Coulter, robbed and stabbed to death 70-year-old Tommie Willie and used the stolen money to purchase cocaine. It seems Elizabeth confessed to the crime once arrested by police. A Hamilton County jury found Green guilty of murder and the trial court sentenced her to death. On appeal, Associate Justice Pfeifer of the Supreme Court of Ohio dissented in affirming her conviction and death sentence and held that "Green's extraordinarily low IQ, relatively young age, chemical dependency, and terrible childhood and adolescence, are not outweighed by the aggravating circumstance present in this case."[73] Governor Celeste commuted Green's death sentence to life in prison without parole because of her low IQ. She is serving her sentence at the Ohio Reformatory for Women.

In 1991, a Hamilton County jury found Beatrice Lampkin guilty in the murder-for-hire of her husband, John D. Lampkin. Apparently, the Lampkins had a very troubled 25-year marriage with Beatrice suffering physical and emotional abuse. Beatrice hired John Curry for $10,000 and he shot John Lampkin in the forehead while John took out the garbage from the family residence. Beatrice eventually confessed to the crime after a two-month police investigation. The trial court sentenced Beatrice to death. Governor Celeste commuted Beatrice's death sentence to life without parole at the Ohio Reformatory for Women in Marysville because she was a battered wife. John Curry is serving a life sentence at the Warren Correctional Institution in Lebanon, Ohio.

Like many death row women, Guinevere Falakassa Garcia's childhood was horrific. At the tender age of 18 months old, Guinevere witnessed her mother commit suicide by jumping from the balcony of the family's apartment. Guinevere's father abandoned her leaving grandparents and an uncle to raise her. When Guinevere was six-years-old, her uncle gave her alcohol to calm her while he raped her, all with the knowledge of her grandmother. Reportedly, Guinevere's grandmother witnessed her son raping Guinevere, "but instead of stopping it, walked out of the room, closing the door behind her." Guinevere was an alcoholic by the age of 11 years old and was gang-raped at 15 years old. An Iranian who needed to marry a citizen paid Guinevere's grandfather $1,500 to do so and then immediately divorced the teenager. At 16, she was a prostitute, and by her seventeenth birthday, she was married and pregnant. Guinevere gave birth to Sara, and fearing child protective services would give Sara to her grandparents and uncle to relive her own experiences, Guinevere suffocated the eleven-month-old child. Guinevere confessed to the killing of her child when arrested on unrelated grounds and served 10 years of a 20-year prison sentence. While in prison, Guinevere married George Garcia, an acquaintance from her time as a prostitute. They had a tragic marriage in which George physically and sexually abused Guinevere. George reportedly mutilated Guinevere's genitalia with a broken beer bottle. A short four months after her release from prison for the murder of Sara, Guinevere shot and killed her husband with a .357 magnum while drunk in the parking lot of his Chicago suburban condominium ostensibly for a $30,000 life insurance policy. A jury found Guinevere guilty of first-degree murder and the trial judge, John J. Nelligan, sentenced her to death in the state's electric chair. In 1996, however, Illinois Governor Jim Edgar commuted Guinevere Garcia's death sentence to life in prison without parole and she currently resides at the Dwight Correctional Center. Edgar's reason for the commutation was that Guinevere's punishment of death was inappropriate for the crime she committed given the severity of her marital abuse.

In 1982, at the age of 17 and pregnant with twins, Judith Ann Neelley and her abusive husband, Alvin Howard Neelley, abducted 13-year-old Lisa Ann Millican from Riverbend Mall in Rome, Georgia. At the time of her abduction, Lisa was on an outing to a shopping center along with five other girls from the Ethel Harbst Home for neglected girls in Cedartown.

The couple took Lisa to a hotel where Alvin and Judith had sex with her over several days while Lisa remained handcuffed to the bed. The two then drove Lisa to a secluded area, handcuffed her to a tree, injected her six times with Liquid Plumber and Drano in the neck, arm, and buttocks, and when the child failed to succumb to the poison, Judith shot her three times in the back and dumped her body down an 80-foot cliff at Little River Canyon in Fort Payne, Alabama. Lisa's torture-murder was part of a crime spree in which Judith and Alvin also kidnapped and murdered Janice Kay Chatman. Tennessee authorities arrested the couple on an unrelated charge but extradited them to Alabama once officials connected the Neelley's to Millican's killing.

At trial, Judith's attorney raised issues concerning her deprived childhood that her mother and sister were excessively promiscuous, and that at 15 years of age Judith ran away from home and married Alvin Neelley, a 26-year-old ex-convict. Defense counsel explained how Judith was physically beaten and sexually abused, and how "she was brainwashed, and reduced to a vegetable and an instrument and extension of her husband," and as such, "Alvin forced her to procure young girls with small sex organs for him." The defense also claimed that Alvin subjected Judith "to such violent and gross mental, emotional, physical, and sexual abuse that she would have done anything, and did do everything he asked." Prosecutors painted a picture of Alvin as Frankenstein and Mrs. Neelley as The Bride of Frankenstein and exposed the jury to "accounts of putrid, pornographic, degrading, disgusting sex as Mrs. Neelley testified how she had been dominated, manipulated, and trained like an animal." She described herself as feeling like a piece of meat and it was argued that she had been reduced to a nonhuman. It is also troubling that Judith's defense counsel sexually harassed Judith with lewd and sexual remarks during interviews prior to trial.

Alvin Neelley was serving a life sentence in Georgia for Chatman's murder until he died in October 2005 at Bostic State Prison. A DeKalb County jury found Judith guilty of murder in March 1983 and recommended a sentence of life in prison without parole. Presiding Judge Randall Cole, however, overruled the jury's recommendation and sentenced Judith to die in the state's electric chair. All appellate courts including the U.S. Supreme Court rejected her appeals, but in January 1999, as he was leaving office, Alabama Governor Forrest "Fob" James commuted Judith's sentence to life in prison with the possibility of parole. James commuted Judith's sentence after receiving letters of appeal from Episcopal Church leaders, a former prosecution witness, and Judith's relatives. He was also concerned that Judge Cole had overruled a jury recommendation of life imprisonment for Judith. Other than these concerns, Governor James gave no public reason for granting clemency to Judith at the time. In later interviews, however, the former governor said he commuted Judith's sentence because the jury had recommended life without parole and not the death sentence. After considerable controversy concerning Judith's potential parole in 2014, the state legislature passed legislation concluding that a sentence of life without parole is automatic when commuting a death sentence. Legislators made the law retroactive to September 1998 to ensure Judith's lifelong incarceration. The Alabama Department of Corrections has removed her name from a list of potentially eligible parolees. She remains incarcerated at the Tutwiler Prison for Women in Wetumpka, Alabama.

Four women were among the 167 inmates that Governor George Ryan commuted in January 2003, including Bernina Mata (Latina), Latasha Pulliam (black), Dorothy Williams (black), and Jacqueline Annette Williams (black). The appellate record for Bernina Mata shows she had an exceedingly troubled history. Bernina suffered from chronic depression, mental illness, drug and alcohol abuse, her stepfather sexually abused as a child, and she was on anti-psychotic medication. A Boone County jury found Bernina guilty of the murder of John Draheim after an evening of drinking. Bernina had taken John back to her apartment and after a sexual encounter stabbed him repeatedly in the chest resulting in his death. Bernina's roommate Russell Grundmeier helped her dispose of Draheim's body by dumping it along a rural road in a nearby county. Grundmeier also helped Bernina clear the bedroom where she had killed Draheim, including painting the walls and removing the blood-soaked bed. Authorities eventually arrested Bernina and charged her with one count of first-degree murder and the trial court sentenced her to death. Her co-defendant received a sentence of four years in prison.

Bernina's case illustrates the sexuality bias plaguing Illinois, if not the nation's, capital sentencing scheme that Governor Ryan condemned when he commuted the sentences of death row prisoners—that Bernina was a Mexican lesbian who killed a heterosexual white male played heavily in her conviction and imposed death sentence particularly since the Illinois Governor's Commission on the Death Penalty specifically recommended abolition of sexual orientation as an aggravating factor in death penalty cases. The most daunting aspect of Bernina's trial was the state attorney's unrelenting reference to Bernina's lesbianism as the motive behind Draheim's killing. Prosecutor Owens referred to Bernina as a "hard core" lesbian and a "man-hating lesbian" who was more likely to kill a man who made an unwanted pass at her than a heterosexual woman—that is, "a normal heterosexual woman would not be so offended by such conduct as to murder." To make the case against Bernina as a cold and calculating lesbian murderer, Owen literally bombarded every stage of the trial with his lesbian fanaticism; he referenced Bernina's lesbianism 17 times throughout the trial. To make the jury believe Bernina was executable, Owen called witnesses to confirm her lesbianism and used reading material found in her apartment to evidence her motive to kill. Yet, to Bernina's appellate attorney, Joey Mogul, with the People's Law Office in Chicago,

> Ms. Mata's lesbianism was not probative of her alleged intent or motive to kill nor should it have been proof of an aggravating circumstance. The State offered no scientific evidence or expert testimony to substantiate its theory that lesbians are predisposed to hate men or kill. As we all know, a defendant's heterosexual orientation is not useful fodder for the State to exploit in a murder case. In fact, it would be absurd for a prosecutor to argue a defendant's heterosexuality caused that person to kill. It should have been impermissible for this prosecutor to argue Ms. Mata's sexual orientation caused her to kill. But as late as 1999, prosecutors advanced this precise argument to excuse the admission of a wealth of prejudicial irrelevant evidence to taint Ms. Mata before the jury.[74]

In the child murder case of Latasha Pulliam, medical experts testified that she is brain damaged from fetal alcohol syndrome and a premature birth, she has febrile seizures, and anoxia due to submersion in a bathtub, ingesting of iron and lead, blows to the head, and illicit drug use. Latasha suffered severe sexual abuse at the hands of her mother and her mother's boyfriends, and as a teenager, Latacha bore children by two of her mother's boyfriends. Latasha is mildly retarded with an IQ of 69 and she was drug-crazed when in March 1991 in Chicago, Latasha and her boyfriend, codefendant Dwight Jordan, kidnapped six-year-old Shenosha Richard while she played in her South Side Chicago neighborhood with promises to the child of snacks and a movie. The couple committed atrocious sexual acts against young Shenosha. Latasha gave a signed, court-reported confession following her arrest for murder. Latasha confessed to authorities that she had taken young Shenosha to her apartment's bedroom. Afterwards, Latasha went to the kitchen to use cocaine, and when she returned to bedroom, Shenosha was on the floor crying with her underwear down to her knees and Jordan was behind her attempting to attain an erection. Jordan then picked up a shoe polish bottle and inserted it into the Shenosha's rectum. Latasha placed the straight end of a hammer into Shenosha's vagina while Jordan continued inserting the shoe polish bottle into her rectum. Shenosha was crying, and when Latasha put her hand over Shenosha's mouth, Shenosha attempted to scream. Defendant took an electrical cord, wrapped it around Shenosha's neck, and began strangling her. Latasha then took Shenosha to an empty apartment in the building and continued strangling her with the cord for 10 minutes until she heard a knock at the door at the apartment. Latasha put Shenosha in a closet in the vacant apartment. Returning to the closet, Latasha found Shenosha was not breathing and then hit Shenosha over the head several times with a hammer. Latasha then put Shenosha's lifeless body in a garbage can, struck her repeatedly in the head with a two-by-four, and covered Shenosha's body with garbage.

Medical evidence showed that Shenosha suffered 42 injuries including two puncture wounds to her chest that damaged her lungs and coronary artery, and lacerations on her head that perforated her skull. Shenosha also suffered from numerous lacerations to her anus and vagina. Cook County authorities indicted Latasha for murder, aggravated criminal sexual assault, aggravated kidnapping, and aggravated unlawful restraint. A Dade County jury convicted Latasha of murder, aggravated criminal sexual assault, and aggravated kidnapping. The trial judge sentenced Latasha to death for the murder conviction and to three consecutive prison terms of 60 years, 30 years, and 15 years on the remaining convictions. Governor Ryan's commutation ensures that Latasha will not suffer execution, but she will certainly spend the rest of her life in prison with no possibility of parole.

In November 1995, Jacqueline Annette Williams, her cousin Levern Ward, and her boyfriend Fedell Caffey, shot and stabbed to death Deborah Evans and her children, 10-year-old Samantha, seven-year-old Joshua, and two-year-old Jordan in their apartment in Addison, Illinois. Deborah Evans was nine months pregnant when the defendants cut the baby she was carrying from her womb. Levern Ward was Deborah's ex-boyfriend and the unborn baby's father. They killed Samantha in the apartment and left Jordan alone with his dead mother and sister. Authorities found Joshua's body discarded in an alleyway a day after the killings. Acting on a tip, police found and arrested Jacqueline with the new born. After nearly five hours of deliberation, a DuPage County jury found Jacqueline guilty of the first-degree murders of the Evans family and for the aggravated kidnappings of Joshua and the newborn named Elijah. The presiding circuit court Judge Peter Dockery sentenced Jacqueline to death and consecutive 15-year sentences for the other offenses. Levern Ward and Fedell Caffey are serving life sentences at the Menard Correctional Facility and both are ineligible for parole. Jacqueline remains housed at the state's Dwight Correctional Center and is ineligible for parole.

In 1985, Gaile Kirksey Owens solicited several men to kill her husband, Ronald (Ryan) Owens. One of the men was Sidney Porterfield, who Gaile met with on three separate occasions to discuss the murder and to whom she offered to pay $17,000. In February of that year, Porterfield brutally and savagely killed Ronald in the family's home. Porterfield hit Ronald 21 times over the head with a tire iron and with such force that he fragmented Ronald's skull, drove those pieces into his brain, and drove his face into the floor. A pathologist's report showed extensive injuries to Ronald's hands, indicating that he had been trying to cover his head with his hands during the savage attack. Police learned of the murder-for-hire when another man that Gaile had solicited, George James, feared that he might be a murder suspect and contacted police. Gaile ultimately confessed to hiring Porterfield to commit the murder and explained to police that she had Ronald killed because "we've just had a bad marriage over the years, and I just felt like he had been cruel to me. There was very little physical violence." The prosecution offered both Gaile and Porterfield a life sentence in return for a guilty plea so long as both of them accepting the plea. Gaile accepted the district attorney's offer but Porterfield refused. As a result, the prosecutor withdrew the offer and tried Gaile and Porterfield jointly for first-degree murder. A Shelby County jury found Gaile guilty of two aggravating circumstances, murder-for-hire, and a murder that was "especially heinous, atrocious, or cruel" convicted Gaile and Porterfield of first-degree murder and the trial court sentenced them to death. By December 2008, Gaile had lost all appeals and Tennessee had scheduled her for execution.

The Shelby County jury that convicted Gaile K. Owens of murder in 1988 heard little of the mental, physical, and sexual cruelty she suffered at the hands of her husband, Ronald (Ryan) Owens. Responding to her appeal before the Sixth Circuit of the U.S. Court of Appeals, Justice Gil Merritt claimed that the majority opinion "slants and misconceives relevant facts and law in this case on each of the three major issues in order to uphold the death penalty." Justice Merritt's passionate dissent criticized his fellow justices for disregarding a prosecutorial cover-up of exculpatory evidence concerning Ronald Owens's marital infidelities, the failure of defense counsel to adequately investigate and develop a battered-wife defense, and the refusal of the Memphis trial court to allow evidence of a battered-wife defense.

Justice Merritt's first claim was that the Memphis district attorney's office engaged in systemic falsehoods during the period of Gaile's trial; the prosecution blatantly lied to the trial court that it did not have in its possession sexually explicit love letters between Ronald Owens and one of his many girlfriends, Gayla Scott. Gaile had requested from the state prosecutor any information it had in its possession that her husband "had numerous girlfriends, extra-marital sexual affairs involving unusual sexual proclivities and/or perversions." The evidentiary value of these letters to Gaile's potential battered-wife defense was that "these proclivities, perversions and affairs were flaunted and visited upon [Gaile] with such regularity and in such ways as to contribute to [her] state of mind and mental condition." The state's attorney clearly denied Gaile her rights under *Brady* when he argued before the trial court that "everything we have in the way of any kind of physical evidence, any piece of paper, any notebook—anything along those lines, letters and etc. that we have, we have made available to them [to Gaile and her lawyer]." Thus, as Justice Merritt points out, "rather than tell the jury the truth about the matter, the prosecution told the jury that she killed her husband to get insurance money." Second, had defense lawyers performed an adequate investigation of Gaile's case as required by the American Bar Association and well-established case law, Justice Merritt explicated the evidence that counsel could have presented to the jury:

> Ron Owens was abusive toward Ms. Owens. He subjected her to physical, emotional, and sexual abuse beginning with their wedding night when he was forceful and impatient, demanding sex immediately upon entering their hotel room. When Ms. Owens revealed to her new husband that she was in great pain and bleeding profusely, he called her frigid, and angrily left the hotel room stating that "If you won't, I know where I can find someone who will."
> Ron Owens inserted large objects into Ms. Owens's vagina and rectum, causing her pain and bleeding. At one point, Mr. Owens inserted a wine bottle into Ms. Owens's vagina and manipulated it with such vigor that it broke inside her. Mr. Owens also used a penis-shaped marijuana pipe to penetrate Ms. Owens's vagina which caused her pain and humiliation.
> Ron Owens's sexually abusive behavior not only placed Ms. Owens at risk, but also risked the life of their unborn son. The night before the birth of her second son, Ron Owens forced Ms. Owens to engage in such brutal sexual intercourse that Ms. Owens's placenta partially detached, requiring an emergency C-section to save Ms. Owens and her son.
> Ron Owens not only sexually abused Ms. Owens, but was also emotionally abusive toward her. Upon the birth of her children, Mr. Owens accused Ms. Owens of not taking properly her birth control pills and complained that the children would be an unbearable financial burden. In addition, Mr. Owens regularly berated Ms. Owens telling her, among other things, that "she did not sweat much for a fat person."
> Ron Owens was also deceitful and unfaithful to Ms. Owens. Mr. Owens had lied to Ms. Owens and to others about his background, falsely claiming that he volunteered to serve as a medic in

Vietnam, and that he was shot twice and contacted Malaria while in Vietnam. Moreover, Mr. Owens had lied about his credentials on a job application at Baptist Hospital, stating that he had a B.S. degree when he did not.

What's more, defense counsel failed to hire expert witnesses to explain that Gaile suffered from a recognized personality disorder of battered wife syndrome and that "the traumatic treatment Mrs. Owens experienced in childhood and as the wife a sadistic husband created an intense anxiety disorder resulting in impulsive actions in conflict with her core values and beliefs." Because of incompetent and ineffective counsel in her capital case, Gaile's jury heard nothing about her "family history or the sadistic treatment she received at the hands of her husband." Justice Merritt passionately scolded his colleagues in the majority for not recognizing that "any relevant mitigating evidence" is admissible at a capital sentencing hearing. To Justice Merritt, the majority mistakenly claimed that Gaile's "failed plea negotiations" with the state's attorney could not constitute mitigating evidence, and so doing, the trial court unconstitutionally prevented Gaile from offering testimony that she accepted the state's plea negotiation of a guilty verdict in return for a life sentence.[75] Governor Phil Bredesen commuted Gaile Owens' death sentence to life in prison. He did so because of a plea bargain offer that the state later rescinded, and to make Gaile's sentence consistent with verdicts delivered in similar cases in Tennessee. Authorities housed Gaile at the Tennessee Prison for Women until her release on parole in September 2011. Sidney Porterfield remains on death row at the Riverbend Maximum Security Institution.

Espy's inventory identifies Pima County officials in territorial Arizona hanging a white woman named Dolores Moore in 1865 for murder. Yet, another source explains that an Arizona judge sentenced Dolores to hang for the murder of her husband but that the territorial governor commuted her sentence to life in prison. Her name does not appear in territorial prison records, however. To one researcher, Dolores was an unmarried Mexican girl who lived with her mother or aunt when officials convicted her of murder and sentenced her to hang. The territorial governor commuted her sentence conditioned upon Dolores leaving the country and she and her companion return to Mexico.

Concluding Remarks

Scholars have overlooked the historical contours of executive clemency granted explicitly to condemned women in the United States. The construction of a preliminary inventory of that population reveals relatively few condemned women have benefited from executive clemency though modernly women are more likely than men to garner the attention of state governors. Still, nearly a fifth of those clemency decisions involved pardons for women unjustly jailed and executed for witchcraft. Many of the cases in the inventory reveal that executive clemency often has to do with the individual characteristics of women such as "a fit object for mercy," offenders' age, impoverishment, pregnancy, remorsefulness, and mental and physical health. Speculation about a female defendant's guilt and evidentiary problems, or that the death sentence was patently unfair or disproportionately severe, weighed heavily with state governors and their willingness to grant clemency to women. Governors also seem cognizant that women often lash out against abusive husbands in domestic violence cases and commuted those sentences accordingly. Not surprisingly, most state governors apparently held little notions of chivalry against executing women; chivalry appears to be more of a rational driving public sentiment about executing women than the sentiment of state governors. State governors commuted the death sentences of women when public dissent challenged a woman's death sentence or prolonged prison term.

Such dissention may have caused states' governors to take pause that should they not act, public opposition may pose a threat to their chances for re-election. This is a popular notion based upon conjecture, however, since recent research shows that governors actually do not endure "any measurable political consequences for granting clemency to death row inmates."[76] Still, this may not be the case historically.

> "The rarity of women on death row may come down to the powerlessness of women in the context of patriarchy."[1]

9

The Female Death Row Population

As a guiding principal in death penalty cases, the U.S. Supreme Court made it clear in *Kennedy v. Louisiana* that "capital punishment must be limited to those offenders who commit a narrow category of the most serious crimes and whose extreme culpability makes them the most deserving of execution."[2] Though the victims of current death row women have suffered extreme cruelty and at times grotesque physical mutilation, condemned women are not categorically murderers of the most evil sort—*the worst of the worst*. Women on the nation's death rows are not particularly different from women who have committed similar crimes but escaped the death penalty. Atwell has put the issue succinctly:

> [T]he small percentage of accused women murderers who are subjected to capital punishment are distinguished not by the atrociousness of their crimes, but instead by the ways in which their alleged offenses and their character as presented by the media, the prosecution, and often even by their defense attorneys, violated norms of the patriarchal society. These women were not the worst of the worst. Rather they represented the worst kind of failure to live up to gendered expectation. They were portrayed by the prosecution as bad mothers, unfaithful wives, greedy bitches, promiscuous hussies, or lesbians. And although such personal behaviors, if true, do not qualify as aggravating circumstances in the criminal courts, they often served to stigmatize the accused and position her as an unworthy outsider.[3]

Actually, justice authorities have sentenced most female killers to prison terms or stays in mental institutions. Yet, as one legal expert explains, "the notion that society is capable of selecting the worst of the worst to have their lives extinguished is fundamentally flawed.... The system is absolutely incapable of [discerning] which offender is deserving of the ultimate penalty."[4] The penalty of death is not limited to the most egregious of cases and "tend[s] to be a fairly random selection from all those arrested for homicide ... a selection skewed by race, sex, poverty level, and just the luck of the draw as to who has been their judge, jury, and defense counsel."[5] In a recent study of Connecticut's death penalty scheme, for instance, Stanford Law Professor John Donohue showed that over a 34-year period ending in 2007, "inmates on death row are indistinguishable from equally violent offenders who escape that penalty. It shows that the process in Connecticut—similar to those in other death penalty states—is utterly arbitrary and discriminatory." Clearly, Connecticut has not limited imposition of the death penalty to the worst of the worst "since many equally egregious or more egregious cases result in non-death sentences."[6] Florida too does not limit imposition of the death penalty to those women who commit the worst of the worst murders. In 2014, for instance, Circuit Judge Randell H. Rowe III sentenced Angela Stoldt to life in prison without parole for the ghoulish killing of her neighbor. Apparently, Angela stabbed her neighbor in the eye with an ice pick and strangled him, dismembered his body, cooked the body parts in her kitchen, and then distributed the parts through Volusia County.

The Tennessee cases of Mary Freeman Winkler and Gaile Kirksey Owens demonstrate how state justice systems render different punishments in similar cases. A Tennessee court convicted Mary Winkler of voluntary manslaughter in the shotgun killing of her minister husband in 2006 and sentenced her to 67 days in a mental health facility. Authorities eventually released Mary. In contrast, a Tennessee court convicted Gaile Owens of first-degree murder and sentenced her to death. Gaile had hired Sidney Porterfield to kill her husband Ronald. Porterfield beat Ronald to death with a tire iron. Governor Phil Bredesen granted Gaile executive clemency due to her age and mental capacity and authorities released her from custody in September 2011. If not for Governor Bredesen's commutation of Gaile's death sentence, she would have died in the state's death chamber. There are stark similarities between these cases that challenge notions of justice in women's death sentences. As one commentator points out, "The dramatic difference in the sentences received by Winkler and Owens relates directly to the manner in which the two cases were tried, how their separate teams of lawyers handled their cases and how two different judges dealt with their battered woman defenses."[7] For one, Mary took the witness stand in her defense and told the trial jury about her years of mental and sexual abuse by her husband. Gaile, however, chose not to take the witness stand and inform the jury of her decades of physical and emotional abuse to protect her children from knowing of the abuse she suffered from their father. For another, Mary's trial attorneys were familiar with the "battered woman defense" and used it to convince a jury that Mary did not deserve punishment from the courts, but help from mental health professionals. Gaile's lawyers were unfamiliar with the defense. It was only after appeals lawyers took over the case did one hear of her victimization at the hands of her husband. In other words, the level of legal competency of female capital defendants' lawyers often dictates whether a state will condemn and execute a woman defendant. Journalist John Seigenthaler differentiated the two condemned women this way:

> Both women, raised as fundamentalist Christians, suffered severe physical, sexual and emotional abuse from the spouses they killed; Both had small children—all younger than 12 at the time of the murders; Both of them were examined—some 20 years apart—by the same psychologist, Dr. Lynne Zager of Memphis, who said that both suffered from battered woman's syndrome—a condition that courts have recognized as "a female who is the victim of consistent, severe domestic violence;" Both had concealed from relatives and close friends the suffering they endured at the hands of their husbands; both minimized the abuse when first questioned by police; Both were in financially troubled marriages and constantly were blamed by their husbands for being "spendthrift wives." Winkler had kited checks and argued with her husband about money the night before she killed him. Owens had stolen money from her employer, a doctor; both women confessed when questioned by police, and both told the officers they blamed themselves for problems in their marriage; in both cases, the spousal abuse included lurid sexual details. In Owens' case, the sexual encounters were more violent and involved her husband's extramarital affairs.[8]

Seigenthaler identifies nine other Tennessee cases where courts have imposed disparate levels of punishment to female killers.[9] Of the nine cases, courts granted the murderers full probation, in one case a court sentenced a woman to a life sentence but commuted the sentence to 18 months imprisonment and probation. In another case, a court sentenced the female killer to a 15-year prison term but she received early parole. Courts sentenced four of the nine women to life sentences, two of whom authorities have paroled and the two others are entitled to parole hearings. Only Gaile Owens received a death sentence and a scheduled execution. All nine cases involved brutal murders of husbands and illustrate "the failure of some defense lawyers to effectively present battered woman syndrome testimony."[10]

Institutional Indifference

There is an institutional disregard for the safety and welfare of death row women. The American Civil Liberties Union (ACLU) has detailed the systemic oppression faced daily by death row women. To gain insight into the lives of condemned women, legal researchers consulted court opinions, newspaper articles, defense attorneys, research compiled by a national clearinghouse, and survey questionnaires of death row women. Accordingly, *legal factors* determinative of whether women end up on death row include ineffective assistance of counsel, official misconduct of prosecutors and law enforcement, and the culpability and lenient treatment of co-defendants. *Social factors* leading to capital convictions of women include the sexual orientation of female defendants, childhood and adult victimization, alcohol and drug addiction, and mental illness. The report found that death row women live in isolation, are mistreated by prison guards, sexually harassed and assaulted by prison staff, lack adequate access to medical and mental health care, live in indecent and unsanitary prison conditions, have restricted visits and telephone contacts, and denied access to religious and recreational programs and activities.

A U.S. Department of Justice study in August 2010 complements the findings revealed in the ACLU study. This research showed that female inmates are more than twice as likely as male inmates to report experiencing inmate-on-inmate sexual victimization but less likely than male inmates to report sexual activity with facility staff. The institutional victimization of death row women essentially continues their life-long patterns of sexual abuse beginning at very young ages, including rape as young as 10 years old. One consistent characteristic among women prisoners is that they share "early lives of abuse so severe that most people can't grasp its impact."[11] The sadistic abuse suffered by women during childhood followed them into adult relationships with violent partners. Death row women invariably suffer from disabling mental illnesses because of their continued sexual and physical victimization.

The ACLU published another report in July 2013 concerning the psychological and psychiatric effects of years of solitary confinement on death row prisoners. Researchers surveyed capital defense attorneys who regularly visit prisoners on death row and, in some limited cases, other persons with direct knowledge of death row conditions. The report reveals that 93 percent of states lock up their death row prisoners for 22 or more hours per day. Human contact for death row is generally restricted to brief interactions with corrections officers and, for some prisoners, occasional encounters with healthcare providers or attorneys. A majority of states do not allow death row prisoners to have access to work or employment opportunities, or provide access to educational or vocational programming of any kind. The negative physiological and psychological effects of solitary confinement on death row inmates are extreme and increase risks of inmate suicide and self-mutilization.

In a more recent study on the unique psychological and psychiatric harmful effects of solitary confinement of women in prisons and jails nationwide, researchers explain that such confinement exacerbates mental illnesses among women and often re-traumatizes women with histories of past abuse. Women in solitary confinement are often more vulnerable to abuse by correctional officers who often use solitary confinement to punish women who report abusive treatment while in prison. Solitary confinement puts at risk the relationship between mothers and their children and specifically harms children. At particular risk of the psychological harms of solitary confinement are pregnant female inmates because of the lack of access to prenatal care.

California's treatment of female death row inmates is far poorer than the treatment of death row men. California prison officials lock 66-year-old Maureen McDermott inside a six by 12 foot cell with solid steel doors for 23 hours a day. She has no contact with other inmates and lives a life of almost complete isolation. On an average day, she leaves her cell for about an hour, only to exercise alone on a small patch of black top behind the prison. Prison guards allow Maureen to leave her cell three times a week for showers. In contrast, guards allow male death row inmates to leave their cells for as long as six hours to play cards or table tennis, or just meander about walkways and visit with other inmates. On the yard, condemned male inmates can play basketball, lift weights or work out on punching bags. They also have access to typewriters and allowed contact visits. McDermott and other death row women must communicate by telephone with visitors because of a glass separation. This unequal treatment permeates the American prison system—"Correctional officials throughout the country have argued that the number of females in the general prison population is so small that it is not economically feasible to provide programs—such as job training and recreational facilities—comparable to the men's prisons."[12] Sixty-nine-year-old Donna Roberts faces similar conditions in Ohio's death row where officials treat her differently than condemned male inmates. From a human rights perspective, conditions on America's death rows for women amount to "cruel, inhumane, or degrading treatment, and could also constitute torture."[13]

Women Foreign Nationals

Pursuant to Article 36 of the Vienna Convention on Consular Relations and Optional Protocols (VCCR) of 1963, local arresting authorities of all 172 signatories are required to notify without delay detained foreign nationals of their right to communicate with their respective consular representative. Ratified by the U.S. Senate in 1969, the provision assures that unfamiliar legal systems do not subject foreign nationals to trial and condemn them to death without the benefit of support from authorities of their native countries. Though United States authorities insist that foreign governments promptly advise the more than 6,000 Americans jailed in foreign countries of their right to contact their consular representative, state and federal officials regularly ignore consulate rights to foreign nationals arrested in the United States. Many states also do not comply with the treaty. Of the foreign national death penalty cases reviewed by the organization, 95 percent of state cases and 75 percent of federal cases have not met the requirements of the treaty. The federal government and 16 states presently house 141 foreign nationals representing 31 different nationalities on death row. Most of these foreign prisoners are Mexican nationals held in California, Texas, and Florida. Two of these foreign national prisoners are women, Linda Anita Carty (Britain) and Dora Gudiño Zamudio (Mexico).

A Harris County grand jury in Texas indicted Linda Carty in 2001 for the murder of Joana Rodriquez during the course of a kidnapping of Rodriguez and her newborn son. In the early morning hours of May 2001, Chris Robinson, Gerald Anderson, and Carlos William broke down the door of Raymundo Cabrera and Joana Rodriguez's apartment in Houston. Cabrera's cousin, Rigoberto Cardenas, shared the apartment with the couple and their newborn baby boy, Ray Cabrera. The intruders pistol-whipped Cabrera, Cardenas, and demanded drugs and money. Finding little money and no drugs, the gunmen abducted Joana and the baby. Police investigations reveal that Linda Carty planned and orchestrated the ghoulish plot to kidnap and murder Joana Rodriguez and abduct her baby because Linda wanted the infant as her own after she had suffered several miscarriages. Upon her arrest, Linda told police they could find the infant in northeast Houston. Police found the baby in a car with its engine running and Joana's body in the trunk of another car parked nearby where her murderer had suffocated her with duct-tape over her mouth and a plastic bag placed around her head.

Linda is a foreign national from St. Kitt in the British West Indies and holds both British and United States citizenship. The British consulate did not learn of Linda's legal troubles until 2002, more than a year after she was already on death row. Since Linda is a foreign national,

Texas authorities were required to notify the British consulate of Linda's arrest "without delay," and appellate lawyers claim the outcome of Linda's trial would have been different had she been afforded the protections of the British government. The British press has been exceedingly critical of Linda's trial, calling it "catastrophically flawed." Defense attorney Jerry Guerinot poorly represented Linda at trial; he met with Linda for only 15 minutes two weeks before her trial, he failed to call witnesses who could have testified on Linda's behalf, and he neglected to contact the British Consulate for legal assistance. To one commentator, "It is no exaggeration to suggest that Mr. Guerinot has perhaps the worst record of any capital lawyer in the United States."[14] One uncalled witness was Charlie Mathis, a Drug Enforcement Agency officer for whom Linda claimed she had worked as an informant. The DEA claimed at one of her appeals that the association did not believe Linda murdered Joana Rodriguez. In 2009, Linda filed a habeas petition under the Antiterrorism and Effective Death Penalty Act in the U.S. District Court for the Southern District of Texas but the court affirmed the district court's judgment denying Linda habeas relief. In 2010, the U.S. Supreme Court rejected Linda's application to review her conviction and death sentence. Linda has lost all appeals and authorities anticipate that state officials will soon set her execution date.

Dora Buenrostro is a condemned foreign national from Mexico. Dora killed her three children in late October 1994; she stabbed her four-year-old daughter Deidra in her throat with a ballpoint pen as she sat in a child safety seat in an abandoned car. Days later, police reported that Dora also murdered her nine-year-old daughter Susana and eight-year-old son Vincente by stabbing them in the throat as they slept in the living room of their San Jacinto apartment in southern California. After killing the children, Dora reported to police that her husband, Alejandro Buenrostro, had murdered their children. A Riverside County jury found Dora guilty of first-degree murder of her children and recommended the death penalty. Superior Court Judge Patrick Magers found the murders particularly callous and sentenced Dora to death. Dora may have murdered her children to inflame her husband. Dora is mentally ill and suffering from paranoia, psychosis, and hallucinations, but the trial jury ignored defense counsel's claim that Dora was mentally incompetent. Consular violations are prevalent in her case, and the California Supreme Court has yet to hear an appeal.

Deaths of Condemned Women by Natural Causes

Two death row women have died of natural causes in Nevada and California in recent years while awaiting execution. Priscilla Joyce Ford (Black) and Caroline Young (Brazilian) died in 2005. On Thanksgiving Day in 1980, Priscilla Ford intentionally drove her Lincoln Continental onto a crowded sidewalk in Reno, Nevada, killing seven people and injuring more than 20 others. After a four-month trial, a Washoe County jury found Priscilla guilty of murder and attempted murder and District Court Judge John W. Barrett sentenced Priscilla to death on the murder convictions and consecutive sentences of 20 years' imprisonment on each of the convictions for attempted murder. The Supreme Court of Nevada affirmed the first-degree and attempted murder counts and found that Priscilla's death sentence was not excessive and proportionate to the penalty imposed in similar cases in Nevada.

Priscilla's mental competency was an issue at her trial, but expert medical testimony claimed that although Priscilla was suffering from several mental illnesses, she nonetheless knew the difference between right and wrong. Priscilla died in late January 2005 at the age of 75 while on death row at the Southern Nevada Women's Correctional Center in Las Vegas. She had been suffering from emphysema. Priscilla had exhausted her state appeals and had federal appeals forthcoming to challenge her death sentence. Priscilla was a Michigan native with an IQ of 140 who had earned a bachelor's degree in education and worked for several years as a schoolteacher. Priscilla had moved to Reno from Maine about three weeks before the rampage. She apparently moved back to Reno after seven years to look for her missing daughter, Wynter Scott, whom authorities had placed in a foster home in 1973 after Priscilla's arrest for trespassing. At the time of the Reno incident, Priscilla worked at a Macy's department store in Reno as a gift-wrapper. In the 1970s, Priscilla sought treatment for mental illness when mental health experts diagnosed her as a paranoid schizophrenic with violent tendencies.

After a short deliberation in 1995, an Alameda County (California) jury convicted Caroline Young of the stabbing murders two years earlier of her six-year-old grandson Darin Torres and her four-year-old granddaughter Dai-Zshia Torres. Superior Court Judge Stanley Golden sentenced Caroline to death. There is no available appellate record of the case but alternative sources provide some details of the facts surrounding the murders. O'Shea notes that Caroline was distraught over losing custody of the children to their father; she was caring for the children because authorities deemed their mother, Vanessa, unfit to care for the children given a jail sentence for prostitution and drug dealing. The children's father was to take custody of the children the day Caroline killed them. She first slit Darin's throat, and while Vanessa called police, Caroline stabbed Dai-Zshia and then stabbed herself in the abdomen. Caroline suffered from mental illness. While serving her death sentence, Caroline died of kidney failure in September 2005 at the age of 61 at Fresno's University Medical Center.

Characteristics of the Female Death Row Population

The historical data on men under death sentences is mostly uninterrupted since 1880, yet there is little information on death row women throughout much of the nation's criminal justice past. For that reason, it is difficult to paint much of a historical portrait of America's female death row population. Even so, the fragmented information on death row women reveals that females have historically comprised a very small proportion of the nation's condemned prisoner population. Available historical corrections data show that two women were under death sentences in 1880, one in 1890, two in 1904, and none in 1910. Women were 2.5 percent of the nation's death row population in 1880, 0.6 percent in 1890, and 1.9 percent in 1904. Records on the number of women received under death sentences from 1911 through 1929 are unavailable though prison officials received 17 death row women in the 1930s. In the 1930s, excluding 1933 where data on female death row inmates is unavailable, on average women comprised 1.8 percent of the total number of persons received under sentences of death. The 11 condemned women on death row from 1940 to 1946 were slightly more than 2.0 percent of the nation's total death row population. One should note that female death row figures from 1930 to 1946 do not include condemned women housed in Alabama, Mississippi, Idaho, Georgia and South Carolina. Data on death row women are unavailable from 1947 to 1952 and from 1956 to 1960, but state and federal prisons held eight women under sentences of death from 1953 to 1955 and five women in the 1960s. Women increased their average percentage of the greater death row population from 1953 to 1955 to 2.9 percent, but then decreased to 1.3 percent in the 1960s. Researchers identify several states that held women under death sentences in the early decades of the 20th century, but state governors and appellate courts commuted the women's death sentences to prison terms.[15] Historical corrections data also reveal that jurisdictions sentenced fewer women to death than the number of women executed—this irregularity in the data most probably results from state and local jurisdictions providing more complete data on female executions than on women sentenced to death. Since 1973, jurisdictions have sentenced 178 women to death as of December 2012, comprising about 2.1 percent of all persons received by state and federal prisons under sentences of death.

Currently, there are 51 women on state and federal death rows. Table 9-1 comprises an inventory of condemned women as of November 2015. Table 9-1 includes the names of death row women, their ages at the time of the crime, their dates of birth, race, and the offenses for which jurisdictions have sentenced women to death, the state and county of conviction, the race and sex of condemned women's victims, and whether women murderers had a male accomplice when they killed. White women comprise the majority of death row women in the United States; 30 white women are 58.8 percent of the female death row population, 12 black women are 22 percent, eight Latinas are 15.6 percent, two Asian (one Vietnamese and one Taiwanese) women are 3.9 percent, and the one American Indian female prisoner is 1.9 percent of the population. Twenty-six (50.9 percent) death row women committed predatory murders aggravated by robbery, burglary, and kidnapping; 17 women (33.3 percent) murdered their own children or other's children, in two (3.9 percent) cases condemned women murdered entire families; and six (11.7 percent) condemned women killed their spouses. In several cases women murdered spouses for pecuniary gain. Frequently wives had male accomplices or hired "hit men" to do the actual killing of their husbands; some 57 percent of condemned female inmates had male accomplices. Nearly 30 percent of the 75 victims of death row women were white males and slightly more than 21 percent were white females. Latinos comprise the next largest category of victims murdered by death row women; 17.3 percent were Latin males and 8.0 percent were Latin females. Black males and females comprise nearly 7 percent of the death row women's victims, and Asian males and females are about 8 percent. About 54 percent of victims murdered by death row women were men.

The average age of death row women at the time of committing their crimes was slightly younger than 30 years old. Though the one American Indian woman on death row in North Carolina was 20 years old at the time of her crime, black females and Latinas were on the average slightly older than 30 years of age, white women were slightly older than 33 years of age, and the two Asian women on death row in California were slightly older than 34 years of age when they committed their crimes. At 81 years old, Blanch Kiser Moore in North Carolina is the oldest living female death row inmate, and 31-year-old Emilia Lily Carr held in Florida is the youngest condemned female inmate. Currently, the average age of female death row inmates is slightly older than 48 years old. This means that the costs associated with maintaining a growing elderly female death row population is going to increase significantly over the next few decades. One recent report points out that the annual costs to state budgets associated incarcerating prisoners age 55 and older with illnesses are *two to three times* that of the expense for all other inmates.[16] The average number of years condemned women have spent on death row is just under 12 years. Debra Denise Brown has spent 28 years as a condemned inmate and holds the dubious distinction of being the longest serving death row female. Kimberly Diane Cargill, imprisoned on death row in Texas since June 2012, has spent the least amount of time of death row.

Predatory Murderers

Official justice figures show that women are about 10 percent of offenders arrested annually for murder and non-negligent manslaughter and account for about 2 percent of death sentences imposed by trial courts. Of the current female death row population, women are nearly *twice* as likely to have committed predatory murders as child murders and nearly *four times* as likely to have committed murders of spouses. Predatory murders often involved condemned women killing former spouses, boyfriends, and other intimates.

Shawna Forde is one of two death row women in Arizona. In February 2011, a Pima County Superior Court jury in Tucson convicted her of masterminding the 2009 home invasion murder

Table 9-1: Women Currently on Death Row in the United States

Name of Female Offender	Age at Crime	Date of Birth	Offense	Race of Offender	Date of Crime	Date of Sentence	State of Conviction	County of Prosecution	Race/Sex of Victim(s)	Male Abettor
Blackmon, Patricia	29	3-Nov-69	Child Murder	Black	29-May-99	7-Jul-02	Alabama	Houston	Black female	No
Gobble, Tierra Capri	21	18-Apr-83	Child Murder	White	15-Dec-04	1-Dec-05	Alabama	Houston	White male	Yes
Scott, Christie Michelle	30	10-Aug-78	Child Murder	White	16-Aug-08	5-Aug-09	Alabama	Franklin	White male	No
Andriano, Wendi Elizabeth	30	6-Aug-70	Spousal Murder	White	8-Oct-00	22-Dec-04	Arizona	Maricopa	Latin male	No
Forde, Shawna	41	6-Dec-67	Predatory Murder	White	30-May-09	23-Feb-11	Arizona	Pima	Latin male & Latin female	Yes
Alfaro, Maria Del Rosio	18	12-Oct-71	Child Murder	Latina	15-Jun-90	14-Jul-92	California	Orange	White female	No
Buenrostro, Dora Luz [FN]	34	1960	Child Murder	Latina	25-Oct-94	2-Oct-98	California	Riverside	2 Latin female & Latin male	No
Caro, Socorro Susan	42	27-Mar-57	Child Murder	Latina	22-Nov-99	5-May-02	California	Ventura	3 Latin males	No
Carrington, Celeste Simone	30	1961	Predatory Murder	Black	11-Mar-92	23-Nov-94	California	San Mateo	Latin male & White female	No
Coffman, Cynthia Lynn	24	19-Jan-62	Predatory Murder	White	7-Nov-86	31-Aug-89	California	San Bernardino	White female	Yes
Dalton, Kerry Lyn	35	1-Apr-53	Predatory Murder	White	26-Jun-88	23-May-95	California	San Diego	White female	Yes
Eubanks, Susan Dianne	32	26-Jun-64	Child Murder	White	27-Oct-96	13-Oct-99	California	San Diego	4 White males	No
Gonzales, Veronica Utilia	26	1968	Child Murder	Latina	21-Jul-95	20-Jul-98	California	San Diego	Latin female	Yes
Martin, Valerie Dee	35	16-Sep-67	Predatory Murder	White	28-Apr-85	26-Mar-10	California	Los Angeles	Non-White male	Yes
McDermott, Maureen	37	15-May-47	Predatory Murder	White	28-Apr-85	8-Jun-90	California	Los Angeles	White male	Yes
Michaud, Michele Lyn	38	7-Nov-58	Predatory Murder	White	2-Dec-97	25-Sep-02	California	Alameda	White female	Yes
Nelson, Tanya Jaime	41	1964	Predatory Murder	Vietnamese	21-Apr-05	26-Mar-10	California	Orange	2 Vietnamese females	Yes
Nieves, Sandi Dawn	34	1964	Child Murder	White	30-Jun-98	6-Oct-00	California	Los Angeles	4 White females	No
Rodriguez, Angelina	32	1968	Spousal Murder	Latina	9-Sep-00	12-Jan-04	California	Los Angeles	Latin male	No
Rottiers, Brooke Marie	26	1980	Predatory Murder	White	28-Aug-06	22-Oct-10	California	Riverside	2 Latin males	Yes
Samuels, Mary Ellen	42	3-Sep-47	Spousal Murder	White	27-Jun-89	16-Sep-94	California	Los Angeles	2 White males	Yes
Sarinana, Cathy Lynn	29	6-Jul-76	Child Murder	White	25-Dec-05	26-Jun-09	California	Riverside	Latin male	Yes
Snyder, Janeen Marie	21	26-Sep-79	Child Murder	White	17-Apr-01	7-Sep-06	California	Riverside	White female	Yes
Thompson, Catherine	42	24-Sep-47	Spousal Murder	Black	14-Jun-90	20-Jun-93	California	Los Angeles	Black male	Yes
Williams, Manling Tsang	28	1979	Family Murder	Taiwanese	7-Aug-07	Jan-12	California	Los Angeles	3 Taiwanese males	No
Allen, Margaret Ann	39	23-Jan-66	Predatory Murder	Black	8-Feb-05	19-May-11	Florida	Duval	White female	Yes
Brown, Tina Lasonya	39	19-Jul-70	Predatory Murder	Black	10-Mar-10	28-Sep-12	Florida	Escambia	Black female	No
Carr, Emilia Lily	24	4-Aug-84	Predatory Murder	Latina	14-Feb-09	2-Feb-11	Florida	Miami-Dade	White female	Yes
Cole, Tiffany Ann	23	3-Dec-81	Predatory Murder	White	8-Jul-05	6-Mar-08	Florida	Duval	White male/White female	Yes
Cardona, Ana Marie	29	26-Nov-61	Child Murder	Latina	2-Nov-90	1992/2011	Florida	Miami-Dade	Latin male	Yes
Row, Robin Lee	35	12-Sep-57	Family Murder	White	10-Feb-92	16-Dec-93	Idaho	Ada	2 White males/White female	No
Brown, Debra Denise	21	11-Nov-62	Child Murder	Black	18-Jun-84	23-Jun-86	Indiana	Gary	Black female	Yes

Foreign national.

Name of Female Offender	Age at Crime	Date of Birth	Offense	Race of Offender	Date of Crime	Date of Sentence	State of Conviction	County of Prosecution	Race/Sex of Victim(s)	Male Abettor
Caudill, Virginia Susan	37	10-Sep-60	Predatory Murder	White	15-Mar-98	24-Mar-00	Kentucky	Fayette	Black female	Yes
Frank, Antoinette	22	30-Apr-71	Predatory Murder	Black	4-Mar-94	13-Sep-95	Louisiana	Orleans Parish	Viet male & female/ White male	Yes
Holmes, Brandy Aileen	23	25-Jun-79	Predatory Murder	White	1-Jan-03	21-Feb-06	Louisiana	Caddo Parrish	White male	Yes
Chamberlin, Lisa Jo	33	30-Nov-72	Predatory Murder	White	20-Mar-04	4-Aug-06	Mississippi	Forrest	White male/White female	Yes
Moore, Blanche Kiser (Taylor)	53	17-Feb-33	Predatory Murder	White	7-Oct-86	18-Jan-91	North Carolina	Alamance	White male	No
Parker, Carlette Elizabeth	34	12-Jun-63	Predatory Murder	Black	12-May-98	1-Apr-99	North Carolina	Wake	White female	No
Roberts, Donna Marie	58	22-May-44	Spousal Murder	White	11-Dec-01	21-Jun-03	Ohio	Trumbull	White male	Yes
Andrew, Brenda Evers	38	16-Dec-63	Spousal Murder	White	20-Nov-01	22-Sep-04	Oklahoma	Oklahoma City	White male	Yes
McAnulty, Angela Darlene	41	2-Oct-68	Child Murder	White	9-Dec-09	24-Feb-11	Oregon	Lane	White female	No
Tharp, Michelle Sue	29	20-Jan-69	Child Murder	White	18-Apr-98	14-Nov-00	Pennsylvania	Washington	White female	Yes
Walter, Shonda Dee	23	16-Jul-79	Predatory Murder	Black	25-Mar-03	19-Apr-05	Pennsylvania	Clinton	White male	No
Pike, Christa Gail	18	10-Mar-76	Predatory Murder	White	12-Jan-95	29-Mar-96	Tennessee	Knox	Latin female	Yes
Cargill, Kimberly Diane	43	10-Nov-66	Predatory Murder	White	18-Jun-10	7-Jun-12	Texas	Smith	White female	No
Carty, Linda Anita [FN]	42	5-Oct-58	Predatory Murder	Black	15-May-01	21-Feb-02	Texas	Harris	Latin female	Yes
Holberg, Brittany Marlowe	23	1-Jan-73	Predatory Murder	White	13-Nov-96	27-Mar-98	Texas	Randall	White male	No
Lucio, Melissa Elizabeth	38	18-Jul-68	Child Murder	Latina	17-Feb-07	12-Aug-08	Texas	Cameron	Latin female	Yes
Routier, Darlie Lynn	26	4-Jan-70	Child Murder	White	6-Jun-96	4-Feb-97	Texas	Dallas	2 White males	No
Sheppard, Erica Yvonne	19	1-Sep-73	Predatory Murder	Black	30-Jun-93	3-Mar-95	Texas	Harris	White female	Yes
Montgomery, Lisa Marie	36	27-Feb-68	Predatory Murder	White	16-Jul-04	4-Apr-08	Federal/Texas	Fort Worth	White female	No

of Raul "Junior" Flores and his nine-year-old daughter, Brisenia Flores. Flores's wife and Brisenia's mother, Gina Marie Gonzales, was seriously wounded but survived the shooting. Judge John S. Leonardo sentenced Shawna to die by lethal injection. Apparently, Shawna and two others stormed the Flores' trailer home in Arivaca, just north of the U.S.-Mexico border in Arizona, looking for drugs and money to support their fledging anti-immigrant Minuteman American Defense vigilante group to which she was ostensibly a founding member. Shawna gained entry to the Flores' home under the ruse of law enforcement in search of fugitives. Shawna's co-defendants in the murder were Jason Eugene "Gunny" Bush, a White supremacist, and Albert Robert Gaxiola, a convicted drug dealer who reportedly wanted Raul Flores dead because he was a rival drug dealer. Officials have yet to arrest a fourth assailant. Bush is also responsible for the 1997 stabbing death of a homeless Mexican man named Hector Lopez Padilla in Wenatchee, Washington. In April 2011, a jury found Bush guilty of the Flores' murders and Judge John Leonardo sentenced him to death. Bush reportedly was the actual killer of the Flores. The same judge sentenced Gaxiola to "natural life" in prison.

Shawna never had a chance at a normal life; she had a deeply troubled childhood marked by repeated instances of sexual and physical abuse, neglect, abandonment, and dominated by religious fanaticism. Shawna was one of nine children of the same mother, Rena Caudle, but of five different fathers. At 10 months old, Caudle gave Shawna to relatives who had molested her as a child and by the age of five, she had lived in several homes and had been molested and abused. Shawna's adoptive father, Jeep Breightam, routinely molested Shawna while her adoptive mother worked at a bowling alley in the late afternoons. Breightam apparently professed his love for young Shawna and took her on trips where he insisted the youngster ride naked in the passenger seat. By the age of 12, Shawna stole clothes from large retail outlets, frequently ran away from home, and had stays in homes for troubled youth. As a teenager, Shawna was living on the streets of Seattle as a prostitute and addicted to cocaine and powerful prescription drugs. As an adult, Shawna attempted suicide with drug overdoses on three separate occasions; she had married and divorced five husbands. Shawna remains jailed at the Arizona State Prison Complex at Perryville while her case proceeds through the appeals process.

California houses eight women convicted of predatory murders on death row. In each case, the women had extremely troubling childhoods. Celeste Simone Carrington's childhood horrors began at the age of seven with sexual abuse including habitual rapes from her father and at 14 became pregnant with her father's child, which she aborted. Celeste and her siblings suffered extreme parental abuse and neglect. According to mental health specialists, Celeste was genetically predisposed to depression and had environmental difficulties, and that both conditions contributed to her mental state. She felt worthless and hopeless, and had become withdrawn and isolated. A jury, however, rejected this evidence as mitigating factors of Celeste's crimes. One commentator pointed out that Celeste's defense lawyer claimed that her robbery and murder spree resulted from a desire to satisfy the materialistic demands of a lesbian lover.

In January 1992, Celeste burglarized Sam and Libby's office building in an industrial park in San Carlos that resulted in her murdering Victor Esparza. Reportedly, Celeste had previously had worked on the premises as a janitor and had a key to the building. Armed with a .357 magnum revolver, Celeste used the key to enter the building but inadvertently set off an alarm. While cleaning the facility, janitor Victor Esparza observed Celeste in an office cubicle. Pulling the gun on Esparza, Celeste demanded his personal identification number (PIN) to an automated teller machine (ATM) card and then shot and killed Esparza with a single gunshot to his head. She later attempted to use his ATM card, but the PIN proved invalid. Upon her arrest, Celeste admitted that she intended to kill Esparza, and that the experience was exciting and made her feel powerful. She told police, "That was the first time I had shot anybody.... Being honest with you, I can't say it was an accident ... I wanted to see what it would be like to shoot someone.... It was just one of those things. I just turned and did it, hoping to hit him.... I didn't realize I was such a good shot."

In March 1992, Celeste burglarized an office building in Palo Alto where she murdered property manager Carolyn Gleason. Celeste admitted to police that she previously worked in the property management firm as a janitor and had a key that she used to enter the building. Celeste apparently herded Gleason into an office where shot Gleason execution style. The same month Celeste burglarized a medical office building where she previously worked as a janitor in Redwood City. There, Celeste found the outside doors to the building unlocked but she was unable to open any of the internal offices. She hid in a closet for a few hours and then saw Dr. Marks leaving his office after a late appointment. While attempting to rob Marks, the two struggled over the gun in which Celeste pulled the trigger three times resulting in a gunshot to Marks' shoulder. Marks managed to force her out of the office and locked the door. In late 1994, a San Mateo County jury found Celeste guilty of the first-degree murders of Victor Esparza and Caroline Gleason and the attempted murder of Dr. Marks. The jury returned a death verdict, and the trial judge sentenced Celeste to die by lethal injection. The California Supreme Court affirmed the convictions and death sentence, and the U.S. Supreme Court has denied Celeste a writ of certiorari. Celeste awaits execution while imprisoned at the Central California Women's Facility at Chowchilla.

Cynthia Lynn Coffman and James Gregory Marlow kidnapped a young college student named Lynn Murray in November 1986 from a drycleaners where she worked in Huntington Beach, California. The two drove Murray to a house where court records reveal that when officials found Murray her head was in six inches of water in the bathtub; her head and face were bound with towel strips, and two gags were in and over her mouth. Her right arm was secured to a towel binding her waist, her right leg lay across the toilet, and her left leg rested on the floor in front of the toilet. Her ankles were bound with duct tape. Murray's bra, pantyhose and one earring were missing; evidence also suggested she had been raped, sodomized, and possibly urinated on. She had suffered blunt force trauma to the head, midsection injuries, bruising of the legs and two black eyes consistent with having suffered blows before death. Cynthia and Marlow pawned Murray's typewriter and swapped her answering machine for methamphetamine. Also in November of that year, officials found the body Corinna Novis buried in a shallow grave in a vineyard in Fontana in San Bernardino County. Cynthia and Marlow had strangled Corinna to death and Marlow had sodomized her since forensic experts found sperm in her rectum. Cynthia and Marlow abducted Novis from a shopping center in Redlands where she had gone after leaving her job at a State Farm Insurance office. Cynthia and Marlow gained access to Corrina's bank account.

Authorities linked Cynthia and Marlow to the murders after an assistant manager at a Taco Bell restaurant in Laguna Beach discovered items belonging to Corrina in a trash receptacle behind the restaurant, including her checkbook, a bank card, identification cards, and papers belonging to Cynthia and Marlow. In August 1989, a San Bernardino County jury convicted Cynthia and Marlow of murder, kidnapping, kidnapping for robbery, robbery, residential burglary, and forcible sodomy. San Bernardino County Superior Court Judge Don A. Turner sentenced Cynthia and Marlow to death. *The court rejected Cynthia's claims based upon testimony of psychologist Dr. Lenore Walker that she suffered from battered woman syndrome, post-traumatic stress disorder, and depression with dysthymia.* On appeal, the state's Supreme Court affirmed Cynthia's conviction and death sentences. The U.S. Supreme Court denied Cynthia certiorari in May 2005, and in October 2006, the California Supreme Court denied Cynthia habeas corpus review. Cynthia remains on death row at California's Institute for Women.

A San Diego County jury deliberated for one day before finding Kerry Lyn Dalton guilty in May 1995 torture-murder Irene "Melanie" Louise May, a young wife and mother of three. Kerry was Irene's ex-roommate. Kerry had two accomplices, Sheryl Ann Baker and Mark Lee Thompkins, who pleaded guilty to the killing to avoid the death penalty and are serving long prison terms. In the June 1988 methamphetamine-fueled torture slaying, the three murderers shocked May with electric wires, injected her with battery acid, and beat her with a metal bar and kitchen skillet before stabbing her to death with a knife and screwdriver. Authorities never found May's body; one defendant claimed they dismembered the body and buried it on different Indian reservations while another defendant claimed they burned the body. The motive for killing the victim apparently derived from some jewelry May had supposedly stolen from Kerry. The case is still undergoing initial appeals.

In late March 2010, a Los Angeles County jury found Valerie Dee Martin guilty of the February 2003 robbery, kidnapping, and murder of her boyfriend, William Whiteside, an Antelope Valley Hospital maintenance worker in Lancaster. Valerie worked at the same hospital in housekeeping. Authorities found Whiteside's battered body inside the trunk of his burned car. Investigators suggested that he was unconscious but still alive when Valerie and her accomplices put Whiteside into the trunk of the car and then set fire to the car. Valerie's three co-defendants were all aspiring member of the White supremacist group Metal Mindz and methamphetamine users: Valerie's 17-year-old son Ronald Kupsch, 15-year-old Bradley Zoda, and Christopher Lee Kennedy, an ex-convict. Authorities tried Kupsch as an adult and sentenced him to life in prison without the possibility of parole. Zoda accepted a first-degree murder "juvenile" conviction and sentenced to a ten-year prison term in exchange for his testimony against the others. Kennedy is serving a life term without parole. Valerie, sentenced to death, has yet to file her direct appeal before the California Supreme Court.

A Los Angeles County jury found Maureen McDermott guilty of the 1985 murder of her boyfriend, Stephen Eldridge, a self-employed landscaper with whom Maureen owned a home. Stating that "the circumstances of the crime demonstrate that Miss McDermott had a complete disregard for human life," Superior Court Judge Alan B. Haber sentenced Maureen to death. Maureen hired a co-worker, James Luna, who in turn hired two others, brothers Marvin and Dondell Lee, to kill Eldridge so she could obtain sole ownership of the house and collect a substantial life insurance policy.[17] McDermott offered Luna $50,000 to kill Eldridge with a knife and make it look like a "homosexual murder" by carving the word "gay" into his body and cutting off his penis. On the night of the killing, Eldridge died from 44 stab wounds and the killers cut off his penis postmortem. Police took Luna into custody for questioning, released him soon thereafter, but rearrested Luna a few weeks later and charged him for the first-degree murder of Eldridge. Police also arrested Maureen in August 1985 and charged her with attempted murder, and murder with special circumstances allegations of murder for financial gain and lying in wait. Officials granted Marvin Lee, who was in custody for an unrelated offense, immunity from prosecution for Eldridge's murder in exchange for his confession and truthful testimony against Maureen. Authorities also granted immunity to Dondell Lee. Luna entered into a plea agreement of first-degree murder and agreed to testify truthfully in the prosecution of defendant. In 2002, the California Supreme Court upheld Maureen's conviction and death sentence and denied her habeas corpus petition in May 2008. The U.S. Supreme Court denied certiorari in 2003.

Though the California Supreme Court summarily dismissed the claims, Maureen asserted the prosecutor and defense lawyer engaged in official misconduct during her closing argument at the penalty phase of Maureen's murder trial. She claimed her trial was characterized by inflammatory epithets, absence of mitigation evidence, that defense counsel fabricated evidence, references to the Bible, misstating the law, misstating the evidence, arguing defendant's character as aggravating, engaging in bad faith by arguing defendant would be dangerous in prison, making a plea to impose the death penalty based upon gut instinct, and asserting that Maureen was *more deserving of the death penalty because she is a woman*. Maureen also cites as improper the prosecutor's comments in closing argument describing her as *a mutation of a human being*, a *wolf in sheep's clothing*, a person who *stalked people like animals*, and someone who had *resigned from the human race*. Defendant asserts that the prosecutor committed misconduct by comparing her to a *Nazi working in the crematorium by day and listening to Mozart by night*. Finally, defendant claims the prosecutor committed misconduct by comparing defendant to a *germ*, a *mad dog*, and a *snake*. McDermott is locked inside a six by 12 foot cell with solid steel doors almost 23 hours a day. She has no contact with other inmates, and lives a life of almost complete isolation. On the average day, she leaves her cell for about an hour, only to exercise alone on a small patch of black top behind the prison. She is allowed to leave her cell three times a week for showers.

In September 2002, an Alameda County jury in California found Michelle Lyn Michaud, a mother of two, guilty of her confessed involvement in helping her boyfriend James Anthony Daveggio, a registered sex offender, to kidnap, rape, and kill Vanessa Lei Samson. The jury recommended death and Superior Court Judge Larry Goodman supported the death sentence claiming that death is an appropriate penalty since Vanessa's slaying and torture was "vile, cruel, senseless, depraved, brutal, evil and vicious." Five years earlier Michelle and Daveggio repeatedly raped and tortured Vanessa in the back of a Dodge Caravan rigged with hooks and ropes as the couple drove to Lake Tahoe. Afterwards, the couple strangled and dumped the woman's body in an Alpine County snow bank. Authorities believe the couple committed a string of unresolved violent sex crimes, some of whom were relatives of the defendants. At trial, James Anthony Daveggio's 16-year-old daughter told a grand jury that in November 1997 her father asked if she would like to help kidnap a vulnerable victim off the street and kill her. According to one commentator, Daveggio and Michaud were methamphetamine users who modeled their crimes after those of Gerald and Charlene Gallego, a Sacramento couple whose "sex slave murders" made headlines in the late 1970s. Michelle's defense lawyers claimed she was a battered woman who would do anything to please Daveggio. In 2001, the Ninth Circuit of Appeals confirmed Michelle's conviction and death sentence, and in 2002, the U.S. Supreme Court denied certiorari.

In March 2010, an Orange County jury in California found Tanya Jaime Nelson (also known as Phuong Thao Nguyen) guilty of the 2005 stabbing murder of a popular Little Saigon fortune teller, Vietnamese American Ha "Jade" Smith, and her college-student daughter Anita Nhi Vo. Her co-defendant was Phillipe Zamora who Tanya lured to fly from North Carolina to California to commit the murders. After the killings, Tanya stole Smith's credit cards, cell phones, jewelry, and expensive luggage, but she did not find $568,000 in cash hidden in a vacuum cleaner and coffee maker. Using the credit cards, Tanya purchased $3,000 in clothing, airline tickets, electronics, and meals at restaurants. Police apprehended Tanya at a local hotel five weeks after the killings and charged her with fraud, burglary, conspiracy, and murder. Prosecutors claimed that Tanya committed the murders because a fortune she received from Smith did not materialize. Zamora pled guilty to the murders and received a sentence of 27 years to life, but Superior Court judge Frank F. Fasel sentenced Tanya to death. Tanya was the youngest child of a wealthy Vietnamese family that immigrated to the United States in 1979, and there is no information in the public record that Tanya suffered from childhood trauma. Officials house Tanya at the Central California Women's Facility in Chowchilla, California, while she undergoes the state and federal appeals process.

In October 2010, a Riverside County jury convicted Brooke Marie Rottiers, a mother of four, of masterminding the robbery-murder of two Mexican day laborers, Marvin Gabriel and Milton Chavez. Describing the crimes as "cold, callous, brutal and particularly cruel," Superior Court Judge Helios J. Hernandez sentenced Brooke to die by lethal injection in the state's death chamber. Separate juries also found Brooke's co-defendants, her boyfriend Omar Tyree Hutchinson and a female accomplice named Franchune Dyuel Epps, guilty of the same murders. Since the state did not seek the death penalty against Hutchinson and Epps, Judge Hernandez sentenced them to life in prison without parole. Reportedly, Chavez and Gabriel met Brooke and Epps while drinking after work at a bar. Believing they were going to have sex with Brooke, the two victims apparently followed her and Epps back to a motel where she lived with Hutchinson. Once inside the motel room, Epps pulled a gun and held it on the victims while Brooke and Hutchinson stripped them and stole their money and valuables. Brooke, a large woman, beat Chavez then bound him and Gabriel with electrical cords, phone cords, bras, and panties. The assailants covered the victims' mouths and noses with tape and they smothered to death, they wrapped the bodies in bed sheets and transported them to a remote area of Riverside where a local resident found the decomposed bodies days later. Brooke's lawyer argued at trial that she suffered sexual abuse as a child and had a long history of drug addiction.

In May 2011, a Brevard County judge in Florida sentenced Margaret Ann Allen to death for the February 2005 torture and strangulation murder of Wenda Wright who was Margaret's friend and housekeeper. Margaret erroneously believed that Wright had stolen her purse containing $2,000. Margaret reportedly poured bleach, nail-polish remover, and ammonia over Wright's face and choked her to death with a belt. Along with her nephew, Quinton Allen, Margaret buried Wright's body in a shallow grave in the northern part of the county. Later, Quinton reported Wright's murder to police, confessed to his part in the killing, and showed officials where he and Margaret buried the body. Margaret's roommate, James Martin pleaded guilty as an accomplice after the fact for his participation in helping Margaret and Quinton bury Wright's body and received a five-year prison term. Judge George Maxwell sentenced Quinton Allen to a 15-year prison term after he pleaded guilty to second-degree murder and testified against Margaret. Trial testimony revealed that Margaret suffered physical and sexual abuse as a child and that she grew up in a violent neighborhood. A family member once beat young Margaret so badly she required hospitalization and suffered brain damage. A recent federal district court ruling may ultimately have implications in Margaret Allen's death sentences. In a habeas corpus petition involving Paul H. Evans in a murder-for-hire case, United States District Court Jose E. Martinez ruled in June 2011 that Florida's death penalty statute is unconstitutional because it violates the 2002 U.S. Supreme Court decision in *Ring v. Arizona* that only a jury can decide critical issues in death penalty cases.

The most recent female death row inmate to join Florida's death row at Lowell Correctional Institutional Annex in Ocala is Tina Lasonya Brown. In late March 2010, Tina, her 16-year-old daughter Britnee Miller, and a neighbor, Heather Trinee Lee, lured 19-year-old Audreanna Zimmerman, a mother of two, to a wooded area near a trailer park in Pensacola where they all lived. The defendants wanted to confront the victim who was feuding with Britnee about a man. Audreanna suffered a violent death. The three defendants beat the young girl with a crowbar, hit her with a stun gun, doused her with an accelerant and then set her on fire. Audreanna was able to get away from her assailants and ran to a neighbor's house who called police. Emergency personnel transported Audreanna to the University of South Alabama Center in Mobile where she died 16 days later. She had suffered burns over 60 percent of her body. Audreanna was able to give police details of the attack and identified her attackers before physicians put her in a medically induced coma. In June 2012, an Escambia County jury took only an hour to return a first-degree murder verdict and a recommendation of death sentence. Circuit Judge Gary Bergosh sentenced her to death by lethal injection in September calling the killing "heinous, atrocious and cruel" and done with premeditation. Since Britnee was a minor at the time of the murder, she cannot be sentenced to life in prison under a recent ruling from the Supreme Court. In the penalty phase of her trial, Brown's family members and doctors testified that she had lived a hard life full of drugs and sexual abuse.

Marion County Circuit Judge Willard Pope sentenced Emilia Lily Carr to death in February 2011 for the kidnapping and murder of Heather Strong in a love triangle turned deadly in 2009. Emilia's co-defendant was Joshua Damien Fulgham, her estranged husband and the father of Heather's two young children. Emilia was eight-months pregnant with Fulgham's child at the time of Heather's murder. Emilia had three other children who did not live with her. Fulgham had an arrest record of five domestic violence occurrences against Heather. Reportedly, Emilia and Fulgham lured Heather into a storage trailer behind Emilia's mother's house, duct-taped her down to a chair, and then suffocated Heather to death with a plastic bag over her head. The killers buried Heather's body in a shallow grave where police found her a month later. Emilia ultimately confessed to the murder. Emilia testified at trial to her disadvantaged upbringing and sexual abuse by her father and grandfather since the age of four. Emilia apparently has above average intelligence but suffers from a post-traumatic-stress disorder.

In July 2005, Tiffany Ann Cole and accomplices Michael James Jackson, Bruce Kent Nixon, and Alan Lyndell Wade robbed, kidnapped, and murdered an elderly couple in poor health, Carol and James "Reggie" Sumner of Jacksonville, Florida. Tiffany had met the Sumners in Ladson, South Carolina, where her stepfather was their neighbor. The Sumners had recently moved to Jacksonville. Tiffany became familiar with the Sumners once they moved to Jacksonville and along with her accomplices planned the robbery and murder of the Sumners. In preparation for the robbery, the foursome dug a grave just over the Florida-Georgia state line in St. George.

While Tiffany held a flashlight, Jackson, Wade, and Nixon dug the hole, approximately four feet deep and six feet square. On the night of the crime, the four entered the Sumners' house, held them at gunpoint using a toy gun, took the victims to a bedroom, and bound them with duct tape. They then took the Sumners to the garage of the house and forced them into the trunk of their Lincoln Town Car. With the Sumners in the Lincoln's trunk, the group drove to the remote Georgia location, buried the victim's alive, and then abandoned the Sumners' car. While at the Sumners' house, one of the defendants gained access to the Sumners' personal identification number for their bank account and after committing the killings withdrew thousands of dollars from an automatic teller machine. An investigation of the Sumners' killings began once their daughter contacted law enforcement about her missing parents.

At the penalty phase of her trial, psychiatrist Dr. Earnest Miller testified on behalf of the defense that Tiffany suffered from poly-substance and alcohol abuse, chronic depression, and a personality disorder. He testified that Tiffany had witnessed abuse to family members and pets, that her father had sexually abused Tiffany, and that she had been in abusive relationships with two boyfriends. He also testified that Tiffany knew right from wrong and that she is of higher than average intelligence. Tried separately from her accomplices, a jury found Tiffany guilty of the crimes committed against the Sumners and recommended the death penalty. Judge Michael Weatherby sentenced Tiffany to death for each murder, life imprisonment for each kidnapping, and 15 years' imprisonment for each robbery. Judge Weatherby explained that he sentenced Tiffany harshly because there were multiple victims she helped to kidnap and then kill in a cold, calculated, and premeditated manner for financial gain. Tiffany remains at Lowell Correctional Annex near Ocala while she appeals her conviction and death sentence. Tried separately, juries convicted Jackson and Wade of two counts of first-degree murder and received two death sentences. Nixon pleaded guilty to two counts of second-degree murder. After testifying against Jackson, Tiffany, and Wade, Nixon received two concurrent sentences of 45 years' imprisonment.

Virginia Caudill is the only woman on Kentucky's death row. In March 2000, a Fayette County jury convicted Virginia, along with accomplice Johnathon Wayne "Heavy" Goforth, of murder, robbery, burglary, arson, and tampering with physical evidence. Circuit Court Judge John R. Adams sentenced both defendants to death. Goforth and Virginia had long criminal records; Virginia's record includes convictions for prostitution. Two years earlier, Virginia and Goforth bludgeoned to death an elderly Black woman named Lonetta White with a roofers hammer in her home in Lexington, Kentucky. The apparent motive for the killing was to get money to buy crack cocaine. They ransacked the house and stole two guns, jewelry, and a mink coat. Authorities found White's body in the trunk of her burning automobile in a field several miles away. Upon their arrest, Virginia and Goforth admitted to the commission of the crimes, although each accused the other of murdering and robbing White and of setting fire to the automobile. Virginia was an ex-girlfriend of White's son, Steve White, with whom she was engaged but he broke off the engagement days before the murder because of her drug use. The Kentucky Supreme Court affirmed Virginia and Goforth's convictions and death sentences and the U.S. Supreme Court denied petitions for a writ of certiorari in April 2010.

Antoinette Frank is one of two women on Louisiana's death row where courts found the women criminally liable for predatory murders. Orleans Parish juries convicted Antoinette and her co-defendant Roger LaCaze on three counts of first-degree murder in July 1995 and recommended the death penalty. Criminal District Court Judge Frank J. Marullo sentenced Antoinette to death. Antoinette was a New Orleans police officer who murdered two members of the Vu family and Officer Ronald Williams of the New Orleans police department. The Vus owned and operated the Kim Anh Vietnamese Restaurant, located in Eastern New Orleans. Officer

Williams was working a security detail at the restaurant the night of the murders. In a robbery of the restaurant, Antoinette and LaCaze shot to death Ha Vu, Cuong Vu, and Officer Williams. They shot Ha Vu on the top and back of the head, Cuong Vu suffered gunshot wounds to the back of the head, and they shot Officer Williams at close range to the right side of the victim's neck, under and beneath his ear, which severed the spinal column and exited just below his left ear. During the mêlée, Antoinette and LaCaze stole the day's receipts.

Antoinette became involved with LaCaze in November of 1994 when she responded to a report of a disturbance and encountered a gunshot LaCaze. She followed his medical progress, then called and visited him after his discharge from the hospital. Antoinette began giving him money, buying him gifts and clothes, tried to get him a job, and saw to it that LaCaze got a high school equivalency. In 2006, the Louisiana Supreme Court overturned Antoinette's death sentence because the state denied her funding for psychiatric evaluation in preparation for the sentencing phase of the trial. The same court in 2008, however, affirmed the death sentence and the U.S. Supreme Court has denied certiorari. The state supreme court also affirmed LaCaze's murder conviction and death sentence. Antoinette remains incarcerated at the Louisiana Correctional Institute for Women just outside of Baton Rouge.

In February 2006, a Caddo Parish jury found Brandy Aileen Holmes guilty of the January 2003 murder and robbery of a retired minister, Julian L. Brandon, Jr., and the attempted murder of his wife, Alice Brandon. The jury recommended the court sentence Brandy to death for the crimes and the state's Supreme Court affirmed the conviction and sentence. Brandy and her boyfriend accomplice, Robert Coleman, forced their way into the Brandon's rural home and shot Reverend Brandon in the underside of his jaw with a .38-caliber handgun. The two then took Mrs. Brandon to a bedroom in the residence and demanded her valuables, cash, and credit cards. They placed a pillow over Mrs. Brandon's face and shot her in the head; she survived the shooting but remains permanently disabled and requires constant care. After shooting Mrs. Brandon, Brandy and Coleman heard Reverend Brandon struggling with his wounds. It was then that the two retrieved knives from the kitchen and stabbed and slashed him to death. They inflicted slashing cuts to his nose and face and stabbing wounds on the top and rear of his head and chest. The offenders cut Reverend Brandon's throat several times.

Upon her arrest, Brandy not only admitted to her participation in Brandon's murder, but that she also participated in an earlier murder of Terrance Blaze and directed police to his body. Evidence showed that Brandy was enrolled in special education classes when she was in school and that she became institutionalized for several months when she was 12 years old after being raped. Brandy suffered organic brain impairment because of fetal alcohol syndrome and functions mentally at a seventh grade level. Brandy had several felony convictions by the age of 15. A juvenile court sentenced her to the Jetson Correctional Center for Youth until she was 21 years old. While she was in juvenile prison, officials charged her with several counts of battery. She is housed at the Louisiana Correctional Institute for Women.

In 2006, a Forrest County jury convicted Lisa Jo Chamberlin of the gruesome 2004 robbery-murders of Linda Heintzelman and Vernon Hullett. County Circuit Court Judge Robert B. Helfrich sentenced Lisa to death. Another jury later found Chamberlin's boyfriend and co-defendant, Roger Lee Gillett, guilty of the murders and the court sentenced him to be executed. In early 2004, the Kansas Bureau of Investigation received a report that Lisa and Gillett had a stolen vehicle and were manufacturing methamphetamine at the abandoned Gillett's farm in Russell County, Kansas. Armed with warrants, investigators searched the property and found methamphetamine and other drug paraphernalia resulting in Lisa and Gillett's arrests. Meanwhile, officers continued searching the Gillette property and discovered a white Dodge Dakota pickup truck with Mississippi license plates parked in a metal shed and a white freezer that was taped shut with duct tape inside a wooden granary. Police discovered a dismembered body and a black plastic trash bag containing severed body parts in the freezer. When officers pulled the male body out of the freezer, they discovered another body frozen in a liquid at the bottom of the freezer. The officers thawed the contents of the freezer and extracted a second body. Officials later identified the remains of those of Linda Heintzelman and Vernon Hullett.

During police interviews, Lisa agreed to show officers where in the Russell County dump she and Gillette had disposed of physical evidence. Officers recovered seven plastic trash bags containing personal items belong to the dead couple. During interviews, Lisa explained her relationship with Gillett and their robbery and murder of Hullett and Heintzelman. Apparently, Lisa met Gillett in Oregon where she was born and raised and the two lived together before moving to Russell, Kansas. Later, Lisa and Gillett moved to Hattiesburg, Mississippi, where they stayed with Gillett's cousin, Vernon Hullett, and his live-in girlfriend, Linda Heintzelman. Shortly after arriving in Hattiesburg, Gillett and Lisa wrecked their car while following Hullett and Heintzelman in Heintzelman's pickup truck. Gillett's car was badly damaged, but Heintzelman's truck sustained only minor damage. After the accident, Hullett and Heintzelman suggested that Gillett and Lisa get their own place to live. Lisa agreed, but Gillett wanted to stay at Hullett's and they argued about moving. Unable to drive her car in its damaged condition, Lisa left on foot and returned that evening to find Gillett standing on the front porch smoking a cigarette. When Lisa and Gillett entered the house, Gillett became violent with Heintzelman. Gillett instructed Lisa to get his gun from under the mattress in the bedroom. She complied. Lisa and Gillett cut the telephone wires so that Hullett and Heintzelman could not call the police. Gillett fired one round inside the house to scare Hullett and Heintzelman. Gillett punched and hit Hullett several times in an attempt to get the combination to Hullett's safe. Upon discovering that there was no beer in the house, Lisa left to get more beer and when Lisa returned found Heintzelman bent over the safe and not wearing any pants. Lisa inquired as to whether Gillett had raped Heintzelman. Gillett explained that he wanted to "break her," so he made her take her clothes off and used a beer bottle to rape her. Still unsuccessful in opening the safe, Lisa became impatient and told Gillett something similar to "let's just kill them and get out of here." Gillett bashed Hullett in the head with a hammer while Hullett was sitting in a chair in the living room. Gillett also slashed Hullett's throat. Lisa went out of the house and came back in a number of times over several hours while Heintzelman was lying on the floor, injured but "still breathing." Lisa and Gillett worked together to bind Heintzelman's hands behind her back so that she could not struggle with them. Gillett lifted Heintzelman's head, and Lisa placed a bag over it. Lisa was unable to complete the asphyxiation of Heintzelman and went outside. She said that Heintzelman was still breathing when she went outside, but when she returned, Heintzelman was dead. Lisa assisted in cleaning up the murder scene. She helped move the bodies to the bathroom, where Gillett cut off Hullett's head and arms and she held garbage bags open while Gillett placed Hullett's arms inside the bags. Lisa described how she assisted in loading Heintzelman's body and then Hullett's body, along with the black trash bag, into the freezer and how she taped the freezer shut as Gillett stood on top of the freezer to hold it closed. Lisa and Gillett took Hullett's pickup truck and transported the freezer containing the two bodies on the back of that truck from Hullett's house to Kansas. After arriving in Kansas, they unloaded the freezer and plugged it in at the Gillett farm. She indicated that they took the items they transported from Hullett's house and disposed of them at the Russell dump. Also, she agreed to cook some methamphetamine for $500 because they needed money. She described how they discarded the trash from making methamphetamine at the public swimming pool and how on the next day she and Gillett were arrested. The Mississippi Supreme Court upheld both Lisa and Gillett's murder convictions and death sentences, and the U.S. Supreme Court has declined to hear their appeals.

In October 1990, a Forsyth County jury convicted Blanche Kiser Moore of the first-degree murder of her boyfriend Raymond C. Reid and Superior Court Judge Freeman sentenced Moore to death based upon the jury's recommendation. In May 1989, physicians at North Carolina Memorial Hospital in Chapel Hill diagnosed and treated the Reverend Dwight D. Moore, Blanche's husband at the time, for arsenic poisoning. As part of an investigation into Moore's poisoning, authorities exhumed the bodies of Blanche's father, P.D. Kiser, Sr., her first husband James N. Taylor, and her ex-boyfriend Raymond Reid and found that the bodies tested positive for arsenic poisoning. The investigation revealed that Blanche Moore had murdered the victims and committed a felonious assault on Reverend Moore. In 1994, the North Carolina Supreme Court affirmed Blanche's conviction and death sentence. Some have argued that Blanche killed the men in her life because of a deep seeded hate of her Depression-era alcoholic father that forced her into prostitution to help pay the family bills. Others claim that Blanche killed for pecuniary gain. In any event, the trial court found that Reid's murder was "especially heinous, atrocious or cruel"; Reid suffered prolonged physical agony, including paralysis, skin splitting and multiple systems failure. Officials house Blanche at the North Carolina Correctional Institution for Women in Raleigh.

A Wake County jury in North Carolina found Carlette Elizabeth Parker guilty of first-degree murder and first-degree-kidnapping in April 1999. The jury found that Carlette committed the murder for pecuniary gain. The jury recommended death and Superior Court Judge Osmond W. Smith entered judgment accordingly. The jury found mitigating factors: the death of her mother when Carlette was five years old seriously effected Carlett's emotional development, and that Carlette suffered from a mental defect. In May 1998, Carlette kidnapped and drowned 86-year-old Alice Covington, a resident of the Springmoor Retirement Village in Raleigh where Carlette worked as a health-care worker. Carlette kidnapped Alice from a Kroger parking lot after a struggle, drove her to a bank and withdrew $2,500 from her account. Carlette then drove Alice to her trailer in Angier, North Carolina, where she drowned her in a bathtub. Carlette left Alice's body in the Kroger's parking lot where she had kidnapped Alice. Passersby found Alice's body and notified police. In interviews with state investigators, Carlette admitted to the events surrounding Alice's death. Police discovered that Carlette had a history of fraudulently obtaining money from elderly persons under her care. In 2001, the North Carolina Supreme Court upheld Carlette's conviction and death sentence and the U.S. Supreme Court denied certiorari in 2002. Again, in 2013, the North Caroline Supreme Court denied her certiorari.

In mid–September 1993, Lebanon County prison officials in Pennsylvania gave Bradley A. Martin a prison visitation pass that allowed him to leave the prison for two hours. Martin failed to return to the prison as required by his visitation pass, he was serving a two year sentence for theft, burglary and related charges. Martin had met and begun a romantic relationship with Carolyn Ann King. The couple traveled to Palmyra in Lebanon County to visit an acquaintance of Martin's, 74-year-old retired florist Guy Goodman. Once at Goodman's home, Martin struck him over the head with a vase and then bound him with duct tape. The two carried Goodman to the basement where they tied him more securely, wrapped him in a bedspread, and then left him to suffocate while they stole his checkbook and credit card and fled in his car. Goodman suffocated to death. Carolyn and Martin used Goodman's credit card and checks to pay their expenses as they traveled to Arizona. While in route, Carolyn and Martin also kidnapped and shot to death a 59-year-old North Dakota woman named Donna Mae Martz, a tour guide. Arizona police apprehended Carolyn and Martin; both provided authorities with tape-recorded confessions to their involvement in Goodman's murder. A Lebanon County jury found Carolyn and Martin guilty of first-degree murder, aggravated assault, robbery, and theft by unlawful taking, flight to avoid apprehension, escape, and conspiracy. In her mitigation case at the penalty phase of the trial, Carolyn's attorney presented evidence concerning her age at the time of the crime, her relatively minor role in the homicide, and factors relating to her character and the circumstances of the offense. Still, in November 1994, the jury returned a death sentence for each defendant and both received a life sentence for the kidnapping and murder of Donna Martz.

Judge Robert J. Eby of the Lebanon County court had appointed M. Jannifer Weiss to represent Carolyn at trial; a family law attorney with little to no experience representing criminal defendants and was not familiar with the state's death penalty statute. Weiss conducted no mitigation investigation and was unaware that the sentencing hearing would be held immediately after the guilty verdict was returned. Consequently, Weiss failed to discover or present evidence to the jury of Carolyn's history of post-traumatic stress disorder, sexual abuse, child abuse, domestic violence, depression, and drug abuse. On appeal, Carolyn challenged the constitutionality of her representation in post-conviction proceedings claiming that the trial judge appointed a civil practitioner with no relevant experience or training as a trial lawyer and thus was constructively denied her Sixth Amendment right to counsel. Most recently, on review to the Supreme Court of Pennsylvania of the guilt-phase claims in Carolyn's case, the court found no ineffectiveness of trial counsel. The U.S. Supreme Court denied Carolyn's request for certiorari. In 2000, the U.S. Supreme Court refused to hear Carolyn's appeal, but in 2010, the Court of Common Pleas for Lebanon County granted her a new sentencing hearing. In March 2015, Carolyn pled guilty to murder and received a life sentence.

In April 2005, a Clinton County jury took less than 30 minutes to convict Shonda Walter of first-degree murder for the 2003 hatchet killing of 83-year-old James Sementelli, widower and a Pearl Harbor survivor, who lived across the street from Shonda. Reportedly, she engaged in the virtual slaughter of Sementelli to gain entry into the infamous Bloods street gang. Sementelli suffered a brutal attack, sustaining over 60 wounds, 18 fractures, and 45 bruises to various parts of his body, many of them to his head, face, and neck. His left ear was nearly severed from his head, his nasal bone and skull were fractured, his right eye was punctured, and he had numerous defensive wounds on his arms and hands and multiple gaping chop wounds all over his body. State witnesses testified that Shonda described to them how Sementelli pleaded with her to call 911, but she instead watched a game show on television, smoked a cigarette and then left in his car. The Pennsylvania Supreme Court upheld Shonda's conviction and death sentence. Authorities scheduled Shonda's execution for April 22, 2010, but Clinton County Judge J. Michael Williamson judge granted her a stay of execution to allow time for attorney Tracy Ulstad to prepare Shonda's post-conviction claims. In March 2010, the U.S. District Court for Pennsylvania granted Shonda's motion to seek that relief.

Christa Pike is the only woman on death row in Tennessee. In January 1995, Christa killed a fellow student and romantic rival, Colleen Slemmer, at a now defunct Federal Job Corps Center at Fort Sanders. Christa claimed she killed Slemmer because she "had just felt mean that day." Actually, there was a love triangle working between Christa and her 17-year-old boyfriend Tadaryl Shipp who had told Christa that Slemmer was interested in him. With Shipp's help and that of 18-year-old Shadolla Peterson, the three lured Slemmer to a remote spot at the University of Tennessee. Trial evidence shows that on the day of the murder, Christa confessed to fellow students that she had killed Slemmer. Christa showed the students a piece of Slemmer's skull she brought back as a souvenir and detailed how she cut Slemmer's throat six times, beat her, and threw a large piece of asphalt at Slemmer's head. She also told the students that she used a meat cleaver to cut Slemmer's back and a box cutter to cut her throat. Christa claimed that she carved a pentagram into Slemmer's forehead and chest. While relating the events of the killing to her fellow students, Christa danced in a circle, smiling, and singing "la, la, la."

On the day of the murder, an employee of the University of Tennessee Grounds Department discovered Slemmer's semi-nude, slashed, and badly beaten body in a remote area of the University. The body was so badly beaten that the grounds man at first mistook the corpse for a dead animal. Once the grounds man saw that the corpse was a human female, he notified Knoxville and campus police. Once arrested, Christa waived her *Miranda* rights and explained in detail to investigators how she killed Slemmer. Investigators tape-recorded and transcribed Christa's statement in some 46 pages. Christa explained that she and Slemmer had a troubled relationship and that Slemmer had tried to get Christa removed from the Job Corps program. Christa directed investigators to the location where she had left Slemmer's body. Forensic evidence substantiated Christa's story of the killing. While the trial court sentenced Christa to death, Shipp received a life sentence and Peterson, who turned state witness, got probation.

At her penalty trial, expert witnesses concluded that Christa suffers from a severe borderline personality disorder and is dependent on marijuana and inhalants. Psychologists claimed that Christa is not so dysfunctional that she requires institutionalization, but does exhibit a multiplicity of problems in interpersonal relationships, in controlling her behavior, and in achieving vocational and academic goals. Christa experienced no maternal bonding since her family has a difficult history of substance abuse and Christa's maternal grandmother was an alcoholic and verbally abused Christa. Following the death of Christa's paternal grandmother, she shuffled between her mother and father. Her mother's home was dirty and unkempt and she set no rules for Christa's behavior. Clinical evaluations found Christa child-like and preferred to play Barbie and dress-up. Despite her severe personality disorder, a Knox County jury convicted Christa of Slemmer's murder, recommended death by electrocution, and Judge Mary Beth Leibowitz entered a judgment in accordance with the jury's verdict. The Court of Criminal Appeals affirmed the conviction and death sentence and after reviewing the trial record, the Tennessee Supreme Court affirmed the judgment of the Court of Criminal Appeals. The U.S. Supreme Court has denied Christa certiorari. While incarcerated at the Tennessee Prison for Women in Knoxville in 2001, Christa strangled inmate Patricia Jones with a shoestring nearly choking her to death. A court convicted Christa of attempted first-degree murder on August 2004. The Tennessee Court of Criminal Appeals has denied Christa's claim that 18-year-old killers with mental problems should be exempt for the death penalty in April 2011 claiming that it would not exempt older adolescents who are cognitively impaired.

In June 2010, 43-year-old Kimberly Cargill, a mother of four sons, murdered Cherry Diane Walker, her 29-year-old mentally challenged baby sitter to keep her from testifying in a Child Protection Services hearing regarding Kimberly's four-year-old son. Cherry, an African American woman, was scheduled to testify in a child-removal hearing in which state officials were to present police reports containing child-abuse allegations against Kimberly. When prosecutors filed murder charges against Kimberly, she was already in jail on a charge of injury to her son. At trial, Kimberly testified that she was with Cherry in a vehicle when Cherry suffered a seizure. Kimberly supposedly panicked and dumped Cherry's body along the side of a county road and set the body on fire. Passing motorists found Cherry's body and contacted authorities. Defense lawyers presented evidence of Kimberly's very lengthy history of violence, arrests, abuse allegations, prescription drugs abuse, and mental disorders including an anxiety disorder with symptoms of major depression, intermittent explosive disorder and borderline personality disorder. Court records and psychological evaluations show detailed custody battles with ex-husbands. Kimberly's lawyers have yet to begin the appeals process.

To one commentator, Brittany Holberg's status as a crack-addicted prostitute was central to how the jury reacted to her claims of self-defense in her murder trial. In March 1998, a Randall County jury convicted Brittany of the 1996 robbery and murder of 80-year-old A.B. Towery in his home and recommended a death sentence. After 11 hours of deliberation, jurors claimed that there were no mitigating factors warranting a lesser sentence and they argued that Brittany posed a continuing threat to society. Judge Patrick Pirtle affirmed the jury's verdict and suggested sentence. The facts of the case show that Brittany met Towery as he left a grocery store and walked home. She gained entry into Towery's apartment by feigning a need to use the telephone. Once inside the apartment, Brittany demanded money from Towery. When Towery refused her money, Brittany struck him with a hammer and stabbed him 58 times with a paring knife, a butcher knife, a grapefruit knife, and a fork. Brittany then shoved a lamp pole more than five inches down the Towery's throat. Brittany's defense attorney, Catherine Brown Dodson, argued at trial that Towery had hired Brittany as a prostitute and she acted in self-defense when Towery attacked her. Reportedly, Brittany was high on crack cocaine at the time of the killing. In a 2003 interview with Brittany, writer Claudia Dreifus revealed that Brittany suffers from *battered wife syndrome, post-traumatic stress disorder, and a cocaine addiction.*[18] On appeal to the Texas Court of Criminal Appeals, the court rejected all 47 issues and affirmed the conviction and death sentence. In October 2001, the U.S. Supreme Court denied Brittany's petition for certiorari. In 2011, the Texas Court of Criminal Appeals denied Brittany post-conviction relief.

In March 1995, a Houston jury convicted Erica Sheppard, a 24-year-old mother of three, of her participation in the 1993 stabbing, smothering, and bludgeoning death of Marilyn Sage Meagher, a 48-year-old real estate agent and mother of two. Her co-defendant, James Dickerson, also received a death sentence. It seems that Erica and Dickerson spotted a woman carrying clothing from her Mazda into her apartment and decided to steal the car. The pair tackled Meagher inside her apartment, and while she begged for her life, slashed her throat with knives five times. The two then wrapped her head in a plastic bag and struck her in the head with a ten-pound statue. Erica had confessed to "her part in the slaying, to the grisly details that portrayed her as an all too willing accomplice to a robbery that had spun violently out of control." At her trial, the state's attorney characterized Erica as a "jackal" and a "predator." Erica claimed that Dickerson threatened to kill her and her baby if she did not help in the robbery-murder of Meagher. At one point Erica had waived her rights to appeal, but after a religious experience she changed her mind after a visit from the Reverend Jessie Jackson. In 1997, the Court of Criminal Appeals upheld Erica's conviction and death sentence. By admission, Erica's trial attorneys were grossly incompetent in defending Erica's right to a fair trial. Her lead attorney, Chris Brown, had never before been lead counsel on a death-penalty case and his assistant attorneys had less experience. Brown did little to put on a defense in Erica's trial. Her newly appointed appeals lawyer and private investigator provide considerable mitigating evidences that the trial jury never heard:

> Erica Yvonne Sheppard grew up hard, raised in Bay City just outside Houston by an abusive mother who moved constantly between homes and lovers. As a young child, she was sexually assaulted and forced to perform oral sex on a babysitter's boyfriend who threatened to kill her mother if Erica told anyone.... Her mother ... would beat her so hard that her grandmother had to intervene. Her mother also had a series of lesbian lovers who were also abusive to Sheppard.... As a teenager, Sheppard was sexually assaulted twice, once by a man who forced her to perform oral sex at knifepoint.... Erica dropped out of high school in the 10th grade ... she got pregnant again.... [A husband] would beat her mercilessly, watching Sheppard cower as he held a knife to her throat or stuck a .45 revolver in her face.[19]

In her latest appeal to the Texas Court of Criminal Appeals, the court held that even though her lawyers failed to fully present mitigating evidence, that does not constitute ineffective assistance. Erica remains incarcerated on death row.

In April 2008, U.S. District Judge Gary A. Fenner sentenced Lisa Montgomery to death for the kidnapping and stabbing murder of Bobbie Jo Stinnett who was eight months pregnant. The apparent motive for the murder was Lisa's desire to have a child. It seems Lisa went to Stinnett's home in Skidmore, Missouri, under the ruse of purchasing a rat terrier. Once there, Lisa strangled Stinnett to death and cut the premature infant from Stinnett's womb. Later, Lisa attempted to pass the infant girl off as her own child. Police recovered the infant, named Victoria Jo Stinnett, and arrested Lisa for Stinnett's murder. Authorities returned the infant to her father. Lisa had a long history of physical and sexual abuse by her stepfather and had a tumultuous relationship with her mother. Lisa married her step-brother when she was 18 years old, and had a child a year later. She had three more children in the following years and underwent a sterilization procedure in 1990. Psychiatrists have diagnosed Lisa with depression, borderline personality disorder, post-traumatic stress disorder, and pseudocyesis—"a false belief of being pregnant that is associated with objective signs of pregnancy." In April 2011, a U.S. Court of Appeals affirmed Lisa's conviction and death sentence, and in 2012 the U.S. Supreme Court denied Lisa writ of certiorari. Lisa remains housed at the Federal Medical Center in Carswell, Texas.

Child Murderers

There are no steadfast figures on the number of children murdered by their mothers in the United States, though estimates suggest that hundreds of children die at the hands of their mothers every year in this country. Government figures show that mothers murder roughly one-third of children killed by their parents and about 5 percent of child homicides result from a female acquaintance. Contrary to popular belief, child homicide is not the province of mothers; fathers are at least as likely to murder their young children though the research literature is much more focused on maternal filicide. Interestingly, though courts are more apt to impose hospitalization than imprisonment to mothers convicted of murdering their children compared to fathers convicted of murdering their children, only about one-fifth of women convicted of murdering their children receive any form of mental health treatment. Yet, there is an important body of psychiatric and psychological research largely overlooked by justice professionals showing that mothers who murder their children suffer from severe mental disorders. The literature on mental illness among women who murder their children reveals that maternal filicide mostly involves married women older than 25 years of age who suffer from extreme psychiatric illnesses, depression, schizophrenia, or mental retardation. The motives for murdering children are usually altruistic—the need to relieve children's real or believed suffering from social and family stress. Forensic psychologists point out that the mental health issues of most murderous mothers are coupled with extreme personal problems that emotionally overwhelm these women at the time of their crimes. It is inconceivable that state prosecutors ignore the scientific research on maternal filicide and continue to seek capital sentences in such cases knowing that these women suffer from extreme psychiatric and psychological disorders. Rapaport may have put it best when she explained, while our society professes a commitment toward shielding children "our practice reveals an unimpressive record of child protection and abiding anxieties about female sexuality and motherhood."[20] As the narratives on the 17 death row women convicted and sentenced to death for murdering children reveal, these women have extensive childhood and adult histories of extreme physical, sexual, and psychological abuse.

In April 2002, a Houston County jury in Alabama found Patricia Blackmon guilty of murdering Dominiqua Bryant, her 28-month-old adopted daughter. The jury recommended that Patricia should die for her crime. Finding young Dominiqua's death particularly "heinous, atrocious and cruel," the court sentenced Patricia to death. It seems that in May 1999, Patricia summoned paramedics to her mobile home claiming that her daughter was not breathing. Patricia told police that Dominiqua fell from a bed and hit a bedpost. Emergency personnel arriving at the home found the baby's lifeless body lying on the floor in the master bedroom; she was covered in vomit and wearing only a diaper and blood-soaked socks. Paramedics transported Dominiqua to a hospital where an emergency room physician pronounced her dead. A pediatrician examined the child and found she had multiple bruises and contusions and an imprint of the sole of a shoe on her chest. Testimony later showed that the sole print on the child's chest matched sandals worn by Patricia. Authorities found Dominiqua's blood on several items in the house including a broken pool cue, a child's T-shirt, a pink flat bed sheet, a quilt, and two napkins. A medical examiner found Dominiqua had died from multiple blunt-force injuries to her head, chest, abdomen, and extremities.

The Court of Criminal Appeals of Alabama in August 2005 denied Patricia's request for a new trial. A year later, the same court reheard Patricia's appeal because the state had suspended her trial counsel from the practice of law and the court allowed her new attorney to file a brief that raised new issues. Patricia claimed that the district attorney's discriminatory removal of black jurors at her trial violated *Batson*, but the Court found that the state's attorney gave legally sufficient race-neutral reasons for removing each of the black jurors. The court revealed the state's attorney removed black jurors who expressed opposition to the death penalty, jurors with family members with felony convictions, jurors who knew witnesses in the case, and jurors with imprisoned relatives. The court found no intentional or purposeful discrimination. The Court entertained no claims of mental incapacity and affirmed Patricia's conviction and death sentence. The U.S. Supreme Court denied certiorari in 2009 and Patricia remains on death row in Tutwiler Prison for Women while undergoing further appeals of her death sentence.

Another Houston County jury in Alabama convicted Tierra Capri Gobble in October 2005 of killing her four-month-old son, Phoenix Jordan Cody Parrish, in December 2004 and recommended the court sentence her to death. The circuit court judge followed the jury's recommendation and sentenced Tierra to die by lethal injection. Reportedly, paramedics rushed Phoenix to the emergency room at Southeast Alabama Medical Center in Dothan where physicians found the child not breathing and with no pulse. Attempts to resuscitate young Phoenix were unsuccessful and the emergency room physician pronounced him dead shortly after the child arrived at the hospital. An autopsy showed that Phoenix died from blunt-force trauma to his head consistent with abuse. Phoenix not only had a fractured skull, but the child suffered from fractured ribs, a fracture to his right arm, fractures to both wrists, multiple bruises on his face, head, neck, and chest and a tear in the inside his mouth that was consistent with a bottle having been shoved into his mouth. To one physician who testified on the state's behalf, Phoenix undoubtedly suffered a horrifically painful death.

Strangely enough, social services in Florida had removed Phoenix and Tierra's first child, 18-month-old Jewell, from her care and placed him with a paternal uncle, Edgar Parrish. At the time of Phoenix's death, Tierra was under a court order to have no contact with her children. Houston County Sheriffs arrested Tierra shortly after paramedics rushed Phoenix to the hospital and questioned her about the child's death. Tierra told police that she often became frustrated with Phoenix when he would not go to sleep, that she could have broken his ribs from holding him too tightly, and that when she was holding Phoenix she leaned down in the crib to get his blanket quickly and Phoenix's head might have struck the side of the crib. Tierra claimed that her boyfriend, Samuel David Hunter, was abusive and domineering. Florida protective services had instructed Parrish not to leave the state or allow any contact between the infant and his parents. Parrish violated both of these instructions by moving to Alabama and allowing Tierra to move in with him. The state attorney claimed that other adults living in the trailer, namely Parrish and Hunter, were abusive to the child as well; they are both serving long prison terms. The month of Phoenix's death, authorities had initiated proceedings to terminate Tierra's parental rights.

In the sentencing phase of Tierra's trial, the defense introduced mitigating evidence that she grew up in a neglectful, abusive, and dangerous environment. She experienced emotional neglect and her mother was physically abusive. As a result of these childhood traumas, Tierra suffers from postpartum depression and an attention deficit hyperactivity disorder. The unresolved issues in her childhood meant that Tierra failed to learn appropriate coping skills as a child and internalized her anger that in turn caused her to suffer from a severe depression disorder.

In February 2010, the Court of Criminal Appeals of Alabama affirmed Tierra's murder conviction, but remanded the case back to the trial court to correct for discrepancies in the penalty phase of her trial, but in April 2010 the same court affirmed Tierra's death sentence.

In August 2009, a Franklin County jury in Alabama convicted Christie Michelle Scott of capital murder for killing of her autistic six-year-old-son, Mason Scott, when she set the family's Russellville home on fire in the pre-dawn hours in August 2008. The jury recommended life in prison without parole by a seven to five vote over the death penalty, but Circuit Judge Terry Dempsey overrode the jury's recommendation and sentenced Christie to death by lethal injection. Judge Dempsey stated in his sentencing order, "Killing your own child for money by burning him alive is too much to overcome." Christie worked as an agent for Alfa Insurance and started the fire to collect two substantial life insurance policies on her son, one of which she purchased hours before the child's death. The Court of Criminal Appeals of Alabama has denied Christie an initial round of state appeals where she argued, among a myriad of other legal issues, that the circuit court failed to consider mitigating evidence that Christie suffers from an anxiety disorder, the hardships she had experienced in life, and a childhood attention deficit disorder. The court affirmed her conviction and death sentence and awaits execution at the Julia Tutwiler maximum security prison in Wetumpka, Alabama.

Orange County Superior Court Judge Ted Millard upheld a jury's recommendation in June 1992 that Maria Del Rosio Alfaro, a mother of four, should die in California's death chamber for the 1990 murder of nine-year-old Autumn Carol Wallace who Maria stabbed to death during a home invasion burglary and robbery to get money for drugs. At her arrest, Maria confessed to police of murdering the child who was home alone at the time of the killing. She had stabbed the child more than 50 times. At the penalty phase of her trial, testimony from family, friends, and expert witnesses showed that Maria had an extremely impoverished and violent childhood while raised in an Anaheim barrio. Maria's father was an alcoholic who often was violent toward Maria and her mother, and at times threw the family out of the house during drunken rages. A friend of her fathers raped Maria when she was nine years old and afterwards she developed emotional problems, including depression associated with trauma. Maria's father abandoned the family when she was 14 years old. Maria had a troubled history of drug abuse beginning in the sixth grade. She dropped out of school at the seventh grade and began running away from home. It was then that Maria started injecting a mixture of heroin and cocaine, commonly known as "speed balls," as much as 50 times each day. At the age of 13, Maria became a prostitute and engaged in petty thefts to support her drug habit. Her mother often found her on the streets, dirty, hungry, and shoeless. Maria was pregnant at 14 years old. Expert testimony showed that Maria suffered from an ongoing organic mental disorder, including attention deficit disorder, learning disabilities, a conduct disorder characterized by childhood antisocial behavior, an adjustment disorder characterized by anxiety and depression, and a dependent personality disorder that were exacerbated by her traumatic childhood. Maria's intellectual functions are "borderline," she has an IQ of 78, and she is a passive and dependent person with low impulse control. Despite this evidence, the California Supreme Court affirmed the verdict and death sentence in August 2007 and rejected Maria's habeas corpus petition in November of that year. In March 2008, the U.S. Supreme Court denied certiorari in her case.

In April 2002, Ventura County Judge Donald Coleman sentenced to death Socorro Susan Caro, a housewife, former nurse, and church-going wife of a respected physician for the November 1999 shooting death of her three young boys while they slept and then wounding herself at their Santa Rosa Valley home in California. Socorro murdered 11-year-old Xavier "Joey" Caro Jr., in his bedroom, eight-year-old Michael Anthony Caro and five-year-old Christopher Laurence Caro in the bedroom they shared. She killed the boys with a .38-caliber handgun. Gabriel, a 13-month-old infant was unharmed. Authorities found Socorro in the house bleeding from a gunshot wound to the head. The family lived in a 4,800-square-foot, 5-bedroom home in an affluent gated community. Xavier Caro was a respected physician of rheumatology and clinical immunology at Northridge Hospital Medical Center, where he had worked for more than 20 years. Xavier Caro had recently fired his wife as an office manager in his practice and had taken away her checkbook and credit cards. Socorro believed her husband was having an affair and they quarreled just before killing the boys. Socorro once abused her husband so badly that he required surgery for a damaged eye. After the murders, Xavier Caro filed for divorce and has custody of the couple's youngest son. Prosecutors maintained that Socorro was a selfish and spiteful woman who was angry with her husband because he cut off her lavish spending. Socorro claimed insanity at her trial. The California Supreme Court has yet to hear an appeal from Socorro.

In October 1997, Susan Dianne Eubanks shot her four young sons in the head with a .38-caliber revolver. The four dead were four-year-old Matthew D. Eubanks, six-year-old Brigham "Reno" Eubanks, seven-year-old Austin C. Eubanks, and 14-year-old Brandon C. Armstrong. Susan left uninjured a five-year-old nephew named Aaron Storm Stanley who authorities found sitting on a bed traumatized. Susan then shot herself in the stomach. Police went to the Eubanks' home shortly after her estranged husband Eric Dale Eubanks, the father of the three youngest boys, called emergency services after he received a troubling voice-mail from this his wife. Susan was living with her boyfriend Rene Dodson and her nephew in a small house in San Marcos, California, at the time she killed her children. Susan and her boyfriend had a disturbed relationship, as well as with her previous husband. At one point, Susan had suffered a job-related back injury that required surgery and began abusing prescription medications and alcohol; police found more than 50 bottles of prescription medications in her home after the murders. Relatives and friends testified at Susan's trial that she was "tortured" during her childhood. A jury found Eubanks guilty of the multiple murders and Superior Court Judge Joan Weber sentenced her to death. The California Supreme Court affirmed Susan's guilty verdict and death sentence in December 2011. Susan remains on death row awaiting execution at the Central California Women's Facility in Chowchilla.

San Diego Superior Court juries found Veronica Gonzales and her husband Ivan of the July 1995 torture-mayhem-murder of their four-year-old niece, Genny Rojas, in their home in Chula Vista, California. At Veronica's trial, jurors issued a statement that the "numerous and horrific acts of violence" committed against young Genny far outweighed any mitigating factors offered during the trial. The Gonzaleses not only submerged the child in a bathtub of scalding water so hot that it peeled the skin from her body after she spilled some of the Gonzales's drugs. They waited hours before calling police and medical personnel and the child died shortly thereafter. During the six month ordeal in which young Genny lived with the Gonzaleses, the couple forced little Genny to live a box in a closet with her feet and hands bound, blindfolded, and they starved, beat, and burned Genny's face with a hand-held hair dryer and curling iron while she hanged from a hook in the closet. The Gonzaleses so often and violently rammed the child's body into the closet wall that her head put a hole in the wall. The jury recommended that the court sentence Veronica to death and San Diego Superior Court Judge Michael Wellington carried out the jury's recommendation that the state execute her for Genny's murder. Judge Wellington had sentenced Ivan Gonzales to death six months earlier for the child's murder. The Gonzales's have the dubious distinction of being the first married couple in state's history to serve on death row together. At the penalty phase of her trial, Veronica testified at length about her childhood emotional and physical abuse inflicted by her mother and of the sexual abuse she suffered at the hands of her stepfather. Other testimony found that Veronica's abuse contributed to her low self-esteem and she became a battered woman. In 2011, the California Supreme Court affirmed Veronica's guilty verdict and death sentence, and the U.S. Supreme Court denied her a writ of certiorari in 2012.

After deliberating for just five hours in August 2000, a San Fernando Superior Court jury in California found Sandi Nieves guilty of the 1998 arson murder of her four daughters and the attempted murder of her 14-year-old son David when she set fire to her Santa Clarita home. Superior Court Judge L. Jeffrey Wiatt sentenced Sandi to death for the killing of five-year-old Jaqlene Marie Folden, seven-year-old Kristl Dawn Folden, 11-year-old Rashel Holly Nieves, and 12-year-old Nikolet Amber Nieves who were wearing pajamas and tucked in sleeping bags when their bodies were found. The girls died from inhaling soot, smoke, and carbon monoxide. Sandi's first husband, Fernando Nieves, fathered her three eldest children and her second husband, Dave Folden, also her former stepfather, fathered the two youngest daughters. Sandi, who was angry at her two ex-husbands, told her children that she was holding a family slumber party, then used gasoline to start fires in the house and prevented her children from leaving. The California Supreme Court has yet to hear an appeal of Sandi's murder conviction and death sentence.

A Riverside County jury in California convicted Cathy Sarinana in March 2009, along with her husband, Raul Ricardo Sarinana (also known as Ruben Osvaldo Parra), for the torture-murder of their 11-year-old nephew, Ricky Morales. The child died in a closet at the Sarinanas' duplex on Christmas Day 2005 after Raul Sarinana kicked and beat him for cleaning a bathroom too slowly. Police also found Ricky's 13-year-old brother, Conrad Morales, dead, entombed in concrete inside a small garbage can, and brought from Washington where prosecutors suspect the Sarinanas killed the child before moving to Corona. The children were staying with their aunt and uncle because their parents could no longer support the children. The Sarinanas have two children of their own, a two-year-old girl, and a 13-month-old boy. The jury recommended that the state should execute Sarinana for her complicity in the torture-murder of her nephew, and Superior Court Judge Paul E. Zellerbach agreed with the jury's instruction and sentenced Sarinana to death claiming that a dominant factor in his decision was the way she repeatedly abused Ricky. A pathologist testified at trial that new and old scabs, bruises, and scars covered the boy's body and that he had cracked ribs and a torn lung. It is noteworthy that Riverside County Deputy District Attorney John Aki, who prosecuted the Sarinanas, recently won a national award in part for winning death penalty convictions against the Sarinanas. The coveted award among state's attorneys may be premature since no appeals court has yet to take any action on the case.

Police in Riverside County, California, charged Janeen Marie Snyder and her boyfriend, Michael Forrest Thornton, for the kidnapping and shooting death of a 16-year-old Las Vegas girl named Michelle Leann Curran taken from her Las Vegas neighborhood while on her way to school in late March 2001. Police investigators found Michelle's bruised, nude body crammed inside a compartment of a horse trailer. Authorities believe that ligature marks on Michelle's wrists and ankles may have indicated that the defendants strung her up using harnesses and other equestrian equipment stored in a tack room on the same property in which they found the young girl. After the couple had used Michelle as a sex slave, Janeen shot her once in the head. The two faced prosecution for first-degree murder, kidnapping, rape, and torture of the young girl. According to prosecutors, Janeen and Thornton had "an insatiable appetite for drugs, guns and sex with underage girls." Several friends and acquaintances testified that the couple engaged in "a no-questions-asked netherworld of almost nonstop partying that included watching pornographic movies for hours on end and ingesting huge amounts of marijuana, cocaine and methamphetamine." Two young women testified that as young teenagers, Janeen and Thornton "held them against their will and used drugs, fear and mind-control techniques to force them to participate in sexual threesomes."[21] In May 2006, a jury convicted Janeen and Thornton of Michelle's murder and Superior Court Judge Paul E. Zellerbach sentenced the two to death. Zellerback explained that Janeen and Thornton held Michelle captive for 14 days during which they gave her drugs, intimidated her with firearms and sexually exploited her. Authorities believe that Michelle's death is one in a long string of attacks committed by the couple. Officials suspected Janeen and Thornton stalked and assaulted other girls. The state's Supreme Court has yet to hear an appeal on Janeen's case.

Ana Cardona was the defendant in a horrific child murder case in Florida in early November 1990 involving the death of her three-year-old son, Lazaro Figueroa. Police nicknamed the child "Baby Lollipops" because of the shirt he was wearing when a utility crew working in the area discovered his emaciated body in the bushes near Miami Beach. Authorities identified the young boy as Ana's youngest child. Trial evidence revealed that before Lazaro's birth, Ana and her two older children lived with her boyfriend Fidel Figueroa, a well-off drug dealer, and Lazaro's father. The family lived in a luxurious apartment and had an extravagant lifestyle. A month before Lazaro's birth, Fidel was a murder victim and left a $100,000 estate that Ana squandered in less than a year. When Ana became insolvent, she sent Lazaro and his older sister to live with friends and relatives but eventually child protective services took the children. In late 1998, the children returned to Ana's custody, at the time young Lazaro was a healthy eleven-month-old child. Ana soon developed a lesbian relationship with Olivia Gonzalez-Mendoza and lived with the children in a series of cut-rate hotels. Ana and Olivia were mostly unemployed and supported themselves, the children, and their drug addictions largely by shoplifting. Ana blamed young Lazaro for her economic plight and often referred to him as a "bad birth."

Almost immediately after Ana gained custody of her children, she beat, choked, starved, confined, emotionally abused, and tortured Lazaro. The child spent much of the time tied to a bed, left in a bathtub with the hot or cold-water running, or locked in a closet. To avoid changing Lazaro's diaper for as long as possible, Cardona often wrapped duct tape around the child's diaper to hold in the excrement. Gonzalez-Mendoza often participated in Lazaro's abuse because it pleased Ana. Then, in late October 1990, Ana beat Lazaro with a baseball bat, splitting open the child's head. Ana locked Lazaro in a closet where she restrained him for at least two months. At one point, Gonzalez-Mendoza opened the closet door and quieted Lazaro by frightening him with the baseball bat and when Lazaro screamed at the sight of Ana, she grabbed the bat from Gonzalez-Mendoza and killed Lazaro. The two women dressed Lazaro's dead body and abandoned him in bushes near a residence. Police arrested Ana and Gonzalez-Mendoza in St. Cloud, Florida, where they had fled after learning that authorities had discovered Lazaro's beaten body. Police charged both women with first-degree murder. Gonzalez-Mendoza testified against Ana in return for a charge of second-degree murder and aggravated child abuse. Gonzalez-Mendoza served 19 years of a 40-year sentence and prison authorities released her in January 2008. A Miami-Dade County jury found Ana guilty of Lazaro's murder and recommended a capital sentence. Weighing the aggravating and mitigating circumstances, the court concluded that the aggravating circumstance of heinous, atrocious, or cruel "is overwhelming and of enormous weight," considering the "long period of time over which this baby was subject to torture, abuse, pain, and suffering." The trial court followed the jury's recommendation and sentenced Ana to die in the state's electric chair.

In 2002, the Florida Supreme Court granted Ana a new trial citing prosecutorial misconduct in her original trial when state prosecutors failed to disclose criminal investigation reports of extensive interviews with Olivia Gonzalez-Mendoza, thus denying defense lawyers an opportunity to cross-examine her testimony. In July 2010, Florida officials retried Ana and won a second murder conviction. At the penalty phase of the trial, the same jury recommended the court sentence Ana to death. Judge Reemberto Diaz handed down the death sentence recommended by the second jury. The state avoided any discussion of Ana's troubled childhood while growing up in Cuba that may explain her sadistic conduct toward Lazaro. Ana is a non–English speaking, illiterate Cuban immigrant from Miami who was raped as a young teenager in Cuba.

Ana moved to the United States when she was 19 years old. Ana complained about her inability to understand what was going on at her trial: "I did not understand what was said in my trial. The translator told me it was not important, and the lawyers I had did not speak Spanish."

Debra Brown is the only woman on death row in Indiana. In 1990, Lake County Superior Court juries convicted Debra and her companion, Alton Coleman, for stomping a seven-year-old child, Tamika Turks, to death and attempting to choke to death Tamika's nine-year-old niece, Annie, with a belt after sexually assaulting the child. In a separate trial, District Court Judge Richard J. Conroy sentenced Debra to death for murder, rape and attempted murder and an additional 40 years on charges of kidnapping and child-molesting. Reportedly, Tamika and Annie were walking back from a store to their home when Brown and Coleman confronted them and convinced the children to walk into the woods to play a game. Once there, Debra and Coleman removed Tamika's shirt and tore it into strips which they used to bind and gag the children. When Tamika began to cry, Debra held her nose and mouth while Coleman stomped on her chest. After carrying Tamika a short distance away, Debra and Coleman forced Annie to perform oral sex on the couple, then Coleman raped her. Debra and Coleman choked Annie until she was unconscious. Annie's cuts were so deep that her intestines were protruding into her vagina. Officials found Tamika's dead body in nearby bushes, strangled with an elastic strip of bed sheet. Authorities believe that the crimes against Tamika and Annie were part of a 53-day crime spree across Wisconsin, Illinois, Indiana, Ohio, Michigan and Kentucky wherein Debra and Coleman committed eight murders, seven rapes, three kidnappings, and 14 armed robberies.

Debra was one of 11 children who had a troubled childhood with a father who had severe mental problems, drank excessively, and physically abused Debra. She used drugs regularly and was hospitalized in 1980 for a drug overdose. Debra's personality changed radically after she met Coleman who completely dominated her, physically abused her, and used her as a prostitute. Debra suffered a severe head trauma as a child and is borderline mentally retarded. Ohio tried the couple first where courts found them guilty of murder and sentenced them to death. In late April 2002, Ohio executed Alton Coleman by lethal injection at the Southern Ohio Correctional Facility near Lucasville. Ohio Governor Richard Celeste commuted Debra's Ohio death sentence to life imprisonment in 1991. She is now facing execution on death row in Indiana.

In late February 2011, Lane County Circuit Judge Kip Leonard sentenced Angela Darlene McAnulty to death after she pleaded guilty to the torture murder of her 15-year-old daughter, Jeanette Marie Maple. Emergency personnel found the teenager's emaciated dead body in a bathtub in her home shortly before Christmas 2009 after her stepfather reported that she was not breathing. Jeanette died from prolonged starvation, dehydration, physical injuries and localized infections though officials could not establish an exact cause of death. As a result of her neglect, mistreatment, maiming and torture, Jenette reportedly weighed 50 pounds at the time of her death. At Angela's trial, relatives, friends, a school counselor, and a child protection officer testified about their suspicions of the abuse suffered by Jeanette. The teenager's estate recently settled a $1.5 million lawsuit against the Oregon Department of Human Services that admitted it had not followed its own policies in dealing with the allegations of child abuse against Jeanette. Angela had a violent and abusive childhood herself. Her mother was stabbed to death when she was five years old. Angela and her siblings went to live with their abusive father who withheld food and beat them. After high school, she traveled with a carnival worker and started using drugs. She had two sons and a daughter in a later marriage but California child protection agents removed the children from Angela's care for neglect and abuse. Angela had another daughter, recovered the daughter taken by state officials, and eventually married a long-haul trucker. The stepfather is serving a life sentence after pleading guilty to murder by abuse. Angela is on death row at the Coffee Creek Correction Facility in Wilsonville where Oregon houses its entire female prison population. Most recently, the Oregon Supreme Court upheld Angela's the conviction and sentence despite "harmless error" when the trial judge should have granted a motion to suppress some statements Angela made to investigators after invoking her right to remain silent.

In November 2000, a Washington County jury in Pennsylvania found Michelle Sue Tharp and her live-in boyfriend, Douglas James Bittinger, guilty of the starvation murder of Michelle's seven-year-old daughter, Tausha Lee Lanham. Common Pleas Judge Paul Pozonsky sentenced Michelle to death by lethal injection and Bittinger to 15 to 30 years in prison for his part in the murder. Tausha weighed less than 12 pounds when she died. A medical examiner testified that Tausha's body showed numerous signs of severe malnutrition; the body had almost no fat in parts of the body where the accumulation of fatty tissue is normally found, there was extreme wear on the grinding surface of Tausha's teeth, a common occurrence in instances of juvenile starvation, and that Tausha had not eaten for several days. Reportedly, Michelle forced the child to forage for food in garbage cans and to drink from the toilet. The couple wrapped the corpse in a sheet, stuffed it into garbage bags, dumped the body along a West Virginia road in a wooded area, and then reported Tausha missing from an Ohio shopping mall. The Pennsylvania Supreme Court affirmed Michelle's verdict and death sentence in 2003 and the U.S. Supreme Court refused to review the case in 2004. Recently, federal public defender attorneys asked Judge Pozonsky to overturn Michelle's conviction and death sentence because her attorney, Glenn Alterio, failed to present evidence in the sentencing phase to the trial of Michelle's brain damage, low IQ, traumatic upbringing, and violent abuse by former boyfriends. The attorneys also pointed out that prosecutors reduced the prison term for Douglas Bittinger in exchange for false testimony. Judge Pozonsky rejected the appeal. In September 2014, however, the Pennsylvania Supreme Court ordered a new penalty hearing on precisely those grounds claimed by the federal public defenders. That is, the 60-page opinion ordered the new hearing "on the grounds that her attorney failed to present evidence that may have persuaded a jury to spare her life, such as a history of mental illness, abuse throughout her childhood and borderline intellectual function."[22]

A Cameron County jury in Texas convicted Melissa Elizabeth Lucio, a mother of 14 children, for the torture and beating death of her two-and-a-half-year-old daughter Mariah Alvarez. The court also sentenced Melissa's common-law husband, Roberto Antonio Alvarez, to four years in prison for failing to prevent the beatings suffered by Mariah. Emergency personnel found the child with purple and green bruises on her entire torso, head, face, and right shoulder upon arriving at Lucio's home in February 2007. The child died from brain damage. Defense attorneys argued that Lucio is impoverished and suffers from battered women's syndrome. There is evidence that Melissa is mentally retarded. Child Protective Services had removed children from her home from 2004 to 2006 for allegations of physical neglect and neglectful supervision. The Texas Court of Criminal Appeals upheld the conviction and death sentence in 2011. The U.S. Supreme Court denied Melissa a writ of certiorari in 2012. In a writ of habeas corpus heard in January 2013, the court reviewed 10 allegations challenging the validity of Melissa's conviction and sentence and held with the trial court's findings and conclusions. Melissa Lucio remains on death row at the Mountain View facility in Gatesville.

A Kerr County jury in Texas convicted housewife Darlie Lynn Routier in June 1996 for the stabbing death of her two sons, five-year-old Damon Routier and six-year-old Devon Routier, and recommended a death sentence. Darlie left a younger son unharmed. Prosecutors sought a conviction only on Damon's murder. Judge Mark Stenson Tolle sentenced Darlie to death. At trial, Darlie testified that she was sleeping on a couch in the family room in the downstairs of her home and that her sons were asleep on the floor in front of the television. She awoke to discover a stranger departing through the kitchen and utility room and out through the garage, leaving a bloody butcher knife from the kitchen behind on the utility room floor. She suffered a number of wounds, including a slash across her neck that came perilously close to severing her carotid artery. She denied having stabbed her sons. The state's prosecutor presented circumstantial evidence suggesting that there was no intruder, that the crime scene had been "staged," that Darlie had inflicted the wounds on herself, and that she had some pecuniary motive to murder her children. A physician found amphetamines in Darlie's blood on the night of the children's murders. Prosecutors explained that she was suffering financial problems and was upset because she could not lose weight after giving birth to her third child. The Texas Court of Criminal Appeals upheld Routier's conviction and sentence in May 2003, and the same court denied a writ of habeas corpus in December 2004. In May 2004, the U.S. Supreme Court denied Darlie certiorari. Dallas Judge Robert Francis denied Darlie's request for DNA testing in early 2007, but the Court of Criminal Appeals overruled Judge Francis and allowed Darlie limited DNA testing. The same denied a rehearing in September 2008. Court reporting problems hindered the case; a certified court reporter directed to correct the *Routier* transcript found some 18,000 errors in 6,000 pages of transcript. Recently, the U.S. District Court in San Antonio has allowed a new trial request from Darlie's attorneys.

Spousal Murderers

Acts of intimate violence—murder and non-negligent manslaughter—account for about 16 percent of all homicides in the United States. Men are far more likely to victimize women than are women to victimize men; roughly 70 percent of intimate partner homicide victims are female. This difference in intimate partner homicides means that spouses and boyfriends (as well as former spouses and boyfriends) are more than *twice* as likely to kill women as are women to kill men. Experts claim that the proportion at which males kill females in intimate partner relationships has remained unchanged over the last few decades although the actual number of homicide victims in intimate partner relationships has decreased substantially. The number of women killed by an intimate partner decreased by 26 percent from 2,200 in 1993 to 1,640 in 2007, while the number of men killed by intimate partners over the same period decreased by 36 percent from 1,100 in 1993 to 700 in 2007. The percent decrease in the number of black female homicide victims killed by intimate partners fell by 39 percent over the same period. Despite the substantial decrease in the numbers of black women murder victims killed by intimate partners over the period, data on intimate partner victimization show that among women, being black, young, divorced or separated, earning a lower income, living in rental housing, and living in an urban area are associated with higher rates of intimate partner victimization.

Scholars have addressed the acute inadequacy of the American criminal justice system to effectively deal with violence against women. One noted expert explains that the American justice system remains "a bastion of male supremacy" particularly within the context of battered women who suffer sexual, physical, and severe psychological abuse from intimate partners. About half of all victims of intimate partner violence report the violence to law enforcement and black women tend to report their victimization to police at higher rates than white women and Latinas. The most common reasons for women not reporting intimate victimization to police include the notion that it is a personal or private matter, their afraid of reprisal, it's a minor crime, police will not bother, wanted to protect the offender, police bias, inconvenience, police ineffectiveness, and a belief that intimate violence is not clearly a crime. Yet, studies suggest that judges and juries are more likely to convict and send black women to prison than white women. Scholars have addressed the severe inadequacy of state justice systems to effectively deal with domestic violence:

[I]n the incidents of violence against women, at every step of the way, the criminal justice system poses significant hurdles for victims. The gender biases within state law enforcement and the state judicial systems prevent the existing laws from being adequately and evenly enforced, especially those concerning domestic violence.... [I]n many incidents of domestic violence police may refuse to take reports; prosecutors may encourage defendants to plead to minor offenses; judges may rule against victims on evidentiary matters. This response to domestic violence cases commonly stems from the misperception of the victim's situation and the belief that the woman should simply leave her abuser. In the rare case where a domestic violence victim's attacker is brought to justice, it is important to recognize that the criminal system's remedies and the battered women's needs may not correspond.[23]

It is still a popular notion in American society to limit understanding of spousal violence to crimes of husbands against wives. The dimensions of spousal violence far exceed this conventional imagery and continue to blind us as a nation to the view that women are regularly the aggressors in domestic violence. Intimate violence against men is a severe problem in this country and it is only recently that scholars have started recognizing domestic violence against men as a severe social problem. Researchers explain that society must overcome gender-stereotypes about domestic violence, conduct accurate studies, and enact responsible legislation if our society is going to address legitimately the problem of male victimization in domestic situations. Researchers have found that women are regularly the aggressors in domestic violence. Some scholars explain that *facts* about domestic violence *contradict* our fixed notions about the problem:

Half of spousal murders are committed by wives, a statistic that has been stable over time. The 1985 National Family Violence Survey, funded by the National Institute of Mental Health and supported by many other surveys, revealed that women and men were physically abusing one another in roughly equal numbers. Wives reported that they were more often the aggressors. Using weapons to make up for physical disadvantage, they were not just fighting back. The Journal for the National Association of Social Workers found in 1986 that among teenagers who date, young women were violent more frequently than boys.... Because men have been taught to 'take it like a man' and are ridiculed when they reveal they have been battered by women, women are nine times more likely to report their abusers to the authorities.[24]

Remarkably, nearly a third of American women experience some form of intimate partner violence in their lifetimes resulting in such significant health issues as personal injury, death, sexually transmitted diseases, unintended pregnancy, psychological distress, and premature births. Researchers exploring the rationales of why women kill their husbands have found a striking parallel between the frequency of marital rape and spousal murder. One study found that more than 75 percent of women murderers killed husbands who forced sexual intercourse with many women killers reportedly raped more than 20 times by their husbands. Other studies show that significant numbers of women raped by their husbands also threaten to kill them. Threatening to kill their wives is a major reason for women killing their husbands especially if women attempt to leave the troubled relationship. Women who cannot easily leave relationship often contemplate suicide. Drug and alcohol abuse precipitate domestic violence with twice as many men killed by their wives when the husband is drunk.

Nine condemned women are on America's death rows for murdering their husbands and currently housed in correctional facilities in Arizona, California, Georgia, Mississippi, North Carolina, Ohio, and Oklahoma. In November 2004, a Maricopa County jury in Arizona found Wendi Elizabeth Andriano guilty of the first-degree murder of her husband Joseph Andriano and recommended a death sentence finding the killing "especially cruel." Superior Court Judge Brian Ishikawa agreed with the jury's finding and sentenced Wendi to die by lethal injection. Wendi had bludgeoned Joseph to death with a bar stool and a lamp. Joseph was terminally ill at the time and the couple had two small children. Wendi called paramedics in October 2000 claiming her husband was having a heart attack. When emergency personnel arrived at the home they found Joseph lying on the floor of the couple's apartment in a fetal position in a pool of blood. Joseph had vomited, was weak and having difficulty breathing. Police found a broken bar stool covered in blood near Joseph's body, pieces of a lamp, a kitchen knife with blood on the sharp edge, a bloody pillow, and a belt. Wendi had beaten Joseph mercilessly. A medical examiner determined that Joseph sustained brain hemorrhaging from more than 20 blows to the back of his head. Joseph had defensive wounds on his hands and wrists. Joseph also sustained a stab wound to the left side of his neck. What's more, forensic specialists found traces of sodiumazide (a poison) present in Joseph's blood. Phoenix police detectives searched the Andrianos' storage unit and found 500 grams of sodiumazide and traces of the chemical in kitchen utensils.

Wendi's defense attorney claimed that she was a battered wife whose husband verbally, physically, and sexually abused her. The court found that this mitigating evidence was not substantial because Wendi did not kill her husband while defending against a domestic violence attack. Any sexual abuse was far too remote for the court to consider and minimally relevant. In contrast, the state's attorney depicted Wendi as a greedy, cheating wife who killed her cancer-stricken husband in a "shockingly evil" way. The prosecution asserted that while Joseph was undergoing chemotherapy, Wendi had affairs with two men and recruited other men to pose as Joe in a plan to fraudulently obtain a one million dollar life insurance policy and forged a business license to buy the poison used to kill her husband. To her defense team, however, Juan Martinez's portrayal of Wendi as a cheating wife was tantamount to prosecutor misconduct that unfairly prejudiced the jury; "he took every opportunity to infuse the trial with marginally relevant information about Andriano's partying and man-chasing."[25] The Arizona Supreme Court has rejected all contentions in Wendi's appeals and upheld her guilty verdict and death sentence. The U.S. Supreme Court denied Wendi's writ of certiorari in October 2007.

In January 2004, a Los Angeles County jury found Angelina Rodriguez guilty of the October 2000 poison-murder of her husband, Jose Francisco "Frank" Rodriguez and recommended the court sentence her to death. The jury deliberated for about a day. The jury also convicted Angelina of threatening a witness to whom she had revealed her plan to kill Jose. Superior Court Judge William Pounders ordered Angelina sent to the women's prison in Chowchilla and once she has exhausted her automatic court appeals, authorities are to transfer her to San Quentin for execution. Frank Rodriguez was Angelina's fifth husband and a special education teacher for the Los Angeles Unified School District. Apparently, Angelina put enough poisonous oleanders in her husband's meals to hospitalize him and then killed him at home by lacing Gatorade with antifreeze. She hoped to collect on a $250,000 life insurance policy. After hearing the testimony and evidence in Angelina's trial, Judge Pounders was convinced that she had also killed her 13-month-old daughter, Alicia Nicole Fuller, in 1993 while living in Santa Barbara though authorities have not charged Angelina in the child's death. Angelina and her then-husband received a $710,000 settlement from the Gerber Company after the child ostensibly chocked to death when a pacifier nibble became lodged in her throat. The state's Supreme Court has yet to hear a direct appeal.

Angelina led an exceedingly troubled life. She grew up in a working-class neighborhood in Queens, New York. Her father was a Puerto Rican–born truck and cabdriver who abandoned the family and her mother was a nurse who worked long hours to support the family. As a young child, her paternal grandfather sexually abused her from the time she was two years old, the abuse continued through high school and resulted in an abortion. Angelina attempted suicide at eight years old, and at 16 years old, she was hospitalized for an overdose of sleeping pills. Though of above average intelligence, for most her life Angelina "lived amid emotional chaos, overwhelmed by self-loathing and shame, the result of repeated incest and molestation in childhood." Angelina suffered from depression and anxiety disorders as a child, with symptoms of manic and borderline personality disorders in adulthood. To one commentator, there was no physical evidence linking Angelina to her husband's death. "Instead, it was her bizarre behavior that convinced [police and jury] of her guilt and ultimately resulted in a death sentence." Another commentator supports this notion with the argument the *Los Angeles Times* coverage of Angelina's story did nothing more than perpetuate negative stereotypes about female violence and gender roles; "society tends to assign unattractive and negative traits to females who commit acts of violence, in order to rationalize the use of the death penalty." Accordingly, the *Los Angeles Times* was more attentive to Angelina's past relationships and demeanor than on the facts of the case.

A Los Angeles County jury convicted Mary Ellen Samuels in July 1994 of two counts of first-degree murder, solicitation of murder, and conspiracy to commit murder. Mary Ellen orchestrated the murder of her husband, Robert Samuels, and the murder of the hit man she hired to kill her husband, James Bernstein. Robert was an assistant cinematographer who worked on the films "Lethal Weapon" and "Heaven Can Wait." In 1987, Mary Ellen began soliciting people to murder Robert and eventually was successful in recruiting Bernstein who was dating Mary Ellen's daughter, Nicole Samuels-Moroianu. Bernstein, in turn, solicited Mike Silva who killed Robert with a shotgun blast fired into his head at close range in early December of the following year. It was then that Mary Ellen and Nicole called paramedics to Robert's house in Northridge and found him dead. Before calling medical personnel, however, the two had arranged the house to make it appear that a struggle had taken place. Later, Mary Ellen and Nicole told police that they had discovered Robert's body while dropping off the family dog. To complete the ruse, Mary Ellen left a message on Robert's answering machine about her plan to drop off the dog. Upon Robert's death, Mary Ellen collected more than $200,000 on several life insurance policies, $70,000 in proceeds from the sale of a sandwich shop owned by Robert, she kept Robert's car, received about $6,000 in uncashed payroll checks of Robert's, and that she refinanced the family home for nearly $200,000. Mary Ellen began living a lavish lifestyle after Robert's murder.

Mary Ellen became troubled with Bernstein believing that he was about to go to police and disclose her involvement in Robert's murder. In early 1989, she solicited Paul Gaul to murder Bernstein claiming that he was blackmailing her about Robert's killing and that Bernstein was a drug dealer who sold drugs to children. Gaul and a friend named Darryl Ray Edwards beat and strangled Bernstein to death in a car on a dirt road in June 1989. They dumped Bernstein's body along an isolated stretch of highway. The two murdered Bernstein for $5,000 while Mary Ellen was away in Cancun, Mexico. In September 1994, Judge Michael R. Hoff followed the jury's recommendation and sentenced Mary Ellen to death for her involvement in Robert's murder. Paul Gaul and Darryl Edwards pleaded guilty to second-degree murder in Bernstein's killing and are serving prison terms of 15 years to life. Gaul was released on parole in 2009. Gaul and Edwards testified against Mary Ellen. Mary Ellen claimed that Robert was an abusive husband when he drank, and that he molested and sexually abused her daughter Nicole who also testified that Robert began fondling her when she was 12 years old, and raped her eight times between the ages of 13 and 16 when she left home to escape the abuse. The California Supreme Court affirmed Mary Ellen's conviction and death sentence, and the U.S. Supreme Court has denied her certiorari.

In June 1993, a Los Angeles County jury convicted Catherine Thompson of masterminding the 1990 murder of her husband, Melvin Thompson, the owner of a transmission repair shop, to collect on a $400,000 life insurance policy. Catherine had hired a hit man to kill Melvin. The perpetrator shot Melvin between the eyes, in the mouth, and in the chest. Police originally suspected robbery as the motive for Melvin's murder since assailants killed him while he closed his shop in West Los Angeles; his Rolex watch was missing along with an undetermined amount of cash. Superior Court Judge George Trammell sentenced Thompson to death and sentenced three others involved in the murder scheme to lengthy prison sentences—Phillip Conrad Sanders, the gunman; Carolyn Sanders, who picked up an advance payment for the killing; and Carolyn Sanders' son Robert Lewis Jones, who drove the getaway car.

In 1998, a Gwinnett County jury in Georgia convicted Kelly Renee Gissendaner, a mother of three of young children, for the murder of her husband Douglas Gissendaner. In early February 1997, while her parents cared for her children, Kelly drove her boyfriend, Gregory Bruce Owen, to her family home so he could murder Douglas. Kelly gave Owen a nightstick and a large knife and left him inside the house to wait for Douglas to arrive home. Meanwhile, Kelly went night-clubbing with friends. When Douglas arrived home later in the evening, Owen confronted Douglas with a knife to his throat, forced him to drive to a remote location, forced him to walk into the woods and kneel, and then killed him by striking him with the nightstick and then stabbing him repeatedly in the back and neck with the knife. Owen took Douglas's watch and wedding ring before killing him to make the murder appear like a robbery. Kelly returned home from the nightclub and then drove to the crime scene. Owen burned Douglas's Chevrolet Caprice with kerosene and the two returned to their respective homes in Kelly's car. The apparent motive for Kelly arranging the killing of her husband was to collect on a $10,000 life insurance policy and the couple's $80,000 house. Owen confessed to the murder after his arrest and implicated Kelly as the mastermind of the plan to kill Douglas. As part of a plea bargain, Owen testified against Kelley and received a life sentence, sparing him a death sentence. Superior Court Judge Homer Stark sentenced her to death. Georgia's Supreme Court upheld Kelly's murder conviction and death sentence in July 2000. In March 2012, a United States District Court denied Kelly's claims of ineffective assistance of counsel because her trial lawyers failed to investigate an alleged history of sexual abuse and mental health problems suffered by Kelly and of prosecutorial misconduct when the state suppressed exculpatory evidence, presented false evidence, and manufactured evidence against Kelly at trial. There is evidence that men in Kelly's childhood sexually victimized her to the extent that she likely suffered from mental health problems. One commentator writes:

> Her stepfather began molesting her when she was 10 years old. He slept alongside her for six months, using the guise of an uncomfortable new bed to make bad things happen "almost every night." Shortly thereafter, a neighbor's stepfather raped her. When she was 12, she spent a summer with her grandmother. Her uncle began molesting her there and did it for three years. During her senior year of high school, she was date raped by a man who "had been taking drugs and drinking heavily." Nine months later—two weeks after graduation—her first son was born.[26]

In February 2015, officials postponed Kelly's execution due to a winter storm that hit the area prohibiting some witnesses to safely get to the prison where the execution was to take place. In early March 2015, officials observed that the execution drug had a 'cloudy' appearance and they postponed her death until a future unspecified date. Georgia officials executed Kelly by lethal injection in September 2015.

In June 2003, a Trumbull County jury convicted Donna Roberts of murdering her ex-husband, Robert Fingerhut, for which the trial court sentenced her to death. Robert and Donna were married in 1983 but soon divorced for financial and business reasons to protect assets in the event his business failed. Robert owned a Greyhound bus terminal in Ohio. Despite the divorce, the couple continued as husband and wife and both considered themselves married. Even so, Donna began an affair with Nathaniel Jackson who became a co-defendant in Robert's murder. In early December 2001, Donna summoned emergency personnel to the couple's home claiming something was seriously wrong with Robert. Police found his body on the kitchen floor and forensic reports showed that Robert had sustained lacerations and abrasions to his left hand and head, as well as multiple gunshot wounds to his head, chest, and back. Police investigators learned that Robert had taken out two life insurance policies on his life amounting to $550,000 and naming Donna as sole beneficiary. Letters recovered by police from the home and monitored telephone conversations between Donna and Nathaniel while he was in prison for a short time revealed the plot to murder Robert. A grand jury indicted both Donna and Nathaniel for Robert's murder. On appeal, the Ohio Supreme Court upheld both the verdict and death sentence of Nathaniel Jackson but reversed Donna's death sentence and remanded her case back to the trial court for reconsideration of the death sentence. The court vacated Donna's death sentence because the trial judge permitted the state's prosecutor to help prepare his sentencing opinion on Donna. Apparently, while the court read aloud its sentencing opinion and imposed the death penalty, defense counsel noticed the prosecutor reading a document and was reading along with the trial judge. Defense counsel objected to the prosecution's involvement with the sentencing opinion. The trial judge conceded that the prosecution had participated in the drafting of the opinion without the knowledge of defense counsel. The trial judge apologized to defense counsel for not providing them with a copy of the opinion before the sentencing hearing. The justices of the state's Supreme Court unanimously ruled that the trial judge acted in violation of Ohio law. Donna remains on death row at the Ohio Reformatory for Women in Marysville, but in May 2013, Donna's defense attorneys argued before the Ohio Supreme Court that the trial judge also failed to consider her mental illness, low intelligence, and other mitigating factors before sentencing her to death in 2007. Donna's attorney claims that she suffers from bipolar disorder, depression, and that her I.Q. is 55. In October 2013, the Ohio Supreme Court overturned Donna's death sentence and remanded the case back to the trial court for consideration of all mitigating evidence pertinent to the case. The American Civil Liberties Union reported in March 2011 of the horrifying conditions of confinement under which Donna lives out her life on death row:

> Donna Marie Roberts, the single woman on the state's death row, was housed in a segregation cell formerly reserved to punish inmates who commit disciplinary infractions, which was smaller than those on men's death row. Unlike the men, Roberts did not have a window or a working TV. She had to bang on the door to get the guard's attention to bring her food, dispose of trash, or receive medication. As the only woman, she would take her one hour of recreation, five days a week in the prison yard all by herself.[27]

Oklahoma also has one female death row inmate sentenced to death for spousal murder. In 2004, an Oklahoma County jury convicted Brenda Evers Andrew of 2002 murder of her husband Robert Andrew, an advertising executive, and District Court Judge Susan W. Bragg sentenced her to death. Brenda and Robert had separated when Robert went to the family home to pick up the two minor children, 10-year-old Tricity and seven-year-old Parker, for visitation over the Thanksgiving holiday. Brenda asked Robert into the garage to light the pilot light on the furnace. While doing so, Brenda's paramour, James Pavatt entered the garage and shot Robert to death with a 16-gauge shotgun to the abdomen. As a ruse, Pavatt shot Brenda in the arm with a .22-caliber pistol and then claimed to police that two masked men entered the garage and fired their guns at Robert. Apparently, Pavatt, a life insurance agent, set up a life insurance policy worth approximately $800,000. In September 2001, Robert moved out of the family home and Brenda initiated divorce proceedings. Brenda and Pavatt had met at church and had begun a sexual relationship. Shortly after Robert's death, Brenda, along with Pavatt and the children went to Mexico and became the subject of an international search. Authorities apprehended them when attempted to re-enter the United States in February 2002. After police apprehended Brenda and placed her in the Oklahoma County jail, she confessed to a jailhouse informant who later testified against Brenda that she and Pavatt killed her husband for the money, the children, and each other. In 2007, the Court of Criminal Appeals for Oklahoma affirmed Brenda's murder conviction and death sentence, and in 2008, the U.S. Supreme Court denied Brenda certiorari. Brenda remains on death row at the Mabel Bassett Correctional Center in McLoud, Oklahoma.

In January 2012, a Pomona Superior Court jury in California convicted Manling Tsang Williams, of Taiwanese descent, of the August 2007 murder of her husband and two young sons at the family's condominium in Rowland Heights. Judge Robert Martinez sentenced Manling to death. Manling had been involved with another man who wanted her to divorce before continuing the relationship. Authorities claim that Manling smothered her two sleeping children with pillows, seven-year-old Devon and three-year-old Ian. After killing her children, Manling went out with friends and after returning home, Manling hacked to death her sleeping husband, Neal Williams, with a katana sword. She had hit Neal with the sword more than 97 times. Trial evidence suggests that Manling had an extremely troubled childhood, the Department of Children and Family Services found excessive abuse in young Manling's home. Defense attorneys characterized Manling's actions as a fit of uncontrollable rage brought on by an abusive childhood and mistreatment by her husband. This case is just beginning the state and federal appeals process.

In early March 1993, an Ada County jury convicted Robin Row of the first-degree arson murder of her husband Randy Row and of her two young children, 10-year-old Joshua and eight-year-old Tabitha. The trial judge sentenced Robin to death. All three victims died from carbon monoxide poisoning. District Court Judge Alan Schwartzman characterized Robin's premeditated arson murders as "the final betrayal of motherhood" and "a descent into the blackened heart of darkness." Robin and Randy were separated at the time of the killings; Robin was staying with a friend while Randy remained in their apartment duplex in Boise, Idaho, with the children. Robin was having an affair with another man at the time. Robin had set two fires, one where the apartment joined the garage, and a second fire in some clothes piled in the living room where she used a liquid accelerant. Robin had disabled the smoke detector in the apartment before setting the fires cutting the power to the apartment from a circuit breaker. A police investigation into her family's deaths revealed that Robin had recently taken out six insurance policies on their lives, naming herself as beneficiary of nearly $300,000. Robin obtained the most recent policy 17 days before the fire. The investigation also discovered that in 1977, Robin had a daughter succumb to Sudden Infant Death Syndrome and that her son Keith had died in a house fire in California in 1980. In March 1998, the Idaho Supreme Court upheld Robin's conviction and death sentence. Robin remains the only female death row inmate housed at the Pocatello Woman's Correctional Center in Pocatello, Idaho.

Trial testimony revealed that Robin had a troubled childhood. Her parents fought often and divorced when Robin was a teenager. Robin was not close to her mother who was an unloving person. A step-grandfather sexually abused Robin and Randy was physically abusive to her during their marriage with serious beatings, kidnappings, and rapes. A psychological evaluation of Robin showed that she suffered from a pathological condition leaving her unable to express her emotions. Robin had an antisocial personality disorder coupled with chronic depression. The trial court dismissed these mitigating factors to Robin's liability for her family's deaths when the court stated, "the murders of Randy, Joshua and Tabitha weigh like a boulder over against the pebbles of those mitigating circumstances." Robin has raised a number of substantive procedural issues on appeal but courts have consistently denied her claims.

Life Without Parole

Following the U.S. Supreme Court's decision in *Furman v. Georgia* rendering unconstitutional the imposition of the death penalty as then applied to capital offenders, state legislatures began passing "life without parole" (LWOP) statutes. Before *Furman* only seven states had LWOP statutes as part of their sentencing structures though authorities rarely imposed the sentence. From 1971 to 1990, however, 25 states and the District of Columbia enacted LWOP statutes and over the last two decades another 17 states have enacted LWOP statutes. Except for Alaska, all death penalty states now authorize LWOP sentencing. The expansion of LWOP sentences reflects draconian sentencing policies developed in the 1970s and 1980s during which states shifted from rehabilitation sentencing measures toward more punitive sentencing structures. The shift in sentencing policy stems mostly from a growing public fear of crime "crystallized by sensationalized media accounts of formerly incarcerated persons reoffending."[28] States now utilize the sentencing scheme extensively. Consequently, roughly 31 percent of people in prison are currently serving LWOP with black inmates comprising 58 percent of this population. Well over half of all LWOP sentences are represented in just five states—Florida, Pennsylvania, Louisiana, California and Michigan. Several states house LWOP inmates convicted of non-homicide offenses where tough drug laws require LWOP for anyone with two previous felony convictions. To death penalty scholar David R. Dow, "sending a prisoner to die behind bars with no hope of release is a sentence that denies the possibility of redemption every bit as much as strapping a murderer to the gurney and filling them with poison."[29] Remarkably, the United States is the only country in the world that imposes LWOP sentences.

According to the Sentencing Project, some 1,600 women are currently serving LWOP. Of that female prisoner population, 63 women are serving LWOP for crimes committed as juveniles.[30] Recently, the U.S. Supreme Court addressed whether states can enforce LWOP statutes to persons who committed crimes as juveniles. In 2010, the Court in *Graham v. Florida* held LWOP sentences for juveniles convicted in non-homicide cases unconstitutional "because developmental and scientific research demonstrates how juveniles—including those who commit violent crimes—possess a greater capacity for rehabilitation, change, and growth than adults do, and are less blameworthy for their criminal conduct."[31] Two years later in *Miller v. Alabama*, the Court determined that the mandatory imposition of LWOP sentences for juveniles, regardless of the crime, violates the U.S. Constitution. The Court suggested in *Miller* that a "judge or jury must have the opportunity to consider mitigating circumstances before imposing the harshest possible penalty for juveniles."[32] Two substantive issues remain unresolved concerning LWOP sentences to juveniles, however; the Court has yet to address non-mandatory imposition of LWOP sentences and whether remedies are available to inmates already serving such sentences. Human rights observers assert that "thousands of people in the United States are still serving these sentences for crimes they committed as children ... either because they were sentenced for homicide cases, they were given these sentences even though they were not mandatory, or the states that imposed their sentences contend that the *Miller* decision is not retroactive."[33] Several states have construed *Miller* as retroactive and have reformed their juvenile sentencing laws. The Court will address specifically whether *Miller* is retroactive in *Toca v. Alabama* in 2015.

Researchers with the Equal Justice Initiative explain that many women and young girls serving LWOP for juvenile crimes have suffered extreme sexual and physical abuse as children whose parents neglected and abandoned them to violence prone, poor neighborhoods. What's more, their parents are often prostitutes, drug addicts, alcoholics, and crack dealers. Take the case of now 29-year-old Ashley Jones serving LWOP at Tutwiler Prison in Alabama:

> Ashley Jones is the only girl in Alabama sentenced to death in prison for an offense when she was 14 years old. From the time she was an infant, Ashley was terrorized by abusive and violent adults. Her addicted mother abandoned Ashley in crack houses while she was still in diapers and on several occasions threatened her at gunpoint. Her father assaulted her, resulting in a hospitalization. Her stepfather sexually assaulted her when she was 11. Relentless violence in her home left Ashley

depressed, traumatized, and suicidal. At 14, Ashley tried to escape the violence and abuse by running away with an older boyfriend who shot and killed her grandfather and aunt. Her grandmother and sister, who were injured during the offense, want Ashley to come home. But Alabama's mandatory sentencing law does not recognize mitigation, mercy, or the abusive dysfunction that lead to her crime. Instead, it condemns Ashley to die in prison despite the fact that today, at 22, she has matured into a remarkable young woman who is incredibly bright and promising.[34]

Concluding Remarks

The historical record is mostly silent on death row women throughout much of the nation's criminal justice past. Even so, one can discern that women have historically comprised a small percentage of death row inmates. One discernable factor of death row women is that sentencing disparity across jurisdictions renders women on death row no different from women where jurisdictions have not imposed death sentences. When one looks deeper into the particulars among women where jurisdictions do not impose death sentences, one sees that death row women are not *the worst of the worst*. There is a complete disregard for the safety and welfare of death row women by the very institutions responsible for their care. Several nationwide studies of women residing on death rows reveal grotesque patterns of maltreatment of death row women by prison guards and other inmates. Two foreign national women remain on death row and denied their right to communicate with their respective consular representatives. In this regard, federal and several state governments continue to violate international treaty laws by ignoring consulate rights of female foreign nationals arrested in the United States. It is troubling that two death row women have died of natural causes in recent years while awaiting execution. One final discernable factor about death row women is that most have lived extremely troubling lives where their physical, sexual, and psychological abuse began in early childhood. These are essentially discarded women abandoned by brutal parents and society at large.

> "It is well past time for social scientists and other researchers to take the analytical step of assessing in empirical and theoretical detail why and how the construction and operation of the criminal justice system itself is centrally white-[male] crafted and fundamentally white-[male] controlled."[1]

Conclusion

While at the School of Criminal Justice at the University of Albany, Professor Charles Lanier critiqued *Women and the Death Penalty in the United States, 1900–1998* for the *Journal of Criminal Justice and Popular Culture*.[2] In "Adding to the Story of What We Know About Capital Punishment," Professor Lanier maintained that the work could have made a more useful contribution to what scholars know about capital punishment had it probed several queries about women and capital punishment in a final chapter. One can summarize his suggestions into four probative questions: Why is it important to understand the circumstances of female death sentences and executions to appreciate the history of women in our criminal justice system? Why is it important that the capital justice system sentences women to death given the infrequency with which the event takes place? What are the policy implications arising from the historical record on female executions? What is the direction research on women and the death penalty should take in the future, and how might that research help the plight of women on death row? Accordingly, the purpose of this final chapter is to address these concerns of one of the country's foremost capital punishment scholars.

Why is it important to understand the circumstances of female death sentences and executions to appreciate the history of women in our criminal justice system?

Probing the contextual history of female death sentences and executions reveals much about the history of women in the American criminal justice system. It is clear from studying the history of women and capital punishment that the criminal justice system originated as a male-dominated institution aimed, in part, at controlling women and reinforcing society's patriarchal order. Analysis of women and capital justice reveals that early in its development an important feature of the justice system was to ensure the second class status of women. Still today, preserving the patriarchal order of American society remains a central component of the capital justice system.

The First Historical Trend

Throughout much of the first historical trend in female executions, white women lived under the influence of fanatical religious orders that consigned them to the subservience and subjugation of men—women were servants and the chattel property of men. As one scholar notes, "the model English woman was weak, submissive, charitable, virtuous, and modest. Her mental and physical activity was limited to keeping the home in order, cooking, and bearing and rearing children."[3] Colonial governments used harsh corporal punishments to ensure women's compliance to their repressed position in the patriarchal order. Penalties for nonconforming women were brutal, they endured the pillory, whippings, ears hacked off, noses slit, and tongues pierced. Horatio Rogers' observation is worth repeating here, "[d]efenseless women, maidens and matrons, were stripped naked to the waist, and, thus exposed to the public gaze, were beaten with whips of threefold knotted cord until the blood ran down their bare backs and bosoms."[4] Capital justice delivered barbaric and agonizing deaths when women challenged the patriarchal order of colonial society.

Colonial leaders dealt with four major societal crises (crime waves) accenting early American life by imposing cruel penalties to women who failed to conform to the patriarchal order. These crises involved the Antinomian controversy, the Quaker intrusion, the witchcraft frenzy, and the curse of infanticide. The sizeable increases in female criminal conviction rates during the antinomian period reveal that church leaders imprisoned women whose conduct directly challenged the gendered order of early America—antinomianism threatened the dominion of the established authority of male religious leaders. Quaker women suffered physical torment when their religious practices threatened the patriarchal authority of ministers and magistrates—officials went so far as to hang Mary Dyer for her religious "heresies." Witchcraft accusations rendered propertied women without male heirs particularly vulnerable to capital justice since colonial leaders sought to keep real property in the hands of men. Infanticide cases largely resulted from colonial leaders criminalizing child illegitimacy to ensure that the care of unwanted children did not burden public coffers. Poor indentured servant women suffered the wrath of penalties for fornication and adultery that often produced unwanted pregnancies. Young unmarried servant girls killed their unwanted infants to avoid public scorn, prolonged indentures, fines and whippings. Colonial women regularly hanged for infanticide though officials rarely indicted fathers for infanticide though they frequently acted in concert with mothers in killing unwanted children. In one case, a mother hanged for the murder of her infant twin daughters when it was the father who viciously murdered the children. Masters of indentured women commonly fathered illegitimate children with legal impunity. Adulterous wives murdered their newborns in fear of public shame and dishonor—a clear indication of the disobedience of women to the community standards of marriage fidelity and virtue.

Colonial wives retaliated against the patriarchal authority of abusive husbands. The justice systems of early colonies subjected wives to harsh punishments when they reacted violently to the physical or psychological ill-treatment of their husbands; and when domestic assaults ended in a husband's death, the law demanded action for *petit treason*—an aggravated form of murder punishable by burning. Catharine Bevan burned alive in 1731 for killing her husband. A double standard of justice accented the penalty for petite treason since no law demanded a similar punishment for husbands who killed their wives. The legal doctrine also warranted the execution of poorly treated servant women convicted of killing abusive masters. The master-servant relationship accounts for most murders in early America—a testament to the hostility and conflict accenting the relations. Indentured women retaliated violently against abusive masters and the state killed women by burning for murdering their sadistic masters—servant woman Esther Anderson burned to death for murdering her master in 1746.

Discerning the particularities giving rise to slave women's death sentences and executions in the early colonial period furthers understanding of the intersection of the oppression of black women and capital justice. Though there is little in the historical record regarding the treatment of slave women in the earliest periods of colonial America, some evidence suggests that slave women suffered extreme cruelty when they reacted violently to white male oppression. Slave traders subjected slave women and young girls to brutal rapes, sadistic sexual assaults, and ferocious attacks against their womanhood. Though jurisdictions put to death relatively few slave women in the earliest decades of slavery, criminal justice measures developed quickly to reinforce slavery as a societal system of domination, degradation, and subordination of slave women. Slave women violently resisted the brutal treatment of white masters, and colonial governments retaliated with sadistic execution methods to kill slave women—one slave woman roasting alive over a fire for several hours until she burned to ashes for killing her abusive master and two other slave women suffered quartering for the same offense.

Executions of American Indian women in the early colonial period are difficult to distinguish apart from the genocidal practices of early colonial governments to dispossess indigenous peoples of their sacred tribal territories and the disruption of their traditional cultures. The historical record on American Indian female executions reveals that colonial officials largely overlooked the behavior of American Indian women unless their conduct directly challenged the greater societal interest of white male hegemony over the newly conquered territories. Unlike African slave women, American Indian women had neither labor value to early colonists nor were they "potential breeders of negotiable property."

The Second Historical Trend

The criminal justice patterns of white women executions accenting early America continued throughout the decades in the second historical trend in female executions though there were far fewer in number. One can argue that criminal justice actors became far too troubled with serving the institutionalized white male interests of slavery through much of the period and were less concerned with white female criminality. Still, women were typically no different from the women subjected to criminal sanctions in previous decades when corporal punishments accented the lives of marginalized women as a means of patriarchal control. Though the strict religious code of early colonial life no longer controlled women, the crimes of executed white women were largely a response to the dire social conditions occasioned by extreme labor exploitation, daunting family disintegration, rampant crime, and unabashed human degradation accenting their lives in the period. Again, justice officials mostly subjected young, illiterate, and poor servant immigrant girls and women to the severities of the criminal justice system. White female executions for spousal killings increased significantly during the period and undoubtedly were the result of the severe social hardships challenging women's physical and mental stability. Though officials blamed poor whites for a rise in violent crime and implemented harsh measures to counter their criminality, relatively few white women suffered executions for predatory murders. Similarly, though justice authorities prosecuted white women for infanticide and child murders, most jurisdictions did not execute women charged with the crimes. Still, the callousness with which criminal justice agents imposed death to women resulted in authorities executing mentally challenged women, women dead from suicide, innocent women, and pregnant women.

By the antebellum period, slavery had evolved as a social institution accented by a rigid legal structure empowering landowning white males to manage slave women as chattel property. The severity of punishments increased for bondwomen as slavery expanded throughout southern states. Slave women were the primary targets of brutal criminal justice practices and the number of female slave executions increased dramatically over the period. Slave women bore the vicious maltreatment of white slaveholders and revolted violently against their ill-treatment. Executed slave women strangled, clubbed, stabbed, burned, shot, poisoned, or hacked to death their white masters, mistresses, overseers, and their owner's children. Slave women also resisted viciously against the brutal tactics of other white persons of authority, including hirers, overseers, and constables. Justice officials hanged, burned or roasted alive, gibbeted, quartered, and hung in chains slave women for killing abusive masters, mistresses, and slave masters' families. Slave women endured similar execution methods for poisoning masters, burglary, arson, theft, slave revolts, and other crimes of slave resistance. Much of the criminal justice control over slave women took place on plantations by white male slave owners who viciously punished slave women for even the most minor of indiscretions. Mistresses also killed female slaves with impunity; one mistress beat to death a young slave girl for allowing the mistresses baby to cry at night. Sexual control over slave women by owners was also critical to slavery and owners relied upon the routine sexual abuse of slave women to ensure their subservience to white male control within the slave institution. The rape of slave women by white male masters often resulted in infanticide cases for which state's regularly executed slave women—slave children were "negotiable property." Infanticide was part of slave women's resistance to their oppression and to keep their children from becoming slaves.

The decades immediately following the War Between the States ushered in one of the most turbulent and violent periods in United States history in which criminal justice authorities executed few women. Fewer black female executions resulted from an increase in black women prison populations in southern states, an increase in white vigilante violence toward black people as a related means of capital justice, and the development of a convict lease system. Black females comprised overwhelming numbers of women committed to southern penitentiaries. Their incarceration rates increased primarily because of their close contact with whites as servants and housemaids. Although imprisoned black women committed mostly property crimes, black female violence against their white oppressors was still common. Mob violence also protected the patriarchal order of American society; lynchings maintained social control over women by continuing their economic, political, and social subjugation and thereby ensuring the gender caste structure and the advantaged social position of white men. Though black female executions diminished in the period, the 1890s and the 1910s were pivotal decades for white terrorist violence against black women. The convict lease system allowed landowning white males to use vagrancy laws to create a neo-slavery institution where overseers stripped naked black women for whippings when they resisted physical and sexual exploitation. By the 1890s, southern society had fully established the legal separation of blacks from white society; Jim Crow segregation took hold as an institutional means of subordinating black women to white male oppression.

Jurisdictions executed Mexican women once the United State annexed much of Mexico's northernmost territories during the colonialization process and after the Mexican-American War in 1848. To many scholars studying the criminal justice history of the American southwest, the United States engaged in nothing less than an extermination process calculated to solidify the theft of more than one-third of Mexico's territory, Mexican women were undoubtedly victims of this outright ethnic cleansing. In most cases of Mexican women executions, racist courts allowed officials to prosecute Mexican women on exaggerated charges and sheriffs to execute innocent Mexican women.

The Third Historical Trend

There was little change for women early in the third historical trend in female executions. Impoverished and socially maligned women still suffered the wrath of capital justice in the United States. Large numbers of European immigrant women landed in the most impoverished regions of the industrial northeast where they quickly became disengaged economically and remained poor for decades after their arrival to the United States. Foreign-born immigrant women experienced high poverty rates, low wages and long hours, joblessness, ever-increasing costs of living, raging labor activism, homelessness, and unhealthy and hazardous working conditions that often resulted in workplace deaths. Black women suffered mass layoffs in the service and manufacturing sectors of the economy and white women often displaced them from traditionally held domestic worker jobs; white society essentially excluded black women from the urban industrial workplace. Undoubtedly, these social conditions gave rise to discontent and violent outrage against oppression. Jurisdictions mostly executed white women for predatory murders and officials largely executed black women for robbery-murder in the period. Most black women executed during the early 20th century were domestic workers whose offenses involved crimes of resistance against white aggression similarly experienced by slave women generations earlier. Virginia Christian's killing of her white employer stands out as a familiar story of executed black women in southern society.

Women's dire impoverishment fueled the social conditions ripe for increased crime rates. Homicides among women increased appreciably in the early 1930s and doubled by the late 1950s. Despite increased female homicide rates, jurisdictions executed relatively few women, most female murderers received less than life in prison. Women comprised a miniscule proportion of the more than 8,000 executions in the United States throughout the 20th century. Ironically, public sentiment on capital punishment for women increased over the last few decades in the period when more than two-thirds of American favored capital punishment for women but opposed the penalty for juveniles, mentally retarded persons, and the mentally ill.

In the later decades of female capital sentencing in the United States, the white male-controlled capital justice system marginalized women from their constitutional protections of due process and equal protection of the law. The gendered oppression of white criminal justice actors rendered women ever more vulnerable to the death penalty. The major obstacles to implementing procedural and substantive protections intended to minimize gender bias in the capital justice system included the chronic underfunding of indigent defense services by state and local governments, the unbridled discretion of state prosecutors in filing capital charges against women, the consistent marginalization of lesbian defendants to juries by prosecutors, the prosecution of mentally retarded and insane women in capital cases, prosecutorial lawlessness in female capital cases, and the continued use of judicial overrides in female capital cases. Until the American criminal justice system rectifies these constitutional challenges to capital justice, the status of the justice system as a primary enforcer of patriarchal rule in this country will not diminish.

Why is it important that the capital justice system sentences women to death given the infrequency with which the event takes place?

The sentencing of women to death throughout American criminal justice history is indeed an extraordinary event. Though the historical record is mostly silent on the sentencing of women to death (as opposed to the actual execution of women) throughout much of the nation's criminal justice past, inconsistent and unreliable data still show that women have comprised a very small percentage of overall death sentences. More intelligible data on female death sentences in the modern era of capital sentencing confirm the same result, however. Despite the infrequency with which jurisdictions sentence women to death, the importance of the capital justice system sentencing women to death is found in the defective procedures commonly used to determine female death sentences. The extant literature reveals a contemptuous record of an intrinsically flawed capital justice system heightened by a culture of lawlessness and indifference to the legal mandates intended to preserve due process and the equal protection of law to female capital defendants.

Pursuant to judicial holdings, women sentenced to death must be noticeably deserving of death given the severity of their crimes—women sentenced to death must be *the worst of the worst*. Yet, women sentenced to death are essentially indistinguishable from women who have committed similar crimes but escaped death sentences. The profiles of current female death row inmates, of women wrongfully convicted of potentially capital offenses, of women whose capital sentences have been reversed by appellate courts, and of women whose capital sentences have warranted executive clemency reveal a commonality of flawed procedures accounting for why some women occupy death rows while similarly situated women are not on death rows. The profiles of women in the capital justice system reveal a comprehensive inventory of procedural failures precluding fairness and evenhandedness in the capital sentencing of American women. The record of procedural failures in female capital cases reveals the consistent marginalization of lesbian defendants to juries by prosecutors, the prosecution of mentally impaired women, prosecutorial lawlessness (misconduct), and the biased use of judicial override. Women receive death sentences because of juror bias against minorities and lesbians, judicial bias against women, incompetent defense lawyers, homophobic prosecutors, and the continued victimization of innocent women by state and federal appellate courts that regularly rely on "the harmless error rule to dismiss the grounds upon which a wrongful conviction or prosecution is challenged." Courts rely on the "unpublished opinion" to curtail public interest in particular appeals to conceal the resolution of important capital justice issues.

In his address before a Joint Committee on the Judiciary of the Massachusetts Legislature in July 2005 concerning a house bill to reinstate capital punishment in the Commonwealth, Columbia Law Professor Jeffrey Fagan noted, "[w]hen only a tiny proportion of the individuals who commit murder are sentenced to death, capital punishment is unconstitutionally irrational because it serves no identifiable penal function."[5] Professor Fagan's statement is particularly applicable to female capital justice in the United States. Women offenders comprise a small fraction of all executed persons, and as a result it is difficult to identify a legitimate punitive function of the death penalty to women. Preserving the patriarchal order of American society is *not* a justifiable penal function though the historical record on female executions reveals that capital punishment serves that function. Any policy considerations stemming from the historical record on female executions must focus on moderating the effects the capital justice system has in perpetuating the systemic oppression of women within the American patriarchal social order. Public policy that would go far to correct for the exploitation of women within the capital justice system is for states to create strong legislation correcting for the systemic problems identified in the above paragraphs.

What are the policy implications arising from the historical record on female executions?

In 2004, the American Civil Liberties Union put forth several important policy proposals, which if implemented, would ensure that every female capital defendant receives a fair and adequate defense.[6] One suggestion is that *defense lawyers representing female capital defendants be adequately trained in how to raise evidence of abuse as part of a self-defense claim in spousal murder cases and how to raise abuse as a mitigating factor in other types of murders.* This proposition is an important policy consideration because poor and marginalized women disproportionately populate death rows and are without the economic resources to pay for private attorneys who are far more likely to succeed in mitigating female capital sentences. Impoverished women charged with capital offenses must rely on public defenders or other appointed lawyers. Yet, there is chronic underfunding of indigent defense services by state and local governments charged with providing poor and marginalized women with a legal defense. Public defenders are often inexperienced and underpaid lawyers with enormous caseloads and often without the funding essential to paying for investigators and expert witnesses. Ineffective assistance of counsel for women charged in capital cases results largely from governments failing to adequately fund indigent defense services. A significant proportion of defense lawyers charged with representing indigent female capital offenders are so inadequate that they are subjected to disciplinary actions of disbarment or suspension by state bar associations. It is this crude lawyering that concerned Justice Marshall when he remarked that these are the same attorneys who fail to present mitigating evidence on behalf of their clients simply because they fail to read state sentencing statutes and do not know what to offer in defense of their clients. Defense lawyers are often unfamiliar with the battered woman defense, for instance, that goes far to mitigate the killing of violent husbands. Incompetent defense lawyers often leave female capital clients unable to put forth clear and convincing evidence to juries showing that they suffer from deeply troubled childhoods often marked by chronic sexual and physical abuse, child neglect and abandonment, prostitution, and alcohol and drug abuse. As adults, these women experience attempted suicides, repeated jail stays, battered woman syndrome, post-traumatic stress disorder, depression, brain damage, bipolar and other personality disorders and organic brain impairments from fetal alcohol syndrome. An inadequate legal defense is one of the more important factors contributing to the wrongful conviction of capitally sentenced women.

Another policy consideration is that *defense attorneys should receive adequate training to identify mental retardation and mental illness among female capital defendants.* Despite the contention of the United States Supreme Court that the imposition of the death penalty to mentally retarded defendants constitutes cruel and unusual punishment, jurisdictions continue to sentence women to death who suffer from severe intellectual disabilities. There are several reasons why states continue to sentence mentally retarded women to death despite its unconstitutionality pursuant to *Atkins*, but the more important reason is that the Court left it up to states to determine the parameters of mental retardation so long as they conform to the clinical definition of intellectual disability established by national psychiatric associations. The result has been that there are significant variations among states in determining which capital defendants warrant the exemption from execution. Researchers suggest that "[t]his troubling array allows a defendant who would be ineligible for execution in one state to be eligible for execution in another."[7] In contrast, the Supreme Court has not barred death penalty jurisdictions from executing persons with mental illnesses unless defendant's mental illness renders them insane. Mental illnesses are pervasive among female capital defendants and suffer from bipolar disorders, personality disorders, post-traumatic stress disorders, schizo-affective disorders, schizophrenia, depression, and suicidal tendencies. Betty Lou Beets and Christina Riggs are at least two women who states have put to death despite severe intellectual disabilities. Thus, another recommendation is that defense attorneys receive adequate training to identify mental retardation and mental illness among female capital defendants. Death penalty jurisdictions must provide the financial resources necessary to ensure that defense attorneys have adequate access to expert witnesses and mitigation specialists and the required training to raise these issues at trial. Other capital justice actors such as judges, prosecutors, and police should also receive training to identify mental retardation and mental illness among female capital defendants. This may be especially the case with law enforcement because there is a link between mentally retarded and mentally ill women who police frequently persuade to give false confessions.[8]

Another important proposition is that *jurisdictions develop meaningful policies that curb the lawlessness of state prosecutors in female capital cases.* The unbridled and biased discretion of state prosecutors in filing capital charges against women is a major obstacle to ensuring fairness in capital sentencing to women. The unfettered discretion of prosecutors to selecting death penalty cases means that prosecutors can breach ethical rules of professional conduct and deliberately deny indigent defendants constitutional protections with impunity. One contemptible feature of prosecutorial discretion in seeking capital sentences to women is that homophobia accents the capital justice system. Homophobia often informs prosecutorial decisions to seek the death penalty and defendants' sexuality becomes central to capital trials involving lesbian defendants. A result of prosecutors exploiting lesbianism to denigrate women in capital cases is that lesbians disproportionately occupy death row. Prosecutors use lesbian women's transgression of feminine stereotypes to show the dangerousness of lesbian capital defendants and that lesbian killers deserve the death penalty.

Prosecutors regularly engage in other forms of unscrupulous conduct in capital cases involving female defendants, including improper behavior in grand jury proceedings; dismissing potential jurors based in race, ethnicity, or gender; unprofessional behavior toward defendants and defense attorneys; knowingly use false or misleading evidence; suppress exculpatory evidence (i.e., *Brady* violation); withhold information about offers of immunity from prosecution and other rewards to witnesses testifying against accused persons; use improper closing arguments; make provocative comments during trial; mischaracterize the facts or evidence in cases; mismanaging evidence; and threaten and harass witnesses. The illegitimate use of peremptory challenges by state attorneys in capital cases to openly discriminate against black persons in jury selection is a technique of the white male-controlled capital justice system to deny due process and equal protection to female black defendants. Despite the *Batson* holding, blatant racial discrimination against black female capital defendants endures when prosecutors abuse peremptory challenges to exclude blacks as potential jurors. The problem is made worse by judicial officers that allow for any justification for peremptory challenges of black persons from juries no matter how arbitrary and irrational. Prosecutorial lawlessness pervades female capital justice. State prosecutors frequently suppress exculpatory evidence, knowingly use false testimony, intimidate witnesses, give improper closing arguments, give false statements to the jury, conceal or fabricate evidence, and use threats against defendants or their family members to coerce confessions. Efforts to deter prosecutorial misconduct in capital cases have proven largely ineffective. Voters can usurp the political power of potential candidates from gaining elected positions who have done little to curb prosecutorial lawlessness in the capital justice system. In states like California, for instance, prosecutorial lawlessness is so rampant that one federal judge referred to it as an "epidemic." Still, state prosecutors, judges, the State Bar and even the state's attorney general who is seeking a Senatorial seat in the U.S. Congress, Kamala Harris, have done absolutely nothing to stop prosecutorial misconduct.[9]

State and federal jurisdictions should eliminate judicial override in capital cases. Judicial override of jury sentencing recommendations allows for judicial bias in sentencing women to death. Judicial override is particularly problematic in Alabama, Delaware and Florida. Judicial override was at issue in appellate court reversals in at least three women sentenced to death (Louise Harris, Doris Carlson, Carla Caillier), and the executive clemency granted to Judith Neelley. Another victim of judicial override is Christie Scott who awaits execution on Alabama's death row. In these cases, judicial override allowed trial judges to disregard jury recommendations of life in prison and use their own biased discretion to sentence these women to death.

What is the direction research on women and the death penalty should take in the future, and how might that research help the plight of women on death row?

Scholars argue that there is a serious lack of academic efforts to identifying the demographic, intellectual, educational, neurological, and psychological profiles of death row women. Indeed, many death row women suffered harrowing physical, sexual, and psychological abuse as children and developed extreme neuropsychological abnormalities as adults. The harsh conditions of death row experienced by women certainly exacerbate condemned women's mental disorders that experts argue should preclude their execution. Death row women are isolated and suffer mistreatment by prison staff, they are sexually harassed and accosted by prison officers, they lack required health care access, and often live in indecent and unsanitary conditions. Justice professionals must develop far more exact methods of assessing the guilt of female capital defendants suffering from severe mental incapacities. Given the U.S. Supreme Court's "evolving standard of decency" test, it seems reasonable that a standard of decency for our society is to cease sentencing to death and executing women with extreme mental incapacities resulting from life times of abuse and ill-treatment.

Chapter Notes

Chapter 1

1. Kathleen O'Shea, *Women and the Death Penalty in the United States, 1900–1998* (Westport: Praeger, 1999).
2. Greg Barak, Jeanne M. Flavin, and Paul S. Leighton, *Class, Race, Gender, and Crime: Social Realities of Justice in America* (Los Angeles: Roxbury, 2001), p. 136.
3. Jessica Salvucci, "Femininity and the Electric Chair: An Equal Protection Challenge to Texas's Death Penalty Statute," *Boston College Third World Law Journal*, 31 (2011): 405–437, p. 410.
4. Andrea Shapiro, "Unequal Before the Law: Men, Women and the Death Penalty," *American University Journal of Gender, Social Policy and the Law*, 8 (2000): 427–470, p. 457.
5. Joan W. Howarth, "Executing White Masculinities: Learning from Karla Faye Tucker," *Oregon Law Review*, 81 (2002): 183–229, p. 214.
6. Dorie Klein, "The Etiology of Female Crime: A Review of the Literature," in Barbara Raffel Price and Natalie Sokoloff, eds., *Criminal Justice System and Women*, pp. 3–30 (New York: McGraw Hill, 1995), p. 10.
7. Linda L. Ammons, "Mules, Madonnas, Babies, Bathwater, Racial Imagery and Stereotypes: The African-American Woman and the Battered Woman Syndrome," *Wisconsin Law Review*, 1995 (1994): 1003–1080, p. 1036.
8. "A Chivalrous Judge," *New York Times* (November 2, 1876), p. 1.
9. "General," *Indiana Progress* [Indiana, Pennsylvania] (November 9, 1876), p. 8.
10. Jenny E. Carroll, "Images of Women and Capital Sentencing Among Female Offenders: Exploring the Outer Limits of the Eighth Amendment and Articulated Theories of Justice," *Texas Law Review*, 75 (1997): 1413–1452, pp. 1421–1422.
11. *Tucker v. State*, 771 S.W.2d 523 (Tex. Crim. App. 1988).
12. Ibid.
13. Tony Snow, "Oppose Capital Punishment Because It Is Wrong to Kill," *St. Louis Post-Dispatch* (February 6, 1998), p. C19.
14. Salvucci, "Femininity and the Electric Chair," p. 421.
15. Winthrop D. Jordan, *White Over Black: American Attitudes Toward the Negro, 1550–1812* (New York: Norton, 1968), p. 238.
16. Jacklyn Huey and Michael J. Lynch, "The Image of Black Women in Criminology: Historical Stereotypes as Theoretical Foundation," in Shaun L. Gabbidon and Helen T. Greene, eds., *Race, Crime, and Justice: A Reader*, pp. 127–140 (New York: Routledge, 2005), p. 137.
17. Raymund A. Paredes, "The Origins of Anti-Mexican Sentiment in the United States," in Manuel G. Gonzales and Cynthia M. Gonzales, eds., *En Aquel Entonces: Readings in Mexican-American History* (Bloomington: Indiana University Press, 2000), pp. 45–52.
18. Tomás Almaguer, *Racial Fault Lines: The Historical Origins of White Supremacy in California* (Berkeley: University of California Press, 1994), p. 62.
19. Joe R. Feagin and Clairece Booher Feagin, *Racial and Ethnic Relations* (Upper Saddle River: Prentice Hall, 2011), p. 144.
20. David E. Stannard, *American Holocaust: The Conquest of the New World* (New York: Oxford University Press, 1992), p. 119.
21. Susan Brownmiller, *Against Our Will: Men, Women and Rape* (New York: Fawcett, 1975), p. 162.
22. Elizabeth Rapaport, "Some Questions About Gender and the Death Penalty," *Golden Gate University Law Review*, 20 (1990): 501–565, pp. 512–513.
23. Renee Herberle, "Disciplining Gender: Or, Are Women Getting Away with Murder?" *Signs: Journal of Women in Culture and Society*, 24 (1999): 1103–1112, p. 1106.
24. Kate Millett, *Sexual Politics* (New York: Doubleday, 1970), p. 25.
25. Gerda Lerner, *The Creation of Patriarchy* (New York: Oxford University Press, 1986), p. 239.
26. Martin N. Marger, *Social Inequality: Patterns and Processes* (New York: McGraw-Hill, 2014), p. 17.
27. Richard Quinney, *Class, State, and Crime: On the Theory and Practice of Criminal Justice* (New York: D. McKay, 1977), p. 45.
28. Randall Kennedy, *Race, Crime, and the Law* (New York: Pantheon, 1997), p. 311.
29. Lawrence Friedman, *Crime and Punishment in American History* (New York: Basic Books, 1993), p. 84.
30. Robert Staples, "White Racism, Black Crime and American Justice: An Application of the Colonial Model to Explain Crime and Race," *Phylon*, 36 (1975): 14–22, p. 18.
31. Friedman, *Crime and Punishment in American History*.
32. William Bowers and Glenn Pierce, "Arbitrariness and Discrimination Under Post-*Furman* Capital Statutes," *Crime and Delinquency*, 26 (1980): 563–635, p. 573.
33. Michael Foley, *Arbitrary and Capricious: The Supreme Court, the Constitution, and the Death Penalty* (Westport: Praeger, 2003), pp. 2–3.
34. *Furman v. Georgia*, 408 U.S. 238, 242.
35. *Furman v. Georgia*, 408 U.S. 238, 365, Justice Marshall concurring.
36. *McCleskey v. Kemp*, 481 U.S. 279 (1987).
37. Gerald Terkel, *Law and Society: Critical Approaches* (Upper Saddle River: Allyn and Bacon, 1995), p. 177.
38. Michael J. Klarman, *From Jim Crow to Civil Rights: The Supreme Court and the Struggle for Racial Equality* (New York: Oxford University Press, 2004), pp. 117–118.
39. Phillip Barron, "Gender Discrimination in the U.S. Death Penalty System," *Radical Philosophy Review*, 1 (2000): 89–96, p. 90.
40. Robert Sherrill, "Death Trip: The American Way of Execution," *The Nation* (January 8, 2001), available at http://www.thenation.com/doc/20010108/sherrill.

41. David C. Baldus, Charles Pulaski, and George Woodworth, "Comparative Review of Death Sentences: An Empirical Study of the Georgia Experience (Symposium on Current Death Penalty Issues)," *Journal of Criminal Law and Criminology*, 74 (1983): 661–753.

42. Bryan A. Stevenson and Ruth E. Friedman, "Deliberate Indifference: Judicial Tolerance of Racial Bias in Criminal Justice," *Washington and Lee Law Review*, 51 (1994): 509–527, p. 510.

43. Adam Liptak, "New Look at Death Sentences and Race," *New York Times* (April 29, 2008), available at http://www.nytimes.com/2008/04/29/us/29bar.html?_r=2&.

44. Carol S. Steiker and Jordan M. Steiker, "Sober Second Thoughts: Reflections on Two Decades of Constitutional Regulation of Capital Punishment," *Harvard Law Review*, 109 (1995): 357–438, p. 436.

45. Barron, "Gender Discrimination in the U.S. Death Penalty System," p. 91.

46. Douglas W. Vick, "Poorhouse Justice: Underfunded Indigent Defense Services and Arbitrary Death Sentences," *Buffalo Law Review*, 43 (1995): 329–460, p. 334.

47. *Furman v. Georgia*, 408 U.S. 238 (1972), pp. 251–252.

48. *Final Report of the Pennsylvania Supreme Court Committee on Racial and Gender Bias in the Justice System* (2003), available at http://nicic.gov/Library/019106.

49. Matthew J. Fogelman, "Justice Asleep Is Justice Denied: Why Dozing Defense Attorneys Demean the Sixth Amendment and Should Be Deemed Per Se Prejudicial," *Journal of Legal Profession*, 26 (2002): 67–100, p. 75.

50. Henry Weinstein, "A Sleeping Lawyer And A Ticket to Death Row," *Los Angeles Times* (July 15, 2000), available at http://articles.latimes.com/2000/jul/15/news/mn-53250.

51. Erica Sanders, "Inadequate Legal Counsel a Key Concern in Death Penalty Cases," *Death Penalty Focus* (September 30, 2010), available at http://www.deathpenalty.org/article.php?id=521.

52. Richard C. Reuben, "Marshall Urges Competency from Death-Penalty Counsel," *Los Angeles Daily Journal* (August 7, 1990), p. 10.

53. Thurgood Marshall, "Remarks on the Death Penalty Made at the Judicial Conference of the Second Circuit," *Columbia Law Review*, 86 (1986): 1–8.

54. American Civil Liberties Union, *Inadequate Representation* (October 8, 2003), available at http://www.aclu.org/news/NewsPrint.cfm?ID=9313&c=62.

55. American Civil Liberties Union, *The Forgotten Population*, p. 23, available at https://www.aclu.org/sites/default/files/FilesPDFs/womenondeathrow.pdf.

56. Death Penalty Information Center, *Update: Texas Woman Faces Execution Despite Questions Regarding Her Guilt* (2005), available at http://www.deathpenaltyinfo.org/article.php?did=1545&scid=64.

57. Ira Mickenberg, "Drunk, Sleeping, and Incompetent Lawyers: Is it Possible to Keep Innocent People Off Death Row?" *Dayton Law Review*, 29 (2004): 319–327, p. 322.

58. *Ibid.*, p. 323.

59. *DeGarno v. Texas*, 474 U.S. 973, 975 (1985), J. Brennan dissenting.

60. Arthur L. Burnett, Sr., "Permeation of Race, National Origin and Gender Issues from Initial Law Enforcement Contact Through Sentencing: The Need for Sensitivity, Equalitarianism and Vigilance in the Criminal Justice System," *American Criminal Law Review*, 31 (1994): 1153–1173, p. 1167.

61. Kevin Nunn, "The 'Darden Dilemma': Should African Americans Prosecute Crime?" *Fordham Law Review*, 68 (2000): 1473–1508, p. 1498.

62. Jeffrey J. Pokorak, "Probing the Capital Prosecutor's Perspective: Race of the Discretionary Actor," *Cornell Law Review*, 83 (1998): 1811–1820, p. 1811.

63. James Bravin, "Surprise: Judges Hand Out Most Punitive Awards," *Wall Street Journal* (June 12, 2000), p. B4.

64. Janice L. Kopec, "Avoiding a Death Sentence in the American Legal System: Get a Woman to Do It," *Capital Defense Journal*, 15 (2003): 353–362.

65. Ryan Patrick Alford, "Appellate Review of Racist Summations: Redeeming the Promise of Searching Analysis," *Michigan Journal of Law and Race*, 11 (2006): 325–365, p. 342.

66. Sally Kohn, "Greasing the Wheel: How the Criminal Justice System Hurts Gay, Lesbian, Bisexual and Transgendered People and Why Hate Crime Laws Won't Save Them," *New York University Review of Law and Social Change*, 27 (2001/2002): 257–280, p. 264.

67. Joey Mogul, "Lesbians and the Death Penalty: Comments from 'Race, Class, Gender and the PIC,'" available at http://womenandprison.org/sexuality/view/lesbians_and_the_death_penalty_comments_from_race_class_gender_and_the_pic/.

68. Bruce Shapiro, "Rethinking the Death Penalty," *The Nation* (July 22, 2002), available at http://www.thenation.com/doc.mhtml?i=20020722&s=shapiro.

69. Amnesty International, *United States of America: The Execution of Mentally Ill Offenders* (January 2006), available at http://amnesty.org/en/library/asset/AMR51/002/2006/en/8bad94ee-d46f-11dd-8743-d305bea2b2c7/amr510022006en.html.

70. Mark D. Cunningham and Mark P. Vigen, "Death Row Inmate Characteristics, Adjustment and Confinement: A Critical Review of the Literature," *Behavioral Sciences and the Law*, 20 (2002): 191–210, pp. 196–198.

71. Dorothy Otnow Lewis, Jonathan H. Pincus, Marilyn Feldman, Lori Jackson, and Barbara Bard, "Psychiatric, Neurological, and Psychoeducational Characteristics of 15 Death Row Inmates in the United States," *American Journal Psychiatry*, 143 (1986): 838–845, pp. 841–842.

72. Stephanie Zywien, "Executing the Insane: A Look at Death Penalty Schemes in Arkansas, Georgia and Texas," *Suffolk Journal of Trial and Appellate Advocacy*, 12 (2007): 93–119, p. 96.

73. Christopher Slobogin, "Mental Illness and the Death Penalty," *California Criminal Law Review*, 2 (2000): 1–24, p. 24.

74. Welsh S. White, "Fact-Finding and the Death Penalty: The Scope of a Capital Defendant's Right to Jury Trial," *Notre Dame Law Review*, 65 (1989): 1–31, p. 11.

75. Paige Williams, "Double Jeopardy," *The New Yorker* (November 17, 2014), available at http://www.newyorker.com/magazine/2014/11/17/double-jeopardy-3.

76. Paul Brech and Steven L. Harmon, "Pacheco Must Go," *Riverside Press-Enterprise* (May 30, 2012), p. B6.

77. Center for Prosecutor Integrity, "An Epidemic of Prosecutor Misconduct," White Paper (2013), p. 1, available at http://www.prosecutorintegrity.org/wp-content/uploads/EpidemicofProsecutorMisconduct.pdf.

78. Molly Hennessy-Fiske, "Wrongful Conviction Inquiry," *Los Angeles Times* (February 13, 2012), p. A7.

79. John Flannery, "Former Federal Prosecutor Criticizes the Withholding of Critical Evidence," Death Penalty Information Center, New Voices (August 20, 2005), available at http://www.deathpenaltyinfo.org/node/326.

80. Texas Defender Service, *A State of Denial: Texas Justice and the Death Penalty* (2000), available at http://www.texasdefender.org/publications.htm.

81. V.A. Richelle, "Racism as a Strategic Tool at Trial: Appealing Race-Based Prosecutorial Misconduct," *Tulane Law Review*, 67 (1993): 2357–2370, p. 2357.

82. Arielle Siebert, "*Batson v. Kentucky*: Application to Whites and the Effect on the Peremptory Challenge System," *Columbia Journal of Law and Social Problems*, 32 (1999): 307–330, p. 312.

83. Steve McGonigle, Holly Becka, Jennifer LaFleur, and Tim Wyatt, "Race Bias Pervades Jury Selection: Prosecutors Routinely Bar Blacks, Study Finds," *Dallas Morning News* (March 9, 2005), p. 1A.

84. *Strauder v. West Virginia*, 100 U.S. 303 (1880), p. 308.

85. Antony Page, "*Batson's* Blind-Spot: Unconscious Stereotyping and the Peremptory Challenge," *Boston University Law Review*, 85 (2005): 155–262, p. 259.
86. McGonigle et al., 2005.
87. Barbara Allen Babcock, "A Place in the Palladium: Women's Rights and Jury Service," *University of Cincinnati Law Review*, 61 (1993): 1139–1180, p. 1145.
88. Clay S. Conrad, *Jury Nullification: The Evolution of a Doctrine* (Durham: Carolina Academic Press, 1998), p. 190.
89. *Batson v. Kentucky* (1986), Justice Marshall dissenting, p. 105.

Chapter 2

1. Elizabeth Rapaport and Victor Streib, "Death Penalty for Women in North Carolina," *Elton Law Review*, 1 (2009): 65–94, p. 68.
2. M. Watt Espy and John Ortiz Smykla, *Executions in the United States, 1608–2002: The Espy File* [computer file], 4th ICPS ed., comp. Espy and John Ortiz Smykla, University of Alabama (Ann Arbor, MI: Inter-University Consortium for Political and Social Research [producer and distributor], 2004).
3. Victor L. Streib, "American Executions of Female Offenders: An Inventory of Names, Dates, and Other Information," 7th ed., July 1, 2005 (unpublished research report) (on file with author).
4. Kathleen O'Shea, *Women and the Death Penalty in the United States, 1900–1998* (Westport: Praeger, 1999).
5. Marvin Shipman, *The Penalty of Death: U.S. Newspaper Coverage of Women's Executions* (Columbia: University of Missouri Press, 2002).
6. Elizabeth Rapaport and Victor Streib, "Death Penalty for Women in North Carolina," *Elton Law Review*, 1 (2009): 65–94; Lewis Laska, *Legal Executions in Tennessee: A Comprehensive Registry, 1782–2009* (Jefferson: McFarland, 2011).
7. Daniel Allen Hearn, *Legal Executions in New England: A Comprehensive Reference, 1623–1960* (Jefferson: McFarland, 1999); Daniel Allen Hearn, *Legal Executions in New Jersey: A Comprehensive Registry, 1691–1963* (Jefferson: McFarland, 2005); Daniel Allen Hearn, *Legal Executions in New York State: A Comprehensive Reference, 1639–1963* (Jefferson: McFarland, 1997); Daniel Allen Hearn, *Legal Executions in North Carolina and South Carolina: A Comprehensive Registry, 1866–1962* (Jefferson: McFarland, 2015).
8. John Bessler, *Legacy of Violence: Lynch Mobs and Executions in Minnesota* (Minneapolis: University of Minnesota Press, 2003); Sheila O'Hare, Irene Berry, and Jesse Silva, *Legal Executions in California. A Comprehensive Registry, 1851–2005* (Jefferson: McFarland, 2006).
9. Harriett Frazier, *Death Penalty in Missouri, 1803–2005: A History and Comprehensive Registry of Legal Executions, Pardons, and Commutations* (Jefferson: McFarland, 2006); West Gilbreath, *Death on the Gallows: The Story of Legal Hangings in New Mexico, 1847–1923* (Silver City: High Lonesome Books, 2002); Robert Tórrez, *Myth of the Hanging Tree: Stories of Crime and Punishment in Territorial New Mexico* (Albuquerque: University of New Mexico Press, 2008).
10. L. Kay Gillespie, *Dancehall Ladies: The Crimes and Executions of America's Condemned Women* (New York: University Press of America, 1997); L. Kay Gillespie, *Executed Women of 20th and 21st Centuries* (Lanham: University Press of America, 2009).
11. Kerry Segrave, *Women and Capital Punishment in America, 1840–1899: Death Sentences and Executions in the United States and Canada* (Jefferson: McFarland, 2008).
12. George C. Wright, *Racial Violence in Kentucky, 1865–1940: Lynchings, Mob Rule, and Legal Lynchings* (Baton Rouge: Louisiana State University Press, 1990); George C. Wright, "By the Book: The Legal Executions of Kentucky Blacks," in W. Fitzhugh Brundage, ed., *Under Sentence of Death, Lynchings in the South*, pp. 250–270 (Chapel Hill: University of North Carolina Press, 1997).
13. Ann Jones, *Women Who Kill* (Boston: Beacon Press, 1996); Mary Atwell, *Wretched Sisters: Examining Gender and Capital Punishment* (New York: Peter Lang, 2008).
14. Victor Streib, *The Fairer Death: Executing Women in Ohio* (Athens: Ohio University Press, 2006).
15. Heritage Archives, available at http://heritagearchives.org/Resources.aspx; Colonial Williamsburg Foundation, available at http://research.history.org/DigitalLibrary/BrowseVG.cfm.
16. Accessible Archives, available at http://www.accessible-archives.com/.
17. The Digital Library on American Slavery at the University of North Carolina, Greensboro, available at http://library.uncg.edu/slavery/petitions/results.aspx?s=3&sid=129.
18. Newspaper Archive, available at http://newspaperarchive.com/.
19. Death Penalty Information Center, available at http://www.deathpenaltyinfo.org/.
20. Kenneth Stampp, *The Peculiar Institution: Slavery in the Ante-Bellum South* (New York: Vintage, 1956).
21. Jim Runkle, "Facing the Death Sentence," *The Express* (March 20, 2010), available at http://www.lockhaven.com/page/content.detail/id/517003.html.
22. "Hammer Slayer Must Die in Chair," *Pittsburg Press* (December 19, 1945), p. 4.
23. "Two Prisoners Get Suspension of Sentence," *Biloxi Daily Herald* [Biloxi, Mississippi] (January 2, 1925), p. 5.
24. C. Ashley Ellefson, "Espy File," H-Law, available at http://h-net.msu.edu/cgi-bin/logbrowse.pl?trx=vx&list=H-Law&month=0209&week=c&msg=EJPWuwIr%2BPM7cw43J3wydA&user=&pw.
25. Frank E. Hartung, "Trends in the Use of Capital Punishment," *Annals of the American Academy of Political and Social Sciences*, 284 (1952): 8–19, p. 17.
26. Terri L. Snyder, "As If There Was Not Master or Woman in the Land," in Christine Daniels and Michael V. Kennedy, eds., *Over the Threshold: Intimate Violence in Early America* (New York: Rutledge, 1999), p. 221.

Chapter 3

1. Lyle Koehler, "The Case of the American Jezebels: Anne Hutchinson and Female Agitation During the Years of Antinomian Turmoil, 1636–1640," *William and Mary Quarterly*, 31 (1974): 55–78, p. 57.
2. Page Smith, *Daughters of the Promised Land: Women in American History* (Boston: Little, Brown, 1970), p. 40.
3. Kathryn Preyer, "Penal Measures in the American Colonies: An Overview," *American Journal of Legal History*, 26 (1982): 326–353, p. 347.
4. Daniel Deville, "White Slavery in America: A Brief History," *Vanguard News Network Forum*, available at http://www.vnnforum.com/showthread.php?t=79466.
5. Ann Jones, *Women Who Kill* (Boston: Beacon Press, 1996), p. 21.
6. Edward Shorter, *A History of Psychiatry: From the Era of the Asylum to the Age of Prozac* (New York: John Wiley, 1997), p. 6.
7. Cited in Jones, *Women Who Kill*, p. 23.
8. Caryl Rivers, "The Real Bias That Divides Us," *Los Angeles Times* (December 12, 2014), p. A27.
9. William J. Chambliss, "Functional and Conflict Theories of Crime: The Heritage of Émile Durkheim and Karl Marx," in William J. Chambliss and Milton Mankoff, eds., *Whose Law, What Order? A Conflict Approach to Criminology*, pp. 1–28 (New York: Wiley, 1976), p. 11.
10. Mary Beth Norton, "The Evolution of White Women's Experience in Early America," *American History Review*, 89 (1984): 593–619.
11. Raymond Michaelowski, *Order, Law and Crime: An Introduction to Criminology* (New York: Random House, 1985), p. 230.

12. Randall G. Sheldon, *Controlling the Dangerous Classes: A Critical Introduction to the History of Criminal Justice* (Boston: Allyn and Bacon, 2001), pp. 120–121.

13. Ann Fairfax Withington and Jack Schwartz, "The Political Trial of Anne Hutchinson," *New England Quarterly*, 51 (1978): 226–240, p. 277.

14. Chambliss, "Functional and Conflict Theories of Crime," p. 13.

15. J. H. Parry, *The Establishment of the European Hegemony 1415–1715: Trade and Exploration in the Age of the Renaissance* (New York: Harper & Row, 1961), p. 104.

16. C. Dallett Hemphill, "Women in Court: Sex-Role Differentiation in Salem, Massachusetts, 1636 to 1683," *William and Mary Quarterly*, 39 (1982): 164–175, pp. 171–172.

17. Mary Maples Dunn, "Saints and Sisters: Congregational and Quaker Women in the Early Colonial Period," *American Quarterly*, 30 (1978): 582–601, p. 586.

18. Koehler, "The Case of the American Jezebels," p. 64.

19. *Ibid.*, p. 57.

20. Bradley Chapin, *Criminal Justice in Colonial America, 1606–1660* (Atlanta: University of Georgia Press, 1983), pp. 103–104.

21. James M. Inverarity, Pat Lauderdal, and Barry C. Feld, *Law and Society: Sociological Perspectives on Criminal Law* (Boston: Little, Brown, 1983), p. 143.

22. *Ibid.*

23. Karlsen, *The Devil in the Shape of a Woman*, p. 19.

24. Inverarity et al., *Law and Society*, p. 144.

25. Daniel Allan Hearn, *Legal Executions in New England: A Comprehensive Reference, 1623–1960* (Jefferson: McFarland, 1999), p. 33.

26. Horatio Rogers, *Mary Dyer of Rhode Island: The Quaker Martyr That Was Hanged on Boston Common, June 1, 1660* (2002), p. 3, available at http://kobek.com/marydyer.pdf.

27. Sheldon, *Controlling the Dangerous Classes*, p. 237.

28. Karlsen, *The Devil in the Shape of a Woman*, p. 48.

29. Hearn, *Legal Executions in New England*, p. 14.

30. David D. Hall, *Witch-Hunting in Seventeenth Century New England: A Documentary History 1638–1693* (Durham: Duke University Press, 1991), p. 21.

31. *Ibid.*, pp. 23–24.

32. Eve LaPlante, *American Jezebel: The Uncommon Life of Anne Hutchinson, the Woman Who Defied the Puritans* (New York: HarperCollins, 2004), p. 46.

33. Hall, *Witch-Hunting in Seventeenth Century New England*, p. 26.

34. Hearn, *Legal Executions in New England*, p. 33.

35. *Ibid.*, p. 38.

36. *Ibid.*

37. Drake, "Witchcraft in the American Colonies," p. 51.

38. *Ibid.*

39. Hall, *Witch-Hunting in Seventeenth Century New England*, p. 21.

40. Hearn, *Legal Executions in New England*, p. 29.

41. Don Jordan and Michael Walsh, *White Cargo: The Forgotten History of Britain's White Slaves in America* (New York: New York University Press, 2007), pp. 151–153.

42. *Ibid.*

43. "226 Years Later, A 'Witch' Not Guilty," *Los Angeles Times* (August 28, 2008).

44. Linnda Caporael, "Ergotism: The Satan Loosed in Salem?" *Science*, 192 (1976): 21–26.

45. Jane Campbell Moriarty, "Wonders of the Invisible World: Prosecutorial Syndrome and Profile Evidence in the Salem Witchcraft Trials," *Vermont Law Review*, 26 (2001): 43–99, p. 49.

46. Chambliss, "Functional and Conflict Theories of Crime," p. 14.

47. Moriarty, "Wonders of the Invisible World," p. 50.

48. Karlsen, *The Devil in the Shape of a Woman*, p. 47.

49. *Ibid.*, p. 118.

50. *Ibid.*

51. Chambliss, "Functional and Conflict Theories of Crime," pp. 14–15.

52. Karlsen, *The Devil in the Shape of a Woman*, p. 51.

53. Anne L. Barstow, *Witchcraze: A New History of European Witch Hunts* (New York: Pandora, 1994), p. 154.

54. Karlsen, *The Devil in the Shape of a Woman*, p. 116.

55. *Ibid.*

56. Marianne Hester, "The Witchcraze in Sixteenth and Seventeenth Century England as Social Control of Women," in Jill Radford and Diane E. H. Russell, eds., *Femicide: The Politics of Woman Killing* (New York: Twayne, 1992), p. 36.

57. Amrita Chakrabarti Myers, "Sisters in Arms: Slave Women's Resistance to Slavery in the United States," *Past Imperfect*, 5 (1996): 141–174, p. 145.

58. Julia Cherry Spruill, *Women's Life and Work in the Southern Colonies* (New York: W.W. Norton, 1972), p. 329.

59. Ian Shapira, "After Toil and Trouble, Witch Is Cleared," *Washington Post* (July 12, 2006), p. B01.

60. Jones, *Women Who Kill*, p. 20.

61. Spruill, *Women's Life and Work in the Southern Colonies*, p. 314.

62. Jones, *Women Who Kill*, p. 42.

63. Roslyn Fraad Baxandall and Linda Gordon, *America's Working Women: A Documentary History—1600 to the Present* (New York: W.W. Norton, 1995), p. 27.

64. Lois Green Carr and Lorena S. Walsh, "The Planter's Wife: The Experiences of White Women in Seventeenth-Century Maryland," *William and Mary Quarterly*, 34 (1977): 542–571, p. 549.

65. A. Leon Higginbotham, *In the Matter of Color: Race and the American Legal Process—the Colonial Period* (New York: Oxford University Press, 1978), p. 43.

66. Sharon Ann Burnston, "Babies in the Well: An Underground Insight Into Deviant Behavior in Eighteenth-Century Philadelphia," *The Pennsylvania Magazine of History and Biography*, 106 (1982): 151–186, p. 174.

67. Laurel Thatcher Ulrich, *Goodwives: Image and Reality in the Lives of Women in Northern New England, 1650–1750* (New York: Alfred A. Knopf, 1982), p. 196.

68. Peter C. Hoffer and N.E.H. Hull, *Murdering Mothers: Infanticide in England and New England, 1558–1803* (New York: New York University Press, 1984), p. 145.

69. *Ibid.*, p. 157.

70. Gail Stuart Rowe, "Infanticide, Its Judicial Resolution, and Criminal Code Revision in Early Pennsylvania," *Proceedings of the American Philosophical Society*, 135 (1991): 200–232, p. 204.

71. Hoffer and Hull, *Murdering Mothers*, p. 44.

72. *Ibid.*, p. 49.

73. Michelee Oberman, "Mothers Who Kill: Coming to Terms with Modern American Infanticide," *DePaul Journal of Health Care Law*, 8 (2004): 3–107, p. 12.

74. Jack D. Marietta and Gail Stuart Rowe, *Troubled Experiment: Crime and Justice in Philadelphia, 1682–1800* (Philadelphia: University of Pennsylvania Press, 2006), p. 117.

75. Collier C. Harris, *Public Goal Historical Report, Block 27 Building 2* (originally entitled *A Manual for the Public Goal*), Colonial Williamsburg Foundation Library Research Report Series—1628, Colonial Williamsburg Foundation Library Williamsburg, Virginia, p. 43, available at http://research.history.org/DigitalLibrary/View/index.cfm?doc=ResearchReports%5CRR1628.xml.

76. Amanda Lea Miracle, *Rape and Infanticide in Maryland, 1634–1689: Gender and Class in the Courtroom Contestation of Patriarchy on the Edge of the English Atlantic*, unpublished doctoral dissertation, Bowling Green State University, 2008, p. 289, available at http://gradworks.umi.com/33/75/3375053.html.

77. Raphael Semmes, *Crime and Punishment in Early Maryland* (Baltimore: John Hopkins University Press, 1938), p. 290, note 7.

78. Hearn, *Legal Executions in New England*, p. 8.

79. Koehler, "The Case of the American Jezebels," p. 70.
80. Ibid.
81. *Peine forte et dure*, a form of judicial torture, refers to pressing to death using heavy stones. The practice began in 1426 in England when those charged with a felony and refused to enter plea of guilty or not guilty were pressed until they did plea. American colonial leaders lacked jurisdiction over a criminal defendant until the defendant entered a plea of guilt or innocence to the court. Where a defendant stood mute and refused to plea, courts would subject the defendant to having heavier and heavier stones placed upon the defendant's chest until a plea was entered or the defendant suffocated to death. Giles Corey (the husband of Martha Corey) is the only person known to have suffered pressing when, in September 1692, he refused to plea to a charge of witchcraft. It is a misguided notion to argue, as some authorities claim, that Giles Corey refused to confess to witchcraft. Giles *refused to plea* to a charge of witchcraft.
82. Jones, *Women Who Kill*, p. 47.
83. Hearn, *Legal Executions in New England*, p. 44.
84. Ibid., p. 56–57.
85. Hearn, *Legal Executions in New England*, p. 106.
86. Sylvester Judd, *History of Hadley: Including the Early History of Hatfield, South Hadley, Amherst, and Granby Massachusetts* (Springfield: H.R. Huntting, 1905), p. 261.
87. Hearn, *Legal Executions in New England*, p. 116.
88. Ibid., p. 124.
89. "1739: Penelope Kenny and Sarah Simpson," ExecutedTodaywww (December 2007), available at http://www.executedtoday.com/2007/12/27/1739-penelope-kenny-and-sarah-simpson.
90. Stuart Banner, *The Death Penalty: An American History* (Cambridge: Harvard University Press, 2002), p. 25.
91. Ibid., p. 41.
92. Henry Ashmead, "Crimes and punishments." *History of Delaware County, Pennsylvania* (Philadelphia: L.H. Everts & Co., 1884), p. 163, available at http://www.pa-roots.com/index.php/delaware-county/204-history-of-delaware-county-pennsylvania/765-historyofdelawarecountychapter18.
93. Hangings in Berks County, Pa., available at http://freepages.genealogy.rootsweb.ancestry.com/~genphotos2/hangings.html.
94. Daniel Allan Hearn, *Legal Executions in New Jersey: A Comprehensive Registry, 1691–1963* (Jefferson: McFarland, 2005), p. 9.
95. Henry Onderdonk, *Long Island and New York in Olden Times, Being Newspaper Extracts and Historical Sketches*, Long Island Genealogy (1851), available at http://longislandgenealogy.com/OldenTimes.pdf.
96. Terry Snyder, "As If There Was Not Master or Woman in the Land: Gender, Dependency, and Household Violence in Virginia, 1646–1720," in C. Daniels and M. Kennedy, eds., *Over the Threshold: Intimate Violence in Early America*, pp. 219–236 (New York: Routledge, 1999), p. 220.
97. Rowe, "Women's Crime and Criminal Administration in Pennsylvania," note 15.
98. Hearn, *Legal Executions in New England*, p.
99. Hearn, *Legal Executions in New England*, p. 109.
100. Jones, *Women Who Kill*, p. 38.
101. Anna Neuzil, *The Plymouth Colony Archieve Project: Women in Plymouth Colony, 1633–1668* (1998), available at www.histarch.uiuc.edu/plymouth/PCR.htm.
102. Ibid.
103. Clarice Feinman, "An Historical Overview of the Treatment of Incarcerated Women: Myths and Realities of Rehabilitation, *Prison Journal*, 63 (1984): 12–26, p. 13.
104. Chapin, *Criminal Justice in Colonial America*, p. 114.
105. David Rauch, "Visitors Become Jurors at Pennsbury Manor," *Bucks County Courier Times* (July 14, 2008), available at http://www.phillyburbs.com/pb-dyn/news/111-07142008-1562712.html.
106. Daniel Allan Hearn, *Legal Executions in New York State* (Jefferson: McFarland, 2007), p. 6.
107. L. Kay Gillespie, *Dancehall Ladies: The Crimes and Executions of America's Condemned Women* (New York: University Press of America, 1997), p. 102.
108. Archives of Maryland Online, *Proceedings of the Council of Maryland, 1732–1753*, Volume 28, p. 576, available at http://aomol.msa.maryland.gov/000001/000028/html/am28-576.html.
109. Leopold Launitz-Schurer, Jr., "Slave Resistance in Colonial New York: An Interpretation of Daniel Horsmanden's New York Conspiracy," *Phylon*, 41 (1980): 137–152, p. 147.
110. Paula C. Johnson, "At the Intersection of Injustice: Experience of African American Women in Crime and Sentencing," *The American University Journal of Gender and the Law*, 4 (1995): 1–76, p. 15, note 84.
111. bell hooks, *Ain't I a Woman: Black Women and Feminism* (Boston: South End Press, 1981), p. 19.
112. Ibid., pp. 18–19.
113. Marcus Rediker, *The Slave Ship: A Human History* (New York: Viking, 2007), p. 40.
114. David Richardson, "Shipboard Revolts, African Authority, and the Atlantic Slave Trade," *William and Mary Quarterly*, 58 (2001): 69–92, p. 73.
115. Rediker, *The Slave Ship*, p. 16.
116. "The Trial of Captain John Kimber," *American Memory, Slaves and the Courts, 1740–1860* (June 7, 1792), available at http://memory.loc.gov/cgi-bin/query/r?ammem/llst:@field(DOCID+@lit(llst061div0)).
117. Emma Christopher, *Slave Ship Sailors and Their Captive Cargoes, 1730–1807* (New York: Cambridge University Press, 2006), p. 187.
118. Edward Baptist. *The Half Has Never Been Told: Slavery and the Making of American Capitalism* (New York: Basic Books, 2014), p. 99.
119. Ira Berlin, "Time, Space, and the Evolution of Afro-American Society in British Mainland North America," *American History Review*, 85 (1980): 44–78.
120. Lawrence Friedman, *A History of American Law* (New York: Simon & Schuster, 1985), p. 33.
121. Ulrich B. Phillips, *American Negro Slavery: A Survey of Supply, Employment, Control of Negro Labor as Determined by the Plantation Regime* (New York: D. Appleton, 1918), p. 454.
122. Myers, "Sisters in Arms," p. 142.
123. Hearn, *Legal Executions in New York State*, p. 6.
124. Ibid.
125. Daniel Allan Hearn, *Legal Executions in New Jersey: A Comprehensive Registry, 1691–1963* (Jefferson: McFarland, 2005), p. 5.
126. Phillip J. Schwarz, *Twice Condemned: Slaves and the Criminal Laws of Virginia, 1705–1865* (Union: Lawbook Exchange, 1998), p. 81.
127. Ibid., note 31.
128. Ibid., p. 92.
129. Milton Ready, *The Tar Heel State: A History of North Carolina* (Columbia: University of South Carolina Press, 2005), p. 80.
130. Ibid.
131. Hoffer and Hull, *Murdering Mothers*, p. 48.
132. Jones, *Women Who Kill*, p. 366.
133. Hearn, *Legal Executions in New England*, pp. 111–112.
134. Schwarz, *Twice Condemned*, pp. 115–116.
135. A. Leon Higginbotham, *Shades of Freedom: Racial Politics and Presumptions of the American Legal Process* (New York: Oxford University Press, 1996), p. 75.
136. Herbert Aptheker, *American Negro Slave Revolts* (New York: International, 1993), p. 190.
137. Gwendolyn Midlo Hall, *Africans in Colonial Louisiana: The Development of Afro-Creole Culture in the Eighteenth Century* (Baton Rouge: Louisiana State University Press, 1992), p. 108.
138. Aptheker, *American Negro Slave Revolts*, p. 182.
139. Robert Perkinson, *Texas Tough: The Rise of America's Prison Empire* (New York: Picador, 2010), p. 63.
140. Hoffer and Hull, *Murdering Mothers*, p. 48.

Chapter 4

1. Laura James, *Women and the Death Penalty in New Mexico, A Historical Review: The Twice-Hanged Angel* (2005), available at http://laurajames.typepad.com/clews/2005/11/women_and_the_d.html.
2. Joan M. Jensen, *Loosening the Bonds: Mid-Atlantic Farm Women 1750–1850* (New Haven: Yale University Press, 1986), p. 69.
3. Jay P. Dolan, *The Irish American, A History* (New York: Bloomsbury, 2008), p. 25.
4. Charles E. Hurst, *Social Inequality: Forms, Causes, and Consequences* (Boston: Allyn & Bacon, 2010), pp. 284–285.
5. *Ibid.*
6. *Ibid.*
7. Daniel Allen Hearn, *Legal Executions in New England: A Comprehensive Reference, 1623–1960* (Jefferson: McFarland, 1999), p. 158.
8. Ann Jones, *Women Who Kill* (Boston: Beacon Press, 1996), p. 59.
9. "Trial of Bathsheba Spooner: 1778—Bathsheba Plots to Kill Her Husband, The Soldiers Are Arrested and Confession," *Great American Trials*, Volume 1, available at http://law.jrank.org/pages/2374/Trial-Bathsheba-Spooner-et-al-1778.html.
10. Deborah Navas, *Murdered by His Wife: A History with Documentation of the Joshua Spooner Murder and Execution of His Wife, Bathsheba, Who Was Hanged in Worcester, Massachusetts, 2 July 1778* (Amherst: University of Massachusetts Press, 1999).
11. Death Penalty in Delaware, 1650–1849, Genealogy Trails History Group, available at http://genealogytrails.com/del/executions1650_1849.html#kirk.
12. Gabriele Gottlieb, *Theater of Death: Capital Punishment in Early America, 1750–1800*, unpublished doctoral dissertation, University of Pittsburgh (2005), p. 21, available at http://etd.library.pitt.edu/ETD/available/etd-12082005-165901/unrestricted/gottlieb.pdf.
13. William Henry Tippetts, *Herkimer County Murders: This Book Contains an Accurate Account of the Capital Crimes Committed in the County of Herkimer, From the Year 1783 Up to the Present Time. Among Those of Recent Date Are the Wishart Murder, the Druse Butchery, and the Middleville Tragedy. The Facts Were Gathered from the Official Records of Herkimer County, and Other Reliable Sources* (Herkimer: H. P. Witherstine, Steam Book and Job Printers, 1885).
14. Lewis L. Lawes, *Legal Executions in Tennessee: A Comprehensive Registry, 1782–2009* (Jefferson: McFarland, 2011), p. 24.
15. Rachel Jennings, "Celtic Women and White Guilt: Frankie Silver and Chipita Rodriguez in Folk Memory," *MELUS*, 28 (2003), pp. 17–37, p. 20.
16. Hearn, *Legal Executions in New York State*, p. 50.
17. Jones, *Women Who Kill*, p. 179.
18. *Ibid.*, p. 181.
19. *Ibid.*, p. 182.
20. Shipman, *The Penalty Is Death*, p. 248.
21. "Died on the Scaffold," *Newark Daily Advocate* [Newark, Ohio] (March 1, 1887), p. 1.
22. "Roxalana Druse Hanged," *New York Times* (February 28, 1887), p. 1.
23. Shipman, *The Penalty Is Death*, p. 35.
24. Merril D. Smith, "Unnatural Mothers: Infanticide, Motherhood, and Class in the Mid-Atlantic, 1730–1830," in Christine Daniels and Michael V. Kennedy, eds., *Over the Threshold: Intimate Violence in Early America*, pp. 173–184 (New York: Routledge, 1999), p. 177.
25. *Ibid.*, p. 179.
26. Rowe, "Infanticide," p. 204.
27. Roxie J. Zwicker, *Haunted Portsmouth: Spirits and Shadows of the Past* (Charleston: History Press, 2007), p. 47.
28. Hearn, *Legal Executions in New England*, p. 273.
29. *Ibid.*, p. 174.
30. Hearn, *Legal Executions in New Jersey*, pp. 25–26.
31. Henry Graham Ashmead, *History of Delaware County, Pennsylvania* (1884), p. 165, available at http://www.delcohistory.org/ashmead/ashmead_pg165.htm.
32. Jack D. Marietta and G. S. Rowe, *Troubled Experiment: Crime and Justice in Philadelphia, 1682–1800* (Philadelphia: University of Pennsylvania Press 2006), p. 118.
33. *Ibid.*
34. Hearn, *Legal Executions in New York State*, p. 24.
35. *Ibid.*, p. 37.
36. *Ibid.*
37. Hearn, *Legal Executions in New York State*, pp. 92–93.
38. Negley Teeters, "Public Executions in Pennsylvania, 1682–1834: With Annotated Lists of Persons Executed and of Delays, Pardons and Reprieves of Persons Sentenced to Death in Pennsylvania, 1682–1834," *Journal of the Lancaster County Historical Society*, 64 (1960): 85–164, p. 106.
39. Harriet C. Frazier, *Slavery and Crime in Missouri, 1773–1865* (Jefferson: McFarland, 2001), p. 150.
40. Jones, *Women Who Kill*, p. 195.
41. Hearn, *Legal Executions in New Jersey*, p. 126.
42. Jones, *Women Who Kill*, p. 199.
43. Hearn, *Legal Executions in New Jersey*, p. 127.
44. Jones, *Woman Who Kill*, p. 202.
45. J. W. Thompson, *Execution. The Life, Trial, and Behaviour of That Unfortunate Young Woman, Mary Johnson, 22 Years of Age, Who Was Executed at Gloucester on Saturday Last, 1831 for the Murder of Her Master and Mistress, John and Anna Robinson* (Library of Congress, 1831), available at http://memory.loc.gov/cgi-bin/query/r?ammem/rbpebib:@field(NUMBER+@band(rbpe+05500900)).
46. Hearn, *Legal Executions in New York State*, p. 16.
47. Katy Berry, Historical Female Pirates, available at http://www.katyberry.com/Dorianne/pirates.html.
48. Hearn, *Legal executions in New England*, pp. 175–176.
49. Samuel Walker, *Popular Justice: A History of American Criminal Justice* (New York: Oxford University Press, 1998), p. 18.
50. Gottlieb, *Theater of Death*, p. 215.
51. Patrick M Hendrix, Heather Spires, Toni Hendrix, and Judy Corbett, *Murder and Mayhem in Holy City* (Charleston: History Press, 2006), pp. 26–34.
52. Elizabeth Trindal, *Mary Surratt: An American Tragedy* (Gretna: Pelican, 1996), pp. 673–674.
53. Shipman, *The Penalty Is Death*, p. 128.
54. *Ibid.*
55. Shipman, *The Penalty Is Death*, p. 241.
56. Deborah G. White, *Ar'n't I a Woman? Female Slaves in the Plantation South* (New York: W.W. Norton, 1998), p. 62.
57. Phillip J. Schwarz, *Twice Condemned: Slaves and the Criminal Laws of Virginia, 1705–1865* (Union: Lawbook Exchange, 1998), p. 15.
58. Michael S. Hindus, "Black Justice Under White Law: Criminal Prosecutions of Blacks in Antebellum South Carolina," *Journal of American History*, 63 (1976): 575–599.
59. Phillip J. Schwarz, *Slave Laws in Virginia* (Athens: University of Georgia Press, 1996).
60. Thomas D. Morris, *Southern Slavery and the Law: 1619–1860* (Chapel Hill: University of North Carolina, 1996), p. 277.
61. Marvin L. Kay and Lorin Lee Cary, *Slavery in North Carolina, 1748–1775* (Chapel Hill: University of North Carolina Press, 1995), p. 79.
62. Digital Library on American Slavery, University of North Carolina at Greensboro, PAR Number 11378503, available at http://library.uncg.edu/slavery/details.aspx?pid=1067.
63. Helen Tunnicliff Catterall, *Judicial Cases Concerning American Slavery and the Negro*, Volume 4 (Washington, D.C.: Carnegie Institution of Washington, 1936), pp. 442–443.
64. Schwarz, *Twice Condemned*, pp. 115–116.
65. Schwarz, *Slave Laws in Virginia*, p. 116.

66. Catterall, *Judicial Cases Concerning American Slavery and the Negro*, p. 38.
67. Gottlieb, *Theater of Death*, p. 30.
68. Aptheker, *American Negro Slave Revolts*, p. 145.
69. Schwarz, *Twice Condemned*, p. 115.
70. Silas Farmer, *The History of Detroit and Michigan* (Detroit: Silas Farmer, 1884), p. 173.
71. "Three Days in Camp with the Robeson County Chain Gang," *The Robesonian* [Lumberton, North Carolina] (September 9, 1902), p. 3; Doris Evans, "Lawson Murder a Great Shock," *The Robesonian* (February 4, 1938), p. 1; W. S. Wishart, "First Hanging in Robeson County," *The Robesonian* (April 1, 1935), p. 12.
72. Schwarz, *Twice Condemned*, p. 237.
73. *Ibid.*, p. 239.
74. "The Execution of Pauline," *The Daily Picayune* (March 29, 1846), p. 2.
75. Digital Library on American Slavery, University of North Carolina at Greensboro, PAR Number 11585901, available at http://library.uncg.edu/slavery/details.aspx?pid=2176.
76. McNair, *Criminal Injustice*, pp. 100–102.
77. *Ibid.*, p. 75.
78. Hearn, *Legal Executions in New Jersey*, pp. 80–81.
79. Nancy Lougbridge, "Chloe's Story," available at www.carothersonline.com/Chloes%20Story.html.
80. Shipman, *The Penalty Is Death*, p. 149.
81. Digital Library on American Slavery, University of North Carolina at Greensboro, PAR Number 11282304, available at http://library.uncg.edu/slavery/details.aspx?pid=858.
82. "The Death Penalty," *Galveston Daily News* (August 28, 1880), p. 1.
83. Laura James, "Women and the Death Penalty in Ohio, an Historical Review: Proving Pearson's Theorem," available at http://laurajames.typepad.com/clews/2005/10/women_and_the_d.html.
84. Paula C. Johnson, "At the Intersection of Injustice: Experiences of African American Women in Crime and Sentencing," *The American University Journal of Gender and the Law*, 4 (1995): 1–76, p. 22.
85. Digital Library on American Slavery, University of North Carolina at Greensboro, PAR Number 11279304, available at http://library.uncg.edu/slavery/details.aspx?pid=668.
86. McNair, "Slave Women, Capital Crime, and Criminal Justice in Georgia," p. 143.
87. Frazier, *Slavery and Crime in Missouri*, p. 168.
88. Oscar Reiss, *Blacks in Colonial America* (Jefferson: McFarland, 1997), p. 198.
89. Morris, *Southern Slavery and the Law*, p. 301.
90. Frazier, *Slavery and Crime in Missouri*, pp. 168–169.
91. Teeters, "Public Executions in Pennsylvania," p. 107.
92. Digital Library on American Slavery, University of North Carolina at Greensboro, PAR Number 11382407, available at http://library.uncg.edu/slavery/details.aspx?pid=596.
93. Michael P. Johnson, "Smothered Slave Infants: Were Slave Mothers at Fault?" *The Journal of Southern History*, 47 (1981): 493–520.
94. Schwarz, *Twice Condemned*, pp. 253–254.
95. Kenneth Milton Stampp, *The Peculiar Institution: Slavery in the Antebellum South* (New York: Vintage, 1956), p. 113.
96. Johnson, "At the Intersection of Injustice," p. 22.
97. White, *Ar'n't I a Woman?*, p. 71.
98. Susan Brownmiller, *Against Our Will: Men, Women and Rape* (New York: Bantam, 1975), p. 153.
99. Angela Davis, *Women, Race, and Class* (New York: Vintage, 1981), p. 175.
100. Davis, *Women, Race, and Class*, p. 9.
101. *Ibid.*
102. Fogel, *Without Consent or Contract*, p. 181.
103. *Ibid.*, p. 166.
104. Kolchin, *American Slavery*, p. 124.
105. Wilma King, "Mad Enough to Kill: Enslaved Women, Murder, and Southern Courts," *The Journal of African American History*, 92 (2007): 37–56, p. 38.
106. Melton Alonza McLaurin, *Celia, a Slave* (Athens: University of Georgia Press, 1991), p. 109.
107. Joan R. Tarpley, "Black Women, Sexual Myth, and Jurisprudence," *Temple Law Review*, 69 (1996): 1343–1388, p. 1353.
108. Paul Finkelman, "The Color of Race," *Tulane Law Review*, 67 (1993): 2063–2112, p. 2084.
109. bell hooks, *Ain't I a Woman: Black Women and Feminism* (Boston: South End Press, 1981), pp. 36–37.
110. Cited in Kolchin, *American Slavery*, p. 58.
111. Cited in Sheri Lynn Johnson, "Symposium on Race and Criminal Law: *Batson* Ethics for Prosecutors and Trial Court Judges," *Chicago-Kent Law Review*, 73 (1998): 475–507, p. 491.
112. A. Leon Higginbotham, *In The Matter of Color: Race and the American Legal Process—the Colonial Period* (New York: Oxford University Press, 1978), p. 289.
113. Streib and Sametz, "Executing Female Juveniles," p. 11.
114. Denise Morgan, "Jack Johnson Versus the American Racial Hierarchy," in Annette Gordon-Reed, ed., *Race on Trial: Law and Justice in American History*, pp. 77–102 (New York: Oxford University Press, 2002), p. 77.
115. Douglas A. Blackmon, *Slavery by Another Name: The Re-Enslavement of Black Americans from the Civil War to World War II* (New York: Doubleday, 2008), p. 57.
116. Perkinson, *Texas Tough*, p. 94.
117. Philip Dray, *At the Hands of Persons Unknown: The Lynching of Black America* (New York: Random House, 2003), p. 49.
118. Davis, *Women, Race, and Class*, pp. 89–90.
119. Elliot Jaspin, *Buried in the Bitter Waters: The Hidden History of Racial Cleansing in America* (New York: Basic Books, 2007), p. 61.
120. Perkinson, *Texas Tough*, p. 87.
121. Joe R. Feagin, *Racist America: Roots, Current Realities, and Future Reparations* (New York: Routledge, 2000), p. 58.
122. Nicole Hahn Rafter, *Partial Justice: Women, Prisons, and Social Control* (New Brunswick, NJ: Transaction, 2004), p. 145.
123. Hearn, *Legal Executions in New Jersey*, p. 76.
124. Harvard Sitkoff, *The Struggle for Black Equality, 1954–1980* (New York: Hill & Wang, 1981), pp. 3–4.
125. Leon F. Litwack, *North of Slavery: The Negro in the Free States, 1790–1860* (Chicago: University of Chicago Press, 1961), p. 97.
126. Walter White, *Rope and Faggot: Biography of Judge Lynch* (New York: Arno Press, 1929), p. 81.
127. Segrave, *Women and Capital Punishment in America*, p. 125.
128. Cited in Segrave, *Women and Capital Punishment in America*, p. 125.
129. "Margaret Harris Meets Her Death Firmly at Calhoun, GA," *New York Times* (October 20, 1883), p. 2.
130. "Died on the Scaffold," *Millbrook Round Table* (October 15, 1892).
131. Antonia I. Castañeda, "Presidarias Y Pobladoras, The Journey North and Life in Frontier California," in Manuel G. Gonzales and Cynthia M. Gonzales, eds., *En Aquel Entonces: Readings in Mexican-American History* (Bloomington: Indiana University Press, 2000), pp. 5–21, p. 6.
132. *Ibid.*, pp. 5–6.
133. Rick Halperin, "Death Penalty News," September 22, 2007, available at http://lists.washlaw.edu/pipermail/deathpenalty/2007-September/007008.html.
134. Pat Chin, "The African Slave Trade and the Drive for Limitless Profits," *Workers World* (1998), available at http://www.workers.org/ww/1998/slaves0122.php.
135. Gilbreath, *Death on the Gallows*, p. 136.
136. James, *Women and the Death Penalty in New Mexico*.
137. Wallace L. McKeehan, *The Hanging of Chepita Ro-*

driquez (2006), available at www.tamu.edu/ccbn/dewitt/irish chipita.htm.

138. Hearn, *Legal Executions in New England*, p. 169.
139. *A New York Correction History Society Timeline on Executions by Hanging in New York State* (1813–1815), p. 7, available at http://www.correctionhistory.org/hangings/hangdates7.html.
140. Karen Halttunen, "Divine Providence and Dr. Parkman's Jawbone: The Cultural Construction of Murder As Mystery," *Ideas* (September 1996), National Humanities Center, North Carolina, available at http://nationalhumanitiescenter.org/ideasv41/halttun4.htm.

Chapter 5

1. Warden Lawes of Sing Sing Prison, quoted in L. Kay Gillespie, *Dancehall Ladies: The Crimes and Executions of America's Condemned Women* (New York: University Press of America, 1997), pp. 35–36.
2. Philip Perlmutter, *Divided We Fall: A History of Ethnic, Religious, and Racial Prejudice in America* (Ames: Iowa State University Press, 1992), p. 171.
3. John Mack Faragher, Mary Jo Buhle, Daniel Czitrom, and Susan H. Armitrage, *Out of Many: A History of the American People* (Upper Saddle River: Prentice Hall, 2001), pp. 647–648.
4. Robert L. Boyd, "Race, Labor Market Disadvantage, and Survivalist Entrepreneurship: Black Women in the Urban North During the Great Depression," *Sociological Forum*, 15 (2000): 647–670, p. 650.
5. Quoted in Gillespie, *Dancehall Ladies*, p. 5.
6. Kathleen A. O'Shea, *Women and the Death Penalty in the United States, 1900–1998* (Westport: Praeger, 1999), p. 96.
7. Gillespie, *Dancehall Ladies*, p. 33.
8. Noted in Gillespie, *Dancehall Ladies*, pp. 35–36.
9. "Woman, in Coma, Is Wheeled to Electric Chair—Guards Lift Unconscious Slayer of Lover's Wife to Death Seat; Man Follows Here," *Nevada State Journal* [Reno, Nevada] (July 17, 1936), p. 1.
10. Vivien Miller, "The Vestige of Institutional Sexism? Paternalism, Equal Rights and the Death Penalty in Twentieth and Twenty-First Century Sunbelt America: The Case of Florida," *Journal of American Studies*, 38 (2004): 391–424, p. 391.
11. *State v. Henry*, 196 La. 217 (1941), at 266–267, Justice Odum concurring.
12. Jack Bass and Marilyn W. Thompson, *STROM: The Complicated Personal and Political Life of Strom Thurmond* (New York: Public Affairs, 2005), p. 68.
13. Mark Cado, "The Lonely Hearts Killers," *Crime Library*, available at http://www.crimelibrary.com/serial_killers/partners/fernandez/1.html.
14. Shipman, *The Penalty Is Death*, pp. 197–198.
15. Clark Howard, "The True Story of Barbara Graham" (2003), available at http://murderpedia.org/female.G/g/graham-barbara.htm.
16. Teree E. Foster, "I Want to Live! Federal Judicial Values in Death Penalty Cases: Preservation of Rights or Punctuality of Execution?" *Oklahoma City University Law Review*, 22 (1997): 63–87, pp. 86–87.
17. Howard, "The True Story of Barbara Graham."
18. *Tucker v. State*, 771 S.W.2d 523 (1988), p. 526.
19. *Ibid.*, p. 527.
20. "Oppose Capital Punishment Because It Is Wrong to Kill," *St. Louis Post-Dispatch* (February 6, 1998), p. C19.
21. Atwell, Mary, *Wretched Sisters: Examining Gender and Capital Punishment* (New York: Peter Lang, 2007), p. 188.
22. David Krajicek, "Sue Basso," *Crime Library*, available at http://www.crimelibrary.com/notorious_murders/women/suzanne_basso/index.html.
23. Gabriel Black, "Texas Executes Suzanne Basso, Despite Claims of Mental Incompetency," *World Socialist Web Site* (February 7, 2014), available at http://www.wsws.org/en/articles/2014/02/07/exec-f07.html.
24. Stephen Millies, "What They Don't Want You to Know," *Workers World* (June 23, 2010), available at http://www.workers.org/2010/world/korea_0701/.
25. Douglas Linder, "The Rosenberg trial. Famous Trials" (2008), at http://law2.umkc.edu/faculty/projects/ftrials/rosenb/ROSENB.HTM.
26. *Ibid.*
27. Tom Eley, "Declassified Grand Jury Transcripts Confirm Frame-Up of Ethel Rosenberg," *World Socialist Web Site*, available at http://www.wsws.org/en/articles/2008/09/rose-s13.html.
28. *Glass v. Louisiana*, 471 U.S. 1080 (1985).
29. Cited in Hugo Bedau, "Habeas Corpus and Other Constitutional Conversies," in Hugo Bedau, *The Death Penalty in America: Current Controversies*, pp. 238–245 (New York: Oxford University Press, 1997), p. 242.
30. "Was Ethel Rosenberg Wrong?" *Los Angeles Times* (September 12, 2008), available at http://articles.latimes.com/2008/sep/12/nation/na-rosenberg12.
31. Michael Meeropol and Robert Meeropol, "The Essential Lessons of the Rosenberg Case," *Los Angeles Times* (October 5, 2008), available at http://articles.latimes.com/2008/oct/05/opinion/oe-meeropol5.
32. Robert Meeropol, "Kinship With Manning," *Los Angeles Times* (August 12, 2013), p. A13.
33. Jeffrey S. Adler, "'I Love Joe, but I Had to Shoot Him': Homicide by Women in Turn-of-the-Century Chicago," *The Journal of Criminal Law and Criminology*, 92 (2002): 867–898, p. 888.
34. *Ibid.*
35. Lawrence M. Freedmen and William E. Haverman, "The Rise and Fall of the Unwritten Law: Sex, Patriarchy, and Vigilante Justice in American Courts," *Buffalo Law Review*, 61 (2013): 997–1056, p. 998.
36. Adler, "'I Love Joe,'" p. 884.
37. *Ibid.*
38. David M. Oshinsky, *Worse Than Slavery: Parchman Farm and the Ordeal of Jim Crow Justice* (New York: Free Press, 1996), p. 175–176.
39. "Did Mary Rogers Deserve Hanging?" *Times Argus* [Montpelier, Vermont] (June 12, 2005), available at http://www.timesargus.com/apps/pbcs.dll/article?AID=/20050612/NEWS/506120319/1013/FEATURES04.
40. Daniel Allen Hearn, *Legal Executions in New England: A Comprehensive Reference, 1623–1960* (Jefferson: McFarland, 1999), p. 305.
41. Daniel Allen Hearn, *Legal Executions in New York State: A Comprehensive Reference, 1639–1963* (Jefferson: McFarland, 1997), p. 200.
42. Jones, *Women Who Kill*, p. 267.
43. Gillespie, *Dancehall Ladies*, p. 32.
44. *People v. Saetta*, 264 N.Y. 640, 191 N.E. 604 (1934); *People v. Antonio*, 265 N.Y. 247, 192 N.E. 311 (1934); *People v. Antonio*, 265 N.Y. 246, 192 N.E. 310 (1934).
45. Hearn, *Legal Executions in New York State*, p. 200.
46. Adler, "'I Love Joe,'" p. 880.
47. Shipman, *The Penalty Is Death*, p. 54.
48. Amnesty International, *USA (Texas) Betty Lou Beets* (January 31, 2000), available at http://www.amnesty.ru/library/print/ENGAMR510192000.
49. Allan Berlow, "Miscarriage of Justice, Texas Style," *Common Dreams, NewsCenter* (February 22, 2000), available at www.commondreams.org/views/022200-101.htm.
50. Cited in Gillespie, *Dancehall Ladies*, p. 90.
51. American Civil Liberties Union, "More Tainted Testimony from Oklahoma Forensics Lab" (May 8, 2001), available at https://www.aclu.org/racial-justice_prisoners-rights_womens-rights_immigrants-rights/more-tainted-testimony-oklahoma-fore.
52. *Lewis v. Commonwealth*, 267 Va. 302, 593 S.E.2d 220 (2004).

53. Dugald McConnell and Brian Todd, "Virginia Puts Woman to Death by Lethal Injection," *CNN* (September 24, 2010), available at http://www.cnn.com/2010/CRIME/09/23/virginia.woman.execution/.

54. Margie Clark, "Mentally Retarded Defendants Still Face Execution," *CQ Researcher*, 20 (November 2010): 976–977.

55. Brian Stull, "Act Now to Save a Virginia Woman on Death Row," ACLU Blog of Rights (August 3, 2010).

56. Dehlia Umunna, "Symposium: Theory and Praxis in Reducing Women's Poverty: Rethinking the Neighborhood Watch: How Lesson from the Nigerian Village Can Creatively Empower the Community to Assist Poor, Single Mothers in America," *American University Journal of Gender, Social Policy & the Law*, 20 (2012): 847–869, p. 851.

57. Amnesty International, "Document—USA (Arkansas): Death penalty/Legal concern: Christina Marie Riggs," available at http://www.amnesty.org/fr/library/asset/AMR51/058/2000/fr/07a71ad6-df5c-11dd-acaa-7d9091d4638f/amr510582000en.html.

58. Robert Anthony Phillips, "Mom Who Killed Kids Is Eager to Die," *APBNews Online* (April 30, 2000), available at http://murderpedia.org/female.R/r/riggs-christina.htm.

59. Trina N. Seitz, "The Wounds of Savagery: Negro Primitivism, Gender Parity, and the Execution of Rosanna Lightner Phillips," *Women and Criminal Justice*, 16 (2005), 29–64, p. 41.

60. Victor L. Streib and Lynn Sametz, "Executing Female Juveniles," *Connecticut Law Review*, 22 (1989): 3–59, p. 26.

61. Ibid., p. 25.

62. Ibid.

63. Ibid.

64. Quoted in Irene Diggs, "DuBois and Children," *Phylon*, 37 (1976): 370–399, p. 372.

65. "1903: Dora Wright, in Indian Territory," ExecutedToday.com, available at http://murderpedia.org/female.W/w/wright-dora.htm.

66. "Indicted by Grand Jury, Sentenced to Death, All Within Six Hours," *Hattiesburg American* [Hattiesburg, Mississippi] (October 4, 1921), p. 1.

67. Seitz, "The Wounds of Savagery," p. 56.

68. David Staba, "Falls Murder Case Presents Contrast to Northrup Verdict," *Niagara Falls Reporter* (December 4, 2001), at www.niagarafallsreporter.com/fowler.html.

69. Lela Bond Phillips, "Execution in a Small Town—The Lena Baker Story," *Justice Denied: The Magazine for the Wrongfully Convicted* 29 (2005): 8.

70. Carla Campos and Bill Torpy, "Post-Execution Pardon; One-Day Trial in 1945 Sent Georgia Woman to Electric Chair," *The Atlanta Journal Constitution* (August 16, 2005), p. 4.

71. *Commonwealth v. Sykes*, 353 Pa. 392 (1946).

72. Vertamae Grosvenor, *Remembering Corrine Sykes*, National Public Radio (NPR) All Things Considered (April 3, 1998), Transcript No. 98040320-212, Linda Wertheimer, reporting.

73. Shipman, *The Penalty Is Death*, p. 165.

74. Joe R. Feagin, *Racist America: Roots, Current Realities, and Future Reparations* (New York: Routledge, 2000), p. 242.

75. Michele Goodwin, "Gender, Race, and Mental Illness: The Case of Wanda Jean Allen," in A. Wing, ed., *Critical Race Feminism: A Reader*, pp. 228–237 (New York: New York University Press, 2003), p. 229.

76. Janice L. Kopec, "Avoiding a Death Sentence in the American Legal System: Get a Woman to Do It," *Capital Defense Journal*, 15 (2003): 353–382, p. 362.

77. Sally Kohn, "Greasing the Wheel: How the Criminal Justice System Hurts Gay, Lesbian, Bisexual and Transgendered People and Why Hate Crime Laws Won't Save Them," *New York University Review of Law and Social Change*, 27 (2001): 257–280, p. 264.

78. Sheri Lynn Johnson, "Racial Derogation in Prosecutors' Closing Arguments," in Dragan Milovanovic and Katheryn K. Russell, eds., *Petit Apartheid in the U.S. Criminal Justice System: The Dark Figure of Racism*, pp. 79–102 (Durham: Carolina Academic Press, 2001).

79. Ryan Patrick Alford, "Appellate Review of Racist Summations: Redeeming the Promise of Searching Analysis," *Michigan Journal of Race and Law*, 11 (2006): 325–365, p. 327.

80. David R. Dow and Jared Tyler, *Ex parte Francis Elaine Newton*, Application for Postconviction Writ of Habeas Corpus and Motion for Stay of Execution, in the 263rd Judicial District, Texas, and in the Court of Criminal Appeals of Texas, p. 8 (July 27, 2005), available at http://www.victimsofthestate.org/TX/Newton2.htm.

81. Tom Dart, "Texas Set to Execute Lisa Coleman for Gruesome Murder of Child," *The Guardian* (September 17, 2014), available at http://www.theguardian.com/world/2014/sep/17/texas-execute-lisa-coleman-lethal-injection-woman.

82. William Bowers, *Legal Homicide: Death as Punishment in America, 1864–1982* (Boston: Northeastern University Press, 1984).

83. David M. Oshinsky, *Capital Punishment on Trial: Furman v. Georgia and the Death Penalty in Modern America* (Lawrence: University Press of Kansas, 2010), p. 10.

Chapter 6

1. *King v. Kentucky*, No. 2012-CA-001985-MR (July 18, 2014).

2. Edwin M. Borchard, *Convicting the Innocent: Sixty-Five Actual Errors of Criminal Justice* (New York: Garden City, 1932).

3. Steven A. Drizin and Richard A. Leo, "The Problem of False Confessions in the Post-DNA World," *North Carolina Law Review*, 82 (2004): 891–1007, p. 901.

4. Samuel R. Gross, Kristen Jacoby, Daniel J. Matheson, Nicholas Montgomery, and Sujat Patil, "Exonerations in the United States 1989 Through 2003," *Journal of Criminal Law and Criminology*, 95 (2005): 523–555.

5. Ibid., p. 532.

6. Samuel R. Gross and Michael Shaffer, "Exonerations in the United States, 1989–2012. Report by the National Registry of Exonerations," available at http://www.law.umich.edu/special/exoneration/Documents/exonerations_us_1989_2012_full_report.pdf.

7. Samuel R. Gross, Barbara O'Brien, Chen Hu, and Edward H. Kennedy, "Rate of False Conviction of Criminal Defendants Who Are Sentenced to Death," *Proceedings of the National Academy of Sciences of the United States of America*, 111 (2014): 7230–7235.

8. Alan Berlow, "The Wrong Man," *Atlantic Monthly*, 284 (November 1999): 66–91.

9. Rodney Uphoff, "Convicting the Innocent: Aberration or Systemic Problem?" *Wisconsin Law Review*, 2006 (2006): 739–842, pp. 779–810.

10. Hans Sherrer, "The Complicity of Judges in the Generation of Wrongful Convictions," *Northern Kentucky Law Review*, 30 (2003): 539–583, pp. 565–575.

11. Kathleen M. Ridolfi and Maurice Possley, *Preventable Error: A Report on Prosecutorial Misconduct in California* (2010), p. 2, available at http://digitalcommons.law.scu.edu/cgi/viewcontent.cgi?article=1001&context=ncippubs; see also Center for Prosecutor Integrity, "An Epidemic of Prosecutor Misconduct," (December 2013), available at www.prosecutorintegrity.org.

12. National Registry of Exonerations, available at http://www.law.umich.edu/special/exoneration/Pages/about.aspx.

13. Bedau and Radelet, "Miscarriages of Justice in Potentially Capital Cases," p. 33.

14. "Exonerations in All States," Center on Wrongful Convictions, available at http://www.law.northwestern.edu/wrongfulconvictions/exonerations/usIndex.htm.

15. *Perry v. New Hampshire*, 132 S.Ct. 716 (2012), J. Sotomajor dissenting, p. 739.

16. Dara Kim, "Justice Pariente Beats Drum for Eyewitness Expert Testimony," News Service of Florida (June 26, 2014), available at http://miami.cbslocal.com/2014/06/26/justice-pariente-beats-drum-for-eyewitness-expert-testimony/.
17. National Registry of Exonerations, Glossary, available at http://www.law.umich.edu/special/exoneration/Pages/glossary.aspx#FC.
18. National Registry of Exonerations, Glossary, available at http://www.law.umich.edu/special/exoneration/Pages/glossary.aspx.
19. Brandon L. Garrett and Peter J. Neufeld, "Invalid Forensic Science Testimony and Wrongful Convictions," *Virginia Law Review*, 95 (2009): 1–97.
20. Diane R. Follingstad, Regina D. Shillinglaw, Dana D. DeHart, and Kathryn L. Kleinfelter, "The Impact of Elements of Self-Defense and Objective versus Subjective Instructions on Jurors' Verdicts for Battered Women Defendants," *Journal of Interpersonal Violence*, 12 (1997): 729–747.
21. Center for Wrongful Convictions, *Joyce Ann Brown*, available at http://www.law.northwestern.edu/wrongfulconvictions/exonerations/txBrownJSummary.html.
22. Stanley Z. Fisher, "Convictions of Innocent Persons in Massachusetts: An Overview," *Boston University Public Interest Law Journal*, 12 (2002): 1–72, pp. 30–31.
23. Brandon L. Garrett, "The Substance of False Confessions," *Stanford Law Review*, 62 (2010): 1051–1119.
24. Radelet, Bedau, and Putnam, *In Spite of Innocence*, p. 170.
25. Bedau and Radelet, "Miscarriages of Justice in Potentially Capital Cases," p. 142.
26. Samuel R. Gross, "The Risks of Death: Why Erroneous Convictions Are Common in Capital Cases," *Buffalo Law Review*, 44 (1996): 469–500, note 89.
27. Hans Sherrer, "Good Samaritan Freed 16 years After One Juror Saved Her from a Death Sentence," *Justice Denied: The Magazine for the Wrongfully Convicted*, available at http://forejustice.org/wc/ellen_reasonover.htm.
28. "Policewoman Sentenced in Lovers' Murder," *Indiana Gazette* [Indiana, Pennsylvania] (July 26, 1984), p. 4.
29. *Woods v. State*, 101 Nev. 128 (1985), p. 131.
30. Devin C. Daines, "*State v. Harden*: Muddying the Waters of Self-Defense Law in West Virginia," *West Virginia Law Review*, 113 (2011): 971–1000, p. 999.
31. *State v. Harden*, 223 W. Va. 796 (2009).
32. Bedau and Radelet, "Miscarriages of Justice in Potentially Capital Cases," p. 161.
33. Robert Perske, "False Confessions from 53 Persons with Intellectual Disabilities: The List Keeps Growing," *Intellectual and Developmental Disabilities*, 46 (2008): 468–479, p. 471.
34. Borchard, *Convicting the Innocent*, pp. 40–45.
35. *People v. Ehlert*, 274 Ill. App. 3d 1026 (1995).
36. *State v. Ashley N. Hepburn*, Appellate Case No. 2011-190695 (February 11, 2013).
37. Wrongfully convicted database, available at http://forejustice.org/db/Labastida-Kriseya-.html.
38. *Labastida v. Nevada*, 112 Nev. 1502; 931 P.2d 1334 (1996), J. Springer dissenting, p. 1517.
39. Renae Merle, "Texas Child Killer's Guilt in Doubt," *Dallas Morning News* (January 16, 1999), available at http://www.texas-justice.com/dalnews/earle990116.html.
40. Hans Sherrer, "Medell Banks Jrs.' Conviction for Killing a Non-Existent Child Is Thrown Out as a 'Manifest Injustice,'" *Justice Denied Magazine*, 2 (2002), available at http://www.justicedenied.org/choctawthree.htm.
41. Tom Jackman, "Shaken Baby Syndrome Itself Is Put on Trial in Fairfax Court," *Washington Post* (January 19, 2010), p. B01.
42. Lawrence J. Goodrich, "Bay State Court Reverses Conviction of Christian Scientists," *Christian Science Monitory* (August 13, 1993).
43. Debra Barayuga, "'Ice' Addict Cleared of Lilling Newborn," StarBulletin.com (November 30, 2005), available at http://archives.starbulletin.com/2005/11/30/news/story02.html.
44. *King v. Kentucky*, No. 2012-CA-001985-MR. (July 18, 2014).
45. "My New Baby Was Torn from My Arms," *London Daily Mail* (December 6, 1994).

Chapter 7

1. Death Penalty Information Center, *What's New*, Washington Governor John Inslee (February 11, 2014), available at http://www.deathpenaltyinfo.org/.
2. Karl S. Myers, "Practical Lackey: The Impact of Holding Execution After a Long Stay on Death Row Unconstitutional Under *Lackey v. Texas*," *Dickinson Law Review*, 106 (2002): 647–677, p. 658.
3. Jack Greenberg, "Capital Punishment as a System," *Yale Law Review*, 91 (1982): 908–936, p. 910.
4. Ibid.
5. *Jane (a Slave) v. State*, 3 Mo. 61 (1831).
6. Frazier, *Slavery and Crime in Missouri*, pp. 175–182.
7. *People v. Fair*, 43 Cal. 137 (1872).
8. *Hartung v. People*, 22 N.Y. 95 (1860).
9. Fort Smith National Historic Site, "Parker's Sentencing of Mary Kettenring, 1895," n.d., available at http://www.nps.gov/fosm/historyculture/parker-sentencing-of-mary-kettenring-1895.htm.
10. "A Missouri Sensation," *Moberly Weekly Monitor* (November 21, 1901), p. 1.
11. *State v. Nesenhener*, 164 Mo. 461 (1901).
12. "The Girl Who Never Had a Chance Ordered to the Gallows," *Muskogee Times Democrat* [Muskogee, Oklahoma] (December 1, 1913), p. 2.
13. Richard Dugsdale, *The Jukes: A Study in Crime, Pauperism, Disease and Heredity* (New York: Putnam's, 1877).
14. David J. Krajicek, "Suffragists Back Wife Who Murdered Husband in 1913 Love Triangle," *New York Daily News* (August 22, 2010), available at http://www.nydailynews.com/news/crime/suffragists-back-wife-murdered-husband-1913-love-triangle-article-1.203509.
15. Ken Silverstein, "The Judge as Lynch Mob: How Alabama Judges Use Judicial Override to Disregard Juries and Impose Death Sentences," *The American Prospect* (May 6, 2001), available at http://prospect.org/article/judge-lynch-mob.
16. American Civil Liberties Union, *The Forgotten Population: A Look at Death Row in the United States Through the Experiences of Women* (December 2004), available at http://www.aclu.org/files/FilesPDFs/womenondeathrow.pdf.
17. *Witherspoon v. Illinois*, 391 U.S. 510, 522 (1968).
18. Charlotte Sutton, "Death Row Is Path Few Women Tread," *St. Petersburg Times* (June 17, 1990).
19. Chimène I. Keitner, "Victim or Vamp? Images of Violent Women in the Criminal Justice System," *Columbia Journal of Gender and Law*, 11 (2002): 38–87.
20. Leigh B. Bienen, *The Status of the Death Penalty in Illinois, as of January 13, 2003*, Northwestern University School of Law, available at http://www.law.northwestern.edu/faculty/fulltime/bienen/bienen_report.pdf.
21. Matthew MacEgan, "Mississippi Throws Out Murder Conviction of Death Row Inmate Michelle Byrom," *World Socialist Web Site* (April 2, 2014), available at http://www.wsws.org/en/articles/2014/04/02/byro-a02.html.
22. Barry Scheck, "Stunning New Case Highlights How Race Bias Corrupts Juries," Salon (April 15, 2014), available at http://www.salon.com/2014/04/15/barry_scheck_stunning_new_case_highlights_how_race_bias_corrupts_juries/.
23. *State v. Young*, 1988 Ohio App. LEXIS 3347 (1988).
24. *State v. Roberts*, 137 Ohio St.3d 230 (2013).
25. *Michelle Ann Binsz and Steven William Binsz v. State*, 1984 OK CR 28; 675 P.2d 448; 1984 Okla. Crim. App. LEXIS 137.
26. Death Penalty Information Center, "Texas Court

Grants Stay on Basis of Possible Innocence," available at http://www.deathpenaltyinfo.org/node/2120.

27. *Richardson v. Texas*, 2008 Tex. Crim. App. Unpub. LEXIS 35 (2008).

Chapter 8

1. *Herrera v. Collins*, 506 U.S. 390, 415 (1993).
2. Michael L. Radelet and Barbara A. Zsembik, "Executive Clemency in Post-*Furman* Capital Cases," *University of Richmond Law Review*, 27 (1993): 289–314, pp. 289–290.
3. *Ibid.*, p. 290.
4. Stuart Banner, *The Death Penalty: An American History* (Cambridge: Harvard University Press, 2002), p. 55.
5. Michael Heise, "Mercy by the Numbers: An Empirical Analysis of Clemency and Its Structure," *Virginia Law Review*, 89: 101–169.
6. Victoria J. Palacios, "Faith in Fantasy: The Supreme Court's Reliance on Commutation to Ensure Justice in Death Penalty Cases," *Vanderbilt Law Review*, 49 (1996): 311–372, p. 332.
7. Austin Sarat, "Memorializing Miscarriages of Justice: Clemency Petitions in the Killing State," *Law and Society*, 42 (2008): 183–224, p. 189.
8. *Ibid.*, pp. 189–190.
9. *Ibid.*
10. Allan Barlow, "The Texas Clemency Memos," *Atlantic Monthly* (July/August 2003), available at http://www.theatlantic.com/magazine/archive/2003/07/the-texas-clemency-memos/2755/?single_page=true.
11. American Bar Association, Death Penalty Due Process Review Project, *The State of the Modern Death Penalty in America: Key Findings of State Death Penalty Assessments 2006-2013*, available at http://www.americanbar.org/content/dam/aba/administrative/death_penalty_moratorium/aba_state_of_modern_death_penalty_web_file.authcheckdam.pdf.
12. *Ibid.*, p. 11.
13. John Kraemer, "An Empirical Examination of the Factors Associated with the Commutation of State Death Row Prisoners' Sentences Between 1986 and 2005," *American Criminal Law Review*, 45 (2008): 1389–1417, p. 1409.
14. Lorraine Schmall, "Forgiving Guin Garcia: Women, the Death Penalty and Commutation," *Wisconsin Women's Law Journal*, 11 (1996): 283–326.
15. Laura M. Argys and H. Naci Mocan, "Who Shall Live and Who Shall Die? An Analysis of Prisoners on Death Row in the United States," *Journal of Legal Studies*, 33 (2004): 255–282, p. 281.
16. Heise, "Mercy by the Numbers," p. 137.
17. Robert M. Ireland, "The Libertine Must Die: Sexual Dishonor and the Unwritten Law in the Nineteenth-Century United States," *Journal of Social History*, 23 (1989): 27–44, p. 27.
18. *Ibid.*, pp. 36–37.
19. Edwin F. Johnson, "Selective Factors in Capital Punishment," *Social Forces*, 36 (1957): 165–169, p. 167.
20. James R. Acker and Charles S. Lanier, "May God—or the Governor—Have Mercy: Executive Clemency and Executions in Modern Death-Penalty Systems," *Criminal Law Bulletin*, 36 (2000): 200–237, p. 215.
21. Radelet and Zsembik, "Executive Clemency in Post-*Furman* Capital Cases."
22. Adam C. Ortiz, "Clemency and Consequences: State Governors and the Impact of Granting Clemency to Death Row Inmates," American Bar Association (July 2002), available at http://www.americanbar.org/content/dam/aba/publishing/criminal_justice_section_newsletter/crimjust_juvjus_jdpclemeffect02.authcheckdam.pdf.
23. Salem Witch Trials: Documentary Archive and Transcription Project, University of Virginia, available at http://salem.lib.virginia.edu/home.html.
24. *Petitions for Compensation and Decision Concerning Compensation, 1710–1711*, Salem Witchcraft Trials 1692, available at http://law2.umkc.edu/faculty/projects/ftrials/salem/SAL_PET.HTM.
25. Ansel Judd Northrup, *Slavery in New York: A Historical Sketch* (Albany: University of the State of New York, 1900), p. 269.
26. Negley K. Teeters, "Public Executions in Pennsylvania 1682 to 1834 with Annotated Lists of Persons Executed, and of Delays, Pardons and Reprieves of Persons Sentenced to Death in Pennsylvania 1682 to 1834," *Journal of the Lancaster County Historical Society*, 64 (1960): 85–164.
27. Teeters, *Public Executions in Pennsylvania*, p. 158.
28. Laura T. Keenan, "Reconstructing Rachel: A Case of Infanticide in the Eighteenth-Century Mid-Atlantic and the Vagaries of Historical Research," *The Pennsylvania Magazine of History and Biography*, 130 (2006): 361–385, p. 384.
29. Karen Halttunen, *Murder Most Foul: The Killer and the American Gothic Imagination* (Cambridge: Harvard University Press, 1998), p. 282, note 39.
30. Jack D. Marietta and Gail Stuart Rowe, *Troubled Experiment: Crime and Justice in Pennsylvania 1682–1800* (Philadelphia: University of Pennsylvania Press, 2006), p. 259.
31. J. Smith Futhey and Gilbert Cope, *History of Chester County, Pennsylvania with Biographical and Genealogical Sketches* (Philadelphia: Louis H. Everts, 1881), p. 407.
32. Marietta and Rowe, *Troubled Experiment*, pp. 242–243.
33. Archives of Maryland Online, "Capital Crimes: Hanged, Pardoned, and Reprieved. All Classes by Name 1726–1775," July 24, 2009, available at http://aomol.msa.maryland.gov/megafile/msa/speccol/sc2900/sc2908/000001/000819/pdf/chart1.pdf.
34. *Minutes of the Provincial Council of Pennsylvania From the Organization to the Termination of the Proprietary Government* (Harrisburg: Theo Fenn, 1852), p. 666.
35. Joshua D. Rothman, *Notorious in the Neighborhood: Sex and Families Across The Color Line in Virginia, 1787–1861* (Chapel Hill: University of North Carolina Press, 2003), pp. 1–2, see p. 245, notes 1–5.
36. "Squaw Murderess to Hang," *Connersville Daily Examiner* [Connersville, Indiana] (March 25, 1889), p. 3.
37. John Y. Simon, ed., *The Papers of Ulysses S. Grant, Volume 28, November 1, 1876–September 30, 1878* (Carbondale: Southern Illinois University Press, 2005), p. 487.
38. "A Murderess Reprieved," *New York Times* (July 27, 1869), p. 1.
39. "Noted Female Prisoner," *Bedford Democrat* [Bedford, Indiana] (December 26, 1899), p. 16.
40. *Centinel* [Gettysburg, Pennsylvania] (September 10, 1806), p. 7.
41. Sarah Barringer Gordon, "Law and Everyday Death: Infanticide and the Hester Vaughn Case," in Austin Sarat, Lawrence Douglas, and Martha Merrill Umphrey, eds., *Lives in the Law*, pp. 55–81 (Ann Arbor: University of Michigan Press, 2002), p. 63.
42. Howard O. Sprogle, *The Philadelphia Police, Past and Present* (Philadelphia, 1887), p. 42–43, available at https://archive.org/details/philadelphiapoli00sproiala.
43. David M. Oshinsky, *Worse Than Slavery: Parchman Farm and the Ordeal of Jim Crow Justice* (New York: Free Press, 1996), p. 169.
44. Harriet C. Frazier, *Death Sentences in Missouri, 1803–2005: A History and Comprehensive Registry of Legal Executions, Pardons, and Commutations* (Jefferson: McFarland, 2006), pp. 151–152.
45. Frazier, *Death Penalty in Missouri*.
46. *Ibid.*, p. 153.
47. *Ibid.*, pp. 152–153.
48. Martha Anne Turner, *Sam Houston and His Twelve Women: The Ladies Who Influenced the Life of Texas' Greatest Statesmen* (Austin: Pemberton Press, 1966).

49. "Chiara Cignarale Must Hang," *Boston Daily Globe* (June 8, 1888), p. 12.
50. "Saved from the Gallows," *New York Times* (April 13, 1884).
51. "Woman to Be Executed," *Goshen Daily Democrat* [Goshen, Indiana] (December 30, 1897), p. 7.
52. "A 12-Year-Old Girl to Hang," *New Philadelphia Ohio Democrat* [New Philadelphia, Ohio] (July 28, 1887), p. 3.
53. Wilma King, "Mad Enough to Kill: Enslaved Women, Murder, and Southern courts," *The Journal of African American History*, 92 (2007): 37–56, p. 47.
54. "A Missouri Woman Convicted," *Reno Evening Gazette* (May 21, 1897), p. 1.
55. Robert J. Tórrez, *Myth of the Hanging Tree: Stories of Crime and Punishment in Territorial New Mexico* (Albuquerque: University of New Mexico Press, 2008), pp. 119–130.
56. *Ibid.*, p. 121.
57. Robert J. Tórrez, "Hillsboro Murder, 1907," New Mexico Office of the State Historian, available at http://dev.newmexicohistory.org/filedetails.php?fileID=21648.
58. Tórrez, *Myth of the Hanging Tree*, p. 125.
59. "Rapid Change of Faces Seen in Death Row," *Panama City News Herald* [Panama City, Florida] (April 14, 1957), p. 16.
60. "Two Pennsylvania Women Seeking Reprieve from Board of Pardons," *Gettysburg Times* (August 3, 1925), p. 2.
61. Kathleen A. Cairns, "Nellie May Madison," American National Biography Online, available at http://www.anb.org/articles/20/20–01909.html.
62. "Highball Slayer Granted Pardon," *Uniontown Morning Herald* [Uniontown, Pennsylvania] (July 10, 1935), p. 14.
63. Gary Younge, "Pardon for Maid Executed in 1945: Campaigners Celebrate Clemency for Woman Who Killed Employer," *The Guardian* (August 17, 2005), p. 14.
64. James W. Marquart, Sheldon Ekland-Olson, and Jonathan R. Sorensen, *The Rope, The Chair, and the Needle: Capital Punishment in Texas, 1923–1990* (Austin: University of Texas Press, 1994), p. 107.
65. Marquart et al., *The Rope, the Chair, and the Needle*, p. 108.
66. "Gov. Craig Commutes Sentence to Life," *The Hammond Times* (December 11, 1956), p. 1.
67. Linda L. Ammons, "Why Do You Do the Things You Do? Clemency for Battered Incarcerated Women, A Decade's Review," *American University Journal of Gender, Social Policy and the Law*, 11 (2003): 533–565, p. 545, pp. 552–556.
68. Maria L. LaGanza, "Execution Moratorium Declared," *Los Angeles Times* (February 12, 2014), p. A7.
69. Cited in Radelet and Zsembik, "Executive Clemency in Post-*Furman* Capital Cases," p. 290.
70. "The Death Penalty: I Want to Die, Doris Foster," *Time* (January 24, 1983).
71. Joe Hallett, "Death Row Decision Gets No Forgiveness," *Plain Dealer* (January 5, 1997).
72. Radelet and Zsembik, "Executive Clemency in Post-*Furman* Capital Cases," pp. 306–307.
73. *State v. Green*, 66 Ohio St. 3d 141; 1993 Ohio 26; 609 N.E.2d 1253; 1993 Ohio LEXIS 729 (1993).
74. Joey Mogul, "The Dykier, the Butcher, the Better: The State's Use of Homophobia and Sexism to Execute Women in the United States," *New York City Law Review*, 8 (2005): 473–493, at 488.
75. *Owens v. Guida*, 549 F.3d 399; 2008 U.S. App. LEXIS 24987; 2008 FED App. 0440P (6th Cir.). J. Merritt dissenting.
76. Ortiz, "Clemency and Consequences."

Chapter 9

1. DeAnna M. Horne, "Either Way It Goes Down: America's 54 Women on Death Row in the Context of Patriarchy," *Women and the Law* (2002): 1–47, p. 28, available at http://law.uoregon.edu/assets/facultydocs/cforell/EitherWayitGoesDown.pdf.
2. *Kennedy v. Louisiana*, 554 U.S. 407, 420 (2008).
3. Mary Atwell, "Gender and Capital Punishment: The Case of Teresa Lewis," paper presented at the American Bar Association Fall Conference, Washington D.C., 2012.
4. Joseph Schlesinger, Center on Constitutional Rights. *Discrimination, Torture, and Execution: A Human Rights Analysis of the Death Penalty in California and Louisiana* (2013), p. 19, available at http://ccrjustice.org/files/2013-Death-Penalty-Report.pdf.
5. Victor Streib, "Classic Arguments for and Against the Death Penalty," *Elton Law Review*, 1 (2009): 1–16, at pp. 9–10.
6. John J. Donohue, "Capital Punishment in Connecticut, 1973–2007: A Comprehensive Evaluation from 4,686 Murders to One Execution," Stanford Law School, National Bureau of Economic Research (June 8, 2013) (unpublished manuscript), pp. 5–6, available at http://works.bepress.com/cgi/viewcontent.cgi?article=1095&context=john_donohue.
7. John Seigenthaler, "The Uneven Hand of Justice in TN Murders," *The Tennessean* [Nashville, Tennessee] (December 21, 2009).
8. *Ibid.*
9. John Seigenthaler, "Deeper Look Shows Even More Cases of Unequal Justice," *The Tennessean* (January 10, 2010), available at http://gaile-owens.blogspot.com/2010/01/deeper-look-shows-even-more-cases-of.html.
10. Seigenthaler, "The Uneven Hand of Justice in TN Murders."
11. Kathryn Kahler, "Women on Death Row," *Syracuse Herald Journal* (April 18, 1993), p. 11.
12. Michael Corwin, "Waiting in Isolation: Punishment," *Los Angeles Times* (January 25, 1991), p. A3.
13. Schlesinger, *Discrimination, Torture, and Execution*, p. 4.
14. Ruth Hill, "Linda Carty: 'Someone Is Trying to Take My Life for Someone Else's Crime,'" *The Observer* (June 27, 2010).
15. William Alex Pridemore, "An Empirical Examination of Commutations and Executions in Post-*Furman* Capital Cases," *Justice Quarterly*, 17 (2000): 159–183, p. 163.
16. The Pew Charitable Trusts, "State Prison Health Care Spending," July 2014, p. 9.
17. *People v. McDermott*, 28 Cal. 4th 946 (2002).
18. Claudia Dreifus, "Women on Death Row," *Ms. Magazine* (Spring 2003).
19. Muriel L. Sims, "Deathtrap," *Dallas Observer* (July 9, 1998), available at http://www.dallasobserver.com/1998-07-09/news/deathtrap/.
20. Elizabeth Rapaport, "Mad Women and Desperate Girls: Infanticide and Child Murder in Law and Myth," *Fordham Urban Law Review*, 33 (2006): 527–569, p. 530.
21. Sandra Stokley, "Prosecution Rests Its Case; Rialto Couple Is on Trial in Shooting Death of Las Vegas Teen," *Riverside Press Enterprise* (March 15, 2006).
22. "New Sentencing Ordered for Pennsylvania Woman on Death Row," *Associated Press* (September 25, 2014), available at http://www.pennlive.com/midstate/index.ssf/2014/09/new_sentencing_ordered_for_pen.html.
23. Jennifer R. Hagan, "Can We Lose the Battle and Still Win the War? The Fight Against Domestic Violence After the Death of Title III of the Violence Against Women Act," *DePaul Law Review*, 50 (2001): 919–991, at pp. 933–934.
24. R.L. McNeely and Gloria Robinson-Simpson, "The Truth About Domestic Violence: A Falsely Framed Issue," *Social Work*, 32 (1984): 485–490.
25. *State of Arizona v. Wendi Elizabeth Andriano*, No. CR-05-0005-AP (July 09, 2007), p. 11.
26. Tyler Estep, "The Life of the Damned: Kelly Gissendaner's Path to Execution," *Gwinnett Daily Post* (February 25,

2015) availabe at http://www.gwinnettdailypost.com/news/2015/feb/23/the-life-of-the-damned-kelly-gissendaner8217s/.

27. Anna Arceneaux, "Women on Death Row," American Civil Liberties Union (March 30, 2011), available at https://www.aclu.org/blog/capital-punishment-womens-rights/women-death-row.

28. The Sentencing Project, "Life Goes On: The Historic Rise in Life Sentences in America," 2013, p. 4, available at http://sentencingproject.org/doc/publications/inc_Life%20Goes%20On%202013.pdf.

29. David R. Row, "Life Without Parole: A Different Death Penalty," *The Nation* (October 26, 2012), available at http://www.thenation.com/article/170852/life-without-parole-different-death-penalty#.

30. The Sentencing Project, "Life Goes On," Table G, p. 11.

31. Juvenile Law Center, "Juvenile Life Without Parole (JLWOP)," available at http://www.jlc.org/current-initiatives/promoting-fairness-courts/juvenile-life-without-parole-jlwop.

32. Ibid.

33. Human Rights Watch, "End Juvenile Life-Without-Parole Sentences," March 25, 2014, available at http://www.hrw.org/news/2014/03/25/usoas-end-juvenile-life-without-parole-sentences.

34. Equal Justice Initiative, "Cruel and Unusual Punishment: Sentencing 13 and 14-Year-Old Children to Die in Prison," January 2008, p. 25, available at http://www.eji.org/files/Cruel%20and%20Unusual%202008_0.pdf.

Chapter 10

1. Joe R. Feagin, "Race and Justice: Wrongful Convictions of African American Men," *Contemporary Sociology: A Journal of Reviews*, 42 (2013): 81–83, p. 83.

2. Charles S. Lanier, "Adding to the Story of What We Know About Capital Punishment: A Review of *Women and the Death Penalty* and *Deathquest*," *Journal of Criminal Justice and Popular Culture*, 7 (1999): 30–37.

3. Lyle Koehler, "The Case of the American Jezebels: Anne Hutchinson and Female Agitation During the Years of Antinomian Turmoil, 1636–1640," *William and Mary Quarterly*, 31 (1974): 55–78, p. 57.

4. Horatio Rogers, *Mary Dyer of Rhode Island: The Quaker Martyr That Was Hanged on Boston Common, June 1, 1660*, 2002, p. 3, available at http://kobek.com/marydyer.pdf.

5. Jeffrey Fagan, Testimony before the Joint Committee on the Judiciary of the Massachusetts Legislature on House Bill 3834, "An Act Reinstating Capital Punishment in the Commonwealth," July 14, 2005, available at http://www.deathpenaltyinfo.org/MassTestimonyFagan.pdf.

6. American Civil Liberties Union, *The Forgotten Population: A Look at Death Row in the United States Through the Experiences of Women*, a Death Penalty Report, December 2004. available at https://www.aclu.org/sites/default/files/field_document/womenondeathrow.pdf.

7. John Blume, Sheri Lynn, and Christopher Seeds, "Of Atkins and Men: Deviations from Clinical Definitions of Mental Retardation in Death Penalty Cases," *Cornell Journal of Law and Public Policy*, 18 (2009): 689–733, p. 693.

8. *Ibid.*, pp. 18–19.

9. Ken Broader, "Kamala Harris Flips on Murder Case after Federal Judges Rip Prosecutorial Misconduct," ALLGOV, February 4, 2015, available at http://www.allgov.com/usa/ca/news/california-and-the-nation/kamala-harris-flips-on-murder-case-after-federal-court-rips-prosecutorial-misconduct-150204?news=855570.

Bibliography

Abelson, Elaine. "Women Who Have No Men to Work for Them: Gender and Homelessness in the Great Depression, 1930–1934." *Feminist Studies*, 29 (2003), 104–127.
Accessible Archives. http://www.accessible-archives.com/.
"Accused Slayer of Husbands Bought Boyfriend New Car." *El Paso Herald Post*, May 8, 1958.
Acker, James, and Charles Lanier. "May God—or the Governor—Have Mercy: Executive Clemency and Executions in Modern Death-Penalty Systems." *Criminal Law Bulletin*, 36 (2000), 200–237.
ACLU Press Release. "ACLU of Arizona Strongly Condemns Maricopa County Attorney's Decision to Retry Debra Milke." American Civil Liberties Union, July 9, 2013. Available at http://acluaz.org/issues/press-releases/2013-07/3911.
Adam, Charles. *Murder by the Bay: Historic Homicide in and About the City of San Francisco*. Sanger: Quill Driver Books, 2005.
Adams, Brooks. *The Emancipation of Massachusetts: The Dream and the Reality*. 1887. Boston: Houghton Mifflin, 1962.
Adams, Kenneth. "Adjusting to Prison Life." *Crime and Justice*, 16 (1992), 275–359.
Adler, Jeffrey. "'I Love Joe, but I Had to Shoot Him': Homicide by Women in Turn-of-the-Century Chicago." *Journal of Criminal Law and Criminology*, 92 (2002), 867–898.
"Aged Murderess of 5 Is Near Death." *Bridgeport Telegram* [Bridgeport, Connecticut], March 15, 1962.
"Aged Murderess Saved from Hanging." *Goshen Daily Democrat* [Goshen, Indiana], April 2, 1898.
"Agent Cleared in Dugas Death." *Baytown Sun* [Baytown, Texas], August 10, 1983.
Aguirre, Adalberto, and David Baker. *Race, Racism and the Death Penalty in the United States*. Berrien Springs: Vande Vere, 1991.
Ahern, Tony. "Crime of Century Now 50 Years Old." *The Madras Pioneer* [Madras, Oregon], August 3, 2011.
"Ala. Governor Commutes Axe-Murder Sentences." *Biloxi Daily Herald* [Biloxi, Mississippi], August 6, 1925.
Alabama Department of Corrections. Inmate Search. http://www.doc.state.al.us/.
Alexander, Ann. *Race Man: The Rise and Fall of the "Fighting Editor" John Mitchell, Jr*. Charlottesville: University of Virginia Press, 2002.
Alfaro v. California, 552 U.S. 1245 (2008).
Alford, Ryan. "Appellate Review of Racist Summations: Redeeming the Promise of Searching Analysis." *Michigan Journal of Law and Race*, 11 (2006), 325–365.
Allcensus. "Early Ancestors." Available at http://www.allcensus.com/earlygeor/pafg58.htm.
Allen v. Massie, 2000 U.S. App. LEXIS 316 (2000).
Allen v. State, 871 P.2d 79 (1994).
Almaguer, Tomás. *Racial Fault Lines: The Historical Origins of White Supremacy in California*. Berkeley: University of California Press, 1994.
Alvarez, Yazmen. "Ex Corona Prostitute Sentenced to Death for Torturing, Murdering Two Men." *Southwest Riverside News Network*, October 22, 2010. Available at http://www.swrnn.com/2010/10/22/ex-corona-prostitute-sentenced-to-death-for-torturing-murdering-two-men/.
"American Borgia: The Execution of Martha Grinder." *New York Times*, January 20, 1866.
Ammons, Linda. "Mules, Madonnas, Babies, Bathwater, Racial Imagery and Stereotypes: The African-American Woman and the Battered Woman Syndrome." *Wisconsin Law Review*, 1995 (1994), 1003–1080.
_____. "Why Do You Do the Things You Do? Clemency for Battered Incarcerated Women, a Decade's Review." *American University Journal of Gender, Social Policy and the Law*, 11 (2003), 533–565.
Amon, Elizabeth. "Prosecutors Attack Death Row Clemencies." *The National Law Journal*, January 21, 2003.
Anders, Roger. "The Rosenberg Case Revisited: The Greenglass Testimony and the Protection of Atomic Secrets." *The American Historical Review*, 83 (1978), 388–400.
Anderson, Daniel. *One Hundred Oklahoma Outlaws, Gangsters, and Lawmen, 1839–1939*. Gretna: Pelican Press, 2007.
Anderson, Etta. "The Chivalrous Treatment of the Female Offender in the Arms of the Criminal Justice System: A Review of the Literature." *Social Problems*, 23 (1976), 350–357.
Anderson, Michelle. "From Chastity Requirement to Sexuality License: Sexual Consent and a New Rape Shield Law." *George Washington Law Review*, 70 (2002), 51–199.
Anderson v. Warden, 2005 U.S. Dist. LEXIS 30446 (1999).
Andrew v. State, 2007 OK CR 23 (2007).
Andriano v. Arizona, 552 U.S. 923 (2007).
"Anna Tribble Hanged for the Murder of Her New Born Babe." *The State*, October 8, 1892. Available at http://genealogytrails.com/scar/newberry/hanging.htm.
"Annie Cutler to Hang in May." *Boston Daily Globe*, October 17, 1885.
Annual Reports of the Departments and Benevolent Institutions of the State of Mississippi for the Year Ending December 31, 1876. Jackson: Power & Barksdale, 1877.
Aptheker, Herbert. *American Negro Slave Revolts*. New York: International, 1993.
_____. *Anti-Racism in U.S. History: The First Two Hundred Years*. Westport: Praeger, 1992.
Arceneaux, Anna. "Women on Death Row." American Civil Liberties Union, March 30, 2011. Available at https://www.aclu.org/blog/capital-punishment-womens-rights/women-death-row.
Archives of Maryland Online. "Capital Crimes: Hanged, Pardoned, and Reprieved. All Classes by Name 1726–1775." July 24, 2009. Available at http://aomol.msa.maryland.gov/megafile/msa/speccol/sc2900/sc2908/000001/000819/pdf/chart1.pdf.
_____. *Proceedings of the Council of Maryland, 1732–1753*. Volume 28, 1752. Available at http://aomol.msa.maryland.gov/000001/000028/html/am28-576.html.

Argys, Laura, and H. Naci Mocan. "Who Shall Live and Who Shall Die? An Analysis of Prisoners on Death Row in the United States." *Journal of Legal Studies*, 33 (2004), 255–282.

Arizona v. Carlson, 202 Ariz. 570 (2002).

Arkansas Department of Corrections. Inmate Search. http://www.adc.arkansas.gov/inmate_info/index.html.

Arkin, Marc. "Rethinking the Constitutional Right to a Criminal Appeal." *University of California Los Angeles Law Review*, 39 (1992), 503–580.

Armstrong, Ken, and Maurice Possley. "Trial and Error: How Prosecutors Sacrifice Justice to Win (Series: Tribune Investigative Report: The Failure of the Death Penalty in Illinois, Parts I–V)." *Chicago Tribune*, January 14, 1999.

Arrington v. State, 233 So. 2d 634 (1970).

"Ashley, Girlfriend Sentenced to Die." *Abilene Reporter-News* [Abilene, Texas], January 15, 1963.

Ashley and Lima v. State, 319 F.2d 80 (1963).

Ashmead, Henry. "Crimes and Punishments." *History of Delaware County, Pennsylvania*. Philadelphia: L.H. Everts & Co., 1884. Available at http://www.pa-roots.com/index.php/delaware-county/204-history-of-delaware-county-pennsylvania/765-historyofdelawarecountychapter18.

"Asks Prison Board to Commute Sentence." *Bedford Gazette* [Bedford, Pennsylvania], October 22, 1952.

Asser, Seth, and Rita Swan. "Child Fatalities from Religion Motivated Medical Neglect." *Pediatrics*, 101 (1998), 625–629.

Atkins v. Virginia, 536 U.S. 304 (2002).

Atwell, Mary. "Gender and Capital Punishment: The Case of Teresa Lewis." Paper presented at the American Bar Association Fall Conference, Washington, D.C., 2012.

_____. *Wretched Sisters: Examining Gender and Capital Punishment*. New York: Peter Lang, 2008.

Avery, Mary. "Frankie Silver Was Tried and Hanged in 1833." *Statesville Landmark* [Statesville, North Carolina], April 25, 1933.

Babcock, Barbara. "A Place in the Palladium: Women's Rights and Jury Service." *University of Cincinnati Law Review*, 61 (1993), 1139–1180.

"'Baby Killer' Clears Her Name at Last." *London Daily Mail*, December 3, 1994.

Bachman, Ronet, Heather Zaykowski, Rachel Kallmyer, Margarita Poteyeva, and Christina Lanier. *Violence Against American Indian and Alaska Native Women and the Criminal Justice Response: What Is Known*. United States Department of Justice, August 2008. Available at http://www.ncjrs.gov/pdffiles1/nij/grants/223691.pdf.

Baim, Tracy. "Death Penalty Shocker." *Windy City Times*, January 1, 2003. Available at http://www.windycitymediagroup.com/gay/lesbian/news/ARTICLE.php?AID=1636.

Baker, David. "American Indian Executions in Historical Context." *Criminal Justice Studies: A Critical Journal of Crime, Law and Society*, 20 (2007), 315–373.

_____. "Historical Forces Governing Hispanic Injustice: Repressive Practices Against Persons of Mexican Descent in the Borderlands of the American Southwest, 1848–1929." In Martin Guevara Urbina, ed., *Hispanics in the U.S. Criminal Justice System: The New American Demography* (pp. 113–130). Springfield: Charles C. Thomas, 2012.

Bakken, Gordon, and Brenda Farrington. *Women Who Kill Men: California Courts, Gender, and the Press*. Lincoln: University of Nebraska Press, 2009.

Baldus, David, Charles Pulaski, and George Woodworth. "Comparative Review of Death Sentences: An Empirical Study of the Georgia Experience (Symposium on Current Death Penalty Issues)." *Journal of Criminal Law and Criminology*, 74 (1983), 661–753.

_____, _____, and _____. *Equal Justice and the Death Penalty: A Legal and Empirical Analysis*. Boston: Northeastern University Press, 1983.

Baldus, David, George Woodworth, David Zuckenan, Neil Alan Weiner, and Barbara Broffit. "Use of Peremptory Challenges in Capital Murder Trials: A Legal and Empirical Analysis." *University of Pennsylvania Journal of Constitutional Law*, 3 (2001), 3–170.

Balfour v. State, 598 So. 2d 731 (1992).

Ballenger v. Mississippi, 518 U.S. 1025 (1996).

Ballenger v. State, 667 So. 2d 1242 (1995).

Ballenger v. State, 761 So. 2d 214 (2000).

Banks v. Alabama, 845 So. 2d 9 (2002).

Banner, Stuart. *The Death Penalty: An American History*. Cambridge: Harvard University Press. 2002.

_____. "Traces of Slavery." In Charles J. Ogletree, Jr., and Austin Sarat, eds., *From Lynch Mobs to the Killing State: Race and the Death Penalty in America* (pp. 96–113). New York: New York University Press, 2006.

Baptist, Edward. *The Half Has Never Been Told: Slavery and the Making of American Capitalism*. New York: Basic Books, 2014.

Barak, Greg, Jeanne Flavin, and Paul Leighton. *Class, Race, Gender, and Crime: Social Realities of Justice in America*. Los Angeles: Roxbury, 2001.

Barayuga, Debra. "'Ice' Addict Cleared of Killing Newborn." *StarBulletinwww*, November 30, 2005. Available at http://archives.starbulletin.com/2005/11/30/news/story02.html.

"Barbara Miller Goes to the Scaffold Chanting Negro Hymns." *Washington Post*, September 15, 1883.

"Barbara Miller Hanged." *New York Times*, September 15, 1883.

"Barbara Miller's Last Day Among the Living." *Boston Daily Globe*, September 14, 1883.

Barfield v. Woodard, 748 F.2d 844 (5th Cir. 1984).

Barlow, Allan. "The Texas Clemency Memos." *Atlantic Monthly*, July/August 2003. Available at http://www.theatlantic.com/magazine/archive/2003/07/the-texas-clemency-memos/2755/?single_page=true.

Barnes, Kathie. "Mary Farmer Took an Ax." *Watertown Daily Times*, 2000. Available at http://freepages.genealogy.rootsweb.ancestry.com/~twigs2000/Murder.html.

Barron, Chana. "The Evil Woman: The Impact of Gender Roles and Expectations on Appellate Outcomes in Women's Capital Convictions." Paper presented at the annual meeting of Law and Society, J.W. Marriott Resort, Las Vegas, Nevada, September 2008.

_____. "Gendered Definitions and Expectations: Their Influence on Outcomes in Women's Death Penalty Appeals." Paper presented at the annual meeting of the American Society of Criminology, Royal York, Toronto, November 2005.

Barron, Phillip. "Gender Discrimination in the U.S. Death Penalty System." *Radical Philosophy Review*, 1 (2000), 89–96.

Barstow, Anne. *Witchcraze: A New History of European Witch Hunts*. New York: Pandora, 1994.

Baskervill, Bill. "AP Interview: Virginia's Only Woman on Death Row Says Sentence Unfair in Murder-For-Hire Scheme." *Associated Press*, June 11, 2004.

Bass, Jack, and Marilyn Thompson. *STROM: The Complicated Personal and Political Life of Strom Thurmond*. New York: Public Affairs, 2005.

Basso v. Texas, 540 U.S. 864 (2003).

Basso v. Thaler, 359 Fed. Appx. 504 (2010).

Batson v. Kentucky, 476 U.S. 79 (1986).

Batts, Denise. "The 'Witch of Pungo' Pardoned After 300 Years." *Justice Denied: The Magazine for the Wrongfully Convicted*, 33 (2006), 17. Available at http://justicedenied.org/issue/issue_33/grace_sherwood.pdf.

Baxandall, Roslyn, and Linda Gordon. *America's Working Women: A Documentary History—1600 to the Present*. New York: W.W. Norton, 1995.

Beauge, John. "Gang Rite Motivated Killing, Says Prosecutor." *Patriot News* [Harrisburg, Pennsylvania], April 12, 2005.

_____. "Woman Convicted in Hatchet Slaying." *Patriot News* [Harrisburg, Pennsylvania], April 19, 2005.

Beck, Allen, and Paige Harrison. *Sexual Victimization in Prisons and Jails Reported by Inmates, 2008–09: National Inmate Survey, 2008–2009*. U.S. Department of Justice, Bureau of

Justice Statistics, August 2010. Available at http://bjs.ojp.usdoj.gov/content/pub/pdf/svpjri0809.pdf.

Beck, E. M., James Massey, and Stewart Tolnay. "The Gallows, the Mob, the Vote: Lethal Sanctioning of Blacks in North Carolina and Georgia, 1882 to 1930." *Law and Society Review*, 23 (1989), 317–331.

Beck, E. M., and Stewart Tolnay. "The Killing Fields of the Deep South: The Market for Cotton and the Lynching of Blacks, 1882–1930." *American Sociological Review*, 55 (1990), 526–539.

Becka, Holly. "Woman Found Guilty of Killing Elderly Victim; Jury to Decide If She'll Get Death Penalty." *Dallas Morning News*. November 18, 1998.

_____. "Woman Not a Brutal Killer, Supporters Say; She's Described at Sentencing Hearing as Good Mom Despite Drug Problem." *Dallas Morning News*, November 19, 1998.

_____. "Woman Preyed on Elderly, Prosecutor Says; Therapist on Trial in Deaths of 3 People." *Dallas Morning News*, November 12, 1998.

Bedau, Hugo. "Capital Punishment in Oregon." *Oregon Law Review*, 45 (1965), 1–39.

_____. *The Death Penalty in America: Current Controversies.* New York: Oxford University Press, 1997.

_____. "Death Sentences in New Jersey, 1907–1960." *Rutgers Law Review*, 19 (1964), 1–64.

_____. "The Decline of Executive Clemency in Capital Cases." *New York University Review of Law and Social Change*, 18 (1990), 255–272.

_____. "Habeas Corpus and Other Constitutional Controversies." In Hugo Bedau, ed., *The Death Penalty in America: Current Controversies* (pp. 238–245). New York: Oxford University Press, 1997.

_____, and Michael Radelet. *Miscarriages of Justice in Potentially Capital Cases.* Stanford: Stanford University, 1987.

Bell, Derrick. *Race, Racism and American Law.* New York: Aspen, 2004.

"Bell Refused to Interfere." *Auburn Citizen* [Auburn, New York], December 8, 1905.

Ben-Yehuda, Nachman. "The European Witch Craze of the 14th and 17th Centuries: A Sociologist's Perspective." *American Journal of Sociology*, 1 (1980), 1–31.

Benjamin, Lois. *The Black Elite: Facing the Color Line in the Twilight of the Twentieth Century.* Chicago: Nelson-Hall, 1991.

Bennett, Lerone. *Before the Mayflower: A History of Black America.* New York: Penguin, 1982.

Bennett, Mark. "Town Prepares for First Festival Based Around a Hanging." *Tribune-Star* [Terre Haute, Indiana], May 24, 2007.

Benokraitis, Nijole, and Joe R. Feagin. *Modern Sexism, Blatant, Subtle, and Covert Discrimination.* Englewood Cliffs: Prentice Hall, 1995.

Berg, Manfred. *Popular Justice: A History of Lynching in America.* Chicago: Ivan R. Dee, 2011.

Berke, Ronnie. "58 Years Later, Records Unsealed in Rosenberg Spy Case." CNNwww, July 22, 2008. Available at http://www.cnn.com/2008/CRIME/07/23/rosenberg.hearing/index.html.

Berks County Legends. *Susannah Cox Saga.* Available at freepages.genealogy.rootsweb.ancestry.com/~genphotos2/legends.html#cox.

Berlin, Ira. *Many Thousands Gone: The First Two Centuries of Slavery in North America.* Cambridge: Harvard University Press, 1998.

_____. "Time, Space, and the Evolution of Afro-American Society in British Mainland North America." *American History Review*, 85 (1980), 44–78.

Berlin, Leonard. "Malpractice Issues in Radiology: Defending the Missed Radiographic Diagnosis." *American Journal of Roentgenology*, 176 (2001), 317–322.

Berlow, Allan. "Miscarriage of Justice, Texas Style." *Common Dreams, NewsCenter*, February 22, 2000. Available at www.commondreams.org/views/022200-101.htm.

Berry v. State, 233 S.W.3d 847 (2007).

"Bessie Wakefield Is Granted a Full Pardon for the Murder of Her Mate." *Morning Avalance* [Lubbock, Texas], November 8, 1933.

Bessler, John. *Legacy of Violence: Lynch Mobs and Executions in Minnesota.* Minneapolis: University of Minnesota Press, 2003.

Bienen, Leigh. *The Status of the Death Penalty in Illinois.* Northwestern University School of Law, January 13, 2003. Available at http://www.law.northwestern.edu/faculty/fulltime/bienen/bienen_report.pdf.

Biffle, Kent. *A Month of Sundays.* Denton: University of Texas Press, 1993.

"Birmingham Negro Captured After Two Attacks with an Axe." *Thomasville Daily Times Enterprise* [Thomasville, Georgia], May 26, 1924.

Black, Charles. *Capital Punishment: The Inevitability of Caprice and Mistake.* New York: W.W. Norton, 1974.

Black, Gabriel. "Texas Executes Suzanne Basso, Despite Claims of Mental Incompetency." *World Socialist Web Site*, February 7, 2014. Available at http://www.wsws.org/en/articles/2014/02/07/exec-f07.html.

"Black Woman's Long Ordeal Ends." *Morning Herald* [Hagerstown, Maryland], January 23, 1974.

Blackman, Paul, and Vance McLaughlin. "Mass Legal Executions of Blacks in the United States, 17th–20th Centuries." *Homicide Studies*, 7 (2003), 235–262.

Blackmon, Douglas. *Slavery by Another Name: The Re-Enslavement of Black Americans from the Civil War to World War II.* New York: Doubleday, 2008.

Blackmon v. State, 7 So. 3d 397 (2006).

Blauner, Robert. *Racial Oppression in America.* New York: Harper and Row, 1972.

"Blease Pardons 100 Convicts." *Muskogee Times Democrat* [Muskogee, Oklahoma], November 25, 1913.

Bledsoe, Jerry. *Death Sentence: The True Story of Velma Barfield's Life, Crimes, and Execution.* New York: Penguin Putnam, 1998.

Block, Sharron. *Rape and Sexual Power in Early America.* Chapel Hill: North Carolina University Press, 2006.

Block, William. "Myth of Texas Executions Debunked: Slave Lucy Was First Woman to Die." *Beaumont Enterprise* [Beaumont, Texas], September 13, 1978.

Blume, John, Sheri Lynn, and Christopher Seeds. "Of Atkins and Men: Deviations from Clinical Definitions of Mental Retardation in Death Penalty Cases." *Cornell Journal of Law and Public Policy*, 18 (2009), 689–733.

"Board Commutes Death Sentences of Four Persons." *Evening Independent* [Massillon, Ohio], March 20, 1929.

"Board Ruling Okayed by Governor." *San Antonio Light*, June 29, 1951.

"Board to Hear Woman's Appeal." *Gettysburg Star and Sentinel* [Gettysburg, Pennsylvania], September 19, 1925.

Bobby v. Bies, 556 U.S. 825 (2009).

Bonham, Nick. "Mandatory Life Without Parole Sentences for the Intellectually Disabled: A Violation of the Eighth Amendment." *Cardozo Public Law, Policy and Ethics Journal*, 12 (2014), 737–775.

Borchard, Edwin. *Convicting the Innocent: Sixty-Five Actual Errors of Criminal Justice.* New York: Garden City, 1932.

_____. "European Systems of State Indemnity for Errors of Criminal Justice." *Journal of the American Institute of Criminal Law and Criminology*, 3 (1913), 684–718.

Bork, June. "The Hanging of Crawford and Lavinia Burnett." June 2001. Available at http://listsearches.rootsweb.com/th/read/BURNETT/2001-06/0993963523.

Bowen, Rebekah. "A Murder in Jackson County." *The Missouri State Archives Newsletter*, Spring 2009. Available at http://www.sos.mo.gov/archives/newsletter/2009_Spring.pdf.

Bowers, William, and Glenn Pierce. "Arbitrariness and Discrimination Under Post-*Furman* Capital Statutes." *Crime and Delinquency*, 26 (1980), 563–635.

Bowers, William, Benjamin Steiner, and Marla Sandys. "Death Sentencing in Black and White: An Empirical Analysis of the Role of Jurors' Race and Racial Jury Composition." *University of Pennsylvania Journal of Constitutional Law*, 3 (2001), 171–274.

Bowman, Frank. "Stories of Crimes, Trials, and Appeals in Civil War Era Missouri." *Marquette Law Review*, 93 (2009), 349–377.

Boyd, Robert. "Race, Labor Market Disadvantage, and Survivalist Entrepreneurship: Black Women in the Urban North During the Great Depression." *Sociological Forum*, 15 (2000), 647–670.

Bracewell v. Alabama, 549 U.S. 1129 (2007).

Bracewell v. State, 401 So. 2d 119 (1978).

Bracewell v. State, 475 So. 2d 616 (1984).

Bravin, James. "Surprise: Judges Hand Out Most Punitive Awards." *Wall Street Journal*, June 12, 2000.

Brech, Paul, and Steven Harmon. "Pacheco Must Go." *Riverside Press-Enterprise*, May 30, 2012.

Brewer, Steven. "Childhood of Indignities: Basso's Daughter Tells of Abuse by Mother Now on Death Row." *Houston Chronicle*, September 5, 1999.

"Bride Kills Paraplegic Husband and Three Members of His Family." *Lebanon Daily News* [Lebanon, Pennsylvania], May 28, 1956.

"Bride Slays Husband, His Mother, 2 Sisters." *Post-Standard* [Syracuse, New York], May 27, 1956.

Bridgewater, Pamela. "Un/Re/Discovering Slave Breeding in Thirteenth Amendment Jurisprudence." *Washington and Lee Race and Ethnic Ancestry Law Journal*, 7 (2001), 11–43.

Bright, Stephen. "Counsel for the Poor: The Death Sentence Not for the Worst Crime but for the Worst Lawyer." *Yale Law Journal*, 103 (1994), 1835–1883.

_____. "Discrimination, Death and Denial: The Tolerance of Racial Discrimination in Infliction of the Death Penalty." *Santa Clara Law Review*, 35 (1995), 433–483.

_____, and Patrick Keenan. "Judges and the Politics of Death: Deciding Between the Bill of Rights and the Next Election in Capital Cases." *Boston University Law Review*, 75 (1995), 760–835.

Broader, Ken. "Kamala Harris Flips on Murder Case After Federal Judges Rip Prosecutorial Misconduct." ALLGOV, February 4, 2015. Available at http://www.allgov.com/usa/ca/news/california-and-the-nation/kamala-harris-flips-on-murder-case-after-federal-court-rips-prosecutorial-misconduct-150204?news=855570.

Broderick, Raymond. "Why the Peremptory Challenge Should Be Abolished." *Temple Law Review*, 65 (1992), 369–423.

Brodhead, Michael. *Issac C. Parker: Federal Justice on the Frontier*. Norman: University of Oklahoma Press, 2003.

Brodie, Janet. *Contraception and Abortion in Nineteenth Century America*. Ithaca: Cornell University Press, 1994.

Brooks, Richard, and Steven Raphael. "Life Terms or Death Sentences: The Uneasy Relationship Between Judicial Elections and Capital Punishment." *Journal of Criminal Law & Criminology*, 92 (2002), 609–639.

Brower, Todd. "Multistable Figures: Sexual Orientation Visibility and Its Effects on the Experiences of Sexual Minorities in the Courts." *Pace Law Review*, 27 (2005), 141–198.

Brown, Angela. *When Battered Women Kill*. New York: Free Press, 1997.

Brown, David. "The Forfeitures at Salem, 1692." *William and Mary Quarterly*, 50 (1993), 85–111.

Brown, Dee. *The Gentle Tamers: Women of the Old West*. New York: Putnam, 1958.

Brown v. Board of Education, 347 U.S. 483 (1954).

Brown v. Indiana, 698 N.E.2d 1132 (1998).

Brown v. Mississippi, 297 U.S. 278 (1936).

Browne, William. *Proceedings of the Council of Maryland, April 15, 1761–September 24, 1770*. Baltimore: Maryland Historical Society, 1912.

Brownmiller, Susan. *Against Our Will: Men, Women and Rape*. New York: Fawcett, 1975.

Brundage, W. Fitzhugh. *Lynching in the New South: Georgia and Virginia, 1880–1930*. Urbana: University of Illinois Press, 1993.

"Brutal Society." *World Socialist Web Site*, February 4, 1998. Available at https://www.wsws.org/en/articles/1998/02/tuck-f04.html.

Bryant v. State, Casteel v. State, Irvine v. State, Rhodes v. State, 565 So. 2d 1298 (1990).

Buenoano v. Singletary, 963 F.2d 1433 (1992).

Buenoano v. Singletary, 519 U.S. 1012 (1996).

Buenoano v. State, 527 So. 2d 194 (1988).

Burnett, Arthur. "Permeation of Race, National Origin and Gender Issues from Initial Law Enforcement Contact Through Sentencing: The Need for Sensitivity, Equalitarianism and Vigilance in the Criminal Justice System." *American Criminal Law Review*, 31 (1994), 1153–1173.

"Burnett Avoids Death Penalty After Murder Conviction." *New Braunfels Herald-Zeitung* [New Braunfels, Texas], August 18, 1983.

Burnett v. State, 642 S.W.2d 765 (1982).

Burnett v. State, 754 S.W.2d 437 (1988).

Burnston, Sharon. "Babies in the Well: An Underground Insight into Deviant Behavior in Eighteenth-Century Philadelphia." *The Pennsylvania Magazine of History and Biography*, 106 (1982), 151–186.

Burr, George. "Grace Sherwood, the Witch of Virginia." In *Narratives of the Witchcraft Cases* (pp. 435–442). New York: Scribner's, 1914.

"Burroughs Murder." *New York Times*, May 5, 1872.

"Burroughs Murder." *New York Times*, May 19, 1872.

Bush, Jonathan. "The First Slave (And Why He Matters)." *Cardozo Law Review*, 18 (1996), 599–629.

Butler, Anne. "Still in Chains: Black Women in Western Prisons, 1865–1910." *Western Historical Quarterly*, 20 (1989), 18–35.

Butler, Brooke. "Death Qualification and Prejudice: The Effect of Implicit Racism, Sexism, and Homophobia on Capital Defendants' Right to Due Process." *Behavioral Sciences and the Law*, 25 (2007), 857–867.

Butler, James. "British Convicts Shipped to American Colonies." *The American Historical Review*, 2 (1896), 12–33.

Buttrum v. Black, 721 F. Supp. 1268 (1989).

Buttrum v. State, 249 Ga. 652 (1982).

Byrom v. State, 927 So. 2d 709 (2006).

Cacy v. Texas, 901 S.W.2d 691 (1995).

Cado, Mark. "The Lonely Hearts Killers." *Crime Library*. Available at http://www.crimelibrary.com/serial_killers/partners/fernandez/1.html.

Cahalan, Margaret. *Historical Corrections Statistics in the United States, 1850–1984*. Bureau of Justice Statistics, U.S. Department of Justice, Table 2–7 & Table 2–8, December 1986. Available at http://www.ncjrs.gov/pdffiles1/pr/102529.pdf.

Cahill, Thomas. "Why Do We Keep Executing People?" Special to CNN Opinion, June 24, 2013. Available at http://www.cnn.com/2013/06/24/opinion/cahill-death-penalty/index.html.

Cahn, Mark. "Punishment, Discretion, and the Codification of Prescribed Penalties in Colonial Massachusetts." *The American Journal of Legal History*, 33 (1989), 107–136.

Caillier v. Florida, 523 So. 2d 158 (1988).

Cairns, Kathleen. "Nellie May Madison." American National Biography Online. Available at http://www.anb.org/articles/20/20-01909.html.

_____. *Proof of Guilt: Barbara Graham and the Politics of Executing Women in America*. Lincoln: University of Nebraska Press, 2013.

Campbell, Jane. "Wonders of the Invisible World: Prosecutorial Syndrome and Profile Evidence in the Salem Witchcraft Trials." *Vermont Law Review*, 26 (2001), 43–99.

Campos, Carla, and Bill Torpy. "Post-Execution Pardon; One-Day Trial in 1945 Sent Georgia Woman to Electric Chair." *Atlanta Journal Constitution,* August 16, 2005.

Cannady v. State, 455 So.2d 713 (1984).

"Capital Crimes: Hanged, Pardoned, and Reprieved. All Classes by Name 1726–1775." Available at http://aomol.msa.maryland.gov/megafile/msa/speccol/sc2900/sc2908/000001/000819/pdf/chart1.pdf.

Capital Punishment in Context. "The Case of Aileen Wuornos: The Facts, the Trial, and Post-Trial Period." Available at http://www.capitalpunishmentincontext.org/cases/wuornos.

Caplan, Lincoln. "The Random Horror of the Death Penalty." *New York Times,* January 7, 2012.

Caporael, Linnda. "Ergotism: The Satan Loosed in Salem?" *Science* 192 (1976), 21–26.

Cardenas v. Texas, 2007 Tex. App. LEXIS 4517 (2007).

Cardona v. Florida, 826 So. 2d 968 (2002).

Cardona v. Florida, 641 So. 2d 361 (2004).

Cardyn, Lisa. "Sexualized Racism/Gendered Violence: Outraging the Body Politic in the Reconstruction South." *Michigan Law Review,* 100 (2002), 675–867.

"Carolyn Ann Lima Freed After Sex Slaying Term." *Abilene Reporter-News* [Abilene, Texas], April 4, 1965.

"Carolyn Lima Gets Five-Year Prison Term." *Abilene Reporter-News* [Abilene, Texas], February 29, 1964.

Carr, Lois, and Lorena Walsh. "The Planter's Wife: The Experiences of White Women in Seventeenth-Century Maryland." *William and Mary Quarterly,* 34 (1977), 542–571.

Carrigan, William. *The Making of a Lynching Culture: Violence and Vigilantism in Central Texas, 1836–1916.* Urbana: University of Illinois Press, 2004.

Carroll, Jenny. "Images of Women and Capital Sentencing Among Female Offenders: Exploring the Outer Limits of the Eighth Amendment and Articulated Theories of Justice." *Texas Law Review,* 75 (1997), 1413–1452.

Carty v. Quarterman, 2008 U.S. Dist. LEXIS 110017 (2008).

Carty v. Quarterman, 2008 U.S. Dist. LEXIS 112260 (2008).

Carty v. Quarterman, 345 Fed. Appx. 897 (2009).

Carty v. Thaler, 583 F.3d 244 (2009).

Carty v. Thaler, 130 S. Ct. 3538 (2010).

Carty v. Thaler, 2010 U.S. LEXIS 3735 (2010).

"Case of Mary Hartung." *New York Times,* November 10, 1895.

Cashin, Sheryll. *The Failures of Integration: How Race and Class Are Undermining the American Dream.* New York: Public Affairs, 2004.

Castañeda, Antonia. "Presidarias Y Pobladoras, the Journey North and Life in Frontier California." In Manuel G. Gonzales and Cynthia M. Gonzales, eds., *En Aquel Entonces, Readings in Mexican-American History* (pp. 5–21). Bloomington: Indiana University Press, 2000.

Castro, Diego. "Hot Blood and Easy Virtue: Mass Media and the Making of Racist Latino/A Stereotypes." In Coramae Richey Mann, Marjorie S. Zatz and Nancy Rodriquez, eds., *Images of Color, Images of Crime* (pp. 88–101). Los Angeles: Roxbury, 2006.

Catalano, Shannon. *Criminal Victimization, 2004.* Department of Justice, Bureau of Justice Statistics, September 2005. Available at http://bjs.ojp.usdoj.gov/index.cfm?ty=pbdetail&iid=1054.

_____. *Intimate Partner Violence in the United States.* U.S. Department of Justice, Bureau of Justice Statistics, December 2007. Available at http://bjs.ojp.usdoj.gov/index.cfm?ty=pbdetail&iid=1000.

_____, Erica Smith, Howard Snyder, and Michael Rand. *Female Victims of Violence.* U.S. Department of Justice, Bureau of Justice Statistics, October 2009. Available at http://bjs.ojp.usdoj.gov/content/pub/pdf/fvv.pdf.

Catterall, Helen. *Judicial Cases Concerning American Slavery and the Negro.* Washington, D.C.: Carnegie Institution of Washington, 1936.

Caudill v. Commonwealth, 120 S.W.3d 635 (2003).

Caudill v. Commonwealth, 130 S. Ct. 2345 (2010).

Caulkins, Frances. *History of New London, Connecticut. from the First Survey of the Coast in 1612 to 1860.* New London: H.D. Utley, 1895.

CBS News. "Capital Punishment Timeline." CBS News, October 16, 2007. Available at http://www.cbsnews.com/elements/2007/10/16/in_depth_us/frameset3374729.shtml.

Ceasar, Stephen. "Exonerated Woman Sues Detective." *Los Angeles Times,* April 24, 2015.

Cedar Rapids Evening Gazette [Cedar Rapids, Iowa], September 29, 1891.

Center for Constitutional Rights. *Discrimination, Torture, and Execution.* 2013. Available at http://ccrjustice.org/files/2013-Death-Penalty-Report.pdf.

Center for Prosecutor Integrity. *An Epidemic of Prosecutor Misconduct.* 2013. Available at http://www.prosecutorintegrity.org/wp-content/uploads/EpidemicofProsecutorMisconduct.pdf.

Center for Wrongful Convictions. "Exonerations in All States." Available at http://www.law.northwestern.edu/wrongfulconvictions/exonerations/usIndex.html.

_____. *Fourteen Illinois Death Sentences Predicated on Confessions Allegedly Extracted by Torture.* June 2, 2003. Available at http://www.law.northwestern.edu/depts/clinic/wrongful/documents/PoliceTorture.htm.

_____. "Joyce Ann Brown." Available at http://www.law.northwestern.edu/wrongfulconvictions/exonerations/txBrownJSummary.html.

_____. "Mississippi." Available at http://www.law.northwestern.edu/legalclinic/wrongfulconvictions/exonerations/.

_____. "Sonia Jacobs: Exonerated While Co-Defendant, Convicted on Similar Evidence, Went to the Electric Chair." Available at http://www.law.northwestern.edu/wrongfulconvictions/exonerations/usIndex.html.

Centinel [Gettysburg, Pennsylvania], September 10, 1806.

Chamberlin v. Mississippi, 129 S. Ct. 908 (2009).

Chamberlin v. State, 989 So. 2d 320 (2008).

Chambliss, William. "Functional and Conflict Theories of Crime: The Heritage of Émile Durkheim and Karl Marx." In William J. Chambliss and Milton Mankoff, eds., *Whose Law, What Order? A Conflict Approach to Criminology* (pp. 1–28). New York: Wiley, 1976.

Chapin, Bradley. *Criminal Justice in Colonial America, 1606–1660.* Atlanta: University of Georgia Press, 1983.

Charbonneau v. Delaware, 904 A.2d 295 (2006).

"Charged with Murder." *Portsmouth Herald* [Portsmouth, New Hampshire], October 18, 1910.

"Charges Dropped in Stop Sign Death Case." *Daily Herald Suburban Chicago* [Arlington Heights, Illinois], May 22, 2001.

Cheever, Joan. *Back from the Dead: One Woman's Search for the Men Who Walked Off America's Death Row.* Hoboken: John Wiley, 2006.

Chester, Alden. *Legal and Judicial History of New York.* New York: North Americana Society, 1911.

Chester Historical Society. *The Hanging of Abiel Converse.* March 2002. Available at http://www.chestermass.com/Chester_Historical_Society/Newsletter/2002_March.pdf.

"Chiara Cignarale Must Hang." *Boston Daily Globe,* June 8, 1888.

Child Welfare Information Gateway. *Child Abuse and Neglect Fatalities 2011: Statistics and Intervention,* February 6, 1936. Available at https://www.childwelfare.gov/pubs/factsheets/fatality.pdf.

"Children at Murder Trial." *Iola Daily Register* [Iola, Kansas], June 8, 1905.

"Chilling Account of the Disturbing Life of Kim Cargill." *Tyler Morning Telegraph,* May 18, 2012.

Chin, Pat. "The African Slave Trade and the Drive for Limitless Profits." *Workers World* 1998. Available at http://www.workers.org/ww/1998/slaves0122.php.

"Chivalrous Judge." *New York Times,* November 2, 1876.

Christopher, Emma. *Slave Ship Sailors and Their Captive Cargoes, 1730–1807.* New York: Cambridge University Press, 2006.

"City Briefs." *Newport Mercury* [Newport, Rhode Island], December 26, 1885.
Clark, Elizabeth. "The Sacred Rights of the Weak: Pain, Sympathy, and the Culture of Individual Rights in the Antebellum America." *Journal of American History*, 82 (1995), 463–493.
Clark, Margie. "Mentally Retarded Defendants Still Face Execution." *Cq Researcher*, 20 (2010), 976–977.
Clark, Richard. "Toni Jo Henry, a Love Worth Dying For?" Capital Punishment UK. Available at http://www.capitalpunishmentuk.org/tonijo.html.
Clarke, James. "Without Fear or Shame: Lynching, Capital Punishment and the Subculture of Violence in the American South." *British Journal of Political Science,* 28 (1998), 269–289.
Clarke, Kevin. "Suspended Sentence: How the U.S. Almost Put Capital Punishment to Death." *Claretian Publications* 1998. Available at http://salt.claretianpubs.org/issues/deathp/hiscap.html.
Clayton, Molly. "Forgiving the Unforgivable: Reinvigorating the Use of Executive Clemency in Capital Cases." *Boston College Law Review*, 54 (2013), 751–788.
"Clemency." Death Penalty Information Center. Available at http://www.deathpenaltyinfo.org/clemency.
"Clemency Letter for Francis Newton." American Civil Liberties Union, December 3, 2004. Available at https://www.aclu.org/capital-punishment/clemency-letter-frances-newton.
Clevenger, Andrew. "Lecco Avoids Death Penalty in Latest Drug Sentence." *Gazette-Mail* [East Charlestown, West Virginia], May 3, 2010.
Cohen, Andrew. "Why Does Mississippi Want to Execute Michelle Byrom?" *The Atlantic*, March 24, 2014. Available at http://www.theatlantic.com/national/archive/2014/03/why-does-mississippi-want-to-execute-michelle-byrom/284577/.
Cohen, William. "Negro Involuntary Servitude in the South, 1865–1940." *Journal of Southern History*, 42 (1976), 31–60.
Colbert, Douglas. "Challenging the Challenge: Thirteenth Amendment as a Prohibition Against Racial Use of Peremptory Challenges." *Cornell Law Review,* 76 (1990), 1–128.
Coker, Matt. "Tanya Jaime Nelson Gets Death." *Orange County Weekly,* April 23, 2010.
Coker v. Georgia, 433 U.S. 584 (1977).
Cole v. Florida, 2010 Fla. LEXIS 359 (2010).
Coleman v. State, 2009 Tex. Crim. App. Unpub. LEXIS 792 (2009).
Coleman v. Thaler, 716 F.3d 895 (2013).
Collins, Patricia. *Black Feminist Thought: Knowledge, Consciousness, and the Politics of Empowerment*. Boston: Unwin-Hyman, 1990.
Collins v. Beto, 348 F.2d 823 (1965).
Collins v. Indiana, 420 N.E.2d 880 (1981).
"Collins' Wife's Life." *Atlanta Constitution,* July 13, 1890.
Colonial Williamsburg Foundation. Available at http://research.history.org/DigitalLibrary/BrowseVG.cfm.
"Colored Murderess Hanged." *New York Times,* April 23, 1881.
"Colored Women Out of Penitentiary." *Santa Fe New Mexican* [Santa Fe, New Mexico], May 19, 1919.
Commonwealth v. Dobrolenski, 460 Pa. 630 (1975).
Commonwealth v. Giovanetti, 341 Pa. 345 (1941).
Commonwealth v. Greason, 204 Pa. 64 (1914).
Commonwealth v. Hill, 542 Pa. 291 (1995).
Commonwealth v. Hill & King, 554 Pa. 331 (1998).
Commonwealth v. Housman, 986 A.2d 822 (2009).
Commonwealth v. Jones, 280 Pa. 368 (1924).
Commonwealth v. Jones, 283 Pa. 564 (1925).
Commonwealth v. King, 57 A.3d 607 (2012).
Commonwealth v. King, 2012 Pa. LEXIS 2744 (2012).
Commonwealth v. Markman, 591 Pa. 249 (2007).
Commonwealth v. O'Donnell, 559 Pa. 320 (1999).
Commonwealth v. Rivers, 23 Phila. 242 (1991).
Commonwealth v. Rivers, 537 Pa. 394 (1994).
Commonwealth v. Schroeder, 302 Pa. 1 (1930).
Commonwealth v. Sykes, 353 Pa. 392 (1946).
Commonwealth v. Tharp, 574 Pa. 202 (2003).
Commonwealth v. Thomas, 282 Pa. 20 (1929).
Commonwealth v. Twitchell, 416 Mass. 114 (1993).
Commonwealth v. Walter, 600 Pa. 392 (2009).
"Commutations in Capital Cases on Humanitarian Grounds." Death Penalty Information Center. Available at http://www.deathpenaltyinfo.org/clemency.
"Commute Sentence." *Kingsport Times* [Kingsport, Tennessee], March 20, 1929.
"Condemned Ask Pardons." *Indiana Evening Gazette* [Indiana, Pennsylvania], September 17, 1941.
"Condemned Mother and Son Find Solace in Religion as Time Nears for Execution." *Ada Evening News* [Ada, Oklahoma], June 5, 1935.
"Condemned Woman Saved from Death as Governor Acts." *Palm Beach Post,* January 11, 1933.
"Condemned Woman Wins Stay." *The Bee* [Portland, Oregon], September 21, 1928.
Conrad, Clay. *Jury Nullification: The Evolution of a Doctrine*. Durham: Carolina Academic Press, 1998.
Cooper, James. "Anne Hutchinson and the Lay Rebellion Against the Clergy." *New England Quarterly*, 61 (1988), 381–397.
Cooper v. State, 540 N.E.2d 1216 (1989).
Copeland v. Washington, 1999 U.S. Dist. LEXIS 22404 (1999).
Coppedge, Clay. "Texas Trails: The Woman from San Patrico." *Country World,* September 18, 2010. Available at http://www.countryworldnews.com/news/texas-trails/702-texas-trails-the-woman-from-san-patrico.html.
Corlett, Celeste. "Impact of the 2000 Child Labor Treaty on United States Child Laborers." *Arizona Journal of International and Comparative Law,* 19 (2002), 713–739.
"Corrine Sykes Second Woman to Die in Chair." *Chester Times* [Chester, Pennsylvania], October 14, 1946.
Corwin, Michael. "Waiting in Isolation: Punishment." *Los Angeles Times,* January 25, 1991.
Costo, Rupert, and Jeannette Costo. *The Missions of California: A Legacy of Genocide*. San Francisco: Indian Historian Press, 1987.
Couloumbis, Angela. "Nelson Is Again Spared Execution." *Philadelphia Inquirer*, July 31, 2002.
"Couple Must Die in Chair." *Hammond Times* [Munster, Indiana], February 12, 1936.
"Couple on Death Row Together." *Riverside Press-Enterprise* [Riverside, California], July 21, 1998.
"Court Orders New Trial for Woman." *Indiana Gazette* [Indiana, Pennsylvania], February 23, 2009.
"Court Upholds Collins Verdict." *Big Spring Herald* [Big Spring, Texas], October 2, 1961.
Cox, Oliver. "Lynching and the Status Quo." *The Journal of Negro Education*, 14 (1945), 576–588.
Craker, Wendel. "Spectral Evidence, Non-Spectral Acts of Witchcraft, and Confession at Salem in 1692." *The Historical Journal*, 40 (1997), 331–358.
Crocker, Phyllis. "Is the Death Penalty Good for Women?" *Buffalo Criminal Law Review*, 4 (2001), 917–965.
Cuevas, Carlos, and Chiara Sabina. *Sexual Assault Among Latinos (Salas) Study*. National Institute of Justice, Office of Justice Programs, U.S. Department of Justice, April 2010. Available at http://www.ncjrs.gov/pdffiles1/nij/grants/230445.pdf.
Cunningham, Mark, and Mark P. Vigen. "Death Row Inmate Characteristics, Adjustment and Confinement: A Critical Review of the Literature." *Behavioral Sciences and the Law*, 20 (2002), 191–210.
Cunningham v. State, 248 Ga. 558 (1981).
Cunningham v. State, 248 Ga. 835 (1982).
"Cusumano Slayer Dies." *New York Times,* June 6, 1912.
"D.A. Fighting Mum Witness." *New Braunfels Herald-Zeitung* [New Braunfels, Texas], July 7, 1982.

Daily Commercial Register [Sandusky, Ohio], July 27, 1852.

Daines, Devin. "*State v. Harden*: Muddying the Waters of Self-Defense Law in West Virginia." *West Virginia Law Review*, 113 (2011), 971–1000.

Daly, Frederica. "Perspectives of Native American Women on Race and Gender." In Ethel Tobach and Betty Rosoff, eds., *Challenging Racism and Sexism: Alternatives to Genetic Explanations* (pp. 231–255). New York: Feminist Press, 1994.

Daly, Katheleen, and Meda Chesney-Lind. "Feminism and Criminology." *Justice Quarterly*, 5 (1988), 497–538.

Daniels, Roger. *Coming to America: A History of Immigration and Ethnicity in American Life.* New York: HarperCollins, 2002.

Dart, Tom. "Texas Set to Execute Lisa Coleman for Gruesome Murder of Child." *The Guardian*, September 17, 2014. Available at http://www.theguardian.com/world/2014/sep/17/texas-execute-lisa-coleman-lethal-injection-woman

Davidson, James. *Mediating Race and Class Through the Death Experience: Power Relations and Resistance Strategies of an African-American Community, Dallas, Texas (1869–1907).* Unpublished doctoral dissertation, University of Texas, 2004.

Davis, Angela. *Women, Race, and Class.* New York: Vintage, 1981.

"Day After the Murder." *New York Times*, February 12, 1879.

Dayton, Cornelia. "Taking the Trade: Abortion and Gender Relations in an Eighteenth-Century New England Village." *William and Mary Quarterly*, 48, 19–49 (1991).

_____. *Women Before the Bar: Gender, Law, and Society in Connecticut, 1639–1789.* Chapel Hill: University of North Carolina Press, 1995.

De León, Arnoldo. *They Called Them Greasers, Anglo Attitudes Toward Mexicans in Texas, 1821–1900.* Austin: The University of Texas Press, 1983.

Dean v. State, 173 Miss. 254 (1935).

"Death Before Dying: Solitary Confinement on Death Row." American Civil Liberties Union, July 2013. Available at http://www.aclu.org/files/assets/deathbeforedying-report.pdf.

"Death of a Murderess." *Tioga County Arbitrator* [New York], November 29, 1855.

"Death Penalty." *Galveston Daily News* [Galveston, Texas], August 28, 1880.

"Death Penalty Bid for Pomona Woman." *Corona Daily Independent* [Corona, California], October 5, 1976.

"Death Penalty: I Want to Die, Doris Foster" *Time Magazine.* January 24, 1983.

Death Penalty in Delaware, 1650–1849. Genealogy Trails History Group, 2015. Available at http://genealogytrails.com/del/executions1650_1849.html#kirk.

"Death Penalty in Flux." Death Penalty Information Center, February 6, 2007. Available at http://www.deathpenaltyinfo.org/death-penalty-flux.

"Death Penalty Retrial Delayed." Wcfcourierwww. Available at http://wcfcourier.com/news/local/death-penalty-retrial-delayed/article_e948857a-cd6f-5880-8dab-1c071b951ea0.html April 4, 2013.

"Death Row Inmate Ford Dies." ReviewJournalwww, January 30, 2005. Available at http://www.reviewjournal.com/lvrj_home/2005/Jan-30-Sun-2005/news/25766120.html.

"Death Row Women." Available at http://www.raulmalo.com/forum/index.php?topic=83075.0;wap2.

"Death Sentence on Woman Commuted." *Daily News* [New York], April 25, 1913.

"Death Sentence Pronounced." *Newark Daily Advocate*, September 13, 1890.

"Death Sentence Recommended for Woman Who Paid for Two Murder Plots." *Associated Press*, July 22, 1994.

"Debra Jean Milke Death Sentence, Conviction Overturned." *Associated Press*, March 14, 2013.

Decanter Morning Review, October 21, 1883.

DeGarno v. Texas, 474 U.S. 973.

Del Castillo, Richard. "Manifest Destiny: The Mexican-American War and the Treaty of Guadalupe Hidalgo." *Southwestern Journal of Law and Trade in the Americas*, 5 (1998), 31–43.

Del Mar, David. *What Trouble I Have Seen: A History of Violence Against Wives.* Cambridge: Harvard University Press, 1996.

"Delaware Prepares to Hang Mother, 52, and Her Son, 27." *Chillicothe Constitution-Tribune* [Chillicothe, Missouri], May 22, 1935.

Delfino, Michelangelo and Mary Day. *Death Penalty USA, 2001–2002.* Tampa: MoBeta, 2009.

DeLongoria, Maria. *Stranger Fruit: The Lynching of Black Women, the Cases of Rosa Jefferson and Marie Scott.* Unpublished doctoral dissertation, University of Missouri–Columbia, 2006.

D'Emilio, John, and Estelle B. Freedman. *Intimate Matters: A History of Sexuality in America.* Chicago: University of Chicago Press, 1997.

Demos, John. *Entertaining Satan: Witchcraft and the Culture of Early New England.* New York: Oxford University Press, 2004.

DeNavas-Walt, Carmen, Bernadette Proctor, and Jessica Smith. *Income, Poverty, and Health Insurance Coverage in the United States, 2010.* Current Population Reports, U.S. Census Bureau. September, 2011.

Dennis, Debra. "Mother Pleads Guilty in Starvation of Boy, 9 Fort Worth." *Dallas Morning News*, September 21, 2006.

Dennison v. State, 259 Ala. 424 (1953).

Denno, Deborah. "Getting to Death: Are Executions Constitutional." *Iowa Law Review*, 82 (1997), 319–464.

Detschelt, Alexander. "Recognizing Domestic Violence Directed Towards Men: Overcoming Societal Perceptions, Conducting Accurate Studies, and Enacting Responsible Legislation." *Kansas Journal of Law and Public Policy*, 12 (2003), 249–272.

Deville, Daniel. "White Slavery in America: A Brief History." *Vanguard News Network Forum*, September 6, 2008. Available at http://www.vnnforum.com/showthread.php?t=79466.

Dickie, Lance. "Rethinking How the Law Deals with Mentally Ill Criminals." *Seattle Times*, January 21, 2010. Available at http://www.seattleTimes, com/opinion/rethinking-how-the-law-deals-with-mentally-ill-criminals/.

"Did Mary Rogers Deserve Hanging?" *Times Argus* [Montpelier, Vermont], June 12, 2005. Available at http://www.timesargus.com/apps/pbcs.dll/article?AID=/20050612/NEWS/506120319/1013/FEATURES04.

"Died on the Scaffold." *Newark Daily Advocate*, March 1, 1887.

Dieter, Richard. *The Death Penalty in Black and White: Who Lives, Who Dies, Who Decides.* Death Penalty Information Center, 1998 Available at http://www.deathpenaltyinfo.org/article.php?scid=45&did=539.

Diggs, Irene. "Dubois and Children." *Phylon*, 37 (1976), 370–399.

Digital Library on American Slavery. University of North Carolina at Greensboro. PAR Number 11279304. Available at http://library.uncg.edu/slavery/details.aspx?pid=668.

_____. University of North Carolina at Greensboro. PAR Number 11378503. Available at http://library.uncg.edu/slavery/details.aspx?pid=1067.

_____. University of North Carolina at Greensboro. PAR Number 11382115. Available at http://library.uncg.edu/slavery/details.aspx?pid=1359.

_____. University of North Carolina at Greensboro. PAR Number 11585901. Available at http://library.uncg.edu/slavery/details.aspx?pid=2176.

_____. University of North Carolina at Greensboro. PAR Number 11282304. Available at http://library.uncg.edu/slavery/details.aspx?pid=858.

_____. University of North Carolina at Greensboro. PAR Number 11086402. Available at http://library.uncg.edu/slavery/details.aspx?pid=596.

Digital Library on American Slavery at the University of North Carolina, Greensboro. Available at http://library.uncg.edu/slavery/petitions/results.aspx?s=3&sid=129.

Dihoff, Debra. "Law Needed for When Courts Deal with Mental Illness." *Fayetteville Observer* [Fayetteville, North Carolina], April 6, 2010. Available at http://www.fayobserver.com/Articles/2010/04/06/988086.

Dimick, Augustus. *Private History and Confession of Pamela Lee, Who Was Convicted at Pittsburgh, Pa., December 19th, 1851, for the Willful Murder of Her Husband and Sentenced to Be Hanged on the 30th Day of January, A.D. 1852. Written at Her Request and According to Her Dictation, and Prepared by the Rev. Augustus Dimick, Pittsburgh, Pa.* 1852. Available at http://www.archive.org/details/privatehistoryco00leep.

DiSalle, Michael. "The Governor Goes into Action." *The News Journal*, April 14, 1966.

_____. "The Jeers Turn into Cheers." *The News Journal*, April 13, 1966.

_____. "The Lovesick Den Mother." *The Daily Reporter*, April 12, 1966.

"Discretion in Pardoning." *New York Times*, April 26, 1880.

Dishneau, David. "Witchcraft Trials Are Part of Md., Va. History." *The Herald-Mail Online*, October 10, 2004. Available at http://www.herald-mail.com/?cmd=displaystory&story_id=92195&format=html.

Dobrolenski v. State, 328 A.2d 447 (1974).

Dobson, Velma, and Bruce Sales. "The Science of Infanticide and Mental Illness." *Psychology, Public Policy and Law*, 6 (2000), 1098–1112.

"Dr. Ruth Dean Is Sentenced to Life in Jail." *Anniston Star* [Anniston, Alabama], March 3, 1934.

"Document—USA (Arkansas): Death Penalty/Legal Concern: Christina Marie Riggs." Amnesty International, April 14, 2000. Available at http://www.amnesty.org/fr/library/asset/AMR51/058/2000/fr/07a71ad6-df5c-11dd-acaa-7d9091d4638f/amr510582000en.html.

Dodge, L. Mara. "One Female Prisoner Is of More Trouble Than Twenty Males: Women Convicts in Illinois Prisons, 1835–1896." *Journal of Social History*, 32 (1999), 907–930.

Dolan, Jay. *The Irish American, a History*. New York: Bloomsbury Press, 2008.

Dolan v. U.S., 218 F.2d 454 (1955).

Donohue, John. "Capital Punishment in Connecticut, 1973–2007: A Comprehensive Evaluation from 4,686 Murders to One Execution." Stanford Law School, National Bureau of Economic Research (unpublished manuscript), June 8, 2013. Available at http://works.bepress.com/cgi/viewcontent.cgi?article=1095&context=john_donohue.

"Don't Limit Death-Penalty Appeals Process." *Wichita Eagle*, March 26, 2014.

"Doom Pair in Love Slaying." *Salamanca Republican Press* [Salamanca, New York], February 11, 1936.

"Doomed to Die, Says She Will Not." *The Bee* [Portland, Oregon], October 14, 1926.

Dorn, T. Felder. *The Guns of Meeting Street, a Southern Tragedy*. Columbia: South Carolina University Press, 2001.

"Double Hanging." *Daily Journal* [New Jersey], January 23, 1892.

"Double Hanging." *Muskogee Daily Phoenix* [Muskogee, Indian Territory], July 18, 1903.

Douglas, Carole, Priya Verma, Katherine Goktepe, Laura Nixon, and Jen Harris. "United States: Women on Death Row Suffer Harsher Conditions Than Male Inmates." *Off Our Backs*, 35 (2005), 10.

Dow, David, and Jared Tyler. *Ex Parte Francis Elaine Newton*, Application for Postconviction Writ of Habeas Corpus and Motion for Stay of Execution. In the 263rd Judicial District, Texas, and in the Court of Criminal Appeals of Texas, July 27, 2005, p. 8. Available at http://www.victimsofthestate.org/TX/Newton2.htm.

Downey, Harris. "The Hand and Head of Molly Glass." *The Kenyon Review*, 23 (1961), 229–254.

Drake, Frederick. "Witchcraft in the American Colonies, 1647–62." *American Quarterly*, 20 (1968), 694–725.

Dray, Philip. *At the Hands of Persons Unknown: The Lynching of Black America*. New York: Random House, 2003.

Dreifus, Claudia. "Women on Death Row." *Ms. Magazine*, Spring 2003.

Dressler, Joshua. "The Wisdom and Morality of Present-Day Criminal Sentencing." *Akron Law Review*, 38 (2005), 853–865.

Drizin, Steven, and Richard Leo. "The Problem of False Confessions in the Post–DNA World." *North Carolina Law Review*, 82 (2004), 891–1007.

DuBois, Steven. "Oregon Supreme Court Upholds Sentence for Only Woman on State's Death Row." *Daily Reporter* [Greenfield, Indiana], October 30, 2014. Available at http://www.greenfieldreporter.com/view/story/9432e3ec7bb343f3842061ee2357bce0/OR-Torture-Death-Sentence-Upheld.

Dudley v. State, 545 So. 2d 857 (1989).

Dugan v. State, 36 Ariz. 36 (1929).

Dugsdale, Richard. *The Jukes: A Study in Crime, Pauperism, Disease and Heredity*. New York: Putnam's, 1877.

Duncan, Gerald. "Books Closed on Arsenic Incorporated." *The American Weekly*, October 7, 1945.

Dunham, Robert. "The First 100 Re-Sentencings: Subsequent Dispositions of Pennsylvania Capital Cases Reversed in Post-Conviction," 2013. Available at http://www.deathpenaltyinfo.org/documents/RDunhamPaReversals.pdf.

Dunn, Mary. "Saints and Sisters: Congregational and Quaker Women in the Early Colonial Period." *American Quarterly*, 30 (1978), 582–601.

Dunphy, Jack. "Cowardice Masquerading as Courage." In Evan J. Mandery, ed., *Capital Punishment: A Balanced Examination* (pp. 607–608). Boston: Jones and Bartlett, 2005.

"Earle Frees Freda Trost." *Chester Times* [Chester, Pennsylvania], May 6, 1938.

"Earliest Perceptions: The Right of the Discover [Conqueror], *Johnson v. McIntosh*, Supreme Court of the United States Decided: February 28, 1823, 21 U.S. 543 (8 Wheat)." In Adalberto Aguirre and David V. Baker, eds., *Structure Inequality in the United States: Critical Discussion on the Continuing Significance of Race, Ethnicity, and Gender* (pp. 9–13). Upper Saddle River: Prentice Hall, 2008.

"Edmonds Acquitted in Oktibbeha County Murder." *Associated Press*. November 1, 2008.

Edmonds v. Deppisch, 313 F.3d 997 (2002).

Edwards, Holly. "Killer Mom Gets Death." *The Daily News of Los Angeles*, October 7, 2000.

Ekirch, A. Roger. "Bound for America: A Profile of British Convicts Transported to the Colonies, 1718–1775." *William and Mary Quarterly*, 42 (1987), 184–200.

_____. "Great Britain's Secret Convict Trade to America, 1783–1784." *American History Review*, 89 (1984), 1285–1291.

_____. "The Transportation of Scottish Criminals to America During the Eighteenth Century." *Journal of British Studies*, 24 (1985), 366–374.

Eley, Tom. "Declassified Grand Jury Transcripts Confirm Frame-Up of Ethel Rosenberg." *World Socialist Web Site*, 2008. Available at http://www.wsws.org/en/articles/2008/09/rose-s13.html. 2008.

Ellefson, Ashley. "Espy File." H-Law, September 19, 2002. Available at http://h-net.msu.edu/cgi-bin/logbrowse.pl?trx=vx&list=H-Law&month=0209&week=c&msg=EJPWuwIr%2BPM7cw43J3wydA&user=&pw.

Ellefson, C. Ashley. "Seven Hangman of Colonial Maryland." Archives of Maryland, 2009. Available at http://aomol.msa.maryland.gov/megafile/msa/speccol/sc2900/sc2908/000001/000819/pdf/am819.pdf.

Elliot, Andrea, and Benjamin Weiser. "When Prosecutors Err, Others Pay the Price." *New York Times*, March 21, 2004.

Elliott, Jack. "Byrom Seeks OK to Chase Retrial in Husband's Death." *Associated Press*, October 19, 2013.

_____. "Mississippi High Court Upholds Death Sentence in Tishomingo Murder." *Associated Press*, October 13, 2013.
Elliott, Ray. "The Hanging of Elizabeth Reed." *Tales Press*, 2002. Available at http://www.talespress.com/column_reed.html.
Ellsworth, Phoebe, and Samuel Gross. "Hardening of the Attitudes: Americans' Views on the Death Penalty." In Hugo Adam Bedau, ed., *The Death Penalty in America: Current Controversies* (pp. 90–115). New York: Oxford University Press, 1997.
Eltis, David. "Free and Coerced Transatlantic Migrations: Some Comparisons." *American History Review*, 88 (1983), 251–280.
_____, and Stanley Engerman. "Fluctuations in Sex and Age Ratios in the Transatlantic Slave Trade, 1663–1864." *The Economic History Review*, 46 (1993), 308–323.
_____, and _____. "Was the Slave Trade Dominated by Men?" *Journal of Interdisciplinary History*, 23 (1992), 237–257.
Emma Oliver v. State, 155 Tex. Crim. 461 (1950).
"End Juvenile Life-Without-Parole Sentences." Human Rights Watch, March 25, 2014. Available at http://www.hrw.org/news/2014/03/25/usoas-end-juvenile-life-without-parole-sentences.
Equal Justice Initiative. "Cruel and Unusual Punishment: Sentencing 13 and 14-Year-Old Children to Die in Prison." January 2008. Available at Http://Www.Eji.Org/Files/Cruel%20and%20Unusual%202008_0.Pdf.
_____. "U.S. Supreme Court Lets Stand Decision Holding *Miller v. Alabama* Is Retroactive." October 6, 2014Available at http://www.Eji.Org/Node/977.
Erikson, Kai. *Wayward Puritans: A Study in the Sociology of Deviance*. New York: Wiley, 1966.
"Escapee Charged with Murder." *Indiana Gazette* [Indiana, Pennsylvania], October 4, 1993.
Espy, M. Watt, and John Smykla. *Executions in the United States, 1608–2002: The Espy File* [computer file], 4th ICPS ed M. Watt Espy and John Ortiz Smykla, University of Alabama, comps. Ann Arbor: Inter-University Consortium for Political and Social Research [producer and distributor], 2004.
Essen, Allen. "Doctor Testifies Abuse Was Worst He's Seen." *Rio Grande Valley Monitor* [Rio Grande, Texas], July 1, 2008.
"Eula Elrod Thompson Given Life Sentence in Slaying of Brother." *Chatsworth Times* [Chatsworth, Georgia], August 14, 1941.
"Eula Thompson Tells New Story." *Atlanta Constitution*, August 28, 1928.
Evans, Doris. "Lawson Murder a Great Shock." *The Robesonian*, February 4, 1938.
Evans v. McNeil, 08-14402 (2011).
Everson, Elisa. *A Little Labor of Love: The Extraordinary Career of Dorothy Ripley, Female Evangelist in Early America*. Unpublished doctoral dissertation, Georgia State University, 2007.
ExecutedToday.com. "1739: Penelope Kenny and Sarah Simpson." December 2007. Available at http://www.executedtoday.com/2007/12/27/1739-penelope-kenny-and-sarah-simpson.
Execution List 2014. Death Penalty Information Center, 2014. Available at http://www.deathpenaltyinfo.org/execution-list-2014.
"Execution of a Woman." *Defiance Democrat* [Defiance, Ohio], November 6, 1858.
"Execution of Bridget Durgan for the Murder of Mrs. Corriell—Her Confession." *Sullivan Democrat* [Sullivan, Indiana], September 12, 1867.
"Execution of Henry Hallenschied, at Hermann, Missouri, Yesterday." *New Albany Daily Ledger Standard* [New Albany, Indiana], December 18, 1875.
"Execution of Pauline." *Daily Picayune* [New Orleans, Louisiana], March 29, 1846.
"Execution to Be Postponed." *New York Times*, April 8, 1884.

Executions in the U.S. from 1976 to 1986. Death Penalty Information Center. Available at http://www.deathpenaltyinfo.org/executions-us-1976-1986.
Executions in the United States. Death Penalty Information Center. Available at http://www.deathpenaltyinfo.org/article.php?did=414&scid=8.
Executive Minutes of Governor John Andrew Shulze 1826–1832. Pennsylvania Achieves, Series 9, Volume IX. Available at http://www.fold3.com/document/197460/.
Ex Parte Brittany Marlowe Holberg, 2008 Tex. Crim. App. Unpub. LEXIS 25 (2008).
Ex Parte Emma Oliver, 156 Tex. Crim. 235 (1951).
Ex Parte Jackson, 459 So.2d 969 (Ala. 1984).
Ex Parte Joseph F. Selby, Sr., 169 Tex. Crim. 157 (1960).
Ex Parte Judy M. Haney;, 603 So. 2d 412 (1992) (*Re: Judy M. Haney v. State of Alabama*).
Ex Parte Kimberly Lagayle McCarthy, 2007 Tex. Crim. App. Unpub. LEXIS 543 (2007).
Ex Parte Kimberly Lagayle McCarthy, 2013 Tex. Crim. App. Unpub. LEXIS 731 (2013).
Ex Parte Lisa Ann Coleman, 2010 Tex. Crim. App. Unpub. LEXIS 424 (2010).
Ex Parte Louise Harris, 632 So. 2d 543 (1993).
Ex Parte Melissa Elizabeth Lucio, 2013 Tex. Crim. App. Unpub. LEXIS 54 (2013).
Ex Parte: State of Alabama Ex Rel: Attorney General, 401 So. 2d 123 (1979) (*In Re: Debra Bracewell, Alias v. State of Alabama*).
Ex Parte State of Alabama, 2006 Ala. LEXIS 277 (2006) (*In Re: Shonda Nicole Johnson v. State of Alabama*).
"Expert Testimony." *Lowell Sun* [Lowell, Massachusetts], February 17, 1911.
EyeWitness to History. http://www.eyewitnesstohistory.com.
"Face Death Chair Does Fair Madeline." *Fort Wayne Daily News* [Fort Wayne, Indiana], January 30, 1913.
"Faces in the News." *Salina Journal* [Salina, Kansas], December 23, 1971.
Fagan, Jeffrey. "An Act Reinstating Capital Punishment in the Commonwealth." Testimony before the Joint Committee on the Judiciary of the Massachusetts Legislature on House Bill 3834, July 14, 2005. Available at http://www.deathpenaltyinfo.org/MassTestimonyFagan.pdf.
Fanny v. State, 6 Mo. 122 (1839).
Faragher, John, Mary Jo Buhle, Daniel Czitrom, and Susan Armitrage. *Out of Many: A History of the American People*. Upper Saddle River: Prentice Hall, 2001.
Farless, Patricia. "Hester Vaughan: Infanticide, Woman's Rights, and Melodrama." University of Central Florida, 2005. Available at http://fch.fiu.edu/FCH-2005/Farless-Hester%20Vaughan.htm#_edn50.
Farmer, Silas. *History of Detroit and Wayne County and Early Michigan, a Chronological Cyclopedia of the Past and Present*. Detroit: Silas Farmer, 1884.
Farr, Kathryn. "Defeminizing and Dehumanizing Female Murderers: Depictions of Lesbians on Death Row." In B. Prices and N. Sokoloff, eds., *The Criminal Justice System and Women: Offenders, Prisoners, Victims and Workers* (pp. 249–260). New York: McGraw-Hill, 2004.
Feagin, Joe. *Racist America: Roots, Current Realities, and Future Reparations*. New York: Routledge, 2000.
_____. "Race and Justice: Wrongful Convictions of African American Men." *Contemporary Sociology: A Journal of Reviews*, 42 (2013), 81–83.
_____, and Clairece Feagin. *Racial and Ethnic Relations*. Upper Saddle River: Prentice Hall, 2011.
Feagin, Joe, and Melvin P. Sikes. *Living with Racism: The Black Middle-Class Experience*. Boston: Beacon, 1994.
Fede, Andrew. "Gender in the Law of Slavery in the Antebellum United States." *Cardozo Law Review*, 18 (1996), 411–432.
_____. "Legitimized Violent Slave Abuse in the American South, 1619–1865: A Case Study of Law and Social Change

in Six Southern States." *American Journal of Legal History*, 29 (1985), 93–150.

Federal Bureau of Prisons. "Inmate Locator." Available at http://www.bop.gov/iloc2/LocateInmate.jsp.

Federal Death Row Prisoners. Death Penalty Information Center, June 6, 2015. Available at http://www.deathpenaltyinfo.org/federal-death-row-prisoners#cases.

Feimster, Crystal. *Ladies and Lynching: The Gendered Discourse of Mob Violence in the New South, 1880–1930*. Unpublished doctoral dissertation, Princeton University, 2000.

_____. *Southern Horrors: Women and the Politics of Rape and Lynching*. Cambridge: Harvard University Press, 2009.

Feinman, Clarice. "An Historical Overview of the Treatment of Incarcerated Women: Myths and Realities of Rehabilitation." *Prison Journal*, 63 (1984), 12–26.

Fettig, Amy. "Women Prisoners: Altering the Cycle of Abuse." *Human Rights Magazine*, Spring 2009. Available at http://www.americanbar.org/publications/human_rights_magazine_home/human_rights_vol36_2009/spring2009/women_prisoners_altering_the_cycle_of_abuse.html.

Fiebert, Martin. *References Examining Assaults by Women on Their Spouses or Male Partners: An Annotated Bibliography*. May 2008. Available at http://www.falseallegations.com/references-assaults-by-women-on-spouses-male-partners.htm.

"5th Circuit Orders New Trial for Female Death Row Inmate." *Texas City Sun* [Texas City, Texas], March 3, 2000.

Final Report of the Pennsylvania Supreme Court Committee on Racial and Gender Bias in the Justice System. 2003. Available at http://nicic.gov/Library/019106.

Finkelman, Paul. "The Color of Race." *Tulane Law Review*, 67 (1993), 2063–2112.

Fins, Deborah. *Death Row U.S.A., a Quarterly Report by the Capital Punishment Project of the NAACP Legal Defense and Educational Fund, Inc.* October 1, 2014. Available at http://www.deathpenaltyinfo.org/documents/DRUSAFall2014.pdf.

Finz, Stacy. "Prosecutors' Call for Death Penalty Rare for Women." *The Daily News of Los Angeles*, January 13, 1997.

Fisher, Kirsten. *Suspect Relations: Sex, Race, and Resistance in Colonial North Carolina*. Ithaca: Cornell University Press, 2002.

Fisher, Stanley. "Convictions of Innocent Persons in Massachusetts: An Overview." *Boston University Public Interest Law Journal*, 12 (2002), 1–72.

Flannery, John. "Former Federal Prosecutor Criticizes the Withholding of Critical Evidence." Death Penalty Information Center, August 20, 2005. Available at http://www.deathpenaltyinfo.org/node/326.

"Florida Woman's Death Penalty Overturned." *News 4 Jax*, February 28, 2008. Available at http://www.news4jax.com.

Fogel, Robert. *Without Consent or Contract: The Rise and Fall of American Slavery*. New York: W.W. Norton, 1989.

_____, and Stanley Engerman. *Time on the Cross: The Economics of American Negro Slavery*. Boston: Little, Brown, 1974.

Fogleman, Aaron. "Migrations to the Thirteen British North American Colonies: New Estimates." *Journal of Interdisciplinary History*, 22 (1992), 691–709.

Fogelman, Matthew. "Justice Asleep Is Justice Denied: Why Dozing Defense Attorneys Demean the Sixth Amendment and Should Be Deemed Per Se Prejudicial." *Journal of Legal Profession*, 26 (2002), 67–100.

Foley, Michael. *Arbitrary and Capricious: The Supreme Court, the Constitution, and the Death Penalty*. Westport: Praeger, 2003.

Follingstad, Diane, Regina Shillinglaw, Dana DeHart, and Kathryn Kleinfelter. "The Impact of Elements of Self-Defense and Objective Versus Subjective Instructions on Jurors' Verdicts for Battered Women Defendants." *Journal of Interpersonal Violence*, 12 (1997), 729–747.

Foner, Eric. *Reconstruction: America's Unfinished Revolution*. New York: Harper & Row, 1988.

Ford v. State, 102 Nev. 126 (1986).

"Forgotten Population: A Look at Death Row in the United States Through the Experiences of Women." American Civil Liberties Union, December 2004. Available at http://www.aclu.org/files/FilesPDFs/womenondeathrow.pdf.

"Former FBI Chief Sessions Calls for Innocence Commission in Texas." Death Penalty Information Center, May 13, 2003. Available at http://www.deathpenaltyinfo.org/node/816.

"Former Spaghetti Salesman Given Respite by James." *Altoona Mirror* [Altoona, Pennsylvania], June 20, 1941.

Fort Wayne Daily Gazette [Fort Wayne, Indiana], April 21, 1871.

Fort Wayne Daily Gazette [Fort Wayne, Indiana], June 24, 1882.

"Foss Has Pardoned 132." *New York Times*, July 8, 1912.

Foster and Powell v. Commonwealth, 827 S.W.2d 670 (1991).

Foster v. State, 297 Md. 191 (1984).

Foster v. State, 285 Ark. 363 (1985).

Foster v. State, 304 Md. 439 (1985).

Foster v. State, 290 Ark. 495 (1986).

Foster, Teree. "I Want to Live! Federal Judicial Values in Death Penalty Cases: Preservation of Rights or Punctuality of Execution?" *Oklahoma City University Law Review*, 22 (1997), 63–87.

"Found Guilty of the Crime." *Xenia Daily Gazette* [Xenia, Ohio], June 12, 1905.

"Francis Elaine Newton." Amnesty International, November 19, 2004. Available at http://www.amnesty.org/en/library/asset/AMR51/163/2004/en/dom-AMR511632004en.pdf.

Frank v. Louisiana, 552 U.S. 1189 (2008).

Fraser, Caroline. "Suffering Children and the Christian Science Church." *The Atlantic Online*, April 1995. Available at http://www.theatlantic.com/past/docs/unbound/flashbks/xsci/suffer.htm.

Frazell, Dayrl. "Murder Most Ordinary Can Be Quite Chilling." *St. Petersburg Times* [St. Petersburg, Florida], January 21, 1990.

Frazier, Harriett. *Death Penalty in Missouri, 1803–2005: A History and Comprehensive Registry of Legal Executions, Pardons, and Commutations*. Jefferson: McFarland, 2006.

_____. *Slavery and Crime in Missouri, 1773–1865*. Jefferson: McFarland, 2001.

Frazier, Martin. "Slavery in New York: Uncovering the Brutal Truth." *People's World*, December 2, 2005. Available at http://www.peoplesworld.org/slavery-in-new-york-uncovering-the-brutal-truth/.

"Freda Frost Refused Application for Pardon." *Lebanon Daily News* [Lebanon, Pennsylvania], November 26, 1926.

Freedmen, Lawrence, and William Haverman. "The Rise and Fall of the Unwritten Law: Sex, Patriarchy, and Vigilante Justice in American Courts." *Buffalo Law Review*, 61 (2013), 997–1056.

Friedman, Lawrence. *Crime and Punishment in American History*. New York: Basic Books, 1993.

_____. *A History of American Law*. New York: Simon & Schuster, 1985.

Friedman, Susan, Sara Horwitz and Phillip Resnick. "Child Murder by Mothers: A Critical Analysis of the Current State of Knowledge and a Research Agenda." *The American Journal of Psychiatry*, 162 (2005), 1578–1587.

Freilich, Joshua, and Craig J. Rivera. "Mercy, Death, and Politics: An Analysis of Executions and Commutations in New York State, 1935–1963." *American Journal of Criminal Justice*, 24 (1999), 15–29.

"Fueling the Fire Over Halcion." *Newsweek*, May 25, 1992. Available at http://www.newsweek.com/1992/05/24/fueling-the-fire-over-halcion.html.

"Fugitive Couple Sought in Slaying of Elderly Lexington Woman." *Associated Press*, October 29, 1998.

"Fugitive Marie Arrington Arrested." *News Herald* [Florida], December 23, 1971.

Fulgham v. State, 46 So.3d 315 (2010).

Furman v. Georgia, 408 U.S. 238 (1972).

Futhey, J. Smith, and Gilbert Cope. *History of Chester County*,

Pennsylvania with Genealogical and Biographical Sketches. Philadelphia: Louis H. Everts, 1881.

Gado, Mark. *Death Row Women: Murder, Justice and the New York Press.* Westport: Praeger, 2008.

Gallagher, Brian. "A Brief History of Institutionalized Child Abuse." *Boston Third World Law Journal,* 17 (1997), 1–30.

"Gallows in Maryland, the Execution of Mary Wallis." *New York Herald,* February 11, 1871.

"Gallows for a Woman." *Daily Republican* [Marion, Illinois], May 22, 1897.

Gallup. *Death Penalty.* Available at http://www.gallup.com/Poll/1606/Death-Penalty.Aspx.

Galonska, Juliet. "First Woman Sentenced to Hang in Fort Smith." National Park Service, Fort Smith. February 1995. Available at http://www.nps.gov/fosm/learn/historyculture/first-woman-sentenced-to-hang.htm.

Galveston Daily News [Galveston, Texas], July 21, 1885.

Garcia, Edwina. "Child Removed from Home in 2004." *Valley Morning Star* [Harlingen, Texas], February 23, 2007.

"Garrabrant Case." *Trenton Times* [Trenton, New Jersey], December 23, 1905.

Garrett, Brandon. "The Substance of False Confessions." *Stanford Law Review,* 62 (2010), 1051–1119.

Garrett, Brandon, and Peter Neufeld. "Invalid Forensic Science Testimony and Wrongful Convictions." *Virginia Law Review,* 95 (2009), 1–97.

Gates, Gary, and Frank Newport. "Special Report: 3.4% of U.S. Adults Identify as LGBT." Gallup, October 18, 2012. Available at http://www.gallup.com/poll/158066/special-report-adults-identify-lgbt.aspx.

Gazlay, Kristin. "Legends Haunt Women's Death Row." *Paris Press,* March 10, 1982.

Geggus, David. "Sex Ratio, Age and Ethnicity in the Atlantic Slave Trade: Data from French Shipping and Plantation Records." *The Journal of African History,* 30 (1989), 23–44.

"General." *Indiana Progress* [Indiana, Pennsylvania], November 9, 1876.

"General News." *Fort Wayne Daily Democrat* [Fort Wayne, Indiana], July 27, 1869.

Genovese, Eugene. *Roll Jordan, Roll: The World the Slaves Made.* New York: Basic Books, 1974.

"George Coyer—1 of 12 Men Convicted of Murder in Cattaraugus and Executed." New York Correction History Society. Available at http://www.correctionhistory.org/html/timeline/cattaraugus/georgecoyer.html.

George, Whitney. "Women on Death Row," *Off Our Backs,* 28 (1998), 16–17.

"Georgia Poison Case." *Ogden Standard Examiner* [Ogden, Utah], September 23, 1959.

Geringer, Joseph. "Winnie Ruth Judd: The Trunk Murderess in Perspective." *TrueTv Crime Library.* Available at http://www.trutv.com/library/crime/notorious_murders/women/judd/1.html.

Gerlach, Don. "Black Arson in Albany, New York: November 1793." *Journal of Black Studies,* 7 (1977), 301–312.

German, Norman. *A Savage Wisdom.* Thibodaux: Thunder Rain, 2010.

Ghiotto, Gene. "Trial Begins for Couple in Nephew's Death." *Riverside Press Enterprise,* January 20, 2009.

Giardini, G., and R. Farrow. "The Paroling of Capital Offenders." *Annals of the American Academy of Political and Social Science,* 284 (1952), 85–94.

Gibson v. Turpin, 270 Ga. 855 (1999).

Gilbreath, West. *Death on the Gallows: The Story of Legal Hangings in New Mexico, 1847–1923.* Silver City: High Lonesome Books, 2002.

Giles v. Harris, 189 U.S. 475 (1903).

Gillespie, L. Kay. *Dancehall Ladies: The Crimes and Executions of America's Condemned Women.* Lanham: University Press of America, 1997.

_____. *Executed Women of 20th and 21st Centuries.* Lanham: University Press of America, 2009.

"Girl Who Never Had a Chance Ordered to the Gallows." *Muskogee Times Democrat* [Muskogee, Oklahoma], December 1, 1913.

Gissendaner v. State, 272 Ga. 704 (2000).

Glass v. Louisiana, 471 U.S. 1080 (1985).

Gobble v. Alabama, 2010 Ala. Crim. App. LEXIS 8 (2010).

Gobble v. Alabama, 2010 Ala. Crim. App. LEXIS 34 (2010).

Godsey, Mark, and Thomas Pulley. "The Innocence Revolution and Our Evolving Standards of Decency in Death Penalty Jurisprudence." *University of Dayton Law Review,* 29 (2004), 265–292.

Goldfarb, Phyllis. "Pedagogy of the Oppressed: A Class on Race and the Death Penalty." Boston College Law School, Research Paper 129, March 31, 2007. Available at http://papers.ssrn.com/sol3/papers.cfm?abstract_id=977779.

Goldsmith, Barbara. *Other Powers: The Age of Suffrage, Spiritualism, and the Scandalous Victoria Woodhull.* New York: Alfred A. Knopf, 1998.

Gonzales v. California, 132 S. Ct. 1639 (2012).

Gonzalez, John. "Doctor Says Routier Had Taken Pills." *Altoona Mirror* [Altoona, Pennsylvania], January 9, 1997.

Goodell, Abner. *The Trial and Execution, for Petite Treason, of Marc and Phillis, Slaves of Capt. John Codman, Who Murdered Their Master at Charlestown, Mass. in 1755; for Which the Man Was Hanged and Gibbeted, and the Woman Was Burned to Death.* Cambridge: John Wilson, 1883. Available at http://www.gutenberg.org/files/26446/26446-h/26446-h.htm.

Gooding, Ed, and Robert Nieman. *Ed Gooding: Soldier, Texas Ranger.* Longview: Ranger, 2001.

Goodrich, Lawrence. "Bay State Court Reverses Conviction of Christian Scientists." *Christian Science Monitor,* August 14, 1993.

Goodwin, Michele. "Gender, Race, and Mental Illness: The Case of Wanda Jean Allen." In Adrien Wing, ed., *Critical Race Feminism: A Reader* (pp. 228–237). New York: New York University Press, 2003.

Gordon, Sarah. "Law and Everyday Death: Infanticide and the Hester Vaughn Case." In Austin Sarat, Lawrence Douglas and Martha Umphrey, eds., *Lives in the Law* (pp. 55–81). Ann Arbor: University of Michigan Press, 2002.

Gordon-Reed, Annette. "Celia's Case (1857)." In Annette Gordon-Reed, ed., *Race on Trial: Law and Justice in American History* (pp. 48–60). New York: Oxford University Press, 2002.

Gottlieb, Gabriele. *Theater of Death: Capital Punishment in Early America, 1750–1800.* Unpublished Doctoral Dissertation, University of Pittsburgh, 2005.

Gould, Jon, and Richard Leo. "Centennial Symposium: A Century of Criminal Justice: II. 'Justice' in Action: One Hundred Years Later: Wrongful Convictions After a Century of Research." *Journal of Criminal Law & Criminology,* 100 (2010), 825–868.

"Gov. Craig Commutes Sentence to Life." *Hammond Times* [Munster, Indiana], December 11, 1956.

"Gov. Marmaduke May Save Her." *Amsterdam Daily Democrat* [Amsterdam, New York], January 4, 1886.

"Governor Commutes Death Sentence of Woman Slayer." *Daily Leader-Times* [West Point, Mississippi], November 22, 1928.

Graczyk, Michael. "Arlington Woman Executed for Abused Boy's Death." *Star-Telegram,* September 17, 2014. Available at http://www.star-telegram.com/2014/09/17/6129167/arlington-woman-executed-for-abused.html?rh=1.

Graham, Troy. "Nelson Gets Life in Police Slayings." *Philadelphia Inquirer.* June 16, 2007.

"Grandmother Arrested in Slaying of Children." *Santa Ana Orange County Register* [California], June 19, 1993.

Granger v. State, 653 S.W.2d 868 (1983).

Granger v. State, 683 S.W.2d 387 (1984).

"Greason Case Again Before Pardon Board." *Reading Eagle* [Reading, Pennsylvania], September 21, 1904.

Green, Aimee. "Court Says Sleep-Driving Strikes Quickly: Teen Driver Who Killed Motorcyclist Gets Case Overturned." *The Oregonian* [Portland], January 29, 2014.

Green, Ashbel. "Court Overturns Manslaughter Conviction of Daughter Accused of Neglect." *The Oregonian* [Portland], March 1, 2007.

Green, Frank. "Woman's Execution Date Set; Teresa Lewis Set to Die Sept. 23 for Role in 2 Pittsylvania Slayings." *Richmond Times Dispatch*, July 30, 2010.

Greenberg, Douglas. "Crime, Law Enforcement, and Social Control in Colonial America." *American Journal of Legal History*, 26 (1982), 293–325.

Greenberg, Jack. "Capital Punishment as a System." *Yale Law Review*, 91 (1982), 908–936.

Greenspan, Stephen. "Posthumous Pardons Granted in American History." Unpublished paper, Department of Psychiatry, University of Colorado, March 2011. Available at http://www.deathpenaltyinfo.org/documents/PosthumousPardons.pdf.

Gribben, Mark. "Alton Coleman and Debra Brown." *True Crime Library*. Available at http://www.trutv.com/library/crime/serial_killers/partners/coleman/index_1.html.

Griffin, Patricia. "Jumping on the Ban Wagon: Minetos v. City University of New York and the Future of the Peremptory Challenge." *Minnesota Law Review*, 81 (1997), 1237–1270.

Grisham, John. "Teresa Lewis Didn't Pull the Trigger. Why Is She on Death Row." *Washington Post*, September 12, 2010.

Grissom, Brandi. "Woman Charged with Murder Campaigns for Innocence." *Texas Tribune*, September 29, 2010. Available at http://www.texastribune.org/texas-dept-criminal-justice/innocence-project-of-texas/woman-charged-with-murder-campaigns-for-innocence/.

Gross, Samuel. "Race and Death: The Judicial Evaluation of Evidence of Discrimination in Capital Sentencing." *University of California Davis Law Review*, 18 (1985), 1275–1325.

———. "The Risks of Death: Why Erroneous Convictions Are Common in Capital Cases." *Buffalo Law Review*, 44 (1996), 469–500.

———, Kristen Jacoby, Daniel J. Matheson, Nicholas Montgomery and Sujat Patil. "Exonerations in the United States 1989 Through 2003." *Journal of Criminal Law and Criminology*, 95 (2005), 523–555.

Gross, Samuel, and Robert Mauro. "Patterns of Death: An Analysis of Racial Disparities in Capital Sentencing and Homicide Victimization." *Stanford Law Review*, 37 (1984), 27–153.

Gross, Samuel, Barbara O'Brien, Chen Hu and Edward H. Kennedy. "Rate of False Conviction of Criminal Defendants Who Are Sentenced to Death." *Proceedings of the National Academy of Sciences of the United States of America*, 111 (2004), 7230–7235.

Gross, Samuel, and Michael Shaffer. "Exonerations in the United States, 1989–2012. Report by the National Registry of Exonerations." June 2012. Available at http://www.law.umich.edu/special/exoneration/Documents/exonerations_us_1989_2012_full_report.pdf.

Grosvenor, Vertamae. "Remembering Corrine Sykes." National Public Radio (NPR) *All Things Considered*, April 3, 1998. Transcript No. 98040320-212. Linda Wertheimer, Reporting.

Guarino, Mark. "As Arizona Woman Exits Prison Pending Retrial, Questions About Confessions." *Christian Science Monitor*, September 6, 2013. Available at http://www.csmonitor.com/USA/Justice/2013/0906/As-Arizona-woman-exits-prison-pending-retrial-questions-about-confessions-video.

"Guilty in Death of Husband." *Press-Telegram* [Long Beach, California], July 16, 1975.

"Guilty Mom Kills Herself, Wacaser Takes Own Life After Drawing Conviction." *Ottawa Herald*, May 11, 1992.

Gutman, Herbert. *The Black Family in Slavery and Freedom: 1750–1925.* New York: Vintage, 1977.

Haas, Brian, and Brandon Gee. "Gaile Owens Granted Parole." *The Tennessean*, September 28, 2011.

Hagan, Jennifer. "Can We Lose the Battle and Still Win the War? The Fight Against Domestic Violence After the Death of Title III of the Violence Against Women Act." *DePaul Law Review*, 50 (2001), 919–991.

Haines, Herbert. *Against Capital Punishment: The Anti-Death Penalty Movement in America, 1972–1994.* New York: Oxford University Press, 1996.

Haines, Max. "Killer Inferno a Tragic April Fool's Day Fire in Youngstown, Ohio, Was No Joke." *Toronto Sun*, May 23, 1999.

———. "Parting Shot; Only One Thing Stood in the Way of Dee and Kosta Living the Good Life—His Wife." *Toronto Sun*, March 26, 1995.

Hall, David. *Witch-Hunting in Seventeenth Century New England: A Documentary History 1638–1693.* Durham: Duke University Press, 1991.

Hall, Dee. "High Court Won't Hear Edmund's Case, the Action Leaves in Place an Appeals Court Ruling Overturning Her Conviction." *Wisconsin State Journal*, April 18, 2008. Available at http://host.madison.com/news/article_9473cbc8-f7ed-5f91-b475-edb992f3ad7d.html.

Hall, Gwendolyn. *Africans in Colonial Louisiana: The Development of Afro-Creole Culture in the Eighteenth Century.* Baton Rouge: Louisiana State University Press, 1992.

Hall, John. "Arizona Prosecutor Plans to Seek Gallows for Ruth Judd" *Coshocton Tribune* [Coshocton, Ohio], October 24, 1931.

Hallett, Joe. "Death Row Decision Gets No Forgiveness." *Plain Dealer* [Cleveland, Ohio], January 5, 1997.

Halperin, Rick. "Death Penalty News." September 22, 2007. Available at http://lists.washlaw.edu/pipermail/deathpenalty/2007-September/007008.html.

Halsey v. Texas, 68 S.W.3d 81 (2001).

Halttunen, Karen. "Divine Providence and Dr. Parkman's Jawbone: The Cultural Construction of Murder as Mystery." *Ideas*. National Humanities Center, North Carolina, 1996. Available at http://nationalhumanitiescenter.org/ideasv41/halttun4.htm.

Halttunen, Karen. *Murder Most Foul: The Killer and the American Gothic Imagination.* Cambridge: Harvard University Press, 1998.

Hamby, Sherry. *Sexual Victimization in Indian Country: Barriers and Resources for Native Women Seeking Help.* Applied Research Forum, May 2004. Available at http://www.unified-solutions.org/Pubs/sexual_victimization_in_indian_country.pdf.

"Hammer Slayer Must Die in Chair." *Pittsburg Press*, December 19, 1945.

Haney v. Alabama, 1991 Ala. Crim. App. LEXIS 2692 (1991).
Haney v. Alabama, 603 So. 2d 368 (1991).

"Hanging of Susan Eberhart." *Webster County Georgia Archives News*, May 9, 1873. Available at http://files.usgwarchives.org/ga/webster/newspapers/nw1240hangingo.txt.

"Hanging of Women." *Lebanon Boone County Pioneer* [Lebanon, Indiana], December 26, 1968.

Hangings in Berks County, Pa. Available at http://freepages.genealogy.rootsweb.ancestry.com/~genphotos2/hangings.html.

Hannaford, Alex. "Did Death Row Inmate Linda Carty Get a Fair Trial." *Texas Observer*, January 10, 2012.

Hansen, Mark. "Why Are Iowa's Babies Dying." *American Bar Association Journal*, 84 (1998), 74–78.

Hardin, Jason. "Parole Rejected for Woman in 1989 Murder Conviction." News-Recordwww, March 30, 2009. Available at http://www.news-record.com/content/2009/03/30/article/parole_rejected_for_woman_in_1989_murder_conviction.

Hardy, James. "The Transportation of Convicts to Colonial Louisiana." *Louisiana History: The Journal of the Louisiana Historical Association*, 7 (1966), 207–220.

Hargroder, Charles. *Ada and the Doc: An Account of the Ada LeBoeuf-Thomas Dreher Murder Case*. Lafayette: Center for Louisiana Studies, 2000.

Harjo, Suzan. "Redskins, Savages, and Other Indian Enemies: A Historical Overview of American Media Coverage of Native People." In Coramae Richey Mann, Marjorie Zatz and Nancy Rodriquez, *Images of Color, Images of Crime* (pp. 62–77). Los Angeles: Roxbury, 2006.

Harman, S.W. *Hell on the Border*. Fort Smith: Phoenix, 1898.

Harris, Angela. "Race and Essentialism in Feminist Legal Theory." *Stanford Law Review*, 42 (199), 581–616.

Harris, Collier. *Public Goal Historical Report, Block 27 Building 2*. Colonial Williamsburg Foundation Library Research Report Series—1628, Colonial Williamsburg Foundation Library Williamsburg, Virginia, 1990. Available at http://research.history.org/DigitalLibrary/View/index.cfm?doc=ResearchReports%5CRR1628.xml.

Harris, Daisey. "Women on Death Row." *Ebony*, February 1980.

Harris, Jonathan, and Lothlorien Redmond. "Executive Clemency: The Lethal Absence of Hope." *Criminal Law Brief*, 3 (2007), 2–11.

Harris v. Alabama, 513 U.S. 504 (1995).

Harris v. State, 632 So. 2d 503 (1992).

Harris v. State, 947 So. 2d 1079 (2004).

Harrison, D. "179 Persons in United States Face Legal Executions in Balance of 1935." *Waterloo Daily Courier* [Waterloo, Iowa], January 27, 1935.

Harrison, M. Leigh. "A Study of the Earliest Reported Decisions of the South Carolina Courts of Law." *American Journal of Legal History*, 16 (1972), 51–70.

Hart, Albert, and Herbert Ferleger. *The Roosevelt Web Book*. New York: Theodore Roosevelt Association, 1989. Available at http://www.theodoreroosevelt.org/tr%20web%20book/TR_CD_to_HTML1273.html.

Hartog, Hendrik. "Lawyering, Husbands' Rights, and the Unwritten Law in Nineteenth Century America." *Journal of American History*, 84 (1997), 67–96.

Hartung, Frank. "Trends in the Use of Capital Punishment." *Annals of the American Academy of Political and Social Sciences*, 284 (1952), 8–19.

Hartung v. People, 22 N.Y. 95 (1860).

Hartung v. People, 26 N.Y. 154 (1862).

Hartung v. People, 28 N.Y. 400 (1863).

Hatfield, Steven. "Criminal Punishment in America: From the Colonial to the Modern Era." *United States Air Force Academy Journal of Legal Studies*, 1 (1990), 139–154.

Hawaii v. Aiwohi, 109 Hawai'i 115 (2005).

Hawkins, Gains. "Mother Without Mercy: The Life, Abuse and Death of Paula Houston in RFD Mississippi." *Washington Post*, January 11, 1986.

Hawkins v. State, 7 Mo. 190 (1841).

Hearn, Daniel. *Legal Executions in New England: A Comprehensive Reference, 1623–1960*. Jefferson: McFarland, 1999.

_____. *Legal Executions in New Jersey: A Comprehensive Registry, 1691–1963*. Jefferson: McFarland, 2005.

_____. *Legal Executions in New York State: A Comprehensive Reference, 1639–1963*. Jefferson: McFarland, 1997.

_____. *Legal Executions in North Carolina and South Carolina: A Comprehensive Registry, 1866–1962*. Jefferson: McFarland, 2015.

Heise, Michael. "Mercy by the Numbers: An Empirical Analysis of Clemency and Its Structure." *Virginia Law Review*, 89 (2003), 101–169.

Helena Independent, October 17, 1883.

Hemphill, C. Dallett. "Women in Court: Sex-Role Differentiation in Salem, Massachusetts, 1636 to 1683." *William and Mary Quarterly*, 39 (1982), 164–175.

Henderson v. State, 583 So.2d 276 (1990).

Hendrix, Patrick, Heather Spires, Toni Hendrix, and Judy Corbett. *Murder and Mayhem in Holy City*. Charleston: History Press, 2006.

Henigman, Laura. *Coming into Communion: Pastoral Dialogues in Colonial New England*. Albany: State University of New York Press, 1999.

Hendrickson v. State, 290 Ark. 319 (1986).

Henrickson v. Norris, 224 F.3d 748 (2000).

Hennessy-Fiske, Molly. "Wrongful Conviction Inquiry." *Los Angeles Times*, February 13, 2012.

Henry White v. the State, 52 Miss. 216 (1876).

Herberle, Renee. "Disciplining Gender: Or, Are Women Getting Away with Murder?" *Signs: Journal of Women in Culture and Society*, 24 (1999), 1103–1112.

Herbert, Bob. "An Imaginary Homicide." *New York Times*, August 15, 2002.

_____. "When Justice Is Mocked." *New York Times*, August 19, 2002.

Heritage Archives. http://heritagearchives.org/Resources.aspx.

Hermanson v. Florida, 570 So. 2d 322 (1990).

Hermanson v. Florida, 604 So. 2d 775 (1992).

Herrera v. Collins, 506 U.S. 390, 415 (1993).

Herzog, Sergio, and Shaul Oreg. "Chivalry and the Moderating Effect of Ambivalent Sexism: Individual Differences in Crime Seriousness Judgments." *Law and Society Review*, 42 (2008), 45–73.

Herzog, Werner. "On Death Row: A Conversation with Linda Carty." Broadcast on Discovery Channel's Investigation, March 16, 2012.

Hess, David. "Case of Two Awaiting Chair Tests Death Penalty Law." *Santa Ana Orange County Register* [Santa Ana, California], October 29, 1977.

Hester, Marianne. "The Witchcraze in Sixteenth and Seventeenth Century England as Social Control of Women." In Jill Radford and Diane E. H. Russell, eds., *Femicide: The Politics of Woman Killing*. New York: Twayne, 1992.

Higginbotham, A. Leon. *In the Matter of Color: Race and the American Legal Process-The Colonial Period*. New York: Oxford University Press, 1978.

_____. *Shades of Freedom: Racial Politics and Presumptions of the American Legal Process*. New York: Oxford University Press, 1996.

_____, and Anne Jacobs. "The 'Law Only as an Enemy': The Legitimization of Racial Powerlessness Through the Colonial and Antebellum Criminal Laws of Virginia." *North Carolina Law Review*, 70 (1992), 969–1070.

Higginbotham, A. Leon, and Barbara Kopytoff. "Property First, Humanity Second: The Recognition of the Slave's Human Nature in Virginia Civil Law." *Ohio State Law Journal*, 50 (1989), 511–540.

"Highball Slayer Granted Pardon." *Uniontown Morning Herald* [Uniontown, Pennsylvania], July 10, 1935.

Hill, Ruth. "Linda Carty: 'Someone Is Trying to Take My Life for Someone Else's Crime.'" *The Guardian*, June 27, 2010. Available at http://www.theguardian.com/world/2010/jun/27/linda-carty-death-row-texas.

Hindman, Hugh. *Child Labor: An American History*. Armonk: M.E. Sharpe, 2002.

Hindus, Michael. "Black Justice Under White Law: Criminal Prosecutions of Blacks in Antebellum South Carolina." *Journal of American History*, 63 (1976), 575–599.

_____. *Prison and Plantation: Crime, Justice, and Authority in Massachusetts and South Carolina, 1767–1878*. Chapel Hill: University of North Carolina, 1980.

"History of the Clemency Movement in California." Free Battered Women. Available at http://www.freebatteredwomen.org/resources.html.

Hoffer, Peter. *The Great New York Conspiracy of 1741: Slavery, Crime, and Colonial Law*. Lawrence: University Press of Kansas, 2003.

_____, and N.E.H. Hull. *Murdering Mothers: Infanticide in England and New England, 1558–1803*. New York: New York University Press, 1984.

Hoffman, Alice. "Honoring Labor's Martyred Heroes." *Los Angeles Times*, March 20, 2011.

Hoffman, Dennis. "Racial Disparities Without Racism: This Is How We Do It in Criminal Justice." Paper presented at the 70th annual meeting of the American Society of Criminology in San Francisco, California. November 19–22, 2014.

Hoffman, Michael. *They Were White and They Were Slaves: The Untold History of the Enslavement of Whites in Early America*. New York: Wiswell Ruffin House, 1992.

Holberg v. Texas, 38 S.W.3d 137 (2000).

____, 534 U.S. 972 (2001).

Holmes, Ronald and Stephen Holmes. *Murder in America*. Thousand Oaks: Sage, 2001.

"Homicide Suspects Return to Pennsylvania." *Indiana Gazette* [Indiana, Pennsylvania], October 10, 1993.

hooks, bell. *Ain't I a Woman: Black Women and Feminism*. Boston: South End Press, 1981.

Horne, DeAnna. "Either Way It Goes Down: America's 54 Women on Death Row in the Context of Patriarchy." Unpublished manuscript, Women and the Law Student Papers, University of Oregon School of Law, 2002 Available at http://law.uoregon.edu/assets/facultydocs/cforell/EitherWayitGoesDown.pdf.

"Horrible Murder." *Dubuque Daily Herald* [Dubuque, Iowa], July 23, 1868.

"Horrible Poisoning Case at Danville, Pennsylvania." *Whitewater Register* [Whitewater, Wisconsin], May 30, 1857.

Houston v. State, 531 So. 2d 598 (1988).

"How the Arizona Cowboy Sheriff Solved the Ranchman's Murder." *San Antonio Light*, April 8, 1928.

Howard, Clark. "The True Story of Barbara Graham." 2003. Available at http://murderpedia.org/female.G/g/graham-barbara.htm.

Howarth, Joan. "Executing White Masculinities: Learning from Karla Faye Tucker." *Oregon Law Review*, 81 (2002), 183–229.

____. "Feminism, Lawyering, and Death Row." *Southern California Review of Law and Women's Studies*, 2 (1992), 401–425.

Hoyt, Charles. *Witchcraft*. Carbondale: Southern Illinois University Press, 1981.

Huey, Jacklyn and Michael J. Lynch. "The Image of Black Women in Criminology: Historical Stereotypes as Theoretical Foundation." In Shaun Gabbidon and Helen Greene, eds., *Race, Crime, and Justice: A Reader* (pp. 127–140). New York: Routledge, 2005.

Huey, Laura. "The Abolition of Capital Punishment as a Feminist Issue." *Feminist Review*, 78 (2004), 175–180.

Hunt v. State, 753 So. 2d 609 (2000).

Huntingdon Journal [Huntingdon, Pennsylvania], December 4, 1885.

Hurst, Charles. *Social Inequality: Forms, Causes, and Consequences*. Boston: Allyn & Bacon, 2010.

"Husband and Wife, Leaving Baby Boy, Will Die Together in Electric Chair." *Logansport Weekly Reporter* [Logansport, Indiana], November 17, 1908.

"Husband Killer Asked Freedom After Escape" *Tyrone Daily* [Tyrone, Pennsylvania], January 27, 1987.

Hutchinson, Darren. "Ignoring the Sexualization of Race: Heteronormativity, Critical Race Theory and Anti-Racist Politics." *Buffalo Law Review*, 47 (1999), 1–116.

Hytrek, Nick. "Death Penalty Sought Against Iowa Woman." *Sioux City Journal*, June 19, 2012.

"I See by the Papers." *Ukiah Republican Press* [Ukiah, California], September 25, 1935.

Illinois v. Montanez, 273 Ill. App. 3d 844 (1995).

Illinois v. Pulliam, 176 Ill. 2d 261 (1997).

Illinois v. Pulliam, 206 Ill. 2d 218 (2002).

"Inadequate Representation." American Civil Liberties Union, October 18, 2003. Available at http://www.aclu.org/news/NewsPrint.cfm?ID=9313&c=62.

In Re Carty, 2004 Tex. Crim. App. LEXIS 1510 (2004).

In Re Catherine Thompson on Habeas Corpus, 2012 Cal. LEXIS 2526 (2012).

In Re Darlie Lynn Routier, 2008 Tex. Crim. App. LEXIS 1168 (2008).

In Re Maria Del Rosio Alfaro on Habeas Corpus, 2007 Cal. LEXIS 13400 (2007).

In the Matter of Sarah M. Victor, 31 Ohio St. 206 (1877).

"Indicted by Grand Jury, Sentenced to Death, All Within Six Hours." *Hattiesburg American* [Hattiesburg, Mississippi], October 4, 1921.

"Information Set for Release." *Lethbridge Herald,* July 9, 1992.

Ingersoll, Thomas. "Riches and Honor Were Rejected by Them as Loathsome Vomit: The Fear of Leveling in New England." In Carla Gardina Pestana and Sharon V. Salinger, eds., *Inequality in Early America* (pp. 46–66). Hanover: University Press of New England, 1999.

"Innocent but in Prison." *Los Angeles Times,* May 31, 2010.

Inverarity, James, Pat Lauderdale, and Barry Feld. *Law and Society: Sociological Perspectives on Criminal Law*. Boston: Little, Brown, 1983.

"Iowa Woman Removed from Death Row." *Cedar Rapids Gazette* [Cedar Rapids, Iowa], March 14, 2012.

Ireland, M. "Insanity and the Unwritten Law." *The American Journal of Legal History*, 32 (1988), 157–172.

Ireland, Robert. "The Libertine Must Die: Sexual Dishonor and the Unwritten Law in the Nineteenth-Century United States." *Journal of Social History*, 23 (1989), 27–44.

Jackman, Tom. "Shaken Baby Syndrome Itself Is Put on Trial in Fairfax Court." *Washington Post,* January 19, 2010.

Jackson, Daniel. "Last Woman Hanged in North Carolina Executed in Dallas." *Gaston Gazette*, August 1, 2008. Available at www.gastongazette.com/news/shipp_23338_article.html/gallows_county.html.

Jackson II, 547 So. 2d (1989).

Jackson III, 648 So. 2d 90 (1997).

Jackson IV, 704 So. 2d 501 (2000).

Jackson v. Alabama, 470 U.S. 1034 (1985).

Jackson v. Dugger, 547 So. 2d 1197 (1989).

Jackson v. Herring, 42 F.3d 1350 (1995).

Jackson v. State, 213 Ala. 143 (1925).

Jackson v. State, 158 So. 2d 133 (1963).

Jackson v. State, 459 So.2d 963 (1984).

Jackson v. State, 498 So. 2d 406 (1986).

Jackson v. State, 648 So. 2d 85 (1994).

James, Laura. "Women and the Death Penalty in New Mexico, a Historical Review: The Twice-Hanged Angel." 2005. Available at http://laurajames.typepad.com/clews/2005/11/women_and_the_d.html.

____. "Women and the Death Penalty in Ohio, an Historical Review: Proving Pearson's Theorem." 2005. Available at http://Laurajames.Typepad.Com/Clews/2005/10/Women_And_The_D.Html.

____. "Women and the Death Penalty in Alabama—Part 1: The Rare Victorian Hanging." Available at http://www.laurajames.com/Clews/2005/11/Women_And_The_D_1.Html. 2005.

Jane v. State, 3 Mo. 61 (1831) (*A Slave*).

Jaspin, Elliot. *Buried in the Bitter Waters: The Hidden History of Racial Cleansing in America*. New York: Basic Books, 2007.

Jennings, Rachel. "Celtic Women and White Guilt: Frankie Silver and Chipita Rodriguez in Folk Memory." *Melus*, 28 (2003), 17–37.

Jensen, Joan. *Loosening the Bonds: Mid-Atlantic Farm Women 1750–1850*. New Haven: Yale University Press, 1986.

Johnson, Edwin. "Selective Factors in Capital Punishment." *Social Forces*, 36 (1957), 165–169.

Johnson, Michael. "Smothered Slave Infants: Were Slave Mothers at Fault?" *The Journal of Southern History*, 47 (1981), 493–520.

Johnson, Paula. "At the Intersection of Injustice: Experience of African American Women in Crime and Sentencing." *The American University Journal of Gender and the Law*, 4 (1995), 1–76.

_____. *Inner Lives: Voices of African-American Women in Prison.* New York: New York University Press, 1995.
Johnson, Sheri. "Black Innocence and the White Jury." *Michigan Law Review,* 83 (1985), 1611–1708.
_____. "Racial Derogation in Prosecutors' Closing Arguments." In Dragan Milovanovic and Katheryn K. Russell, eds., *Petit Apartheid in the U.S. Criminal Justice System: The Dark Figure of Racism* (pp. 79–102). Durham: Carolina Academic Press, 2001.
Johnson, Sheri. "Symposium on Race and Criminal Law: *Batson* Ethics for Prosecutors and Trial Court Judges." *Chicago-Kent Law Review,* 73 (1998), 475–507.
Johnson v. State, 196 Miss. 402 (1944).
Johnson v. State, 261 Ga. 419 (1991).
Johnson v. State, 2005 Ala. Crim. App. LEXIS 58; (2005).
Johnson v. State, 2009 Ala. Crim. App. LEXIS 124 (2009).
Johnson v. United States, 860 F. Supp. 2d 663 (2012).
Jones, Ann. *Women Who Kill.* Boston: Beacon, 1996.
Jones, J. Harry, and Lola Sherman. "Four Beautiful Boys Are Dead." *San Diego Union-Tribune,* October 28, 1997.
Jones, Jeffrey. *The Death Penalty.* August 30, 2002. Available at http://www.gallup.com/poll/9913/Death-Penalty.aspx#1.
Jones v. Barnes, 463 U.S. 745 (1983).
Jones v. State, 1995 OK CR 81 (1995).
Jonsson, Patrick. "North Carolina Creates a New Route to Exoneration: An Official Innocence Commission Can Revisit Death Penalty Convictions." *The Christian Science Monitor,* October 10, 2006. Available at http://www.csmonitor.com/2006/0810/p01s01-usju.html?s=hns.
Jordon, Don, and Michael Walsh. *White Cargo: The Forgotten History of Britain's White Slaves in America.* New York: New York University Press, 2007.
Jordan, Emma. "Crossing the River of Blood Between Us: Lynching, Violence, Beauty, and the Paradox of Feminist History." *Journal of Gender, Race and Justice,* 3 (2000), 545–580.
Jordan, Winthrop. *White Over Black: American Attitudes Toward the Negro, 1550–1812.* New York: W.W. Norton, 1968.
"Josiah and Elizabeth Potts." Nevada State Library and Archives. Available at http://nevadaculture.org/docs/nsla/archives/prison/case27.htm.
Journal of the First Session of the House of Representatives of the Commonwealth of Pennsylvania. 1942. https://archive.org/details/journalofhouseof179899penn.
Journal of the Senate. April 12, 1935. Available at http://archive.flsenate.gov/data/Historical/Senate%20Journals/1930s/1935/8A/4_12_35.pdf.
Joyce, Fay. "Georgia Man Becomes Second Executed in 26 Days." *New York Times,* December 16, 1983.
Judd v. State, 41 Ariz. 176 (1932).
Judd, Sylvester. *History of Hadley: Including the Early History of Hatfield, South Hadley, Amherst, and Granby Massachusetts.* Springheld: H.R. Huntting, 1905.
"Judge Nixes Pa. Mom's Death Row Appeal in Starving." *The Sentinel* [Carlisle, Pennsylvania], September 1, 2011.
"Judge: No License for Teen Driver Who Hit, Killed Motorcyclist." *Curry Coastal Pilot* [Brookings, Oregon], May 4, 2011.
"Jury Convicts Couple of Murder." *Indiana Gazette* [Indiana, Pennsylvania], October 12, 1994.
"Jury Decides Woman Guilty of Poisoning." *Circleville Herald* [Circleville, Ohio], March 4, 1934.
"Jury May Give Woman Death Penalty." *Gettysburg Times* [Gettysburg, Pennsylvania], November 19, 1984.
"Jury Rules for Death Penalty in Spousal-Poisoning Case." *North County Times* [Escondido, California], November 13, 2003. Available at http://www.ncTimes, com/news/state-and-regional/article_657d545a-afee-522a-8d70-be03d4ffa95c.html.
"Jury Says Death for Woman Who Stomped Her Child to Death." *Gastonia Gaston Gazette* [Gastonia, North Carolina], April 21, 2002.
"Jury Sentences Kristi Fulgham to Death for Killing Husband." *Associated Press,* December 10, 2006.
"Just Sentence." *Connersville Daily Examiner* [Connersville, Indiana], September 13, 1890.
"Justice Canady Signs Order Creating Fla. Innocence Commission." *Theleger.com,* July 2, 2010.
"Justice for Margaret." *Spotsylvania Memory,* October 12, 2011. Available at http://spotsylvaniamemory.blogspot.com/2011/10/justice-for-margaret.html.
"Justice Stevens Harshly Critical of the Death Penalty." Death Penalty Information Center, August 7, 2005. Available at http://www.deathpenaltyinfo.org/node/498.
"Juvenile Life Without Parole (JLWOP)." Juvenile Law Center, November 28, 2013. Available at http://www.jlc.org/current-initiatives/promoting-fairness-courts/juvenile-life-without-parole-jlwop.
Kaczor, Bill. "Only Fla. Woman on Death Row Appeals Sentence." *Associated Press,* October 6, 2009.
_____. "Only Woman on Florida's Death Row Loses Appeal." *Associated Press,* March 11, 2010.
Kahler, Kathryn. "Women on Death Row." *Syracuse Herald Journal,* April 18, 1993.
Kaplan, David. "Capital Cases." *The National Law Journal,* 3 (February 18, 1985).
Kaplan, Steven. "Why Death Is Different: Minnesota's Experiment with Capital Punishment." *William Mitchell Law Review,* 30 (2004), 1113–1142.
Karlsen, Carol. *The Devil in the Shape of a Woman: Witchcraft in Colonial New England.* New York: W. W. Norton, 1998.
Katz, Michael, and Mark J. Stern. *Poverty in Twentieth-Century America.* America at the Millennium Project, Working Paper #7, November 2001. Available at http://www.sp2.upenn.edu/america2000/wp7all.pdf.
Kay, Marvin, and Lorin Cary. *Slavery in North Carolina, 1748–1775.* Chapel Hill: University of North Carolina Press, 1995.
Keeman, Susan. "Females on Death Row: Profiles of Two Females Currently on Death Row." *Associated Content,* May 25, 2006. Available at http://www.associatedcontent.com/article/33947/females_on_death_row_pg2.html?cat=17.
Keenan, Laura. "Reconstructing Rachel: A Case of Infanticide in the Eighteenth-Century Mid-Atlantic and the Vagaries of Historical Research." *The Pennsylvania Magazine of History and Biography,* 130 (2006), 361–385.
Keene, Michael. "The Woman Who Poisoned Her Family." *Rochester Crime History Examiner,* May 17, 2012. Available at http://www.examiner.com/article/the-woman-who-poisoned-her-family.
Keitner, Chimène. "Victim or Vamp? Images of Violent Women in the Criminal Justice System." *Columbia Journal of Gender and Law,* 11 (2002), 38–87.
Kelley, Lane. "Chaplain Guilty in Jail Escape Try." *Sun Sentinel,* September 24, 1992. Available at http://articles.sun-sentinel.com/1992-09-24/news/9201230388_1_prison-chaplain-inmate-sentence.
Kelly, Linda. "Disabusing the Definition of Domestic Abuse: How Women Batter Men and the Role of the Feminist State." *Florida State University Law Review,* 30 (2003), 791–855.
Kennedy, Randall. *Race, Crime, and the Law.* New York: Pantheon Books, 1997.
_____. *Interracial Intimacies: Sex, Marriage, Identity, and Adoption.* New York: Pantheon Books, 2003.
Kennedy, Raquel. *Wife Rape: Understanding the Response of Survivors and Service Providers.* Thousand Oaks: Sage, 1996.
Kennedy v. Louisiana, 554 U.S. 407 (2008).
Kerber, Linda and Jane DeHart. *Women's America: Refocusing the Past.* New York: Oxford University Press, 1991.
Kiefer, Michael. "Arizona Woman Released After Decades on Death Row." *Arizona Republic,* September 6, 2013. Available at http://www.azcentral.com/news/arizona/articles/20130906arizona-debra-milke-case-release-retrial-murder-trial-son.html.

Kiefer, Michael. "The Gray Area of Courtroom Conduct." *Arizona Republic*, October 28–29, 2013. Available at http://www.azcentral.com/news/arizona/articles/20131027milkekrone-prosecutors-conduct-day1.html.

"Killed Her Baby and Cooked It." *Orleans Democrat*, December 13, 1892.

Kim, Dara. "Justice Pariente Beats Drum for Eyewitness Expert Testimony." *News Service of Florida*, June 26, 2014. Available at http://miami.cbslocal.com/2014/06/26/justice-pariente-beats-drum-for-eyewitness-expert-testimony/.

Kimbrough, Pat. "Date Set for Baby Sitter's Murder Trial." *High Point Enterprise* [High Point, North Carolina], March 13, 2007.

King, Wilma. "Mad Enough to Kill: Enslaved Women, Murder, and Southern Courts." *The Journal of African American History*, 92 (2007), 37–56.

King v. Kentucky, No. 2012-CA-001985-MR (July 18, 2014).

Kirchmeier, Jeffrey. "Dead Innocent: The Death Penalty Abolitionist Search for a Wrongful Execution." *Tulsa Law Review*, 42 (2006), 403–435.

_____, Stephen Greenwald, Harold Reynolds, and Jonathan Sussman. "Vigilante Justice: Prosecutor Misconduct in Capital Cases." *Wayne Law Review*, 55 (2010), 1327–1385.

Kirkpatrick, James. "Case Provides Chilling Glimpse of a Teenage Murderer." *The Capital*, May 13, 1996.

Klarman, Michael. *From Jim Crow to Civil Rights: The Supreme Court and the Struggle for Racial Equality*. New York: Oxford University Press, 2004.

Klein, Dorie. "The Etiology of Female Crime: A Review of the Literature." In Barbara Price and Natalie Sokoloff, eds., *Criminal Justice System and Women* (pp. 3–30). New York: McGraw Hill, 1995.

Koehler, Lyle. "The Case of the American Jezebels: Anne Hutchinson and Female Agitation During the Years of Antinomian Turmoil, 1636–1640." *William and Mary Quarterly*, 31 (1974), 55–78.

Koepplinger, Susanne. "Sex Trafficking of American Indian Women and Girls in Minnesota." *University of St. Thomas Law Review*, 6 (2008), 129–137.

Kohn, Sally. "Greasing the Wheel: How the Criminal Justice System Hurts Gay, Lesbian, Bisexual and Transgendered People and Why Hate Crime Laws Won't Save Them." *New York University Review of Law and Social Change*, 27 (2002), 257–280.

Kolchin, Peter. *American Slavery: 1619–1877*. New York: Hill and Wang, 2003.

Kopec, Janice. "Avoiding a Death Sentence in the American Legal System: Get a Woman to Do It." *Capital Defense Journal*, 15 (2003), 353–362.

Korengold, Michael, Todd Noteboom, and Sara Gurwitch. "And Justice for Few: The Collapse of the Capital Clemency System in the United States." *Hamline Law Review*, 20 (1996), 349–369.

Kraemer, John. "An Empirical Examination of the Factors Associated with the Commutation of State Death Row Prisoners' Sentences Between 1986 and 2005." *American Criminal Law Review*, 45 (2008), 1389–1417.

Kraybill, Jeanine. "Death Penalty: How Newspaper Coverage Has Perpetuated Negative Stereotypes About Female Violence & Gender Roles." Thinking Gender Papers, UCLA Center for the Study of Women, University of California, Los Angeles, February 1, 2009. Available at http://escholarship.org/uc/item/8rm5m2dq.

Krajicek, David. "Sue Basso." *Crime Library*. Available at http://www.crimelibrary.com/notorious_murders/women/suzanne_basso/index.html.

_____. "Suffragists Back Wife Who Murdered Husband in 1913 Love Triangle." *New York Daily News*, August 22, 2010. Available at http://www.nydailynews.com/news/crime/suffragists-back-wife-murdered-husband-1913-love-triangle-article-1.203509.

Kroll, Michael. *Killing Justice: Government Misconduct and the Death Penalty*. 1992. Available at www.deathpenaltyinfo.org/article.php?scid=45&did=529.

Kubik, Jeffrey, and John Moran. "Lethal Elections: Gubernatorial Politics and the Timing of Executions." *Journal of Law and Economics*, 46 (2003), 1–25.

Kudlac, Christopher. *Public Executions: The Death Penalty and the Media*. Westport: Praeger, 2007.

Kuncl, Tom. *Death Row Women: The Shocking True Stories of America's Most Vicious Female Killers*. New York: Pocket Books, 1994.

KVAL.com. "Prosecutors Allege Girl Died After Being Tortured." December 11, 2009. Available at http://www.kval.com/news/local/79003987.html.

"Ky. Supreme Court Upholds 3 Convictions." *Associated Press*, April 23, 2009.

Labastida v. Nevada, 112 Nev. 1502 (1996).

Ladd, Donna. "Miss. Supreme Court Reverses Michelle Byrom's Conviction, Delays Second Execution." *Jackson Free Press*, March 31, 2014. Available at http://www.jacksonfreepress.com/news/2014/mar/31/miss-supreme-court-reverses-michelle-byroms-convic/.

LaGanza, Maria. "Execution Moratorium Declared." *Los Angeles Times*, February 12, 2014.

Landress v. State, 600 N.E.2d 938 (1992).

Landress v. State, 638 N.E.2d 787 (1994).

Lang, Andrew. "Man Killed by Police; Girl Held." *Evening Capital* [Pennsylvania], January 6, 1972.

Lanier, Charles. "Adding to the Story of What We Know About Capital Punishment: A Review of *Women and the Death Penalty* and *Deathquest*." *Journal of Criminal Justice and Popular Culture*, 7 (1999), 30–37.

LaPlante, Eve. *American Jezebel: The Uncommon Life of Anne Hutchinson, the Woman Who Defied the Puritans*. New York: HarperCollins, 2004.

Larson, Kate. *The Assassin's Accomplice: Mary Surratt and the Plot to Kill Abraham Lincoln*. Philadelphia: Basic Books, 2008.

Larzelere v. State, 676 So. 2d 394 (1996).

Laska, Lewis. "Fact-Based Death Penalty Research." *Tennessee Journal of Law and Policy*, 4 (2007), 103–112.

_____. *Legal Executions in Tennessee: A Comprehensive Registry, 1782–2009*. Jefferson: McFarland, 2011.

"Last Week's Ft. Smith Letters." *Indian Chieftain* [Vinita, Indian Territory], March 5, 1896.

Latimer, John. "Defense of Convicted Killer Bradley Martin to Cost Lebanon County Taxpayers." *Lebanon Daily News* [Lebanon, Pennsylvania], June 6, 2013. Available at http://www.ldnews.com/latestnews/ci_23403842/defense-convicted-killer-bradley-martin-cost-lebanon-county.

Launitz-Schurer, Leopold. "Slave Resistance in Colonial New York: An Interpretation of Daniel Horsmanden's New York Conspiracy." *Phylon*, 41 (1980), 137–152.

"Law Will Not Execute Woman." *Washington Herald* [Washington, Indiana], June 6, 1912.

Lawes, Lewis. *Legal Executions in Tennessee: A Comprehensive Registry, 1782–2009*. Jefferson: McFarland, 2011.

Leadership Conference on Civil Rights. *The Bush Administration Takes Aim: Civil Rights Under Attack*. 2003. Available at www.civilrights.org/publications/reports/taking_aim/bush_takes_aim.pdf.

Lear, Calvin. "The LA Execution of Toni Jo Hood." *The Advocate*, September 22, 1995.

"Louise Thomas, Phila., Is to Be Electrocuted." *Lebanon Semi-Weekly News* [Lebanon, Pennsylvania], September 15, 1924.

Lee, Alfred. *History of the City of Columbus, Capital of Ohio*. New York: Munsell, 1892.

Lee, Henry. "Sex-Torture Duo Get Death Penalty." *San Francisco Chronicle*, September 26, 2002.

Lee, Jean. "The Problem of Slave Community in the Eighteenth-Century Chesapeake." *The William and Mary Quarterly*, 43 (1986), 334–361.

Lee, Renee. "Supreme Court Rejects Plea from British Woman on Death Row." *Houston and Texas News*, May 3, 2010.

Lee, Suevon. "Death Sentence for Emilia Carr." *Ocala Star Banner*, February 22, 2011.
Legislative Council of Maryland. *Report of the Legislative Council Committee on Capital Punishment*. 1962. Available at https://search.library.wisc.edu/catalog/99100739240021 21.
Leon, Luis. "Radical Feminists Jeopardize Feminism." *Miami Herald*, August 12, 1994.
Lerner, Gerda. *The Creation of Patriarchy*. New York: Oxford University Press, 1986.
Lester, Will. "Jurors Say They Follow Beliefs, Not Instructions." *Chicago Sun Times*, October 24, 1998.
Leve, Ariel. "The Pink Mile." *Sunday Times* (London), August 31, 2008.
Lewis, Dorothy, Jonathan H. Pincus, Marilyn Feldman, Lori Jackson, and Barbara Bard. "Psychiatric, Neurological, and Psychoeducational Characteristics of 15 Death Row Inmates in the United States." *American Journal Psychiatry*, 143 (1986), 838–845.
Lewis v. Commonwealth, 267 Va. 302, 593 S.E.2d 220 (2004).
Lewis v. Virginia, 267 Va. 302 (2004).
Lewis v. Virginia, 543 U.S. 904 (2004).
Lewis v. Warden of the Fluvanna Correctional Center, 2007 Va. LEXIS 68 (2007).
LibertadLatino. http://www.libertadlatina.org/Index.htm.
Liebman, James, Jeffrey Fagan, Valerie West, and Jonathan Lloyd. "Capital Attrition, Error Rates in Capital Cases, 1973–1995." *Texas Law Review*, 78 (2000), 1839–1865.
"Life Goes On: The Historic Rise in Life Sentences in America." The Sentencing Project, 2013. Available at http://sentencingproject.org/Doc/Publications/Inc_Life%20Goes %20On%202013.Pdf.
Lindell, Chuck. "Henderson Granted New Trial in Baby's 1994 Death." *Austin American-Statesman* [Austin, Texas], December 5, 2010. Available at http://www.statesman.com/news/news/local/henderson-granted-new-trial-in-babys-1994-death/nTNRC/.
Lindemann, Barbara. "To Ravish and Carnally Know: Rape in Eighteenth-Century Massachusetts." *Signs: Journal of Women, Culture, and Society*, 10 (1984), 63–82.
Lindenmeyer, Kriste. *A Right to Childhood: The U.S. Children's Bureau and Child Welfare, 1912–1946*. Urbana: University of Illinois Press, 1997.
Linder, Douglas. "The Rosenberg Trial. Famous Trials." 2008. Available at Http://Law2.Umkc.Edu/Faculty/Projects/Ftrials/Rosenb/ROSENB.HTM.
Linders, Annulla, and Alana Van Gundy-Yoder. "Gall, Gallantry, and the Gallows: Capital Punishment and the Social Construction of Gender, 1840–1920." *Gender and Society*, 22 (2008), 324–348.
Lindsey, Linda. *Gender Roles: A Sociological Perspective*. New York: Pearson, 1997.
Liptak, Adam. "A Lawyer Known Best for Losing Capital Cases." *New York Times*, May 18, 2010.
———. "New Look at Death Sentences and Race." *New York Times*, April 28, 2008. Available at http://www.nyTimes.com/2008/04/29/us/29bar.html?_r=2&.
Lisa Marie Roberts v. Nancy Howton, No. 3-08-cv-01433-MA (April 29, 2014).
Litchfield, Lynn. "Unfit for Execution." *Newsweek*, August 27, 2010. Available at http://www.newsweek.com/2010/08/27/my-turn-teresa-lewis-doesn-t-deserve-to-die.html.
Litwack, Leon. *North of Slavery: The Negro in the Free States, 1790–1860*. Chicago: University of Chicago Press, 1961.
"Lizzie Halliday Dead." *New York Times*, June 19, 1918.
"Lizzie Halliday's Bad Temper." *New York Times*, September 2, 1895.
Lockett v. Ohio, 438 U.S. 586 (1978).
Lofquist, William. "Putting Them There, Keeping Them There, and Killing Them: An Analysis of State-Level Variations in Death Penalty Intensity." *Iowa Law Review*, 87 (2002), 1505–1557.

"Lois A. Thacker." Indiana Department of Corrections. Available at http://www.in.gov/apps/indcorrection/ofs/ofs?lname=Thacker&fname=Lois&search1.x=26&search1.y=8.
"Louisiana Couple Admit They Killed Husband." *Burlington Daily Times* [Burlington, North Carolina], July 9, 1927.
Logue, Victoria, and Frank Logue. *Touring the Back Roads of North and South Georgia*. Winston-Salem: John F. Blair, 1997.
Lohr, David. "The True Story of Ray and Faye Copeland." *True Crime Library*. Available at http://www.crimelibrary.com/serial_killers/partners/copelands/index.html.
Lougbridge, Nancy. "Chloe's Story." Available at www.carothersonline.com/Chloes%20Story.html.
Louisiana Ex Rel. Francis v. Resweber, 329 U.S. 459 (1947).
Louisiana v. LaCraze, 99-0584 (La. 01/25/02).
Lucio v. State, 351 S.W.3d 878 (2011).
Lucio v. Texas, 132 S. Ct. 2712 (2012).
Lucy v. State, 8 Mo. 134 (1843).
Lujan, Carol. "Women Warriors: American Indian Women, Crime and Alcohol." *Women and Criminal Justice*, 7 (1995), 1–9.
Luo, Michael. "Small Town Justice." *Del Rio News Herald* [Del Rio, Texas], July 16–18, 2002.
MacEgan, Matthew. "Mississippi Throws Out Murder Conviction of Death Row Inmate Michelle Byrom." *World Socialist Web Site*, April 2, 2004. Available at http://www.wsws.org/en/articles/2014/04/02/byro-a02.html.
MacKinnon, Catherine. "Toward Feminist Jurisprudence." *Stanford Law Review*, 34 (1983), 703–737.
"Man Gets Death in Slaying." *Oxnard Press-Courier* [Oxnard, California], October 25, 1975.
"Man Gets 25-Year Term in Wealthy Widow's Death." *St. Petersburg Times* [Florida], July 8, 1987.
Mandery, Evan. *Capital Punishment: A Balanced Examination*. Sudbury: Jones & Bartlett Publishers, 2005.
"Margaret Harris Meets Her Death Firmly at Calhoun, GA." *New York Times*, October 20, 1883.
Marger, Martin. *Social Inequality: Patterns and Processes*. New York: McGraw-Hill, 2014.
"Maria Is Told the News." *New York Times*, April 22, 1896.
Marietta, Jack, and Gail Rowe. *Troubled Experiment: Crime and Justice in Philadelphia, 1682–1800*. Philadelphia: University of Pennsylvania Press, 2006.
"Marilyn Plantz Clemency Letter." American Civil Liberties Union, April 19, 2001. Available at https://www.aclu.org/capital-punishment/marilyn-plantz-clemency-letter.
Mario Dion Woodward v. Alabama, 571 U. S. _ Justice Sotomayor dissenting. 2013.
Marshall, Peter. "A Comparative Analysis of the Right to Appeal." *Duke Journal of Comparative & International Law*, 22 (2011), 1–45.
Marshall, Thurgood. "Remarks on the Death Penalty Made at the Judicial Conference of the Second Circuit." *Columbia Law Review*, 86 (1986), 1–8.
Marin, Carol. "A Commuted Sentence, and a Life Reborn." *Chicago Sun-Times*, June 8, 2008.
Martin, John. *Chester (And Its Vicinity) Delaware County, in Pennsylvania: With Genealogical Sketches of Some Old Families Philadelphia*. 1923.
Martinez, Laura. "Harlingen Woman to Stay on Death Row." *Brownsville Herald*, February 15, 2011.
Marquart, James, Sheldon Ekland-Olson, and Jonathan Sorensen. *The Rope, the Chair, and the Needle: Capital Punishment in Texas, 1923–1990*. Austin: University of Texas Press, 1994.
Marshall, Lawrence. "The Innocence Revolution and the Death Penalty." *Ohio State Journal of Criminal Law*, 1 (2004), 573–584.
"Martha Bassett and Mary Powell." *Pennsylvania Gazette*, January 6, 1752.
Martin, William. *History of Franklin County: A Collection of Reminiscences of The Early Settlement of the County*. Columbus: Follett, Foster, 1858.

"Mary Booth's Sentence Commuted." *New York Times,* November 16, 1882.

"Mary Farmer Dies in Electric Chair." *San Francisco Call,* March 30, 1909.

Mary v. State, 5 Mo. 71 (1837).

Maryland Gazette, April 22, 1746.

Maryland Gazette, January 2, 16, 23, 1752.

Massillon Independent [Massillon, Ohio], December 14, 1896.

Mathieson, Anna-Rose, and Samuel R. Gross. "Review for Error." *Law Probability & Risk,* 2 (2003), 259–268.

Maxwell-Stuart, P. G. *Witchcraft in Europe and the New World.* New York: Palgrave, 2001.

Mays, Dorothy. *Women in Early America: Struggle, Survival and Freedom in a New World.* Santa Barbara: ABC-CLIO, 2004.

McCarthy v. Texas, 65 S.W.3d 47 (2001).

McCarthy v. Texas, 536 U.S. 972 (2002).

McCarthy v. Texas, 545 U.S. 1117 (2005).

McCarthy v. Thaler, 2011 U.S. Dist. LEXIS 49798 (2011).

McCartney, Martha. *A Study of the Africans and African Americans on Jamestown Island and at Green Spring, 1619–1803.* February 2003. Williamsburg: Colonial Williamsburg Foundation. Available at http://www.nps.gov/jame/history culture/upload/African%20Americans%20on%20James town%20Island.pdf.

McCleskey v. Kemp, 481 U.S. 279 (1987).

McCollum v. State, 74 So. 2d 74 (1954).

McConnell, Dugald, and Brian Todd. "Virginia Puts Woman to Death by Lethal Injection." CNNwww, September 4, 2010. Available at http://www.cnn.com/2010/CRIME/09/23/virginia.woman.execution/.

McCord, David. "Lightning Still Strikes: Evidence from the Popular Press That Death Sentencing Continues to Be Unconstitutionally Arbitrary More Than Three Decades After *Furman.*" *Brook Law Review,* 71 (2005), 797–927.

McCormick, John. "Why Parents Kill." *Newsweek.* November 14, 1994.

McCowan, Karen. "Child Killer Gets Death." *The Register-Guard* [Eugene, Oregon], February 25, 2011.

———. "Testimony: Many Reported Suspicions of Sbuse." *The Register-Guard* [Eugene, Oregon], February 16, 2011.

McDonough, Daniel. *Christopher Gadsden and Henry Laurens: The Parallel Lives of Two American Patriots.* Sellinsgrove: Susquehanna University Press, 2000.

McGonigle, Steve, Holly Becka, Jennifer LaFleur and Tim Wyatt. "Race Bias Pervades Jury Selection: Prosecutors Routinely Bar Blacks, Study Finds." *Dallas Morning News,* March 9, 2005.

McKane v. Durston, 153 U.S. 684 (1894).

McKeehan, Wallace. *The Hanging of Chipita Rodriquez.* 2006. Available at www.tamu.edu/ccbn/dewitt/irishchipita.htm.

McKenna, B. "Jim Moss, a Negro League Player, Executed." *Baseball History,* May 5, 2010. Available at http://baseballhistoryblog.com/tag/jim-moss/.

McLaurin, Melton. *Celia, a Slave.* Athens: University of Georgia Press, 1991.

McMahon, Kathy. "The Invisible Women of the Great Depression." EzineArticleswww, January 2009. Available at http://ezinearticles.com/?The-Invisible-Women-of-the-Great—Depression&id=1888970.

McManus, Melanie. "Oh, Baby: Audrey Edmunds Is Rebuilding Her Life After Her Murder Conviction Was Overturned." *Madison Magazine,* July 2009. Available at http://www.madisonmagazine.com/Madison-Magazine/July-2009/Oh-Baby/.

McNair, Glenn. *Criminal Injustice: Slaves and Free Blacks in Georgia's Criminal Justice System.* Charlottesville: University of Virginia Press, 2009.

———. "Slave Women, Capital Crime, and Criminal Justice in Georgia." *Georgia Historical Quarterly,* 93 (2009), 135–158.

McNeely, R. L., and Gloria Robinson-Simpson. "The Truth About Domestic Violence: A Falsely Framed Issue," *Social Work,* 32 (1984), 485–490.

McPherson, James. "Comparing the Two Reconstructions." *Princeton Alumni Weekly,* 16 (1999), 18–19.

McRae, Sherwin. *Calendar of Virginia State Papers and Other Manuscripts from August 11, 1792 to December 31, 1793, Volume VI.* Richmond: A.R. Micou, 1886.

McRoberts, Susan. "Woman Gets Death for Poisoning." *San Gabriel Valley Tribune* [California], January 12, 2004.

Medrano, Lourdes. "Arizona Justice: Shawna Forde Death Sentence a Rebuke to Border Vigilantes." *Christian Science Monitor,* February 23, 2011.

Meeropol, Michael, and Robert Meeropol. "The Essential Lessons of the Rosenberg Case." *Los Angeles Times,* October 5, 2008. Available at http://articles.laTimes,com/2008/oct/05/opinion/oe-meeropol5.

Meeropol, Robert. "Kinship with Manning." *Los Angeles Times,* August 12, 2013.

Menard, Russell. "The Maryland Slave Population, 1658 to 1730: A Demographic Profile of Blacks in Four Counties." *The William and Mary Quarterly,* 32 (1975), 29–54.

Mental Illness and the Death Penalty. Death Penalty Information Center, July 18, 2012. Retrieved from http://www.death penaltyinfo.org/mental-illness-and-death-penalty?did=782&scid=66.

Merle, Renae. "Texas Child Killer's Guilt in Doubt." *Dallas Morning News,* January 16, 1999. Available at http://www.texas-justice.com/dalnews/earle990116.html.

Michaelowski, Raymond. *Order, Law and Crime, An Introduction to Criminology.* New York: Random House, 1985.

Michaud v. U.S., 537 U.S. 867 (2002).

Michelle Ann Binsz and Steven William Binsz v. State, 1984 OK CR 28 (1984).

Mickenberg, Ira. "Drunk, Sleeping, and Incompetent Lawyers: Is It Possible to Keep Innocent People Off Death Row?" *Dayton Law Review,* 29 (2004), 319–327.

Middlesboro Daily News. "Horse Tonic Becomes Focus in Widow's Arsenic Trial." July 24, 1980.

"Milestones." *Time Magazine.* January 30, 1933.

Milke v. Ryan, 2010 U.S. Dist. LEXIS 12881 (2010).

Millbrook Round Table. "Died on the Scaffold." October 15, 1892.

Miller and Sanders v. State, 1977 OK CR 14 (1977).

Miller v. State, 782 So. 2d 426 (2001).

Miller, Barbara. "Woman Convicted in Palmyra Murder to Get New Penalty Hearing." Pennlivewww. Available at http://www.pennlive.com/midstate/index.ssf/2010/08/new_penalty_hearing_ordered_fo.html. August 4, 2010.

Miller, Vivien. "The Vestige of Institutional Sexism? Paternalism, Equal Rights and the Death Penalty in Twentieth and Twenty-First Century Sunbelt America: The Case of Florida." *Journal of American Studies,* 38 (2004), 391–424.

———. "Wife-Killers and Evil Temptresses: Gender, Pardons and Respectability in Florida, 1889–1914." *The Florida Historical Quarterly,* 75 (1996), 44–68.

———. *Crime, Sexual Violence and Clemency: Florida's Pardon Board and Penal System in the Progressive Era.* Gainesville: University Press of Florida, 2000.

Millett, Kate. *Sexual Politics.* New York: Doubleday. 1970.

Millies, Stephen. "What They Don't Want You to Know." *Workers World,* June 23, 2010. Available at http://www.workers.org/2010/world/korea_0701/.

Milner, Paul. "Irish Immigration to North America: Before, During, and After the Famine." 2011. Available at http://broadcast.lds.org/elearning/FHD/Community/en/Community/Paul_Milner/Irish_Migration_to_NA-2011.pdf.

Minutes of the Provincial Council of Pennsylvania, from the Organization to the Termination of the Proprietary Government [March 10, 1683–September 27, 1775]. 1851–1852. Philadelphia: J. Steverns. Available at www.archive.org/stream/minutesofprovinc00penn#page/n5/mode/1up.

Mintz, Jonathan. "Note: *Batson v. Kentucky*: A Half Step in the Right Direction (Racial Discrimination and Peremptory Challenges Under the Heavier Confines of Equal Protection)." *Cornell Law Review,* 72 (1987), 1026–1046.

Miracle, Amanda. *Rape and Infanticide in Maryland, 1634–1689: Gender and Class in the Courtroom Contestation of Patriarchy on the Edge of the English Atlantic.* Unpublished doctoral dissertation, Bowling Green State University, 2008.

"Missouri Sensation." *Moberly Weekly Monitor* [Moberly, Missouri], November 21, 1901.

"Missouri Woman Convicted." *Reno Evening Gazette*, May 21, 1897.

Mitchell, Mitch. "Arlington Woman's Execution Set for Wednesday." *Star-Telegram*, September 16, 2014. Available at http://www.star-telegram.com/2014/09/15/6122414/arlington-womans-execution-set.html?rh=1.

Mogul, Joey. "The Dykier, the Butcher, the Better: The State's Use of Homophobia and Sexism to Execute Women in the United States." *New York City Law Review*, 8 (2005), 473–493.

_____. "Lesbians and the Death Penalty: Comments from 'Race, Class, Gender and the PIC.'" Available at http://womenandprison.org/sexuality/view/lesbians_and_the_death_penalty_comments_from_race_class_gender_and_the_pic/.

_____, Andrea Ritchie, and Kay Whitlock. *Queer (In)Justice: The Criminalization of the LGBT People in the United States.* New York: Beacon, 2011.

"Mom Gets Death Penalty for Daughter's Slaying." *Associated Press*, July 11, 2008.

"Mom Loses Custody, Kills Kids." *Daily Herald* [Chicago], August 31, 1987.

"Mom to Die for Starving Her Daughter to Death." *Titusville Herald* [Titusville, Pennsylvania], November 15, 2000.

Moore v. Dempsey, 261 U.S. 86 (1923).

Moran, Jack. "Long Route to Ultimate Penalty." *The Register-Guard* [Eugene, Oregon], February 26, 2011.

"More Tainted Testimony from Oklahoma Forensics Lab." American Civil Liberties Union, May 8, 2001. Available at https://www.aclu.org/racial-justice_prisoners-rights_womens-rights_immigrants-rights/more-tainted-testimony-oklahoma-fore.

Morgan, Denise. "Jack Johnson Versus the American Racial Hierarchy." In Annette Gordon-Reed (Ed.) *Race on Trial: Law and Justice in American History* (pp. 77–102). New York: Oxford University Press, 2002.

Morgan, Kenneth. "Shipping Patterns and the Atlantic Trade of Bristol, 1749–1770." *William and Mary Quarterly*, 46 (1989), 506–538.

_____. "Slave Sales in Colonial Charleston." *The English Historical Review*, 113 (1998), 905–927.

Morgan v. Illinois, 504 U.S. 719 (1992).

Morgan v. State, 171 Tex. Crim. 187 (1961).

Moriarty, Jane. "Wonders of the Invisible World: Prosecutorial Syndrome and Profile Evidence in the Salem Witchcraft Trials." *Vermont Law Review*, 26 (2001), 43–99.

Moriarty, Linnda. "Ergotism: The Satan Loosed in Salem?" *Science*, 192 (1976), 21–26.

Morin, Monte. "Domestic Violence Checkup." *Los Angeles Times*, January 22, 2013.

Morris, Robert, and Elizabeth Nuxoll. *The Papers of Robert Morris: January 1–October 30, 1784, Volume 9.* Pittsburgh: University of Pittsburgh Press, 1995.

Morris, Thomas. *Southern Slavery and the Law: 1619–1860.* Chapel Hill: University of North Carolina, 1996.

Moskowitz, Seymour. "Dickens Redux: How American Child Labor Law Became a Con Game." *Whittier Journal of Child and Family Advocacy*, 10 (2010), 89–154.

Mosley, Joe. "Freed Death Row Inmate Back in Prison." *Eugene Register-Guard* [Eugene, Oregon], May 18, 2002.

"Mother and Son Both on Death Row." *Jacksonville Journal Courier* [Jacksonville, Illinois], May 29, 1977.

"Mother and Son Sentenced to Death." *Palo Alto Pilot*, December 9, 1875.

"Mother Gets Death Penalty." *New York Times*, October 23, 1983.

"Mother Guilty in Slaying of 2 Sons for Insurance." *New York Times*, October 15, 1983.

Moten, Derryn. *A Gruesome Warning to Black Girls: The August 16, 1912, Execution of Virginia Christian.* Unpublished doctoral dissertation, University of Iowa, 1997.

Mott, Ronni. "An Innocent Woman? Michelle Byrom Vs. Mississippi." *Jackson Free Press*, March 19, 2014. Available at http://www.jacksonfreepress.com/news/2014/mar/19/innocent-woman-michelle-byrom-vs-mississippi/.

Moyer, Virginia. "Screening for Intimate Partner Violence and Abuse of Elderly and Vulnerable Adults: A U.S. Preventive Services Task Force Recommendation Statement." *Annals of Internal Medicine*, January 2013. Available at http://www.uspreventiveservicestaskforce.org/uspstf12/ipvelder/ipvelderfinalrs.pdf.

"Mrs. Agnes Meyers' Life in the Hands of Governor Folk." *Washington Post*, July 15, 1906.

"Mrs. Dolbow on Stand at Trial." *Chester Times* [Chester, Pennsylvania], February 6, 1936.

"Mrs. Eula Thompson to Marry Newbutcher." *Burlington Daily Times* [Burlington, North Carolina], November 23, 1928.

"Mrs. Farmer Dies Praying in Chair." *New York Times*, March 30, 1909.

"Mrs. Farmer Seventh Woman to Be Executed in New York." *New Castle News* [New Castle, Pennsylvania], March 29, 1909.

"Mrs. Frost and Guenkel Held." *Gettysburg Times* [Gettysburg, Pennsylvania], August 14, 1912.

"Mrs. Gulligan Found Guilty of Murder." *Lowell Sun* [Lowell, Massachusetts], July 14, 1917.

"Mrs. Rogers Hanged, Bell Upholding Law." *New York Times*, December 9, 1905.

"Mrs. Ruth Judd Gives Up and Pleads Self Defense in Confession of Murder." *Coshocton Tribune* [Coshocton, Ohio], October 24, 1931.

"Mrs. Smith Pleads Not Guilty." *New York Times*, October 16, 1878.

"Mrs. Wakefield Found Guilty." *New Brunswick Times* [New Brunswick, New Jersey], November 1, 1913.

"Murder Born in Home of Poverty." *La Crosse Tribune* [La Crosse, Wisconsin], November 19, 1913.

"Murderer of Her Husband to Die for Love Crime." *Laredo Times* [Laredo, Texas], March 1, 1931.

"Murderess Is Spared Execution." *Beckley Post-Herald* [Beckley, West Virginia], October 16, 1959.

"Murderess Reprieved." *New York Times*, July 27, 1869.

"Murderess Reprieved." *Fitchburg Sentinel* [Fitchburg, Massachusetts], August 20, 2005.

"Murderess Saved from Death Chair." *New Brunswick Times* [New Brunswick, New Jersey], April 25, 1913.

"Murderess Seeks Release." *New York Times*, January 23, 1914.

Murrin, John. "Things Fearful to Name: Bestiality in Early America." *Explorations in Early American Culture Pennsylvania History: A Journal of Mid-Atlantic Studies*, 65 (1998), 8–43.

"My 11 Years' Turmoil, by Wife Cleared of Killing Girl." *London Times*, December 6, 1994.

"My New Baby Was Torn from My Arms." *London Daily Mail*, December 6, 1994.

Myers, Amrita. "Sisters in Arms: Slave Women's Resistance to Slavery in the United States." *Past Imperfect*, 5 (1996), 141–174.

Myers, Karl. "Practical Lackey: The Impact of Holding Execution After a Long Stay on Death Row Unconstitutional Under *Lackey v. Texas*." *Dickinson Law Review*, 106 (2002), 647–677.

Myers, Ryan. "Kenisha Berry Faces New Charges for Second Infant." *Beaumont Enterprise* [Beaumont, Texas], November 13, 2007. Available at http://www.tdcaa.com/node/1480.

National Registry of Exonerations. Available at http://www.law.umich.edu/special/exoneration/Pages/about.aspx.

National Registry of Exonerations. Glossary. Available at http://www.law.umich.edu/special/exoneration/Pages/glossary.aspx#FC.

Navas, Deborah. *Murdered by His Wife: A History with Documentation of the Joshua Spooner Murder and Execution of His Wife, Bathsheba, Who Was Hanged in Worcester, Massachusetts, 2 July 1778.* Amherst: University of Massachusetts Press, 1999.

Neelley v. State, 642 So. 2d 494 (1993).

"Negress, Two Negro Men Go to Gas Chamber; Two Confess, One Denies." *Burlington Daily Times* [Burlington, North Carolina], December 29, 1944.

"Negro Girl Hanged." *Newark Daily Advocate*, October 13, 1888.

Nelson v. State, 155 N.J. 487 (1998).

Nelson, William. *The Common Law of Colonial America, Volume 1, the Chesapeake and New England, 1607–1660.* New York: Oxford University Press, 2008.

Nesbitt, J. "Classic Arsenic and Old Lace Murderess a Victim, Too?" *Orlando Sentinel Journal.* November 9, 1984.

Neuzil, Anna. *The Plymouth Colony Archive Project: Women in Plymouth Colony, 1633–1668.* 1998. Available at www.histarch.uiuc.edu/plymouth/PCR.htm.

Nevada Department of Corrections. Available at http://www.doc.nv.gov/notis/detail.php?offender_id=19090.

Neville, John. *The Press, the Rosenbergs, and the Cold War.* Westport: Greenwood, 1995

"New Evidence of Frances Newton's Innocence Ignored by Courts and TX Governor." *Justice Denied: The Magazine for the Wrongfully Convicted*, 29 (2005), 4–5.

"New Jersey Justice." *New York Times*, June 26, 1872.

New Jersey v. Antonio Fiore, 85 N.J.L. 311 (1913).

"New Mode of Hanging," *Adams Sentinel* [Gettysburg, Pennsylvania], November 29, 1847.

"New Sentencing Ordered for Pennsylvania Woman on Death Row." *Associated Press*, September 25, 2014. Available at http://www.pennlive.com/midstate/index.ssf/2014/09/new_sentencing_ordered_for_pen.html.

New York Correction History Society Timeline on Executions by Hanging in New York State. 1813–1815, 7. Available at http://www.correctionhistory.org/hangings/hangdates7.html.

New York v. Maria Barberi, 149 N.Y. 256 (1896).

Newman, Sandra, Eric Rayz, and Scott Friedman. "Capital Sentencing: The Effect of Adding Aggravators to Death Penalty Statutes in Pennsylvania." *University of Pittsburg Law Review*, 65 (2004), 457–506.

"News." *Delphi Carroll County Citizen* [Delphi, Indiana], December 17, 1892.

"News by Mail." *Galveston Flakes Semi Weekly* [Galveston, Texas], December 9, 1868.

"News of This Week." *Humeston New Era* [Humeston, Iowa], September 1, 1887.

Newspaper Archive. http://newspaperarchive.com/.

Newton v. Dretke, 371 F.3d 250 (2004).

Nies, Judith. *Nine Women: Portraits from the American Radical Tradition.* Berkeley: University of California Press, 1977.

"1903: Dora Wright, in Indian Territory." ExecutedToday.com. Available at http://murderpedia.org/female.W/w/wright-dora.htm.

"No Death Penalty in Henderson Retrial, DA Says." *Austin-American Statesman* [Austin, Texas], September 9, 2013. Available at http://www.mystatesman.com/news/news/local/no-death-penalty-in-henderson-retrial-da-says/nZrY2/.

Noble, John. "The Case of Maria in the Court of Assistants in 1681." *Publications of the Colonial Society of Massachusetts*, 6 (1904), 323–336.

Norris, Teresa. "Summaries of Successful Ineffective Assistance of Counsel Claims Including and Following *Wiggins v. Smith* Involving Capital Sentencing Phase Errors." December 6, 2010. Available at http://www.docstoc.com/docs/85087949/SUMMARIES-OF-SUCCESSFUL-INEFFECTIVE-ASSISTANCE-OF-COUNSEL-CLAIMS.

Norris v. Alabama. 294 U.S. 587 (1935).

North, Beverly. "The Petrillo Poison Ring, Pennsylvania 1932–1938." *Malice, Madness, and Mayhem: An Eclectic Collection of American Infamy.* 2010. Available at http://www.flexassistant.com/images/Petrillo.pdf.

North Carolina Department of Corrections. Available at http://webapps6.doc.state.nc.us/opi/viewoffender.do?method=view&offenderID=198138

North Carolina v. Parker, 743 S.E.2d 180 (2013).

Northrup, Ansel. *Slavery in New York: A Historical Sketch.* Albany: University of the State of New York, 1900.

Norton, Mary. "The Evolution of White Women's Experience in Early America." *American History Review*, 89 (1984), 593–619.

Nostrand, Richard. "Mexican Americans Circa 1850." *Annals of the Association of American Geographers*, 65 (1975), 378–390.

"Noted Female Prisoner." *Bedford Democrat* [Bedford, Indiana], December 26, 1899.

Nunn, Kevin. "The 'Darden Dilemma': Should African Americans Prosecute Crime?" *Fordham Law Review*, 68 (2000), 1473–1508.

Nwokeji, G. Ugo. "African Conceptions of Gender and the Slave Traffic." *William and Mary Quarterly*, 58 (2001), 47–68.

Oberman, Michelle. "Mothers Who Kill. Coming to Terms with Modern American Infanticide." *DePaul Journal of Health Care Law*, 8 (2004), 3–107.

_____. "Understanding Infanticide in Context: Mothers Who Kill, 1870–1930 and Today." *Journal of Criminal Law and Criminology*, 92 (2002), 707–737.

O'Bryan v. Commonwealth, 634 S.W.2d 153 (1982).

"Odds and Ends and Things." *Clearfield Progress* [Clearfield, Pennsylvania], January 16, 1928.

Ogletree, Charles,. "Black Man's Burden: Race and the Death Penalty in America." *Oregon Law Review*, 81 (2002), 15–38.

O'Hare, Sheila, Irene Berry, and Jesse Silva. *Legal Executions in California: A Comprehensive Registry, 1851–2005.* Jefferson: McFarland, 2006.

Ohio Legislative Service Commission. *Capital Punishment, Staff Research Report, No. 46.* 1961.

Ohio v. Grant, 67 Ohio St. 3d 465 (1993).

Ohio v. Lampkin, 1990 Ohio App. LEXIS 4315 (1990).

"Ohio's Female Death Row Inmate Describes Conditions." *Bryan Times* [Bryan, Ohio], November 3, 2003.

Olasky, Marvin. *Abortion Rites: A Social History of Abortion in America.* Wheaton: Crossways Books, 1992.

Oldfather, Chad. "Error Correction." *Indiana Law Journal*, 85 (2010), 49–85.

Oldman, James. *Trial by Jury: The Seventh Amendment and Anglo-American Special Juries.* New York: New York University Press, 2006.

Olivas, Michael. "The Chronicles, My Grandfather's Stories, and Immigration Law: The Slave Traders Chronicle as Racial History." In Richard Delgado and Jean Stephanic, eds., *Critical Race Theory: The Cutting Edge* (pp. 9–20). New Haven: Yale University Press, 2000.

Omalza, Floyd, and Flippo v. State, 1995 OK CR 80 (1995).

Onderdonk, Henry. *Long Island and New York in Olden Times, Being Newspaper Extracts and Historical Sketches.* 1851. Long Island Genealogy. Available at http://longislandgenealogy.com/OldenTimes.pdf.

"167 Murders Go to Chair." *Gettysburg Times* [Gettysburg, Pennsylvania], June 24, 1926.

"One Man and Two Women Hanged." *New York Times*, October 8, 1892.

"Opening Arguments Allege Sex Murder Glorification." *Berkeley Daily Planet*, February 6, 2002.

"Oppose Capital Punishment Because It Is Wrong to Kill." *St. Louis Post-Dispatch*, February 6, 1998.

"Opposition to Hanging Denied by Governor." *Oakland Tribune*, October 2, 1935.

Oregon v. Crosby, 204 Ore. App. 75 (2006).
Oregon v. Crosby, 342 Ore. 419 (2007).
Oregon v. Freeman, 232 Ore. 267 (1962).
Ortiz, Adam. "Clemency and Consequences: State Governors and the Impact of Granting Clemency to Death Row Inmates." American Bar Association, July 2002. Available at http://www.americanbar.org/content/dam/aba/publishing/criminal_justice_section_newsletter/crimjust_juvjus_jdpclemeffect02.authcheckdam.pdf.
Osgood Et Al. v. the State of Georgia, 63 Ga. 791 (1879).
O'Shea, Kathleen. *Women and the Death Penalty in the United States, 1900–1998*. Westport: Praeger Press, 1999.
———. *Women on Death Row: Revelations from Both Sides of the Bars*. New York: Firebrand Books, 2000.
Oshinsky, David. *Capital Punishment on Trial: Furman v. Georgia and the Death Penalty in Modern America*. Austin: University of Texas, 2010.
———. *Worse than Slavery: Parchman Farm and the Ordeal of Jim Crow Justice*. New York: Free Press, 1996.
"Ought to Be Pardoned." *Daily Kennebec Journal* [Augusta, Maine], November 17, 1885.
Ovalle, David. "'Baby Lollipops' Mother Receives Death Penalty for Killing Toddler Son." *Miami Herald*, June 10, 2011.
Owen, Barbara. "The Case of the Women: Gendered Harm in the Contemporary Prison." In John Irwin, *The Warehouse Prison: Disposal of the New Dangerous Class* (pp. 261–289). Los Angeles: Roxbury, 2005.
Owens v. Guida, 2006 U.S. Dist. LEXIS 35465 (2006).
Owens v. Guida, 549 F.3d 399 (2008).
Owens v. State, 908 S.W.2d 923 (1995).
Owens v. State, 13 S.W.3d 742 (1999).
Owens v. Tennessee, 531 U.S. 846 (2000).
Oxford Mirror [Oxford, Iowa], November 28, 1895.
Page, Antony. "Batson's Blind-Spot: Unconscious Stereotyping and the Peremptory Challenge." *Boston University Law Review*, 85 (2005), 155–262.
Palacios, Victoria. "Faith in Fantasy: The Supreme Court's Reliance on Commutation to Ensure Justice in Death Penalty Cases." *Vanderbilt Law Review*, 49 (1996), 311–372.
Pallone, Greg. "Convicted Killer Margaret Allen Sentenced to Death." 13 *News*, May 19, 2011.
"Pardon Board Holds Secret Conference." *Sarasota Herald-Tribune* [Sarasota, Florida], March 21, 1929.
"Pardoned Convict Dies of Consumption." *New York Times*, October 14, 1903.
"Pardons for July 4." *St. Louis Republic*. July 4, 1901.
Paredes, Raymund,. "The Origins of Anti-Mexican Sentiment in the United States." In Manuel G. Gonzales and Cynthia M. Gonzales (Eds.) *En Aquel Entonces, Readings in Mexican-American History* (pp. 45–52). Bloomington: Indiana University Press, 2000.
Parker, Linda. "Murderous Women and Mild Justice: A Look at Female Violence in Pre-1910 San Diego, San Luis Obispo and Tuolumne Counties." *The Journal of San Diego History*, 1992, 38. Available at http://www.sandiegohistory.org/journal/92winter/women.htm.
Parker, Paul, and Ben Coate. "Whose Justice? Prosecution and Defense Reactions to Capital Case Reversals." *The Justice System Journal*, 29 (2008), 367–384.
Parker v. North Carolina, 535 U.S. 1114 (2002).
"Parker's Sentencing of Mary Kettenring, 1895." Fort Smith National Historic Site. Available at http://www.nps.gov/fosm/historyculture/parker-sentencing-of-mary-kettenring-1895.htm.
Parkes, Walter. "Parallel in Approaching Doom of 'Triangle' Murder Couples." *The Hope Star* [Hope, Arkansas], June 10, 1936.
Parrish, Michael. "Cold War Justice: The Supreme Court and the Rosenbergs." *The American Historical Review*, 82 (1977), 805–842.
———. "Revisited: The Rosenberg 'Atom Spy' Case." *University of Missouri Kansas City Law Review*, 68 (2000), 601–621.
Parry, J. H. *The Establishment of the European Hegemony 1415–1715: Trade and Exploration in the Age of the Renaissance*. New York: Harper & Row, 1961.
"Patrolman Slain Probing Robbery." *Gastonia Gazette*. [Gastonia, North Carolina], September 3, 1975.
Patterson, Orlando. *Rituals of Blood: Consequences of Slavery in Two American Centuries*. New York: Basic Civitas, 1998.
Paulson, Morris, Robert Coombs, and John Landsverk. "Youth Who Physically Assault Their Parents." *Journal of Family Violence*, 5 (1990), 121–133.
"Penalty for Murder." *New York Times*, June 10, 1879.
"Pennsylvania Escapee Charged with Murder." *Gettysburg Times* [Gettysburg, Pennsylvania], October 4, 1993.
Pennsylvania Gazette, February 5, 1751.
Pennsylvania Gazette, February 19, 1751.
Pennsylvania Gazette, May 16, 1754.
Pennsylvania v. Walter, 600 Pa. 392 (2009).
People v. Alfaro, 41 Cal. 4th 1277 (2007).
People v. Anderson, 6 Cal.3d 628 (1972).
People v. Antonio, 265 N.Y. 247 (1934).
People v. Antonio, 265 N.Y. 246 (1934).
People v. Caffey, 205 Ill. 2d 52 (2001).
People v. Caro, 2010 Cal. LEXIS 11276 (2010) (*Socorro Susan*).
People v. Cignarale, 110 N.Y. 23 (1888).
People v. Coo, 267 N.Y. 556 (1935).
People v. Ehlert, 274 Ill. App. 3d 1026 (1995).
People v. Eubanks, 53 Cal. 4th 110 (2011).
People v. Fair, 43 Cal. 137 (1872).
People v. Farmer, 194 N.Y. 251 (1909).
People v. Gonzales, 51 Cal. 4th 894 (2011).
People v. Helen Fowler and George F. Knight, 293 N.Y. 721 (1944).
People v. John A. Santos, Et Al. 43 Cal. 2d 319 (1954).
People v. Madison, 3 Cal.2d 668 (1935).
People v. Mata, 819 N.E.2d 1261 (2004).
People v. McDermott, 28 Cal. 4th 946 (2002).
People v. Nieves, 2010 Cal. LEXIS 8582 (2010).
People v. Place, 11 E.H. Smith 584 (1899).
People v. Saetta, 264 N.Y. 640 (1934).
People v. Samuels, 36 Cal. 4th 96 (2005).
People v. Williams, 193 Ill. 2d 306 (2000).
Perea, Juan, Richard Delgado, Angela Harris, Stephanie Wildman, and Jean Stephancic. *Race and Races: Cases and Resources for a Diverse America*. St. Paul, MN: West Group, 2000.
Perillo v. Johnson, 79 F.3d 441 (1996).
Perillo v. Johnson, 205 F.3d 775 (2000).
Perillo v. State, 656 S.W.2d 78 (1983).
Perillo v. State, 758 S.W.2d 567 (1988).
Perkinson, Robert. *Texas Tough: The Rise of America's Prison Empire*. New York: Picador, 2010.
Perlmutter, Philip. *Divided We Fall: A History of Ethnic, Religious, and Racial Prejudice in America*. Ames: Iowa State University Press, 1992.
Perry v. New Hampshire, 132 S.Ct. 716 (2012).
Perske, Robert. "False Confessions from 53 Persons with Intellectual Disabilities: The List Keeps Growing." *Intellectual and Developmental Disabilities*, 46 (2008), 468–479.
Pestana, Carla. "The City Upon a Hill Under Siege: The Puritan Perception of the Quaker Threat to Massachusetts Bay, 1656–1661." *New England Quarterly*, 56 (1983), 323–353.
———. "The Quaker Executions in Myth and History." *Journal of American History*, 80 (1993), 441–469.
Petersburg Index-Appeal [Virginia], December 25, 1878.
Philadelphia Gazette, April 15, 1736.
Philadelphia Gazette, May 26, 1737.
"Philadelphia Ring Slayer Is Convicted." *Syracuse Herald-Journal*, December 1, 1950.
"Philadelphia Woman Murdered Husband." *Janesville Daily Gazette* [Janesville, Wisconsin], December 14, 1912.
Phillips, Charles. "Exploring Relations Among Forms of Social Control: The Lynching and Execution of Blacks in North

Carolina, 1889–1918." *Law and Society Review*, 21 (1987), 361–374.

Phillips, Lela. "Execution in a Small Town—The Lena Baker Story." *Justice Denied: The Magazine for the Wrongfully Convicted*, 29 (2005), 8.

Phillips, Nancy. "In Life and Death Cases, Costly Mistakes." *Philadelphia Inquirer*, October 23, 2011.

Phillips, Robert. "Mom Who Killed Kids Is Eager to Die." APBNews Online, April 30, 2000. Available at http://murderpedia.org/female.R/r/riggs-christina.htm.

Phillips, Ulrich. American *Negro Slavery: A Survey of Supply, Employment, Control of Negro Labor as Determined by the Plantation Regime*. New York: D. Appleton, 1918.

Phillips, Ulrich. "Slave Crime in Virginia." *American Historical Review*, 20 (1915), 336–340.

Piccalo, Gina. "Fatal Lies: Angelina Rodriguez Is Many Things. Wife, Mother, Sister, Daughter. She Is Also a Convicted Killer." *Los Angeles Times*, March 9, 2005.

Pierson, Gerald. "Extralegal Crimes, Extralegal Punishments: Justice on the Antebellum Plantation." April 2007. Available at http://works.bepress.com/gerald_pierson/1/.

Pike v. Tennessee, 526 U.S. 1147 (1999).

Pike v. Tennessee, 2011 Tenn. Crim. App. LEXIS 285 (2011).

Pillemer, Karl, and David Finkehor. "Prevalence of Elder Abuse: A Random Sample Survey." *The Gerontologist*, 28 (1988), 51–57.

Pinkham, Paul. "Female Murderer Cole Receives Death Sentence; She Will Join Two of Her Three Partners on State's Death Row." *Florida Times-Union*, March 7, 2008.

Pittman, Craig. "Interest Points to Death Row's Lack of Equality." *St. Petersburg Times* [Florida], January 18, 1998.

Plantz v. Massie, 2000 U.S. App. LEXIS 13017 (2000).

Plantz v. State, 876 P2d 268 (1994).

Plantz v. State, 936 P2d 339 (1997).

"Plea for Mercy." *Decatur Daily Review* [Decatur, Illinois], June 26, 1887.

Plessey v. Ferguson, 163 U.S. 537 (1896).

Pokorak, Jeffrey. "Probing the Capital Prosecutor's Perspective: Race of the Discretionary Actor." *Cornell Law Review*, 83 (1998), 1811–1820.

"Police Officer Killed." *Santa Fé New Mexican Review* [Santa Fe, New Mexico], October 9, 1883.

"Policewoman Sentenced in Lovers' Murder." *Indiana Gazette* [Indiana, Pennsylvania], July 26, 1984.

"Polly Barclay—Another Murderous Woman?" *Your Peachy Past*, May 16, 2011. Available at Http://Peachypast.Blog spot.Com/2011/05/Polly-Barclay-Another-Murderous-Woman.Html.

Ponce, Pedro. "Trouble for the Spanish, the Pueblo Revolt of 1680." *Humanities*, 23 (2002), 20–24.

Port, Bob. "Killer Details How He Shot Lover's Mate." *St. Petersburg Times* [Florida], March 19, 1987.

Powell v. Alabama, 294 U.S. 600 (1935).

Powers, Edwin. *Crime and Punishment in Early Massachusetts 1620–1692: A Documentary History*. Boston: Beacon, 1966.

Preyer, Kathryn. "Penal Measures in the American Colonies: An Overview." *American Journal of Legal History*, 26 (1982), 326–353.

Pridemore, Amelia. "Mom Cleared of Murder to Appear on TV." *Beckley Register Herald* [Beckley, West Virginia], May 7, 2010.

Pridemore, William. "An Empirical Examination of Commutations and Executions in Post–*Furman* Capital Cases." *Justice Quarterly*, 17 (2000), 159–183.

Prison Talk. Execution a Tough Sell When Killer Is a Woman—"Rebecca Smith's Horrendous Case." August 2002. Available at http://www.prisontalk.com/forums/showthread.php?t=15679.

"Prosecutor to Get National Award." *Riverside Press-Enterprise* [Riverside, California], August 24, 2010.

"Prosecutors Winds Up Case in Baby Sitter's Murder Trial." *Cedar Rapids Gazette* [Cedar Rapids, Iowa], February 27, 1997.

Provincial Council of Pennsylvania. *Minutes of the Provincial Council of Pennsylvania from the Organization to the Termination of the Proprietary Government*. Harrisburg: Theo Fenn, 1852.

Provincial Court Proceedings of 1671 Found in the Archives of Maryland, Vol. 51. Available at http://aomol.msa.maryland.gov/html/volumes.html.

Puit, Glenn. "Binion Trial Verdict: Reversal of Fortunes." *Las Vegas Review Journal*, November 24, 2004.

Puit, Glenn, and J. M. Kalil. "Murder Convictions in Binion Case Overturned." *Las Vegas Review Journal*, July 15, 2003.

Pulliam v. Illinois, 522 U.S. 921 (1997).

Quigley, William. "Work or Starve: Regulation of the Poor in Colonial America." *University of San Francisco Law Review*, 35 (1996), 35–83.

"Quinn Signs Bill Abolishing Death Penalty in Illinois." Fox Chicago News, March 10, 2011. Available at http://www.myfoxchicago.com/dpp/news/metro/death-penalty-execution-abolished-illinois-pat-quinn-sign-bill-20110309.

Quinney, Richard. *Class, State, and Crime: On the Theory and Practice of Criminal Justice*. New York: D. McKay, 1977.

Race of Death Row Inmates Executed Since 1976. Death Penalty Information Center, July 15, 2015. Available at http://www.deathpenaltyinfo.org/article.php?scid=5&did=184.

Radelet, Michael, and Barbara A. Zsembik. "Executive Clemency in Post-*Furman* Capital Cases. *University of Richmond Law Review*, 27 (1993), 289–314.

Rafter, Nicole. *Partial Justice: Women, Prisons, and Social Control*. New Brunswick: Transaction, 2004.

_____. "Prisons for Women, 1790–1980." *Crime and Justice*, 5 (1983), 129–181.

Ramsey, Carolyn. "Intimate Homicide: Gender and Crime Control, 1880–1920." *University of Colorado Law Review*, 77 (2006), 101–190.

Ramsland, Katherine. "Nightrider and Lady Sundown: The Bonnie and Clyde of Georgia." *Women Who Kill, True Crime*. Available at http://www.trutv.com/library/crime/notorious_murders/women/neelley/1.html.

Randall, Kate. "Commutation of Death Sentences in Illinois Deals Blow to Capital Punishment." *World Socialist Website*, January 23, 2003. Available at http://www.wsws.org/articles/jan2003/ryan-j23.shtml.

_____. "A Grim Milestone: Texas Carries Out 500th Execution." *World Socialist Web Site*, June 27, 2013. Available at http://www.wsws.org/en/articles/2013/06/27/exec-j27.html.

Rankin, Hugh. *Criminal Trial Proceedings in the General Court of Colonial Virginia*. Charlottesville: University Press of Virginia, 1965.

Rapaport, Elizabeth. "Mad Women and Desperate Girls: Infanticide and Child Murder in Law and Myth." *Fordham Urban Law Review*, 33 (2006), 527–569.

_____. "Some Questions About Gender and the Death Penalty." *Golden Gate University Law Review*, 20 (1990), 501–565.

_____. "Straight Is the Gate: Capital Clemency in the United States from *Gregg* to *Atkins*." *New Mexico Law Review*, 33 (2003), 349–376.

_____, and Victor Streib. "Death Penalty for Women in North Carolina." *Elton Law Review*, 1 (2009), 65–94.

"Rapid Change of Faces Seen in Death Row." *Panama City News Herald* [Panama City, Florida], April 14, 1957.

Rauch, David. "Visitors Become Jurors at Pennsbury Manor." *Bucks County Courier Times*, July 14, 2008. Available at http://www.phillyburbs.com/pb-dyn/news/111-07142008-1562712.html.

Ray, Angela. "Representing the Working Class in Early U.S. Feminist Media: The Case of Hester Vaughn." *Women's Studies in Communication*, 26 (2003), 1–26.

Ray, Phil. "Judge Allows New Trial Request for Routier Case." *Altoona Mirror* [Altoona, Pennsylvania], February 9, 2014. Available at http://www.altoonamirror.com/page/content.detail/id/578587/.

Ready, Milton. *The Tar Heel State: A History of North Carolina.* Columbia: University of South Carolina Press, 2005.
"Recorder Goffs Errors." *New York Times,* April 22, 1896.
Reddick v. State, 190 So. 2d 340 (1966).
Rediker, Marcus. *The Slave Ship: A Human History.* New York: Viking, 2007.
Reich, Jerome. *Colonial America.* Upper Saddle River: Prentice Hall, 1989.
Reimer, Norman. "Capital Punishment in America: A Steady Decline—But Still a Long Way to Go." *Champion,* 38 (2014), 7–18.
Reis, Elizabeth. *Damned Women: Sinners and Witches in Puritan New England.* New York: Cornell University Press, 1997.
Reiss, Oscar. *Blacks in Colonial America.* Jefferson: McFarland, 1997.
Reissmann, Kelly. "Our System Is Broken: A Study of the Crisis Facing the Death-Eligible Defendant." *Northern Illinois University Law Review,* 23 (2002), 43–79.
Rennison, Callie. *Intimate Partner Violence, 1993–2001.* U.S. Department of Justice, Bureau of Justice Statistics, February 2003. Available at http://bjs.ojp.usdoj.gov/content/pub/pdf/ipv01.pdf.
Rennison, Callie, and Sarah Wellchans. *Intimate Partner Violence, Special Report.* U.S. Department of Justice, Bureau of Justice Statistics, January 2002. Available at http://bjs.ojp.usdoj.gov/content/pub/pdf/ipv.pdf.
"Replica Prison Cell Highlights Briton's Death Row Plight." UK Press Association, August 10, 2010. Available at http://www.google.com/hostednews/ukpress/article/ALeqM5jqjVSQvMltotWEh1Atbdz4Lt2GjA.
Report on Sexual Victimization in Prisons and Jails: Review Panel on Prison Rape. U.S. Department of Justice, April 2012. Available at http://www.ojp.usdoj.gov/reviewpanel/pdfs/prea_finalreport_2012.pdf.
"Reprieve Issues New Report on Foreign Nationals on Death Row in U.S." Death Penalty Information Center, November 2012. Available at http://www.deathpenaltyinfo.org/foreign-nationals-reprieve-issues-new-report-foreign-nationals-death-row-us.
Resnick, Phillip. "Child Murder by Parents: A Psychiatric Review of Filicide." *American Journal of Psychiatry,* 126 (1969), 325–334.
Resnick, Phillip. "Murder of the Newborn: A Psychiatric Review of Neonaticide." *American Journal of Psychiatry,* 126 (1970), 1414–1420.
Reuben, Richard. "Marshall Urges Competency from Death-Penalty Counsel." *Los Angeles Daily Journal,* August 7, 1990.
Reza, Elizabeth. "Gender Bias in North Carolina's Death Penalty." *Duke Journal Gender Law and Policy,* 12 (2005), 179–214.
Richardson, David. "Shipboard Revolts, African Authority, and the Atlantic Slave Trade." *William and Mary Quarterly,* 58 (2001), 69–92.
Richardson, Howard. "In America 3 to 5 Children Are Killed by Their Mothers Daily." *Suite,* January 1, 2011. Available at https://suite101.com/a/in-america-3-to-5-children-are-killed-by-their-parents-daily-a326523.
Richardson v. Texas, 129 S. Ct. 49 (2008).
Richardson v. Texas, 2008 Tex. Crim. App. Unpub. LEXIS 35 (2008).
Richelle, V.A. "Racism as a Strategic Tool at Trial: Appealing Race-Based Prosecutorial Misconduct." *Tulane Law Review,* 67 (1993), 2357–2370.
Ridolfi, Kathleen, Tiffany Joslyn, and Todd Fries. *Material Indifference: How Courts Are Impeding Fair Disclosure in Criminal Case.* National Association of Criminal Defense Lawyers and the Veritas Initiative, November 17, 2014. Available at http://www.nacdl.org/discoveryreform/materialindifference/.
Ridolfi, Kathleen, and Maurice Possley. *Preventable Error: A Report on Prosecutorial Misconduct in California 1997–2009.* October 1, 2010. Available at http://digitalcommons.law.scu.edu/cgi/viewcontent.cgi?article=1001&context=ncippubs.
Riggs v. Branch, 1976 OK CR 216 (1976).
Ring v. Arizona, 536 U.S. 584 (2002).
Rivers, Caryl. "The Real Bias That Divides Us." *Los Angeles Times,* December 12, 2014.
Roberts, Dorothy. "Crime, Race, and Reproduction." *Tulane Law Review,* 67 (1993), 1945–1977.
Roberts v. Louisiana, 428 U.S. 325 (1976).
Robertson, Cassandra. "The Right to Appeal." *North Carolina Law Review,* 91 (2013), 1219–1281.
Robinson, Alicia. "Sentence Is Death for Boy's Killers." *Riverside Press Enterprise,* June 27, 2009.
———. "Verdict in Uncle's Trial Reached." *Riverside Press Enterprise,* March 25, 2009.
Robinson, Conway. "Notes from Council and General Court Records." *The Virginia Magazine of History and Biography,* 13 (1906), 389–401.
Robinson, W. Scott. *History of the City of Cleveland: Its Settlement Rise and Progress.* Cleveland: Robison & Cockett, 1887.
Robson, Ruthann. "Lesbianism and the Death Penalty: A Hard Core Case." *Women's Studies Quarterly,* 3 (2004), 181–191.
Rogers, George. *Charleston in the Age of Pinckneys.* Columbia: University of South Carolina Press, 1980.
Rogers, Horatio. *Mary Dyer of Rhode Island: The Quaker Martyr That Was Hanged on Boston Common, June 1, 1660.* 1896. Providence: Preston and Rounds. Available at https://archive.org/details/marydyerofrhodeis00roge.
Rogers v. Peck, 199 U.S. 425 (1905).
Rogers v. State, 77 Vt. 454 (1905).
Roper v. Simmons, 543 U.S. 551 (2005).
Rosales, F. Arturo. *Pobre Raza: Violence, Justice, and Mobilization Among México Lindo Immigrants, 1900–1936.* Austin: University of Texas Press, 1999.
Rosenmeier, Jesper. "New England's Perfection: The Image of Adam and the Image of Christ in the Antinomian." *William and Mary Quarterly,* 27 (1970), 435–459.
Rosenthal, Andrew. "Death Penalty Death Watch: Angela Johnson." *New York Times,* March 26, 2010. Available at http://www.takingnote.blogs.nyTimes, com/2012/03/26/death-penalty-death-watch-angela-johnson/.
Roth, Alex. "Eubanks to Die for Killing Sons." *San Diego Union-Tribune,* October 14, 1999.
Roth, Randolph. "Spousal Murder in Northern New England, 1776–1865." In Christine Daniels and Michael V. Kennedy, eds., *Over the Threshold: Intimate Violence in Early America* (pp. 65–93). New York: Routledge, 1999.
Rothermel, J. "Truth Telling Drug Solves 15 Ax Murders." *Sandusky Star Journal* [Sandusky, Ohio], January 14, 1924.
Rothman, Joshua. *Notorious in the Neighborhood: Sex and Families Across the Color Line in Virginia, 1787–1861.* Chapel Hill: University of North Carolina Press, 2003.
Routier v. Texas, 541 U.S. 1040 (2004).
Routier v. Texas, 273 S.W.3d 241 (2008).
Row v. Idaho, 131 Idaho 303 (1998).
Row v. Idaho, 525 U.S. 967 (1998).
Row v. Underwood, 2007 U.S. Dist. LEXIS 41571 (2007).
Row v. Underwood, 2008 U.S. Dist. LEXIS 77899 (2008).
Row v. Underwood, 2011 U.S. Dist. LEXIS 97287 (2011).
Row, David. "Life Without Parole: A Different Death Penalty." *The Nation,* October 26, 2012. Available at http://www.thenation.com/article/170852/life-without-parole-different-death-penalty#.
Rowe, Gail. "Infanticide, Its Judicial Resolution, and Criminal Code Revision in Early Pennsylvania." *Proceedings of the American Philosophical Society,* 135 (1991), 200–232.
———. "Women's Crime and Criminal Administration in Pennsylvania, 1763–1790." *Pennsylvania Magazine of History and Biography,* 109 (1985), 335–368.
———, and Jack Marietta. "Personal Violence in a 'Peaceable Kingdom." In Christine Daniels and Michale V. Kennedy,

eds., *Over the Threshold: Intimate Violence in Early America* (pp. 22–44). New York: Routledge, 1999.

"Roxalana Druse Hanged." *New York Times,* February 28, 1887.

"Ruby Mccollum Freed 20 Years After Crime." *Harrisonburg Daily News Record* [Harrisonburg, Virginia], January 23, 1974.

Ruckman, P. "The Study of Mercy: What Political Scientists Know (And Don't Know) About the Pardon Power." *University of Saint Thomas Law Journal,* 9 (2013), 783–837.

Runkle, Jim. "Facing the Death Sentence." *The Express,* March 20, 2010. Available at http://www.lockhaven.com/page/content.detail/id/517003.html.

_____. "Shonda Walter Granted Stay of Execution." *The Express,* April 1, 1010. Available at http://www.lockhaven.com/page/content.detail/id/517257.html.

"Ruth Judd Gives Long Written Confession to Trunk Murders." *Coshocton Tribune* [Coshocton, Ohio], October 24, 1931.

Ryan, Cy. "Court Rejects Appeal of Sandra Murphy." *Las Vegas Sun,* November 18, 2008.

Salem Witch Trials: Documentary Archive and Transcription Project. University of Virginia, 2002. Available at http://salem.lib.virginia.edu/home.html.

Salem Witchcraft Trials 1692. *Magistrates Hold a Hearing, Jails Fill with Accused, Evidence Questioned.* Available at http://law.jrank.org/pages/2340/Salem-Witchcraft-Trials-1692.html.

_____. *Petitions for Compensation and Decision Concerning Compensation, 1710–1711.* University of Missouri–Kansas City School of Law. Available at http://law2.umkc.edu/faculty/projects/ftrials/salem/SAL_PET.HTM.

Salinas, Lupe. "Latinos and Criminal Justice in Texas: Has the New Millennium Brought Progress?" *Thurgood Marshall Law Review,* 30 (2005), 289–346.

Salmon, Marylynn. "The Legal Status of Women in Early America: A Reappraisal." *Law and History Review,* 1 (1983), 129–151.

Salvucci, Jessica. "Femininity and the Electric Chair: An Equal Protection Challenge to Texas's Death Penalty Statute." *Boston College Third World Law Journal,* 31 (2011), 405–437.

Samuels v. California, 547 U.S. 1073 (2006).

Sanders, Erica. "Inadequate Legal Counsel a Key Concern in Death Penalty Cases." *Death Penalty Focus,* September 30, 2010. Available at http://www.deathpenalty.org/article.php?id=521.

Sarat, Austin. "Memorializing Miscarriages of Justice: Clemency Petitions in the Killing State." *Law and Society,* 42 (2008), 183–224.

Satterfield, Jamie. "Christa Pike's Appeal of Death Sentence Falls Short." Knoxnews.com, April 28, 2011. Available at http://www.knoxnews.com/news/local-news/death-row-inmates-appeal-falls-short.

Savage, David. "Justices Weight State's Jury Selection Law." *Los Angeles Times,* April 19, 2005.

"Saved from the Gallows." *New York Times,* April 13, 1884.

Savitt, Todd. *Medicine and Slavery: The Diseases and Health Care of Blacks in Antebellum Virginia.* Urbana: University of Illinois Press, 2002.

"Scared of Science: Crime Labs' Work Is Rarely Challenged by Defense Lawyers." National Fire and Arson Report, 15 (1997), 4.

Scheck, Barry. "Stunning New Case Highlights How Race Bias Corrupts Juries." *Salon,* April 15, 2014. Available at http://www.salon.com/2014/04/15/barry_scheck_stunning_new_case_highlights_how_race_bias_corrupts_juries/.

Scheffel, David. "*Harris v. Alabama*: A Portrait of Deference to the States in Capital Punishment." *Thomas Jefferson Law Review,* 19 (1997), 39–62.

Schlesinger, Joseph. *Discrimination, Torture, and Execution: A Human Rights Analysis of the Death Penalty in California and Louisiana.* Center for Constitutional Rights, 2013. Available at http://ccrjustice.org/files/2013-Death-Penalty-Report.pdf.

Schmall, Lorraine. "Forgiving Guin Garcia: Women, the Death Penalty and Commutation." *Wisconsin Women's Law Journal,* 11 (1996), 283–326.

Schriro v. Summerlin, 542 U.S. 348 (2004).

Schulz, Janice. "Edythe Klumpp and the Case of the Century." February 24, 2012. Available at http://www.libraries.uc.edu/liblog/2012/02/24/edythe-klumpp-and-the-case-of-the-century/.

Schwarz, Phillip. *Slave Laws in Virginia.* Athens: University of Georgia Press, 1996.

_____. *Twice Condemned: Slaves and the Criminal Laws of Virginia, 1705–1865.* Union: Lawbook Exchange, 1998.

Schwartz, Bernard. *Constitutional Law, a Textbook.* New York: Macmillan, 1972.

Scott v. Alabama, 2012 Ala. Crim. App. LEXIS 82 (2012).

"Second Woman to the Electric Chair." *Indiana Evening Gazette* [Indiana, Pennsylvania], April 2, 1927.

"Seek Pardon for Condemned Woman." *Gettysburg Times* [Gettysburg, Pennsylvania], August 8, 1912.

"Seeking Mercy." *Elkhart Sentinel* [Elkhart, Indiana], August 1, 1889.

Segrave, Kerry. *Women and Capital Punishment in America, 1840–1899: Death Sentences and Executions in the United States and Canada.* Jefferson: McFarland, 2008.

Seigenthaler, John. "Deeper Look Shows Even More Cases of Unequal Justice." *The Tennessean* [Nashville, Tennessee], January 10, 2010.

_____. "The Uneven Hand of Justice in TN Murders." *The Tennessean* [Nashville, Tennessee], December 21, 2009.

Seitz, Trina. "The Wounds of Savagery: Negro Primitivism, Gender Parity, and the Execution of Rosanna Lightner Phillips." *Women and Criminal Justice,* 16 (2005), 29–64.

Sellin, Thorsten. "The Philadelphia Gibbet Iron." *Journal of Criminal Law, Criminology, and Police Science,* 46 (1955), 11–25.

Semmes, Raphael. *Crime and Punishment in Early Maryland.* Baltimore: John Hopkins University Press, 1938.

"Sensational Murder Trial Figure Dies." *Daily Herald* [Biloxi-Gulfport, Mississippi], December 6, 1977.

"Sentence Given." *Oxnard Press-Courier* [Oxnard, California], May 14, 1975.

"Sentence of a Murderess." *Greencastle Weekly Indiana Press* [Greencastle, Indiana], November 18, 1868.

"Sentence Reversals in Intellectual Disability Cases." Death Penalty Information Center, July 19, 2012. Available at http://www.deathpenaltyinfo.org/sentence-reversals-intellectual-disability-cases.

"7 Charged with Killing 2 Nightclub Dancers" *Herald-Sun* [Durham, North Carolina], August 21, 1998.

Sewall, Samuel, and Melvin Yazawa. *The Diary and Life of Samuel Sewall.* Boston: Bedford, 1998.

Shaffer, Josh. "Convicted Murderer Spared Death Penalty After 23 Years." NewsObserverwww, June 30, 2013. Available at http://www.newsobserver.com/2013/06/20/2978300/convicted-murderer-spared-death.html.

Shallus, Francis. *Chronological Tables for Every Day in the Year.* Philadelphia: Merritt Printer, 1817.

Shapira, Ian. "After Toil and Trouble, Witch Is Cleared." *Washington Post,* July 12, 2006.

Shapiro, Andrea. "Unequal Before the Law: Men, Women and the Death Penalty." *American University Journal of Gender, Social Policy and the Law,* 8 (2000), 427–470.

Shapiro, Bruce. "Rethinking the Death Penalty." *The Nation,* July 22, 2002. Available at http://www.thenation.com/doc.mhtml?i=20020722&s=shapiro.

Shatz, Steven, and Naomi Shatz. "Chivalry Is Not Dead: Murder, Gender, and the Death Penalty." *Berkeley Journal of Gender, Law & Justice,* 27 (2012), 64–112.

Shaw, Renee. "Ban Death Penalty for Severely Mentally Ill?" *Public News Service* [Boulder, Colorado], August 13, 2010.

"She Must Soon Die." *Ironwood News Record* [Ironwood, Michigan], September 14, 1895.

Sheeran, Thomas. "Third Husband's Poisoning Brings Sentence of Death." *Sarasota Herald-Tribune*, September 13, 1980.

Shefts, Kimberly. "*People v. Pulliam*: Legislative Standards Needed for an *Atkins* Hearing to Determine Whether a Defendant Is Mentally Retarded and, Therefore, May Not Be Put to Death." *Journal of the DuPage County Bar Association*, January 2003. Available at http://www.dcba.org/brief/janissue/2003/art60103.htm.

Sheldon, Randall. *Controlling the Dangerous Classes: A Critical Introduction to the History of Criminal Justice*. Boston: Allyn and Bacon, 2001.

_____, and William B. Brown. *The New American Apartheid*. 2007. Available at http://www.sheldensays.com/Res-five.htm.

Sherrer, Hans. "The Complicity of Judges in the Generation of Wrongful Convictions." *Northern Kentucky Law Review*, 30 (2003), 539–583.

_____. "Good Samaritan Freed 16 Years After One Juror Saved Her from a Death Sentence." *Justice Denied: The Magazine for the Wrongfully Convicted*, Vol. 1. Available at http://forejustice.org/wc/ellen_reasonover.htm.

_____. "'Medell Banks Jr.' Conviction for Killing a Non-Existent Child Is Thrown Out as a 'Manifest Injustice.'" *Justice Denied: The Magazine for the Wrongfully Convicted*, Vol. 2. Available at http://www.justicedenied.org/choctawthree.htm.

Sherrill, Robert. "Death Trip: The American Way of Execution." *The Nation*, January 8, 2001. Available at http://www.thenation.com/doc/20010108/sherrill.

Shielded from Justice: Police Brutality and Accountability in the United States. Human Rights Watch, June 1998. Available at http://www.hrw.org/reports98/police/index.htm.

Shipley, Stacey, and Bruce A. Arrigo. *The Female Homicide Offender: Serial Murder and the Case of Aileen Wuornos*. Upper Saddle River: Prentice Hall, 2004.

Shipman, Marvin. *The Penalty of Death: U.S. Newspaper Coverage of Women's Executions*. Columbia: University of Missouri Press, 2002.

Shorter, Edward. *A History of Psychiatry: From the Era of the Asylum to the Age of Prozac*. New York: John Wiley, 1997.

Shortnacy, Michael. "Guilty and Gay, a Recipe for Execution in American Courtrooms: Sexual Orientation as a Tool for Prosecutorial Misconduct in Death Penalty Cases." *American University Law Review*, 51 (2001), 309–365.

"Shot Dead by a Jealous Woman." *Jeffersonville Daily Evening News* [Jeffersonville, Indiana], April 25, 1885.

Siciliano, Karen. "The Kate Southern Trial: Explaining and Punishing Female Criminal Behavior in Georgia, 1878." *Gender and Legal History Papers*. Georgetown Law Library, 2000. Available at http://www.law.georgetown.edu/library/collections/gender-legal-history/glh-summary.cfm?glhid=68beb8bb-0182-a0aa-7b1cd0145723e13c.

Siebert, Arielle. "*Batson v. Kentucky*: Application to Whites and the Effect on the Peremptory Challenge System." *Columbia Journal of Law and Social Problems*, 32 (1999), 307–330.

Siegel, Barry. "Judging Parents as Murderers on 4 Specks of Blood." *Los Angeles Times*, July 11, 1999.

Siegel, Reva. "Why Equal Protection No Longer Protects: The Evolving Forms of Status-Enforcing State Action." *Stanford Law Review*, 49 (1987), 1111–1148.

Sigler, Mary. "Mercy, Clemency, and the Case of Karla Faye Tucker." *Ohio State Journal of Criminal Law*, 4 (2007), 455–486.

Silver, Ann. "The Woman Must Pay." *Charlestown Gazette* [Charlestown, West Virginia], September 8, 1931.

Silver, Jonathan. "Mother of Starved Girl Guilty of Murder." *Pittsburgh Post-Gazette*, November 20, 2000.

Silverstein, Ken. "The Judge as Lynch Mob: How Alabama Judges Use Judicial Override to Disregard Juries and Impost Death Sentences." *The American Prospect*, May 6, 2001. Available at http://prospect.org/article/judge-lynch-mob.

Simmons v. South Carolina, 512 U.S. 154 (1994).

Simon, John, ed. *The Papers of Ulysses S. Grant, Volume 28, November 1, 1876–September 30, 1878*. Carbondale: Southern Illinois University Press, 2005.

Simon, Richard. "This Should Never Happen Again." *Los Angeles Times*, April 20, 2014.

Simon, Rita. "American Women and Crime." *Annals of the American Academy of Political and Social Science*, 423 (1976), 31–46.

Sims, Muriel. "Deathtrap." *Dallas Observer*, July 9, 1998. Available at http://www.dallasobserver.com/1998-07-09/news/deathtrap/.

"Singular Decision." *New York Times*, June 29, 1877.

Sitkoff, Harvard. *The Struggle for Black Equality, 1954–1980*. New York: Hill and Wang, 1981.

"Six Murderers Hanged." *New York Times*, February 4, 1881.

Slave Rebellion Website. "Slave Insurrections in the United States: An Overview." Available at http://slaverebellion.org/index.php?page=united-states-insurrections.

_____. "Slave Revolt on the Robert 1721." Available at http://slaverebellion.org/index.php?page=slave-revolt-on-the-robert-1721.

"Slayer Sentenced." *Press-Courier* [Oxnard, California], November 12, 1976.

"Slaying Lover Names Wife as Crime Plotter." *New Smyrna Daily News* [New Smyrna Beach, Florida], June 12, 1926.

Slobogin, Christopher. "Mental Illness and the Death Penalty." *California Criminal Law Review*, 2 (2000), 1–24.

Smith, Abbot. "The Transportation of Convicts to the American Colonies in the Seventeenth Century." *American History Review*, 39 (1934), 232–249.

Smith, Andrea. *Conquest: Sexual Violence and American Indian Genocide*. New York: South End Press, 2005.

Smith, Bruce. "The History of Wrongful Executions." *Hastings Law Journal*, 56 (2005), 1185–1233.

Smith and Bennett v. State, 41 N.J.L. 370 (1879).

Smith and Bennett v. State, 41 N.J.L. 598 (1879).

Smith v. Georgia, 429 U.S. 932 (1976).

Smith v. Georgia, 429 U.S. 1055 (1977).

Smith v. Georgia, 434 U.S. 878 (1977).

Smith, Daniel, and Michael Hindus. "Premarital Pregnancy in America 1640–1971: An Overview and Interpretation." *Journal of Interdisciplinary History*, 4 (1975), 537–570.

Smith, Jean. *John Marshall: Definer of a Nation*. New York: Henry Holt and Company, 1996.

Smith, Lois. Clark County Prosecutor. Available at http://www.clarkprosecutor.org/html/death/US/smith746.htm.

Smith, Merril. "Unnatural Mothers: Infanticide, Motherhood, and Class in the Mid-Atlantic, 1730–1830." In Christine Daniels and Michael V. Kennedy, eds., *Over the Threshold: Intimate Violence in Early America* (pp. 173–184). New York: Routledge, 1999.

Smith, Page. *Daughters of the Promised Land: Women in American History*. Boston: Little, Brown, 1970.

Smith, Raymond. "Mom to Die for Killing Her 3 Kids." *Riverside Press-Enterprise* [Riverside, California], October 3, 1998.

Smith, Robert, Sophie Cull, and Zoë Robinson. "The Failure of Mitigation." *Hastings Law Review*, 65 (2014), 1221–1255.

Smith v. Massey, 235 F.3d 1259 (2000).

Smith v. Oklahoma, 519 U.S. 970 (1996).

Smith v. State, 236 Ga. 12 (1976).

Smith v. State, 238 Ga. 655 (1977).

Smith v. State, 1986 OK CR 158 (1986).

Smith v. State, 1996 OK CR 13 (1996).

Smylie, Vernon. *A Noose for Chipita*. Corpus Christi: Texas News Syndicate Press, 1970.

Snell, Tracy. *Capital Punishment, 2009—Statistical Tables*. Bureau of Justice Statistics, U.S. Department of Justice,

December 2010. Available at http://bjs.ojp.usdoj.gov/content/pub/pdf/cp09st.pdf.
Snow, Tony. "Oppose Capital Punishment Because It Is Wrong to Kill." *St. Louis Post-Dispatch*, February 6, 1998.
Snyder, Terri. "As If There Was Not Master or Woman in the Land." In Christine Daniels and Michael V. Kennedy, eds., *Over the Threshold: Intimate Violence in Early America* (pp. 219–236). New York: Routledge, 1999.
Sonia Jacobs A/K/A Sonia Linder v. Singletary, 952 F.2d 1282 (1992).
Sonia Jacobs A/K/A Sonia Linder v. State, 357 So. 2d 169 (1978).
Soteropoulos, Jacqueline. "Female Death-Row Inmate Is Resentenced to Life in Prison." *Philadelphia Inquirer*, July 1, 2005.
Soto v. State, 252 Ga. 164 (1984).
South Carolina Department of Corrections. Incarcerated Inmate Search. http://www.doc.sc.gov/InmateSearchDisclaimer.jsp.
"Special to Washington Post." *Washington Post*, July 15, 1906.
Spindel, Donna, and Stewart Thomas. "Crime and Society in North Carolina, 1663–1740." *Journal of Social History*, 49 (1983), 233–244.
"Split Decision—Court Overturns Sentence." *Daily News* [New York], March 10, 1982.
Sprogle, Howard. *The Philadelphia Police, Past and Present*. Philadelphia, 1887. Available at https://archive.org/details/philadelphiapoli00sproiala.
Spruill, Julia. *Women's Life and Work in the Southern Colonies*. New York: W.W. Norton, 1972.
Spunaugle v. State, 1997 OK CR 47 (1997).
"Squaw Murderess to Hang." *Connersville Daily Examiner* [Connersville, Indiana], March 25, 1889.
Stanley, Alessandra. "K.G.B. Agent Plays Down Atom Role of Rosenbergs." *New York Times*, March 16, 1997.
Staba, David. "Falls Murder Case Presents Contrast to Northrup Verdict." *Niagara Falls Reporter*, December 4, 2001. Available at www.niagarafallsreporter.com/fowler.html.
Stampp, Kenneth. *The Peculiar Institution: Slavery in the Ante-Bellum South*. New York: Vintage Books, 1956.
Stannard, David. *American Holocaust: The Conquest of the New World*. New York: Oxford University Press, 1992.
Staples, Robert. "White Racism, Black Crime and American Justice: An Application of the Colonial Model to Explain Crime and Race." *Phylon*, 36 (1975), 14–22.
Stapleton, Annie. "Woman Sentenced to Death Walks Free, Thanks in Part to Victim's Grandson." CNN, June 18, 2013. Available at Http://Www.Cnn.Com/2013/06/17/Justice-/Death-Row-Freedom/Index.Html?Hpt=Hp_T1.
Starr, Allison. "Women or Machines? Pregnancy and Its Importance in the Life of a Slave Woman." *Quaestio*, 11 (2004), 55–59.
Starr, Linda. *Commentary from My Clark/Moorman File*. 1996. Available at http://homepages.rootsweb.ancestry.com/~lksstarr/reports/july96.txt.
State Ex Rel. Maurer Et Al., Appellants, v. Sheward, Judge, Appellee. Wilkinson, Dir., Et Al., Appellants, v. Maurer Et Al., Appellees Nos. 92-1350, 93-1165, 71 Ohio St. 3d 513 (1994).
State Ex Rel. Murphy v. Woodard, 134 Ohio St. 521 (1938).
"State Nears Close of Its Murder Case." *Racine Journal-Times* [Racine, Wisconsin], January 31, 1936.
State of Arizona v. Wendi Elizabeth Andriano, No. CR-05-0005-AP (July 9, 2007).
State of Denial: Texas Justice and the Death Penalty. Texas Defender Service, 2000. Available at http://www.texasdefender.org/publications.htm.
State of Oregon v. S.N.R., No. A148495 (2014, January 29) (Ore. Ct. of Appeals).
"State of the Modern Death Penalty in America: Key Findings of State Death Penalty Assessments 2006–2013." American Bar Association. Death Penalty Due Process Review Project, 2013. Available at http://www.americanbar.org/content/dam/aba/administrative/death_penalty_moratorium/aba_state_of_modern_death_penalty_web_file.authcheckdam.pdf.
"State Prison Health Care Spending." Pew Charitable Trusts, July, 2014.
"State-Sponsored Horror in Oklahoma." *New York Times*, April 30, 2014.
State v. Amanda Gutweiler, 06-561; 940 So. 2d 160 (2006) (La.App. 3 Cir. September 27, 2006).
State v. Amanda Gutweiler, 06-2596; 979 So. 2d 469 (2008) (La. April 8, 2008).
State v. Anderson, 350 N.C. 152 (1999).
State v. Andriano, 215 Ariz. 497 (2007).
State v. Ashley N. Hepburn, Appellate Case No. 2011-190695 (February 11, 2013).
State v. Barfield, 259 S.E.2d 510 (N.C. 1979).
State v. Boykin, 291 N.C. 264 (1976).
State v. Brown, 292 N.C. 494 (1977).
State v. Brown, 38 Ohio St. 3d 305 (1988).
State v. Buffom, 214 N.Y. 53 (1915).
State v. Carey Et Al., 6 W.W.Harr. 521 (1935).
State v. Carter, 1890 Ohio Misc. LEXIS 172 (1890).
State v. Copeland, 928 S.W.2d 828 (1996).
State v. Detter, 298 N.C. 604 (1979).
State v. Diar, 120 Ohio St. 3d 460 (2008).
State v. Dolbow and Driscoll, 117 N.J.L. 560 (1937).
State v. Edmunds, 229 Wis. 2d 67 (1999).
State v. Edmunds, 2008 Wisc. App. LEXIS 91 (2008).
State v. Evans, 107 N.J.L. 474 (1931).
State v. Ferola, 215 N.Y. 285 (1915).
State v. Fiore, 85 N.J.L. 311 (1913).
State v. Frances Silver, 14 N.C. 332 (1832).
State v. Funicello, 60 N.J. 60 (1972).
State v. Galligan, 92 Conn. 526 (1919).
State v. Gay, 334 N.C. 467 (1993).
State v. Green, 66 Ohio St. 3d 141 (1993).
State v. Hahn, 1937 Ohio Misc. LEXIS 1255 (1937).
State v. Harden, 223 W. Va. 796 (2009).
State v. Hayes, 89 Mo. 262 (1886).
State v. Henry, 196 La. 217 (1941).
State v. Henry, 197 La. 999 (1941).
State v. Henry, 200 La. 875 (1942).
State v. Holmes, 06-2988 (La. 12/02/08).
State v. Hunt, 289 N.C. 403 (1976).
State v. Isa, 850 S.W.2d 876 (1993).
State v. Jennings, 333 N.C. 579 (1993).
State v. John Fisher, 2 Nott & McC. 261 (1820).
State v. Kemmerlin, 356 N.C. 446 (2002).
State v. Larzelere, 979 So. 2d 195 (2008).
State v. Lockett, 49 Ohio St. 2d 48 (1976).
State v. Mahaley, 332 N.C. 583 (1992).
State v. Mahaley, 122 N.C. App. 490 (1996).
State v. Mantich, 842 N.W.2d 716 (2014).
State v. McAnulty, 356 Or 432 (2014).
State v. McKown, 475 N.W.2d 63 (1991).
State v. Milke, 177 Ariz. 118 (1993).
State v. Moore, 113 N.J. 239 (1988).
State v. Moore, 335 N.C. 567 (1994).
State v. Myers, 198 Mo. 225 (1906).
State v. Nesenhener, 164 Mo. 461 (1901).
State v. Osborne, 49 Ohio St. 2d 135 (1976).
State v. Osborne, 1976 Ohio App. LEXIS 6149 (1976).
State v. Parker, 354 N.C. 268 (2001).
State v. Phillips, 222 N.C. 440 (1942).
State v. Potts Et Al., 20 Nev. 389 (1889).
State v. Ralph Thompson, Cleve Bryant Johnson, Bessie Mae Williams, and Annie Mae Allision, 224 N.C. 661 (1944).
State v. Roach, 2009 N.C. App. LEXIS 1602 (2009).
State v. Roach, 364 N.C. 440 (2010).
State v. Robert Dunlap, 7 Tenn. 90 (1823).

State v. Roberts, 137 Ohio St.3d 230 (2013).
State v. Scott, 177 Ariz. 131 (1993).
State v. Smith, 309 S.C. 442 (1992).
State v. Smith, 177 Ill. 2d 53 (1997).
State v. Stager, 329 N.C. 278 (1991).
State v. Styers, 177 Ariz. 104 (1993).
State v. Twenter, 818 S.W.2d 628 (1991).
State v. Umble, 115 Mo. 452 (1893).
State v. Underdown, 107 N.J.L. 486 (1931).
State v. Wacaser, 794 S.W.2d 190 (1990).
State v. Wakefield, 88 Conn. 164 (1914).
State v. Walters, 357 N.C. 68 (2003).
State v. Ward, 286 N.C. 304 (1974).
State v. Ware, 282 Ga. 676 (2007).
State v. Weaver, 554 N.W.2d 240 (1996).
State v. Wernert, 1979 Ohio App. LEXIS 9325 (1976).
State v. Wernert, 1982 Ohio App. LEXIS 15689 (1982).
State v. Wernert, 1984 Ohio App. LEXIS 11006 (1984).
State v. Williams, 161 Ill. 2d 1 (1994).
State v. Windsor, 110 Idaho 410 (1985).
State v. Young, 1986 Ohio App. LEXIS 6788 (1986).
State v. Young, 1988 Ohio App. LEXIS 3347 (1988).
"Stay in Prison Ends on Pretty Day for Murderess." *Pampa Daily News* [Pampa, Texas], April 4, 1965.
Stebbing v. State, 299 Md. 331 (1984).
Steiker, Carol, and Jordan Steiker. "Sober Second Thoughts: Reflections on Two Decades of Constitutional Regulation of Capital Punishment." *Harvard Law Review*, 109 (1995), 357–438.
Steinmetz, Katy, and Alex Altman. "In Virginia, a Women on the Verge of Execution." *Time* Magazine, September 10, 2010.
"Stephens Pardons Three." *Kansas City Star*, November 24, 1898.
Stevenson, Bryan, and Ruth Friedman. "Deliberate Indifference: Judicial Tolerance of Racial Bias in Criminal Justice." *Washington and Lee Law Review*, 51 (1994), 509–527.
Stewart, Les. "Killer's Bid for a New Trial Fails." *Lebanon Daily News* [Lebanon, Pennsylvania], August 3, 2010. Available at http://www.ldnews.com/news/ci_15659121.
Stokley, Sandra. "Prosecution Rests Its Case; Rialto Couple Is on Trial in Shooting Death of Las Vegas Teen." *Riverside Press Enterprise* [Riverside, California], March 15, 2006.
"Story of the Crime for Which Mrs. Nobles Has Been Condemned to Hang." *Atlanta Constitution*. December 12, 1897.
Strauder v. West Virginia, 100 U.S. 303 (1880).
Straus, Murray. "Women's Violence Towards Men Is a Serious Social Problem." In Donileen Loseke, Richard Gelles and Mary Cavanaugh (Eds.) *Current Controversies on Family Violence* (pp. 55–78). Thousand Oaks: Sage Publication, 2005.
Streib, Victor. "American Executions of Female Offenders: An Inventory of Names, Dates, and Other Information." Unpublished research report (on file with author), July 1, 2005.
Streib, Victor. "Classic Arguments for and Against the Death Penalty." *Elton Law Review*, 1 (2009), 1–16.
_____. *The Fairer Death: Executing Women in Ohio*. Athens: Ohio University Press, 2006.
_____, and Lynn Sametz. "Executing Female Juveniles." *Connecticut Law Review*, 22 (1989), 3–16.
Stull, Brian. "Act Now to Save a Virginia Woman on Death Row." American Civil Liberties Union, August 3, 2010. Available at https://www.aclu.org/blog/capital-punishment/act-now-save-virginia-woman-death-row.
Sutton, Charlotte. "Death Row Is Path Few Women Tread." *St. Petersburg Times,* June 17, 1990.
Sweeney, Joseph. "Guantanamo and U.S. Law." *Fordham International Law Journal*, 30 (2007), 673–779.
Tabish and Murphy v. Nevada, 119 Nev. 293 (2003).
Tagaki, Midori. *Rearing Wolves to Our Own Destruction: Slavery in Richmond, Virginia, 1782–1865*. Charlottesville: University Press of Virginia, 1999.

Talley, Tim. "Prosecutor Says Insurance Policy Was Motive for Murder." *Associated Press*, June 17, 2004.
Talley, William. "Briefs from History of Bath Co., KY 1876." July 10, 2010. Available at http://spotisadog.wordpress.com/2010/07/10/george-lansdowne-prince-william-county-virginia-to-bath-county-kentucky/.
Tarpley, John. "Black Women, Sexual Myth, and Jurisprudence." *Temple Law Review*, 69 (1996), 1343–1388.
Tatum, Georgia. *Disloyalty in the Confederacy*. Chapel Hill: University of North Carolina Press, 1934.
Taylor, John. *The Witchcraft Delusion in Colonial Connecticut (1647–1697)*. 1908. Project Gutenberg. Available at http://www.gutenberg.org/etext/12288.
Teeters, Negley. "Public Executions in Pennsylvania, 1682–1834: With Annotated Lists of Persons Executed and of Delays, Pardons and Reprieves of Persons Sentenced to Death in Pennsylvania, 1682–1834." *Journal of the Lancaster County Historical Society*, 64 (1960), 85–164.
Tennessee v. Pike, 1997 Tenn. Crim. App. LEXIS 1186 (1997).
Terkel, Gerald. *Law and Society: Critical Approaches*. Upper Saddle River: Allyn and Bacon, 1995.
"Territorial Topics." *Fort Smith Elevator*, August 3, 1884.
Terzano, John, Joyce McGee, and Alanna Holt. *Improving Prosecutorial Accountability, A Policy Review*. The Justice Project, 2009. Available at http://www.truthinjustice.org/prosecutorial-accountability1.pdf.
"Texas Court Grants Stay on Basis of Possible Evidence." Death Penalty Information Center. Available at http://www.deathpenaltyinfo.org/node/2120. June 11, 2007
"Texas Court Grants Stay on Basis of Possible Evidence." Death Penalty Information Center. Available at http://www.deathpenaltyinfo.org/node/2120. June 12, 2007.
"Texas Jury Sentences Woman to Death." *Associated Press*, March 27, 1998.
"Texas Woman Charged in Death of Baby Sitter." *Port Arthur News* [Port Arthur, Texas], July 31, 2010.
"Texas Woman Faces Execution Despite Questions Regarding Her Guilt." Death Penalty Information Center, August 25 2005. Available at http://www.deathpenaltyinfo.org/node/1509.
"Texas Woman, 25, Gets Death Sentence." *Austin-American Statesman* [Austin, Texas], March 28, 1998.
"Texas Woman's Execution Halted; DA Won't Appeal." *Associated Press*, January 29, 2013.
Thacker v. State, 578 N.E.2d 351 (1993).
Tharp v. Pennsylvania, 541 U.S. 1045 (2004).
Theroux, Joseph. "A Short History of Hawaiian Executions, 1826–1947." *The Hawaiian Journal of History*, 25 (1991), 147–159.
"Third Murder Trial to Open." *Cedar Rapids Gazette* [Cedar Rapids, Iowa], February 17, 1997.
"32 Men and One Woman in Death Row at State Prison." *News Tribune*, October 23, 1963.
Thomas, Franklin. "Reminiscences of Medina County Bench and Bar." *The Western Reserve Law Journal*, 2 (1896), 187–190.
Thomas, George. "Colonial Criminal Law and Procedure: The Royal Colony of New Jersey 1749–57." *New York University Journal of Law and Liberty*, 1 (2005), 671–711.
Thompson, A. C., Joseph Shapiro, Sandra Bartlett, and Chisun Lee. "The Child Cases: Guilty Until Proved Innocent." *National Public Radio*. Available at http://www.npr.org/2011/06/28/137454415/the-child-cases-guilty-until-proven-innocent?ps=cprs. June 28, 2011.
Thompson, J. W. *Execution. the Life, Trial, and Behaviour of That Unfortunate Young Woman, Mary Johnson, 22 Years of Age, Who Was Executed at Gloucester on Saturday Last, 1831 for the Murder of Her Master and Mistress, John and Anna Robinson*. 1831. Available at http://memory.loc.gov/cgi-bin/query/r?ammem/rbpebib:@field(NUMBER+@band(rbpe+05500900)). 1831.
Thompson v. State, 166 Ga. 512 (1928).

Thompson v. State, 166 Ga. 758 (1928).

"Three Convicted of Manslaughter for Sign Theft." *Altoona Mirror* [Altoona, Pennsylvania], May 16, 1997.

"Three Days in Camp with the Robeson County Chain Gang." *Robesonian* [Lumberton, North Carolina], September 9, 1902.

"Three Defendants Sentenced in Stop Sign Case." *Joplin Globe* [Joplin, Missouri], June 21, 1997.

"Three Young Negroes Executed, Sentence of Young Girl Commuted." *The Robesonian* [Lumberton, North Carolina], January 1, 1945.

Tiede, Tom. "Are Women Barred from Execution?" *Sunday Herald.* August 3, 1980.

"Texas: The Imperfect Crime." *Time Magazine.* August 15, 1960.

Tindall, George and David Shi. *America: A Narrative History.* New York: W.W. Norton, 1997.

Tippetts, William. *Herkimer County Murders: This Book Contains an Accurate Account of the Capital Crimes Committed in the County of Herkimer, from the Year 1783 Up to the Present Time. Among Those of Recent Date Are the Wishart Murder, the Druse Butchery, and the Middleville Tragedy. The Facts Were Gathered from the Official Records of Herkimer County, and Other Reliable Sources.* Herkimer: H. P. Witherstine, Steam Book and Job Printers, 1885.

"To Be Hanged." *Hutchinson Daily News* [Hutchinson, Kansas], July 21, 1887.

"To Save Her from the Gallows." *Boston Daily Globe*, November 17, 1885.

"Today's Answers to Questions." *Independent Helena Montana,* October 20, 1941.

Tolnay, Stewart, and E. M. Beck. *A Festival of Violence: An Analysis of Southern Lynchings, 1882–1930.* Urbana: University of Illinois Press, 1995.

_____, and _____. "Racial Violence of Black Migration in the American South, 1910 to 1930." *American Sociological Review,* 57 (1992), 103–116.

Tolnay, Stewart, E. M. Beck, and James Massey. "Black Competition and White Vengeance: Legal Execution of Blacks as Social Control in the Cotton South, 1890 to 1929." *Social Science Quarterly,* 73 (1992), 627–644.

_____, _____, and _____. "Black Lynchings: The Power Threat Hypothesis Revisited." *Social Forces,* 67 (1989), 605–623.

Tórrez, Robert. "Hillsboro Murder, 1907." New Mexico Office of the State Historian. Available at http://dev.newmexicohistory.org/filedetails.php?fileID=21648.

_____. *Myth of the Hanging Tree: Stories of Crime and Punishment in Territorial New Mexico.* Albuquerque: University of New Mexico Press, 2008.

Touré. "Put to Death for Being Black: New Hope Against Judicial System Bias." *Time Magazine,* May 3, 2012. Available at http://ideas.time.com/2012/05/03/put-to-death-for-being-black-new-hope-against-judicial-system-bias/.

"Train Boy Still Love Eula." *Evening Independent* [Massillon, Ohio], December 3, 1928.

Tran, My-Thuan. "Fortuneteller, Daughter Killed Over Fortunetelling, O.C. Jury Told." *Los Angeles Times,* February 12, 2010.

Treleven, Ed. "No Second Trial in Baby-Shaking Case So Conviction of a Former Waunakee Women Who Spent 11 Years in Prison No Longer Stands." *Washington State Journal,* July 12, 2008. Available at http://host.madison.com/news/article_24f9c42f-22b5-593e-93fc-eeee1585a017.html.

"Trial of Bathsheba Spooner: 1778—Bathsheba Plots to Kill Her Husband, the Soldiers Are Arrested and Confession." Great American Trials. Available at http://law.jrank.org/pages/2374/Trial-Bathsheba-Spooner-et-al-1778.html.

"Trial of Captain John Kimber." American Memory, Slaves and the Courts, 1740–1860. June 7, 1792. Available at http://memory.loc.gov/cgi-bin/query/r?ammem/llst:@field(DOCID+@lit(llst061div0)).

"Trial of Henrietta Robinson for the Murder of Timothy Lannagan." *New York Daily Times,* May 26, 1854.

"Triple Execution." *Galveston Daily News* [Galveston, Texas], July 12, 1884.

Trindal, Elizabeth. *Mary Surratt: An American Tragedy.* Gretna: Pelican, 1996.

Trotti, Michael. *The Body in the Reservoir: Murder and Sensationalism in the South.* Chapel Hill: University of North Carolina Press, 2008.

"Trucker Held on Murder Charges." *Santa Fe New Mexican* [Santa Fe, New Mexico], March 29, 1979.

Tucker v. State, 771 S.W.2d 523 (Tex. Crim. App. 1988).

Tuerkheimer, Deborah. "The Next Innocence Project: Shaken Baby Syndrome and the Criminal Courts." *Washington University Law Review,* 87 (2009), 1–58.

_____. "Science-Dependent Prosecution and the Problem of Epistemic Contingency: A Study of Shaken Baby Syndrome." *Alabama Law Review,* 62 (2011), 513–569.

Tufts, Meredity. "A Matter of Context: Elizabeth Wilson Revisited." *Pennsylvania Magazine of History and Biography,* 131 (2007), 149–176.

Turner, Allan, and Cynthia Garza. "Newton Is Executed for Slaying Her Family: She Is the First Black Woman Put to Death in Texas Since Civil War." Chroniclewww. Available at http://www.chron.com/news/article/Frances-Newton-executed-for-slaying-her-family-1649278.php. 2005.

Turner, Martha. *Sam Houston and His Twelve Women: The Ladies Who Influenced the Life of Texas' Greatest Statesmen.* Austin: Pemberton Press, 1966.

Turner, Jonathan, Royce Singleton and David Musick. *Oppression: A Socio-History of Black-White Relations in America.* Chicago: Nelson Hall, 1984.

Twelfth Annual Report of the Massachusetts Board of Prison Commissioners. Boston: Wright & Potter Printing, 1913.

"12-Year-Old Girl to Hang." *New Philadelphia Ohio Democrat* [New Philadelphia, Ohio], July 28, 1887.

"24 Sentences Commuted by Pryor." *Hope Star* [Hope, Arkansas], October 17, 1975.

"23 Women Pay Death Penalty for Their Crimes." *Sheboygan Press* [Sheboygan, Wisconsin], February 1, 1929.

"226 Years Later, a 'Witch' Not Guilty." *Los Angeles Times,* August 28, 2008.

"Two Pennsylvania Women Seeking Reprieve from Board of Pardons." *Gettysburg Times* [Gettysburg, Pennsylvania], August 3, 1925.

"Two Prisoners Get Suspension of Sentence." *Biloxi Daily Herald* [Biloxi, Mississippi], January 2, 1925.

"Two Women Accused of Killing Five People in Drunken Spree." *Logansport Pharos Tribune* [Logansport, Indiana], June 28, 1985.

"Two Women Face Chair in Florida." *Waterloo Evening Courier* [Waterloo, Iowa], February 8, 1927.

"Two Women Sentenced to Die." *Clearfield Progress* [Clearfield, Pennsylvania], October 26, 1940.

Twombly, Robert and Robert H. Moore. "Black Puritan: The Negro in Seventeenth-Century Massachusetts." *William and Mary Quarterly,* 24 (1967), 224–242.

Tyler v. Kemp, 755 F.2d 741 (1985).

Tyler v. State, 247 Ga. 119 (1981).

Uelmen, Gerald. "California Death Penalty Laws and the California Supreme Court: A Ten-Year Perspective." *Crime and Social Justice,* 25 (1986), 78–93.

Ulrich, Laurel. *Goodwives: Image and Reality in the Lives of Women in Northern New England, 1650–1750.* New York: Alfred A. Knopf, 1982.

Umunna, Dehlia. "Symposium: Theory and Praxis in Reducing Women's Poverty: Rethinking the Neighborhood Watch: How Lesson from the Nigerian Village Can Creatively Empower the Community to Assist Poor, Single Mothers in America." *American University Journal of Gender, Social Policy & the Law,* 20 (2012), 847–869.

"Uncertain Justice." *Alton Weekly Courier* [Illinois], April 17, 1856.

Underwood, Barbara. "Ending Race Discrimination in Jury Selection: Whose Right Is It Anyway?" *Columbia Law Review,* 92 (1992), 725–774.
United States of America: The Execution of Mentally Ill Offenders." Amnesty International, January 2006. Available at http://amnesty.org/en/library/asset/AMR51/002/2006/en/8bad94ee-d46f-11dd-8743-d305bea2b2c7/amr510022006en.html.
United States v. Isa, 923 F.2d 1300 (1991).
United States v. Jackson, 390 U.S. 570 (1968).
United States v. Michaud, 268 F.3d 728 (2001).
United States v. Montgomery, 635 F.3d 1074 (2011).
Uphoff, Rodney. "Convicting the Innocent: Aberration or Systemic Problem?" *Wisconsin Law Review,* 2006 (2006), 739–842.
U.S. Bureau of the Census. "Population Censuses Taken in the Colonies and States During the Colonial and Pre-Federal Period: 1624–25 to 1786." *Historical Statistics of the United States, Colonial Times to 1970, Bicentennial Edition, Part 1.* Washington, D.C., 1975. Available at available at http://www2.census.gov/prod2/statcomp/documents/CT1970p2-13.pdf.
U.S. Commission on Civil Rights. Office of Civil Rights Evaluation. *Redefining Rights in America: The Civil Rights Record of the George W. Bush Administration, 2001–2004.* Draft Report of the Commissioners' Review, 2004. Available at http://www.usccr.gov/pubs/bush/bush04.pdf.
"US Death Row to Haunt Trafalgar Square Replica Highlights Case of Linda Carty, British Woman Who Faces Execution." UK Press Association, August 10, 2010. Available at http://www.londonnet.co.uk/news/2010/aug/us-death-row-haunt-trafalgar-square.html.
"Usa (Texas) Betty Lou Beets." Amnesty International, January 31, 2000. Available at http://www.amnesty.org.ru/library/print/ENGAMR510192000.
Valentine, Paul. "MD Court of Appeals Upholds Death Penalty." *Washington Post,* April 17, 1984.
Valery, Chantal. "U.S. States Mulling Old Execution Methods Amid Drug Shortage." *The Nation,* February 5, 2014. Available at http://www.nation.com.pk/international/05-Feb-2014/us-states-mulling-old-execution-methods-amid-drug-shortage.
Vandiver, Margaret. "The Quality of Mercy: Race and Clemency in Florida Death Penalty Cases, 1924–1966." *University of Richmond Law Review,* 27 (1993), 315–343.
"Veiled Murderess Dies with 50 Years' Secret." *New York Times,* May 15, 1905.
Vick, Douglas. "Poorhouse Justice: Underfunded Indigent Defense Services and Arbitrary Death Sentences." *Buffalo Law Review,* 43 (1995), 329–460.
Virginia Beach Historical Society. *Grace Sherwood and the Witch of Pungo.* Available at http://www.virginiabeachhistory.org/kyle.html.
Virginia Gazette, November 5, 1736.
Virginia Gazette, November 26, 1736.
Virginia Gazette, November 2, 1739.
Virginia Gazette, November 26, 1739.
Virginia Gazette, May 23, 1755.
Virginia Gazette, June 11, 1767.
Virginia Gazette, June 2, 1774.
Virginia Gazette, January 14, 1775.
Voorhees, Betsy. *Two Famous Murder Trials: Trial of Roxalana Druse in Herkimer.* October 1999. Available at http://herkimer.nygenweb.net/herktown/gillette.html.
Wade, Wyn. *The Fiery Cross: The Ku Klux Klan in America.* New York: Oxford University Press, 1987.
"Wakefield Verdict Is Prison for Life." *New York Times,* July 31, 1914.
Walker, Candace, and David Nichols. "Meet Eva Dugan, the Last Woman Hanged in Arizona." HLN. Available at http://www.hlntv.com/video/2013/05/07/meet-eva-dugan-last-woman-hanged-arizona?clusterId=121#videoplayer. May 7, 2013.
Walker, Lenore. "Racism and Violence Against Women." In Jeanne Adleman and Gloria Enguídanos, eds., *Racism in the Lives of Women: Testimony, Theory, and Guides to Antiracist Practice* (pp. 239–250). New York: Harrington Park Press, 1995.
Walker, Samuel. *Popular Justice: A History of American Criminal Justice.* New York: Oxford University Press, 1998.
Walker v. Alabama, 611 So. 2d 1133 (1992).
Walker v. Alabama, 919 So. 2d 1235 (2004).
Walker v. Alabama, 544 U.S. 925 (2005).
Walker v. State, 586 So. 2d 49 (1991).
Wallace, L.J., Alice D. Calhoun, Kenneth E. Powell, Joanne O'Neil, and Stephen P. James. *Homicide and Suicide Among Native Americans, 1979–1992.* Centers for Disease Control and Prevention. National Center for Injury Prevention and Control. Violence Surveillance Summary Series, No. 2, 1996 Available at Stacks.Cdc.Gov/View/Cdc/11253/Cdc_11253_Ds1.Pdf.
Walters, Ryan. "Raise It or Waive It? Addressing the Federal and State Split in Authority on Whether a Conviction Under an Unconstitutional Statute Is a Jurisdictional Defect." *Baylor Law Review,* 62 (2010), 909–942.
"Wanda Jean Allen Clemency Letter." American Civil Liberties Union, January 3, 2001. Available at https://www.aclu.org/capital-punishment/wanda-jean-allen-clemency-letter.
Ward, Megan. "Choked to Death by Law: *Gastonia Gazette* Story from Jan. 28, 1892." *Gaston Gazette,* August 11, 2008. Available at http://www.gastongazette.com/news/article_23343_article.html/gazette_gastonia.html.
Ward, Paula. "Washington County Woman Who Starved Daughter Gets New Hearing." *Pittsburgh Post-Gazette,* September 25, 2014. Available at http://www.post-gazette.com/local/south/2014/09/25/Washington-County-woman-who-starved-daughter-to-death-gets-new-sentencing-hearing/stories/201409240205.
"Was Ethel Rosenberg Wrong?" *Los Angeles* Times, September 12, 2008. Available at http://articles.laTimes, com/2008/sep/12/nation/na-rosenberg12.
"Washington Governor John Inslee." Death Penalty Information Center, February 11, 2014. Available at http://www.deathpenaltyinfo.org/.
Websdale, Neil. "Reviewing Domestic Violence Deaths." *National Institute of Justice Journal,* 2003. Available at http://www.ncjrs.gov/pdffiles1/jr000250g.pdf.
Weicek, William. "The Origins of the Law of Slavery in British North America." *Cardozo Law Review,* 17 (1996), 1711–1792.
Weinberg, Steve. "A Short History of Exposing Misconduct." The Center for Public Integrity, June 26, 2003. Available at http://www.publicintegrity.org/2003/06/26/5528/short-history-exposing-misconduct.
Weinstein, Henry. "A Sleeping Lawyer and a Ticket to Death Row." *Los Angeles Times,* July 15, 2000. Available at http://articles.laTimes, com/2000/jul/15/news/mn-53250.
Weithorn, Lois. "Protecting Children from Exposure to Domestic Violence: The Use and Abuse of Child Maltreatment." *Hastings Law Journal,* 53 (2001), 53–154.
Welborn, Larry. "Woman Convicted in Fortune-Teller Murders." *Orange County Register.* February 16, 2010.
———. "Woman Enticed Accomplice into Murder Plot, Prosecutor Says." *Orange County Register,* January 14, 2010.
Welsch, Elizabeth. *Peete Louise—Duchess of Death.* Serial Killer True Library, 2005. Available at http://www.crimezzz.net/serialkillers/P/PEETE_louise.php.
Welsh, John. "Pair Sentenced to Death." *Riverside Press Enterprise,* January 8, 2006.
Welsh-Huggins, Andrew. *No Winners Here Tonight: Race, Politics, and Geography in One of the Country's Busiest Death Penalty States.* Athens: Ohio University Press, 2009.
Wernert v. Arn, 819 F.2d 613 (1987).
West, Sara, Susan Friedman, and Phillip Resnick. "Fathers Who Kill Their Children: An Analysis of the Literature." *Journal of Forensic Sciences,* 54 (2009), 463–468.

"What Do You Want to Know." *Madison Wisconsin State Journal*, September 1, 1932.

Wheeler, Kenneth. "Infanticide in Nineteenth-Century Ohio." *Journal of Social History*, 31 (1997), 407–418.

White, Deborah. *Ar'n't I a Woman? Female Slaves in the Plantatio South*. New York: W.W. Norton, 1998.

White, Jerry. "Texas Executes 62-Year-Old Great Grandmother Betty Lou Beets." *World Socialist Web Site*, February 26, 2000. Available at http://www.wsws.org/articles/2000/feb 2000/exec-f26.shtml.

White, Penny. "Errors and Ethics: Dilemmas in Death." *Hofstra Law Review*, 29 (2001), 1265–1299.

White, Walter. *Rope and Faggot: Biography of Judge Lynch*. New York: Arno Press, 1929.

White, Welsh. "Fact-Finding and the Death Penalty: The Scope of a Capital Defendant's Right to Jury Trial." *Notre Dame Law Review*, 65 (1989), 1–31.

Whittington v. State, 252 Ga. 168 (1984).

Wholuba, Anita. *A Generation of Witnesses: Neo-Testimonial Practices in Flight to Canada, Dessa Rose, Beloved, Kindred, and the Chaneysville Incident*. Unpublished doctoral dissertation, Florida State University, 2007.

"Why Didn't I Confess Before? Sobs the Condemned Cowgirl Murderess." *Salt Lake Tribune*, August 18, 1935.

"Widow Fights Death Decree as Vague Law." *Piqua Daily Call* [Piqua, Ohio], Febuary 21, 1936.

"Widow Hears Death Verdict." *San Antonio Light*, September 22, 1939.

William John Clark v. the Commonwealth, 29 Pa. 129 (1858).

Williams, Carol. "Briton Seeks Stay in Texas Murder Case. Linda Carty Sits on Death Row. the Supreme Court May Decide Her Fate." *Los Angeles Times*, May 3, 2010.

_____. "The Nation; Briton Loses Death Penalty Appeal; the Supreme Court Refuses to Hear the Texas Inmate's Case." *Los Angeles Times*, May 4, 2010.

Williams, Paige. "Double Jeopardy." *The New Yorker*. Available at http://www.newyorker.com/magazine/2014/11/17/double-jeopardy-3. November 17 2014.

Williams v. Mississippi, 170 U.S. 213 (1898).

Williamson v. State, 512 So. 2d 868 (1987).

Willingham, Robert. *An Overview of Local History*. 2004. Available at http://www.rootsweb.ancestry.com/~gawilkes/localhst.htm.

Wills, Christopher. "Illinois Death Penalty Abolished: Pat Quinn Signs Death Penalty Ban, Clears Death Row." *Huffington Post*, March 9, 2011. Available at http://www.huffingtonpost.com/2011/03/08/illinois-death-penalty-ab_n_83 3250.html.

Wilson, Kate. "Magical Mystery Tower: Where's the Evidence Rod Underhill Said He Had That Compelled Lisa Roberts to Confess to Strangling Her Girlfriend?" *Willamette Week*, June 11, 2014. Available at http://www.wweek.com/portland/article-22676-magical_mystery_tower.html.

Wilson, R. Michael. *Crime and Punishment in Early Arizona*. Las Vegas: Stagecoach Books, 2004.

_____. Michael. *Encyclopedia of Murder and Execution in the Wild West*. Las Vegas: Stagecoach Books, 2006.

Wing, Adrien. "Examining the Correlation Between Disability and Poverty: A Comment from a Critical Race Feminist Perspective—Helping the Joneses to Keep Up!" *Journal of Gender, Race and Justice*, 8 (2005), 655–666.

"Wins Fight to Escape Execution." *Chester Times* [Chester, Pennsylvania], June 30, 1941.

Wisconsin v. Edmunds, 2008 WI App 33 (2008).

Wish, Harvey. "American Slave Insurrections Before 1861." *Journal of Negro History*, 22 (1937), 299–320.

Wishart, W. S. "First Hanging in Robeson County." *The Robesonian*. April 1, 1935.

Witherspoon v. Illinois, 391 U.S. 510 (1968).

Withington, Ann, and Jack Schwartz. "The Political Trial of Anne Hutchinson." *New England Quarterly*, 51 (1978), 226–240.

Witkowski, Monica. *Justice Without Partiality: Women and the Law in Colonial Maryland, 1648–1715*. Unpublished doctoral dissertation, Marquette University, 2010.

Wolf, Leslie. "Veronica Gonzales to Join Her Husband on Death Row." *San Diego Union-Tribune*, July 21, 1998.

Wolmack, Amy. "Machetti: Once Only Woman in GA. Death Row Released After 36 Years." Maconwww, July 3, 2010. Available at http://www.macon.com/2010/07/03/1184127/machetti-released-from-prison.html.

"Woman Accused of Poisoning Inmate of Her Home." *Lowell Sun* [Lowell, Massachusetts], May 9, 1916.

"Woman and Man Sentenced to Be Hanged Together." *Moberly Weekly Monitor* [Moberly, Missouri], November 7, 1913.

"Woman Asking to Be Hanged." *Cedar Rapids Republican* [Cedar Rapids, Iowa], February 22, 1901.

"Woman Asks $50,000 for Husband's Death." *Sarasota Herald-Tribune* [Sarasota, Florida], July 12, 1929.

"Woman Charged with Arsenic Killing of Four." *Galveston Daily News* [Galveston, Texas], May 7, 1958.

"Woman Charged with Embracery." *Daily News* [New York], October 12, 1935.

"Woman Confined to Death Cell." *Paris News* [Paris, Texas], September 10, 1978.

"Woman Convicted in Murder Syndicate Trial." *Orleans Times-Herald*. September 22, 1939.

"Woman Convicted of Burning 2 Sons." *Washington Post*, October 14, 1983.

"Woman Could Get the Death Penalty." *Brownsville Daily Heral,*. March 3, 1995.

"Woman Dies on Gallows." *Auburn Citizen* [Auburn, New York], December 8, 1905.

"Woman Doctor Goes on Trial in Mississippi." *New Castle News* [New Castle, Pennsylvania], January 29, 1934.

"Woman Escapes Chair." *New York Tribune*, June 6, 1912.

"Woman Faces Death Penalty Trial." *Associated Press*, June 14, 2004.

"Woman Faces Gallows for Slaying Mate." *Oakland Tribune*, June 23, 1934.

"Woman Found Guilty in Slay of Son." *Lawrence Daily Journal World* [Lawrence, Kansas], June 8, 1988.

"Woman Freed from Prison." *Monessen Valley Independent* [Monessen, Pennsylvania], December 27, 1993.

"Woman Gets Death for Killing Family." *Riverside Press-Enterprise* [Riverside, California], January 20, 2012.

"Woman Gets Death for Killing Lover's Wife." *Northwest Florida Daily News* [Fort Walton Beach, Florida], February 23, 2011.

"Woman Gets Death Sentence." *Associated Galveston Daily News*, March 4, 1995.

"Woman Hanging." *Sullivan Democrat* [Sullivan, Indiana], September 19, 1867.

"Woman, in Coma, Is Wheeled to Electric Chair—Guards Lift Unconscious Slayer of Lover's Wife to Death Seat; Man Follows Here." *Nevada State Journal* [Reno, Nevada], July, 17, 1936.

"Woman in Jury Box, Another Is Convicted." *Bridgeport Telegram* [Bridgeport, Connecticut], December 15, 1923.

"Woman Once Sentenced to Die Faces Trial in Brother's Slaying," *Albuquerque Journal*, August 10, 1941.

"Woman Pleads Innocent in Fire That Killed Her Children." *Gastonia Gaston Gazette* [Gastonia, North Carolina], May 4, 2002.

"Woman Saved from Death for Murder." *Syracuse Herald*, October 24, 1931.

"Woman Sentenced to Be Hung." *Williamsport Warren Republican* [Williamsport, Indiana], February 28, 1856.

"Woman Sentenced to Death." *San Mateo Times* [San Mateo, California], October 22, 1975.

"Woman Sentenced to Death." *Logansport Pharos Tribune* [Logansport, Indiana], June 27, 1989.

"Woman Sentenced to Death for Arranging Slayings of Husband, Hitman." *Associated Press*, September 17, 1994.

"Woman Sentenced to Death for Murdering Little Girl During Robbery." *Associated Press*, July 14, 1992.//
"Woman to Be Executed." *Goshen Daily Democrat* [Goshen, Indiana], December 30, 1897.
"Woman to Be Hanged." *New Albany Daily Ledger* [New Albany, Indiana], April 30, 1864.
"Woman to Die in Chair." *Indiana Evening Gazette* [Indiana, Pennsylvania], September 17, 1924.
"Woman to Stand Trial in Husband's Killing." *Los Angeles Times*, February 6, 1991.
"Woman's Death Sentence Upheld by State Supreme Court." *Associated Press*, June 28, 2005.
"Woman's First Husband Attends Murder Trial." *Altoona Mirror* [Altoona, Pennsylvania], July 26, 1980.
Women and the Death Penalty. Death Penalty Information Center. http://www.deathpenaltyinfo.org/women-and-death-penalty.
"Women as Criminals." *Logansport Chronicle* [Logansport, Indiana], August 3, 1895.
"Women and Girls Executed for Murder in America." Available at http://www.sonic.net/~msnyder/femvio/executed-US.htm.
"Women Facing Death Penalty." *New Castle News* [New Castle, Pennsylvania], March 12, 1940.
"Women Fight to Prevent Hanging." *La Crosse Tribune* [La Crosse, Wisconsin], November 15, 1913.
"Women Given Death in Rifle Slaying." *The Bee* [Portland, Oregon], December 10, 1975.
"Women Save Mrs. Ferola." *New York Times*, July 22, 1915.
"Women Sentenced to Death but Not Executed." *Miami Herald*, October 14, 2010.
"Women's Mass Meeting in New York." *Galveston Daily News* [Galveston, Texas], December 13, 1868.
Wood, Betty. "Some Aspects of Female Resistance to Chattel Slavery in Low Country Georgia, 1763–1815." *The Historical Journal*, 30 (1987), 603–622.
Woods v. State, 101 Nev. 128 (1985).
Woodson v. North Carolina, 428 U.S. 280 (1976).
Worchel, Dayna. "Kimberly Cargill Murder Trial Set for May." *Tyler Morning Telegraph*, April 30, 2010.
Worral, Arthur. *Quakers in the Colonial Northeast*. Hanover: University Press of New England, 1980.
"Worse than Second-Class: Solitary Confinement of Women in the United States." American Civil Liberties Union, April 2014. Available at https://www.aclu.org/worse-second-class.
Wright, Donald. *African Americans in the Colonial Era: From African Origins Through the American Revolution*. Arlington Heights: Harlan Davidson, 1991.
Wright, George. "By the Book: The Legal Executions of Kentucky Blacks." In W. Fitzhugh Brundage, ed., *Under Sentence of Death, Lynchings in the South* (pp. 250–270). Chapel Hill: University of North Carolina Press, 1997.
_____. *Racial Violence in Kentucky, 1865–1940: Lynchings, Mob Rule, and Legal Lynchings*. Baton Rouge: Louisiana State University Press, 1990.
Wright, Richard. "Women as Victims and Resisters: Depictions of the Oppression of Women Criminology Textbooks." *Teaching Sociology*, 23 (1995), 111–121.
Wright, Scott. "No Parole for Judith Ann Neelley—Ever." *The Post Online*, July 15, 2013. Available at http://www.postpaper.com/neelley071513.htm.
Wrongfully Convicted Data Base. http://forejustice.org/db/Labastida—Kriseya-.html. n
"W.Va. Man Again Guilty in Federal Capital Case." *Associated Press*, April 27, 2010.
Wyatt, Tim. "Retrial Yields Guilty Verdict; Lancaster Woman Could Get Death Sentence for Killing Neighbor in '97." *Dallas Morning News*, October 30, 2002.
Yang, Sandy. "Ariz. Woman Gets Death in Husband's Murder." *Associated Press*, December 22, 2004.
Yegge, Kathryn. "4 Held in Mansfield Couple's Slayings Son Among Suspects Charged with Capital Murder Solicitation." *Dallas Morning News*, April 8, 2004. Available at http://www.freerepublic.com/focus/f-news/1114026/posts.
Young, Robert. "Arsenic and No Lace: The Bizarre Tale of a Philadelphia Murder Ring." *Pennsylvania History*, 67 (2000), 397–414.
Young, Vernetta. "Gender Expectations and Their Impact on Black Female Offenders and Victims." *Justice Quarterly*, 3 (1986), 305–327.
Younge, Gary. "Pardon for Maid Executed in 1945: Campaigners Celebrate Clemency for Woman Who Killed Employer." *The Guardian*, August 17, 2005.
Zalman, Marvin. "Edwin Borchard and the Limits of Innocence Reform." In C. Ronald Huff and Martin Killias, eds., *Wrongful Convictions and Miscarriages of Justice: Causes and Remedies in North American and European Criminal Justice Systems* (pp. 329–355). New York: Routledge, 2013.
Zanger, Jules. "Crime and Punishment in Early Massachusetts." *William and Mary Quarterly*, 22 (1965), 471–477.
Zangrando, Robert. *The Naacp Crusade Against Lynching, 1909–1950*. Philadelphia: Temple University Press, 1980.
Zywien, Stephanie. "Executing the Insane: A Look at Death Penalty Schemes in Arkansas, Georgia and Texas." *Suffolk Journal of Trial and Appellate Advocacy*, 12 (2007), 93–119.
Zwicker, Roxie. *Haunted Portsmouth: Spirits and Shadows of the Past*. Charleston: History Press, 2007.

Index

Abigail, slave to Gysbert Vaninburgh 87
Accessible Archives 32
Action Committee for Women in Prison 19
Admiralty Court 8
Alfaro, Maria Del Rosio 358
Alito, Justice Samuel 21
Agar, Agnes 311
age of defendant 36
Ailey, slave to Edna McMichael 112
Alexander, slave ship 83
Allen, Margaret Ann 347
Allen, Wanda Jean 20, 23, 24, 28, 42, 135, 166–168
Allison, Annie Mae 322
Allyn, Thomas 69
American Bar Association 22, 29, 291, 298
American Civil Liberties Union 337, 378
American Indian women 1, 7–9, 35–37, 39–41, 90–91, 131–132, 186–187, 233, 375
American League to Abolish Capital Punishment 174
Amnesty International 25
Amsterdam, Anthony 17
Amy, slave to Maj. A.C. Spain 121
Anaca, slave to Ellis Palmer 117
Anderson, Esther 81
Andrew, Brenda Evers 369
Andrews, Mary 103
Andrews, Susanna 77
Andriano, Wendi Elizabeth 365–366
Angel, Paula 129
Anglo intolerance 8
Ann, slave to Dr. William S. Croxton 112
Ann, slave to John Easton 88
Annice, slave to Jeremiah Prior 117
Annis, slave Henry Ormond 109
antebellum slavery 3, 41, 111–121, 132
Anthony, Susan B. 306
anti-Catholicism 8
Antinomianism 66
Antinomian controversy 65–67
Antiterrorism and Effective Death Penalty Act 339
Antoine, Mary 131
Antonio, Anna 153–154
Arden, slave woman 114
Ardner, Sally 95
Arnett, Mary 103

Arthur, Pres. Chester 303
Ashcroft, Gov. John 325
Atkins, Daryl Reynard 24
Atkins v. Virginia 24–25, 379
Atkinson, Gov. William 312
Atwell, Mary Welek 32, 335
Atwood, Elizabeth 77
Axell, Mary 75
Aztecs 128

Baker, Lena 163–164, 322
Baldus, David 16
Barclay, Polly 95
Barfield, Velma Margie 136, 146–147
Barnes, Mary 69
Barnett, Angelica 302
Bassett, Goodwife 68
Bassett, Martha 81–82
Bassett, Thomas 68
Basso, Suzanne Margaret 32, 136, 148–150
Batson v. Kentucky 29, 357, 380
battered woman syndrome 20, 25, 183, 195, 197, 199, 291, 336, 345, 379
"Beatrice Six" 189
Beck, slave to Sarah Taylor 115
Bedau, Hugo 174
Beets, Betty Lou 25, 156, 379
Bell, Christiana 79
benefit of clergy 104
benefit-of-linen 74
Berlow, Alan 175, 291
Bertrand, Delphine 181, 184
Bess, slave to Joseph Warnock 109
Bessler, John 32
Bett, slave to Wilhelmus Houghtaling 90
Betty, slave to Isaac Winslow 88
Betty, slave to Smith 115
Bevan, Catharine 80, 95
Bevers (Beaver), Sarah 301
Bigler, Gov. William 307
Bilansky, Mary Ann 97–98
Bill of Rights 12, 26
Bishop, Alice (Allis) Martin Clark 76
Bishop, Bridget Playfer 70, 299
bipolar disorder 26, 379
black codes 121
black inferiority 21
Black Nationalism 165
Blackmon, Patricia 356–357
Blackmun, Justice Harry 17
Blackwood, Gov. Ibar C. 320

Blay, Ruth 100
Blease, Gov. Cole L. 314
Block, Lynda Lyon 25, 148
Bolton, Mildred Mary 141, 321
Boon, Emily 304
Booth, Mary 313
Borchard, Edwin Montefiore 174
Bowen, Anne 82
Boxley, Tucker 36
Bradbury, Mary Perkins 299
Bradley, Sarah Jane 123
Brady v. Maryland 28, 380
Bramble, Sarah 78
Brandon, Gov. William W. 318
Brandstad, Gov. Terry 325
Brazier, Susannah 101
Bredesen, Gov. Phil 333
Brennan, Justice William 17, 21
Brian, Mary 302
Briggs, Ruth 78
British mainland colonies 64, 83, 290
Bronson, Catherine 104
Brooks, Jane 311
Broughton, Gov. J. Melville 322
Brown, Debra Denise 184–185, 326–327, 341, 362
Brown, Joyce Ann 181, 185
Brown, Milbry 127
Brown, Tina Lasonya 348
Brown v. Board of Education 165
Brumbaugh, Gov. Martin G. 317
Bryan, Sheila 185
Buenoano (Welty), Judy Ann 155–156
Buenrostro, Dora 339
Bullingnee, Ann 301
Bullock, Gov. Rufus B. 304
Burleigh, Charles C. 174
Burnett, Judge Arthur L. 21
Burnett, Lavinia 106
Bush, George W. 291
Bushnell, Gov. Asa Smith 305
Butler, Betty Evelyn 165
Butler, Louise 181
Butler, Sabrina 20
Buzard, Anne 79

Caillier, Carla Ann 27
Caine, Margaret 82
Calef, Robert 70
Callogharne, Margaret 77
Calvert, Gov. Charles 301
Cameron, Gov. William Evelyn 313
Campbell, Gov. James Edwin 305
Canen, Lana 182, 186

Cantero, Justice Raoul 19
capital justice 10; and the modern era 1, 18–30; and the U.S. Supreme Court 12–18
Cardona, Ana 361–362
Carey, May (Mary) H. 138–139
Cargill, Kimberly Diane 341, 354
Carlson, Doris Ann 27
Caro, Socorro Susan 358
Caroline, slave to William Rogus 112
Carr, Emilia Lily 341, 348
Carrier, Martha Allen 70, 299
Carrington, Celeste Simone 344–345
Carrington, Joan 69, 72
Carter, Elizabeth "Lizzie" 305
Carter, Matilda 126
Carty, Linda Anita 338–339
Cash, Martha 301
Cashiere, Catharine 114
Caty, slave to Linah Harwell 112
Caudill, Virginia 349
Cela, slave to Wyat Smith 117
Celeste, Gov. Richard F. 315, 325–327
Celia, slave to Daughtry 112
Celia, slave to Robert Newsom 119
Centurion Ministries 185, 197
Chamberlain, Sarah 75, 103
Chamberlin, Lisa Jo 350–351
Chamblitt, Rebeckah 77–78
Champion, June 2, 32, 75
Champion, Percival 75
characteristics of female executions 33–40
Charity, slave ship 73
Chase, Auriela 115
Chasity, slave to Lawson 116
Cherry, Axey 312
Chiles, Gov. Lawton 325
chivalry theory 2, 6–7, 64
Chloe, slave to Andrew Carothers 113
Choctaw Indians 110
Christian, Virginia 160–161
Ciccone, Maddalena 317
Cignarale, Chiara 310
Cinda, slave to Lubbock 116
Civil Rights Act of 1875 124
Civil Rights Act of 1965 165
Civil Rights Cases 124
civil rights movement 10
Civil War 13, 99
Clark, Sarah 105
Clarke, Gov. George 300–302
class hierarchy 10
clemency 290
Cleveland, Gov. Grover 311
Clifton, Alice 300
Clinton, Gov. Dewitt 310
Cody, Amanda 126
Coffman, Cynthia Lynn 345
Cole, Tiffany Ann 348
Coleman, Lisa Ann 169
Collar, Magdalen 75
Colledge, Joan 75
Collins, Opal 323
colonial conquest 8–9
colonial slavery 41, 85–86, 88–89, 91, 108–111, 132, 293
Colonial Williamsburg Foundation 32
Colored Woman's League 315
Colquitt, Gov. Alfred H. 304
Colson, Elizabeth 88

Comfort, Abiah (Nantucket Indian) 90
commutations 290
Congress of Racial Equality 165
Connelly, Ann 105
Conner, Gov. Martin Sennett 321
Connor, Catherine 83, 301
convict farms 122
Coo, Eva 139, 172
Corey, Martha Rich 70, 299
Cornish, Goodwife 80
covenant of grace 66
covenant of works 66
Cox, Susannah 101
Craig, Gov. George N. 323
Craig, Sarah 302
Creasy, slave to Mrs. Morrisett 114
Creese, slave to Fisher 116
Creighton, Mary Frances 139–140
crime waves 65
criminal offenses 36
criminology 8
critical perspective 10–12
Croy, Norma Jean 186–187
Cruce, Gov. Lee 314
cruel and unusual punishment 14, 196, 379
Cunningham, Alice 82
Cusumano, Lena 316
Cutler, Annie E. 307

Dailey, Mary 104
Dalton, Kerry Lyn 345
Daniels, Gov. Price 324
Daphne, slave to Edward Travis 111
Davis, Gray 291
Dayon, slave to Abraham Bruyn 113
Dean, Dovie Blanche 154–155
Dean, Jerry Lynn 8, 147
Dean, Dr. Sarah Ruth 320
Death Penalty Information Center 32, 176
de Gálvez, Visitor-General José 128
DeGarno v. Texas 21
Degoe, Hannah 88
Dennison, Earle 159
de Portolá, Gaspar 128
Deukmejian, George 291
Dickinson, Gov. John 302
Dickson, Mary 300
Digital Library on American Slavery 32
Dinah, slave to Peter Damon 110
Dinah, slave woman 115
DiSalle, Gov. Michael V. 323
Disney Corporation 9
Dix, Gov. John 311
Dockery, Gov. Alexander M. 315
Dodds, Catherine "Kitty" 325–326
Dolbow, Marguerite Fox 321
Dolly, slave to James Sands 109
Donohue, Prof. John 335
Douglas, Justice William 13
Dower 72
Dred Scott v. Sandford 17
Druse, Roxalana 98–99
Dudley, Gov. Joseph 299
due process of law 12–13, 26, 28, 30, 196–197, 229, 267, 279, 289, 377, 380
Dugan, Eva 137
Duncan, Elizabeth Ann 136, 146

Durgan, Bridget 103
Dyer, Mary Barrett 68, 374

Eagle, slave ship 84
Eames, Rebecca Blake 299
Earle, Gov. George E. 316
Early Jim Crow 124–128
Eastman Race Riot 125–126
Easty, Mary Towne 70, 299
Eberhart, Susan 107
Echols, Fannie 303
economic deprivation 1
Eden, Gov. Robert 301–302
Edgar, Gov. Jim 325, 328
Edwards, Gov. Edwin 325–326
Edwards, Gov. John C. 307
Edwards, Kate 317
Eighth Amendment 16–17, 26
Eliza, slave to Dr. William S. Croxton 112
Eliza, slave to Griffin 115
Elizabethan England 8
Elkins, Jane 114
Ellison, Ella Mae 187
emancipation 13
Emerson, Elizabeth 77
English common law 290
Equal Justice Initiative 371
equal protection of the law 13–14, 16, 26, 30, 229, 241, 289, 377, 380
equality theory 2, 9–10
Erwin, Elizabeth 101
Espy, M. Watt 31
Esther, slave to Blount 111
Esther, slave to Wise 109
ethnic chauvinism 8
Eubanks, Susan Dianne 359
Evans, Harriet 319–320
Eve, slave to Peter Montague 87, 108
evil woman theory 2, 7–9
Ewing, Jane 101
execution methods 37
execution of dead women 95
execution of pregnant women 94
exonerations 174–228

Facteau, Peggy 102
Factors Contributing to False Convictions 180–184
Fagan, Prof. Jeffrey 378
false confessions 181
false eyewitness identification 180–181
false forensic evidence 182–183
Fanny, slave woman 115
Farmer, Mary O'Brien 136–137
Faulkner, Abigail 299
Fava, Italian ambassador baron 310
female-headed households 11
female slaves as breeders 118
female subordination 10
Fennison, Margaret 78
Fenton, Gov. Rueben 311
Ferola, Madeline 318
Fielder, Gov. James F. 317
Fisher, Lavinia 105–106
fit object of mercy 300
Flower, Gov. Roswell P. 311–312
Folk, Gov. Joseph W. 315
Foraker, Gov. Joseph B. 305
Ford, Priscilla Joyce 341–344
"Ford Heights Four" 189

Index

Forde, Shawna 341–342
forensic DNA evidence 184
forgotten population 2
Foss, Gov. Eugene N. 314, 317
Foster, Anne Alcock 299
Foster, Doris Ann 326
Foster, Esther 114
Fourteenth Amendment 12, 15–17, 125, 229, 275, 279
Fowler, Helen Ray 163
Fowler, Rebecca 72
Fowlkes, Lucinda 123–124
Frances, slave to Berry 116
Francisca, María 38, 128
Francisco, Rachel 300
Frank, Antoinette 340–350
Franklin, Gov. Benjamin 300
Franklin (Hoag, Frisch), Polly 311
Frazier, Harriet 32
Fredenburg, Lodicia 310
Free, Marvin 176
Freeman, Elizabeth 123
Freeman, Jeannace June 324
Fritz, Judith 181
Furman, William Henry 14
Furman v. Georgia 14–15, 18, 314, 370, 371

Garcia, Guinevere Falakassa 328
Garrabrant, Elizabeth "Libbie" 308
Garrett, Daniel Ryan 147
Garrett, Katherine (Pequot Indian) 39
Garrett, Mary 305
Geary, Gov. John W. 306
gender bias 11–12
gender discrimination 11
gender disparity 6
gender inequality 10–11
gender oppression 1–2, 10–12, 22, 30
gender stratification 10–11
genocide 9
George, Cynthia 184, 187–188
Gideon's Trumpet 19
Gilbert, Lydia 69
Gilbreath, West 32
Gillespie, Ellenor 95
Gillespie, L. Kay 32
Gilmore, Selina 161
Ginsburg, Justice Ruth Bader 20
Given, Margaret 207
Glass, Maria 110
Glover, Anne 69, 71
Gobble, Tierra Capri 357
Godman, Elizabeth 72
Goeldi, Anna 70
Goldman, Steven 28
Gonzales, Alberto R. 291
Gonzales, Kathy 183, 188–189
Gonzales, Veronica 359
Gooch, Gov. William 302
Good, Dorcas 70
Good, Sarah Solart Poole 70, 299
Goodwin, John 70
Goodwin, Martha 70
Gordon, Elizabeth 82
Gordon, Gov. John B. 304
Gordon, Lt. Gov. Patrick 300–301
Grace, Nancy 27
Grace, slave to James Taylor 88
Grace, slave to Joseph Galloway 110
Grady, Katharine 39
Graham, Barbara 144–146

Graham v. Florida 371
Grant, Elizabeth 302
Grant, Rosalie 326–327
Grant, Pres. Ulysses S. 7, 304
Grauel, Elizabeth Learch 79
Gray, Paula 25, 181
Greeley, Horace 30, 174
Green, Elizabeth 326–327
Greene, Elizabeth 75
Greenley, Elizabeth 8
Greensmith, Rebecca 69, 71
Gregg, Troy Leon 1
Gregg v. Georgia 1, 14–15, 19, 33, 146, 229, 240, 325
Grier (Crittenden), Harriet 304
Grinder, Martha 107
Grover, Mary 30
Gryce, Deborah 7

Hagar, slave to James Sherron 8
Hagerman, Gov. Herbert J. 316
Hahn, Anna Marie 140
Haight, Angenette B. 310
Hall, Bertha 31
Hall, Mary 302
Hall, Paula 184, 189–191
Hall, Phyllis 184, 189–190
Hall, Gov. Willard P. 308
Hallenschied, Anna 308
Halliday, Elizabeth "Lizzie" 312
Hamilton, Gov. James 300, 302
Hampton, Mary Kathryn 183
Hannah, slave to Charles Clagget 302
Hannah, slave to George Walker 90
Hannah, slave to Moses Atwater 87
Hannah, slave to Nicholas Summer 110
Hardin, Gov. Charles H. 308
Hardman, Gov. Lamaratine G. 319
Harker, Elizabeth 306
Harrill, Clinton 36
Harris, Alcee 123
Harris, Louise 20, 27
Harris, Margaret 126–127
Harris v. Alabama 27
Harrison, Pres. Benjamin 303
Hatch, Margaret 75
Hatfield, Gov. Mark 324
Havard, Kenny 291
Hawaiian women 35–39, 41, 92, 132, 180
Hawkins, Rebecca 307
Haycraft, Sarah 308
Hayes, Gov. Rutherford B. 304–305
Hayes (Hill), Sadie 313
Heady, Bonnie Brown 144
Hearn, Daniel Allen 32
Hendricks, Angel 79
Henry, Annie Beatrice (aka Toni Jo Henry) 141–142
Heritage Microfilm 32
Herrera v. Collins 290
Hibbins, Anne 69
Hill, Christina 182
Hispanophobia 8
historical contours of female executions 40–42
Hoag, Anna 97
Hoar, Dorcas 299
Hoffman, Gov. Harold G. 321
Holberg, Brittany 354–355
Holmes, Brandy Aileen 350

Holmes, Mary 161–162
Holmes, Gov. Robert D. 314
Holt, Susanne 301
Horner, Elizabeth 302
Horner, Gov. Henry 320–321
The Horse 122
Houghson, Sarah 300
Houghtaling, Margaret 102, 176
Houston, Gen. Sam 309
Howe, Elizabeth Jackson 70, 299
Howells, William 174
Huckabee, Mike 291
Hudibras, slave ship 85
Huff, Jane 112
Hughes, Gov. Harry 326
Hughes, Polly 95
Hughson, Sarah 83
Hunt, Ann 123
Hunt, Martha 301
Hunter, Gov. Robert 300
Huson, Anne 301
Hutchinson, Anne 66–68
Hutchinson, Susanna 67
Hutter, Margaret Ann 113–114

indentured servants 40, 64–65, 69, 73–75, 81–82, 86, 90, 93, 95, 109–110, 126, 374
ineffective assistance of counsel 19–21, 156, 183, 205, 212, 244, 264, 289, 291, 337, 368, 378
Ingram, Margaret 301
Innocence Project 176
Inslee, Gov. Jay 325
insufficient evidence 184
Irish 64–65, 70, 74, 81–83, 92–93, 95, 97, 103, 105, 107, 134, 136, 312

"Jack the Ripper" 312
Jackson, Annie Mae "Billy" 319
Jackson, Effie 315
Jackson, Pearl 318
Jacobs, Sonia 27
James, Elsie (Chickasaw Indian) 303
James, Gov. Forrest "Fob" 329
Jane, slave to Henry Brite 233
Jaspin, Elliot 122
J.E.M. v. Alabama 29
Jenny, slave to Hugh Anderson 108
Jenny, slave to Jones 116
Jenny, slave to Joseph Galloway 110
Jenny, slave woman 109, 117
Jezebel 8, 119
Jim Crow 3, 10, 13, 29, 41, 92, 108, 124–128, 132, 163–165, 181, 322, 376
Joan of Arc 68
Johnson, Catherine 311
Johnson, Emma 191
Johnson, Eveline 311
Johnson, Mary 68, 71–72, 104, 176
Johnson (James), Mildred Louise 162–163
Johnson, Sophia 191
Jones, Ann 32
Jones, Ashley 371–372
Jones, Gov. Brereton 325
Jones, Charlotte 106
Jones, Margaret 69, 72
Jordan, Winthrop 8

Josefa, María 38, 128
Josephine, slave to William Rogus 112
Judd, Winnie Ruth (McKinnell) 324
judicial override 10, 26–27
Judith, slave to Edward Harris 37
jurisdiction of execution 38–39
jury nullification 23

Kaine, Gov. Tim 72, 299
Kaomali 38, 39, 132
Karibi-Ikiriko, Abere Biobele 191–192
Kate, slave to Thomas Belding 88
Keen, Rosanne 116
Keith, Gov. William 300–301
Kendall, Elizabeth 3, 69, 175
Kennedy, Mary 105
Kennedy v. Louisiana 335
Kenny, Penelope 78
Killian, Gloria 192
Kimbler, Captain John 85
King, Wilma 313
King Kamehameha III 132
Kirchin, Margaretta Catherine 300
Kirk, Eleanor 306
Kirk, Sarah 94–95
Klumpp, Edythe Margaret 323
Knapp, Goodwife (Elizabeth) 69
Knight, Ann 161
Knights of the White Camellias 122
Konvisser, Zieva Dauber 176
Ku Klux Klan 122

LaBatte, Beth 182, 192–193
Lacey, Mary 299
Lake, Alice 69
Lake, Henry 69
Lamar, Mirabeau B. 309
Lampkin, Beatrice 326, 328
Lanier, Prof. Charles 373
Larrazolo, Gov. Octaviano A. 316
Larson, Gov. Morgan F. 320
Lashley, Margaret 126
Laska, Lewis L. 32
Latham, Mary 81
Lawes, Lewis 174
Leathers, Gloria 23
LeBoeuf, Ada Bonner 153
Leddra, William 68
Lee, Gov. Henry 302
Lee, Mary 39, 73
lesbian capital defendants 23, 277, 379
lethal violence 10
Letty, slave to Robert Hartford 313
Lewis, Anthony 19
Lewis, Hannah 306
Lewis, Teresa Wilson Bean 157–159
Liberty, slave ship 85
Life After Exoneration Program 176
Linehan (Hughes), Mechele 193–194
Livingston, Edward 174
Logue, Sue Stidham 142
Louisiana Correctional Institute for Women 326
Lowry, Gov. Robert 307
Lucas, Margaret 194–195
Lucio, Melissa Elizabeth 363
Lucy, slave to Bouligny 115
Lucy, slave to Dr. Mathew Hardy 87
Lucy, slave to Mrs. Maria Dougherty 112
Lucy, slave to Richard Randolph 87
Lucy, slave to Thomas Balton 118

Lucy, slave to Wyriot Ormond 109
Lunt, Mary 75
Lyles, Anjette Donovan 323
lynchings 13, 122
Lyons, Alma 316

Madison, Nellie May 320
Madrid, Valentina 316
male domination 10
Malina, slave woman 116
Mammy 8
Mann, Pamela (Pamelia) Dickinson 309
Marja, slave woman 89
Marshall, Justice Thurgood 13, 18, 19, 30, 302, 378
Martin, Eve 132
Martin, Gov. John W. 319
Martin, Mary 76, 306
Martin, Rhonda Bell 155
Martin, Susannah North 70, 299
Martin, Valerie Dee 345
Mary, slave to Brinker 113
Mary, slave woman 90, 111
massiveness of racial discrimination 166
Mata, Bernina 24, 329
material wealth 10
Mathers, Cotton 68, 76
Matowa 9
matriarchal 8
Matthews, Constantine 104
Matthews, Margaret 302
Matts, Sarah 104, 302
Maze, Elizabeth 75
McAnulty, Angela Darlene 362–363
McCarthy, Kimberly 42, 135, 168–169
McCarty, Carrie 36
McClellan, Gov. George B. 309
McCleskey, Warren 15
McCleskey v. Kemp 15
McCoy, Catherine 308
McCoy, Pauline 127
McDermott, Maureen 337, 346
McDonald, Rebecca 301
McKay, Hannah 111
McKean, Gov. Thomas 306
McKeithen, Shellie 36
McShane, Kate 38
Meaker, Emeline 38, 100–101
Meierhoeffer, Margaret Klem 99
Melvaine, slave Florentine Frivaz 114
Mental Health America 26
mental illnesses 337, 339, 379
mental retardation 20, 21, 25–26, 33, 158, 166–168, 242, 272, 289, 298, 300, 356, 379
Merriam, Gov. Frank Finley 320
Merrill, Gov. Steve 325
Mesca, Francesca 132
Mexican women 1, 7–9, 39–40, 92, 128–130, 293, 376
Meyers, Maggie (Agnes or Aggie) 315
Michaud, Michelle Lyn 346
Micke, William J. 14
Millay, slave to Robe 116
Miller, Barbara 126
Miller, Catharine 98
Miller, Hannah 117
Miller, Lena 176
Miller v. Alabama 371
Milley, slave to Hanley 117

Mily, slave to Fox 115
Minutes of the Provincial Council of Pennsylvania 300
Miranda v. Arizona 353
Mitchell, Anne 301
Mitchell, Minnie 141, 321
Mol, slave Jeremiah Pattison 37
Molly, slave to Clark 111
Molly, slave to Marshall 120
Monroe, Beverly 195
Montgomery, Lisa 355–356
Moody, Deborah 66
Moore, Blanche Kiser Taylor 20, 341, 351–352
Moore, Bob Durwood 15
Moore, Dolores 39, 333
Moore, Elizabeth 117
Moore, Ella 125–126
Moore, Julia 170
Morgan, Gov. Edwin D. 311
Morgan, Margaret "Maggie" 324
Moss, Rebecca 79
Murphy, Elizabeth 78
Murray, Mary 82
Murrell, Henrietta 127

Nan, slave to Smith 120
Nan, slave to Sutton 111
Nancy, slave to Rhodes 116
Nancy, slave woman 114
National Registry of Exonerations 176, 182
Neelley, Judith Ann 27, 328–329
Nelly, slave to Daniel Braine 116
Nelly, slave to Henry Edwards 307
Nelly, slave to William Rogus 112
Nelly, slave woman 111
Nelson, Tanya Jaime 347
Neptune, slave ship 85
Newton, Frances Elaine 20, 42, 135, 168
Nieves, Sandi 360
Ninth U.S. Circuit Court of Appeals 19
no crime cases 183–184
Nobles (Scarborough), Elizabeth 312
Northern California Innocence Project 175
Norton, Mary Beth 65
Nurse, Rebeccah Towne 70, 299

O'Cammon, Mary 38
occupation of offender 39–40
occupational segregation 11
occupational structure 11
O'Connor, Justice Sandra Day 16
Ocuish, Hannah 131
official misconduct 183
O'Hare, Sheila 32
Olge, Gov. Samuel 301
Oliver, Emma 322
Oliver, Mary 66
Olson, Gov. Culbert 320
Ortiz, Sandra 195
Osgood, Ellen 125
O'Shea, Kathleen 32
Oshinsky, David 307
Ottley, Ann 82
Owens, Gaile Kirksey 331–333, 336

Pacheco, Rod 27
Parchman Penitentiary 307

pardons 290
Pariente, Justice Barbara 180–181
Parker, Alice 70, 299
Parker, Carlette Elizabeth 352
Parker, Mary 70
Parker, Judge Isaac 303
Parker, Jane 302
Parsons, Mary 72, 76–77
Pataki, Gov. George 325
patriarchal social order 10, 66–67, 73, 79, 91, 306
Pattison, Gov. Robert E. 307
Pauline, slave to Rabbeneck 112
Pavlinac, Laverne 181, 195–196
Peabody, Gov. Endicott 314
Peasley, Kenneth 28
Peete, Louise 142–143
Peggin, Hannah 131
Peine forte et dure 76
Penelope, slave to Copeland 111
Penn, Lt. Gov. John 302
Penn, Gov. Richard 300
Penn, William 82
Pennsylvania Committee on Racial and Gender Bias in the Justice System 18
Pennypacker, Gov. Samuel W. 317
Peppers, Catherine 101
Pequot Indians 66, 69
Perdue, Pattie 161
peremptory challenge 10
perjury 145, 182
Perry, Mary 83
personality disorders 26, 250, 289, 367, 379
Petersen v. Florida 180
petit treason 79–80, 95, 115, 374
Pettit, Leona 196
Phillipps, Samuel March 174
Phillips, Rosana Lightner 162
Phillis, slave to Captain John Codman 108
Phillis, slave to John Greenleaf 88
Phips, Gov. William 299
Phoebe, slave to Joseph Richardson 110
Phyllis, slave woman 109
Pike, Christa 353–354
Pinchot, Gov. Gifford 321
Pineda, Lisa 196
Place, Martha Savacool 102
place of execution 38
Plantz, Marilyn 156–157
pleading her belly 75, 300
Pleasant, Gov. James 313
Plunkett, Anne 82
Pocahontas 9
political powerlessness 1
Polk, James K. 129
Poll, slave to Bobbitt 115, 117
Pompilla v. Beard 21
Pongas, slave ship 84
Porter, Marie 140–141
Post, Mary 299
post-traumatic stress disorder 20, 25–26, 119, 156, 196, 243, 248, 250, 282, 345, 348, 353, 355–356, 379
Poteat, Milly (Millie) 313
Potts, Elizabeth 107
poverty 18–21
Powell, Justice Lewis 16

Powell, Mary 81–82
Powell v. Alabama 21
preindustrial colonial America 64
Proceedings of the National Academy of Sciences 174
Proctor, Elizabeth Bassett 299
prosecutorial discretion 10, 20–23
prosecutorial homophobia 23–24
prosecutorial lawlessness 10, 27–29
prosecutorial misconduct 10
prostitution of slaves 119
Pudeator, Ann Greenslit 70, 299
Puhae, Gertrude 141, 320
Pulliam, Latasha 329–330
Purnell, Lucy 124
Puritan women 64–68

Quaker intrusion 67–68, 91
Quinn, Gov. Patrick 315

race of the defendant 14
race of the victim 14, 39
racial bias 13
Radelet, Michael 174
Rapaport, Elizabeth 32
Rauch, Margaret 101
Raynolds, Acting Gov. James W. 316
Reardon, Sarah 301
Reasonover, Ellen 28–29, 196–197
Reconstruction 10, 41, 92, 121–124, 132, 171, 307
Recovery, slave ship 85
Red Shirts 122
Redd, Wilmot 299
Reed, Elizabeth "Betsey" 96
Reed, Wilmot 70
regional variation in female executions 37–38
Rehnquist, Justice William 16
Renah, slave woman 115
Reynolds, Catherine 300
Reynolds, Gov. Thomas 307
Rhodie, slave woman 115
Richards, Gov. Ann 290
Richardson, Elizabeth 39, 73
Richardson, Gov. John 313
Riggs, Christina Marie 25, 159–160, 379
Rimby, Elizabeth 305
Ring v. Arizona 25, 27, 348
Roberta, slave woman 115
Roberts, slave ship 84
Roberts, Gov. Barbara 325
Roberts, Donna Marie 338, 368–369
Robinson, Elizabeth 83
Robinson, Henrietta 310
Robinson, William 68
Rockefeller, Gov. Winthrop 314
Rocky Mountain Innocence Center 185
Rodríguez, Angelina 366–367
Rodríguez, Chipita 39, 130
Roe, Judith 82
Rogers, Esther 77
Rogers, Horatio 374
Rogers, Mary Mabel 152–153
Roman Catholic Church 68, 83
Romer, Gov. Roy 325
Romualdo, Josephine 321
Rooney v. North Dakota 38
Roosevelt, Theodore 103
Rose, slave woman 110

Rose, Ernestine L. 306
Rosenberg, Ethel 38, 150–151
Ross, Gov. George 302
Rottiers, Brooke Marie 347
Routier, Darlie Lynn 363–364
Row, Robin 370
Ruesink, Mitch 176
runaway servants 105
runaway slaves 118, 302
Runkle, Mary Alice 97
Ryan, Gov. George 314–315, 329
Ryley, Alice 82, 95

Salem witchcraft trials 68, 299
Sall, slave woman 114
Sampson, Patience 39, 90
Samuels, Mary Ellen 367
Sandoval, Pablita 39
Sanford, Mary 69
Santiago, supply ship 128
Sarah, slave woman 87, 89, 111–112, 116
Sarah Artch, slave ship 73
Sarinana, Cathy 360
Scales, Gov. Alfred M. 313
Scalia, Justice Antonin 16
Schaefer, Gov. William 325
Schmidt, Eve Mary 83
Schroeder, Irene Crawford 137–138
Scott, Christie Michelle 27, 358
Scott, Margaret 70, 299
Seaborn, Margaret 105
Seaborn (Beck), Martha Jule 143–144
Seigenthaler, John 336
selective incorporation doctrine 12
Sephens, Gov. Lawrence V. 313–314
Serra, Junípero 128
sex discrimination 16
sex trafficking 9
sexism 11–12, 18
sexist ideology 11, 31
Sexton, Margaret 103
sexual control of slave women 118, 376
Seymour, Gov. Horatio 310–311
Sharp, Martha 101
Sharpe, Gov. Horatio 301
Shaw, Elizabeth 78
Shelden, Debra 183, 187–188
Sheppard, Erica 355
Sherrer, Hans 176
Sherwood, Grace White 72, 299
Shipman, Marlin 32
Shipp, Caroline 127–128
Shitts, Margaret 300
Shivers, Gov. Allan 322
Shultz, Gov. John Andrew 306
Siggins, Margaret 104
Silver, Frances "Frankie" 96
Silvy, slave woman 115
Simmons, Fred Edward 15
Simpson, Sarah 78
Sitty, slave woman 110
Siwanoy Indians 67
Sixth Amendment 12, 19, 22, 167, 353
slave markets 135
Smiley, Judge Prentiss 24
Smith, Jennie R. 309
Smith, Lois Nadean 169–170
Smith, Sarah 77
Smykla, John Ortiz 31
Snipes, Beatrice Ferguson 320

Snodgrass, Mary 103
Snyder, Janeen Marie 360–361
Snyder, Ruth Brown 153
social hierarchy 10
social inequality 11
social opportunities 10
social status or social prestige 10–11
social vulnerability 1
societal privilege 10
Sorubiero, Margaret 83
Sotomayor, Justice Sonia 180
Southern, Catherine "Kate" 304
Southern Christian Leadership Conference 165
Spain 128
Spanish Mexico 8
Spearman, Mary 301
Spinelli, Eithel 140
Spooner, Bathsheba Ruggles 39, 94
Sproul, Gov. William C. 317
Spurrier, Elizabeth 82
Stanton, Elizabeth Cady 306
state sanctioned violence 11
Stevens, Justice John Paul 17, 29
Stevenson, Marmaduke 68
Stewart, Gov. Robert M. 308
Stiles, Henry 69
Stillwell, Barbara 102
Stinette, Rose Marie 165
Stone, Gov. William J. 31
Stonehouse, Carol 183, 197 Stratton, Alice 69
Strauder v. West Virginia 29
Streamline Procedures Act of 2005 28
Streib, Victor 31–32
Strickland v. Washington 21
Stuart, Gov. Edwin S. 317
Student Nonviolent Coordinating Committee 165
Sucky, slave woman 110
sudden infant death syndrome 117, 370
Sue, slave to Constant Chapman 301
Sue, slave woman 301
Sullivan, Catherine 75
Surratt, Mary 38, 106–107
Susan, servant girl 123
Susan, slave woman 112
Sykes, Corrine 164–165

Tafero, Jesse 27
Talbye, Dorothy 66, 76
Talmadge, Gov. Eugene 319
Tandy, Ann 75
Taylor, Ada JoAnn 183, 187–188
Teasdale, Lucinda 126
Teeters, Negley 300
Tener, Gov. John K. 316–317
Terkel, Louis 1
Texas Court of Criminal Appeals 19
Texas Defenders Service 20

Thames, slave ship 85
Tharp, Michelle Sue 363
Theory of Presumptive Proof 174
Thirteenth Amendment 121
Thomas, Cherice 198
Thomas, Deputy Gov. George 301
Thomas, Teresa 198
Thompson, Abigail 80
Thompson, Catherine 367–368
Thompson, Eula Mae 319
Thornton, Deborah Ruth Davis 8, 147
Threeneedles, Sarah 77
Thurmond, Strom 142
Tilden, Gov. Samuel 310–311
Tituba, slave woman 71
Toca v. Alabama 371
Tórrez, Robert 32, 316
Tracy, Sarah 82
Treaty of Guadalupe Hidalgo 129
trial by touch 80
Triangle Shirtwaist Factory 134
Tribble, Anna 128
Trost, Freida Hartmann 316
Trusler, Eleanor 66
Truth in Justice 176
Tucker, Karla Faye 7–8, 147–148
Turbin, Johanna 7, 303
Turner, Mary 122
Twiggs, Mary 97
Twopence, Elizabeth 75
Tyson, Betty 181, 198–199

Umble, Amanda 315
Underdown, Martha 300
unidentified slave women and girls 40, 86–87, 89–90, 108–111, 116–119, 130
U.S. Calvary 9
U.S. Department of Justice 22
United States v. Jackson 240
Unjust Conviction and Imprisonment Act 199
Utah's Post-Conviction Remedies Act 185

valued resources 11
Vandiver, Gov. Ernest 323
van Valkenburgh, Elizabeth 96–97
Vaughn, Elizabeth 101
Vaughn, Hester 306
Venus, slave to Catherine Ball 110, 121
Verrin, Jane 66
victims of the State 176
Victor, Sarah M. 304
Vienna Convention on Consular Relations and Optional Protocols 338
Vina, slave Joseph Wynn 113
Violet, slave to Sawyer 110
Voinovich, Gov. George V. 327
Voting Rights Act of 1964 165

Waisoiusksquaw (Mohegan-Pequot Indian) 90
Wakefield, Elizabeth 75
Walker, Dr. Lenore 345
Wall, Rachel 105
Wallens Ridge State Prison 24
Wallis, Mary 123
Walter, Shonda 352
Wardell, Sarah 299
Warren, Justice Earl 12
Washington, Booker T. 317
Washington, David Leroy 21
Washington, George 94
Waters, Pearl 314
Watkins, Cathy 199
Weick, Wilhemine 311
Weld, Gov. William 325
welfare mom 8
Westerdon, Jemmina 79
White, Justice Byron 16
white male interests 18
Whiteling, Sarah Jane 99
Whitman, Gov. Charles S. 318
Wiggins v. Smith 21
Wilde, Sarah Averill 70, 299
Wiles, Sarah 70
Williams, Bessie Mae 163, 322, 331
Williams, Dorothy 329
Williams, Jacqueline Annette 329
Williams, Gov. John R. 325
Williams, Manling Tsang 370
Williams, Sarah 300
Wilson, Elizabeth 101, 175
Wilson, Gov. Pete 291, 325
Winfrey, Megan 199–200
Winkler, Mary Freeman 336
Winney, slave to John Knox 114
Winthrop, John 67–68, 76–77, 80–81
witchcraft 68–73
Witherspoon v. Illinois 240
Women Foreign Nationals 338–339
Wood, Cindy 200–201
Wood, Sylvia 95
Woodson v. North Carolina 240
Woolvin, Mary 301
Working Women's National Association 306
Worms, Pamela Lee 97
Wright, Dora 39, 161
wrongful convictions 10, 174–228
Wuornos, Aileen Carol 25, 148
Wyley, Ann 110–111

Yarber, Parmelia 103
Yausley, Isabella 75
Young, Caroline 339
Youngs, Alse 68, 72

Zamudio, Dora Gudiño 338